INSTITUTES

OF

THE CHRISTIAN RELIGION

By

JOHN CALVIN

Translated by

HENRY BEVERIDGE

VOLUME II

1957

WM. B. EERDMANS PUBLISHING COMPANY

Grand Rapids, Michigan

This printing 1957

PHOTOLITHOPRINTED BY CUSHING - MALLOY, INC.
ANN ARBOR, MICHIGAN, UNITED STATES OF AMERICA
1957

OUTLINE OF THE INSTITUTES

Book One: Knowledge of God, the Father

chs. 1-2	The Nature of Religious Knowledge
chs. 3-5	Knowledge of God in the Works of Creation
chs. 6-9	Knowledge of God in Scripture.
chs. 10	A summary of the knowledge of God in Creation and Scripture
Chs. 11-12	Quality of the true knowledge of God.
chs. 13	The Trinity
chs. 14-15	Creation
chs. 16-18	Providence

Book Two: Knowledge of God, the Redeemer

chs. 1-5	Sin occasion for Redemption
chs. 6-11	Gospel and Law.
chs. 12-14	The Person of Christ
chs. 15-17	The Work of Christ

Book Three: On The Holy Spirit

1	Introductory
2	Faith
3-5	Repentance
6-10	The Christian Life
11-18	Justification
19	Christian Liberty
20	Prayer
21-24	Election - the last implicate of faith
25	Eschatology

Book Four: On the Outward Aids by Which God Invites Us Into the Fellowship of the Church

1-13	The Church
14-17	The Sacraments
18-19	On the Mass - On False Sacraments
20	Civil Government - the State.

CONTENTS OF THE SECOND VOLUME.

*** The Division and Arrangement of the Chapters of the Institutes will be found under No. VI.

The Sections are introduced at the commencement of each Chapter.

INSTITUTES

OF

THE CHRISTIAN RELIGION.

BOOK THIRD

CONTINUED.

CHAPTER VI.

THE LIFE OF A CHRISTIAN MAN. SCRIPTURAL ARGUMENTS EXHORTING TO IT.

This and the four following chapters treat of the Life of the Christian, and are so arranged as to admit of being classed under two principal heads.

First, it must be held to be a universally acknowledged point, that no man is a Christian who does not feel some special love for righteousness, chap. vi. Secondly, in regard to the standard by which every man ought to regulate his life, although it seems to be considered in chap. vii. only, yet the three following chapters also refer to it. For it shows that the Christian has two duties to perform. First, the observance being so arduous, he needs the greatest patience. Hence chap. viii. treats professedly of the utility of the cross, and chap. ix. invites to meditation on the future life. Lastly, chap. x. clearly shows, as in no small degree conducive to this end, how we are to use this life and its comforts without abusing them.

This sixth chapter consists of two parts,—I. Connection between this treatise on the Christian Life and the doctrine of Regeneration and Repentance. Arrangement of the treatise, sec. 1–3. II. Extremes to be avoided; 1. False Christians denying Christ, by their works condemned, sec. 4. 2, Christians should not despair, though they have not attained perfection, provided they make daily progress in piety and righteousness.

Sections.

1. Connection between this chapter and the doctrine of Regeneration. Necessity of the doctrine concerning the Christian Life. The brevity of this treatise: The method of it. Plainness and unadorned simplicity of the Scripture system of morals.
2. Two divisions. First, Personal holiness. 1. Because God is holy. 2. Because of our communion with his saints.
3. Second division, relating to our Redemption. Admirable moral system of Scripture. Five special inducements or exhortations to a Christian Life.
4. False Christians who are opposed to this life censured. 1. They have not truly learned Christ. 2. The Gospel not the guide of their words or actions. 3. They do not imitate Christ the Master. 4. They would separate the Spirit from his word.
5. Christians ought not to despond: Provided, 1. They take the word of God for their guide. 2. Sincerely cultivate righteousness. 3. Walk, according to their capacity, in the ways of the Lord. 4. Make some progress. 5. Persevere.

1. We have said that the object of regeneration is to bring the life of believers into concord and harmony with the righteousness of God, and so confirm the adoption by which they have been received as sons. But although the law comprehends within it that new life by which the image of God is restored in us, yet, as our sluggishness stands greatly in need both of helps and incentives, it will be useful to collect out of Scripture a true account of this reformation, lest any who have a heartfelt desire of repentance should in their zeal go astray. Moreover, I am not unaware that, in undertaking to describe the life of the Christian, I am entering on a large and extensive subject, one which, when fully considered in all its parts, is sufficient to fill a large volume. We see the length to which the Fathers, in treating of individual virtues, extend their exhortations. This they do, not from mere loquaciousness; for whatever be the virtue which you undertake to recommend, your pen is spontaneously led by the copiousness of the matter so to amplify, that you seem not to have discussed it properly if you have not done it at length. My intention, however, in the plan of life which I now propose to give, is not to extend it so far as to treat of each virtue specially, and expatiate in exhortation. This must be sought in the writings of others, and particularly in the Homilies of the Fathers.[1] For me it will be sufficient to point out the method by which a pious man may be taught how to frame his life aright, and briefly lay down some universal rule by which he may not improperly regulate his conduct. I shall one day possibly find time for more ample discourse [or leave others to perform an office for which I am not so fit. I have a natural love of brevity, and, perhaps, any attempt of mine at copiousness would not succeed. Even if I could gain the highest applause by being more prolix, I would scarcely be disposed to attempt it],[2] while the nature of my present work requires me to glance at simple doctrine with as much brevity as possible. As philosophers have certain definitions of rectitude and honesty, from which they derive particular duties and the whole train of virtues; so in this respect Scripture is not without order, but presents a most beautiful arrangement, one too which is every way much more certain than that of philosophers. The only difference is, that they, under the influence of ambition, constantly affect an exquisite perspicuity of arrangement, which may serve to display their genius, whereas the Spirit of God, teaching without affectation, is not so perpetually observant of exact method, and yet by observing it at times sufficiently intimates that it is not to be neglected.

2. The Scripture system of which we speak aims chiefly at two objects. The former is, that the love of righteousness, to which we are by no means naturally inclined, may be instilled and implanted into our minds. The latter is (see chap. vii.), to prescribe a rule

1 The French adds, "C'est a dire, sermons populaires;"—that is to say, popular sermons.
2 The passage in brackets is omitted in the French.

which will prevent us while in the pursuit of righteousness from going astray. It has numerous admirable methods of recommending righteousness.[1] Many have been already pointed out in different parts of this work; but we shall here also briefly advert to some of them. With what better foundation can it begin than by reminding us that we must be holy, because "God is holy"? (Lev. xix. 1; 1 Pet. i. 16.) For when we were scattered abroad like lost sheep, wandering through the labyrinth of this world, he brought us back again to his own fold. When mention is made of our union with God, let us remember that holiness must be the bond; not that by the merit of holiness we come into communion with him (we ought rather first to cleave to him, in order that, pervaded with his holiness, we may follow whither he calls), but because it greatly concerns his glory not to have any fellowship with wickedness and impurity. Wherefore he tells us that this is the end of our calling, the end to which we ought ever to have respect, if we would answer the call of God. For to what end were we rescued from the iniquity and pollution of the world into which we were plunged, if we allow ourselves, during our whole lives, to wallow in them? Besides, we are at the same time admonished, that if we would be regarded as the Lord's people, we must inhabit the holy city Jerusalem (Isaiah xxxv. 8, *et alibi*), which, as he hath consecrated it to himself, it were impious for its inhabitants to profane by impurity. Hence the expressions, "Who shall abide in thy tabernacle? who shall dwell in thy holy hill? He that walketh uprightly, and worketh righteousness" (Ps. xv. 1, 2; xxiv. 3, 4); for the sanctuary in which he dwells certainly ought not to be like an unclean stall.

3. The better to arouse us, it exhibits God the Father, who, as he hath reconciled us to himself in his Anointed, has impressed his image upon us, to which he would have us to be conformed (Rom. v. 4). Come, then, and let them show me a more excellent system among philosophers, who think that they only have a moral philosophy duly and orderly arranged. They, when they would give excellent exhortations to virtue, can only tell us to live agreeably to nature. Scripture derives its exhortations from the true source,[2] when it not only enjoins us to regulate our lives with a view to God its author to whom it belongs; but after showing us that we have degenerated from our true origin—viz. the law of our Creator, adds, that Christ, through whom we have returned to favour with God, is set before us as a model, the image of which our lives should express. What do you require more effectual than this? Nay, what do you require beyond this? If the Lord adopts us for his sons on the condition that our life be a representation of Christ, the bond of our

1 The French begins the sentence thus, "Quant est du premier poinct;"—As to the former point.

2 Mal. i. 6; Eph. v. 1; 1 John iii. 1, 3; Eph. v. 26; Rom. vi. 1–4; 1 Cor. vi. 11; 1 Pet. i. 15, 19; 1 Cor. vi. 15; John xv. 3; Eph. v. 2, 3; Col. iii. 1, 2; 1 Cor. iii. 16; vi. 17; 2 Cor. vi. 16; 1 Thess. v. 23.

adoption,—then, unless we dedicate and devote ourselves to righteousness, we not only, with the utmost perfidy, revolt from our Creator, but also abjure the Saviour himself. Then, from an enumeration of all the blessings of God, and each part of our salvation, it finds materials for exhortation. Ever since God exhibited himself to us as a Father, we must be convicted of extreme ingratitude if we do not in turn exhibit ourselves as his sons. Ever since Christ purified us by the laver of his blood, and communicated this purification by baptism, it would ill become us to be defiled with new pollution. Ever since he ingrafted us into his body, we, who are his members, should anxiously beware of contracting any stain or taint. Ever since he who is our head ascended to heaven, it is befitting in us to withdraw our affections from the earth, and with our whole soul aspire to heaven. Ever since the Holy Spirit dedicated us as temples to the Lord, we should make it our endeavour to show forth the glory of God, and guard against being profaned by the defilement of sin. Ever since our soul and body were destined to heavenly incorruptibility and an unfading crown, we should earnestly strive to keep them pure and uncorrupted against the day of the Lord. These, I say, are the surest foundations of a well-regulated life, and you will search in vain for anything resembling them among philosophers, who, in their commendation of virtue, never rise higher than the natural dignity of man.

4. This is the place to address those who, having nothing of Christ but the name and sign, would yet be called Christians. How dare they boast of this sacred name? None have intercourse with Christ but those who have acquired the true knowledge of him from the Gospel. The Apostle denies that any man truly has learned Christ who has not learned to put off "the old man, which is corrupt according to the deceitful lusts, and put on Christ" (Eph. iv. 22). They are convicted, therefore, of falsely and unjustly pretending a knowledge of Christ, whatever be the volubility and eloquence with which they can talk of the Gospel. Doctrine is not an affair of the tongue, but of the life; is not apprehended by the intellect and memory merely, like other branches of learning; but is received only when it possesses the whole soul, and finds its seat and habitation in the inmost recesses of the heart. Let them, therefore, either cease to insult God, by boasting that they are what they are not, or let them show themselves not unworthy disciples of their divine Master. To doctrine in which our religion is contained we have given the first place, since by it our salvation commences; but it must be transfused into the breast, and pass into the conduct, and so transform us into itself, as not to prove unfruitful. If philosophers are justly offended, and banish from their company with disgrace those who, while professing an art which ought to be the mistress of their conduct, convert it into mere loquacious sophistry, with how much better reason shall we detest those flimsy sophists who are contented to let the Gospel play upon their lips, when, from its efficacy, it ought to penetrate the inmost affections

of the heart, fix its seat in the soul, and pervade the whole man a hundred times more than the frigid discourses of philosophers?

5. I insist not that the life of the Christian shall breathe nothing but the perfect Gospel, though this is to be desired, and ought to be attempted. I insist not so strictly on evangelical perfection, as to refuse to acknowledge as a Christian any man who has not attained it. In this way all would be excluded from the Church, since there is no man who is not far removed from this perfection, while many, who have made but little progress, would be undeservedly rejected. What then? Let us set this before our eye as the end at which we ought constantly to aim. Let it be regarded as the goal towards which we are to run. For you cannot divide the matter with God, undertaking part of what his word enjoins, and omitting part at pleasure. For, in the first place, God uniformly recommends integrity as the principal part of his worship, meaning by integrity real singleness of mind, devoid of gloss and fiction, and to this is opposed a double mind; as if it had been said that the spiritual commencement of a good life is when the internal affections are sincerely devoted to God, in the cultivation of holiness and justice. But seeing that, in this earthly prison of the body, no man is supplied with strength sufficient to hasten in his course with due alacrity, while the greater number are so oppressed with weakness, that hesitating, and halting, and even crawling on the ground, they make little progress, let every one of us go as far as his humble ability enables him, and prosecute the journey once begun. No one will travel so badly as not daily to make some degree of progress. This, therefore, let us never cease to do, that we may daily advance in the way of the Lord; and let us not despair because of the slender measure of success. How little soever the success may correspond with our wish, our labour is not lost when to-day is better than yesterday, provided with true singleness of mind we keep our aim, and aspire to the goal, not speaking flattering things to ourselves, nor indulging our vices, but making it our constant endeavour to become better, until we attain to goodness itself. If during the whole course of our life we seek and follow, we shall at length attain it, when relieved from the infirmity of flesh we are admitted to full fellowship with God.

CHAPTER VII.

A SUMMARY OF THE CHRISTIAN LIFE. OF SELF-DENIAL.[1]

The divisions of the chapter are,—I. The rule which permits us not to go astray in the study of righteousness, requires two things—viz. that man, abandoning his own will, devote himself entirely to the service of God; whence it follows, that we must seek not our own things, but the things of God, sec. 1, 2. II. A description of this renovation or Christian life taken from the Epistle to Titus, and accurately explained under certain special heads, sec. 3 to end.

Sections.

1. Consideration of the second general division in regard to the Christian life. Its beginning and sum. A twofold respect. 1. We are not our own. Respect to both the fruit and the use. Unknown to philosophers, who have placed reason on the throne of the Holy Spirit.
2. Since we are not our own, we must seek the glory of God, and obey his will. Self-denial recommended to the disciples of Christ. He who neglects it, deceived either by pride or hypocrisy, rushes on destruction.
3. Three things to be followed, and two to be shunned in life. Impiety and worldly lusts to be shunned. Sobriety, justice, and piety, to be followed. An inducement to right conduct.
4. Self-denial the sum of Paul's doctrine. Its difficulty. Qualities in us which make it difficult. Cures for these qualities. 1. Ambition to be suppressed. 2. Humility to be embraced. 3. Candour to be esteemed. 4. Mutual charity to be preserved. 5. Modesty to be sincerely cultivated.
5. The advantage of our neighbour to be promoted. Here self-denial most necessary, and yet most difficult. Here a double remedy. 1. The benefits bestowed upon us are for the common benefit of the Church. 2. We ought to do all we can for our neighbour. This illustrated by analogy from the members of the human body. This duty of charity founded on the divine command.
6. Charity ought to have for its attendants patience and kindness. We should consider the image of God in our neighbours, and especially in those who are of the household of faith. Hence a fourfold consideration which refutes all objections. A common objection refuted.
7. Christian life cannot exist without charity. Remedies for the vices opposed to charity. 1. Mercy. 2. Humility. 3. Modesty. 4. Diligence. 5. Perseverance.
8. Self-denial, in respect of God, should lead to equanimity and tolerance. 1. We are always subject to God. 2. We should shun avarice and ambition. 3. We should expect all prosperity from the blessing of God, and entirely depend on him.
9. We ought not to desire wealth or honours without the divine blessing, nor follow the arts of the wicked. We ought to cast all our care upon God, and never envy the prosperity of others.
10. We ought to commit ourselves entirely to God. The necessity of this doctrine. Various uses of affliction. Heathen abuse and corruption.

1 On this and the three following chapters, which contain the second part of the Treatise on the Christian Life, see Augustin. De Moribus Ecclesiæ Catholicæ, and Calvin de Scandalis.

1. ALTHOUGH the Law of God contains a perfect rule of conduct admirably arranged, it has seemed proper to our divine Master to train his people by a more accurate method, to the rule which is enjoined in the Law; and the leading principle in the method is, that it is the duty of believers to present their "bodies a living sacrifice, holy and acceptable unto God, which is their reasonable service" (Rom. xii. 1). Hence he draws the exhortation: "Be not conformed to this world: but be ye transformed by the renewing of your mind, that ye may prove what is that good, and acceptable, and perfect will of God." The great point, then, is, that we are consecrated and dedicated to God, and therefore should not henceforth think, speak, design, or act, without a view to his glory. What he hath made sacred cannot, without signal insult to him, be applied to profane use. But if we are not our own, but the Lord's, it is plain both what error is to be shunned, and to what end the actions of our lives ought to be directed. We are not our own; therefore, neither is our own reason or will to rule our acts and counsels. We are not our own; therefore, let us not make it our end to seek what may be agreeable to our carnal nature. We are not our own; therefore, as far as possible, let us forget ourselves and the things that are ours. On the other hand, we are God's; let us, therefore, live and die to him (Rom. xiv. 8). We are God's; therefore, let his wisdom and will preside over all our actions. We are God's; to him, then, as the only legitimate end, let every part of our life be directed. O how great the proficiency of him who, taught that he is not his own, has withdrawn the dominion and government of himself from his own reason that he may give them to God! For as the surest source of destruction to men is to obey themselves, so the only haven of safety is to have no other will, no other wisdom, than to follow the Lord wherever he leads. Let this, then, be the first step, to abandon ourselves, and devote the whole energy of our minds to the service of God. By service, I mean not only that which consists in verbal obedience, but that by which the mind, divested of its own carnal feelings, implicitly obeys the call of the Spirit of God. This transformation (which Paul calls *the renewing of the mind*, Rom. xii. 2; Eph. iv. 23), though it is the first entrance to life, was unknown to all the philosophers. They give the government of man to reason alone, thinking that she alone is to be listened to; in short, they assign to her the sole direction of the conduct. But Christian philosophy bids her give place, and yield complete submission to the Holy Spirit, so that the man himself no longer lives, but Christ lives and reigns in him (Gal. ii. 20).

2. Hence follows the other principle, that we are not to seek our own, but the Lord's will, and act with a view to promote his glory. Great is our proficiency, when, almost forgetting ourselves, certainly postponing our own reason, we faithfully make it our study to obey God and his commandments. For when Scripture enjoins us to lay aside private regard to ourselves, it not only divests our minds of an excessive longing for wealth, or power, or human favour, but eradi-

cates all ambition and thirst for worldly glory, and other more secret pests. The Christian ought, indeed, to be so trained and disposed as to consider, that during his whole life he has to do with God. For this reason, as he will bring all things to the disposal and estimate of God, so he will religiously direct his whole mind to him. For he who has learned to look to God in everything he does, is at the same time diverted from all vain thoughts. This is that self-denial which Christ so strongly enforces on his disciples from the very outset (Matth. xvi. 24), which, as soon as it takes hold of the mind, leaves no place either, first, for pride, show, and ostentation; or, secondly, for avarice, lust, luxury, effeminacy, or other vices which are engendered by self-love. On the contrary, wherever it reigns not, the foulest vices are indulged in without shame; or, if there is some appearance of virtue, it is vitiated by a depraved longing for applause. Show me, if you can, an individual who, unless he has renounced himself in obedience to the Lord's command, is disposed to do good for its own sake. Those who have not so renounced themselves have followed virtue at least for the sake of praise. The philosophers who have contended most strongly that virtue is to be desired on her own account, were so inflated with arrogance as to make it apparent that they sought virtue for no other reason than as a ground for indulging in pride. So far, therefore, is God from being delighted with these hunters after popular applause with their swollen breasts, that he declares they have received their reward in this world (Matth. vi. 2), and that harlots and publicans are nearer the kingdom of heaven than they (Matth. xxi. 31). We have not yet sufficiently explained how great and numerous are the obstacles by which a man is impeded in the pursuit of rectitude, so long as he has not renounced himself. The old saying is true, There is a world of iniquity treasured up in the human soul. Nor can you find any other remedy for this than to deny yourself, renounce your own reason, and direct your whole mind to the pursuit of those things which the Lord requires of you, and which you are to seek only because they are pleasing to Him.

3. In another passage, Paul gives a brief, indeed, but more distinct account of each of the parts of a well-ordered life: "The grace of God that bringeth salvation hath appeared to all men, teaching us that, denying ungodliness and worldly lusts, we should live soberly, righteously, and godly, in this present world; looking for that blessed hope, and the glorious appearance of the great God and our Saviour Jesus Christ; who gave himself for us, that he might redeem us from all iniquity, and purify to himself a peculiar people, zealous of good works" (Tit. ii. 11—14). After holding forth the grace of God to animate us, and pave the way for His true worship, he removes the two greatest obstacles which stand in the way—viz. ungodliness, to which we are by nature too prone, and worldly lusts, which are of still greater extent. Under *ungodliness*, he includes not merely superstition, but everything at variance with the true fear of God. *Worldly lusts* are equivalent to the lusts of the flesh. Thus he en-

joins us, in regard to both tables of the Law, to lay aside our own mind, and renounce whatever our own reason and will dictate. Then he reduces all the actions of our lives to three branches, sobriety, righteousness, and godliness. *Sobriety* undoubtedly denotes as well chastity and temperance as the pure and frugal use of temporal goods, and patient endurance of want. *Righteousness* comprehends all the duties of equity, in rendering to every one his due. Next follows *godliness*, which separates us from the pollutions of the world, and connects us with God in true holiness. These, when connected together by an indissoluble chain, constitute complete perfection. But as nothing is more difficult than to bid adieu to the will of the flesh, subdue, nay, abjure our lusts, devote ourselves to God and our brethren, and lead an angelic life amid the pollutions of the world, Paul, to set our minds free from all entanglements, recalls us to the hope of a blessed immortality, justly urging us to contend, because as Christ has once appeared as our Redeemer, so on his final advent he will give full effect to the salvation obtained by him. And in this way he dispels all the allurements which becloud our path, and prevent us from aspiring as we ought to heavenly glory; nay, he tells us that we must be pilgrims in the world, that we may not fail of obtaining the heavenly inheritance.

4. Moreover, we see by these words that self-denial has respect partly to men and partly (more especially) to God (sec. 8–10). For when Scripture enjoins us, in regard to our fellow-men, to prefer them in honour to ourselves, and sincerely labour to promote their advantage (Rom. xii. 10; Phil. ii. 3), he gives us commands which our mind is utterly incapable of obeying until its natural feelings are suppressed. For so blindly do we all rush in the direction of self-love, that every one thinks he has a good reason for exalting himself and despising all others in comparison. If God has bestowed on us something not to be repented of, trusting to it, we immediately become elated, and not only swell, but almost burst with pride. The vices with which we abound we both carefully conceal from others, and flatteringly represent to ourselves as minute and trivial, nay, sometimes hug them as virtues. When the same qualities which we admire in ourselves are seen in others, even though they should be superior, we, in order that we may not be forced to yield to them, maliciously lower and carp at them; in like manner, in the case of vices, not contented with severe and keen animadversion, we studiously exaggerate them. Hence the insolence with which each, as if exempted from the common lot, seeks to exalt himself above his neighbour, confidently and proudly despising others, or at least looking down upon them as his inferiors. The poor man yields to the rich, the plebeian to the noble, the servant to the master, the unlearned to the learned, and yet every one inwardly cherishes some idea of his own superiority. Thus each flattering himself, sets up a kind of kingdom in his breast; the arrogant, to satisfy themselves, pass censure on the minds and manners of other men, and when conten-

tion arises, the full venom is displayed. Many bear about with them some measure of mildness so long as all things go smoothly and lovingly with them, but how few are there who, when stung and irritated, preserve the same tenor of moderation? For this there is no other remedy than to pluck up by the roots those most noxious pests, self-love and love of victory (φιλονεικὶα και φιλαυτιὰ). This the doctrine of Scripture does. For it teaches us to remember, that the endowments which God has bestowed upon us are not our own, but His free gifts, and that those who plume themselves upon them betray their ingratitude. "Who maketh thee to differ," saith Paul, "and what hast thou that thou didst not receive? now if thou didst receive it, why dost thou glory, as if thou hadst not received it?" (1 Cor. iv. 7.) Then by a diligent examination of our faults, let us keep ourselves humble. Thus while nothing will remain to swell our pride, there will be much to subdue it. Again, we are enjoined, whenever we behold the gifts of God in others, so to reverence and respect the gifts, as also to honour those in whom they reside. God having been pleased to bestow honour upon them, it would ill become us to deprive them of it. Then we are told to overlook their faults, not, indeed, to encourage by flattering them, but not because of them to insult those whom we ought to regard with honour and good-will.[1] In this way, with regard to all with whom we have intercourse, our behaviour will be not only moderate and modest, but courteous and friendly. The only way by which you can ever attain to true meekness, is to have your heart imbued with a humble opinion of yourself and respect for others.

5. How difficult it is to perform the duty of seeking the good of our neighbour! Unless you leave off all thought of yourself, and in a manner cease to be yourself, you will never accomplish it. How can you exhibit those works of charity which Paul describes unless you renounce yourself, and become wholly devoted to others? "Charity (says he, 1 Cor. xiii. 4) suffereth long, and is kind; charity envieth not; charity vaunteth not itself, is not puffed up, doth not behave itself unseemly, seeketh not her own, is not easily provoked," &c. Were it the only thing required of us to seek not our own, nature would not have the least power to comply: she so inclines us to love ourselves only, that she will not easily allow us carelessly to pass by ourselves and our own interests that we may watch over the interests of others, nay, spontaneously to yield our own right, and resign it to another. But Scripture, to conduct us to this, reminds us, that whatever we obtain from the Lord is granted on the condition of our employing it for the common good of the Church, and that, therefore, the legitimate use of all our gifts is a kind and liberal communication of them with others. There cannot be a surer rule, nor a stronger exhortation to the observance of it, than when we are tauhgt that all the endowments which we possess are divine deposits

[1] Calvin. de Sacerdotiis Eccles. Papal. in fine.

intrusted to us for the very purpose of being distributed for the good of our neighbour. But Scripture proceeds still farther when it likens these endowments to the different members of the body (1 Cor. xii. 12). No member has its function for itself, or applies it for its own private use, but transfers it to its fellow-members; nor does it derive any other advantage from it than that which it receives in common with the whole body. Thus, whatever the pious man can do, he is bound to do for his brethren, not consulting his own interest in any other way than by striving earnestly for the common edification of the Church. Let this, then, be our method of showing good-will and kindness, considering that, in regard to everything which God has bestowed upon us, and by which we can aid our neighbour, we are his stewards, and are bound to give account of our stewardship; moreover, that the only right mode of administration is that which is regulated by love. In this way, we shall not only unite the study of our neighbour's advantage with a regard to our own, but make the latter subordinate to the former. And lest we should have omitted to perceive that this is the law for duly administering every gift which we receive from God, he of old applied that law to the minutest expressions of his own kindness. He commanded the first-fruits to be offered to him as an attestation by the people that it was impious to reap any advantage from goods not previously consecrated to him (Exod. xxii. 29; xxiii. 19). But if the gifts of God are not sanctified to us until we have with our own hand dedicated them to the Giver, it must be a gross abuse that does not give signs of such dedication. It is in vain to contend that you cannot enrich the Lord by your offerings. Though, as the Psalmist says, "Thou art my Lord: my goodness extendeth not unto thee," yet you can extend it "to the saints that are in the earth" (Ps. xvi. 2, 3); and therefore a comparison is drawn between sacred oblations and alms as now corresponding to the offerings under the Law.[1]

6. Moreover, that we may not weary in well-doing (as would otherwise forthwith and infallibly be the case), we must add the other quality in the Apostle's enumeration, "Charity suffereth long, and is kind, is not easily provoked" (1 Cor. xiii. 4). The Lord enjoins us to do good to all without exception, though the greater part, if estimated by their own merit, are most unworthy of it. But Scripture subjoins a most excellent reason, when it tells us that we are not to look to what men in themselves deserve, but to attend to the image of God, which exists in all, and to which we owe all honour and love. But in those who are of the household of faith, the same rule is to be more carefully observed, inasmuch as that image is renewed and restored in them by the Spirit of Christ. Therefore, whoever be the man that is presented to you as needing your assistance, you have no ground for declining to give it to him. Say he is a stranger. The Lord has given him a mark which ought

[1] Heb. xiii. 16; 2 Cor. ix. 12.

to be familiar to you: for which reason he forbids you to despise your own flesh (Gal. vi. 10). Say he is mean and of no consideration. The Lord points him out as one whom he has distinguished by the lustre of his own image (Isaiah lviii. 7). Say that you are bound to him by no ties of duty. The Lord has substituted him as it were into his own place, that in him you may recognise the many great obligations under which the Lord has laid you to himself. Say that he is unworthy of your least exertion on his account; but the image of God, by which he is recommended to you, is worthy of yourself and all your exertions. But if he not only merits no good, but has provoked you by injury and mischief, still this is no good reason why you should not embrace him in love, and visit him with offices of love. He has deserved very differently from me, you will say. But what has the Lord deserved?[2] Whatever injury he has done you, when he enjoins you to forgive him, he certainly means that it should be imputed to himself. In this way only we attain to what is not to say difficult, but altogether against nature,[1] to love those that hate us, render good for evil, and blessing for cursing, remembering that we are not to reflect on the wickedness of men, but look to the image of God in them, an image which, covering and obliterating their faults, should by its beauty and dignity allure us to love and embrace them.

7. We shall thus succeed in mortifying ourselves if we fulfil all the duties of charity. Those duties, however, are not fulfilled by the mere discharge of them, though none be omitted, unless it is done from a pure feeling of love. For it may happen that one may perform every one of these offices, in so far as the external act is concerned, and be far from performing them aright. For you see some who would be thought very liberal, and yet accompany every thing they give with insult, by the haughtiness of their looks, or the violence of their words. And to such a calamitous condition have we come in this unhappy age, that the greater part of men never almost give alms without contumely. Such conduct ought not to have been tolerated even among the heathen; but from Christians something more is required than to carry cheerfulness in their looks, and give attractiveness to the discharge of their duties by courteous language. First, they should put themselves in the place of him whom they see in need of their assistance, and pity his misfortune as if they felt and bore it, so that a feeling of pity and humanity should incline them to assist him just as they would themselves. He who is thus minded will go and give assistance to his brethren, and not only not taint his acts with arrogance or upbraiding, but will neither look down upon the brother to whom he does a kindness, as one who

1 French, "Car si nous disons qu'il n'a merité que mal de nous; Dieu nous pourra demander quel mal il nous a fait, lui dont nous tenons tout notre bien;"—For if we say that he has deserved nothing of us but evil, God may ask us what evil he has done us, he of whom we hold our every blessing.

2 Matth. v. 44; vi. 14; xviii. 35; Luke xvii. 3.

needed his help, or keep him in subjection as under obligation to him, just as we do not insult a diseased member when the rest of the body labours for its recovery, nor think it under special obligation to the other members, because it has required more exertion than it has returned. A communication of offices between members is not regarded as at all gratuitous, but rather as the payment of that which being due by the law of nature it were monstrous to deny. For this reason, he who has performed one kind of duty will not think himself thereby discharged, as is usually the case when a rich man, after contributing somewhat of his substance, delegates remaining burdens to others as if he had nothing to do with them. Every one should rather consider, that however great he is, he owes himself to his neighbours, and that the only limit to his beneficence is the failure of his means. The extent of these should regulate that of his charity.

8. The principal part of self-denial, that which as we have said has reference to God, let us again consider more fully. Many things have already been said with regard to it which it were superfluous to repeat; and, therefore, it will be sufficient to view it as forming us to equanimity and endurance. First, then, in seeking the convenience or tranquillity of the present life, Scripture calls us to resign ourselves, and all we have, to the disposal of the Lord, to give him up the affections of the heart, that he may tame and subdue them. We have a frenzied desire, an infinite eagerness, to pursue wealth and honour, intrigue for power, accumulate riches, and collect all those frivolities which seem conducive to luxury and splendour. On the other hand, we have a remarkable dread, a remarkable hatred of poverty, mean birth, and a humble condition, and feel the strongest desire to guard against them. Hence, in regard to those who frame their life after their own counsel, we see how restless they are in mind, how many plans they try, to what fatigues they submit, in order that they may gain what avarice or ambition desires, or, on the other hand, escape poverty and meanness. To avoid similiar entanglements, the course which Christian men must follow is this: first, they must not long for, or hope for, or think of any kind of prosperity apart from the blessing of God; on it they must cast themselves, and there safely and confidently recline. For, however much the carnal mind may seem sufficient for itself when in the pursuit of honour or wealth, it depends on its own industry and zeal, or is aided by the favour of men, it is certain that all this is nothing, and that neither intellect nor labour will be of the least avail, except in so far as the Lord prospers both. On the contrary, his blessing alone makes a way through all obstacles, and brings everything to a joyful and favourable issue. Secondly, though without this blessing we may be able to acquire some degree of fame and opulence (as we daily see wicked men loaded with honours and riches), yet since those on whom the curse of God lies do not enjoy the least particle of true happiness, whatever we obtain without his blessing must turn

out ill. But surely men ought not to desire what adds to their misery.

9. Therefore, if we believe that all prosperous and desirable success depends entirely on the blessing of God, and that when it is wanting all kinds of misery and calamity await us, it follows that we should not eagerly contend for riches and honours, trusting to our own dexterity and assiduity, or leaning on the favour of men, or confiding in any empty imagination of fortune; but should always have respect to the Lord, that under his auspices we may be conducted to whatever lot he has provided for us. First, the result will be, that instead of rushing on regardless of right and wrong, by wiles and wicked arts, and with injury to our neighbours, to catch at wealth and seize upon honours, we will only follow such fortune as we may enjoy with innocence. Who can hope for the aid of the divine blessing amid fraud, rapine, and other iniquitous arts? As this blessing attends him only who thinks purely and acts uprightly, so it calls off all who long for it from sinister designs and evil actions. Secondly, a curb will be laid upon us, restraining a too eager desire of becoming rich, or an ambitious striving after honour. How can any one have the effrontery to expect that God will aid him in accomplishing desires at variance with his word? What God with his own lips pronounces cursed, never can be prosecuted with his blessing. Lastly, if our success is not equal to our wish and hope, we shall, however, be kept from impatience and detestation of our condition, whatever it be, knowing that so to feel were to murmur against God, at whose pleasure riches and poverty, contempt and honours, are dispensed. In short, he who leans on the divine blessing in the way which has been described, will not, in the pursuit of those things which men are wont most eagerly to desire, employ wicked arts which he knows would avail him nothing; nor when any thing prosperous befalls him will he impute it to himself and his own diligence, or industry, or fortune, instead of ascribing it to God as its author. If, while the affairs of others flourish, his make little progress, or even retrograde, he will bear his humble lot with greater equanimity and moderation than any irreligious man does the moderate success which only falls short of what he wished; for he has a solace in which he can rest more tranquilly than at the very summit of wealth or power, because he considers that his affairs are ordered by the Lord in the manner most conducive to his salvation. This, we see, is the way in which David was affected, who, while he follows God and gives up himself to his guidance, declares, "Neither do I exercise myself in great matters, or in things too high for me. Surely I have behaved and quieted myself as a child that is weaned of his mother" (Ps. cxxxi. 1, 2).

10. Nor is it in this respect only that pious minds ought to manifest this tranquillity and endurance; it must be extended to all the accidents to which this present life is liable. He alone, therefore, has properly denied himself, who has resigned himself entirely to the Lord, placing all the course of his life entirely at his disposal. Happen

what may, he whose mind is thus composed will neither deem himself wretched or murmur against God because of his lot. How necessary this disposition is will appear, if you consider the many accidents to which we are liable. Various diseases ever and anon attack us: at one time pestilence rages; at another we are involved in all the calamities of war. Frost and hail, destroying the promise of the year, cause sterility, which reduces us to penury; wife, parents, children, relatives, are carried off by death; our house is destroyed by fire. These are the events which make men curse their life, detest the day of their birth, execrate the light of heaven, even censure God, and (as they are eloquent in blasphemy) charge him with cruelty and injustice. The believer must in these things also contemplate the mercy and truly paternal indulgence of God. Accordingly, should he see his house by the removal of kindred reduced to solitude, even then he will not cease to bless the Lord; his thought will be, Still the grace of the Lord, which dwells within my house, will not leave it desolate. If his crops are blasted, mildewed, or cut off by frost, or struck down by hail,[1] and he sees famine before him, he will not however despond or murmur against God, but maintain his confidence in him; "We thy people, and sheep of thy pasture, will give thee thanks for ever" (Ps. lxxix. 13); he will supply me with food, even in the extreme of sterility. If he is afflicted with disease, the sharpness of the pain will not so overcome him, as to make him break out with impatience, and expostulate with God; but recognising justice and lenity in the rod, will patiently endure. In short, whatever happens, knowing that it is ordered by the Lord, he will receive it with a placid and grateful mind, and will not contumaciously resist the government of him, at whose disposal he has placed himself and all that he has. Especially let the Christian breast eschew that foolish and most miserable consolation of the heathen, who, to strengthen their mind against adversity, imputed it to fortune, at which they deemed it absurd to feel indignant, as she was ἄσκοπος (aimless) and rash, and blindly wounded the good equally with the bad. On the contrary, the rule of piety is, that the hand of God is the ruler and arbiter of the fortunes of all, and, instead of rushing on with thoughtless violence, dispenses good and evil with perfect regularity.

1 The French is, "Soit que ses bleds et vignes soyent gastées et destruites par gelée, gresle, ou autre tempeste;"—whether his corn and vines are hurt and destroyed by frost, hail, or other tempest.

CHAPTER VIII.

OF BEARING THE CROSS—ONE BRANCH OF SELF-DENIAL.

The four divisions of this chapter are,—I. The nature of the cross, its necessity and dignity, sec. 1, 2. II. The manifold advantages of the cross described, sec. 3–6. III. The form of the cross the most excellent of all, and yet it by no means removes all sense of pain, sec 7, 8. IV. A description of warfare under the cross, and of true patience (not that of philosophers), after the example of Christ, sec. 9–11.

Sections.

1. What the cross is By whom, and on whom, and for what cause imposed. Its necessity and dignity.
2. The cross necessary: 1. To humble our pride. 2. To make us apply to God for aid. Example of David. 3. To give us experience of God's presence.
3. Manifold uses of the cross 1. Produces patience, hope, and firm confidence in God, gives us victory and perseverance. Faith invincible.
4. 2. Frames us to obedience. Example of Abraham. This training how useful.
5. The cross necessary to subdue the wantonness of the flesh. This portrayed by an apposite simile. Various forms of the cross.
6. 3. God permits our infirmities, and corrects past faults, that he may keep us in obedience. This confirmed by a passage from Solomon and an Apostle.
7. Singular consolation under the cross, when we suffer persecution for righteousness. Some parts of this consolation
8. This form of the cross most appropriate to believers, and should be borne willingly and cheerfully. This cheerfulness is not unfeeling hilarity, but, while groaning under the burden, waits patiently for the Lord.
9. A description of this conflict. Opposed to the vanity of the Stoics. Illustrated by the authority and example of Christ
10. Proved by the testimony and uniform experience of the elect. Also by the special example of the Apostle Peter. The nature of the patience required of us.
11. Distinction between the patience of Christians and philosophers. The latter pretend a necessity which cannot be resisted. The former hold forth the justice of God and his care of our safety A full exposition of this difference.

1. THE pious mind must ascend still higher—namely, whither Christ calls his disciples when he says, that every one of them must "take up his cross" (Matth. xvi. 24). Those whom the Lord has chosen and honoured with his intercourse must prepare for a hard, laborious, troubled life, a life full of many and various kinds of evils: it being the will of our heavenly Father to exercise his people in this way while putting them to the proof. Having begun this course with Christ the first-born, he continues it towards all his children. For though that Son was dear to him above others, the Son in whom he was "well pleased," yet we see, that far from being treated gently and indulgently, we may say, that not only was he subjected to a perpetual cross while he dwelt on earth, but his whole life was nothing else than a kind of perpetual cross. The Apostle assigns the reason, "Though he was a Son, yet learned he obedience by the things which he suffered" (Heb. v. 8). Why then should we exempt ourselves

from that condition to which Christ our Head behoved to submit; especially since he submitted on our account, that he might in his own person exhibit a model of patience? Wherefore, the Apostle declares, that all the children of God are destined to be conformed to him. Hence it affords us great consolation in hard and difficult circumstances, which men deem evil and adverse, to think that we are holding fellowship with the sufferings of Christ; that as he passed to celestial glory through a labyrinth of many woes, so we too are conducted thither through various tribulations. For, in another passage, Paul himself thus speaks, "we must through much tribulation enter the kingdom of God" (Acts xiv. 22); and again, "that I may know him, and the power of his resurrection, and the fellowship of his sufferings, being made conformable unto his death" (Rom. viii. 29). How powerfully should it soften the bitterness of the cross, to think that the more we are afflicted with adversity, the surer we are made of our fellowship with Christ; by communion with whom our sufferings are not only blessed to us, but tend greatly to the furtherance of our salvation.

2. We may add, that the only thing which made it necessary for our Lord to undertake to bear the cross, was to testify and prove his obedience to the Father; whereas there are many reasons which make it necessary for us to live constantly under the cross. Feeble as we are by nature, and prone to ascribe all perfection to our flesh, unless we receive as it were ocular demonstration of our weakness, we readily estimate our virtue above its proper worth, and doubt not that, whatever happens, it will stand unimpared and invincible against all difficulties. Hence we indulge a stupid and empty confidence in the flesh, and then trusting to it wax proud against the Lord himself; as if our own faculties were sufficient without his grace. This arrogance cannot be better repressed than when He proves to us by experience, not only how great our weakness, but also our frailty is. Therefore, he visits us with disgrace, or poverty, or bereavement, or disease, or other afflictions. Feeling altogether unable to support them, we forthwith, in so far as regards ourselves, give way, and thus humbled learn to invoke his strength, which alone can enable us to bear up under a weight of affliction. Nay, even the holiest of men, however well aware that they stand not in their own strength, but by the grace of God, would feel too secure in their own fortitude and constancy, were they not brought to a more thorough knowledge of themselves by the trial of the cross. This feeling gained even upon David, "In my prosperity I said, I shall never be moved. Lord, by thy favour thou hast made my mountain to stand strong: thou didst hide thy face, and I was troubled" (Ps. xxx. 6, 7). He confesses that in prosperity his feelings were dulled and blunted, so that, neglecting the grace of God, on which alone he ought to have depended, he leant to himself, and promised himself perpetuity. If it so happened to this great prophet, who of us should not fear and study caution?

Though in tranquillity they flatter themselves with the idea of greater constancy and patience, yet, humbled by adversity, they learn the deception. Believers, I say, warned by such proofs of their diseases, make progress in humility, and, divesting themselves of a depraved confidence in the flesh, betake themselves to the grace of God, and, when they have so betaken themselves, experience the presence of the divine power, in which is ample protection.

3. This Paul teaches, when he says that tribulation worketh patience, and patience experience. God having promised that he will be with believers in tribulation, they feel the truth of the promise; while supported by his hand, they endure patiently. This they could never do by their own strength. Patience, therefore, gives the saints an experimental proof that God in reality furnishes the aid which he has promised whenever there is need. Hence also their faith is confirmed, for it were very ungrateful not to expect that in future the truth of God will be, as they have already found it, firm and constant. We now see how many advantages are at once produced by the cross. Overturning the overweening opinion we form of our own virtue, and detecting the hypocrisy in which we delight, it removes our pernicious carnal confidence, teaching us, when thus humbled, to recline on God alone, so that we neither are oppressed nor despond. Then victory is followed by hope, inasmuch as the Lord, by performing what he has promised, establishes his truth in regard to the future. Were these the only reasons, it is surely plain how necessary it is for us to bear the cross. It is of no little importance to be rid of your self-love and made fully conscious of your weakness; so impressed with a sense of your weakness as to learn to distrust yourself—to distrust yourself so as to transfer your confidence to God, reclining on him with such heartfelt confidence as to trust in his aid, and continue invincible to the end, standing by his grace so as to perceive that he is true to his promises, and so assured of the certainty of his promises as to be strong in hope.

4. Another end which the Lord has in afflicting his people is to try their patience, and train them to obedience—not that they can yield obedience to him except in so far as he enables them; but he is pleased thus to attest and display striking proofs of the graces which he has conferred upon his saints, lest they should remain within unseen and unemployed. Accordingly, by bringing forward openly the strength and constancy of endurance with which he has provided his servants, he is said to try their patience. Hence the expressions that God tempted Abraham (Gen. xxi. 1, 12), and made proof of his piety by not declining to sacrifice his only son. Hence, too, Peter tells us that our faith is proved by tribulation, just as gold is tried in a furnace of fire. But who will say it is not expedient that the most excellent gift of patience which the believer has received from his God should be applied to use, by being made sure and manifest? Otherwise men would never value it according to its worth. But if God himself, to prevent the virtues which he has conferred upon believers from

lurking in obscurity, nay, lying useless and perishing, does aright in supplying materials for calling them forth, there is the best reason for the afflictions of the saints, since without them their patience could not exist. I say, that by the cross they are also trained to obedience, because they are thus taught to live not according to their own wish, but at the disposal of God. Indeed, did all things proceed as they wish, they would not know what it is to follow God. Seneca mentions (De Vit. Beata, cap. xv.) that there was an old proverb when any one was exhorted to endure adversity, "*Follow God;*" thereby intimating, that men truly submitted to the yoke of God only when they gave their back and hand to his rod. But if it is most right that we should in all things prove our obedience to our heavenly Father, certainly we ought not to decline any method by which he trains us to obedience.

5. Still, however, we see not how necessary that obedience is, unless we at the same time consider how prone our carnal nature is to shake off the yoke of God whenever it has been treated with some degree of gentleness and indulgence. It just happens to it as with refractory horses, which, if kept idle for a few days at hack and manger, become ungovernable, and no longer recognise the rider, whose command before they implicitly obeyed. And we invariably become what God complains of in the people of Israel—waxing gross and fat, we kick against him who reared and nursed us (Deut. xxxii. 15). The kindness of God should allure us to ponder and love his goodness; but since such is our malignity, that we are invariably corrupted by his indulgence, it is more than necessary for us to be restrained by discipline from breaking forth into such petulance. Thus, lest we become emboldened by an over-abundance of wealth; lest elated with honour, we grow proud; lest inflated with other advantages of body, or mind, or fortune, we grow insolent, the Lord himself interferes as he sees to be expedient by means of the cross, subduing and curbing the arrogance of our flesh, and that in various ways, as the advantage of each requires. For as we do not all equally labour under the same disease, so we do not all need the same difficult cure. Hence we see that all are not exercised with the same kind of cross. While the heavenly Physician treats some more gently, in the case of others he employs harsher remedies, his purpose being to provide a cure for all. Still none is left free and untouched, because he knows that all, without a single exception, are diseased.

6. We may add, that our most merciful Father requires not only to prevent our weakness, but often to correct our past faults, that he may keep us in due obedience. Therefore, whenever we are afflicted we ought immediately to call to mind our past life. In this way we will find that the faults which we have committed are deserving of such castigation. And yet the exhortation to patience is not to be founded chiefly on the acknowledgment of sin. For Scripture supplies a far better consideration when it says, that in adversity "we are chastened of the Lord, that we should not be condemned with the

world" (1 Cor. xi. 32). Therefore, in the very bitterness of tribulation we ought to recognise the kindness and mercy of our Father, since even then he ceases not to further our salvation. For he afflicts, not that he may ruin or destroy, but rather that he may deliver us from the condemnation of the world. Let this thought lead us to what Scripture elsewhere teaches: "My son, despise not the chastening of the Lord; neither be weary of his correction: For whom the Lord loveth he correcteth; even as a father the son in whom he delighteth" (Prov. iii. 11, 12). When we perceive our Father's rod, is it not our part to behave as obedient docile sons, rather than rebelliously imitate desperate men, who are hardened in wickedness? God dooms us to destruction, if he does not, by correction, call us back when we have fallen off from him, so that it is truly said, "If ye be without chastisement," "then are ye bastards, and not sons" (Heb. xii. 8). We are most perverse then if we cannot bear him while he is manifesting his good-will to us, and the care which he takes of our salvation. Scripture states the difference between believers and unbelievers to be, that the latter, as the slaves of inveterate and deep-seated iniquity, only become worse and more obstinate under the lash; whereas the former, like free-born sons, turn to repentance. Now, therefore, choose your class. But as I have already spoken of this subject, it is sufficient to have here briefly adverted to it.

7. There is singular consolation, moreover, when we are persecuted for righteousness' sake. For our thought should then be, How high the honour which God bestows upon us in distinguishing us by the special badge of his soldiers. By suffering persecution for righteousness' sake, I mean not only striving for the defence of the Gospel, but for the defence of righteousness in any way. Whether, therefore, in maintaining the truth of God against the lies of Satan, or defending the good and innocent against the injuries of the bad, we are obliged to incur the offence and hatred of the world, so as to endanger life, fortune, or honour, let us not grieve or decline so far to spend ourselves for God; let us not think ourselves wretched in those things in which he with his own lips has pronounced us blessed (Matth. v. 10). Poverty, indeed, considered in itself, is misery; so are exile, contempt, imprisonment, ignominy: in fine, death itself is the last of all calamities. But when the favour of God breathes upon us, there is none of these things which may not turn out to our happiness. Let us then be contented with the testimony of Christ rather than with the false estimate of the flesh, and then, after the example of the Apostles, we will rejoice in being "counted worthy to suffer shame for his name" (Acts v. 41). For why? If, while conscious of our innocence, we are deprived of our substance by the wickedness of man, we are, no doubt, humanly speaking, reduced to poverty; but in truth our riches in heaven are increased: if driven from our homes, we have a more welcome reception into the family of God; if vexed and despised, we are more firmly rooted in Christ; if stigmatised by disgrace and ignominy, we have a higher place in the kingdom of God;

and if we are slain, entrance is thereby given us to eternal life. The Lord having set such a price upon us, let us be ashamed to estimate ourselves at less than the shadowy and evanescent allurements of the present life.

8. Since by these, and similar considerations, Scripture abundantly solaces us for the ignominy or calamities which we endure in defence of righteousness, we are very ungrateful if we do not willingly and cheerfully receive them at the hand of the Lord, especially since this form of the cross is the most appropriate to believers, being that by which Christ desires to be glorified in us, as Peter also declares (1 Pet. iv. 11, 14). But as to ingenuous natures, it is more bitter to suffer disgrace than a hundred deaths, Paul expressly reminds us that not only persecution, but also disgrace awaits us, "because we trust in the living God" (1 Tim. iv. 10). So in another passage he bids us, after his example, walk "by evil report and good report" (2 Cor. vi. 8). The cheerfulness required, however, does not imply a total insensibility to pain. The saints could show no patience under the cross if they were not both tortured with pain and grievously molested. Were there no hardship in poverty, no pain in disease, no sting in ignominy, no fear in death, where would be the fortitude and moderation in enduring them? But while every one of these, by its inherent bitterness, naturally vexes the mind, the believer in this displays his fortitude, that though fully sensible of the bitterness, and labouring grievously, he still withstands and struggles boldly; in this displays his patience, that though sharply stung, he is however curbed by the fear of God from breaking forth into any excess; in this displays his alacrity, that though pressed with sorrow and sadness, he rests satisfied with spiritual consolation from God.

9. This conflict which believers maintain against the natural feeling of pain, while they study moderation and patience, Paul elegantly describes in these words: "We are troubled on every side, yet not distressed; we are perplexed, but not in despair; persecuted, but not forsaken; cast down, but not destroyed" (2 Cor. iv. 8, 9). You see that to bear the cross patiently is not to have your feelings altogether blunted, and to be absolutely insensible to pain, according to the absurd description which the Stoics of old gave of their hero as one who, divested of humanity, was affected in the same way by adversity and prosperity, grief and joy; or rather, like a stone, was not affected by anything. And what did they gain by that sublime wisdom? they exhibited a shadow of patience, which never did, and never can, exist among men. Nay, rather by aiming at a too exact and rigid patience, they banished it altogether from human life. Now also we have among Christians a new kind of Stoics, who hold it vicious not only to groan and weep, but even to be sad and anxious. These paradoxes are usually started by indolent men who, employing themselves more in speculation than in action, can do nothing else for us than beget such paraxoxes. But we have nothing to do with

that iron philosophy which our Lord and Master condemned—not only in word, but also by his own example. For he both grieved and shed tears for his own and others' woes. Nor did he teach his disciples differently: "Ye shall weep and lament, but the world shall rejoice" (John xvi. 20). And lest any one should regard this as vicious, he expressly declares, "Blessed are they that mourn" (Matth. v. 4). And no wonder. If all tears are condemned, what shall we think of our Lord himself, whose "sweat was as it were great drops of blood falling down to the ground"? Luke xxii. 44; Matth. xxvi. 38.) If every kind of fear is a mark of unbelief, what place shall we assign to the dread which, it is said, in no slight degree amazed him; if all sadness is condemned, how shall we justify him when he confesses, "My soul is exceeding sorrowful, even unto death"?

10. I wished to make these observations to keep pious minds from despair, lest, from feeling it impossible to divest themselves of the natural feeling of grief, they might altogether abandon the study of patience. This must necessarily be the result with those who convert patience into stupor, and a brave and firm man into a block. Scripture gives saints the praise of endurance when, though afflicted by the hardships they endure, they are not crushed; though they feel bitterly, they are at the same time filled with spiritual joy; though pressed with anxiety, breathe exhilarated by the consolation of God. Still there is a certain degree of repugnance in their hearts, because natural sense shuns and dreads what is adverse to it, while pious affection, even through these difficulties, tries to obey the divine will. This repugnance the Lord expressed when he thus addressed Peter: "Verily, verily, I say unto thee, When thou wast young, thou girdedst thyself and walkedst whither thou wouldest: but when thou shalt be old, thou shalt stretch forth thy hands, and another shall gird thee, and carry thee whither thou wouldest not" (John xxi. 18). It is not probable, indeed, that when it became necessary to glorify God by death, he was driven to it unwilling and resisting; had it been so, little praise would have been due to his martyrdom. But though he obeyed the divine ordination with the greatest alacrity of heart, yet, as he had not divested himself of humanity, he was distracted by a double will. When he thought of the bloody death which he was to die, struck with horror, he would willingly have avoided it: on the other hand, when he considered that it was God who called him to it, his fear was vanquished and suppressed, and he met death cheerfully. It must therefore be our study, if we would be disciples of Christ, to imbue our minds with such reverence and obedience to God as may tame and subjugate all affections contrary to his appointment. In this way, whatever be the kind of cross to which we are subjected, we shall in the greatest straits firmly maintain our patience. Adversity will have its bitterness, and sting us. When afflicted with disease, we shall groan and be disquieted, and long for health; pressed with

poverty, we shall feel the stings of anxiety and sadness, feel the pain of ignominy, contempt, and injury, and pay the tears due to nature at the death of our friends; but our conclusion will always be, The Lord so willed it, therefore let us follow his will. Nay, amid the pungency of grief, among groans and tears, this thought will necessarily suggest itself, and incline us cheerfully to endure the things for which we are so afflicted.

11. But since the chief reason for enduring the cross has been derived from a consideration of the divine will, we must in few words explain wherein lies the difference between philosophical and Christian patience. Indeed, very few of the philosophers advanced so far as to perceive that the hand of God tries us by means of affliction, and that we ought in this matter to obey God. The only reason which they adduce is, that *so it must be.* But is not this just to say, that we must yield to God, because it is in vain to contend against him? For if we obey God only because it is necessary, provided we can escape, we shall cease to obey him. But what Scripture calls us to consider in the will of God is very different—namely, first justice and equity, and then a regard to our own salvation. Hence Christian exhortations to patience are of this nature, Whether poverty, or exile, or imprisonment, or contumely, or disease, or bereavement, or any such evil affects us, we must think that none of them happens except by the will and providence of God; moreover, that everything he does is in the most perfect order. What! do not our numberless daily faults deserve to be chastised, more severely, and with a heavier rod than his mercy lays upon us? Is it not most right that our flesh should be subdued, and be, as it were, accustomed to the yoke, so as not to rage and wanton as it lists? Are not the justice and the truth of God worthy of our suffering on their account?[1] But if the equity of God is undoubtedly displayed in affliction, we cannot murmur or struggle against them without iniquity. We no longer hear the frigid cant, Yield, because it is necessary; but a living and energetic precept, Obey, because it is unlawful to resist; bear patiently, because impatience is rebellion against the justice of God. Then as that only seems to us attractive which we perceive to be for our own safety and advantage, here also our heavenly Father consoles us, by the assurance, that in the very cross with which he afflicts us he provides for our salvation. But if it is clear that tribulations are salutary to us, why should we not receive them with calm and grateful minds? In bearing them patiently we are not submitting to necessity, but resting satisfied with our own good. The effect of these thoughts is, that to whatever extent our minds are contracted by the bitterness which we naturally feel under the cross, to the same extent will they be expanded with spiritual joy. Hence arises thanksgiving, which cannot exist unless joy be felt. But if the praise of the Lord

[1] See end of sec. 4, and sec. 5, 7, 8.

and thanksgiving can emanate only from a cheerful and gladdened breast, and there is nothing which ought to interrupt these feelings in us, it is clear how necessary it is to temper the bitterness of the cross with spiritual joy.

CHAPTER IX.

OF MEDITATING ON THE FUTURE LIFE.

The three divisions of this chapter,—I. The principal use of the cross is, that it in various ways accustoms us to despise the present, and excites us to aspire to the future life, sec. 1, 2. II. In withdrawing from the present life we must neither shun it nor feel hatred for it; but desiring the future life, gladly quit the present at the command of our sovereign Master, sec. 3, 4. III. Our infirmity in dreading death described. The correction and safe remedy, sec. 6.

Sections.

1. The design of God in afflicting his people. 1. To accustom us to despise the present life. Our infatuated love of it. Afflictions employed as the cure. 2. To lead us to aspire to heaven.
2. Excessive love of the present life prevents us from duly aspiring to the other. Hence the disadvantages of prosperity. Blindness of the human judgment. Our philosophising on the vanity of life only of momentary influence. The necessity of the cross.
3. The present life an evidence of the divine favour to his people; and, therefore, not to be detested. On the contrary, should call forth thanksgiving. The crown of victory in heaven after the contest on earth.
4. Weariness of the present life how to be tempered. The believer's estimate of life. Comparison of the present and the future life. How far the present life should be hated.
5. Christians should not tremble at the fear of death. Two reasons. Objection. Answer. Other reasons.
6. Reasons continued. Conclusion.

1. WHATEVER be the kind of tribulation with which we are afflicted, we should always consider the end of it to be, that we may be trained to despise the present, and thereby stimulated to aspire to the future life. For since God well knows how strongly we are inclined by nature to a slavish love of this world, in order to prevent us from clinging too strongly to it, he employs the fittest reason for calling us back, and shaking off our lethargy. Every one of us, indeed, would be thought to aspire and aim at heavenly immortality during the whole course of his life. For we would be ashamed in no respect to excel the lower animals; whose condition would not be at all inferior to ours, had we not a hope of immortality beyond the grave. But when you attend to the plans, wishes, and actions of each, you see nothing in them but the earth. Hence our stupidity; our minds being so dazzled with the glare of wealth, power, and honours, that they can see no farther. The heart also, engrossed with avarice, ambition, and lust, is weighed down and cannot rise above them. In short, the whole soul, ensnared by the allurements of the flesh, seeks its happiness on the earth. To meet this disease, the Lord makes his people sensible of the vanity of the present life,

by a constant proof of its miseries. Thus, that they may not promise themselves deep and lasting peace in it, he often allows them to be assailed by war, tumult, or rapine, or to be disturbed by other injuries. That they may not long with too much eagerness after fleeting and fading riches, or rest in those which they already possess, he reduces them to want, or, at least, restricts them to a moderate allowance, at one time by exile, at another by sterility, at another by fire, or by other means. That they may not indulge too complacently in the advantages of married life, he either vexes them by the misconduct of their partners, or humbles them by the wickedness of their children, or afflicts them by bereavement. But if in all these he is indulgent to them, lest they should either swell with vain-glory, or be elated with confidence, by diseases and dangers he sets palpably before them how unstable and evanescent are all the advantages competent to mortals. We duly profit by the discipline of the cross, when we learn that this life, estimated in itself, is restless, troubled, in numberless ways wretched, and plainly in no respect happy; that what are estimated its blessings are uncertain, fleeting, vain, and vitiated by a great admixture of evil. From this we conclude, that all we have to seek or hope for here is contest; that when we think of the crown we must raise our eyes to heaven. For we must hold, that our mind never rises seriously to desire and aspire after the future, until it has learned to despise the present life.

2. For there is no medium between the two things: the earth must either be worthless in our estimation, or keep us enslaved by an intemperate love of it. Therefore, if we have any regard to eternity, we must carefully strive to disencumber ourselves of these fetters. Moreover, since the present life has many enticements to allure us, and great semblance of delight, grace, and sweetness to soothe us, it is of great consequence to us to be now and then called off from its fascinations.[1] For what, pray, would happen, if we here enjoyed an uninterrupted course of honour and felicity, when even the constant stimulus of affliction cannot arouse us to a due sense of our misery? That human life is like smoke or a shadow, is not only known to the learned; there is not a more trite proverb among the vulgar. Considering it a fact most useful to be known, they have recommended it in many well-known expressions. Still there is no fact which we ponder less carefully, or less frequently remember. For we form all our plans just as if we had fixed our immortality on the earth. If we see a funeral, or walk among graves, as the image of death is then present to the eye, I admit we philosophise

1 French, "Or pource que la vie presente a tousiours force de delices pour nous attraire, et a grande apparence d'amenité, de grace et de douceur pour nous amieller, il nous est bien mestier d'estre retiré d'heure en d'heure, à ce que nous ne soyons point abusez, et comme ensorcelez de telles flatteries;"—Now because the present life has always a host of delights to attract us, and has great appearance of amenity, grace, and sweetness to entice us, it is of great importance to us to be hourly withdrawn, in order that we may not be deceived, and, as it were, bewitched with such flattery.

admirably on the vanity of life. We do not indeed always do so, for those things often have no effect upon us at all. But, at the best, our philosophy is momentary. It vanishes as soon as we turn our back, and leaves not the vestige of remembrance behind; in short, it passes away, just like the applause of a theatre at some pleasant spectacle. Forgetful not only of death, but also of mortality itself, as if no rumour of it had ever reached us, we indulge in supine security as expecting a terrestrial immortality. Meanwhile, if any one breaks in with the proverb, that man is the creature of a day,[1] we indeed acknowledge its truth, but, so far from giving heed to it, the thought of perpetuity still keeps hold of our minds. Who then can deny that it is of the highest importance to us all, I say not, to be admonished by words, but convinced by all possible experience of the miserable condition of our earthly life; since even when convinced we scarcely cease to gaze upon it with vicious, stupid admiration, as if it contained within itself the sum of all that is good? But if God finds it necessary so to train us, it must be our duty to listen to him when he calls, and shakes us from our torpor, that we may hasten to despise the world, and aspire with our whole heart to the future life.

3. Still the contempt which believers should train themselves to feel for the present life, must not be of a kind to beget hatred of it or ingratitude to God. This life, though abounding in all kinds of wretchedness, is justly classed among divine blessings which are not to be despised. Wherefore, if we do not recognise the kindness of God in it, we are chargeable with no little ingratitude towards him. To believers, especially, it ought to be a proof of divine benevolence, since it is wholly destined to promote their salvation. Before openly exhibiting the inheritance of eternal glory, God is pleased to manifest himself to us as a Father by minor proofs—viz. the blessings which he daily bestows upon us. Therefore, while this life serves to acquaint us with the goodness of God, shall we disdain it as if it did not contain one particle of good? We ought, therefore, to feel and be affected towards it in such a manner as to place it among those gifts of the divine benignity which are by no means to be despised. Were there no proofs in Scripture (they are most numerous and clear), yet nature herself exhorts us to return thanks to God for having brought us forth into light, granted us the use of it, and bestowed upon us all the means necessary for its preservation. And there is a much higher reason when we reflect that here we are in a manner prepared for the glory of the heavenly kingdom. For the Lord hath ordained, that those who are ultimately to be crowned in heaven must maintain a previous warfare on the earth, that they may not triumph before they have overcome the difficulties of war, and obtained the victory. Another reason is, that we here begin to experience in various ways a foretaste of the divine benignity, in

1 Latin, "Animal esse ἐφήμερον;"—is an ephemeral animal.

20–24). Wherefore, if it becomes us to live and die to the Lord, let us leave the period of our life and death at his disposal. Still let us ardently long for death, and constantly meditate upon it, and in comparison with future immortality, let us despise life, and, on account of the bondage of sin, long to renounce it whenever it shall so please the Lord.

5. But, most strange to say, many who boast of being Christians, instead of thus longing for death, are so afraid of it that they tremble at the very mention of it as a thing ominous and dreadful. We cannot wonder, indeed, that our natural feelings should be somewhat shocked at the mention of our dissolution. But it is altogether intolerable that the light of piety should not be so powerful in a Christian breast as with greater consolation to overcome and suppress that fear. For if we reflect that this our tabernacle, unstable, defective, corruptible, fading, pining, and putrid, is dissolved, in order that it may forthwith be renewed in sure, perfect, incorruptible, in fine, in heavenly glory, will not faith compel us eagerly to desire what nature dreads? If we reflect that by death we are recalled from exile to inhabit our native country, a heavenly country, shall this give us no comfort? But everything longs for permanent existence. I admit this, and therefore contend that we ought to look to future immortality, where we may obtain that fixed condition which nowhere appears on the earth. For Paul admirably enjoins believers to hasten cheerfully to death, not because they "would be unclothed, but clothed upon" (2 Cor. v. 2). Shall the lower animals, and inanimate creatures themselves, even wood and stone, as conscious of their present vanity, long for the final resurrection, that they may with the sons of God be delivered from vanity (Rom. viii. 19); and shall we, endued with the light of intellect, and more than intellect, enlightened by the Spirit of God, when our essence is in question, rise no higher than the corruption of this earth? But it is not my purpose, nor is this the place, to plead against this great perverseness. At the outset, I declared that I had no wish to engage in a diffuse discussion of common-places. My advice to those whose minds are thus timid is to read the short treatise of Cyprian De Mortalitate, unless it be more accordant with their deserts to send them to the philosophers, that by inspecting what they say on the contempt of death, they may begin to blush. This, however, let us hold as fixed, that no man has made much progress in the school of Christ who does not look forward with joy to the day of death and final resurrection (2 Tim. iv. 18; Tit. ii. 13); for Paul distinguishes all believers by this mark; and the usual course of Scripture is to direct us thither whenever it would furnish us with an argument for substantial joy. "Look up," says our Lord, "and lift up your heads: for your redemption draweth nigh" (Luke xxi. 28). Is it reasonable, I ask, that what he intended to have a powerful effect in stirring us up to alacrity and exultation should produce nothing but sadness and consternation? If it is so, why do we still glory in him as our Master?

Therefore, let us come to a sounder mind, and how repugnant so ever the blind and stupid longing of the flesh may be, let us doubt not to desire the advent of the Lord not in wish only, but with earnest sighs, as the most propitious of all events. He will come as a Redeemer to deliver us from an immense abyss of evil and misery, and lead us to the blessed inheritance of his life and glory.

6. Thus, indeed, it is; the whole body of the faithful, so long as they live on the earth, must be like sheep for the slaughter, in order that they may be conformed to Christ their head (Rom. viii. 36). Most deplorable, therefore, would their situation be did they not, by raising their mind to heaven, become superior to all that is in the world, and rise above the present aspect of affairs (1 Cor. xv. 19). On the other hand, when once they have raised their head above all earthly objects, though they see the wicked flourishing in wealth and honour, and enjoying profound peace, indulging in luxury and splendour, and revelling in all kinds of delights, though they should moreover be wickedly assailed by them, suffer insult from their pride, be robbed by their avarice, or assailed by any other passion, they will have no difficulty in bearing up under these evils. They will turn their eye to that day (Isaiah xxv. 8; Rev. vii. 17) on which the Lord will receive his faithful servants, wipe away all tears from their eyes, clothe them in a robe of glory and joy, feed them with the ineffable sweetness of his pleasures, exalt them to share with him in his greatness; in fine, admit them to a participation in his happiness. But the wicked who may have flourished on the earth, he will cast forth in extreme ignominy, will change their delights into torments, their laughter and joy into wailing and gnashing of teeth, their peace into the gnawing of conscience, and punish their luxury with unquenchable fire. He will also place their necks under the feet of the godly, whose patience they abused. For, as Paul declares, "it is a righteous thing with God to recompense tribulation to them that trouble you; and to you who are troubled rest with us, when the Lord Jesus shall be revealed from heaven" (2 Thess. i. 6, 7). This, indeed, is our only consolation; deprived of it, we must either give way to despondency, or resort to our destruction to the vain solace of the world. The Psalmist confesses, "My feet were almost gone, my steps had well nigh slipt: for I was envious at the foolish when I saw the prosperity of the wicked" (Psalm lxxiii. 3, 4); and he found no resting-place until he entered the sanctuary, and considered the latter end of the righteous and the wicked. To conclude in one word, the cross of Christ then only triumphs in the breasts of believers over the devil and the flesh, sin and sinners, when their eyes are directed to the power of his resurrection.

CHAPTER X.

HOW TO USE THE PRESENT LIFE, AND THE COMFORTS OF IT.

The divisions of this chapter are,—I. The necessity and usefulness of this doctrine. Extremes to be avoided, if we would rightly use the present life and its comforts, sec. 1, 2. II. One of these extremes—viz. the intemperance of the flesh—to be carefully avoided. Four methods of doing so described in order, sec. 3–6.

Sections.

1. Necessity of this doctrine. Use of the goods of the present life. Extremes to be avoided. 1. Excessive austerity. 2. Carnal intemperance and lasciviousness.
2. God, by creating so many mercies, consulted not only for our necessities, but also for our comfort and delight. Confirmation from a passage in the Psalms, and from experience.
3. Excessive austerity, therefore, to be avoided. So also must the wantonness of the flesh. 1. The creatures invite us to know, love, and honour the Creator. 2. This not done by the wicked, who only abuse these temporal mercies.
4. All earthly blessings to be despised in comparison of the heavenly life. Aspiration after this life destroyed by an excessive love of created objects. First, Intemperance.
5. Second, Impatience and immoderate desire. Remedy of these evils. The creatures assigned to our use. Man still accountable for the use he makes of them.
6. God requires us in all our actions to look to his calling. Use of this doctrine. It is full of comfort.

1. By such rudiments we are at the same time well instructed by Scripture in the proper use of earthly blessings, a subject which, in forming a scheme of life, is by no means to be neglected. For if we are to live, we must use the necessary supports of life; nor can we even shun those things which seem more subservient to delight than to necessity. We must therefore observe a mean, that we may use them with a pure conscience, whether for necessity or for pleasure. This the Lord prescribes by his word, when he tells us that to his people the present life is a kind of pilgrimage by which they hasten to the heavenly kingdom. If we are only to pass through the earth, there can be no doubt that we are to use its blessings only in so far as they assist our progress, rather than retard it. Accordingly, Paul, not without cause, admonishes us to use this world without abusing it, and to buy possessions as if we were selling them (1 Cor. vii. 30, 31). But as this is a slippery place, and there is great danger of falling on either side, let us fix our feet where we can stand safely. There have been some good and holy men who, when they saw intemperance and luxury perpetually carried to excess, if not strictly curbed, and were desirous to correct so pernicious an evil, imagined that there was no other method than to allow man to use corporeal goods

only in so far as they were necessaries: a counsel pious indeed, but unnecessarily austere; for it does the very dangerous thing of binding consciences in closer fetters than those in which they are bound by the word of God. Moreover, necessity, according to them,[1] was abstinence from everything which could be wanted, so that they held it scarcely lawful to make any addition to bread and water. Others were still more austere, as is related of Cratetes the Theban, who threw his riches into the sea, because he thought that unless he destroyed them they would destroy him. Many also in the present day, while they seek a pretext for carnal intemperance in the use of external things, and at the same time would pave the way for licentiousness, assume for granted, what I by no means concede, that this liberty is not to be restrained by any modification, but that it is to be left to every man's conscience to use them as far as he thinks lawful. I indeed confess that here consciences neither can nor ought to be bound by fixed and definite laws; but that Scripture having laid down general rules for the legitimate use, we should keep within the limits which they prescribe.

2. Let this be our principle, that we err not in the use of the gifts of Providence when we refer them to the end for which their author made and destined them, since he created them for our good, and not for our destruction. No man will keep the true path better than he who shall have this end carefully in view. Now then, if we consider for what end he created food, we shall find that he consulted not only for our necessity, but also for our enjoyment and delight. Thus, in clothing, the end was, in addition to necessity, comeliness and honour; and in herbs, fruits, and trees, besides their various uses, gracefulness of appearance and sweetness of smell. Were it not so, the Prophet would not enumerate among the mercies of God "wine that maketh glad the heart of man, and oil to make his face to shine" (Ps. civ. 15). The Scriptures would not everywhere mention, in commendation of his benignity, that he had given such things to men. The natural qualities of things themselves demonstrate to what end, and how far, they may be lawfully enjoyed. Has the Lord adorned flowers with all the beauty which spontaneously presents itself to the eye, and the sweet odour which delights the sense of smell, and shall it be unlawful for us to enjoy that beauty and this odour? What? Has he not so distinguished colours as to make some more agreeable than others? Has he not given qualities to gold and silver, ivory and marble, thereby rendering them precious above other metals or stones? In short, has he not given many things a value without having any necessary use?

3. Have done, then, with that inhuman philosophy which, in allowing no use of the creatures but for neccessity, not only maliciously deprives us of the lawful fruit of the divine beneficence, but cannot be realised without depriving man of all his senses, and reducing him

1 See Chrysost. ad Heb. xi. As to Cratetes the Theban, see Plutarch, Lib. de Vitand.ære alien. and Philostratus in Vita Apollonii.

to a block. But, on the other hand, let us with no less care guard against the lusts of the flesh, which, if not kept in order, break through all bounds, and are, as I have said, advocated by those who, under pretence of liberty, allow themselves every sort of licence. First, one restraint is imposed when we hold that the object of creating all things was to teach us to know their author, and feel grateful for his indulgence. Where is the gratitude, if you so gorge or stupify yourself with feasting and wine as to be unfit for offices of piety, or the duties of your calling? Where the recognition of God, if the flesh, boiling forth in lust through excessive indulgence, infects the mind with its impurity, so as to lose the discernment of honour and rectitude? Where thankfulness to God for clothing, if on account of sumptuous raiment we both admire ourselves and disdain others? if, from a love of show and splendour, we pave the way for immodesty? Where our recognition of God, if the glare of these things captivates our minds? For many are so devoted to luxury in all their senses, that their mind lies buried: many are so delighted with marble, gold, and pictures, that they become marble-hearted—are changed as it were into metal, and made like painted figures. The kitchen, with its savoury smells, so engrosses them that they have no spiritual savour. The same thing may be seen in other matters. Wherefore it is plain that there is here great necessity for curbing licentious abuse, and conforming to the rule of Paul, "make not provision for the flesh to fulfil the lusts thereof" (Rom. xiii. 14). Where too much liberty is given to them, they break forth without measure or restraint.

4. There is no surer or quicker way of accomplishing this than by despising the present life and aspiring to celestial immortality. For hence two rules arise: First, "it remaineth, that both they that have wives be as though they had none;" "and they that use this world, as not abusing it" (1 Cor. vii. 29, 31). Secondly, we must learn to be no less placid and patient in enduring penury, than moderate in enjoying abundance. He who makes it his rule to use this world as if he used it not, not only cuts off all gluttony in regard to meat and drink, and all effeminacy, ambition, pride, excessive show, and austerity, in regard to his table, his house, and his clothes, but removes every care and affection which might withdraw or hinder him from aspiring to the heavenly life, and cultivating the interest of his soul.[1] It was well said by Cato: Luxury causes great care, and produces great carelessness as to virtue; and it is an old proverb,—Those who are much occupied with the care of the body, usually give little care to the soul. Therefore, while the liberty of the Christian in external matters is not to be tied down to a strict rule, it is, however, subject to this law—he must indulge as little as possible; on the other hand,

[1] French, "Parer notre ame de ses vrais ornemens;"—deck our soul with its true ornaments.

it must be his constant aim, not only to curb luxury, but to cut off all show of superfluous abundance, and carefully beware of converting a help into a hinderance.

5. Another rule is, that those in narrow and slender circumstances should learn to bear their wants patiently, that they may not become immoderately desirous of things, the moderate use of which implies no small progress in the school of Christ. For in addition to the many other vices which accompany a longing for earthly good, he who is impatient under poverty almost always betrays the contrary disease in abundance. By this I mean, that he who is ashamed of a sordid garment will be vain-glorious of a splendid one; he who not contented with a slender, feels annoyed at the want of a more luxurious supper, will intemperately abuse his luxury if he obtains it; he who has a difficulty, and is dissatisfied in submitting to a private and humble condition, will be unable to refrain from pride if he attain to honour. Let it be the aim of all who have any unfeigned desire for piety to learn, after the example of the Apostle, "both to be full and to be hungry, both to abound and to suffer need" (Philip. iv. 12). Scripture, moreover, has a third rule for modifying the use of earthly blessings. We have already adverted to it when considering the offices of charity. For it declares that they have all been given us by the kindness of God, and appointed for our use under the condition of being regarded as trusts, of which we must one day give account. We must, therefore, administer them as if we constantly heard the words sounding in our ears, "Give an account of your stewardship." At the same time, let us remember by whom the account is to be taken—viz. by him who, while he so highly commends abstinence, sobriety, frugality, and moderation, abominates luxury, pride, ostentation, and vanity; who approves of no administration but that which is combined with charity, who with his own lips has already condemned all those pleasures which withdraw the heart from chastity and purity, or darken the intellect.

6. The last thing to be observed is, that the Lord enjoins every one of us, in all the actions of life, to have respect to our own calling. He knows the boiling restlessness of the human mind, the fickleness with which it is borne hither and thither, its eagerness to hold opposites at one time in its grasp, its ambition. Therefore, lest all things should be thrown into confusion by our folly and rashness, he has assigned distinct duties to each in the different modes of life. And that no one may presume to overstep his proper limits, he has distinguished the different modes of life by the name of callings. Every man's mode of life, therefore, is a kind of station assigned him by the Lord, that he may not be always driven about at random. So necessary is this distinction, that all our actions are thereby estimated in his sight, and often in a very different way from that in which human reason or philosophy would estimate them. There is no more illustrious deed even among philosophers than to free one's country from tyranny, and yet the private individual who stabs the tyrant is

openly condemned by the voice of the heavenly Judge. But I am unwilling to dwell on particular examples; it is enough to know that in everything the call of the Lord is the foundation and beginning of right action. He who does not act with reference to it will never, in the discharge of duty, keep the right path. He will sometimes be able, perhaps, to give the semblance of something laudable, but whatever it may be in the sight of man, it will be rejected before the throne of God; and besides, there will be no harmony in the different parts of his life. Hence, he only who directs his life to this end will have it properly framed; because, free from the impulse of rashness, he will not attempt more than his calling justifies, knowing that it is unlawful to overleap the prescribed bounds. He who is obscure will not decline to cultivate a private life, that he may not desert the post at which God has placed him. Again, in all our cares, toils, annoyances, and other burdens, it will be no small alleviation to know that all these are under the superintendence of God. The magistrate will more willingly perform his office, and the father of a family confine himself to his proper sphere. Every one in his particular mode of life will, without repining, suffer its inconveniences, cares, uneasiness, and anxiety, persuaded that God has laid on the burden. This, too, will afford admirable consolation, that in following your proper calling, no work will be so mean and sordid as not to have a splendour and value in the eye of God.

CHAPTER XI.

OF JUSTIFICATION BY FAITH. BOTH THE NAME AND THE REALITY DEFINED.

In this chapter and the seven which follow, the doctrine of Justification by Faith is expounded, and opposite errors refuted. The following may be regarded as the arrangement of these chapters:—Chapter XI. states the doctrine, and the four subsequent chapters, by destroying the righteousness of works, confirm the righteousness of faith, each in the order which appears in the respective titles of these chapters. In Chapter XII. the doctrine of Justification is confirmed by a description of perfect righteousness; in Chapter XIII. by calling attention to two precautions; in Chapter XIV. by a consideration of the commencement and progress of regeneration in the regenerate; and in Chapter XV. by two very pernicious effects which constantly accompany the righteousness of works. The three other chapters are devoted to refutation; Chapter XVI. disposes of the objections of opponents; Chapter XVII. replies to the arguments drawn from the promises of the Law or the Gospel; Chapter XVIII. refutes what is said in support of the righteousness of faith from the promise of reward.

There are three principal divisions in the Eleventh Chapter. I. The terms used in this discussion are explained, sec. 1–4. II. Osiander's dream as to essential righteousness impugned, sec. 5–13. III. The righteousness of faith established in opposition to the righteousness of works.

Sections.

14. Sophistical evasion by giving the same name to different things: Two answers.
15. Second evasion: Two answers. First answer. Pernicious consequences resulting from this evasion.
16. Second answer, showing wherein, according to Scripture, Justification consists.
17. In explanation of this doctrine of Justification, two passages of Scripture produced.
18. Another passage of Scripture.
19. Third evasion. Papistical objection to the doctrine of Justification by Faith *alone:* Three answers. Fourth evasion: Three answers.
20. Fifth evasion, founded on the application of the term Righteousness to good works, and also on their reward· Answer, confirmed by the invincible argument of Paul. Sixth evasion: Answer.
21. Osiander and the Sophists being thus refuted, the accuracy of the definition of Justification by Faith established.
22. Definition confirmed. 1. By passages of Scripture. 2. By the writings of the ancient Fathers.
23. Man justified by faith, not because by it he obtains the Spirit, and is thus made righteous, but because by faith he lays hold of the righteousness of Christ. An objection removed. An example of the doctrine of Justification by Faith from the works of Ambrose.

1. I TRUST I have now sufficiently shown[1] how man's only resource for escaping from the curse of the law, and recovering salvation, lies in faith; and also what the nature of faith is, what the benefits which it confers, and the fruits which it produces. The whole may be thus summed up: Christ given to us by the kindness of God is apprehended and possessed by faith, by means of which we obtain in particular a twofold benefit: first, being reconciled by the righteousness of Christ, God becomes, instead of a judge, an indulgent Father; and, secondly, being sanctified by his Spirit, we aspire to integrity and purity of life. This second benefit—viz. regeneration—appears to have been already sufficiently discussed. On the other hand, the subject of justification was discussed more cursorily, because it seemed of more consequence first to explain that the faith by which alone, through the mercy of God, we obtain free justification, is not destitute of good works; and also to show the true nature of these good works on which this question partly turns. The doctrine of Justification is now to be fully discussed, and discussed under the conviction, that as it is the principal ground on which religion must be supported, so it requires greater care and attention. For unless you understand first of all what your position is before God, and what the judgment which he passes upon you, you have no foundation on which your salvation can be laid, or on which piety towards God can be reared. The necessity of thoroughly understanding this subject will become more apparent as we proceed with it.

2. Lest we should stumble at the very threshold (this we should do were we to begin the discussion without knowing what the subject is), let us first explain the meaning of the expressions, *To be justified in the sight of God, To be justified by faith or by works.* A man is said to be justified in the sight of God when in the judgment of God he is deemed righteous, and is accepted on account of his righteous-

1 See Institutes, Book II. chap. vi. and vii., and Book III. from the commencement to the present chapter.

ness; for as iniquity is abominable to God, so neither can the sinner find grace in his sight, so far as he is and so long as he is regarded as a sinner. Hence, wherever sin is, there also are the wrath and vengeance of God. He, on the other hand, is justified who is regarded not as a sinner, but as righteous, and as such stands acquitted at the judgment-seat of God, where all sinners are condemned. As an innocent man, when charged before an impartial judge, who decides according to his innocence, is said to be justified by the judge, so a man is said to be justified by God when, removed from the catalogue of sinners, he has God as the witness and assertor of his righteousness. In the same manner, a man will be said to be *justified by works*, if in his life there can be found a purity and holiness which merits an attestation of righteousness at the throne of God, or if by the perfection of his works he can answer and satisfy the divine justice. On the contrary, a man will be *justified by faith* when, excluded from the righteousness of works, he by faith lays hold of the righteousness of Christ, and clothed in it appears in the sight of God not as a sinner, but as righteous. Thus we simply interpret justification, as the acceptance with which God receives us into his favour as if we were righteous; and we say that this justification consists in the forgiveness of sins and the imputation of the righteousness of Christ (see sec. 21 and 23).

3. In confirmation of this there are many clear passages of Scripture. First, it cannot be denied that this is the proper and most usual signification of the term. But as it were too tedious to collect all the passages, and compare them with each other, let it suffice to have called the reader's attention to the fact: he will easily convince himself of its truth. I will only mention a few passages in which the justification of which we speak is expressly handled. First, when Luke relates that all the people that heard Christ "justified God" (Luke vii. 29), and when Christ declares, that "Wisdom is justified of all her children" (Luke vii. 35), Luke means not that they conferred righteousness, which always dwells in perfection with God, although the whole world should attempt to wrest it from him, nor does Christ mean that the doctrine of salvation is made just: this it is in its own nature; but both modes of expression are equivalent to attributing due praise to God and his doctrine. On the other hand, when Christ upbraids the Pharisees for justifying themselves (Luke xvi. 15), he means not that they acquired righteousness by acting properly, but that they ambitiously courted a reputation for righteousness of which they were destitute. Those acquainted with Hebrew understand the meaning better; for in that language the name of wicked is given not only to those who are conscious of wickedness, but to those who receive sentence of condemnation. Thus, when Bathsheba says, "I and my son Solomon shall be counted offenders," she does not acknowledge a crime, but complains that she and her son will be exposed to the disgrace of being numbered among reprobates and criminals (1 Kings i. 21). It is, indeed, plain from the

context that the term even in Latin[1] must be thus understood—viz. *relatively*—and does not denote any quality. In regard to the use of the term with reference to the present subject, when Paul speaks of the Scripture, "foreseeing that God would justify the heathen through faith" (Gal. iii. 8), what other meaning can you give it than that God imputes righteousness by faith? Again, when he says "that he (God) might be just, and the justifier of him who believeth in Jesus" (Rom. iii. 26), what can the meaning be, if not that God, in consideration of their faith, frees them from the condemnation which their wickedness deserves? This appears still more plainly at the conclusion, when he exclaims, "Who shall lay anything to the charge of God's elect? It is God that justifieth. Who is he that condemneth? It is Christ that died, yea rather, that is risen again, who is even at the right hand of God, who also maketh intercession for us" (Rom. viii. 33, 34). For it is just as if he had said, Who shall accuse those whom God has acquitted? Who shall condemn those for whom Christ pleads? *To justify*, therefore, is nothing else than to acquit from the charge of guilt, as if innocence were proved. Hence, when God justifies us through the intercession of Christ, he does not acquit us on a proof of our own innocence, but by an imputation of righteousness, so that though not righteous in ourselves, we are deemed righteous in Christ. Thus it is said in Paul's discourse, in the Acts, "Through this man is preached unto you the forgiveness of sins; and by him all that believe are justified from all things from which ye could not be justified by the law of Moses" (Acts xiii. 38, 39). You see that after remission of sins justification is set down by way of explanation; you see plainly that it is used for acquittal; you see how it cannot be obtained by the works of the law; you see that it is entirely through the interposition of Christ; you see that it is obtained by faith; you see, in fine, that satisfaction intervenes, since it is said that we are justified from our sins by Christ. Thus when the publican is said to have gone down to his house "justified" (Luke xviii. 14), it cannot be held that he obtained this justification by any merit of works. All that is said is, that after obtaining the pardon of sins he was regarded in the sight of God as righteous. He was justified, therefore, not by any approval of works, but by gratuitous acquittal on the part of God. Hence Ambrose elegantly terms confession of sins "legal justification" (Ambrose on Psalm cxviii. Serm. x.).

4. Without saying more about the term, we shall have no doubt as to the thing meant if we attend to the description which is given of it. For Paul certainly designates justification by the term *acceptance*, when he says to the Ephesians, "Having predestinated us unto the adoption of children by Jesus Christ to himself, according to the good pleasure of his will, to the praise of the glory of his grace, wherein he

[1] Latin, "etiam dum Latine legitur."—French, "mesme en Grec et en Latin;" even in Greek and Latin.

hath made us accepted in the Beloved" (Eph. i. 5, 6). His meaning is the very same as where he elsewhere says, "being justified freely by his grace" (Rom. iii. 24). In the fourth chapter of the Epistle to the Romans, he first terms it the *imputation* of righteousness, and hesitates not to place it in forgiveness of sins: "Even as David also describeth the blessedness of the man unto whom God imputeth righteousness without works, saying, Blessed are they whose iniquities are forgiven" &c. (Rom. iv. 6–8). There, indeed, he is not speaking of a part of justification, but of the whole. He declares, moreover, that a definition of it was given by David, when he pronounced him *blessed* who has obtained the *free* pardon of his sins. Whence it appears that this righteousness of which he speaks is simply opposed to judicial guilt.[1] But the most satisfactory passage on this subject is that in which he declares the sum of the Gospel message to be reconciliation to God, who is pleased, through Christ, to receive us into favour by not imputing our sins (2 Cor v. 18–21). Let my readers carefully weigh the whole context. For Paul shortly after adding, by way of explanation, in order to designate the mode of reconciliation, that Christ who knew no sin was made sin for us, undoubtedly understands by reconciliation nothing else than justification. Nor, indeed, could it be said, as he elsewhere does, that we are made righteous "by the obedience" of Christ (Rom. v. 19), were it not that we are deemed righteous in the sight of God in him and not in ourselves.

5. But as Osiander has introduced a kind of monstrosity termed *essential righteousness*, by which, although he designed not to abolish free righteousness, he involves it in darkness, and by that darkness deprives pious minds of a serious sense of divine grace;[2] before I pass to other matters, it may be proper to refute this delirious dream. And, first, the whole speculation is mere empty curiosity. He, indeed, heaps together many passages of Scripture showing that Christ is one with us, and we likewise one with him, a point which needs no proof; but he entangles himself by not attending to the bond of this unity. The explanation of all difficulties is easy to us, who hold that we are united to Christ by the secret agency of his Spirit, but he had formed some idea akin to that of the Manichees, desiring to transfuse the divine essence into men.[3] Hence his other notion, that Adam was formed in the image of God, because even before the fall Christ was destined to be the model of human nature. But as I study brevity, I will confine myself to the matter in hand. He says, that we are one with Christ. This we admit, but still we deny that

1 French, "Dont il appert qu'il note ces deux choses comme opposites, Estre justifies et Estre tenu coulpable; à ce que le proces soit fait à l'homme qui aura failli;"—whence it appears that he sets down as opposites the two things, To be justified, and To be held guilty, in that the process is brought against man who has failed.

2 French, "Que les poures ames ne sauroyent comprendre en telle obscurité la grace de Christ;"—that poor souls cannot in such obscurity comprehend the grace of Christ.

3 French, "C'est, que l'ame est de l'essence de Dieu;"—that is, that the soul is of the essence of God.

the essence of Christ is confounded with ours. Then we say that he absurdly endeavours to support his delusions by means of this principle: that Christ is our righteousness, because he is the eternal God, the fountain of righteousness, the very righteousness of God. My readers will pardon me for now only touching on matters which method requires me to defer to another place. But although he pretends that, by the term essential righteousness, he merely means to oppose the sentiment that we are reputed righteous on account of Christ, he however clearly shows, that not contented with that righteousness, which was procured for us by the obedience and sacrificial death of Christ, he maintains that we are substantially righteous in God by an infused essence as well as quality. For this is the reason why he so vehemently contends, that not only Christ but the Father and the Spirit dwell in us. The fact I admit to be true, but still I maintain it is wrested by him. He ought to have attended to the mode of dwelling—viz. that the Father and the Spirit are in Christ; and as in him the fulness of the Godhead dwells, so in him we possess God entire. Hence, whatever he says separately concerning the Father and the Spirit, has no other tendency than to lead away the simple from Christ. Then he introduces a substantial mixture, by which God, transfusing himself into us, makes us as it were a part of himself. Our being made one with Christ by the agency of the Spirit, he being the head and we the members, he regards as almost nothing unless his essence is mingled with us. But, as I have said, in the case of the Father and the Spirit he more clearly betrays his views—namely, that we are not justified by the mere grace of the Mediator, and that righteousness is not simply or entirely offered to us in his person, but that we are made partakers of divine righteousness when God is essentially united to us.

6. Had he only said, that Christ by justifying us becomes ours by an essential union, and that he is our head not only in so far as he is man, but that as the essence of the divine nature is diffused into us, he might indulge his dreams with less harm, and perhaps, it were less necessary to contest the matter with him; but since this principle is like a cuttle-fish, which, by the ejection of dark and inky blood, conceals its many tails,[1] if we would not knowingly and willingly allow ourselves to be robbed of that righteousness which alone gives us full assurance of our salvation, we must strenuously resist. For, in the whole of this discussion, the noun *righteousness*, and the verb *to justify*, are extended by Osiander to two parts; to be justified being not only to be reconciled to God by a free pardon, but also to be made just; and righteousness being not a free impu-

1 French, "Mais comme le principe qu'il prend est comme une seche, laquelle en jettant son sang qui est noir comme encre, trouble l'eau d'alentour pour cacher une grande multitude de queues;"—But as the principle which he adopts is like a cuttle-fish, which, casting out its blood, which is black as ink, troubles the water all around, to hide a great multitude of tails.

tation, but the holiness and integrity which the divine essence dwelling in us inspires. And he vehemently asserts (see sec. 8) that Christ is himself our righteousness, not in so far as he, by expiating sins, appeased the Father, but because he is the eternal God and life. To prove the first point—viz. that God justifies not only by pardoning but by regenerating—he asks, whether he leaves those whom he justifies as they were by nature, making no change upon their vices? The answer is very easy: as Christ cannot be divided into parts, so the two things, justification and sanctification, which we perceive to be united together in him, are inseparable. Whomsoever, therefore, God receives into his favour, he presents with the Spirit of adoption, whose agency forms them anew into his image. But if the brightness of the sun cannot be separated from its heat, are we therefore to say, that the earth is warmed by light and illumined by heat? Nothing can be more apposite to the matter in hand than this simile. The sun by its heat quickens and fertilises the earth; by its rays enlightens and illumines it. Here is a mutual and undivided connection, and yet reason itself prohibits us from transferring the peculiar properties of the one to the other. In the confusion of a twofold grace, which Osiander obtrudes upon us, there is a similar absurdity. Because those whom God freely regards as righteous, he in fact renews to the cultivation of righteousness, Osiander confounds that free acceptance with this gift of regeneration, and contends that they are one and the same. But Scripture, while combining both, classes them separately, that it may the better display the manifold grace of God. Nor is Paul's statement superfluous, that Christ is made unto us "righteousness and sanctification" (1 Cor. i. 30). And whenever he argues from the salvation procured for us, from the paternal love of God and the grace of Christ, that we are called to purity and holiness, he plainly intimates, that to be justified is something else than to be made new creatures. Osiander on coming to Scripture corrupts every passage which he quotes. Thus when Paul says, "to him that worketh not, but believeth on him that justifieth the ungodly, his faith is counted for righteousness," he expounds *justifying* as *making just*. With the same rashness he perverts the whole of the fourth chapter to the Romans. He hesitates not to give a similar gloss to the passage which I lately quoted, "Who shall lay any thing to the charge of God's elect? It is God that justifieth." Here it is plain that guilt and acquittal simply are considered, and that the Apostle's meaning depends on the antithesis. Therefore his futility is detected both in his argument and his quotations for support from Scripture. He is not a whit sounder in discussing the term righteousness, when it is said, that faith was imputed to Abraham for righteousness after he had embraced Christ (who is the righteousness of God and God himself), and was distinguished by excellent virtues. Hence it appears, that two things which are perfect are viciously converted by him into one which is corrupt. For the righteousness which is there mentioned pertains not to the whole course of life; or rather, the Spirit testifies, that though Abraham greatly excelled in virtue, and by long perseverance in it had made so much progress, the only way in which he pleased God was by receiving the grace which was offered by the promise, in faith. From this it follows, that, as Paul justly maintains, there is no room for works in justification.

7. When he objects that the power of justifying exists not in faith, considered in itself, but only as receiving Christ, I willingly admit it. For did faith justify of itself, or (as it is expressed) by its own intrinsic virtue, as it is always weak and imperfect, its efficacy would be partial, and thus our righteousness being maimed, would give us only a portion of salvation. We indeed imagine nothing of the kind, but say, that, properly speaking, God alone justifies. The same thing we likewise transfer to Christ, because he was given to us for righteousness; while we compare faith to a kind of vessel, because we are incapable of receiving Christ, unless we are emptied and come with open mouth to receive his grace. Hence it follows, that we do not withdraw the power of justifying from Christ, when we hold that, previous to his righteousness, he himself is received by faith. Still, however, I admit not the tortuous figure of the sophist, that faith is Christ; as if a vessel of clay were a treasure, because gold is deposited in it.[1] And yet this is no reason why faith, though in itself of no dignity or value, should not justify us by giving Christ; just as such a vessel filled with coin may give wealth. I say, therefore, that faith, which is only the instrument for receiving justification, is ignorantly confounded with Christ, who is the material cause, as well as the author and minister of this great blessing. This disposes of the difficulty—viz. how the term *faith* is to be understood when treating of justification.

8. Osiander goes still farther in regard to the mode of receiving Christ, holding, that by the ministry of the external word the internal word is received; that he may thus lead us away from the priesthood of Christ, and his office of Mediator, to his eternal divinity.[2] We, indeed, do not divide Christ, but hold that he who, reconciling us to God in his flesh, bestowed righteousness upon us, is the eternal Word of God; and that he could not perform the office of Mediator, nor acquire righteousness for us, if he were not the eternal God. Osiander will have it, that as Christ is God and man, he was made our righteousness in respect not of his human but of his divine nature. But if this is a peculiar property of the Godhead, it will not be peculiar to Christ, but common to him with the Father and the Spirit, since

1 French, "Quant à d'autres folies extravagantes d'Osiander, tout homme de sain jugement les rejettera; comme quand il dit que la foy est Jesus Christ, autant que s'il disoit, qu'un pot de terre est le thresor qui est caché dedans;"—As to the other extravagant follies of Osiander, every man of sound judgment will reject them; for instance, when he says that faith is Jesus Christ, as much as if he said, that an earthen pot is the treasure which is hidden in it.

2 French, "Faisant semblant de les rauir à la divinité d'icelui;"—under pretence of leading them to his divinity.

their righteousness is one and the same. Thus it would be incongruous to say, that that which existed naturally from eternity was made ours. But granting that God was made unto us righteousness, what are we to make of Paul's interposed statement, that he was so made by God? This certainly is peculiar to the office of Mediator, for although he contains in himself the divine nature, yet he receives his own proper title, that he may be distinguished from the Father and the Spirit. But he makes a ridiculous boast of a single passage of Jeremiah, in which it is said, that Jehovah will be our righteousness (Jer. xxiii. 6; xxxiii. 16). But all he can extract from this is, that Christ, who is our righteousness, was God manifest in the flesh. We have elsewhere quoted from Paul's discourse, that God purchased the Church with his own blood (Acts xx. 28). Were any one to infer from this that the blood by which sins were expiated was divine, and of a divine nature, who could endure so foul a heresy? But Osiander, thinking that he has gained the whole cause by this childish cavil, swells, exults, and stuffs whole pages with his bombast, whereas the solution is simple and obvious—viz. that Jehovah, when made of the seed of David, was indeed to be the righteousness of believers, but in what sense Isaiah declares, "By his knowledge shall my righteous servant justify many" (Isa. liii. 11). Let us observe that it is the Father who speaks. He attributes the office of justifying to the Son, and adds the reason—because he is "righteous." He places the method, or *medium* (as it is called), in the doctrine by which Christ is known. For the word דעת is more properly to be understood in a passive sense. Hence I infer, first, that Christ was made righteousness when he assumed the form of a servant; secondly, that he justified us by his obedience to the Father; and, accordingly, that he does not perform this for us in respect of his divine nature, but according to the nature of the dispensation laid upon him. For though God alone is the fountain of righteousness, and the only way in which we are righteous is by participation with him, yet as by our unhappy revolt we are alienated from his righteousness, it is necessary to descend to this lower remedy, that Christ may justify us by the power of his death and resurrection.

9. If he objects, that this work by its excellence transcends human, and therefore can only be ascribed to the divine nature; I concede the former point, but maintain, that on the latter he is ignorantly deluded. For although Christ could neither purify our souls by his own blood, nor appease the Father by his sacrifice, nor acquit us from the charge of guilt, nor, in short, perform the office of priest, unless he had been very God, because no human ability was equal to such a burden, it is however certain that he performed all these things in his human nature. If it is asked, in what way we are justified? Paul answers, *by the obedience of Christ.* Did he obey in any other way than by assuming the form of a servant? We infer, therefore, that righteousness was manifested to us in his flesh. In like manner, in another passage (which I greatly wonder that Osiander does not

blush repeatedly to quote), he places the fountain of righteousness entirely in the incarnation of Christ, "He hath made him to be sin for us who knew no sin, that we might be made the righteousness of God in him" (2 Cor. v. 21). Osiander in turgid sentences lays hold of the expression, *righteousness of God*, and shouts victory! as if he had proved it to be his own phantom of essential righteousness,[1] though the words have a very different meaning—viz. that we are justified through the expiation made by Christ. That the righteousness of God is used for the righteousness which is approved by God, should be known to mere tyros, as in John, the praise of God is contrasted with the praise of men[2] (John xii. 43). I know that by the righteousness of God is sometimes meant that of which God is the author, and which he bestows upon us; but that here the only thing meant is, that being supported by the expiation of Christ, we are able to stand at the tribunal of God, sound readers perceive without any observation of mine. The word is not of so much importance, provided Osiander agrees with us in this, that we are justified by Christ in respect he was made an expiatory victim for us. This he could not be in his divine nature. For which reason also, when Christ would seal the righteousness and salvation which he brought to us, he holds forth the sure pledge of it in his flesh. He indeed calls himself "living bread," but, in explanation of the mode, adds, "my flesh is meat indeed, and my blood is drink indeed" (John vi. 55). The same doctrine is clearly seen in the sacraments; which, though they direct our faith to the whole, not to a part of Christ, yet, at the same time, declare that the materials of righteousness and salvation reside in his flesh; not that the mere man of himself justifies or quickens, but that God was pleased, by means of a Mediator, to manifest his own hidden and incomprehensible nature. Hence I often repeat, that Christ has been in a manner set before us as a fountain, whence we may draw what would otherwise lie without use in that deep and hidden abyss which streams forth to us in the person of the Mediator.[3] In this way, and in this meaning, I deny not that Christ, as he is God and man, justifies us; that this work is common also to

1 French, "Il magnifie la justice de Dieu tant et plus; mais c'est pour triompher comme s'il auoit gagné ce poinct, que la justice de Dieu nous est essencielle;"—He magnifies the righteousness of God above measure; but it is to triumph, as if he had gained this point, that the righteousness of God is essential to us.

2 The French adds, "signifiant, que ceux desquels il parle ont nagé entre deux eaux; pource qu'ils aimoyent mieux garder leur bonne reputation au monde, que d'etre priser devant Dieu;"—meaning, that those of whom he speaks were swimming between two streams; that they preferred keeping their good reputation in the world, to being prized in the sight of God.

3 French, "Pour ceste cause j'ay accoustume de dire que Christ nous est comme une fontaine, dont chacun peut puiser et boire à son aise et à souhait; et que par son moyen les biens celestes sourdent et decoulent à nous, lesquels ne nous profiteroyent rien demeurans en la majesté de Dieu, qui est comme une source profonde;"—For this cause I am accustomed to say, that Christ is to us like a fountain, of which every man may draw and drink at his ease, and to the fill; and that by his means heavenly blessings rise and flow to us, which blessings would profit us nothing, remaining in the majesty of God, which is, as it were, a profound abyss.

the Father and the Holy Spirit; in fine, that the righteousness of which God makes us partakers is the eternal righteousness of the eternal God, provided effect is given to the clear and valid reasons to which I have adverted.

10. Moreover, lest by his cavils he deceive the unwary, I acknowledge that we are devoid of this incomparable gift until Christ become ours. Therefore, to that union of the head and members, the residence of Christ in our hearts, in fine, the mystical union, we assign the highest rank, Christ when he becomes ours making us partners with him in the gifts with which he was endued. Hence we do not view him as at a distance and without us, but as we have put him on, and been ingrafted into his body, he deigns to make us one with himself, and, therefore, we glory in having a fellowship of righteousness with him. This disposes of Osiander's calumny, that we regard faith as righteousness; as if we were robbing Christ of his rights when we say, that, destitute in ourselves, we draw near to him by Faith, to make way for his grace, that he alone may fill us. But Osiander, spurning this spiritual union, insists on a gross mixture of Christ with believers; and, accordingly, to excite prejudice, gives the name of Zuinglians[1] to all who subscribe not to his fanatical heresy of essential righteousness, because they do not hold that, in the supper, Christ is eaten substantially. For my part, I count it the highest honour to be thus assailed bya haughty man, devoted to his own impostures; though he assails not me only, but writers of known reputation throughout the world, and whom it became him modestly to venerate. This, however, does not concern me, as I plead not my own cause, and plead the more sincerely that I am free from every sinister feeling. In insisting so vehemently on essential righteousness, and an essential inhabitation of Christ within us, his meaning is, first, that God by a gross mixture[2] transfuses himself into us, as he pretends that there is a carnal eating in the supper; and, secondly, that by instilling his own righteousness into us, he makes us really righteous with himself, since, according to him, this righteousness is as well God himself as the probity, or holiness, or integrity of God. I will not spend much time in disposing of the passages of Scripture which he adduces, and which, though used in reference to the heavenly life, he wrests to our present state. Peter says, that through the knowledge of Christ "are given unto us exceeding great and precious promises, that by them ye might be partakers of the divine nature" (2 Pet. i. 4);[3] as if we now were what the gospel promises we shall be at the final advent of Christ; nay, John reminds us, that "when he shall appear we shall be like him,

1 The Latin, "ideo Zuinglianos odiose nominat;" is in the French simply, "condamne furieusement;"—furiously condemns.

2 Latin, "crassa mixtura;"—French, "mixtion telle que les viandes que nous mangeons;"—mixture such as the victuals we eat.

3 The French adds, "Osiander tire de la que Dieu a meslée son essence avec la nostre;"—Osiander implies from this that God has mingled his essence with ours.

for we shall see him as he is" (1 John iii. 2). I only wished to give my readers a slender specimen of Osiander, it being my intention to decline the discussion of his frivolities, not because there is any difficulty in disposing of them, but because I am unwilling to annoy the reader with superfluous labour.

11. But more poison lurks in the second branch, when he says that we are righteous together with God. I think I have already sufficiently proved, that although the dogma were not so pestiferous, yet because it is frigid and jejune, and falls by its own vanity, it must justly be disrelished by all sound and pious readers. But it is impossible to tolerate the impiety which, under the pretence of a twofold righteousness, undermines our assurance of salvation, and, hurrying us into the clouds, tries to prevent us from embracing the gift of expiation in faith, and invoking God with quiet minds. Osiander derides us for teaching, that *to be justified* is a forensic term, because it behoves us to be in reality just: there is nothing also to which he is more opposed than the idea of our being justified by a free imputation. Say, then, if God does not justify us by acquitting and pardoning, what does Paul mean when he says, "God was in Christ reconciling the world unto himself, not imputing their trespasses unto them"? "He made him to be sin for us who knew no sin; that we might be made the righteousness of God in him" (2 Cor. v. 19, 21). Here I learn, first, that those who are reconciled to God are regarded as righteous: then the method is stated, God justifies by pardoning; and hence, in another place, justification is opposed to accusation (Rom. viii. 33); this antithesis clearly demonstrating that the mode of expression is derived from forensic use. And, indeed, no man, moderately versant in the Hebrew tongue (provided he is also of sedate brain), is ignorant that this phrase thus took its rise, and thereafter derived its tendency and force. Now, then, when Paul says that David "describeth the blessedness of the man unto whom God imputeth righteousness without works, saying, Blessed are they whose iniquities are forgiven" (Rom. iv. 6, 7; Ps. xxxii. 1), let Osiander say whether this is a complete or only a partial definition. He certainly does not adduce the Psalmist as a witness that pardon of sins is a part of righteousness, or concurs with something else in justifying, but he includes the whole of righteousness in gratuitous forgiveness, declaring those to be blessed "whose iniquities are forgiven, and whose sins are covered," and "to whom the Lord will not impute sin." He estimates and judges of his happiness from this, that in this way he is righteous not in reality, but by imputation.

Osiander objects that it would be insulting to God, and contrary to his nature, to justify those who still remain wicked. But it ought to be remembered, as I already observed, that the gift of justification is not separated from regeneration, though the two things are distinct. But as it is too well known by experience, that the remains of sin always exist in the righteous, it is necessary that justification should be something very different from reformation to newness of life. This latter God begins in his elect, and carries on during the whole course of life, gradually and sometimes slowly, so that if placed at his judgment-seat they would always deserve sentence of death. He justifies not partially, but freely, so that they can appear in the heavens as if clothed with the purity of Christ. No portion of righteousness could pacify the conscience. It must be decided that we are pleasing to God, as being without exception righteous in his sight. Hence it follows that the doctrine of justification is perverted and completely overthrown whenever doubt is instilled into the mind, confidence in salvation is shaken, and free and intrepid prayer is retarded; yea, whenever rest and tranquillity with spiritual joy are not established. Hence Paul argues against objectors, that "if the inheritance be of the law, it is no more of promise" (Gal. iii. 18), that in this way faith would be made vain; for if respect be had to works it fails, the holiest of men in that case finding nothing in which they can confide. This distinction between justification and regeneration (Osiander confounding the two, calls them a twofold righteousness) is admirably expressed by Paul. Speaking of his real righteousness, or the integrity bestowed upon him (which Osiander terms his essential righteousness), he mournfully exclaims, "O wretched man that I am! who shall deliver me from the body of this death?" (Rom. vii. 24); but betaking himself to the righteousness which is founded solely on the mercy of God, he breaks forth thus magnificently into the language of triumph: "Who shall lay any thing to the charge of God's elect? It is God that justifieth." "Who shall separate us from the love of Christ? shall tribulation, or distress, or persecution, or famine, or nakedness, or peril, or sword?" (Rom. viii. 33, 35.) He clearly declares that the only righteousness for him is that which alone suffices for complete salvation in the presence of God, so that that miserable bondage, the consciousness of which made him a little before lament his lot, derogates not from his confidence, and is no obstacle in his way. This diversity is well known, and indeed is familiar to all the saints who groan under the burden of sin, and yet with victorious assurance rise above all fears. Osiander's objection as to its being inconsistent with the nature of God, falls back upon himself; for though he clothes the saints with a twofold righteousness as with a coat of skins, he is, however, forced to admit, that without forgiveness no man is pleasing to God. If this be so, let him at least admit, that with reference to what is called the proportion of imputation, those are regarded as righteous who are not so in reality. But how far shall the sinner extend this gratuitous acceptance, which is substituted in the room of righteousness? Will it amount to the whole pound, or will it be only an ounce? He will remain in doubt, vibrating to this side and to that, because he will be unable to assume to himself as much righteousness as will be necessary to give confidence. It is well that he who would prescribe a law to God is not the judge in this cause. But this saying will ever stand true, "That thou mightest be justified when thou speakest, and be clear when thou judgest" (Ps. li. 4).

What arrogance to condemn the Supreme Judge when he acquits freely, and try to prevent the response from taking effect: "I will have mercy on whom I will have mercy." And yet the intercession of Moses, which God calmed by this answer, was not for pardon to some individual, but to all alike, by wiping away the guilt to which all were liable. And we, indeed, say, that the lost are justified before God by the burial of their sins; for (as he hates sin) he can only love those whom he justifies. But herein is the wondrous method of justification, that, clothed with the righteousness of Christ, they dread not the judgment of which they are worthy; and while they justly condemn themselves, are yet deemed righteous out of themselves.

12. I must admonish the reader carefully to attend to the mystery which he boasts he is unwilling to conceal from them. For after contending with great prolixity that we do not obtain favour with God through the mere imputation of the righteousness of Christ, because (to use his own words) it were impossible for God to hold those as righteous who are not so, he at length concludes that Christ was given to us for righteousness, in respect not of his human, but of his divine nature; and though this can only be found in the person of the Mediator, it is, however, the righteousness not of man, but of God. He does not now twist his rope of two righteousnesses, but plainly deprives the human nature of Christ of the office of justifying. It is worth while to understand what the nature of his argument is. It is said in the same passage that Christ is made unto us *wisdom* (1 Cor. i. 30); but this is true only of the eternal Word, and, therefore, it is not the man Christ that is made *righteousness*. I answer, that the only-begotten Son of God was indeed his eternal wisdom, but that this title is applied to him by Paul in a different way—viz. because "in him are hid all the treasures of wisdom and righteousness" (Col. ii. 3). That, therefore, which he had with the Father he manifested to us; and thus Paul's expression refers not to the essence of the Son of God, but to our use, and is fitly applied to the human nature of Christ; for although the light shone in darkness before he was clothed with flesh, yet he was a hidden light until he appeared in human nature as the *Sun of Righteousness*, and hence he calls himself the *light of the world*. It is also foolishly objected by Osiander, that justifying far transcends the power both of men and angels, since it depends not on the dignity of any creature, but on the ordination of God. Were angels to attempt to give satisfaction to God, they could have no success, because they are not appointed for this purpose, it being the peculiar office of Christ, who "hath redeemed us from the curse of the law, being made a curse for us" (Gal. iii. 13). Those who deny that Christ is our righteousness, in respect of his divine nature, are wickedly charged by Osiander with leaving only a part of Christ, and (what is worse) with making two Gods; because, while admitting that God dwells in us, they still insist that we are not justified by the righteousness of God. For

though we call Christ the author of life, inasmuch as he endured death that he might destroy him who had the power of death (Heb. ii. 14), we do not thereby rob him of this honour, in his whole character as God manifested in the flesh. We only make a distinction as to the manner in which the righteousness of God comes to us, and is enjoyed by us,—a matter as to which Osiander shamefully erred. We deny not that that which was openly exhibited to us in Christ flowed from the secret grace and power of God; nor do we dispute that the righteousness which Christ confers upon us is the righteousness of God, and proceeds from him. What we constantly maintain is, that our righteousness and life are in the death and resurrection of Christ. I say nothing of that absurd accumulation of passages with which, without selection or common understanding, he has loaded his readers, in endeavouring to show, that whenever mention is made of righteousness, this essential righteousness of his should be understood; as when David implores help from the righteousness of God. This David does more than a hundred times, and as often Osiander hesitates not to pervert his meaning. Not a whit more solid is his objection, that the name of righteousness is rightly and properly applied to that by which we are moved to act aright, but that it is God only that worketh in us both to will and to do (Phil. ii. 13). For we deny not that God by his Spirit forms us anew to holiness and righteousness of life; but we must first see whether he does this of himself, immediately, or by the hand of his Son, with whom he hath deposited all the fulness of the Holy Spirit, that out of his own abundance he may supply the wants of his members. Then, although righteousness comes to us from the secret fountain of the Godhead, it does not follow that Christ, who sanctified himself in the flesh on our account, is our righteousness in respect of his divine nature (John xvii. 19). Not less frivolous is his observation, that the righteousness with which Christ himself was righteous was divine; for had not the will of the Father impelled him, he could not have fulfilled the office assigned him. For although it has been elsewhere said that all the merits of Christ flow from the mere good pleasure of God, this gives no countenance to the phantom by which Osiander fascinates both his own eyes and those of the simple. For who will allow him to infer, that because God is the source and commencement of our righteousness, we are essentially righteous, and the essence of the divine righteousness dwells in us? In redeeming us, says Isaiah, "he (God) put on righteousness as a breastplate, and an helmet of salvation upon his head" (Isaiah lix. 17), was this to deprive Christ of the armour which he had given him, and prevent him from being a perfect Redeemer? All that the Prophet meant was, that God borrowed nothing from an external quarter, that in redeeming us he received no external aid. The same thing is briefly expressed by Paul in different terms, when he says that God set him forth "to declare his righteousness for the remission of sins." This is not the least repugnant to his doctrine: in another place, that "by the obedience of one shall many be made righteous" (Rom. v. 19). In short, every one who, by the entanglement of a twofold righteousness, prevents miserable souls from resting entirely on the mere mercy of God, mocks Christ by putting on him a crown of plaited thorns.

13. But since a great part of mankind imagine a righteousness compounded of faith and works, let us here show that there is so wide a difference between justification by faith and by works, that the establishment of the one necessarily overthrows the other. The Apostle says, "Yea doubtless, and I count all things but loss for the excellency of the knowledge of Christ Jesus my Lord: for whom I have suffered the loss of all things, and do count them but dung, that I may win Christ, and be found in him, not having mine own righteousness, which is of the law, but that which is through the faith of Christ, the righteousness which is of God by faith" (Phil. iii. 8, 9). You here see a comparison of contraries, and an intimation that every one who would obtain the righteousness of Christ must renounce his own. Hence he elsewhere declares the cause of the rejection of the Jews to have been, that "they being ignorant of God's righteousness, and going about to establish their own righteousness, have not submitted themselves unto the righteousness of God" (Rom. x. 3). If we destroy the righteousness of God by establishing our own righteousness, then, in order to obtain his righteousness, our own must be entirely abandoned. This also he shows, when he declares that boasting is not excluded by the Law, but by faith (Rom. iii. 27). Hence it follows, that so long as the minutest portion of our own righteousness remains, we have still some ground for boasting. Now if faith utterly excludes boasting, the righteousness of works cannot in any way be associated with the righteousness of faith. This meaning is so clearly expressed in the fourth chapter to the Romans as to leave no room for cavil or evasion. "If Abraham were justified by works, he hath whereof to glory;" and then it is added, "but not before God" (Rom. iv. 2). The conclusion therefore is, that he was not justified by works. He then employs another argument from contraries—viz. when *reward* is paid to works, it is done *of debt*, not *of grace;* but the righteousness of faith is of grace: therefore it is not of the merit of works. Away, then, with the dream of those who invent a righteousness compounded of faith and works, (see Calvin. ad Concilium Tridentinum).

14. The Sophists, who delight in sporting with Scripture and in empty cavils, think they have a subtle evasion when they expound *works* to mean, such as unregenerated men do literally, and by the effect of free will, without the grace of Christ, and deny that these have any reference to spiritual works.[1] Thus, according to them, man is justified by faith as well as by works, provided these are not

[1] French, "Ainsi ils disent que cela n'appartient de rien aux bonnes œuvres des fideles qui se font par la vertu du Sainct Esprit;"—Thus they say that that has no reference at all to the good works of believers, which are done by the power of the Holy Spirit.

his own works, but gifts of Christ and fruits of regeneration; Paul's only object in so expressing himself being to convince the Jews, that in trusting to their own strength they foolishly arrogated righteousness to themselves, whereas it is bestowed upon us by the Spirit of Christ alone, and not by studied efforts of our own nature. But they observe not that in the antithesis between Legal and Gospel righteousness, which Paul elsewhere introduces, all kinds of works, with whatever name adorned, are excluded (Gal. iii. 11, 12). For he says that the righteousness of the Law consists in obtaining salvation by doing what the Law requires, but that the righteousness of faith consists in believing that Christ died and rose again (Rom. x. 5–9). Moreover, we shall afterwards see, at the proper place, that the blessings of sanctification and justification, which we derive from Christ, are different. Hence it follows, that not even spiritual works are taken into account when the power of justifying is ascribed to faith. And, indeed, the passage above quoted, in which Paul declares that Abraham had no ground of glorying before God, because he was not justified by works, ought not to be confined to a literal and external form of virtue, or to the effort of free will. The meaning is, that though the life of the Patriarch had been spiritual and almost angelic, yet he could not by the merit of works have procured justification before God.

15. The Schoolmen treat the matter somewhat more grossly by mingling their preparations with it; and yet the others instil into the simple and unwary a no less pernicious dogma, when, under cover of the Spirit and grace, they hide the divine mercy, which alone can give peace to the trembling soul. We, indeed, hold with Paul, that those who fulfil the Law are justified by God; but because we are all far from observing the Law, we infer that the works which should be most effectual to justification are of no avail to us, because we are destitute of them. In regard to vulgar Papists or Schoolmen, they are here doubly wrong, both in calling faith assurance of conscience while waiting to receive from God the reward of merits, and in interpreting divine grace to mean not the imputation of gratuitous righteousness, but the assistance of the Spirit in the study of holiness. They quote from an Apostle: "He that cometh to God must believe that he is, and that he is the rewarder of them that diligently seek him" (Heb. xi. 6). But they observe not what the method of seeking is. Then in regard to the term *grace*, it is plain from their writings that they labour under a delusion. For Lombard holds that justification is given to us by Christ in two ways. "First," says he (Lombard, Sent. Lib. iii. Dist. 16, c. 11), "the death of Christ justifies us when by means of it the love by which we are made righteous is excited in our hearts; and, secondly, when by means of it sin is extinguished, sin by which the devil held us captive, but by which he cannot now procure our condemnation." You see here that the chief office of divine grace in our justification he considers to be its directing us to good works by the agency of the Holy Spirit. He intended, no doubt, to follow the opinion of Augustine, but he follows it at a distance,

and even wanders far from a true imitation of him, both obscuring what was clearly stated by Augustine, and making what in him was less pure more corrupt. The Schools have always gone from worse to worse, until at length, in their downward path, they have degenerated into a kind of Pelagianism. Even the sentiment of Augustine, or at least his mode of expressing it, cannot be entirely approved of. For although he is admirable in stripping man of all merit of righteousness, and transferring the whole praise of it to God, yet he classes the grace by which we are regenerated to newness of life under the head of sanctification.

16. Scripture, when it treats of justification by faith, leads us in a very different direction. Turning away our view from our own works, it bids us look only to the mercy of God and the perfection of Christ. The order of justification which it sets before us in this: first, God of his mere gratuitous goodness is pleased to embrace the sinner, in whom he sees nothing that can move him to mercy but wretchedness, because he sees him altogether naked and destitute of good works. He, therefore, seeks the cause of kindness in himself, that thus he may affect the sinner by a sense of his goodness, and induce him, in distrust of his own works, to cast himself entirely upon his mercy for salvation. This is the meaning of faith by which the sinner comes into the possession of salvation, when, according to the doctrine of the Gospel, he perceives that he is reconciled by God; when, by the intercession of Christ, he obtains the pardon of his sins, and is justified; and, though renewed by the Spirit of God, considers that, instead of leaning on his own works, he must look solely to the righteousness which is treasured up for him in Christ. When these things are weighed separately, they will clearly explain our view, though they may be arranged in a better order than that in which they are here presented. But it is of little consequence, provided they are so connected with each other as to give us a full exposition and solid confirmation of the whole subject.

17. Here it is proper to remember the relation which we previously established between faith and the Gospel; faith being said to justify because it receives and embraces the righteousness offered in the Gospel. By the very fact of its being said to be offered by the Gospel, all consideration of works is excluded. This Paul repeatedly declares, and in two passages, in particular, most clearly demonstrates. In the Epistle to the Romans, comparing the Law and the Gospel, he says, "Moses describeth the righteousness which is of the law, That the man which doeth those things shall live by them. But the righteousness which is of faith speaketh on this wise,—If thou shalt confess with thy mouth the Lord Jesus, and shalt believe in thine heart that God hath raised him from the dead, thou shalt be saved" (Rom. x. 5, 6, 9). Do you see how he makes the distinction between the Law and the Gospel to be, that the former gives justification to works, whereas the latter bestows it freely without any help from works? This is a notable passage, and may free us from many difficulties if

we understand that the justification which is given us by the Gospel is free from any terms of Law. It is for this reason he more than once places the promise in diametrical opposition to the Law. "If the inheritance be of the law, it is no more of promise" (Gal. iii. 18). Expressions of similar import occur in the same chapter. Undoubtedly the Law also has its promises; and, therefore, between them and the Gospel promises there must be some distinction and difference, unless we are to hold that the comparison is inept. And in what can the difference consist unless in this, that the promises of the Gospel are gratuitous, and founded on the mere mercy of God, whereas the promises of the Law depend on the condition of works? But let no prater here allege that only the righteousness which men would obtrude upon God of their own strength and free will is repudiated; since Paul declares, without exception, that the Law gained nothing by its commands, being such as none, not only of mankind in general, but none even of the most perfect, are able to fulfil. Love assuredly is the chief commandment in the Law; and since the Spirit of God trains us to love, it cannot but be a cause of righteousness in us, though that righteousness even in the saints is defective, and therefore of no value as a ground of merit.

18. The second passage is, "That no man is justified by the law in the sight of God, it is evident: for, The just shall live by faith. And the law is not of faith: but, The man that doeth them shall live in them" (Gal. iii. 11, 12; Hab. ii. 4). How could the argument hold unless it be true that works are not to be taken into account, but are to be altogether separated? The Law, he says, is different from faith. Why? Because to obtain justification by it, works are required; and hence it follows, that to obtain justification by the Gospel they are not required. From this statement, it appears that those who are justified by faith are justified independent of, nay, in the absence of, the merit of works, because faith receives that righteousness which the Gospel bestows. But the Gospel differs from the Law in this, that it does not confine justification to works, but places it entirely in the mercy of God. In like manner, Paul contends, in the Epistle to the Romans, that Abraham had no ground of glorying, because faith was imputed to him for righteousness (Rom. iv. 2); and he adds in confirmation, that the proper place for justification by faith is where there are no works to which reward is due. "To him that worketh is the reward not reckoned of grace, but of debt." What is given to faith is gratuitous, this being the force of the meaning of the words which he there employs. Shortly after he adds, "Therefore it is of faith, that it might be by grace" (Rom. iv. 16); and hence infers that the inheritance is gratuitous because it is procured by faith. How so but just because faith, without the aid of works, leans entirely on the mercy of God? And in the same sense, doubtless, he elsewhere teaches, that the righteousness of God without the Law was manifested, being witnessed by the Law and the Prophets (Rom. iii. 21); for excluding the Law, he

declares that it is not aided by works, that we do not obtain it by working, but are destitute when we draw near to receive it.

19. The reader now perceives with what fairness the Sophists of the present day cavil at our doctrine, when we say that a man is justified by faith alone (Rom. iv. 2). They dare not deny that *he is justified by faith*, seeing Scripture so often declares it; but as the word *alone* is nowhere expressly used, they will not tolerate its being added.[1] Is it so? What answer, then, will they give to the words of Paul, when he contends that righteousness is not of faith unless it be gratuitous? How can it be gratuitous, and yet by works? By what cavils, moreover, will they evade his declaration in another place, that in the Gospel the righteousness of God is manifested? (Rom. i. 17.) If righteousness is manifested in the Gospel, it is certainly not a partial or mutilated, but a full and perfect righteousness. The Law, therefore, has no part in it, and their objection to the exclusive word *alone* is not only unfounded, but is obviously absurd. Does he not plainly enough attribute everything to faith alone when he disconnects it with works? What, I would ask, is meant by the expressions, "The righteousness of God without the law is manifest;" "Being justified freely by his grace;" "Justified by faith without the deeds of the law"? (Rom. iii. 21, 24, 28). Here they have an ingenious subterfuge, one which, though not of their own devising, but taken from Origen and some ancient writers, is most childish. They pretend that the works excluded are ceremonial, not moral works. Such profit do they make by their constant wrangling, that they possess not even the first elements of logic. Do they think the Apostle was raving when he produced, in proof of his doctrine, these passages? "The man that doeth them shall live in them" (Gal. iii. 12). "Cursed is every one that continueth not in all things that are written in the book of the law to do them" (Gal. iii. 10). Unless they are themselves raving, they will not say that life was promised to the observers of ceremonies, and the curse denounced only against the transgressors of them. If these passages are to be understood of the Moral Law, there cannot be a doubt that moral works also are excluded from the power of justifying. To the same effect are the arguments which he employs. "By the deeds of the law there shall no flesh be justified in his sight: for by the law is the knowledge of sin" (Rom. iii. 20). "The law worketh wrath" (Rom. iv. 15), and therefore not righteousness. "The law cannot pacify the conscience," and therefore cannot confer righteousness. "Faith is imputed for righteousness," and therefore righteousness is not the reward of works, but is given without being due. Because "we are justified by faith," boasting is excluded. "Had there been a law given which could have given life, verily righteousness should

1 French. "Mais pource que ce mot Seule, n'y est point exprimé, ils nous reprochent qu'il est adjousté du notre;" —but because this word Alone is not expressed, they upbraid us with having it added of our own accord.

have been by the law. But the Scripture hath concluded all under sin, that the promise by faith of Jesus Christ might be given to them that believe" (Gal. iii. 21, 22). Let them maintain, if they dare, that these things apply to ceremonies, and not to morals, and the very children will laugh at their effrontery. The true conclusion therefore is, that the whole Law is spoken of when the power of justifying is denied to it.

20. Should any one wonder why the Apostle, not contented with having named works, employs this addition, the explanation is easy. However highly works may be estimated, they have their whole value more from the approbation of God than from their own dignity. For who will presume to plume himself before God on the righteousness of works, unless in so far as He approves of them? Who will presume to demand of Him a reward except in so far as He has promised it? It is owing entirely to the goodness of God that works are deemed worthy of the honour and reward of righteousness; and, therefore, their whole value consists in this, that by means of them we endeavour to manifest obedience to God. Wherefore, in another passage, the Apostle, to prove that Abraham could not be justified by works, declares, "that the covenant, that was confirmed before of God in Christ, the law, which was four hundred and thirty years after, cannot disannul, that it should make the promise of none effect" (Gal. iii. 17). The unskilful would ridicule the argument that there could be righteous works before the promulgation of the Law, but the Apostle, knowing that works could derive this value solely from the testimony and honour conferred on them by God, takes it for granted that, previous to the Law, they had no power of justifying. We see why he expressly terms them works of Law when he would deny the power of justifying to them—viz. because it was only with regard to such works that a question could be raised; although he sometimes, without addition, excepts all kinds of works whatever, as when on the testimony of David he speaks of the man to whom the Lord imputeth righteousness without works (Rom. iv. 5, 6). No cavils, therefore, can enable them to prove that the exclusion of works is not general. In vain do they lay hold of the frivolous subtilty, that the *faith alone*, by which we are justified, "*worketh by love*," and that love, therefore, is the foundation of justification. We, indeed, acknowledge with Paul, that the only faith which justifies is that which works by love (Gal. v. 6); but love does not give it its justifying power. Nay, its only means of justifying consists in its bringing us into communication with the righteousness of Christ. Otherwise the whole argument, on which the Apostle insists with so much earnestness, would fall. "To him that worketh is the reward not reckoned of grace, but of debt. But to him that worketh not, but believeth on him that justifieth the ungodly, his faith is counted for righteousness." Could he express more clearly than in this way, that there is justification in faith only where there are no works to which reward is due, and that

faith is imputed for righteousness only when righteousness is conferred freely without merit?

21. Let us now consider the truth of what was said in the definition—viz. that justification by faith is reconciliation with God, and that this consists solely in the remission of sins. We must always return to the axiom, that the wrath of God lies upon all men so long as they continue sinners. This is elegantly expressed by Isaiah in these words: "Behold, the Lord's hand is not shortened, that it cannot save; neither his ear heavy, that it cannot hear: but your iniquities have separated between you and your God, and your sins have hid his face from you, that he will not hear" (Isaiah lix. 1, 2). We are here told that sin is a separation between God and man; that His countenance is turned away from the sinner; and that it cannot be otherwise, since to have any intercourse with sin is repugnant to his righteousness. Hence the Apostle shows that man is at enmity with God until he is restored to favour by Christ (Rom. v. 8–10). When the Lord, therefore, admits him to union, he is said to justify him, because he can neither receive him into favour, nor unite him to himself, without changing his condition from that of a sinner into that of a righteous man. We add, that this is done by remission of sins. For if those whom the Lord hath reconciled to himself are estimated by works, they will still prove to be in reality sinners, while they ought to be pure and free from sin. It is evident, therefore, that the only way in which those whom God embraces are made righteous, is by having their pollutions wiped away by the remission of sins, so that this justification may be termed in one word the remission of sins.

22. Both of these become perfectly clear from the words of Paul: "God was in Christ reconciling the world unto himself, not imputing their trespasses unto them; and hath committed unto us the word of reconciliation." He then subjoins the sum of his embassy: "He hath made him to be sin for us who knew no sin; that we might be made the righteousness of God in him" (2 Cor. v. 19–21). He here uses righteousness and reconciliation indiscriminately, to make us understand that the one includes the other. The mode of obtaining this righteousness he explains to be, that our sins are not imputed to us. Wherefore, you cannot henceforth doubt how God justifies us when you hear that he reconciles us to himself by not imputing our faults. In the same manner, in the Epistle to the Romans, he proves, by the testimony of David, that righteousness is imputed without works, because he declares the man to be blessed "whose transgression is forgiven, whose sin is covered," and "unto whom the Lord imputeth not iniquity" (Rom. iv. 6; Ps. xxxii. 1, 2). There he undoubtedly uses blessedness for righteousness; and as he declares that it consists in forgiveness of sins, there is no reason why we should define it otherwise. Accordingly, Zacharias, the father of John the Baptist, sings that the knowledge of salvation consists in the forgiveness of sins (Luke i. 77). The same course

was followed by Paul when, in addressing the people of Antioch, he gave them a summary of salvation. Luke states that he concluded in this way: "Through this man is preached unto you the forgiveness of sins, and by him all that believe are justified from all things from which ye could not be justified by the law of Moses" (Acts xii. 38, 39). Thus the Apostle connects forgiveness of sins with justification in such a way as to show that they are altogether the same; and hence he properly argues that justification, which we owe to the indulgence of God, is gratuitous. Now should it seem an unusual mode of expression to say that believers are justified before God not by works, but by gratuitous acceptance, seeing it is frequently used in Scripture, and sometimes also by ancient writers. Thus Augustine says: "The righteousness of the saints in this world consists more in the forgiveness of sins than the perfection of virtue" (August. de Civitate Dei, Lib. xix. cap. 27). To this corresponds the well-known sentiment of Bernard: "Not to sin is the righteousness of God, but the righteousness of man is the indulgence of God" (Bernard, Serm. xxii. xxiii. in Cant.). He previously asserts that Christ is our righteousness in absolution, and, therefore, that those only are just who have obtained pardon through mercy.

23. Hence also it is proved, that it is entirely by the intervention of Christ's righteousness that we obtain justification before God. This is equivalent to saying that man is not just in himself, but that the righteousness of Christ is communicated to him by imputation, while he is strictly deserving of punishment. Thus vanishes the absurd dogma, that man is justified by faith, inasmuch as it brings him under the influence of the Spirit of God by whom he is rendered righteous. This is so repugnant to the above doctrine that it never can be reconciled with it. There can be no doubt that he who is taught to seek righteousness out of himself does not previously possess it in himself.[1] This is most clearly declared by the Apostle, when he says, that he who knew no sin was made an expiatory victim for sin, that we might be made the righteousness of God in him (2 Cor. v. 21). You see that our righteousness is not in ourselves, but in Christ; that the only way in which we become possessed of it is by being made partakers with Christ, since with him we possess all riches. There is nothing repugnant to this in what he elsewhere says: "God sending his own Son in the likeness of sinful flesh, and for sin condemned sin in the flesh: that the righteousness of the law might be fulfilled in us" (Rom. viii. 3, 4). Here the only fulfilment to which he refers is that which we obtain by imputation. Our Lord Jesus Christ communicates his righteousness to us, and so by some wondrous way, in so far as pertains to the

1 French, "Ceci est fort contraire a la doctrine ci dessus mise: car il n'y a nulle doute que celui qui doit cercher justice hors de soy-mesme, ne soit desnué de la sienne propre;"—This is quite contrary to the doctrine above laid down; for there is no doubt, that he who is to seek righteousness out of himself, is devoid of righteousness in himself.

justice of God, transfuses its power into us. That this was the Apostle's view is abundantly clear from another sentiment which he had expressed a little before: "As by one man's disobedience many were made sinners, so by the obedience of one shall many be made righteous" (Rom. v. 19). To declare that we are deemed righteous, solely because the obedience of Christ is imputed to us as if it were our own, is just to place our righteousness in the obedience of Christ. Wherefore, Ambrose appears to me to have most elegantly adverted to the blessing of Jacob as an illustration of this righteousness, when he says that as he who did not merit the birthright in himself personated his brother, put on his garments, which gave forth a most pleasant odour, and thus introduced himself to his father that he might receive a blessing to his own advantage, though under the person of another, so we conceal ourselves under the precious purity[1] of Christ, our first-born brother, that we may obtain an attestation of righteousness from the presence of God. The words of Ambrose are, —"Isaac's smelling the odour of his garments, perhaps means that we are justified not by works, but by faith, since carnal infirmity is an impediment to works, but errors of conduct are covered by the brightness of faith, which merits the pardon of faults" (Ambrose de Jacobo et Vita Beata, Lib. ii. c. 2). And so indeed it is; for in order to appear in the presence of God for salvation, we must send forth that fragrant odour, having our vices covered and buried by his perfection.

[1] French, "Sous la robbe;"—under the robe.

CHAPTER XII.

NECESSITY OF CONTEMPLATING THE JUDGMENT-SEAT OF GOD, IN ORDER TO BE SERIOUSLY CONVINCED OF THE DOCTRINE OF GRATUITOUS JUSTIFICATION.

The divisions of this chapter are,—I. A consideration of the righteousness of God overturns the righteousness of works, as is plain from passages of Scripture, and the confession and example of the saints, sec. 1–3. II. The same effect produced by a serious examination of the conscience, and a constant citation to the divine tribunal, sec. 4 and 5. III. Hence arises, in the hearts of the godly, not hypocrisy, or a vain opinion of merit, but true humility. This illustrated by the authority of Scripture and the example of the Publican, sec. 6, 7. IV. Conclusion—arrogance and security must be discarded, every man throwing an impediment in the way of the divine goodness in proportion as he trusts to himself.

Sections.

1. Source of error on the subject of Justification. Sophists speak as if the question were to be discussed before some human tribunal. It relates to the majesty and justice of God. Hence nothing accepted without absolute perfection. Passages confirming this doctrine. If we descend to the righteousness of the Law, the curse immediately appears.
2. Source of hypocritical confidence. Illustrated by a simile. Exhortation. Testimony of Job, David, and Paul.
3. Confession of Augustine and Bernard.
4. Another engine overthrowing the righteousness of works—viz. a serious examination of the conscience, and a comparison between the perfection of God and the imperfection of man.
5. How it is that we so indulge this imaginary opinion of our own works. The proper remedy to be found in a consideration of the majesty of God and our own misery. A description of this misery.
6. Christian humility consists in laying aside the imaginary idea of our own righteousness, and trusting entirely to the mercy of God, apprehended by faith in Christ. This humility described. Proved by passages of Scripture.
7. The parable of the Publican explained.
8. Arrogance, security, and self-confidence, must be renounced. General rule, or summary of the above doctrine.

1. Although the perfect truth of the above doctrine is proved by clear passages of Scripture, yet we cannot clearly see how necessary it is, before we bring distinctly into view the foundations on which the whole discussion ought to rest. First, then, let us remember that the righteousness which we are considering is not that of a human, but of a heavenly tribunal; and so beware of employing our own little standard to measure the perfection which is to satisfy the justice of God. It is strange with what rashness and presumption this is commonly defined. Nay, we see that none talk more confidently, or, so to speak, more blusteringly, of the righteousness of works, than those whose diseases are most palpable, and blemishes most apparent. This

they do because they reflect not on the righteousness of Christ, which, if they had the slightest perception of it, they would never treat with so much insult. It is certainly undervalued, if not recognised to be so perfect that nothing can be accepted that is not in every respect entire and absolute, and tainted by no impurity; such indeed as never has been, and never will be, found in man. It is easy for any man, within the precincts of the schools, to talk of the sufficiency of works for justification; but when we come into the presence of God there must be a truce to such talk. The matter is there discussed in earnest, and is no longer a theatrical logomachy. Hither must we turn our minds if we would inquire to any purpose concerning true righteousness; the question must be, How shall we answer the heavenly Judge when he calls us to account? Let us contemplate that Judge, not as our own unaided intellect conceives of him, but as he is pourtrayed to us in Scripture (see especially the Book of Job), with a brightness which obscures the stars, a strength which melts the mountains, an anger which shakes the earth, a wisdom which takes the wise in their own craftiness, a purity before which all things become impure, a righteousness to which not even angels are equal (so far is it from making the guilty innocent), a vengeance which once kindled burns to the lowest hell (Exod. xxxiv. 7; Nahum i. 3; Deut. xxxii. 22). Let him, I say, sit in judgment on the actions of men, and who will feel secure in sisting himself before his throne? "Who among us," says the prophet, "shall dwell with the devouring fire? who among us shall dwell with everlasting burnings? He that walketh righteously, and speaketh uprightly," &c. (Isaiah xxxiii. 14, 15). Let whoso will come forth. Nay, the answer shows that no man can. For, on the other hand, we hear the dreadful voice: "If thou, Lord, shouldst mark our iniquities, O Lord, who shall stand?" (Ps. cxxx. 3.) All must immediately perish, as Job declares, "Shall mortal man be more just than God? shall a man be more pure than his Maker? Behold, he put no trust his servants; and his angels he charged with folly: How much less in in them that dwell in houses of clay, whose foundation is in the dust, which are crushed before the moth? They are destroyed from morning to evening" (Job iv. 17–20). Again, "Behold, he putteth no trust in his saints; yea, the heavens are not clean in his sight. How much more abominable and filthy is man, which drinketh iniquity like water?" (Job xv. 15, 16.) I confess, indeed, that in the Book of Job reference is made to a righteousness of a more exalted description than the observance of the Law. It is of importance to attend to this distinction; for even could a man satisfy the Law, he could not stand the scrutiny of that righteousness which transcends all our thoughts. Hence, although Job was not conscious of offending, he is still dumb with astonishment, because he sees that God could not be appeased even by the sanctity of angels, were their works weighed in that supreme balance. But to advert no farther to this righteousness, which is incomprehensible,

I only say, that if our life is brought to the standard of the written law, we are lethargic indeed if we are not filled with dread at the many maledictions which God has employed for the purpose of arousing us, and among others, the following general one: "Cursed be he that confirmeth not all the words of this law to do them" (Deut. xxvii. 26). In short, the whole discussion of this subject will be insipid and frivolous, unless we sist ourselves before the heavenly Judge, and, anxious for our acquittal, voluntarily humble ourselves, confessing our nothingness.

2. Thus, then, must we raise our eyes that we may learn to tremble instead of vainly exulting. It is easy, indeed, when the comparison is made among men, for every one to plume himself on some quality which others ought not to despise; but when we rise to God that confidence instantly falls and dies away. The case of the soul with regard to God is very analogous to that of the body in regard to the visible firmament. The bodily eye, while employed in surveying adjacent objects, is pleased with its own perspicacity; but when directed to the sun, being dazzled and overwhelmed by the refulgence, it becomes no less convinced of its weakness than it formerly was of its power in viewing inferior objects. Therefore, lest we deceive ourselves by vain confidence, let us recollect that even though we deem ourselves equal or superior to other men, this is nothing to God, by whose judgment the decision must be given. But if our presumption cannot be tamed by these considerations, he will answer us as he did the Pharisees, "Ye are they which justify yourselves before men; but God knoweth your hearts: for that which is highly esteemed among men is abomination in the sight of God" (Luke xvi. 15). Go now and make a proud boast of your righteousness among men, while God in heaven abhors it. But what are the feelings of the servants of God, of those who are truly taught by his Spirit? "Enter not into judgment with thy servant; for in thy sight shall no man living be justified" (Ps. cxliii. 2). Another, though in a sense somewhat different, says, "How should man be just with God? If he will contend with him he cannot answer him one of a thousand" (Job ix. 2, 3). Here we are plainly told what the righteousness of God is—namely, a righteousness which no human works can satisfy, which charges us with a thousand sins, while not one sin can be excused. Of this righteousness Paul, that chosen vessel of God, had formed a just idea, when he declared, "I know nothing by myself, yet am I not hereby justified" (1 Cor. iv. 4).

3. Such examples exist not in the sacred volume only; all pious writers show that their sentiment was the same. Thus, Augustine says, "Of all pious men groaning under this burden of corruptible flesh, and the infirmities of this life, the only hope is, that we have one Mediator Jesus Christ the righteous, and that he intercedes for our sins" (August. ad Bonif. Lib. iii. c. 5). What do we hear? If this is their only hope, where is their confidence in works? When

he says *only*, he leaves no other. Bernard says, "And, indeed, where have the infirm firm security and safe rest, but in the wounds of the Saviour? Hold it then the more securely, the more powerful he is to save. The world frowns, the body presses, the devil lays snares: I fall not, because I am founded on a firm rock. I have sinned a grievous sin: conscience is troubled, but it shall not be overwhelmed, for I will remember the wounds of the Lord." He afterwards concludes, "My merit, therefore, is the compassion of the Lord; plainly I am not devoid of merit so long as he is not devoid of commiseration. But if the mercies of the Lord are many, equally many are my merits. Shall I sing of my own righteousness? O Lord, I will make mention of thy righteousness alone. That righteousness is mine also, being made mine by God" (Bernard, Serm. 61, in Cantic). Again, in another passage, "Man's whole merit is to place his whole hope in him who makes the whole man safe" (in Psal. Qui Habitat. Serm. 15). In like manner, reserving peace to himself, he leaves the glory to God: "Let thy glory remain unimpaired: it is well with me if I have peace; I altogether abjure boasting, lest if I should usurp what is not mine, I lose also what is offered" (Serm. 13, in Cantic). He says still more plainly in another place: "Why is the Church solicitous about merits? God purposely supplies her with a firmer and more secure ground of boasting. There is no reason for asking by what merits may we hope for blessings, especially when you hear in the prophet, 'Thus saith the Lord God, I do not this for your sakes, O house of Israel, but for mine holy name's sake' (Ezek. xxxvi. 22, 32). It is sufficient for merit to know that merits suffice not; but as it is sufficient for merit not to presume on merit, so to be without merits is sufficient for condemnation" (Bernard, Serm. 68). The free use of the term merits for good works must be pardoned to custom. Bernard's purpose was to alarm hypocrites, who turned the grace of God into licentiousness, as he shortly after explains: "Happy the church which neither wants merit without presumption, nor presumption without merit. It has ground to presume, but not merit. It has merit, merit to deserve, not presume. Is not the absence of presumption itself a merit? He, therefore, to whom the many mercies of the Lord furnish ample grounds of boasting, presumes the more securely that he presumes not" (Bernard, Serm. 68).

4. Thus, indeed, it is. Aroused consciences, when they have to do with God, feel this to be the only asylum in which they can breathe safely. For if the stars which shine most brightly by night lose their brightness on the appearance of the sun, what think we will be the case with the highest purity of man when contrasted with the purity of God? For the scrutiny will be most strict, penetrating to the most hidden thoughts of the heart. As Paul says, it "will bring to light the hidden things of darkness, and will make manifest the counsels of the heart" (1 Cor. iv. 5); will compel the reluctant and dissembling conscience to bring forward everything,

even things which have now escaped our memory. The devil, aware of all the iniquities which he has induced us to perpetrate, will appear as accuser; the external show of good works, the only thing now considered, will then be of no avail; the only thing demanded will be the true intent of the will. Hence hypocrisy, not only that by which a man, though consciously guilty before God, affects to make an ostentatious display before man, but that by which each imposes upon himself before God (so prone are we to soothe and flatter ourselves), will fall confounded, how much soever it may now swell with pride and presumption. Those who do not turn their thoughts to this scene, may be able for the moment calmly and complacently to rear up a righteousness for themselves; but this the judgment of God will immediately overthrow, just as great wealth amassed in a dream vanishes the moment we awake. Those who, as in the presence of God, inquire seriously into the true standard of righteousness, will certainly find that all the works of men, if estimated by their own worth, are nothing but vileness and pollution, that what is commonly deemed justice is with God mere iniquity; what is deemed integrity is pollution; what deemed glory is ignominy.

5. Let us not decline to descend from this contemplation of the divine perfection, to look into ourselves without flattery or blind self-love. It is not strange that we are so deluded in this matter, seeing none of us can avoid that pestilential self-indulgence, which, as Scripture proclaims, is naturally inherent in all: "Every way of a man is right in his own eyes," says Solomon (Prov. xxi. 2). And again, "All the ways of a man are clean in his own eyes" (Prov. xvi. 2). What then? does this hallucination excuse him? No, indeed, as Solomon immediately adds, "The Lord weigheth the spirits;" that is, while man flatters himself by wearing an external mask of righteousness, the Lord weighs the hidden impurity of the heart in his balance. Seeing, therefore, that nothing is gained by such flattery, let us not votuntarily delude ourselves to our own destruction. To examine ourselves properly, our conscience must be called to the judgment-seat of God. His light is necessary to disclose the secret recesses of wickedness, which otherwise lie too deeply hid. Then only shall we clearly perceive what the value of our works is; that man, so far from being just before God, is but rottenness and a worm, abominable and vain, drinking in "iniquity like water." For "who can bring a clean thing out of an unclean? not one" (Job xiv. 5). Then we shall experience the truth of what Job said of himself: "If I justify myself, mine own mouth shall condemn me: if I say I am perfect, it shall prove me perverse" (Job. ix. 20). Nor does the complaint which the prophet made concerning Israel apply to one age only. It is true of every age, that "all we like sheep have gone astray; we have turned every one to his own way" (Isaiah liii. 6). Indeed, he there comprehends all to whom the gift of redemption was to come. And the strictness of the examination ought to be

continued until it have completely alarmed us, and in that way prepared us for receiving the grace of Christ. For he is deceived who thinks himself capable of enjoying it, until he have laid aside all loftiness of mind. There is a well-known declaration, "God resisteth the proud, but giveth grace to the humble" (1 Pet. v. 5).

6. But what means is there of humbling us if we do not make way for the mercy of God, by our utter indigence and destitution? For I call it not humility, so long as we think there is any good remaining in us. Those who have joined together the two things, to think humbly as ourselves before God and yet hold our own righteousness in some estimation, have hitherto taught a pernicious hypocrisy. For if we confess to God contrary to what we feel, we wickedly lie to him; but we cannot feel as we ought without seeing that everything like a ground of boasting is completely crushed. Therefore, when you hear from the prophet, "thou wilt save the afflicted people; but wilt bring down high looks" (Ps. xviii. 27), consider, first, that there is no access to salvation unless all pride is laid aside and true humility embraced; secondly, that that humility is not a kind of moderation by which you yield to God some article of your right (thus men are called humble in regard to each other when they neither conduct themselves haughtily nor insult over other, though they may still entertain some consciousness of their own excellence), but that it is the unfeigned submission of a mind overwhelmed by a serious conviction of its want and misery. Such is the description everywhere given by the word of God. When in Zephaniah the Lord speaks thus, "I will take away out of the midst of thee them that rejoice in thy pride, and thou shalt no more be haughty because of my holy mountain. I will also leave in the midst of thee an afflicted and poor people, and they shall trust in the name of the Lord" (Zeph. iii. 11, 12), does he not plainly show who are the humble—viz. those who lie afflicted by a knowledge of their poverty? On the contrary, he describes the proud as rejoicing (*exultantes*), such being the mode in which men usually express their delight in prosperity. To the humble, whom he designs to save, he leaves nothing but hope in the Lord. Thus, also, in Isaiah, "To this man will I look, even to him that is poor and of a contrite spirit, and trembleth at my word" (Isaiah lxvi. 2). Again, "Thus saith the high and lofty One that inhabiteth eternity, whose name is Holy; I dwell in the high and holy place, with him also that is of a contrite and humble spirit, to revive the spirit of the humble, and to revive the heart of the contrite ones" (Isaiah lvii. 15). By the term *contrition*, which you so often hear, understand a wounded heart, which, humbling the individual to the earth, allows him not to rise. With such contrition must your heart be wounded, if you would, according to the declaration of God, be exalted with the humble. If this is not your case, you shall be humbled by the mighty hand of God to your shame and disgrace.

7. Our divine Master, not confining himself to words, has by a parable set before us, as in a picture, a representation of true humility. He brings forward a publican, who standing afar off, and not daring to lift up his eyes to heaven, smites upon his breast, laments aloud, and exclaims, "God be merciful to me a sinner" (Luke xviii. 13). Let us not suppose that he gives the signs of a fictitious modesty when he dares not come near or lift up his eyes to heaven, but, smiting upon his breast, confesses himself a sinner; let us know that these are the evidences of his internal feeling. With him our Lord contrasts the Pharisee, who thanks God "I am not as other men are, extortioners, unjust, adulterers, or even as this publican. I fast twice in the week, I give tithes of all that I possess." In this public confession he admits that the righteousness which he possesses is the gift of God; but because of his confidence that he is righteous, he departs from the presence of God unaccepted and abominated. The publican acknowledging his iniquity is justified. Hence we may see how highly our humility is valued by the Lord: our breast cannot receive his mercy until deprived completely of all opinion of its own worth. When such an opinion is entertained, the door of mercy is shut. That there might be no doubt on this matter, the mission on which Christ was sent into the world by his Father was "to preach good tidings to the meek," "to bind up the broken-hearted, to proclaim liberty to the captives, and the opening of the prison to them that are bound; to proclaim the acceptable year of the Lord, and the day of vengeance of our God; to comfort all that mourn; to appoint unto them that mourn in Zion, to give unto them beauty for ashes, the oil of joy for mourning, the garment of praise for the spirit of heaviness" (Isa. lxi. 1–3). In fulfilment of that mission, the only persons whom he invites to share in his beneficence are the "weary and heavy laden." In another passage he says, "I am not come to call the righteous, but sinners to repentance" (Matth. xi. 28; ix. 13).

8. Therefore, if we would make way for the call of Christ, we must put far from us all arrogance and confidence. The former is produced by a foolish persuasion of self-righteousness, when a man thinks that he has something in himself which deservedly recommends him to God; the latter may exist without any confidence in works.[1] For many sinners, intoxicated with the pleasures of vice, think not of the judgment of God. Lying stupified, as it were, by a kind of lethargy, they aspire not to the offered mercy. It is not less necessary to shake off torpor of this description than every kind of confidence in ourselves, in order that we may haste to Christ unencumbered, and while hungry and empty be filled with his blessings. Never shall we have suffici-

[1] French, "Par arrogance j'enten l'orgueil qui s'engendre d'une fole persuasion de justice, quand l'homme pense avoir quelque chose, dont il merite d'estre agreable à Dieu; par presomption j'enten une nonchalance charnelle, qui peut estre sans aucune fiance des œuvres;"—by arrogance I mean the pride which is engendered by a foolish persuasion of righteousness, when man thinks he has something for which he deserves to be agreeable to God. By presumption I understand a carnal indifference, which may exist without any confidence in works.

ent confidence in him unless utterly distrustful of ourselves; never shall we take courage in him until we first despond of ourselves; never shall we have full consolation in him until we cease to have any in ourselves. When we have entirely discarded all self-confidence, and trust solely in the certainty of his goodness, we are fit to apprehend and obtain the grace of God. "When" (as Augustine says) "forgetting our own merits, we embrace the gifts of Christ, because if he should seek for merits in us we should not obtain his gifts" (August. de Verb. Apost. 8). With this Bernard admirably accords, comparing the proud, who presume in the least on their merits, to unfaithful servants, who wickedly take the merit of a favour merely passing through them, just as if a wall were to boast of producing the ray which it receives through the window (Bernard, Serm. 13, in Cant.). Not to dwell longer here, let us lay down this short but sure and general rule, That he is prepared to reap the fruits of the divine mercy who has thoroughly emptied himself, I say not of righteousness (he has none), but of a vain and blustering show of righteousness; for to whatever extent any man rests in himself, to the same extent he impedes the beneficence of God.

CHAPTER XIII.

TWO THINGS TO BE OBSERVED IN GRATUITOUS JUSTIFICATION.

The divisions of this chapter are,—I. The glory of God, and peace of conscience, both secured by gratuitous justification. An insult to the glory of God to glory in ourselves and seek justification out of Christ, whose righteousness, apprehended by faith, is imputed to all the elect for reconciliation and eternal salvation, sec. 1, 2. II. Peace of conscience cannot be obtained in any other way than by gratuitous justification. This fully proved, sec. 3–5.

Sections.

1. The glory of God remains untarnished, when he alone is acknowledged to be just. This proved from Scripture.
2. Those who glory in themselves glory against God. Objection. Answer, confirmed by the authority of Paul and Peter.
3. Peace of conscience obtained by free justification only. Testimony of Solomon, of conscience itself, and the Apostle Paul, who contends that faith is made vain if righteousness come by the law.
4. The promise confirmed by faith in the mercy of Christ. This is confirmed by Augustine and Bernard, is in accordance with what has been above stated, and is illustrated by clear predictions of the prophets.
5. Farther demonstration by an Apostle. Refutation of a sophism.

1. HERE two ends must be kept specially in view—namely, that the glory of God be maintained unimpaired, and that our consciences, in the view of his tribunal, be secured in peaceful rest and calm tranquillity. When the question relates to righteousness, we see how often and how anxiously Scripture exhorts us to give the whole praise of it to God. Accordingly, the Apostle testifies that the purpose of the Lord in conferring righteousness upon us in Christ, was to demonstrate his own righteousness. The nature of this demonstration he immediately subjoins—viz. "that he might be just, and the justifier of him which believeth in Jesus" (Rom. iii. 25). Observe, that the righteousness of God is not sufficiently displayed, unless He alone is held to be righteous, and freely communicates righteousness to the undeserving. For this reason it is his will, that "every mouth may be stopped, and all the world may become guilty before God" (Rom. iii. 19). For so long as a man has anything, however small, to say in his own defence, so long he deducts somewhat from the glory of God. Thus, we are taught in Ezekiel how much we glorify his name by acknowledging our iniquity: "Then shall ye remember your ways and all your doings, wherein ye have been defiled; and ye shall loathe yourselves in your own sight, for all your evils that ye have committed. And ye shall know that I am the Lord, when I have wrought with you for my name's sake, not according to your

wicked ways, nor according to your corrupt doings" (Ezek. xx. 43, 44). If part of the true knowledge of God consists in being oppressed by a consciousness of our own iniquity, and in recognising him as doing good to those who are unworthy of it, why do we attempt, to our great injury, to steal from the Lord even one particle of the praise of unmerited kindness? In like manner, when Jeremiah exclaims, "Let not the wise man glory in his wisdom, neither let the mighty man glory in his might, let not the rich man glory in his riches: but let him that glorieth glory" in the Lord (Jer. ix. 23, 24), does he not intimate, that the glory of the Lord is infringed when man glories in himself? To this purpose, indeed, Paul accommodates the words when he says, that all the parts of our salvation are treasured up with Christ, that we may glory only in the Lord (1 Cor. i. 29). For he intimates, that whosoever imagines he has anything of his own, rebels against God, and obscures his glory.

2. Thus, indeed, it is: we never truly glory in him until we have utterly discarded our own glory. It must, therefore, be regarded as an universal proposition, that whoso glories in himself glories against God. Paul indeed considers, that the whole world is not made subject to God until every ground of glorying has been withdrawn from men (Rom. iii. 19). Accordingly, Isaiah, when he declares that "in the Lord shall all the seed of Israel be justified," adds, "and shall glory" (Isa. xlv. 25); as if he had said, that the elect are justified by the Lord, in order that they may glory in him, and in none else. The way in which we are to glory in the Lord he had explained in the preceding verse, "Unto me every knee shall bow, every tongue shall swear;" "Surely, shall one say, in the Lord have I righteousness and strength, even to him shall men come." Observe, that the thing required is not simple confession, but confession confirmed by an oath, that it might not be imagined that any kind of fictitious humility might suffice. And let no man here allege that he does not glory, when without arrogance he recognises his own righteousness; such a recognition cannot take place without generating confidence, nor such confidence without begetting boasting. Let us remember, therefore, that in the whole discussion concerning justification the great thing to be attended to is, that God's glory be maintained entire and unimpaired; since, as the Apostle declares, it was in demonstration of his own righteousness that he shed his favour upon us; it was "that he might be just, and the justifier of him which believeth in Jesus" (Rom. iii. 26). Hence, in another passage, having said that the Lord conferred salvation upon us, in order that he might show forth the glory of his name (Eph. i. 6), he afterwards, as if repeating the same thing, adds, "By grace are ye saved through faith; and that not of yourselves: it is the gift of God: not of works, lest any man should boast" (Eph. ii. 8). And Peter, when he reminds us that we are called to the hope of salvation, "that ye should show forth the praises of him who hath called you out of darkness into his marvellous light" (1 Pet. ii. 9), doubtless intends thus to proclaim

in the ears of believers only the praises of God, that they may bury in profound silence all arrogance of the flesh. The sum is, that man cannot claim a single particle of righteousness to himself, without at the same time detracting from the glory of the divine righteousness.

3. If we now inquire in what way the conscience can be quieted as in the view of God, we shall find that the only way is by having righteousness bestowed upon us freely by the gift of God. Let us always remember the words of Solomon, "Who can say I have made my heart clean, I am free from my sin?" (Prov. xx. 9). Undoubtedly, there is not one man who is not covered with infinite pollutions. Let the most perfect man descend into his own conscience, and bring his actions to account, and what will the result be? Will he feel calm and quiescent, as if all matters were well arranged between himself and God; or will he not rather be stung with dire torment, when he sees that the ground of condemnation is within him if he be estimated by his works? Conscience, when it beholds God, must either have sure peace with his justice, or be beset by the terrors of hell. We gain nothing, therefore, by discoursing of righteousness, unless we hold it to be a righteousness stable enough to support our souls before the tribunal of God. When the soul is able to appear intrepidly in the presence of God, and receive his sentence without dismay, then only let us know that we have found a righteousness that is not fictitious. It is not, therefore, without cause, that the Apostle insists on this matter. I prefer giving it in his words rather than my own: "If they which are of the law be heirs, faith is made void, and the promise made of no effect" (Rom. iv. 14). He first infers that faith is made void if the promise of righteousness has respect to the merit of our works, or depends on the observance of the law. Never could any one rest securely in it, for never could he feel fully assured that he had fully satisfied the law; and it is certain that no man ever fully satisfies it by works. Not to go far for proof of this, every one who will use his eyes aright may be his own witness. Hence it appears how deep and dark the abyss is into which hypocrisy plunges the minds of men, when they indulge so securely as, without hesitation, to oppose their flattery to the judgment of God, as if they were relieving him from his office as judge. Very different is the anxiety which fills the breasts of believers, who sincerely examine themselves.[1] Every mind, therefore, would first begin to hesitate, and at length to despair, while each determined for itself with how great a load of debt it was still oppressed, and how far it was from coming up to the enjoined condition. Thus, then, faith would be oppressed and extinguished. To have faith is not to fluctuate, to vary, to be carried up and down, to hesitate, remain in suspense, vacillate, in fine, to despair; it is to possess sure certainty and complete security of mind, to have whereon to rest and fix your foot.

[1] The two previous sentences are omitted in the French.

4. Paul, moreover, adds, that the promise itself would be rendered null and void. For if its fulfilment depends on our merit, when, pray, will we be able to come the length of meriting the favour of God? Nay, the second clause is a consequence of the former, since the promise will not be fulfilled unless to those who put faith in it. Faith therefore failing, no power will remain in the promise. "Therefore it is of faith, that it might be by grace, to the end the promise might be sure to all the seed" (Rom. iv. 16). It was abundantly confirmed when made to rest on the mercy of God alone, for mercy and truth are united by an indissoluble tie; that is, whatever God has mercifully promised he faithfully performs. Thus David, before he asks salvation according to the word of God, first places the source of it in his mercy. "Let, I pray thee, thy merciful kindness be for my comfort, according to thy word unto thy servant" (Ps. cxix. 76). And justly, for nothing but mere mercy induces God to promise. Here, then, we must place, and, as it were, firmly fix our whole hope, paying no respect to our works, and asking no assistance from them. And lest you should suppose that there is anything novel in what I say, Augustine also enjoins us so to act. "Christ," says he, "will reign for ever among his servants. This God has promised, God has spoken; if this is not enough, God has sworn. Therefore, as the promise stands firm, not in respect of our merits, but in respect of his mercy, no one ought to tremble in announcing that of which he cannot doubt" (August. in Ps. lxxxviii. Tract. 1). Thus Bernard also, "Who can be saved? ask the disciples of Christ. He replies, With men it is impossible, but not with God. This is our whole confidence; this our only consolation; this the whole ground of our hope: but being assured of the possibility, what are we to say as to his willingness? Who knows whether he is deserving of love or hatred? (Eccles. ix. 1.) 'Who hath known the mind of the Lord that he may instruct him?' (1 Cor. ii. 16.) Here it is plain, faith must come to our aid: here we must have the assistance of truth, in order that the secret purpose of the Father respecting us may be revealed by the Spirit, and the Spirit testifying may persuade our hearts that we are the sons of God. But let him persuade by calling and justifying freely by faith: in these there is a kind of transition from eternal predestination to future glory" (Berd. in Dedica. Templi. Serm. 5). Let us thus briefly conclude: Scripture indicates that the promises of God are not sure, unless they are apprehended with full assurance of conscience; it declares that wherever there is doubt or uncertainty, the promises are made void; on the other hand, that they can only waver and fluctuate if they depend on our works. Therefore, either our righteousness must perish, or without any consideration of our works, place must be given to faith alone, whose nature it is to prick up the ear, and shut the eye; that is, to be intent on the promise only, to give up all idea of any dignity or merit in man. Thus is fulfilled the celebrated prophecy of Zechariah: "I will remove the iniquity of that land in one day. In that

day, saith the Lord of hosts, shall ye call every man his neighbour under the vine, and under the fig-tree" (Zech. iii. 9, 10). Here the prophet intimates that the only way in which believers can enjoy true peace, is by obtaining the remission of their sins. For we must attend to this peculiarity in the prophets, that when they discourse of the kingdom of Christ, they set forth the external mercies of God as types of spiritual blessings. Hence Christ is called *the Prince of Peace, and our peace* (Isaiah ix. 6; Eph. ii. 14), because he calms all the agitations of conscience. If the method is asked, we must come to the sacrifice by which God was appeased, for no man will ever cease to tremble, until he hold that God is propitiated solely by that expiation in which Christ endured his anger. In short, peace must be sought no where but in the agonies of Christ our Redeemer.

5. But why employ a more obscure testimony? Paul uniformly declares that the conscience can have no peace or quiet joy until it is held for certain that we are justified by faith. And he at the same time declares whence this certainty is derived—viz. when "the love of God is shed abroad in our hearts by the Holy Ghost" (Rom. v. 5); as if he had said, that our souls cannot have peace until we are fully assured that we are pleasing to God. Hence he elsewhere exclaims in the person of believers in general, "Who shall separate us from the love of Christ?" (Rom. viii. 35). Until we have reached that haven, the slightest breeze will make us tremble, but so long as the Lord is our Shepherd, we shall walk without fear in the valley of the shadow of death (Ps. xxiii.). Thus those who pretend that justification by faith consists in being regenerated and made just, by living spiritually, have never tasted the sweetness of grace in trusting that God will be propitious. Hence also, they know no more of praying aright than do the Turks or any other heathen people. For, as Paul declares, faith is not true, unless it suggest and dictate the delightful name of Father; nay, unless it open our mouths and enable us freely to cry, Abba, Father. This he expresses more clearly in another passage, "In whom we have boldness and access with confidence by the faith of him" (Eph. iii. 12). This, certainly, is not obtained by the gift of regeneration, which, as it is always defective in the present state, contains within it many grounds of doubt. Wherefore, we must have recourse to this remedy; we must hold that the only hope which believers have of the heavenly inheritance is, that being ingrafted into the body of Christ, they are justified freely. For, in regard to justification, faith is merely passive, bringing nothing of our own to procure the favour of God, but receiving from Christ everything that we want.

CHAPTER XIV.

THE BEGINNING OF JUSTIFICATION. IN WHAT SENSE PROGRESSIVE.

To illustrate what has been already said, and show what kind of righteousness man can have during the whole course of his life, mankind are divided into four classes. I. First class considered, sec. 1–6. II. Second and third classes considered together, sec. 7, 8. III. Fourth class considered, sec. 9 to end.

Sections.

1. Men either idolatrous, profane, hypocritical, or regenerate. 1. Idolaters void of righteousness, full of unrighteousness, and hence in the sight of God altogether wretched and undone.
2. Still a great difference in the characters of men. This difference manifested. 1. In the gifts of God. 2. In the distinction between honourable and base. 3. In the blessings of the present life.
3. All human virtue, how praiseworthy soever it may appear, is corrupted. 1. By impurity of heart. 2. By the absence of a proper nature.
4. By the want of Christ, without whom there is no life.
5. Natural condition of man as described by Scripture. All men dead in sins before regeneration.
6. Passages of Scripture to this effect. Vulgar error confounding the righteousness of works with the redemption purchased by Christ.
7. The second and third classes of men, comprehending hypocrites and Christians in name only. Every action of theirs deserves condemnation. Passage from Haggai. Objection. Answer.
8. Other passages. Quotations from Augustine and Gregory.
9. The fourth class—viz. the regenerate. Though guided by the Spirit, corruption adheres to all they do, especially when brought to the bar of God.
10. One fault sufficient to efface all former righteousness. Hence they cannot possibly be justified by works.
11. In addition to the two former arguments, a third adduced against the Sophists, to show that whatever be the works of the regenerate, they are justified solely by faith and the free imputation of Christ's righteousness.
12. Sophism of the Schoolmen in opposition to the above doctrine. Answer.
13. Answer explained. Refutation of the fiction of partial righteousness, and compensation by works of supererogation. This fiction necessarily falls with that of satisfaction.
14. Statement of our Saviour—viz. that after we have done all, we are still unprofitable servants.
15. Objection founded on Paul's boasting. Answer, showing the Apostle's meaning. Other answers, stating the general doctrine out of Chrysostom. Third answer, showing that supererogation is the merest vanity.
16. Fourth answer, showing how Scripture dissuades us from all confidence in works. Fifth answer, showing that we have no ground of boasting.
17. Sixth answer, showing in regard to four different causes, that works have no part in procuring our salvation. 1. The efficient cause is the free love of the Father, 2. The material cause is Christ acquiring righteousness for us. 3. The instrumental cause is faith 4. The final cause the display of the divine justice and praise of the divine goodness.
18. A second objection, founded on the glorying of saints. An answer, explaining these modes of expression. How the saints feel in regard to the certainty of salvation. The opinion they have of their own works as in the sight of God.
19. Another answer—viz. that the elect, by this kind of glorying, refer only to their adoption by the Father as proved by the fruits of their calling. The order of this glorying. Its foundation, structure, and parts.
20. Conclusion. The saints neither attribute anything to the merits of works, nor

derogate in any degree from the righteousness which they obtain in Christ. Confirmation from a passage of Augustine, in which he gives two reasons why no believer will presume to boast before God of his works.

21. A third objection—viz. that the good works of believers are the causes of divine blessings. Answer. There are inferior causes, but these depend on free justification, which is the only true cause why God blesses us. These modes of expression designate the order of sequence rather than the cause.

1. In farther illustration of the subject, let us consider what kind of righteousness man can have, during the whole course of his life, and for this purpose let us make a fourfold division. Mankind, either endued with no knowledge of God, are sunk in idolatry; or, initiated in the sacraments, but by the impurity of their lives denying him whom they confess with their mouths, are Christians in name only; or they are hypocrites, who with empty glosses hide the iniquity of the heart; or they are regenerated by the Spirit of God, and aspire to true holiness. In the first place, when men are judged by their natural endowments, not an iota of good will be found from the crown of the head to the sole of the foot, unless we are to charge Scripture with falsehood, when it describes all the sons of Adam by such terms as these: "The heart is deceitful above all things, and desperately wicked." "The imagination of man's heart is evil from his youth." "The Lord knoweth the thoughts of man that they are vanity." "They are all gone aside: they are altogether become filthy; there is none that doeth good, no, not one." In short, that they are *flesh*, under which name are comprehended all those works which are enumerated by Paul; adultery, fornication, uncleanness, lasciviousness, idolatry, witchcraft, hatred, variance, emulation, wrath, strife, seditions, heresies, envyings, murders, drunkenness, revellings, and all kinds of pollution and abomination which it is possible to imagine.[1] Such, then, is the worth on which men are to plume themselves. But if any among them possess an integrity of manners which presents some semblance of sanctity among men, yet because we know that God regards not the outward appearance, we must penetrate to the very source of action, if we would see how far works avail for righteousness. We must, I say, look within, and see from what affection of the heart these works proceed. This is a very wide field of discussion, but as the matter may be explained in few words, I will use as much brevity as I can.

2. First, then, I deny not, that whatever excellent endowments appear in unbelievers [2] are divine gifts. Nor do I set myself so much in opposition to common sense, as to contend that there was no difference between the justice, moderation, and equity of Titus and Trajan, and the rage, intemperance, and cruelty of Caligula, Nero, and Domitian; between the continence of Vespasian, and the obscene lusts of Tiberius; and (not to dwell on single virtues and vices) be-

[1] Jer. xvii. 9; Gen. viii. 21; Ps. xciv. 11; xxxvi. 2; xiv. 2, 3; Gen. vi. 3; Gal. v. 19.

[2] Latin, "in incredulis." French, "en la vie des infideles et idolatres;"—in the life of infidels and idolaters.

tween the observance of law and justice, and the contempt of them. So great is the difference between justice and injustice, that it may be seen even where the former is only a lifeless image. For what order would remain in the world if we were to confound them? Hence this distinction between honourable and base actions God has not only engraven on the minds of each, but also often confirms in the administration of his providence. For we see how he visits those who cultivate virtue with many temporal blessings. Not that that external image of virtue in the least degree merits his favour, but he is pleased thus to show how much he delights in true righteousness, since he does not leave even the outward semblance of it to go unrewarded. Hence it follows, as we lately observed, that those virtues, or rather images of virtues, of whatever kind, are divine gifts, since there is nothing in any degree praiseworthy which proceeds not from him.

3. Still the observation of Augustine is true, that all who are strangers to the true God, however excellent they may be deemed on account of their virtues, are more deserving of punishment than of reward, because, by the pollution of their heart, they contaminate the pure gifts of God (August. contra Julian. Lib. iv.). For though they are instruments of God to preserve human society by justice, continence, friendship, temperance, fortitude, and prudence, yet they execute these good works of God in the worst manner, because they are kept from acting ill, not by a sincere love of goodness, but merely by ambition or self-love, or some other sinister affection. Seeing then that these actions are polluted as in their very source, by impurity of heart, they have no better title to be classed among virtues than vices, which impose upon us by their affinity or resemblance to virtue. In short, when we remember that the object at which righteousness always aims is the service of God, whatever is of a different tendency deservedly forfeits the name. Hence, as they have no regard to the end which the divine wisdom prescribes, although from the performance the act seems good, yet from the perverse motive it is sin. Augustine, therefore, concludes that all the Fabriciuses, the Scipios, and Catos,[1] in their illustrious deeds, sinned in this, that, wanting the light of faith, they did not refer them to the proper end, and that, therefore, there was no true righteousness in them, because duties are estimated not by acts but by motives.

4. Besides, if it is true, as John says, that there is no life without the Son of God (1 John v. 12), those who have no part in Christ, whoever they be, whatever they do or devise, are hastening on, during their whole career, to destruction and the judgment of eternal death. For this reason, Augustine says, "Our religion distinguishes the righteous from the wicked, by the law, not of works but of faith, without which works which seem good are converted into sins" (August. ad Bonif. Lib. iii. c. v.). He finely expresses the same

1 Latin, "omnes Fabricios, Scipiones, Catones." French, "tous ceux qui ont esté prisez entre les Pagans;"—all those who have been prized among the Heathen.

idea in another passage, when he compares the zeal of such men to those who in a race mistake the course (August. Præf. in Ps. xxxi.). He who is off the course, the more swiftly he runs is the more distant from the goal; and, therefore, the more unhappy. It is better to limp in the way than run out of the way. Lastly, as there is no sanctification without union with Christ, it is evident that they are bad trees which are beautiful and fair to look upon, and may even produce fruit, sweet to the taste, but are still very far from good. Hence we easily perceive that everything which man thinks, designs, and performs, before he is reconciled to God by faith, is cursed, and not only of no avail for justification, but merits certain damnation. And why do we talk of this as if it were doubtful, when it has already been proved by the testimony of an apostle, that "without faith it is impossible to please God"? (Heb. xi. 6.)

5. But the proof will be still clearer if divine grace is set in opposition to the natural condition of man. For Scripture everywhere proclaims that God finds nothing in man to induce him to show kindness, but that he prevents him byfree liberality. What can a dead man do to obtain life? But when he enlightens us with the knowledge of himself, he is said to raise us from the dead, and make us new creatures (John v. 25). On this ground we see that the kindness of God toward us is often commended, especially by the apostle: "God," says he, "who is rich in mercy, for his great love wherewith he loved us, even when we were dead in sins, hath quickened us together with Christ" (Eph. ii. 4). In another passage, when treating of the general call of believers under the type of Abraham, he says, "God quickeneth the dead, and calleth those things which be not as though they were" (Rom. iv. 17). If we are nothing, what, pray, can we do? Wherefore, in the Book of Job the Lord sternly represses all arrogance in these words, "Who hath prevented me, that I should repay him? whatsoever is under the whole heaven is mine" (Job xli. 11). Paul explaining this sentence applies it in this way,—Let us not imagine that we bring to the Lord anything but the mere disgrace of want and destitution (Rom. xi. 35). Wherefore, in the passage above quoted, to prove that we attain to the hope of salvation, not by works but only by grace, he affirms that "we are his workmanship, created in Christ Jesus unto good works, which God hath before ordained that we should walk in them" (Eph. ii. 10); as if he had said, Who of us can boast of having challenged God by his righteousness, seeing our first power to act aright is derived from regeneration? For, as we are formed by nature, sooner shall oil be extracted from stone than good works from us. It is truly strange how man, convicted of such ignominy, dares still to claim anything as his own. Let us acknowledge, therefore, with that chosen vessel, that God "hath called us with an holy calling, not according to our works, but according to his own purpose and grace;" and "that the kindness and love of God our Saviour toward men appeared not by works of righteousness which we have done,

but according to his mercy he saved us;" that being justified by his grace, we might become the heirs of everlasting life (2 Tim. i. 9; Tit. iii. 4, 5). By this confession we strip man of every particle of righteousness, until by mere mercy he is regenerated unto the hope of eternal life, since it is not true to say we are justified by grace, if works contribute in any degree to our justification. The apostle undoubtedly had not forgotten himself in declaring that justification is gratuitous, seeing he argues in another place, that if works are of any avail, "grace is no more grace" (Rom xi. 6). And what else does our Lord mean, when he declares, "I am not come to call the righteous, but sinners to repentance"? (Matth. ix. 13). If sinners alone are admitted, why do we seek admission by means of fictitious righteousness?

6. The thought is ever and anon recurring to me, that I am in danger of insulting the mercy of God by labouring with so much anxiety to maintain it, as if it were doubtful or obscure. Such, however, is our malignity in refusing to concede to God what belongs to him until most strongly urged, that I am obliged to insist at greater length. But as Scripture is clear enough on this subject, I shall contend in its words rather than my own. Isaiah, after describing the universal destruction of the human race, finely subjoins the method of restitution. "The Lord saw it, and it displeased him that there was no judgment. And he saw that there was no man, and wondered that there was no intercessor: therefore his arm brought salvation unto him; and his righteousness, it sustained him" (Isaiah lix. 15, 16). Where is our righteousness, if the prophet says truly, that no man in recovering salvation gives any assistance to the Lord? Thus another prophet, introducing the Lord as treating concerning the reconciliation of sinners, says, "I will betroth thee unto me for ever; yea, I will betroth thee unto me in righteousness, and in judgment, and in loving-kindness, and in mercies." "I will have mercy upon her that had not obtained mercy" (Hosea ii. 19, 23). If a covenant of this kind, evidently forming our first union with God, depends on mercy, there is no foundation left for our righteousness. And, indeed, I would fain know, from those who pretend that man meets God with some righteousness of works, whether they imagine there is any kind of righteousness save that which is acceptable to Him. If it were insane to think so, can anything agreeable to God proceed from his enemies, whom he abominates with all their deeds? Truth declares that we are all the avowed and inveterate enemies of God until we are justified and admitted to his friendship (Rom. v. 6; Col. i. 21). If justification is the beginning of love, how can the righteousness of works precede it? Hence John, to put down the arrogant idea, carefully reminds us that God first loved us (1 John iv. 10). The Lord had formerly taught the same thing by his prophet: "I will love them freely: for mine anger is turned away from him" (Hosea xiv. 4). Assuredly he is not influenced by works if his love turns to us spontaneously. But the rude and vulgar idea

entertained is, that we did not merit the interposition of Christ for our redemption, but that we are aided by our works in obtaining possession of it. On the contrary, though we may be redeemed by Christ, still, until we are ingrafted into union with him by the calling of the Father, we are darkness, the heirs of death, and the enemies of God. For Paul declares that we are not purged and washed from our impurities by the blood of Christ until the Spirit accomplishes that cleansing in us (1 Cor. vi. 11). Peter, intending to say the same thing, declares that the sanctification of the Spirit avails "unto obedience and sprinkling of the blood of Jesus Christ" (1 Pet. i. 2). If the sprinkling of the blood of Christ by the Spirit gives us purification, let us not think that, previous to this sprinkling, we are anything but sinners without Christ. Let us, therefore, hold it as certain, that the beginning of our salvation is as it were a resurrection from death unto life, because, when it is given us on behalf of Christ to believe on him (Phil. i. 29), then only do we begin to pass from death unto life.

7. Under this head the second and third class of men noted in the above division is comprehended. Impurity of conscience proves that as yet neither of these classes is regenerated by the Spirit of God. And, again, their not being regenerated proves their want of faith. Whence it is clear that they are not yet reconciled, not yet justified, since it is only by faith that these blessings are obtained. What can sinners, alienated from God, produce save that which is abominable in his sight? Such, however, is the stupid confidence entertained by all the wicked, and especially by hypocrites, that however conscious that their whole heart teems with impurity, they yet deem any spurious works which they may perform as worthy of the approbation of God. Hence the pernicious consequence, that though convicted of a wicked and impious mind, they cannot be induced to confess that they are devoid of righteousness. Even acknowledging themselves to be unrighteous, because they cannot deny it, they yet arrogate to themselves some degree of righteousness. This vanity the Lord admirably refutes by the prophet: "Ask now the priests concerning the law, saying, If one bear holy flesh in the skirt of his garment, and with his skirt do touch bread, or pottage, or wine, or oil, or any meat, shall it be holy? And the priests answered and said, No. Then said Haggai, If one that is unclean by a dead body touch any of these, shall it be unclean? And the priests answered and said, It shall be unclean. Then answered Haggai, and said, So is this people, and so is this nation before me, saith the Lord; and so is every work of their hands; and that which they offer there is unclean" (Haggai ii. 11–14). I wish these sentiments could obtain full credit with us, and be deeply fixed on our memories. For there is no man, however flagitious the whole tenor of his life may be, who will allow himself to be convinced of what the Lord here so clearly declares. As soon as any person, even the most wicked, has performed some one duty of the law, he hesitates not to impute it to

himself for righteousness; but the Lord declares that no degree of holiness is thereby acquired, unless the heart has previously been made pure. And not contented with this, he declares that all the works performed by sinners are contaminated by impurity of heart. Let us cease then to give the name of righteousness to works which the mouth of the Lord condemns as polluted. How well is this shown by that elegant similitude? It might be objected, that what the Lord has commanded is inviolably holy. But he, on the contrary, replies, that it is not strange that those things which are sanctified in the law are contaminated by the impurity of the wicked, the unclean hand profaning that which is sacred by handling it.

8. The same argument is admirably followed out by Isaiah: "Bring no more vain oblations; incense is an abomination unto me; the new moons and sabbaths, the calling of assemblies, I cannot away with; it is iniquity, even the solemn meeting. Your new moons and your appointed feasts my soul hateth: they are a trouble unto me; I am weary to bear them. And when ye spread forth your hands, I will hide mine eyes from you; yea, when ye make many prayers, I will not hear: your hands are full of blood. Wash you, make you clean; put away the evil of your doings from before mine eyes" (Isaiah i. 13–16, compared with lviii.). What is meant by the Lord thus nauseating the observance of his law? Nay, indeed, he does not repudiate anything relating to the genuine observance of the law, the beginning of which is, as he uniformly declares, the sincere fear of his name. When this is wanting, all the services which are offered to him are not only nugatory, but vile and abominable. Let hypocrites now go, and while keeping depravity wrapt up in their heart, study to lay God under obligation by their works. In this way they will only offend him more and more. "The sacrifice of the wicked is an abomination to the Lord; but the prayer of the upright is his delight" (Prov. xv. 8). We hold it, therefore, as indubitable, indeed it should be notorious to all tolerably versant with Scripture, that the most splendid works performed by men, who are not yet truly sanctified, are so far from being righteousness in the sight of the Lord, that he regards them as sins. And, therefore, it is taught with perfect truth, that no man procures favour with God by means of works, but that, on the contrary, works are not pleasing to God unless the person has previously found favour in his sight.[1] Here we should carefully observe the order which Scripture sets before us. Moses says, that "the Lord had respect unto Abel and to his offering" (Gen. iv. 4). Observe how he says that the Lord was propitious (had respect) to Abel, before he had respect to his works. Wherefore, purification of heart ought to precede, in order that the works performed by us may be graciously accepted by God: for the saying of Jeremiah is always true, "O Lord, are not thine eyes upon the truth?" (Jer. v. 3). Moreover, the Holy Spirit declared by the mouth of

[1] See August. Lib. de Pœnit., and Gregory, whose words are quoted, Sent. Lib. iii. Quæst. 7.

Peter, that it is by faith alone the heart is purified (Acts xv. 9). Hence it is evident, that the primary foundation is in true and living faith.

9. Let us now see what kind of righteousness belongs to those persons whom we have placed in the fourth class. We admit, that when God reconciles us to himself by the intervention of the righteousness of Christ, and bestowing upon us the free pardon of sins regards us as righteous, his goodness is at the same time conjoined with mercy, so that he dwells in us by means of his Holy Spirit, by whose agency the lusts of our flesh are every day more and more mortified, while that we ourselves are sanctified; that is, consecrated to the Lord for true purity of life, our hearts being trained to the obedience of the law. It thus becomes our leading desire to obey his will, and in all things advance his glory only. Still, however, while we walk in the ways of the Lord, under the guidance of the Holy Spirit, lest we should become unduly elated, and forget ourselves, we have still remains of imperfection which serve to keep us humble: "There is no man that sinneth not," saith Scripture (1 Kings viii. 46). What righteousness then can men obtain by their works? First, I say, that the best thing which can be produced by them is always tainted and corrupted by the impurity of the flesh, and has, as it were, some mixture of dross in it. Let the holy servant of God, I say, select from the whole course of his life the action which he deems most excellent, and let him ponder it in all its parts; he will doubtless find in it something that savours of the rottenness of the flesh, since our alacrity in well-doing is never what it ought to be, but our course is always retarded by much weakness. Although we see that the stains by which the works of the righteous are blemished are by no means unapparent, still, granting that they are the minutest possible, will they give no offence to the eye of God, before which even the stars are not clean? We thus see, that even saints cannot perform one work which, if judged on its own merits, is not deserving of condemnation.

10. Even were it possible for us to perform works absolutely pure, yet one sin is sufficient to efface and extinguish all remembrance of former righteousness, as the prophet says (Ezek. xviii. 24). With this James agrees, "Whosoever shall keep the whole law, and yet offend in one point, is guilty of all" (James ii. 10). And since this mortal life is never entirely free from the taint of sin, whatever righteousness we could acquire would ever and anon be corrupted, overwhelmed, and destroyed, by subsequent sins, so that it could not stand the scrutiny of God, or be imputed to us for righteousness. In short, whenever we treat of the righteousness of works, we must look not to the legal work but to the command. Therefore, when righteousness is sought by the Law, it is in vain to produce one or two single works; we must show an uninterrupted obedience. God does not (as many foolishly imagine) impute that forgiveness of sins, once for all, as righteousness; so that having obtained the pardon of our past

life we may afterwards seek righteousness in the Law. This were only to mock and delude us by the entertainment of false hopes. For since perfection is altogether unattainable by us, so long as we are clothed with flesh, and the Law denounces death and judgment against all who have not yielded a perfect righteousness, there will always be ground to accuse and convict us unless the mercy of God interpose, and ever and anon absolve us by the constant remission of sins. Wherefore the statement with which we set out is always true, If we are estimated by our own worthiness, in everything that we think or devise, with all our studies and endeavours we deserve death and destruction.

11. We must strongly insist on these two things: That no believer ever performed one work which, if tested by the strict judgment of God, could escape condemnation; and, moreover, that were this granted to be possible (though it is not), yet the act being vitiated and polluted by the sins of which it is certain that the author of it is guilty, it is deprived of its merit. This is the cardinal point of the present discussion. There is no controversy between us and the sounder Schoolmen as to the beginning of justification.[1] They admit that the sinner, freely delivered from condemnation, obtains justification, and that by forgiveness of sins; but under the term justification they comprehend the renovation by which the Spirit forms us anew to the obedience of the Law; and in describing the righteousness of the regenerate man, maintain that being once reconciled to God by means of Christ, he is afterwards deemed righteous by his good works, and is accepted in consideration of them. The Lord, on the contrary, declares, that he imputed Abraham's faith for righteousness (Rom. iv. 3), not at the time when he was still a worshipper of idols, but after he had been many years distinguished for holiness. Abraham had long served God with a pure heart, and performed that obedience of the Law which a mortal man is able to perform: yet his righteousness still consisted in faith. Hence we infer, according to the reasoning of Paul, that it was *not of works*. In like manner, when the prophet says, "The just shall live by his faith" (Hab. ii. 4), he is not speaking of the wicked and profane, whom the Lord justifies by converting them to the faith: his discourse is directed to believers, and life is promised to them by faith. Paul also removes every doubt, when in confirmation of this sentiment he quotes the words of David, "Blessed is he whose transgression is forgiven, whose sin is covered"

1 The following sentence is added in the French:—"Il est bien vray que le poure monde a esté seduit jusques la, de penser que l'homme se preparast de soy-mesme pour estre justifié de Dieu : et que ce blaspheme a regné communement tant en predications qu'aux escoles; comme encore aujourdhui il est soustenue de ceux qui veulent maintenir toutes les abominations de la Papauté."—It is very true that the poor world has been seduced hitherto, to think that man could of himself prepare to be justified by God, and that this blasphemy has commonly reigned both in sermons and schools, as it is still in the present day asserted by those who would maintain all the abominations of the Papacy.

(Ps. xxxii. 1). It is certain that David is not speaking of the ungodly, but of believers such as he himself was, because he was giving utterance to the feelings of his own mind. Therefore we must have this blessedness not once only, but must hold it fast during our whole lives. Moreover, the message of free reconciliation with God is not promulgated for one or two days, but is declared to be perpetual in the Church (2 Cor. v. 18, 19). Hence believers have not even to the end of life any other righteousness than that which is there described. Christ ever remains a Mediator to reconcile the Father to us, and there is a perpetual efficacy in his death—viz. ablution, satisfaction, expiation; in short, perfect obedience, by which all our iniquities are covered. In the Epistle to the Ephesians, Paul says not that the beginning of salvation is of grace, but "by grace are ye saved," "not of works, lest any man should boast" (Eph. ii. 8, 9).

12. The subterfuges by which the Schoolmen here endeavour to escape will not disentangle them. They say that good works are not of such intrinsic worth as to be sufficient to procure justification, but it is owing to accepting grace that they have this effect. Then because they are forced to confess that here the righteousness of works is always imperfect, they grant that so long as we are in this life we stand in need of the forgiveness of sin in order to supply the deficiency of works, but that the faults which are committed are compensated by works of supererogation. I answer, that the grace which they call accepting, is nothing else than the free goodness with which the Father embraces us in Christ when he clothes us with the innocence of Christ, and accepts it as ours, so that in consideration of it he regards us as holy, pure, and innocent. For the righteousness of Christ (as it alone is perfect, so it alone can stand the scrutiny of God) must be sisted for us, and as a surety represent us judicially. Provided with this righteousness, we constantly obtain the remission of sins through faith. Our imperfection and impurity, covered with this purity, are not imputed, but are as it were buried, so as not to come under judgment until the hour arrive when the old man being destroyed, and plainly extinguished in us, the divine goodness shall receive us into beatific peace with the new Adam, there to await the day of the Lord, on which, being clothed with incorruptible bodies, we shall be translated to the glory of the heavenly kingdom.

13. If these things are so, it is certain that our works cannot in themselves make us agreeable and acceptable to God, and even cannot please God, except in so far as being covered with the righteousness of Christ we thereby please him, and obtain forgiveness of sins. God has not promised life as the reward of certain works, but only declares, "which if a man do, he shall live in them" (Lev. xviii. 5), denouncing the well-known curse against all who do not continue in all things that are written in the book of the Law to do them. In this way is completely refuted the fiction of a partial righteousness, the only righteousness acknowledged in heaven being the perfect observance of the law. There is nothing more solid in their dogma

of compensation by means of works of supererogation. For must they not always return to the proposition which has already been disproved—viz. that he who observes the Law in part is so far justified by works? This, which no man of sound judgment will concede to them, they are not ashamed to take for granted. The Lord having so often declared that he recognises no justification by works unless they be works by which the Law is perfectly fulfilled,—how perverse is it, while we are devoid of such works, to endeavour to secure some ground of glorying to ourselves; that is, not to yield it entirely to God, by boasting of some kind of fragments of works, and trying to supply the deficiency by other satisfactions? Satisfactions have already been so completely disposed of, that we ought never again even to dream of them. Here all I say is, that those who thus trifle with sin do not at all consider how execrable it is in the sight of God; if they did, they would assuredly understand, that all the righteousness of men collected into one heap would be inadequate to compensate for a single sin. For we see that by one sin man was so cast off and forsaken by God, that he at the same time lost all power of recovering salvation. He was, therefore, deprived of the power of giving satisfaction. Those who flatter themselves with this idea will never satisfy God, who cannot possibly accept or be pleased with any thing that proceeds from his enemies. But all to whom he imputes sin are enemies, and, therefore, our sins must be covered and forgiven before the Lord has respect to any of our works. From this it follows, that the forgiveness of sins is gratuitous, and this forgiveness is wickedly insulted by those who introduce the idea of satisfaction. Let us, therefore, after the example of the Apostle, "forgetting those things which are behind, and reaching forth unto those things which are before," "press toward the mark for the prize of the high calling of God in Jesus Christ" (Philip. iii. 13, 14).

14. How can boasting in works of supererogation agree with the command given to us: "When ye shall have done all those things which are commanded you, say, We are unprofitable servants: we have done that which was our duty to do"? (Luke xvii. 10.) To *say* or speak in the presence of God is not to feign or lie, but to declare what we hold as certain. Our Lord, therefore, enjoins us sincerely to feel and consider with ourselves that we do not perform gratuitous duties, but pay him service which is due. And truly. For the obligations of service under which we lie are so numerous, that we cannot discharge them though all our thoughts and members were devoted to the observance of the Law; and, therefore, when he says, "When ye shall have done all those things which are commanded you," it is just as if he had said, that all the righteousness of men would not amount to one of these things. Seeing, then, that every one is very far distant from that goal, how can we presume to boast of having accumulated more than is due? It cannot be objected that a person, though failing in some measure in what is necessary, may yet in intention go beyond what is necessary. For it must

ever be held, that in whatever pertains to the worship of God, or to charity, nothing can ever be thought of that is not comprehended under the Law. But if it is part of the Law, let us not boast of voluntary liberality in matters of necessary obligation.

15. On this subject, they causelessly allege the boast of Paul, that among the Corinthians he spontaneously renounced a right which, if he had otherwise chosen, he might have exercised (1 Cor. ix. 15); thus not only paying what he owed them in duty, but gratuitously bestowing upon them more than duty required. They ought to have attended to the reason there expressed, that his object was to avoid giving offence to the weak. For wicked and deceitful workmen employed this pretence of kindness that they might procure favour to their pernicious dogmas, and excite hatred against the Gospel, so that it was necessary for Paul either to peril the doctrine of Christ, or to thwart their schemes. Now, if it is a matter of indifference to a Christian man whether or not he cause a scandal when it is in his power to avoid it, then I admit that the Apostle performed a work of supererogation to his Master; but if the thing which he did was justly required in a prudent minister of the Gospel, then I say he did what he was bound to do. In short, even when no such reason appears, yet the saying of Chrysostom is always true, that everything which we have is held on the same condition as the private property of slaves; it is always due to our Master. Christ does not disguise this in the parable; for he asks in regard to the master who, on return from his labour, requires his servant to gird himself and serve him, "Does he thank that servant because he did the things that were commanded him? I trow not" (Luke xvii. 9). But possibly the servant was more industrious than the master would have ventured to exact. Be it so: still he did nothing to which his condition as a servant did not bind him, because his utmost ability is his master's. I say nothing as to the kind of supererogations on which these men would plume themselves before God. They are frivolities which he never commanded, which he approves not, and will not accept when they come to give in their account. The only sense in which we admit works of supererogation is that expressed by the prophet, when he says, "Who hath required this at your hand?" (Isaiah i. 12). But let them remember what is elsewhere said of them: "Wherefore do ye spend money for that which is not bread? and your labour for that which satisfieth not?" (Isaiah lv. 2). It is, indeed, an easy matter for these indolent Rabbins to carry on such discussions sitting in their soft chairs under the shade; but when the Supreme Judge shall sit on his tribunal, all these blustering dogmas will behove to disappear.[1] This, this I say, was the true question: not what we can fable and talk in schools and corners, but what ground of defence we can produce at his judgment-seat.

1 French, "Tout ce qu'ils auront determiné ne profitera gueres, ains s'evanouisra comme fumee;"—All their decisions will scarcely avail them, but will vanish like smoke.

16. In this matter the minds of men must be specially guarded against two pestiferous dogmas—viz. against putting any confidence in the righteousness of works, or ascribing any glory to them. From all such confidence the Scriptures uniformly dissuade us when they declare that our righteousness is offensive in the sight of God unless it derives a sweet odour from the purity of Christ: that it can have no other effect than to excite the divine vengeance unless sustained by his indulgent mercy. Accordingly, the only thing they leave to us is to deprecate our Judge with that confession of David: "Enter not into judgment with thy servant: for in thy sight shall no living be justified" (Psalm cxliii. 2). And when Job says, "If I be wicked, woe unto me: and if I be righteous, yet will I not lift up my head" (Job x. 15). Although he refers to that spotless righteousness of God, before which even angels are not clean, he however shows, that when brought to the bar of God, all that mortals can do is to stand dumb. He does not merely mean that he chooses rather to give way spontaneously than to risk a contest with the divine severity, but that he was not conscious of possessing any righteousness that would not fall the very first moment it was brought into the presence of God. Confidence being banished, all glorying must necessarily cease. For who can attribute any merit of righteousness to works, which instead of giving confidence, only make us tremble in the presence of God? We must, therefore, come to what Isaiah invites us: "In the Lord shall all the seed of Israel be justified, and shall glory" (Isaiah xlv. 25); for it is most true, as he elsewhere says, that we are "the planting of the Lord, that he might be glorified" (Isaiah lxi. 3). Our soul, therefore, will not be duly purified until it ceases to have any confidence, or feel any exultation in works. Foolish men are puffed up to this false and lying confidence by the erroneous idea that the cause of their salvation is in works.

17. But if we attend to the four kinds of causes which philosophers bring under our view in regard to effects, we shall find that not one of them is applicable to works as a cause of salvation. The efficient cause of our eternal salvation the Scripture uniformly proclaims to be the mercy and free love of the heavenly Father towards us; the material cause to be Christ, with the obedience by which he purchased righteousness for us; and what can the formal or instrumental cause be but faith? John includes the three in one sentence when he says, "God so loved the world, that he gave his only begotten Son, that whosoever believeth in him should not perish, but have everlasting life" (John iii. 16). The Apostle, moreover, declares that the final cause is the demonstration of the divine righteousness and the praise of his goodness. There also he distinctly mentions the other three causes; for he thus speaks to the Romans: "All have sinned, and come short of the glory of God; being justified freely by his grace" (Rom. iii. 23, 24). You have here the head and primary source—God has embraced us with free mercy. The next words are, "through the redemption that is in Christ Jesus;" this is as it were the material

cause by which righteousness is procured for us. "Whom God hath set forth to be a propitiation through faith." Faith is thus the instrumental cause by which righteousness is applied to us. He lastly subjoins the final cause when he says, "To declare at this time his righteousness; that he might be just, and the justifier of him that believeth in Jesus." And to show by the way that this righteousness consists in reconciliation, he says that Christ was "set forth to be a propitiation." Thus also, in the Epistle to the Ephesians, he tells us that we are received into the favour of God by mere mercy; that this is done by the intervention of Christ; that it is apprehended by faith; the end of all being that the glory of the divine goodness may be fully displayed. When we see that all the parts of our salvation thus exist without us, what ground can we have for glorying or confiding in our works? Neither as to the efficient nor the final cause can the most sworn enemies of divine grace raise any controversy with us unless they would abjure the whole of Scripture. In regard to the material or formal cause they make a gloss, as if they held that our works divide the merit with faith and the righteousness of Christ. But here also Scripture reclaims, simply affirming that Christ is both righteousness and life, and that the blessing of justification is possessed by faith alone.

18. When the saints repeatedly confirm and console themselves with the remembrance of their innocence and integrity, and sometimes even abstain not from proclaiming them, it is done in two ways: either because by comparing their good cause with the bad cause of the ungodly, they thence feel secure of victory, not so much from commendation of their own righteousness, as from the just and merited condemnation of their adversaries; or because, reviewing themselves before God, even without any comparison with others, the purity of their conscience gives them some comfort and security. The former reason will afterwards be considered (chap. xvii. sec. 14, and chap. xx. sec. 10); let us now briefly show, in regard to the latter, how it accords with what we have above said, that we can have no confidence in works before the bar of God, that we cannot glory in any opinion of their worth. The accordance lies here, that when the point considered is the constitution and foundation of salvation, believers, without paying any respect to works, direct their eyes to the goodness of God alone. Nor do they turn to it only in the first instance, as to the commencement of blessedness, but rest in it as the completion. Conscience being thus founded, built up, and established, is farther established by the consideration of works, inasmuch as they are proofs of God dwelling and reigning in us. Since, then, this confidence in works has no place unless you have previously fixed your whole confidence on the mercy of God, it should not seem contrary to that on which it depends. Wherefore, when we exclude confidence in works, we merely mean, that the Christian mind must not turn back to the merit of works as an aid to salvation, but must dwell entirely on the free promise of justification. But we forbid no

believer to confirm and support this faith by the signs of the divine favour towards him. For if when we call to mind the gifts which God has bestowed upon us, they are like rays of the divine countenance, by which we are enabled to behold the highest light of his goodness; much more is this the case with the gift of good works, which shows that we have received the Spirit of adoption.

19. When believers, therefore, feel their faith strengthened by a consciousness of integrity, and entertain sentiments of exultation, it is just because the fruits of their calling convince them that the Lord has admitted them to a place among his children. Accordingly, when Solomon says, "In the fear of the Lord is strong confidence" (Prov. xiv. 26), and when the saints sometimes beseech the Lord to hear them, because they walked before his face in simplicity and integrity (Gen. xxiv. 10; 2 Kings xx. 3), these expressions apply not to laying the foundation of a firm conscience, but are of force only when taken *a posteriori*.[1] For there is nowhere such a fear of God as can give full security, and the saints are always conscious that any integrity which they may possess is mingled with many remains of the flesh. But as the fruits of regeneration furnish them with a proof of the Holy Spirit dwelling in them, experiencing God to be a Father in a matter of so much moment, they are strengthened in no slight degree to wait for his assistance in all their necessities. Even this they could not do, had they not previously perceived that the goodness of God is sealed to them by nothing but the certainty of the promise. Should they begin to estimate it by their good works, nothing will be weaker or more uncertain; works, when estimated by themselves, no less proving the divine displeasure by their imperfection, than his good-will by their incipient purity. In short, while proclaiming the mercies of the Lord, they never lose sight of his free favour, with all its "breadth and length, and depth and height," testified by Paul (Eph. iii. 18); as if he had said, Whithersoever the believer turns, however loftily he climbs, however far and wide his thoughts extend, he must not go farther than the love of Christ, but must be wholly occupied in meditating upon it, as including in itself all dimensions. Accordingly, he declares that it "passeth knowledge," that "to know the love of Christ" is to "be filled with all the fulness of God" (Eph. iii. 19). In another passage, where he glories that believers are victorious in every contest, he adds the reason, "through him that loved us" (Rom. viii. 37).

20. We now see that believers have no such confidence in works as to attribute any merit to them (since they regard them only as divine gifts, in which they recognise his goodness and signs of calling, in which they discern their election); nor such confidence as to derogate in any respect from the free righteousness of Christ; since on this it depends, and without this cannot subsist. The same thing is briefly but elegantly expressed by Augustine when he says, "I do

[1] Latin, "a posteriori;" French, "comme enseigne de la vocation de Dieu;"—as a sign of the calling of God.

not say to the Lord, Despise not the works of my hands; I have sought the Lord with my hands, and have not been deceived. But I commend not the works of my hands, for I fear that when thou examinest them thou wilt find more faults than merits. This only I say, this ask, this desire, Despise not the works of thy hands. See in me thy work, not mine. If thou seest mine, thou condemnest; if thou seest thine own, thou crownest. Whatever good works I have are of thee" (August. in Ps. cxxxvii.). He gives two reasons for not venturing to boast of his works before God: first, that if he has any good works, he does not see in them anything of his own; and, secondly, that these works are overwhelmed by a multitude of sins. Whence it is, that the conscience derives from them more fear and alarm than security. Therefore, the only way in which he desires God to look at any work which he may have done aright is, that he may therein see the grace of his calling, and perfect the work which he has begun.

21. Moreover, when Scripture intimates that the good works of believers are causes why the Lord does them good, we must still understand the meaning so as to hold unshaken what has previously been said—viz. that the efficient cause of our salvation is placed in the love of God the Father; the material cause in the obedience of the Son; the instrumental cause in the illumination of the Spirit, that is, in faith; and the final cause in the praise of the divine goodness. In this, however, there is nothing to prevent the Lord from embracing works as inferior causes. But how so? In this way: Those whom in mercy he has destined for the inheritance of eternal life, he, in his ordinary adminstration, introduces to the possession of it by means of good works. What precedes in the order of administration is called the cause of what follows. For this reason, he sometimes makes eternal life a consequent of works; not because it is to be ascribed to them, but because those whom he has elected he justifies, that he may at length glorify (Rom. viii. 30); he makes the prior grace to be a kind of cause, because it is a kind of step to that which follows. But whenever the true cause is to be assigned, he enjoins us not to take refuge in works, but to keep our thoughts entirely fixed on the mercy of God; "The wages of sin is death; but the gift of God is eternal life" (Rom. vi. 23). Why, as he contrasts life with death, does he not also contrast righteousness with sin? Why, when setting down sin as the cause of death, does he not also set down righteousness as the cause of life? The antithesis which would otherwise be complete is somewhat marred by this variation; but the Apostle employed the comparison to express the fact, that death is due to the deserts of men, but that life was treasured up solely in the mercy of God. In short, by these expressions, the order rather than the cause is noted.[1] The Lord adding grace to

[1] French, "Brief, en toutes ces façons de parler, ou il est fait mention de bonnes œuvres, il n'est pas question de la cause pourquoy Dieu fait bien aux siens, mais seule-

grace, takes occasion from a former to add a subsequent, so that he may omit no means of enriching his servants. Still, in following out his liberality, he would have us always look to free election as its source and beginning. For although he loves the gifts which he daily bestows upon us, inasmuch as they proceed from that fountain, still our duty is to hold fast by that gratuitous acceptance, which alone can support our souls; and so to connect the gifts of the Spirit which he afterwards bestows, with their primary cause, as in no degree to detract from it.

ment de l'ordre qu'il y tient;"—In short, in all those forms of expression in which mention is made of good works, there is no question as to the cause why God does good to his people, but only to the order which he observes in it.

CHAPTER XV.

THE BOASTED MERIT OF WORKS SUBVERSIVE BOTH OF THE GLORY OF GOD, IN BESTOWING RIGHTEOUSNESS, AND OF THE CERTAINTY OF SALVATION.

The divisions of this chapter are,—I. To the doctrine of free justification is opposed the question, Whether or not works merit favour with God, sec. 1. This question answered, sec. 2 and 3. II. An exposition of certain passages of Scripture produced in support of the erroneous doctrine of merit, sec. 4 and 5. III. Sophisms of Semi-pelagian Schoolmen refuted, sec. 6 and 7. IV. Conclusion, proving the sufficiency of the orthodox doctrine, sec. 8.

Sections.

1. After a brief recapitulation, the question, Whether or not good works merit favour with God, considered.
2. First answer, fixing the meaning of the term Merit. This term improperly applied to works, but used in a good sense, as by Augustine, Chrysostom, Bernard.
3. A second answer to the question. First by a negative, then by a concession. In the rewarding of works what to be attributed to God, and what to man. Why good works please God, and are advantageous to those who do them. The ingratitude of seeking righteousness by works. This shown by a double similitude.
4. First objection taken from Ecclesiasticus. Second objection from the Epistle to the Hebrews. Two answers to both objections. A weak distinction refuted.
5. A third and most complete answer, calling us back to Christ as the only foundation of salvation. How Christ is our righteousness. Whence it is manifest that we have all things in Christ and he nothing in us.
6. We must abhor the sophistry which destroys the merit of Christ, in order to establish that of man. This impiety refuted by clear passages of Scripture.
7. Errors of the younger Sophists extracted from Lombard. Refuted by Augustine. Also by Scripture.
8. Conclusion, showing that the foundation which has been laid is sufficient for doctrine, exhortation, and comfort. Summary of the orthodox doctrine of Justification.

1. THE principal point in this subject has been now explained: as justification, if dependant upon works, cannot possibly stand in the sight of God, it must depend solely on the mercy of God and communion with Christ, and therefore on faith alone. But let us carefully attend to the point on which the whole subject hinges, lest we get entangled in the common delusion, not only of the vulgar, but of the learned. For the moment the question is raised as to the justification by faith or works, they run off to those passages which seem to ascribe some merit to works in the sight of God, just as if justification by works were proved whenever it is proved that works have any value with God. Above we have clearly shown that justification by works consists only in a perfect and absolute fulfilment of the law; and that, therefore, no man is justified by works unless he

has reached the summit of perfection, and cannot be convicted of even the smallest transgression. But there is another and a separate question, Though works by no means suffice to justify, do they not merit favour with God?

2. First, I must premise with regard to the term Merit, that he, whoever he was, that first applied it to human works, viewed in reference to the divine tribunal, consulted very ill for the purity of the faith. I willingly abstain from disputes about words, but I could wish that Christian writers had always observed this soberness—that when there was no occasion for it, they had never thought of using terms foreign to the Scriptures—terms which might produce much offence, but very little fruit. I ask, what need was there to introduce the word Merit, when the value of works might have been fully expressed by another term, and without offence? The quantity of offence contained in it the world shows to its great loss. It is certain that, being a high sounding term, it can only obscure the grace of God, and inspire men with pernicious pride. I admit it was used by ancient ecclesiastical writers, and I wish they had not by the abuse of one term furnished posterity with matter of heresy, although in some passages they themselves show that they had no wish to injure the truth. For Augustine says, "Let human merits, which perished by Adam, here be silent, and let the grace of God reign by Jesus Christ" (August. de. Prædest. Sanct.). Again, "The saints ascribe nothing to their merits; every thing will they ascribe solely to thy mercy, O God" (August. in Psal. cxxxix.). Again, "And when a man sees that whatever good he has he has not of himself, but of his God, he sees that every thing in him which is praised is not of his own merits, but of the divine mercy" (August. in Psal. lxxxviii.). You see how he denies man the power of acting aright, and thus lays merit prostrate. Chrysostom says, "If any works of ours follow the free calling of God, they are return and debt; but the gifts of God are grace, and beneficence, and great liberality." But to say nothing more of the name, let us attend to the thing. I formerly quoted a passage from Bernard: "As it is sufficient for merit not to presume on merit, so to be without merit is sufficient for condemnation" (Bernard in Cantic. Serm. 98). He immediately adds an explanation which softens the harshness of the expression, when he says, "Hence be careful to have merits; when you have them, know that they were given; hope for fruit from the divine mercy, and you have escaped all the perils of poverty, ingratitude, and presumption. Happy the Church which neither wants merit without presumption, nor presumption without merit." A little before he had abundantly shown that he used the words in a sound sense, saying, "Why is the Church anxious about merits? God has furnished her with a firmer and surer ground of boasting. God cannot deny himself; he will do what he has promised. Thus there is no reason for asking by what merits may we hope for blessings; especially when you hear, 'Thus saith the Lord God; I do not this for your sakes, O house of Israel,

but for mine holy name's sake' (Ezek. xxxvi. 22). It suffices for merit to know that merits suffice not."

3. What all our works can merit Scripture shows when it declares that they cannot stand the view of God, because they are full of impurity; it next shows what the perfect observance of the law (if it can anywhere be found) will merit when it enjoins, "So likewise ye, when ye shall have done all those things which are commanded you, say, We are unprofitable servants, we have done that which was our duty to do" (Luke xvii. 10); because we make no free-offering to God, but only perform due service by which no favour is deserved. And yet those good works which the Lord has bestowed upon us he counts ours also, and declares, that they are not only acceptable to him, but that he will recompense them. It is ours in return to be animated by this great promise, and to keep up our courage, that we may not weary in well-doing, but feel duly grateful for the great kindness of God. There cannot be a doubt, that everything in our works which deserves praise is owing to divine grace, and that there is not a particle of it which we can properly ascribe to ourselves. If we truly and seriously acknowledge this, not only confidence, but every idea of merit vanishes. I say we do not, like the Sophists, share the praise of works between God and man, but we keep it entire and unimpaired for the Lord. All we assign to man is, that, by his impurity, he pollutes and contaminates the very works which were good. The most perfect thing which proceeds from man is always polluted by some stain. Should the Lord, therefore, bring to judgment the best of human works, he would indeed behold his own righteousness in them; but he would also behold man's dishonour and disgrace. Thus good works please God, and are not without fruit to their authors, since, by way of recompense, they obtain more ample blessings from God, not because they so deserve, but because the divine benignity is pleased of itself to set this value upon them. Such, however, is our malignity, that, not contented with this liberality on the part of God, which bestows rewards on works that do not at all deserve them, we with profane ambition maintain that that which is entirely due to the divine munificence is paid to the merit of works. Here I appeal to every man's common sense. If one who by another's liberality possesses the usufruct of a field, rear up a claim to the property of it, does he not by his ingratitude deserve to lose the possession formerly granted? In like manner, if a slave, who has been manumitted, conceals his humble condition of freedman, and gives out that he was free-born, does he not deserve to be reduced to his original slavery? A benefit can only be legitimately enjoyed when we neither arrogate more to ourselves than has been given, nor defraud the author of it of his due praise; nay, rather when we so conduct ourselves as to make it appear that the benefit conferred still in a manner resides with him who conferred it. But if this is the moderation to be observed towards men, let every one reflect and consider for himself what is due to God.

4. I know that the Sophists abuse some passages in order to prove that the Scriptures use the term *merit* with reference to God. They quote a passage from Ecclesiasticus: "Mercy will give place to every man according to the merit of his works" (Ecclesiasticus xvi. 14); and from the Epistle to the Hebrews: "To do good and communicate forget not; for with such sacrifices God is well pleased" (Heb. xiii. 16). I now renounce my right to repudiate the authority of Ecclesiasticus; but I deny that the words of Ecclesiasticus, whoever the writer may have been, are faithfully quoted. The Greek is as follows: Πάσῃ ἐλεημοσύνῃ ποιήσει τόπον· ἕκαστος γὰρ κατὰ τὰ ἔργα αὐτοῦ εὑρήσει. "He will make room for all mercy: for each shall find according to his works." That this is the genuine reading, and has been corrupted in the Latin version, is plain, both from the very structure of the sentence, and from the previous context. In the Epistle to the Hebrews there is no room for their quibbling on one little word, for in the Greek the Apostle simply says, that *such sacrifices are pleasing* and acceptable to God. This alone should amply suffice to quell and beat down the insolence of our pride, and prevent us from attaching value to works beyond the rule of Scripture. It is the doctrine of Scripture, moreover, that our good works are constantly covered with numerous stains by which God is justly offended and made angry against us, so far are they from being able to conciliate him, and call forth his favour towards us; and yet because of his indulgence, he does not examine them with the utmost strictness, he accepts them just as if they were most pure; and therefore rewards them, though undeserving, with innumerable blessings, both present and future. For I admit not the distinction laid down by otherwise learned and pious men, that good works merit the favours which are conferred upon us in this life, whereas eternal life is the reward of faith only. The recompense of our toils, and crown of our contest, our Lord almost uniformly places in heaven. On the other hand, to attribute to the merit of works, so as to deny it to grace, that we are loaded with other gifts from the Lord, is contrary to the doctrine of Scripture. For though Christ says, "Unto every one that hath shall be given;" "thou hast been faithful over a few things, I will make thee ruler over many things" (Matth. xxv. 29, 21), he, at the same time, shows that all additional gifts to believers are of his free benignity: "Ho, every one that thirsteth, come ye to the waters, and he that hath no money, come ye, buy, and eat: yea, come, buy wine and milk, without money and without price" (Isaiah lv. 1). Therefore, every help to salvation bestowed upon believers, and blessedness itself, are entirely the gift of God, and yet in both the Lord testifies that he takes account of works, since to manifest the greatness of his love toward us, he thus highly honours not ourselves only, but the gifts which he has bestowed upon us.

5. Had these points been duly handled and digested in past ages, never could so many tumults and dissensions have arisen. Paul says, that in the architecture of Christian doctrine, it is necessary to

retain the foundation which he had laid with the Corinthians, "Other foundation can no man lay than that which is laid, which is Jesus Christ" (1 Cor. iii. 11). What then is our foundation in Christ? Is it that he begins salvation and leaves us to complete it? Is it that he only opened up the way, and left us to follow it in our own strength? By no means, but as Paul had a little before declared, it is to acknowledge that he has been given us for righteousness. No man, therefore, is well founded in Christ who has not entire righteousness in him, since the Apostle says not that he was sent to assist us in procuring, but was himself to be our righteousness. Thus it is said that God "hath chosen us in him before the foundation of the world" not according to our merit, but "according to the good pleasure of his will;" that in him "we have redemption through his blood, even the forgiveness of sins;" that peace has been made "through the blood of his cross;" that we are reconciled by his blood; that, placed under his protection, we are delivered from the danger of finally perishing; that thus ingrafted into him we are made partakers of eternal life, and hope for admission into the kingdom of God.[1] Nor is this all. Being admitted to participation in him, though we are still foolish, he is our wisdom; though we are still sinners, he is our righteousness; though we are unclean, he is our purity; though we are weak, unarmed, and exposed to Satan, yet ours is the power which has been given him in heaven and in earth, to bruise Satan under our feet, and burst the gates of hell (Matth. xxviii. 18); though we still bear about with us a body of death, he is our life; in short, all things of his are ours, we have all things in him, he nothing in us. On this foundation, I say, we must be built, if we would grow up into a holy temple in the Lord.

6. For a long time the world has been taught very differently. A kind of good works called *moral* has been found out, by which men are rendered agreeable to God before they are ingrafted into Christ; as if Scripture spoke falsely when it says, "He that hath the Son hath life, and he that hath not the Son of God hath not life" (1 John v. 12). How can they produce the materials of life if they are dead? Is there no meaning in its being said, that "whatsoever is not of faith is sin"? (Rom. xiv. 23); or can good fruit be produced from a bad tree? What have these most pestilential Sophists left to Christ on which to exert his virtue? They say that he merited for us the first grace, that is, the occasion of meriting, and that it is our part not to let slip the occasion thus offered. O the daring effrontery of impiety! Who would have thought that men professing the name of Christ would thus strip him of his power, and all but trample him under foot? The testimony uniformly borne to him in Scripture is, that whoso believeth in him is justified; the doctrine of these men is, that the only benefit which proceeds from him is to open up a way for each to justify himself. I wish they could get a taste of what is

[1] 1 Cor. i. 30; Eph. i. 3–5; Col. i. 14, 20; John i. 12; x. 28.

meant by these passages: "He that hath the Son hath life." "He that heareth my word, and believeth on him that sent me," "is passed from death unto life." Whoso believeth in him "is passed from death unto life." "Being justified freely by his grace, through the redemption that is in Christ Jesus." "He that keepeth his commandments dwelleth in him, and he in him." God "hath raised us up together, and made us sit together in heavenly places in Christ." "Who hath delivered us from the power of darkness, and hath translated us into the kingdom of his dear Son."[1] There are similar passages without number. Their meaning is not, that by faith in Christ an opportunity is given us of procuring justification, or acquiring salvation, but that both are given us. Hence, so soon as you are ingrafted into Christ by faith, you are made a son of God, an heir of heaven, a partaker of righteousness, a possessor of life, and (the better to manifest the false tenets of these men) you have not obtained an opportunity of meriting), but all the merits of Christ, since they are communicated to you.

7. In this way the schools of Sorbonne, the parents of all heresies, have deprived us of justification by faith, which lies at the root of all godliness. They confess, indeed, in word, that men are justified by a formed faith, but they afterwards explain this to mean that of faith they have good works, which avail to justification, so that they almost seem to use the term faith in mockery, because they were unable, without incurring great obloquy, to pass it in silence, seeing it is so often repeated by Scripture. And yet not contented with this, they by the praise of good works transfer to man what they steal from God. And seeing that good works give little ground for exultation, and are not even properly called merits, if they are regarded as the fruits of divine grace, they derive them from the power of free-will; in other words, extract oil out of stone. They deny not that the principal cause is in grace; but they contend that there is no exclusion of free-will through which all merit comes. This is the doctrine, not only of the later Sophists, but of Lombard their Pythagoras (Sent. Lib. ii. Dist. 28), who, in comparison of them, may be called sound and sober. It was surely strange blindness, while he had Augustine so often in his mouth, not to see how cautiously he guarded against ascribing a single particle of praise to man because of good works. Above, when treating of free-will, we quoted some passages from him to this effect, and similar passages frequently occur in his writings (see in Psal. civ.; Ep. cv.), as when he forbids us ever to boast of our merits, because they themselves also are the gifts of God, and when he says that all our merits are only of grace, are not provided by our sufficiency, but are entirely the production of grace, &c. It is less strange that Lombard was blind to the light of Scripture, in which it is obvious that he had not been a very successful student.[2]

[1] 1 John v. 12; John v. 24; Rom. iii. 24; 1 John iii. 24; Eph. ii. 6; Col. i. 13.

[2] French, "d'autant qu'il n'y estoit gueres exercité;"—inasmuch as he was little versant in it.

Still there cannot be a stronger declaration against him and his disciples than the words of the Apostle, who, after interdicting all Christians from glorying, subjoins the reason why glorying is unlawful: "For we are his workmanship, created in Christ Jesus unto good works, which God hath before ordained that we should walk in them" (Eph. ii. 10). Seeing, then, that no good proceeds from us unless in so far as we are regenerated—and our regeneration is without exception wholly of God—there is no ground for claiming to ourselves one iota in good works. Lastly, while these men constantly inculcate good works, they, at the same time, train the conscience in such a way as to prevent it from venturing to confide that works will render God favourable and propitious. We, on the contrary, without any mention of merit, give singular comfort to believers when we teach them that in their works they please, and doubtless are accepted of God. Nay, here we even insist that no man shall attempt or enter upon any work without faith, that is, unless he previously have a firm conviction that it will please God.

8. Wherefore, let us never on any account allow ourselves to be drawn away one nail's breadth[1] from that only foundation. After it is laid, wise architects build upon it rightly and in order. For whether there is need of doctrine or exhortation, they remind us that "for this purpose the Son of God was manifested, that he might destroy the works of the devil;" that "whosoever is born of God doth not commit sin;" that "the time past of our life may suffice us to have wrought the will of the Gentiles;" that the elect of God are vessels of mercy, appointed "to honour," purged, "sanctified, and meet for the Master's use, and prepared unto every good work." The whole is expressed at once, when Christ thus describes his disciples, "If any man will come after me, let him deny himself, and take up his cross daily, and follow me."[2] He who has denied himself has cut off the root of all evil, so as no longer to seek his own; he who has taken up his cross has prepared himself for all meekness and endurance. The example of Christ includes this and all offices of piety and holiness. He obeyed his Father even unto death; his whole life was spent in doing the works of God; his whole soul was intent on the glory of his Father; he laid down his life for the brethren; he did good to his enemies, and prayed for them. And when there is need of comfort, it is admirably afforded in these words: "We are troubled on every side, yet not distressed; we are perplexed, but not in despair; persecuted, but not forsaken; cast down, but not destroyed; always bearing about in the body the dying of the Lord Jesus, that the life also of Jesus might be made manifest in our body." "For if we be dead with him, we shall also live with him; if we suffer, we shall also reign with him;" by means of "the fellowship of his sufferings, being made conformable unto his death;" the Father having predestinated us "to be conformed to the image

1 French, "ne fust ce que de la pointe d'une espingle;"—were it only a pin's point.
2 1 John iii. 8; 1 Pet. iv. 3; 2 Tim. ii. 20, 21; Luke ix. 23.

of his Son, that he might be the first-born among many brethren." Hence it is, that "neither death, nor life, nor angels, nor principalities, nor powers, nor things present, nor things to come, nor height, nor depth, nor any other creature, shall be able to separate us from the love of God which is in Christ Jesus our Lord;"[1] nay, rather all things will work together for our good. See how it is that we do not justify men before God by works, but say, that all who are of God are regenerated and made new creatures, so that they pass from the kingdom of sin into the kingdom of righteousness. In this way they make their calling sure, and, like trees, are judged by their fruits.

[1] 2 Cor. iv. 8; 2 Tim. ii. 11; Phil. iii. 10; Rom. viii. 29, 39.

CHAPTER XVI.

REFUTATION OF THE CALUMNIES BY WHICH IT IS ATTEMPTED TO THROW ODIUM ON THIS DOCTRINE.

The divisions of this chapter are,—I. The calumnies of the Papists against the orthodox doctrine of Justification by Faith are reduced to two classes. The first class, with its consequences, refuted, sec. 1–3. II. The second class, which is dependant on the first, refuted in the last section.

Sections.

1. Calumnies of the Papists. 1. That we destroy good works, and give encouragement to sin. Refutation of the first calumny. 1. Character of those who censure us. 2. Justification by faith establishes the necessity of good works.
2. Refutation of a consequent of the former calumny—viz. that men are dissuaded from well-doing when we destroy merit. Two modes of refutation. First mode confirmed by many invincible arguments.
3. The Apostles make no mention of merit, when they exhort us to good works. On the contrary, excluding merit, they refer us entirely to the mercy of God. Another mode of refutation.
4. Refutation of the second calumny and of an inference from it—viz. that the obtaining righteousness is made too easy, when it is made to consist in the free remission of sins.

1. Our last sentence may refute the impudent calumny of certain ungodly men, who charge us, first, with destroying good works, and leading men away from the study of them, when we say, that men are not justified, and do not merit salvation by works; and, secondly, with making the means of justification too easy, when we say that it consists in the free remission of sins, and thus alluring men to sin to which they are already too much inclined. These calumnies, I say, are sufficiently refuted by that one sentence; however, I will briefly reply to both. The allegation is, that justification by faith destroys good works. I will not describe what kind of zealots for good works the persons are who thus charge us. We leave them as much liberty to bring the charge, as they take licence to taint the whole world with the pollution of their lives.[1] They pretend to lament[2] that when faith is so highly extolled, works are deprived of their proper place. But what if they are rather ennobled and established? We dream not of a faith which is devoid of good works, nor of a justification which can exist without them: the only difference is, that while we acknowledge that faith and works are necessarily connected, we, however, place justification in faith, not in works. How this is done is easily explained, if we turn to Christ only, to whom our faith is directed, and from whom it derives all its power. Why, then, are

1 This sentence is wholly omitted in the French.
2 Latin, "Dolere sibi simulant."—French, "Ils alleguent;"—they allege.

we justified by faith? Because by faith we apprehend the righteousness of Christ, which alone reconciles us to God. This faith, however, you cannot apprehend without at the same time apprehending sanctification; for Christ "is made unto us wisdom, and righteousness, and sanctification, and redemption" (1 Cor. i. 30). Christ, therefore, justifies no man without also sanctifying him. These blessings are conjoined by a perpetual and inseparable tie. Those whom he enlightens by his wisdom he redeems; whom he redeems he justifies; whom he justifies he sanctifies. But as the question relates only to justification and sanctification, to them let us confine ourselves. Though we distinguish between them, they are both inseparably comprehended in Christ. Would ye then obtain justification in Christ? You must previously possess Christ. But you cannot possess him without being made a partaker of his sanctification: for Christ cannot be divided. Since the Lord, therefore, does not grant us the enjoyment of these blessings without bestowing himself, he bestows both at once, but never the one without the other. Thus it appears how true it is that we are justified not without, and yet not by works, since in the participation of Christ, by which we are justified, is contained not less sanctification than justification.

2. It is also most untrue that men's minds are withdrawn from the desire of well-doing when we deprive them of the idea of merit. Here, by the way, the reader must be told that those men absurdly infer merit from reward, as I will afterwards more clearly explain. They thus infer, because ignorant of the principle that God gives no less a display of his liberality when he assigns reward to works, than when he bestows the faculty of well-doing. This topic it will be better to defer to its own place. At present, let it be sufficient merely to advert to the weakness of their objection. This may be done in two ways.[1] For, *first*, they are altogether in error when they say that, unless a hope of reward is held forth, no regard will be had to the right conduct of life. For if all that men do when they serve God is to look to the reward, and hire out or sell their labour to him, little is gained: he desires to be freely worshipped, freely loved: I say he approves the worshipper who, even if all hope of reward were cut off, would cease not to worship him. Moreover, when men are to be urged, there cannot be a stronger stimulus than that derived from the end of our redemption and calling, such as the word of God employs when it says, that it were the height of impiety and ingratitude not to "love him who first loved us;" that by "the blood of Christ" our conscience is purged "from dead works to serve the living God;" that it were impious sacrilege in any one to count "the blood of the covenant, wherewith he was sanctified, an unholy thing;" that we have been "delivered out of the hands of our enemies," that we "might serve him without fear, in holiness and righteousness before him, all the days of our life;" that being "made free from sin," we

[1] All the previous sentences of this section, except the first, are omitted in the French.

"become the servants of righteousness;" "that our old man is crucified with him," in order that we might rise to newness of life. Again, "if ye then be risen with Christ (as becomes his members), seek those things which are above," living as pilgrims in the world, and aspiring to heaven, where our treasure is. "The grace of God hath appeared to all men, bringing salvation, teaching us that, denying ungodliness and worldly lusts, we should live soberly, righteously, and godly, in this present world; looking for that blessed hope, and the glorious appearing of the great God and our Saviour Jesus Christ." "For God hath not appointed us to wrath, but to obtain salvation through our Lord Jesus Christ." "Know ye not that ye are the temples of the Holy Spirit," which it were impious to profane? "Ye were sometimes darkness, but now are ye light in the Lord: walk as the children of light." "God hath not called us unto uncleanness, but unto holiness." "For this is the will of God, even your sanctification, that ye should abstain" from all illicit desires: ours is a "holy calling," and we respond not to it except by purity of life. "Being then made free from sin, ye became the servants of righteousness." Can there be a stronger argument in exciting us to charity than that of John? "If God so loved us, we ought also to love one another." "In this the children of God are manifest, and the children of the devil: whosoever doeth not righteousness is not of God, neither he that loveth not his brother." Similar is the argument of Paul, "Know ye not that your bodies are the members of Christ?" "For as the body is one, and hath many members, and all the members of that one body being many, are one body, so also is Christ." Can there be a stronger incentive to holiness than when we are told by John, "Every man that hath this hope in him purifieth himself, even as he is pure"? and by Paul, "Having, therefore, these promises, dearly beloved, cleanse yourselves from all filthiness of the flesh and spirit;" or when we hear our Saviour hold forth himself as an example to us that we should follow his steps?[1]

3. I have given these few passages merely as a specimen; for were I to go over them all, I should form a large volume. All the Apostles abound in exhortations, admonitions, and rebukes, for the purpose of training the man of God to every good work, and that without any mention of merit. Nay, rather their chief exhortations are founded on the fact, that without any merit of ours, our salvation depends entirely on thme ercy of God. Thus Paul, who during a whole Epistle had maintained that there was no hope of life for us save in the righteousness of Christ, when he comes to exhortation, beseeches us by the mercy which God has bestowed upon us (Rom. xii. 1). And, indeed, this one reason ought to have been sufficient, that God may be glorified in us. But if any are not so ardently desirous to promote

[1] 1 John iv. 10, 19; Heb. ix. 14; x. 29; Luke i. 74, 75; Rom. vi. 18; Col. iii. 1; Tit. ii. 11; 1 Thess. v. 9; 1 Cor. iii. 16; Eph. ii. 21; v. 8; 2 Cor. vi. 16; 1 Thess. iv. 3, 7; 2 Tim. i. 9; Rom. vi. 18; 1 John iv. 10; iii. 11; 1 Cor. vi. 15, 17; xii. 12; 1 John iii. 3; 2 Cor. vii. 1; John xv. 10.

the glory of God, still the remembrance of his kindness is most sufficient to incite them to do good (see Chrysost. Homil. in Genes.). But those men,[1] because, by introducing the idea of merit, they perhaps extract some forced and servile obedience of the Law, falsely allege, that as we do not adopt the same course, we have no means of exhorting to good works. As if God were well pleased with such services when he declares that he loves a cheerful giver, and forbids anything to be given him grudgingly or of necessity (2 Cor. ix. 7). I say not that I would reject that or omit any kind of exhortation which Scripture employs, its object being not to leave any method of animating us untried. For it states, that the recompense which God will render to every one is *according to his deeds;* but, first, I deny that that is the only, or, in many instances, the principal motive ; and, secondly, I admit not that it is the motive with which we are to begin. Moreover, I maintain that it gives not the least countenance to those merits which these men are always preaching. This will afterwards be seen. Lastly, there is no use in this recompense, unless we have previously embraced the doctrine that we are justified solely by the merits of Christ as apprehended by faith, and not by any merit of works; because the study of piety can be fitly prosecuted only by those by whom this doctrine has been previously imbibed. This is beautifully intimated by the Psalmist when he thus addresses God. "There is forgiveness with thee, that thou mayest be feared" (Ps. cxxx. 4). For he shows that the worship of God cannot exist without acknowledging his mercy, on which it is founded and established. This is specially deserving of notice, as showing us not only that the beginning of the due worship of God is confidence in his mercy ; but that the fear of God (which Papists will have to be meritorious) cannot be entitled to the name of merit, for this reason, that it is founded on the pardon and remission of sins.

4. But the most futile calumny of all is, that men are invited to sin when we affirm that the pardon in which we hold that justification consists is gratuitous. Our doctrine is, that justification is a thing of such value, that it cannot be put into the balance with any good quality of ours ; and, therefore, could never be obtained unless it were gratuitous: moreover, that it is gratuitous to us, but not also to Christ, who paid so dearly for it—namely, his own most sacred blood, out of which there was no price of sufficient value to pay what was due to the justice of God. When men are thus taught, they are reminded that it is owing to no merit of theirs that the shedding of that most sacred blood is not repeated every time they sin. Moreover, we say that our pollution is so great, that it can never be washed away save in the fountain of his pure blood. Must not those who are thus addressed conceive a greater horror of sin than if it were said to be wiped off by a sprinkling of good works? If they have any reverence for God, how can they, after being once purified, avoid shuddering

[1] French, "ces Pharisiens;"—those Pharisees.

at the thought of again wallowing in the mire, and as much as in them lies troubling and polluting the purity of this fountain? "I have washed my feet" (says the believing soul in the Song of Solomon, v. 3), "how shall I defile them?" It is now plain which of the two makes the forgiveness of sins of less value, and derogates from the dignity of justification. They pretend that God is appeased by their frivolous satisfactions; in other words, by mere dross. We maintain that the guilt of sin is too heinous to be so frivolously expiated; that the offence is too grave to be forgiven to such valueless satisfactions; and, therefore, that forgiveness is the prerogative of Christ's blood alone. They say that righteousness, wherever it is defective, is renewed and repaired by works of satisfaction. We think it too precious to be balanced by any compensation of works, and, therefore, in order to restore it, recourse must be had solely to the mercy of God. For the other points relating to the forgiveness of sins, see the following chapter.

CHAPTER XVII.

THE PROMISES OF THE LAW AND THE GOSPEL RECONCILED.

In the following chapter, the arguments of Sophists, who would destroy or impair the doctrine of Justification by Faith, are reduced to two classes. The former is general, the latter special, and contains some arguments peculiar to itself. I. The first class, which is general, and in a manner contains the foundation of all the arguments, draws an argument from the promises of the law. This is considered from sec. 1–3. II. The second class following from the former, and containing special proofs. An argument drawn from the history of Cornelius explained, sec. 4, 5. III. A full exposition of those passages of Scripture which represent God as showing mercy and favour to the cultivators of righteousness, sec. 6. IV. A third argument from the passages which distinguish good works by the name of righteousness, and declare that men are justified by them, sec. 7, 8. V. The adversaries of justification by faith placed in a dilemma. Their partial righteousness refuted, sec. 9, 10. VI. A fourth argument, setting the Apostle James in opposition to Paul, considered, sec. 11, 12. VII. Answer to a fifth argument, that, according to Paul, not the hearers but the doers of the law are justified, sec. 13. VIII. Consideration of a sixth argument, drawn from those passages in which believers boldly submit their righteousness to the judgment of God, and ask him to decide according to it, sec. 14. IX. Examination of the last argument, drawn from passages which ascribe righteousness and life to the ways of believers, sec. 15.

Sections.

1. Brief summary of Chapters xv. and xvi. Why justification is denied to works. Argument of opponents founded on the promises of the law. The substance of this argument. Answer. Those who would be justified before God must be exempted from the power of the law. How this is done.
2. Confirmation of the answer *ab impossibili*, and from the testimony of an Apostle and of David.
3. Answer to the objection, by showing why these promises were given. Refutation of the sophistical distinction between the *intrinsic* value of works, and their value *ex pacto*.
4. Argument from the history of Cornelius. Answer, by distinguishing between two kinds of acceptance. Former kind. Sophistical objection refuted.
5. Latter kind. Plain from this distinction that Cornelius was accepted freely before his good works could be accepted. Similar explanations to be given of the passage in which God is represented as merciful and propitious to the cultivators of righteousness.
6. Exposition of these passages. Necessary to observe whether the promise is legal or evangelical. The legal promise always made under the condition that we "do," the evangelical under the condition that we "believe."
7. Argument from the passages which distinguish good works by the name of righteousness, and declare that man is justified by them. Answer to the former part of the argument respecting the name. Why the works of the saints called works of righteousness. Distinction to be observed.
8. Answer to the second part of the argument—viz. that man is justified by works. Works of no avail by themselves; we are justified by faith only. This kind of righteousness defined. Whence the value set on good works.
9. Answer confirmed and fortified by a dilemma.
10. In what sense the partial imperfect righteousness of believers accepted. Conclusion of the refutation.
11. Argument founded on the Epistle of James. First answer. One Apostle cannot be opposed to another. Second answer. Third answer, from the scope of James

A double paralogism in the term Faith. In James the faith said not to justify is a mere empty opinion; in Paul it is the instrument by which we apprehend Christ our righteousness.

12. Another paralogism on the word *justify*. Paul speaks of the cause, James of the effects, of justification. Sum of the discussion.
13. Argument founded on Rom. ii. 13. Answer, explaining the Apostle's meaning. Another argument, containing a *reductio ad impossibili*. Why Paul used the argument.
14. An argument founded on the passages in which believers confidently appeal to their righteousness. Answer, founded on a consideration of two circumstances. 1. They refer only to a special cause. 2. They claim righteousness in comparison with the wicked.
15. Last argument from those passages which ascribe righteousness and life to the ways of believers. Answer. This proceeds from the paternal kindness of God. What meant by the perfection of saints.

1. LET us now consider the other arguments which Satan by his satellites invents to destroy or impair the doctrine of Justification by Faith. I think we have already put it out of the power of our calumniators to treat us as if we were the enemies of good works—justification being denied to works, not in order that no good works may be done, or that those which are done may be denied to be good; but only that we may not trust or glory in them, or ascribe salvation to them. Our only confidence and boasting, our only anchor of salvation is, that Christ the Son of God is ours, and that we are in him sons of God and heirs of the heavenly kingdom, being called, not by our worth, but the kindness of God, to the hope of eternal blessedness. But since, as has been said, they assail us with other engines, let us now proceed to demolish them also. First, they recur to the legal promises which the Lord proclaimed to the observers of the law, and they ask us whether we hold them to be null or effectual. Since it were absurd and ridiculous to say they are null, they take it for granted that they have some efficacy. Hence they infer that we are not justified by faith only. For the Lord thus speaks: "Wherefore it shall come to pass, if ye hearken to these judgments, and keep and do them, that the Lord thy God shall keep unto thee the covenant and the mercy which he sware unto thy fathers; and he will love thee, and bless thee, and multiply thee" (Deut. vii. 12, 13). Again, "If ye thoroughly amend your ways and your doings: if ye thoroughly execute judgment between a man and his neighbour; if ye oppress not the stranger, the fatherless, and the widow, and shed not innocent blood in this place, neither walk after other gods to your hurt: then will I cause you to dwell in this place, in the land that I gave to your fathers, for ever and ever" (Jer. vii. 5–7). It were to no purpose to quote a thousand similar passages, which, as they are not different in meaning, are to be explained on the same principle. In substance, Moses declares that in the law is set down "a blessing and a curse," life and death (Deut. xi. 26); and hence they argue, either that that blessing is become inactive and unfruitful, or that justification is not by faith only. We have already shown,[1] that if

[1] See Book II. chap. vii: sec. 2–8, 15; chap. viii. sec. 3; chap. xi. sec. 8; Book III. chap. xix. sec. 2.

we cleave to the law we are devoid of every blessing, and have nothing but the curse denounced on all transgressors. The Lord does not promise anything except to the perfect observers of the law; and none such are anywhere to be found. The result, therefore, is, that the whole human race is convicted by the law, and exposed to the wrath and curse of God: to be saved from this they must escape from the power of the law, and be as it were brought out of bondage into freedom,—not that carnal freedom which indisposes us for the observance of the law, tends to licentiousness, and allows our passions to wanton unrestrained with loosened reins; but that spiritual freedom which consoles and raises up the alarmed and smitten conscience, proclaiming its freedom from the curse and condemnation under which it was formerly held bound. This freedom from subjection to the law, this manumission, if I may so express it, we obtain when by faith we apprehend the mercy of God in Christ, and are thereby assured of the pardon of sins, with a consciousness of which the law stung and tortured us.

2. For this reason, the promises offered in the law would all be null and ineffectual, did not God in his goodness send the Gospel to our aid, since the condition on which they depend, and under which only they are to be performed—viz. the fulfilment of the law—will never be accomplished. Still, however, the aid which the Lord gives consists not in leaving part of justification to be obtained by works, and in supplying part out of his indulgence, but in giving us Christ as in himself alone the fulfilment of righteousness. For the Apostle, after premising that he and the other Jews, aware that "a man is not justified by the works of the law," had "believed in Jesus Christ," adds as the reason, not that they might be assisted to make up the sum of righteousness, by faith in Christ, but that they "might be justified by the faith of Christ, and not by the works of the law" (Gal. ii. 16). If believers withdraw from the law to faith, that in the latter they may find the justification which they see is not in the former, they certainly disclaim justification by the law. Therefore, whoso will, let him amplify the rewards which are said to await the observer of the law, provided he at the same time understand that, owing to our depravity, we derive no benefit from them until we have obtained another righteousness by faith. Thus David, after making mention of the reward which the Lord has prepared for his servants (Ps. xxv. almost throughout), immediately descends to an acknowledgment of sins, by which the reward is made void. In Psalm xix., also, he loudly extols the benefits of the law; but immediately exclaims, "Who can understand his errors? cleanse thou me from secret faults" (Ps. xix. 12). This passage perfectly accords with the former, when, after saying, "All the paths of the Lord are mercy and truth unto such as keep his covenant and his testimonies," he adds, "For thy name's sake, O Lord, pardon mine iniquity: for it is great" (Ps. xxv. 10, 11). Thus, too, we ought not to acknowledge that the favour of God is offered to us in the law, provided by our works we can

deserve it; but that it never actually reaches us through any such desert.

3. What then? Were the promises given that they might vanish away without fruit? I lately declared that this is not my opinion. I say, indeed, that their efficacy does not extend to us so long as they have respect to the merit of works, and therefore that, considered in themselves, they are in some sense abolished. Hence the Apostle shows, that the celebrated promise, "Ye shall therefore keep my statutes and my judgments: which if a man do, he shall live in them" (Levit. xviii. 5; Ezek. xx. 10), will, if we stop at it, be of no avail, and will profit us not a whit more than if it were not given, being inaccessible even to the holiest servants of God, who are all far from fulfilling the law, being encompassed with many infirmities. But when the Gospel promises are substituted, promises which announce the free pardon of sins, the result is not only that our persons are accepted of God, but his favour also is shown to our works, and that not only in respect that the Lord is pleased with them, but also because he visits them with the blessings which were due by agreement to the observance of his law. I admit, therefore, that the works of the faithful are rewarded with the promises which God gave in his law to the cultivators of righteousness and holiness; but in this reward we should always attend to the cause which procures favour to works. This cause, then, appears to be threefold. First, God turning his eye away from the works of his servants which merit reproach more than praise, embraces them in Christ, and by the intervention of faith alone reconciles them to himself without the aid of works. Secondly, the works not being estimated by their own worth, he, by his fatherly kindness and indulgence, honours so far as to give them some degree of value. Thirdly, he extends his pardon to them, not imputing the imperfection by which they are all polluted, and would deserve to be regarded as vices rather than virtues. Hence it appears how much Sophists[1] were deluded in thinking they admirably escaped all absurdities when they said, that works are able to merit salvation, not from their intrinsic worth, but according to agreement, the Lord having, in his liberality, set this high value upon them. But, meanwhile, they observed not how far the works which they insisted on regarding as meritorious must be from fulfilling the condition of the promises, were they not preceded by a justification founded on faith alone, and on forgiveness of sins—a forgiveness necessary to cleanse even good works from their stains. Accordingly, of the three causes of divine liberality to which it is owing that good works are accepted, they attended only to one; the other two, though the principal causes, they suppressed.

4. They quote the saying of Peter as given by Luke in the Acts, "Of a truth I perceive that God is no respector of persons: but in every nation he that feareth him, and worketh righteousness, is ac-

1 French, "Les Sophistes de Sorbonne;"—the Sophists of Sorbonne.

cepted with him" (Acts x. 34, 35). And hence they infer, as a thing which seems to them beyond a doubt, that if man by right conduct procures the favour of God, his obtaining salvation is not entirely the gift of God. Nay, that when God in his mercy assists the sinner, he is inclined to mercy by works. There is no way of reconciling the passages of Scripture unless you observe that man's acceptance with God is twofold. As man is by nature, God finds nothing in him which can incline him to mercy, except merely his wretchedness. If it is clear then that man, when God first interposes for him, is naked and destitute of all good, and, on the other hand, loaded and filled with all kinds of evil,—for what quality, pray, shall we say that he is worthy of the heavenly kingdom? Where God thus clearly displays free mercy, have done with that empty imagination of merit. Another passage in the same book—viz. where Cornelius hears from the lips of an angel, "Thy prayer and thine alms are come up for a memorial before God" (Acts x. 4), is miserably wrested to prove that man is prepared by the study of good works to receive the favour of God. Cornelius being endued with true wisdom, in other words, with the fear of God, must have been enlightened by the Spirit of wisdom, and, being an observer of righteousness, must have been sanctified by the same Spirit; righteousness being, as the Apostle testifies, one of the most certain fruits of the Spirit (Gal. v. 5). Therefore all those qualities by which he is said to have pleased God he owed to divine grace: so far was he from preparing himself by his own strengh to receive it. Indeed not a syllable of Scripture can be produced which does not accord with the doctrine, that the only reason why God receives man into his favour is, because he sees that he is in every respect lost when left to himself; lost, if he does not display his mercy in delivering him. We now see that in thus accepting, God looks not to the righteousness of the individual, but merely manifests the divine goodness towards miserable sinners, who are altogether undeserving of this great mercy.

5. But after the Lord has withdrawn the sinner from the abyss of perdition, and set him apart for himself by means of adoption, having begotten him again and formed him to newness of life, he embraces him as a new creature, and bestows the gifts of his Spirit. This is the acceptance to which Peter refers, and by which believers after their calling are approved by God even in respect of works; for the Lord cannot but love and delight in the good qualities which he produces in them by means of his Spirit. But we must always bear in mind, that the only way in which men are accepted of God in respect of works is, that whatever good works he has conferred upon those whom he admits to favour, he by an increase of liberality honours with his acceptance. For whence their good works, but just that the Lord having chosen them as vessels of honour, is pleased to adorn them with true purity? And how are their actions deemed good as if there was no deficiency in them, but just that their merciful Father indulgently pardons the spots and blemishes which adhere to them?

In one word, the only meaning of acceptance in this passage is, that God accepts and takes pleasure in his children, in whom he sees the traces and lineaments of his own countenance. We have elsewhere said, that regeneration is a renewal of the divine image in us. Since God therefore, whenever he beholds his own face, justly loves it and holds it in honour, the life of believers, when formed to holiness and justice, is said, not without cause, to be pleasing to him. But because believers, while encompassed with mortal flesh, are still sinners, and their good works only begun savour of the corruption of the flesh, God cannot be propitious either to their persons or their works, unless he embraces them more in Christ than in themselves. In this way are we to understand the passages in which God declares that he is clement and merciful to the cultivators of righteousness. Moses said to the Israelites, "Know, therefore, that the Lord thy God, he is God, the faithful God, which keepeth covenant and mercy with them that love him and keep his commandments, to a thousand generations." These words afterwards became a common form of expression among the people. Thus Solomon in his prayer at the dedication says, "Lord God of Israel, there is no God like thee, in heaven above, or on earth beneath, who keepest covenant and mercy with thy servants that walk before thee with all their heart" (1 Kings viii. 23). The same words are repeated by Nehemiah (Neh. i. 5). As the Lord in all covenants of mercy stipulates on his part for integrity and holiness of life in his servants (Deut. xxix. 18), lest his goodness might be held in derision, or any one, puffed up with exultation in it, might speak flatteringly to his soul while walking in the depravity of his heart, so he is pleased that in this way those whom he admits to communion in the covenant should be kept to their duty. Still, however, the covenant was gratuitous at first, and such it ever remains. Accordingly, while David declares, "according to the cleanness of my hands hath he recompensed me," yet does he not omit the fountain to which I have referred; "he delivered me, because he delighted in me" (2 Sam. xxii. 20, 21). In commending the goodness of his cause, he derogates in no respect from the free mercy which takes precedence of all the gifts of which it is the origin.

6. Here, by the way, it is of importance to observe how those forms of expression differ from legal promises. By legal promises, I mean not those which lie scattered in the books of Moses (for there many Evangelical promises occur), but those which properly belong to the legal dispensation. All such promises, by whatever name they may be called, are made under the condition that the reward is to be paid on the things commanded being done. But when it is said that the Lord keeps a covenant of mercy with those who love him, the words rather demonstrate what kind of servants those are who have sincerely entered into the covenant, than express the reason why the Lord blesses them. The nature of the demonstration is this: As the end for which God bestows upon us the gift of eternal life is, that he may be loved, feared, and worshipped by us, so the end of all the promises

of mercy contained in Scripture justly is, that we may reverence and serve their author. Therefore, whenever we hear that he does good to those that observe his law, let us remember that the sons of God are designated by the duty which they ought perpetually to observe, that his reason for adopting us is, that we may reverence him as a father. Hence, if we would not deprive ourselves of the privilege of adoption, we must always strive in the direction of our calling. On the other hand, however, let us remember, that the completion of the Divine mercy depends not on the works of believers, but that God himself fulfils the promise of salvation to those who by right conduct correspond to their calling, because he recognises the true badges of sons in those only who are directed to good by his Spirit. To this we may refer what is said of the members of the Church, "Lord, who shall abide in thy tabernacle? who shall dwell in thy holy hill? He that walketh uprightly, and worketh righteousness, and speaketh the truth in his heart," &c. (Ps. xv. 1, 2). Again, in Isaiah, "Who among us shall dwell with the devouring fire? who among us shall dwell with everlasting burnings? He that walketh righteously," &c. (Isa. xxxiii. 14, 15). For the thing described is not the strength with which believers can stand before the Lord, but the manner in which our most merciful Father introduces them into his fellowship, and defends and confirms them therein. For as he detests sin and loves righteousness, so those whom he unites to himself he purifies by his Spirit, that he may render them conformable to himself and to his kingdom. Therefore, if it be asked, What is the first cause which gives the saints free access to the kingdom of God, and a firm and permanent footing in it? the answer is easy. The Lord in his mercy once adopted and ever defends them. But if the question relates to the manner, we must descend to regeneration, and the fruits of it, as enumerated in the fifteenth Psalm.

7. There seems much more difficulty in those passages which distinguish good works by the name of righteousness, and declare that man is justified by them. The passages of the former class are very numerous, as when the observance of the commandments is termed justification or righteousness. Of the other classes we have a description in the words of Moses, "It shall be our righteousness, if we observe to do all these commandments" (Deut. vi. 25). But if you object, that it is a legal promise, which, having an impossible condition annexed to it, proves nothing, there are other passages to which the same answer cannot be made; for instance, "If the man be poor," "thou shalt deliver him the pledge again when the sun goeth down:" "and it shall be righteousness unto thee before the Lord thy God" (Deut. xxiv. 13). Likewise the words of the prophet, "Then stood up Phinehas, and executed judgment: and so the plague was stayed. And that was counted unto him for righteousness unto all generations for evermore" (Psal. cvi. 30, 31). Accordingly, the Pharisees of our day think they have here full scope for exultation.[1] For, as

1 French, "de crier contre nous en cest endroit;"—here to raise an outcry against us.

we say, that when justification by faith is established, justification by works falls; they argue on the same principle, If there is a justification by works, it is false to say that we are justified by faith only. When I grant that the precepts of the law are termed righteousness, I do nothing strange: for they are so in reality. I must, however, inform the reader, that the Hebrew word חקים has been rendered by the Septuagint, not very appropriately, δικαιώματα, *justifications*, instead of *edicts*.[1] But I readily give up any dispute as to the word. Nor do I deny that the Law of God contains a perfect righteousness. For although we are debtors to do all the things which it enjoins, and therefore, even after a full obedience, are unprofitable servants; yet, as the Lord has deigned to give it the name of righteousness, it is not ours to take from it what he has given. We readily admit, therefore, that the perfect obedience of the law is righteousness, and the observance of any precept a part of righteousness, the whole substance of righteousness being contained in the remaining parts. But we deny that any such righteousness ever exists. Hence we discard the righteousness of the law, not as being in itself maimed and defective, but because of the weakness of our flesh it nowhere appears. But then Scripture does not merely call the precepts of the law righteousness, it also gives this name to the works of the saints: as when it states that Zacharias and his wife "were both righteous before God, walking in all the commandments and ordinances of the Lord blameless" (Luke i. 6). Surely when it thus speaks, it estimates works more according to the nature of the law than their own proper character. And here, again, I must repeat the observation which I lately made, that the law is not to be ascertained from a careless translation of the Greek interpreter. Still, as Luke chose not to make any change on the received version, I will not contend for this. The things contained in the law God enjoined upon man for righteousness, but that righteousness we attain not unless by observing the whole law: every transgression whatever destroys it. While, therefore, the law commands nothing but righteousness, if we look to itself, every one of its precepts is righteousness: if we look to the men by whom they are performed, being transgressors in many things, they by no means merit the praise of righteousness for one work, and that a work which, through the imperfection adhering to it, is always in some respect vicious.[2]

8. I come to the second class (sec. 1, 7, ad init.), in which the

1 French, "Edits ou Statuts;"—Edicts or Statutes.

2 The French here adds the two following sentences:—"Nostre response donc est, que quand les œuvres des saincts sont nommées justice, cela ne vient point de leurs merites: mais entant qu'elles tendent à la justice que Dieu nous a commandee, laquelle est nulle, si elle n'est parfaite. Or elle ne se trouve parfaite en nul homme de monde; pourtant faut conclure, q'une bonne œuvre de soy ne merite pas le nom de justice."—Our reply then is, that when the works of the saints are called righteousness, it is not owing to their merits, but is in so far as they tend to the righteousness which God has commanded, and which is null if it be not perfect. Now it is not found perfect in any man in the world. Hence we must conclude, that no good work merits in itself the name of righteousness.

chief difficulty lies. Paul finds nothing stronger to prove justification by faith than that which is written of Abraham, he "believed God, and it was counted unto him for righteousness" (Rom. iv. 3; Gal. iii. 6). Therefore, when it is said that the achievement of Phinehas "was counted unto him for righteousness" (Psal. cvi. 30, 31), we may argue that what Paul contends for respecting faith applies also to works. Our opponents, accordingly, as if the point were proved, set it down that though we are not justified without faith, it is not by faith only; that our justification is completed by works. Here I beseech believers, as they know that the true standard of righteousness must be derived from Scripture alone, to consider with me seriously and religiously, how Scripture can be fairly reconciled with that view. Paul, knowing that justification by faith was the refuge of those who wanted righteousness of their own, confidently infers, that all who are justified by faith are excluded from the righteousness of works. But as it is clear that this justification is common to all believers, he with equal confidence infers that no man is justified by works; nay, more, that justification is without any help from works. But it is one thing to determine what power works have in themselves, and another to determine what place they are to hold after justification by faith has been established. If a price is to be put upon works according to their own worth, we hold that they are unfit to appear in the presence of God: that man, accordingly, has no works in which he can glory before God, and that hence, deprived of all aid from works, he is justified by faith alone. Justification, moreover, we thus define: The sinner being admitted into communion with Christ is, for his sake, reconciled to God; when purged by his blood he obtains the remission of sins, and clothed with righteousness, just as if it were his own, stands secure before the judgment-seat of heaven. Forgiveness of sins being previously given, the good works which follow have a value different from their merit, because whatever is imperfect in them is covered by the perfection of Christ, and all their blemishes and pollutions are wiped away by his purity, so as never to come under the cognisance of the divine tribunal. The guilt of all transgressions, by which men are prevented from offering God an acceptable service, being thus effaced, and the imperfection which is wont to sully even good works being buried, the good works which are done by believers are deemed righteous, or, which is the same thing, are imputed for righteousness.

9. Now, should any one state this to me as an objection to justification by faith, I would first ask him, Whether a man is deemed righteous for one holy work or two, while in all the other acts of his life he is a transgressor of the law? This were, indeed, more than absurd. I would next ask, Whether he is deemed righteous on account of many good works if he is guilty of transgression in some one part? Even this he will not venture to maintain in opposition to the authority of the law, which pronounces, "Cursed be he that

confirmeth not all the words of this law to do them" (Deut xxvii. 26). I would go still farther and ask, Whether there be any work which may not justly be convicted of impurity or imperfection? How, then, will it appear to that eye before which even the heavens are not clean, and angels are chargeable with folly? (Job. iv. 18.) Thus he will be forced to confess that no good work exists that is not defiled, both by contrary transgression and also by its own corruption, so that it cannot be honoured as righteousness. But if it is certainly owing to justification by faith that works, otherwise impure, unclean, defective, unworthy of the sight, not to say of the love of God, are imputed for righteousness, why do they by boasting of this imputation aim at the destruction of that justification, but for which the boast were vain? Are they desirous of having a viper's birth?[1] To this their ungodly language tends. They cannot deny that justification by faith is the beginning, the foundation, the cause, the subject, the substance, of works of righteousness, and yet they conclude that justification is not by faith, because good works are counted for righteousness. Let us have done then with this frivolity, and confess the fact as it stands; *if* any righteousness which works are supposed to possess depends on justification by faith, this doctrine is not only not impaired, but on the contrary confirmed, its power being thereby more brightly displayed. Nor let us suppose, that after free justification works are commended, as if they afterwards succeeded to the office of justifying, or shared the office with faith. For did not justification by faith always remain entire, the impurity of works would be disclosed. There is nothing absurd in the doctrine, that though man is justified by faith, he is himself not only not righteous, but the righteousness attributed to his works is beyond their own deserts.

10. In this way we can admit not only that there is a partial righteousness in works (as our adversaries maintain), but that they are approved by God as if they were absolutely perfect. If we remember on what foundation this is rested, every difficulty will be solved. The first time when a work begins to be acceptable is when it is received with pardon. And whence pardon, but just because God looks upon us and all that belongs to us as in Christ? Therefore, as we ourselves when ingrafted into Christ appear righteous before God, because our iniquities are covered with his innocence; so our works are, and are deemed righteous, because everything otherwise defective in them being buried by the purity of Christ is not imputed. Thus we may justly say, that not only ourselves, but our works also, are justified by faith alone. Now, if that righteousness of works, whatever it be, depends on faith and free justification, and is produced by it, it ought to be included under it, and, so to speak, made subordinate to it, as the effect to its cause; so far is it from

1 French, " Voudrions nous faire une lignee serpentine, que les enfans meurtrissent leur mere?"—Would we have a viperish progeny, where the children murder the parent?

being entitled to be set up to impair or destroy the doctrine of justification.[1] Thus Paul, to prove that our blessedness depends not on our works, but on the mercy of God, makes special use of the words of David, "Blessed is he whose transgression is forgiven, whose sin is covered;" "Blessed is the man unto whom the Lord imputeth not iniquity." Should any one here obtrude the numberless passages in which blessedness seems to be attributed to works, as "Blessed is the man that feareth the Lord;" "He that hath mercy on the poor, happy is he;" "Blessed is the man that walketh not in the counsel of the ungodly," and "that endureth temptation;" "Blessed are they that keep judgment," that are "pure in heart," "meek," "merciful," &c.,[2] they cannot make out that Paul's doctrine is not true. For seeing that the qualities thus extolled never all so exist in man as to obtain for him the approbation of God, it follows, that man is always miserable until he is exempted from misery by the pardon of his sins. Since, then, all the kinds of blessedness extolled in the Scripture are vain, so that man derives no benefit from them until he obtains blessedness by the forgiveness of sins, a forgiveness which makes way for them, it follows that this is not only the chief and highest, but the only blessedness, unless you are prepared to maintain that it is impaired by things which owe their entire existence to it. There is much less to trouble us in the name of *righteous* which is usually given to believers. I admit that they are so called from the holiness of their lives, but as they rather exert themselves in the study of righteousness than fulfil righteousness itself, any degree of it which they possess must yield to justification by faith, to which it is owing that it is what it is.

11. But they say that we have a still more serious business with James, who in express terms opposes us. For he asks, "Was not Abraham our father justified by works?" and adds, "You see then how that by works a man is justified, and not by faith only" (James ii. 21, 24). What then? Will they engage Paul in a quarrel with James? If they hold James to be a servant of Christ, his sentiments must be understood as not dissenting from Christ speaking by the mouth of Paul. By the mouth of Paul the Spirit declares that Abraham obtained justification by faith, not by works; we also teach that all are justified by faith without the works of the law. By James the same Spirit declares that both Abraham's justification and ours consists of works, and not of faith only. It is certain that the Spirit cannot be at variance with himself. Where, then, will be the agree-

1 The whole sentence in French stands thus :—"Or si cette justice des œuvres telle quelle procede de la foy et de la justification gratuite, il ne faut pas qu'on la prenne pour destruire ou obscurcir la grace dont elle depend; mais plustost doit estre enclose en icelle, comme le fruict à l'arbre."—Now, if this righteousness of works, such as it is, proceeds from faith and free justification, it must not be employed to destroy or obscure the grace on which it depends, but should rather be included in it, like the fruit in the tree.

2 Rom. iv. 7; Ps xxxii. 1, 2; cxii. 1; Prov. xiv. 21; Ps. i. 1; cvi. 3; cxix. 11; Matth. v. 3.

ment? It is enough for our opponents, provided they can tear up that justification by faith which we regard as fixed by the deepest roots:[1] to restore peace to the conscience is to them a matter of no great concern. Hence you may see, that though they indeed carp at the doctrine of justification by faith, they meanwhile point out no goal of righteousness at which the conscience may rest. Let them triumph then as they will, so long as the only victory they can boast of is, that they have deprived righteousness of all its certainty. This miserable victory they will indeed obtain when the light of truth is extinguished, and the Lord permits them to darken it with their lies. But wherever the truth of God stands they cannot prevail. I deny, then, that the passage of James which they are constantly holding up before us as if it were the shield of Achilles, gives them the slightest countenance. To make this plain, let us first attend to the scope of the Apostle, and then show wherein their hallucination consists. As at that time (and the evil has existed in the Church ever since) there were many who, while they gave manifest proof of their infidelity, by neglecting and omitting all the works peculiar to believers, ceased not falsely to glory in the name of faith. James here dissipates their vain confidence. His intention therefore is, not to derogate in any degree from the power of true faith, but to show how absurdly these triflers laid claim only to the empty name, and resting satisfied with it, felt secure in unrestrained indulgence in vice. This state of matters being understood, it will be easy to see where the error of our opponents lies. They fall into a double paralogism, the one in the term *faith*, the other in the term *justifying*. The Apostle, in giving the name of *faith* to an empty opinion altogether differing from true faith, makes a concession which derogates in no respect from his case. This he demonstrates at the outset by the words, "What doth it profit, my brethren, though a man say he hath faith, and have not works?" (James ii. 14). He says not, "If a man *have* faith without works," but "if he say that he has." This becomes still clearer when a little after he derides this faith as worse than that of devils, and at last when he calls it "dead." You may easily ascertain his meaning by the explanation, "Thou believest that there is one God." Surely if all which is contained in that faith is a belief in the existence of God, there is no wonder that it does not justify. The denial of such a power to it cannot be supposed to derogate in any degree from Christian faith, which is of a very different description. For how does true faith justify unless by uniting us to Christ, so that being made one with him, we may be admitted to a participation in his righteousness? It does not justify because it forms an idea of the divine existence, but because it reclines with confidence on the divine mercy.

1 French, "Il suffit à nos adversaires s'ils peuvent deraciner la justice de foy, laquelle nous voulons estre plantee au profond du cœur."—It is enough for our opponents if they can root up justification by faith, which we desire to be planted at the bottom of the heart.

12. We have not made good our point until we dispose of the other paralogism: since James places a part of justification in works. If you would make James consistent with the other Scriptures and with himself, you must give the word *justify*, as used by him, a different meaning from what it has with Paul. In the sense of Paul we are said to be justified when the remembrance of our unrighteousness is obliterated, and we are counted righteous. Had James had the same meaning it would have been absurd for him to quote the words of Moses, "Abraham believed God," &c. The context runs thus: "Was not Abraham our father justified by works when he had offered Isaac his son upon the altar? Seest thou how faith wrought with his works, and by works was faith made perfect? And the Scripture was fulfilled which saith, Abraham believed God, and it was imputed unto him for righteousness." If it is absurd to say that the effect was prior to its cause, either Moses falsely declares in that passage that Abraham's faith was imputed for righteousness, or Abraham, by his obedience in offering up Isaac, did not merit righteousness. Before the existence of Ishmael, who was a grown youth at the birth of Isaac. Abraham was justified by his faith. How then can we say that he obtained justification by an obedience which followed long after? Wherefore, either James erroneously inverts the proper order (this it were impious to suppose), or he meant not to say that he was justified, as if he deserved to be deemed just. What then? It appears certain that he is speaking of the manifestation, not of the imputation of righteousness, as if he had said, Those who are justified by true faith prove their justification by obedience and good works, not by a bare and imaginary semblance of faith. In one word, he is not discussing the mode of justification, but requiring that the justification of believers shall be operative. And as Paul contends that men are justified without the aid of works, so James will not allow any to be regarded as justified who are destitute of good works. Due attention to the scope will thus disentangle every doubt; for the error of our opponents lies chiefly in this, that they think James is defining the mode of justification, whereas his only object is to destroy the depraved security of those who vainly pretended faith as an excuse for their contempt of good works. Therefore, let them twist the words of James as they may, they will never extract out of them more than the two propositions: That an empty phantom of faith does not justify, and that the believer, not contented with such an imagination, manifests his justification by good works.

13. They gain nothing by quoting from Paul to the same effect, that "not the hearers of the law are just before God, but the doers of the law shall be justified" (Rom. ii. 13). I am unwilling to evade the difficulty by the solution of Ambrose, that Paul spoke thus because faith in Christ is the fulfilment of the law. This I regard as a mere subterfuge, and one too for which there is no occasion, as the explanation is perfectly obvious. The Apostle's object is to suppress the absurd confidence of the Jews, who gave out that they alone had

a knowledge of the law, though at the very time they were its greatest despisers. That they might not plume themselves so much on a bare acquaintance with the law, he reminds them that when justification is sought by the law, the thing required is not the knowledge but the observance of it. We certainly mean not to dispute that the righteousness of the law consists in works, and not only so, but that justification consists in the dignity and merits of works. But this proves not that we are justified by works unless they can produce some one who has fulfilled the law. That Paul had no other meaning is abundantly obvious from the context. After charging Jews and Gentiles in common with unrighteousness, he descends to particulars, and says, that "as many as have sinned without law shall also perish without law," referring to the Gentiles; and that "as many as have sinned in the law shall be judged by the law," referring to the Jews. Moreover, as they, winking at their transgressions, boasted merely of the law, he adds most appropriately, that the law was passed with the view of justifying not those who only heard it, but those only who obeyed it; as if he had said, Do you seek righteousness in the law? do not bring forward the mere hearing of it, which is in itself of little weight, but bring works by which you may show that the law has not been given to you in vain. Since in these they were all deficient, it followed that they had no ground of boasting in the law. Paul's meaning, therefore, rather leads to an opposite argument. The righteousness of the law consists in the perfection of works; but no man can boast of fulfilling the law by works, and therefore there is no righteousness by the law.

14. They now betake themselves to those passages in which believers boldly submit their righteousness to the judgment of God, and wish to be judged accordingly; as in the following passages: "Judge me, O Lord, according to my righteousness, and according to mine integrity that is in me." Again, "Hear the right, O Lord;" "Thou hast proved mine heart; thou hast visited me in the night; thou hast tried me, and shalt find nothing." Again, "The Lord rewarded me according to my righteousness; according to the cleanness of my hands hath he recompensed me. For I have kept the ways of the Lord, and have not wickedly departed from my God." "I was also upright before him, and I kept myself from mine iniquity." Again, "Judge me, O Lord; for I have walked in mine integrity;" "I have not sat with vain persons; neither will I go in with dissemblers;" "Gather not my soul with sinners, nor my life with bloody men; in whose hands is mischief, and their right hand is full of bribes. But as for me, I will walk in mine integrity."[1] I have already spoken of the confidence which the saints seem to derive simply from works. The passages now quoted will not occasion much difficulty, if we attend to their περίστασις, their connection, or (as it is commonly called) special circumstances. These are of two kinds; for those who use

[1] Ps. vii. 9; xvii. 1; xviii. 20; xxvi. 1, 9, 10. Farther on, see Chap. xiv. s. 18; Chap. xx. s. 10.

them have no wish that their whole life should be brought to trial, so that they may be acquitted or condemned according to its tenor; all they wish is, that a decision, should be given on the particular case; and even here the righteousness which they claim is not with reference to the divine perfection, but only by comparison with the wicked and profane. When the question relates to justification, the thing required is not that the individual have a good ground of acquittal in regard to some particular matter, but that his whole life be in accordance with righteousness. But when the saints implore the divine justice in vindication of their innocence, they do not present themselves as free from fault, and in every respect blameless, but while placing their confidence of salvation in the divine goodness only, and trusting that he will vindicate his poor when they are afflicted contrary to justice and equity, they truly commit to him the cause in which the innocent are oppressed. And when they sist themselves with their adversaries at the tribunal of God, they pretend not to an innocence corresponding to the divine purity were inquiry strictly made, but knowing that in comparison of the malice, dishonesty, craft, and iniquity of their enemies, their sincerity, justice, simplicity, and purity, are ascertained and approved by God, they dread not to call upon him to judge between them. Thus when David said to Saul, "The Lord render to every man his righteousness and his faithfulness" (1 Sam. xxvi. 23), he meant not that the Lord should examine and reward every one according to his deserts, but he took the Lord to witness how great his innocence was in comparison of Saul's injustice. Paul, too, when he indulges in the boast, "Our rejoicing is this, the testimony of our conscience, that in simplicity and godly sincerity, not with fleshly wisdom, but by the grace of God, we have had our conversation in the world, and more abundantly to you-ward" (2 Cor. i. 12), means not to call for the scrutiny of God, but compelled by the calumnies of the wicked he appeals, in contradiction of all their slanders, to his faith and probity, which he knew that God had indulgently accepted. For we see how he elsewhere says, "I know nothing by myself; yet am I not hereby justified" (1 Cor. iv. 4); in other words, he was aware that the divine judgment far transcended the blind estimate of man. Therefore, however believers may, in defending their integrity against the hypocrisy of the ungodly, appeal to God as their witness and judge, still when the question is with God alone, they all with one mouth exclaim, "If thou, Lord, should mark iniquities, O Lord, who shall stand?" Again, "Enter not into judgment with thy servant; for in thy sight shall no man living be justified." Distrusting their own works, they gladly exclaim, "Thy loving-kindness is better than life" (Ps. cxxx. 3; cxliii. 2; lxiii. 3).

15. There are other passages not unlike those quoted above, at which some may still demur. Solomon says, "The just man walketh in his integrity" (Prov. xx. 7). Again, "In the way of righteousness is life; and in the pathway thereof there is no death" (Prov.

xii. 28). For this reason Ezekiel says, He that "hath walked in my statutes, and hath kept my judgments to deal truly; he is just, he shall surely live" (Ezek. xviii. 9, 21; xxxiii. 15). None of these declarations do we deny or obscure. But let one of the sons of Adam come forward with such integrity. If there is none, they must perish from the presence of God, or betake themselves to the asylum of mercy. Still we deny not that the integrity of believers, though partial and imperfect, is a step to immortality. How so, but just that the works of those whom the Lord has assumed into the covenant of grace, he tries not by their merit, but embraces with paternal indulgence. By this we understand not with the Schoolmen, that works derive their value from accepting grace. For their meaning is, that works otherwise unfit to obtain salvation in terms of law, are made fit for such a purpose by the divine acceptance. On the other hand, I maintain that these works being sullied both by other transgressions and by their own deficiencies, have no other value than this, that the Lord indulgently pardons them; in other words, that the righteousness which he bestows on man is gratuitous. Here they unseasonably obtrude those passages in which the Apostle prays for all perfection to believers, "To the end he may establish your hearts unblameable in holiness before God, even our Father" (1 Thess. iii. 13, and elsewhere). These words were strongly urged by the Celestines of old, in maintaining the perfection of holiness in the present life. To this we deem it sufficient briefly to reply with Augustine, that the goal to which all the pious ought to aspire is, to appear in the presence of God without spot and blemish; but as the course of the present life is at best nothing more than progress, we shall never reach the goal until we have laid aside the body of sin, and been completely united to the Lord. If any one choose to give the name of perfection to the saints, I shall not obstinately quarrel with him, provided he defines this perfection in the words of Augustine, "When we speak of the perfect virtue of the saints, part of this perfection consists in the recognition of our imperfection both in truth and in humility" (August. ad Bonif. Lib. iii. c. 7).

CHAPTER XVIII.

THE RIGHTEOUSNESS OF WORKS IMPROPERLY INFERRED FROM REWARDS.

There are three divisions in this chapter,—I. A solution of two general objections which are urged in support of justification by works. First, That God will render to every one according to his works, sec. 1. Second that the reward of works is called eternal, sec. 2-6. II. Answer to other special objections derived from the former, and a perversion of passages of Scripture, sec. 6-9. III. Refutation of the sophism that faith itself is called a work, and therefore justification by it is by works, sec. 10.

Sections.

1. Two general objections. The former solved and explained. What meant by the term *working*.
2. Solution of the second general objection. 1. Works not the cause of salvation. This shown from the name and nature of inheritance. 2. A striking example that the Lord rewards the works of believers with blessings which he had promised before the works were thought of.
3. First reason why eternal life said to be the reward of works. This confirmed by passages of Scripture. The concurrence of Ambrose. A rule to be observed. Declarations of Christ and an Apostle.
4. Other four reasons. Holiness the way to the kingdom, not the cause of obtaining it. Proposition of the Sophists.
5. Objection that God crowns the works of his people. Three answers from Augustine. A fourth from Scripture.
6. First special objection—viz. that we are ordered to lay up treasure in heaven. Answer, showing in what way this can be done.
7. Second objection—viz. that the righteous enduring affliction are said to be worthy of the kingdom of heaven. Answer. What meant by righteousness.
8. A third objection founded on three passages of Paul. Answer.
9. Fourth objection founded on our Saviour's words, "If ye would enter into life, keep the commandments." Answer, giving an exposition of the passage.
10. Last objection—viz. that faith itself is called a work. Answer—it is not as a work that faith justifies.

1. Let us now proceed to those passages which affirm that God will render to every one according to his deeds. Of this description are the following: "We must all appear before the judgment-seat of Christ; that every one may receive the things done in his body, according to that he hath done, whether it be good or bad;" "Who will render to every man according to his deeds: to them who by patient continuance in well-doing seek for glory, and honour, and immortality, eternal life;" but "tribulation and anguish upon every soul of man that doeth evil;" "They that have done good, unto the resurrection of life; and they that have done evil, unto the resurrection of damnation;" "Come, ye blessed of my Father;" "For I was an hungered, and ye gave me meat; I was thirsty, and ye gave me drink," &c. To these we may add the passages which describe eter-

nal life as the reward of works, such as the following: "The recompense of a man's hands shall be rendered unto him;" "He that feareth the commandment shall be rewarded;" "Rejoice and be exceeding glad, for great is your reward in heaven;" "Every man shall receive his own reward, according to his own labour."[1] The passages in which it is said that God will reward every man according to his works are easily disposed of. For that mode of expression indicates not the cause but the order of sequence. Now, it is beyond a doubt that the steps by which the Lord in his mercy consummates our salvation are these, "Whom he did predestinate, them he also called; and whom he called, them he also justified; and whom he justified, them he also glorified" (Rom. viii. 30). But though it is by mercy alone that God admits his people to life, yet as he leads them into possession of it by the course of good works, that he may complete his work in them in the order which he has destined, it is not strange that they are said to be crowned according to their works, since by these doubtless they are prepared for receiving the crown of immortality. Nay, for this reason they are aptly said to work out their own salvation (Phil. ii. 12), while by exerting themselves in good works they aspire to eternal life, just as they are elsewhere told to labour for the meat which perisheth not (John vi. 27), while they acquire life for themselves by believing in Christ; and yet it is immediately added, that this meat "the Son of man shall give unto you." Hence it appears, that *working* is not at all opposed to *grace*, but refers to pursuit,[2] and therefore it follows not that believers are the authors of their own salvation, or that it is the result of their works. What then? The moment they are admitted to fellowship with Christ, by the knowledge of the gospel, and the illumination of the Holy Spirit, their eternal life is begun, and then He which hath begun a good work in them "will perform it until the day of Jesus Christ" (Phil. i. 6). And it is performed when in righteousness and holiness they bear a resemblance to their heavenly Father, and prove that they are not degenerate sons.

2. There is nothing in the term *reward* to justify the inference that our works are the cause of salvation. First, let it be a fixed principle in our hearts, that the kingdom of heaven is not the hire of servants, but the inheritance of sons (Eph. i. 18); an inheritance obtained by those only whom the Lord has adopted as sons, and obtained for no other cause than this adoption, "The son of the bond-woman shall not be heir with the son of the free-woman" (Gal. iv. 30). And hence in those very passages in which the Holy Spirit promises eternal glory as the reward of works, by expressly calling it an inheritance, he demonstrates that it comes to us from some other quarter. Thus Christ enumerates the works for which he bestows

[1] Matth. xvi. 27; 2 Cor. v. 10; Rom. ii. 6; John v. 29: Matth. xxv. 34; Prov. xii. 14; xiii. 13; Matth. v. 12; Luke vi. 23; 1 Cor. iii. 8.

[2] French, "mais seulement emporte zele et estude;"—but only imports zeal and study.

heaven as a recompense, while he is calling his elect to the possession of it, but he at the same time adds, that it is to be possessed by right of inheritance (Matth. xxv. 34). Paul, too, encourages servants, while faithfully doing their duty, to hope for reward from the Lord, but adds, "of the inheritance" (Col. iii. 24). You see how, as it were, in formal terms they carefully caution us to attribute eternal blessedness not to works, but to the adoption of God. Why then do they at the same time make mention of works? This question will be elucidated by an example from Scripture (Gen. xv. 5; xvii. 1). Before the birth of Isaac, Abraham had received promise of a seed in whom all the families of the earth should be blessed; the propagation of a seed that for number should equal the stars of heaven, and the sand of the sea, &c. Many years after he prepares, in obedience to a divine message, to sacrifice his son. Having done this act of obedience, he receives the promise, "By myself have I sworn, saith the Lord, for because thou hast done this thing, and hast not withheld thy son, thine only son; that in blessing I will bless thee, and in multiplying I will multiply thy seed as the stars of the heaven, and as the sand which is upon the sea-shore, and thy seed shall possess the gate of his enemies; and in thy seed shall all the nations of the earth be blessed, because thou hast obeyed my voice" (Gen. xxii. 16–18). What is it we hear? Did Abraham by his obedience merit the blessing which had been promised him before the precept was given? Here assuredly we see without ambiguity that God rewards the works of believers with blessings which he had given them before the works were thought of, there still being no cause for the blessings which he bestows but his own mercy.

3. And yet the Lord does not act in vain, or delude us when he says, that he renders to works what he had freely given previous to works. As he would have us to be exercised in good works, while aspiring to the manifestation, or, if I may so speak, the fruition of the things which he has promised, and by means of them to hasten on to the blessed hope set before us in heaven, the fruit of the promises is justly ascribed to those things by which it is brought to maturity. Both things were elegantly expressed by the Apostle, when he told the Colossians to study the offices of charity, "for the hope which is laid up for you in heaven, whereof ye heard before in the word of the truth of the gospel" (Col. i. 5). For when he says that the gospel informed them of the hope which was treasured up for them in heaven, he declares that it depends on Christ alone, and not at all upon works. With this accords the saying of Peter, that believers "are kept by the power of God through faith unto salvation, ready to be revealed in the last time" (1 Pet. i. 5). When he says that they strive on account of it, he intimates that believers must continue running during the whole course of their lives, in order that they may attain it. But to prevent us from supposing that the reward which is promised becomes a kind of merit, our Lord introduced a parable, in which he represented himself as a householder,

who sent all the labourers whom he met to work in his vineyard, some at the first hour of the day, others at the second, others at the third, some even at the eleventh; at evening he paid them all alike. The interpretation of this parable is briefly and truly given by that ancient writer (whoever he was) who wrote the book *De Vocatione Gentium*, which goes under the name of Ambrose. I will give it in his words rather than my own:[1] "By means of this comparison, our Lord represented the many various modes of calling as pertaining to grace alone, where those who were introduced into the vineyard at the eleventh hour, and made equal to those who had toiled the whole day, doubtless represent the case of those whom the indulgence of God, to commend the excellence of grace, has rewarded in the decline of the day and the conclusion of life; not paying the price of labour, but shedding the riches of his goodness on those whom he chose without works; in order that even those who bore the heat of the day, and yet received no more than those who came last, may understand that they received a gift of grace, not the hire of works" (Lib. i. cap. 5). Lastly, it is also worthy of remark, that in those passages in which eternal life is called the reward of works, it is not taken simply for that communion which we have with God preparatory to a blessed immortality, when with paternal benevolence he embraces us in Christ, but for the possession, or, as it is called, the fruition of blessedness, as the very words of Christ express it, "in the world to come eternal life" (Mark x. 30); and elsewhere, "Come, ye blessed of my Father, inherit the kingdom," &c. (Matth. xxv. 34). For this reason also, Paul gives the name of *adoption* to that revelation of adoption which shall be made at the resurrection; and which adoption he afterwards interprets to mean, the redemption of our body (Rom. viii. 23). But, otherwise, as alienation from God is eternal death,—so when man is received into favour by God that he may enjoy communion with him and become one with him, he passes from death unto life. This is owing to adoption alone. Although after their manner they pertinaciously urge the term *reward*, we can always carry them back to the declaration of Peter, that eternal life is the reward of faith (1 Pet. i. 9).

4. Let us not suppose, then, that the Holy Spirit, by this promise, commends the dignity of our works, as if they were deserving of such a reward. For Scripture leaves us nothing of which we may glory in the sight of God. Nay, rather its whole object is to repress, humble, cast down, and completely crush our pride. But in this way help is given to our weakness, which would immediately give way were it not sustained by this expectation, and soothed by this comfort. First, let every man reflect for himself how hard it is not only to leave all things, but to leave and abjure one's self. And yet

1 French, "Pource que c'est un Docteur ancien, j'aime mieux user de ses paroles que des miennes;"—Because he is an ancient Doctor, I prefer making use of his words rather than my own.

this is the training by which Christ initiates his disciples, that is, all the godly. Secondly, he thus keeps them all their lifetime under the discipline of the cross, lest they should allow their heart to long for or confide in present good. In short, his treatment is usually such, that wherever they turn their eyes, as far as this world extends, they see nothing before them but despair; and hence Paul says, "If in this life only we have hope in Christ, we are of all men most miserable" (1 Cor. xv. 19). That they may not fail in these great straits, the Lord is present reminding them to lift their head higher and extend their view farther, that in him they may find a happiness which they see not in the world: to this happiness he gives the name of reward, hire, recompense, not as estimating the merit of works, but intimating that it is a compensation for their straits, sufferings, and affronts, &c. Wherefore, there is nothing to prevent us from calling eternal life a recompense after the example of Scripture, because in it the Lord brings his people from labour to quiet, from affliction to a prosperous and desirable condition, from sorrow to joy, from poverty to affluence, from ignominy to glory; in short, exchanges all the evils which they endured for blessings. Thus there will be no impropriety in considering holiness of life as the way, not indeed the way which gives access to the glory of the heavenly kingdom; but a way by which God conducts his elect to the manifestation of that kingdom, since his good pleasure is to glorify those whom he has sanctified (Rom. viii. 30). Only let us not imagine that merit and hire are correlative terms, a point on which the Sophists absurdly insist, from not attending to the end to which we have adverted. How preposterous is it when the Lord calls us to one end to look to another? Nothing is clearer than that a reward is promised to good works, in order to support the weakness of our flesh by some degree of comfort; but not to inflate our minds with vain glory. He, therefore, who from merit infers reward, or weighs works and reward in the same balance, errs very widely from the end which God has in view.

5. Accordingly, when the Scripture speaks of "a crown of righteousness which God the righteous Judge shall give" "at that day" (2 Tim. iv. 8), I not only say with Augustine, "To whom could the righteous Judge give the crown if the merciful Father had not given grace, and how could there have been righteousness but for the precedence of grace which justifies the ungodly? how could these be paid as things due were not things not due previously given?" (August. ad Valent. de Grat. et Lib. Art.); but I also add, how could he impute righteousness to our works, did not his indulgence hide the unrighteousness that is in them? How could he deem them worthy of reward, did he not with boundless goodness destroy what is unworthy in them? Augustine is wont to give the name of grace to eternal life, because, while it is the recompense of works, it is bestowed by the gratuitous gifts of God. But Scripture humbles us more, and at the same time elevates us. For besides forbidding us to glory in works, because they are the gratuitous gifts of God, it tells us that they are

always defiled by some degrees of impurity, so that they cannot satisfy God when they are tested by the standard of his justice; but that, lest our activity should be destroyed, they please merely by pardon. But though Augustine speaks somewhat differently from us, it is plain from his words that the difference is more apparent than real. After drawing a contrast between two individuals, the one with a life holy and perfect almost to a miracle; the other honest indeed, and of pure morals, yet not so perfect as not to leave much room for desiring better, he at length infers, "He who seems inferior in conduct, yet on account of the true faith in God by which he lives (Hab. ii. 4), and in conformity to which he accuses himself in all his faults, praises God in all his good works, takes shame to himself, and ascribes glory to God, from whom he receives both forgiveness for his sins, and the love of well-doing, the moment he is set free from this life is translated into the society of Christ. Why, but just on account of his faith? For though it saves no man without works (such faith being reprobate and not working by love), yet by means of it sins are forgiven; for the just lives by faith: without it works which seem good are converted into sins" (August. ad Bonifac., Lib. iii. c. 5). Here he not obscurely acknowledges what we so strongly maintain, that the righteousness of good works depends on their being approved by God in the way of pardon.[1]

6. In a sense similar to the above passages our opponents quote the following: "Make to yourselves friends of the mammon of unrighteousness; that when ye fail, they may receive you into everlasting habitations" (Luke xvi. 9). "Charge them that are rich in this world, that they be not high-minded, nor trust in uncertain riches, but in the living God, who giveth us richly all things to enjoy: that they do good, that they be rich in good works, ready to distribute, willing to communicate; laying up in store for themselves a good foundation against the time to come, that they may lay hold on eternal life" (1 Tim. vi. 17-19). For the good works which we enjoy in eternal blessedness are compared to riches. I answer, that we shall never attain to the true knowledge of these passages unless we attend to the scope of the Spirit in uttering them. If it is true, as Christ says, "Where your treasure is, there will your heart be also" (Matth. vi. 21), then, as the children of the world are intent on providing those things which form the delight of the present life, so it is the duty of believers, after they have learned that this life will shortly pass away like a dream, to take care that those things which they would truly enjoy be transmitted thither where their entire life is to be spent. We must, therefore, do like those who begin to remove to any place where they mean to fix their abode. As they send forward their effects, and grudge not to want them for a season, because they think the more they have in their future residence the happier they are; so, if we think that heaven is our country, we should send our

[1] The French adds, "C'est à dire, en misericorde, et non pas en jugement;"—that is to say, in mercy, and not in judgment.

wealth thither rather than retain it here, where on our sudden departure it will be lost to us. But how shall we transmit it? By contributing to the necessities of the poor, the Lord imputing to himself whatever is given to them. Hence that excellent promise, "He that hath pity on the poor lendeth to the Lord" (Prov. xix. 17; Matth. xxv. 40); and again, "He which soweth bountifully shall reap also bountifully" (2 Cor. ix. 6). What we give to our brethren in the exercise of charity is a deposit with the Lord, who, as a faithful depositary, will ultimately restore it with abundant interest. Are our duties, then, of such value with God that they are as a kind of treasure placed in his hand? Who can hesitate to say so when Scripture so often and so plainly attests it? But if any one would leap from the mere kindness of God to the merit of works,[1] his error will receive no support from these passages. For all you can properly infer from them is the inclination on the part of God to treat us with indulgence. For, in order to animate us in well-doing, he allows no act of obedience, however unworthy of his eye, to pass unrewarded.

7. But they insist more strongly on the words of the apostle when, in consoling the Thessalonians under their tribulations, he tells them that these were sent, "that ye may be counted worthy of the kingdom of God, for which ye also suffer; seeing it is a righteous thing with God to recompense tribulation to them that trouble you; and to you who are troubled, rest with us, when the Lord Jesus shall be revealed from heaven with his mighty angels" (2 Thess. i. 5–7). The author of the Epistle to the Hebrews says, "God is not unrighteous to forget your work and labour of love, which ye have showed towards his name, in that ye have ministered to the saints, and do minister" (Heb. vi. 10). To the former passage I answer, that the worthiness spoken of is not that of merit, but as God the Father would have those whom he has chosen for sons to be conformed to Christ the first born, and as it behoved him first to suffer, and then to enter into his glory, so we also, through much tribulation, enter the kingdom of heaven. Therefore, while we suffer tribulation for the name of Christ, we in a manner receive the marks with which God is wont to stamp the sheep of his flock (Gal. vi. 17). Hence we are counted worthy of the kingdom of God, because we bear in our body the marks of our Lord and Master, these being the insignia of the children of God. In this sense are we to understand the passages: "Always bearing about in the body the dying of the Lord Jesus, that the life also of Jesus might be made manifest in our body" (2 Cor. iv. 10). "That I may know him and the power of his resurrection, and the fellowship of his sufferings, being made conformable unto his death" (Phil. iii. 10). The reason which is subjoined is intended not to prove any merit, but to confirm our hope of the kingdom of God; as if he had said, As it is befitting the just judgment of God to take vengeance

[1] French, "Mais si quelcun pour obscurcir la benignité de Dieu veut establir la dignité des œuvres;"—but if any one to obscure the benignity of God would establish the dignity of works.

on your enemies for the tribulation which they have brought upon you, so it is also befitting to give you release and rest from these tribulations. The other passage, which speaks as if it were becoming the justice of God not to overlook the services of his people, and almost insinuates that it were unjust to forget them, is to be thus explained: God, to arouse us from sloth, assures us that every labour which we undertake for the glory of his name shall not be in vain. Let us always remember that this promise, like all other promises, will be of no avail unless it is preceded by the free covenant of mercy, on which the whole certainty of our salvation depends. Trusting to it, however, we ought to feel secure that, however unworthy our services, the liberality of God will not allow them to pass unrewarded. To confirm us in this expectation, the Apostle declares that God is not unrighteous; but will act consistently with the promise once given. Righteousness, therefore, refers rather to the truth of the divine promise than to the equity of paying what is due. In this sense there is a celebrated saying of Augustine, which, as containing a memorable sentiment, that holy man declined not repeatedly to employ, and which I think not unworthy of being constantly remembered: "Faithful is the Lord, who hath made himself our debtor, not by receiving anything from us, but by promising us all things" (August. in Ps. xxxii., cix., *et alibi*).

8. Our opponents also adduce the following passages from Paul: "Though I have all faith so that I could remove mountains, and have not charity, I am nothing" (1 Cor. xiii. 2). Again, "Now abideth faith, hope, charity, these three; but the greatest of these is charity" (1 Cor. 13). "Above all these things put on charity, which is the bond of perfectness" (Col. iii. 14). From the two first passages our Pharisees[1] contend that we are justified by charity rather than by faith, charity being, as they say, the better virtue. This mode of arguing is easily disposed of. I have elsewhere shown that what is said in the first passage refers not to true faith. In the second passage we admit that charity is said to be greater than true faith, but not because charity is more meritorious, but because it is more fruitful, because it is of wider extent, of more general service, and always flourishes, whereas the use of faith is only for a time. If we look to excellence, the love of God undoubtedly holds the first place. Of it, however, Paul does not here speak; for the only thing he insists on is, that we should by mutual charity edify one another in the Lord. But let us suppose that charity is in every respect superior to faith, what man of sound judgment, nay, what man with any soundness in his brain, would argue that it therefore does more to justify? The power of justifying which belongs to faith consists not in its worth as a work. Our justification depends entirely on the mercy of God and the merits of Christ: when faith apprehends these,

1 See Calvin's Answer to Sadolet, who had said that charity is the first and principal cause of our salvation.

it is said to justify. Now, if you ask our opponents in what sense they ascribe justification to charity, they will answer, Being a duty acceptable to God, righteousness is in respect of its merit imputed to us by the acceptance of the divine goodness. Here you see how beautifully the argument proceeds. We say that faith justifies not because it merits justification for us by it own worth, but because it is an instrument by which we freely obtain the righteousness of Christ. They, overlooking the mercy of God, and passing by Christ, the sum of righteousness, maintain that we are justified by charity as being superior to faith; just as if one were to maintain that a king is fitter to make a shoe than a shoemaker, because the king is infinitely the superior of the two. This one syllogism is ample proof that all the schools of Sorbonne have never had the slightest apprehension of what is meant by justification by faith. Should any disputant here interpose, and ask why we give different meanings to the term faith as used by Paul in passages so near each other, I can easily show that I have not slight grounds for so doing. For while those gifts which Paul enumerates are in some degree subordinate to faith and hope, because they relate to the knowledge of God, he by way of summary comprehends them all under the name of faith and hope; as if he had said, Prophecy and tongues, and the gift of interpreting, and knowledge, are all designed to lead us to the knowledge of God. But in this life it is only by faith and hope that we acknowledge God. Therefore, when I name faith and hope, I at the same time comprehend the whole. "Now abideth faith, hope, charity, these three;" that is, how great soever the number of the gifts, they are all to be referred to them; but "the greatest of these is charity." From the third passage they infer, If charity is the bond of perfection, it must be the bond of righteousness, which is nothing else than perfection. First, without objecting that the name of perfection is here given by Paul to proper union among the members of a rightly constituted church, and admitting that by charity we are perfected before God, what new result do they gain by it? I will always object in reply, that we never attain to that perfection unless we fulfil all the parts of charity; and will thence infer, that as all are most remote from such fulfilment, the hope of perfection is excluded.

9. I am unwilling to discuss all the things which the foolish Sorbonnists have rashly laid hold of in Scripture as it chanced to come in their way, and throw out against us. Some of them are so ridiculous, that I cannot mention them without laying myself open to a charge of trifling. I will, therefore, conclude with an exposition of one of our Saviour's expressions with which they are wondrously pleased. When the lawyer asked him, "Good Master, what good thing shall I do, that I may have eternal life?" he answers, "If thou wilt enter into life, keep the commandments" (Matth. xix. 16, 17). What more (they ask) would we have, when the very author of grace bids us acquire the kingdom of heaven by the observance of the commandments? As if it were not plain that Christ adapted his answers

to the characters of those whom he addressed. Here he is questioned by a Doctor of the Law as to the means of obtaining eternal life; and the question is not put simply, but is, What can men do to attain it? Both the character of the speaker and his question induced our Lord to give this answer. Imbued with a persuasion of legal righteousness, the lawyer had a blind confidence in works. Then all he asked was, what are the works of righteousness by which salvation is obtained? Justly, therefore, is he referred to the law, in which there is a perfect mirror of righteousness. We also distinctly declare, that if life is sought in works, the commandments are to be observed. And the knowledge of this doctrine is necessary to Christians; for how should they betake themselves to Christ, unless they perceived that they had fallen from the path of life over the precipice of death? Or how could they understand how far they have wandered from the way of life unles sthey previously understand what that way is? Then only do they feel that the asylum of safety is in Christ when they see how much their conduct is at variance with the divine righteousness, which consists in the observance of the law. The sum of the whole is this, If salvation is sought in works, we must keep the commandments, by which we are instructed in perfect righteousness. But we cannot remain here unless we would stop short in the middle of our course; for none of us is able to keep the commandments. Being thus excluded from the righteousness of the law, we must betake ourselves to another remedy—viz. to the faith of Christ. Wherefore, as a teacher of the law, whom our Lord knew to be puffed up with a vain confidence in works, was here directed by him to the law, that he might learn he was a sinner exposed to the fearful sentence of eternal death; so others, who were already humbled with this knowledge, he elsewhere solaces with the promise of grace, without making any mention of the law. "Come unto me, all ye that labour and are heavy laden, and I will give you rest." "Take my yoke upon you, and learn of me; for I am meek and lowly in heart: and ye shall find rest unto your souls" (Matth. xi. 28, 29).

10. At length, after they have wearied themselves with perverting Scripture, they have recourse to subtleties and sophisms. One cavil is, that faith is somewhere called a work (John vi. 29); hence they infer that we are in error in opposing faith to works; as if faith, regarded as obedience to the divine will, could by its own merit procure our justification, and did not rather, by embracing the mercy of God, thereby seal upon our hearts the righteousness of Christ, which is offered to us in the preaching of the Gospel. My readers will pardon me if I stay not to dispose of such absurdities; their own weakness, without external assault, is sufficient to destroy them. One objection, however, which has some semblance of reason, it will be proper to dispose of in passing, lest it give any trouble to those less experienced. As common sense dictates that contraries must be tried by the same rule, and as each sin is charged against us as unright-

eousness, so it is right (say our opponents) that each good work should receive the praise of righteousness. The answer which some give, that the condemnation of men proceeds on unbelief alone, and not on particular sins, does not satisfy me. I agree with them, indeed, that infidelity is the fountain and root of all evil; for it is the first act of revolt from God, and is afterwards followed by particular transgressions of the law. But as they seem to hold, that in estimating righteousness and unrighteousness, the same rule is to be applied to good and bad works, in this I dissent from them.[1] The righteousness of works consists in perfect obedience to the law. Hence you cannot be jusitfied by works unless you follow this straight line (if I may so call it) during the whole course of your life. The moment you decline from it you have fallen into unrighteousness. Hence it appears, that righteousness is not obtained by few works, but by an indefatigable and inflexible observance of the divine will. But the rule with regard to unrighteousness is very different. The adulterer or the thief is by one act guilty of death, because he offends against the majesty of God. The blunder of these arguers of ours lies here: they attend not to the words of James, "Whosoever shall keep the whole law, and yet offend in one point, he is guilty of all. For he that said, Do not commit adultery, said also, Do not kill," &c. (James ii. 10, 11). Therefore, it should not seem absurd when we say that death is the just recompense of every sin, because each sin merits the just indignation and vengeance of God. But you reason absurdly if you infer the converse, that one good work will reconcile a man to God notwithstanding of his meriting wrath by many sins.

1 French, "Mais touchant ce qu'ils semblent advis contrepoiser en une mesme balance les bonnes œuvres et les mauvaises, pour estimer la justice ou l'injustice de l'homme, en cela je suis contreint de leur repugner."—But as they seem disposed to put good and bad works into the opposite scales of the same balance, in order to estimate the righteousness or unrighteousness of man, in this I am forced to dissent from them.

CHAPTER XIX.

OF CHRISTIAN LIBERTY.

The three divisions of this chapter are,—1. Necessity of the doctrine of Christian Liberty, sec. 1. The principal parts of this liberty explained, sec. 2–8. II. The nature and efficacy of this liberty against the Epicureans and others who take no account whatever of the weak, sec. 9 and 10. III. Of offence given and received. A lengthened and not unnecessary discussion of this subject, sec. 11–16.

Sections.

1. Connection of this chapter with the previous ones on Justification. A true knowledge of Christian liberty useful and necessary. 1. It purifies the conscience. 2. It checks licentiousness. 3. It maintains the merits of Christ, the truth of the Gospel, and the peace of the soul.
2. This liberty consists of three parts. First, Believers renouncing the righteousness of the law, look only to Christ. Objection. Answer, distinguishing between Legal and Evangelical righteousness.
3. This first part clearly established by the whole Epistle to the Galatians.
4. The second part of Christian liberty—viz. that the conscience, freed from the yoke of the law, voluntarily obeys the will of God. This cannot be done so long as we are under the law. Reason.
5. When freed from the rigorous exactions of the law, we can cheerfully and with much alacrity answer the call of God.
6. Proof of this second part from an Apostle. The end of this liberty.
7. Third part of liberty—viz. the free use of things indifferent. The knowledge of this part necessary to remove despair and superstition. Superstition described.
8. Proof of this third part from the Epistle to the Romans. Those who observe it not only use evasion. 1. Despisers of God. 2. The desperate. 3. The ungrateful. The end and scope of this third part.
9. Second part of the chapter, showing the nature and efficacy of Christian liberty, in opposition to the Epicureans. Their character described. Pretext and allegation. Use of things indifferent. Abuse detected. Mode of correcting it.
10. This liberty maintained in opposition to those who pay no regard to the weak. Error of this class of men refuted. A most pernicious error. Objection. Reply.
11. Application of the doctrine of Christian liberty to the subject of offences. These of two kinds. Offence given. Offence received. Of offence given, a subject comprehended by few. Of Pharisaical offence, or offence received.
12. Who are to be regarded as weak and Pharisaical. Proved by examples and the doctrine of Paul. The just moderation of Christian liberty. Necessity of vindicating it. No regard to be paid to hypocrites. Duty of edifying our weak neighbours.
13. Application of the doctrine to things indifferent. Things necessary not to be omitted from any fear of offence.
14. Refutation of errors in regard to Christian liberty. The consciences of the godly not to be fettered by human traditions in matters of indifference.
15. Distinction to be made between Spiritual and Civil government. These must not be confounded. How far conscience can be bound by human constitutions. Definition of conscience. Definition explained by passages from the Apostolic writings.
16. The relation which conscience bears to external obedience: first, in things good and evil; secondly, in things indifferent.

1. We are now to treat of Christian Liberty, the explanation of which certainly ought not to be omitted by any one proposing to give

a compendious summary of Gospel doctrine. For it is a matter of primary necessity, one without the knowledge of which the conscience can scarcely attempt anything without hesitation, in many must demur and fluctuate, and in all proceed with fickleness and trepidation. In particular, it forms a proper appendix to Justification, and is of no little service in understanding its force. Nay, those who seriously fear God will hence perceive the incomparable advantages of a doctrine which wicked scoffers are constantly assailing with their jibes; the intoxication of mind under which they labour leaving their petulance without restraint. This, therefore, seems the proper place for considering the subject. Moreover, though it has already been occasionally adverted to, there was an advantage in deferring the fuller consideration of it till now, for the moment any mention is made of Christian liberty lust begins to boil, or insane commotions arise, if a speedy restraint is not laid on those licentious spirits by whom the best things are perverted into the worst. For they either, under pretext of this liberty, shake off all obedience to God, and break out into unbridled licentiousness, or they feel indignant, thinking that all choice, order, and restraint, are abolished. What can we do when thus encompassed with straits? Are we to bid adieu to Christian liberty, in order that we may cut off all opportunity for such perilous consequences? But, as we have said, if the subject be not understood, neither Christ, nor the truth of the Gospel, nor the inward peace of the soul, is properly known. Our endeavour must rather be, while not suppressing this very necessary part of doctrine, to obviate the absurd objections to which it usually gives rise.

2. Christian liberty seems to me to consist of three parts. First, the consciences of believers, while seeking the assurance of their justification before God, must rise above the law, and think no more of obtaining justification by it. For while the law, as has already been demonstrated (*supra*, chap. xvii. sec. 1), leaves not one man righteous, we are either excluded from all hope of justification, or we must be loosed from the law, and so loosed as that no account at all shall be taken of works. For he who imagines that in order to obtain justification he must bring any degree of works whatever, cannot fix any mode or limit, but makes himself debtor to the whole law. Therefore, laying aside all mention of the law, and all idea of works, we must in the matter of justification have recourse to the mercy of God only; turning away our regard from ourselves, we must look only to Christ. For the question is, not how we may be righteous, but how, though unworthy and unrighteous, we may be regarded as righteous. If consciences would obtain any assurance of this, they must give no place to the law. Still it cannot be rightly inferred from this that believers have no need of the law. It ceases not to teach, exhort, and urge them to good, although it is not recognised by their consciences before the judgment-seat of God. The two things are very different, and should be well and carefully distinguished. The whole lives of Christians ought to be a kind of aspiration after piety, seeing they

are called unto holiness (Eph. i. 4; 1 Thess. iv. 5). The office of the law is to excite them to the study of purity and holiness, by reminding them of their duty. For when the conscience feels anxious as to how it may have the favour of God, as to the answer it could give, and the confidence it would feel, if brought to his judgment-seat, in such a case the requirements of the law are not to be brought forward, but Christ, who surpasses all the perfection of the law, is alone to be held forth for righteousness.

3. On this almost the whole subject of the Epistle to the Galatians hinges; for it can be proved from express passages that those are absurd interpreters who teach that Paul there contends only for freedom from ceremonies. Of such passages are the following: "Christ hath redeemed us from the curse of the law, being made a curse for us." "Stand fast, therefore, in the liberty wherewith Christ has made us free, and be not entangled again with the yoke of bondage. Behold, I Paul say unto you, that if ye be circumcised, Christ shall profit you nothing. For I testify again to every man that is circumcised, that he is a debtor to do the whole law. Christ is become of no effect unto you, whosoever of you are justified by the law; ye are fallen from grace" (Gal. iii. 13; v. 1–4). These words certainly refer to something of a higher order than freedom from ceremonies. I confess, indeed, that Paul there treats of ceremonies, because he was contending with false apostles, who were plotting to bring back into the Christian Church those ancient shadows of the law which were abolished by the advent of Christ. But, in discussing this question, it was necessary to introduce higher matters, on which the whole controversy turns. First, because the brightness of the Gospel was obscured by those Jewish shadows, he shows that in Christ we have a full manifestation of all those things which were typified by Mosaic ceremonies. Secondly, as those impostors instilled into the people the most pernicious opinion, that this obedience was sufficient to merit the grace of God, he insists very strongly that believers shall not imagine that they can obtain justification before God by any works, far less by those paltry observances. At the same time, he shows that by the cross of Christ they are free from the condemnation of the law, to which otherwise all men are exposed, so that in Christ alone they can rest in full security. This argument is pertinent to the present subject (Gal. iv. 5, 21, &c.). Lastly, he asserts the right of believers to liberty of conscience, a liberty which may not be restrained without necessity.

4. Another point which depends on the former is, that consciences obey the law, not as if compelled by legal necessity; but being free from the yoke of the law itself, voluntarily obey the will of God. Being constantly in terror so long as they are under the dominion of the law, they are never disposed promptly to obey God, unless they have previously obtained this liberty. Our meaning shall be explained more briefly and clearly by an example. The command of the law is, "Thou shalt love the Lord thy God with all thine heart,

and with all thy soul, and with all thy might" (Deut. vi. 5). To accomplish this, the soul must previously be divested of every other thought and feeling, the heart purified from all its desires, all its powers collected and united on this one object. Those who, in comparison of others, have made much progress in the way of the Lord, are still very far from this goal. For although they love God in their mind, and with a sincere affection of heart, yet both are still in a great measure occupied with the lusts of the flesh, by which they are retarded and prevented from proceeding with quickened pace towards God. They indeed make many efforts, but the flesh partly enfeebles their strength, and partly binds them to itself. What can they do while they thus feel that there is nothing of which they are less capable than to fulfil the law? They wish, aspire, endeavour; but do nothing with the requisite perfection. If they look to the law, they see that every work which they attempt or design is accursed. Nor can any one deceive himself by inferring that the work is not altogether bad, merely because it is imperfect, and, therefore, that any good which is in it is still accepted of God. For the law demanding perfect love condemns all imperfection, unless its rigour is mitigated. Let any man therefore consider his work which he wishes to be thought partly good, and he will find that it is a transgression of the law by the very circumstance of its being imperfect.

5. See how our works lie under the curse of the law if they are tested by the standard of the law. But how can unhappy souls set themselves with alacrity to a work from which they cannot hope to gain anything in return but cursing? On the other hand, if freed from this severe exaction, or rather from the whole rigour of the law, they hear themselves invited by God with paternal lenity, they will cheerfully and alertly obey the call, and follow his guidance. In one word, those who are bound by the yoke of the law are like servants who have certain tasks daily assigned them by their masters. Such servants think that nought has been done; and they dare not come into the presence of their masters until the exact amount of labour has been performed. But sons who are treated in a more candid and liberal manner by their parents, hesitate not to offer them works that are only begun or half finished, or even with something faulty in them, trusting that their obedience and readiness of mind will be accepted, although the performance be less exact than was wished. Such should be our feelings, as we certainly trust that our most indulgent Parent will approve our services, however small they may be, and however rude and imperfect. Thus He declares to us by the prophet, "I will spare them as a man spareth his own son that serveth him" (Mal. iii. 17); where the word *spare* evidently means indulgence, or connivance at faults, while at the same time service is remembered. This confidence is necessary in no slight degree, since without it everything should be attempted in vain; for

God does not regard any work of ours as done to himself, unless truly done from a desire to serve him. But how can this be amidst these terrors, while we doubt whether God is offended or served by our work?

6. This is the reason why the author of the Epistle to the Hebrews ascribes to faith all the good works which the holy patriarchs are said to have performed, and estimates them merely by faith (Heb. xi. 2). In regard to this liberty there is a remarkable passage in the Epistle to the Romans, where Paul argues, "Sin shall not have dominion over you; for ye are not under the law, but under grace" (Rom. vi. 14). For after he had exhorted believers, "Let not sin therefore reign in your mortal body, that ye should obey it in the lusts thereof: Neither yield ye your members as instruments of unrighteousness unto sin; but yield yourselves unto God, as those that are alive from the dead, and your members as instruments of righteousness unto God;" they might have objected that they still bore about with them a body full of lust, that sin still dwelt in them. He therefore comforts them by adding, that they are freed from the law; as if he had said, Although you feel that sin is not yet extinguished, and that righteousness does not plainly live in you, you have no cause for fear and dejection, as if God were always offended because of the remains of sin, since by grace you are freed from the law, and your works are not tried by its standard. Let those, however, who infer that they may sin because they are not under the law, understand that they have no right to this liberty, the end of which is to encourage us in well-doing.

7. The third part of this liberty is, that we are not bound before God to any observance of external things which are in themselves indifferent (ἀδιάφορα), but that we are now at full liberty either to use or omit them. The knowledge of this liberty is very necessary to us; where it is wanting our consciences will have no rest, there will be no end of superstition. In the present day many think us absurd in raising a question as to the free eating of flesh, the free use of dress and holidays, and similar frivolous trifles, as they think them; but they are of more importance than is commonly supposed. For when once the conscience is entangled in the net, it enters a long and inextricable labyrinth, from which it is afterwards most difficult to escape. When a man begins to doubt whether it is lawful for him to use linen for sheets, shirts, napkins, and handkerchiefs, he will not long be secure as to hemp, and will at last have doubts as to tow; for he will revolve in his mind whether he cannot sup without napkins, or dispense with handkerchiefs. Should he deem a daintier food unlawful, he will afterwards feel uneasy for using loaf-bread and common eatables, because he will think that his body might possibly be supported on a still meaner food. If he hesitates as to a more genial wine, he will scarcely drink the worst with a good conscience; at last he will not dare to touch water if more than

usually sweet and pure. In fine, he will come to this, that he will deem it criminal to trample on a straw lying in his way. For it is no trivial dispute that is here commenced, the point in debate being, whether the use of this thing or that is in accordance with the divine will, which ought to take precedence of all our acts and counsels. Here some must by despair be hurried into an abyss, while others, despising God and casting off his fear, will not be able to make a way for themselves without ruin. When men are involved in such doubts, whatever be the direction in which they turn, everything they see must offend their conscience.

8. "I know," says Paul, "that there is nothing unclean of itself" (by unclean meaning unholy); "but to him that esteemeth anything to be unclean, to him it is unclean" (Rom. xiv. 14). By these words he makes all external things subject to our liberty, provided the nature of that liberty approves itself to our minds as before God. But if any superstitious idea suggests scruples, those things which in their own nature were pure are to us contaminated. Wherefore the apostle adds, "Happy is he that condemneth not himself in that which he alloweth. And he that doubteth is damned if he eat, because he eateth not of faith: for whatsoever is not of faith is sin" (Rom. xiv. 22, 23). When men, amid such difficulties, proceed with greater confidence, securely doing whatever pleases them, do they not in so far revolt from God? Those who are thoroughly impressed with some fear of God, if forced to do many things repugnant to their conscience, are discouraged and filled with dread. All such persons receive none of the gifts of God with thanksgiving, by which alone Paul declares that all things are sanctified for our use (1 Tim. iv. 5). By thanksgiving I understand that which proceeds from a mind recognising the kindness and goodness of God in his gifts. For many, indeed, understand that the blessings which they enjoy are the gifts of God, and praise God in their works; but not being persuaded that these have been given to them, how can they give thanks to God as the giver? In one word, we see whither this liberty tends—viz. that we are to use the gifts of God without any scruple of conscience, without any perturbation of mind, for the purpose for which he gave them: in this way our souls may both have peace with him, and recognise his liberality towards us. For here are comprehended all ceremonies of free observance, so that while our consciences are not to be laid under the necessity of observing them, we are also to remember that, by the kindness of God, the use of them is made subservient to edification.

9. It is, however, to be carefully observed, that Christian liberty is in all its parts a spiritual matter, the whole force of which consists in giving peace to trembling consciences, whether they are anxious and disquieted as to the forgiveness of sins, or as to whether their imperfect works, polluted by the infirmities of the flesh, are pleasing to God, or are perplexed as to the use of things indifferent. It is, therefore, perversely interpreted by those who use it as a cloak for

their lusts, and they may licentiously abuse the good gifts of God, or who think there is no liberty unless it is used in the presence of men, and, accordingly, in using it pay no regard to their weak brethren. Under this head, the sins of the present age are more numerous. For there is scarcely any one whose means allow him to live sumptuously, who does not delight in feasting, and dress, and the luxurious grandeur of his house, who wishes not to surpass his neighbour in every kind of delicacy, and does not plume himself amazingly on his splendour. And all these things are defended under the pretext of Christian liberty. They say they are things indifferent: I admit it, provided they are used indifferently. But when they are too eagerly longed for, when they are proudly boasted of, when they are indulged in luxurious profusion, things which otherwise were in themselves lawful are certainly defiled by these vices. Paul makes an admirable distinction in regard to things indifferent: "Unto the pure all things are pure: but unto them that are defiled and unbelieving is nothing pure; but even their mind and conscience is defiled" (Tit. i. 15). For why is a woe pronounced upon the rich who have received their consolation? (Luke vi. 24), who are full, who laugh now, who "lie upon beds of ivory, and stretch themselves upon their couches;" "join house to house," and "lay field to field;" "and the harp and the viol, the tabret and pipe, and wine, are in their feasts?" (Amos. vi. 6; Is. v. 8, 10). Certainly ivory and gold, and riches, are the good creatures of God, permitted, nay, destined, by divine providence for the use of man; nor was it ever forbidden to laugh, or to be full, or to add new to old and hereditary possessions, or to be delighted with music, or to drink wine. This is true, but when the means are supplied, to roll and wallow in luxury, to intoxicate the mind and soul with present, and be always hunting after new pleasures, is very far from a legitimate use of the gifts of God. Let them, therefore, suppress immoderate desire, immoderate profusion, vanity, and arrogance, that they may use the gifts of God purely with a pure conscience. When their mind is brought to this state of soberness, they will be able to regulate the legitimate use. On the other hand, when this moderation is wanting, even plebeian and ordinary delicacies are excessive. For it is a true saying, that a haughty mind often dwells in a coarse and homely garb, while true humility lurks under fine linen and purple. Let every one then live in his own station, poorly or moderately, or in splendour; but let all remember that the nourishment which God gives is for life, not luxury, and let them regard it as the law of Christian liberty, to learn with Paul in whatever state they are, "therewith to be content," to know "both how to be abased," and "how to abound," "to be full and to be hungry, both to abound and to suffer need" (Phil. iv. 11).

10. Very many also err in this: as if their liberty were not safe and entire, without having men to witness it, they use it indiscriminately and imprudently, and in this way often give offence to weak brethren. You may see some in the present day who cannot think

they possess their liberty unless they come into possession of it by eating flesh on Friday. Their eating I blame not, but this false notion must be driven from their minds: for they ought to think that their liberty gains nothing new by the sight of men, but is to be enjoyed before God, and consists as much in abstaining as in using. If they understand that it is of no consequence in the sight of God whether they eat flesh or eggs, whether they are clothed in red or in black, this is amply sufficient. The conscience to which the benefit of this liberty was due is loosed. Therefore, though they should afterwards, during their whole life, abstain from flesh, and constantly wear one colour, they are not less free. Nay, just because they are free, they abstain with a free conscience. But they err most egregiously in paying no regard to the infirmity of their brethren, with which it becomes us to bear, so as not rashly to give them offence. But[1] it is sometimes also of consequence that we should assert our liberty before men. This I admit: yet must we use great caution in the mode, lest we should cast off the care of the weak whom God has specially committed to us.

11. I will here make some observations on offences, what distinctions are to be made between them, what kind are to be avoided and what disregarded. This will afterwards enable us to determine what scope there is for our liberty among men. We are pleased with the common division into *offence given* and *offence taken*, since it has the plain sanction of Scripture, and not improperly expresses what is meant. If from unseasonable levity or wantonness, or rashness, you do anything out of order or not in its own place, by which the weak or unskilful are offended, it may be said that offence has been *given* by you, since the ground of offence is owing to your fault. And in general, offence is said to be *given* in any matter where the person from whom it has proceeded is in fault. Offence is said to be *taken* when a thing otherwise done, not wickedly or unseasonably, is made an occasion of offence from malevolence or some sinister feeling. For here offence was not given, but sinister interpreters causelessly take offence. By the former kind, the weak only, by the latter, the ill-tempered and Pharisaical are offended. Wherefore, we shall call the one the offence of the weak, the other the offence of Pharisees, and we will so temper the use of our liberty as to make it yield to the ignorance of weak brethren, but not to the austerity of Pharisees. What is due to infirmity is fully shown by Paul in many passages. "Him that is weak in the faith receive ye." Again, "Let us not judge one another any more: but judge this rather, that no man put a stumbling-block, or an occasion to fall, in his brother's way;" and many others to the same effect in the same place, to which, instead of quoting them here, we refer the reader. The sum is, "We then that are strong ought to bear the infirmities of the weak, and not to please ourselves. Let every one of us please his neighbour for his

1 French, "Mais quelcun dira;"—But some one will say.

good to edification." Elsewhere he says, "Take heed lest by any means this liberty of yours become a stumbling-block to them that are weak." Again, "Whatsoever is sold in the shambles, that eat, asking no question for conscience sake." "Conscience, I say, not thine own, but of the other." Finally, "Give none offence, neither to the Jews, nor to the Gentiles, nor to the Church of God." Also in another passage, "Brethren, ye have been called into liberty, only use not liberty for an occasion to the flesh, but by love serve one another."[1] Thus, indeed, it is: our liberty was not given us against our weak neighbours, whom charity enjoins us to serve in all things, but rather that, having peace with God in our minds, we should live peaceably among men. What value is to be set upon the offence of the Pharisees we learn from the words of our Lord, in which he says, "Let them alone: they be blind leaders of the blind" (Matth. xv. 14). The disciples had intimated that the Pharisees were offended at his words. He answers, that they are to be let alone, that their offence is not to be regarded.

12. The matter still remains uncertain, unless we understand who are the weak and who the Pharisees; for if this distinction is destroyed, I see not how, in regard to offences, any liberty at all would remain without being constantly in the greatest danger. But Paul seems to me to have marked out most clearly, as well by example as by doctrine, how far our liberty, in the case of offence, is to be modified or maintained. When he adopts Timothy as his companion, he circumcises him: nothing can induce him to circumcise Titus (Acts xvi. 3; Gal. ii. 3). The acts are different, but there is no difference in the purpose or intention; in circumcising Timothy, as he was free from all men, he made himself the servant of all: "Unto the Jews I became as a Jew, that I might gain the Jews; to them that are under the law, as under the law, that I might gain them that are under the law; to them that are without law, as without law (being not without law to God, but under the law to Christ), that I might gain them that are without law. To the weak became I as weak, that I might gain the weak: I am made all things to all men, that I might by all means save some" (1 Cor. ix. 20-22). We have here the proper modification of liberty, when in things indifferent it can be restrained with some advantage. What he had in view in firmly resisting the circumcision of Titus, he himself testifies when he thus writes: "But neither Titus, who was with me, being a Greek, was compelled to be circumcised: and that because of false brethren unawares brought in, who came in privily to spy out our liberty which we have in Christ Jesus, that they might bring us into bondage: to whom we gave place by subjection, no, not for an hour, that the truth of the gospel might continue with you" (Gal. ii. 3-5). We here see the necessity of vindicating our liberty when, by the unjust exactions of false apostles, it is

[1]Rom. xiv. 1, 13; xv. 1; 1 Cor. viii. 9; x. 25, 29, 32; Gal. v. 13.

brought into danger with weak consciences. In all cases we must study charity, and look to the edification of our neighbour. "All things are lawful for me," says he, "but all things are not expedient; all things are lawful for me, but all things edify not. Let no man seek his own, but every man another's wealth" (1 Cor. x. 23, 24). There is nothing plainer than this rule, that we are to use our liberty if it tends to the edification of our neighbour, but if inexpedient for our neighbour, we are to abstain from it. There are some who pretend to imitate this prudence of Paul by abstinence from liberty, while there is nothing for which they less employ it than for purposes of charity. Consulting their own ease, they would have all mention of liberty buried though it is not less for the interest of our neighbour to use liberty for their good and edification, than to modify it occasionally for their advantage. It is the part of a pious man to think, that the free power conceded to him in external things is to make him the readier in all offices of charity.

13. Whatever I have said about avoiding offences, I wish to be referred to things indifferent.[1] Things which are necessary to be done cannot be omitted from any fear of offence. For as our liberty is to be made subservient to charity, so charity must in its turn be subordinate to purity of faith. Here, too, regard must be had to charity, but it must go as far as the altar; that is, we must not offend God for the sake of our neighbour. We approve not of the intemperance of those who do everything tumultuously, and would rather burst through every restraint at once than proceed step by step. But neither are those to be listened to who, while they take the lead in a thousand forms of impiety, pretend that they act thus to avoid giving offence to their neighbour, as if in the meantime they did not train the consciences of their neighbours to evil, especially when they always stick in the same mire without any hope of escape. When a neighbour is to be instructed, whether by doctrine or by example, then smooth-tongued men say that he is to be fed with milk, while they are instilling into him the worst and most pernicious opinions. Paul says to the Corinthians, "I have fed you with milk, and not with meat" (1 Cor. iii. 2); but had there then been a Popish mass among them, would he have sacrificed as one of the modes of giving them milk? By no means: milk is not poison. It is false then to say they nourish those whom, under a semblance of soothing, they cruelly murder. But granting that such dissimulation may be used for a time, how long are they to make their pupils drink that kind of milk? If they never grow up so as to be able to bear at least some gentle food, it is certain that they have never been reared on milk.[2] Two reasons prevent me from now entering farther into contest with these people: first, their follies are scarcely worthy of refutation, seeing all men of sense must nauseate them; and,

1 The French adds, "Lesquelles ne sont de soy ne bonnes ne mauvais;"—which in themselves are neither good nor bad.

2 French, "de bon laict;"—good milk.

secondly, having already amply refuted them in special treatises, I am unwilling to do it over again.[1] Let my readers only bear in mind, first, that whatever be the offences by which Satan and the world attempt to lead us away from the law of God, we must nevertheless strenuously proceed in the course which he prescribes; and, secondly, that whatever dangers impend, we are not at liberty to deviate one nail's breadth from the command of God, that on no pretext is it lawful to attempt anything but what he permits.

14. Since by means of this privilege of liberty which we have described, believers have derived authority from Christ not to entangle themselves by the observance of things in which he wished them to be free, we conclude that their consciences are exempted from all human authority. For it were unbecoming that the gratitude due to Christ for his liberal gift should perish, or that the consciences of believers should derive no benefit from it. We must not regard it as a trivial matter when we see how much it cost our Saviour, being purchased not with silver or gold, but with his own blood (1 Pet. i. 18, 19); so that Paul hesitates not to say that Christ has died in vain, if we place our souls under subjection to men (Gal. v. 1, 4; 1 Cor. vii. 23). Several chapters of the Epistle to the Galatians are wholly occupied with showing that Christ is obscured, or rather extinguished to us, unless our consciences maintain their liberty; from which they have certainly fallen, if they can be bound with the chains of laws and constitutions at the pleasure of men. But as the knowledge of this subject is of the greatest importance, so it demands a longer and clearer exposition. For the moment the abolition of human constitutions is mentioned, the greatest disturbances are excited, partly by the seditious, and partly by calumniators, as if obedience of every kind were at the same time abolished and overthrown.

15. Therefore, lest this prove a stumbling-block to any, let us observe that in man government is twofold: the one spiritual, by which the conscience is trained to piety and divine worship; the other civil, by which the individual is instructed in those duties which, as men and citizens, we are bound to perform (see Book IV. chap. x. sec. 3–6). To these two forms are commonly given the not inappropriate names of spiritual and temporal jurisdiction, intimating that the former species has reference to the life of the soul, while the latter relates to matters of the present life, not only to food and clothing, but to the enacting of laws which require a man to live among his fellows purely, honourably, and modestly. The former has its seat within the soul, the latter only regulates the external conduct. We may call the one the spiritual, the other the civil kingdom. Now, these two, as we have divided them, are always to be viewed apart from each other. When the one is considered, we should call off our minds, and not allow them to think of the other.

1 See Epist. de Fugiendis Impiorum Illicitis Sacris. Also Epist. de Abjiciendis vel Administrandis Sacerdotiis Also the short treatise, De Vitandis Superstitionibus.

For there exists in man a kind of two worlds, over which different kings and different laws can preside. By attending to this distinction, we will not erroneously transfer the doctrine of the gospel concerning spiritual liberty to civil order, as if in regard to external government Christians were less subject to human laws, because their consciences are unbound before God, as if they were exempted from all carnal service, because in regard to the Spirit they are free. Again, because even in those constitutions which seem to relate to the spiritual kingdom, there may be some delusion, it is necessary to distinguish between those which are to be held legitimate as being agreeable to the word of God, and those, on the other hand, which ought to have no place among the pious. We shall elsewhere have an opportunity of speaking of civil government (see Book IV. chap. xx.). For the present, also, I defer speaking of ecclesiastical laws, because that subject will be more fully discussed in the Fourth Book when we come to treat of the Power of the Church. We would thus conclude the present discussion. The question, as I have said, though not very obscure, or perplexing in itself, occasions difficulty to many, because they do not distinguish with sufficient accuracy between what is called the external *forum*, and the *forum* of conscience. What increases the difficulty is, that Paul commands us to obey the magistrate, "not only for wrath, but also for conscience sake" (Rom. xiii. 1, 5). Whence it follows that civil laws also bind the conscience. Were this so, then what we said a little ago, and are still to say of spiritual government, would fall. To solve this difficulty, the first thing of importance is to understand what is meant by *conscience*. The definition must be sought in the etymology of the word. For as men, when they apprehend the knowledge of things by the mind and intellect, are said to know, and hence arises the term knowledge or *science*, so when they have a sense of the divine justice added as a witness which allows them not to conceal their sins, but drags them forward as culprits to the bar of God, that sense is called *conscience*. For it stands as it were between God and man, not suffering man to suppress what he knows in himself; but following him on even to conviction. It is this that Paul means when he says, "Their conscience also bearing witness, and their thoughts the meanwhile accusing, or else excusing one another" (Rom. ii. 15). Simple knowledge may exist in man, as it were shut up; therefore this sense, which sists man before the bar of God, is set over him as a kind of sentinel to observe and spy out all his secrets, that nothing may remain buried in darkness. Hence the ancient proverb, Conscience is a thousand witnesses. For the same reason Peter also employs the expression, "the answer of a good conscience" (1 Pet. iii. 21), for tranquillity of mind; when persuaded of the grace of Christ, we boldly present ourselves before God. And the author of the Epistle to the Hebrews says, that we have "no more conscience of sins" (Heb. x. 2), that we are held as freed or acquitted, so that sin no longer accuses us.

16. Wherefore, as works have respect to men, so conscience bears reference to God, a good conscience being nothing else than inward integrity of heart. In this sense Paul says, that "the end of the commandment is charity, out of a pure heart, and of a good conscience, and of faith unfeigned" (1 Tim. i. 5). He afterwards, in the same chapter, shows how much it differs from intellect when he speaks of "holding faith, and a good conscience; which some having put away, have made shipwreck" (1 Tim. i. 19). For by these words he intimates, that it is a lively inclination to serve God, a sincere desire to live in piety and holiness. Sometimes, indeed, it is even extended to men, as when Paul testifies, "Herein do I exercise myself, to have always a conscience void of offence toward God, and toward men" (Acts xxiv. 16). He speaks thus, because the fruits of a good conscience go forth and reach even to men. But, as I have said, properly speaking, it refers to God only. Hence a law is said to bind the conscience, because it simply binds the individual, without looking at men, or taking any account of them. For example, God not only commands us to keep our mind chaste and pure from lust, but prohibits all external lasciviousness or obscenity of language. My conscience is subjected to the observance of this law, though there were not another man in the world, and he who violates it sins not only by setting a bad example to his brethren, but stands convicted in his conscience before God. The same rule does not hold in things indifferent. We ought to abstain from everything that produces offence, but with a free conscience. Thus Paul, speaking of meat consecrated to idols, says, "If any man say unto you, This is offered in sacrifice unto idols, eat not for his sake that showed it, and for conscience sake:" "Conscience, I say, not thine own, but of the other" (1 Cor. x. 28, 29). A believer, after being previously admonished, would sin were he still to eat meat so offered. But though abstinence, on his part, is necessary, in respect of a brother, as it is prescribed by God, still he ceases not to retain liberty of conscience. We see how the law, while binding the external act, leaves the conscience unbound.

CHAPTER XX.

OF PRAYER—A PERPETUAL EXERCISE OF FAITH. THE DAILY BENEFITS DERIVED FROM IT.

The principal divisions of this chapter are,—I. Connection of the subject of prayer with the previous chapters. The nature of prayer, and its necessity as a Christian exercise, sec. 1, 2. II. To whom prayer is to be offered. Refutation of an objection which is too apt to present itself to the mind, sec. 3. III. Rules to be observed in prayer, sec. 4–16. IV. Through whom prayer is to be made, sec. 17–19. V. Refutation of an error as to the doctrine of our Mediator and Intercessor, with answers to the leading arguments urged in support of the intercession of saints, sec. 20–27. VI. The nature of prayer, and some of its accidents, sec. 28–33. VII. A perfect form of invocation, or an exposition of the Lord's Prayer, sec. 34–50. VIII. Some rules to be observed with regard to prayer, as time, perseverance, the feeling of the mind, and the assurance of faith, sec. 50–52.

Sections.

1. A general summary of what is contained in the previous part of the work. A transition to the doctrine of prayer. Its connection with the subject of faith.
2. Prayer defined. Its necessity and use.
3. Objection, that prayer seems useless, because God already knows our wants. Answer, from the institution and end of prayer. Confirmation by example. Its necessity and propriety. Perpetually reminds us of our duty, and leads to meditation on divine providence. Conclusion. Prayer a most useful exercise. This proved by three passages of Scripture.
4. Rules to be observed in prayer. First, reverence to God. How the mind ought to be composed.
5. All giddiness of mind must be excluded, and all our feelings seriously engaged. This confirmed by the form of lifting the hand in prayer. We must ask only in so far as God permits. To help our weakness, God gives the Spirit to be our guide in prayer. What the office of the Spirit in this respect. We must still pray both with the heart and the lips.
6. Second rule of prayer, a sense of our want. This rule violated, 1. By perfunctory and formal prayer. 2. By hypocrites, who have no sense of their sins. 3. By giddiness in prayer. Remedies.
7. Objection, that we are not always under the same necessity of praying. Answer, we must pray always. This answer confirmed by an examination of the dangers by which both our life and our salvation are every moment threatened. Confirmed farther by the command and permission of God, by the nature of true repentance, and a consideration of impenitence. Conclusion.
8. Third rule, the suppression of all pride. Examples. Daniel, David, Isaiah, Jeremiah, Baruch.
9. Advantage of thus suppressing pride. It leads to earnest entreaty for pardon, accompanied with humble confession and sure confidence in the Divine mercy. This may not always be expressed in words. It is peculiar to pious penitents. A general introduction to procure favour to our prayers never to be omitted.
10. Objection to the third rule of prayer. Of the glorying of the saints. Answer. Confirmation of the answer.
11. Fourth rule of prayer,—a sure confidence of being heard animating us to prayer. The kind of confidence required—viz. a serious conviction of our misery, joined with sure hope. From these true prayer springs. How diffidence impairs prayer. In general, faith is required.
12. This faith and sure hope regarded by our opponents as most absurd. Their error

described and refuted by various passages of Scripture, which show that acceptable prayer is accompanied with these qualities. No repugnance between this certainty and an acknowledgment of our destitution.

13. To our unworthiness we oppose, 1. The command of God. 2. The promise. Rebels and hypocrites completely condemned. Passages of Scripture confirming the command to pray.
14. Other passages respecting the promises which belong to the pious when they invoke God. These realised though we are not possessed of the same holiness as other distinguished servants of God, provided we indulge no vain confidence, and sincerely betake ourselves to the mercy of God. Those who do not invoke God under urgent necessity are no better than idolaters. This concurrence of fear and confidence reconciles the different passages of Scripture, as to humbling ourselves in prayer, and causing our prayers to ascend.
15. Objection founded on some examples—viz. that prayers have proved effectual, though not according to the form prescribed. Answer. Such examples, though not given for our imitation, are of the greatest use. 2. Objection, the prayers of the faithful sometimes not effectual. Answer confirmed by a noble passage of Augustine. Rule for right prayer.
16. The above four rules of prayer not so rigidly exacted, as that every prayer deficient in them in any respect is rejected by God. This shown by examples. Conclusion, or summary of this section.
17. Through whom God is to be invoked—viz. Jesus Christ. This founded on a consideration of the divine majesty, and the precept and promise of God himself. God therefore to be invoked only in the name of Christ.
18. From the first all believers were heard through him only: yet this specially restricted to the period subsequent to his ascension. The ground of this restriction.
19. The wrath of God lies on those who reject Christ as a Mediator. This excludes not the mutual intercession of saints on the earth.
20. Refutation of errors interfering with the intercession of Christ. 1. Christ the Mediator of redemption; the saints mediators of intercession. Answer confirmed by the clear testimony of Scripture, and by a passage from Augustine. The nature of Christ's intercession.
21. Of the intercession of saints living with Christ in heaven. Fiction of the Papists in regard to it. Refuted. 1. Its absurdity. 2. It is nowhere mentioned by Scripture. 3. Appeal to the conscience of the superstitious. 4. Its blasphemy. Exception. Answers.
22. Monstrous errors resulting from this fiction. Refutation. Exception by the advocates of this fiction. Answer.
23. Arguments of the Papists for the intercession of saints. 1. From the duty and office of angels. Answer. 2. From an expression of Jeremiah respecting Moses and Samuel. Answer, retorting the argument. 3. The meaning of the prophet confirmed by a similar passage in Ezekiel, and the testimony of an apostle.
24. 4. Fourth papistical argument from the nature of charity, which is more perfect in the saints in glory. Answer.
25. Argument founded on a passage in Moses. Answer.
26. Argument from its being said that the prayers of saints are heard. Answer, confirmed by Scripture, and illustrated by examples.
27. Conclusion, that the saints cannot be invoked without impiety. 1. It robs God of his glory. 2. Destroys the intercession of Christ. 3. Is repugnant to the word of God. 4. Is opposed to the due method of prayer. 5. Is without approved example. 6. Springs from distrust. Last objection. Answer.
28. Kinds of prayer. Vows. Supplications. Petitions. Thanksgiving. Connection of these, their constant use and necessity. Particular explanation confirmed by reason, Scripture, and example. Rule as to supplication and thanksgiving.
29. The accidents of prayer—viz. private and public, constant, at stated seasons, &c. Exception in time of necessity. Prayer without ceasing. Its nature. Garrulity of Papists and hypocrites refuted. The scope and parts of prayer. Secret prayer. Prayer at all places. Private and public prayer.
30. Of public places or churches in which common prayers are offered up. Right use of churches. Abuse.
31. Of utterance and singing. These of no avail if not from the heart. The use of the voice refers more to public than private prayer.
32. Singing of the greatest antiquity, but not universal. How to be performed.
33. Public prayers should be in the vulgar, not in a foreign tongue. Reason, 1. The

nature of the Church. 2. Authority of an apostle. Sincere affection always necessary. The tongue not always necessary. Bending of the knee, and uncovering of the head.

34. The form of prayer delivered by Christ displays the boundless goodness of our heavenly Father. The great comfort thereby afforded.
35. Lord's Prayer divided into six petitions. Subdivision into two principal parts, the former referring to the glory of God, the latter to our salvation.
36. The use of the term Father implies, 1. That we pray to God in the name of Christ alone. 2. That we lay aside all distrust. 3. That we expect everything that is for our good.
37. Objection, that our sins exclude us from the presence of him whom we have made a Judge, not a Father. Answer, from the nature of God, as described by an apostle, the parable of the prodigal son, and from the expression, *Our* Father. Christ the earnest, the Holy Spirit the witness, of our adoption.
38. Why God is called generally, Our Father.
39. We may pray specially for ourselves and certain others, provided we have in our mind a general reference to all.
40. In what sense God is said to be *in heaven*. A threefold use of this doctrine for our consolation. Three cautions. Summary of the preface to the Lord's Prayer.
41. The necessity of the first petition a proof of our unrighteousness. What meant by the name of God. How it is hallowed. Parts of this hallowing. A deprecation of the sins by which the name of God is profaned.
42. Distinction between the first and second petitions. The kingdom of God, what. How said to come. Special exposition of this petition. It reminds us of three things. Advent of the kingdom of God in the world.
43. Distinction between the second and third petitions. The will here meant not the secret will or good pleasure of God, but that manifested in the word. Conclusion of the three first petitions.
44. A summary of the second part of the Lord's Prayer. Three petitions. What contained in the first. Declares the exceeding kindness of God, and our distrust. What meant by *bread*. Why the petition for bread precedes that for the forgiveness of sins. Why it is called ours. Why to be sought *this day*, or *daily*. The doctrine resulting from this petition, illustrated by an example. Two classes of men sin in regard to this petition. It what sense it is called, our bread. Why we ask God to give it to us.
45. Close connection between this and the subsequent petition. Why our sins are called debts. This petition violated, 1. By those who think they can satisfy God by their own merits, or those of others. 2. By those who dream of a perfection which makes pardon unnecessary. Why the elect cannot attain perfection in this life. Refutation of the libertine dreamers of perfection. Objection refuted. In what sense we are said to forgive those who have sinned against us. How the condition is to be understood.
46. The sixth petition reduced to three heads. 1. The various forms of temptation. The depraved conceptions of our minds. The wiles of Satan, on the right hand and on the left. 2. What it is to be led into temptation. We do not ask not to be tempted of God. What meant by evil, or the evil one. Summary of this petition. How necessary it is. Condemns the pride of the superstitious. Includes many excellent properties. In what sense God may be said to lead us into temptation.
47. The last three petitions show that the prayers of Christians ought to be public. The conclusion of the Lord's Prayer. Why the word Amen is added.
48. The Lord's Prayer contains everything that we can or ought to ask of God. Those who go beyond it sin in three ways.
49. We may, after the example of the saints, frame our prayers in different words, provided there is no difference in meaning.
50. Some circumstances to be observed. Of appointing special hours of prayer. What to be aimed at, what avoided. The will of God, the rule of our prayers.
51. Perseverance in prayer especially recommended, both by precept and example. Condemnatory of those who assign to God a time and mode of hearing.
52. Of the dignity of faith, through which we always obtain, in answer to prayer, whatever is most expedient for us. The knowledge of this most necessary.

1. From the previous part of the work we clearly see how com-

pletely destitute man is of all good, how devoid of every means of procuring his own salvation. Hence, if he would obtain succour in his necessity, he must go beyond himself, and procure it in some other quarter. It has farther been shown that the Lord kindly and spontaneously manifests himself in Christ, in whom he offers all happiness for our misery, all abundance for our want, opening up the treasures of heaven to us, so that we may turn with full faith to his beloved Son, depend upon him with full expectation, rest in him, and cleave to him with full hope. This, indeed, is that secret and hidden philosophy which cannot be learned by syllogisms, a philosophy thoroughly understood by those whose eyes God has so opened as to see light in his light. But after we have learned by faith to know that whatever is necessary for us or defective in us is supplied in God and in our Lord Jesus Christ, in whom it hath pleased the Father that all fulness should dwell, that we may thence draw as from an inexhaustible fountain, it remains for us to seek and in prayer implore of him what we have learned to be in him. To know God as the sovereign disposer of all good, inviting us to present our requests, and yet not to approach or ask of him, were so far from availing us, that it were just as if one told of a treasure were to allow it to remain buried in the ground. Hence the Apostle, to show that a faith unaccompanied with prayer to God cannot be genuine, states this to be the order: As faith springs from the Gospel, so by faith our hearts are framed to call upon the name of God (Rom. x. 14). And this is the very thing which he had expressed some time before—viz. that the *Spirit of adoption*, which seals the testimony of the Gospel on our hearts, gives us courage to make our requests known unto God, calls forth groanings which cannot be uttered, and enables us to cry, Abba, Father (Rom. viii. 26). This last point, as we have hitherto only touched upon it slightly in passing, must now be treated more fully.

2. To *prayer*, then, are we indebted for penetrating to those riches which are treasured up for us with our heavenly Father. For there is a kind of intercourse between God and men, by which, having entered the upper sanctuary, they appear before Him and appeal to his promises, that when necessity requires, they may learn by experience, that what they believed merely on the authority of his word was not in vain. Accordingly, we see that nothing is set before us as an object of expectation from the Lord which we are not enjoined to ask of Him in prayer, so true it is that prayer digs up those treasures which the Gospel of our Lord discovers to the eye of faith. The necessity and utility of this exercise of prayer no words can sufficiently express. Assuredly it is not without cause our heavenly Father declares that our only safety is in calling upon his name, since by it we invoke the presence of his providence to watch over our interests, of his power to sustain us when weak and almost fainting, of his goodness to receive us into favour, though miserably loaded with sin; in fine, call upon him to manifest himself to us in all his

perfections. Hence, admirable peace and tranquillity are given to our consciences; for the straits by which we were pressed being laid before the Lord, we rest fully satisfied with the assurance that none of our evils are unknown to him, and that he is both able and willing to make the best provision for us.

3. But some one will say, Does he not know without a monitor both what our difficulties are, and what is meet for our interest, so that it seems in some measure superfluous to solicit him by our prayers, as if he were winking, or even sleeping, until aroused by the sound of our voice?[1] Those who argue thus attend not to the end for which the Lord taught us to pray. It was not so much for his sake as for ours. He wills indeed, as is just, that due honour be paid him by acknowledging that all which men desire or feel to be useful, and pray to obtain, is derived from him. But even the benefit of the homage which we thus pay him redounds to ourselves. Hence the holy patriarchs, the more confidently they proclaimed the mercies of God to themselves and others, felt the stronger incitement to prayer. It will be sufficient to refer to the example of Elijah, who being assured of the purpose of God, had good ground for the promise of rain which he gives to Ahab, and yet prays anxiously upon his knees, and sends his servant seven times to inquire (1 Kings xviii. 42); not that he discredits the oracle, but because he knows it to be his duty to lay his desires before God, lest his faith should become drowsy or torpid. Wherefore, although it is true that while we are listless or insensible to our wretchedness, he wakes and watches for us, and sometimes even assists us unasked; it is very much for our interest to be constantly supplicating him: first, that our heart may always be inflamed with a serious and ardent desire of seeking, loving, and serving him, while we accustom ourselves to have recourse to him as a sacred anchor in every necessity; secondly, that no desire, no longing whatever, of which we are ashamed to make him the witness, may enter our minds, while we learn to place all our wishes in his sight, and thus pour out our heart before him; and, lastly, that we may be prepared to receive all his benefits with true gratitude and thanksgiving, while our prayers remind us that they proceed from his hand. Moreover, having obtained what we asked, being persuaded that he has answered our prayers, we are led to long more earnestly for his favour, and at the same time have greater pleasure in welcoming the blessings which we perceive to have been obtained by our prayers. Lastly, use and experience confirm the thought of his providence in our minds in a manner adapted to our weakness, when we understand that he not only promises that he will never fail us, and spontaneously gives us access to approach him in every time of need,

[1] French, "Dont il sembleroit que ce fust chose superflue de le soliciter par prieres; veu que nous avons accoustumé de soliciter ceux qui ne pensent à nostre affaire, et qui sont endormis."—Whence it would seem that it was a superfluous matter to solicit him by prayer; seeing we are accustomed to solicit those who think not of our business, and who are slumbering.

but has his hand always stretched out to assist his people, not amusing them with words, but proving himself to be a present aid. For these reasons, though our most merciful Father never slumbers nor sleeps he very often seems to do so, that thus he may exercise us, when we might otherwise be listless and slothful, in asking, entreating, and earnestly beseeching him to our great good. It is very absurd, therefore, to dissuade men from prayer, by pretending that Divine Providence, which is always watching over the government of the universe, is in vain importuned by our supplications, when, on the contrary, the Lord himself declares, that he is "nigh unto all that call upon him, to all that call upon him in truth" (Ps. cxlv. 18). No better is the frivolous allegation of others, that it is superfluous to pray for things which the Lord is ready of his own accord to bestow; since it is his pleasure that those very things which flow from his spontaneous liberality should be acknowledged as conceded to our prayers. This is testified by that memorable sentence in the psalm, to which many others correspond, "The eyes of the Lord are upon the righteous, and his ears are open unto their cry" (Ps. xxxiv. 15), This passage, while extolling the care which Divine Providence spontaneously exercises over the safety of believers, omits not the exercise of faith by which the mind is aroused from sloth. The eyes of God are awake to assist the blind in their necessity, but he is likewise pleased to listen to our groans, that he may give us the better proof of his love. And thus both things are true, "He that keepeth Israel shall neither slumber nor sleep" (Ps. cxxi. 4); and yet whenever he sees us dumb and torpid, he withdraws as if he had forgotten us.

4. Let the first rule of right prayer then be, to have our heart and mind framed as becomes those who are entering into converse with God. This we shall accomplish in regard to the mind, if, laying aside carnal thoughts and cares which might interfere with the direct and pure contemplation of God, it not only be wholly intent on prayer, but also, as far as possible, be borne and raised above itself. I do not here insist on a mind so disengaged as to feel none of the gnawings of anxiety; on the contrary, it is by much anxiety that the fervour of prayer is inflamed. Thus we see that the holy servants of God betray great anguish, not to say solicitude, when they cause the voice of complaint to ascend to the Lord from the deep abyss and the jaws of death. What I say is, that all foreign and extraneous cares must be dispelled by which the mind might be driven to and fro in vague suspense, be drawn down from heaven, and kept grovelling on the earth. When I say it must be raised above itself, I mean that it must not bring into the presence of God any of those things which our blind and stupid reason is wont to devise, nor keep itself confined within the little measure of its own vanity, but rise to a purity worthy of God.

5. Both things are specially worthy of notice. First, let every one in professing to pray turn thither all his thoughts and feelings, and be not (as is usual) distracted by wandering thoughts; because

nothing is more contrary to the reverence due to God than that levity which bespeaks a mind too much given to license and devoid of fear. In this matter we ought to labour the more earnestly the more difficult we experience it to be; for no man is so intent on prayer as not to feel many thoughts creeping in, and either breaking off the tenor of his prayer, or retarding it by some turning or digression. Here let us consider how unbecoming it is when God admits us to familiar intercourse, to abuse his great condescension by mingling things sacred and profane, reverence for him not keeping our minds under restraint; but just as if in prayer we were conversing with one like ourselves, forgetting him, and allowing our thoughts to run to and fro. Let us know, then, that none duly prepare themselves for prayer but those who are so impressed with the majesty of God that they engage in it free from all earthly cares and affections. The ceremony of lifting up our hands in prayer is designed to remind us that we are far removed from God, unless our thoughts rise upward: as it is said in the psalm, "Unto thee, O Lord, do I lift up my soul" (Psalm xxv. 1). And Scripture repeatedly uses the expression to *raise our prayer*, meaning, that those who would be heard by God must not grovel in the mire. The sum is, that the more liberally God deals with us, condescendingly inviting us to disburden our cares into his bosom, the less excusable we are if this admirable and incomparable blessing does not in our estimation outweigh all other things, and win our affection, that prayer may seriously engage our every thought and feeling. This cannot be unless our mind, strenuously exerting itself against all impediments, rise upward.

Our second proposition was, that we are to ask only in so far as God permits. For though he bids us pour out our hearts (Ps. lxii. 8), he does not indiscriminately give loose reins to foolish and depraved affections; and when he promises that he will grant believers their wish, his indulgence does not proceed so far as to submit to their caprice. In both matters grevious delinquencies are everywhere committed. For not only do many without modesty, without reverence, presume to invoke God concerning their frivolities, but impudently bring forward their dreams, whatever they may be, before the tribunal of God. Such is the folly or stupidity under which they labour, that they have the hardihood to obtrude upon God desires so vile, that they would blush exceedingly to impart them to their fellow-men. Profane writers have derided and even expressed their detestation of this presumption, and yet the vice has always prevailed. Hence, as the ambitious adopted Jupiter as their patron; the avaricious, Mercury; the literary aspirants, Apollo and Minerva; the warlike, Mars; the licentious, Venus: so in the present day, as I lately observed, men in prayer give greater license to their unlawful desires than if they were telling jocular tales among their equals. God does not suffer his condescension to be thus mocked, but vindicating his own right, places our wishes under the restraint of his authority. We must, therefore, attend to the observation of John,

"This is the confidence that we have in him, that if we ask anything according to his will, he heareth us" (1 John v. 14).

But as our faculties are far from being able to attain to such high perfection, we must seek for some means to assist them. As the eye of our mind should be intent upon God, so the affection of our heart ought to follow in the same course. But both fall far beneath this, or rather, they faint and fail, and are carried in a contrary direction. To assist this weakness, God gives us the guidance of the Spirit in our prayers to dictate what is right, and regulate our affections. For seeing "we know not what we should pray for as we ought," "the Spirit itself maketh intercession for us with groanings which cannot be uttered" (Rom. viii. 26); not that he actually prays or groans, but he excites in us sighs, and wishes, and confidence, which our natural powers are not at all able to conceive. Nor is it without cause Paul gives the name of *groanings which cannot be uttered* to the prayers which believers send forth under the guidance of the Spirit. For those who are truly exercised in prayer are not unaware that blind anxieties so restrain and perplex them, that they can scarcely find what it becomes them to utter; nay, in attempting to lisp they halt and hesitate. Hence it appears that to pray aright is a special gift. We do not speak thus in indulgence to our sloth, as if we were to leave the office of prayer to the Holy Spirit, and give way to that carelessness to which we are too prone. Thus we sometimes hear the impious expression, that we are to wait in suspense until he take possession of our minds while otherwise occupied. Our meaning is that, weary of our own heartlessness and sloth, we are to long for the aid of the Spirit. Nor indeed does Paul, when he enjoins us to pray *in the Spirit* (1 Cor. xiv. 15), cease to exhort us to vigilance, intimating, that while the inspiration of the Spirit is effectual to the formation of prayer, it by no means impedes or retards our own endeavours; since in this matter God is pleased to try how efficiently faith influences our hearts.

6. Another rule of prayer is, that in asking we must always truly feel our wants, and seriously considering that we need all the things which we ask, accompany the prayer with a sincere, nay, ardent desire of obtaining them. Many repeat prayers in a perfunctory manner from a set form, as if they were performing a task to God; and though they confess that this is a necessary remedy for the evils of their condition, because it were fatal to be left without the divine aid which they implore, it still appears that they perform the duty from custom, because their minds are meanwhile cold, and they ponder not what they ask. A general and confused feeling of their necessity leads them to pray, but it does not make them solicitous as in a matter of present consequence, that they may obtain the supply of their need. Moreover, can we suppose anything more hateful or even more execrable to God than this fiction of asking the pardon of sins, while he who asks at the very time either thinks that he is not a sinner or at least is not thinking that he is a sinner; in other words, a fiction by

which God is plainly held in derision? But mankind, as I have lately said, are full of depravity, so that in the way of perfunctory service they often ask many things of God which they think come to them without his beneficence, or from some other quarter, or are already certainly in their possession. There is another fault which seems less heinous, but is not to be tolerated. Some murmur out prayers without meditation, their only principle being that God is to be propitiated by prayer. Believers ought to be specially on their guard never to appear in the presence of God with the intention of presenting a request unless they are under some serious impression, and are, at the same time, desirous to obtain it. Nay, although in these things which we ask only for the glory of God, we seem not at first sight to consult for our necessity, yet we ought not to ask with less fervour and vehemency of desire. For instance, when we pray that his name be hallowed, that hallowing must, so to speak, be earnestly hungered and thirsted after.

7. If it is objected, that the necessity which urges us to pray is not always equal, I admit it, and this distinction is profitably taught us by James: "Is any among you afflicted? let him pray. Is any merry? let him sing psalms" (James v. 13). Therefore, common sense itself dictates, that as we are too sluggish, we must be stimulated by God to pray earnestly whenever the occasion requires. This David calls a time when God "may be found" (a seasonable time); because, as he declares in several other passages, that the more hardly grievances, annoyances, fears, and other kinds of trial press us, the freer is our access to God, as if he were inviting us to himself. Still not less true is the injunction of Paul to pray "always" (Eph. vi. 18); because, however prosperously, according to our view, things proceed, and however we may be surrounded on all sides with grounds of joy, there is not an instant of time during which our want does not exhort us to prayer. A man abounds in wheat and wine; but as he cannot enjoy a morsel of bread, unless by the continual bounty of God, his granaries or cellars will not prevent him from asking for daily bread. Then, if we consider how many dangers impend every moment, fear itself will teach us that no time ought to be without prayer. This, however, may be better known in spiritual matters. For when will the many sins of which we are conscious allow us to sit secure without suppliantly entreating freedom from guilt and punishment? When will temptation give us a truce, making it unnecessary to hasten for help? Moreover, zeal for the kingdom and glory of God ought not to seize us by starts, but urge us without intermission, so that every time should appear seasonable. It is not without cause, therefore, that assiduity in prayer is so often enjoined.. I am not now speaking of perseverance, which shall afterwards be considered; but Scripture, by reminding us of the necessity of constant prayer, charges us with sloth, because we feel not how much we stand in need of this care and assiduity. By this rule hypocrisy and the device of lying to God are restrained, nay, altogether banished from prayer. God promises

that he will be near to those who call upon him in truth, and declares that those who seek him with their whole heart will find him: those, therefore, who delight in their own pollution cannot surely aspire to him.

One of the requisites of legitimate prayer is repentance. Hence the common declaration of Scripture, that God does not listen to the wicked; that their prayers, as well as their sacrifices, are an abomination to him. For it is right that those who seal up their hearts should find the ears of God closed against them, that those who, by their hard-heartedness, provoke his severity should find him inflexible. In Isaiah he thus threatens: "When ye make many prayers, I will not hear: your hands are full of blood" (Isaiah i. 15). In like manner, in Jeremiah, "Though they shall cry unto me, I will not hearken unto them" (Jer. xi. 7, 8, 11); because he regards it as the highest insult for the wicked to boast of his covenant while profaning his sacred name by their whole lives. Hence he complains in Isaiah: "This people draw near to me with their mouth, and with their lips do honour me; but have removed their heart far from me" (Isaiah xxix. 13). Indeed, he does not confine this to prayers alone, but declares that he abominates pretence in every part of his service. Hence the words of James, "Ye ask and receive not, because ye ask amiss, that ye may consume it upon your lusts" (James iv. 3). It is true indeed (as we shall again see in a little) that the pious, in the prayers which they utter, trust not to their own worth; still the admonition of John is not superfluous: "Whatsoever we ask, we receive of him, because we keep his commandments" (1 John iii. 22); an evil conscience shuts the door against us. Hence it follows, that none but the sincere worshippers of God pray aright, or are listened to. Let every one, therefore, who prepares to pray feel dissatisfied with what is wrong in his condition, and assume, which he cannot do without repentance, the character and feelings of a poor suppliant.

8. The third rule to be added is, that he who comes into the presence of God to pray must divest himself of all vain-glorious thoughts, lay aside all idea of worth; in short, discard all self-confidence, humbly giving God the whole glory, lest by arrogating anything, however little, to himself, vain pride cause him to turn away his face. Of this submission, which casts down all haughtiness, we have numerous examples in the servants of God. The holier they are, the more humbly they prostrate themselves when they come into the presence of the Lord. Thus Daniel, on whom the Lord himself bestowed such high commendation, says, "We do not present our supplications before thee for our righteousness, but for thy great mercies. O Lord, hear; O Lord, forgive; O Lord, hearken and do; defer not, for thine own sake, O my God: for thy city and thy people are called by thy name." This he does not indirectly in the usual manner, as if he were one of the individuals in a crowd: he rather confesses his guilt apart, and as a suppliant betaking himself to the asylum of pardon, he distinctly declares that he was confessing his own sin, and

the sin of his people Israel (Dan. ix. 18-20). David also sets us an example of this humility: "Enter not into judgment with thy servant: for in thy sight shall no man living be justified" (Psalm cxliii. 2). In like manner, Isaiah prays, "Behold, thou art wroth; for we have sinned: in those is continuance, and we shall be saved. But we are all as an unclean thing, and all our righteousness are as filthy rags; and we all do fade as a leaf; and our iniquities, like the wind, have taken us away. And there is none that calleth upon thy name that stirreth up himself to take hold of thee: for thou hast hid thy face from us, and hast consumed us, because of our iniquities. But now, O Lord, thou art our Father; we are the clay, and thou our potter; and we all are the work of thy hand. Be not wroth very sore, O Lord, neither remember iniquity for ever: Behold, see, we beseech thee, we are all thy people" (Isa. lxiv. 5-9). You see how they put no confidence in anything but this: considering that they are the Lord's, they despair not of being the objects of his care. In the same way, Jeremiah says, "O Lord, though our iniquities testify against us, do thou it for thy name's sake" (Jer. xiv. 7). For it was most truly and piously written by the uncertain author (whoever he may have been) that wrote the book which is attributed to the prophet Baruch,[1] "but the soul that is greatly vexed, which goeth stooping and feeble, and the eyes that fail, and the hungry soul, will give thee praise and righteousness, O Lord. Therefore, we do not make our humble supplication before thee, O Lord our God, for the righteousness of our fathers, and of our kings." "Hear, O Lord, and have mercy; for thou art merciful: and have pity upon us, because we have sinned before thee" (Baruch ii. 18, 19; iii. 2).

9. In fine, supplication for pardon, with humble and ingenuous confession of guilt, forms both the preparation and commencement of right prayer. For the holiest of men cannot hope to obtain anything from God until he has been freely reconciled to him. God cannot be propitious to any but those whom he pardons. Hence it is not strange that this is the key by which believers open the door of prayer, as we learn from several passages in The Psalms. David, when presenting a request on a different subject, says, "Remember not the sins of my youth, nor my transgressions; according to thy mercy remember me, for thy goodness sake, O Lord" (Psalm xxv. 7). Again, "Look upon my affliction and my pain, and forgive my sins" (Psalm xxv. 18). Here also we see that it is not sufficient to call ourselves to account for the sins of each passing day; we must also call to mind those which might seem to have been long before buried in oblivion. For in another passage the same prophet, confessing one grievous crime, takes occasion to go back to his very birth, "I was shapen in iniquity, and in sin did my mother conceive me" (Psalm

[1] French, "Pourtant ce qui est escrit en la prophetie qu'on attribue à Baruch, combien que l'autheur soit incertain, est tres sainctement dit;"—However, what is written in the prophecy which is attributed to Baruch, though the author is uncertain, is very holily said.

li. 5); not to extenuate the fault by the corruption of his nature, but as it were to accumulate the sins of his whole life, that the stricter he was in condemning himself, the more placable God might be. But although the saints do not always in express terms ask forgiveness of sins, yet if we carefully ponder those prayers as given in Scripture, the truth of what I say will readily appear—namely, that their courage to pray was derived solely from the mercy of God, and that they always began with appeasing him. For when a man interrogates his conscience, so far is he from presuming to lay his cares familiarly before God, that if he did not trust to mercy and pardon, he would tremble at the very thought of approaching him. There is, indeed, another special confession. When believers long for deliverance from punishment, they at the same time pray that their sins may be pardoned;[1] for it were absurd to wish that the effect should be taken away while the cause remains. For we must beware of imitating foolish patients, who, anxious only about curing accidental symptoms, neglect the root of the disease.[2] Nay, our endeavour must be to have God propitious even before he attests his favour by external signs, both because this is the order which he himself chooses, and it were of little avail to experience his kindness, did not conscience feel that he is appeased, and thus enable us to regard him as altogether lovely. Of this we are even reminded by our Saviour's reply. Having determined to cure the paralytic, he says, "Thy sins are forgiven thee;" in other words, he raises our thoughts to the object which is especially to be desired—viz. admission into the favour of God—and then gives the fruit of reconciliation by bringing assistance to us. But besides that special confession of present guilt which believers employ, in supplicating for pardon of every fault and punishment, that general introduction which procures favour for our prayers must never be omitted, because prayers will never reach God unless they are founded on free mercy. To this we may refer the words of John, "If we confess our sins, he is faithful and just to forgive us our sins, and to cleanse us from all unrighteousness" (1 John i. 9). Hence under the law it was necessary to consecrate prayers by the expiation of blood, both that they might be accepted, and that the people might be warned that they were unworthy of the high privilege, until being purged from their defilements, they founded their confidence in prayer entirely on the mercy of God.

10. Sometimes, however, the saints, in supplicating God, seem to appeal to their own righteousness, as when David says, "Preserve my soul; for I am holy" (Ps. lxxxvi. 2). Also Hezekiah, "Remember now, O Lord, I beseech thee, how I have walked before thee in truth, and with a perfect heart, and have done that which is good in

1 French, "il recognoissent le chastiement qu'ils ont merité;"—they acknowledge the punishment which they have deserved.

2 The French adds, "Ils voudront qu'on leur oste le mal de teste et des reins, et seront contens qu'on ne touche point a la fievre;"—They would wish to get quit of the pain in the head and the loins, and would be contented to leave the fever untouched.

thy sight" (Is. xxxviii. 3). All they mean by such expressions is, that regeneration declares them to be among the servants and children to whom God engages that he will show favour. We have already seen how he declares by the Psalmist that his eyes "are upon the righteous, and his ears are open unto their cry" (Ps. xxxiv. 16): and again by the apostle, that "whatsoever we ask of him we obtain, because we keep his commandments" (John iii. 22). In these passages he does not fix a value on prayer as a meritorious work, but designs to establish the confidence of those who are conscious of an unfeigned integrity and innocence, such as all believers should possess. For the saying of the blind man who had received his sight is in perfect accordance with divine truth—"God heareth not sinners" (John ix. 31)—provided we take the term sinners in the sense commonly used by Scripture to mean those who, without any desire for righteousness, are sleeping secure in their sins; since no heart will ever rise to genuine prayer that does not at the same time long for holiness. Those supplications in which the saints allude to their purity and integrity correspond to such promises, that they may thus have, in their own experience, a manifestation of that which all the servants of God are made to expect. Thus they almost always use this mode of prayer when before God they compare themselves with their enemies, from whose injustice they long to be delivered by his hand. When making such comparisons, there is no wonder that they bring forward their integrity and simplicity of heart, that thus, by the justice of their cause, the Lord may be the more disposed to give them succour. We rob not the pious breast of the privilege of enjoying a consciousness of purity before the Lord, and thus feeling assured of the promises with which he comforts and supports his true worshippers, but we would have them to lay aside all thought of their own merit, and found their confidence of success in prayer solely on the divine mercy.

11. The fourth rule of prayer is, that notwithstanding of our being thus abased and truly humbled, we should be animated to pray with the sure hope of succeeding. There is, indeed, an appearance of contradiction between the two things, between a sense of the just vengeance of God and firm confidence in his favour, and yet they are perfectly accordant, if it is the mere goodness of God that raises up those who are overwhelmed by their own sins. For, as we have formerly shown (chap. iii. sec. 1, 2) that repentance and faith go hand in hand, being united by an indissoluble tie, the one causing terror, the other joy, so in prayer they must both be present. This concurrence David expresses in a few words: "But as for me, I will come into thy house in the multitude of thy mercy; and in thy fear will I worship toward thy holy temple" (Ps. v. 7). Under the goodness of God he comprehends faith, at the same time not excluding fear; for not only does his majesty compel our reverence, but our own unworthiness also divests us of all pride and confidence, and keeps us in fear. The confidence of which I speak is not one which

frees the mind from all anxiety, and soothes it with sweet and perfect rest, such rest is peculiar to those who, while all their affairs are flowing to a wish, are annoyed by no care, stung with no regret, agitated by no fear. But the best stimulus which the saints have to prayer is when, in consequence of their own necessities, they feel the greatest disquietude, and are all but driven to despair, until faith seasonably comes to their aid; because in such straits the goodness of God so shines upon them, that while they groan, burdened by the weight of present calamities, and tormented with the fear of greater, they yet trust to this goodness, and in this way both lighten the difficulty of endurance, and take comfort in the hope of final deliverance. It is necessary, therefore, that the prayer of the believer should be the result of both feelings, and exhibit the influence of both—namely, that while he groans under present and anxiously dreads new evils, he should, at the same time, have recourse to God, not at all doubting that God is ready to stretch out a helping hand to him. For it is not easy to say how much God is irritated by our distrust, when we ask what we expect not of his goodness. Hence nothing is more accordant to the nature of prayer than to lay it down as a fixed rule, that it is not to come forth at random, but is to follow in the footsteps of faith. To this principle Christ directs all of us in these words, "Therefore, I say unto you, What things soever ye desire, when ye pray, believe that ye receive them, and ye shall have them" (Mark xi. 24). The same thing he declares in another passage, "All things, whatsoever ye shall ask in prayer, believing, ye shall receive" (Matth. xxi. 22). In accordance with this are the words of James, "If any of you lack wisdom, let him ask of God, that giveth to all men liberally, and upbraideth not, and it shall be given him. But let him ask in faith, nothing wavering" (James i. 5). He most aptly expresses the power of faith by opposing it to wavering. No less worthy of notice is his additional statement, that those who approach God with a doubting, hesitating mind, without feeling assured whether they are to be heard or not, gain nothing by their prayers. Such persons he compares to a wave of the sea, driven with the wind and tossed. Hence in another passage he terms genuine prayer "the prayer of faith" (James v. 15). Again, since God so often declares that he will give to every man according to his faith, he intimates that we cannot obtain anything without faith. In short, it is faith which obtains everything that is granted to prayer. This is the meaning of Paul in the well-known passage to which dull men give too little heed, "How then shall they call upon him in whom they have not believed? and how shall they believe in him of whom they have not heard?" "So then faith cometh by hearing, and hearing by the word of God" (Rom. x. 14, 17). Gradually deducing the origin of prayer from faith, he distinctly maintains that God cannot be invoked sincerely except by those to whom, by the preaching of the Gospel, his mercy and willingness have been made known, nay, familiarly explained.

12. This necessity our opponents do not at all consider. Therefore, when we say that believers ought to feel firmly assured, they think we are saying the absurdest thing in the world. But if they had any experience in true prayer, they would assuredly understand that God cannot be duly invoked without this firm sense of the Divine benevolence. But as no man can well perceive the power of faith, without at the same time feeling it in his heart, what profit is there in disputing with men of this character, who plainly show that they have never had more than a vain imagination? The value and necessity of that assurance for which we contend is learned chiefly from prayer. Every one who does not see this gives proof of a very stupid conscience. Therefore, leaving those who are thus blinded, let us fix our thoughts on the words of Paul, that God can only be invoked by such as have obtained a knowledge of his mercy from the Gospel, and feel firmly assured that that mercy is ready to be bestowed upon them. What kind of prayer would this be? "O Lord, I am indeed doubtful whether or not thou art inclined to hear me; but being oppressed with anxiety, I fly to thee, that if I am worthy, thou mayest assist me." None of the saints whose prayers are given in Scripture thus supplicated. Nor are we thus taught by the Holy Spirit, who tells us to "come boldly unto the throne of grace, that we may obtain mercy, and find grace to help in time of need" (Heb. iv. 16); and elsewhere teaches us to "have boldness and access with confidence by the faith of Christ" (Eph. iii. 12). This confidence of obtaining what we ask, a confidence which the Lord commands, and all the saints teach by their example, we must therefore hold fast with both hands, if we would pray to any advantage. The only prayer acceptable to God is that which springs (if I may so express it) from this presumption of faith, and is founded on the full assurance of hope. He might have been contented to use the simple name of faith, but he adds not only confidence, but liberty or boldness, that by this mark he might distinguish us from unbelievers, who indeed like us pray to God, but pray at random. Hence the whole Church thus prays, "Let thy mercy, O Lord, be upon us, according as we hope in thee" (Ps. xxxiii. 22). The same condition is set down by the Psalmist in another passage, "When I cry unto thee, then shall mine enemies turn back: this I know, for God is for me" (Ps. lvi. 9). Again, "In the morning will I direct my prayer unto thee, and will look up" (Ps. v. 3). From these words we gather, that prayers are vainly poured out into the air unless accompanied with faith, in which, as from a watch-tower, we may quietly wait for God. With this agrees the order of Paul's exhortation. For before urging believers to pray in the Spirit always, with vigilance and assiduity, he enjoins them to take "the shield of faith," the helmet of salvation, and the sword of the Spirit, which is the word of God" (Eph. vi. 16–18).

Let the reader here call to mind what I formerly observed, that faith by no means fails, though accompanied with a recognition of our wretchedness, poverty, and pollution. How much soever believers may feel that they are oppressed by a heavy load of iniquity, and are not only devoid of everything which can procure the favour of God for them, but justly burdened with many sins which make him an object of dread, yet they cease not to present themselves, this feeling not deterring them from appearing in his presence, because there is no other access to him. Genuine prayer is not that by which we arrogantly extol ourselves before God, or set a great value on any thing of our own, but that by which, while confessing our guilt, we utter our sorrows before God, just as children familiarly lay their complaints before their parents. Nay, the immense accumulation of our sins should rather spur us on and incite us to prayer. Of this the Psalmist gives us an example, "Heal my soul: for I have sinned against thee" (Ps. xli. 4). I confess, indeed, that these stings would prove mortal darts, did not God give succour; but our heavenly Father has, in ineffable kindness, added a remedy, by which, calming all perturbation, soothing our cares, and dispelling our fears, he condescendingly allures us to himself; nay, removing all doubts, not to say obstacles, makes the way smooth before us.

13. And first, indeed, in enjoining us to pray, he by the very injunction convicts us of impious contumacy if we obey not. He could not give a more precise command than that which is contained in the psalm, "Call upon me in the day of trouble" (Ps. l. 15). But as there is no office of piety more frequently enjoined by Scripture, there is no occasion for here dwelling longer upon it. "Ask," says our Divine Master, "and it shall be given you; seek, and ye shall find; knock, and it shall be opened unto you" (Matth. vii. 7). Here, indeed, a promise is added to the precept, and this is necessary. For though all confess that we must obey the precept, yet the greater part would shun the invitation of God, did he not promise that he would listen and be ready to answer. These two positions being laid down, it is certain that all who cavillingly allege that they are not to come to God directly, are not only rebellious and disobedient, but are also convicted of unbelief, inasmuch as they distrust the promises. There is the more occasion to attend to this, because hypocrites, under a pretence of humility and modesty, proudly contemn the precept, as well as deny all credit to the gracious invitation of God; nay, rob him of a principal part of his worship. For when he rejected sacrifices, in which all holiness seemed then to consist, he declared that the chief thing, that which above all others is precious in his sight, is to be invoked in the day of necessity. Therefore, when he demands that which is his own, and urges us to alacrity in obeying, no pretexts for doubt, how specious soever they may be, can excuse us. Hence all the passages throughout Scripture in which we are commanded to pray, are set up before our eyes as so many banners, to inspire us with confidence. It were presumption to go forward into the presence of God, did he not anticipate us by his invitation. Accordingly, he opens up the way for us by his own voice,

"I will say, It is my people: and they shall say, The Lord is my God" (Zech. xiii. 9). We see how he anticipates his worshippers, and desires them to follow, and therefore we cannot fear that the melody which he himself dictates will prove unpleasing. Especially let us call to mind that noble description of the divine character, by trusting to which we shall easily overcome every obstacle: "O thou that hearest prayer, unto thee shall all flesh come" (Ps. lxv. 2). What can be more lovely or soothing than to see God invested with a title which assures us that nothing is more proper to his nature than to listen to the prayers of suppliants? Hence the Psalmist infers, that free access is given not to a few individuals, but to all men, since God addresses all in these terms, "Call upon me in the day of trouble: I will deliver thee, and thou shalt glorify me" (Ps. l. 15). David, accordingly, appeals to the promise thus given, in order to obtain what he asks: "Thou, O Lord of hosts, God of Israel, hast revealed to thy servant, saying, I will build thee an house: therefore hath thy servant found in his heart to pray this prayer unto thee" (2 Sam. vii. 27). Here we infer, that he would have been afraid but for the promise which emboldened him. So in another passage he fortifies himself with the general doctrine, "He will fulfil the desire of them that fear him" (Ps. cxlv. 19). Nay, we may observe in The Psalms, how the continuity of prayer is broken, and a transition is made at one time to the power of God, at another to his goodness, at another to the faithfulness of his promises. It might seem that David, by introducing these sentiments, unseasonably mutilates his prayers; but believers well know by experience, that their ardour grows languid unless new fuel be added, and, therefore, that meditation as well on the nature as the word of God during prayer, is by no means superfluous. Let us not decline to imitate the example of David, and introduce thoughts which may reanimate our languid minds with new vigour.

14. It is strange that these delightful promises affect us coldly, or scarcely at all, so that the generality of men prefer to wander up and down, forsaking the fountain of living waters, and hewing out to themselves broken cisterns, rather than embrace the divine liberality voluntarily offered to them. "The name of the Lord," says Solomon, "is a strong tower; the righteous runneth into it, and is safe." Joel, after predicting the fearful disaster which was at hand, subjoins the following memorable sentence: "And it shall come to pass, that whosoever shall call on the name of the Lord shall be delivered." This we know properly refers to the course of the Gospel. Scarcely one in a hundred is moved to come into the presence of God, though he himself exclaims by Isaiah, "And it shall come to pass, that before they call, I will answer; and while they are yet speaking, I will hear." This honour he elsewhere bestows upon the whole Church in general, as belonging to all the members of Christ: "He shall call upon me, and I will answer him: I will be with him in trouble;

I will deliver him, and honour him."[1] My intention, however, as I already observed, is not to enumerate all, but only select some admirable passages as a specimen how kindly God allures us to himself, and how extreme our ingratitude must be when with such powerful motives our sluggishness still retards us. Wherefore, let these words always resound in our ears: "The Lord is nigh unto all them that call upon him, to all that call upon him in truth" (Ps. cxlv. 18). Likewise those passages which we have quoted from Isaiah and Joel, in which God declares that his ear is open to our prayers, and that he is delighted as with a sacrifice of sweet savour when we cast our cares upon him. The special benefit of these promises we receive when we frame our prayer, not timorously or doubtingly, but when trusting to his word whose majesty might otherwise deter us, we are bold to call him Father, he himself deigning to suggest this most delightful name. Fortified by such invitations, it remains for us to know that we have therein sufficient materials for prayer, since our prayers depend on no merit of our own, but all their worth and hope of success are founded and depend on the promises of God, so that they need no other support, and require not to look up and down on this hand and on that. It must therefore be fixed in our minds, that though we equal not the lauded sanctity of patriarchs, prophets, and apostles, yet as the command to pray is common to us as well as them, and faith is common, so if we lean on the word of God, we are in respect of this privilege their associates. For God declaring, as has already been seen, that he will listen and be favourable to all, encourages the most wretched to hope that they shall obtain what they ask; and, accordingly, we should attend to the general forms of expression, which, as it is commonly expressed, exclude none from first to last; only let there be sincerity of heart, self-dissatisfaction, humility, and faith, that we may not, by the hypocrisy of a deceitful prayer, profane the name of God. Our most merciful Father will not reject those whom he not only encourages to come, but urges in every possible way. Hence David's method of prayer to which I lately referred: "And now, O Lord God, thou art that God, and thy words be true, and thou hast promised this goodness unto thy servant, that it may continue for ever before thee" (2 Sam. vii. 28). So also, in another passage, "Let, I pray thee, thy merciful kindness be for my comfort, according to thy word unto thy servant" (Psalm cxix. 76). And the whole body of the Israelites, whenever they fortify themselves with the remembrance of the covenant, plainly declare, that since God thus prescribes they are not to pray timorously (Gen. xxxii. 10). In this they imitated the example of the patriarchs, particularly Jacob, who, after confessing that he was unworthy of the many mercies which he had received of the Lord's hand, says, that he is encouraged to make still larger requests, because God had promised that he would grant them. But whatever be the pretexts

[1] Jer. ii. 13; Prov. xviii. 10; Joel ii. 32; Is. lxv. 24; Ps. xci. 15; cxlv. 18.

which unbelievers employ, when they do not flee to God as often as necessity urges, nor seek after him, nor implore his aid, they defraud him of his due honour just as much as if they were fabricating to themselves new gods and idols, since in this way they deny that God is the author of all their blessings. On the contrary, nothing more effectually frees pious minds from every doubt, than to be armed with the thought that no obstacle should impede them while they are obeying the command of God, who declares that nothing is more grateful to him than obedience. Hence, again, what I have previously said becomes still more clear—namely, that a bold spirit in prayer well accords with fear, reverence, and anxiety, and that there is no inconsistency when God raises up those who had fallen prostrate. In this way forms of expression apparently inconsistent admirably harmonise. Jeremiah and David speak of humbly laying their supplications[1] before God. In another passage Jeremiah says, "Let, we beseech thee, our supplication be accepted before thee, and pray for us unto the Lord thy God, even for all this remnant." On the other hand, believers are often said to *lift up prayer*. Thus Hezekiah speaks, when asking the prophet to undertake the office of interceding. And David says, "Let my prayer be set forth before thee as incense; and the lifting up of my hands as the evening sacrifice."[2] The explanation is, that though believers, persuaded of the paternal love of God, cheerfully rely on his faithfulness, and have no hesitation in imploring the aid which he voluntarily offers, they are not elated with supine or presumptuous security; but climbing up by the ladder of the promises, still remain humble and abased suppliants.

15. Here, by way of objection, several questions are raised. Scripture relates that God sometimes complied with certain prayers which had been dictated by minds not duly calmed or regulated. It is true, that the cause for which Jotham imprecated on the inhabitants of Shechem the disaster which afterwards befell them was well founded; but still he was inflamed with anger and revenge (Judges ix. 20); and hence God, by complying with the execration, seems to approve of passionate impulses. Similar fervour also seized Samson when he prayed, "Strengthen me, I pray thee, only this once, O God, that I may be at once avenged of the Philistines for my two eyes" (Judges xvi. 28). For although there was some mixture of good zeal, yet his ruling feeling was a fervid, and therefore vicious longing for vengeance. God assents, and hence apparently it might be inferred that prayers are effectual, though not framed in conformity to the rule of the word. But I answer, *first*, that a perpetual law is not abrogated by singular examples; and, *secondly*, that special suggestions have sometimes been made to a few individuals,

[1] Latin, "prosternere preces." French, "mettent bas leurs prieres;"—lay low their prayers.

[2] Jer. xlii. 9; Dan. ix. 18; Jer. xlii. 2; 2 Kings xix. 4; Ps. cxliv. 2.

whose case thus becomes different from that of the generality of men. For we should attend to the answer which our Saviour gave to his disciples when they inconsiderately wished to imitate the example of Elias, "Ye know not what manner of spirit ye are of" (Luke ix. 55). We must, however, go farther and say, that the wishes to which God assents are not always pleasing to him; but he assents, because it is necessary, by way of example, to give clear evidence of the doctrine of Scripture—viz. that he assists the miserable, and hears the groans of those who unjustly afflicted implore his aid: and, accordingly, he executes his judgments when the complaints of the needy, though in themselves unworthy of attention, ascend to him. For how often, in inflicting punishment on the ungodly for cruelty, rapine, violence, lust, and other crimes, in curbing audacity and fury, and also in overthrowing tyrannical power, has he declared that he gives assistance to those who are unworthily oppressed, though they by addressing an unknown deity only beat the air? There is one psalm which clearly teaches that prayers are not without effect, though they do not penetrate to heaven by faith (Ps. cvii.). For it enumerates the prayers which, by natural instinct, necessity extorts from unbelievers not less than from believers, and to which it shows by the event, that God is, notwithstanding, propitious. Is it to testify by such readiness to hear that their prayers are agreeable to him? Nay; it is, first, to magnify or display his mercy by the circumstance, that even the wishes of unbelievers are not denied; and, secondly, to stimulate his true worshippers to more urgent prayer, when they see that sometimes even the wailings of the ungodly are not without avail. This, however, is no reason why believers should deviate from the law divinely imposed upon them, or envy unbelievers, as if they gained much in obtaining what they wished. We have observed (chap. iii. sec. 25), that in this way God yielded to the feigned repentance of Ahab, that he might show how ready he is to listen to his elect when, with true contrition, they seek his favour. Accordingly he upbraids the Jews, that shortly after experiencing his readiness to listen to their prayers, they returned to their own perverse inclinations. It is also plain from the Book of Judges that, whenever they wept, though their tears were deceitful, they were delivered from the hands of their enemies. Therefore, as God sends his sun indiscrimately on the evil and on the good, so he despises not the tears of those who have a good cause, and whose sorrows are deserving of relief. Meanwhile, though he hears them, it has no more to do with salvation than the supply of food which he gives to other despisers of his goodness.

There seems to be a more difficult question concerning Abraham and Samuel, the one of whom, without any instructions from the word of God, prayed in behalf of the people of Sodom, and the other, contrary to an express prohibition, prayed in behalf of Saul (Gen. xviii. 23; 1 Sam. xv. 11). Similar is the case of Jeremiah, who prayed that the city might not be destroyed (Jer. xxxii. 16). It is true their prayers were refused, but it seems harsh to affirm that they prayed without faith. Modest readers will, I hope, be satisfied with this solution—viz. that leaning to the general principle on which God enjoins us to be merciful even to the unworthy, they were not altogether devoid of faith, though in this particular instance their wish was disappointed. Augustine shrewdly remarks, "How do the saints pray in faith when they ask from God contrary to what he has decreed? Namely, because they pray according to his will, not his hidden and immutable will, but that which he suggests to them, that he may hear them in another manner; as he wisely distinguishes" (August. de Civit. Dei, Lib. xxii. c. 2). This is truly said: for, in his incomprehensible counsel, he so regulates events, that the prayers of the saints, though involving a mixture of faith and error, are not in vain. And yet this no more sanctions imitation than it excuses the saints themselves, who I deny not exceeded due bounds. Wherefore, whenever no certain promise exists, our request to God must have a condition annexed to it. Here we may refer to the prayer of David, "Awake for me to the judgment that thou hast commanded" (Ps. vii. 6); for he reminds us that he had received special instruction to pray for a temporal blessing.[1]

16. It is also of importance to observe, that the four laws of prayer of which I have treated are not so rigorously enforced, as that God rejects the prayers in which he does not find perfect faith or repentance, accompanied with fervent zeal and wishes duly framed. We have said (sec. 4), that though prayer is the familiar intercourse of believers with God, yet reverence and modesty must be observed: we must not give loose reins to our wishes, nor long for anything farther than God permits; and, moreover, lest the majesty of God should be despised, our minds must be elevated to pure and chaste veneration. This no man ever performed with due perfection. For, not to speak of the generality of men, how often do David's complaints savour of intemperance? Not that he actually means to expostulate with God, or murmur at his judgments, but failing, through infirmity, he finds no better solace than to pour his griefs into the bosom of his heavenly Father. Nay, even our stammering is tolerated by God, and pardon is granted to our ignorance as often as anything rashly escapes us: indeed, without this indulgence, we should have no freedom to pray. But although it was David's intention to submit himself entirely to the will of God, and he prayed with no less patience than fervour, yet irregular emotions appear, nay, sometimes burst forth,—emotions not a little at variance with the first law which we laid down. In particular, we may see in a clause of the thirty-ninth Psalm, how this saint was carried away by the vehemence of his grief, and unable to keep within bounds. "O spare me,[2] that I may recover strength, before I go hence, and be no more" (Ps. xxxix. 13).

1 The French adds, "duquel il n'eust pas autrement esté asseuré;"—of which he would not otherwise have felt assured

2 Latin, "Desine a me." French, "Retire-toy;"—Withdraw from me.

You would call this the language of a desperate man, who had no other desire than that God should withdraw and leave him to perish in his distresses. Not that his devout mind rushes into such intemperance, or that, as the reprobate are wont, he wishes to have done with God; he only complains that the divine anger is more than he can bear. During those trials, wishes often escape which are not in accordance with the rule of the word, and in which the saints do not duly consider what is lawful and expedient. Prayers contaminated by such faults, indeed, deserve to be rejected; yet provided the saints lament, administer self-correction, and return to themselves, God pardons.

Similar faults are committed in regard to the second law (as to which, see sec. 6), for the saints have often to struggle with their own coldness, their want and misery not urging them sufficiently to serious prayer. It often happens, also, that their minds wander, and are almost lost; hence in this matter also there is need of pardon, lest their prayers, from being languid or mutilated, or interrupted and wandering, should meet with a refusal. One of the natural feelings which God has imprinted on our mind is, that prayer is not genuine unless the thoughts are turned upward. Hence the ceremony of raising the hands, to which we have adverted, a ceremony known to all ages and nations, and still in common use. But who, in lifting up his hands, is not conscious of sluggishness, the heart cleaving to the earth? In regard to the petition for remission of sins (sec. 8), though no believer omits it, yet all who are truly exercised in prayer feel that they bring scarcely a tenth of the sacrifice of which David speaks, "The sacrifices of God are a broken spirit: a broken and a contrite heart, O God, thou wilt not despise" (Ps. li. 17). Thus a twofold pardon is always to be asked. first, because they are conscious of many faults, the sense of which, however, does not touch them so as to make them feel dissatisfied with themselves as they ought; and, secondly, in so far as they have been enabled to profit in repentance and the fear of God, they are humbled with just sorrow for their offences, and pray for the remission of punishment by the judge. The thing which most of all vitiates prayer, did not God indulgently interpose, is weakness or imperfection of faith; but it is not wonderful that this defect is pardoned by God, who often exercises his people with severe trials, as if he actually wished to extinguish their faith. The hardest of such trials is when believers are forced to exclaim, "O Lord God of hosts, how long wilt thou be angry against the prayer of thy people?" (Ps. lxxx. 4), as if their very prayers offended him. In like manner, when Jeremiah says, "Also when I cry and shout, he shutteth out my prayer" (Lam. iii. 8), there cannot be a doubt that he was in the greatest perturbation. Innumerable examples of the same kind occur in the Scriptures, from which it is manifest that the faith of the saints was often mingled with doubts and fears, so that while believing and hoping, they however betrayed some degree of unbelief.

But because they do not come so far as were to be wished, that is only an additional reason for their exerting themselves to correct their faults, that they may daily approach nearer to the perfect law of prayer, and at the same time feel into what an abyss of evils those are plunged, who, in the very cures they use, bring new diseases upon themselves: since there is no prayer which God would not deservedly disdain, did he not overlook the blemishes with which all of them are polluted. I do not mention these things that believers may securely pardon themselves in any faults which they commit, but that they may call themselves to strict account, and thereby endeavour to surmount these obstacles; and though Satan endeavours to block up all the paths in order to prevent them from praying, they may, nevertheless, break through, being firmly persuaded that though not disencumbered of all hinderances, their attempts are pleasing to God, and their wishes are approved, provided they hasten on and keep their aim, though without immediately reaching it.

17. But since no man is worthy to come forward in his own name, and appear in the presence of God, our heavenly Father, to relieve us at once from fear and shame, with which all must feel oppressed,[1] has given us his Son, Jesus Christ our Lord, to be our Advocate and Mediator, that under his guidance we may approach securely, confiding that with him for our Intercessor nothing which we ask in his name will be denied to us, as there is nothing which the Father can deny to him (1 Tim. ii. 5; 1 John ii. 1; see sec. 36, 37). To this it is necessary to refer all that we have previously taught concerning faith; because, as the promise gives us Christ as our Mediator, so, unless our hope of obtaining what we ask is founded on him, it deprives us of the privilege of prayer. For it is impossible to think of the dread majesty of God without being filled with alarm; and hence the sense of our own unworthiness must keep us far away, until Christ interpose, and convert a throne of dreadful glory into a throne of grace; as the Apostle teaches that thus we can "come boldly unto the throne of grace, that we may obtain mercy, and find grace to help in time of need" (Heb. iv. 16). And as a rule has been laid down as to prayer, as a promise has been given that those who pray will be heard, so we are specially enjoined to pray in the name of Christ, the promise being that we shall obtain what we ask in his name. "Whatsoever ye shall ask in my name," says our Saviour, "that will I do; that the Father may be glorified in the Son;" "Hitherto ye have asked nothing in my name; ask, and ye shall receive, that your joy may be full" (John xiv. 13; xvi. 24). Hence it is incontrovertibly clear that those who pray to God in any other name than that of Christ contumaciously falsify his orders, and regard his will as nothing, while they have no promise that they shall obtain. For, as Paul says, "All the promises of God in him

1 French, "Confusion que nous avons, ou devons avoir en nousmesmes;"—confusion which we have, or ought to have, in ourselves.

are yea, and in him amen;" that is, are confirmed and fulfilled in him.

18. And we must carefully attend to the circumstance of time. Christ enjoins his disciples to have recourse to his intercession after he shall have ascended to heaven: "At that day ye shall ask in my name" (John xvi. 26). It is certain, indeed, that from the very first all who ever prayed were heard only for the sake of the Mediator. For this reason God had commanded in the Law, that the priest alone should enter the sanctuary, bearing the names of the twelve tribes of Israel on his shoulders, and as many precious stones on his breast, while the people were to stand at a distance in the outer court, and thereafter unite their prayers with the priest. Nay, the sacrifice had even the effect of ratifying and confirming their prayers. That shadowy ceremony of the Law therefore taught, first, that we are all excluded from the face of God, and, therefore, that there is need of a Mediator to appear in our name, and carry us on his shoulders, and keep us bound upon his breast, that we may be heard in his person; and, secondly, that our prayers, which, as has been said, would otherwise never be free from impurity, are cleansed by the sprinkling of his blood. And we see that the saints, when they desired to obtain anything, founded their hopes on sacrifices, because they knew that by sacrifice all prayers were ratified: "Remember all thy offerings," says David, "and accept thy burnt sacrifice" (Ps. xx. 3). Hence we infer, that in receiving the prayers of his people, God was from the very first appeased by the intercession of Christ. Why then does Christ speak of a new period ("at that day") when the disciples were to begin to pray in his name, unless it be that this grace, being now more brightly displayed, ought also to be in higher estimation with us? In this sense he had said a little before, "Hitherto ye have asked nothing in my name; ask." Not that they were altogether ignorant of the office of Mediator (all the Jews were instructed in these first rudiments), but they did not clearly understand that Christ by his ascent to heaven would be more the advocate of the Church than before. Therefore, to solace their grief for his absence by some more than ordinary result, he asserts his office of advocate, and says, that hitherto they had been without the special benefit which it would be their privilege to enjoy, when aided by his intercession they should invoke God with greater freedom. In this sense the Apostle says, that we have "boldness to enter into the holiest by the blood of Jesus, by a new and living way, which he hath consecrated for us" (Heb. x. 19, 20). Therefore, the more inexcusable we are, if we do not with both hands (as it is said) embrace the inestimable gift which is properly destined for us.

19. Moreover, since he himself is the only way and the only access by which we can draw near to God, those who deviate from this way, and decline this access, have no other remaining; his throne presents nothing but wrath, judgment, and terror. In short, as the Father has consecrated him our guide and head, those who abandon or turn

aside from him in any way endeavour, as much as in them lies, to sully and efface the stamp which God has impressed. Christ, therefore, is the only Mediator by whose intercession the Father is rendered propitious and exorable (1 Tim. ii. 5). For though the saints are still permitted to use intercessions, by which they mutually beseech God in behalf of each other's salvation, and of which the Apostle makes mention (Eph. vi. 18, 19; 1 Tim. ii. 1); still these depend on that one intercession, so far are they from derogating from it. For as the intercessions which as members of one body we offer up for each other, spring from the feeling of love, so they have reference to this one head. Being thus also made in the name of Christ, what more do they than declare that no man can derive the least benefit from any prayers without the intercession of Christ? As there is nothing in the intercession of Christ to prevent the different members of the Church from offering up prayers for each other, so let it be held as a fixed principle, that all the intercessions thus used in the Church must have reference to that one intercession. Nay, we must be specially careful to show our gratitude on this very account, that God pardoning our unworthiness, not only allows each individual to pray for himself, but allows all to intercede mutually for each other. God having given a place in his Church to intercessors who would deserve to be rejected when praying privately on their own account, how presumptuous were it to abuse this kindness by employing it to obscure the honour of Christ.

20. Moreover, the Sophists are guilty of the merest trifling when they allege that Christ is the Mediator of *redemption*, but that believers are mediators of *intercession*; as if Christ had only performed a temporary mediation, and left an eternal and imperishable mediation to his servants. Such, forsooth, is the treatment which he receives from those who pretend only to take from him a minute portion of honour. Very different is the language of Scripture, with whose simplicity every pious man will be satisfied, without paying any regard to those impostors. For when John says, "If any man sin, we have an advocate with the Father, Jesus Christ the righteous" (1 John ii. 1), does he mean merely that we once had an advocate; does he not rather ascribe to him a perpetual intercession? What does Paul mean when he declares that he "is even at the right hand of God, who also maketh intercession for us"? (Rom. viii. 32.) But when in another passage he declares that he is the only Mediator between God and man (1 Tim. ii. 5), is he not referring to the supplications which he had mentioned a little before? Having previously said that prayers were to be offered up for all men, he immediately adds, in confirmation of that statement, that there is one God, and one Mediator between God and man. Nor does Augustine give a different interpretation when he says, "Christian men mutually recommend each other in their prayers. But he for whom none intercedes, while he himself intercedes for all, is the only true Mediator. Though the Apostle Paul was under the head a principal

member, yet because he was a member of the body of Christ, and knew that the most true and High Priest of the Church had entered not by figure into the inner veil to the holy of holies, but by firm and express truth into the inner sanctuary of heaven to holiness, holiness not imaginary, but eternal, he also commends himself to the prayers of the faithful. He does not make himself a mediator between God and the people, but asks that all the members of the body of Christ should pray mutually for each other, since the members are mutually sympathetic: if one member suffers, the others suffer with it. And thus the mutual prayers of all the members still labouring on the earth ascend to the Head, who has gone before into heaven, and in whom there is propitiation for our sins. For if Paul were a mediator, so would also the other apostles, and thus there would be many mediators, and Paul's statement could not stand, 'There is one God, and one Mediator between God and men, the man Christ Jesus;' in whom we also are one if we keep the unity of the faith in the bond of peace"[1] (August. Contra Parmenian, Lib. ii. cap. 8). Likewise in another passage Augustine says, "If thou requirest a priest, he is above the heavens, where he intercedes for those who on earth died for thee" (August. in Ps. xciv.). We imagine not that he throws himself before his Father's knees, and suppliantly intercedes for us; but we understand with the Apostle, that he appears in the presence of God, and that the power of his death has the effect of a perpetual intercession for us; that having entered into the upper sanctuary, he alone continues to the end of the world to present the prayers of his people, who are standing far off in the outer court.

21. In regard to the saints who having died in the body live in Christ, if we attribute prayer to them, let us not imagine that they have any other way of supplicating God than through Christ who alone is the way, or that their prayers are accepted by God in any other name. Wherefore, since the Scripture calls us away from all others to Christ alone, since our heavenly Father is pleased to gather together all things in him, it were the extreme of stupidity, not to say madness, to attempt to obtain access by means of others, so as to be drawn away from him without whom access cannot be obtained. But who can deny that this was the practice for several ages, and is still the practice, wherever Popery prevails? To procure the favour of God, human merits are ever and anon obtruded, and very frequently while Christ is passed by, God is supplicated in their name. I ask if this is not to transfer to them that office of sole intercession which we have above claimed for Christ? Then what angel or devil ever announced one syllable to any human being concerning that fancied intercession of theirs? There is not a word on the subject in Scripture. What ground then was there for the fiction? Certainly, while the human mind thus seeks help for itself in which it is not sanctioned by the word of God, it plainly manifests its distrust

[1] Heb. ix. 11, 24; Rom. xv. 30; Eph. vi. 19; Col. iv. 3; 1 Cor. xii. 25; 1 Tim. ii. 5; Eph. iv. 3.

(see s. 27). But if we appeal to the consciences of all who take pleasure in the intercession of saints, we shall find that their only reason for it is, that they are filled with anxiety, as if they supposed that Christ were insufficient or too rigorous. By this anxiety they dishonour Christ, and rob him of his title of sole Mediator, a title which being given him by the Father as his special privilege, ought not to be transferred to any other. By so doing they obscure the glory of his nativity and make void his cross; in short, divest and defraud of due praise everything which he did or suffered, since all which he did and suffered goes to show that he is and ought to be deemed sole Mediator. At the same time, they reject the kindness of God in manifesting himself to them as a Father, for he is not their Father if they do not recognise Christ as their brother. This they plainly refuse to do if they think not that he feels for them a brother's affection; affection than which none can be more gentle or tender. Wherefore Scripture offers him alone, sends us to him, and establishes us in him. "He," says Ambrose, "is our mouth by which we speak to the Father; our eye by which we see the Father; our right hand by which we offer ourselves to the Father. Save by his intercession neither we nor any saints have any intercourse with God" (Ambros. Lib. de Isaac et Anima). If they object that the public prayers which are offered up in churches conclude with the words, *through Jesus Christ our Lord*, it is a frivolous evasion; because no less insult is offered to the intercession of Christ by confounding it with the prayers and merits of the dead, than by omitting it altogether, and making mention only of the dead. Then, in all their litanies, hymns, and proses, where every kind of honour is paid to dead saints, there is no mention of Christ.

22. But here stupidity has proceeded to such a length as to give a manifestation of the genius of superstition, which, when once it has shaken off the rein, is wont to wanton without limit. After men began to look to the intercession of saints, a peculiar administration was gradually assigned to each, so that, according to diversity of business, now one, now another, intercessor was invoked. Then individuals adopted particular saints, and put their faith in them, just as if they had been tutelar deities. And thus not only were gods set up according to the number of the cities (the charge which the prophet brought against Israel of old, Jer. ii. 28; xi. 13), but according to the number of individuals. But while the saints in all their desires refer to the will of God alone, look to it, and acquiesce in it, yet to assign to them any other prayer than that of longing for the arrival of the kingdom of God, is to think of them stupidly, carnally, and even insultingly. Nothing can be farther from such a view than to imagine that each, under the influence of private feeling, is disposed to be most favourable to his own worshippers. At length vast numbers have fallen into the horrid blasphemy of invoking them not merely as helping but presiding over their salvation. See the depth to which miserable men fall when they forsake their proper station,

that is, the word of God. I say nothing of the more monstrous specimens of impiety in which, though detestable to God, angels, and men, they themselves feel no pain or shame. Prostrated at a statue or picture of Barbara or Catherine, and the like, they mutter a *Pater Noster;*[1] and so far are their pastors[2] from curing or curbing this frantic course, that, allured by the scent of gain, they approve and applaud it. But while seeking to relieve themselves of the odium of this vile and criminal procedure, with what pretext can they defend the practice of calling upon Eloy or Medard to look upon their servants, and send them help from heaven? or the Holy Virgin to order her Son to do what they ask?[3] The Council of Carthage forbade direct prayer to be made at the altar to saints. It is probable that these holy men, unable entirely to suppress the force of depraved custom, had recourse to this check, that public prayers might not be vitiated with such forms of expression as *Sancti Petre, ora pro nobis —St Peter, pray for us.* But how much farther has this devilish extravagance proceeded when men hesitate not to transfer to the dead the peculiar attributes of Christ and God?

23. In endeavouring to prove that such intercession derives some support from Scripture they labour in vain. We frequently read (they say) of the prayers of angels; and not only so, but the prayers of believers are said to be carried into the presence of God by their hands. But if they would compare saints who have departed this life with angels, it will be necessary to prove that saints are ministering spirits, to whom has been delegated the office of superintending our salvation, to whom has been assigned the province of guiding us in all our ways, of encompassing, admonishing, and comforting us, of keeping watch over us. All these are assigned to angels, but none of them to saints. How preposterously they confound departed saints with angels is sufficiently apparent from the many different offices

1 Erasmus, though stumbling and walking blindfold in clear light, ventures to write thus in a letter to Sadolet, 1530: "Primum, constat nullum esse locum in divinis voluminibus, qui permittat invocare divos, nisi fortasse detorquere huc placet, quod dives in Evangelica parabola implorat opem Abrahæ. Quanquam autem in re tanta novare quicquam præter auctoritatem Scripturæ, merito periculosum videri possit, tamen invocationem divorum nusquam improbo," &c.—First, it is clear that there is no passage in the Sacred Volume which permits the invocation of saints, unless we are pleased to wrest to this purpose what is said in the parable as to the rich man imploring the help of Abraham. But though in so weighty a matter it may justly seem dangerous to introduce anything without the authority of Scripture, I by no means condemn the invocation of saints, &c.

2 Latin, "Pastores;"—French, "ceux qui se disent prelats, curés, ou precheurs;"—those who call themselves prelates, curates, or preachers.

3 French, "Mais encore qu'ils taschent de laver leur mains d'un si vilain sacrilege, d'autant qu'il ne se commet point en leurs messes ni en leurs vespres; sous quelle couleur defendront ils ces blasphemes qu'il lisent a pleine gorge, où ils prient St Eloy ou St Medard, de regarder du ciel leurs serviteurs pour les aider? mesmes où ils supplient la vierge Maire de commander a son fils qu'il leur ottroye leur requestes?—But although they endeavour to wash their hands of the vile sacrilege, inasmuch as it is not committed in their masses or vespers, under what pretext will they defend those blasphemies which they repeat with full throat, in which they pray St Eloy or St Medard to look from heaven upon their servants and assist them; even supplicate the Virgin Mary to command her Son to grant their requests?

by which Scripture distinguishes the one from the other. No one unless admitted will presume to perform the office of pleader before an earthly judge; whence then have worms such licence as to obtrude themselves on God as intercessors, while no such office has been assigned them? God has been pleased to give angels the charge of our safety. Hence they attend our sacred meetings, and the Church is to them a theatre in which they behold the manifold wisdom of God (Eph. iii. 10). Those who transfer to others this office which is peculiar to them, certainly pervert and confound the order which has been established by God and ought to be inviolable. With similar dexterity they proceed to quote other passages. God said to Jeremiah, "Though Moses and Samuel stood before me, yet my mind could not be toward this people" (Jer. xv. 1). How (they ask) could he have spoken thus of the dead but because he knew that they interceded for the living? My inference, on the contrary, is this: since it thus appears that neither Moses nor Samuel interceded for the people of Israel, there was then no intercession for the dead. For who of the saints can be supposed to labour for the salvation of the people, while Moses who, when in life, far surpassed all others in this matter, does nothing? Therefore, if they persist in the paltry quibble, that the dead intercede for the living, because the Lord said, "*If they stood before me*" (*intercesserint*), I will argue far more speciously in this way: Moses, of whom it is said, *if he interceded*, did not intercede for the people in their extreme necessity: it is probable, therefore, that no other saint intercedes, all being far behind Moses in humanity, goodness, and paternal solicitude. Thus all they gain by their cavilling is to be wounded by the very arms with which they deem themselves admirably protected. But it is very ridiculous to wrest this simple sentence in this manner; for the Lord only declares that he would not spare the iniquities of the people, though some Moses or Samuel, to whose prayers he had shown himself so indulgent, should intercede for them. This meaning is most clearly elicited from a similar passage in Ezekiel: "Though these three men, Noah, Daniel, and Job, were in it, they should deliver but their own souls by their righteousness, saith the Lord God" (Ezek. xiv. 14). Here there can be no doubt that we are to understand the words as if it had been said, If two of the persons named were again to come alive; for the third was still living—namely, Daniel, who it is well known had then in the bloom of youth given an incomparable display of piety. Let us therefore leave out those whom Scripture declares to have completed their course. Accordingly, when Paul speaks of David, he says not that by his prayers he assisted posterity, but only that he "served his own generation" (Acts xiii. 36).

24. They again object, Are those, then, to be deprived of every pious wish, who, during the whole course of their lives, breathed nothing but piety and mercy? I have no wish curiously to pry into what they do or meditate; but the probability is, that instead of

being subject to the impulse of various and particular desires, they, with one fixed and immoveable will, long for the kingdom of God, which consists not less in the destruction of the ungodly, than in the salvation of believers. If this be so, there cannot be a doubt that their charity is confined to the communion of Christ's body, and extends no farther than is compatible with the nature of that communion. But though I grant that in this way they pray for us, they do not, however, lose their quiescence so as to be distracted with earthly cares: far less are they, therefore, to be invoked by us. Nor does it follow that such invocation is to be used, because, while men are alive upon the earth, they can mutually commend themselves to each other's prayers. It serves to keep alive a feeling of charity when they, as it were, share each other's wants, and bear each other's burdens. This they do by the command of the Lord, and not without a promise, the two things of primary importance in prayer. But all such reasons are inapplicable to the dead, with whom the Lord, in withdrawing them from our society, has left us no means of intercourse (Eccles. ix. 5, 6), and to whom, so far as we can conjecture, he has left no means of intercourse with us. But if any one allege that they certainly must retain the same charity for us, as they are united with us in one faith, who has revealed to us that they have ears capable of listening to the sounds of our voice, or eyes clear enough to discern our necessities. Our opponents, indeed, talk in the shade of their schools of some kind of light which beams upon departed saints from the divine countenance, and in which, as in a mirror, they, from their lofty abode, behold the affairs of men; but to affirm this with the confidence which these men presume to use, is just to desire, by means of the extravagant dreams of our own brain, and without any authority, to pry and penetrate into the hidden judgments of God, and trample upon Scripture, which so often declares that the wisdom of our flesh is at enmity with the wisdom of God, utterly condemns the vanity of our mind, and humbling our reason, bids us look only to the will of God.

25. The other passages of Scripture which they employ to defend their error are miserably wrested. Jacob (they say) asks for the sons of Joseph, "Let my name be named on them, and the name of my fathers, Abraham and Isaac" (Gen. xlviii. 16). First, let us see what the nature of this invocation was among the Israelites. They do not implore their fathers to bring succour to them, but they beseech God to remember his servants, Abraham, Isaac, and Jacob. Their example, therefore, gives no countenance to those who use addresses to the saints themselves. But such being the dulness of these blocks, that they comprehend not what it is to invoke the name of Jacob, nor why it is to be invoked, it is not strange that they blunder thus childishly as to the mode of doing it. The expression repeatedly occurs in Scripture. Isaiah speaks of women being called by the name of men, when they have them for husbands and live under their protection (Isa. iv. 1). The calling of the name of Abraham

over the Israelites consists in referring the origin of their race to him, and holding him in distinguished remembrance as their author and parent. Jacob does not do so from any anxiety to extend the celebrity of his name, but because he knows that all the happiness of his posterity consisted in the inheritance of the covenant which God had made with them. Seeing that this would give them the sum of all blessings, he prays that they may be regarded as of his race, this being nothing else than to transmit the succession of the covenant to them. They again, when they make mention of this subject in their prayers, do not betake themselves to the intercession of the dead, but call to remembrance that covenant in which their most merciful Father undertakes to be kind and propitious to them for the sake of Abraham, Isaac, and Jacob. How little, in other respects, the saints trusted to the merits of their fathers, the public voice of the Church declares in the prophet, "Doubtless thou art our Father, though Abraham be ignorant of us, and Israel acknowledge us not; thou, O Lord, art our Father, our Redeemer" (Isa. lxiii. 16). And while the Church thus speaks, she at the same time adds, "Return for thy servants' sake," not thinking of anything like intercession, but adverting only to the benefit of the covenant. Now, indeed, when we have the Lord Jesus, in whose hand the eternal covenant of mercy was not only made but confirmed, what better name can we bear before us in our prayers? And since those good Doctors would make out by these words that the Patriarchs are intercessors, I should like them to tell me why, in so great a multitude,[1] no place whatever is given to Abraham, the father of the Church? We know well from what a crew they select their intercessors.[2] Let them then tell me what consistency there is in neglecting and rejecting Abraham, whom God preferred to all others, and raised to the highest degree of honour. The only reason is, that as it was plain there was no such practice in the ancient Church, they thought proper to conceal the novelty of the practice by saying nothing of the Patriarchs: as if by a mere diversity of names they could excuse a practice at once novel and impure. They sometimes, also, object that God is entreated to have mercy on his people "for David's sake" (Ps. cxxxii. 1, 10; see Calv. Com.). This is so far from supporting their error, that it is the strongest refutation of it. We must consider the character which David bore. He is set apart from the whole body of the faithful to establish the covenant which God made in his hand. Thus regard is had to the covenant rather than to the individual. Under him as a type the sole intercession of Christ is asserted. But what was peculiar to David as a type of Christ is certainly inapplicable to others.

26. But some seem to be moved by the fact, that the prayers of

1 The French adds, "et quasi en une fourmiliere de saincts;"—and as it were a swarm of saints.

2 "C'est chose trop notoire de quel bourbieu ou de quelle racaille ils tirent leur saincts."—It is too notorious out of what mire or rubbish they draw their saints.

saints are often said to have been heard. Why? Because they prayed. "They cried unto thee" (says the Psalmist), "and were delivered: they trusted in thee, and were not confounded" (Ps. xxii. 5). Let us also pray after their example, that like them we too may be heard. Those men, on the contrary, absurdly argue that none will be heard but those who have been heard already. How much better does James argue, "Elias was a man subject to like passions as we are, and he prayed earnestly that it might not rain: and it rained not on the earth by the space of three years and six months. And he prayed again, and the heaven gave rain, and the earth brought forth her fruit" (James v. 17, 18). What? Does he infer that Elias possessed some peculiar privilege, and that we must have recourse to him for the use of it? By no means. He shows the perpetual efficacy of a pure and pious prayer, that we may be induced in like manner to pray. For the kindness and readiness of God to hear others is malignantly interpreted, if their example does not inspire us with stronger confidence in his promise, since his declaration is not that he will incline his ear to one or two, or a few individuals, but to all who call upon his name. In this ignorance they are the less excusable, because they seem as it were avowedly to contemn the many admonitions of Scripture. David was repeatedly delivered by the power of God. Was this to give that power to him that we might be delivered on his application? Very different is his affirmation: "The righteous shall compass me about; for thou shalt deal bountifully with me" (Ps. cxlii. 7). Again, "The righteous also shall see, and fear, and shall laugh at him" (Ps. lii. 6). "This poor man cried, and the Lord heard him, and saved him out of all his troubles" (Ps. xxxiv. 6). In The Psalms are many similar prayers, in which David calls upon God to give him what he asks, for this reason—viz. that the righteous may not be put to shame, but by his example encouraged to hope. Here let one passage suffice, "For this shall every one that is godly pray unto thee in a time when thou mayest be found" (Ps. xxxii. 6, Calv. Com.). This passage I have quoted the more readily, because those ravers who employ their hireling tongues in defence of the Papacy, are not ashamed to adduce it in proof of the intercession of the dead. As if David intended anything more than to show the benefit which he shall obtain from the divine clemency and condescension when he shall have been heard. In general, we must hold that the experience of the grace of God, as well towards ourselves as towards others, tends in no slight degree to confirm our faith in his promises. I do not quote the many passages in which David sets forth the loving-kindness of God to him as a ground of confidence, as they will readily occur to every reader of The Psalms. Jacob had previously taught the same thing by his own example, "I am not worthy of the least of all thy mercies, and of all the truth which thou hast showed unto thy servant: for with my staff I passed over this Jordan; and now I am become two bands" (Gen. xxxii. 10). He, indeed, alleges the promise, but not the promise only; for he at the same time adds the effect, to animate him with greater confidence in the future kindness of God. God is not like men who grow weary of their liberality, or whose means of exercising it become exhausted; but he is to be estimated by his own nature, as David properly does when he says, "Thou hast redeemed me, O Lord God of truth" (Ps. xxxi. 5). After ascribing the praise of his salvation to God, he adds that he is true: for were he not ever like himself, his past favour would not be an infallible ground for confidence and prayer. But when we know that as often as he assists us, he gives us a specimen and proof of his goodness and faithfulness, there is no reason to fear that our hope will be ashamed or frustrated.

27. On the whole, since Scripture places the principal part of worship in the invocation of God (this being the office of piety which he requires of us in preference to all sacrifices), it is manifest sacrilege to offer prayer to others. Hence it is said in the psalm: "If we have forgotten the name of our God, or stretched out our hands to a strange God, shall not God search this out?" (Ps. xliv. 20, 21.) Again, since it is only in faith that God desires to be invoked, and he distinctly enjoins us to frame our prayers according to the rule of his word: in fine, since faith is founded on the word, and is the parent of right prayer, the moment we decline from the word, our prayers are impure. But we have already shown, that if we consult the whole volume of Scripture, we shall find that God claims this honour to himself alone. In regard to the office of intercession, we have also seen that it is peculiar to Christ, and that no prayer is agreeable to God which he as Mediator does not sanctify. And though believers mutually offer up prayers to God in behalf of their brethren, we have shown that this derogates in no respect from the sole intercession of Christ, because all trust to that intercession in commending themselves as well as others to God. Moreover, we have shown that this is ignorantly transferred to the dead, of whom we nowhere read that they were commanded to pray for us. The Scripture often exhorts us to offer up mutual prayers; but says not one syllable concerning the dead; nay, James tacitly excludes the dead, when he combines the two things, to "confess our sins one to another, and to pray one for another" (James v. 16). Hence it is sufficient to condemn this error, that the beginning of right prayer springs from faith, and that faith comes by the hearing of the word of God, in which there is no mention of fictitious intercession, superstition having rashly adopted intercessors who have not been divinely appointed. While the Scripture abounds in various forms of prayer, we find no example of this intercession, without which Papists think there is no prayer. Moreover, it is evident that this superstition is the result of distrust, because they are either not contented with Christ as an intercessor, or have altogether robbed him of this honour. This last is easily proved by their effrontery in maintaining, as the strongest of all their arguments for the intercession of the saints, that we are

unworthy of familiar access to God. This, indeed, we acknowledge to be most true, but we thence infer that they leave nothing to Christ, because they consider his intercession as nothing, unless it is supplemented by that of George and Hypolyte, and similar phantoms.

28. But though prayer is properly confined to vows and supplications, yet so strong is the affinity between petition and thanksgiving, that both may be conveniently comprehended under one name. For the forms which Paul enumerates (1 Tim. ii. 1) fall under the first member of this division. By prayer and supplication we pour out our desires before God, asking as well those things which tend to promote his glory and display his name, as the benefits which contribute to our advantage. By thanksgiving we duly celebrate his kindnesses toward us, ascribing to his liberality every blessing which enters into our lot. David accordingly includes both in one sentence, "Call upon me in the day of trouble: I will deliver thee, and thou shalt glorify me" (Ps. l. 15). Scripture, not without reason, commands us to use both continually. We have already described the greatness of our want, while experience itself proclaims the straits which press us on every side to be so numerous and so great, that all have sufficient ground to send forth sighs and groans to God without intermission, and suppliantly implore him. For even should they be exempt from adversity, still the holiest ought to be stimulated first by their sins, and, secondly, by the innumerable assaults of temptation, to long for a remedy. The sacrifice of praise and thanksgiving can never be interrupted without guilt, since God never ceases to load us with favour upon favour, so as to force us to gratitude, however slow and sluggish we may be. In short, so great and widely diffused are the riches of his liberality towards us, so marvellous and wondrous the miracles which we behold on every side, that we never can want a subject and materials for praise and thanksgiving.

To make this somewhat clearer: since all our hopes and resources are placed in God (this has already been fully proved), so that neither our persons nor our interests can prosper without his blessing, we must constantly submit ourselves and our all to him. Then whatever we deliberate, speak, or do, should be deliberated, spoken, and done under his hand and will; in fine, under the hope of his assistance. God has pronounced a curse upon all who, confiding in themselves or others, form plans and resolutions, who, without regarding his will, or invoking his aid, either plan or attempt to execute (James iv. 14; Isaiah xxx. 1; xxxi. 1). And since, as has already been observed, he receives the honour which is due when he is acknowledged to be the author of all good, it follows that, in deriving all good from his hand, we ought continually to express our thankfulness, and that we have no right to use the benefits which proceed from his liberality, if we do not assiduously proclaim his praise, and give him thanks, these being the ends for which they are given. When Paul declares that every creature of God "is sanctified by the word of God and prayer" (1 Tim. iv. 5), he intimates that without the word and prayer, none of them are holy and pure, *word* being used metonymically for *faith.* Hence David, on experiencing the loving-kindness of the Lord, elegantly declares, "He hath put a new song in my mouth" (Ps. xl. 3); intimating, that our silence is malignant when we leave his blessings unpraised, seeing every blessing he bestows is a new ground of thanksgiving. Thus Isaiah, proclaiming the singular mercies of God, says, "Sing unto the Lord a new song." In the same sense David says in another passage, "O Lord, open thou my lips; and my mouth shall show forth thy praise" (Ps. li. 15). In like manner, Hezekiah and Jonah declare that they will regard it as the end of their deliverance "to celebrate the goodness of God with songs in his temple" (Is. xxxviii. 20; Jonah ii. 10). David lays down a general rule for all believers in these words, "What shall I render unto the Lord for all his benefits toward me? I will take the cup of salvation, and call upon the name of the Lord" (Ps. cxvi. 12, 13). This rule the Church follows in another psalm, "Save us, O Lord our God, and gather us from among the heathen, to give thanks unto thy holy name, and to triumph in thy praise" (Ps. cvi. 47). Again, "He will regard the prayer of the destitute, and not despise their prayer. This shall be written for the generation to come: and the people which shall be created shall praise the Lord." "To declare the name of the Lord in Zion, and his praise in Jerusalem" (Ps. cii. 18, 21). Nay, whenever believers beseech the Lord to do anything *for his own name's sake,* as they declare themselves unworthy of obtaining it in their own name, so they oblige themselves to give thanks, and promise to make the right use of his loving-kindness by being the heralds of it. Thus Hosea, speaking of the future redemption of the Church, says, "Take away all iniquity, and receive us graciously; so will we render the calves of our lips" (Hos. xiv. 2). Not only do our tongues proclaim the kindness of God, but they naturally inspire us with love to him. "I love the Lord, because he hath heard my voice and my supplications" (Ps. cxvi. 1). In another passage, speaking of the help which he had experienced, he says, "I will love thee, O Lord, my strength" (Ps. xviii. 1). No praise will ever please God that does not flow from this feeling of love. Nay, we must attend to the declaration of Paul, that all wishes are vicious and perverse which are not accompanied with thanksgiving. His words are, "In everything by prayer and supplication with thanksgiving let your requests be made known unto God" (Phil. iv. 6). Because many, under the influence of moroseness, weariness, impatience, bitter grief and fear, use murmuring in their prayers, he enjoins us so to regulate our feelings as cheerfully to bless God even before obtaining what we ask. But if this connection ought always to subsist in full vigour between things that are almost contrary, the more sacred is the tie which binds us to celebrate the praises of God whenever he grants our requests. And as we have already shown that our prayers, which otherwise would be polluted, are sanctified by the intercession of Christ, so the Apostle, by enjoining us "to offer the sacrifice of praise to God continually" by Christ (Heb. xiii. 15), reminds us, that without the intervention of his priesthood our lips are not pure enough to celebrate the name of God. Hence we infer that a monstrous delusion prevails among Papists, the great majority of whom wonder when Christ is called an intercessor. The reason why Paul enjoins, "Pray without ceasing; in everything give thanks" (1 Thess. v. 17, 18), is, because he would have us with the utmost assiduity, at all times, in every place, in all things, and under all circumstances, direct our prayers to God, to expect all the things which we desire from him, and when obtained ascribe them to him; thus furnishing perpetual grounds for prayer and praise.

29. This assiduity in prayer, though it specially refers to the peculiar private prayers of individuals, extends also in some measure to the public prayers of the Church. These, it may be said, cannot be continual, and ought not to be made, except in the manner which, for the sake of order, has been established by public consent. This I admit, and hence certain hours are fixed beforehand, hours which, though indifferent in regard to God, are necessary for the use of man, that the general convenience may be consulted, and all things be done in the Church, as Paul enjoins, "decently and in order" (1 Cor. xiv. 40). But there is nothing in this to prevent each church from being now and then stirred up to a more frequent use of prayer, and being more zealously affected under the impulse of some greater necessity. Of perseverance in prayer, which is much akin to assiduity, we shall speak towards the close of the chapter (sec. 51, 52). This assiduity, moreover, is very different from the Βαττολογία, *vain speaking*, which our Saviour has prohibited (Matth. vi. 7). For he does not there forbid us to pray long or frequently, or with great fervour, but warns as against supposing that we can extort anything from God by importuning him with garrulous loquacity, as if he were to be persuaded after the manner of men. We know that hypocrites, because they consider not that they have to do with God, offer up their prayers as pompously as if it were part of a triumphal show. The pharisee, who thanked God that he was not as other men, no doubt proclaimed his praises before men, as if he had wished to gain a reputation for sanctity by his prayers. Hence that *vain speaking*, which for a similar reason prevails so much in the Papacy in the present day, some vainly spinning out the time by a reiteration of the same frivolous prayers, and others employing a long series of verbiage for vulgar display.[1] This childish garrulity being a mockery of God, it is not

1 French, "Cette longueur de priere a aujourd'hui sa vogue en la Papauté, et procede de cette mesme source; c'est que les uns barbotant force Ave Maria, et reiterant cent fois un chapelet, perdent une partie du temps; les autres, comme les chanoines et caphars, en abayant le parchemin jour et nuict, et barbotant leur breviaire vendent leur coquilles au peuple."—This long prayer is at present in vogue among the Papists, and proceeds from the same cause: some muttering a host of Ave Marias, and going over their beads a hundred times, lose part of their time; others, as the canons and monks, grumbling over their parchment night and day, and muttering their breviary, sell their cockleshells to the people.

strange that it is prohibited in the Church, in order that every feeling there expressed may be sincere, proceeding from the inmost heart. Akin to this abuse is another which our Saviour also condemns—namely, when hypocrites for the sake of ostentation court the presence of many witnesses, and would sooner pray in the market place than pray without applause. The true object of prayer being, as we have already said (sec. 4, 5), to carry our thoughts directly to God, whether to celebrate his praise or implore his aid, we can easily see that its primary seat is in the mind and heart, or rather that prayer itself is properly an effusion and manifestation of internal feeling before Him who is the searcher of hearts. Hence (as has been said), when our divine Master was pleased to lay down the best rule for prayer, his injunction was, "Enter into thy closet, and when thou hast shut thy door, pray to thy Father which is in secret, and thy Father which seeth in secret shall reward thee openly" (Matth. vi. 6). Dissuading us from the example of hypocrites, who sought the applause of men by an ambitious ostentation in prayer, he adds the better course—enter thy chamber, shut thy door, and there pray. By these words (as I understand them) he taught us to seek a place of retirement which might enable us to turn all our thoughts inwards, and enter deeply into our hearts, promising that God would hold converse with the feelings of our mind, of which the body ought to be the temple. He meant not to deny that it may be expedient to pray in other places also, but he shows that prayer is somewhat of a secret nature, having its chief seat in the mind, and requiring a tranquillity far removed from the turmoil of ordinary cares. And hence it was not without cause that our Lord himself, when he would engage more earnestly in prayer, withdrew into a retired spot beyond the bustle of the world, thus reminding us by his example that we are not to neglect those helps which enable the mind, in itself too much disposed to wander, to become sincerely intent on prayer. Meanwhile, as he abstained not from prayer when the occasion required it, though he were in the midst of a crowd, so must we, whenever there is need, lift up "pure hands" (1 Tim. ii. 8) at all places. And hence we must hold that he who declines to pray in the public meeting of the saints, knows not what it is to pray apart, in retirement, or at home. On the other hand, he who neglects to pray alone and in private, however sedulously he frequents public meetings, there gives his prayers to the wind, because he defers more to the opinion of man than to the secret judgment of God. Still, lest the public prayers of the Church should be held in contempt, the Lord anciently bestowed upon them the most honourable appellation, especially when he called the temple the "*house of prayer*" (Isa. lvi. 7). For by this expression he both showed that the duty of prayer is a principal part of his worship, and that to enable believers to engage in it with one consent his temple is set up before them as a kind of banner. A noble promise was also added, "Praise waiteth for thee, O God, in Sion:

and unto thee shall the vow be performed"[1] (Ps. lxv. 1). By these words the Psalmist reminds us that the prayers of the Church are never in vain; because God always furnishes his people with materials for a song of joy. But although the shadows of the law have ceased, yet because God was pleased by this ordinance to foster the unity of the faith among us also, there can be no doubt that the same promise belongs to us—a promise which Christ sanctioned with his own lips, and which Paul declares to be perpetually in force.

30. As God in his word enjoins common prayer, so public temples are the places destined for the performance of them, and hence those who refuse to join with the people of God in this observance have no ground for the pretext, that they enter their chamber in order that they may obey the command of the Lord. For he who promises to grant whatsoever two or three assembled in his name shall ask (Matth. xviii. 20), declares, that he by no means despises the prayers which are publicly offered up, provided there be no ostentation, or catching at human applause, and provided there be a true and sincere affection in the secret recesses of the heart.[2] If this is the legitimate use of churches (and it certainly is), we must, on the other hand, beware of imitating the practice which commenced some centuries ago, of imagining that churches are the proper dwellings of God, where he is more ready to listen to us, or of attaching to them some kind of secret sanctity, which makes prayer there more holy. For seeing we are the true temples of God, we must pray in ourselves if we would invoke God in his holy temple. Let us leave such gross ideas to the Jews or the heathen, knowing that we have a command to pray, without distinction of place, "in spirit and in truth" (John iv. 23). It is true that by the order of God the temple was anciently dedicated for the offerings of prayers and sacrifices, but this was at a time when the truth (which being now fully manifested, we are not permitted to confine to any material temple) lay hid under the figure of shadows. Even the temple was not represented to the Jews as confining the presence of God within its walls, but was meant to train them to contemplate the image of the true temple. Accordingly, a severe rebuke is administered both by Isaiah and Stephen, to those who thought that God could in any way dwell in temples made with hands (Isa. lxvi. 2; Acts vii. 48).

31. Hence it is perfectly clear that neither words nor singing (if used in prayer) are of the least consequence, or avail one iota with God, unless they proceed from deep feeling in the heart. Nay, rather they provoke his anger against us, if they come from the lips and throat only, since this is to abuse his sacred name, and hold his majesty in derision. This we infer from the words of Isaiah, which,

1 Calvin translates, "Te expectat Deus, laus in Sion;"—God, the praise in Sion waiteth for thee.

2 See Book I. chap. xi. sec. 7, 13, on the subject of images in churches. Also Book IV. chap. iv. sec. 8, and chap. v. sec. 18, as to the ornaments of churches.

though their meaning is of wider extent, go to rebuke this vice also: "Forasmuch as this people draw near me with their mouth, and with their lips do honour me, but have removed their heart far from me, and their fear toward me is taught by the precept of men: therefore, behold, I will proceed to do a marvellous work among this people, even a marvellous work and a wonder: for the wisdom of their wise men shall perish, and the understanding of their prudent men shall be hid" (Isa. xxix. 13). Still we do not condemn words or singing, but rather greatly commend them, provided the feeling of the mind goes along with them. For in this way the thought of God is kept alive on our minds, which, from their fickle and versatile nature, soon relax, and are distracted by various objects, unless various means are used to support them. Besides, since the glory of God ought in a manner to be displayed in each part of our body, the special service to which the tongue should be devoted is that of singing and speaking, inasmuch as it has been expressly created to declare and proclaim the praise of God. This employment of the tongue is chiefly in the public services which are performed in the meeting of the saints. In this way the God whom we serve in one spirit and one faith, we glorify together as it were with one voice and one mouth; and that openly, so that each may in turn receive the confession of his brother's faith, and be invited and incited to imitate it.

32. It is certain that the use of singing in churches (which I may mention in passing) is not only very ancient, but was also used by the Apostles, as we may gather from the words of Paul, "I will sing with the spirit, and I will sing with the understanding also" (1 Cor. xiv. 15). In like manner he says to the Colossians, "Teaching and admonishing one another in psalms, and hymns, and spiritual songs, singing with grace in your hearts to the Lord" (Col. iii. 16). In the former passage, he enjoins us to sing with the voice and the heart; in the latter, he commends spiritual songs, by which the pious mutually edify each other. That it was not a universal practice, however, is attested by Augustine (Confess. lib. ix. cap. 7), who states that the church of Milan first began to use singing in the time of Ambrose, when the orthodox faith being persecuted by Justina, the mother of Valentinian, the vigils of the people were more frequent than usual;[1] and that the practice was afterwards followed by the other Western churches. He had said a little before that the custom came from the East.[2] He also intimates (Retract. Lib. ii.) that it was received in Africa in his own time. His words are, "Hilarius, a man of tribunitial rank, assailed with the bitterest invectives he could use the custom which then began to exist at Carthage, of singing hymns from the book of Psalms at the altar, either before the oblation, or when it was distributed to the people; I answered him, at the request of my brethren."[3] And certainly if singing is

1 This clause of the sentence is omitted in the French.
2 The French adds, "où on en avoit tousjours usé;"—where it had always been used.
3 The whole of this quotation is omitted in the French.

tempered to a gravity befitting the presence of God and angels, it both gives dignity and grace to sacred actions, and has a very powerful tendency to stir up the mind to true zeal and ardour in prayer. We must, however, carefully beware, lest our ears be more intent on the music than our minds on the spiritual meaning of the words. Augustine confesses (Confess. Lib. x. cap. 33) that the fear of this danger sometimes made him wish for the introduction of a practice observed by Athanasius, who ordered the reader to use only a gentle inflection of the voice, more akin to recitation than singing. But on again considering how many advantages were derived from singing, he inclined to the other side.[1] If this moderation is used, there cannot be a doubt that the practice is most sacred and salutary. On the other hand, songs composed merely to tickle and delight the ear are unbecoming the majesty of the Church, and cannot but be most displeasing to God.

33. It is also plain that the public prayers are not to be couched in Greek among the Latins, nor in Latin among the French or English (as hitherto has been everywhere practised), but in the vulgar tongue, so that all present may understand them, since they ought to be used for the edification of the whole Church, which cannot be in the least degree benefited by a sound not understood. Those who are not moved by any reason of humanity or charity, ought at least to be somewhat moved by the authority of Paul, whose words are by no means ambiguous: "When thou shalt bless with the spirit, how shall he that occupieth the room of the unlearned say, Amen, at thy giving of thanks, seeing he understandeth not what thou sayest? For thou verily givest thanks, but the other is not edified" (1 Cor. xiv. 16, 17). How then can one sufficiently admire the unbridled licence of the Papists, who, while the Apostle publicly protests against it, hesitate not to brawl out the most verbose prayers in a foreign tongue, prayers of which they themselves sometimes do not understand one syllable, and which they have no wish that others should understand?[2] Different is the course which Paul prescribes, "What is it then? I will pray with the spirit, and I will pray with the understanding also; I will sing with the spirit, and I will sing with the understanding also:" meaning by the *spirit* the special gift of tongues, which some who had received it abused when they dissevered

1 French, "Mais il adjouste d'autre part, que quand il se souvenoit du fruict et de l'edification qu'il avoit recue en oyant chanter à l'Église il enclinoit plus à l'autre partie, c'est, approuver le chant;"—but he adds on the other hand, that when he called to mind the fruit and edification which he had received from hearing singing in the church, he inclined more to the other side; that is, to approve singing.

2 French, "Qui est-ce donc qui se pourra assez esmerveiller d'une audace tant effrenee qu'ont eu les Papistes et ont encore, qui contre la defense de l'Apostre, chantent et brayent de langue estrange et inconnue, en laquelle le plus souvent ils n'entendent pas eux mesmes une syllabe, et ne veulent que les autres y entendent?"—Who then can sufficiently admire the unbridled audacity which the Papists have had, and still have, who, contrary to the prohibition of the Apostle, chant and bray in a foreign and unknown tongue, in which, for the most part, they do not understand one syllable, and which they have no wish that others understand?

it from the mind, that is, the understanding. The principle we must always hold is, that in all prayer, public and private, the tongue without the mind must be displeasing to God. Moreover, the mind must be so incited, as in ardour of thought far to surpass what the tongue is able to express. Lastly, the tongue is not even necessary to private prayer, unless in so far as the internal feeling is insufficient for incitement, or the vehemence of the incitement carries the utterance of the tongue along with it. For although the best prayers are sometimes without utterance, yet when the feeling of the mind is overpowering, the tongue spontaneously breaks forth into utterance, and our other members into gesture. Hence that dubious muttering of Hannah (1 Sam. i. 13), something similar to which is experienced by all the saints when concise and abrupt expressions escape from them. The bodily gestures usually observed in prayer, such as kneeling and uncovering of the head (Calv. in Acts xx. 36), are exercises by which we attempt to rise to higher veneration of God.

34. We must now attend not only to a surer method, but also form of prayer, that—namely, which our heavenly Father has delivered to us by his beloved Son, and in which we may recognise his boundless goodness and condescension (Matth. vi. 9; Luke xi. 2). Besides admonishing us and exhorting us to seek him in our every necessity (as children are wont to betake themselves to the protection of their parents when oppressed with any anxiety), seeing that we are not fully aware how great our poverty was, or what was right or for our interest to ask, he has provided for this ignorance; that wherein our capacity failed he has sufficiently supplied. For he has given us a form in which is set before us as in a picture everything which it is lawful to wish, everything which is conducive to our interest, everything which it is necessary to demand. From his goodness in this respect we derive the great comfort of knowing, that as we ask almost in his words, we ask nothing that is absurd, or foreign, or unseasonable; nothing, in short, that is not agreeable to him. Plato, seeing the ignorance of men in presenting their desires to God, desires which if granted would often be most injurious to them, declares the best form of prayer to be that which an ancient poet has furnished: "O king Jupiter, give what is best, whether we wish it or wish it not; but avert from us what is evil even though we ask it" (Plato, Alcibid. i.). This heathen shows his wisdom in discerning how dangerous it is to ask of God what our own passion dictates; while, at the same time, he reminds us of our unhappy condition in not being able to open our lips before God without danger, unless his Spirit instruct us how to pray aright (Rom. viii. 26). The higher value, therefore, ought we to set on the privilege, when the only begotten Son of God puts words into our lips, and thus relieves our minds of all hesitation.

35. This form or rule of prayer is composed of *six petitions*. For I am prevented from agreeing with those who divide it into *seven* by the adversative mode of diction used by the Evangelist, who appears

to have intended to unite the two members together: as if he had said, Do not allow us to be overcome by temptation, but rather bring assistance to our frailty, and deliver us that we may not fall. Ancient writers[1] also agree with us, that what is added by Matthew as a seventh head is to be considered as explanatory of the sixth petition.[2] But though in every part of the prayer the first place is assigned to the glory of God, still this is more especially the object of the three first petitions, in which we are to look to the glory of God alone, without any reference to what is called our own advantage. The three remaining petitions are devoted to our interest, and properly relate to things which it is useful for us to ask. When we ask that the name of God may be hallowed, as God wishes to prove whether we love and serve him freely, or from the hope of reward, we are not to think at all of our own interest; we must set his glory before our eyes, and keep them intent upon it alone. In the other similar petitions, this is the only manner in which we ought to be affected. It is true, that in this way our own interest is greatly promoted, because, when the name of God is hallowed in the way we ask, our own sanctification is also thereby promoted. But in regard to this advantage, we must, as I have said, shut our eyes, and be in a manner blind, so as not even to see it; and hence were all hope of our private advantage cut off, we still should never cease to wish and pray for this hallowing, and everything else which pertains to the glory of God. We have examples in Moses and Paul, who did not count it grievous to turn away their eyes and minds from themselves, and with intense and fervent zeal long for death, if by their loss the kingdom and glory of God might be promoted (Exod. xxxii. 32; Rom. ix. 3). On the other hand, when we ask for daily bread, although we desire what is advantageous for ourselves we ought also especially to seek the glory of God, so much so that we would not ask at all unless it were to turn to his glory. Let us now proceed to an exposition of the Prayer.

OUR FATHER WHICH ART IN HEAVEN.

36. The first thing suggested at the very outset is, as we have already said (sec. 17–19), that all our prayers to God ought only to be presented in the name of Christ, as there is no other name which can recommend them. In calling God our Father, we certainly plead the name of Christ. For with what confidence could any man call God his Father? Who would have the presumption to arrogate

1 August. in Enchirid. ad Laurent. cap. 116. Chrysost. in an imperfect work. See end of sec. 53.

2 "Dont il est facile de juger que ce qui est adjousté en S. Matthieu, et qu'aucuns ont pris pour une septieme requeste, n'est qu'un explication de la sixieme, et se doit a icelle rapporter;"—Whence it is easy to perceive that what is added in St Matthew, and which some have taken for a seventh petition, is only an explanation of the sixth, and ought to be referred to it.

to himself the honour of a son of God were we not gratuitously adopted as his sons in Christ? He being the true Son, has been given to us as a brother, so that that which he possesses as his own by nature becomes ours by adoption, if we embrace this great mercy with firm faith. As John says, "As many as receive him, to them gave he power to become the sons of God, even to them that believe in his name" (John i. 12). Hence he both calls himself our Father, and is pleased to be so called by us, by this delightful name relieving us of all distrust, since nowhere can a stronger affection be found than in a father. Hence, too, he could not have given us a stronger testimony of his boundless love than in calling us his sons. But his love towards us is so much the greater and more excellent than that of earthly parents, the farther he surpasses all men in goodness and mercy (Isaiah lxiii. 18). Earthly parents, laying aside all paternal affection, might abandon their offspring; he will never abandon us (Ps. xxvii. 10), seeing he cannot deny himself. For we have his promise, "If ye then, being evil, know how to give good gifts unto your children, how much more shall your Father which is in heaven give good things to them that ask him?" (Matth. vii. 11.) In like manner in the prophet, "Can a woman forget her sucking child, that she should not have compassion on the son of her womb? Yea, they may forget, yet will not I forget thee" (Isaiah xlix. 15). But if we are his sons, then as a son cannot betake himself to the protection of a stranger and a foreigner without at the same time complaining of his father's cruelty or poverty, so we cannot ask assistance from any other quarter than from him, unless we would upbraid him with poverty, or want of means, or cruelty and excessive austerity.

37. Nor let us allege that we are justly rendered timid by a consciousness of sin, by which our Father, though mild and merciful, is daily offended. For if among men a son cannot have a better advocate to plead his cause with his father, and cannot employ a better intercessor to regain his lost favour, than if he come himself suppliant and downcast, acknowledging his fault, to implore the mercy of his father, whose paternal feelings cannot but be moved by such entreaties, what will that "Father of all mercies, and God of all comfort," do? (2 Cor. i. 3.) Will he not rather listen to the tears and groans of his children, when supplicating for themselves (especially seeing he invites and exhorts us to do so), than to any advocacy of others to whom the timid have recourse, not without some semblance of despair, because they are distrustful of their father's mildness and clemency? The exuberance of his paternal kindness he sets before us in the parable (Luke xv. 20; see Calv. Comm.), when the father with open arms receives the son who had gone away from him, wasted his substance in riotous living, and in all ways grievously sinned against him. He waits not till pardon is asked in words, but, anticipating the request, recognises him afar off, runs to meet him, consoles him, and restores him to favour. By setting before us this admirable example of mildness in a man, he de-

signed to show in how much greater abundance we may expect it from him who is not only a Father, but the best and most merciful of all fathers, however ungrateful, rebellious, and wicked sons we may be, provided only we throw ourselves upon his mercy. And the better to assure us that he is such a Father if we are Christians, he has been pleased to be called not only a Father, but OUR Father, as if we were pleading with him after this manner, O Father, who art possessed of so much affection for thy children, and art so ready to forgive, we thy children approach thee and present our requests, fully persuaded that thou hast no other feelings towards us than those of a father, though we are unworthy of such a parent.[1] But as our narrow hearts are incapable of comprehending such boundless favour, Christ is not only the earnest and pledge of our adoption, but also gives us the Spirit as a witness of this adoption, that through him we may freely cry aloud, Abba, Father. Whenever, therefore, we are restrained by any feeling of hesitation, let us remember to ask of him that he may correct our timidity, and placing us under the magnanimous guidance of the Spirit, enable us to pray boldly.

38. The instruction given us, however, is not that every individual in particular is to call him Father, but rather that we are all in common to call him Our Father. By this we are reminded how strong the feeling of brotherly love between us ought to be, since we are all alike, by the same mercy and free kindness, the children of such a Father. For if He from whom we all obtain whatever is good is our common Father (Matth. xxiii. 9), everything which has been distributed to us we should be prepared to communicate to each other, as far as occasion demands. But if we are thus desirous, as we ought, to stretch out our hand, and give assistance to each other, there is nothing by which we can more benefit our brethren than by committing them to the care and protection of the best of parents, since if He is propitious and favourable nothing more can be desired. And, indeed, we owe this also to our Father. For as he who truly and from the heart loves the father of a family, extends the same love and good-will to all his household, so the zeal and affection which we feel for our heavenly Parent it becomes us to extend towards his people, his family, and, in fine, his heritage, which he has honoured so highly as to give them the appellation of the "fulness" of his only begotten Son (Eph. i. 23). Let the Christian, then, so regulate his prayers as to make them common, and embrace all who are his brethren in Christ; not only those whom at present he sees and knows to be such, but all men who are alive upon the earth. What God has determined with regard to them is beyond our knowledge, but to wish and hope the best concerning them is both pious and humane. Still it becomes us to regard with special affection those who are of the household of faith, and whom the

[1] French, "Quelque mauvaistié qu'ayons euë, ou quelque imperfection ou poureté qui soit en nous;"—whatever wickedness we may have done, or whatever imperfection or poverty there may be in us.

Apostle has in express terms recommended to our care in everything (Gal. vi. 10). In short, all our prayers ought to bear reference to that community which our Lord has established in his kingdom and family.

39. This, however, does not prevent us from praying specially for ourselves, and certain others, provided our mind is not withdrawn from the view of this community, does not deviate from it, but constantly refers to it. For prayers, though couched in special terms, keeping that object still in view, cease not to be common. All this may easily be understood by analogy. There is a general command from God to relieve the necessities of all the poor, and yet this command is obeyed by those who with that view give succour to all whom they see or know to be in distress, although they pass by many whose wants are not less urgent, either because they cannot know or are unable to give supply to all. In this way there is nothing repugnant to the will of God in those who, giving heed to this common society of the Church, yet offer up particular prayers, in which, with a public mind, though in special terms, they commend to God themselves or others, with whose necessity he has been pleased to make them more familiarly acquainted. It is true that prayer and the giving of our substance are not in all respects alike. We can only bestow the kindness of our liberality on those of whose wants we are aware, whereas in prayer we can assist the greatest strangers, how wide soever the space which may separate them from us. This is done by that general form of prayer which, including all the sons of God, includes them also. To this we may refer the exhortation which Paul gave to the believers of his age, to lift up "holy hands, without wrath and doubting" (1 Tim. ii. 8). By reminding them that dissension is a bar to prayer, he shows it to be his wish that they should with one accord present their prayers in common.

40. The next words are, WHICH ART IN HEAVEN. From this we are not to infer that he is enclosed and confined within the circumference of heaven, as by a kind of boundaries. Hence Solomon confesses, "The heaven of heavens cannot contain thee" (1 Kings viii. 27); and he himself says by the Prophet, "The heaven is my throne, and the earth is my footstool" (Isa. lxvi. 1); thereby intimating, that his presence, not confined to any region, is diffused over all space. But as our gross minds are unable to conceive of his ineffable glory, it is designated to us by *heaven*, nothing which our eyes can behold being so full of splendour and majesty. While, then, we are accustomed to regard every object as confined to the place where our senses discern it, no place can be assigned to God; and hence, if we would seek him, we must rise higher than all corporeal or mental discernment. Again, this form of expression reminds us that he is far beyond the reach of change or corruption, that he holds the whole universe in his grasp, and rules it by his power. The effect of the expression, therefore, is the same as if it had been said, that he is of infinite majesty, incomprehensible essence,

boundless power, and eternal duration. When we thus speak of God, our thoughts must be raised to their highest pitch; we must not ascribe to him anything of a terrestrial or carnal nature, must not measure him by our little standards, or suppose his will to be like ours. At the same time, we must put our confidence in him, understanding that heaven and earth are governed by his providence and power. In short, under the name of Father is set before us that God, who hath appeared to us in his own image, that we may invoke him with sure faith; the familiar name of Father being given not only to inspire confidence, but also to curb our minds, and prevent them from going astray after doubtful or fictitious gods. We thus ascend from the only begotten Son to the supreme Father of angels and of the Church. Then when his throne is fixed in heaven, we are reminded that he governs the world, and, therefore, that it is not in vain to approach him whose present care we actually experience. "He that cometh to God," says the Apostle, "must believe that he is, and that he is a rewarder of them that diligently seek him" (Heb. xi. 6). Here Christ makes both claims for his Father, *first*, that we place our faith in him; and, *secondly*, that we feel assured that our salvation is not neglected by him, inasmuch as he condescends to extend his providence to us. By these elementary principles Paul prepares us to pray aright; for before enjoining us to make our requests known unto God, he premises in this way, "The Lord is at hand. Be careful for nothing" (Phil. iv. 5, 6). Whence it appears that doubt and perplexity hang over the prayers of those in whose minds the belief is not firmly seated, that "the eyes of the Lord are upon the righteous" (Ps. xxxiv. 15).

41. The first petition is, HALLOWED BE THY NAME. The necessity of presenting it bespeaks our great disgrace. For what can be more unbecoming than that our ingratitude and malice should impair, our audacity and petulance should as much as in them lies destroy, the glory of God? But though all the ungodly should burst with sacrilegious rage, the holiness of God's name still shines forth. Justly does the Psalmist exclaim, "According to thy name, O God, so is thy praise unto the ends of the earth" (Ps. xlviii. 10). For wherever God hath made himself known, his perfections must be displayed, his power, goodness, wisdom, justice, mercy, and truth, which fill us with admiration, and incite us to show forth his praise. Therefore, as the name of God is not duly hallowed on the earth, and we are otherwise unable to assert it, it is at least our duty to make it the subject of our prayers. The sum of the whole is, It must be our desire that God may receive the honour which is his due: that men may never think or speak of him without the greatest reverence. The opposite of this reverence is profanity, which has always been too common in the world, and is very prevalent in the present day. Hence the necessity of the petition, which, if piety had any proper existence among us, would be superfluous. But if the name of God is duly hallowed only when separated from all other names it alone is glori-

fied, we are in the petition enjoined to ask not only that God would vindicate his sacred name from all contempt and insult, but also that he would compel the whole human race to reverence it. Then since God manifests himself to us partly by his word, and partly by his works, he is not sanctified unless in regard to both of these we ascribe to him what is due, and thus embrace whatever has proceeded from him, giving no less praise to his justice than to his mercy. On the manifold diversity of his works he has inscribed the marks of his glory, and these ought to call forth from every tongue an ascription of praise. Thus Scripture will obtain its due authority with us, and no event will hinder us from celebrating the praises of God, in regard to every part of his government. On the other hand, the petition implies a wish that all impiety which pollutes this sacred name may perish and be extinguished, that everything which obscures or impairs his glory, all detraction and insult, may cease; that all blasphemy being suppressed, the divine majesty may be more and more signally displayed.

42. The second petition is, THY KINGDOM COME. This contains nothing new, and yet there is good reason for distinguishing it from the first. For if we consider our lethargy in the greatest of all matters, we shall see how necessary it is that what ought to be in itself perfectly known should be inculcated at greater length. Therefore, after the injunction to pray that God would reduce to order, and at length completely efface every stain which is thrown on his sacred name, another petition, containing almost the same wish, is added—viz. Thy kingdom come. Although a definition of this kingdom has already been given, I now briefly repeat that God reigns when men, in denial of themselves, and contempt of the world and this earthly life, devote themselves to righteousness and aspire to heaven (see Calvin, Harm. Matth. vi.). Thus this kingdom consists of two parts: the first is, when God by the agency of his Spirit corrects all the depraved lusts of the flesh, which in bands war against Him; and the second, when he brings all our thoughts into obedience to his authority. This petition, therefore, is duly presented only by those who begin with themselves; in other words, who pray that they may be purified from all the corruptions which disturb the tranquillity and impair the purity of God's kingdom. Then as the word of God is like his royal sceptre, we are here enjoined to pray that he would subdue all minds and hearts to voluntary obedience. This is done when by the secret inspiration of his Spirit he displays the efficacy of his word, and raises it to the place of honour which it deserves. We must next descend to the wicked, who perversely and with desperate madness resist his authority. God, therefore, sets up his kingdom, by humbling the whole world, though in different ways, taming the wantonness of some, and breaking the ungovernable pride of others. We should desire this to be done every day, in order that God may gather churches to himself from all quarters of the world, may extend and increase their numbers, enrich them with his gifts,

establish due order among them; on the other hand, beat down all the enemies of pure doctrine and religion, dissipate their counsels, defeat their attempts. Hence it appears that there is good ground for the precept which enjoins daily progress, for human affairs are never so prosperous as when the impurities of vice are purged away, and integrity flourishes in full vigour. The completion, however, is deferred to the final advent of Christ, when, as Paul declares, "God will be all in all" (1 Cor. xv. 28). This prayer, therefore, ought to withdraw us from the corruptions of the world which separate us from God, and prevent his kingdom from flourishing within us; secondly, it ought to inflame us with an ardent desire for the mortification of the flesh; and, lastly, it ought to train us to the endurance of the cross; since this is the way in which God would have his kingdom to be advanced. It ought not to grieve us that the outward man decays, provided the inner man is renewed. For such is the nature of the kingdom of God, that while we submit to his righteousness he makes us partakers of his glory. This is the case when continually adding to his light and truth, by which the lies and the darkness of Satan and his kingdom are dissipated, extinguished, and destroyed, he protects his people, guides them aright by the agency of his Spirit, and confirms them in perseverance; while, on the other hand, he frustrates the impious conspiracies of his enemies, dissipates their wiles and frauds, prevents their malice, and curbs their petulance, until at length he consume Antichrist "with the spirit of his mouth," and destroy all impiety "with the brightness of his coming" (2 Thess. ii. 8, Calv. Com.).

43. The third petition is, THY WILL BE DONE ON EARTH AS IT IS IN HEAVEN. Though this depends on his kingdom, and cannot be disjoined from it, yet a separate place is not improperly given to it on account of our ignorance, which does not at once or easily apprehend what is meant by God reigning in the world. This, therefore, may not improperly be taken as the explanation, that God will be King in the world when all shall subject themselves to his will. We are not here treating of that secret will by which he governs all things, and destines them to their end (see chap. xxiv. s. 17). For although devils and men rise in tumult against him, he is able by his incomprehensible counsel not only to turn aside their violence, but make it subservient to the execution of his decrees. What we here speak of is another will of God—namely, that of which voluntary obedience is the counterpart; and, therefore, heaven is expressly contrasted with earth, because, as is said in The Psalms, the angels "do his commandments, hearkening unto the voice of his word" (Ps ciii. 20). We are, therefore, enjoined to pray that as everything done in heaven is at the command of God, and the angels are calmly disposed to do all that is right, so the earth may be brought under his authority, all rebellion and depravity having been extinguished. In presenting this request we renounce the desires of the flesh, because he who does not entirely resign his affections to God, does as much as in him lies

to oppose the divine will, since everything which proceeds from us is vicious. Again, by this prayer we are taught to deny ourselves, that God may rule us according to his pleasure; and not only so, but also having annihilated our own may create new thoughts and new minds, so that we shall have no desire save that of entire agreement with his will; in short, wish nothing of ourselves, but have our hearts governed by his Spirit, under whose inward teaching we my learn to love those things which please and hate those things which displease him. Hence also we must desire that he would nullify and suppress all affections which are repugnant to his will.

Such are the three first heads of the prayer, in presenting which we should have the glory of God only in view, taking no account of ourselves, and paying no respect to our own advantage, which, though it is thereby greatly promoted, is not here to be the subject of request. And though all the events prayed for must happen in their own time, without being either thought of, wished, or asked by us, it is still our duty to wish and ask for them. And it is of no slight importance to do so, that we may testify and profess that we are the servants and children of God, desirous by every means in our power to promote the honour due to him as our Lord and Father, and truly and thoroughly devoted to his service. Hence if men, in praying that the name of God may be hallowed, that his kingdom may come, and his will be done, are not influenced by this zeal for the promotion of his glory, they are not to be accounted among the servants and children of God; and as all these things will take place against their will, so they will turn out to their confusion and destruction.

44. Now comes the second part of the prayer, in which we descend to our own interests, not, indeed, that we are to lose sight of the glory of God (to which, as Paul declares, we must have respect even in meat and drink, 1 Cor. x. 31), and ask only what is expedient for ourselves; but the distinction, as we have already observed, is this: God claiming the three first petitions as specially his own, carries us entirely to himself, that in this way he may prove our piety. Next he permits us to look to our own advantage, but still on the condition, that when we ask anything for ourselves it must be in order that all the benefits which he confers may show forth his glory, there being nothing more incumbent on us than to live and die to him.

By the first petition of the second part, GIVE US THIS DAY OUR DAILY BREAD, we pray in general that God would give us all things which the body requires in this sublunary state, not only food and clothing, but everything which he knows will assist us to eat our bread in peace. In this way we briefly cast our care upon him, and commit ourselves to his providence, that he may feed, foster, and preserve us. For our heavenly Father disdains not to take our body under his charge and protection, that he may exercise our faith in those minute matters, while we look to him for everything, even to a morsel of bread and a drop of water. For since, owing to some strange inequality, we feel more concern for the body than for the soul, many who can trust the latter to God still continue anxious about the former, still hesitate as to what they are to eat, as to how they are to be clothed, and are in trepidation whenever their hands are not filled with corn, and wine, and oil (Ps. iv. 8): so much more value do we set on this shadowy, fleeting life, than on a blessed immortality. But those who, trusting to God, have once cast away that anxiety about the flesh, immediately look to him for greater gifts, even salvation and eternal life. It is no slight exercise of faith, therefore, to hope in God for things which would otherwise give us so much concern; nor have we made little progress when we get quit of this unbelief, which cleaves, as it were, to our very bones.

The speculations of some concerning supersubstantial bread seem to be very little accordant with our Saviour's meaning; for our prayer would be defective were we not to ascribe to God the nourishment even of this fading life. The reason which they give is heathenish—viz. that it is inconsistent with the character of sons of God, who ought to be spiritual, not only to occupy their mind with earthly cares, but to suppose God also occupied with them. As if his blessing and paternal favour were not eminently displayed in giving us food, or as if there were nothing in the declaration that godliness hath "the promise of the life that now is, and of that which is to come" (1 Tim. iv. 8). But although the forgiveness of sins is of far more importance than the nourishment of the body, yet Christ has set down the inferior in the prior place, in order that he might gradually raise us to the other two petitions, which properly belong to the heavenly life,—in this providing for our sluggishness. We are enjoined to ask *our bread*, that we may be contented with the measure which our heavenly Father is pleased to dispense, and not strive to make gain by illicit arts. Meanwhile, we must hold that the title by which it is ours is donation, because, as Moses says (Levit. xxvi. 20; Deut. viii. 17), neither our industry, nor labour, nor hands, acquire anything for us, unless the blessing of God be present; nay, not even would abundance of bread be of the least avail were it not divinely converted into nourishment. And hence this liberality of God is not less necessary to the rich than the poor, because, though their cellars and barns were full, they would be parched and pine with want did they not enjoy his favour along with their bread. The terms *this day*, or, as it is in another Evangelist, *daily*, and also the epithet *daily*, lay a restraint on our immoderate desire of fleeting good—a desire which we are extremely apt to indulge to excess, and from which other evils ensue: for when our supply is in richer abundance we ambitiously squander it in pleasure, luxury, ostentation, or other kinds of extravagance. Wherefore, we are only enjoined to ask as much as our necessity requires, and as it were for each day, confiding that our heavenly Father, who gives us the supply of to-day, will not fail us on the morrow. How great soever our abundance may be, however well filled our cellars and granaries, we must still always ask for daily bread, for we must feel assured that all substance is nothing, unless in so far as the Lord, by pouring out his blessing, make it fruitful during its whole progress; for even that which is in our hand is not ours except in so far as he every hour portions it out, and permits us to use it. As nothing is more difficult to human pride than the admission of this truth, the Lord declares that he gave a special proof for all ages, when he fed his people with manna in the desert (Deut. viii. 3), that he might remind us that "man shall not live by bread alone, but by every word that proceedeth out of the mouth of God" (Matth. iv. 4). It is thus intimated, that by his power alone our life and strength are sustained, though he ministers supply to us by bodily instruments. In like manner, whenever it so pleases, he gives us a proof of an opposite description, by breaking the strength, or, as he himself calls it, the *staff* of bread (Levit. xxvi. 26), and leaving us even while eating to pine with hunger, and while drinking to be parched with thirst. Those who, not contented with daily bread, indulge an unrestrained insatiable cupidity, or those who are full of their own abundance, and trust in their own riches, only mock God by offering up this prayer. For the former ask what they would be unwilling to obtain, nay, what they most of all abominate—namely, daily bread only—and as much as in them lies disguise their avarice from God, whereas true prayer should pour out the whole soul and every inward feeling before him. The latter, again, ask what they do not at all expect to obtain—namely, what they imagine that they in themselves already possess. In its being called *ours*, God, as we have already said, gives a striking display of his kindness, making that to be ours to which we have no just claim. Nor must we reject the view to which I have already adverted—viz. that this name is given to what is obtained by just and honest labour, as contrasted with what is obtained by fraud and rapine, nothing being our own which we obtain with injury to others. When we ask God to *give us*, the meaning is, that the thing asked is simply and freely the gift of God, whatever be the quarter from which it comes to us, even when it seems to have been specially prepared by our own art and industry, and procured by our hands, since it is to his blessing alone that all our labours owe their success.

45. The next petition is, FORGIVE US OUR DEBTS. In this and the following petition our Saviour has briefly comprehended whatever is conducive to the heavenly life, as these two members contain the spiritual covenant which God made for the salvation of his Church, "I will put my law in their inward parts, and write it on their hearts." "I will pardon all their iniquities" (Jer. xxxi. 33; xxxiii. 8). Here our Saviour begins with the forgiveness of sins, and then adds the subsequent blessing—viz. that God would protect us by the power, and support us by the aid of his Spirit, so that we may stand invincible against all temptations. To sins he gives the name of *debts*, because

we owe the punishment due to them, a debt which we could not possibly pay were we not discharged by this remission, the result of his free mercy, when he freely expunges the debt, accepting nothing in return; but of his own mercy receiving satisfaction in Christ, who gave himself a ransom for us (Rom. iii. 24). Hence, those who expect to satisfy God by merits of their own or of others, or to compensate and purchase forgiveness by means of satisfactions, have no share in this free pardon, and while they address God in this petition, do nothing more than subscribe their own accusation, and seal their condemnation by their own testimony. For they confess that they are debtors, unless they are discharged by means of forgiveness. This forgiveness, however, they do not receive, but rather reject, when they obtrude their merits and satisfactions upon God, since by so doing they do not implore his mercy, but appeal to his justice. Let those, again, who dream of a perfection which makes it unnecessary to seek pardon, find their disciples among those whose itching ears incline them to imposture[1] (see Calv. on Dan. ix. 20); only let them understand that those whom they thus acquire have been carried away from Christ, since he, by instructing all to confess their guilt, receives none but sinners, not that he may soothe, and so encourage them in their sins, but because he knows that believers are never so divested of the sins of the flesh as not to remain obnoxious to the justice of God. It is, indeed, to be wished, it ought even to be our strenuous endeavour, to perform all the parts of our duty, so as truly to congratulate ourselves before God as being pure from every stain; but as God is pleased to renew his image in us by degrees, so that to some extent there is always a residue of corruption in our flesh, we ought by no means to neglect the remedy. But if Christ, according to the authority given him by his Father, enjoins us, during the whole course of our lives, to implore pardon, who can tolerate those new teachers who, by the phantom of perfect innocence, endeavour to dazzle the simple, and make them believe that they can render themselves completely free from guilt? This, as John declares, is nothing else than to make God a liar (1 John i. 10). In like manner, those foolish men mutilate the covenant in which we have seen that our salvation is contained by concealing one head of it, and so destroying it entirely; being guilty not only of profanity in that they separate things which ought to be indissolubly connected; but also of wickedness and cruelty in overwhelming wretched souls with despair—of treachery also to themselves and their followers, in that they encourage themselves in a carelessness diametrically opposed to the mercy of God. It is excessively childish to object that when they long for the advent of the kingdom of God, they at the same time pray for the abolition of sin. In the former division of the prayer absolute perfection is set before us; but in the latter our own weakness. Thus the two fitly correspond to each other—we strive for the

1 French, "Telles disciples qu'ils voudront;"—such disciples as they will.

goal, and at the same time neglect not the remedies which our necessities require.

In the next part of the petition we pray to be forgiven, "*as we forgive our debtors;*" that is, as we spare and pardon all by whom we are in any way offended, either in deed by unjust, or in word by contumelious treatment. Not that we can forgive the guilt of a fault or offence: this belongs to God only; but we can forgive to this extent; we can voluntarily divest our minds of wrath, hatred, and revenge, and efface the remembrance of injuries by a voluntary oblivion. Wherefore, we are not to ask the forgiveness of our sins from God, unless we forgive the offences of all who are or have been injurious to us. If we retain any hatred in our minds, if we meditate revenge, and devise the means of hurting; nay, if we do not return to a good understanding with our enemies, perform every kind of friendly office, and endeavour to effect a reconciliation with them, we by this petition beseech God not to grant us forgiveness. For we ask him to do to us as we do to others. This is the same as asking him not to do unless we do also. What, then, do such persons obtain by this petition but a heavier judgment? Lastly, it is to be observed that the condition of being forgiven as we forgive our debtors, is not added because by forgiving others we deserve forgiveness, as if the cause of forgiveness were expressed; but by the use of this expression the Lord has been pleased partly to solace the weakness of our faith, using it as a sign to assure us that our sins are as certainly forgiven as we are certainly conscious of having forgiven others, when our mind is completely purged from all envy, hatred, and malice; and partly using as a badge by which he excludes from the number of his children all who, prone to revenge and reluctant to forgive, obstinately keep up their enmity, cherishing against others that indignation which they deprecate from themselves; so that they should not venture to invoke him as a Father. In the Gospel of Luke we have this distinctly stated in the words of Christ.

46. The sixth petition corresponds (as we have observed) to the promise[1] of *writing the law upon our hearts;* but because we do not obey God without a continual warfare, without sharp and arduous contests, we here pray that he would furnish us with armour, and defend us by his protection, that we may be able to obtain the victory. By this we are reminded that we not only have need of the gift of the Spirit inwardly to soften our hearts, and turn and direct them to the obedience of God, but also of his assistance, to render us invincible by all the wiles and violent assaults of Satan. The forms of temptation are many and various. The depraved conceptions of our minds provoking us to transgress the law—conceptions which our concupiscence suggests or the devil excites, are temptations; and things which in their own nature are not evil, become temptations by the wiles of the devil, when they are presented to our eyes in such

1 The French adds, "que Dieu nous a donnee et faite;"—which God has given and performed to us.

a way that the view of them makes us withdraw or decline from God.[1] These temptations are both on the right hand and on the left. On the right, when riches, power, and honours, which by their glare, and the semblance of good which they present, generally dazzle the eyes of men, and so entice by their blandishments, that, caught by their snares, and intoxicated by their sweetness, they forget their God: on the left, when offended by the hardship and bitterness of poverty, disgrace, contempt, afflictions, and other things of that description, they despond, cast away their confidence and hope, and are at length totally estranged from God. In regard to both kinds of temptation, which either enkindled in us by concupiscence, or presented by the craft of Satan, war against us, we pray God the Father not to allow us to be overcome, but rather to raise and support us by his hand, that strengthened by his mighty power we may stand firm against all the assaults of our malignant enemy, whatever be the thoughts which he sends into our minds; next we pray that whatever of either description is allotted us, we may turn to good, that is, may neither be inflated with prosperity, nor cast down by adversity. Here, however, we do not ask to be altogether exempted from temptation, which is very necessary to excite, stimulate, and urge us on, that we may not become too lethargic. It was not without reason that David wished to be tried, nor is it without cause that the Lord daily tries his elect, chastising them by disgrace, poverty, tribulation, and other kinds of cross.[2] But the temptations of God and Satan are very different: Satan tempts, that he may destroy, condemn, confound, throw headlong; God, that by proving his people he may make trial of their sincerity, and by exercising their strength confirm it; may mortify, tame, and cauterise their flesh, which, if not curbed in this manner, would wanton and exult above measure. Besides, Satan attacks those who are unarmed and unprepared, that he may destroy them unawares; whereas, whatever God sends, he "will with the temptation also make a way to escape, that ye may be able to bear it." Whether by the term *evil* we understand the devil or sin, is not of the least consequence. Satan is indeed the very enemy who lays snares for our life, but it is by sin that he is armed for our destruction.

Our petition, therefore, is, that we may not be overcome or overwhelmed with temptation, but in the strength of the Lord may stand firm against all the powers by which we are assailed; in other words, may not fall under temptation: that being thus taken under his charge and protection, we may remain invincible by sin, death, the gates of hell, and the whole power of the devil; in other words, be delivered from evil. Here it is carefully to be observed, that we have no strength to contend with such a combatant as the devil, or to

1 James i. 2, 14; Matth. iv. 1, 3; 1 Thess. iii. 5; 2 Cor. vi. 7, 8.

2 Ps. xxvi. 2; Gen. xxii. 1; Deut. viii. 2; xiii. 3; 1 Cor. x. 13; 2 Pet. ii. 9; 1 Pet. v. 8. For the sense in which God is said to lead us into temptation, see the end of this section.

sustain the violence of his assault. Were it otherwise, it would be mockery of God to ask of him what we already possess in ourselves. Assuredly those who in self-confidence prepare for such a fight, do not understand how bold and well-equipped the enemy is with whom they have to do. Now we ask to be delivered from his power, as from the mouth of some furious raging lion, who would instantly tear us with his teeth and claws, and swallow us up, did not the Lord rescue us from the midst of death; at the same time knowing that if the Lord is present and will fight for us while we stand by, through him "we shall do valiantly" (Ps. lx. 12). Let others if they will confide in the powers and resources of their free will which they think they possess; enough for us that we stand and are strong in the power of God alone. But the prayer comprehends more than at first sight it seems to do. For if the Spirit of God is our strength in waging the contest with Satan, we cannot gain the victory unless we are filled with him, and thereby freed from all infirmity of the flesh. Therefore, when we pray to be delivered from sin and Satan, we at the same time desire to be enriched with new supplies of divine grace, until completely replenished with them, we triumph over every evil. To some it seems rude and harsh to ask God not to lead us into temptation, since, as James declares (James i. 13), it is contrary to his nature to do so. This difficulty has already been partly solved by the fact that our concupiscence is the cause, and therefore properly bears the blame of all the temptations by which we are overcome. All that James means is, that it is vain and unjust to ascribe to God vices which our own consciousness compels us to impute to ourselves. But this is no reason why God may not when he sees it meet bring us into bondage to Satan, give us up to a reprobate mind and shameful lusts, and so by a just, indeed, but often hidden judgment, lead us into temptation. Though the cause is often concealed from men, it is well known to him. Hence we may see that the expression is not improper, if we are persuaded that it is not without cause he so often threatens to give sure signs of his vengeance, by blinding the reprobate, and hardening their hearts.

47. These three petitions, in which we specially commend ourselves and all that we have to God, clearly show what we formerly observed (sec. 38, 39), that the prayers of Christians should be public, and have respect to the public edification of the Church and the advancement of believers in spiritual communion. For no one requests that anything should be given to him as an individual, but we all ask in common for daily bread and the forgiveness of sins, not to be led into temptation, but delivered from evil. Moreover, there is subjoined the reason for our great boldness in asking and confidence of obtaining (sec. 11, 36). Although this does not exist in the Latin copies, yet as it accords so well with the whole, we cannot think of omitting it.

The words are, THINE IS THE KINGDOM, AND THE POWER, AND THE GLORY, FOR EVER. Here is the calm and firm assurance of our faith.

For were our prayers to be commended to God by our own worth, who would venture even to whisper before him? Now, however wretched we may be, however unworthy, however devoid of commendation, we shall never want a reason for prayer, nor a ground of confidence, since the kingdom, power, and glory, can never be wrested from our Father. The last word is AMEN, by which is expressed the eagerness of our desire to obtain the things which we ask, while our hope is confirmed, that all things have already been obtained, and will assuredly be granted to us, seeing they have been promised by God, who cannot deceive. This accords with the form of expression to which we have already adverted: "Grant, O Lord, for thy name's sake, not on account of us or of our righteousness." By this the saints not only express the end of their prayers, but confess that they are unworthy of obtaining did not God find the cause in himself, and were not their confidence founded entirely on His nature.

48. All things that we ought, indeed all that we are able, to ask of God, are contained in this formula, and as it were rule, of prayer delivered by Christ, our divine Master, whom the Father has appointed to be our teacher, and to whom alone he would have us to listen (Matth. xvii. 5). For he ever was the eternal wisdom of the Father, and being made man, was manifested as the Wonderful, the Counsellor (Isa. xi. 2). Accordingly, this prayer is complete in all its parts, so complete, that whatever is extraneous and foreign to it, whatever cannot be referred to it, is impious and unworthy of the approbation of God. For he has here summarily prescribed what is worthy of him, what is acceptable to him, and what is necessary for us; in short, whatever he is pleased to grant. Those, therefore, who presume to go further and ask something more from God, first seek to add of their own to the wisdom of God (this it is insane blasphemy to do); secondly, refusing to confine themselves within the will of God, and despising it, they wander as their cupidity directs; lastly, they will never obtain anything, seeing they pray without faith. For there cannot be a doubt that all such prayers are made without faith, because at variance with the word of God, on which if faith do not always lean it cannot possibly stand. Those who, disregarding the Master's rule, indulge their own wishes, not only have not the word of God, but as much as in them lies oppose it. Hence Tertullian (De Fuga in Persequutione) has not less truly than elegantly termed it *Lawful Prayer*, tacitly intimating that all other prayers are lawless and illicit.

49. By this, however, we would not have it understood that we are so astricted to this form of prayer as to make it unlawful to change a word or syllable of it. For in Scripture we meet with many prayers differing greatly from it in word, yet written by the same Spirit, and capable of being used by us with the greatest advantage. Many prayers also are continually suggested to believers by the same Spirit, though in expression they bear no great resemblance to it. All we mean to say is, that no man should wish, expect, or ask anything

which is not summarily comprehended in this prayer. Though the words may be very different, there must be no difference in the sense. In this way, all prayers, both those which are contained in the Scripture, and those which come forth from pious breasts, must be referred to it, certainly none can ever equal it, far less surpass it in perfection. It omits nothing which we can conceive in praise of God, nothing which we can imagine advantageous to man, and the whole is so exact that all hope of improving it may well be renounced. In short, let us remember that we have here the doctrine of heavenly wisdom. God has taught what he willed; he willed what was necessary.

50. But although it has been said above (sec. 7, 27, &c.) that we ought always to raise our minds upwards towards God, and pray without ceasing, yet such is our weakness, which requires to be supported, such our torpor, which requires to be stimulated, that it is requisite for us to appoint special hours for this exercise, hours which are not to pass away without prayer, and during which the whole affections of our minds are to be completely occupied—namely, when we rise in the morning, before we commence our daily work, when we sit down to food, when by the blessing of God we have taken it, and when we retire to rest. This, however, must not be a superstitious observance of hours, by which, as it were, performing a task to God, we think we are discharged as to other hours; it should rather be considered as a discipline by which our weakness is exercised, and ever and anon stimulated. In particular, it must be our anxious care, whenever we are ourselves pressed, or see others pressed by any strait, instantly to have recourse to him not only with quickened pace, but with quickened minds; and again, we must not in any prosperity of ourselves or others omit to testify our recognition of his hand by praise and thanksgiving. Lastly, we must in all our prayers carefully avoid wishing to confine God to certain circumstances, or prescribe to him the time, place, or mode of action. In like manner, we are taught by this prayer not to fix any law or impose any condition upon him, but leave it entirely to him to adopt whatever course of procedure seems to him best, in respect of method, time, and place. For before we offer up any petition for ourselves, we ask that his will may be done, and by so doing place our will in subordination to his, just as if we had laid a curb upon it, that, instead of presuming to give law to God, it may regard him as the ruler and disposer of all its wishes.

51. If, with minds thus framed to obedience, we allow ourselves to be governed by the laws of Divine Providence, we shall easily learn to persevere in prayer, and suspending our own desires wait patiently for the Lord, certain, however little the appearance of it may be, that he is always present with us, and will in his own time show how very far he was from turning a deaf ear to prayers, though to the eyes of men they may seem to be disregarded. This will be a very present consolation, if at any time God does not grant an immediate answer to our prayers, preventing us from fainting or giving way to despond

ency, as those are wont to do who, in invoking God, are so borne away by their own fervour, that unless he yield on their first importunity and give present help, they immediately imagine that he is angry and offended with them, and abandoning all hope of success cease from prayer. On the contrary, deferring our hope with well tempered equanimity, let us insist with that perseverance which is so strongly recommended to us in Scripture. We may often see in The Psalms how David and other believers, after they are almost weary of praying, and seem to have been beating the air by addressing a God who would not hear, yet cease not to pray, because due authority is not given to the word of God, unless the faith placed in it is superior to all events. Again, let us not tempt God, and by wearying him with our importunity, provoke his anger against us. Many have a practice of formally bargaining with God on certain conditions, and, as if he were the servant of their lusts, binding him to certain stipulations; with which if he do not immediately comply, they are indignant and fretful, murmur, complain, and make a noise. Thus offended, he often in his anger grants to such persons what in mercy he kindly denies to others. Of this we have a proof in the children of Israel, for whom it had been better not to have been heard by the Lord, than to swallow his indignation with their flesh (Num. xi. 18, 33).

52. But if our sense is not able till after long expectation to perceive what the result of prayer is, or experience any benefit from it, still our faith will assure us of that which cannot be perceived by sense—viz. that we have obtained what was fit for us, the Lord having so often and so surely engaged to take an interest in all our troubles from the moment they have been deposited in his bosom. In this way we shall possess abundance in poverty, and comfort in affliction. For though all things fail, God will never abandon us, and he cannot frustrate the expectation and patience of his people. He alone will suffice for all, since in himself he comprehends all good, and will at last reveal it to us on the day of judgment, when his kingdom shall be plainly manifested. We may add, that although God complies with our request, he does not always give an answer in the very terms of our prayer, but while apparently holding us in suspense, yet in an unknown way, shows that our prayers have not been in vain. This is the meaning of the words of John, "If we know that he hear us, whatsoever we ask, we know that we have the petitions that we desired of him" (1 John v. 15). It might seem that there is here a great superfluity of words, but the declaration is most useful—namely, that God, even when he does not comply with our requests, yet listens and is favourable to our prayers, so that our hope founded on his word is never disappointed. But believers have always need of being supported by this patience, as they could not stand long if they did not lean upon it. For the trials by which the Lord proves and exercises us are severe, nay, he often drives us to extremes, and when driven allows us long to stick fast in the mire

before he gives us any taste of his sweetness. As Hannah says, "The Lord killeth, and maketh alive; he bringeth down to the grave, and bringeth up" (1 Sam. ii. 6). What could they here do but become dispirited and rush on despair, were they not, when afflicted, desolate, and half dead, comforted with the thought that they are regarded by God, and that there will be an end to their present evils. But however secure their hopes may stand, they in the meantime cease not to pray, since prayer unaccompanied by perseverance leads to no result.

CHAPTER XXI.

OF THE ETERNAL ELECTION, BY WHICH GOD HAS PREDESTINATED SOME TO SALVATION, AND OTHERS TO DESTRUCTION.

The divisions of this chapter are,—I. The necessity and utility of the doctrine of eternal Election explained. Excessive curiosity restrained, sec. 1, 2. II. Explanation to those who through false modesty shun the doctrine of Predestination, sec. 3, 4. III. The orthodox doctrine expounded.

Sections.

1. The doctrine of Election and Predestination. It is useful, necessary, and most sweet. Ignorance of it impairs the glory of God, plucks up humility by the roots, begets and fosters pride. The doctrine establishes the certainty of salvation, peace of conscience, and the true origin of the Church. Answer to two classes of men: 1. The curious.
2. A sentiment of Augustine confirmed by an admonition of our Saviour and a passage of Solomon.
3. An answer to a second class—viz. those who are unwilling that the doctrine should be adverted to. An objection founded on a passage of Solomon, solved by the words of Moses.
4. A second objection—viz. That this doctrine is a stumbling-block to the profane. Answer 1. The same may be said of many other heads of doctrine. 2. The truth of God will always defend itself. Third objection—viz. That this doctrine is dangerous even to believers. Answer 1. The same objection made to Augustine. 2. We must not despise anything that God has revealed. Arrogance and blasphemy of such objections.
5. Certain cavils against the doctrine. 1. Prescience regarded as the cause of predestination. Prescience and predestination explained. Not prescience, but the good pleasure of God the cause of predestination. This apparent from the gratuitous election of the posterity of Abraham and the rejection of all others.
6. Even of the posterity of Abraham some elected and others rejected by special grace.
7. The Apostle shows that the same thing has been done in regard to individuals under the Christian dispensation.

1. THE covenant of life is not preached equally to all, and among those to whom it is preached, does not always meet with the same reception. This diversity displays the unsearchable depth of the divine judgment, and is without doubt subordinate to God's purpose of eternal election. But if it is plainly owing to the mere pleasure of God that salvation is spontaneously offered to some, while others have no access to it, great and difficult questions immediately arise, questions which are inexplicable, when just views are not entertained concerning election and predestination. To many this seems a perplexing subject, because they deem it most incongruous that of the great body of mankind some should be predestinated to salvation, and others to destruction. How causelessly they entangle themselves will appear as we proceed. We may add, that in the very obscurity

which deters them, we may see not only the utility of this doctrine, but also its most pleasant fruits. We shall never feel persuaded as we ought that our salvation flows from the free mercy of God as its fountain, until we are made acquainted with his eternal election, the grace of God being illustrated by the contrast—viz. that he does not adopt promiscuously to the hope of salvation, but gives to some what he denies to others. It is plain how greatly ignorance of this principle detracts from the glory of God, and impairs true humility. But though thus necessary to be known, Paul declares that it cannot be known unless God, throwing works entirely out of view, elect those whom he has predestined. His words are, "Even so then at this present time also, there is a remnant according to the election of grace. And if by grace, then it is no more of works: otherwise grace is no more grace. But if it be of works, then it is no more grace: otherwise work is no more work" (Rom. xi. 6). If to make it appear that our salvation flows entirely from the good mercy of God, we must be carried back to the origin of election, then those who would extinguish it, wickedly do as much as in them lies to obscure what they ought most loudly to extol, and pluck up humility by the very roots. Paul clearly declares that it is only when the salvation of a remnant is ascribed to gratuitous election, we arrive at the knowledge that God saves whom he wills of his mere good pleasure, and does not pay a debt, a debt which never can be due. Those who preclude access, and would not have any one to obtain a taste of this doctrine, are equally unjust to God and men, there being no other means of humbling us as we ought, or making us feel how much we are bound to him. Nor, indeed, have we elsewhere any sure ground of confidence. This we say on the authority of Christ, who, to deliver us from all fear, and render us invincible amid our many dangers, snares, and mortal conflicts, promises safety to all that the Father hath taken under his protection (John x. 26). From this we infer, that all who know not that they are the peculiar people of God, must be wretched from perpetual trepidation, and that those, therefore, who, by overlooking the three advantages which we have noted, would destroy the very foundation of our safety, consult ill for themselves and for all the faithful. What? Do we not here find the very origin of the Church, which, as Bernard rightly teaches (Serm. in Cantic.), could not be found or recognised among the creatures, because it lies hid (in both cases wondrously) within the lap of blessed predestination, and the mass of wretched condemnation?

But before I enter on the subject, I have some remarks to address to two classes of men. The subject of predestination, which in itself is attended with considerable difficulty, is rendered very perplexed, and hence perilous by human curiosity, which cannot be restrained from wandering into forbidden paths, and climbing to the clouds, determined if it can that none of the secret things of God shall remain unexplored. When we see many, some of them in other respects not bad men, everywhere rushing into this audacity and wickedness, it is necessary to remind them of the course of duty in this matter. First, then, when they inquire into predestination, let them remember that they are penetrating into the recesses of the divine wisdom, where he who rushes forward securely and confidently instead of satisfying his curiosity will enter an inextricable labyrinth.[1] For it is not right that man should with impunity pry into things which the Lord has been pleased to conceal within himself, and scan that sublime eternal wisdom which it is his pleasure that we should not apprehend but adore, that therein also his perfections may appear. Those secrets of his will, which he has seen it meet to manifest, are revealed in his word—revealed in so far as he knew to be conducive to our interest and welfare.

2. "We have come into the way of faith," says Augustine: "let us constantly adhere to it. It leads to the chambers of the king, in which are hidden all the treasures of wisdom and knowledge. For our Lord Jesus Christ did not speak invidiously to his great and most select disciples when he said, 'I have yet many things to say unto you, but ye cannot bear them now' (John xvi. 12). We must walk, advance, increase, that our hearts may be able to comprehend those things which they cannot now comprehend. But if the last day shall find us making progress, we shall there learn what here we could not" (August. Hom. in Joann.). If we give due weight to the consideration, that the word of the Lord is the only way which can conduct us to the investigation of whatever it is lawful for us to hold with regard to him—is the only light which can enable us to discern what we ought to see with regard to him, it will curb and restrain all presumption. For it will show us that the moment we go beyond the bounds of the word we are out of the course, in darkness, and must every now and then stumble, go astray, and fall. Let it, therefore, be our first principle that to desire any other knowledge of predestination than that which is expounded by the word of God, is no less infatuated than to walk where there is no path, or to seek light in darkness. Let us not be ashamed to be ignorant in a matter in which ignorance is learning. Rather let us willingly abstain from the search after knowledge, to which it is both foolish as well as perilous, and even fatal to aspire. If an unrestrained imagination urges us, our proper course is to oppose it with these words, "It is not good to eat much honey: so for men to search their own glory is not glory" (Prov. xxv. 27). There is good reason to dread a presumption which can only plunge us headlong into ruin.

3. There are others who, when they would cure this disease, recommend that the subject of predestination should scarcely if ever be mentioned, and tell us to shun every question concerning it as we would a rock. Although their moderation is justly commendable in thinking that such mysteries should be treated with moderation, yet

1 Thus Eck boasts that he had written of predestination to exercise his youthful spirits.

because they keep too far within the proper measure, they have little influence over the human mind, which does not readily allow itself to be curbed. Therefore, in order to keep the legitimate course in this matter, we must return to the word of God, in which we are furnished with the right rule of understanding. For Scripture is the school of the Holy Spirit, in which as nothing useful and necessary to be known has been omitted, so nothing is taught but what it is of importance to know. Everything, therefore, delivered in Scripture on the subject of predestination, we must beware of keeping from the faithful lest we seem either maliciously to deprive them of the blessing of God, or to accuse and scoff at the Spirit, as having divulged what ought on any account to be suppressed. Let us, I say, allow the Christian to unlock his mind and ears to all the words of God which are addressed to him, provided he do it with this moderation—viz. that whenever the Lord shuts his sacred mouth, he also desists from inquiry. The best rule of sobriety is, not only in learning to follow wherever God leads, but also when he makes an end of teaching, to cease also from wishing to be wise. The danger which they dread is not so great that we ought on account of it to turn away our minds from the oracles of God. There is a celebrated saying of Solomon, "It is the glory of God to conceal a thing" (Prov. xxv. 2). But since both piety and common sense dictate that this is not to be understood of everything, we must look for a distinction, lest under the pretence of modesty and sobriety we be satisfied with a brutish ignorance. This is clearly expressed by Moses in a few words, "The secret things belong unto the Lord our God: but those things which are revealed belong unto us, and to our children for ever" (Deut. xxix. 29). We see how he exhorts the people to study the doctrine of the law in accordance with a heavenly decree, because God has been pleased to promulgate it, while he at the same time confines them within these boundaries, for the simple reason that it is not lawful for men to pry into the secret things of God.

4. I admit that profane men lay hold of the subject of predestination to carp, or cavil, or snarl, or scoff. But if their petulance frightens us, it will be necessary to conceal all the principal articles of faith, because they and their fellows leave scarcely one of them unassailed with blasphemy. A rebellious spirit will display itself no less insolently when it hears that there are three persons in the divine essence, than when it hears that God when he created man foresaw everything that was to happen to him. Nor will they abstain from their jeers when told that little more than five thousand years have elapsed since the creation of the world. For they will ask, Why did the power of God slumber so long in idleness? In short, nothing can be stated that they will not assail with derision. To quell their blasphemies, must we say nothing concerning the divinity of the Son and Spirit? Must the creation of the world be passed over in silence? No! The truth of God is too powerful, both here and everywhere, to dread the slanders of the ungodly, as Augustine powerfully maintains

in his treatise, De Bono Perseverantiæ (cap. xiv.–xx.). For we see that the false apostles were unable, by defaming and accusing the true doctrine of Paul, to make him ashamed of it. There is nothing in the allegation that the whole subject is fraught with danger to pious minds, as tending to destroy exhortation, shake faith, disturb and dispirit the heart. Augustine disguises not that on these grounds he was often charged with preaching the doctrine of predestination too freely, but, as it was easy for him to do, he abundantly refutes the charge. As a great variety of absurd objections are here stated, we have thought it best to dispose of each of them in its proper place (see chap. xxiii.). Only I wish it to be received as a general rule, that the secret things of God are not to be scrutinised, and that those which he has revealed are not to be overlooked, lest we may, on the one hand, be chargeable with curiosity, and, on the other, with ingratitude. For it has been shrewdly observed by Augustine (de Genesi ad Literam, Lib. v.), that we can safely follow Scripture, which walks softly, as with a mother's step, in accommodation to our weakness. Those, however, who are so cautious and timid, that they would bury all mention of predestination in order that it may not trouble weak minds, with what colour, pray, will they cloak their arrogance, when they indirectly charge God with a want of due consideration, in not having foreseen a danger for which they imagine that they prudently provide? Whoever, therefore, throws obloquy on the doctrine of predestination, openly brings a charge against God, as having inconsiderately allowed something to escape from him which is injurious to the Church.

5. The predestination by which God adopts some to the hope of life, and adjudges others to eternal death, no man who would be thought pious ventures simply to deny; but it is greatly cavilled at, especially by those who make prescience its cause. We, indeed, ascribe both prescience and predestination to God; but we say that it is absurd to make the latter subordinate to the former (see chap. xxii. sec. 1). When we attribute prescience to God, we mean that all things always were, and ever continue, under his eye; that to his knowledge there is no past or future, but all things are present, and indeed so present, that it is not merely the idea of them that is before him (as those objects are which we retain in our memory), but that he truly sees and contemplates them as actually under his immediate inspection. This prescience extends to the whole circuit of the world, and to all creatures. By predestination we mean the eternal decree of God, by which he determined with himself whatever he wished to happen with regard to every man. All are not created on equal terms, but some are preordained to eternal life, others to eternal damnation; and, accordingly, as each has been created for one or other of these ends, we say that he has been predestinated to life or to death. This God has testified, not only in the case of single individuals; he has also given a specimen of it in the whole posterity of Abraham, to make it plain

that the future condition of each nation was entirely at his disposal: "When the Most High divided to the nations their inheritance, when he separated the sons of Adam, he set the bounds of the people according to the number of the children of Israel. For the Lord's portion is his people; Jacob is the lot of his inheritance" (Deut. xxxii. 8, 9). The separation is before the eyes of all; in the person of Abraham, as in a withered stock, one people is specially chosen, while the others are rejected; but the cause does not appear, except that Moses, to deprive posterity of any handle for glorying, tells them that their superiority was owing entirely to the free love of God. The cause which he assigns for their deliverance is, "Because he loved thy fathers, therefore he chose their seed after them" (Deut. iv. 37); or more explicitly in another chapter, "The Lord did not set his love upon you, nor choose you, because you were more in number than any people: for ye were the fewest of all people: but because the Lord loved you" (Deut. vii. 7, 8). He repeatedly makes the same intimation, "Behold, the heaven, and the heaven of heavens, is the Lord's thy God, the earth also, with all that therein is. Only the Lord had a delight in thy fathers to love them, and he chose their seed after them" (Deut. x. 14, 15). Again, in another passage, holiness is enjoined upon them, because they have been chosen to be a peculiar people; while in another, love is declared to be the cause of their protection (Deut. xxiii. 5). This, too, believers with one voice proclaim, "He shall choose our inheritance for us, the excellency of Jacob, whom he loved" (Ps. xlvii. 4). The endowments with which God had adorned them, they all ascribe to gratuitous love, not only because they knew that they had not obtained them by any merit, but that not even was the holy patriarch endued with a virtue that could procure such distinguished honour for himself and his posterity. And the more completely to crush all pride, he upbraids them with having merited nothing of the kind, seeing they were a rebellious and stiff-necked people (Deut. ix. 6). Often, also, do the prophets remind the Jews of this election by way of disparagement and opprobrium, because they had shamefully revolted from it. Be this as it may, let those who would ascribe the election of God to human worth or merit come forward. When they see that one nation is preferred to all others, when they hear that it was no feeling of respect that induced God to show more favour to a small and ignoble body, nay, even to the wicked and rebellious, will they plead against him for having chosen to give such a manifestation of mercy? But neither will their obstreperous words hinder his work, nor will their invectives, like stones thrown against heaven, strike or hurt his righteousness; nay, rather they will fall back on their own heads. To this principle of a free covenant, moreover, the Israelites are recalled whenever thanks are to be returned to God, or their hopes of the future to be animated. "The Lord he is God," says the Psalmist; "it is he that hath made us, and not we ourselves: we are his people, and the sheep of his pasture" (Ps. c. 3; xcv. 7). The negation which is added, "not we ourselves," is not superfluous, to teach us that God is not only the author of all the good qualities in which men excel, but that they originate in himself, there being nothing in them worthy of so much honour. In the following words also they are enjoined to rest satisfied with the mere good pleasure of God: "O ye seed of Abraham, his servant; ye children of Jacob, his chosen" (Ps. cv. 6). And after an enumeration of the continual mercies of God as fruits of election, the conclusion is, that he acted thus kindly because he remembered his covenant. With this doctrine accords the song of the whole Church, "They got not the land in possession by their own sword, neither did their own arm save them; but thy right hand, and thine arm, and the light of thy countenance, because thou hadst a favour unto them" (Ps. xliv. 3). It is to be observed, that when the land is mentioned, it is a visible symbol of the secret election in which adoption is comprehended. To like gratitude David elsewhere exhorts the people, "Blessed is the nation whose God is the Lord, and the people whom he hath chosen for his own inheritance" (Ps. xxxiii. 12). Samuel thus animates their hopes, "The Lord will not forsake his people for his great name's sake: because it hath pleased the Lord to make you his people" (1 Sam. xii. 22). And when David's faith is assailed, how does he arm himself for the battle? "Blessed is the man whom thou choosest, and causest to approach unto thee, that he may dwell in thy courts" (Ps. lxv. 4). But as the hidden election of God was confirmed both by a first and second election, and by other intermediate mercies, Isaiah thus applies the term, "The Lord will have mercy on Jacob, and will yet choose Israel" (Isa. xiv. 1). Referring to a future period, the gathering together of the dispersion, who seemed to have been abandoned, he says, that it will be a sign of a firm and stable election, notwithstanding of the apparent abandonment. When it is elsewhere said, "I have chosen thee, and not cast thee away" (Isa. xli. 9), the continual course of his great liberality is ascribed to paternal kindness. This is stated more explicitly in Zechariah by the angel, the Lord "shall choose Jerusalem again," as if the severity of his chastisements had amounted to reprobation, or the captivity had been an interruption of election, which, however, remains inviolable, though the signs of it do not always appear.

6. We must add a second step of a more limited nature, or one in which the grace of God was displayed in a more special form, when of the same family of Abraham God rejected some, and by keeping others within his Church showed that he retained them among his sons. At first Ishmael had obtained the same rank with his brother Isaac, because the spiritual covenant was equally sealed in him by the symbol of circumcision. He is first cut off, then Esau, at last an innumerable multitude, almost the whole of Israel. In Isaac was the seed called. The same calling held good in the case of Jacob. God gave a similar example in the rejection of Saul. This is also celebrated in the psalm, "Moreover, he refused the tabernacle of

Joseph, and chose not the tribe of Ephraim: but chose the tribe of Judah" (Ps. lxxviii. 67, 68). This the sacred history sometimes repeats, that the secret grace of God may be more admirably displayed in that change. I admit that it was by their own fault Ishmael, Esau, and others, fell from their adoption; for the condition annexed was, that they should faithfully keep the covenant of God, whereas they perfidiously violated it. The singular kindness of God consisted in this, that he had been pleased to prefer them to other nations; as it is said in the psalm, "He hath not dealt so with any nation: and as for his judgments, they have not known them" (Ps. cxlvii. 20). But I had good reason for saying that two steps are here to be observed; for in the election of the whole nation, God had already shown that in the exercise of his mere liberality he was under no law, but was free, so that he was by no means to be restricted to an equal division of grace, its very inequality proving it to be gratuitous. Accordingly, Malachi enlarges on the ingratitude of Israel, in that being not only selected from the whole human race, but set peculiarly apart from a sacred household, they perfidiously and impiously spurn God their beneficent parent. "Was not Esau Jacob's brother? saith the Lord: yet I loved Jacob, and I hated Esau" (Mal. i. 2, 3). For God takes it for granted, that as both were the sons of a holy father, and successors of the covenant, in short, branches from a sacred root, the sons of Jacob were under no ordinary obligation for having been admitted to that dignity; but when by the rejection of Esau the first-born, their progenitor though inferior in birth was made heir, he charges them with double ingratitude, in not being restrained by a double tie.

7. Although it is now sufficiently plain that God by his secret counsel chooses whom he will while he rejects others, his gratuitous election has only been partially explained until we come to the case of single individuals, to whom God not only offers salvation, but so assigns it, that the certainty of the result remains not dubious or suspended.[1] These are considered as belonging to that one seed of which Paul makes mention (Rom. ix. 8; Gal. iii. 16, &c.). For although adoption was deposited in the hand of Abraham, yet as many of his posterity were cut off as rotten members, in order that election may stand and be effectual, it is necessary to ascend to the head in whom the heavenly Father hath connected his elect with each other, and bound them to himself by an indissoluble tie. Thus in the adoption of the family of Abraham, God gave them a liberal display of favour which he has denied to others; but in the members of Christ there is a far more excellent display of grace, because those ingrafted into him as their head never fail to obtain salvation.

1 On predestination, see the pious and very learned observations of Luther, tom. i. p. 86, fin., and p. 87, fin. Tom. iii. ad Psal. xxii. 8. Tom. v. in Joann. cxvii. Also his Prefatio in Epist. ad Rom. and Adv. Erasmum de Servo Arbitrio, p. 429, sqq. 452, 463. Also in Psal. cxxxix.

Hence Paul skilfully argues from the passage of Malachi which I quoted (Rom. ix. 13; Mal. i. 2), that when God, after making a covenant of eternal life, invites any people to himself, a special mode of election is in part understood, so that he does not with promiscuous grace effectually elect all of them. The words, "Jacob have I loved," refer to the whole progeny of the patriarch, which the prophet there opposes to the posterity of Esau. But there is nothing in this repugnant to the fact, that in the person of one man is set before us a specimen of election, which cannot fail of accomplishing its object. It is not without cause Paul observes, that these are called *a remnant* (Rom. ix. 27; xi. 5); because experience shows that of the general body many fall away and are lost, so that often a small portion only remains. The reason why the general election of the people is not always firmly ratified, readily presents itself—viz. that on those with whom God makes the covenant, he does not immediately bestow the Spirit of regeneration, by whose power they persevere in the covenant even to the end. The external invitation, without the internal efficacy of grace which would have the effect of retaining them, holds a kind of middle place between the rejection of the human race and the election of a small number of believers. The whole people of Israel are called the Lord's inheritance, and yet there were many foreigners among them. Still, because the covenant which God had made to be their Father and Redeemer was not altogether null, he has respect to that free favour rather than to the perfidious defection of many; even by them his truth was not abolished, since by preserving some residue to himself, it appeared that his calling was without repentance. When God ever and anon gathered his Church from among the sons of Abraham rather than from profane nations, he had respect to his covenant, which, when violated by the great body, he restricted to a few, that it might not entirely fail. In short, that common adoption of the seed of Abraham was a kind of visible image of a greater benefit which God deigned to bestow on some out of many. This is the reason why Paul so carefully distinguishes between the sons of Abraham according to the flesh and the spiritual sons, who are called after the example of Isaac. Not that simply to be a son of Abraham was a vain or useless privilege (this could not be said without insult to the covenant), but that the immutable counsel of God, by which he predestinated to himself whomsoever he would, was alone effectual for their salvation. But until the proper view is made clear by the production of passages of Scripture, I advise my readers not to prejudge the question. We say, then, that Scripture clearly proves this much, that God by his eternal and immutable counsel determined once for all those whom it was his pleasure one day to admit to salvation, and those whom, on the other hand, it was his pleasure to doom to destruction. We maintain that this counsel, as regards the elect, is founded on his free mercy, without any respect to human worth, while those whom he dooms to destruction are excluded from access to life by a just and blameless, but at the same time incomprehensible judgment. In regard to the elect, we regard calling as the evidence of election, and justification as another symbol of its manifestation, until it is fully accomplished by the attainment of glory. But as the Lord seals his elect by calling and justification, so by excluding the reprobate either from the knowledge of his name or the sanctification of his Spirit, he by these marks in a manner discloses the judgment which awaits them. I will here omit many of the fictions which foolish men have devised to overthrow predestination. There is no need of refuting objections which the moment they are produced abundantly betray their hollowness. I will dwell only on those points which either form the subject of dispute among the learned, or may occasion any difficulty to the simple, or may be employed by impiety as specious pretexts for assailing the justice of God.

CHAPTER XXII.

THIS DOCTRINE CONFIRMED BY PROOFS FROM SCRIPTURE.

The divisions of this chapter are,—I. A confirmation of the orthodox doctrine in opposition to two classes of individuals. This confirmation founded on a careful exposition of our Saviour's words, and passages in the writings of Paul, sec. 1–7. II. A refutation of some objections taken from ancient writers, Thomas Aquinas, and more modern writers, sec. 8–10. III. Of reprobation, which is founded entirely on the righteous will of God, sec. 11.

Sections.

1. Some imagine that God elects or reprobates according to a foreknowledge of merit. Others make it a charge against God that he elects some and passes by others. Both refuted, 1. By invincible arguments; 2. By the testimony of Augustine.
2. Who are elected, when, in whom, to what, for what reason.
3. The reason is the good pleasure of God, which so reigns in election that no works, either past or future, are taken into consideration. This proved by notable declarations of our Saviour and passages of Paul.
4. Proved by a striking discussion in the Epistle to the Romans. Its scope and method explained. The advocates of foreknowledge refuted by the Apostle, when he maintains that election is special and wholly of grace.
5. Evasion refuted. A summary and analysis of the Apostle's discussion.
6. An exception, with three answers to it. The efficacy of gratuitous election extends only to believers, who are said to be elected according to foreknowledge. This foreknowledge or prescience is not speculative but active.
7. This proved from the words of Christ. Conclusion of the answer, and solution of the objection with regard to Judas.
8. An objection taken from the ancient fathers. Answer from Augustine, from Ambrose, as quoted by Augustine, and an invincible argument by an Apostle. Summary of this argument.
9. Objection from Thomas Aquinas. Answer.
10. Objection of more modern writers. Answers. Passages in which there is a semblance of contradiction reconciled. Why many called and few chosen. An objection founded on mutual consent between the word and faith. Solution confirmed by the words of Paul, Augustine, and Bernard. A clear declaration by our Saviour.
11. The view to be taken of reprobation. It is founded on the righteous will of God.

1. MANY controvert all the positions which we have laid down, especially the gratuitous election of believers, which however cannot be overthrown. For they commonly imagine that God distinguishes between men according to the merits which he foresees that each individual is to have, giving the adoption of sons to those whom he foreknows will not be unworthy of his grace, and dooming those to destruction whose dispositions he perceives will be prone to mischief and wickedness. Thus by interposing foreknowledge as a veil, they not only obscure election, but pretend to give it a different origin. Nor is this the commonly received opinion of the vulgar merely, for

it has in all ages had great supporters (see sec. 8). This I candidly confess, lest any one should expect greatly to prejudice our cause by opposing it with their names. The truth of God is here too certain to be shaken, too clear to be overborne by human authority. Others, who are neither versed in Scripture, nor entitled to any weight, assail sound doctrine with a petulance and improbity which it is impossible to tolerate.[1] Because God of his mere good pleasure electing some passes by others, they raise a plea against him. But if the fact is certain, what can they gain by quarrelling with God? We teach nothing but what experience proves to be true—viz. that God has always been at liberty to bestow his grace on whom he would. Not to ask in what respect the posterity of Abraham excelled others, if it be not in a worth, the cause of which has no existence out of God, let them tell why men are better than oxen or asses. God might have made them dogs when he formed them in his own image. Will they allow the lower animals to expostulate with God, as if the inferiority of their condition were unjust? It is certainly not more equitable that men should enjoy the privilege which they have not acquired by any merit, than that he should variously distribute favours as seems to him meet. If they pass to the case of individuals where inequality is more offensive to them, they ought at least, in regard to the example of our Saviour, to be restrained by feelings of awe from talking so confidently of this sublime mystery. He is conceived a mortal man of the seed of David; what, I would ask them, are the virtues by which he deserved to become in the very womb, the head of angels, the only begotten Son of God, the image and glory of the Father, the light, righteousness, and salvation of the world? It is wisely observed by Augustine,[2] that in the very head of the Church we have a bright mirror of free election, lest it should give any trouble to us the members—viz. that he did not become the Son of God by living righteously, but was freely presented with this great honour, that he might afterwards make others partakers of his gifts. Should any one here ask, why others are not what he was, or why we are all at so great a distance from him, why we are all corrupt while he is purity, he would not only betray his madness, but his effrontery also. But if they are bent on depriving God of the free right of electing and reprobating, let them at the same time take away what has been given to Christ. It will now be proper to attend to what Scripture declares concerning each. When Paul declares that we were chosen in Christ before the foundation of the world (Eph. i. 4), he certainly shows that no regard is had to our

[1] French, "Il y en a d'aucuns, lesquels n'estans exercés en l'Ecriture ne sont dignes d'aucun credit ne reputation; et toutes fois sont plus hardis et temeraires à diffamer la doctrine qui leur est incognue; et ainsi ce n'est pas raison que leur arrogance soit supportée."—There are some who, not being exercised in Scripture, are not worthy of any credit or reputation, and yet are more bold and presumptuous in defaming the doctrine which is unknown to them, and hence their arrogance is insupportable.

[2] August. de Corrept. et Gratia ad Valent. c. 15. Hom. de Bono Perseveran. c. 8. Item, de Verbis Apost. Serm. viii.

own worth; for it is just as if he had said, Since in the whole seed of Adam our heavenly Father found nothing worthy of his election, he turned his eye upon his own Anointed, that he might select as members of his body those whom he was to assume into the fellowship of life. Let believers, then, give full effect to this reason—viz. that we were in Christ adopted unto the heavenly inheritance, because in ourselves we were incapable of such excellence. This he elsewhere observes in another passage, in which he exhorts the Colossians to give thanks that they had been made meet to be partakers of the inheritance of the saints (Col. i. 12). If election precedes that divine grace by which we are made fit to obtain immortal life, what can God find in us to induce him to elect us? What I mean is still more clearly explained in another passage: God, says he, "hath chosen us in him before the foundation of the world, that we might be holy and without blame before him in love: having predestinated us unto the adoption of children by Jesus Christ to himself, according to the good pleasure of his will" (Eph. i. 4, 5). Here he opposes the good pleasure of God to our merits of every description.

2. That the proof may be more complete, it is of importance to attend to the separate clauses of that passage. When they are connected together they leave no doubt. From giving them the name of elect, it is clear that he is addressing believers, as indeed he shortly after declares. It is, therefore, a complete perversion of the name to confine it to the age in which the gospel was published. By saying they were elected before the foundation of the world, he takes away all reference to worth. For what ground of distinction was there between persons who as yet existed not, and persons who were afterwards like them to exist in Adam? But if they were elected in Christ, it follows not only that each was elected on some extrinsic ground, but that some were placed on a different footing from others, since we see that all are not members of Christ. In the additional statement that they were elected that they might be holy, the apostle openly refutes the error of those who deduce election from prescience, since he declares that whatever virtue appears in men is the result of election. Then, if a higher cause is asked, Paul answers that God so predestined, and predestined according to the good pleasure of his will. By these words, he overturns all the grounds of election which men imagine to exist in themselves. For he shows that whatever favours God bestows in reference to the spiritual life flow from this one fountain, because God chose whom he would, and before they were born had the grace which he designed to bestow upon them set apart for their use.

3. Wherever this good pleasure of God reigns, no good works are taken into account. The Apostle, indeed, does not follow out the antithesis, but it is to be understood, as he himself explains it in another passage, "Who hath called us with a holy calling, not according to our works, but according to his own purpose and grace, which was given us in Christ Jesus before the world began" (1 Tim.

ii. 9). We have already shown that the additional words, "that we might be holy," remove every doubt. If you say that he foresaw they would be holy, and therefore elected them, you invert the order of Paul. You may, therefore, safely infer, If he elected us that we might be holy, he did not elect us because he foresaw that we would be holy. The two things are evidently inconsistent—viz. that the pious owe it to election that they are holy, and yet attain to election by means of works. There is no force in the cavil to which they are ever recurring, that the Lord does not bestow election in recompense of preceding, but bestows it in consideration of future merits. For when it is said that believers were elected that they might be holy, it is at the same time intimated that the holiness which was to be in them has its origin in election. And how can it be consistently said, that things derived from election are the cause of election? The very thing which the Apostle had said, he seems afterwards to confirm by adding, "According to his good pleasure which he hath purposed in himself" (Eph. i. 9); for the expression that God "purposed in himself," is the same as if it had been said, that in forming his decree he considered nothing external to himself; and, accordingly, it is immediately subjoined, that the whole object contemplated in our election is, that "we should be to the praise of his glory." Assuredly divine grace would not deserve all the praise of election, were not election gratuitous; and it would not be gratuitous, did God in electing any individual pay regard to his future works. Hence, what Christ said to his disciples is found to be universally applicable to all believers, "Ye have not chosen me, but I have chosen you" (John xv. 16). Here he not only excludes past merits, but declares that they had nothing in themselves for which they could be chosen, except in so far as his mercy anticipated. And how are we to understand the words of Paul, "Who hath first given to him, and it shall be recompensed unto him again?" (Rom. xi. 35). His meaning obviously is, that men are altogether indebted to the preventing goodness of God, there being nothing in them, either past or future, to conciliate his favour.

4. In the Epistle to the Romans (Rom. ix. 6), in which he again treats this subject more reconditely and at greater length, he declares that "they are not all Israel which are of Israel;" for though all were blessed in respect of hereditary right, yet all did not equally obtain the succession. The whole discussion was occasioned by the pride and vain-glorying of the Jews, who, by claiming the name of the Church for themselves, would have made the faith of the Gospel dependent on their pleasure; just as in the present day the Papists would fain under this pretext substitute themselves in place of God. Paul, while he concedes that in respect of the covenant they were the holy offspring of Abraham, yet contends that the greater part of them were strangers to it, and that not only because they were degenerate, and so had become bastards instead of sons, but because the principal point to be considered was the special election of God, by which alone his adop-

tion was ratified. If the piety of some established them in the hope of salvation, and the revolt of others was the sole cause of their being rejected, it would have been foolish and absurd in Paul to carry his readers back to a secret election. But if the will of God (no cause of which external to him either appears or is to be looked for) distinguishes some from others, so that all the sons of Israel are not true Israelites, it is vain for any one to seek the origin of his condition in himself. He afterwards prosecutes the subject at greater length, by contrasting the cases of Jacob and Esau. Both being sons of Abraham, both having been at the same time in the womb of their mother, there was something very strange in the change by which the honour of the birthright was transferred to Jacob, and yet Paul declares that the change was an attestation to the election of the one and the reprobation of the other.

The question considered is the origin and cause of election. The advocates of foreknowledge insist that it is to be found in the virtues and vices of men. For they take the short and easy method of asserting, that God showed in the person of Jacob, that he elects those who are worthy of his grace; and in the person of Esau, that he rejects those whom he foresees to be unworthy. Such is their confident assertion; but what does Paul say? "For the children being not yet born, neither having done any good or evil, that the purpose of God according to election might stand, not of works, but of him that calleth; it was said unto her [Rebecca], The elder shall serve the younger. As it is written, Jacob have I loved, but Esau have I hated" (Rom. ix. 11—13). If foreknowledge had anything to do with this distinction of the brothers, the mention of time would have been out of place. Granting that Jacob was elected for a worth to be obtained by future virtues, to what end did Paul say that he was not yet born? Nor would there have been any occasion for adding, that as yet he had done no good, because the answer was always ready, that nothing is hid from God, and that therefore the piety of Jacob was present before him. If works procure favour, a value ought to have been put upon them before Jacob was born, just as if he had been of full age. But in explaining the difficulty, the Apostle goes on to show, that the adoption of Jacob proceeded not on works but on the calling of God. In works he makes no mention of past or future, but distinctly opposes them to the calling of God, intimating, that when place is given to the one the other is overthrown; as if he had said, The only thing to be considered is what pleased God, not what men furnished of themselves. Lastly, it is certain that all the causes which men are wont to devise as external to the secret counsel of God, are excluded by the use of the terms *purpose* and *election.*

5. Why should men attempt to darken these statements by assigning some place in election to past or future works? This is altogether to evade what the Apostle contends for—viz. that the distinction between the brothers is not founded on any ground of works, but on

the mere calling of God, inasmuch as it was fixed before the children were born. Had there been any solidity in this subtlety, it would not have escaped the notice of the Apostle, but being perfectly aware that God foresaw no good in man, save that which he had already previously determined to bestow by means of his election, he does not employ a preposterous arrangement which would make good works antecedent to their cause. We learn from the Apostle's words, that the salvation of believers is founded entirely on the decree of divine election, that the privilege is procured not by works but free calling. We have also a specimen of the thing itself set before us. Esau and Jacob are brothers, begotten of the same parents, within the same womb, not yet born. In them all things are equal, and yet the judgment of God with regard to them is different. He adopts the one and rejects the other. The only right of precedence was that of primogeniture; but that is disregarded, and the younger is preferred to the elder. Nay, in the case of others, God seems to have disregarded primogeniture for the express purpose of excluding the flesh from all ground of boasting. Rejecting Ishmael he gives his favour to Isaac, postponing Manasseh he honours Ephraim.

6. Should any one object that these minute and inferior favours do not enable us to decide with regard to the future life, that it is not to be supposed that he who received the honour of primogeniture was thereby adopted to the inheritance of heaven (many objectors do not even spare Paul, but accuse him of having in the quotation of these passages wrested Scripture from its proper meaning); I answer as before, that the Apostle has not erred through inconsideration, or spontaneously misapplied the passages of Scripture; but he saw (what these men cannot be brought to consider) that God purposed under an earthly sign to declare the spiritual election of Jacob, which otherwise lay hidden at his inaccessible tribunal. For unless we refer the primogeniture bestowed upon him to the future world, the form of blessing would be altogether vain and ridiculous, inasmuch as he gained nothing by it but a multitude of toils and annoyances, exile, sharp sorrows, and bitter cares. Therefore, when Paul knew beyond a doubt that by the external, God manifested the spiritual and unfading blessings, which he had prepared for his servant in his kingdom, he hesitated not in proving the latter to draw an argument from the former. For we must remember that the land of Canaan was given in pledge of the heavenly inheritance; and that therefore there cannot be a doubt that Jacob was like the angels ingrafted into the body of Christ, that he might be a partaker of the same life. Jacob therefore is chosen, while Esau is rejected; the predestination of God makes a distinction where none existed in respect of merit. If you ask the reason the Apostle gives it, "For he saith to Moses, I will have mercy on whom I will have mercy, and I will have compassion on whom I will have compassion" (Rom. ix. 15). And what, pray, does this mean? It is just a clear declaration by the Lord that he finds nothing in men themselves to induce him to show kind-

ness, that it is owing entirely to his own mercy, and accordingly that their salvation is his own work. Since God places your salvation in himself alone, why should you descend to yourself? Since he assigns you his own mercy alone, why will you recur to your own merits? Since he confines your thoughts to his own mercy, why do you turn partly to the view of your own works?

We must therefore come to that smaller number whom Paul elsewhere describes as foreknown of God (Rom. xi. 2); not foreknown, as these men imagine, by idle, inactive comtemplation, but in the sense which it often bears. For surely when Peter says that Christ was "delivered by the determinate counsel and foreknowledge of God" (Acts ii. 23), he does not represent God as contemplating merely, but as actually accomplishing our salvation. Thus also Peter, in saying that the believers to whom he writes are elect "according to the foreknowledge of God" (1 Pet. i. 2), properly expresses that secret predestination by which God has sealed those whom he has been pleased to adopt as sons. In using the term *purpose* as synonymous with a term which uniformly denotes what is called a fixed determination, he undoubtedly shows that God, in being the author of our salvation, does not go beyond himself. In this sense he says in the same chapter, that Christ as "a lamb" "was foreordained before the creation of the world" (1 Pet. i. 19, 20). What could have been more frigid or absurd than to have represented God as looking from the height of heaven to see whence the salvation of the human race was to come? By a people foreknown, Peter means the same thing as Paul does by a remnant selected from a multitude falsely assuming the name of God. In another passage, to suppress the vain boasting of those who, while only covered with a mask, claim for themselves in the view of the world a first place among the godly, Paul says, "The Lord knoweth them that are his" (2 Tim. ii. 19). In short, by that term he designates two classes of people, the one consisting of the whole race of Abraham, the other a people separated from that race, and though hidden from human view, yet open to the eye of God. And there is no doubt that he took the passage from Moses, who declares that God would be merciful to whomsoever he pleased (although he was speaking of an elect people whose condition was apparently equal); just as if he had said, that in a common adoption was included a special grace which he bestows on some as a holier treasure, and that there is nothing in the common covenant to prevent this number from being exempted from the common order. God being pleased in this matter to act as a free dispenser and disposer, distinctly declares, that the only ground on which he will show mercy to one rather than to another is his sovereign pleasure; for when mercy is bestowed on him who asks it, though he indeed does not suffer a refusal, he however either anticipates or partly acquires a favour, the whole merit of which God claims for himself.

7. Now, let the supreme Judge and Master decide on the whole case. Seeing such obduracy in his hearers, that his words fell upon

the multitude almost without fruit, he, to remove this stumbling-block, exclaims, "All that the Father giveth me shall come to me." "And this is the Father's will which hath sent me, that of all which he hath given me I should lose nothing" (John vi. 37, 39). Observe that the donation of the Father is the first step in our delivery into the charge and protection of Christ. Some one, perhaps, will here turn round and object, that those only peculiarly belong to the Father who make a voluntary surrender by faith. But the only thing which Christ maintains is, that though the defections of vast multitudes should shake the world, yet the counsel of God would stand firm, more stable than heaven itself, that his election would never fail. The elect are said to have belonged to the Father before he bestowed them on his only begotten Son. It is asked if they were his by nature? Nay, they were aliens, but he makes them his by delivering them. The words of Christ are too clear to be rendered obscure by any of the mists of caviling. "No man can come to me except the Father which hath sent me draw him." "Every man, therefore, that hath heard and learned of the Father cometh unto me" (John vi. 44, 45). Did all promiscuously bend the knee to Christ, election would be common; whereas now in the small number of believers a manifest diversity appears. Accordingly our Saviour, shortly after declaring that the disciples who were given to him were the common property of the Father, adds, "I pray not for the world, but for them which thou hast given me; for they are thine" (John xvii. 9). Hence it is that the whole world no longer belongs to its Creator, except in so far as grace rescues from malediction, divine wrath, and eternal death, some, not many, who would otherwise perish, while he leaves the world to the destruction to which it is doomed. Meanwhile, though Christ interpose as a Mediator, yet he claims the right of electing in common with the Father, "I speak not of you all: I know whom I have chosen" (John xiii. 18). If it is asked whence he hath chosen them, he answers in another passage, "Out of the world;" which he excludes from his prayers when he commits his disciples to the Father (John xv. 19). We must indeed hold, when he affirms that he knows whom he has chosen, first, that some individuals of the human race are denoted; and, secondly, that they are not distinguished by the quality of their virtues, but by a heavenly decree. Hence it follows, that since Christ makes himself the author of election, none excel by their own strength or industry. In elsewhere numbering Judas among the elect, though he was a devil (John vi. 70), he refers only to the apostolical office, which, though a bright manifestation of divine favour (as Paul so often acknowledges it to be in his own person), does not however contain within itself the hope of eternal salvation. Judas, therefore, when he discharged the office of Apostle perfidiously, might have been worse than a devil; but not one of those whom Christ has once ingrafted into his body will he ever permit to perish, for in securing their salvation, he will perform what he has promised; that is, exert a divine power greater than all (John x. 28). For when he says, "Those that thou gavest me I have kept, and none of them is lost but the son of perdition" (John xvii. 12), the expression, though there is a catachresis in it, is not at all ambiguous. The sum is, that God by gratuitous adoption forms those whom he wishes to have for sons; but that the intrinsic cause is in himself, because he is contented with his secret pleasure.

8. But Ambrose, Origen, and Jerome, were of opinion, that God dispenses his grace among men according to the use which he foresees that each will make of it. It may be added, that Augustine also was for some time of this opinion; but after he had made greater progress in the knowledge of Scripture, he not only retracted it as evidently false, but powerfully confuted it (August. Retract. Lib. i. c. 13). Nay, even after the retractation, glancing at the Pelagians who still persisted in that error, he says, "Who does not wonder that the Apostle failed to make this most acute observation? For after stating a most startling proposition concerning those who were not yet born, and afterwards putting the question to himself by way of objection, 'What then? Is there unrighteousness with God?' he had an opportunity of answering, that God foresaw the merits of both, he does not say so, but has recourse to the justice and mercy of God" (August. Epist. 106, ad Sixtum). And in another passage, after excluding all merit before election, he says, "Here, certainly, there is no place for the vain argument of those who defend the foreknowledge of God against the grace of God, and accordingly maintain that we were elected before the foundation of the world, because God foreknew that we would be good, not that he himself would make us good. This is not the language of him who says, 'Ye have not chosen me, but I have chosen you' (John xv. 16). For had he chosen us because he foreknew that we would be good, he would at the same time also have foreknown that we were to choose him" (August. in Joann. viii.; see also what follows to the same effect). Let the testimony of Augustine prevail with those who willingly acquiesce in the authority of the Fathers; although Augustine allows not that he differs from the others,[1] but shows by clear evidence that the difference which the Pelagians invidiously objected to him is unfounded. For he quotes from Ambrose (Lib. de Prædest. Sanct. cap. 19), "Christ calls whom he pities." Again, "Had he pleased, he could have made them devout instead of undevout; but God calls whom he deigns to call, and makes religious whom he will." Were we disposed to frame an entire volume out of Augustine, it were easy to show the reader that I have no occasion to use any other words than his: but I am unwilling to burden him with a prolix statement. But assuming that the fathers did not speak thus, let us attend to the thing itself. A difficult question had been raised—viz. Did God do justly in bestowing his grace on certain individuals? Paul might

1 Latin, "a reliquis;" French, "les autre Docteurs anciens;"—the other ancient Doctors.

have disencumbered himself of this question at once by saying, that God had respect to works. Why does he not do so? Why does he rather continue to use a language which leaves him exposed to the same difficulty? Why, but just because it would not have been right to say it. There was no obliviousness on the part of the Holy Spirit, who was speaking by his mouth. He therefore answers without ambiguity, that God favours his elect, because he is pleased to do so, and shows mercy because he is pleased to do so. For the words, "I will be gracious to whom I will be gracious, and show mercy on whom I will show mercy" (Exod. xxxiii. 19), are the same in effect as if it had been said, God is moved to mercy by no other reason than that he is pleased to show mercy. Augustine's declaration, therefore, remains true. The grace of God does not find, but makes persons fit to be chosen.

9. Nor let us be detained by the subtlety of Thomas, that the foreknowledge of merit is the cause of predestination, not indeed in respect of the predestinating act, but that on our part it may in some sense be so called—namely, in respect of a particular estimate of predestination; as when it is said, that God predestinates man to glory according to his merit, inasmuch as he decreed to bestow upon him the grace by which he merits glory. For while the Lord would have us to see nothing more in election than his mere goodness, for any one to desire to see more is preposterous affectation. But were we to make a trial of subtlety, it would not be difficult to refute the sophistry of Thomas. He maintains that the elect are in a manner predestinated to glory on account of their merits, because God predestines to give them the grace by which they merit glory. What if I should, on the contrary, object that predestination to grace is subservient to election unto life, and follows as its handmaid; that grace is predestined to those to whom the possession of glory was previously assigned, the Lord being pleased to bring his sons by election to justification? For it will hence follow that the predestination to glory is the cause of the predestination to grace, and not the converse. But let us have done with these disputes as superfluous among those who think that there is enough of wisdom for them in the word of God. For it has been truly said by an old ecclesiastical writer, Those who ascribe the election of God to merits, are wise above what they ought to be (Ambros. de Vocat. Gentium, Lib. i. c. 2).

10. Some object that God would be inconsistent with himself, in inviting all without distinction while he elects only a few. Thus, according to them, the universality of the promise destroys the distinction of special grace. Some moderate men speak in this way, not so much for the purpose of suppressing the truth, as to get quit of puzzling questions, and curb excessive curiosity. The intention is laudable, but the design is by no means to be approved, dissimulation being at no time excusable. In those again who display their petulance, we see only a vile cavil or a disgraceful error. The mode in which Scripture reconciles the two things—viz. that by external

preaching all are called to faith and repentance, and that yet the Spirit of faith and repentance is not given to all—I have already explained, and will again shortly repeat. But the point which they assume I deny as false in two respects: for he who threatens that when it shall rain on one city there will be drought in another (Amos iv. 7); and declares in another passage, that there will be a famine of the word (Amos viii. 11), does not lay himself under a fixed obligation to call all equally. And he who, forbidding Paul to preach in Asia, and leading him away from Bithynia, carries him over to Macedonia (Acts xvi. 6), shows that it belongs to him to distribute the treasure in what way he pleases. But it is by Isaiah he more clearly demonstrates how he destines the promises of salvation specially to the elect (Isa. viii. 16); for he declares that his disciples would consist of them only, and not indiscriminately of the whole human race. Whence it is evident that the doctrine of salvation, which is said to be set apart for the sons of the Church only, is abused when it is represented as effectually available to all. For the present let it suffice to observe, that though the word of the gospel is addressed generally to all, yet the gift of faith is rare. Isaiah assigns the cause when he says, that the arm of the Lord is not revealed to all (Isa. liii. 1). Had he said, that the gospel is malignantly and perversely contemned, because many obstinately refuse to hear, there might perhaps be some colour for this universal call. It is not the purpose of the Prophet, however, to extenuate the guilt of men, when he states the source of their blindness to be, that God deigns not to reveal his arm to them; he only reminds us that since faith is a special gift, it is in vain that external doctrine sounds in the ear. But I would fain know from those doctors whether it is mere preaching or faith that makes men sons of God. Certainly when it is said, "As many as received him, to them gave he power to become the sons of God, even to them that believe on his name" (John i. 12), a confused mass is not set before us, but a special order is assigned to believers, who are "born not of blood, nor of the will of the flesh, nor of the will of man, but of God."

But it is said, there is a mutual agreement between faith and the word. That must be wherever there is faith. But it is no new thing for the seed to fall among thorns or in stony places; not only because the majority appear in fact to be rebellious against God, but because all are not gifted with eyes and ears. How, then, can it consistently be said, that God calls while he knows that the called will not come? Let Augustine answer for me: "Would you dispute with me? Wonder with me, and exclaim, O the depth! Let us both agree in dread, lest we perish in error" (August. de Verb. Apost. Serm. xi.). Moreover, if election is, as Paul declares, the parent of faith, I retort the argument, and maintain that faith is not general, since election is special. For it is easily inferred from the series of causes and effects, when Paul says, that the Father "hath blessed us with all spiritual blessings in heavenly places in Christ, according as he hath chosen us in him before the foundation of the world" (Eph. i. 3, 4), that these riches are not common to all, because God has chosen only whom he would. And the reason why in another passage he commends the faith of the elect is, to prevent any one from supposing that he acquires faith of his own nature; since to God alone belongs the glory of freely illuminating those whom he had previously chosen (Tit. i. 1). For it is well said by Bernard, "His friends hear apart when he says to them, Fear not, little flock: to you it is given to know the mysteries of the kingdom. Who are these? Those whom he foreknew and predestinated to be conformed to the image of his Son. He has made known his great and secret counsel. The Lord knoweth them that are his, but that which was known to God was manifested to men; nor, indeed, does he deign to give a participation in this great mystery to any but those whom he foreknew and predestinated to be his own" (Bernard. ad Thomam Præpos. Benerlae. Epist. 107). Shortly after he concludes, "The mercy of the Lord is from everlasting to everlasting upon them that fear him; from everlasting through predestination, to everlasting through glorification: the one knows no beginning, the other no end." But why cite Bernard as a witness, when we hear from the lips of our Master, "Not that any man hath seen the Father, save he which is of God"? (John vi. 46). By these words he intimates that all who are not regenerated by God are amazed at the brightness of his countenance. And, indeed, faith is aptly conjoined with election, provided it hold the second place. This order is clearly expressed by our Saviour in these words, "This is the Father's will which hath sent me, that of all which he hath given me I should lose nothing;" "And this is the will of him that sent me, that every one which seeth the Son, and believeth on him, may have everlasting life" (John vi. 39, 40). If he would have all to be saved, he would appoint his Son their guardian, and would ingraft them all into his body by the sacred bond of faith. It is now clear that faith is a singular pledge of paternal love, treasured up for the sons whom he has adopted. Hence Christ elsewhere says, that the sheep follow the shepherd because they know his voice, but that they will not follow a stranger, because they know not the voice of strangers (John x. 4). But whence that distinction, unless that their ears have been divinely bored? For no man makes himself a sheep, but is formed by heavenly grace. And why does the Lord declare that our salvation will always be sure and certain, but just because it is guarded by the invincible power of God? (John x. 29.) Accordingly, he concludes that unbelievers are not of his sheep (John x. 16). The reason is, because they are not of the number of those who, as the Lord promised by Isaiah, were to be his disciples. Moreover, as the passages which I have quoted imply perseverance, they are also attestations to the inflexible constancy of election.

11. We come now to the reprobate, to whom the Apostle at the same time refers (Rom. ix. 13). For as Jacob, who as yet had

merited nothing by good works, is assumed into favour; so Esau, while as yet unpolluted by any crime, is hated. If we turn our view to works, we do injustice to the Apostle, as if he had failed to see the very thing which is clear to us. Moreover, there is complete proof of his not having seen it, since he expressly insists that when as yet they had done neither good nor evil, the one was elected, the other rejected, in order to prove that the foundation of divine predestination is not in works. Then after starting the objection, Is God unjust? instead of employing what would have been the surest and plainest defence of his justice—viz. that God had recompensed Esau according to his wickedness—he is contented with a different solution—viz. that the reprobate are expressly raised up, in order that the glory of God may thereby be displayed. At last, he concludes that God hath mercy on whom he will have mercy, and whom he will he hardeneth (Rom. ix. 18). You see how he refers both to the mere pleasure of God. Therefore, if we cannot assign any reason for his bestowing mercy on his people, but just that it so pleases him, neither can we have any reason for his reprobating others but his will. When God is said to visit in mercy or harden whom he will, men are reminded that they are not to seek for any cause beyond his will.

CHAPTER XXIII.

REFUTATION OF THE CALUMNIES BY WHICH THIS DOCTRINE IS ALWAYS UNJUSTLY ASSAILED.

This chapter consists of four parts, which refute the principal objections to this doctrine, and the various pleas and exceptions founded on these objections. These are preceded by a refutation of those who hold election but deny reprobation, sec. 1. Then follows, I. A refutation of the first objection to the doctrine of reprobation and election, sec. 2–5. II. An answer to the second objection, sec. 6–9. III A refutation of the third objection. IV. A refutation of the fourth objection; to which is added a useful and necessary caution, sec. 12–14.

Sections.

1. Error of those who deny reprobation. 1. Election opposed to reprobation. 2. Those who deny reprobation presumptuously plead with God, whose counsels even angels adore. 3. They murmur against God when disclosing his counsels by the Apostle. Exception and answer. Passage of Augustine.
2. First objection—viz. that God is unjustly offended with those whom he dooms to destruction without their own desert. First answer, from the consideration of the divine will. The nature of this will, and how to be considered.
3. Second answer. God owes nothing to man. His hatred against those who are corrupted by sin is most just. The reprobate convinced in their own consciences of the just judgment of God.
4. Exception—viz. that the reprobate seem to have been preordained to sin. Answer. Passage of the Apostle vindicated from calumny.
5. Answer, confirmed by the authority of Augustine. Illustration. Passage of Augustine.
6. Objection, that God ought not to impute the sins rendered necessary by his predestination. First answer, by ancient writers. This not valid. Second answer also defective. Third answer, proposed by Valla, well founded.
7. Objection, that God did not decree that Adam should perish by his fall, refuted by a variety of reasons. A noble passage of Augustine.
8. Objection, that the wicked perish by the permission, not by the will of God. Answer. A pious exhortation.
9. Objection and answer.
10. Objection, that, according to the doctrine of predestination, God is a respecter of persons. Answer.
11. Objection, that sinners are to be punished equally, or the justice of God is unequal. Answer. Confirmed by passages of Augustine.
12. Objection, that the doctrine of predestination produces overweening confidence and impiety. Different answers.
13. Another objection, depending on the former. Answer. The doctrine of predestination to be preached, not passed over in silence.
14. How it is to be preached and delivered to the people. Summary of the orthodox doctrine of predestination, from Augustine.

1. THE human mind, when it hears this doctrine, cannot restrain its petulance, but boils and rages as if aroused by the sound of a trumpet. Many professing a desire to defend the Deity from an invidious charge admit the doctrine of election, but deny that any one

is reprobated (Bernard, in Die Ascensionis, Serm. 2). This they do ignorantly and childishly, since there could be no election without its opposite reprobation. God is said to set apart those whom he adopts for salvation. It were most absurd to say, that he admits others fortuitously, or that they by their industry acquire what election alone confers on a few. Those, therefore, whom God passes by he reprobates, and that for no other cause but because he is pleased to exclude them from the inheritance which he predestines to his children. Nor is it possible to tolerate the petulance of men, in refusing to be restrained by the word of God, in regard to his incomprehensible counsel, which even angels adore. We have already been told that hardening is not less under the immediate hand of God than mercy. Paul does not, after the example of those whom I have mentioned, labour anxiously to defend God, by calling in the aid of falsehood; he only reminds us that it is unlawful for the creature to quarrel with its Creator. Then how will those who refuse to admit that any are reprobated by God explain the following words of Christ? "Every plant which my heavenly Father hath not planted shall be rooted up" (Matth. xv. 13). They are plainly told that all whom the heavenly Father has not been pleased to plant as sacred trees in his garden, are doomed and devoted to destruction. If they deny that this is a sign of reprobation, there is nothing, however clear, that can be proved to them. But if they will still murmur, let us in the soberness of faith rest contented with the admonition of Paul, that it can be no ground of complaint that God, "willing to show his wrath, and to make his power known, endured with much long-suffering the vessels of wrath fitted for destruction: and that he might make known the riches of his glory on the vessels of mercy, which he had afore prepared unto glory" (Rom. ix. 22, 23). Let my readers observe that Paul, to cut off all handle for murmuring and detraction, attributes supreme sovereignty to the wrath and power of God; for it were unjust that those profound judgments, which transcend all our powers of discernment, should be subjected to our calculation. It is frivolous in our opponents to reply, that God does not altogether reject those whom in lenity he tolerates, but remains in suspense with regard to them, if peradventure they may repent; as if Paul were representing God as patiently waiting for the conversion of those whom he describes as fitted for destruction. For Augustine, rightly expounding this passage, says, that where power is united to endurance, God does not permit, but rules (August. Cont. Julian., Lib. v. c. 5). They add also, that it is not without cause the vessels of wrath are said to be fitted for destruction, and that God is said to have prepared the vessels of mercy, because in this way the praise of salvation is claimed for God, whereas the blame of perdition is thrown upon those who of their own accord bring it upon themselves. But were I to concede that by the different forms of expression Paul softens the harshness of the former clause, it by no means follows, that he transfers the preparation for destruction to any other cause than the secret counsel of God. This, indeed, is asserted in the preceding context, where God is said to have raised up Pharaoh, and to harden whom he will. Hence it follows, that the hidden counsel of God is the cause of hardening. I at least hold with Augustine, that when God makes sheep out of wolves, he forms them again by the powerful influence of grace, that their hardness may thus be subdued, and that he does not convert the obstinate, because he does not exert that more powerful grace, a grace which he has at command, if he were disposed to use it (August. de Prædest. Sanct., Lib. i. c. 2).

2. These observations would be amply sufficient for the pious and modest, and such as remember that they are men. But because many are the species of blasphemy which these virulent dogs utter against God, we shall, as far as the case admits, give an answer to each. Foolish men raise many grounds of quarrel with God, as if they held him subject to their accusations. First, they ask why God is offended with his creatures, who have not provoked him by any previous offence; for to devote to destruction whomsoever he pleases, more resembles the caprice of a tyrant than the legal sentence of a judge; and, therefore, there is reason to expostulate with God, if at his mere pleasure men are, without any desert of their own, predestinated to eternal death. If at any time thoughts of this kind come into the minds of the pious, they will be sufficiently armed to repress them, by considering how sinful it is to insist on knowing the causes of the divine will, since it is itself, and justly ought to be, the cause of all that exists. For if his will has any cause, there must be something antecedent to it, and to which it is annexed; this it were impious to imagine. The will of God is the supreme rule of righteousness,[1] so that everything which he wills must be held to be righteous by the mere fact of his willing it. Therefore, when it is asked why the Lord did so, we must answer, Because he pleased. But if you proceed farther to ask why he pleased, you ask for something greater and more sublime than the will of God, and nothing such can be found. Let human temerity then be quiet, and cease to inquire after what exists not, lest perhaps it fails to find what does exist. This, I say, will be sufficient to restrain any one who would reverently contemplate the secret things of God. Against the audacity of the wicked, who hesitate not openly to blaspheme, God will sufficiently defend himself by his own righteousness, without our assistance, when depriving their consciences of all means of evasion, he shall hold them under conviction, and make them feel their guilt. We, however, give no countenance to the fiction of absolute power,[2] which, as it is heathenish, so it ought justly to be held in detestation by us. We do not imagine God to be lawless. He is a law to himself; because, as Plato says, men labouring under the influence of concupiscence

[1] This is taken from Auguste Dein Gen. cont. Manich., Lib. i. c. 3.

[2] French, "Toutesfois en parlant ainsi, nous n'approuvons pas la reverie des theologiens Papistes touchant la puissance absolue de Dieu;"—still in speaking thus, we approve not of the reverie of the Popish theologians touching the absolute power of God.

need law; but the will of God is not only free from all vice, but is the supreme standard of perfection, the law of all laws. But we deny that he is bound to give an account of his procedure; and we moreover deny that we are fit of our own ability to give judgment in such a case. Wherefore, when we are tempted to go farther than we ought, let this consideration deter us, Thou shalt be "justified when thou speakest, and be clear when thou judgest" (Ps. li. 4).

3. God may thus quell his enemies by silence. But lest we should allow them with impunity to hold his sacred name in derision, he supplies us with weapons against them from his word. Accordingly, when we are accosted in such terms as these, Why did God from the first predestine some to death, when, as they were not yet in existence, they could not have merited sentence of death? let us by way of reply ask in our turn, What do you imagine that God owes to man, if he is pleased to estimate him by his own nature? As we are all vitiated by sin, we cannot but be hateful to God, and that not from tyrannical cruelty, but the strictest justice. But if all whom the Lord predestines to death are naturally liable to sentence of death, of what injustice, pray, do they complain? Should all the sons of Adam come to dispute and contend with their Creator, because by his eternal providence they were before their birth doomed to perpetual destruction, when God comes to reckon with them, what will they be able to mutter against this defence? If all are taken from a corrupt mass, it is not strange that all are subject to condemnation. Let them not, therefore, charge God with injustice, if by his eternal judgment they are doomed to a death to which they themselves feel that whether they will or not they are drawn spontaneously by their own nature. Hence it appears how perverse is this affectation of murmuring, when of set purpose they suppress the cause of condemnation which they are compelled to recognise in themselves, that they may lay the blame upon God. But though I should confess a hundred times that God is the author (and it is most certain that he is), they do not, however, thereby efface their own guilt, which, engraven on their own consciences, is ever and anon presenting itself to their view.

4. They again object, Were not men predestinated by the ordination of God to that corruption which is now held forth as the cause of condemnation? If so, when they perish in their corruption, they do nothing else than suffer punishment for that calamity, into which, by the predestination of God, Adam fell, and dragged all his posterity headlong with him. Is not he, therefore, unjust in thus cruelly mocking his creatures? I admit that by the will of God all the sons of Adam fell into that state of wretchedness in which they are now involved; and this is just what I said at the first, that we must always return to the mere pleasure of the divine will, the cause of which is hidden in himself. But it does not forthwith follow that God lies open to this charge. For we will answer with Paul in these words, "Nay but, O man, who art thou that repliest against God? Shall the thing formed say to him that formed it, Why hast thou made me

thus? Hath not the potter power over the clay, of the same lump to make one vessel unto honour, and another unto dishonour?" (Rom. ix. 20, 21). They will deny that the justice of God is thus truly defended, and will allege that we seek an evasion, such as those are wont to employ who have no good excuse. For what more seems to be said here than just that the power of God is such as cannot be hindered, so that he can do whatsoever he pleases? But it is far otherwise. For what stronger reason can be given than when we are ordered to reflect who God is? How could he who is the Judge of the world commit any unrighteousness? If it properly belongs to the nature of God to do judgment, he must naturally love justice and abhor injustice. Wherefore, the Apostle did not, as if he had been caught in a difficulty, have recourse to evasion; he only intimated that the procedure of divine justice is too high to be scanned by human measure, or comprehended by the feebleness of human intellect. The Apostle, indeed, confesses that in the divine judgments there is a depth in which all the minds of men must be engulfed if they attempt to penetrate into it. But he also shows how unbecoming it is to reduce the works of God to such a law as that we can presume to condemn them the moment they accord not with our reason. There is a well-known saying of Solomon (which, however, few properly understand), "The great God that formed all things both rewardeth the fool and rewardeth transgressors" (Prov. xxvi. 10). For he is speaking of the greatness of God, whose pleasure it is to inflict punishment on fools and transgressors, though he is not pleased to bestow his Spirit upon them. It is a monstrous infatuation in men to seek to subject that which has no bounds to the little measure of their reason. Paul gives the name of *elect* to the angels who maintained their integrity. If their steadfastness was owing to the good pleasure of God, the revolt of the others proves that they were abandoned.[1] Of this no other cause can be adduced than reprobation, which is hidden in the secret counsel of God.

5. Now, should some Manes or Cœlestinus[2] come forward to arraign Divine Providence (see sec. 8), I say with Paul, that no account of it can be given, because by its magnitude it far surpasses our understanding. Is there anything strange or absurd in this? Would we have the power of God so limited as to be unable to do more than our mind can comprehend? I say with Augustine, that the Lord has created those who, as he certainly foreknew, were to go to destruction, and he did so because he so willed. Why he willed it is not ours to ask, as we cannot comprehend, nor can it become us even to raise a controversy as to the justice of the divine will. Whenever we speak of it, we are speaking of the supreme standard of justice. (See August. Ep. 106). But when justice clearly appears, why

1 French, "Si leur constance et fermeté a eté fondee au bon plaisir de Dieu, la revolte des diables monstre qu'ils n'ont pas eté retenus, mais plustost delaissez;"—if their constancy and firmness was founded on the good pleasure of God, the revolt of the devils shows that they were not restrained, but rather abandoned.

2 The French adds, "ou autre heretique;"—or other heretic.

should we raise any question of injustice? Let us not, therefore, be ashamed to stop their mouths after the example of Paul. Whenever they presume to carp, let us begin to repeat: Who are ye, miserable men, that bring an accusation against God, and bring it because he does not adapt the greatness of his works to your meagre capacity? As if everything must be perverse that is hidden from the flesh. The immensity of the divine judgments is known to you by clear experience. You know that they are called "a great deep" (Ps. xxxvi. 6). Now, look at the narrowness of your own mind, and say whether it can comprehend the decrees of God. Why then should you, by infatuated inquisitiveness, plunge yourselves into an abyss which reason itself tells you will prove your destruction? Why are you not deterred, in some degree at least, by what the Book of Job, as well as the Prophetical books, declare concerning the incomprehensible wisdom and dreadful power of God? If your mind is troubled, decline not to embrace the counsel of Augustine, "You a man expect an answer from me: I also am a man. Wherefore, let us both listen to him who says, 'O man, who art thou?' Believing ignorance is better than presumptuous knowledge. Seek merits; you will find nought but punishment. O the height! Peter denies, a thief believes. O the height! Do you ask the reason? I will tremble at the height. Reason you, I will wonder; dispute you, I will believe. I see the height; I cannot sound the depth. Paul found rest, because he found wonder. He calls the judgments of God 'unsearchable;' and have you come to search them? He says that his ways are 'past finding out,' and do you seek to find them out?" (August. de Verb. Apost. Serm. 20). We shall gain nothing by proceeding farther. For neither will the Lord satisfy the petulance of these men, nor does he need any other defence than that which he used by his Spirit, who spoke by the mouth of Paul. We unlearn the art of speaking well when we cease to speak with God.

6. Impiety starts another objection, which however seeks not so much to criminate God as to excuse the sinner; though he who is condemned by God as a sinner cannot ultimately be acquitted without impugning the judge. This, then, is the scoffing language which profane tongues employ. Why should God blame men for things the necessity of which he has imposed by his own predestination? What could they do? Could they struggle with his decrees? It were in vain for them to do it, since they could not possibly succeed. It is not just, therefore, to punish them for things the principal cause of which is in the predestination of God. Here I will abstain from a defence to which ecclesiastical writers usually recur, that there is nothing in the prescience of God to prevent him from regarding man as a sinner, since the evils which he foresees are man's, not his. This would not stop the caviller, who would still insist that God might, if he had pleased, have prevented the evils which he foresaw, and not having done so, must with determinate counsel have created man for the very purpose of so acting on the earth. But if by the providence

of God man was created, on the condition of afterwards doing whatever he does, then that which he cannot escape, and which he is constrained by the will of God to do, cannot be charged upon him as a crime. Let us, therefore, see what is the proper method of solving the difficulty. First, all must admit what Solomon says, "The Lord hath made all things for himself; yea, even the wicked for the day of evil" (Prov. xvi. 4). Now, since the arrangement of all things is in the hand of God, since to him belongs the disposal of life and death, he arranges all things by his sovereign counsel, in such a way that individuals are born, who are doomed from the womb to certain death, and are to glorify him by their destruction. If any one alleges that no necessity is laid upon them by the providence of God, but rather that they are created by him in that condition, because he foresaw their future depravity, he says something, but does not say enough. Ancient writers, indeed, occasionally employ this solution, though with some degree of hesitation. The Schoolmen, again, rest in it as if it could not be gainsayed. I, for my part, am willing to admit, that mere prescience lays no necessity on the creatures; though some do not assent to this, but hold that it is itself the cause of things. But Valla, though otherwise not greatly skilled in sacred matters, seems to me to have taken a shrewder and more acute view, when he shows that the dispute is superfluous, since life and death are acts of the divine will rather than of prescience. If God merely foresaw human events, and did not also arrange and dispose of them at his pleasure, there might be room for agitating the question, how far his foreknowledge amounts to necessity; but since he foresees the things which are to happen, simply because he has decreed that they are so to happen, it is vain to debate about prescience, while it is clear that all events take place by his sovereign appointment.

7. They deny that it is ever said in distinct terms, God decreed that Adam should perish by his revolt.[1] As if the same God, who is declared in Scripture to do whatsoever he pleases, could have made the noblest of his creatures without any special purpose. They say that, in accordance with free-will, he was to be the architect of his own fortune, that God had decreed nothing but to treat him according to his desert. If this frigid fiction is received, where will be the omnipotence of God, by which, according to his secret counsel on which everything depends, he rules over all? But whether they will allow it or not, predestination is manifest in Adam's posterity. It was not owing to nature that they all lost salvation by the fault of one parent. Why should they refuse to admit with regard to one man that which against their will they admit with regard to the whole human race? Why should they in cavilling lose their labour? Scripture proclaims that all were, in the person of one, made liable to eternal death. As this cannot be ascribed to nature, it is plain that it is owing to the wonderful counsel of God. It is very absurd

1 See Calvin, De Prædestinatione.

in these worthy defenders of the justice of God to strain at a gnat and swallow a camel. I again ask how it is that the fall of Adam involves so many nations with their infant children in eternal death without remedy, unless that it so seemed meet to God? Here the most loquacious tongues must be dumb. The decree, I admit, is dreadful; and yet it is impossible to deny that God foreknew what the end of man was to be before he made him, and foreknew, because he had so ordained by his decree. Should any one here inveigh against the prescience of God, he does it rashly and unadvisedly. For why, pray, should it be made a charge against the heavenly Judge, that he was not ignorant of what was to happen? Thus, if there is any just or plausible complaint, it must be directed against predestination. Nor ought it to seem absurd when I say, that God not only foresaw the fall of the first man, and in him the ruin of his posterity; but also at his own pleasure arranged it. For as it belongs to his wisdom to foreknow all future events, so it belongs to his power to rule and govern them by his hand. This question, like others, is skilfully explained by Augustine: "Let us confess with the greatest benefit, what we believe with the greatest truth, that the God and Lord of all things, who made all things very good, both foreknew that evil was to arise out of good, and knew that it belonged to his most omnipotent goodness to bring good out of evil, rather than not permit evil to be, and so ordained the life of angels and men as to show in it, first, what free-will could do; and, secondly, what the benefit of his grace and his righteous judgment could do" (August. Enchir. ad Laurent.).

8. Here they recur to the distinction between will and permission, the object being to prove that the wicked perish only by the permission, but not by the will of God. But why do we say that he permits, but just because he wills? Nor, indeed, is there any probability in the thing itself—viz. that man brought death upon himself, merely by the permission, and not by the ordination of God; as if God had not determined what he wished the condition of the chief of his creatures to be. I will not hesitate, therefore, simply to confess with Augustine that the will of God is necessity, and that everything is necessary which he has willed; just as those things will certainly happen which he has foreseen (August. de Gen. ad Lit., Lib. vi. cap. 15). Now, if in excuse of themselves and the ungodly, either the Pelagians, or Manichees, or Anabaptists, or Epicureans (for it is with these four sects we have to discuss this matter), should object the necessity by which they are constrained, in consequence of the divine predestination, they do nothing that is relevant to the cause. For if predestination is nothing else than a dispensation of divine justice, secret indeed, but unblameable, because it is certain that those predestinated to that condition were not unworthy of it, it is equally certain, that the destruction consequent upon predestination is also most just. Moreover, though their perdition depends on the predestination of God, the cause and matter of it is in themselves. The

first man fell because the Lord deemed it meet that he should: why he deemed it meet, we know not. It is certain, however, that it was just, because he saw that his own glory would thereby be displayed. When you hear the glory of God mentioned, understand that his justice is included. For that which deserves praise must be just. Man therefore falls, divine providence so ordaining, but he falls by his own fault. The Lord had a little before declared that all the things which he had made were very good (Gen. i. 31). Whence then the depravity of man, which made him revolt from God? Lest it should be supposed that it was from his creation, God had expressly approved what proceeded from himself. Therefore, man's own wickedness corrupted the pure nature which he had received from God, and his ruin brought with it the destruction of all his posterity. Wherefore, let us in the corruption of human nature contemplate the evident cause of condemnation (a cause which comes more closely home to us), rather than inquire into a cause hidden and almost incomprehensible in the predestination of God. Nor let us decline to submit our judgment to the boundless wisdom of God, so far as to confess its insufficiency to comprehend many of his secrets. Ignorance of things which we are not able, or which it is not lawful to know, is learning, while the desire to know them is a species of madness.

9. Some one, perhaps, will say, that I have not yet stated enough to refute this blasphemous excuse. I confess that it is impossible to prevent impiety from murmuring and objecting; but I think I have said enough, not only to remove the ground, but also the pretext for throwing blame upon God. The reprobate would excuse their sins by alleging that they are unable to escape the necessity of sinning, especially because a necessity of this nature is laid upon them by the ordination of God. We deny that they can thus be validly excused, since the ordination of God, by which they complain that they are doomed to destruction, is consistent with equity,—an equity, indeed, unknown to us, but most certain. Hence we conclude, that every evil which they bear is inflicted by the most just judgment of God. Next we have shown that they act preposterously when, in seeking the origin of their condemnation, they turn their view to the hidden recesses of the divine counsel, and wink at the corruption of nature, which is the true source. They cannot impute this corruption to God, because he bears testimony to the goodness of his creation. For though, by the eternal providence of God, man was formed for the calamity under which he lies, he took the matter of it from himself, not from God, since the only cause of his destruction was his degenerating from the purity of his creation into a state of vice and impurity.

10. There is a third absurdity by which the adversaries of predestination defame it. As we ascribe it entirely to the counsel of the divine will, that those whom God adopts as the heirs of his kingdom are exempted from universal destruction, they infer that he is an accepter of persons; but this Scripture uniformly denies: and, therefore, Scripture is either at variance with itself, or respect is had to

merit in election. First, the sense in which Scripture declares that God is not an acceptor of persons, is different from that which they suppose: since the term *person* means not *man*, but those things which, when conspicuous in a man, either procure favour, grace, and dignity, or, on the contrary, produce hatred, contempt, and disgrace. Among these are, on the one hand, riches, wealth, power, rank, office, country, beauty, &c.; and, on the other hand, poverty, want, mean birth, sordidness, contempt, and the like. Thus Peter and Paul say, that the Lord is no accepter of persons, because he makes no distinction between the Jew and the Greek; does not make the mere circumstance of country the ground for rejecting one or embracing the other (Acts x. 34; Rom. ii. 10; Gal. iii. 28). Thus James also uses the same words, when he would declare that God has no respect to riches in his judgment (James ii. 5). Paul also says in another passage, that in judging God has no respect to slavery or freedom (Eph. vi. 9; Col. iii. 25). There is nothing inconsistent with this when we say, that God, according to the good pleasure of his will, without any regard to merit, elects those whom he chooses for sons, while he rejects and reprobates others. For fuller satisfaction the matter may be thus explained (see August. Epist. 115, et ad Bonif., Lib. ii. cap. 7). It is asked, how it happens that of two, between whom there is no difference of merit, God in his election adopts the one, and passes by the other? I, in my turn, ask, Is there anything in him who is adopted to incline to God towards him? If it must be confessed that there is nothing, it will follow, that God looks not to the man, but is influenced entirely by his own goodness to do him good. Therefore, when God elects one and rejects another, it is owing not to any respect to the individual, but entirely to his own mercy, which is free to display and exert itself when and where he pleases. For we have elsewhere seen, that in order to humble the pride of the flesh, "not many wise men after the flesh, not many mighty, not many noble, are called" (1 Cor. i. 26); so far is God in the exercise of his favour from showing any respect to persons.

11. Wherefore, it is false and most wicked to charge God with dispensing justice unequally, because in this predestination he does not observe the same course towards all. If (say they) he finds all guilty, let him punish all alike: if he finds them innocent, let him relieve all from the severity of judgment. But they plead with God as if he were either interdicted from showing mercy, or were obliged, if he show mercy, entirely to renounce judgment. What is it that they demand? That if all are guilty, all shall receive the same punishment. We admit that the guilt is common, but we say, that God in mercy succours some. Let him (they say) succour all. We object, that it is right for him to show by punishing that he is a just judge. When they cannot tolerate this, what else are they attempting than to deprive God of the power of showing mercy; or, at least, to allow it to him only on the condition of altogether renouncing judgment? Here the words of Augustine most admirably apply:

"Since in the first man the whole human race fell under condemnation, those vessels which are made of it unto honour, are not vessels of self-righteousness, but of divine mercy. When other vessels are made unto dishonour, it must be imputed not to injustice, but to judgment" (August. Epist. 106, De Prædest. et Gratia; De Bono Persever., cap. 12). Since God inflicts due punishment on those whom he reprobates, and bestows unmerited favour on those whom he calls, he is free from every accusation; just as it belongs to the creditor to forgive the debt to one, and exact it of another. The Lord therefore may show favour to whom he will, because he is merciful; not show it to all, because he is a just judge. In giving to some what they do not merit, he shows his free favour; in not giving to all, he declares what all deserve. For when Paul says, "God hath concluded them all in unbelief, that he might have mercy upon all" it ought also to be added, that he is debtor to none; for "who hath first given to him, and it shall be recompensed unto him again?" (Rom. xi. 32, 35.)

12. Another argument which they employ to overthrow predestination is, that if it stand, all care and study of well-doing must cease. For what man can hear (say they) that life and death are fixed by an eternal and immutable decree of God, without immediately concluding that it is of no consequence how he acts, since no work of his can either hinder or further the predestination of God? Thus all will rush on, and like desperate men plunge headlong wherever lust inclines. And it is true that this is not altogether a fiction; for there are multitudes of a swinish nature who defile the doctrine of predestination by their profane blasphemies, and employ them as a cloak to evade all admonition and censure. "God knows what he has determined to do with regard to us: if he has decreed our salvation, he will bring us to it in his own time; if he has doomed us to death, it is vain for us to fight against it." But Scripture, while it enjoins us to think of this high mystery with much greater reverence and religion, gives very different instruction to the pious, and justly condemns the accursed licence of the ungodly. For it does not remind us of predestination to increase our audacity, and tempt us to pry with impious presumption into the inscrutable counsels of God, but rather to humble and abase us, that we may tremble at his judgment, and learn to look up to his mercy. This is the mark at which believers will aim. The grunt of these filthy swine is duly silenced by Paul. They say that they feel secure in vice, because, if they are of the number of the elect, their vices will be no obstacle to the ultimate attainment of life. But Paul reminds us that the end for which we are elected is, "that we should be holy, and without blame before him" (Eph. i. 4). If the end of election is holiness of life, it ought to arouse and stimulate us strenuously to aspire to it, instead of serving as a pretext for sloth. How wide the difference between the two things, between ceasing from well-doing because election is sufficient for salvation, and its being the very end of election, that we

should devote ourselves to the study of good works. Have done, then, with blasphemies which wickedly invert the whole order of election. When they extend their blasphemies farther, and say that he who is reprobated by God will lose his pains if he studies to approve himself to him by innocence and probity of life, they are convicted of the most impudent falsehood. For whence can any such study arise but from election? As all who are of the number of the reprobate are vessels formed unto dishonour, so they cease not by their perpetual crimes to provoke the anger of God against them, and give evident signs of the judgment which God has already passed upon them; so far is it from being true that they vainly contend against it.

13. Another impudent and malicious calumny against this doctrine is, that it destroys all exhortations to a pious life. The great odium to which Augustine was at one time subjected on this head he wiped away in his treatise De Correptione et Gratia, to Valentinus, a perusal of which will easily satisfy the pious and docile. Here, however, I may touch on a few points, which will, I hope, be sufficient for those who are honest and not contentious. We have already seen how plainly and audibly Paul preaches the doctrine of free election: is he, therefore, cold in admonishing and exhorting? Let those good zealots compare his vehemence with theirs, and they will find that they are ice, while he is all fervour. And surely every doubt on this subject should be removed by the principles which he lays down, that God hath not called us to uncleanness; that every one should possess his vessel in honour; that we are the workmanship of God, "created in Christ Jesus unto good works, which God hath before ordained that we should walk in them" (1 Thess iv. 4, 7; Eph. ii. 10). In one word, those who have any tolerable acquaintance with the writings of Paul will understand, without a long demonstration, how well he reconciles the two things which those men pretend to be contradictory to each other. Christ commands us to believe in him, and yet there is nothing false or contrary to this command in the statement which he afterwards makes: "No man can come unto me, except it were given him of my Father" (John vi. 65). Let preaching then have its free course, that it may lead men to faith, and dispose them to persevere with uninterrupted progress. Nor, at the same time, let there be any obstacle to the knowledge of predestination, so that those who obey may not plume themselves on anything of their own, but glory only in the Lord. It is not without cause our Saviour says, "Who hath ears to hear, let him hear" (Matth. xiii. 9). Therefore, while we exhort and preach, those who have ears willingly obey: in those, again, who have no ears is fulfilled what is written: "Hear ye indeed, but understand not" (Isaiah vi. 9). "But why (says Augustine) have some ears, and others not? Who hath known the mind of the Lord? Are we, therefore, to deny what is plain because we cannot comprehend what is hid?" This is a faithful quotation from Augustine; but because his words will perhaps have more

authority than mine, let us adduce the following passage from his treatise, De Bono Persever., cap. 15.

"Should some on hearing this turn to indolence and sloth, and, leaving off all exertion, rush headlong into lust, are we therefore to suppose that what has been said of the foreknowledge of God is not true? If God foreknew that they would be good, will they not be good, however great their present wickedness? and if God foreknew that they would be wicked, will they not be wicked, how great soever the goodness now seen in them? For reasons of this description, must the truth which has been stated on the subject of divine foreknowledge be denied or not mentioned? and more especially when, if it is not stated, other errors will arise?" In the sixteenth chapter he says, "The reason for not mentioning the truth is one thing, the necessity for telling the truth is another. It were tedious to inquire into all the reasons for silence. One however is, lest those who understand not become worse, while we are desirous to make those who understand better informed. Now, such persons, when we say anything of this kind, do not indeed become better informed, but neither do they become worse. But when the truth is of such a nature, that he who cannot comprehend it becomes worse by our telling it, and he who can comprehend it becomes worse by our not telling it, what think ye ought we to do? Are we not to tell the truth, that he who can comprehend may comprehend, rather than not tell it, and thereby not only prevent both from comprehending, but also make the more intelligent of the two to become worse, whereas if he heard and comprehended others might learn through him? And we are unwilling to say what, on the testimony of Scripture, it is lawful to say. For we fear lest, when we speak, he who cannot comprehend may be offended; but we have no fear lest, while we are silent, he who can comprehend the truth be involved in falsehood." In chapter twentieth, glancing again at the same view, he more clearly confirms it. "Wherefore, if the apostles and teachers of the Church who came after them did both; if they discoursed piously of the eternal election of God, and at the same time kept believers under the discipline of a pious life, how can those men of our day, when shut up by the invincible force of truth, think they are right in saying, that what is said of predestination, though it is true, must not be preached to the people? Nay, it ought indeed to be preached, that whoso hath ears to hear may hear. And who hath ears if he hath not received them from him who has promised to give them? Certainly, let him who receives not, reject. Let him who receives, take and drink, drink and live. For as piety is to be preached, that God may be duly worshipped; so predestination also is to be preached, that he who hath ears to hear may, in regard to divine grace, glory not in himself, but in God."

14. And yet as that holy man had a singular desire to edify, he so regulates his method of teaching as carefully, and as far as in him lay, to avoid giving offence. For he reminds us, that those things

which are truly should also be fitly spoken. Were any one to address the people thus: If you do not believe, the reason is, because God has already doomed you to destruction: he would not only encourage sloth, but also give countenance to wickedness. Were any one to give utterance to the sentiment in the future tense, and say, that those who hear will not believe because they are reprobates, it were imprecation rather than doctrine. Wherefore, Augustine not undeservedly orders such, as senseless teachers or sinister and ill-omened prophets, to retire from the Church. He, indeed, elsewhere truly contends that "a man profits by correction only when He who causes those whom He pleases to profit without correction, pities and assists. But why is it thus with some, and differently with others? Far be it from us to say that it belongs to the clay and not to the potter to decide." He afterwards says, "When men by correction either come or return to the way of righteousness, who is it that works salvation in their hearts but he who gives the increase, whoever it be that plants and waters? When he is pleased to save, there is no free-will in man to resist. Wherefore, it cannot be doubted that the will of God (who hath done whatever he hath pleased in heaven and in earth, and who has even done things which are to be) cannot be resisted by the human will, or prevented from doing what he pleases, since with the very wills of men he does so." Again, "When he would bring men to himself, does he bind them with corporeal fetters? He acts inwardly, inwardly holds, inwardly moves their hearts, and draws them by the wills which he has wrought in them." What he immediately adds must not be omitted: "Because we know not who belongs to the number of the predestinated, or does not belong, our desire ought to be that all may be saved; and hence every person we meet, we will desire to be with us a partaker of peace. But our peace will rest upon the sons of peace. Wherefore, on our part, let correction be used as a harsh yet salutary medicine for all, that they may neither perish, nor destroy others. To God it will belong to make it available to those whom he has foreknown and predestinated."

CHAPTER XXIV.

ELECTION CONFIRMED BY THE CALLING OF GOD. THE REPROBATE BRING UPON THEMSELVES THE RIGHTEOUS DESTRUCTION TO WHICH THEY ARE DOOMED.

The title of this chapter shows that it consists of two parts,—I. The case of the Elect, from sec. 1–11. II. The case of the Reprobate, from sec. 12–17.

Sections.

1. The election of God is secret, but is manifested by effectual calling. The nature of this effectual calling. How election and effectual calling are founded on the free mercy of God. A cavil of certain expositors refuted by the words of Augustine. An exception disposed of.
2. Calling proved to be free, 1. By its nature and the mode in which it is dispensed. 2. By the word of God. 3. By the calling of Abraham, the father of the faithful. 4. By the testimony of John. 5. By the example of those who have been called.
3. The pure doctrine of the calling of the elect misunderstood, 1. By those who attribute too much to the human will. 2. By those who make election dependent on faith. This error amply refuted.
4. In this and the five following sections the certainty of election vindicated from the assaults of Satan. The leading arguments are: 1. Effectual calling. 2. Christ apprehended by faith. 3. The protection of Christ, the guardian of the elect. We must not attempt to penetrate to the hidden recesses of the divine wisdom, in order to learn what is decreed with regard to us at the judgment-seat. We must begin and end with the call of God. This confirmed by an apposite saying of Bernard.
5. Christ the foundation of this calling and election. He who does not lean on him alone cannot be certain of his election. He is the faithful interpreter of the eternal counsel in regard to our salvation.
6. Another security of our election is the protection of Christ our Shepherd. How it is manifested to us. Objection 1. As to the future state. 2. As to perseverance. Both objections refuted.
7. Objection, that those who seem elected sometimes fall away. Answer. A passage of Paul dissuading us from security explained. The kind of fear required in the elect.
8. Explanation of the saying, that many are called, but few chosen. A twofold call.
9. Explanation of the passage, that none is lost but the son of perdition. Refutation of an objection to the certainty of election.
10. Explanation of the passages urged against the certainty of election. Examples by which some attempt to prove that the seed of election is sown in the hearts of the elect from their very birth. Answer 1. One or two examples do not make the rule. 2. This view opposed to Scripture. 3. Is expressly opposed by an apostle.
11. An explanation and confirmation of the third answer.
12. Second part of the chapter, which treats of the reprobate. Some of them God deprives of the opportunity of hearing his word. Others he blinds and stupifies the more by the preaching of it.
13. Of this no other account can be given than that the reprobate are vessels fitted for destruction. This confirmed by the case of the elect; of Pharaoh and of the Jewish people both before and after the manifestation of Christ.
14. Question, Why does God blind the reprobate? Two answers. These confirmed by different passages of Scripture. Objection of the reprobate. Answer.
15. Objection to this doctrine of the righteous rejection of the reprobate. The first founded on a passage in Ezekiel. The passage explained.
16. A second objection founded on a passage in Paul. The apostle's meaning explained. A third objection and fourth objection answered.

17. A fifth objection—viz. that there seems to be a twofold will in God. Answer. Other objections and answers. Conclusion.

1. But that the subject may be more fully illustrated, we must treat both of the calling of the elect, and of the blinding and hardening of the ungodly. The former I have already in some measure discussed (chap. xxii. sec. 10, 11), when refuting the error of those who think that the general terms in which the promises are made place the whole human race on a level. The special election which otherwise would remain hidden in God, he at length manifests by his calling. "For whom he did foreknow, he also did predestinate to be conformed to the image of his Son." Moreover, "whom he did predestinate, them he also called; and whom he called, them he also justified," that he may one day glorify (Rom. viii. 29, 30). Though the Lord, by electing his people, adopted them as his sons, we however see that they do not come into possession of this great good until they are called; but when called, the enjoyment of their election is in some measure communicated to them. For which reason the Spirit which they receive is termed by Paul both the "Spirit of adoption," and the "seal" and "earnest" of the future inheritance; because by his testimony he confirms and seals the certainty of future adoption on their hearts. For although the preaching of the gospel springs from the fountain of election, yet being common to them with the reprobate, it would not be in itself a solid proof. God, however, teaches his elect effectually when he brings them to faith, as we formerly quoted from the words of our Saviour, "Not that any man hath seen the Father, save he which is of God, he hath seen the Father" (John vi. 46). Again, "I have manifested thy name unto the men which thou gavest me out of the world" (John xvii. 6). He says in another passage, "No man can come to me except the Father which hath sent me draw him" (John vi. 44). This passage Augustine ably expounds in these words: "If (as Truth says) every one who has learned cometh, then every one who does not come has not learned. It does not therefore follow, that he who can come does come, unless he have willed and done it; but every one who hath learned of the Father, not only can come, but also comes; the antecedence of possibility,[1] the affection of will, and the effect of action being now present" (August. de Grat. Chr. Cont. Pelag., Lib. i. c. 14, 31). In another passage, he says still more clearly, "What means, Every one that hath heard and learned of the Father cometh unto me, but just that there is no one who hears and learns of the Father that does not come to me? For if every one who has heard and learned, comes; assuredly every one who does not come, has neither heard nor learned of the Father; for if he had heard and learned, he would come. Far removed from carnal sense is this school in which the Father is heard and teaches us to come to the Son" (August. de Prædes. Sanct. c. 8). Shortly after, he says, "This grace, which is secretly imparted to the hearts of men, is not

1 Latin, "possibilitatis profectus."—French, "l'avancement de possibilité.

received by any hard heart; for the reason for which it is given is, that the hardness of the heart may first be taken away. Hence, when the Father is heard within, he takes away the stony heart, and gives a heart of flesh. Thus he makes them sons of promise and vessels of mercy, which he has prepared for glory. Why then does he not teach all to come to Christ, but just because all whom he teaches he teaches in mercy, while those whom he teaches not he teaches not in judgment? for he pities whom he will, and hardens whom he will." Those, therefore, whom God has chosen he adopts as sons, while he becomes to them a Father. By calling, moreover, he admits them to his family, and unites them to himself, that they may be one with him. When calling is thus added to election, the Scripture plainly intimates that nothing is to be looked for in it but the free mercy of God. For if we ask whom it is he calls, and for what reason, he answers, it is those whom he had chosen. When we come to election, mercy alone everywhere appears; and, accordingly, in this the saying of Paul is truly realised, "So then, it is not of him that willeth, nor of him that runneth, but of God that showeth mercy" (Rom. ix. 16); and that not as is commonly understood by those who share the result between the grace of God and the will and agency of man. For their exposition is, that the desire and endeavour of sinners are of no avail by themselves, unless accompanied by the grace of God, but that when aided by his blessing, they also do their part in procuring salvation. This cavil I prefer refuting in the words of Augustine rather than my own: "If all that the apostle meant is, that it is not alone of him that willeth, or of him that runneth, unless the Lord be present in mercy, we may retort and hold the converse, that it is not of mercy alone, unless willing and running be present" (August. Enchir. ad Laurent. c. 31). But if this is manifestly impious, let us have no doubt that the apostle attributes all to the mercy of the Lord, and leaves nothing to our wills or exertions. Such were the sentiments of that holy man. I set not the value of a straw on the subtlety to which they have recourse—viz. that Paul would not have spoken thus had there not been some will and effort on our part. For he considered not what might be in man; but seeing that certain persons ascribed a part of salvation to the industry of man, he simply condemned their error in the former clause, and then claimed the whole substance of salvation for the divine mercy. And what else do the prophets than perpetually proclaim the free calling of God?

2. Moreover, this is clearly demonstrated by the nature and dispensation of calling, which consists not merely of the preaching of the word, but also of the illumination of the Spirit. Who those are to whom God offers his word is explained by the prophet, "I am sought of them that asked not for me: I am found of them that sought me not: I said, Behold me, behold me, unto a nation that was not called by my name" (Isaiah lxv. 1). And lest the Jews

should think that that mercy applied only to the Gentiles, he calls to their remembrance whence it was he took their father Abraham when he condescended to be his friend (Isaiah xxiv. 3)—namely, from the midst of idolatry, in which he was plunged with all his people. When he first shines with the light of his word on the undeserving, he gives a sufficiently clear proof of his free goodness. Here, therefore, boundless goodness is displayed, but not so as to bring all to salvation, since a heavier judgment awaits the reprobate for rejecting the evidence of his love. God also, to display his own glory, withholds from them the effectual agency of his Spirit. Therefore, this inward calling is an infallible pledge of salvation. Hence the words of John, "Hereby we know that he abideth in us by the Spirit which he hath given us" (1 John iii. 24). And lest the flesh should glory, in at least responding to him, when he calls and spontaneously offers himself, he affirms that there would be no ears to hear, no eyes to see, did not he give them. And he acts not according to the gratitude of each, but according to his election. Of this you have a striking example in Luke, when the Jews and Gentiles in common heard the discourse of Paul and Barnabas. Though they were all instructed in the same word, it is said, that "as many as were ordained to eternal life believed" (Acts xiii. 48). How can we deny that calling is gratuitous, when election alone reigns in it even to its conclusion?

3. Two errors are here to be avoided. Some make man a fellow-worker with God in such a sense, that man's suffrage ratifies election, so that, according to them, the will of man is superior to the counsel of God. As if Scripture taught that only the power of being able to believe is given us, and not rather faith itself. Others, although they do not so much impair the grace of the Holy Spirit, yet, induced by what means I know not, make election dependent on faith, as if it were doubtful and ineffectual till confirmed by faith. There can be no doubt, indeed, that in regard to us it is so confirmed. Moreover, we have already seen, that the secret counsel of God, which lay concealed, is thus brought to light, by this nothing more being understood than that that which was unknown is proved, and as it were sealed. But it is false to say that election is then only effectual after we have embraced the gospel, and that it thence derives its vigour. It is true that we must there look for its certainty, because, if we attempt to penetrate to the secret ordination of God, we shall be engulfed in that profound abyss. But when the Lord hath manifested it to us, we must ascend higher in order that the effect may not bury the cause. For what can be more absurd and unbecoming, than while Scripture teaches that we are illuminated as God has chosen us, our eyes should be so dazzled with the brightness of this light, as to refuse to attend to election? Meanwhile, I deny not that, in order to be assured of our salvation, we must begin with the word, and that our confidence ought to go no farther than the word when we invoke God the Father. For some, to obtain more certainty of the counsel of God (which is nigh us in our mouth, and in our hearts, Deut. xxx.

14), absurdly desire to fly above the clouds. We must, therefore, curb that temerity by the soberness of faith, and be satisfied to have God as the witness of his hidden grace in the external word; provided always that the channel in which the water flows, and out of which we may freely drink, does not prevent us from paying due honour to the fountain.

4. Therefore, as those are in error who make the power of election dependent on the faith by which we perceive that we are elected, so we shall follow the best order, if, in seeking the certainty of our election, we cleave to those posterior signs which are sure attestations to it. Among the temptations with which Satan assaults believers, none is greater or more perilous, than when disquieting them with doubts as to their election, he at the same time stimulates them with a depraved desire of inquiring after it out of the proper way. (See Luther in Genes. cap. xxvi.) By inquiring out of the proper way, I mean when puny man endeavours to penetrate to the hidden recesses of the divine wisdom, and goes back even to the remotest eternity, in order that he may understand what final determination God has made with regard to him. In this way he plunges headlong into an immense abyss, involves himself in numberless inextricable snares, and buries himself in the thickest darkness. For it is right that the stupidity of the human mind should be punished with fearful destruction, whenever it attempts to rise in its own strength to the height of divine wisdom. And this temptation is the more fatal, that it is the temptation to which of all others almost all of us are most prone. For there is scarcely a mind in which the thought does not sometimes rise, Whence your salvation but from the election of God? But what proof have you of your election? When once this thought has taken possession of any individual, it keeps him perpetually miserable, subjects him to dire torment, or throws him into a state of complete stupor. I cannot wish a stronger proof of the depraved ideas, which men of this description form of predestination, than experience itself furnishes, since the mind cannot be infected by a more pestilential error than that which disturbs the conscience, and deprives it of peace and tranquillity in regard to God. Therefore, as we dread shipwreck, we must avoid this rock, which is fatal to every one who strikes upon it. And though the discussion of predestination is regarded as a perilous sea, yet in sailing over it the navigation is calm and safe, nay, pleasant, provided we do not voluntarily court danger. For as a fatal abyss engulfs those who, to be assured of their election, pry into the eternal counsel of God without the word, yet those who investigate it rightly, and in the order in which it is exhibited in the word, reap from it rich fruits of consolation.

Let our method of inquiry then be, to begin with the calling of God and to end with it. Although there is nothing in this to prevent believers from feeling that the blessings which they daily receive from the hand of God originate in that secret adoption, as they themselves express it in Isaiah, "Thou hast done wonderful things; thy counsels of old are faithfulness and truth" (Isa. xxv. 1). For with this as a pledge, God is pleased to assure us of as much of his counsel as can be lawfully known. But lest any should think that testimony weak, let us consider what clearness and certainty it gives us. On this subject there is an apposite passage in Bernard. After speaking of the reprobate, he says, "The purpose of God stands, the sentence of peace on those that fear him also stands, a sentence concealing their bad and recompensing their good qualities; so that, in a wondrous manner, not only their good but their bad qualities work together for good. Who will lay anything to the charge of God's elect? It is completely sufficient for my justification to have him propitious against whom only I have sinned. Everything which he has decreed not to impute to me, is as if it had never been." A little after he says, "O the place of true rest, a place which I consider not unworthy of the name of inner-chamber, where God is seen, not as if disturbed with anger, or distracted by care, but where his will is proved to be good, and acceptable, and perfect. That vision does not terrify but soothe, does not excite restless curiosity but calms it, does not fatigue but tranquillises the senses. Here is true rest. A tranquil God traquillises all things; and to see him at rest, is to be at rest" (Bernard, super Cantic. Serm. xiv.).

5. First, if we seek for the paternal mercy and favour of God, we must turn our eyes to Christ, in whom alone the Father is well pleased (Matth. iii. 17). When we seek for salvation, life, and a blessed immortality, to him also must we betake ourselves, since he alone is the fountain of life, and the anchor of salvation, and the heir of the kingdom of heaven. Then what is the end of election, but just that, being adopted as sons by the heavenly Father, we may by his favour obtain salvation and immortality? How much soever you may speculate and discuss, you will perceive that in its ultimate object it goes no farther. Hence, those whom God has adopted as sons, he is said to have elected, not in themselves, but in Christ Jesus (Eph. i. 4); because he could love them only in him, and only as being previously made partakers with him, honour them with the inheritance of his kingdom. But if we are elected in him, we cannot find the certainty of our election in ourselves; and not even in God the Father, if we look at him apart from the Son. Christ, then, is the mirror in which we ought, and in which, without deception, we may contemplate our election. For since it is into his body that the Father has decreed to ingraft those whom from eternity he wished to be his, that he may regard as sons all whom he acknowledges to be his members, if we are in communion with Christ, we have proof sufficiently clear and strong that we are written in the Book of Life. Moreover, he admitted us to sure communion with himself, when, by the preaching of the gospel, he declared that he was given us by the Father, to be ours with all his blessings (Rom. viii. 32). We are said to be clothed with him, to be one with him, that we may live, because he himself lives. The doctrine is often repeated, "God so

loved the world, that he gave his only begotten Son, that whosoever believeth in him should not perish, but have everlasting life" (John iii. 16). He who believes in him is said to have passed from death unto life (John v. 24). In this sense he calls himself the *bread of life*, of which if a man eat, he shall never die (John vi. 35). He, I say, was our witness, that all by whom he is received in faith will be regarded by our heavenly Father as sons. If we long for more than to be regarded as sons of God and heirs, we must ascend above Christ. But if this is our final goal, how infatuated is it to seek out of him what we have already obtained in him, and can only find in him? Besides, as he is the Eternal Wisdom, the Immutable Truth, the Determinate Counsel of the Father, there is no room for fear that anything which he tells us will vary in the minutest degree from that will of the Father after which we inquire. Nay, rather he faithfully discloses it to us as it was from the beginning, and always will be. The practical influence of this doctrine ought also to be exhibited in our prayers. For though a belief of our election animates us to invoke God, yet when we frame our prayers, it were preposterous to obtrude it upon God, or to stipulate in this way, "O Lord, if I am elected, hear me." He would have us to rest satisfied with his promises, and not to inquire elsewhere whether or not he is disposed to hear us. We shall thus be disentangled from many snares, if we know how to make a right use of what is rightly written; but let us not inconsiderately wrest it to purposes different from that to which it ought to be confined.

6. Another confirmation tending to establish our confidence is, that our election is connected with our calling. For those whom Christ enlightens with the knowledge of his name, and admits into the bosom of his Church, he is said to take under his guardianship and protection. All whom he thus receives are said to be committed and intrusted to him by the Father, that they may be kept unto life eternal. What would we have? Christ proclaims aloud that all whom the Father is pleased to save he hath delivered into his protection (John vi. 37–39; xvii. 6, 12). Therefore, if we would know whether God cares for our salvation, let us ask whether he has committed us to Christ, whom he has appointed to be the only Saviour of all his people. Then, if we doubt whether we are received into the protection of Christ, he obviates the doubt when he spontaneously offers himself as our Shepherd, and declares that we are of the number of his sheep if we hear his voice (John x. 3, 16). Let us, therefore, embrace Christ, who is kindly offered to us, and comes forth to meet us: he will number us among his flock, and keep us within his fold. But anxiety arises as to our future state.[1] For as Paul teaches, that those are called who were previously elected, so our

[1] French, "Mas quelcun dira qu'il nous faut soucier de ce qui peut nous advenir: et quand nous pensons au temps futur que nostre imbecilité nous admoneste d'etre en solicitude;"—But some one will say, that we must feel anxious as to what may happen to us; and that when we think on the future, our weakness warns us to be solicitous.

Saviour shows that many are called, but few chosen (Matth. xxii. 14). Nay, even Paul himself dissuades us from security, when he says, "Let him that thinketh he standeth take heed lest he fall" (1 Cor. x. 12). And again, "Well, because of unbelief they were broken off, and thou standest by faith. Be not high-minded, but fear: for if God spared not the natural branches, take heed lest he also spare not thee" (Rom. xi. 20, 21). In fine, we are sufficiently taught by experience itself, that calling and faith are of little value without perseverance, which, however, is not the gift of all. But Christ has freed us from anxiety on this head; for the following promises undoubtedly have respect to the future: "All that the Father giveth me shall come to me, and him that cometh to me I will in no wise cast out." Again, "This is the will of him that sent me, that of all which he hath given me I should lose nothing; but should raise it up at the last day" (John vi. 37, 39). Again, "My sheep hear my voice, and I know them, and they follow me: and I give unto them eternal life, and they shall never perish, neither shall any man pluck them out of my hand. My Father which gave them me is greater than all: and no man is able to pluck them out of my Father's hand" (John x. 27, 28). Again, when he declares, "Every plant which my heavenly Father hath not planted shall be rooted up" (Matth. xv. 13), he intimates conversely that those who have their root in God can never be deprived of their salvation. Agreeable to this are the words of John, "If they had been of us, they would no doubt have continued with us" (1 John ii. 19). Hence, also, the magnificent triumph of Paul over life and death, things present, and things to come (Rom. viii. 38). This must be founded on the gift of perseverance. There is no doubt that he employs the sentiment as applicable to all the elect. Paul elsewhere says, "Being confident of this very thing, that he who hath begun a good work in you will perform it until the day of Jesus Christ" (Phil. i. 6). David, also, when his faith threatened to fail, leant on this support, "Forsake not the works of thy hands." Moreover, it cannot be doubted, that since Christ prays for all the elect, he asks the same thing for them as he asked for Peter—viz. that their faith fail not (Luke xxii. 32). Hence we infer, that there is no danger of their falling away, since the Son of God, who asks that their piety may prove constant, never meets with a refusal. What then did our Saviour intend to teach us by this prayer, but just to confide, that whenever we are his our eternal salvation is secure?

7. But it daily happens that those who seemed to belong to Christ revolt from him and fall away: Nay, in the very passage where he declares that none of those whom the Father hath given to him have perished, he excepts the son of perdition. This, indeed, is true; but it is equally true that such persons never adhered to Christ with that heartfelt confidence by which I say that the certainty of our election is established: "They went out from us," says John, "but they were not of us; for if they had been of us, they would, no doubt, have con-

tinued with us" (1 John ii. 19). I deny not that they have signs of calling similar to those given to the elect; but I do not at all admit that they have that sure confirmation of election which I desire believers to seek from the word of the gospel. Wherefore, let not examples of this kind move us away from tranquil confidence in the promise of the Lord, when he declares that all by whom he is received in true faith have been given him by the Father, and that none of them, while he is their Guardian and Shepherd, will perish (John iii. 16; vi. 39). Of Judas we shall shortly speak (sec. 9). Paul does not dissuade Christians from security simply, but from careless, carnal security, which is accompanied with pride, arrogance, and contempt of others, which extinguishes humility and reverence for God, and produces a forgetfulness of grace received (Rom. xi. 20). For he is addressing the Gentiles, and showing them that they ought not to exult proudly and cruelly over the Jews, in consequence of whose rejection they had been substituted in their stead. He also enjoins fear, not a fear under which they may waver in alarm, but a fear which, teaching us to receive the grace of God in humility, does not impair our confidence in it, as has elsewhere been said. We may add, that he is not speaking to individuals, but to sects in general (see 1 Cor. x. 12). The Church having been divided into two parties, and rivalship producing dissension, Paul reminds the Gentiles that their having been substituted in the place of a peculiar and holy people was a reason for modesty and fear. For there were many vain-glorious persons among them, whose empty boasting it was expedient to repress. But we have elsewhere seen, that our hope extends into the future, even beyond death, and that nothing is more contrary to its nature than to be in doubt as to our future destiny.

8. The expression of our Saviour, "Many are called, but few are chosen" (Matth. xxii. 14), is also very improperly interpreted (see Book III. chap. ii. sec. 11, 12). There will be no ambiguity in it if we attend to what our former remarks ought to have made clear—viz. that there are two species of calling;—for there is a universal call, by which God, through the external preaching of the word, invites all men alike, even those for whom he designs the call to be a savour of death, and the ground of a severer condemnation. Besides this there is a special call which, for the most part, God bestows on believers only, when by the internal illumination of the Spirit he causes the word preached to take deep root in their hearts. Sometimes, however, he communicates it also to those whom he enlightens only for a time, and whom afterwards, in just punishment for their ingratitude, he abandons and smites with greater blindness. Now, our Lord seeing that the Gospel was published far and wide, was despised by multitudes, and justly valued by few, describes God under the character of a King, who, preparing a great feast, sends his servants all around to invite a great multitude, but can only obtain the presence of a very few, because almost all allege causes of excuse; at length, in consequence of their refusal, he is obliged to send his

servants out into the highways to invite every one they meet. It is perfectly clear, that thus far the parable is to be understood of external calling. He afterwards adds, that God acts the part of a kind entertainer, who goes round his table and affably receives his guests; but still if he finds any one not adorned with the nuptial garment, he will by no means allow him to insult the festivity by his sordid dress. I admit that this branch of the parable is to be understood of those who, by a profession of faith, enter the Church, but are not at all invested with the sanctification of Christ. Such disgraces to his Church, such cankers God will not always tolerate, but will cast them forth as their turpitude deserves. Few, then, out of the great number of called are chosen; the calling, however, not being of that kind which enables believers to judge of their election. The former call is common to the wicked, the latter brings with it the spirit of regeneration, which is the earnest and seal of the future inheritance by which our hearts are sealed unto the day of the Lord (Eph. i. 13, 14). In one word, while hypocrites pretend to piety, just as if they were true worshippers of God, Christ declares that they will ultimately be ejected from the place which they improperly occupy, as it is said in the psalm, "Lord, who shall abide in thy tabernacle? who shall dwell in thy holy hill? He that walketh uprightly, and worketh righteousness, and speaketh the truth in his heart" (Psalm xv. 1. 2). Again, in another passage, "This is the generation of them that seek him, that seek thy face, O Jacob" (Psalm xxiv. 6). And thus the Spirit exhorts believers to patience, and not to murmur because Ishmaelites are mingled with them in the Church, since the mask will at length be torn off, and they will be ejected with disgrace.

9. The same account is to be given of the passage lately quoted, in which Christ says, that none is lost but the son of perdition (John xvii. 12). The expression is not strictly proper; but it is by no means obscure: for Judas was not numbered among the sheep of Christ, because he was one truly, but because he held a place among them. Then, in another passage, where the Lord says, that he was elected with the apostles, reference is made only to the office, "Have I not chosen you twelve," says he, "and one of you is a devil?" (John vi. 70). That is, he had chosen him to the office of apostle. But when he speaks of election to salvation, he altogether excludes him from the number of the elect, "I speak not of you all: I know whom I have chosen" (John xiii. 18). Should any one confound the term *election* in the two passages, he will miserably entangle himself; whereas if he distinguish between them, nothing can be plainer. Gregory, therefore, is most grievously and perniciously in error, when he says that we are conscious only of our calling, but are uncertain of our election; and hence he exhorts all to fear and trembling, giving this as the reason, that though we know what we are to-day, yet we know not what we are to be (Gregor. Hom. 38). But in that passage he clearly shows how he stumbled on that stone. By suspending election on the merit of works, he had too good a

reason for dispiriting the minds of his readers, while, at the same time, as he did not lead them away from themselves to confidence in the divine goodness, he was unable to confirm them. Hence believers may in some measure perceive the truth of what we said at the outset—viz. predestination duly considered does not shake faith, but rather affords the best confirmation of it. I deny not, however, that the Spirit sometimes accommodates his language to our feeble capacity; as when he says, "They shall not be in the assembly of my people, neither shall they be written in the writing of the house of Israel" (Ezek. xiii. 9). As if God were beginning to write the names of those whom he counts among his people in the Book of Life; whereas we know, even on the testimony of Christ, that the names of the children of God were written in the Book of Life from the beginning (Luke x. 20). The words simply indicate the abandonment of those who seemed to have a chief place among the elect, as is said in the psalm, "Let them be blotted out of the Book of the Living, and not be written with the righteous" (Psalm lxix. 28).

10. For the elect are brought by calling into the fold of Christ, not from the very womb, nor all at the same time, but according as God sees it meet to dispense his grace. Before they are gathered to the supreme Shepherd they wander dispersed in a common desert, and in no respect differ from others, except that by the special mercy of God they are kept from rushing to final destruction. Therefore, if you look to themselves, you will see the offspring of Adam giving token of the common corruption of the mass. That they proceed not to extreme and desperate impiety is not owing to any innate goodness in them, but because the eye of God watches for their safety, and his hand is stretched over them. Those who dream of some seed of election implanted in their hearts from their birth, by the agency of which they are ever inclined to piety and the fear of God, are not supported by the authority of Scripture, but refuted by experience. They, indeed, produce a few examples to prove that the elect before they were enlightened were not aliens from religion; for instance, that Paul led an unblemished life during his Pharisaism, that Cornelius was accepted for his prayers and alms, and so forth (Phil. iii. 5; Acts x. 2). The case of Paul we admit, but we hold that they are in error as to Cornelius; for it appears that he was already enlightened and regenerated, so that all which he wanted was a clear revelation of the Gospel. But what are they to extract from these few examples? Is it that all the elect were always endued with the spirit of piety? Just as well might any one, after pointing to the integrity of Aristides, Socrates, Xenocrates, Scipio, Curius, Camillus, and others (see Book II. c. iv. sec. 4), infer that all who are left in the blindness of idolatry are studious of virtue and holiness. Nay, even Scripture is plainly opposed to them in more passages than one. The description which Paul gives of the state of the Ephesians before regeneration shows not one grain of this seed. His words are, "You hath he quickened, who were dead in trespasses and sins; wherein

in time past ye walked according to the course of this world, according to the prince of the power of the air, the spirit that now worketh in the children of disobedience: among whom also we all had our conversation in times past in the lusts of our flesh, fulfilling the desires of the flesh and of the mind; and were by nature the children of wrath, even as others" (Eph. ii. 1—3). And again, "At that time ye were without Christ," "having no hope, and without God in the world" (Eph. ii. 12). Again, "Ye were sometimes darkness, but now are ye light in the Lord: walk as children of light" (Eph. v. 8). But perhaps they will insist that in this last passage reference is made to that ignorance of the true God, in which they deny not that the elect lived before they were called. Though this is grossly inconsistent with the Apostle's inference, that they were no longer to lie or steal (Eph. iv. 28). What answer will they give to other passages; such as that in which, after declaring to the Corinthians that "neither fornicators, nor idolaters, nor adulterers, nor effeminate, nor abusers of themselves with mankind, nor thieves, nor covetous, nor drunkards, nor revilers, nor extortioners, shall inherit the kingdom of God," he immediately adds, "Such were some of you: but ye are washed, but be are sanctified, but ye are justified in the name of the Lord Jesus, and by the Spirit of our God"? (1 Cor. vi. 9—11.) Again, he says to the Romans, "As ye have yielded your members servants to uncleanness and to iniquity unto iniquity; even so now yield your members servants to righteousness unto holiness. For when ye were the servants of sin, ye were free from righteousness. What fruit had ye then in those things whereof ye are now ashamed?" (Rom. vi. 19—21.)

11. Say, then, what seed of election germinated in those who, contaminated in various ways during their whole lives, indulged as with desperate wickedness in every kind of abomination? Had Paul meant to express this view, he ought to have shown how much they then owed to the kindness of God, by which they had been preserved from falling into such pollution. Thus, too, Peter ought to have exhorted his countrymen to gratitude for a perpetual seed of election. On the contrary, his admonition is, "The time past of our life may suffice us to have wrought the will of the Gentiles" (1 Pet. iv. 3). What if we come to examples? Was there any germ of righteousness in Rahab the harlot before she believed? (Josh. ii. 4); in Manasseh when Jerusalem was dyed and almost deluged with the blood of the prophets? (2 Kings xxiii. 16); in the thief who only with his last breath thought of repentance? (Luke xxiii. 42.) Have done, then, with those arguments which curious men of themselves rashly devise without any authority from Scripture. But let us hold fast what Scripture states—viz. that "All we like sheep have gone astray, we have turned every one to his own way" (Isa. liii. 6); that is, to perdition. In this gulf of perdition God leaves those whom he has determined one day to deliver until his own time arrive; he only preserves them from plunging into irremediable blasphemy.

12. As the Lord by the efficacy of his calling accomplishes towards his elect the salvation to which he had by his eternal counsel destined them, so he has judgments against the reprobate, by which he executes his counsel concerning them. Those, therefore, whom he has created for dishonour during life and destruction at death, that they may be vessels of wrath and examples of severity, in bringing to their doom, he at one time deprives of the means of hearing his word, at another by the preaching of it blinds and stupifies them the more. The examples of the former case are innumerable, but let us select one of the most remarkable of all. Before the advent of Christ, about four thousand years passed away, during which he hid the light of saving doctrine from all nations. If any one answer, that he did not put them in possession of the great blessing, because he judged them unworthy, then their posterity will be in no respect more worthy. Of this in addition to experience, Malachi is a sufficient witness; for while charging them with mixed unbelief and blasphemy, he yet declares that the Redeemer will come. Why then is he given to the latter rather than to the former? They will in vain torment themselves in seeking for a deeper cause than the secret and inscrutable counsel of God. And there is no occasion to fear lest some disciple of Porphyry with impunity arraign the justice of God, while we say nothing in its defence. For while we maintain that none perish without deserving it, and that it is owing to the free goodness of God that some are delivered, enough has been said for the display of his glory; there is not the least occasion for our cavilling. The Supreme Disposer then makes way for his own predestination, when depriving those whom he has reprobated of the communication of his light, he leaves them in blindness. Every day furnishes instances of the latter case, and many of them are set before us in Scripture. Among a hundred to whom the same discourse is delivered, twenty, perhaps, receive it with the prompt obedience of faith; the others set no value upon it, or deride, or spurn, or abominate it. If it is said that this diversity is owing to the malice and perversity of the latter, the answer is not satisfactory: for the same wickedness would possess the minds of the former, did not God in his goodness correct it. And hence we will always be entangled until we call in the aid of Paul's question, "Who maketh thee to differ?" (1 Cor. iv. 7), intimating that some excel others, not by their own virtue, but by the mere favour of God.

13. Why, then, while bestowing grace on the one, does he pass by the other? In regard to the former, Luke gives the reason, Because they "were ordained to eternal life" (Acts xiii. 48). What, then, shall we think of the latter, but that they are vessels of wrath unto dishonour? Wherefore, let us not decline to say with Augustine, "God could change the will of the wicked into good, because he is omnipotent. Clearly he could. Why, then, does he not do it? Because he is unwilling. Why he is unwilling remains with himself" (August. de Genes. ad Lit. Lib. ii.). We should not attempt to be

wise above what is meet, and it is much better to take Augustine's explanation, than to quibble with Chrysostom, "that he draws him who is willing, and stretching forth his hand" (Chrysost. Hom. de Convers. Pauli), lest the difference should seem to lie in the judgment of God, and not in the mere will of man. So far is it, indeed, from being placed in the mere will of man, that we may add, that even the pious, and those who fear God, need this special inspiration of the Spirit. Lydia, a seller of purple, feared God, and yet it was necessary that her heart should be opened, that she might attend to the doctrine of Paul, and profit in it (Acts xvi. 14). This was not said of one woman only, but to teach us that all progress in piety is the secret work of the Spirit. Nor can it be questioned, that God sends his word to many whose blindness he is pleased to aggravate. For why does he order so many messages to be taken to Pharaoh? Was it because he hoped that he might be softened by the repetition? Nay, before he began he both knew and had foretold the result: "The Lord said unto Moses, When thou goest to return into Egypt, see that thou do all those wonders before Pharaoh, which I have put in thine hand: but I will harden his heart, that he will not let the people go" (Exod iv. 21). So when he raises up Ezekiel, he forewarns him, "I send thee to the children of Israel, to a rebellious nation that hath rebelled against me." "Be not afraid of their words." "Thou dwellest in the midst of a rebellious house, which hath eyes to see, and see not; they have ears to hear, and hear not" (Ezek. ii. 3, 6; xii. 2). Thus he foretells to Jeremiah that the effect of his doctrine would be, "to root out, and pull down, and to destroy" (Jer. i. 10). But the prophecy of Isaiah presses still more closely; for he is thus commissioned by the Lord, "Go and tell this people, Hear ye indeed, but understand not, and see ye indeed, but perceive not. Make the heart of this people fat, and make their ears heavy, and shut their eyes; lest they see with their eyes, and hear with their ears, and understand with their heart, and convert and be healed" (Isa. vi. 9, 10). Here he directs his voice to them, but it is that they may turn a deafer ear; he kindles a light, but it is that they may become more blind; he produces a doctrine, but it is that they may be more stupid; he employs a remedy, but it is that they may not be cured. And John, referring to this prophecy, declares that the Jews could not believe the doctrine of Christ, because this curse from God lay upon them. It is also incontrovertible, that to those whom God is not pleased to illumine, he delivers his doctrine wrapt up in enigmas, so that they may not profit by it, but be given over to greater blindness. Hence our Saviour declares that the parables in which he had spoken to the multitude he expounded to the Apostles only, "because it is given unto you to know the mysteries of the kingdom of heaven, but to them it is not given" (Matth. xiii. 11). What, you will ask, does our Lord mean, by teaching those by whom he is careful not to be understood? Consider where the fault lies, and then cease to ask. How obscure soever the word may be, there is always sufficient light in it to convince the consciences of the ungodly.

14. It now remains to see why the Lord acts in the manner in which it is plain that he does. If the answer be given, that it is because men deserve this by their impiety, wickedness, and ingratitude, it is indeed well and truly said; but still, because it does not yet appear what the cause of the difference is, why some are turned to obedience, and others remain obdurate, we must, in discussing it, pass to the passage from Moses, on which Paul has commented—namely, "Even for this same purpose have I raised thee up, that I might show my power in thee, and that my name might be declared throughout all the earth" (Rom. ix. 17). The refusal of the reprobate to obey the word of God when manifested to them, will be properly ascribed to the malice and depravity of their hearts, provided it be at the same time added, that they were adjudged to this depravity, because they were raised up by the just but inscrutable judgment of God, to show forth his glory by their condemnation. In like manner, when it is said of the sons of Eli, that they would not listen to salutary admonitions, "because the Lord would slay them" (1 Sam. ii. 25), it is not denied that their stubbornness was the result of their own iniquity; but it is at the same time stated why they were left to their stubbornness, when the Lord might have softened their hearts—namely, because his immutable decree had once for all doomed them to destruction. Hence the words of John, "Though he had done so many miracles before them, yet they believed not on him; that the saying of Esaias the prophet might be fulfilled which he spake, Lord, who hath believed our report?" (John xii. 37, 38); for though he does not exculpate their perverseness, he is satisfied with the reason that the grace of God is insipid to men, until the Holy Spirit gives it its savour. And Christ, in quoting the prophecy of Isaiah, "They shall be all taught of God" (John vi. 45), designs only to show that the Jews were reprobates and aliens from the Church, because they would not be taught: and gives no other reason than that the promise of God does not belong to them. Confirmatory of this are the words of Paul, "Christ crucified" was "unto the Jews a stumbling-block, and unto the Greeks foolishness; but unto them which are called, both Jews and Greeks, Christ the power of God, and the wisdom of God" (1 Cor. i. 23). For after mentioning the usual result wherever the Gospel is preached, that it exasperates some, and is despised by others, he says, that it is precious to them only who are called. A little before he had given them the name of believers, but he was unwilling to refuse the proper rank to divine grace, which precedes faith; or rather, he added the second term by way of correction, that those who had embraced the Gospel might ascribe the merit of their faith to the calling of God. Thus, also, he shortly after shows that they were elected by God. When the wicked hear these things, they complain that God abuses his inordinate power, to make cruel sport with the miseries of his creatures. But let us, who

know that all men are liable on so many grounds to the judgment of God, that they cannot answer for one in a thousand of their transgressions (Job ix. 3), confess that the reprobate suffer nothing which is not accordant with the most perfect justice. When unable clearly to ascertain the reason, let us not decline to be somewhat in ignorance in regard to the depths of the divine wisdom.

15. But since an objection is often founded on a few passages of Scripture, in which God seems to deny that the wicked perish through his ordination, except in so far as they spontaneously bring death upon themselves in opposition to his warning, let us briefly explain these passages, and demonstrate that they are not adverse to the above view. One of the passages adduced is, "Have I any pleasure at all that the wicked should die? saith the Lord God; and not that he should return from his ways and live?" (Ezek. xviii. 23.) If we are to extend this to the whole human race, why are not the very many whose minds might be more easily bent to obey urged to repentance, rather than those who by his invitations become daily more and more hardened? Our Lord declares that the preaching of the gospel and miracles would have produced more fruit among the people of Nineveh and Sodom than in Judea (Matth. xiii. 23). How comes it, then, that if God would have all to be saved, he does not open a door of repentance for the wretched, who would more readily have received grace? Hence we may see that the passage is violently wrested, if the will of God, which the prophet mentions, is opposed to his eternal counsel, by which he separated the elect from the reprobate.[1] Now, if the genuine meaning of the prophet is inquired into, it will be found that he only means to give the hope of pardon to them who repent. The sum is, that God is undoubtedly ready to pardon whenever the sinner turns. Therefore, he does not will his death, in so far as he wills repentance. But experience shows that this will, for the repentance of those whom he invites to himself, is not such as to make him touch all their hearts. Still, it cannot be said that he acts deceitfully; for though the external word only renders those who hear it, and do not obey it, inexcusable, it is still truly regarded as an evidence of the grace by which he reconciles men to himself. Let us therefore hold the doctrine of the prophet, that God has no pleasure in the death of the sinner: that the godly may feel confident that whenever they repent God is ready to pardon them; and that the wicked may feel that their guilt is doubled, when they respond not to the great mercy and condescension of God. The mercy of God, therefore, will ever be ready to meet the penitent; but all the prophets, and apostles, and Ezekiel himself, clearly tell us who they are to whom repentance is given.

16. The second passage adduced is that in which Paul says that "God will have all men to be saved" (1 Tim. ii. 4). Though the reason here differs from the former, they have somewhat in common.

[1] Bernard, in his Sermon on the Nativity, on 2 Cor. i. 3, quoting the two passages, Rom. ix. 18, and Ezek. xviii. 32, admirably reconciles them.

I answer, first, That the mode in which God thus wills is plain from the context; for Paul connects two things, a will to be saved, and to come to the knowledge of the truth. If by this they will have it to be fixed by the eternal counsel of God that they are to receive the doctrine of salvation, what is meant by Moses in these words, "What nation is there so great, who hath God so nigh unto them?" (Deut. iv. 7.) How comes it that many nations are deprived of that light of the Gospel which others enjoy? How comes it that the pure knowledge of the doctrine of godliness has never reached some, and others have scarcely tasted some obscure rudiments of it? It will now be easy to extract the purport of Paul's statement. He had commanded Timothy that prayers should be regularly offered up in the church for kings and princes; but as it seemed somewhat absurd that prayer should be offered up for a class of men who were almost hopeless (all of them being not only aliens from the body of Christ, but doing their utmost to overthrow his kingdom), he adds, that it was acceptable to God, who will have all men to be saved. By this he assuredly means nothing more than that the way of salvation was not shut against any order of men; that, on the contrary, he had manifested his mercy in such a way, that he would have none debarred from it. Other passages do not declare what God has, in his secret judgment, determined with regard to all, but declare that pardon is prepared for all sinners who only turn to seek after it. For if they persist in urging the words, "God hath concluded all in unbelief, that he might have mercy upon all" (Rom. xi. 32), I will, on the contrary, urge what is elsewhere written, "Our God is in the heavens: he hath done whatsoever he hath pleased" (Ps. cxv. 3). We must, therefore, expound the passage so as to reconcile it with another, I "will be gracious to whom I will be gracious, and will show mercy on whom I will show mercy" (Exod. xxxiii. 19). He who selects those whom he is to visit in mercy does not impart it to all. But since it clearly appears that he is there speaking not of individuals, but of orders of men, let us have done with a longer discussion. At the same time, we ought to observe, that Paul does not assert what God does always, everywhere, and in all circumstances, but leaves it free to him to make kings and magistrates partakers of heavenly doctrine, though in their blindness they rage against it. A stronger objection seems to be founded on the passage in Peter; the Lord is "not willing that any should perish, but that all should come to repentance" (2 Pet. iii. 9). But the solution of the difficulty is to be found in the second branch of the sentence, for his will that they should come to repentance cannot be used in any other sense than that which is uniformly employed. Conversion is undoubtedly in the hand of God, whether he designs to convert all can be learned from himself, when he promises that he will give some a heart of flesh, and leave to others a heart of stone (Ezek. xxxvi. 26). It is true, that if he were not disposed to receive those who implore his mercy, it could not have been said, "Turn ye unto me, saith the Lord of Hosts, and I will turn unto you, saith the

Lord of Hosts" (Zech. i. 3); but I hold that no man approaches God unless previously influenced from above. And if repentance were placed at the will of man, Paul would not say, "If God peradventure will give them repentance" (2 Tim. ii. 25). Nay, did not God at the very time when he is verbally exhorting all to repentance, influence the elect by the secret movement of his Spirit, Jeremiah would not say, "Turn thou me, and I shall be turned; for thou art the Lord my God. Surely after that I was turned, I repented" (Jer. xxxi. 18).

17. But if it is so (you will say), little faith can be put in the Gospel promises, which, in testifying concerning the will of God, declare that he wills what is contrary to his inviolable decree. Not at all; for however universal the promises of salvation may be, there is no discrepancy between them and the predestination of the reprobate, provided we attend to their effect. We know that the promises are effectual only when we receive them in faith, but, on the contrary, when faith is made void, the promise is of no effect. If this is the nature of the promises, let us now see whether there be any inconsistency between the two things—viz. that God, by an eternal decree, fixed the number of those whom he is pleased to embrace in love, and on whom he is pleased to display his wrath, and that he offers salvation indiscriminately to all. I hold that they are perfectly consistent, for all that is meant by the promise is, just that his mercy is offered to all who desire and implore it, and this none do, save those whom he has enlightened. Moreover, he enlightens those whom he has predestinated to salvation. Thus the truth of the promises remains firm and unshaken, so that it cannot be said there is any disagreement between the eternal election of God and the testimony of his grace which he offers to believers. But why does he mention all men? Namely, that the consciences of the righteous may rest the more secure when they understand that there is no difference between sinners, provided they have faith, and that the ungodly may not be able to allege that they have not an asylum to which they may betake themselves from the bondage of sin, while they ungratefully reject the offer which is made to them. Therefore, since by the Gospel the mercy of God is offered to both, it is faith, in other words, the illumination of God, which distinguishes between the righteous and the wicked; the former feeling the efficacy of the Gospel, the latter obtaining no benefit from it. Illumination itself has eternal election for its rule.

Another passage quoted is the lamentation of our Saviour, "O Jerusalem, Jerusalem, how often would I have gathered thy children together, even as a hen gathereth her chickens under her wings, and ye would not!" (Matth. xxiii. 37); but it gives them no support. I admit that here Christ speaks not only in the character of man, but upbraids them with having, in every age, rejected his grace. But this will of God, of which we speak, must be defined. For it is well known what exertions the Lord made to retain that people, and how perversely, from the highest to the lowest, they followed their own wayward desires, and refused to be gathered together. But it does not follow that by the wickedness of men the counsel of God was frustrated. They object that nothing is less accordant with the nature of God than that he should have a double will. This I concede, provided they are sound interpreters. But why do they not attend to the many passages in which God clothes himself with human affections, and descends beneath his proper majesty?[1] He says, "I have spread out my hands all the day unto a rebellious people" (Isa. lxv. 1), exerting himself early and late to bring them back. Were they to apply these qualities without regarding the figure, many unnecessary disputes would arise which are quashed by the simple solution, that what is human is here transferred to God. Indeed, the solution which we have given elsewhere (see Book I. c. xviii. sec. 3; and Book III. c. xx. sec. 43) is amply sufficient—viz. that though to our apprehension the will of God is manifold, yet he does not in himself will opposites, but, according to his manifold wisdom (so Paul styles it, Eph. iii. 10), transcends our senses, until such time as it shall be given us to know how he mysteriously wills what now seems to be adverse to his will. They also amuse themselves with the cavil, that since God is the Father of all, it is unjust to discard any one before he has by his misconduct merited such a punishment. As if the kindness of God did not extend even to dogs and swine. But if we confine our view to the human race, let them tell why God selected one people for himself and became their father, and why, from that one people, he plucked only a small number as if they were the flower. But those who thus charge God are so blinded by their love of evil speaking, that they consider not that as God "maketh his sun to rise on the evil and on the good" (Matth. v. 45), so the inheritance is treasured up for a few to whom it shall one day be said, "Come, ye blessed of my Father, inherit the kingdom," &c. (Matth. xxv. 34). They object, moreover, that God does not hate any of the things which he has made. This I concede, but it does not affect the doctrine which I maintain, that the reprobate are hateful to God, and that with perfect justice, since those destitute of his Spirit cannot produce anything that does not deserve cursing. They add, that there is no distinction of Jew and Gentile, and that, therefore, the grace of God is held forth to all indiscriminately; true, provided they admit (as Paul declares) that God calls as well Jews as Gentiles, according to his good pleasure, without being astricted to any. This disposes of their gloss upon another passage, "God hath concluded all in unbelief, that he might have mercy upon all" (Rom. xi. 32); in other words, he wills that all who are saved should ascribe their salvation to his mercy, although the blessing of salvation is not common to all. Finally, after all that has been adduced

1 The French adds, "pour se conformer à notre rudesse;"—in accommodation to our weakness.

on this side and on that, let it be our conclusion to feel overawed with Paul at the great depth, and if petulant tongues will still murmur, let us not be ashamed to join in his exclamation, "Nay but, O man, who art thou that repliest against God?" (Rom. ix. 20.) Truly does Augustine maintain that it is perverse to measure divine by the standard of human justice (De Prædest. et Gra. c. ii.).

CHAPTER XXV.

OF THE LAST RESURRECTION.

There are four principal heads in this chapter,—I. The utility, necessity, truth, and irrefragable evidence of the orthodox doctrine of a final resurrection—a doctrine unknown to philosophers, sec. 1–4. II. Refutation of the objections to this doctrine by Atheists, Sadducees, Chiliasts, and other fanatics, sec. 5–7. III. The nature of the final resurrection explained, sec. 8, 9. IV. Of the eternal felicity of the elect, and the everlasting misery of the reprobate.

Sections.

1. For invincible perseverance in our calling, it is necessary to be animated with the blessed hope of our Saviour's final advent.
2. The perfect happiness reserved for the elect at the final resurrection unknown to philosophers.
3. The truth and necessity of this doctrine of a final resurrection. To confirm our belief in it we have, 1. The example of Christ; and, 2. The omnipotence of God. There is an inseparable connection between us and our risen Saviour. The bodies of the elect must be conformed to the body of their Head. It is now in heaven. Therefore our bodies also must rise, and, reanimated by their souls, reign with Christ in heaven. The resurrection of Christ a pledge of ours.
4. As God is omnipotent, he can raise the dead. Resurrection explained by a natural process. The vision of dry bones.
5. Second part of the chapter, refuting objections to the doctrine of resurrection. 1. Atheists. 2. Sadducees. 3. Chiliasts. Their evasion. Various answers. 4. Universalists. Answer.
6. Objections continued. 5. Some speculators who imagine that death destroys the whole man. Refutation. The condition and abode of souls from death till the last day. What meant by the bosom of Abraham.
7. Refutation of some weak men and Manichees, pretending that new bodies are to be given. Refutation confirmed by various arguments and passages of Scripture.
8. Refutation of the fiction of new bodies continued.
9. Shall the wicked rise again? Answer in the affirmative. Why the wicked shall rise again. Why resurrection promised to the elect only.
10. The last part of the chapter, treating of eternal felicity; 1. Its excellence transcends our capacity. Rules to be observed. The glory of all the saints will not be equal.
11. Without regarding questions which merely puzzle, an answer given to some which are not without use.
12. As the happiness of the elect, so the misery of the reprobate, will be without measure, and without end.

1. ALTHOUGH Christ, the Sun of righteousness, shining upon us through the gospel, hath, as Paul declares, after conquering death, given us the light of life; and hence on believing we are said to have passed from "death unto life," being no longer strangers and pilgrims, but fellow-citizens with the saints, and of the household of God, who has made us sit with his only begotten Son in heavenly places, so that nothing is wanting to our complete felicity; yet, lest we should feel it grievous to be exercised under a hard warfare, as if the victory obtained by Christ had produced no fruit, we must attend to what is elsewhere taught concerning the nature of hope. For since we hope

for what we see not, and faith, as is said in another passage, is "the evidence of things not seen," so long as we are imprisoned in the body we are absent from the Lord. For which reason Paul says, "Ye are dead, and your life is hid with Christ in God. When Christ, who is our life, shall appear, then shall ye also appear with him in glory." Our present condition, therefore, requires us to "live soberly, righteously, and godly;" "looking for that blessed hope, and the glorious appearing of the great God and our Saviour Jesus Christ." Here there is need of no ordinary patience, lest, worn out with fatigue, we either turn backwards or abandon our post. Wherefore, all that has hitherto been said of our salvation calls upon us to raise our minds towards heaven, that, as Peter exhorts, though we now see not Christ, "yet believing," we may "rejoice with joy unspeakable and full of glory," receiving the end of our faith, even the salvation of our souls.[1] For this reason Paul says, that the faith and charity of the saints have respect to the faith and hope which is laid up for them in heaven (Col. i. 5). When we thus keep our eyes fixed upon Christ in heaven, and nothing on earth prevents us from directing them to the promised blessedness, there is a true fulfilment of the saying, "where your treasure is, there will your heart be also" (Matth. vi. 21). Hence the reason why faith is so rare in the world; nothing being more difficult for our sluggishness than to surmount innumerable obstacles in striving for the prize of our high calling. To the immense load of miseries which almost overwhelm us, are added the jeers of profane men, who assail us for our simplicity, when spontaneously renouncing the allurements of the present life we seem, in seeking a happiness which lies hid from us, to catch at a fleeting shadow. In short, we are beset above and below, behind and before, with violent temptations, which our minds would be altogether unable to withstand, were they not set free from earthly objects, and devoted to the heavenly life, though apparently remote from us. Wherefore, he alone has made solid progress in the gospel who has acquired the habit of meditating continually on a blessed resurrection.

2. In ancient times philosophers discoursed, and even debated with each other, concerning the chief good: none however, except Plato, acknowledged that it consisted in union with God. He could not, however, form even an imperfect idea of its true nature; nor is this strange, as he had learned nothing of the sacred bond of that union. We even in this our earthly pilgrimage know wherein our perfect and only felicity consists,—a felicity which, while we long for it, daily inflames our hearts more and more, until we attain to full fruition. Therefore I said, that none participate in the benefits of Christ save those who raise their minds to the resurrection. This, accordingly, is the mark which Paul sets before believers, and at which he says they are to aim, forgetting everything until they reach it (Phil. iii. 8). The more strenuously, therefore, must we contend for it, lest if

[1] 2 Tim. i. 10; John v. 24; Eph. ii. 6, 19; Rom. viii. 16–18; Heb. xi. 1; 2 Cor. v. 6; Col. iii. 3; Titus ii. 12.

the world engross us we be severely punished for our sloth.[1] Accordingly, he in another passage distinguishes believers by this mark, that their conversation is in heaven, from whence they look for the Saviour (Phil. iii. 20). And that they may not faint in their course, he associates all the other creatures with them. As shapeless ruins are everywhere seen, he says, that all things in heaven and earth struggle for renovation. For since Adam by his fall destroyed the proper order of nature, the creatures groan under the servitude to which they have been subjected through his sin; not that they are at all endued with sense, but that they naturally long for the state of perfection from which they have fallen. Paul therefore describes them as groaning and travailing in pain (Rom. viii. 19); so that we who have received the first-fruits of the Spirit may be ashamed to grovel in our corruption, instead of at least imitating the inanimate elements which are bearing the punishment of another's sin. And in order that he may stimulate us the more powerfully, he terms the final advent of Christ *our redemption*. It is true, indeed, that all the parts of our redemption are already accomplished; but as Christ was once offered for sins (Heb. ix. 28), so he shall again appear without sin unto salvation. Whatever, then, be the afflictions by which we are pressed, let this redemption sustain us until its final accomplishment.

3. The very importance of the subject ought to increase our ardour. Paul justly contends, that if Christ rise not the whole gospel is delusive and vain (1 Cor. xv. 13–17); for our condition would be more miserable than that of other mortals, because we are exposed to much hatred and insult, and incur danger every hour; nay, are like sheep destined for slaughter; and hence the authority of the gospel would fail, not in one part merely, but in its very essence, including both our adoption and the accomplishment of our salvation. Let us, therefore, give heed to a matter of all others the most serious, so that no length of time may produce weariness. I have deferred the brief consideration to be given of it to this place, that my readers may learn, when they have received Christ, the author of perfect salvation, to rise higher, and know that he is clothed with heavenly immortality and glory, in order that the whole body may be rendered conformable to the Head. For thus the Holy Spirit is ever setting before us in his person an example of the resurrection. It is difficult to believe that after our bodies have been consumed with rottenness, they will rise again at their appointed time. And hence, while many of the philosophers maintained the immortality of the soul, few of them assented to the resurrection of the body. Although in this they were inexcusable, we are thereby reminded that the subject is too difficult for human apprehension to reach it. To enable faith to surmount the great difficulty, Scripture furnishes two auxiliary proofs, the one the likeness of Christ's resurrection, and the other the omnipotence of God. Therefore, whenever the subject of the resurrection is con-

1 French, "nous recevions un povre salaire de nostre lascheté et paresse;"—we receive a poor salary for our carelessness and sloth.

sidered, let us think of the case of our Saviour, who, having completed his mortal course in our nature which he had assumed, obtained immortality, and is now the pledge of our future resurrection. For in the miseries by which we are beset, we always bear "about in the body the dying of the Lord Jesus, that the life also of Jesus might be made manifest in our mortal flesh" (2 Cor. iv. 10). It is not lawful, it is not even possible, to separate him from us, without dividing him. Hence Paul's argument, "If there be no resurrection of the dead, then is Christ not risen" (1 Cor. xv. 13); for he assumes it as an acknowledged principle, that when Christ was subjected to death, and by rising gained a victory over death, it was not on his own account, but in the Head was begun what must necessarily be fulfilled in all the members, according to the degree and order of each. For it would not be proper to be made equal to him in all respects. It is said in the psalm, "Neither wilt thou suffer thine Holy One to see corruption" (Ps. xvi. 10). Although a portion of this confidence appertain to us according to the measure bestowed on us, yet the full effect appeared only in Christ, who, free from all corruption, resumed a spotless body. Then, that there may be no doubt as to our fellowship with Christ in a blessed resurrection, and that we may be contented with this pledge, Paul distinctly affirms that he sits in the heavens, and will come as a judge on the last day for the express purpose of changing our vile body, "that it may be fashioned like unto his glorious body" (Phil. iii. 21). For he elsewhere says that God did not raise up his Son from death to give an isolated specimen of his mighty power, but that the Spirit exerts the same efficacy in regard to them that believe; and accordingly he says, that the Spirit when he dwells in us is life, because the end for which he was given is to quicken our mortal body (Rom. viii. 10, 11; Col. iii. 4). I briefly glance at subjects which might be treated more copiously, and deserve to be adorned more splendidly, and yet in the little I have said I trust pious readers will find sufficient materials for building up their faith. Christ rose again, that he might have us as partakers with him of future life. He was raised up by the Father, inasmuch as he was the Head of the Church, from which he cannot possibly be dissevered. He was raised up by the power of the Spirit, who also in in us performs the office of quickening. In fine, he was raised up to be the resurrection and the life. But as we have said, that in this mirror we behold a living image of the resurrection, so it furnishes a sure evidence to support our minds, provided we faint not, nor grow weary at the long delay, because it is not ours to measure the periods of time at our own pleasure; but to rest patiently till God in his own time renew his kingdom. To this Paul refers when he says, "But every man in his own order: Christ the first-fruits; afterward they that are Christ's at his coming" (1 Cor. xv. 23).

But lest any question should be raised as to the resurrection of Christ on which ours is founded, we see how often and in what various ways he has borne testimony to it. Scoffing men will deride the narrative which is given by the Evangelist as a childish fable. For what importance will they attach to a message which timid women bring, and the disciples, almost dead with fear, afterwards confirm? Why does not Christ rather place the illustrious trophies of his victory in the midst of the temple and the forum? Why does he not come forth, and in the presence of Pilate strike terror? Why does he not show himself alive again to the priests and all Jerusalem? Profane men will scarcely admit that the witnesses whom he selects are well qualified. I answer, that though at the commencement their infirmity was contemptible, yet the whole was directed by the admirable providence of God, so that partly from love to Christ and religious zeal, partly from incredulity, those who were lately overcome with fear now hurry to the sepulchre, not only that they might be eyewitnesses of the fact, but that they might hear angels announce what they actually saw. How can we question the veracity of those who regarded what the women told them as a fable, until they saw the reality? It is not strange that the whole people and also the governor, after they were furnished with sufficient evidence for conviction, were not allowed to see Christ or the other signs (Matth. xxvii. 66; xxviii. 11). The sepulchre is sealed, sentinels keep watch, on the third day the body is not found. The soldiers are bribed to spread the report that his disciples had stolen the body. As if they had had the means of deforcing a band of soldiers, or been supplied with weapons, or been trained so as to make such a daring attempt. But if the soldiers had not courage enough to repel them, why did they not follow and apprehend some of them by the aid of the populace? Pilate, therefore, in fact, put his signet to the resurrection of Christ, and the guards who were placed at the sepulchre by their silence or falsehood also became heralds of his resurrection. Meanwhile, the voice of angels was heard, "He is not here, but is risen" (Luke xxiv. 6). The celestial splendour plainly shows that they were not men but angels. Afterwards, if any doubt still remained, Christ himself removed it. The disciples saw him frequently; they even touched his hands and his feet, and their unbelief is of no little avail in confirming our faith. He discoursed to them of the mysteries of the kingdom of God, and at length, while they beheld, ascended to heaven. This spectacle was exhibited not to eleven apostles only, but was seen by more than five hundred brethren at once (1 Cor. xv. 6). Then by sending the Holy Spirit he gave a proof not only of life but also of supreme power, as he had foretold, "It is expedient for you that I go away: for if I go not away, the Comforter will not come unto you" (John xvi. 7). Paul was not thrown down on the way by the power of a dead man, but felt that he whom he was opposing was possessed of sovereign authority. To Stephen he appeared for another purpose—viz. that he might overcome the fear of death by the certainty of life. To refuse assent to these numerous and authentic proofs is not diffidence, but depraved and therefore infatuated obstinacy.

4. We have said that in proving the resurrection our thoughts must be directed to the immense power of God. This Paul briefly teaches, when he says that the Lord Jesus Christ "shall change our vile body, that it may be fashioned like unto his glorious body, according to the working of that mighty power whereby he is able even to subdue all things unto himself" (Phil. iii. 21). Wherefore, nothing can be more incongruous than to look here at what can be done naturally when the subject presented to us is an inestimable miracle, which by its magnitude absorbs our senses. Paul, however, by producing a proof from nature, confutes the senselessness of those who deny the resurrection. "Thou fool, that which thou sowest is not quickened except it die" &c. (1 Cor. xv. 36). He says that in seed there is a species of resurrection, because the crop is produced from corruption. Nor would the thing be so difficult of belief were we as attentive as we ought to be to the wonders which meet our eye in every quarter of the world. But let us remember that none is truly persuaded of the future resurrection save he who, carried away with admiration, gives God the glory.

Elated with this conviction, Isaiah exclaims, "Thy dead men shall live, together with my dead body shall they arise. Awake and sing, ye that dwell in dust" (Isaiah xxvi. 19). In desperate circumstances he rises to God, the author of life, in whose hand are "the issues from death" (Psalm lxviii. 20). Job also, when liker a dead body than a living being, trusting to the power of God, hesitates not as if in full vigour to rise to that day: "I know that my Redeemer liveth, and that he will stand at the latter day upon the earth" (that is, that he will there exert his power): "and though after my skin worms destroy this body, yet in my flesh shall I see God; whom I shall see for myself, and mine eyes shall behold, and not another" (Job xix. 25–27). For though some have recourse to a more subtle interpretation, by which they wrest these passages, as if they were not to be understood of the resurrection, they only confirm what they are desirous to overthrow; for holy men, in seeking consolation in their misfortunes, have recourse for alleviation merely to the similitude of a resurrection. This is better learned from a passage in Ezekiel. When the Jews scouted the promise of return, and objected that the probability of it was not greater than that of the dead coming forth from the tomb, there is presented to the prophet in vision a field covered with dry bones, which at the command of God recover sinews and flesh. Though under that figure he encourages the people to hope for return, yet the ground of hope is taken from the resurrection, as it is the special type of all the deliverances which believers experience in this world. Thus Christ declares that the voice of the Gospel gives life; but because the Jews did not receive it, he immediately adds, "Marvel not at this; for the hour is coming in which all that are in the grave shall hear his voice, and shall come forth" (John v. 28, 29). Wherefore, amid all our conflicts let us exult after the example of Paul, that he who has promised us future life "is able to keep that" which "is committed unto him" and thus glory that there is laid up for us "a crown of righteousness, which the Lord, the righteous judge, shall give" (2 Tim. i. 12; iv. 8). Thus all the hardships which we may endure will be a demonstration of our future life, "seeing it is a righteous thing with God to recompense tribulation to them that trouble you; and to you who are troubled rest with us, when the Lord Jesus shall be revealed from heaven with his mighty angels, in flaming fire" (2 Thess. i. 6–8). But we must attend to what he shortly after adds—viz. that he "shall come to be glorified in his saints, and to be admired in all them that believe"—by receiving the Gospel.

5. Although the minds of men ought to be perpetually occupied with this pursuit, yet, as if they actually resolved to banish all remembrance of the resurrection, they have called death the end of all things, the extinction of man. For Solomon certainly expresses the commonly received opinion when he says, "A living dog is better than a dead lion" (Eccl. ix. 4). And again, "Who knoweth the spirit of man that goeth upward, and the spirit of the beast that goeth downward to the earth?"[1] In all ages, a brutish stupor has prevailed, and accordingly it has made its way into the very Church; for the Sadducees had the hardihood openly to profess that there was no resurrection, nay, that the soul was mortal (Mark xii. 18; Luke xx. 27). But that this gross ignorance might be no excuse, unbelievers have always by natural instinct had an image of the resurrection before their eyes. For why the sacred and inviolable custom of burying, but that it might be the earnest of a new life? Nor can it be said that it had its origin in error, for the solemnity of sepulture always prevailed among the holy patriarchs, and God was pleased that the same custom should continue among the Gentiles, in order that the image of the resurrection thus presented might shake off their torpor. But although that ceremony was without profit, yet it is useful to us if we prudently consider its end; because it is no feeble refutation of infidelity that all men agreed in professing what none of them believed. But not only did Satan stupify the senses of mankind, so that with their bodies they buried the remembrance of the resurrection; but he also managed by various fictions so to corrupt this branch of doctrine that it at length was lost. Not to mention that even in the days of Paul he began to assail it (1 Cor. xv.). shortly after the Chiliasts arose, who limited the reign of Christ to a thousand years. This fiction is too puerile to need or to deserve refutation. Nor do they receive any countenance from the Apocalypse, from which it is known that they extracted a gloss for their error (Rev. xx. 4), since the thousand years there mentioned refer not to the eternal blessedness of the Church, but only to the various troubles which await the Church militant in this world. The whole Scripture proclaims that there will be no end either to the happiness of the

1 Calvin translates, "Quis scit an hominis anima ascendit sursum?" &c.—Who knows whether the soul of man goes upward? &c.

elect, or the punishment of the reprobate. Moreover, in regard to all things which lie beyond our sight, and far transcend the reach of our intellect, belief must either be founded on the sure oracles of God, or altogether renounced. Those who assign only a thousand years to the children of God to enjoy the inheritance of future life, observe not how great an insult they offer to Christ and his kingdom. If they are not to be clothed with immortality, then Christ himself, into whose glory they shall be transformed, has not been received into immortal glory; if their blessedness is to have an end, the kingdom of Christ, on whose solid structure it rests, is temporary. In short, they are either most ignorant of all divine things, or they maliciously aim at subverting the whole grace of God and power of Christ, which cannot have their full effect, unless sin is obliterated, death swallowed up, and eternal life fully renewed. How stupid and frivolous their fear that too much severity will be ascribed to God, if the reprobate are doomed to eternal punishment, even the blind may see. The Lord, forsooth, will be unjust if he exclude from his kingdom those who, by their ingratitude, shall have rendered themselves unworthy of it. But their sins are temporary (see Bernard, Epist. 254). I admit it; but then the majesty of God, and also the justice which they have violated by their sins, are eternal. Justly, therefore, the memory of their iniquity does not perish. But in this way the punishment will exceed the measure of the fault. It is intolerable blasphemy to hold the majesty of God in so little estimation, as not to regard the contempt of it as of greater consequence than the destruction of a single soul. But let us have done with these triflers, that we may not seem (contrary to what we first observed) to think their dreams deserving of refutation.

6. Besides these, other two dreams have been invented by men who indulge a wicked curiosity. Some, under the idea that the whole man perishes, have thought that the soul will rise again with the body; while others, admitting that spirits are immortal, hold that they will be clothed with new bodies, and thus deny the resurrection of the flesh. Having already adverted to the former point when speaking of the creation of man, it will be sufficient again to remind the reader how grovelling an error it is to convert a spirit, formed after the image of God, into an evanescent breath, which animates the body only during this fading life, and to reduce the temple of the Holy Spirit to nothing; in short, to rob of the badge of immortality that part of ourselves in which the divinity is most refulgent, and the marks of immortality conspicuous, so as to make the condition of the body better and more excellent than that of the soul. Very different is the course taken by Scripture, which compares the body to a tabernacle, from which it describes us as migrating when we die, because it estimates us by that part which distinguishes us from the lower animals. Thus Peter, in reference to his approaching death, says, "Knowing that shortly I must put off this my tabernacle" (2 Pet. i. 14). Paul, again, speaking of believers, after saying,

"If our earthly house of this tabernacle were dissolved, we have a building of God," adds, "Whilst we are at home in the body, we are absent from the Lord" (2 Cor. v. 1, 6). Did not the soul survive the body, how could it be present with the Lord on being separated from the body? But an Apostle removes all doubt when he says that we go "to the spirits of just men made perfect" (Heb. xii. 23); by these words meaning, that we are associated with the holy patriarchs, who, even when dead, cultivate the same piety, so that we cannot be the members of Christ unless we unite with them. And did not the soul, when unclothed from the body, retain its essence, and be capable of beatific glory, our Saviour would not have said to the thief, "To-day shalt thou be with me in paradise" (Luke xxiii. 43). Trusting to these clear proofs, let us doubt not, after the example of our Saviour, to commend our spirits to God when we come to die, or, after the example of Stephen, to commit ourselves to the protection of Christ, who, with good reason, is called "The Shepherd and Bishop" of our souls (Acts vii. 59; 1 Pet. ii. 25). Moreover, to pry curiously into their intermediate state is neither lawful nor expedient (see Calv. Psychopannychia). Many greatly torment themselves with discussing what place they occupy, and whether or not they already enjoy celestial glory. It is foolish and rash to inquire into hidden things, farther than God permits us to know. Scripture, after telling that Christ is present with them, and receives them into paradise (John xii. 32), and that they are comforted, while the souls of the reprobate suffer the torments which they have merited, goes no farther. What teacher or doctor will reveal to us what God has concealed? As to the place of abode, the question is not less futile and inept, since we know that the dimension of the soul is not the same as that of the body.[1] When the abode of blessed spirits is designated as the *bosom of Abraham*, it is plain that, on quitting this pilgrimage, they are received by the common father of the faithful, who imparts to them the fruit of his faith. Still, since Scripture uniformly enjoins us to look with expectation to the advent of Christ, and delays the crown of glory till that period, let us be contented with the limits divinely prescribed to us—viz. that the souls of the righteous, after their warfare is ended, obtain blessed rest where in joy they wait for the fruition of promised glory, and that thus the final result is suspended till Christ the Redeemer appear. There can be no doubt that the reprobate have the same doom as that which Jude assigns to the devils, they are "reserved in everlasting chains under darkness, unto the judgment of the great day" (Jude, ver. 6).

7. Equally monstrous is the error of those who imagine that the soul, instead of resuming the body with which it is now clothed, will obtain a new and different body. Nothing can be more futile than

1 French, "La question quant au lieu est bien frivole et sotte: veu que nous savons que l'ame n'a pas ses mesures de long et de large, comme le corps;"—the question as to place is very frivolous and foolish, seeing we know that the soul has no measures of length and breadth like the body.

the reason given by the Manichees—viz. that it were incongruous for impure flesh to rise again: as if there were no impurity in the soul; and yet this does not exclude it from the hope of heavenly life. It is just as if they were to say, that what is infected by the taint of sin cannot be divinely purified; for I now say nothing to the delirious dream that flesh is naturally impure as having been created by the devil. I only maintain, that nothing in us at present, which is unworthy of heaven, is any obstacle to the resurrection. But, first, Paul enjoins believers to purify themselves from "all filthiness of the flesh and spirit" (2 Cor. vii. 1); and then denounces the judgment which is to follow, that every one shall "receive the things done in his body, according to that he hath done, whether it be good or bad" (2 Cor. v. 10). With this accords what he says to the Corinthians, "That the life also of Jesus might be made manifest in our body" (2 Cor. iv. 10). For which reason he elsewhere says, "I pray God your whole spirit and soul and body be preserved blameless unto the coming of our Lord Jesus Christ" (1 Thess. v. 23). He says "body" as well as "spirit and soul," and no wonder; for it were most absurd that bodies which God has dedicated to himself as temples should fall into corruption without hope of resurrection. What? are they not also the members of Christ? Does he not pray that God would sanctify every part of them, and enjoin them to celebrate his name with their tongues, lift up pure hands, and offer sacrifices? That part of man, therefore, which the heavenly Judge so highly honours, what madness is it for any mortal man to reduce to dust without hope of revival? In like manner, when Paul exhorts, "Glorify God in your body, and in your spirit, which are God's," he certainly does not allow that that which he claims for God as sacred is to be adjudged to eternal corruption. Nor, indeed, on any subject does Scripture furnish clearer explanation than on the resurrection of our flesh. "This corruptible (says Paul) must put on incorruption, and this mortal must put on immortality" (1 Cor. xv. 53). If God formed new bodies, where would be this change of quality? If it were said that we must be renewed, the ambiguity of the expression might, perhaps, afford room for cavil; but here pointing with the finger to the bodies with which we are clothed, and promising that they shall be incorruptible, he very plainly affirms that no new bodies are to be fabricated. "Nay," as Tertullian says, "he could not have spoken more expressly, if he had held his skin in his hands" (Tertull. de Resurrect. Carnis.). Nor can any cavil enable them to evade the force of another passage, in which saying that Christ will be the Judge of the world, he quotes from Isaiah, "As I live, saith the Lord, every knee shall bow to me" (Rom. xiv. 11; Isa. xix. 18); since he openly declares that those whom he was addressing will have to give an account of their lives. This could not be true if new bodies were to be sisted to the tribunal. Moreover, there is no ambiguity in the words of Daniel, "Many of them that sleep in the dust of the earth shall awake, some to everlasting life, and some to shame and everlasting contempt" (Dan. xii. 2); since he does not bring new matter from the four elements to compose men, but calls forth the dead from their graves. And the reason which dictates this is plain. For if death, which originated in the fall of man, is adventitious, the renewal produced by Christ must be in the same body which began to be mortal. And, certainly, since the Athenians mocked Paul for asserting the resurrection (Acts xvii. 32), we may infer what his preaching was: their derision is of no small force to confirm our faith. The saying of our Saviour also is worthy of observation, "Fear not them which kill the body, but are not able to kill the soul: but rather fear him which is able to destroy both soul and body in hell" (Matth. x. 28). Here there would be no ground for fear, were not the body which we now have liable to punishment. Nor is another saying of our Saviour less obscure, "The hour is coming, in the which all that are in the graves shall hear his voice, and shall come forth; they that have done good, unto the resurrection of life; and they that have done evil, unto the resurrection of damnation" (John v. 28, 29). Shall we say that the soul rests in the grave, that it may there hear the voice of Christ, and not rather that the body shall at his command resume the vigour which it had lost? Moreover, if we are to receive new bodies, where will be the conformity of the Head and the members? Christ rose again. Was it by forming for himself a new body? Nay, he had foretold, "Destroy this temple, and in three days I will raise it up" (John ii. 19). The mortal body which he had formerly carried he again received; for it would not have availed us much if a new body had been substituted, and that which had been offered in expiatory sacrifice been destroyed. We must, therefore, attend to that connection which the Apostle celebrates, that we rise because Christ rose (1 Cor. xv. 12); nothing being less probable than that the flesh in which we bear about the dying of Christ, shall have no share in the resurrection of Christ. This was even manifested by a striking example, when, at the resurrection of Christ, many bodies of the saints came forth from their graves. For it cannot be denied that this was a prelude, or rather earnest, of the final resurrection for which we hope, such as already existed in Enoch and Elijah, whom Tertullian calls *candidates for resurrection*, because, exempted from corruption, both in body and soul, they were received into the custody of God.

8. I am ashamed to waste so many words on so clear a matter; but my readers will kindly submit to the annoyance, in order that perverse and presumptuous minds may not be able to avail themselves of any flaw to deceive the simple. The volatile spirits with whom I now dispute adduce the fiction of their own brain, that in the resurrection there will be a creation of new bodies. Their only reason for thinking so is, that it seems to them incredible that a dead body, long wasted by corruption, should return to its former state. Therefore, mere unbelief is the parent of their opinion. The Spirit of God, on the contrary, uniformly exhorts us in Scripture to hope for the resurrection of our flesh. For this reason Baptism is, according to Paul,

a seal of our future resurrection; and in like manner the holy Supper invites us confidently to expect it, when with our mouths we receive the symbols of spiritual grace. And certainly the whole exhortation of Paul, "Yield ye your members as instruments of righteousness unto God" (Rom. vi. 13), would be frigid, did he not add, as he does in another passage, "He that raised up Christ from the dead shall also quicken your mortal bodies" (Rom. viii. 11). For what would it avail to apply feet, hands, eyes, and tongues, to the service of God, did not these afterwards participate in the benefit and reward? This Paul expressly confirms when he says, "The body is not for fornication, but for the Lord; and the Lord for the body. And God hath both raised up the Lord, and will also raise up us by his own power" (1 Cor. vi. 13, 14). The words which follow are still clearer, "Know ye not that your bodies are the members of Christ?" "Know ye not that your body is the temple of the Holy Ghost?" (1 Cor. vi. 15, 19.) Meanwhile, we see how he connects the resurrection with chastity and holiness, as he shortly after includes our bodies in the purchase of redemption. It would be inconsistent with reason, that the body, in which Paul bore the marks of his Saviour, and in which he magnificently extolled him (Gal. vi. 17), should lose the reward of the crown. Hence he glories thus, "Our conversation is in heaven; from whence also we look for the Saviour, the Lord Jesus Christ: Who shall change our vile body, that it may be fashioned like unto his glorious body" (Phil. iii. 20, 21). As it is true, "That we must through much tribulation enter into the kingdom of God" (Acts xiv. 22); so it were unreasonable that this entrance should be denied to the bodies which God exercises under the banner of the cross, and adorns with the palm of victory.

Accordingly, the saints never entertained any doubt that they would one day be the companions of Christ, who transfers to his own person all the afflictions by which we are tried, that he may show their quickening power.[1] Nay, under the law, God trained the holy patriarch in this belief, by means of an external ceremony. For to what end was the rite of burial, as we have already seen, unless to teach that new life was prepared for the bodies thus deposited? Hence, also, the spices and other symbols of immortality, by which under the law the obscurity of the doctrine was illustrated in the same way as by sacrifices. That custom was not the offspring of superstition, since we see that the Spirit is not less careful in narrating burials than in stating the principal mysteries of the faith. Christ commends these last offices as of no trivial importance (Matth. xvi. 10), and that, certainly, for no other reason than just that they raise our eyes from the view of the tomb, which corrupts and destroys all things, to the prospect of renovation. Besides, that careful observance of the ceremony for which the patriarchs are praised, sufficiently proves that they found in it a special and valuable help to their faith. Nor

[1] Latin, "ut vivificas esse doceat"—French, "pour monstrer quelles nous meinent à vie;"— to show that they conduct us to life.

would Abraham have been so anxious about the burial of his wife (Gen. xxiii. 4, 19), had not the religious view, and something superior to any worldly advantage, been present to his mind; in other words, by adorning her dead body with the insignia of the resurrection, he confirmed his own faith, and that of his family. A clearer proof of this appears in the example of Jacob, who, to testify to his posterity that even death did not destroy the hope of the promised land, orders his bones to be carried thither. Had he been to be clothed with a new body, would it not have been ridiculous in him to give commands concerning a dust which was to be reduced to nothing? Wherefore, if Scripture has any authority with us, we cannot desire a clearer or stronger proof of any doctrine. Even tyros understand this to be the meaning of the words, *resurrection*, and *raising up*. A thing which is created for the first time cannot be said to rise again; nor could our Saviour have said, "This is the father's will which hath sent me, that of all which he hath given me I should lose nothing, but should raise it up again at the last day" (John vi. 39). The same is implied in the word *sleeping*, which is applicable only to the body. Hence, too, the name of cemetery, applied to burying-grounds.

It remains to make a passing remark on the mode of resurrection. I speak thus because Paul, by styling it a mystery, exhorts us to soberness, in order that he may curb a licentious indulgence in free and subtle speculation. First, we must hold, as has already been observed, that the body in which we shall rise will be the same as at present in respect of substance, but that the quality will be different; just as the body of Christ which was raised up was the same as that which had been offered in sacrifice, and yet excelled in other qualities, as if it had been altogether different. This Paul declares by familiar examples (1 Cor. xv. 39). For as the flesh of man and of beasts is the same in substance, but not in quality: as all the stars are made of the same matter, but have different degrees of brightness: so he shows, that though we shall retain the substance of the body, there will be a change, by which its condition will become much more excellent. The corruptible body therefore, in order that we may be raised, will not perish or vanish away, but, divested of corruption, will be clothed with incorruption. Since God has all the elements at his disposal, no difficulty can prevent him from commanding the earth, the fire, and the water, to give up what they seem to have destroyed. This, also, though not without figure, Isaiah testifies, "Behold the Lord cometh out of his place to punish the inhabitants of the earth for their iniquity: the earth also shall disclose her blood, and shall no more cover her slain" (Isa. xxvi. 21). But a distinction must be made between those who died long ago, and those who on that day shall be found alive. For as Paul declares, "We shall not all sleep, but we shall all be changed" (1 Cor. xv. 51); that is, it will not be necessary that a period should elapse between death and the beginning of the second life, for in a moment of time, in the twinkling of an eye, the trumpet shall sound, raising up the dead incorruptible, and, by a sudden change, fitting those who are alive for the same glory. So, in another passage, he comforts believers who were to undergo death, telling them that those who are then alive shall not take precedence of the dead, because those who have fallen asleep in Christ shall rise first (1 Thess. iv. 15). Should any one urge the Apostle's declaration, "It is appointed unto all men once to die" (Heb. ix. 27), the solution is easy, that when the natural state is changed there is an appearance of death, which is fitly so denominated, and therefore there is no inconsistency in the two things—viz. that all when divested of their mortal body shall be renewed by death; and yet that where the change is sudden, there will be no necessary separation between the soul and the body.

9. But a more difficult question here arises, How can the resurrection, which is a special benefit of Christ, be common to the ungodly, who are lying under the curse of God? We know that in Adam all died. Christ has come to be the resurrection and the life (John xi. 25). Is it to revive the whole human race indiscriminately? But what more incongruous than that the ungodly in their obstinate blindness should obtain what the pious worshippers of God receive by faith only? It is certain, therefore, that there will be one resurrection to judgment, and another to life, and that Christ will come to separate the kids from the goats (Matth. xxv. 32). I observe, that this ought not to seem very strange, seeing something resembling it occurs every day. We know that in Adam we were deprived of the inheritance of the whole world, and that the same reason which excludes us from eating of the tree of life, excludes us also from common food. How comes it, then, that God not only makes his sun to rise on the evil and on the good, but that, in regard to the uses of the present life, his inestimable liberality is constantly flowing forth in rich abundance? Hence we certainly perceive, that things which are proper to Christ and his members, abound to the wicked also: not that their possession is legitimate, but that they may thus be rendered more inexcusable. Thus the wicked often experience the beneficence of God, not in ordinary measures, but such as sometimes throw all the blessings of the godly into the shade, though they eventually lead to greater damnation. Should it be objected, that the resurrection is not properly compared to fading and earthly blessings, I again answer, that when the devils were first alienated from God, the fountain of life, they deserved to be utterly destroyed; yet, by the admirable counsel of God, an intermediate state was prepared, where without life they might live in death. It ought not to seem in any respect more absurd that there is to be an adventitious resurrection of the ungodly which will drag them against their will before the tribunal of Christ, whom they now refuse to receive as their master and teacher. To be consumed by death would be a light punishment were they not, in order to the punishment of their rebellion, to be sisted before the Judge whom they have provoked to a vengeance without measure and without

end. But although we are to hold, as already observed, and as is contained in the celebrated confession of Paul to Felix, "That there shall be a resurrection of the dead, both of the just and unjust" (Acts xxiv. 15); yet Scripture more frequently sets forth the resurrection as intended, along with celestial glory, for the children of God only: because, properly speaking, Christ comes not for the destruction, but for the salvation of the world; and, therefore, in the Creed the life of blessedness only is mentioned.

10. But since the prophecy, that death shall be swallowed up in victory (Hosea xiii. 14), will then only be completed, let us always remember that the end of the resurrection is eternal happiness, of whose excellence scarcely the minutest part can be described by all that human tongues can say. For though we are truly told that the kingdom of God will be full of light, and gladness, and felicity, and glory, yet the things meant by these words remain most remote from sense, and as it were involved in enigma, until the day arrive on which he will manifest his glory to us face to face (1 Cor. xv. 54). "Now," says John, "are we the sons of God; and it doth not yet appear what we shall be: but we know that, when he shall appear, we shall be like him; for we shall see him as he is" (1 John iii. 2). Hence, as the prophets were unable to give a verbal description of that spiritual blessedness, they usually delineated it by corporeal objects. On the other hand, because the fervour of desire must be kindled in us by some taste of its sweetness, let us specially dwell upon this thought, If God contains in himself as an inexhaustible fountain all fulness of blessing, those who aspire to the supreme good and perfect happiness must not long for anything beyond him. This we are taught in several passages, "Fear not, Abraham; I am thy shield, and thy exceeding great reward" (Gen. xv. 1). With this accords David's sentiment, "The Lord is the portion of mine inheritance, and of my cup: thou maintainest my lot. The lines are fallen unto me in pleasant places" (Ps. xvi. 5, 6). Again, "I shall be satisfied when I awake with thy likeness" (Ps. xvii. 15). Peter declares that the purpose for which believers are called is, that they may be "partakers of the divine nature" (2 Pet. i. 4). How so? Because "he shall come to be glorified in his saints, and to be admired in all them that believe" (2 Thess. i. 10). If our Lord will share his glory, power, and righteousness with the elect, nay, will give himself to be enjoyed by them; and what is better still, will, in a manner, become one with them, let us remember that every kind of happiness is herein included. But when we have made great progress in thus meditating, let us understand that if the conceptions of our minds be contrasted with the sublimity of the mystery, we are still halting at the very entrance.[1] The more necessary is it for us

[1] French, Et encore quand nous aurons bien profité en cette meditation, si nous faut il entendre que nous sommes encore tout au bas et à la premiere entree, et que jamais nous n'approcherons durant cette vie à la hautesse de ce mystere."—And still, when

to cultivate sobriety in this matter, lest, unmindful of our feeble capacity, we presume to take too lofty a flight, and be overwhelmed by the brightness of the celestial glory. We feel how much we are stimulated by an excessive desire of knowing more than is given us to know, and hence frivolous and noxious questions are ever and anon springing forth: by frivolous, I mean questions from which no advantage can be extracted. But there is a second class which is worse than frivolous; because those who indulge in them involve themselves in hurtful speculations. Hence I call them noxious. The doctrine of Scripture on the subject ought not to be made the ground of any controversy, and it is that as God, in the varied distribution of gifts to his saints in this world, gives them unequal degrees of light, so when he shall crown his gifts, their degrees of glory in heaven will also be unequal. When Paul says, "Ye are our glory and our joy" (2 Thess. ii. 19), his words do not apply indiscriminately to all; nor do those of our Saviour to his apostles, "Ye also shall sit on twelve thrones judging the twelve tribes of Israel" (Matth. xix. 28). But Paul, who knew that as God enriches the saints with spiritual gifts in this world, he will in like manner adorn them with glory in heaven, hesitates not to say, that a special crown is laid up for him in proportion to his labours. Our Saviour, also, to commend the dignity of the office which he had conferred on the apostles, reminds them that the fruit of it is laid up in heaven. This, too, Daniel says, "They that be wise shall shine as the brightness of the firmament; and they that turn many to righteousness as the stars for ever and ever" (Dan. xii. 3). Any one who attentively considers the Scriptures will see not only that they promise eternal life to believers, but a special reward to each. Hence the expression of Paul, "The Lord grant unto him that he may find mercy of the Lord in that day" (2 Tim. i. 18; iv. 14). This is confirmed by our Saviour's promise, that they "shall receive an hundredfold, and shall inherit everlasting life" (Matth. xix. 29). In short, as Christ, by the manifold variety of his gifts, begins the glory of his body in this world, and gradually increases it, so he will complete it in heaven.

11. While all the godly with one consent will admit this, because it is sufficiently attested by the word of God, they will, on the other hand, avoid perplexing questions which they feel to be a hinderance in their way, and thus keep within the prescribed limits. In regard to myself, I not only individually refrain from a superfluous investigation of useless matters, but also think myself bound to take care that I do not encourage the levity of others by answering them. Men puffed up with vain science are often inquiring how great the difference will be between prophets and apostles, and again, between apostles and martyrs; by how many degrees virgins will surpass those who are married; in short, they leave not a corner of heaven un-

we shall have profited much by thus meditating, we must understand that we are still far beneath it, and at the very threshold, and that never during this life shall we approach the height of this mystery.

touched by their speculations. Next it occurs to them to inquire to what end the world is to be repaired, since the children of God will not be in want of any part of this great and incomparable abundance, but will be like the angels, whose abstinence from food is a symbol of eternal blessedness. I answer, that independent of use, there will be so much pleasantness in the very sight, so much delight in the very knowledge, that this happiness will far surpass all the means of enjoyment which are now afforded. Let us suppose ourselves placed in the richest quarter of the globe, where no kind of pleasure is wanting, who is there that is not ever and anon hindered and excluded by disease from enjoying the gifts of God? who does not oftentimes interrupt the course of enjoyment by intemperance? Hence it follows, that fruition, pure and free from all defect, though it be of no use to a corruptible life, is the summit of happiness. Others go further, and ask whether dross and other impurities in metals will have no existence at the restitution, and are inconsistent with it. Though I should go so far as concede this to them, yet I expect with Paul a reparation of those defects which first began with sin, and on account of which the whole creation groaneth and travaileth with pain (Rom. viii. 22). Others go a step further, and ask, What better condition can await the human race, since the blessing of offspring shall then have an end? The solution of this difficulty also is easy. When Scripture so highly extols the blessing of offspring, it refers to the progress by which God is constantly urging nature forward to its goal; in perfection itself we know that the case is different. But as such alluring speculations instantly captivate the unwary, who are afterwards led farther into the labyrinth, until at length, every one becoming pleased with his own view, there is no limit to disputation, the best and shortest course for us will be to rest contented with seeing through a glass darkly until we shall see face to face. Few out of the vast multitude of mankind feel concerned how they are to get to heaven; all would fain know before the time what is done in heaven. Almost all, while slow and sluggish in entering upon the contest, are already depicting to themselves imaginary triumphs.

12. Moreover, as language cannot describe the severity of the divine vengeance on the reprobate, their pains and torments are figured to us by corporeal things, such as darkness, wailing and gnashing of teeth, unextinguishable fire, the ever-gnawing worm (Matth. viii. 12; xxii. 13; Mark ix. 43; Isa. lxvi. 24). It is certain that by such modes of expression the Holy Spirit designed to impress all our senses with dread, as when it is said, "Tophet is ordained of old; yea, for the king it is prepared: he hath made it deep and large; the pile thereof is fire and much wood; the breath of the Lord, like a stream of brimstone, doth kindle it (Isa. xxx. 33). As we thus require to be assisted to conceive the miserable doom of the reprobate, so the consideration on which we ought chiefly to dwell is the fearful consequence of being estranged from all fellowship with God, and not only so, but of feeling that his majesty is

adverse to us, while we cannot possibly escape from it. For, first, his indignation is like a raging fire, by whose touch all things are devoured and annihilated. Next, all the creatures are the instruments of his judgment, so that those to whom the Lord will thus publicly manifest his anger will feel that heaven, and earth, and sea, all beings, animate and inanimate, are, as it were, inflamed with dire indignation against them, and armed for their destruction. Wherefore, the Apostle made no trivial declaration, when he said that unbelievers shall be "punished with everlasting destruction from the presence of the Lord, and from the glory of his power" (2 Thess. i. 9). And whenever the prophets strike terror by means of corporeal figures, although in respect of our dull understanding there is no extravagance in their language, yet they give preludes of the future judgment in the sun and the moon, and the whole fabric of the world. Hence unhappy consciences find no rest, but are vexed and driven about by a dire whirlwind, feeling as if torn by an angry God, pierced through with deadly darts, terrified by his thunderbolt, and crushed by the weight of his hand; so that it were easier to plunge into abysses and whirlpools than endure these terrors for a moment. How fearful, then, must it be to be thus beset throughout eternity! On this subject there is a memorable passage in the ninetieth Psalm: Although God by a mere look scatters all mortals, and brings them to nought, yet as his worshippers are more timid in this world, he urges them the more, that he may stimulate them, while burdened with the cross, to press onward until he himself shall be all in all.

END OF THE THIRD BOOK.

INSTITUTES

OF

THE CHRISTIAN RELIGION.

BOOK FOURTH.

OF THE HOLY CATHOLIC CHURCH.

ARGUMENT.

In the former Books an exposition has been given of the three parts of the Apostles' Creed concerning God the Creator, the Redeemer, and the Sanctifier. It now remains to treat, in this last Book, of the Church and the Communion of Saints, or of the external means or helps by which God invites us to fellowship with Christ, and keeps us in it.

The twenty Chapters of which it consists may be conveniently reduced to three particular heads—viz. I. Of the Church. II. Of the Sacraments. III. Of Civil Government.

The first head occupies the first thirteen chapters; but these may all be reduced to four—viz. I. Of the marks of the Church, or the means by which the Church may be discerned, since it is necessary to cultivate unity with the Church. This is considered in Chapters I. and II.—II. Of the rule or government of the Church. The order of government, Chap. III. The form in use in the primitive Church, Chap. IV. The form at present existing in the Papacy, Chap. V. The primacy of the Pope, Chap. VI. The gradual rise of his usurpation, Chap. VII.—III. Of the power of the Church. The power in relation to doctrine as possessed either by individuals, Chap. VIII.; or universally as in Councils, Chap. IX. The power of enacting laws, Chap. X. The extent of ecclesiastical jurisdiction, Chap. XI.—IV. Of the discipline of the Church. The chief use of discipline, Chap. XII. The abuse of it, Chap. XIII.

The second general head, Of the Sacraments, comprehends three particulars,—I. Of the Sacraments in general, Chap. XIV.—II. Of the two Sacraments in particular. Of Baptism, Chap. XV. Of Pædobaptism, Chap. XVI. Of the Lord's Supper, Chap. XVII. Of profaning the Lord's Supper, Chap. XVIII. Of the five Sacraments falsely so called, Chap. XIX.

The third general head, Of Civil Government. This considered first generally, and then under the separate heads of Magistrates, Laws, and People.

INSTITUTES

OF

THE CHRISTIAN RELIGION.

BOOK FOURTH.

OF THE HOLY CATHOLIC CHURCH.

CHAPTER I.

OF THE TRUE CHURCH. DUTY OF CULTIVATING UNITY WITH HER, AS THE MOTHER OF ALL THE GODLY.

The three divisions of this chapter are,—I. The article of the Creed concerning the Holy Catholic Church and the Communion of Saints briefly expounded. The grounds on which the Church claims our reverence, sec. 1–6. II. Of the marks of the Church, sec. 7–9. III. The necessity of cleaving to the Holy Catholic Church and the Communion of Saints. Refutation of the errors of the Novatians, Anabaptists, and other schismatics, in regard to this matter, sec. 10–29.

Sections.

1. The church now to be considered. With her God has deposited whatever is necessary to faith and good order. A summary of what is contained in this Book. Why it begins with the Church.
2. In what sense the article of the Creed concerning the Church is to be understood. Why we should say, "I believe the Church," not "I believe in the Church." The purport of this article. Why the Church is called Catholic or Universal.
3. What meant by the Communion of Saints. Whether it is inconsistent with various gifts in the saints, or with civil order. Uses of this article concerning the Church and the Communion of Saints. Must the Church be visible in order to our maintaining unity with her?
4. The name of Mother given to the Church shows how necessary it is to know her. No salvation out of the Church.
5. The Church is our mother, inasmuch as God has committed to her the kind office of bringing us up in the faith until we attain full age. This method of education not to be despised. Useful to us in two ways. This utility destroyed by those who despise the pastors and teachers of the Church. The petulance of such despisers repressed by reason and Scripture. For this education of the Church her children enjoined to meet in the sanctuary. The abuse of churches both before and since the advent of Christ. Their proper use.

6. Her ministry effectual, but not without the Spirit of God. Passages in proof of this.
7. Second part of the Chapter. Concerning the marks of the Church. In what respect the Church is invisible. In what respect she is visible.
8. God alone knoweth them that are his. Still he has given marks to discern his children.
9. These marks are the ministry of the word, and administration of the sacraments instituted by Christ. The same rule not to be followed in judging of individuals and of churches.
10. We must on no account forsake the Church distinguished by such marks. Those who act otherwise are apostates, deserters of the truth and of the household of God, deniers of God and Christ, violators of the mystical marriage.
11. These marks to be the more carefully observed, because Satan strives to efface them, or to make us revolt from the Church. The twofold error of despising the true, and submitting to a false Church.
12. Though the common profession should contain some corruption, this is not a sufficient reason for forsaking the visible Church. Some of these corruptions specified. Caution necessary. The duty of the members.
13. The immoral lives of certain professors no ground for abandoning the Church. Error on this head of the ancient and modern Cathari. Their first objection. Answer to it from three of our Saviour's parables.
14. Second objection. Answer from a consideration of the state of the Corinthian Church, and the Churches of Galatia.
15. Third objection and answer.
16. The origin of these objections. A description of Schismatics. Their portraiture by Augustine. A pious counsel respecting these scandals, and a safe remedy against them.
17. Fourth objection and answer. Answer confirmed by the divine promises.
18. Another confirmation from the example of Christ and of the faithful servants of God. The appearance of the Church in the days of the prophets.
19. Appearance of the Church in the days of Christ and the apostles, and their immediate followers.
20. Fifth objection. Answer to the ancient and modern Cathari, and to the Novatians, concerning the forgiveness of sins.
21. Answer to the fifth objection continued. By the forgiveness of sins believers are enabled to remain perpetually in the Church.
22. The keys of the Church given for the express purpose of securing this benefit. A summary of the answer to the fifth objection.
23. Sixth objection, formerly advanced by the Novatians, and renewed by the Anabaptists. This error confuted by the Lord's Prayer.
24. A second answer, founded on some examples under the Old Testament.
25. A third answer, confirmed by passages from Jeremiah, Ezekiel, and Solomon. A fourth answer, derived from sacrifices.
26. A fifth answer, from the New Testament. Some special examples.
27. General examples. A celebrated passage. The arrangement of the Creed.
28. Objection, that voluntary transgression excludes from the Church.
29. Last objection of the Novatians, founded on the solemn renewal of repentance required by the Church for more heinous offences. Answer.

1. In the last Book, it has been shown, that by the faith of the gospel Christ becomes ours, and we are made partakers of the salvation and eternal blessedness procured by him. But as our ignorance and sloth (I may add, the vanity of our mind) stand in need of external helps, by which faith may be begotten in us, and may increase and make progress until its consummation, God, in accommodation to our infirmity, has added such helps, and secured the effectual preaching of the gospel, by depositing this treasure with the Church. He has appointed pastors and teachers, by whose lips he might edify his people (Eph. iv. 11); he has invested them with authority, and, in short, omitted nothing that might conduce to holy consent in the

faith, and to right order. In particular, he has instituted sacraments, which we feel by experience to be most useful helps in fostering and confirming our faith. For seeing we are shut up in the prison of the body, and have not yet attained to the rank of angels, God, in accommodation to our capacity, has in his admirable providence provided a method by which, though widely separated, we might still draw near to him. Wherefore, due order requires that we first treat of the Church, of its Government, Orders, and Power; next, of the Sacraments; and, lastly, of Civil Government;—at the same time guarding pious readers against the corruptions of the Papacy, by which Satan has adulterated all that God had appointed for our salvation. I will begin with the Church, into whose bosom God is pleased to collect his children, not only that by her aid and ministry they may be nourished so long as they are babes and children, but may also be guided by her maternal care until they grow up to manhood, and, finally, attain to the perfection of faith. What God has thus joined, let not man put asunder (Mark x. 9): to those to whom he is a Father, the Church must also be a mother. This was true not merely under the Law, but even now after the advent of Christ; since Paul declares that we are the children of a new, even a heavenly Jerusalem (Gal. iv. 26).

2. When in the Creed we profess to believe the Church, reference is made not only to the visible Church of which we are now treating, but also to all the elect of God, including in the number even those who have departed this life. And, accordingly, the word used is "believe," because oftentimes no difference can be observed between the children of God and the profane, between his proper flock and the untamed herd. The particle *in* is often interpolated, but without any probable ground. I confess, indeed, that it is the more usual form, and is not unsupported by antiquity, since the Nicene Creed, as quoted in Ecclesiastical History, adds the preposition. At the same time, we may perceive from early writers, that the expression received without controversy in ancient times was to believe "the Church," and not "in the Church." This is not only the expression used by Augustine, and that ancient writer, whoever he may have been, whose treatise, *De Symboli Expositione*, is extant under the name of Cyprian, but they distinctly remark that the addition of the preposition would make the expression improper, and they give good grounds for so thinking. We declare that we believe in God, both because our mind reclines upon him as true, and our confidence is fully satisfied in him. This cannot be said of the Church, just as it cannot be said of the forgiveness of sins, or the resurrection of the body. Wherefore, although I am unwilling to dispute about words, yet I would rather keep to the proper form, as better fitted to express the thing that is meant, than affect terms by which the meaning is causelessly obscured. The object of the expression is to teach us, that though the devil leaves no stone unturned in order to destroy the grace of Christ, and the enemies of God rush with insane violence in the same

direction, it cannot be extinguished,—the blood of Christ cannot be rendered barren, and prevented from producing fruit. Hence, regard must be had both to the secret election and to the internal calling of God, because he alone "knoweth them that are his" (2 Tim. ii. 19); and as Paul expresses it, holds them as it were enclosed under his seal, although, at the same time, they wear his insignia, and are thus distinguished from the reprobate. But as they are a small and despised number, concealed in an immense crowd, like a few grains of wheat buried among a heap of chaff, to God alone must be left the knowledge of his Church, of which his secret election forms the foundation. Nor is it enough to embrace the number of the elect in thought and intention merely. By the unity of the Church we must understand a unity into which we feel persuaded that we are truly ingrafted. For unless we are united with all the other members under Christ our head, no hope of the future inheritance awaits us. Hence the Church is called Catholic or Universal (August. Ep. 48), for two or three cannot be invented without dividing Christ; and this is impossible. All the elect of God are so joined together in Christ, that as they depend on one head, so they are as it were compacted into one body, being knit together like its different members; made truly one by living together under the same Spirit of God in one faith, hope, and charity, called not only to the same inheritance of eternal life, but to participation in one God and Christ. For although the sad devastation which everywhere meets our view may proclaim that no Church remains, let us know that the death of Christ produces fruit, and that God wondrously preserves his Church, while placing it as it were in concealment. Thus it was said to Elijah, "Yet I have left me seven thousand in Israel" (1 Kings xix. 18).

3. Moreover, this article of the Creed relates in some measure to the external Church, that every one of us must maintain brotherly concord with all the children of God, give due authority to the Church, and, in short, conduct ourselves as sheep of the flock. And hence the additional expression, the "communion of saints;" for this clause, though usually omitted by ancient writers, must not be overlooked, as it admirably expresses the quality of the Church; just as if it had been said, that saints are united in the fellowship of Christ on this condition, that all the blessings which God bestows upon them are mutually communicated to each other. This, however, is not incompatible with a diversity of graces, for we know that the gifts of the Spirit are variously distributed; nor is it incompatible with civil order, by which each is permitted privately to possess his own means, it being necessary for the preservation of peace among men that distinct rights of property should exist among them. Still a community is asserted, such as Luke describes when he says, "The multitude of them that believed were of one heart and of one soul" (Acts iv. 32); and Paul, when he reminds the Ephesians, "There is one body, and one Spirit, even as ye are called in one hope of your call-

ing" (Eph. iv. 4). For if they are truly persuaded that God is the common Father of them all, and Christ their common head, they cannot but be united together in brotherly love, and mutually impart their blessings to each other. Then it is of the highest importance for us to know what benefit thence redounds to us. For when we believe the Church, it is in order that we may be firmly persuaded that we are its members. In this way our salvation rests on a foundation so firm and sure, that though the whole fabric of the world were to give way, it could not be destroyed. First, it stands with the election of God, and cannot change or fail, any more than his eternal providence. Next, it is in a manner united with the stability of Christ, who will no more allow his faithful followers to be dissevered from him, than he would allow his own members to be torn to pieces. We may add, that so long as we continue in the bosom of the Church, we are sure that the truth will remain with us. Lastly, we feel that we have an interest in such promises as these, "In Mount Zion and in Jerusalem shall be deliverance" (Joel ii. 32; Obad. 17); "God is in the midst of her, she shall not be moved" (Ps. xlvi. 5). So available is communion with the Church to keep us in the fellowship of God. In the very term communion there is great consolation; because, while we are assured that everything which God bestows on his members belongs to us, all the blessings conferred upon them confirm our hope. But in order to embrace the unity of the Church in this manner, it is not necessary, as I have observed, to see it with our eyes, or feel it with our hands. Nay, rather from its being placed in faith, we are reminded that our thoughts are to dwell upon it, as much when it escapes our perception as when it openly appears. Nor is our faith the worse for apprehending what is unknown, since we are not enjoined here to distinguish between the elect and the reprobate (this belongs not to us, but to God only), but to feel firmly assured in our minds, that all those who, by the mercy of God the Father, through the efficacy of the Holy Spirit, have become partakers with Christ, are set apart as the proper and peculiar possession of God, and that as we are of the number, we are also partakers of this great grace.

4. But as it is now our purpose to discourse of the visible Church, let us learn, from her single title of Mother, how useful, nay, how necessary the knowledge of her is, since there is no other means of entering into life unless she conceive us in the womb and give us birth, unless she nourish us at her breasts, and, in short, keep us under her charge and government, until, divested of mortal flesh, we become like the angels (Matth. xxii. 30). For our weakness does not permit us to leave the school until we have spent our whole lives as scholars. Moreover, beyond the pale of the Church no forgiveness of sins, no salvation, can be hoped for, as Isaiah and Joel testify (Isa. xxxvii. 32; Joel ii. 32). To their testimony Ezekiel subscribes, when he declares, "They shall not be in the assembly of my people, neither shall they be written in the writing of the house of Israel"

(Ezek. xiii. 9); as, on the other hand, those who turn to the cultivation of true piety are said to inscribe their names among the citizens of Jerusalem. For which reason it is said in the psalm, "Remember me, O Lord, with the favour that thou bearest unto thy people: O visit me with thy salvation; that I may see the good of thy chosen, that I may rejoice in the gladness of thy nation, that I may glory with thine inheritance" (Ps. cvi. 4, 5). By these words the paternal favour of God and the special evidence of spiritual life are confined to his peculiar people, and hence the abandonment of the Church is always fatal.

5. But let us proceed to a full exposition of this view. Paul says that our Saviour "ascended far above all heavens, that he might fill all things. And he gave some, apostles; and some, prophets; and some, evangelists; and some, pastors and teachers; for the perfecting of the saints, for the work of the ministry, for the edifying of the body of Christ: till we all come in the unity of the faith, and of the knowledge of the Son of God, unto a perfect man, unto the measure of the stature of the fulness of Christ" (Eph. iv. 10–13). We see that God, who might perfect his people in a moment, chooses not to bring them to manhood in any other way than by the education of the Church. We see the mode of doing it expressed; the preaching of celestial doctrine is committed to pastors. We see that all without exception are brought into the same order, that they may with meek and docile spirit allow themselves to be governed by teachers appointed for this purpose. Isaiah had long before given this as the characteristic of the kingdom of Christ, "My Spirit that is upon thee, and my words which I have put in thy mouth, shall not depart out of thy mouth, nor out of the mouth of thy seed, nor out of the mouth of thy seed's seed, saith the Lord, from henceforth and for ever" (Isa. lix. 21). Hence it follows, that all who reject the spiritual food of the soul divinely offered to them by the hands of the Church, deserve to perish of hunger and famine. God inspires us with faith, but it is by the instrumentality of his gospel, as Paul reminds us, "Faith cometh by hearing" (Rom. x. 17). God reserves to himself the power of maintaining it, but it is by the preaching of the gospel, as Paul also declares, that he brings it forth and unfolds it. With this view, it pleased him in ancient times that sacred meetings should be held in the sanctuary, that consent in faith might be nourished by doctrine proceeding from the lips of the priest. Those magnificent titles, as when the temple is called God's rest, his sanctuary, his habitation, and when he is said to dwell between the cherubims (Ps. cxxxii. 13, 14; lxxx. 1), are used for no other purpose than to procure respect, love, reverence, and dignity to the ministry of heavenly doctrine, to which otherwise the appearance of an insignificant human being might be in no slight degree derogatory. Therefore, to teach us that the treasure offered to us in earthen vessels is of inestimable value (2 Cor. iv. 7), God himself appears and, as the author of this ordinance, requires his presence to be recognised in his own institu-

tion. Accordingly, after forbidding his people to give heed to familiar spirits, wizards, and other superstitions (Lev. xix. 30, 31), he adds, that he will give what ought to be sufficient for all—namely, that he will never leave them without prophets. For, as he did not commit his ancient people to angels, but raised up teachers on the earth to perform a truly angelical office, so he is pleased to instruct us in the present day by human means. But as anciently he did not confine himself to the law merely, but added priests as interpreters, from whose lips the people might inquire after his true meaning, so in the present day he would not only have us to be attentive to reading, but has appointed masters to give us their assistance. In this there is a twofold advantage. For, on the one hand, he by an admirable test proves our obedience when we listen to his ministers just as we would to himself; while, on the other hand, he consults our weakness in being pleased to address us after the manner of men by means of interpreters, that he may thus allure us to himself, instead of driving us away by his thunder. How well this familiar mode of teaching is suited to us all the godly are aware, from the dread with which the divine majesty justly inspires them.

Those who think that the authority of the doctrine is impaired by the insignificance of the men who are called to teach, betray their ingratitude; for among the many noble endowments with which God has adorned the human race, one of the most remarkable is, that he deigns to consecrate the mouths and tongues of men to his service, making his own voice to be heard in them. Wherefore, let us not on our part decline obediently to embrace the doctrine of salvation, delivered by his command and mouth; because, although the power of God is not confined to external means, he has, however, confined us to his ordinary method of teaching, which method, when fanatics refuse to observe, they entangle themselves in many fatal snares. Pride, or fastidiousness, or emulation, induces many to persuade themselves that they can profit sufficiently by reading and meditating in private, and thus to despise public meetings, and deem preaching superfluous. But since as much as in them lies they loose or burst the sacred bond of unity, none of them escapes the just punishment of this impious divorce, but become fascinated with pestiferous errors, and the foulest delusions. Wherefore, in order that the pure simplicity of the faith may flourish among us, let us not decline to use this exercise of piety, which God by his institution of it has shown to be necessary, and which he so highly recommends. None, even among the most petulant of men, would venture to say, that we are to shut our ears against God, but in all ages prophets and pious teachers have had a difficult contest to maintain with the ungodly, whose perverseness cannot submit to the yoke of being taught by the lips and ministry of men. This is just the same as if they were to destroy the impress of God as exhibited to us in doctrine. For no other reason were believers anciently enjoined to seek the face of God in the sanctuary (Ps. cv. 4) (an injunction so often repeated in the Law), than because the doctrine of the Law, and the exhortations of the prophets, were to them a living image of God. Thus Paul declares, that in his preaching the glory of God shone in the face of Jesus Christ (2 Cor. iv. 6). The more detestable are the apostates who delight in producing schisms in churches, just as if they wished to drive the sheep from the fold, and throw them into the jaws of wolves. Let us hold, agreeably to the passage we quoted from Paul, that the Church can only be edified by external preaching, and that there is no other bond by which the saints can be kept together than by uniting with one consent to observe the order which God has appointed in his Church for learning and making progress. For this end, especially, as I have observed, believers were anciently enjoined under the Law to flock together to the sanctuary; for when Moses speaks of the habitation of God, he at the same time calls it the place of the name of God, the place where he will record his name (Exod. xx. 24); thus plainly teaching that no use could be made of it without the doctrine of godliness. And there can be no doubt that, for the same reason, David complains with great bitterness of soul, that by the tyrannical cruelty of his enemies he was prevented from entering the tabernacle (Ps. lxxxiv.). To many the complaint seems childish, as if no great loss were sustained, not much pleasure lost, by exclusion from the temple, provided other amusements were enjoyed. David, however, laments this one deprivation, as filling him with anxiety and sadness, tormenting, and almost destroying him. This he does because there is nothing on which believers set a higher value than on this aid, by which God gradually raises his people to heaven. For it is to be observed, that he always exhibited himself to the holy patriarchs in the mirror of his doctrine in such a way as to make their knowledge spiritual. Whence the temple is not only styled his face, but also, for the purpose of removing all superstition, is termed his footstool (Ps. cxxxii. 7; xcix. 5). Herein is the unity of the faith happily realised, when all, from the highest to the lowest, aspire to the head. All the temples which the Gentiles built to God with a different intention were a mere profanation of his worship,—a profanation into which the Jews also fell, though not with equal grossness. With this Stephen upbraids them in the words of Isaiah when he says, "Howbeit the Most High dwelleth not in temples made with hands; as saith the Prophet, Heaven is my throne," &c. (Acts vii. 48). For God only consecrates temples to their legitimate use by his word. And when we rashly attempt anything without his order, immediately setting out from a bad principle, we introduce adventitious fictions, by which evil is propagated without measure. It was inconsiderate in Xerxes when, by the advice of the magians, he burnt or pulled down all the temples of Greece, because he thought it absurd that God, to whom all things ought to be free and open, should be enclosed by walls and roofs, as if it were not in the power of God in a manner to descend to us, that he may be near to us, and yet neither change his place nor affect us by earthly means, but rather, by a kind of vehicles, raise us aloft to his own heavenly glory, which, with its immensity, fills all things, and in height is above the heavens.

6. Moreover, as at this time there is a great dispute as to the efficacy of the ministry, some extravagantly overrating its dignity, and others erroneously maintaining, that what is peculiar to the Spirit of God is transferred to mortal man, when we suppose that ministers and teachers penetrate to the mind and heart, so as to correct the blindness of the one, and the hardness of the other; it is necessary to place this controversy on its proper footing. The arguments on both sides will be disposed of without trouble, by distinctly attending to the passages in which God, the author of preaching, connects his Spirit with it, and then promises a beneficial result; or, on the other hand, to the passages in which God, separating himself from external means, claims for himself alone both the commencement and the whole course of faith. The office of the second Elias was, as Malachi declares, to "turn the heart of the fathers to the children, and the heart of the children to their fathers" (Mal. iv. 6). Christ declares that he sent the Apostles to produce fruit from his labours (John xv. 16). What this fruit is Peter briefly defines, when he says that we are begotten again of incorruptible seed (1 Pet. i. 23). Hence Paul glories, that by means of the Gospel he had begotten the Corinthians, who were the seals of his apostleship (1 Cor. iv. 15); moreover, that his was not a ministry of the letter, which only sounded in the ear, but that the effectual agency of the Spirit was given to him, in order that his doctrine might not be in vain (1 Cor. ix. 2; 2 Cor. iii. 6). In this sense he elsewhere declares that his Gospel was not in word, but in power (1 Thess. i. 5). He also affirms that the Galatians received the Spirit by the hearing of faith (Gal. iii. 2). In short, in several passages he not only makes himself a fellow-worker with God, but attributes to himself the province of bestowing salvation (1 Cor. iii. 9). All these things he certainly never uttered with the view of attributing to himself one iota apart from God, as he elsewhere briefly explains. "For this cause also thank we God without ceasing, because, when ye received the word of God which ye heard of us, ye received it not as the word of men, but (as it is in truth) the word of God, which effectually worketh also in you that believe" (1 Thess. ii. 13). Again, in another place, "He that wrought effectually in Peter to the apostleship of the circumcision, the same was mighty in me toward the Gentiles" (Gal. ii. 8). And that he allows no more to ministers is obvious from other passages. "So then neither is he that planteth anything, neither he that watereth; but God that giveth the increase" (1 Cor. iii. 7). Again, "I laboured more abundantly than they all: yet not I, but the grace of God which was with me" (1 Cor. xv. 10). And it is indeed necessary to keep these sentences in view, since God, in ascribing to himself the illumination of the mind and renewal of the heart, reminds us that it is sacrilege for man to claim any part of either to himself. Still every one who listens with docility to the ministers whom God appoints, will know

by the beneficial result, that for good reason God is pleased with this method of teaching, and for good reason has laid believers under this modest yoke.

7. The judgment which ought to be formed concerning the visible Church which comes under our observation, must, I think, be sufficiently clear from what has been said. I have observed that the Scriptures speak of the Church in two ways. Sometimes when they speak of the Church they mean the Church as it really is before God—the Church into which none are admitted but those who by the gift of adoption are sons of God, and by the sanctification of the Spirit true members of Christ. In this case it not only comprehends the saints who dwell on the earth, but all the elect who have existed from the beginning of the world. Often, too, by the name of Church is designated the whole body of mankind scattered throughout the world, who profess to worship one God and Christ, who by baptism are initiated into the faith; by partaking of the Lord's Supper profess unity in true doctrine and charity, agree in holding the word of the Lord, and observe the ministry which Christ has appointed for the preaching of it. In this Church there is a very large mixture of hypocrites, who have nothing of Christ but the name and outward appearance: of ambitious, avaricious, envious, evil-speaking men, some also of impurer lives, who are tolerated for a time, either because their guilt cannot be legally established, or because due strictness of discipline is not always observed. Hence, as it is necessary to believe the invisible Church, which is manifest to the eye of God only, so we are also enjoined to regard this Church which is so called with reference to man, and to cultivate its communion.

8. Accordingly, inasmuch as it was of importance to us to recognise it, the Lord has distinguished it by certain marks, and as it were symbols. It is, indeed, the special prerogative of God to know those who are his, as Paul declares in the passage already quoted (2 Tim. ii. 19). And doubtless it has been so provided as a check on human rashness, the experience of every day reminding us how far his secret judgments surpass our apprehension. For even those who seemed most abandoned, and who had been completely despaired of, are by his goodness recalled to life, while those who seemed most stable often fall. Hence, as Augustine says, "In regard to the secret predestination of God, there are very many sheep without, and very many wolves within" (August. Hom. in Joan. 45). For he knows, and has his mark on those who know neither him nor themselves. Of those again who openly bear his badge, his eyes alone see who of them are unfeignedly holy, and will persevere even to the end, which alone is the completion of salvation. On the other hand, foreseeing that it was in some degree expedient for us to know who are to be regarded by us as his sons, he has in this matter accommodated himself to our capacity. But as here full certainty was not necessary, he has in its place substituted the judgment of charity, by which we acknowledge all as members of the Church who by confession of faith,

regularity of conduct, and participation in the sacraments, unite with us in acknowledging the same God and Christ. The knowledge of his body, inasmuch as he knew it to be more necessary for our salvation, he has made known to us by surer marks.

9. Hence the form of the Church appears and stands forth conspicuous to our view. Wherever we see the word of God sincerely preached and heard, wherever we see the sacraments administered according to the institution of Christ, there we cannot have any doubt that the Church of God has some existence, since his promise cannot fail, "Where two or three are gathered together in my name, there am I in the midst of them" (Matth. xviii. 20). But that we may have a clear summary of this subject, we must proceed by the following steps:—The Church universal is the multitude collected out of all nations, who, though dispersed and far distant from each other, agree in one truth of divine doctrine, and are bound together by the tie of a common religion. In this way it comprehends single churches, which exist in different towns and villages, according to the wants of human society, so that each of them justly obtains the name and authority of the Church; and also comprehends single individuals, who by a religious profession are accounted to belong to such churches, although they are in fact aliens from the Church, but have not been cut off by a public decision. There is, however, a slight difference in the mode of judging of individuals and of churches. For it may happen in practice that those whom we deem not altogether worthy of the fellowship of believers, we yet ought to treat as brethren, and regard as believers, on account of the common consent of the Church in tolerating and bearing with them in the body of Christ. Such persons we do not approve by our suffrage as members of the Church, but we leave them the place which they hold among the people of God, until they are legitimately deprived of it. With regard to the general body we must feel differently; if they have the ministry of the word, and honour the administration of the sacraments, they are undoubtedly entitled to be ranked with the Church, because it is certain that these things are not without a beneficial result. Thus we both maintain the Church universal in its unity, which malignant minds have always been eager to dissever, and deny not due authority to lawful assemblies distributed as circumstances require.

10. We have said that the symbols by which the Church is discerned are the preaching of the word and the observance of the sacraments, for these cannot anywhere exist without producing fruit and prospering by the blessing of God. I say not that wherever the word is preached fruit immediately appears; but that in every place where it is received, and has a fixed abode, it uniformly displays its efficacy. Be this as it may, when the preaching of the gospel is reverently heard, and the sacraments are not neglected, there for the time the face of the Church appears without deception or ambiguity

and no man may with impunity spurn her authority, or reject her admonitions, or resist her counsels, or make sport of her censures, far less revolt from her, and violate her unity (see Chap. II. sec. 1, 10, and Chap. VIII. sec. 12). For such is the value which the Lord sets on the communion of his Church, that all who contumaciously alienate themselves from any Christian society, in which the true ministry of his word and sacraments is maintained, he regards as deserters of religion. So highly does he recommend her authority, that when it is violated he considers that his own authority is impaired. For there is no small weight in the designation given to her, "the house of God," "the pillar and ground of the truth" (1 Tim. iii. 15). By these words Paul intimates, that to prevent the truth from perishing in the world, the Church is its faithful guardian, because God has been pleased to preserve the pure preaching of his word by her instrumentality, and to exhibit himself to us as a parent while he feeds us with spiritual nourishment, and provides whatever is conducive to our salvation. Moreover, no mean praise is conferred on the Church when she is said to have been chosen and set apart by Christ as his spouse, "not having spot or wrinkle, or any such thing" (Eph. v. 27), as "his body, the fulness of him that filleth all in all" (Eph. i. 23). Whence it follows, that revolt from the Church is denial of God and Christ. Wherefore there is the more necessity to beware of a dissent so iniquitous; for seeing by it we aim as far as in us lies at the destruction of God's truth, we deserve to be crushed by the full thunder of his anger. No crime can be imagined more atrocious than that of sacrilegiously and perfidiously violating the sacred marriage which the only begotten Son of God has condescended to contract with us.

11. Wherefore let these marks be carefully impressed upon our minds, and let us estimate them as in the sight of the Lord. There is nothing on which Satan is more intent than to destroy and efface one or both of them—at one time to delete and abolish these marks, and thereby destroy the true and genuine distinction of the Church; at another, to bring them into contempt, and so hurry us into open revolt from the Church. To his wiles it was owing that for several ages the pure preaching of the word disappeared, and now, with the same dishonest aim, he labours to overthrow the ministry, which, however, Christ has so ordered in his Church, that if it is removed the whole edifice must fall. How perilous, then, nay, how fatal the temptation, when we even entertain a thought of separating ourselves from that assembly in which are beheld the signs and badges which the Lord has deemed sufficient to characterise his Church! We see how great caution should be employed in both respects. That we may not be imposed upon by the name of Church, every congregation which claims the name must be brought to that test as to a Lydian stone. If it holds the order instituted by the Lord in word and sacraments there will be no deception; we may safely pay it the honour due to a church: on the other hand, if it exhibit itself with-

out word and sacraments, we must in this case be no less careful to avoid the imposture than we were to shun pride and presumption in the other.

12. When we say that the pure ministry of the word and pure celebration of the sacraments is a fit pledge and earnest, so that we may safely recognise a church in every society in which both exist, our meaning is, that we are never to discard it so long as these remain, though it may otherwise teem with numerous faults. Nay, even in the administration of word and sacraments defects may creep in which ought not to alienate us from its communion. For all the heads of true doctrine are not in the same position. Some are so necessary to be known, that all must hold them to be fixed and undoubted as the proper essentials of religion: for instance, that God is one, that Christ is God, and the Son of God, that our salvation depends on the mercy of God, and the like. Others, again, which are the subject of controversy among the churches, do not destroy the unity of the faith; for why should it be regarded as a ground of dissension between churches, if one, without any spirit of contention or perverseness in dogmatising, hold that the soul on quitting the body flies to heaven, and another, without venturing to speak positively as to the abode, holds it for certain that it lives with the Lord?[1] The words of the Apostle are, "Let us therefore, as many as be perfect, be thus minded: and if in anything ye be otherwise minded, God shall reveal even this unto you" (Phil. iii. 15). Does he not sufficiently intimate that a difference of opinion as to these matters which are not absolutely necessary, ought not to be a ground of dissension among Christians? The best thing, indeed, is to be perfectly agreed, but seeing there is no man who is not involved in some mist of ignorance, we must either have no church at all, or pardon delusion in those things of which one may be ignorant, without violating the substance of religion and forfeiting salvation. Here, however, I have no wish to patronise even the minutest errors, as if I thought it right to foster them by flattery or connivance; what I say is, that we are not on account of every minute difference to abandon a church, provided it retain sound and unimpaired that doctrine in which the safety of piety consists,[2] and keep the use of the sacraments instituted by the Lord. Meanwhile, if we strive to reform what is offensive, we act in the discharge of duty. To this effect are the words of Paul, "If anything be revealed to another that sitteth by, let the first hold his peace" (1 Cor.

French, "Pour donner exemple, s'il advenoit qu'une Eglise tint que les ames etant separées des corps fussent transferés au ciel incontinent: une autre, sans oser determiner du lieu pensât semplement qu'elles vivent en Dieu; et que telle diversité fut sans contention et sans opiniatreté pourquoy se diviseroient elles d'ensemble?"—To give an example, should one church happen to hold that the soul when separated from the body is forthwith transported to heaven, and should another, without venturing to determine the place, simply think that it lives in God, and should such diversity be without contention and obstinacy, why should they be divided?

2 French, "La doctrine principale de nostre salut;"—the fundamental doctrine of our salvation.

xiv. 30). From this it is evident that to each member of the Church, according to his measure of grace, the study of public edification has been assigned, provided it be done decently and in order. In other words, we must neither renounce the communion of the Church, nor, continuing in it, disturb peace and discipline when duly arranged.[1]

13. Our indulgence ought to extend much farther in tolerating imperfection of conduct. Here there is great danger of falling, and Satan employs all his machinations to ensnare us. For there always have been persons who, imbued with a false persuasion of absolute holiness, as if they had already become a kind of aërial spirits,[2] spurn the society of all in whom they see that something human still remains. Such of old were the Cathari and the Donatists, who were similarly infatuated. Such in the present day are some of the Anabaptists, who would be thought to have made superior progress. Others, again, sin in this respect, not so much from that insane pride as from inconsiderate zeal. Seeing that among those to whom the gospel is preached, the fruit produced is not in accordance with the doctrine, they forthwith conclude that there no church exists. The offence is indeed well founded, and it is one to which in this most unhappy age we give far too much occasion. It is impossible to excuse our accursed sluggishness, which the Lord will not leave unpunished, as he is already beginning sharply to chastise us. Woe then to us who, by our dissolute licence of wickedness, cause weak consciences to be wounded! Still those of whom we have spoken sin intheir turn, by not knowing how to set bounds to their offence. For where the Lord requires mercy they omit it, and give themselves up to immoderate severity. Thinking there is no church where there is not complete purity and integrity of conduct, they, through hatred of wickedness, withdraw from a genuine church, while they think they are shunning the company of the ungodly. They allege that the Church of God is holy. But that they may at the same time understand that it contains a mixture of good and bad, let them hear from the lips of our Saviour that parable in which he compares the Church to a net in which all kinds of fishes are taken, but not separated until they are brought ashore. Let them hear it compared to a field which, planted with good seed, is by the fraud of an enemy mingled with tares, and is not freed of them until the harvest is brought into the barn. Let them hear, in fine, that it is a thrashing-floor in which the collected wheat lies concealed under the chaff, until, cleansed by the fanners and the sieve, it is at length laid up in the granary. If the Lord declares that the Church will labour under the defect of being burdened with a multitude of wicked until the day of judgment, it is in vain to look for a church altogether free from blemish (Matth. xiii.).

1 French, "Et aussi que demeurant en icelle nous ne troublions point la police ni la discipline;"—and also that, remaining in it, we disturb not its order and discipline.

2 French, "Comme s'ils eussent ete quelques anges de Paradis;"—as if they had bean some angels of Paradise.

14. They exclaim that it is impossible to tolerate the vice which everywhere stalks abroad like a pestilence. What if the apostle's sentiment applies here also? Among the Corinthians it was not a few that erred, but almost the whole body had become tainted; there was not one species of sin merely, but a multitude, and those not trivial errors, but some of them execrable crimes. There was not only corruption in manners, but also in doctrine. What course was taken by the holy apostle, in other words, by the organ of the heavenly Spirit, by whose testimony the Church stands and falls? Does he seek separation from them? Does he discard them from the kingdom of Christ? Does he strike them with the thunder of a final anathema? He not only does none of these things, but he acknowledges and heralds them as a Church of Christ, and a society of saints. If the Church remains among the Corinthians, where envyings, divisions, and contentions rage; where quarrels, lawsuits, and avarice prevail; where a crime, which even the Gentiles would execrate, is openly approved; where the name of Paul, whom they ought to have honoured as a father, is petulantly assailed; where some hold the resurrection of the dead in derision, though with it the whole gospel must fall; where the gifts of God are made subservient to ambition, not to charity; where many things are done neither decently nor in order:[1] If there the Church still remains, simply because the ministration of word and sacrament is not rejected, who will presume to deny the title of church to those to whom a tenth part of these crimes cannot be imputed? How, I ask, would those who act so morosely against present churches have acted to the Galatians, who had done all but abandon the gospel (Gal. i. 6), and yet among them the same apostle found churches?[2]

15. They also object, that Paul sharply rebukes the Corinthians for permitting an heinous offender in their communion, and then lays down a general sentence, by which he declares it unlawful even to eat bread with a man of impure life (1 Cor. v. 11, 12). Here they exclaim, If it is not lawful to eat ordinary bread, how can it be lawful to eat the Lord's bread? I admit, that it is a great disgrace if dogs and swine are admitted among the children of God; much more, if the sacred body of Christ is prostituted to them. And, indeed, when churches are well regulated, they will not bear the wicked in their bosom, nor will they admit the worthy and unworthy indiscriminately to that sacred feast. But because pastors are not always sedulously vigilant, are sometimes also more indulgent than they ought, or are prevented from acting so strictly as they could wish; the consequence is, that even the openly wicked are not always excluded from the fellowship of the saints. This I admit to be a vice, and I have no wish to extenuate it, seeing that Paul sharply rebukes it in the Corinthians. But although the Church fail in her

[1] 1 Cor. i. 11; iii. 3; v. 1; vi. 7; ix. 1; xv. 12.

[2] French, "Toutesfois Sainct Paul recognoissoit entre eux quelque Eglise;"—yet St Paul recognised some church among them.

duty, it does not therefore follow that every private individual is to decide the question of separation for himself. I deny not that it is the duty of a pious man to withdraw from all private intercourse with the wicked, and not entangle himself with them by any voluntary tie; but it is one thing to shun the society of the wicked, and another to renounce the communion of the Church through hatred of them. Those who think it sacrilege to partake the Lord's bread with the wicked, are in this more rigid than Paul.[1] For when he exhorts us to pure and holy communion, he does not require that we should examine others, or that every one should examine the whole church, but that each should examine himself (1 Cor. xi. 28, 29). If it were unlawful to communicate with the unworthy, Paul would certainly have ordered us to take heed that there were no individual in the whole body by whose impurity we might be defiled, but now that he only requires each to examine himself, he shows that it does no harm to us though some who are unworthy present themselves along with us. To the same effect he afterwards adds, "He that eateth and drinketh unworthily, eateth and drinketh damnation to himself." He says not *to others*, but *to himself*. And justly; for the right of admitting or excluding ought not to be left to the decision of individuals. Cognisance of this point, which cannot be exercised without due order, as shall afterwards be more fully shown, belongs to the whole church. It would therefore be unjust to hold any private individual as polluted by the unworthiness of another, whom he neither can nor ought to keep back from communion.

16. Still, however, even the good are sometimes affected by this inconsiderate zeal for righteousness, though we shall find that this excessive moroseness is more the result of pride and a false idea of sanctity, than genuine sanctity itself, and true zeal for it. Accordingly, those who are the most forward, and, as it were, leaders in producing revolt from the Church, have, for the most part, no other motive than to display their own superiority by despising all other men. Well and wisely, therefore, does Augustine say, "Seeing that pious reason and the mode of ecclesiastical discipline ought specially to regard the unity of the Spirit in the bond of peace, which the Apostle enjoins us to keep, by bearing with one another (for if we keep it not, the application of medicine is not only superfluous, but pernicious, and therefore proves to be no medicine); those bad sons who, not from hatred of other men's iniquities, but zeal for their own contentions, attempt altogether to draw away, or at least to divide, weak brethren ensnared by the glare of their name, while swollen with pride, stuffed with petulance, insidiously calumnious, and turbulently seditious, use the cloak of a rigorous severity, that they may not seem devoid of the light of truth, and pervert to sacrilegious schism, and purposes of excision, those things which are enjoined in the Holy Scriptures (due regard being had to sincere love, and the

1 See Calvin, Lib. de Cœna Domini; item, Instructio adv. Anabapt.

unity of peace), to correct a brother's faults by the appliance of a moderate cure" (August. Cont. Parmen. cap. i.). To the pious and placid his advice is, mercifully to correct what they can, and to bear patiently with what they cannot correct, in love lamenting and mourning until God either reform or correct, or at the harvest root up the tares, and scatter the chaff (Ibid. cap. ii.). Let all the godly study to provide themselves with these weapons, lest, while they deem themselves strenuous and ardent defenders of righteousness, they revolt from the kingdom of heaven, which is the only kingdom of righteousness. For as God has been pleased that the communion of his Church shall be maintained in this external society, any one who, from hatred of the ungodly, violates the bond of this society, enters on a downward course, in which he incurs great danger of cutting himself off from the communion of saints. Let them reflect, that in a numerous body there are several who may escape their notice, and yet are truly righteous and innocent in the eyes of the Lord. Let them reflect, that of those who seem diseased, there are many who are far from taking pleasure or flattering themselves in their faults, and who, ever and anon aroused by a serious fear of the Lord, aspire to greater integrity. Let them reflect, that they have no right to pass judgment on a man for one act, since the holiest sometimes make the most grievous fall. Let them reflect, that in the ministry of the word and participation of the sacraments, the power to collect the Church is too great to be deprived of all its efficacy, by the fault of some ungodly men. Lastly, let them reflect, that in estimating the Church, divine is of more force than human judgment.

17. Since they also argue that there is good reason for the Church being called holy, it is necessary to consider what the holiness is in which it excels, lest by refusing to acknowledge any church, save one that is completely perfect, we leave no church at all. It is true, indeed, as Paul says, that Christ "loved the church, and gave himself for it, that he might sanctify and cleanse it with the washing of water by the word, that he might present it to himself a glorious church, not having spot, or wrinkle, or any such thing; but that it should be holy and without blemish" (Eph. v. 25–27). Nevertheless, it is true, that the Lord is daily smoothing its wrinkles, and wiping away its spots. Hence it follows, that its holiness is not yet perfect. Such, then, is the holiness of the Church: it makes daily progress, but is not yet perfect; it daily advances, but as yet has not reached the goal, as will elsewhere be more fully explained. Therefore, when the Prophets foretel, "Then shall Jerusalem be holy, and there shall no strangers pass through her any more;"—"It shall be called, The way of holiness; the unclean shall not pass over it" (Joel iii. 17; Isa. xxxv. 8), let us not understand it as if no blemish remained in the members of the Church: but only that with there whole heart they aspire after holiness and perfect purity: and hence, that purity which they have not yet fully attained is, by the kindness of God, attributed to them. And though the indications of such a kind of holiness existing among men

are too rare, we must understand, that at no period since the world began has the Lord been without his Church, nor ever shall be till the final consummation of all things. For although, at the very outset, the whole human race was vitiated and corrupted by the sin of Adam, yet of this kind of polluted mass he always sanctifies some vessels to honour, that no age may be left without experience of his mercy. This he has declared by sure promises, such as the following: "I have made a covenant with my chosen, I have sworn unto David my servant, Thy seed will I establish for ever, and build up thy throne to all generations" (Ps. lxxxix. 3, 4). "The Lord hath chosen Zion; he hath desired it for his habitation. This is my rest for ever; here will I dwell" (Ps. cxxxii. 13, 14). Thus saith the Lord, which giveth the sun for a light by day, and the ordinances of the moon and of the stars for a light by night, which divideth the sea when the waves thereof roar; The Lord of hosts is his name: If those ordinances depart from before me, saith the Lord, then the seed of Israel also shall cease from being a nation before me for ever" (Jer. xxxi. 35, 36).

18. On this head, Christ himself, his apostles, and almost all the prophets, have furnished us with examples. Fearful are the descriptions in which Isaiah, Jeremiah, Joel, Habakkuk, and others, deplore the diseases of the Church of Jerusalem. In the people, the rulers, and the priests, corruption prevailed to such a degree, that Isaiah hesitates not to liken Jerusalem to Sodom and Gomorrah (Isa. i. 10). Religion was partly despised, partly adulterated, while in regard to morals, we everywhere meet with accounts of theft, robbery, perfidy, murder, and similar crimes. The prophets, however, did not therefore either form new churches for themselves, or erect new altars on which they might have separate sacrifices, but whatever their countrymen might be, reflecting that the Lord had deposited his word with them, and instituted the ceremonies by which he was then worshipped, they stretched out pure hands to him, though amid the company of the ungodly. Certainly, had they thought that they thereby contracted any pollution, they would have died a hundred deaths sooner than suffered themselves to be dragged thither. Nothing, therefore, prevented them from separating themselves, but a desire of preserving unity. But if the holy prophets felt no obligation to withdraw from the Church on account of the very numerous and heinous crimes, not of one or two individuals, but almost of the whole people, we arrogate too much to ourselves, if we presume forthwith to withdraw from the communion of the Church, because the lives of all accord not with our judgment, or even with the Christian profession.

19. Then what kind of age was that of Christ and the apostles? Yet neither could the desperate impiety of the Pharisees, nor the dissolute licentiousness of manners which everywhere prevailed, prevent them from using the same sacred rites with the people, and meeting in one common temple for the public exercises of religion. And why so, but just because they knew that those who joined in

these sacred rites with a pure conscience were not at all polluted by the society of the wicked? If any one is little moved by prophets and apostles, let him at least defer to the authority of Christ. Well, therefore, does Cyprian say, "Although tares or unclean vessels are seen in the Church, that is no reason why we ourselves should withdraw from the Church; we must only labour that we may be able to be wheat; we must give our endeavour, and strive as far as we can, to be vessels of gold or silver. But to break the earthen vessels belongs to the Lord alone, to whom a rod of iron has been given: let no one arrogate to himself what is peculiar to the Son alone, and think himself sufficient to winnow the floor and cleanse the chaff, and separate all the tares by human judgment. What depraved zeal thus assumes to itself is proud obstinacy and sacrilegious presumption" (Cyprian, Lib. iii. Ep. v). Let both points, therefore, be regarded as fixed; *first*, that there is no excuse for him who spontaneously abandons the external communion of a church in which the word of God is preached and the sacraments are administered; *secondly*, that notwithstanding of the faults of a few or of many, there is nothing to prevent us from there duly professing our faith in the ordinances instituted by God, because a pious conscience is not injured by the unworthiness of another, whether he be a pastor or a private individual; and sacred rites are not less pure and salutary to a man who is holy and upright, from being at the same time handled by the impure.

20. Their moroseness and pride proceed even to greater lengths. Refusing to acknowledge any church that is not pure from the minutest blemish, they take offence at sound teachers for exhorting believers to make progress, and so teaching them to groan during their whole lives under the burden of sin, and flee for pardon. For they pretend[1] that in this way believers are led away from perfection. I admit that we are not to labour feebly or coldly in urging perfection, far less to desist from urging it; but I hold that it is a device of the devil to fill our minds with a confident belief of it while we are still in our course. Accordingly, in the Creed forgiveness of sins is appropriately subjoined to belief as to the Church, because none obtain forgiveness but those who are citizens, and of the household of the Church, as we read in the Prophet (Is. xxxiii. 24). The first place, therefore, should be given to the building of the heavenly Jerusalem, in which God afterwards is pleased to wipe away the iniquity of all who betake themselves to it. I say, however, that the Church must first be built; not that there can be any church without forgiveness of sins, but because the Lord has not promised his mercy save in the communion of saints. Therefore, our first entrance into the Church and the kingdom of God is by forgiveness of sins, without which we have no covenant nor union with God. For thus he speaks by the Prophet, "In that day will I make a covenant for them

1 Latin, "Jactant."—French, "Ces grands correcteurs leur reprochent;"—those great reformers upbraid them.

with the beasts of the field, and with the fowls of heaven, and with the creeping things of the ground: and I will break the bow, and the sword, and the battle, out of the earth, and will make them to lie down safely. And I will betroth thee unto me for ever; yea, I will betroth thee unto me in righteousness, and in judgment, and in loving-kindness, and in mercies" (Hos. ii. 18, 19). We see in what way the Lord reconciles us to himself by his mercy. So in another passage, where he foretells that the people whom he had scattered in anger will again be gathered together, "I will cleanse them from all their iniquity, whereby they have sinned against me" (Jer. xxxiii. 8). Wherefore, our initiation into the fellowship of the Church is, by the symbol of ablution, to teach us that we have no admission into the family of God, unless by his goodness our impurities are previously washed away.

21. Nor by remission of sins does the Lord only once for all elect and admit us into the Church, but by the same means he preserves and defends us in it. For what would it avail us to receive a pardon of which we were afterwards to have no use? That the mercy of the Lord would be vain and delusive if only granted once, all the godly can bear witness; for there is none who is not conscious, during his whole life, of many infirmities which stand in need of divine mercy. And truly it is not without cause that the Lord promises this gift specially to his own household, nor in vain that he orders the same message of reconciliation to be daily delivered to them. Wherefore, as during our whole lives we carry about with us the remains of sin, we could not continue in the Church one single moment were we not sustained by the uninterrupted grace of God in forgiving our sins. On the other hand, the Lord has called his people to eternal salvation, and therefore they ought to consider that pardon for their sins is always ready. Hence let us surely hold that if we are admitted and ingrafted into the body of the Church, the forgiveness of sins has been bestowed, and is daily bestowed on us, in divine liberality, through the intervention of Christ's merits, and the sanctification of the Spirit.

22. To impart this blessing to us, the keys have been given to the Church (Matth. xvi. 19; xviii. 18). For when Christ gave the command to the apostles, and conferred the power of forgiving sins, he not merely intended that they should loose the sins of those who should be converted from impiety to the faith of Christ;[1] but, moreover, that they should perpetually perform this office among believers. This Paul teaches, when he says that the embassy of reconciliation has been committed to the ministers of the Church, that they may ever and anon in the name of Christ exhort the people to be reconciled to God (2 Cor. v. 20). Therefore, in the communion of saints

1 French, "Ce n'a pas eté seulement afin qu'ils deliassent ceux qui si convertiroient alla foy Christienne, et qu'ils fissent cela pour une fois."—It was not only that they might loose those who should be converted to the Christian faith, and that they should do so once for all.

our sins are constantly forgiven by the ministry of the Church, when presbyters or bishops, to whom the office has been committed, confirm pious consciences, in the hope of pardon and forgiveness by the promises of the gospel, and that as well in public as in private, as the case requires. For there are many who, from their infirmity, stand in need of special pacification, and Paul declares that he testified of the grace of Christ not only in the public assembly, but from house to house, reminding each individually of the doctrine of salvation (Acts xx. 20, 21). Three things are here to be observed. First, Whatever be the holiness which the children of God possess, it is always under the condition, that so long as they dwell in a mortal body, they cannot stand before God without forgiveness of sins. Secondly, This benefit is so peculiar to the Church, that we cannot enjoy it unless we continue in the communion of the Church. Thirdly, It is dispensed to us by the ministers and pastors of the Church, either in the preaching of the Gospel or the administration of the Sacraments, and herein is especially manifested the power of the keys, which the Lord has bestowed on the company of the faithful. Accordingly, let each of us consider it to be his duty to seek forgiveness of sins only where the Lord has placed it. Of the public reconciliation which relates to discipline, we shall speak at the proper place.

23. But since those frantic spirits of whom I have spoken attempt to rob the Church of this the only anchor of salvation, consciences must be more firmly strengthened against this pestilential opinion The Novatians, in ancient times, agitated the Churches with this dogma, but in our day, not unlike the Novatians are some of the Anabaptists, who have fallen into the same delirious dreams. For they pretend that in baptism, the people of God are regenerated to a pure and angelical life, which is not polluted by any carnal defilements. But if a man sin after baptism, they leave him nothing except the inexorable judgment of God. In short, to the sinner who has lapsed after receiving grace they give no hope of pardon, because they admit no other forgiveness of sins save that by which we are first regenerated. But although no falsehood is more clearly refuted by Scripture, yet as these men find means of imposition (as Novatus also of old had very many followers), let us briefly show how much they rave, to the destruction both of themselves and others. In the first place, since by the command of our Lord the saints daily repeat this prayer, "Forgive us our debts" (Matth. vi. 12), they confess that they are debtors. Nor do they ask in vain; for the Lord has only enjoined them to ask what he will give. Nay, while he has declared that the whole prayer will be heard by his Father, he has sealed this absolution with a peculiar promise. What more do we wish? The Lord requires of his saints confession of sins during their whole lives, and that without ceasing, and promises pardon. How presumptuous, then, to exempt them from sin, or when they have stumbled, to exclude them altogether from grace? Then whom does he enjoin us to pardon seventy and seven times? Is it not our brethren? (Matth.

xviii. 22.) And why has he so enjoined but that we may imitate his clemency? He therefore pardons not once or twice only, but as often as, under a sense of our faults, we feel alarmed, and sighing call upon him.

24. And to begin almost with the very first commencement of the Church: the Patriarchs had been circumcised, admitted to a participation in the covenant, and doubtless instructed by their father's care in righteousness and integrity, when they conspired to commit fratricide. The crime was one which the most abandoned robbers would have abominated.[1] At length, softened by the remonstrances of Judah, they sold him; this also was intolerable cruelty. Simeon and Levi took a nefarious revenge on the sons of Sychem, one, too, condemned by the judgment of their father. Reuben, with execrable lust, defiled his father's bed. Judah, when seeking to commit whoredom, sinned against the law of nature with his daughter-in-law. But so far are they from being expunged from the chosen people, that they are rather raised to be its heads. What, moreover, of David? when on the throne of righteousness, with what iniquity did he make way for blind lust, by the shedding of innocent blood? He had already been regenerated, and, as one of the regenerated, received distinguished approbation from the Lord. But he perpetrated a crime at which even the Gentiles would have been horrified, and yet obtained pardon. And not to dwell on special examples, all the promises of divine mercy extant in the Law and the Prophets are so many proofs that the Lord is ready to forgive the offences of his people. For why does Moses promise a future period, when the people who had fallen into rebellion should return to the Lord? "Then the Lord thy God will turn thy captivity, and have compassion upon thee, and will return and gather thee from all the nations whither the Lord thy God hath scattered thee" (Deut. xxx. 3).

25. But I am unwilling to begin an enumeration which never could be finished. The prophetical books are filled with similar promises, offering mercy to a people covered with innumerable transgressions. What crime is more heinous than rebellion? It is styled divorce between God and the Church, and yet, by his goodness, it is surmounted. They say, "If a man put away his wife, and she go from him, and become another man's, shall he return unto her again? shall not that land be greatly polluted? But thou hast played the harlot with many lovers; yet return again unto me, saith the Lord." "Return, thou backsliding Israel, saith the Lord; and I will not cause mine anger to fall upon you; for I am merciful, saith the Lord, and I will not keep anger for ever" (Jer. iii. 1, 12). And surely he could not have a different feeling who declares, "I have no pleasure in the death of him that dieth;" "Wherefore turn yourselves, and live ye" (Ezek. xviii. 23, 32). Accordingly, when Solomon dedicated the temple, one of the uses for which it was destined was, that prayers

1 Gen. xxxvii. 18, 28; xxxiv. 25; xxxv. 22; xxxviii. 16; 2 Sam xi. 4, 15; xii 13.

offered up for the pardon of sins might there be heard. "If they sin against thee (for there is no man that sinneth not), and thou be angry with them, and deliver them to the enemy, so that they carry them away captive unto the land of the enemy, far or near; yet if they shall bethink themselves in the land whither they were carried captives, and repent, and make supplication unto thee in the land of them that carried them captives, saying, We have sinned, and have done perversely, we have committed wickedness; and so return unto thee with all their heart, and with all their soul, in the land of their enemies which led them away captive, and pray unto thee towards their land, which thou gavest unto their fathers, the city which thou hast chosen, and the house which I have built for thy name: then hear thou their prayer and their supplication in heaven thy dwelling-place, and maintain their cause, and forgive thy people that have sinned against thee, and all their transgressions wherein they have transgressed against thee" (1 Kings viii. 46-50). Nor in vain in the Law did God ordain a daily sacrifice for sins. Had he not foreseen that his people were constantly to labour under the disease of sin, he never would have appointed these remedies.

26. Did the advent of Christ, by which the fulness of grace was displayed, deprive believers of this privilege of supplicating for the pardon of their sins? If they offended against the Lord, were they not to obtain any mercy? What were it but to say that Christ came not for the salvation, but for the destruction of his people, if the divine indulgence in pardoning sin, which was constantly provided for the saints under the Old Testament, is now declared to have been taken away? But if we give credit to the Scriptures, when distinctly proclaiming that in Christ alone the grace and loving-kindness of the Lord have fully appeared, the riches of his mercy been poured out, reconciliation between God and man accomplished (Tit. ii. 11; iii. 4; 2 Tim. i. 9, 10), let us not doubt that the clemency of our heavenly Father, instead of being cut off or curtailed, is in much greater exuberance. Nor are proofs of this wanting. Peter, who had heard our Saviour declare that he who did not confess his name before men would be denied before the angels of God, denied him thrice in one night, and not without execration; yet he is not denied pardon (Mark viii. 38). Those who lived disorderly among the Thessalonians, though chastised, are still invited to repentance (2 Thess. iii. 6). Not even is Simon Magus thrown into despair. He is rather told to hope, since Peter invites him to have recourse to prayer (Acts viii. 22).

27. What shall we say to the fact, that occasionally whole churches have been implicated in the grossest sins, and yet Paul, instead of giving them over to destruction, rather mercifully extricated them? The defection of the Galatians was no trivial fault; the Corinthians were still less excusable, the iniquities prevailing among them being more numerous and not less heinous, yet neither are excluded from

the mercy of the Lord. Nay, the very persons who had sinned above others in uncleanness and fornication are expressly invited to repentance. The covenant of the Lord remains, and ever will remain, inviolable, that covenant which he solemnly ratified with Christ the true Solomon, and his members, in these words: "If his children forsake my law, and walk not in my judgments; if they break my statutes, and keep not my commandments; then will I visit their transgression with the rod, and their iniquity with stripes. Nevertheless, my loving-kindness will I not utterly take from him" (Ps. lxxxix. 30–33). In short, by the very arrangement of the Creed, we are reminded that forgiveness of sins always resides in the Church of Christ, for after the Church is as it were constituted, forgiveness of sins is subjoined.

28. Some persons who have somewhat more discernment, seeing that the dogma of Novatus is so clearly refuted in Scripture, do not make every fault unpardonable, but that voluntary transgression of the Law into which a man falls knowingly and willingly. Those who speak thus allow pardon to those sins only that have been committed through ignorance. But since the Lord has in the Law ordered some sacrifices to be offered in expiation of the voluntary sins of believers, and others to redeem sins of ignorance (Lev. iv.), how perverse is it to concede no expiation to a voluntary sin? I hold nothing to be more plain, than that the one sacrifice of Christ avails to remit the voluntary sins of believers, the Lord having attested this by carnal sacrifices as emblems. Then how is David, who was so well instructed in the Law, to be excused by ignorance? Did David, who was daily punishing it in others, not know how heinous a crime murder and adultery was? Did the patriarchs deem fratricide a lawful act? Had the Corinthians made so little proficiency as to imagine that God was pleased with lasciviousness, impurity, whoredom, hatred, and strife? Was Peter, after being so carefully warned, ignorant how heinous it was to forswear his Master? Therefore, let us not by our malice shut the door against the divine mercy, when so benignly manifested.

29. I am not unaware, that by the sins which are daily forgiven to believers, ancient writers have understood the lighter errors which creep in through the infirmity of the flesh, while they thought that the formal repentance which was then exacted for more heinous crimes was no more to be repeated than Baptism. This opinion is not to be viewed as if they wished to plunge those into despair who had fallen from their first repentance, or to extenuate those errors as if they were of no account before God. For they knew that the saints often stumble through unbelief, that superfluous oaths occasionally escape them, that they sometimes boil with anger, nay, break out into open invectives, and labour, besides, under other evils, which are in no slight degree offensive to the Lord; but they so called them to distinguish them from public crimes, which came under the cogni-

sance of the Church, and produced much scandal.[1] The great difficulty they had in pardoning those who had done something that called for ecclesiastical animadversion, was not because they thought it difficult to obtain pardon from the Lord, but by this severity they wished to deter others from rushing precipitately into crimes, which, by their demerit, would alienate them from the communion of the Church. Still the word of the Lord, which here ought to be our only rule, certainly prescribes greater moderation, since it teaches that the rigour of discipline must not be stretched so far as to overwhelm with grief the individual for whose benefit it should specially be designed (2 Cor. ii. 7), as we have above discoursed at greater length.

1 French, "Ils usoient de cette maniere de parler afin de mettre difference autre les fautes privees, et les crimes publiques qui emportoient grands scandales en l'Eglise."—They used this manner of speech, in order to make a difference between private faults and the public crimes which brought great scandals into the Church.

CHAPTER II.

COMPARISON BETWEEN THE FALSE CHURCH AND THE TRUE.

The divisions of the chapter are,—I. Description of a spurious Church, resembling the Papacy vaunting of personal succession, of which a refutation is subjoined, sec. 1–4. II. An answer, in name of the orthodox Churches, to the Popish accusations of heresy and schism. A description of the Churches existing at present under the Papacy.

Sections.

1. How much the ministry of the word and sacraments should weigh with us, and how far reverence for it should extend, so as to be a perpetual badge for distinguishing the Church, has been explained; for we have shown, first, that wherever it exists entire and unimpaired, no errors of conduct, no defects should prevent us from giving the name of Church;[1] and, secondly, that trivial errors in this ministry

[1] French, "Secondement, qu'encore il y ait quelques petites fautes, ou en la doctrine ou aux sacremens qu'icelui no laisse point d'avoir sa vigeur."—Secondly, that though there may be some little faults either in doctrine or in the sacraments, the Church ceases not to be in vigour.

ought not to make us regard it as illegitimate. Moreover, we have shown that the errors to which such pardon is due, are those by which the fundamental doctrine of religion is not injured, and by which those articles of religion, in which all believers should agree, are not suppressed, while, in regard to the sacraments, the defects are such as neither destroy nor impair the legitimate institution of their Author. But as soon as falsehood has forced its way into the citadel of religion, as soon as the sum of necessary doctrine is inverted, and the use of the sacraments is destroyed, the death of the Church undoubtedly ensues, just as the life of man is destroyed when his throat is pierced, or his vitals mortally wounded. This is clearly evinced by the words of Paul when he says, that the Church is "built upon the foundation of the apostles and prophets, Jesus Christ himself being the chief corner-stone" (Eph. ii. 20). If the Church is founded on the doctrine of the apostles and prophets, by which believers are enjoined to place their salvation in Christ alone, then if that doctrine is destroyed, how can the Church continue to stand? The Church must necessarily fall whenever that sum of religion which alone can sustain it has given way. Again, if the true Church is "the pillar and ground of the truth" (1 Tim. iii. 15), it is certain that there is no Church where lying and falsehood have usurped the ascendancy.

2. Since this is the state of matters under the Papacy, we can understand how much of the Church there survives.[1] There, instead of the ministry of the word, prevails a perverted government, compounded of lies, a government which partly extinguishes, partly suppresses, the pure light. In place of the Lord's Supper, the foulest sacrilege has entered, the worship of God is deformed by a varied mass of intolerable superstitions; doctrine (without which Christianity exists not) is wholly buried and exploded, the public assemblies are schools of idolatry and impiety. Wherefore, in declining fatal participation in such wickedness, we run no risk of being dissevered from the Church of Christ. The communion of the Church was not instituted to be a chain to bind us in idolatry, impiety, ignorance of God, and other kinds of evil, but rather to retain us in the fear of God and obedience of the truth. They, indeed, vaunt loudly of their Church,[2] as if there was not another in the world; and then, as if the matter were ended, they make out that all are schismatics who withdraw from obedience to that Church which they thus depict, that all are heretics who presume to whisper against its doctrine (see sec. 5). But by what arguments do they prove their possession of the true Church? They appeal to ancient records which formerly existed in Italy, France, and Spain, pretending to derive their origin from those holy men who, by sound doctrine, founded and raised up churches, confirmed the doctrine, and reared the edifice of the Church

1 See chap. i. sec. 10; ii. sec. 10; viii. sec. 12.

2 French, "Je say bien que les flatteurs du Pape magnifient grandement leur Eglise."—I know that the flatterers of the Pope greatly extol their Church.

with their blood; they pretend that the Church thus consecrated by spiritual gifts and the blood of martyrs was preserved from destruction by a perpetual succession of bishops. They dwell on the importance which Irenæus, Tertullian, Origen, Augustine, and others, attached to this succession (see sec. 3). How frivolous and plainly ludicrous these allegations are, I will enable any, who will for a little consider the matter with me, to understand without any difficulty. I would also exhort our opponents to give their serious attention, if I had any hope of being able to benefit them by instruction; but since they have laid aside all regard to truth, and make it their only aim to prosecute their own ends in whatever way they can, I will only make a few observations by which good men and lovers of truth may disentangle themselves from their quibbles. First, I ask them why they do not quote Africa, and Egypt, and all Asia, just because in all those regions there was a cessation of that sacred succession, by the aid of which they vaunt of having continued churches. They therefore fall back on the assertion, that they have the true Church, because ever since it began to exist it was never destitute of bishops, because they succeeded each other in an unbroken series. But what if I bring Greece before them? Therefore, I again ask them, Why they say that the Church perished among the Greeks, among whom there never was any interruption in the succession of bishops—a succession, in their opinion, the only guardian and preserver of the Church? They make the Greeks schismatics. Why? because, by revolting from the Apostolic See, they lost their privilege. What? Do not those who revolt from Christ much more deserve to lose it? It follows, therefore, that the pretence of succession is vain, if posterity do not retain the truth of Christ, which was handed down to them by their fathers, safe and uncorrupted, and continue in it.

3. In the present day, therefore, the pretence of the Romanists is just the same as that which appears to have been formerly used by the Jews, when the Prophets of the Lord charged them with blindness, impiety, and idolatry. For as the Jews proudly vaunted of their temple, ceremonies, and priesthood, by which, with strong reason, as they supposed, they measured the Church, so, instead of the Church, we are presented by the Romanists with certain external masks, which often are far from being connected with the Church, and without which the Church can perfectly exist. Wherefore, we need no other argument to refute them than that with which Jeremiah opposed the foolish confidence of the Jews—namely, "Trust ye not in lying words, saying, The temple of the Lord, The temple of the Lord, The temple of the Lord are these" (Jer. vii. 4). The Lord recognises nothing as his own, save when his word is heard and religiously observed. Thus, though the glory of God sat in the sanctuary between the cherubim (Ezek. x. 4), and he had promised that he would there have his stated abode, still when the priests corrupted his worship by depraved superstitions, he transferred it elsewhere, and left the place without any sanctity. If that temple which

seemed consecrated for the perpetual habitation of God, could be abandoned by God and become profane, the Romanists have no ground to pretend that God is so bound to persons or places, and fixed to external observances, that he must remain with those who have only the name and semblance of a Church. This is the question which Paul discusses in the Epistle to the Romans, from the ninth to the twelfth chapter. Weak consciences were greatly disturbed, when those who seemed to be the people of God not only rejected, but even persecuted the doctrine of the Gospel. Therefore, after expounding doctrine, he removes this difficulty, denying that those Jews, the enemies of the truth, were the Church, though they wanted nothing which might otherwise have been desired to the external form of the Church. The ground of his denial is, that they did not embrace Christ. In the Epistle to the Galatians, when comparing Ishmael with Isaac, he says still more expressly, that many hold a place in the Church to whom the inheritance does not belong, because they were not the offspring of a free parent. From this he proceeds to draw a contrast between two Jerusalems, because, as the Law was given on Mount Sinai, but the Gospel proceeded from Jerusalem, so many who were born and brought up in servitude confidently boast that they are the sons of God and of the Church; nay, while they are themselves degenerate, proudly despise the genuine sons of God. Let us also, in like manner, when we hear that it was once declared from heaven, "Cast out the bondmaid and her son," trust to this inviolable decree, and boldly despise their unmeaning boasts. For if they plume themselves on external profession, Ishmael also was circumcised: if they found on antiquity, he was the first-born: and yet we see that he was rejected. If the reason is asked, Paul assigns it (Rom. ix. 6), that those only are accounted sons who are born of the pure and legitimate seed of doctrine. On this ground God declares that he was not astricted to impious priests, though he had made a covenant with their father Levi, to be their angel, or interpreter (Mal. ii. 4); nay, he retorts the false boast by which they were wont to rise against the Prophets—namely, that the dignity of the priesthood was to be held in singular estimation. This he himself willingly admits: and he disputes with them, on the ground that he is ready to fulfil the covenant, while they, by not fulfilling it on their part, deserve to be rejected. Here, then, is the value of succession when not conjoined with imitation and corresponding conduct: posterity, as soon as they are convicted of having revolted from their origin, are deprived of all honour; unless, indeed, we are prepared to say, that because Caiaphas succeeded many pious priests (nay, the series from Aaron to him was continuous), that accursed assembly deserved the name of Church. Even in earthly governments, no one would bear to see the tyranny of Caligula, Nero, Heliogabalus, and the like, described as the true condition of a republic, because they succeeded such men as Brutus,

Scipio, and Camillus.[1] That in the government of the Church especially, nothing is more absurd than to disregard doctrine, and place succession in persons. Nor, indeed, was anything farther from the intention of the holy teachers, whom they falsely obtrude upon us, than to maintain distinctly that churches exist, as by hereditary right, wherever bishops have been uniformly succeeded by bishops. But while it was without controversy that no change had been made in doctrine from the beginning down to their day, they assumed it to be a sufficient refutation of all their errors, that they were opposed to the doctrine maintained constantly, and with unanimous consent, even by the apostles themselves. They have, therefore, no longer any ground for proceeding to make a gloss of the name of the Church, which we regard with due reverence; but when we come to definition, not only (to use the common expression) does the water adhere to them, but they stick in their own mire, because they substitute a vile prostitute for the sacred spouse of Christ. That the substitution may not deceive us, let us, among other admonitions, attend to the following from Augustine. Speaking of the Church, he says, "She herself is sometimes obscured, and, as it were, beclouded by a multitude of scandals; sometimes, in a time of tranquillity, she appears quiet and free; sometimes she is covered and tossed by the billows of tribulation and trial."—(August. ad Vincent. Epist. 48). As instances, he mentions that the strongest pillars of the Church often bravely endured exile for the faith, or lay hid throughout the world.

4. In this way the Romanists assail us in the present day, and terrify the unskilful with the name of Church, while they are the deadly adversaries of Christ. Therefore, although they exhibit a temple, a priesthood, and other similar masks, the empty glare by which they dazzle the eyes of the simple should not move us in the least to admit that there is a Church where the word of God appears not. The Lord furnished us with an unfailing test when he said, "Every one that is of the truth heareth my voice" (John xviii. 37). Again, "I am the good shepherd, and know my sheep, and am known of mine." "My sheep hear my voice, and I know them, and they follow me." A little before he had said, when the shepherd "putteth forth his own sheep, he goeth before them, and the sheep follow him; for they know his voice. And a stranger will they not follow, but will flee from him: for they know not the voice of strangers" (John x. 14, 4, 5). Why then do we, of our own accord, form so infatuated an estimate of the Church, since Christ has des-

[1] French, "Or tant s'en faut que cela ait lieu, que mesmes aux gouvernemens terrestres il ne seroit point supportable. Comme il n'y a nul propos de dire que la tyrannie de Caligula, Neron, Heliogabale, et leurs semblables soit le vrai etat de la cité de Rome, pourcequ'ils ont succedé aux bons governeurs qui etoient establis par la peuple."—Now, so far is this from being the case, that even in earthly governments it would not be supportable. As there is no ground for saying that the tyranny of Caligula, Nero, Heliogabalus, and the like, is the true state of the city of Rome, because they succeeded the good governors who were established by the people.

ignated it by a sign in which is nothing in the least degree equivocal, a sign which is everywhere seen, the existence of which infallibly proves the existence of the Church, while its absence proves the absence of everything that properly bears the name of Church? Paul declares that the Church is not founded either upon the judgments of men or the priesthood, but upon the doctrine of the Apostles and Prophets (Eph. ii. 20). Nay, Jerusalem is to be distinguished from Babylon, the Church of Christ from a conspiracy of Satan, by the discriminating test which our Saviour has applied to them, "He that is of God, heareth God's words: ye therefore hear them not, because ye are not of God" (John viii. 47). In short, since the Church is the kingdom of Christ, and he reigns only by his word, can there be any doubt as to the falsehood of those statements by which the kingdom of Christ is represented without his sceptre, in other words, without his sacred word?

5. As to their charge of heresy and schism, because we preach a different doctrine, and submit not to their laws, and meet apart from them for Prayer, Baptism, the administration of the Supper, and other sacred rites, it is indeed a very serious accusation, but one which needs not a long and laboured defence. The name of heretics and schismatics is applied to those who, by dissenting from the Church, destroy its communion. This communion is held together by two chains—viz. consent in sound doctrine and brotherly charity. Hence the distinction which Augustine makes between heretics and schismatics is, that the former corrupt the purity of the faith by false dogmas, whereas the latter sometimes, even while holding the same faith, break the bond of union (August. Lib. Quæst. in Evang. Matth.). But the thing to be observed is, that this union of charity so depends on unity of faith, as to have in it its beginning, its end, in fine, its only rule. Let us therefore remember, that whenever ecclesiastical unity is commended to us, the thing required is, that while our minds consent in Christ, our wills also be united together by mutual good-will in Christ. Accordingly Paul, when he exhorts us to it, takes for his fundamental principle that there is "one God, one faith, one baptism" (Eph. iv. 5). Nay, when he tells us to be "of one accord, of one mind," he immediately adds, "Let this mind be in you which was also in Christ Jesus" (Phil. ii. 2, 5); intimating, that where the word of the Lord is not, it is not a union of believers, but a faction of the ungodly.

6. Cyprian, also, following Paul, derives the fountain of ecclesiastical concord from the one bishopric of Christ, and afterwards adds, "There is one Church, which by increase from fecundity is more widely extended to a multitude, just as there are many rays of the sun, but one light, and many branches of a tree, but one trunk upheld by the tenacious root. When many streams flow from one fountain, though there seems wide spreading numerosity from the overflowing copiousness of the supply, yet unity remains in the origin. Pluck a ray from the body of the sun, and the unity sustains no di-

vision. Break a branch from a tree, and the branch will not germinate. Cut off a stream from a fountain, that which is thus cut off dries up. So the Church, pervaded by the light of the Lord, extends over the whole globe, and yet the light which is everywhere diffused is one" (Cyprian, de Simplicit. Prælat.). Words could not more elegantly express the inseparable connection which all the members of Christ have with each other. We see how he constantly calls us back to the head. Accordingly, he declares that when heresies and schisms arise, it is because men return not to the origin of the truth, because they seek not the head, because they keep not the doctrine of the heavenly Master. Let them now go and clamour against us as heretics for having withdrawn from their Church, since the only cause of our estrangement is, that they cannot tolerate a pure profession of the truth. I say nothing of their having expelled us by anathemas and curses. The fact is more than sufficient to excuse us, unless they would also make schismatics of the apostles, with whom we have a common cause. Christ, I say, forewarned his apostles, "they shall put you out of the synagogues" (John xvi. 2). The synagogues of which he speaks were then held to be lawful churches. Seeing then it is certain that we were cast out, and we are prepared to show that this was done for the name of Christ, the cause should first be ascertained before any decision is given either for or against us. This, however, if they choose, I am willing to leave to them; to me it is enough that we behoved to withdraw from them in order to draw near to Christ.

7. The place which we ought to assign to all the churches on which the tyranny of the Romish idol has seized will better appear if we compare them with the ancient Israelitish Church, as delineated by the prophets. So long as the Jews and Israelites persisted in the laws of the covenant, a true Church existed among them; in other words, they by the kindness of God obtained the benefits of a Church. True doctrine was contained in the law, and the ministry of it was committed to the prophets and priests. They were initiated in religion by the sign of circumcision, and by the other sacraments trained and confirmed in the faith. There can be no doubt that the titles with which the Lord honoured his Church were applicable to their society. After they forsook the law of the Lord, and degenerated into idolatry and superstition, they partly lost the privilege. For who can presume to deny the title of the Church to those with whom the Lord deposited the preaching of his word and the observance of his mysteries? On the other hand, who may presume to give the name of Church, without reservation, to that assembly by which the word of God is openly and with impunity trampled under foot—where his ministry, its chief support, and the very soul of the Church, is destroyed?

8. What then? (some one will say); was there not a particle of the Church left to the Jews from the date of their revolt to idolatry? The answer is easy. First, I say that in the defection itself there

were several gradations; for we cannot hold that the lapses by which both Judah and Israel turned aside from the pure worship of God were the same. Jeroboam, when he fabricated the calves against the express prohibition of God, and dedicated an unlawful place for worship, corrupted religion entirely. The Jews became degenerate in manners and superstitious opinions before they made any improper change in the external form of religion. For although they had adopted many perverse ceremonies under Rehoboam, yet, as the doctrine of the law and the priesthood, and the rites which God had instituted, continued at Jerusalem, the pious still had the Church in a tolerable state. In regard to the Israelites, matters which, up to the time of Ahab, had certainly not been reformed, then became worse. Those who succeeded him, until the overthrow of the kingdom, were partly like him, and partly (when they wished to be somewhat better) followed the example of Jeroboam, while all, without exception, were wicked and idolatrous. In Judea different changes now and then took place, some kings corrupting the worship of God by false and superstitious inventions, and others attempting to reform it, until, at length, the priests themselves polluted the temple of God by profane and abominable rites.

9. Now then let the Papists, in order to extenuate their vices as much as possible, deny, if they can, that the state of religion is as much vitiated and corrupted with them as it was in the kingdom of Israel under Jeroboam. They have a grosser idolatry, and in doctrine are not one whit more pure; rather, perhaps, they are even still more impure. God, nay, even those possessed of a moderate degree of judgment, will bear me witness, and the thing itself is too manifest to require me to enlarge upon it. When they would force us to the communion of their Church, they make two demands upon us—first, that we join in their prayers, their sacrifices, and all their ceremonies; and, secondly, that whatever honour, power, and jurisdiction, Christ has given to his Church, the same we must attribute to theirs. In regard to the first, I admit that all the prophets who were at Jerusalem, when matters there were very corrupt, neither sacrificed apart nor held separate meetings for prayer. For they had the command of God, which enjoined them to meet in the temple of Solomon, and they knew that the Levitical priests, whom the Lord had appointed over sacred matters, and who were not yet discarded, how unworthy soever they might be of that honour, were still entitled to hold it[1] (Exod. xxix. 9). But the principal point in the whole question is, that they were no tcompelled to any superstitious worship, nay, they undertook nothing but what had been instituted by God. But in these men, I mean the Papists, where is the resemblance?

1 French, "Ils savoient que les pretres Levitiques, combien qu'ils fussent indignes d'un tel office, neantmoins pourcequ'ils avoient eté ordonnez de Dieu, et n'etoient point encore deposés, devoient etre recognus pour ministres legitimes, ayant le degré de pretrise."—They knew that the Levitical priests, although they were unworthy of such an office, nevertheless, because they had been ordained of God, and were not yet deposed, were to be recognised as lawful ministers, having the rank of priesthood.

Scarcely can we hold any meeting with them without polluting ourselves with open idolatry. Their principal bond of communion is undoubtedly in the Mass, which we abominate as the greatest sacrilege. Whether this is justly or rashly done will be elsewhere seen (see chap. xviii.; see also Book II., chap. xv., sec. 6). It is now sufficient to show that our case is different from that of the prophets, who, when they were present at the sacred rites of the ungodly, were not obliged to witness or use any ceremonies but those which were instituted by God. But if we would have an example in all respects similar, let us take one from the kingdom of Israel. Under the ordinance of Jeroboam, circumcision remained, sacrifices were offered, the law was deemed holy, and the God whom they had received from their fathers was worshipped; but in consequence of invented and forbidden modes of worship, everything which was done there God disapproved and condemned. Show me one prophet or pious man who once worshipped or offered sacrifice in Bethel. They knew that they could not do it without defiling themselves with some kind of sacrilege. We hold, therefore, that the communion of the Church ought not to be carried so far by the godly as to lay them under a necessity of following it when it has degenerated to profane and polluted rites.

10. With regard to the second point, our objections are still stronger. For when the Church is considered in that particular point of view as the Church, whose judgment we are bound to revere, whose authority acknowledge, whose admonitions obey, whose censures dread, whose communion religiously cultivate in every respect, we cannot concede that they have a Church, without obliging ourselves to subjection and obedience. Still we are willing to concede what the Prophets conceded to the Jews and Israelites of their day, when with them matters were in a similar, or even in a better condition. For we see how they uniformly exclaim against their meetings as profane conventicles, to which it is not more lawful for them to assent than to abjure God (Isa. i. 14). And certainly if those were churches, it follows, that Elijah, Micaiah, and others in Israel, Isaiah, Jeremiah, Hosea, and those of like character in Judah, whom the prophets, priests, and people of their day, hated and execrated more than the uncircumcised, were aliens from the Church of God. If those were churches, then the Church was no longer the pillar of the truth, but the stay of falsehood, not the tabernacle of the living God, but a receptacle of idols. They were, therefore, under the necessity of refusing consent to their meetings, since consent was nothing else than impious conspiracy against God. For this same reason, should any one acknowledge those meetings of the present day, which are contaminated by idolatry, superstition, and impious doctrine, as churches, full communion with which a Christian must maintain so far as to agree with them even in doctrine, he will greatly err. For if they are churches, the power of the keys belongs to them, whereas the keys are inseparably connected with the word which they have

put to flight. Again, if they are churches, they can claim the promise of Christ, "Whatsoever ye bind," &c.; whereas, on the contrary, they discard from their communion all who sincerely profess themselves the servants of Christ. Therefore, either the promise of Christ is vain, or in this respect, at least, they are not churches. In fine, instead of the ministry of the word, they have schools of impiety, and sinks of all kinds of error. Therefore, in this point of view, they either are not churches, or no badge will remain by which the lawful meetings of the faithful can be distinguished from the meetings of Turks.

11. Still, as in ancient times, there remained among the Jews certain special privileges of a Church, so in the present day we deny not to the Papists those vestiges of a Church which the Lord has allowed to remain among them amid the dissipation. When the Lord had once made his covenant with the Jews, it was preserved not so much by them as by its own strength, supported by which it withstood their impiety. Such, then, is the certainty and constancy of the divine goodness, that the covenant of the Lord continued there, and his faith could not be obliterated by their perfidy; nor could circumcision be so profaned by their impure hands as not still to be a true sign and sacrament of his covenant. Hence the children who were born to them the Lord called his own (Ezek. xvi. 20), though, unless by special blessing, they in no respect belonged to him. So having deposited his covenant in Gaul, Italy, Germany, Spain, and England, when these countries were oppressed by the tyranny of Antichrist, He, in order that his covenant might remain inviolable, first preserved baptism there as an evidence of the covenant;—baptism, which, consecrated by his lips, retains its power in spite of human depravity; secondly, He provided by his providence that there should be other remains also to prevent the Church from utterly perishing. But as in pulling down buildings the foundations and ruins are often permitted to remain, so he did not suffer Antichrist either to subvert his Church from its foundation, or to level it with the ground (though, to punish the ingratitude of men who had despised his word, he allowed a fearful shaking and dismembering to take place), but was pleased that amid the devastation the edifice should remain, though half in ruins.

12. Therefore, while we are unwilling simply to concede the name of Church to the Papists, we do not deny that there are churches among them. The question we raise only relates to the true and legitimate constitution of the Church, implying communion in sacred rites, which are the signs of profession, and especially in doctrine.[1] Daniel and Paul foretold that Antichrist would sit in the temple of God (Dan. ix. 27; 2 Thess. ii. 4); we regard the Roman Pontiff as

[1] French, "Mais nous contendons seulement du vrai etat de l'Eglise, qui emporte communion, tant en doctrine, qu'en tout qui appartient à la profession de notre Chretienté;"—but we contend only for the true state of the Church, implying communion, as well as everything which pertains to the profession of our Christianity.

the leader and standard-bearer of that wicked and abominable kingdom.[1] By placing his seat in the temple of God, it is intimated that his kingdom would not be such as to destroy the name either of Christ or of his Church. Hence, then, it is obvious that we do not at all deny that churches remain under his tyranny; churches, however, which by sacrilegious impiety he has profaned, by cruel domination has oppressed, by evil and deadly doctrines like poisoned potions has corrupted and almost slain; churches where Christ lies half-buried, the gospel is suppressed, piety is put to flight, and the worship of God almost abolished; where, in short, all things are in such disorder as to present the appearance of Babylon rather than the holy city of God. In one word, I call them churches, inasmuch as the Lord there wondrously preserves some remains of his people, though miserably torn and scattered, and inasmuch as some symbols of the Church still remain—symbols especially whose efficacy neither the craft of the devil nor human depravity can destroy. But as, on the other hand, those marks to which we ought especially to have respect in this discussion are effaced, I say that the whole body, as well as every single assembly, want the form of a legitimate Church.

1 The French adds, "pour le moins en l'Eglise Occidentale;"—at least in the Western Church.

CHAPTER III.

OF THE TEACHERS AND MINISTERS OF THE CHURCH. THEIR ELECTION AND OFFICE.

The three heads of this chapter are,—I. A few preliminary remarks on Church order, on the end, utility, necessity, and dignity of the Christian ministry, sec. 1–3. II. A separate consideration of the persons performing Ecclesiastical functions, sec. 4–10. III. Of the Ordination or calling of the ministers of the Church, sec. 10–16.

Sections.

1. Summary of the chapter. Reasons why God, in governing the Church, uses the ministry of men. 1. To declare his condescension. 2. To train us to humility and obedience. 3. To bind us to each other in mutual charity. These reasons confirmed by Scripture.
2. This ministry of men most useful to the whole Church. Its advantages enumerated.
3. The honourable terms in which the ministry is spoken of. Its necessity established by numerous examples.
4. Second part of the chapter, treating of Ecclesiastical office-bearers in particular. Some of them, as Apostles, Prophets, and Evangelists, temporary. Others, as Pastors and Teachers, perpetual and indispensable.
5. Considering the office of Evangelist and Apostle as one, we have Pastors corresponding with Apostles, and Teachers with Prophets. Why the name of Apostles specially conferred on the twelve.
6. As to the Apostles so also to Pastors the preaching of the Word and the administration of the sacraments has been committed. How the Word should be preached.
7. Regularly every Pastor should have a separate church assigned to him. This, however, admits of modification, when duly and regularly made by public authority.
8. Bishops, Presbyters, Pastors, and Ministers, are used by the Apostles as one and the same. Some functions, as being temporary, are omitted. Two—namely, those of Elders and Deacons—as pertaining to the ministry of the Word, are retained.
9. Distinction between Deacons. Some employed in distributing alms, others in taking care of the poor.
10. Third part of the chapter, treating of the Ordination or calling of the ministers of the Church.
11. A twofold calling—viz. an external and an internal. Mode in which both are to be viewed.
12. 1. Who are to be appointed ministers? 2. Mode of appointment.
13. 3. By whom the appointment is to be made. Why the Apostles were elected by Christ alone. Of the calling and election of St Paul.
14. Ordinary Pastors are designated by other Pastors. Why certain of the Apostles also were designated by men.
15. The election of Pastors does not belong to one individual. Other Pastors should preside, and the people consent and approve.
16. Form in which the ministers of the Church are to be ordained. No express precept but one. Laying on of hands.

1. We are now to speak of the order in which the Lord has been pleased that his Church should be governed. For though it is right

that he alone should rule and reign in the Church, that he should preside and be conspicuous in it, and that its government should be exercised and administered solely by his word; yet as he does not dwell among us in visible presence, so as to declare his will to us by his own lips, he in this (as we have said) uses the ministry of men, by making them, as it were, his substitutes,[1] not by transferring his right and honour to them, but only doing his own work by their lips, just as an artificer uses a tool for any purpose. What I have previously expounded (chap. i. sec. 5) I am again forced to repeat. God might have acted, in this respect, by himself, without any aid or instrument, or might even have done it by angels; but there are several reasons why he rather chooses to employ men.[2] First, in this way he declares his condescension towards us, employing men to perform the function of his ambassadors in the world, to be the interpreters of his secret will; in short, to represent his own person. Thus he shows by experience that it is not to no purpose he calls us his temples, since by man's mouth he gives responses to men as from a sanctuary. Secondly, it forms a most excellent and useful training to humility, when he accustoms us to obey his word though preached by men like ourselves, or, it may be, our inferiors in worth. Did he himself speak from heaven, it were no wonder if his sacred oracles were received by all ears and minds reverently and without delay. For who would not dread his present power? who would not fall prostrate at the first view of his great majesty? who would not be overpowered by that immeasurable splendour? But when a feeble man, sprung from the dust, speaks in the name of God, we give the best proof of our piety and obedience, by listening with docility to his servant, though not in any respect our superior. Accordingly, he hides the treasure of his heavenly wisdom in frail earthen vessels (2 Cor. iv. 7), that he may have a more certain proof of the estimation in which it is held by us. Moreover, nothing was fitter to cherish mutual charity than to bind men together by this tie, appointing one of them as a pastor to teach the others who are enjoined to be disciples, and receive the common doctrine from a single mouth. For did every man suffice for himself, and stand in no need of another's aid (such is the pride of the human intellect), each would despise all others, and be in his turn despised. The Lord, therefore, has astricted his Church to what he foresaw would be the strongest bond of unity when he deposited the doctrine of eternal life and salvation with men, that by their hands he might communicate it to others. To this Paul had respect when he wrote to the Ephesians, "There is one body, and one Spirit, even as ye are called in one hope of your calling; one Lord, one faith, one baptism, one God and Father of all, who is above all, and through all, and in you all. But unto every one of us is given grace according to the measure of the

1 Latin, "quasi vicariam operam."—French, "les faisans comme ses lieutenans;"—making them as it were his substitutes.

2 See on this subject August. de Doctrina Christiana, Lib. i.

gift of Christ. Wherefore he saith, When he ascended up on high, he led captivity captive, and gave gifts unto men. (Now that he ascended, what is it but that he also descended first into the lower parts of the earth? He that descended is the same also that ascended up far above all heavens, that he might fill all things.) And he gave some, apostles; and some, prophets; and some, evangelists; and some, pastors and teachers; for the perfecting of the saints, for the work of the ministry, for the edifying of the body of Christ: till we all come in the unity of the faith, and of the knowledge of the Son of God, unto a perfect man, unto the measure of the stature of the fulness of Christ: that we henceforth be no more children, tossed to and fro, and carried about with every wind of doctrine, by the sleight of men, and cunning craftiness, whereby they lie in wait to deceive; but speaking the truth in love, may grow up into him in all things, which is the head, even Christ: from whom the whole body fitly joined together and compacted by that which every joint supplieth, according to the effectual working in the measure of every part, maketh increase of the body unto the edifying of itself in love" (Eph. iv. 4–16).

2. By these words he shows that the ministry of men, which God employs in governing the Church, is a principal bond by which believers are kept together in one body. He also intimates, that the Church cannot be kept safe, unless supported by those guards to which the Lord has been pleased to commit its safety. Christ "ascended up far above all heavens, that he might fill all things" (Eph. iv. 10). The mode of filling is this: By the ministers to whom he has committed this office, and given grace to discharge it, he dispenses and distributes his gifts to the Church, and thus exhibits himself as in a manner actually present by exerting the energy of his Spirit in this his institution, so as to prevent it from being vain or fruitless. In this way, the renewal of the saints is accomplished, and the body of Christ is edified; in this way we grow up in all things unto Him who is the Head, and unite with one another; in this way we are all brought into the unity of Christ, provided prophecy flourishes among us, provided we receive his apostles, and despise not the doctrine which is administered to us. Whoever, therefore, studies to abolish this order and kind of government of which we speak, or disparages it as of minor importance, plots the devastation, or rather the ruin and destruction, of the Church. For neither are the light and heat of the sun, nor meat and drink, so necessary to sustain and cherish the present life, as is the apostolical and pastoral office to preserve a Church in the earth.

3. Accordingly, I have observed above, that God has repeatedly commended its dignity by the titles which he has bestowed upon it, in order that we might hold it in the highest estimation, as among the most excellent of our blessings. He declares, that in raising up teachers, he confers a special benefit on men, when he bids his prophet exclaim, "How beautiful upon the mountains are the feet of him that bringeth good tidings, that publisheth peace" (Isa. lii. 7); when

he calls the apostles the light of the world and the salt of the earth (Matth. v. 13, 14). Nor could the office be more highly eulogised than when he said, "He that heareth you heareth me; and he that despiseth you despiseth me" (Luke x. 16). But the most striking passage of all is that in the Second Epistle to the Corinthians, where Paul treats as it were professedly of this question. He contends, that there is nothing in the Church more noble and glorious than the ministry of the Gospel, seeing it is the administration of the Spirit of righteousness and eternal life. These and similar passages should have the effect of preventing that method of governing and maintaining the Church by ministers, a method which the Lord has ratified for ever, from seeming worthless in our eyes, and at length becoming obsolete by contempt. How very necessary it is, he has declared not only by words but also by examples. When he was pleased to shed the light of his truth in greater effulgence on Cornelius, he sent an angel from heaven to despatch Peter to him (Acts x. 3). When he was pleased to call Paul to the knowledge of himself, and ingraft him into the Church, he does not address him with his own voice, but sends him to a man from whom he may both obtain the doctrine of salvation and the sanctification of baptism (Acts ix. 6–20). If it was not by mere accident that the angel, who is the interpreter of God, abstains from declaring the will of God, and orders a man to be called to declare it; that Christ, the only Master of believers, commits Paul to the teaching of a man, that Paul whom he had determined to carry into the third heaven, and honour with a wondrous revelation of things that could not be spoken (2 Cor. xii. 2), who will presume to despise or disregard as superfluous that ministry, whose utility God has been pleased to attest by such evidence?

4. Those who preside over the government of the Church, according to the institution of Christ, are named by Paul, first, *Apostles*; secondly, *Prophets*; thirdly, *Evangelists*; fourthly, *Pastors*; and, lastly, *Teachers* (Eph. iv. 11). Of these, only the two last have an ordinary office in the Church. The Lord raised up the other three at the beginning of his kingdom, and still occasionally raises them up when the necessity of the times requires. The nature of the apostolic function is clear from the command, "Go ye into all the world, and preach the Gospel to every creature" (Mark xvi. 15). No fixed limits are given them, but the whole world is assigned to be reduced under the obedience of Christ, that by spreading the Gospel as widely as they could, they might everywhere erect his kingdom. Accordingly, Paul, when he would approve his apostleship, does not say that he had acquired some one city for Christ, but had propagated the Gospel far and wide—had not built on another man's foundation, but planted churches where the name of his Lord was unheard. The apostles, therefore, were sent forth to bring back the world from its revolt to the true obedience of God, and everywhere establish his kingdom by the preaching of the Gospel; or, if you choose, they were like the first architects of the Church, to lay its foundations

throughout the world. By *Prophets,* he means not all interpreters of the divine will, but those who excelled by special revelation; none such now exist, or they are less manifest. By *Evangelists,* I mean those who, while inferior in rank to the apostles, were next them in office, and even acted as their substitutes. Such were Luke, Timothy, Titus, and the like; perhaps, also, the seventy disciples whom our Saviour appointed in the second place to the apostles (Luke x. 1). According to this interpretation, which appears to me consonant both to the words and the meaning of Paul, those three functions were not instituted in the Church to be perpetual, but only to endure so long as churches were to be formed where none previously existed, or at least where churches were to be transferred from Moses to Christ; although I deny not, that afterward God occasionally raised up Apostles, or at least Evangelists, in their stead, as has been done in our time. For such were needed to bring back the Church from the revolt of Antichrist. The office I nevertheless call extraordinary, because it has no place in churches duly constituted. Next come *Pastors* and *Teachers,* with whom the Church never can dispense, and between whom, I think, there is this difference, that teachers preside not over discipline, or the administration of the sacraments, or admonitions, or exhortations, but the interpretation of Scripture only, in order that pure and sound doctrine may be maintained among believers. But all these are embraced in the pastoral office.

5. We now understand what offices in the government of the Church were temporary, and what offices were instituted to be of perpetual duration. But if we class evangelists with apostles, we shall have two like offices in a manner corresponding to each other. For the same resemblance which our teachers have to the ancient prophets pastors have to the apostles. The prophetical office was more excellent in respect of the special gift of revelation which accompanied it, but the office of teachers was almost of the same nature, and had altogether the same end. In like manner, the twelve, whom the Lord chose to publish the new preaching of the Gospel to the world (Luke vi. 13), excelled others in rank and dignity. For although, from the nature of the case, and etymology of the word, all ecclesiastical officers may be properly called apostles, because they are all sent by the Lord and are his messengers, yet as it was of great importance that a sure attestation should be given to the mission of those who delivered a new and extraordinary message, it was right that the twelve (to the number of whom Paul was afterwards added) should be distinguished from others by a peculiar title. The same name, indeed, is given by Paul to Andronicus and Junia, who, he says, were "of note among the apostles" (Rom. xvi. 7); but when he would speak properly, he confines the term to that primary order. And this is the common use of Scripture. Still pastors (except that each has the government of a particular church assigned to him) have the same function as apostles. The nature of this function let us now see still more clearly.

6. When our Lord sent forth the apostles, he gave them a commission (as has been lately said) to preach the Gospel, and baptise those who believed for the remission of sins. He had previously commanded that they should distribute the sacred symbols of his body and blood after his example (Matth. xxviii. 19; Luke xxii. 19). Such is the sacred, inviolable, and perpetual law, enjoined on those who succeed to the place of the apostles,—they receive a commission to preach the Gospel and administer the sacraments. Whence we infer that those who neglect both of these falsely pretend to the office of apostles. But what shall we say of pastors? Paul speaks not of himself only but of all pastors, when he says, "Let a man so account of us, as of the ministers of Christ, and stewards of the mysteries of God" (1 Cor. iv. 1). Again, in another passage, he describes a bishop as one "holding fast the faithful word as he hath been taught, that he may be able by sound doctrine both to exhort and convince the gainsayers" (Tit. i. 9). From these and similar passages which everywhere occur, we may infer that the two principal parts of the office of pastors are to preach the Gospel and administer the sacraments. But the method of teaching consists not merely in public addresses, it extends also to private admonitions. Thus Paul takes the Ephesians to witness, "I kept back nothing that was profitable to you, but have showed you, and have taught you publicly, and from house to house, testifying both to the Jews, and also to the Greeks, repentance toward God, and faith toward our Lord Jesus Christ." A little after he says, "Remember, that, for the space of three years, I ceased not to warn every one night and day with tears" (Acts xx. 20, 31). Our present purpose, however, is not to enumerate the separate qualities of a good pastor, but only to indicate what those profess who call themselves pastors—viz. that in presiding over the Church they have not an indolent dignity, but must train the people to true piety by the doctrine of Christ, administer the sacred mysteries, preserve and exercise right discipline. To those who are set as watchmen in the Church the Lord declares, "When I say unto the wicked, Thou shalt surely die; and thou givest him not warning, nor speakest to warn the wicked from his wicked way, to save his life; the same wicked man shall die in his iniquity; but his blood will I require at thine hand" (Ezek. iii. 18). What Paul says of himself is applicable to all pastors: "For though I preach the Gospel, I have nothing to glory of: for necessity is laid upon me; yea, woe is unto me if I preach not the Gospel" (1 Cor. ix. 16). In short, what the apostles did to the whole world, every pastor should do to the flock over which he is appointed.

7. While we assign a church to each pastor, we deny not that he who is fixed to one church may assist other churches, whether any disturbance has occurred which requires his presence, or his advice is asked on some doubtful matter. But because that policy is necessary to maintain the peace of the Church, each has his proper duty assigned, lest all should become disorderly, run up and down with-

out any certain vocation, flock together promiscuously to one spot, and capriciously leave the churches vacant, being more solicitous for their own convenience than for the edification of the Church. This arrangement ought, as far as possible, to be commonly observed, that every one, content with his own limits, may not encroach on another's province. Nor is this a human invention. It is an ordinance of God. For we read that Paul and Barnabas appointed presbyters over each of the churches of Lystra, Antioch, and Iconium (Acts xiv. 23); and Paul himself enjoins Titus to ordain presbyters in every town (Tit. i. 5). In like manner, he mentions the bishops of the Philippians, and Archippus, the bishop of the Colossians (Phil. i. 1; Col. iv. 17). And in the Acts we have his celebrated address to the presbyters of the Church of Ephesus (Acts xx. 28). Let every one, then, who undertakes the government and care of one church, know that he is bound by this law of divine vocation, not that he is astricted to the soil (as lawyers speak), that is, enslaved, and, as it were, fixed, as to be unable to move a foot if public utility so require, and the thing is done duly and in order; but he who has been called to one place ought not to think of removing, nor seek to be set free when he deems it for his own advantage. Again, if it is expedient for any one to be transferred to another place, he ought not to attempt it of his own private motive, but to wait for public authority.

8. In giving the name of bishops, presbyters, and pastors, indiscriminately to those who govern churches, I have done it on the authority of Scripture, which uses the words as synonymous. To all who discharge the ministry of the word it gives the name of bishops. Thus Paul, after enjoining Titus to ordain elders in every city, immediately adds, "A bishop must be blameless," &c. (Tit. i. 5, 7). So in another place he salutes several bishops in one church (Phil. i. 1). And in the Acts, the elders of Ephesus, whom he is said to have called together, he, in the course of his address, designates as bishops (Acts xx. 17). Here it is to be observed, that we have hitherto enumerated those offices only which consist in the ministry of the word; nor does Paul make mention of any others in the passage which we have quoted from the fourth chapter of the Epistle to the Ephesians. But in the Epistle to the Romans, and the First Epistle to the Corinthians, he enumerates other offices, as powers, gifts of healing, interpretation, government, care of the poor (Rom. xii. 7: 1 Cor. xii. 28). As to those which were temporary, I say nothing, for it is not worth while to dwell upon them. But there are two of perpetual duration—viz. government and care of the poor. By these governors I understand seniors selected from the people to unite with the bishops in pronouncing censures and exercising discipline. For this is the only meaning which can be given to the passage, "He that ruleth with diligence" (Rom. xii. 8). From the beginning, therefore, each church had its senate,[1] composed of pious, grave, and

[1] Latin, "senatum."—French, "conseil ou consistoire;"—council or consistory.

venerable men, in whom was lodged the power of correcting faults. Of this power we shall afterwards speak. Moreover, experience shows that this arrangement was not confined to one age, and therefore we are to regard the office of government as necessary for all ages.

9. The care of the poor was committed to deacons, of whom two classes are mentioned by Paul in the Epistle to the Romans, "He that giveth, let him do it with simplicity;" "he that showeth mercy, with cheerfulness" (Rom. xii. 8). As it is certain that he is here speaking of public offices of the Church, there must have been two distinct classes. If I mistake not, he in the former clause designates deacons, who administered alms; in the latter, those who had devoted themselves to the care of the poor and the sick. Such were the widows of whom he makes mention in the Epistle to Timothy (1 Tim. v. 10). For there was no public office which women could discharge save that of devoting themselves to the service of the poor. If we admit this (and it certainly ought to be admitted), there will be two classes of deacons, the one serving the Church by administering the affairs of the poor; the other, by taking care of the poor themselves. For although the term διακονία has a more extensive meaning, Scripture specially gives the name of deacons to those whom the Church appoints to dispense alms, and take care of the poor, constituting them as it were stewards of the public treasury of the poor. Their origin, institution, and office, is described by Luke (Acts vi. 3). When a murmuring arose among the Greeks, because in the administration of the poor their widows were neglected, the apostles, excusing themselves that they were unable to discharge both offices, to preach the word and serve tables, requested the multitude to elect seven men of good report, to whom the office might be committed. Such deacons as the Apostolic Church had, it becomes us to have after her example.

10. Now seeing that in the sacred assembly all things ought to be done decently and in order (1 Cor. xiv. 40), there is nothing in which this ought to be more carefully observed than in settling government, irregularity in any respect being nowhere more perilous. Wherefore, lest restless and turbulent men should presumptuously push themselves forward to teach or rule (an event which actually was to happen), it was expressly provided that no one should assume a public office in the Church without a call (Heb. v. 4; Jer. xvii. 16). Therefore, if any one would be deemed a true minister of the Church, he must *first* be duly called; and, *secondly*, he must answer to his calling; that is, undertake and execute the office assigned to him. This may often be observed in Paul, who, when he would approve his apostleship, almost always alleges a call, together with his fidelity in discharging the office. If so great a minister of Christ dares not arrogate to himself authority to be heard in the Church, unless as having been appointed to it by the command of his Lord, and faithfully performing what has been intrusted to him, how great the effrontery for any man, devoid of one or both of them, to demand

for himself such honour. But as we have already touched on the necessity of executing the office, let us now treat only of the call.

11. The subject is comprehended under four heads—viz. *who* are to be appointed ministers, *in what way*, *by whom*, and *with what rite or initiatory ceremony*. I am speaking of the external and formal call which relates to the public order of the Church, while I say nothing of that secret call of which every minister is conscious before God, but has not the Church as a witness of it; I mean, the good testimony of our heart, that we undertake the offered office neither from ambition nor avarice, nor any other selfish feeling, but a sincere fear of God and desire to edify the Church. This, as I have said, is indeed necessary for every one of us, if we would approve our ministry to God. Still, however, a man may have been duly called by the Church, though he may have accepted with a bad conscience, provided his wickedness is not manifest. It is usual also to say, that private men are called to the ministry when they seem fit and apt to discharge it; that is, because learning, conjoined with piety and the other endowments of a good pastor, is a kind of preparation for the office. For those whom the Lord has destined for this great office he previously provides with the armour which is requisite for the discharge of it, that they may not come empty and unprepared. Hence Paul, in the First Epistle to the Corinthians, when treating of the offices, first enumerates the gifts in which those who performed the offices ought to excel. But as this is the first of the four heads which I mentioned, let us now proceed to it.

12. What persons should be elected bishops is treated at length by Paul in two passages (Tit. i. 7; 1 Tim. iii. 1). The substance is, that none are to be chosen save those who are of sound doctrine and holy lives, and not notorious for any defect which might destroy their authority and bring disgrace on the ministry. The description of deacons and elders is entirely similar (see chapter iv. sec. 10–13). We must always take care that they are not unfit for or unequal to the burden imposed upon them; in other words, that they are provided with the means which will be necessary to fulfil their office. Thus our Saviour, when about to send his apostles, provided them with the arms and instruments which were indispensably requisite.[1] And Paul, after portraying the character of a good and genuine bishop, admonishes Timothy not to contaminate himself by choosing an improper person for the office. The expression, *in what way*, I use not in reference to the rite of choosing, but only to the religious fear which is to be observed in election. Hence the fastings and prayers which Luke narrates that the faithful employed when they elected presbyters (Acts xiv. 23). For, understanding that the business was the most serious in which they could engage, they did not venture to act without the greatest reverence and solicitude. But above all, they were earnest in prayer, imploring from God the spirit of wisdom and discernment.

[1] Luke xxi. 15; xxiv. 49; Mark vi. 15; Acts i. 8; 1 Tim. v. 22.

13. The third division which we have adopted is, *by whom* ministers are to be chosen. A certain rule on this head cannot be obtained from the appointment of the apostles, which was somewhat different from the common call of others. As theirs was an extraordinary ministry, in order to render it conspicuous by some more distinguished mark, those who were to discharge it behoved to be called and appointed by the mouth of the Lord himself. It was not, therefore, by any human election, but at the sole command of God and Christ, that they prepared themselves for the work. Hence, when the apostles were desirous to substitute another in the place of Judas, they did not venture to nominate any one certainly, but brought forward two, that the Lord might declare by lot which of them he wished to succeed (Acts i. 23). In this way we ought to understand Paul's declaration, that he was made an apostle, "not of men, neither by man, but by Jesus Christ, and God the Father" (Gal. i. 1). The former —viz. *not of men*—he had in common with all the pious ministers of the word, for no one could duly perform the office unless called by God. The other was proper and peculiar to him. And while he glories in it, he boasts that he had not only what pertains to a true and lawful pastor, but he also brings forward the insignia of his apostleship. For when there were some among the Galatians who, seeking to disparage his authority, represented him as some ordinary disciple, substituted in place of the primary apostles, he, in order to maintain unimpaired the dignity of his ministry, against which he knew that these attempts were made, felt it necessary to show that he was in no respect inferior to the other apostles. Accordingly, he affirms that he was not chosen by the judgment of men, like some ordinary bishop, but by the mouth and manifest oracle of the Lord himself.

14. But no sober person will deny that the regular mode of lawful calling is, that bishops should be designated by men, since there are numerous passages of Scripture to this effect. Nor, as has been said, is there anything contrary to this in Paul's protestation, that he was not sent either of man, or by man, seeing he is not there speaking of the ordinary election of ministers, but claiming for himself what was peculiar to the apostles: although the Lord in thus selecting Paul by special privilege, subjected him in the meantime to the discipline of an ecclesiastical call: for Luke relates, "As they ministered to the Lord, and fasted, the Holy Ghost said, Separate me Barnabas and Saul for the work whereunto I have called them" (Acts xiii. 2). Why this separation and laying on of hands after the Holy Spirit had attested their election, unless that ecclesiastical discipline might be preserved in appointing ministers by men? God could not give a more illustrious proof of his approbation of this order, than by causing Paul to be set apart by the Church after he had previously declared that he had appointed him to be the Apostle of the Gentiles. The same thing we may see in the election of Matthias. As the apostolic office was of such importance that they did not venture to appoint any one to it of their own judgment, they

bring forward two, on one of whom the lot might fall, that thus the election might have a sure testimony from heaven, and, at the same time, the policy of the Church might not be disregarded.

15. The next question is, Whether a minister should be chosen *by the whole Church*, or only by *colleagues* and *elders*, who have the charge of discipline; or whether they may be appointed by the authority of one individual?[1] Those who attribute this right to one individual quote the words of Paul to Titus "For this cause left I thee in Crete, that thou shouldest set in order the things that are wanting, and ordain elders in every city" (Tit. i. 5); and also to Timothy, "Lay hands suddenly on no man" (1 Tim. v. 22). But they are mistaken if they suppose that Timothy so reigned at Ephesus, and Titus in Crete, as to dispose of all things at their own pleasure. They only presided by previously giving good and salutary counsels to the people, not by doing alone whatever pleased them, while all others were excluded. Lest this should seem to be a fiction of mine, I will make it plain by a similar example. Luke relates that Barnabas and Paul ordained elders throughout the churches, but he at the same time marks the plan or mode when he says that it was done by suffrage. The words are, Χειροτονήσαντες πρεσβυτέρους κατ' ἐκκλησιαν (Acts xiv. 23). They therefore selected (*creabant*) two; but the whole body, as was the custom of the Greeks in elections, declared by a show of hands which of the two they wished to have. Thus it is not uncommon for Roman historians to say, that the consul who held the comitia elected the new magistrates, for no other reason but because he received the suffrages, and presided over the people at the election. Certainly it is not credible that Paul conceded more to Timothy and Titus than he assumed to himself. Now we see that his custom was to appoint bishops by the suffrages of the people. We must therefore interpret the above passages, so as not to infringe on the common right and liberty of the Church. Rightly, therefore, does Cyprian contend for it as of divine authority, that the priest be chosen in presence of the people, before the eyes of all, and be approved as worthy and fit by public judgment and testimony, (Cyprian, Lib. i. Ep. 3). Indeed, we see that by the command of the Lord, the practice in electing the Levitical priests was to bring them forward in view of the people before consecration. Nor is Matthias enrolled among the number of the apostles, nor are the seven deacons elected in any other way, than at the sight and approval of the people (Acts vi. 2). "Those examples," says Cyprian, "show that the ordination of a priest behoved not to take place, unless under the consciousness of the people assisting, so that that ordination was just and legitimate which was vouched by the testimony of all." We see, then, that ministers are legitimately called according to the word of God, when those who may have seemed fit are elected on the consent and approbation of the people. Other

1 See chap. iv. sec. 10, 11; chap. v. sec. 2, 3. Also Calv. in Acts vi. 3, and Luther, tom. ii. p. 374.

pastors, however, ought to preside over the election, lest any error should be committed by the general body either through levity, or bad passion, or tumult.

16. It remains to consider the form of ordination, to which we have assigned the last place in the call (see chap. iv., sec. 14, 15). It is certain, that when the apostles appointed any one to the ministry, they used no other ceremony than the laying on of hands. This form was derived, I think, from the custom of the Jews, who, by the laying on of hands, in a manner presented to God whatever they wished to be blessed and consecrated. Thus Jacob, when about to bless Ephraim and Manasseh, placed his hands upon their heads (Gen. xlviii. 14). The same thing was done by our Lord, when he prayed over the little children (Matth. xix. 15). With the same intent (as I imagine), the Jews, according to the injunction of the law, laid hands upon their sacrifices. Wherefore, the apostles, by the laying on of hands, intimated that they made an offering to God of him whom they admitted to the ministry; though they also did the same thing over those on whom they conferred the visible gifts of the Spirit (Acts viii. 17; xix. 6). However this be, it was the regular form, whenever they called any one to the sacred ministry. In this way they consecrated pastors and teachers; in this way they consecrated deacons. But though there is no fixed precept concerning the laying on of hands, yet as we see that it was uniformly observed by the apostles, this careful observance ought to be regarded by us in the light of a precept (see chap. xiv., sec. 29; chap. xix., sec. 31). And it is certainly useful, that by such a symbol the dignity of the ministry should be commended to the people, and he who is ordained, reminded that he is no longer his own, but is bound in service to God and the Church. Besides, it will not prove an empty sign, if it be restored to its genuine origin. For if the Spirit of God has not instituted anything in the Church in vain, this ceremony of his appointment we shall feel not to be useless, provided it be not superstitiously abused. Lastly, it is to observed, that it was not the whole people, but only pastors, who laid hands on ministers, though it is uncertain whether or not several always laid their hands: it is certain, that in the case of the deacons, it was done by Paul and Barnabas, and some few others (Acts vi. 6; xiii. 3). But in another place, Paul mentions that he himself, without any others, laid hands on Timothy. "Wherefore, I put thee in remembrance, that thou stir up the gift of God which is in thee, by the putting on of my hands" (2 Tim. i. 6). For what is said in the First Epistle, of the *laying on of the hands of the presbytery*, I do not understand as if Paul were speaking of the college of Elders. By the expression, I understand the ordination itself; as if he had said, Act so, that the gift which you received by the laying on of hands, when I made you a presbyter, may not be in vain.

CHAPTER IV.

OF THE STATE OF THE PRIMITIVE CHURCH, AND THE MODE OF GOVERNMENT IN USE BEFORE THE PAPACY.

The divisions of this chapter are,—I. The mode of government in the primitive Church, sec 1–10. II. The formal ordination of Bishops and Ministers in the primitive Church, sec. 10–15.

Sections.

1. The method of government in the primitive Church. Not in every respect con formable to the rule of the word of God. Three distinct orders of Ministers.
2. First, the Bishop, for the sake of preserving order, presided over the Presbyters or Pastors. The office of Bishop. Presbyter and Bishop the same. The institution of this order ancient.
3. The office of Bishop and Presbyters. Strictly preserved in the primitive Church.
4. Of Archbishops and Patriarchs. Very seldom used. For what end instituted. Hierarchy an improper name, and not used in Scripture.
5. Deacons, the second order of Ministers in the primitive Church. Their proper office. The Bishop their inspector. Subdeacons, their assistants. Archdeacons, their presidents. The reading of the Gospel, an adventitious office conferred in honour on the Deacons.
6. Mode in which the goods of the Church were anciently dispensed. 1. The support of the poor. 2. Due provision for the ministers of the Church.
7. The administration at first free and voluntary. The revenues of the Church afterwards classed under four heads.
8. A third part of the revenues devoted to the fabric of churches. To this, however, when necessary, the claim of the poor was preferred. Sayings, testimonies, and examples to this effect, from Cyril, Acatius, Jerome, Exuperius, Ambrose.
9. The Clerici, among whom were the Doorkeepers and Acolytes, were the names given to exercises used as a kind of training for tyros.
10. Second part of the chapter, treating of the calling of Ministers. Some error introduced in course of time in respect to celibacy from excessive strictness. In regard to the ordination of Ministers, full regard not always paid to the consent of the people. Why the people less anxious to maintain their right. Ordinations took place at stated times.
11. In the ordination of Bishops the liberty of the people maintained.
12. Certain limits afterwards introduced to restrain the inconsiderate licence of the multitude.
13 This mode of election long prevailed. Testimony of Gregory. Nothing repugnant to this in the decretals of Gratian.
14. The form of ordination in the ancient Church.
15. This form gradually changed.

1. HITHERTO we have discoursed of the order of church government as delivered to us in the pure word of God, and of ministerial offices as instituted by Christ (chap. i. sec. 5, 6 ; chap. iii.). Now that the whole subject may be more clearly and familiarly explained, and also better fixed in our minds, it will be useful to attend to the form of the early church, as this will give us a kind of visible representation of the divine institution. For although the bishops of those

times published many canons, in which they seemed to express more than is expressed by the sacred volume, yet they were so cautious in framing all their economy on the word of God, the only standard, that it is easy to see that they scarcely in any respect departed from it. Even if something may be wanting in these enactments, still, as they were sincerely desirous to preserve the divine institution, and have not strayed far from it, it will be of great benefit here briefly to explain what their observance was. As we have stated that three classes of ministers are set before us in Scripture, so the early Church distributed all its ministers into three orders. For from the order of presbyters, part were selected as pastors and teachers, while to the remainder was committed the censure of manners and discipline. To the deacons belonged the care of the poor and the dispensing of alms. Readers and Acolytes were not the names of certain offices; but those whom they called clergy, they accustomed from their youth to serve the Church by certain exercises, that they might the better understand for what they were destined, and afterwards come better prepared for their duty, as I will shortly show at greater length. Accordingly, Jerome, in setting forth five orders in the Church, enumerates Bishops, Presbyters, Deacons, Believers, Catechumens: to the other Clergy and Monks he gives no proper place [1] (Hieron. in Jes. c. ix.).

2. All, therefore, to whom the office of teaching was committed, they called presbyters, and in each city these presbyters selected one of their number to whom they gave the special title of bishop, lest, as usually happens, from equality dissension should arise. The bishop, however, was not so superior in honour and dignity as to have dominion over his colleagues, but as it belongs to a president in an assembly to bring matters before them, collect their opinions, take precedence of others in consulting, advising, exhorting, guide the whole procedure by his authority, and execute what is decreed by common consent, a bishop held the same office in a meeting of presbyters. And the ancients themselves confess that this practice was introduced by human arrangement, according to the exigency of the times. Thus Jerome, on the Epistle to Titus, cap. i., says, "A bishop is the same as a presbyter. And before dissensions were introduced into religion by the instigation of the devil, and it was said among the people, I am of Paul, and I of Cephas, churches were governed by a common council of presbyters. Afterwards, that the seeds of dissension might be plucked up, the whole charge was devolved upon

1 "Pourtant Sainct Hierome apres avoir divisé l'Eglise en cinq ordres, nomme les Eveques, secondement, les Pretres, tiercement, les Diacres, puis les fideles en commun, finalement, ceux qui n'etoient pas baptisés encore, mais qui s'etoient presentés pour etre instruits en la foy Chretienne; et puis recevoient le baptéme. Ainsi il n'attribue point de certain lieu au reste du Clergé ni aux Moines."—However, St Jerome, after dividing the Church into five orders, names the Bishops, secondly, the Priests, thirdly, the Deacons, then the faithful in common, lastly, those who were not yet baptised, but had presented themselves to be instructed in the Christian faith, and thereafter received baptism. Thus he attributes no certain place to the remainder of the Clergy or to the Monks.

mendatory rescripts, preventions, and the like. But they all conduct one. Therefore, as presbyters know that by the custom of the Church they are subject to him who presides, so let bishops know that they are greater than presbyters more by custom than in consequence of our Lord's appointment, and ought to rule the Church for the common good." In another place he shows how ancient the custom was (Hieron. Epist. ad Evang.). For he says that at Alexandria, from Mark the Evangelist, as far down as Heraclas and Dionysius, presbyters always placed one, selected from themselves, in a higher rank, and gave him the name of bishop. Each city, therefore, had a college of presbyters, consisting of pastors and teachers. For they all performed to the people that office of teaching, exhorting, and correcting, which Paul enjoins on bishops (Tit. i. 9); and that they might leave a seed behind them, they made it their business to train the younger men who had devoted themselves to the sacred warfare. To each city was assigned a certain district which took presbyters from it, and was considered as it were incorporated into that church. Each presbyter, as I have said, merely to preserve order and peace, was under one bishop, who, though he excelled others in dignity, was subject to the meeting of the brethren. But if the district which was under his bishopric was too large for him to be able to discharge all the duties of bishop, presbyters were distributed over it in certain places to act as his substitutes in minor matters. These were called *Chorepiscopi* (rural bishops), because they represented the bishops throughout the province.

3. But, in regard to the office of which we now treat, the bishop as well as the presbyters behoved to employ themselves in the administration of word and sacraments. For, at Alexandria only (as Arius had there troubled the Church), it was enacted, that no presbyter should deliver an address to the people, as Socrates says, Tripartit. Hist. Lib. ix. Jerome does not conceal his dissatisfaction with the enactment (Hieron. Epist. ad Evagr.). It certainly would have been deemed monstrous for one to give himself out as a bishop, and yet not show himself a true bishop by his conduct. Such, then, was the strictness of those times, that all ministers were obliged to fulfil the office as the Lord requires of them. Nor do I refer to the practice of one age only, since not even in the time of Gregory, when the Church had almost fallen (certainly had greatly degenerated from ancient purity), would any bishop have been tolerated who abstained from preaching. In some part of his twenty-fourth Epistle he says, "The priest dies when no sound is heard from him: for he calls forth the wrath of the unseen Judge against him if he walks without the sound of preaching." Elsewhere he says, "When Paul testifies that he is pure from the blood of all men (Acts xx. 26), by his words, we, who are called priests, are charged, are arraigned, are shown to be guilty, since to those sins which we have of our own we add the deaths of other men, for we commit murder as often as lukewarm and silent we see them daily going to destruction" (Gregor. Hom. in

Ezek. xi. 26). He calls himself and others silent when less assiduous in their work than they ought to be. Since he does not spare even those who did their duty partially, what think you would he do in the case of those who entirely neglected it? For a long time, therefore, it was regarded in the Church as the first duty of a bishop to feed the people by the word of God, or to edify the Church, in public and private, with sound doctrine.

4. As to the fact, that each province had an archbishop among the bishops (see chap. vii. sec. 15), and, moreover, that, in the Council of Nice, patriarchs were appointed to be superior to archbishops, in order and dignity, this was designed for the preservation of discipline, although, in treating of the subject here, it ought not to be omitted, that the practice was very rare. The chief reason for which these orders were instituted was, that if anything occurred in any church which could not well be explicated by a few, it might be referred to a provincial synod. If the magnitude or difficulty of the case demanded a larger discussion, patriarchs were employed along with synods,[1] and from them there was no appeal except to a General Council. To the government thus constituted some gave the name of Hierarchy—a name, in my opinion, improper, certainly one not used by Scripture. For the Holy Spirit designed to provide that no one should dream of primacy or domination in regard to the government of the Church. But if, disregarding the term, we look to the thing, we shall find that the ancient bishops had no wish to frame a form of church government different from that which God has prescribed in his word.

5. Nor was the case of deacons then different from what it had been under the apostles (chap. iii. sec. 6). For they received the daily offerings of the faithful, and the annual revenues of the Church, that they might apply them to their true uses; in other words, partly in maintaining ministers, and partly in supporting the poor; at the sight of the bishop, however, to whom they every year gave an account of their stewardship. For, although the canons uniformly make the bishop the dispenser of all the goods of the Church, this is not to be understood as if he by himself undertook that charge, but because it belonged to him to prescribe to the deacon who were to be admitted to the public alimony of the Church, and point out to what persons, and in what portions, the residue was to be distributed, and because he was entitled to see whether the deacon faithfully performed his office. Thus, in the canons which they ascribe to the apostles, it is said, "We command that the bishop have the affairs of the Church under his control. For if the souls of men, which are more precious, have been intrusted to him, much more is he entitled to have the charge of money matters, so that under his control all may be dispensed to the poor by the presbyters and deacons, that the ministra-

[1] French, "La cognoissance venoit aux patriarches, qui assemblerent le concile de tous les eveques respondant a leur primauté;"—the cognisance fell to the patriarchs, who assembled a council of all the bishops corresponding to their precedence.

tion may be made reverently and with due care." And in the Council of Antioch, it was decreed (cap. xxxv.), that bishops, who intermeddled with the effects of the Church, without the knowledge of the presbyters and deacons, should be restrained. But there is no occasion to discuss this point farther, since it is evident, from many of the letters of Gregory, that even at that time, when the ecclesiastical ordinances were otherwise much vitiated, it was still the practice for the deacons to be, under the bishops, the stewards of the poor. It is probable that at the first subdeacons were attached to the deacons, to assist them in the management of the poor; but the distinction was gradually lost. Archdeacons began to be appointed when the extent of the revenues demanded a new and more exact method of administration, though Jerome mentions that it already existed in his day.[1] To them belonged the amount of revenues, possessions, and furniture, and the charge of the daily offerings. Hence Gregory declares to the Archdeacon Solitanus, that the blame rested with him, if any of the goods of the Church perished through his fraud or negligence. The reading of the word to the people, and exhortation to prayer, was assigned to them, and they were permitted, moreover, to give the cup in the sacred Supper; but this was done for the purpose of honouring their office, that they might perform it with greater reverence, when they were reminded by such symbols that what they discharged was not some profane stewardship, but a spiritual function dedicated to God.

6. Hence, also, we may judge what was the use, and of what nature was the distribution of ecclesiastical goods. You may everywhere find, both from the decrees of synods, and from ancient writers, that whatever the Church possessed, either in lands or in money, was the patrimony of the poor. Accordingly, the saying is ever and anon sounded in the ears of bishops and deacons, Remember that you are not handling your own property, but that destined for the necessities of the poor; if you dishonestly conceal or dilapidate it, you will be guilty of blood. Hence they are admonished to distribute them to those to whom they are due, with the greatest fear and reverence, as in the sight of God, without respect of persons. Hence, also, in Chrysostom, Ambrose, Augustine, and other like bishops, those grave obtestations in which they assert their integrity before the people. But since it is just in itself, and was sanctioned by a divine law, that those who devote their labour to the Church shall be supported at the public expense of the Church, and some presbyters in that age having consecrated their patrimony to God, had become voluntarily poor, the distribution was so made that aliment was afforded to ministers, and the poor were not neglected. Meanwhile, it was provided that the ministers themselves, who ought to be an example of frugality to others, should not have so much as might be abused for luxury or delicacy; but only what might be needful to support their wants:

1 Hieronymus, Epist. ad Nepotianum. It is mentioned also by Chrysostom, Epist. ad Innocent.

"For those clergy, who can be supported by their own patrimony," says Jerome, "commit sacrilege if they accept what belongs to the poor, and by such abuse eat and drink judgment to themselves."

7. At first the administration was free and voluntary, when bishops and deacons were faithful of their own accord, and when integrity of conscience and purity of life supplied the place of laws. Afterwards, when, from the cupidity and depraved desires of some, bad examples arose, canons were framed, to correct these evils, and divided the revenues of the Church into four parts, assigning one to the clergy, another to the poor, another to the repair of churches and other edifices, a fourth to the poor, whether[1] strangers or natives. For though other canons attribute this last part to the bishop, it differs in no respect from the division which I have mentioned. For they do not mean that it is his property, which he may devour alone or squander in any way he pleases, but that it may enable him to use the hospitality which Paul requires in that order (1 Tim. iii. 2). This is the interpretation of Gelasius and Gregory. For the only reason which Gelasius gives why the bishop should claim anything to himself is, that he may be able to bestow it on captives and strangers. Gregory speaks still more clearly: "It is the custom of the Apostolic See," says he, "to give command to the bishop who has been ordained, to divide all the revenues into four portions—namely, one to the bishop and his household for hospitality and maintenance, another to the clergy, a third to the poor, a fourth to the repair of churches." The bishop, therefore, could not lawfully take for his own use more than was sufficient for moderate and frugal food and clothing. When any one began to wanton either in luxury or ostentation and show, he was immediately reprimanded by his colleagues, and if he obeyed not, was deprived of his honours.

8. Moreover, the sum expended on the adorning of churches was at first very trifling, and even afterwards, when the Church had become somewhat more wealthy, they in that matter observed mediocrity. Still, whatever money was then collected was reserved for the poor, when any greater necessity occurred. Thus Cyril, when a famine prevailed in the province of Jerusalem, and the want could not otherwise be supplied, took the vessels and robes and sold them for the support of the poor. In like manner, Acatius, Bishop of Amida, when a great multitude of the Persians were almost destroyed by famine, having assembled the clergy, and delivered this noble address, "Our God has no need either of chalices or salvers, for he neither eats nor drinks" (Tripart. Hist. Lib. v. and Lib. xi. c. 16), melted down the plate, that he might be able to furnish food and obtain the means of ransoming the miserable. Jerome also, while inveighing against the excessive splendour of churches, relates that Exuperius, Bishop of Tholouse, in his day, though he carried the

[1] In the Amsterdam edition the words are only "quartam vero advenis pauperibus." The Geneva edition of 1559, the last published under Calvin's own eye, has "quartam vero tam advenis quam indigenis pauperibus." With this Tholuck agrees.

body of the Lord in a wicker basket, and his blood in a glass, nevertheless suffered no poor man to be hungry (Hieron. ad Nepotian). What I lately said of Acatius, Ambrose relates of himself. For when the Arians assailed him for having broken down the sacred vessels for the ransom of captives, he made this most admirable excuse: "He who sent the apostles without gold has also gathered churches without gold. The Church has gold not to keep but to distribute, and give support in necessity. What need is there of keeping what is of no benefit? Are we ignorant how much gold and silver the Assyrians carried off from the temple of the Lord? Is it not better for a priest to melt them for the support of the poor, if other means are wanting, than for a sacrilegious enemy to carry them away? Would not the Lord say, Why have you suffered so many poor to die of hunger, and you certainly had gold wherewith to minister to their support? Why have so many captives been carried away and not redeemed? Why have so many been slain by the enemy? It had been better to preserve living than metallic vessels. These charges you will not be able to answer: for what could you say? I feared lest the temple of God should want ornament. He would answer, Sacraments require not gold, and things which are not bought with gold please not by gold. The ornament of the Sacraments is the ransom of captives" (Ambros. de Offic. Lib. ii. c. 28). In a word, we see the exact truth of what he elsewhere says—viz. that whatever the Church then possessed was the revenue of the needy. Again, A bishop has nothing but what belongs to the poor (Ambros. Lib. v. Ep. 31, 33).

9. We have now reviewed the ministerial offices of the ancient Church. For others, of which ecclesiastical writers make mention, were rather exercises and preparations than distinct offices. These holy men, that they might leave a nursery of the Church behind them, received young men, who, with the consent and authority of their parents, devoted themselves to the spiritual warfare under their guardianship and training, and so formed them from their tender years, that they might not enter on the discharge of the office as ignorant novices. All who received this training were designated by the general name of *Clerks*. I could wish that some more appropriate name had been given them, for this appellation had its origin in error, or at least improper feeling, since the whole church is by Peter denominated κληρος (*clerus*), that is, the inheritance of the Lord (1 Pet. v. 3). It was in itself, however, a most sacred and salutary institution, that those who wished to devote themselves and their labour to the Church should be brought up under the charge of the bishop; so that no one should minister in the Church unless he had been previously well trained, unless he had in early life imbibed sound doctrine, unless by stricter discipline he had formed habits of gravity and severer morals, been withdrawn from ordinary business, and accustomed to spiritual cares and studies. For as tyros in the military art are trained by mock fights for true and serious warfare, so there was a rudimental training by which they were exercised in

clerical duty before they were actually appointed to office. First, then, they intrusted them with the opening and shutting of the church, and called them Ostiarii. Next, they gave the name of Acolytes to those who assisted the bishop in domestic services, and constantly attended him, first, as a mark of respect; and, secondly, that no suspicion might arise.[1] Moreover, that they might gradually become known to the people, and recommend themselves to them, and at the same time might learn to stand the gaze of all, and speak before all, that they might not, when appointed presbyters, be overcome with shame when they came forward to teach, the office of reading in the desk was given them.[2] In this way they were gradually advanced, that they might prove their carefulness in separate exercises, until they were appointed subdeacons. All I mean by this is, that these were rather the rudimentary exercises of tyros than functions which were accounted among the true ministries of the Church.

10. In regard to what we have set down as the first and second heads in the calling of ministers—viz. the persons to be elected and the religious care to be therein exercised—the ancient Church followed the injunction of Paul, and the examples of the apostles. For they were accustomed to meet for the election of pastors with the greatest reverence, and with earnest prayer to God. Moreover, they had a form of examination by which they tested the life and doctrine of those who were to be elected by the standard of Paul (1 Tim. iii. 2); only here they sometimes erred from excessive strictness, by exacting more of a bishop than Paul requires, and especially, in process of time, by exacting celibacy: but in other respects their practice corresponded with Paul's description. In regard to our third head, however—viz. Who were entitled to appoint ministers?—they did not always observe the same rule. Anciently none were admitted to the number of the clergy without the consent of the whole people: and hence Cyprian makes a laboured apology for having appointed Aurelius a reader without consulting the Church, because, although done contrary to custom, it was not done without reason. He thus premises: "In ordaining clergy, dearest brethren, we are wont previously to consult you, and weigh the manners and merits of each by the common advice" (Cyprian. Lib. ii. Ep. 5). But as in these minor exercises[3] there was no great danger, inasmuch as they were appointed to a long probation and unimportant function, the consent of the people ceased to be asked. Afterwards, in other orders also, with the exception of the bishopric, the people usually left the choice and decision to the bishop and presbyters, who thus determined who were fit and worthy, unless, perhaps, when new presbyters were appointed to parishes, for then the express consent of the inhabitants of the place behoved to be given. Nor is it strange that in this matter the people

1 The French adds, "Afin qu'il n'allâ nulle part sans compagnie et sans temoin;"—in order that he might not go anywhere without company and without witness

2 French, "On leur ordonnoit de faire la lecture des Pseaumes au pulpitre;"—they ordered them to read the Psalms in the desk.

3 The French adds, "Comme de Lecteurs et Acolytes;"—as Readers and Acolytes.

were not very anxious to maintain their right, for no subdeacon was appointed who had not given a long proof of his conduct in the clerical office, agreeably to the strictness of discipline then in use. After he had approved himself in that degree, he was appointed deacon, and thereafter, if he conducted himself faithfully, he attained to the honour of a presbyter. Thus none were promoted whose conduct had not, in truth, been tested for many years under the eye of the people. There were also many canons for punishing their faults, so that the Church, if she did not neglect the remedies, was not burdened with bad presbyters or deacons. In the case of presbyters, indeed, the consent of the citizens was always required, as is attested by the canon (Primus Distinct. 67), which is attributed to Anacletus. In fine, all ordinations took place at stated periods of the year, that none might creep in stealthily without the consent of the faithful, or be promoted with too much facility without witnesses.

11. In electing bishops, the people long retained their right of preventing any one from being intruded who was not acceptable to all. Accordingly, it was forbidden by the Council of Antioch to induct any one on the unwilling. This also Leo I. carefully confirms. Hence these passages: "Let him be elected whom the clergy and people or the majority demand." Again, "Let him who is to preside over all be elected by all" (Leo, Ep. 90, cap. 2). He, therefore, who is appointed while unknown and unexamined, must of necessity be violently intruded. Again, "Let him be elected who is chosen by the clergy, and called by the people, and let him be consecrated by the provincials with the judgment of the metropolitan." So careful were the holy fathers that this liberty of the people should on no account be diminished, that when a general council, assembled at Constantinople, were ordaining Nectarius, they declined to do it without the approbation of the whole clergy and people, as their letter to the Roman synod testified. Accordingly, when any bishop nominated his successor, the act was not ratified without consulting the whole people. Of this you have not only an example, but the form, in Augustine, in the nomination of Eradius (August. Ep. 110). And Theodoret, after relating that Peter was the successor nominated by Athanasius, immediately adds, that the sacerdotal order ratified it, that the magistracy, chief men, and whole people, by their acclamation approved.[1]

12. It was, indeed, decreed (and I admit on the best grounds) by the Council of Laodicea (Can. xviii.) that the election should not be left to crowds. For it scarcely ever happens that so many heads, with one consent, settle any affair well. It generally holds true, "Incertum scindi studia in contraria vulgus;"—"Opposing wishes rend the fickle crowd." For, first, the clergy alone selected, and presented him whom they had selected to the magistrate, or senate, and chief men. These, after deliberation, put their signature to the

1 The whole narrative in Theodoret is most deserving of notice. Theodoret. Lib. iv. cap. xx.

election, if it seemed proper, if not, they chose another whom they more highly approved. The matter was then laid before the multitude, who, although not bound by those previous proceedings, were less able to act tumultuously. Or, if the matter began with the multitude, it was only that it might be known whom they were most desirous to have; the wishes of the people being heard, the clergy at length elected. Thus, it was neither lawful for the clergy to appoint whom they chose, nor were they, however, under the necessity of yielding to the foolish desires of the people. Leo sets down this order, when he says, "The wishes of the citizens, the testimonies of the people, the choice of the honourable, the election of the clergy, are to be waited for" (Leo, Ep. 87). Again, "Let the testimony of the honourable, the subscription of the clergy, the consent of the magistracy and people, be obtained; otherwise (says he) it must on no account be done." Nor is anything more intended by the decree of the Council of Laodicea, than that the clergy and rulers were not to allow themselves to be carried away by the rash multitude, but rather by their prudence and gravity to repress their foolish desires whenever there was occasion.

13. This mode of election was still in force in the time of Gregory, and probably continued to a much later period. Many of his letters which are extant clearly prove this, for whenever a new bishop is to be elected, his custom is to write to the clergy, magistrates, and people; sometimes also to the governor, according to the nature of the government. But if, on account of the unsettled state of the Church, he gives the oversight of the election to a neighbouring bishop, he always requires a formal decision confirmed by the subscriptions ot all. Nay, when one Constantius was elected Bishop of Milan, and in consequence of the incursions of the Barbarians many of the Milanese had fled to Genoa, he thought that the election would not be lawful unless they too were called together and gave their assent (Gregor. Lib. ii. Ep. 69). Nay, five hundred years have not elapsed since Pope Nicholas fixed the election of the Roman Pontiff in this way, first, that the cardinals should precede; next, that they should join to themselves the other clergy; and, lastly, that the election should be ratified by the consent of the people. And in the end he recites the decree of Leo, which I lately quoted, and orders it to be enforced in future. But should the malice of the wicked so prevail that the clergy are obliged to quit the city, in order to make a pure election, he, however, orders that some of the people shall, at the same time, be present. The suffrage of the Emperor, as far as we can understand, was required only in two churches, those of Rome and Constantinople, these being the two seats of empire. For when Ambrose was sent by Valentinianus to Milan with authority to superintend the election of a new bishop, it was an extraordinary proceeding, in consequence of the violent factions which raged among the citizens. But at Rome the authority of the Emperor in the election of the bishop was so great, that Gregory says he was appointed to the government

of the Church by his order (Gregor. Lib. i. Ep. 5), though he had been called by the people in regular form. The custom, however, was, that when the magistrates, clergy, and people, nominated any one, he was forthwith presented to the Emperor, who either by approving ratified, or by disapproving annulled the election. There is nothing contrary to this practice in the decretals which are collected by Gratian, where all that is said is, that it was on no account to be tolerated, that canonical election should be abolished, and a king should at pleasure appoint a bishop, and that one thus promoted by violent authority was not to be consecrated by the metropolitans. For it is one thing to deprive the Church of her right, and transfer it entirely to the caprice of a single individual; it is another thing to assign to a king or emperor the honour of confirming a legitimate election by his authority.

14. It now remains to treat of the form by which the ministers of the ancient Church were initiated to their office after election. This was termed by the Latins, Ordination or consecration, and by the Greeks χειροτονία, sometimes also χειροθεσία, though χειροτονία properly denotes that mode of election by which suffrages are declared by a show of hands. There is extant a decree of the Council of Nice, to the effect that the metropolitans, with all the bishops of the province, were to meet to ordain him who was chosen. But if, from distance, or sickness, or any other necessary cause, part were prevented, three at least should meet, and those who were absent signify their consent by letter. And this canon, after it had fallen into desuetude, was afterwards renewed by several councils. All, or at least all who had not an excuse, were enjoined to be present, in order that a stricter examination might be had of the life and doctrine of him who was to be ordained; for the thing was not done without examination. And it appears, from the words of Cyprian, that, in old time, they were not wont to be called after the election, but to be present at the election, and with the view of their acting as moderators, that no disorder might be committed by the crowd. For after saying that the people had the power either of choosing worthy or refusing unworthy priests, he immediately adds, "For which reason, we must carefully observe and hold by the divine and apostolic tradition (which is observed by us also, and almost by all the provinces), that for the due performance of ordinations all the nearest bishops of the province should meet with the people over whom the person is proposed to be ordained, and the bishop should be elected in presence of the people. But as they were sometimes too slowly assembled, and there was a risk that some might abuse the delay for purposes of intrigue, it was thought that it would be sufficient if they came after the designation was made, and on due investigation consecrated him who had been approved.

15. While this was done everywhere without exception, a different custom gradually gained ground—namely, that those who were elected

should go to the metropolitan to obtain ordination. This was owing more to ambition, and the corruption of the ancient custom, than to any good reason. And not long after, the authority of the Romish See being now increased, another still worse custom was introduced, of applying to it for the consecration of the bishops of almost all Italy. This we may observe from the letters of Gregory (Lib. ii. Ep. 69, 76). The ancient right was preserved by a few cities only which had not yielded so easily; for instance, Milan. Perhaps metropolitan sees only retained their privilege. For, in order to consecrate an archbishop, it was the practice for all the provincial bishops to meet in the metropolitan city. The form used was the laying on of hands (chap. xix. sec. 28, 31). I do not read that any other ceremonies were used, except that, in the public meeting, the bishops had some dress to distinguish them from the other presbyters. Presbyters, also, and deacons, were ordained by the laying on of hands; but each bishop, with the college of presbyters, ordained his own presbyters. But though they all did the same act, yet because the bishop presided, and the ordination was performed as it were under his auspices, it was said to be his. Hence ancient writers often say that a presbyter does not differ in any respect from a bishop except in not having the power of ordaining.

CHAPTER V.

THE ANCIENT FORM OF GOVERNMENT UTTERLY CORRUPTED BY THE TYRANNY OF THE PAPACY.

This chapter consists of two parts,—I. Who are called to the ministry under the Papacy, their character, and the ground of their appointment, sec. 1–7. II. How far they fulfil their office, sec. 8–19.

Sections.

1. Who and what kind of persons are uniformly appointed bishops in the Papacy. 1. No inquiry into doctrine. 2. In regard to character, the unlearned and dissolute, boys, or men of wicked lives, chosen.
2. The right of the people taken away, though maintained by Leo, Cyprian, and Councils. It follows, that there is no Canonical election in the Papacy. Two objections answered. Papal elections, what. Kind of persons elected.
3. A fuller explanation of the answer to the second objection, unfolding the errors of people, bishops, and princes.
4. No election of presbyters and deacons in the Papacy. 1. Because they are ordained for a different end. 2. Contrary to the command of Scripture and the Council of Chalcedon, no station is assigned them. 3. Both the name and thing adulterated by a thousand frauds.
5. Refutation of those corruptions. Proper end of ordination. Of trial, and other necessary things. For these, wicked and sanguinary men have substituted vain show and deplorable blindness.
6. Second corruption relating to the assignation of benefices which they call collation. Manifold abuses here exposed. Why the offices of priests are in the Papacy called benefices.
7. One individual appointed over five or six churches. This most shameful corruption severely condemned by many Councils.
8. Second part of the chapter—viz. how the office is discharged. Monks who have no place among Presbyters. Objection answered.
9. Presbyters divided into beneficiaries and mercenaries. The beneficiaries are bishops, parsons, canons, chaplains, abbots, priors. The mercenaries condemned by the word of God.
10. The name of beneficiaries given to idle priests who perform no office in the church. Objection answered. What kind of persons the canons should be. Another objection answered. The beneficiaries not true presbyters.
11. The bishops and rectors of parishes, by deserting their churches, glory only in an empty name.
12. The seeds of this evil in the age of Gregory, who inveighs against mercenaries. More sharply rebuked by Bernard.
13. The supreme Popish administration described. Ridiculous allegation of those so-called ministers of the Church. Answer.
14. Their shameful morals. Scarcely one who would not have been excommunicated or deposed by the ancient canons.
15. No true diaconate existing in the Papacy, though they have still the shadow of it. Corruption of the practice of the primitive Church in regard to deacons.
16. Ecclesiastical property, which was formerly administered by true deacons, plundered by bishops and canons, in defraud of the poor.
17. Blasphemous defence of these robbers. Answer. Kings doing homage to Christ. Theodosius. A saying of Ambrose.
18. Another defence with regard to the adorning of churches. Answer.
19. Concluding answer, showing that the diaconate is completely subverted by the Papacy.

1. It may now be proper to bring under the eye of the reader the order of church government observed by the Roman See and all its satellites, and the whole of that hierarchy, which they have perpetually in their mouths, and compare it with the description we have given of the primitive and early Church, that the contrast may make it manifest what kind of church those have who plume themselves on the very title, as sufficient to outweigh, or rather overwhelm us. It will be best to begin with the call, that we may see who are called to the ministry, with what character, and on what grounds. Thereafter we will consider how far they faithfully fulfil their office. We shall give the first place to the bishops; would that they could claim the honour of holding the first rank in this disscussion! But the subject does not allow me even to touch it lightly, without exposing their disgrace. Still, let me remember in what kind of writing I am engaged, and not allow my discourse, which ought to be framed for simple teaching, to wander beyond its proper limits. But let any of them, who have not laid aside all modesty, tell me what kind of bishops are uniformly elected in the present day. Any examination of doctrine is too old fashioned, but if any respect is had to doctrine, they make choice of some lawyer who knows better how to plead in the forum than to preach in the church. This much is certain, that for a hundred years, scarcely one in a hundred has been elected who had any acquaintance with sacred doctrine. I do not spare former ages because they were much better, but because the question now relates only to the present Church. If morals be inquired into, we shall find few or almost none whom the ancient canons would not have judged unworthy. If one was not a drunkard, he was a fornicator; if one was free from this vice, he was either a gambler or sportsman, or a loose liver in some respect. For there are lighter faults which, according to the ancient canons, exclude from the episcopal office. But the most absurd thing of all is, that even boys scarcely ten years of age are, by the permission of the Pope, made bishops. Such is the effrontery and stupidity to which they have arrived, that they have no dread even of that last and monstrous iniquity, which is altogether abhorrent even from natural feeling. Hence it appears what kind of elections these must have been, when such supine negligence existed.

2. Then in election, the whole right has been taken from the people. Vows, assents, subscriptions, and all things of this sort, have disappeared; the whole power has been given to the canons alone. First, they confer the episcopal office on whomsoever they please; by-and-by they bring him forth into the view of the people, but it is to be adored, not examined. But Leo protests that no reason permits this, and declares it to be a violent imposition (Leo, Ep. 90, cap. 2). Cyprian, after declaring it to be of divine authority, that election should not take place without the consent of the people, shows that a different procedure is at variance with the word of God. Numerous decrees of councils most strictly forbid it to be

otherwise done, and if done, order it to be null. If this is true, there is not throughout the whole Papacy in the present day any canonical election in accordance either with divine or ecclesiastical law. Now, were there no other evil in this, what excuse can they give for having robbed the Church of her right? But the corruption of the times required (they say), that since hatred and party-spirit prevailed with the people and magistrates in the election of bishops more than right and sound judgment, the determination should be confined to a few. Allow that this was the last remedy in desperate circumstances. When the cure was seen to be more hurtful than the disease, why was not a remedy provided for this new evil? But it is said that the course which the Canons must follow is strictly prescribed. But can we doubt, that even in old times the people, on meeting to elect a bishop, were aware that they were bound by the most sacred laws, when they saw a rule prescribed by the word of God? That one sentence in which God describes the true character of a bishop ought justly to be of more weight than ten thousand canons. Nevertheless, carried away by the worst of feelings, they had no regard to law or equity. So in the present day, though most excellent laws have been made, they remain buried in writing. Meanwhile, the general and approved practice is (and it is carried on as it were systematically), that drunkards, fornicators, gamblers, are everywhere promoted to this honour; nay, this is little: bishoprics are the rewards of adulterers and panders: for when they are given to hunters and hawkers, things may be considered at the best. To excuse such unworthy procedure in any way, were to be wicked over much. The people had a most excellent canon prescribed to them by the word of God—viz. that a bishop must be blameless, apt to teach, not a brawler, &c. (1 Tim. iii. 2). Why, then, was the province of electing transferred from the people to these men? Just because among the tumults and factions of the people the word of God was not heard. And, on the other hand, why is it not in the present day transferred from these men, who not only violate all laws, but having cast off shame, libidinously, avariciously, and ambitiously, mix and confound things human and divine?

3. But it is not true to say that the thing was devised as a remedy. We read, that in old times tumults often arose in cities at the election of bishops; yet no one ever ventured to think of depriving the citizens of their right: for they had other methods by which they could either prevent the fault, or correct it when committed. I will state the matter as it truly is. When the people began to be negligent in making their choice, and left the business, as less suited to them, to the presbyters, these abused the opportunity to usurp a domination, which they afterwards established by putting forth new canons. Ordination is now nothing else than a mere mockery. For the kind of examination of which they make a display is so empty and trifling, that it even entirely wants the semblance. Therefore. when sovereigns, by paction with the Roman Pontiffs, obtained for

themselves the right of nominating bishops, the Church sustained no new injury, because the canons were merely deprived of an election which they had seized without any right, or acquired by stealth. Nothing, indeed, can be more disgraceful, than that bishops should be sent from courts to take possession of churches, and pious princes would do well to desist from such corruption. For there is an impious spoliation of the Church whenever any people have a bishop intruded whom they have not asked, or at least freely approved. But that disorderly practice, which long existed in churches, gave occasion to sovereigns to assume to themselves the presentation of bishops. They wished the benefice to belong to themselves, rather than to those who had no better right to it, and who equally abused it.

4. Such is the famous call, on account of which bishops boast that they are the successors of the apostles. They say, moreover, that they alone can competently appoint presbyters. But herein they most shamefully corrupt the ancient institution, that they by their ordination appoint not presbyters to guide and feed the people, but priests to sacrifice. In like manner, when they consecrate deacons, they pay no regard to their true and proper office, but only ordain to certain ceremonies concerning the cup and paten. But in the Council of Chalcedon it was, on the contrary, decreed that there should be no absolute ordinations, that is, ordinations without assigning to the ordained a place where they were to exercise their office. This decree is most useful for two reasons—first, That churches may not be burdened with superfluous expense, nor idle men receive what ought to be distributed to the poor; and, secondly, That those who are ordained may consider that they are not promoted merely to an honorary office, but intrusted with a duty which they are solemnly bound to discharge. But the Roman authorities (who think that nothing is to be cared for in religion but their belly) consider the first title to be a revenue adequate to their support, whether it be from their own patrimony or from the priesthood. Accordingly, when they ordain presbyters or deacons, without any anxiety as to where they ought to minister, they confer the order, provided those ordained are sufficiently rich to support themselves. But what man can admit that the title which the decree of the council requires is an annual revenue for sustenance? Again, when more recent canons made bishops liable in the support of those whom they had ordained without a fit title, that they might thus repress too great facility, a method was devised of eluding the penalty. For he who is ordained promises that whatever be the title named he will be contented with it. In this way he is precluded from an action for aliment. I say nothing of the thousand frauds which are here committed, as when some falsely claim the empty titles of benefices, from which they cannot obtain a sixpence of revenue, and others by secret stipulation obtain a temporary appointment, which they promise that they will immediately restore, but sometimes do not. There are still more mysteries of the same kind.

5. But although these grosser abuses were removed, is it not at all times absurd to appoint a presbyter without assigning him a locality? For when they ordain it is only to sacrifice. But the legitimate ordination of a presbyter is to the government of the Church, while deacons are called to the charge of alms. It is true, many pompous ceremonies are used to disguise the act, that mere show may excite veneration in the simple; but what effect can these semblances have upon men of sound minds, when beneath them there is nothing solid or true? They used ceremonies either borrowed from Judaism or devised by themselves; from these it were better if they would abstain. Of the trial (for it is unnecessary to say anything of the shadow which they retain), of the consent of the people, of other necessary things, there is no mention. By shadow, I mean those ridiculous gesticulations framed in inept and frigid imitation of antiquity. The bishops have their vicars, who, previous to ordination, inquire into doctrine. But what is the inquiry? Is it whether they are able to read their Missals, or whether they can decline some common noun which occurs in the lesson, or conjugate a verb, or give the meaning of some one word? For it is not necessary to give the sense of a single sentence. And yet even those who are deficient in these puerile elements are not repelled, provided they bring the recommendation of money or influence. Of the same nature is the question which is thrice put in an unintelligible voice, when the persons who are to be ordained are brought to the altar—viz. Are they worthy of the honour? One (who never saw them, but has his part in the play, that no form may be wanting) answers, They are worthy.[1] What can you accuse in these venerable fathers save that, by indulging in such sacrilegious sport, they shamelessly laugh at God and man? But as they have long been in possession of the thing, they think they have now a legal title to it. For any one who ventures to open his lips against these palpable and flagrant iniquities is hurried off to a capital trial, like one who had in old time divulged the mysteries of Ceres. Would they act thus if they had any belief in a God?

6. Then in the collation of benefices (which was formerly conjoined with ordination, but is now altogether separate), how much better do they conduct themselves? But they have many reasons to give, for it is not bishops alone who confer the office of priests (and even in their case, where they are called Collators, they have not always the full right), but others have the presentation, while they only retain the honorary title of collations. To these are added nominations from schools, resignations, either simple or by way of exchange, com-

1 "C'est un acte semblable, que quand ceux qu'on doit promouvoir se presentent à l'autel, on demande par trois fois en Latin, s'il ést digne; et quelcun qui ne l'a jamais vue, ou quelque valet de chambre que n'entend point Latin, repond en Latin qu'il est digne: tout ainsi qu'un personnage joueroit son rolle en une farce."—In like manner, when those whom they are to promote present themselves at the altar, they ask, three times in Latin, if he is worthy; and some one who has never seen him, or some valet who does not understand Latin, replies, in Latin, that he is worthy: just as a person would play his part in a farce.

mendatory rescripts, preventions, and the like. But they all conduct themselves in such a way that one cannot upbraid another. I maintain that, in the Papacy in the present day, scarcely one benefice in a hundred is conferred without simony, as the ancients have defined it (Calv. in Art. viii. 21). I say not that all purchase for a certain sum; but show me one in twenty who does not attain to the priesthood by some sinister method. Some owe their promotion to kindred or affinity, others to the influence of their parents, while others procure favour by obsequiousness. In short, the end for which the offices are conferred is, that provision may be made not for churches, but for those who receive them. Accordingly, they call them benefices, by which name they sufficiently declare, that they look on them in no other light than as the largesses by which princes either court the favour or reward the services of their soldiers. I say nothing of the fact, that these rewards are conferred on barbers, cooks, grooms, and dross of that sort. At present, indeed, there are no cases in law courts which make a greater noise than those concerning sacerdotal offices, so that you may regard them as nothing else than game set before dogs to be hunted. Is it tolerable even to hear the name of pastors given to those who have forced their way into the possession of a church as into an enemy's country? who have evicted it by forensic brawls? who have bought it for a price? who have laboured for it by sordid sycophancy? who, while scarcely lisping boys, have obtained it like heritage from uncles and relatives? Sometimes even bastards obtain it from their fathers.

7. Was the licentiousness of the people, however corrupt and lawless, ever carried to such a height? But a more monstrous thing still is, that one man (I say not what kind of man, but certainly one who cannot govern himself) is appointed to the charge of five or six churches. In the courts of princes in the present day, you may see youths who are thrice abbots, twice bishops, once archbishops. Everywhere are Canons loaded with five, six, or seven cures, of not one of which they take the least charge, except to draw the income. I will not object that the word of God cries aloud against this: it has long ceased to have the least weight with them. I will not object that many councils denounce the severest punishment against this dishonest practice; these, too, when it suits them, they boldly contemn. But I say that it is monstrous wickedness, altogether opposed to God, to nature, and to ecclesiastical government, that one thief should lie brooding over several churches, that the name of pastor should be given to one who, even if he were willing, could not be present among his flock, and yet (such is their impudence) they cloak these abominations with the name of church, that they may exempt them from all blame. Nay, if you please, in these iniquities is contained that sacred succession to which, as they boast, it is owing that the Church does not perish.

8. Let us now see, as the second mark for estimating a legitimate pastor, how faithfully they discharge their office. Of the priests

who are there elected, some are called monks, others seculars. The former herd was unknown to the early Church; even to hold such a place in the Church is so repugnant to the monastic profession, that in old times, when persons were elected out of monasteries to clerical offices, they ceased to be monks. And, accordingly, Gregory, though in his time there were many abuses, did not suffer the offices to be thus confounded (Gregor. Lib. iii. Ep. 11). For he insists that those who have been appointed abbots shall resign the clerical office, because no one can be properly at the same time a monk and a clerk, the one being an obstacle to the other. Now, were I to ask how he can well fulfil his office who is declared by the canons to be unfit, what answer, pray, will they give? They will quote those abortive decrees of Innocent and Boniface, by which monks are admitted to the honour and power of the priesthood, though they remain in their monasteries. But is it at all reasonable that any unlearned ass, as soon as he has seized upon the Roman See, may by one little word overturn all antiquity? But of this matter afterwards. Let it now suffice, that in the purer times of the Church it was regarded as a great absurdity for a monk to hold the office of priest. For Jerome declares that he does not the office of priest while he is living among monks, and ranks himself as one of the people to be governed by the priests. But to concede this to them, what duty do they perform? Some of the mendicants preach, while all the other monks chant or mutter masses in their cells; as if either our Saviour had wished, or the nature of the office permits, presbyters to be made for such a purpose. When Scripture plainly testifies that it is the duty of a presbyter to rule his own church (Acts xx. 28), is it not impious profanation to transfer it to another purpose, nay, altogether to change the sacred institution of God? For when they are ordained, they are expressly forbidden to do what God enjoins on all presbyters. For this is their cant, Let a monk, contented with his cell, neither presume to administer the sacraments, nor hold any other public office. Let them deny, if they can, that it is open mockery of God when any one is appointed a presbyter in order to abstain from his proper and genuine office, and when he who has the name is not able to have the thing.

9. I come to the seculars, some of whom are (as they speak) beneficiaries; that is, have offices by which they are maintained, while others let out their services, day by day, to chant or say masses, and live in a manner on a stipend thus collected. Benefices either have a cure of souls, as bishoprics and parochial charges, or they are the stipends of delicate men, who gain a livelihood by chanting; as prebends, canonries, parsonships, deaneries, chaplainships, and the like; although, things being now turned upside down, the offices of abbot and prior are not only conferred on secular presbyters, but on boys also by privilege, that is, by common and usual custom. In regard to the mercenaries who seek their food from day to day, what else could they do than they actually do, in other words, prostitute

themselves in an illiberal and disgraceful manner for gain, especially from the vast multitude of them with which the world now teems? Hence, as they dare not beg openly, or think that in this way they would gain little, they go about like hungry dogs, and by a kind of barking importunity extort from the unwilling what they may deposit in their hungry stomachs. Were I here to attempt to describe how disgraceful it is to the Church, that the honour and office of a presbyter should come to this, I should never have done. My readers, therefore, must not expect from me a discourse which can fully represent this flagitious indignity. I briefly say, that if it is the office of a presbyter (and this both the word of God prescribes (1 Cor. iv. 1) and the ancient canons enjoin) to feed the Church, and administer the spiritual kingdom of Christ, all those priests who have no work or stipend, save in the traffic of masses, not only fail in their office, but have no lawful office to discharge. No place is given them to teach, they have no people to govern. In short, nothing is left them but an altar on which to sacrifice Christ; this is to sacrifice not to God but to demons, as we shall afterwards show (see chap. xviii. sec. 3, 9, 14).

10. I am not here touching on extraneous faults,[1] but only on the intestine evil which lies at the root of the very institution. I will add a sentence which will sound strange in their ears, but which, as it is true, it is right to express, that canons, deans, chaplains, provosts, and all who are maintained in idle offices of priesthood, are to be viewed in the same light. For what service can they perform to the Church? The preaching of the word, the care of discipline, and the administration of the sacraments, they have shaken off as burdens too grievous to be borne. What then remains on which they can plume themselves as being true presbyters? Merely chanting and pompous ceremonies. But what is this to the point? If they allege custom, use, or the long prescription, I, on the contrary, appeal to the definition by which our Saviour has described true presbyters, and shown the qualities of those who are to be regarded as presbyters. But if they cannot endure the hard law of submitting to the rule of Christ, let them at least allow the cause to be decided by the authority of the primitive Church. Their condition will not be one whit improved when decided according to the ancient canons. Those who have degenerated into Canons ought to be presbyters, as they formerly were, to rule the Church in common with the bishop, and be, as it were, his colleagues in the pastoral office. What they call deaneries of the chapter have no concern with the true government of the Church, much less chaplainships and other similar worthless names. In what light then are they all to be regarded? Assuredly, both the word of Christ and the practice of the primitive Church exclude them from the honour of presbyters. They maintain, however, that they are presbyters; but we must unmask them, and we shall find that their whole profession is most alien from the office of presbyters, as that office is described to us by the apostles, and was

1 French, "les vices des personnes;"—the faults of individuals.

discharged in the primitive Church. All such offices, therefore, by whatever titles they are distinguished, as they are novelties, and certainly not supported either by the institution of God or the ancient practice of the Church, ought to have no place in a description of that spiritual government which the Church received, and was consecrated by the mouth of the Lord himself. Or (if they would have me express it in ruder and coarser terms), since chaplains, canons, deans, provosts, and such like lazy-bellies, do not even, with one finger, touch a particle of the office, which is necessarily required in presbyters, they must not be permitted falsely to usurp the honour, and thereby violate the holy institution of Christ.

11. There still remain bishops and rectors of parishes; and I wish that they would contend for the maintenance of their office. I would willingly grant that they have a pious and excellent office if they would discharge it; but when they desert the churches committed to them, and throwing the care upon others, would still be considered pastors, they just act as if the office of pastor were to do nothing. If any usurer, who never stirs from the city, were to give himself out as a ploughman or vine-dresser; or a soldier, who has constantly been in the field or the camp, and has never seen books or the forum, to pass for a lawyer, who could tolerate the absurdity? Much more absurdly do those act who would be called and deemed lawful pastors of the Church, and are unwilling so to be. How few are those who in appearance even take the superintendence of their church? Many spend their lives in devouring the revenues of churches which they never visit even for the purpose of inspection. Some once a-year go themselves or send a steward, that nothing may be lost in the letting of them. When the corruption first crept in, those who wished to enjoy this kind of vacation pleaded privilege, but it is now a rare case for any one to reside in his church. They look upon them merely in the light of farms, over which they appoint their vicars as grieves or husbandmen. But it is repugnant to common sense to regard him as a shepherd who has never seen a sheep of his flock.

12. It appears that in the time of Gregory some of the seeds of this corruption existed, the rulers of churches having begun to be more negligent in teaching; for he thus bitterly complains: "The world is full of priests, and yet labourers in the harvest are rare, for we indeed undertake the office of the priesthood, but we perform not the work of the office" (Gregor. Hom. 17). Again, "As they have no bowels of love, they would be thought lords, but do not at all acknowledge themselves to be fathers. They change a post of humility into the elevation of ascendancy." Again, "But we, O pastors! what are we doing, we who obtain the hire but are not labourers? We have fallen off to extraneous business; we undertake one thing, we perform another; we leave the ministry of the word, and, to our punishment, as I see, are called bishops, holding the honour of the name, not the power." Since he uses such bitterness of expression against those who were only less diligent or sedulous in their office,

what, pray, would he have said if he had seen that very few bishops, if any at all, and scarcely one in a hundred of the other clergy, mounted the pulpit once in their whole lifetime? For to such a degree of infatuation have men come, that it is thought beneath the episcopal dignity to preach a sermon to the people. In the time of Bernard things had become still worse. Accordingly, we see how bitterly he inveighs against the whole order, and yet there is reason to believe that matters were then in a much better state than now.

13. Whoever will duly examine and weigh the whole form of ecclesiastical government as now existing in the Papacy, will find that there is no kind of spoliation in which robbers act more licentiously, without law or measure. Certainly all things are so unlike, nay, so opposed to the institution of Christ, have so degenerated from the ancient customs and practices of the Church, are so repugnant to nature and reason, that a greater injury cannot be done to Christ than to use his name in defending this disorderly rule. We (say they) are the pillars of the Church, the priests of religion, the vicegerents of Christ, the heads of the faithful, because the apostolic authority has come to us by succession. As if they were speaking to stocks, they perpetually plume themselves on these absurdities. Whenever they make such boasts, I, in my turn, will ask, What have they in common with the apostles? We are not now treating of some hereditary honour which can come to men while they are asleep, but of the office of preaching, which they so greatly shun. In like manner, when we maintain that their kingdom is the tyranny of Antichrist, they immediately object that their venerable hierarchy has often been extolled by great and holy men, as if the holy fathers, when they commended the ecclesiastical hierarchy or spiritual government handed down to them by the apostles, ever dreamed of that shapeless and dreary chaos where bishoprics are held for the most part by ignorant asses, who do not even know the first and ordinary rudiments of the faith, or occasionally by boys who have just left their nurse; or if any are more learned (this, however, is a rare case), they regard the episcopal office as nothing else than a title of magnificence and splendour; where the rectors of churches no more think of feeding the flock than a cobbler does of ploughing, where all things are so confounded by a confusion worse than that of Babel, that no genuine trace of paternal government is any longer to be seen.

14. But if we descend to conduct, where is that light of the world which Christ requires, where the salt of the earth, where that sanctity which might operate as a perpetual censorship? In the present day, there is no order of men more notorious for luxury, effeminacy, delicacy, and all kinds of licentiousness; in no order are more apt or skilful teachers of imposture, fraud, treachery, and perfidy; nowhere is there more skill or audacity in mischief, to say nothing of ostentation, pride, rapacity, and cruelty. In bearing these the world is so disgusted, that there is no fear lest I seem to exaggerate. One thing I say, which even they themselves will not be able to deny: Among

bishops there is scarcely an individual, and among the parochial clergy not one in a hundred, who, if sentence were passed on his conduct according to the ancient canons, would not deserve to be excommunicated, or at least deposed from his office. I seem to say what is almost incredible, so completely has that ancient discipline which enjoined strict censure of the morals of the clergy become obsolete; but such the fact really is. Let those who serve under the banner and auspices of the Romish See now go and boast of their sacerdotal order. It is certain that that which they have is neither from Christ, nor his apostles, nor the fathers, nor the early Church.

15. Let the deacons now come forward and show their most sacred distribution of ecclesiastical goods (see chap. xix. sec. 32). Although their deacons are not at all elected for that purpose, for the only injunction which they lay upon them is to minister at the altar, to read the Gospel, or chant and perform I know not what frivolous acts. Nothing is said of alms, nothing of the care of the poor, nothing at all of the function which they formerly performed. I am speaking of the institution itself; for if we look to what they do, theirs, in fact, is no office, but only a step to the priesthood. In one thing, those who hold the place of deacons in the mass exhibit an empty image of antiquity, for they receive the offerings previous to consecration. Now, the ancient practice was, that before the communion of the Supper the faithful mutually kissed each other, and offered alms at the altar; thus declaring their love, first by symbol, and afterwards by an act of beneficence. The deacon, who was steward of the poor, received what was given that he might distribute it. Now, of these alms no more comes to the poor than if they were cast into the sea. They, therefore, delude the Church by that lying deaconship. Assuredly in this they have nothing resembling the apostolical institution or the ancient practice. The very distribution of goods they have transferred elsewhere, and have so settled it that nothing can be imagined more disorderly. For as robbers, after murdering their victims, divide the plunder, so these men, after extinguishing the light of God's word, as if they had murdered the Church, have imagined that whatever had been dedicated to pious uses was set down for prey and plunder. Accordingly, they have made a division, each seizing for himself as much as he could.

16. All those ancient methods which we have explained are not only disturbed but altogether disguised and expunged. The chief part of the plunder has gone to bishops and city presbyters, who, having thus enriched themselves, have been converted into canons. That the partition was a mere scramble is apparent from this, that even to this day they are litigating as to the proportions. Be this as it may, the decision has provided that out of all the goods of the Church not one penny shall go to the poor, to whom at least the half belonged. The canons expressly assign a fourth part to them, while the other fourth they destine to the bishops, that they may expend it in hospitality and other offices of kindness. I say nothing as to what

the clergy ought to do with their portion, or the use to which they ought to apply it, for it has been clearly shown that what is set apart for churches, buildings, and other expenditure, ought in necessity to be given to the poor. If they had one spark of the fear of God in their heart, could they, I ask, bear the consciousness that all their food and clothing is the produce of theft, nay, of sacrilege? But as they are little moved by the judgment of God, they should at least reflect that those whom they would persuade that the orders of their Church are so beautiful and well arranged as they are wont to boast, are men endued with sense and reason. Let them briefly answer whether the diaconate is a licence to rob and steal. If they deny this, they will be forced to confess that no diaconate remains among them, since the whole administration of their ecclesiastical resources has been openly converted into sacrilegious depredation.

17. But here they use a very fair gloss, for they say that the dignity of the Church is not unbecomingly maintained by this magnificence. And certain of their sect are so impudent as to dare openly to boast that thus only are fulfilled the prophecies, in which the ancient prophets describe the splendour of Christ's kingdom, where the sacerdotal order is exhibited in royal attire, that it was not without cause that God made the following promises to his Church: "All kings shall fall down before him: all nations shall serve him" (Ps. lxxii. 11). "Awake, awake; put on thy strength, O Sion; put on thy beautiful garments, O Jerusalem, the holy city" (Isa. lii. 1). "All they from Sheba shall come; they shall bring gold and incense, and they shall show forth the praises of the Lord. All the flocks of Kedar shall be gathered together unto thee" (Isa. lx. 6, 7). I fear I should seem childish were I to dwell long in refuting this dishonesty. I am unwilling, therefore, to use words unnecessarily; I ask, however, were any Jew to misapply these passages, what answer would they give? They would rebuke his stupidity in making a carnal and worldly application of things spiritually said of Christ's spiritual kingdom. For we know that under the image of earthly objects the prophets have delineated to us the heavenly glory which ought to shine in the Church. For in those blessings with these words literally express, the Church never less abounded than under the apostles; and yet all admit that the power of Christ's kingdom was then most flourishing. What, then, is the meaning of the above passages? That everything which is precious, sublime, and illustrious, ought to be made subject to the Lord. As to its being said expressly of kings, that they will submit to Christ, that they will throw their diadems at his feet, that they will dedicate their resources to the Church, when was this more truly and fully manifested than when Theodosius, having thrown aside the purple and left the insignia of empire, like one of the people humbled himself before God and the Church in solemn repentance? than when he and other like pious princes made it their study and their care to preserve pure doctrine in the Church, to cherish and protect sound teachers? But that priests did not

then luxuriate in superfluous wealth is sufficiently declared by this one sentence of the Council of Aquileia, over which Ambrose presided, "*Poverty in the priests of the Lord is glorious.*" It is certain that the bishops then had some means by which they might have rendered the glory of the Church conspicuous, if they had deemed them the true ornaments of the Church. But knowing that nothing was more adverse to the duty of pastors than to plume themselves on the delicacies of the table, on splendid clothes, numerous attendants, and magnificent places, they cultivated and followed the humility and modesty, nay, the very poverty, which Christ has consecrated among his servants.

18. But not to be tedious, let us again briefly sum up and show how far that distribution, or rather squandering, of ecclesiastical goods which now exists differs from the true diaconate, which both the word of God recommends and the ancient Church observed (Book I. chap. xi. sec. 7, 13; Book III. chap. xx. sec. 30; *supra*, chap. iv. sec. 8). I say, that what is employed on the adorning of churches is improperly laid out, if not accompanied with that moderation which the very nature of sacred things prescribes, and which the apostles and other holy fathers prescribed, both by precept and example. But is anything like this seen in churches in the present day? Whatever accords, I do not say with that ancient frugality, but with decent mediocrity, is rejected. Nought pleases but what savours of luxury and the corruption of the times. Meanwhile, so far are they from taking due care of living temples, that they would allow thousands of the poor to perish sooner than break down the smallest cup or platter to relieve their necessity. That I may not decide too severely at my own hand, I would only ask the pious reader to consider what Exuperius, the Bishop of Thoulouse, whom we have mentioned, what Acatius, or Ambrose, or any one like minded, if they were to rise from the dead, would say? Certainly, while the necessities of the poor are so great, they would not approve of their funds being carried away from them as superfluous; not to mention that, even were there no poor, the uses to which they are applied are noxious in many respects and useful in none. But I appeal not to men. These goods have been dedicated to Christ, and ought to be distributed at his pleasure. In vain, however, will they make that to be expenditure for Christ which they have squandered contrary to his commands, though, to confess the truth, the ordinary revenue of the Church is not much curtailed by these expenses. No bishoprics are so opulent, no abbacies so productive, in short, no benefices so numerous and ample, as to suffice for the gluttony of priests. But while they would spare themselves, they induce the people by superstition to employ what ought to have been distributed to the poor in building temples, erecting statues, buying plate, and providing costly garments. Thus the daily alms are swallowed up in this abyss.

19. Of the revenue which they derive from lands and property, what else can I say than what I have already said, and is manifest

before the eyes of all? We see with what kind of fidelity the greatest portion is administered by those who are called bishops and abbots. What madness is it to seek ecclesiastical order here? Is it becoming in those whose life ought to have been a singular example of frugality, modesty, continence, and humility, to rival princes in the number of their attendants, the splendour of their dwellings, the delicacies of dressing and feasting? Can anything be more contrary to the duty of those whom the eternal and inviolable edict of God forbids to long for filthy lucre, and orders to be contented with simple food, not only to lay hands on villages and castles, but also invade the largest provinces, and even seize on empire itself? If they despise the word of God, what answer will they give to the ancient canons of councils, which decree that the bishop shall have a little dwelling not far from the church, a frugal table and furniture? (Conc. Carth. cap. 14, 15). What answer will they give to the declaration of the Council of Aquileia, in which poverty in the priests of the Lord is pronounced glorious? For, the injunction which Jerome gives to Nepotian, to make the poor and strangers acquainted with his table, and have Christ with them as a guest, they would, perhaps, repudiate as too austere. What he immediately adds it would shame them to acknowledge—viz. that the glory of a bishop is to provide for the sustenance of the poor, that the disgrace of all priests is to study their own riches. This they cannot admit without covering themselves with disgrace. But it is unnecessary here to press them so hard, since all we wished was to demonstrate that the legitimate order of deacons has long ago been abolished, and that they can no longer plume themselves on this order in commendation of their Church. This, I think, has been completely established.

CHAPTER VI.

OF THE PRIMACY OF THE ROMISH SEE.

The divisions of this chapter are,—I. Question stated, and an argument for the primacy of the Roman Pontiff drawn from the Old Testament refuted, sec. 1, 2. II. Reply to various arguments in support of the Papacy founded on the words, "Thou art Peter," &c., sec. 3–17.

Sections.

1. Brief recapitulation. Why the subject of primacy not yet mentioned. Represented by Papists as the bond of ecclesiastical unity. Setting out with this axiom, they begin to debate about their hierarchy.
2. Question stated. An attempted proof from the office of High Priest among the Jews. Two answers.
3. Arguments for primacy from the New Testament. Two answers.
4. Another answer. The keys given to the other apostles as well as to Peter. Other two arguments answered by passages of Cyprian and Augustine.
5. Another argument answered.
6. Answer to the argument that the Church is founded on Peter, from its being said, "Upon this rock I will build my Church."
7. Answer confirmed by passages of Scripture.
8. Even allowing Peter's superiority in some respect, this is no proof of the primacy of the Roman Pontiff. Other arguments answered.
9. Distinction between civil and ecclesiastical government. Christ alone the Head of the Church. Argument that there is still a ministerial head answered.
10. Paul, in giving a representation of the Church, makes no mention of this ministerial head.
11. Even though Peter were ministerial head, it does not follow that the Pope is so also. Argument founded on Paul's having lived and died at Rome.
12. On the hypothesis of the Papists, the primacy belongs to the Church of Antioch.
13. Absurdity of the Popish hypothesis.
14. Peter was not the Bishop of Rome.
15. Same subject continued.
16. Argument that the unity of the Church cannot be maintained without a supreme head on earth. Answer, stating three reasons why great respect was paid in early times to the See of Rome.
17. Opinion of early times on the subject of the unity of the Church. No primacy attributed to the Church of Rome. Christ alone regarded as the Head of the Universal Church.

1. HITHERTO we have reviewed those ecclesiastical orders which existed in the government of the primitive Church; but afterwards corrupted by time, and thereafter more and more vitiated, now only retain the name in the Papal Church, and are, in fact, nothing but mere masks, so that the contrast will enable the pious reader to judge what kind of Church that is, for revolting from which we are charged with schism. But, on the head and crown of the whole matter, I mean the primacy of the Roman See, from which they undertake to prove that the Catholic Church is to be found only with them,[1] we

[1] See Calv. Adversus Concilium Tridentinum. Also Adversus Theologos Parisienses.

have not yet touched, because it did not take its origin either in the institution of Christ, or the practice of the early Church, as did those other parts, in regard to which we have shown, that though they were ancient in their origin, they in process of time altogether degenerated, nay, assumed an entirely new form. And yet they endeavour to persuade the world that the chief and only bond of ecclesiastical unity is to adhere to the Roman See, and continue in subjection to it. I say, the prop on which they chiefly lean, when they would deprive us of the Church, and arrogate it to themselves, is, that they retain the head on which the unity of the Church depends, and without which it must necessarily be rent and go to pieces. For they regard the Church as a kind of mutilated trunk if it be not subject to the Romish See as its head. Accordingly, when they debate about their hierarchy they always set out with the axiom: The Roman Pontiff (as the vicar of Christ, who is the Head of the Church) presides in his stead over the universal Church, and the Church is not rightly constituted unless that See hold the primacy over all others. The nature of this claim must, therefore, be considered, that we may not omit anything which pertains to the proper government of the Church.

2. The question, then, may be thus stated, Is it necessary for the true order of the hierarchy (as they term it), or of ecclesiastical order, that one See should surpass the others in dignity and power, so as to be the head of the whole body? We subject the Church to unjust laws if we lay this necessity upon her without sanction from the word of God. Therefore, if our opponents would prove what they maintain, it behoves them first of all to show that this economy was instituted by Christ. For this purpose, they refer to the office of high priest under the law, and the supreme jurisdiction which God appointed at Jerusalem.[1] But the solution is easy, and it is manifold if one does not satisfy them. First, no reason obliges us to extend what was useful in one nation to the whole world; nay, the cases of one nation and of the whole world are widely different. Because the Jews were hemmed in on every side by idolaters, God fixed the seat of his worship in the central region of the earth, that they might not be distracted by a variety of religions; there he appointed one priest to whom they might all look up, that they might be the better kept in unity. But now when the true religion has been diffused over the whole globe, who sees not that it is altogether absurd to give the government of East and West to one individual? It is just as if one were to contend that the whole world ought to be governed by one prefect, because one district has not several prefects.[2] But there is

1 French, "Pour ce faire, ils alleguent la pretrise souveraine qui etoit en la loy, et la jurisdiction souveraine du grand sacrificateur, que Dieu avoit establie en Jerusalem."—For this purpose, they allege the sovereign priesthood which was under the law, and the sovereign jurisdiction of the high priest which God had established at Jerusalem.

2 "Car c'est tout ainsi comme si quelcun debattoit que le monde doit etre gouverné par un baillie ou seneschal parce que chacune province a le sien."—For it is just as if

still another reason why that institution ought not to be drawn into a precedent. Every one knows that the high priest was a type of Christ; now, the priesthood being transferred, that right must also be transferred. To whom, then, was it transferred? certainly not to the Pope, as he dares impudently to boast when he arrogates this title to himself, but to Christ, who, as he alone holds the office without vicar or successor, does not resign the honour to any other. For this priesthood consists not in doctrine only, but in the propitiation which Christ made by his death, and the intercession which he now makes with the Father (Heb. vii. 11).

3. That example, therefore, which is seen to have been temporary, they have no right to bind upon us as by a perpetual law. In the New Testament there is nothing which they can produce in confirmation of their opinion, but its having been said to one, "Thou art Peter, and upon this rock I will build my Church" (Matth. xvi. 18). Again, "Simon, son of Jonas, lovest thou me?" "Feed my lambs" (John xxi. 15). But to give strength to these proofs, they must, in the first place, show, that to him who is ordered to feed the flock of Christ power is given over all churches, and that to bind and loose is nothing else than to preside over the whole world. But as Peter had received a command from the Lord, so he exhorts all other presbyters to feed the Church (1 Pet. v. 2). Hence we are entitled to infer, that, by that expression of Christ, nothing more was given to Peter than to the others, or that the right which Peter had received he communicated equally to others. But not to argue to no purpose, we elsewhere have, from the lips of Christ himself, a clear exposition of what it is to bind and loose. It is just to retain and remit sins (John x. 23). The mode of loosing and binding is explained throughout Scripture: but especially in that passage in which Paul declares that the ministers of the Gospel are commissioned to reconcile men to God, and at the same time to exercise discipline over those who reject the benefit (2 Cor. v. 18; x. 16).

4. How unbecomingly they wrest the passages of binding and loosing I have elsewhere glanced at, and will in a short time more fully explain. It may now be worth while merely to see what they can extract from our Saviour's celebrated answer to Peter. He promised him the keys of the kingdom of heaven, and said, that whatever things he bound on earth should be bound in heaven (Matth. xvi. 19). The moment we are agreed as to the meaning of the keys, and the mode of binding, all dispute will cease. For the Pope will willingly omit that office assigned to the apostles, which, full of labour and toil, would interfere with his luxuries without giving any gain. Since heaven is opened to us by the doctrine of the Gospel, it is by an elegant metaphor distinguished by the name of *keys*. Again, the only mode in which men are bound and loosed is, in the latter case, when they are reconciled to God by faith, and in the former, more

one were to maintain that the whole world ought to be governed by a bailie or seneschal, because each province has its own.

strictly bound by unbelief. Were this all that the Pope arrogated to himself, I believe there would be none to envy him or stir the question. But because this laborious and very far from lucrative succession is by no means pleasing to the Pope, the dispute immediately arises as to what it was that Christ promised to Peter. From the very nature of the case, I infer that nothing more is denoted than the dignity which cannot be separated from the burden of the apostolic office. For, admitting the definition which I have given (and it cannot without effrontery be rejected), nothing is here given to Peter that was not common to him with his colleagues. On any other view, not only would injustice be done to their persons, but the very majesty of the doctrine would be impaired. They object; but what, pray, is gained by striking against this stone? The utmost they can make out is, that as the preaching of the same gospel was enjoined on all the apostles, so the power of binding and loosing was bestowed upon them in common. Christ (they say) constituted Peter prince of the whole Church when he promised to give him the keys. But what he then promised to one he elsewhere delivers, and as it were hands over, to all the rest. If the same right, which was promised to one, is bestowed upon all, in what respect is that one superior to his colleagues? He excels (they say) in this, that he receives both in common, and by himself, what is given to the others in common only. What if I should answer with Cyprian, and Augustine, that Christ did not do this to prefer one to the other, but in order to commend the unity of his Church? For Cyprian thus speaks: "In the person of one man he gave the keys to all, that he might denote the unity of all; the rest, therefore, were the same that Peter was, being admitted to an equal participation of honour and power, but a beginning is made from unity that the Church of Christ may be shown to be one" (Cyprian, de Simplic. Prælat.). Augustine's words are, "Had not the mystery of the Church been in Peter, our Lord would not have said to him, I will give thee the keys. For if this was said to Peter, the Church has them not; but if the Church has them, then when Peter received the keys he represented the whole Church" (August. Hom. in Joann. 50). Again, "All were asked, but Peter alone answers, Thou art the Christ; and it is said to him, I will give thee the keys; as if he alone had received the power of loosing and binding; whereas he both spoke for all, and received in common with all, being, as it were, the representative of unity. One received for all, because there is unity in all" (Hom. 124).

5. But we nowhere read of its being said to any other, "Thou art Peter, and upon this rock I will build my Church"! (Matth. xvi. 18); as if Christ then affirmed anything else of Peter, than Paul and Peter himself affirm of all Christians (Eph. ii. 20; 1 Peter ii. 5). The former describes Christ as the chief corner-stone, on whom are built all who grow up into a holy temple in the Lord; the latter describes us as living stones who are founded on that elect and precious stone, and being so joined and compacted, are united to our God, and

to each other. Peter (they say) is above others, because the name was specially given to him. I willingly concede to Peter the honour of being placed among the first in the building of the Church, or (if they prefer it) of being the first among the faithful; but I will not allow them to infer from this that he has a primacy over others. For what kind of inference is this? Peter surpasses others in fervid zeal, in doctrine, in magnanimity; therefore, he has power over them: as if we might not with greater plausibility infer, that Andrew is prior to Peter in order, because he preceded him in time, and brought him to Christ (John i. 40, 42); but this I omit. Let Peter have the pre-eminence, still there is a great difference between the honour of rank and the possession of power. We see that the Apostles usually left it to Peter to address the meeting, and in some measure take precedence in relating, exhorting, admonishing, but we nowhere read anything at all of power.

6. Though we are not yet come to that part of the discussion, I would merely observe at present, how futilely those argue who, out of the mere name of Peter, would rear up a governing power over the whole Church. For the ancient quibble which they at first used to give a colour—viz. The Church is founded upon Peter, because it is said, "On this rock," &c.—is undeserving of notice, not to say of refutation. Some of the Fathers so expounded![1] But when the whole of Scripture is repugnant to the exposition, why is their authority brought forward in opposition to God? nay, why do we contend about the meaning of these words, as if it were obscure or ambiguous, when nothing can be more clear and certain? Peter had confessed in his own name, and that of his brethren, that Christ was the Son of God (Matth. xvi. 16). On this rock Christ builds his Church, because it is the only foundation; as Paul says, "Other foundation than this can no man lay" (1 Cor. iii. 11). Therefore, I do not here repudiate the authority of the Fathers, because I am destitute of passages from them to prove what I say, were I disposed to quote them; but as I have observed, I am unwilling to annoy my readers by debating so clear a matter, especially since the subject has long ago been fully handled and expounded by our writers.

7. And yet, in truth, none can solve this question better than Scripture, if we compare all the passages in which it shows what office and power Peter held among the apostles, how he acted among them, how he was received by them (Acts xv. 7). Run over all these passages, and the utmost you will find is, that Peter was one of twelve, their equal and colleague, not their master. He indeed brings the matter before the council when anything is to be done, and advises as to what is necessary, but he, at the same time, listens to the others, not only conceding to them an opportunity of expressing their sentiments, but allowing them to decide; and when they have decided, he follows and obeys. When he writes to pastors, he

1 French, "Ils ont pour leur bouclier, qu'aucuns des Peres les ont ainsi exposees."—They regard it as their buckler, that some of the Fathers have so expounded them.

does not command authoritatively as a superior, but makes them his colleagues, and courteously advises as equals are wont to do (1 Pet. v. 1). When he is accused of having gone in to the Gentiles, though the accusation is unfounded, he replies to it, and clears himself (Acts xi. 3). Being ordered by his colleagues to go with John into Samaria, he declines not (Acts viii. 14). The apostles, by sending him, declare that they by no means regard him as a superior, while he, by obeying and undertaking the embassy committed to him, confesses that he is associated with them, and has no authority over them. But if none of these facts existed, the one Epistle to the Galatians would easily remove all doubt, there being almost two chapters in which the whole for which Paul contends is, that in regard to the honour of the apostleship, he is the equal of Peter (Gal. i. 18; ii. 8). Hence he states, that he went to Peter, not to acknowledge subjection, but only to make their agreement in doctrine manifest to all; that Peter himself asked no acknowledgment of the kind, but gave him the right hand of fellowship, that they might be common labourers in the vineyard; that not less grace was bestowed on him among the Gentiles than on Peter among the Jews: in fine, that Peter, when he was not acting with strict fidelity, was rebuked by him, and submitted to the rebuke (Gal. ii. 11). All these things make it manifest, either that there was an equality between Paul and Peter, or, at least, that Peter had no more authority over the rest than they had over him. This point, as I have said, Paul handles professedly, in order that no one might give a preference over him, in respect of apostleship, to Peter or John, who were colleagues, not masters.

8. But were I to concede to them what they ask with regard to Peter—viz. that he was the chief of the apostles, and surpassed the others in dignity—there is no ground for making a universal rule out of a special example, or wresting a single fact into a perpetual enactment, seeing that the two things are widely different. One was chief among the apostles, just because they were few in number. If one man presided over twelve, will it follow that one ought to preside over a hundred thousand? That twelve had one among them to direct all is nothing strange. Nature admits, the human mind requires, that in every meeting, though all are equal in power, there should be one as a kind of moderator to whom the others should look up. There is no senate without a consul, no bench of judges without a president or chancellor, no college without a provost, no company without a master. Thus there would be no absurdity were we to confess that the apostles had conferred such a primacy on Peter. But an arrangement which is effectual among a few must not be forthwith transferred to the whole world, which no one man is able to govern. But (say they) it is observed that not less in nature as a whole, than in each of its parts, there is one supreme head. Proof of this it pleases them to derive from cranes and bees, which always place themselves under the guidance of one, not of several. I admit

the examples which they produce; but do bees flock together from all parts of the world to choose one queen? Each queen is contented with her own hive. So among cranes, each flock has its own king. What can they prove from this, except that each church ought to have its bishop? They refer us to the examples of states, quoting from Homer, Οὐκ ἀγαθον πολυκοιρανιη, "a many-headed rule is not good;" and other passages to the same effect from heathen writers in commendation of monarchy. The answer is easy. Monarchy is not lauded by Homer's Ulysses, or by others, as if one individual ought to govern the whole world; but they mean to intimate that one kingdom does not admit of two kings, and that empire, as one expresses it (Lucan. Lib. i.), cannot bear a partner.

9. Be it, however, as they will have it (though the thing is most absurd; be it), that it were good and useful for the whole world to be under one monarchy, I will not, therefore, admit that the same thing should take effect in the government of the Church. Her only Head is Christ, under whose government we are all united to each other, according to that order and form of policy which he himself has prescribed. Wherefore they offer an egregious insult to Christ, when under this pretext they would have one man to preside over the whole Church, seeing the Church can never be without a head, "even Christ, from whom the whole body fitly joined together, and compacted by that which every joint supplieth, according to the effectual working in the measure of every part, maketh increase of the body" (Eph. iv. 15, 16). See how all men, without exception, are placed in the body, while the honour and name of Head is left to Christ alone. See how to each member is assigned a certain measure, a finite and limited function, while both the perfection of grace and the supreme power of government reside only in Christ. I am not unaware of the cavilling objection which they are wont to urge—viz. that Christ is properly called the only Head, because he alone reigns by his own authority and in his own name; but that there is nothing in this to prevent what they call another *ministerial* head from being under him, and acting as his substitute. But this cavil cannot avail them, until they previously show that this office was ordained by Christ. For the apostle teaches, that the whole subministration is diffused through the members, while the power flows from one celestial Head;[1] or, if they will have it more plainly, since Scripture testifies that Christ is Head, and claims this honour for himself alone, it ought not to be transferred to any other than him whom Christ himself has made his vicegerent. But not only is there no passage to this effect, but it can be amply refuted by many passages.

10. Paul sometimes depicts a living image of the Church, but makes no mention of a single head. On the contrary, we may infer from his description, that it is foreign to the institution of Christ. Christ, by his ascension, took away his visible presence from us, and

1 Eph. i. 22; iv. 15; v. 23; Col. i. 18; ii. 10.

yet he ascended that he might fill all things: now, therefore, he is present in the Church, and always will be. When Paul would show the mode in which he exhibits himself, he calls our attention to the ministerial offices which he employs: "Unto every one of us is given grace according to the measure of the gift of Christ;" "And he gave some, apostles; and some, prophets; and some, evangelists; and some, pastors and teachers."[1] Why does he not say, that one presided over all to act as his substitute? The passage particularly required this, and it ought not on any account to have been omitted if it had been true. Christ, he says, is present with us. How? By the ministry of men whom he appointed over the government of the Church. Why not rather by a ministerial head whom he appointed his substitute? He speaks of unity, but it is in God and in the faith of Christ. He attributes nothing to men but a common ministry, and a special mode to each. Why, when thus commending unity, does he not, after saying, "one body, one Spirit, even as ye are called in one hope of your calling, one Lord, one faith, one baptism" (Eph. iv. 4), immediately add, one Supreme Pontiff to keep the Church in unity? Nothing could have been said more aptly if the case had really been so. Let that passage be diligently pondered, and there will be no doubt that Paul there meant to give a complete representation of that sacred and ecclesiastical government to which posterity have given the name of hierarchy. Not only does he not place a monarchy among ministers, but even intimates that there is none. There can also be no doubt, that he meant to express the mode of connection by which believers unite with Christ the Head. There he not only makes no mention of a ministerial head, but attributes a particular operation to each of the members, according to the measure of grace distributed to each. Nor is there any ground for subtle philosophical comparisons between the celestial and the earthly hierarchy. For it is not safe to be wise above measure with regard to the former, and in constituting the latter, the only type which it behoves us to follow is that which our Lord himself has delineated in his own word.

11. I will now make them another concession, which they will never obtain from men of sound mind—viz. that the primacy of the Church was fixed in Peter, with the view of remaining for ever by perpetual succession. Still how will they prove that his See was so fixed at Rome, that whosoever becomes Bishop of that city is to preside over the whole world? By what authority do they annex this dignity to a particular place, when it was given without any mention of place? Peter, they say, lived and died at Rome. What did Christ himself do? Did he not discharge his episcopate while he lived, and complete the office of the priesthood by dying at Jerusalem? The Prince of pastors, the chief Shepherd, the Head of the Church, could not procure honour for a place, and Peter, so far his inferior, could! Is

[2] Eph. iv. 10, 7, 11.

not this worse than childish trifling? Christ conferred the honour of primacy on Peter. Peter had his See at Rome, therefore he fixed the seat of the primacy there. In this way the Israelites of old must have placed the seat of the primacy in the wilderness, where Moses, the chief teacher and prince of prophets, discharged his ministry and died.

12. Let us see, however, how admirably they reason. Peter, they say, had the first place among the apostles; therefore, the church in which he sat ought to have the privilege. But where did he first sit? At Antioch, they say. Therefore, the church of Antioch justly claims the primacy. They acknowledge that she was once the first, but that Peter, by removing from it, transferred the honour which he had brought with him to Rome. For there is extant, under the name of Pope Marcellus, a letter to the presbyters of Antioch, in which he says, "The See of Peter, at the outset, was with you, and was afterwards, by the order of the Lord, translated hither." Thus the church of Antioch, which was once the first, yielded to the See of Rome. But by what oracle did that good man learn that the Lord had so ordered? For if the question is to be determined in regular form, they must say whether they hold the privilege to be personal, or real, or mixed. One of the three it must be. If they say personal, then it has nothing to do with place; if real, then when once given to a place it is not lost by the death or departure of the person. It remains that they must hold it to be mixed; then the mere consideration of place is not sufficient unless the person also correspond. Let them choose which they will, I will forthwith infer, and easily prove, that Rome has no ground to arrogate the primacy.

13. However, be it so. Let the primacy have been (as they vainly allege) transferred from Antioch to Rome. Why did not Antioch retain the second place? For if Rome has the first, simply because Peter had his See there at the end of his life, to which place should the second be given sooner than to that where he first had his See? How comes it, then, that Alexandria takes precedence of Antioch? How can the church of a disciple be superior to the See of Peter? If honour is due to a church according to the dignity of its founder, what shall we say of other churches? Paul names three individuals who seemed to be pillars—viz. James, Peter, and John (Gal. ii. 9). If, in honour of Peter, the first place is given to the Roman See, do not the churches of Ephesus and Jerusalem, where John and James were fixed, deserve the second and third places? But in ancient times Jerusalem held the last place among the Patriarchates, and Ephesus was not able to secure even the lowest corner. Other churches too have passed away, churches which Paul founded, and over which the apostles presided. The See of Mark, who was only one of the disciples, has obtained honour. Let them either confess that that arrangement was preposterous, or let them concede that it is not always true that each church is entitled to the degree of honour which its founder possessed.

14. But I do not see that any credit is due to their allegation of Peter's occupation of the Roman See. Certainly it is, that the statement of Eusebius, that he presided over it for twenty-five years, is easily refuted. For it appears from the first and second chapters of Galatians, that he was at Jerusalem about twenty years after the death of Christ, and afterwards came to Antioch. How long he remained here is uncertain; Gregory counts seven, and Eusebius twenty-five years. But from our Saviour's death to the end of Nero's reign (under which they state that he was put to death), will be found only thirty-seven years. For our Lord suffered in the eighteenth year of the reign of Tiberius. If you cut off the twenty years, during which, as Paul testifies, Peter dwelt at Jerusalem, there will remain at most seventeen years; and these must be divided between his two episcopates. If he dwelt long at Antioch, his See at Rome must have been of short duration. This we may demonstrate still more clearly. Paul wrote to the Romans while he was on his journey to Jerusalem, where he was apprehended and conveyed to Rome (Rom. xv. 15, 16). It is therefore probable that this letter was written four years before his arrival at Rome. Still there is no mention of Peter, as there certainly would have been if he had been ruling that church. Nay, in the end of the Epistle, where he enumerates a long list of individuals whom he orders to be saluted, and in which it may be supposed he includes all who were known to him, he says nothing at all of Peter. To men of sound judgment, there is no need here of a long and subtle demonstration; the nature of the case itself, and the whole subject of the Epistle, proclaim that he ought not to have passed over Peter if he had been at Rome.

15. Paul is afterwards conveyed as a prisoner to Rome. Luke relates that he was received by the brethren, but says nothing of Peter. From Rome he writes to many churches. He even sends salutations from certain individuals, but does not by a single word intimate that Peter was then there. Who, pray, will believe that he would have said nothing of him if he had been present? Nay, in the Epistle to the Philippians, after saying that he had no one who cared for the work of the Lord so faithfully as Timothy, he complains, that "all seek their own" (Phil. ii. 20). And to Timothy he makes the more grievous complaint, that no man was present at his first defence, that all men forsook him (2 Tim. iv. 16). Where then was Peter? If they say that he was at Rome, how disgraceful the charge which Paul brings against him of being a deserter of the Gospel! For he is speaking of believers, since he adds, "The Lord lay it not to their charge." At what time, therefore, and how long, did Peter hold that See? The uniform opinion of authors is, that he governed that church until his death. But these authors are not agreed as to who was his successor. Some say Linus, others Clement. And they relate many absurd fables concerning a discussion between him and Simon Magus. Nor does Augustine, when treating of superstition, disguise the fact, that owing to an opinion rashly entertained, it had

become customary at Rome to fast on the day on which Peter carried away the palm from Simon Magus (August. ad Januar. Ep. 2). In short, the affairs of that period are so involved from the variety of opinions, that credit is not to be given rashly to anything we read concerning it. And yet, from this agreement of authors, I do not dispute that he died there, but that he was bishop, particularly for a long period, I cannot believe. I do not, however, attach much importance to the point, since Paul testifies, that the apostleship of Peter pertained especially to the Jews, but his own specially to us. Therefore, in order that that compact which they made between themselves, nay, that the arrangement of the Holy Spirit may be firmly established among us, we ought to pay more regard to the apostleship of Paul than to that of Peter, since the Holy Spirit, in allotting them different provinces, destined Peter for the Jews and Paul for us. Let the Romanists, therefore, seek their primacy somewhere else than in the word of God, which gives not the least foundation for it.

16. Let us now come to the Primitive Church, that it may also appear that our opponents plume themselves on its support, not less falsely and unadvisedly than on the testimony of the word of God. When they lay it down as an axiom, that the unity of the Church cannot be maintained unless there be one supreme head on earth whom all the members should obey; and that, accordingly, our Lord gave the primacy to Peter, and thereafter, by right of succession, to the See of Rome, there to remain even to the end, they assert that this has always been observed from the beginning. But since they improperly wrest many passages, I would first premise, that I deny not that the early Christians uniformly give high honour to the Roman Church, and speak of it with reverence. This, I think, is owing chiefly to three causes. The opinion which had prevailed (I know not how), that that Church was founded and constituted by the ministry of Peter, had great effect in procuring influence and authority. Hence, in the East, it was, as a mark of honour, designated the Apostolic See. Secondly, as the seat of empire was there, and it was for this reason to be presumed, that the most distinguished for learning, prudence, skill, and experience, were there more than elsewhere, account was justly taken of the circumstance, lest the celebrity of the city, and the much more excellent gifts of God also, might seem to be despised. To these was added a third cause, that when the churches of the East, of Greece and of Africa, were kept in a constant turmoil by differences of opinion, the Church of Rome was calmer and less troubled. To this it was owing, that pious and holy bishops, when driven from their sees, often betook themselves to Rome as an asylum or haven. For as the people of the West are of a less acute and versatile turn of mind than those of Asia or Africa, so they are less desirous of innovations. It therefore added very great authority to the Roman Church, that in those dubious times it was not so much unsettled as others, and adhered more firmly to the

doctrine once delivered, as shall immediately be better explained. For these three causes, I say, she was held in no ordinary estimation, and received many distinguished testimonies from ancient writers.

17. But since on this our opponents would rear up a primacy and supreme authority over other churches, they, as I have said, greatly err. That this may better appear, I will first briefly show what the views of early writers are as to this unity which they so strongly urge. Jerome, in writing to Nepotian, after enumerating many examples of unity, descends at length to the ecclesiastical hierarchy. He says, "Every bishop of a church, every archpresbyter, every archdeacon, and the whole ecclesiastical order, depends on its own rulers." Here a Roman presbyter speaks and commends unity in ecclesiastical order. Why does he not mention that all the churches are bound together by one Head as a common bond? There was nothing more appropriate to the point in hand, and it cannot be said that he omitted it through forgetfulness; there was nothing he would more willingly have mentioned had the fact permitted. He therefore undoubtedly owns, that the true method of unity is that which Cyprian admirably describes in these words: "The episcopate is one, part of which is held entire by each bishop, and the Church is one, which, by the increase of fecundity, extends more widely in numbers. As there are many rays of the sun and one light, many branches of a tree and one trunk, upheld by its tenacious root, and as very many streams flow from one fountain, and though numbers seem diffused by the largeness of the overflowing supply, yet unity is preserved entire in the source, so the Church, pervaded with the light of the Lord, sends her rays over the whole globe, and yet is one light, which is everywhere diffused without separating the unity of the body, extends her branches over the whole globe, and sends forth flowing streams; still the head is one, and the source one" (Cyprian, de Simplic. Prælat.). Afterwards he says, "The spouse of Christ cannot be an adulteress: she knows one house, and with chaste modesty keeps the sanctity of one bed." See how he makes the bishopric of Christ alone universal, as comprehending under it the whole Church: See how he says that part of it is held entire by all who discharge the episcopal office under this head. Where is the primacy of the Roman See, if the entire bishopric resides in Christ alone, and a part of it is held entire by each? My object in these remarks is, to show the reader, in passing, that that axiom of the unity of an earthly kind in the hierarchy, which the Romanists assume as confessed and indubitable, was altogether unknown to the ancient Church.

CHAPTER VII.

OF THE BEGINNING AND RISE OF THE ROMISH PAPACY, TILL IT ATTAINED A HEIGHT BY WHICH THE LIBERTY OF THE CHURCH WAS DESTROYED, AND ALL TRUE RULE OVERTHROWN.

There are five heads in this chapter. I. The Patriarchate given and confirmed to the Bishop of Rome, first by the Council of Nice, and afterwards by that of Chalcedon, though by no means approved of by other bishops, was the commencement of the Papacy, sec. 1–4. II. The Church at Rome, by taking pious exiles under its protection, and also thereby protecting wicked men who fled to her, helped forward the mystery of iniquity, although at that time neither the ordination of bishops, nor admonitions and censures, nor the right cf convening Councils, nor the right of receiving appeals, belonged to the Roman Bishop, whose profane meddling with these things was condemned by Gregory, sec. 5–13. III. After the Council of Turin, disputes arose as to the authority of Metropolitans. Disgraceful strife between the Patriarchs of Rome and Constantinople. The vile assassin Phocas put an end to these brawls at the instigation of Boniface, sec. 14–18. IV. To the dishonest arts of Boniface succeeded fouler frauds devised in more modern times, and expressly condemned by Gregory and Bernard. sec. 19–21. V. The Papacy at length appeared complete in all its parts, the seat of Antichrist. Its impiety, execrable tyranny, and wickedness, portrayed, sec. 23–30.

Sections.

1. First part of the chapter, in which the commencement of the Papacy is assigned to the Council of Nice. In subsequent Councils other bishops presided. No attempt then made to claim the first place.
2. Though the Roman Bishop presided in the Council of Chalcedon, this was owing to special circumstances. The same right not given to his successors in other Councils.
3. The ancient Fathers did not give the title of Primate to the Roman Bishop.
4. Gregory was vehement in opposition to the title when claimed by the Bishop of Constantinople, and did not claim it for himself.
5. Second part of the chapter, explaining the ambitious attempts of the Roman See to obtain the primacy. Their reception of pious exiles. Hearing the appeals and complaints of heretics. Their ambition in this respect offensive to the African Church.
6. The power of the Roman Bishops in ordaining bishops, appointing councils, deciding controversies, &c., confined to their own Patriarchate.
7. If they censured other bishops, they themselves were censured in their turn.
8. They had no right of calling provincial councils except within their own boundaries. The calling of a universal council belonged solely to the Emperor.
9. Appeal to the Roman See not acknowledged by other bishops. Stoutly resisted by the Bishops of France and Africa. The impudence and falsehood of the Roman Pontiff detected.
10. Proof from history that the Roman had no jurisdiction over other churches.
11. The decretal epistles of no avail in support of this usurped jurisdiction.
12. The authority of the Roman Bishop extended in the time of Gregory. Still it only consisted in aiding other bishops with their own consent, or at the command of the Emperor.
13. Even the extent of jurisdiction, thus voluntarily conferred, objected to by Gregory as interfering with better duties.
14. Third part of the chapter, showing the increase of the power of the Papacy in defining the limits of Metropolitans. This gave rise to the decree of the Council of Turin. This decree haughtily annulled by Innocent.

15. Hence the great struggle for precedency between the Sees of Rome and Constantinople. The pride and ambition of the Roman Bishops unfolded.
16. Many attempts of the Bishop of Constantinople to deprive the Bishop of Rome of the primacy.
17. Phocas murders the Emperor, and gives Rome the primacy.
18. The Papal tyranny shortly after established. Bitter complaints by Bernard.
19. Fourth part of the chapter. Altered appearance of the Roman See since the days of Gregory.
20. The present demands of the Romanists not formerly conceded. Fictions of Gregory IX. and Martin.
21. Without mentioning the opposition of Cyprian, of councils, and historical facts, the claims now made were condemned by Gregory himself.
22. The abuses of which Gregory and Bernard complained now increased and sanctioned.
23. The fifth and last part of the chapter, containing the chief answer to the claims of the Papacy—viz. that the Pope is not a bishop in the house of God. This answer confirmed by an enumeration of the essential parts of the episcopal office.
24. A second confirmation by appeal to the institution of Christ. A third confirmation *e contrario*—viz. That in doctrine and morals the Roman Pontiff is altogether different from a true bishop. Conclusion, that Rome is not the Apostolic See, but the Papacy.
25. Proof from Daniel and Paul that the Pope is Antichrist.
26. Rome could not now claim the primacy, even though she had formerly been the first See, especially considering the base trafficking in which she has engaged.
27. Personal character of Popes. Irreligious opinions held by some of them.
28. John XXII. heretical in regard to the immortality of the soul. His name, therefore, ought to be expunged from the catalogue of Popes, or rather, there is no foundation for the claim of perpetuity of faith in the Roman See.
29. Some Roman Pontiffs atheists, or sworn enemies of religion. Their immoral lives. Practice of the Cardinals and Romish clergy.
30. Cardinals were formerly merely presbyters of the Roman Church, and far inferior to bishops. As they now are, they have no true and legitimate office in the Church. Conclusion.

1. In regard to the antiquity of the primacy of the Roman See, there is nothing in favour of its establishment more ancient than the decree of the Council of Nice, by which the first place among the Patriarchs is assigned to the Bishop of Rome, and he is enjoined to take care of the suburban churches. While the council, in dividing between him and the other Patriarchs, assigns the proper limits of each, it certainly does not appoint him head of all, but only one of the chief. Vitus and Vincentius attended on the part of Julius, who then governed the Roman Church, and to them the fourth place was given. I ask, if Julius was acknowledged the head of the Church, would his legates have been consigned to the fourth place? Would Athanasius have presided in the council where a representative of the hierarchal order should have been most conspicuous? In the Council of Ephesus, it appears that Celestinus (who was then Roman Pontiff) used a cunning device to secure the dignity of his See. For when he sent his deputies, he made Cyril of Alexandria, who otherwise would have presided, his substitute. Why that commission, but just that his name might stand connected with the first See? His legates sit in an inferior place, are asked their opinion along with others, and subscribe in their order, while, at the same time, his name is coupled with that of the Patriarch of Alexandria. What shall I say of the second Council of Ephesus, where, while the deputies of Leo

were present, the Alexandrian Patriarch Dioscorus presided as in his own right? They will object that this was not an orthodox council, since by it the venerable Flavianus was condemned, Eutyches acquitted, and his heresy approved. Yet when the council was met, and the bishops distributed the places among themselves, the deputies of the Roman Church sat among the others just as in a sacred and lawful Council. Still they contend not for the first place, but yield it to another: this they never would have done if they had thought it their own by right. For the Roman bishops were never ashamed to stir up the greatest strife in contending for honours, and for this cause alone, to trouble and harass the Church with many pernicious contests; but because Leo saw that it would be too extravagant to ask the first place for his legates, he omitted to do it.

2. Next came the Council of Chalcedon, in which, by concession of the Emperor, the legates of the Roman Church occupied the first place. But Leo himself confesses that this was an extraordinary privilege; for when he asks it of the Emperor Marcian and Pulcheria Augusta, he does not maintain that it is due to him, but only pretends that the Eastern bishops who presided in the Council of Ephesus had thrown all into confusion, and made a bad use of their power. Therefore, seeing there was need of a grave moderator, and it was not probable that those who had once been so fickle and tumultuous would be fit for this purpose, he requests that, because of the fault and unfitness of others, the office of governing should be transferred to him. That which is asked as a special privilege, and out of the usual order, certainly is not due by a common law. When it is only pretended that there is need of a new president, because the former ones had behaved themselves improperly, it is plain that the thing asked was not previously done, and ought not to be made perpetual, being done only in respect of a present danger. The Roman Pontiff, therefore, holds the first place in the Council of Chalcedon, not because it is due to his See, but because the council is in want of a grave and fit moderator, while those who ought to have presided exclude themselves by their intemperance and passion. This statement the successor of Leo approved by his procedure. For when he sent his legates to the fifth Council, that of Constantinople, which was held long after, he did not quarrel for the first seat, but readily allowed Mennas, the patriarch of Constantinople, to preside. In like manner, in the Council of Carthage, at which Augustine was present, we perceive that not the legates of the Roman See, but Aurelius, the archbishop of the place, presided, although there was then a question as to the authority of the Roman Pontiff. Nay, even in Italy itself, a universal council was held (that of Aquileia), at which the Roman Bishop was not present. Ambrose, who was then in high favour with the Emperor, presided, and no mention is made of the Roman Pontiff. Therefore, owing to the dignity of Ambrose, the See of Milan was then more illustrious than that of Rome.

3. In regard to the mere title of primate and other titles of pride,

of which that pontiff now makes a wondrous boast, it is not difficult to understand how and in what way they crept in. Cyprian often makes mention of Cornelius (Cyprian. Lib. ii. Ep. 2; Lib. iv. Ep. 6), nor does he distinguish him by any other name than that of brother, or fellow bishop, or colleague. When he writes to Stephen, the successor of Cornelius, he not only makes him the equal of himself and others, but addresses him in harsh terms, charging him at one time with presumption, at another with ignorance. After Cyprian, we have the judgment of the whole African Church on the subject. For the Council of Carthage enjoined that none should be called chief of the priests, or first bishop, but only bishop of the first See. But any one who will examine the more ancient records will find that the Roman Pontiff was then contented with the common appellation of brother. Certainly, as long as the true and pure form of the Church continued, all these names of pride on which the Roman See afterwards began to plume itself, were altogether unheard of; none knew what was meant by the supreme Pontiff, and the only head of the Church on earth. Had the Roman Bishop presumed to assume any such title, there were right-hearted men who would immediately have repressed his folly. Jerome, seeing he was a Roman presbyter, was not slow to proclaim the dignity of his church, in as far as fact and the circumstances of the times permitted, and yet we see how he brings it under due subordination. "If authority is asked, the world is greater than a city. Why produce to me the custom of one city? Why vindicate a small number with whom superciliousness has originated against the laws of the Church? Wherever the bishop be, whether at Rome, or Eugubium, or Constantinople, or Rhegium, the merit is the same, and the priesthood the same. The power of riches, or the humbleness of poverty, do not make a bishop superior or inferior" (Hieron. Ep. ad Evagr.).

4. The controversy concerning the title of universal bishop arose at length in the time of Gregory, and was occasioned by the ambition of John of Constantinople. For he wished to make himself universal, a thing which no other had ever attempted. In that controversy, Gregory does not allege that he is deprived of a right which belonged to him, but he strongly insists that the appellation is profane, nay, blasphemous, nay the forerunner of Antichrist. "The whole Church falls from its state, if he who is called universal falls" (Greg. Lib. iv. Ep. 76). Again, "It is very difficult to bear patiently that one who is our brother and fellow bishop should alone be called bishop, while all others are despised. But in this pride of his, what else is intimated but that the days of Antichrist are already near? For he is imitating him, who, despising the company of angels, attempted to ascend the pinnacle of greatness" (Lib. iv. Ep. 76). He elsewhere says to Eulogius of Alexandria and Anastasius of Antioch: "None of my predecessors ever desired to use this profane term: for if one patriarch is called universal, it is derogatory to the name of patriarch in others. But far be it from any Christian mind to wish to arrogate

to itself that which would in any degree, however slight, impair the honour of his brethren" (Lib. iv. Ep. 80). "To consent to that impious term is nothing else than to lose the faith" (Lib. iv. Ep. 83). "What we owe to the preservation of the unity of the faith is one thing, what we owe to the suppression of pride is another. I speak with confidence, for every one that calls himself, or desires to be called, universal priest, is by his pride a forerunner of Antichrist, because he acts proudly in preferring himself to others" (Lib. vii. Ep. 154). Thus, again, in a letter to Anastasius of Antioch, "I said, that he could not have peace with us unless he corrected the presumption of a superstitious and haughty term which the first apostate invented; and (to say nothing of the injury to your honour) if one bishop is called universal, the whole Church goes to ruin when that universal bishop falls" (Lib. vi. Ep. 188). But when he writes, that this honour was offered to Leo in the Council of Chalcedon (Lib. iv. Ep. 76, 80; Lib. vii. Ep. 76), he says what has no semblance of truth; nothing of the kind is found among the acts of that council. And Leo himself, who, in many letters, impugns the decree which was then made in honour of the See of Constantinople, undoubtedly would not have omitted this argument, which was the most plausible of all, if it was true that he himself repudiated what was given to him. One who, in other respects, was rather too desirous of honour, would not have omitted what would have been to his praise. Gregory, therefore, is incorrect in saying, that that title was conferred on the Roman See by the Council of Chalcedon; not to mention how ridiculous it is for him to say, that it proceeded from that sacred council, and yet to term it wicked, profane, nefarious, proud, and blasphemous, nay, devised by the devil, and promulgated by the herald of Antichrist. And yet he adds, that his predecessor refused it, lest by that which was given to one individually, all priests should be deprived of their due honour. In another place, he says, "None ever wished to be called by such a name; none arrogated this rash name to himself, lest, by seizing on the honour of supremacy in the office of the Pontificate, he might seem to deny it to all his brethren" (Gregor. Lib. iv. Ep. 82).

5. I come now to jurisdiction, which the Roman Pontiff asserts as an incontrovertible proposition that he possesses over all churches. I am aware of the great disputes which anciently existed on this subject: for there never was a time when the Roman See did not aim at authority over other churches. And here it will not be out of place to investigate the means by which she gradually attained to some influence. I am not now referring to that unlimited power which she seized at a comparatively recent period. The consideration of that we shall defer to its own place. But it is worth while here briefly to show in what way, and by what means, she formerly raised herself, so as to arrogate some authority over other churches. When the churches of the East were troubled and rent by the fac-

tions of the Arians, under the Emperors Constantius and Constans, sons of Constantine the Great; and Athanasius, the principal defender of the orthodox faith, had been driven from his see, the calamity obliged him to come to Rome, in order that by the authority of this see he might both repress the rage of his enemies, and confirm the orthodox under their distress. He was honourably received by Julius, who was then bishop, and engaged those of the West to undertake the defence of his cause. Therefore, when the orthodox stood greatly in need of external aid, and perceived that their chief protection lay in the Roman See, they willingly bestowed upon it all the authority they could. But the utmost extent of this was, that its communion was held in high estimation, and it was deemed ignominious to be excommunicated by it. Dishonest bad men afterwards added much to its authority, for when they wished to escape lawful tribunals, they betook themselves to Rome as an asylum. Accordingly, if any presbyter was condemned by his bishop, or if any bishop was condemned by the synod of his province, he appealed to Rome. These appeals the Roman bishops received more eagerly than they ought, because it seemed a species of extraordinary power to interpose in matters with which their connection was so very remote. Thus, when Eutyches was condemned by Flavianus, Bishop of Constantinople, he complained to Leo that the sentence was unjust. He, nothing loth, no less presumptuously than abruptly, undertook the patronage of a bad cause, and inveighed bitterly against Flavianus, as having condemned an innocent man without due investigation: and thus the effect of Leo's ambition was, that for some time the impiety of Eutyches was confirmed. It is certain that in Africa the same thing repeatedly occurred, for whenever any miscreant had been condemned by his ordinary judge, he fled to Rome, and brought many calumnious charges against his own people. The Roman See was always ready to interpose. This dishonesty obliged the African bishops to decree that no one should carry an appeal beyond sea under pain of excommunication.

6. Be this as it may, let us consider what right or authority the Roman See then possessed. Ecclesiastical power may be reduced to four heads—viz. ordination of bishops, calling of councils, hearing of appeals (or jurisdiction), inflicting monitory chastisements or censures. All ancient councils enjoin that bishops shall be ordained by their own Metropolitans; they nowhere enjoin an application to the Roman Bishop, except in his own patriarchate. Gradually, however, it became customary for all Italian bishops to go to Rome for consecration, with the exception of the Metropolitans, who did not allow themselves to be thus brought into subjection; but when any Metropolitan was to be ordained, the Roman Bishop sent one of his presbyters merely to be present, but not to preside. An example of this kind is extant in Gregory (Lib. ii. Ep. 68, 70), in the consecration of Constantius of Milan, after the death of Laurence. I do not, however, think that this was a very ancient custom. At first, as a mark

of respect and good-will, they sent deputies to one another to witness the ordination, and attest their communion. What was thus voluntary afterwards began to be regarded as necessary. However this be, it is certain that anciently the Roman Bishop had no power of ordaining except within the bounds of his own patriarchate, that is, as a canon of the Council of Nice expresses it, in suburban churches. To ordination was added the sending of a *synodical epistle*, but this implied no authority. The patriarchs were accustomed, immediately after consecration, to attest their faith by a formal writing, in which they declared that they assented to sacred and orthodox councils. Thus, by rendering an account of their faith, they mutually approved of each other. If the Roman Bishop had received this confession from others, and not given it, he would therein have been acknowledged superior; but when it behoved to give as well as to receive, and to be subject to the common law, this was a sign of equality, not of lordship. Of this we have an example in a letter of Gregory to Anastasius and Cyriac of Constantinople, and in another letter to all the patriarchs together (Gregor. Lib. i. Ep. 24, 25; Lib. vi. Ep. 169).

7. Next come *admonitions* or *censures*. These the Roman Bishops anciently employed towards others, and in their turn received. Irenæus sharply rebuked Victor for rashly troubling the Church with a pernicious schism, for a matter of no moment. He submitted without objecting. Holy bishops were then wont to use the freedom as brethren, of admonishing and rebuking the Roman Prelate when he happened to err. He in his turn, when the case required, reminded others of their duty, and reprimanded them for their faults. For Cyprian, when he exhorts Stephen to admonish the bishops of France, does not found on his larger power, but on the common right which priests have in regard to each other (Cyprian. Lib. iii. Ep. 13). I ask if Stephen had then presided over France, would not Cyprian have said, "Check them, for they are yours"? but his language is very different. "The brotherly fellowship which binds us together requires that we should mutually admonish each other" (Cyprian. ad Pomp. Cont. Epist. Steph.). And we see also with what severity of expression, a man otherwise of a mild temper, inveighs against Stephen himself, when he thinks him chargeable with insolence. Therefore, it does not yet appear in this respect that the Roman Bishop possessed any jurisdiction over those who did not belong to his province.

8. In regard to calling of councils, it was the duty of every Metropolitan to assemble a provincial synod at stated times. Here the Roman Bishop had no jurisdiction, while the Emperor alone could summon a general council. Had any of the bishops attempted this, not only would those out of the province not have obeyed the call, but a tumult would instantly have arisen. Therefore the Emperor gave intimation to all alike to attend. Socrates, indeed, relates that Julius expostulated with the Eastern bishops for not having called

him to the Council of Antioch, seeing it was forbidden by the canons that anything should be decided without the knowledge of the Roman Bishop (Tripart. Hist. Lib. iv.). But who does not perceive that this is to be understood of those decrees which bind the whole Church? At the same time, it is not strange if, in deference both to the antiquity and largeness of the city, and the dignity of the see, no universal decree concerning religion should be made in the absence of the Bishop of Rome, provided he did not refuse to be present. But what has this to do with the dominion of the whole Church? For we deny not that he was one of the principal bishops, though we are unwilling to admit what the Romanists now contend for—viz. that he had power over all.

9. The fourth remaining species of power is that of hearing *appeals*. It is evident that the supreme power belongs to him to whose tribunal appeals are made. Many had repeatedly appealed to the Roman Pontiff. He also had endeavoured to bring causes under his cognisance, but he had always been derided whenever he went beyond his own boundaries. I say nothing of the East and of Greece, but it is certain, that the bishops of France stoutly resisted when he seemed to assume authority over them. In Africa, the subject was long disputed, for in the Council of Milevita, at which Augustine was present, when those who carried appeals beyond seas were excommunicated, the Roman Pontiff attempted to obtain an alteration of the decree, and sent legates to show that the privilege of hearing appeals was given him by the Council of Nice. The legates produced acts of the council drawn from the armoury of their church. The African bishops resisted, and maintained, that credit was not to be given to the Bishop of Rome in his own cause; accordingly, they said that they would send to Constantinople, and other cities of Greece, where less suspicious copies might be had. It was found that nothing like what the Romanists had pretended was contained in the acts, and thus the decree which abrogated the supreme jurisdiction of the Roman Pontiff was confirmed. In this matter was manifested the egregious effrontery of the Roman Pontiff. For when he had fraudulently substituted the Council of Sardis for that of Nice, he was disgracefully detected in a palpable falsehood; but still greater and more impudent was the iniquity of those who added a fictitious letter to the Council, in which some Bishop of Carthage condemns the arrogance of Aurelius his predecessor, in promising to withdraw himself from obedience to the Apostolic See, and making a surrender of himself and his church, suppliantly prays for pardon. These are the noble records of antiquity on which the majesty of the Roman See is founded, while, under the pretext of antiquity, they deal in falsehoods so puerile, that even a blind man might feel them. "Aurelius (says he), elated by diabolical audacity and contumacy, was rebellious against Christ and St Peter, and, accordingly, deserved to be anathematised." What does Augustine say? and what the many Fathers who were present at the Council of Milevita? But what need is

there to give a lengthened refutation of that absurd writing, which not even Romanists, if they have any modesty left them, can look at without a deep feeling of shame? Thus Gratian, whether through malice or ignorance, I know not, after quoting the decree, That those are to be deprived of communion who carry appeals beyond seas, subjoins the exception, Unless, perhaps, they have appealed to the Roman See (Grat. 2, Quæst. 4, cap. Placuit.). What can you make of creatures like these, who are so devoid of common sense that they set down as an exception from the law the very thing on account of which, as everybody sees, the law was made? For the Council, in condemning transmarine appeals, simply prohibits an appeal to Rome. Yet this worthy expounder excepts Rome from the common law.

10. But (to end the question at once) the kind of jurisdiction which belonged to the Roman Bishop one narrative will make manifest. Donatus of Casa Nigra had accused Cecilianus the Bishop of Carthage. Cecilianus was condemned without a hearing: for, having ascertained that the bishops had entered into a conspiracy against him, he refused to appear. The case was brought before the Emperor Constantine, who, wishing the matter to be ended by an ecclesiastical decision, gave the cognisance of it to Melciades, the Roman Bishop, appointing as his colleagues some bishops from Italy, France, and Spain. If it formed part of the ordinary jurisdiction of the Roman See to hear appeals in ecclesiastical causes, why did he allow others to be conjoined with him at the Emperor's discretion? nay, why does he undertake to decide more from the command of the Emperor than his own office? But let us hear what afterwards happened (see August. Ep. 162, *et alibi*). Cecilianus prevails. Donatus of Casa Nigra is thrown in his calumnious action and appeals. Constantine devolves the decision of the appeal on the Bishop of Arles, who sits as judge, to give sentence after the Roman Pontiff.[1] If the Roman See has supreme power not subject to appeal, why does Melciades allow himself to be so greatly insulted as to have the Bishop of Arles preferred to him? And who is the Emperor that does this? Constantine, who they boast not only made it his constant study, but employed all the resources of the empire to enlarge the dignity of that see. We see, therefore, how far in every way the Roman Pontiff was from that supreme dominion, which he asserts to have been given him by Christ over all churches, and which he falsely alleges that he possessed in all ages, with the consent of the whole world.

11. I know how many epistles there are, how many rescripts and edicts in which there is nothing which the pontiffs do not ascribe and confidently arrogate to themselves. But all men of the least intellect and learning know, that the greater part of them are in themselves

1 French. " Voila l'Archeveque d'Arles assis pour retracter; si bon lui semble la sentence de l'Eveque Romain. au moins pour juger par dessus lui."—Here is the Archbishop of Arles seated to recall, if he thinks fit, the sentence of the Bishop of Rome, or at least to judge as his superior.

so absurd, that it is easy at the first sight to detect the forge from which they have come. Does any man of sense and soberness think that Anacletus is the author of that famous interpretation which is given in Gratian, under the name of Anacletus—viz. that Cephas is head? (Dist. 22, cap. Sacrosancta.) Numerous follies of the same kind which Gratian has heaped together without judgment, the Romanists of the present day employ against us in defence of their see. The smoke, by which, in the former days of ignorance, they imposed upon the ignorant, they would still vend in the present light. I am unwilling to take much trouble in refuting things which, by their extreme absurdity, plainly refute themselves. I admit the existence of genuine epistles by ancient Pontiffs, in which they pronounce magnificent eulogiums on the extent of their see. Such are some of the epistles of Leo. For as he possessed learning and eloquence, so he was excessively desirous of glory and dominion; but the true question is, whether or not, when he thus extolled himself, the churches gave credit to his testimony? It appears that many were offended with his ambition, and also resisted his cupidity. He in one place appoints the Bishop of Thessalonica his vicar throughout Greece and other neighbouring regions (Leo, Ep. 85), and elsewhere gives the same office to the Bishop of Arles or some other throughout France (Ep. 83). In like manner, he appointed Hormisdas, Bishop of Hispala, his vicar throughout Spain, but he uniformly makes this reservation, that in giving such commissions, the ancient privileges of the Metropolitans were to remain safe and entire. These appointments, therefore, were made on the condition, that no bishop should be impeded in his ordinary jurisdiction, no Metropolitan in taking cognisance of appeals, no provincial council in constituting churches. But what else was this than to decline all jurisdiction, and to interpose for the purpose of settling discord only, in so far as the law and nature of ecclesiastical communion admit?

12. In the time of Gregory, that ancient rule was greatly changed. For when the empire was convulsed and torn, when France and Spain were suffering from the many disasters which they ever and anon received, when Illyricum was laid waste, Italy harassed, and Africa almost destroyed by uninterrupted calamities, in order that, during these civil convulsions, the integrity of the faith might remain, or at least not entirely perish, the bishops in all quarters attached themselves more to the Roman Pontiff. In this way, not only the dignity, but also the power of the see, exceedingly increased, although I attach no great importance to the means by which this was accomplished. It is certain, that it was then greater than in former ages. And yet it was very different from the unbridled dominion of one ruling others as he pleased. Still the reverence paid to the Roman See was such, that by its authority it could guide and repress those whom their own colleagues were unable to keep to their duty; for Gregory is careful ever and anon to testify that he was not less faithful in preserving the rights of others, that in insisting that his

own should be preserved. "I do not," says he, "under the stimulus of ambition, derogate from any man's right, but desire to honour my brethren in all things" (Gregor. Lib. ii. Ep. 68). There is no sentence in his writings in which he boasts more proudly of the extent of his primacy than the following: "I know not what bishop is not subject to the Roman See, when he is discovered in a fault" (Leo. Lib. ii., Epist. 68). However, he immediately adds, "Where faults do not call for interference, all are equal according to the rule of humility." He claims for himself the right of correcting those who have sinned; if all do their duty, he puts himself on a footing of equality. He, indeed, claimed this right, and those who chose assented to it, while those who were not pleased with it were at liberty to object with impunity; and it is known that the greater part did so. We may add, that he is then speaking of the primate of Byzantium, who, when condemned by a provincial synod, repudiated the whole judgment. His colleagues had informed the Emperor of his contumacy, and the Emperor had given the cognisance of the matter to Gregory. We see, therefore, that he does not interfere in any way with the ordinary jurisdiction, and that, in acting as a subsidiary to others, he acts entirely by the Emperor's command.

13. At this time, therefore, the whole power of the Roman Bishop consisted in opposing stubborn and ungovernable spirits, where some extraordinary remedy was required, and this in order to assist other bishops, not to interfere with them. Therefore, he assumes no more power over others than he elsewhere gives others over himself, when he confesses that he is ready to be corrected by all, amended by all (Lib. ii. Ep. 37). So, in another place, though he orders the Bishop of Aquileia to come to Rome to plead his cause in a controversy as to doctrine which had arisen between himself and others, he thus orders not of his own authority, but in obedience to the Emperor's command. Nor does he declare that he himself will be sole judge, but promises to call a synod, by which the whole business may be determined. But although the moderation was still such, that the power of the Roman See had certain limits which it was not permitted to overstep, and the Roman Bishop himself was not more above than under others, it appears how much Gregory was dissatisfied with this state of matters. For he ever and anon complains, that he, under the colour of the episcopate, was brought back to the world, and was more involved in earthly cares than when living as a laic; that he, in that honourable office, was oppressed by the tumult of secular affairs. Elsewhere he says, "So many burdensome occupations depress me, that my mind cannot at all rise to things above. I am shaken by the many billows of causes, and after they are quieted, am afflicted by the tempests of a tumultuous life, so that I may truly say I am come into the depths of the sea, and the flood has overwhelmed me." From this I infer what he would have said if he had fallen on the present times. If he did not fulfil, he at least did the duty of a pastor. He declined the administration of civil power, and

acknowledged himself subject, like others, to the Emperor. He did not interfere with the management of other churches, unless forced by necessity. And yet he thinks himself in a labyrinth, because he cannot devote himself entirely to the duty of a bishop.

14. At that time, as has already been said, the Bishop of Constantinople was disputing with the Bishop of Rome for the primacy. For after the seat of empire was fixed at Constantinople, the majesty of the empire seemed to demand that that church should have the next place of honour to that of Rome. And certainly, at the outset, nothing had tended more to give the primacy to Rome, than that it was then the capital of the empire. In Gratian (Dist. 80), there is a rescript under the name of Pope Lucinus, to the effect that the only way in which the cities where Metropolitans and Primates ought to preside were distinguished, was by means of the civil government which had previously existed. There is a similar rescript under the name of Pope Clement, in which he says, that patriarchs were appointed in those cities which had previously had the first flamens. Although this is absurd, it was borrowed from what was true. For it is certain, that in order to make as little change as possible, provinces were distributed according to the state of matters then existing, and Primates and Metropolitans were placed in those cities which surpassed others in honours and power. Accordingly, it was decreed in the Council of Turin, that the cities of every province which were first in the civil government should be the first sees of bishops. But if it should happen that the honour of civil government was transferred from one city to another, then the right of the metropolis should be at the same time transferred thither. But Innocent, the Roman Pontiff, seeing that the ancient dignity of the city had been decaying ever since the seat of empire had been transferred to Constantinople, and fearing for his see, enacted a contrary law, in which he denies the necessity of changing metropolitan churches as imperial metropolitan cities were changed. But the authority of a synod is justly to be preferred to the opinion of one individual, and Innocent himself should be suspected in his own cause. However this be, he by his caveat shows the original rule to have been, that Metropolitans should be distributed according to the order of the empire.

15. Agreeably to this ancient custom, the first Council of Constantinople decreed that the bishop of that city should take precedence after the Roman Pontiff, because it was a new Rome. But long after, when a similar decree was made at Chalcedon, Leo keenly protested (Socrat. Hist. Trop. Lib. ix. cap. 13). And not only did he permit himself to set at nought what six hundred bishops or more had decreed, but he even assailed them with bitter reproaches, because they had derogated from other sees in the honour which they had presumed to confer on the Church of Constantinople (in Decr. 22, Distinct. cap. Constantinop.). What, pray, could have incited the man to trouble the world for so small an affair but mere ambition? He says, that what the Council of Nice had once sanctioned

ought to have been inviolable; as if the Christian faith was in any danger if one church was preferred to another; or as if separate Patriarchates had been established on any other grounds than that of policy. But we know that policy varies with times, nay, demands various changes. It is therefore futile in Leo to pretend that the See of Constantinople ought not to receive the honour which was given to that of Alexandria, by the authority of the Council of Nice. For it is the dictate of common sense, that the decree was one of those which might be abrogated, in respect of a change of times. What shall we say to the fact, that none of the Eastern churches, though chiefly interested, objected? Proterius, who had been appointed at Alexandria instead of Dioscorus, was certainly present; other patriarchs whose honour was impaired were present. It belonged to them to interfere, not to Leo, whose station remained entire. While all of them are silent, many assent, and the Roman Bishop alone resists, it is easy to judge what it is that moves him; just because he foresaw what happened not long after, that when the glory of ancient Rome declined, Constantinople, not contented with the second place, would dispute the primacy with her. And yet his clamour was not so successful as to prevent the decree of the council from being ratified. Accordingly, his successors seeing themselves defeated, quietly desisted from that petulance, and allowed the Bishop of Constantinople to be regarded as the second Patriarch.

16. But shortly after, John, who, in the time of Gregory, presided over the church of Constantinople, went so far as to say that he was universal Patriarch. Here Gregory, that he might not be wanting to his See in a most excellent cause, constantly opposed. And certainly it was impossible to tolerate the pride and madness of John, who wished to make the limits of his bishopric equal to the limits of the empire. This, which Gregory denies to another, he claims not for himself, but abominates the title by whomsoever used, as wicked, impious, and nefarious. Nay, he is offended with Eulogius, Bishop of Alexandria, who had honoured him with this title, "See (says he, Lib. vii. Ep. 30) in the address of the letter which you have directed to me, though I prohibited you, you have taken care to write a word of proud signification by calling me universal Pope. What I ask is, that your holiness do not go farther, because, whatever is given to another more than reason demands is withdrawn from you. I do not regard that as honour by which I see that the honour of my brethren is diminished. For my honour is the universal honour of the Church, and entire prerogative of my brethren. If your holiness calls me universal Pope, it denies itself to be this whole which it acknowledges me to be." The cause of Gregory was indeed good and honourable; but John, aided by the favour of the Emperor Maurice, could not be dissuaded from his purpose. Cyriac also, his successor, never allowed himself to be spoken to on the subject.

17. At length Phocas, who had slain Maurice, and usurped his place (more friendly to the Romans, for what reason I know not, or

rather because he had been crowned king there without opposition), conceded to Boniface III. what Gregory by no means demanded—viz. that Rome should be the head of all the churches. In this way the controversy was ended. And yet this kindness of the Emperor to the Romans would not have been of very much avail had not other circumstances occurred. For shortly after Greece and all Asia were cut off from his communion, while all the reverence which he received from France was obedience only in so far as she pleased. She was brought into subjection for the first time when Pepin got possession of the throne. For Zachary, the Roman Pontiff, having aided him in his perfidy and robbery when he expelled the lawful sovereign, and seized upon the kingdom, which lay exposed as a kind of prey, was rewarded by having the jurisdiction of the Roman See established over the churches of France. In the same way as robbers are wont to divide and share the common spoil, those two worthies arranged that Pepin should have the worldly and civil power by spoiling the true prince, while Zachary should become the head of all the bishops, and have the spiritual power. This, though weak at the first (as usually happens with new power), was afterwards confirmed by the authority of Charlemagne for a very similar cause. For he too was under obligation to the Roman Pontiff, to whose zeal he was indebted for the honour of empire. Though there is reason to believe that the churches had previously been greatly altered, it is certain that the ancient form of the Church was then only completely effaced in Gaul and Germany. There are still extant among the archives of the Parliament of Paris short commentaries on those times, which, in treating of ecclesiastical affairs, make mention of the compacts both of Pepin and Charlemagne with the Roman Pontiff. Hence we may infer that the ancient state of matters was then changed.

18. From that time, while everywhere matters were becoming daily worse, the tyranny of the Roman Bishop was established, and ever and anon increased, and this partly by the ignorance, partly by the sluggishness, of the bishops. For while he was arrogating everything to himself, and proceeding more and more to exalt himself without measure, contrary to law and right, the bishops did not exert themselves so zealously as they ought in curbing his pretensions. And though they had not been deficient in spirit, they were devoid of true doctrine and experience, so that they were by no means fit for so important an effort. Accordingly, we see how great and monstrous was the profanation of all sacred things, and the dissipation of the whole ecclesiastical order at Rome, in the age of Bernard. He complains (Lib. i. de Consider. ad Eugen.) that the ambitious, avaricious, demoniacal, sacrilegious, fornicators, incestuous, and similar miscreants, flocked from all quarters of the world to Rome, that by apostolic authority they might acquire or retain ecclesiastical honours: that fraud, circumvention, and violence, prevailed. The mode of judging causes then in use he describes as

execrable, as disgraceful, not only to the Church, but the bar. He exclaims that the Church is filled with the ambitious: that not one is more afraid to perpetrate crimes than robbers in their den when they share the spoils of the traveller. "Few (say he) look to the mouth of the legislator, but all to his hands. Not without cause, however: for their hands do the whole business of the Pope. What kind of thing is it when those are bought by the spoils of the Church, who say to you, Well done, well done? The life of the poor is sown in the highways of the rich: silver glitters in the mire: they run together from all sides: it is not the poorer that takes it up, but the stronger, or, perhaps, he who runs fastest. That custom, however, or rather that death, comes not of you: I wish it would end in you. While these things are going on, you, a pastor, come forth robed in much costly clothing. If I might presume to say it, this is more the pasture of demons than of sheep. Peter, forsooth, acted thus; Paul sported thus. Your court has been more accustomed to receive good men than to make them. The bad do not gain much there, but the good degenerate." Then when he describes the abuses of appeals, no pious man can read them without being horrified. At length, speaking of the unbridled cupidity of the Roman See in usurping jurisdiction, he thus concludes (Lib. iii. de Concil.), "I express the murmur and common complaint of the churches. Their cry is, that they are maimed and dismembered. There are none, or very few, who do not lament or fear that plague. Do you ask what plague? Abbots are encroached upon by bishops, bishops by archbishops, &c. It is strange if this can be excused. By thus acting, you prove that you have the fulness of power, but not the fulness of righteousness. You do this because you are able; but whether you also ought to do it is the question. You are appointed to preserve, not to envy, the honour and rank of each." I have thought it proper to quote these few passages out of many, partly that my readers may see how grievously the Church had then fallen, partly, too, that they may see with what grief and lamentation all pious men beheld this calamity.

19. But though we were to concede to the Roman Pontiff of the present day the eminence and extent of jurisdiction which his see had in the middle ages, as in the time of Leo and Gregory, what would this be to the existing Papacy? I am not now speaking of worldly dominion, or of civil power, which will afterwards be explained in their own place (chap. xi. sec. 8–14); but what resemblance is there between the spiritual government of which they boast and the state of those times? The only definition which they give of the Pope is, that he is the supreme head of the Church on earth, and the universal bishop of the whole globe. The Pontiffs themselves, when they speak of their authority, declare with great superciliousness, that the power of commanding belongs to them,—that the necessity of obedience remains with others,—that all their decrees are to be regarded as confirmed by the divine voice of Peter,—that

provincial synods, from not having the presence of the Pope, are deficient in authority,—that they can ordain the clergy of any church,—and can summon to their See any who have been ordained elsewhere. Innumerable things of this kind are contained in the farrago of Gratian, which I do not mention, that I may not be tedious to my readers. The whole comes to this, that to the Roman Pontiff belongs the supreme cognisance of all ecclesiastical causes, whether in determining and defining doctrines, or in enacting laws, or in appointing discipline, or in giving sentences. It were also tedious and superfluous to review the privileges which they assume to themselves in what they call reservations. But the most intolerable of all things is their leaving no judicial authority in the world to restrain and curb them when they licentiously abuse their immense power. "No man (say they[1]) is entitled to alter the judgment of this See, on account of the primacy of the Roman Church." Again, "The judge shall not be judged either by the emperor, or by kings, or by the clergy, or by the people." It is surely imperious enough for one man to appoint himself the judge of all, while he will not submit to the judgment of any. But what if he tyrannises over the people of God? if he dissipates and lays waste the kingdom of Christ? if he troubles the whole Church? if he convert the pastoral office into robbery? Nay, though he should be the most abandoned of all, he insists that none can call him to account. The language of Pontiffs is, "God has been pleased to terminate the causes of other men by men, but the Prelate of this See he has reserved unquestioned for his own judgment." Again, "The deeds of subjects are judged by us; ours by God only."

20. And in order that edicts of this kind might have more weight, they falsely substituted the names of ancient Pontiffs, as if matters had been so constituted from the beginning, while it is absolutely certain that whatever attributes more to the Pontiff than we have stated to have been given to him by ancient councils, is new and of recent fabrication. Nay, they have carried their effrontery so far as to publish a rescript under the name of Anastasius, the Patriarch of Constantinople, in which he testifies that it was appointed by ancient regulations, that nothing should be done in the remotest provinces without being previously referred to the Roman See. Besides its extreme folly, who can believe it credible that such an eulogium on the Roman See proceeded from an opponent and rival of its honour and dignity? But doubtless it was necessary that those Antichrists should proceed to such a degree of madness and blindness, that their iniquity might be manifest to all men of sound mind who will only open their eyes. The decretal epistles collected by Gregory IX., also the Clementines and Extravagants of Martin, breathe still more plainly, and in more bombastic terms bespeak this boundless ferocity

1 Nicolas, whose view is given in Decretis 17, Quæst. 3, cap. Nemini; Innocent IX. Quæst. 3. cap. Nemo. Symmachi 9. Quæst. 3, cap. Aliorum. Antherius, ibidem, cap. Facta.

and tyranny, as it were, of barbarian kings. But these are the oracles out of which the Romanists would have their Papacy to be judged. Hence have sprung those famous axioms which have the force of oracles throughout the Papacy in the present day—viz. that the Pope cannot err; that the Pope is superior to councils; that the Pope is the universal bishop of all churches, and the chief Head of the Church on earth. I say nothing of the still greater absurdities which are babbled by the foolish canonists in their schools, absurdities, however, which Roman theologians not only assent to, but even applaud in flattery of their idol.

21. I will not treat with them on the strictest terms. In opposition to their great insolence, some would quote the language which Cyprian used to the bishops in the council over which he presided: "None of us styles himself bishop of bishops, or forces his colleagues to the necessity of obeying by the tyranny of terror." Some might object what was long after decreed at Carthage, "Let no one be called the prince of priests or first bishop;" and might gather many proofs from history, and canons from councils, and many passages from ancient writers, which bring the Roman Pontiff into due order. But these I omit, that I may not seem to press too hard upon them. However, let these worthy defenders of the Roman See tell me with what face they can defend the title of universal bishop, while they see it so often anathematised by Gregory. If effect is to be given to his testimony, then they, by making their Pontiff universal, declare him to be Antichrist. The name of *head* was not more approved. For Gregory thus speaks: "Peter was the chief member in the body, John, Andrew, and James, the heads of particular communities. All, however, are under one head members of the Church: nay, the saints before the law, the saints under the law, the saints under grace, all perfecting the body of the Lord, are constituted members: none of them ever wished to be styled universal" (Gregor. Lib. iv. Ep. 83). When the Pontiff arrogates to himself the power of ordering, he little accords with what Gregory elsewhere says. For Eulogius, Bishop of Alexandria, having said that he had received an order from him, he replies in this manner: "This word *order* I beg you to take out of my hearing, for I know who I am, and who you are: in station you are my brethren, in character my fathers. I therefore did not order, but took care to suggest what seemed useful" (Gregor. Lib. vii. Ep. 80). When the Pope extends his jurisdiction without limit, he does great and atrocious injustice not only to other bishops, but to each single church, tearing and dismembering them, that he may build his see upon their ruins. When he exempts himself from all tribunals, and wishes to reign in the manner of a tyrant, holding his own caprice to be his only law, the thing is too insulting, and too foreign to ecclesiastical rule, to be on any account submitted to. It is altogether abhorrent, not only from pious feeling, but also from common sense.

22. But that I may not be forced to discuss and follow out each point singly, I again appeal to those who, in the present day, would

be thought the best and most faithful defenders of the Roman See, whether they are not ashamed to defend the existing state of the Papacy, which is clearly a hundred times more corrupt than in the days of Gregory and Bernard, though even then these holy men were so much displeased with it. Gregory everywhere complains (Lib. i. Ep. 5; *item*, Ep. 7, 25, &c.) that he was distracted above measure by foreign occupations: that under colour of the episcopate he was taken back to the world, being subject to more worldly cares than he remembered to have ever had when a laic; that he was so oppressed by the trouble of secular affairs, as to be unable to raise his mind to things above; that he was so tossed by the many billows of causes, and afflicted by the tempests of a tumultuous life, that he might well say, "I am come into the depths of the sea." It is certain, that amid these worldly occupations, he could teach the people in sermons, admonish in private, and correct those who required it; order the Church, give counsel to his colleagues, and exhort them to their duty. Moreover, some time was left for writing, and yet he deplores it as his calamity, that he was plunged into the very deepest sea. If the administration at that time was a sea, what shall we say of the present Papacy? For what resemblance is there between the periods? Now there are no sermons, no care for discipline, no zeal for churches, no spiritual function; nothing, in short, but the world. And yet this labyrinth is lauded as if nothing could be found better ordered and arranged. What complaints also does Bernard pour forth, what groans does he utter, when he beholds the vices of his own age? What then would he have done on beholding this iron, or, if possible, worse than iron, age of ours? How dishonest, therefore, not only obstinately to defend as sacred and divine what all the saints have always with one mouth disapproved, but to abuse their testimony in favour of the Papacy, which, it is evident, was altogether unknown to them? Although I admit, in respect to the time of Bernard, that all things were so corrupt as to make it not unlike our own. But it betrays a want of all sense of shame to seek any excuse from that middle period—namely, from that of Leo, Gregory, and the like—for it is just as if one were to vindicate the monarchy of the Cæsars by lauding the ancient state of the Roman empire; in other words, were to borrow the praises of liberty in order to eulogise tyranny.

23. Lastly, Although all these things were granted, an entirely new question arises, when we deny that there is at Rome a Church in which privileges of this nature can reside; when we deny that there is a bishop to sustain the dignity of these privileges. Assume, therefore, that all these things are true (though we have already extorted the contrary from them), that Peter was by the words of Christ constituted head of the universal Church, and that the honour thus conferred upon him he deposited in the Roman See, that this was sanctioned by the authority of the ancient Church, and confirmed by long use; that supreme power was always with one consent devolved by all on the Roman Pontiff, that while he was the judge of all causes

and all men, he was subject to the judgment of none. Let even more be conceded to them if they will, I answer, in one word, that none of these things avail if there be not a Church and a Bishop at Rome. They must of necessity concede to me that she is not a mother of churches who is not herself a church, that he cannot be the chief of bishops who is not himself a bishop. Would they then have the Apostolic See at Rome? Let them give me a true and lawful apostleship. Would they have a supreme pontiff, let them give me a bishop. But how? Where will they show me any semblance of a church? They, no doubt, talk of one, and have it ever in their mouths. But surely the Church is recognised by certain marks, and bishopric is the name of an office. I am not now speaking of the people but of the government, which ought perpetually to be conspicuous in the Church. Where, then, is a ministry such as the institution of Christ requires? Let us remember what was formerly said of the duty of presbyters and bishops. If we bring the office of cardinals to that test, we will acknowledge that they are nothing less than presbyters. But I should like to know what one quality of a bishop the Pope himself has? The first point in the office of a bishop is to instruct the people in the word of God; the second and next to it is to administer the sacraments; the third is to admonish and exhort, to correct those who are in fault, and restrain the people by holy discipline. Which of these things does he do? Nay, which of these things does he pretend to do? Let them say, then, on what ground they will have him to be regarded as a bishop, who does not even in semblance touch any part of the duty with his little finger.

24. It is not with a bishop as with a king; the latter, though he does not execute the proper duty of a king, nevertheless retains the title and the honour; but in deciding on a bishop respect is had to the command of Christ, to which effect ought always to be given in the Church. Let the Romanists then untie this knot. I deny that their pontiff is the prince of bishops, seeing he is no bishop. This allegation of mine they must prove to be false if they would succeed in theirs. What then do I maintain? That he has nothing proper to a bishop, but is in all things the opposite of a bishop. But with what shall I here begin? With doctrine or with morals? What shall I say, or what shall I pass in silence, or where shall I end? This I maintain: while in the present day the world is so inundated with perverse and impious doctrines, so full of all kinds of superstition, so blinded by error and sunk in idolatry, there is not one of them which has not emanated from the Papacy, or at least been confirmed by it. Nor is there any other reason why the pontiffs are so enraged against the reviving doctrine of the Gospel, why they stretch every nerve to oppress it, and urge all kings and princes to cruelty, than just that they see their whole dominion tottering and falling to pieces the moment the Gospel of Christ prevails. Leo was cruel and Clement sanguinary, Paul is truculent. But in assailing the truth, it is not so much natural temper that impels them as the conviction

that they have no other method of maintaining their power. Therefore, seeing they cannot be safe unless they put Christ to flight, they labour in this cause as if they were fighting for their altars and hearths, for their own lives and those of their adherents. What then? Shall we recognise the Apostolic See where we see nothing but horrible apostacy? Shall he be the vicar of Christ who, by his furious efforts in persecuting the Gospel, plainly declares himself to be Antichrist? Shall he be the successor of Peter who goes about with fire and sword demolishing everything that Peter built? Shall he be the Head of the Church who, after dissevering the Church from Christ, her only true Head, tears and lacerates her members? Rome, indeed, was once the mother of all the churches, but since she began to be the seat of Antichrist she ceased to be what she was.

25. To some we seem slanderous and petulant, when we call the Roman Pontiff Antichrist. But those who think so perceive not that they are bringing a charge of intemperance against Paul, after whom we speak, nay, in whose very words we speak. But lest any one object that Paul's words have a different meaning, and are wrested by us against the Roman Pontiff, I will briefly show that they can only be understood of the Papacy. Paul says that Antichrist would sit in the temple of God (2 Thess. ii. 4). In another passage, the Spirit, portraying him in the person of Antiochus, says that his reign would be with great swelling words of vanity (Dan. vii. 25). Hence we infer that his tyranny is more over souls than bodies, a tyranny set up in opposition to the spiritual kingdom of Christ. Then his nature is such, that he abolishes not the name either of Christ or the Church, but rather uses the name of Christ as a pretext, and lurks under the name of Church as under a mask. But though all the heresies and schisms which have existed from the beginning belong to the kingdom of Antichrist, yet when Paul foretells that defection will come, he by the description intimates that that seat of abomination will be erected, when a kind of universal defection comes upon the Church, though many members of the Church scattered up and down should continue in the true unity of the faith. But when he adds, that in his own time, the mystery of iniquity, which was afterwards to be openly manifested, had begun to work in secret, we thereby understand that this calamity was neither to be introduced by one man, nor to terminate in one man (see Calv. in 2 Thess. ii. 3; Dan. vii. 9). Moreover, when the mark by which he distinguishes Antichrist is, that he would rob God of his honour and take it to himself, he gives the leading feature which we ought to follow in searching out Antichrist; especially when pride of this description proceeds to the open devastation of the Church. Seeing then it is certain that the Roman Pontiff has impudently transferred to himself the most peculiar properties of God and Christ, there cannot be a doubt that he is the leader and standard-bearer of an impious and abominable kingdom.

26. Let the Romanists now go and oppose us with antiquity; as

if, amid such a complete change in every respect, the honour of the See can continue where there is no See. Eusebius says that God, to make way for his vengeance, transferred the Church which was at Jerusalem to Pella (Euseb. Lib. iii. cap. 5). What we are told was once done may have been done repeatedly. Hence it is too absurd and ridiculous so to fix the honour of the primacy to a particular spot, as that he who is in fact the most inveterate enemy of Christ, the chief adversary of the Gospel, the greatest devastator and waster of the Church, the most cruel slayer and murderer of the saints, should be, nevertheless, regarded as the vicegerent of Christ, the successor of Peter, the first priest of the Church, merely because he occupies what was formerly the first of all sees. I do not say how great the difference is between the chancery of the Pope and well-regulated order in the Church; although this one fact might well set the question at rest. For no man of sound mind will include the episcopate in lead and bulls, much less in that administration of captions and circumscriptions, in which the spiritual government of the Pope is supposed to consist. It has therefore been elegantly said, that that vaunted Roman Church was long ago converted into a temporal court, the only thing which is now seen at Rome. I am not here speaking of the vices of individuals, but demonstrating that the Papacy itself is diametrically opposed to the ecclesiastical system.

27. But if we come to individuals, it is well known what kind of vicars of Christ we shall find. No doubt, Julius and Leo, and Clement and Paul, will be pillars of the Christian faith, the first interpreters of religion, though they knew nothing more of Christ than they had learned in the school of Lucian. But why give the names of three or four pontiffs? as if there were any doubt as to the kind of religion professed by pontiffs, with their College of Cardinals, and professors, in the present day. The first head of the secret theology which is in vogue among them is, that there is no God. Another, that whatever things have been written and are taught concerning Christ are lies and imposture.[1] A third, that the doctrine of a future life and final resurrection is a mere fable. All do not think, few speak thus; I confess it. Yet it is long since this began to be the ordinary religion of pontiffs; and though the thing is notorious to all who know Rome, Roman theologians cease not to boast that by special privilege our Saviour has provided that the Pope cannot err, because it was said to Peter, "I have prayed for thee that thy faith fail not" (Luke xxii. 32). What, pray, do they gain by their effrontery, but to let the whole world understand that they have reached the extreme of wickedness, so as neither to fear God nor regard man?

1 Erasmus, in a letter to Steuchus, says, "It may be that in Germany there are persons who do not refrain from blasphemy against God, but the severest punishment is inflicted on them. But at Rome, I have with my own ears heard men belching out

28. But let us suppose that the iniquity of these pontiffs whom I have mentioned is not known, as they have not published it either in sermons or writings, but betrayed it only at table or in their chamber, or at least within the walls of their court. But if they would have the privilege which they claim to be confirmed, they must expunge from their list of pontiffs John XXII.,[1] who publicly maintained that the soul is mortal, and perishes with the body till the day of resurrection. And to show you that the whole See with its chief props then utterly fell, none of the Cardinals opposed his madness, only the Faculty of Paris urged the king to insist on a recantation. The king interdicted his subjects from communion with him, unless he would immediately recant, and published his interdict in the usual way by a herald. Thus necessitated, he abjured his error. This example relieves me from the necessity of disputing further with my opponents, when they say that the Roman See and its pontiffs cannot err in the faith, from its being said to Peter, "I have prayed for thee that thy faith fail not." Certainly by this shameful lapse he fell from the faith, and became a noted proof to posterity, that all are not Peters who succeed Peter in the episcopate; although the thing is too childish in itself to need an answer: for if they insist on applying everything that was said to Peter to the successors of Peter, it will follow, that they are all Satans, because our Lord once said to Peter, "Get thee behind me, Satan, thou art an offence unto me." It is as easy for us to retort the latter saying as for them to adduce the former.

29. But I have no pleasure in this absurd mode of disputation, and therefore return to the point from which I digressed. To fix down Christ and the Holy Spirit and the Church to a particular spot, so that every one who presides in it, should he be a devil, must still be deemed vicegerent of Christ, and the head of the Church, because that spot was formerly the See of Peter, is not only impious and insulting to Christ, but absurd and contrary to common sense. For a long period, the Roman Pontiffs have either been altogether devoid of religion, or been its greatest enemies. The see which they occupy, therefore, no more makes them the vicars of Christ, than it makes an idol to become God, when it is placed in the temple of God (2 Thess. ii. 4). Then, if manners be inquired into, let the Popes answer for themselves, what there is in them that can make them be recognised for bishops. First, the mode of life at Rome, while they not only connive and are silent, but also tacitly approve, is altogether unworthy of bishops, whose duty it is to curb the licence of the people by the strictness of discipline. But I will not be so rigid with them as to charge them with the faults of others. But when they with their household, with almost the whole College of Cardinals, and the whole body of their clergy, are so devoted to wickedness, obscenity, unclean-

horrid blasphemies against Christ and his apostles, in the presence of many besides myself, and doing it with impunity!"

[1] John Gerson, who lived at the time, attests that John XXII. openly denied the immortality of the soul.

ness, iniquity, and crime of every description, that they resemble monsters more than men, they herein betray that they are nothing less than bishops. They need not fear that I will make a farther disclosure of their turpitude. For it is painful to wade through such filthy mire, and I must spare modest ears. But I think I have amply demonstrated what I proposed—viz. that though Rome was formerly the first of churches, she deserves not in the present day to be regarded as one of her minutest members.

30. In regard to those whom they call Cardinals, I know not how it happened that they rose so suddenly to such a height. In the age of Gregory, the name was applied to bishops only (Gregor. Lib. ii. Ep. 15, 77, 79; Ep. 6, 25). For whenever he makes mention of cardinals, he assigns them not only to the Roman Church, but to every other church, so that, in short, *a Cardinal priest* is nothing else than a bishop. I do not find the name among the writers of a former age. I see, however, that they were inferior to bishops, whom they now far surpass. There is a well-known passage in Augustine: "Although, in regard to terms of honour which custom has fixed in the Church, the office of bishop is greater than that of presbyter, yet in many things, Augustine is inferior to Jerome" (August. ad Hieron. Ep. 19). Here, certainly, he is not distinguishing a presbyter of the Roman Church from other presbyters, but placing all of them alike after bishops. And so strictly was this observed, that at the Council of Carthage, when two legates of the Roman See were present, one a bishop, and the other a presbyter, the latter was put in the lowest place. But not to dwell too much on ancient times, we have account of a Council held at Rome, under Gregory, at which the presbyters sit in the lowest place, and subscribe by themselves, while deacons do not subscribe at all. And, indeed, they had no office at that time, unless to be present under the bishop, and assist him in the administration of word and sacraments. So much is their lot now changed, that they have become associates of kings and Cesars. And there can be no doubt that they have grown gradually with their head, until they reached their present pinnacle of dignity. This much it seemed proper to say in passing, that my readers may understand how very widely the Roman See, as it now exists, differs from the ancient See, under which it endeavours to cloak and defend itself. But whatever they were formerly, as they have no true and legitimate office in the Church, they only retain a colour and empty mask; nay, as they are in all respects the opposite of true ministers, the thing which Gregory so often writes must, of necessity, have befallen them. His words are, "Weeping, I say, groaning, I declare it; when the sacerdotal order has fallen within, it cannot long stand without" (Gregor. Lib. iv. Ep. 55, 56; Lib. v. Ep. 7). Nay, rather what Malachi says of such persons must be fulfilled in them: "Ye are departed out of the way; ye have caused many to stumble at the law; ye have corrupted the covenant of Levi, saith the Lord of hosts. Therefore have I also made you contemptible and base before all the people" (Mal. ii. 8,

9). I now leave all the pious to judge what the supreme pinnacle of the Roman hierarchy must be, to which the Papists, with nefarious effrontery, hesitate not to subject the word of God itself, that word which should be venerable and holy in earth and heaven, to men and angels.

CHAPTER VIII.

OF THE POWER OF THE CHURCH IN ARTICLES OF FAITH. THE UNBRIDLED LICENCE OF THE PAPAL CHURCH IN DESTROYING PURITY OF DOCTRINE.

This chapter is divided into two parts,—I. The limits within which the Church ought to confine herself in matters of this kind, sec. 1–9. II. The Roman Church convicted of having transgressed these limits, sec. 10–16.

Sections.

1. The marks and government of the Church having been considered in the seven previous chapters, the power of the Church is now considered under three heads—viz. Doctrine, Legislation, Jurisdiction.
2. The authority and power given to Church-officers not given to themselves, but their office. This shown in the case of Moses and the Levitical priesthood.
3. The same thing shown in the case of the Prophets.
4. Same thing shown in the case of the Apostles, and of Christ himself.
5. The Church astricted to the written Word of God. Christ the only teacher of the Church. From his lips ministers must derive whatever they teach for the salvation of others. Various modes of divine teaching. 1. Personal revelations.
6. Second mode of teaching—viz. by the Law and the Prophets. The Prophets were, in regard to doctrine, the expounders of the Law. To these were added Historical Narratives and the Psalms.
7. Last mode of teaching by our Saviour himself manifested in the flesh. Different names given to this dispensation, to show that we are not to dream of anything more perfect than the written word.
8. Nothing can be lawfully taught in the Church, that is not contained in the writings of the Prophets and Apostles, as dictated by the Spirit of Christ.
9. Neither the Apostles, nor apostolic men, nor the whole Church, allowed to overstep these limits. This confirmed by passages of Peter and Paul. Argument *a fortiori*.
10. The Roman tyrants have taught a different doctrine—viz. that Councils cannot err, and, therefore, may coin new dogmas.
11. Answer to the Papistical arguments for the authority of the Church. Argument, that the Church is to be led into all truth. Answer. This promise made not only to the whole Church, but to every individual believer.
12. Answers continued.
13. Answers continued.
14. Argument, that the Church should supply the deficiency of the written word by traditions. Answer.
15. Argument founded on Matth. xviii. 17. Answer.
16. Objections founded on Infant Baptism, and the Canon of the Council of Nice, as to the consubstantiality of the Son. Answer.

1. WE come now to the third division—viz. the *Power of the Church*, as existing either in individual bishops, or in councils, whether provincial or general. I speak only of the spiritual power which is proper to the Church, and which consists either in doctrine, or jurisdiction, or in enacting laws. In regard to doctrine, there are two divisions—viz. the authority of delivering dogmas, and the interpretation of them. Before we begin to treat of each in particular, I wish to remind the pious reader, that whatever is taught respecting

the power of the Church, ought to have reference to the end for which Paul declares (2 Cor. x. 8; xiii. 10) that it was given—namely, for edification, and not for destruction, those who use it lawfully deeming themselves to be nothing more than servants of Christ, and, at the same time, servants of the people in Christ. Moreover, the only mode by which ministers can edify the Church is, by studying to maintain the authority of Christ, which cannot be unimpaired, unless that which he received of the Father is left to him—viz. to be the only Master of the Church. For it was not said of any other but of himself alone, "Hear him" (Matth. xvii. 5). Ecclesiastical power, therefore, is not to be mischievously adorned, but it is to be confined within certain limits, so as not to be drawn hither and thither at the caprice of men. For this purpose, it will be of great use to observe how it is described by Prophets and Apostles. For if we concede unreservedly to men all the power which they think proper to assume, it is easy to see how soon it will degenerate into a tyranny which is altogether alien from the Church of Christ.

2. Therefore, it is here necessary to remember, that whatever authority and dignity the Holy Spirit in Scripture confers on priests, or prophets, or apostles, or successors of Apostles, is wholly given not to men themselves, but to the ministry to which they are appointed; or, to speak more plainly, to the word, to the ministry of which they are appointed. For were we to go over the whole in order, we should find that they were not invested with authority to teach or give responses, save in the name and word of the Lord. For whenever they are called to office, they are enjoined not to bring anything of their own, but to speak by the mouth of the Lord. Nor does he bring them forward to be heard by the people, before he has instructed them what they are to speak, lest they should speak anything but his own word. Moses, the prince of all the prophets, was to be heard in preference to others (Exod. iii. 4; Deut. xvii. 9); but he is previously furnished with his orders, that he may not be able to speak at all except from the Lord. Accordingly, when the people embraced his doctrine, they are said to have believed the Lord, and his servant Moses (Exod. xiv. 31). It was also provided under the severest sanctions, that the authority of the priests should not be despised (Exod. xvii. 9). But the Lord, at the same time, shows in what terms they were to be heard, when he says that he made his covenant with Levi, that the law of truth might be in his mouth (Mal. ii. 4–6). A little after he adds, "The priest's lips should keep knowledge, and they should seek the law at his mouth; for he is the messenger of the Lord of hosts." Therefore, if the priest would be heard, let him show himself to be the messenger of God; that is, let him faithfully deliver the commands which he has received from his Maker. When the mode of hearing, then, is treated of, it is expressly said, "According to the sentence of the law which they shall teach thee" (Deut. xvii. 11).

3. The nature of the power conferred upon the prophets in general

is elegantly described by Ezekiel: "Son of man, I have made thee a watchman unto the house of Israel: therefore hear the word at my mouth, and give them warning from me" (Ezek. iii. 17). Is not he who is ordered to hear at the mouth of the Lord prohibited from devising anything of himself? And what is meant by giving a warning from the Lord, but just to speak so as to be able confidently to declare that the word which he delivers is not his own but the Lord's? The same thing is expressed by Jeremiah in different terms, "The prophet that hath a dream, let him tell a dream; and he that hath my word, let him speak my word faithfully" (Jer. xxiii. 28). Surely God here declares the law to all, and it is a law which does not allow any one to teach more than he has been ordered. He afterwards gives the name of chaff to whatever has not proceeded from himself alone. Accordingly, none of the prophets opened his mouth unless preceded by the word of the Lord. Hence we so often meet with the expressions, "The word of the Lord, The burden of the Lord, Thus saith the Lord, The mouth of the Lord hath spoken it."[1] And justly, for Isaiah exclaims that his lips are unclean (Isa. vi. 5); and Jeremiah confesses that he knows not how to speak because he is a child (Jer. i. 6). Could anything proceed from the unclean lips of the one, and the childish lips of the other, if they spoke their own language, but what was unclean or childish? But their lips were holy and pure when they began to be organs of the Holy Spirit. The prophets, after being thus strictly bound not to deliver anything but what they received, are invested with great power and illustrious titles. For when the Lord declares, "See, I have this day set thee over the nations, and over the kingdoms, to root out, and to pull down, and to destroy, and to throw down, to build, and to plant," he at the same time gives the reason, "Behold, I have put my words in thy mouth" (Jer. i. 9, 10).

4. Now, if you look to the apostles, they are commended by many distinguished titles, as the Light of the world, and the Salt of the earth, to be heard in Christ's stead, whatever they bound or loosed on earth being bound or loosed in heaven (Matth. v. 13, 14; Luke x. 16; John xx. 23). But they declare in their own name what the authority was which their office conferred on them—viz. if they are apostles they must not speak their own pleasure, but faithfully deliver the commands of him by whom they are sent. The words in which Christ defined their embassy are sufficiently clear, "Go ye, therefore, and teach all nations, teaching them to observe all things whatsoever I have commanded you" (Matth. xxviii. 19, 20). Nay, that none might be permitted to decline this law, he received it and imposed it on himself. "My doctrine is not mine, but his that sent me" (John vii. 16). He who always was the only and eternal counsellor of the Father, who by the Father was constituted Lord and Master of all, yet because he per-

1 The French adds, "Vision receue du Seigneur; Le Seigneur des armees l'a dit;"—A vision received from the Lord; The Lord of hosts hath spoken it.

formed the ministry of teaching, prescribed to all ministers by his example the rule which they ought to follow in teaching. The power of the Church, therefore, is not infinite, but is subject to the word of the Lord, and, as it were, included in it.

5. But though the rule which always existed in the Church from the beginning, and ought to exist in the present day, is, that the servants of God are only to teach what they have learned from himself, yet, according to the variety of times, they have had different methods of learning. The mode which now exists differs very much from that of former times. First, if it is true, as Christ says, "Neither knoweth any man the Father save the Son, and he to whomsoever the Son will reveal him" (Matth. xi. 27), then those who wish to attain to the knowledge of God behoved always to be directed by that eternal wisdom. For how could they have comprehended the mysteries of God in their mind, or declared them to others, unless by the teaching of him, to whom alone the secrets of the Father are known? The only way, therefore, by which in ancient times holy men knew God, was by beholding him in the Son as in a mirror. When I say this, I mean that God never manifested himself to men by any other means than by his Son, that is, his own only wisdom, light, and truth. From this fountain Adam, Noah, Abraham, Isaac, Jacob, and others, drew all the heavenly doctrine which they possessed. From the same fountain all the prophets also drew all the heavenly oracles which they published. For this wisdom did not always display itself in one manner. With the patriarchs he employed secret revelations, but, at the same time, in order to confirm these, had recourse to signs so as to make it impossible for them to doubt that it was God that spake to them. What the patriarchs received they handed down to posterity, for God had, in depositing it with them, bound them thus to propagate it, while their children and descendants knew by the inward teaching of God, that what they heard was of heaven and not of earth.

6. But when God determined to give a more illustrious form to the Church, he was pleased to commit and consign his word to writing, that the priests might there seek what they were to teach the people, and every doctrine delivered be brought to it as a test (Mal. ii. 7). Accordingly, after the promulgation of the Law, when the priests are enjoined to teach from the mouth of the Lord, the meaning is, that they are not to teach anything extraneous or alien to that kind of doctrine which God had summed up in the Law, while it was unlawful for them to add to it or take from it. Next followed the prophets, by whom God published the new oracles which were added to the Law, not so new, however, but that they flowed from the Law, and had respect to it. For in so far as regards doctrine, they were only interpreters of the Law, adding nothing to it but predictions of future events. With this exception, all that they delivered was pure exposition of the Law. But as the Lord was pleased that doctrine should exist in a clearer and more ample form, the better to satisfy weak

consciences, he commanded the prophecies also to be committed to writing, and to be held part of his word. To these at the same time were added historical details, which are also the composition of prophets, but dictated by the Holy Spirit; I include the Psalms among the Prophecies, the quality which we attribute to the latter belonging also to the former. The whole body, therefore, composed of the Law, the Prophets, the Psalms, and Histories, formed the word of the Lord to his ancient people, and by it as a standard, priests and teachers, before the advent of Christ, were bound to test their doctrine, nor was it lawful for them to turn aside either to the right hand or the left, because their whole office was confined to this—to give responses to the people from the mouth of God. This is gathered from a celebrated passage of Malachi, in which it is enjoined to remember the Law, and give heed to it until the preaching of the Gospel (Mal. iv. 4). For he thus restrains men from all adventitious doctrines, and does not allow them to deviate in the least from the path which Moses had faithfully pointed out. And the reason why David so magnificently extols the Law, and pronounces so many encomiums on it (Ps. xix., cxix.), was, that the Jews might not long after any extraneous aid, all perfection being included in it.

7. But when at length the Wisdom of God was manifested in the flesh, he fully unfolded to us all that the human mind can comprehend, or ought to think of the heavenly Father. Now, therefore, since Christ, the Sun of Righteousness, has arisen, we have the perfect refulgence of divine truth, like the brightness of noon-day, whereas the light was previously dim. It was no ordinary blessing which the apostle intended to publish when he wrote: "God, who at sundry times and in divers manners, spake in time past unto the fathers by the prophets, hath in these last days spoken unto us by his Son" (Heb. i. 1, 2); for he intimates, nay, openly declares, that God will not henceforth, as formerly, speak by this one and by that one, that he will not add prophecy to prophecy, or revelation to revelation, but has so completed all the parts of teaching in the Son, that it is to be regarded as his last and eternal testimony. For which reason, the whole period of the new dispensation, from the time when Christ appeared to us with the preaching of his Gospel, until the day of judgment, is designated by the *last hour*, *the last times*, *the last days*, that, contented with the perfection of Christ's doctrine, we may learn to frame no new doctrine for ourselves, or admit any one devised by others. With good cause, therefore, the Father appointed the Son our teacher, with special prerogative, commanding that he and no human being should be heard. When he said, "Hear him" (Matth. xvii. 5), he commended his office to us, in few words, indeed, but words of more weight and energy than is commonly supposed, for it is just as if he had withdrawn us from all doctrines of man, and confined us to him alone, ordering us to seek the whole doctrine of salvation from him alone, to depend on him alone, and cleave to him alone; in short (as the words express), to listen only to his voice.

And, indeed, what can now be expected or desired from man, when the very Word of life has appeared before us, and familiarly explained himself? Nay, every mouth should be stopped when once he has spoken, in whom, according to the pleasure of our heavenly Father, "are hid all the treasures of wisdom and knowledge" (Col. ii. 3), and spoken as became the Wisdom of God (which is in no part defective) and the Messiah (from whom the revelation of all things was expected) (John iv. 25); in other words, has so spoken as to leave nothing to be spoken by others after him.

8. Let this then be a sure axiom—that there is no word of God to which place should be given in the Church save that which is contained, first, in the Law and the Prophets; and, secondly, in the writings of the Apostles, and that the only due method of teaching in the Church is according to the prescription and rule of his word. Hence also we infer that nothing else was permitted to the apostles than was formerly permitted to the prophets—namely, to expound the ancient Scriptures, and show that the things there delivered are fulfilled in Christ: this, however, they could not do unless from the Lord; that is, unless the Spirit of Christ went before, and in a manner dictated words to them. For Christ thus defined the terms of their embassy, when he commanded them to go and teach, not what they themselves had at random fabricated, but whatsoever he had commanded (Matth. xxviii. 20). And nothing can be plainer than his words in another passage, "Be not ye called Rabbi: for one is your Master, even Christ" (Matth. xxiii. 8–10). To impress this more deeply in their minds, he in the same place repeats it twice. And because from ignorance they were unable to comprehend the things which they had heard and learned from the lips of their Master, the Spirit of truth is promised to guide them unto all truth (John xiv. 26; xvi. 13). The restriction should be carefully attended to. The office which he assigns to the Holy Spirit is to bring to remembrance what his own lips had previously taught.

9. Accordingly, Peter, who was perfectly instructed by his Master as to the extent of what was permitted to him, leaves nothing more to himself or others than to dispense the doctrine delivered by God. "If any man speak, let him speak as the oracles of God" (1 Peter iv. 11); that is, not hesitatingly, as those are wont whose convictions are imperfect, but with the full confidence which becomes a servant of God, provided with a sure message. What else is this than to banish all the inventions of the human mind (whatever be the head which may have devised them), that the pure word of God may be taught and learned in the Church of the faithful,—than to discard the decrees, or rather fictions of men (whatever be their rank), that the decrees of God alone may remain steadfast? These are "the weapons of our warfare," which "are not carnal, but mighty through God to the pulling down of strongholds; casting down imaginations, and every high thing that exalteth itself against the knowledge of God, and bringing into captivity every thought to the obedience of Christ"

(2 Cor. x. 4, 5). Here is the supreme power with which pastors of the Church, by whatever name they are called, should be invested—namely, to dare all boldly for the word of God, compelling all the virtue, glory, wisdom, and rank of the world to yield and obey its majesty; to command all from the highest to the lowest, trusting to its power to build up the house of Christ and overthrow the house of Satan; to feed the sheep and chase away the wolves; to instruct and exhort the docile, to accuse, rebuke, and subdue the rebellious and petulant, to bind and loose; in fine, if need be, to fire and fulminate, but all in the word of God. Although, as I have observed, there is this difference between the apostles and their successors, they were sure and authentic amanuenses of the Holy Spirit; and, therefore, their writings are to be regarded as the oracles of God, whereas others have no other office than to teach what is delivered and sealed in the holy Scriptures. We conclude, therefore, that it does not now belong to faithful ministers to coin some new doctrine, but simply to adhere to the doctrine to which all, without exception, are made subject. When I say this, I mean to show not only what each individual, but what the whole Church, is bound to do. In regard to individuals, Paul certainly had been appointed an apostle to the Corinthians, and yet he declares that he has no dominion over their faith (2 Cor. i. 24). Who will now presume to arrogate a dominion to which the apostle declares that he himself was not competent? But if he had acknowledged such licence in teaching, that every pastor could justly demand implicit faith in whatever he delivered, he never would have laid it down as a rule to the Corinthians, that while two or three prophets spoke, the others should judge, and that, if anything was revealed to one sitting by, the first should be silent (1 Cor. xiv. 29, 30). Thus he spared none, but subjected the authority of all to the censure of the word of God. But it will be said, that with regard to the whole Church the case is different. I answer, that in another place Paul meets the objection also when he says, that faith cometh by hearing, and hearing by the word of God (Rom. x. 17). In other words, if faith depends upon the word of God alone, if it regards and reclines on it alone, what place is left for any word of man? He who knows what faith is can never hesitate here, for it must possess a strength sufficient to stand intrepid and invincible against Satan, the machinations of hell, and the whole world. This strength can be found only in the word of God. Then the reason to which we ought here to have regard is universal: God deprives man of the power of producing any new doctrine, in order that he alone may be our master in spiritual teaching, as he alone is true, and can neither lie nor deceive. This reason applies not less to the whole Church than to every individual believer.

10. But if this power of the church which is here described be contrasted with that which spiritual tyrants, falsely styling themselves bishops and religious prelates, have now for several ages exercised among the people of God, there will be no more agreement

than that of Christ with Belial. It is not my intention here to unfold the manner, the unworthy manner, in which they have used their tyranny; I will only state the doctrine which they maintain in the present day, first, in writing, and then, by fire and sword. Taking it for granted, that a universal council is a true representation of the Church, they set out with this principle, and, at the same time, lay it down as incontrovertible, that such councils are under the immediate guidance of the Holy Spirit, and therefore cannot err. But as they rule councils, nay, constitute them, they in fact claim for themselves whatever they maintain to be due to councils. Therefore, they will have our faith to stand and fall at their pleasure, so that whatever they have determined on either side must be firmly seated in our minds; what they approve must be approved by us without any doubt; what they condemn we also must hold to be justly condemned. Meanwhile, at their own caprice, and in contempt of the word of God, they coin doctrines to which they in this way demand our assent, declaring that no man can be a Christian unless he assent to all their dogmas, affirmative as well as negative, if not with explicit, yet with implicit faith, because it belongs to the Church to frame new articles of faith.

11. First, let us hear by what arguments they prove that this authority was given to the Church, and then we shall see how far their allegations concerning the Church avail them. The Church, they say, has the noble promise that she will never be deserted by Christ her spouse, but be guided by his Spirit into all truth. But of the promises which they are wont to allege, many were given not less to private believers than to the whole Church. For although the Lord spake to the twelve apostles, when he said, "Lo! I am with you alway, even unto the end of the world" (Matth. xxviii. 20); and again, "I will pray the Father, and he shall give you another Comforter, that he may abide with you for ever: even the Spirit of truth" (John xiv. 16, 17), he made these promises not only to the twelve, but to each of them separately, nay, in like manner, to other disciples whom he already had received, or was afterwards to receive. When they interpret these promises, which are replete with consolation, in such a way as if they were not given to any particular Christian but to the whole Church together, what else is it but to deprive Christians of the confidence which they ought thence to have derived, to animate them in their course? I deny not that the whole body of the faithful is furnished with a manifold variety of gifts, and endued with a far larger and richer treasure of heavenly wisdom than each Christian apart; nor do I mean that this was said of believers in general, as implying that all possess the spirit of wisdom and knowledge in an equal degree: but we are not to give permission to the adversaries of Christ to defend a bad cause, by wresting Scripture from its proper meaning. Omitting this, however, I simply hold what is true—viz. that the Lord is always present with his people, and guides them by his Spirit. He is the Spirit,

not of error, ignorance, falsehood, or darkness, but of sure revelation, wisdom, truth, and light, from whom they can, without deception, learn the things which have been given to them (1 Cor. ii. 12); in other words, "what is the hope of their calling, and what the riches of the glory of their inheritance in the saints" (Eph. i. 18). But while believers, even those of them who are endued with more excellent graces, obtain in the present life only the first-fruits, and, as it were, a foretaste of the Spirit, nothing better remains to them than, under a consciousness of their weakness, to confine themselves anxiously within the limits of the word of God, lest, in following their own sense too far, they forthwith stray from the right path, being left without that Spirit, by whose teaching alone truth is discerned from falsehood. For all confess with Paul, that "they have not yet reached the goal" (Phil. iii. 12). Accordingly, they rather aim at daily progress than glory in perfection.

12. But it will be objected, that whatever is attributed in part to any of the saints, belongs in complete fulness to the Church. Although there is some semblance of truth in this, I deny that it is true. God, indeed, measures out the gifts of his Spirit to each of the members, so that nothing necessary to the whole body is wanting, since the gifts are bestowed for the common advantage. The riches of the Church, however, are always of such a nature, that much is wanting to that supreme perfection of which our opponents boast. Still the Church is not left destitute in any part, but always has as much as is sufficient, for the Lord knows what her necessities require. But to keep her in humility and pious modesty, he bestows no more on her than he knows to be expedient. I am aware, it is usual here to object, that Christ hath cleansed the Church "with the washing of water by the word: that he might present it to himself a glorious Church, not having spot or wrinkle" (Eph. v. 26, 27), and that it is therefore called the "pillar and ground of the truth" (1 Tim. iii. 15). But the former passage rather shows what Christ daily performs in it, than what he has already perfected. For if he daily sanctifies all his people, purifies, refines them, and wipes away their stains, it is certain that they have still some spots and wrinkles, and that their sanctification is in some measure defective. How vain and fabulous is it to suppose that the Church, all whose members are somewhat spotted and impure, is completely holy and spotless in every part? It is true, therefore, that the Church is sanctified by Christ, but here the commencement of her sanctification only is seen; the end and entire completion will be effected when Christ, the Holy of holies, shall truly and completely fill her with his holiness. It is true also, that her stains and wrinkles have been effaced, but so that the process is continued every day, until Christ at his advent will entirely remove every remaining defect. For unless we admit this, we shall be constrained to hold with the Pelagians, that the righteousness of believers is perfected in this life: like the Cathari and Donatists we shall tolerate no infirmity in

the Church.[1] The other passage, as we have elsewhere seen (chap. i. sec. 10), has a very different meaning from what they put upon it. For when Paul instructed Timothy, and trained him to the office of a true bishop, he says, he did it in order that he might learn how to behave himself in the Church of God. And to make him devote himself to the work with greater seriousness and zeal, he adds, that the Church is the pillar and ground of the truth. And what else do these words mean, than just that the truth of God is preserved in the Church, and preserved by the instrumentality of preaching; as he elsewhere says, that Christ "gave some, apostles; and some, prophets; and some, evangelists; and some, pastors and teachers;" "that we henceforth be no more children, tossed to and fro, and carried about with every wind of doctrine, by the sleight of men, and cunning craftiness, whereby they lie in wait to deceive; but, speaking the truth in love, may grow up into him in all things, who is the head, even Christ"? (Eph. iv. 11, 14, 15.) The reason, therefore, why the truth, instead of being extinguished in the world, remains unimpaired, is, because he has the Church as a faithful guardian, by whose aid and ministry it is maintained. But if this guardianship consists in the ministry of the Prophets and Apostles, it follows, that the whole depends upon this—viz. that the word of the Lord is faithfully preserved and maintained in purity.

13. And that my readers may the better understand the hinge on which the question chiefly turns, I will briefly explain what our opponents demand, and what we resist. When they deny that the Church can err, their end and meaning are to this effect: Since the Church is governed by the Spirit of God, she can walk safely without the word; in whatever direction she moves, she cannot think or speak anything but the truth, and hence, if she determines anything without or beside the word of God, it must be regarded in no other light than if it were a divine oracle. If we grant the first point—viz. that the Church cannot err in things necessary to salvation—our meaning is, that she cannot err, because she has altogether discarded her own wisdom, and submits to the teaching of the Holy Spirit through the word of God. Here then is the difference. They place the authority of the Church without the word of God; we annex it to the word, and allow it not to be separated from it. And is it strange if the spouse and pupil of Christ is so subject to her lord and master as to hang carefully and constantly on his lips? In every well-ordered house the wife obeys the command of her husband, in every well-regulated school the doctrine of the master only is listened to. Wherefore, let not the Church be wise in herself, nor think any thing of herself, but let her consider her wisdom terminated when he ceases to speak. In this way she will distrust all the inventions of her own reason; and when she leans on the word of God, will not waver in diffidence or hesitation, but rest in full assurance and un-

1 The French adds, "Or, nos adversaires mesmes tiennent tous ceux-la pour heretiques."—Now, our opponents themselves regard all those as heretics.

wavering constancy. Trusting to the liberal promises which she has received, she will have the means of nobly maintaining her faith, never doubting that the Holy Spirit is always present with her to be the perfect guide of her path. At the same time, she will remember the use which God wishes to be derived from his Spirit. "When he, the Spirit of truth, is come, he will guide you into all truth" (John xvi. 13). How? "He shall bring to your remembrance all things whatsoever I have said unto you." He declares, therefore, that nothing more is to be expected of his Spirit than to enlighten our minds to perceive the truth of his doctrine. Hence Chrysostom most shrewdly observes, "Many boast of the Holy Spirit, but with those who speak their own it is a false pretence. As Christ declared that he spoke not of himself (John xii. 50; xiv. 10), because he spoke according to the Law and the Prophets; so, if anything contrary to the Gospel is obtruded under the name of the Holy Spirit, let us not believe it. For as Christ is the fulfilment of the Law and the Prophets, so is the Spirit the fulfilment of the Gospel" (Chrysost. Serm. de Sancto et Adorando Spiritu.) Thus far Chrysostom. We may now easily infer how erroneously our opponents act in vaunting of the Holy Spirit, for no other end than to give the credit of his name to strange doctrines, extraneous to the word of God, whereas he himself desires to be inseparably connected with the word of God; and Christ declares the same thing of him, when he promises him to the Church. And so indeed it is. The soberness which our Lord once prescribed to his Church, he wishes to be perpetually observed. He forbade that anything should be added to his word, and that anything should be taken from it. This is the inviolable decree of God and the Holy Spirit, a decree which our opponents endeavour to annul when they pretend that the Church is guided by the Spirit without the word.

14. Here again they mutter that the Church behoved to add something to the writings of the apostles, or that the apostles themselves behoved orally to supply what they had less clearly taught, since Christ said to them, "I have yet many things to say unto you, but ye cannot bear them now" (John xvi. 12), and that these are the points which have been received, without writing, merely by use and custom. But what effrontery is this? The disciples, I admit, were ignorant and almost indocile when our Lord thus addressed them, but were they still in this condition when they committed his doctrine to writing, so as afterwards to be under the necessity of supplying orally that which, through ignorance, they had omitted to write? If they were guided by the Spirit of truth unto all truth when they published their writings, what prevented them from embracing a full knowledge of the Gospel, and consigning it therein? But let us grant them what they ask, provided they point out the things which behoved to be revealed without writing. Should they presume to attempt this, I will address them in the words of Augustine, "When the Lord is silent, who of us may say, this is, or that is? or if we

should presume to say it, how do we prove it?" (August. in Joann. 96.) But why do I contend superfluously? Every child knows that in the writings of the apostles, which these men represent as mutilated and incomplete, is contained the result of that revelation which the Lord then promised to them.

15. What, say they, did not Christ declare that nothing which the Church teaches and decrees can be gainsayed, when he enjoined that every one who presumes to contradict should be regarded as a heathen man and a publican? (Matth. xviii. 17.) First, there is here no mention of doctrine, but her authority to censure, for correction is asserted, in order that none who had been admonished or reprimanded might oppose her judgment. But to say nothing of this, it is very strange that those men are so lost to all sense of shame, that they hesitate not to plume themselves on this declaration. For what, pray, will they make of it, but just that the consent of the Church, a consent never given but to the word of God, is not to be despised? The Church is to be heard, say they. Who denies this? since she decides nothing but according to the word of God. If they demand more than this, let them know that the words of Christ give them no countenance. I ought not to seem contentious when I so vehemently insist that we cannot concede to the Church any new doctrine; in other words, allow her to teach and oracularly deliver more than the Lord has revealed in his word. Men of sense see how great the danger is if so much authority is once conceded to men. They see also how wide a door is opened for the jeers and cavils of the ungodly, if we admit that Christians are to receive the opinions of men as if they were oracles. We may add, that our Saviour, speaking according to the circumstances of his times, gave the name of Church to the Sanhedrim, that the disciples might learn afterwards to revere the sacred meetings of the Church. Hence it would follow, that single cities and districts would have equal liberty in coining dogmas.

16. The examples which they bring do not avail them. They say that pædobaptism proceeds not so much on a plain command of Scripture, as on a decree of the Church. It would be a miserable asylum if, in defence of pædobaptism, we were obliged to betake ourselves to the bare authority of the Church; but it will be made plain enough elsewhere (chap. xvi.) that it is far otherwise. In like manner, when they object that we nowhere find in the Scriptures what was declared in the Council of Nice—viz. that the Son is consubstantial with the Father (see August. Ep. 178)—they do a grievous injustice to the Fathers, as if they had rashly condemned Arius for not swearing to their words, though professing the whole of that doctrine which is contained in the writings of the Apostles and Prophets. I admit that the expression does not exist in Scripture, but seeing it is there so often declared that there is one God, and Christ is so often called true and eternal God, one with the Father, what do the Nicene Fathers do when they affirm that he is of one essence, than simply

declare the genuine meaning of Scripture? Theodoret relates that Constantine, in opening their meeting, spoke as follows: "In the discussion of divine matters, the doctrine of the Holy Spirit stands recorded. The Gospels and apostolical writings, with the oracles of the prophets, fully show us the meaning of the Deity. Therefore, laying aside discord, let us take the exposition of questions from the words of the Spirit" (Theodoret. Hist. Eccles. Lib. i. c. 5). There was none who opposed this sound advice; none who objected that the Church could add something of her own, that the Spirit did not reveal all things to the apostles, or at least that they did not deliver them to posterity, and so forth. If the point on which our opponents insist is true, Constantine, first, was in error in robbing the Church of her power; and, secondly, when none of the bishops rose to vindicate it, their silence was a kind of perfidy, and made them traitors to Ecclesiastical law. But since Theodoret relates that they readily embraced what the Emperor said, it is evident that this new dogma was then wholly unknown.

CHAPTER IX.

OF COUNCILS AND THEIR AUTHORITY.[1]

Since Papists regard their Councils as expressing the sentiment and consent of the Church, particularly as regards the authority of declaring dogmas and the exposition of them, it was necessary to treat of Councils before proceeding to consider that part of ecclesiastical power which relates to doctrine. I. First, the authority of Councils in delivering dogmas is discussed, and it is shown that the Spirit of God is not so bound to the Pastors of the Church as opponents suppose. Their objections refuted, sec. 1–7. II. The errors, contradictions, and weaknesses, of certain Councils exposed. A refutation of the subterfuge, that those set over us are to be obeyed without distinction, sec. 8–12. III. Of the authority of Councils as regards the interpretation of Scripture, sec. 13. 14.

Sections.

1. The true nature of Councils.
2. Whence the authority of Councils is derived. What meant by assembling in the name of Christ.
3. Objection, that no truth remains in the Church if it be not in Pastors and Councils. Answer, showing by passages from the Old Testament that Pastors were often devoid of the spirit of knowledge and truth.
4. Passages from the New Testament showing that our times were to be subject to the same evil. This confirmed by the example of almost all ages.
5. All not Pastors who pretend to be so.
6. Objection, that General Councils represent the Church. Answer, showing the absurdity of this objection from passages in the Old Testament.
7. Passages to the same effect from the New Testament.
8. Councils have authority only in so far as accordant with Scripture. Testimony of Augustine. Councils of Nice, Constantinople, and Ephesus. Subsequent Councils more impure, and to be received with limitation.
9. Contradictory decisions of Councils. Those agreeing with divine truth to be received. Those at variance with it to be rejected. This confirmed by the example of the Council of Constantinople and the Council of Nice; also of the Council of Chalcedon, and second Council of Ephesus.
10. Errors of purer Councils. Four causes of these errors. An example from the Council of Nice.
11. Another example from the Council of Chalcedon. The same errors in Provincial Councils.
12. Evasion of the Papists. Three answers. Conclusion of the discussion as to the power of the Church in relation to doctrine.
13. Last part of the chapter. Power of the Church in interpreting Scripture. From what source interpretation is to be derived. Means of preserving unity in the Church.
14. Impudent attempt of the Papists to establish their tyranny refuted. Things at variance with Scripture sanctioned by their Councils. Instance in the prohibition of marriage and communion in both kinds.

1. WERE I now to concede all that they ask concerning the Church, it would not greatly aid them in their object. For everything that

[1] See Calvin's Antidote to the Articles of Sorbonne; Letter to Sadolet; Necessity of Reforming the Church; Antidote to the Council of Trent; Remarks on the Paternal Admonition of the Pope.

is said of the Church they immediately transfer to councils, which, in their opinion, represent the Church. Nay, when they contend so doggedly for the power of the Church, their only object is to devolve the whole which they extort on the Roman Pontiff and his conclave. Before I begin to discuss this question, two points must be briefly premised. First, though I mean to be more rigid in discussing this subject, it is not because I set less value than I ought on ancient councils. I venerate them from my heart, and would have all to hold them in due honour.[1] But there must be some limitation, there must be nothing derogatory to Christ. Moreover, it is the right of Christ to preside over all councils, and not share the honour with any man. Now, I hold that he presides only when he governs the whole assembly by his word and Spirit. Secondly, in attributing less to councils than my opponents demand, it is not because I have any fear that councils are favourable to their cause and adverse to ours. For as we are amply provided by the word of the Lord with the means of proving our doctrine and overthrowing the whole Papacy, and thus have no great need of other aid, so, if the case required it, ancient councils furnish us in a great measure with what might be sufficient for both purposes.

2. Let us now proceed to the subject itself. If we consult Scripture on the authority of councils, there is no promise more remarkable than that which is contained in these words of our Saviour, "Where two or three are gathered together in my name, there am I in the midst of them." But this is just as applicable to any particular meeting as to a universal council. And yet the important part of the question does not lie here, but in the condition which is added—viz. that Christ will be in the midst of a council, provided it be assembled in his name. Wherefore, though our opponents should name councils of thousands of bishops it will little avail them; nor will they induce us to believe that they are, as they maintain, guided by the Holy Spirit, until they make it credible that they assemble in the name of Christ: since it is as possible for wicked and dishonest to conspire against Christ, as for good and honest bishops to meet together in his name. Of this we have a clear proof in very many of the decrees which have proceeded from councils. But this will be afterwards seen. At present I only reply in one word, that our Saviour's promise is made to those only who assemble in his name. How, then, is such an assembly to be defined? I deny that those assemble in the name of Christ who, disregarding his command by which he forbids anything to be added to the word of God or taken from it, determine everything at their own pleasure, who, not contented with the oracles of Scripture, that is, with the only rule of perfect wisdom, devise

1 French, "Si je tien ici la bride roide pour ne lascher rien facilement à nos adversaires, ce n'est pas a dire pourtant que je prise les conciles anciens moins que je ne doy. Car je les honore de bonne affection, et desire que chacun les estime, et les ait en reverence."—If I here keep the reins tight, and do not easily yield anything to our opponents, it is not because I prize ancient councils less than I ought. For I honour them sincerely and desire that every man esteem them, and hold them in reverence.

some novelty out of their own head (Deut. iv. 2; Rev. xxii. 18). Certainly, since our Saviour has not promised to be present with all councils of whatever description, but has given a peculiar mark for distinguishing true and lawful councils from others, we ought not by any means to lose sight of the distinction. The covenant which God anciently made with the Levitical priests was to teach at his mouth (Mal. ii. 7). This he always required of the prophets, and we see also that it was the law given to the apostles. On those who violate this covenant God bestows neither the honour of the priesthood nor any authority. Let my opponents solve this difficulty if they would subject my faith to the decrees of man, without authority from the word of God.

3. Their idea that the truth cannot remain in the Church unless it exist among pastors, and that the Church herself cannot exist unless displayed in general councils, is very far from holding true if the prophets have left us a correct description of their own times. In the time of Isaiah there was a Church at Jerusalem which the Lord had not yet abandoned. But of pastors he thus speaks: "His watchmen are blind; they are all ignorant, they are all dumb dogs, they cannot bark; sleeping, lying down, loving to slumber. Yea, they are greedy dogs which never have enough, and they are shepherds that cannot understand: they all look to their own way" (Isa. lvi. 10, 11). In the same way Hosea says, "The watchman of Ephraim was with my God: but the prophet is a snare of a fowler in all his ways, and hatred in the house of his God" (Hosea ix. 8). Here, by ironically connecting them with God, he shows that the pretext of the priesthood was vain. There was also a Church in the time of Jeremiah. Let us hear what he says of pastors: "From the prophet even unto the priest, every one dealeth falsely." Again, "The prophets prophesy lies in my name: I sent them not, neither have I commanded them, neither spake unto them" (Jer. vi. 13; xiv. 14). And not to be prolix with quotations, read the whole of his thirty-third and fortieth chapters. Then, on the other hand, Ezekiel inveighs against them in no milder terms. "There is a conspiracy of her prophets in the midst thereof, like a roaring lion ravening the prey; they have devoured souls." "Her priests have violated my law, and profaned mine holy things" (Ezek. xxii. 25, 26). There is more to the same purpose. Similar complaints abound throughout the prophets; nothing is of more frequent recurrence.

4. But perhaps, though this great evil prevailed among the Jews, our age is exempt from it. Would that it were so; but the Holy Spirit declared that it would be otherwise. For Peter's words are clear, "But there were false prophets among the people, even as there shall be false teachers among you, who privily will bring in damnable heresies" (2 Peter ii. 1). See how he predicts impending danger, not from ordinary believers, but from those who should plume themselves on the name of pastors and teachers. Besides, how often did Christ and his apostles foretell that the greatest dangers with

which the Church was threatened would come from pastors? (Matth. xxiv. 11, 24). Nay, Paul openly declares, that Antichrist would have his seat in the temple of God (2 Thess. ii. 4); thereby intimating, that the fearful calamity of which he was speaking would come only from those who should have their seat in the Church as pastors. And in another passage he shows that the introduction of this great evil was almost at hand. For in addressing the Elders of Ephesus, he says, "I know this, that after my departing shall grievous wolves enter in among you, not sparing the flock. Also of your own selves shall men arise, speaking perverse things, to draw away disciples after them" (Acts xx. 29, 30). How great corruption might a long series of years introduce among pastors, when they could degenerate so much within so short a time? And not to fill my pages with details, we are reminded by the examples of almost every age, that the truth is not always cherished in the bosoms of pastors, and that the safety of the Church depends not on their state. It was becoming that those appointed to preserve the peace and safety of the Church should be its presidents and guardians; but it is one thing to perform what you owe, and another to owe what you do not perform.

5. Let no man, however, understand me as if I were desirous in everything rashly and unreservedly to overthrow the authority of pastors.[1] All I advise is, to exercise discrimination, and not suppose, as a matter of course, that all who call themselves pastors are so in reality. But the Pope, with the whole crew of his bishops, for no other reason but because they are called pastors, shake off obedience to the word of God, invert all things, and turn them hither and thither at their pleasure; meanwhile, they insist that they cannot be destitute of the light of truth, that the Spirit of God perpetually resides in them, that the Church subsists in them, and dies with them, as if the Lord did not still inflict his judgments, and in the present day punish the world for its wickedness, in the same way in which he punished the ingratitude of the ancient people—namely, by smiting pastors with astonishment and blindness (Zech. xii. 4). These stupid men understand not that they are just chiming in with those of ancient times who warred with the word of God. For the enemies of Jeremiah thus set themselves against the truth, "Come, and let us devise devices against Jeremiah; for the law shall not perish from the priest, nor counsel from the wise, nor the word from the prophet" (Jer. xviii. 18).

6. Hence it is easy to reply to their allegation concerning general councils. It cannot be denied, that the Jews had a true Church under the prophets. But had a general council then been composed of the priests, what kind of appearance would the Church have had? We hear the Lord denouncing not against one or two of them, but

1 French, "Toutesfois je ne veux point que ces propos soyent entendus comme si je vouloye amoindrir l'authorité des pasteurs, et induire le peuple à la mepriser legerement."—However, I would not have these statements to be understood as if I wished to lessen the authority of pastors, and induce the people lightly to despise it.

the whole order: "The priests shall be astonished, and the prophets shall wonder" (Jer. iv. 9). Again, "The law shall perish from the priest, and counsel from the ancients" (Ezek. vii. 26). Again, "Therefore night shall be unto you, that ye shall not have a vision; and it shall be dark unto you, that ye shall not divine; and the sun shall go down over the prophets, and the day shall be dark over them," &c. (Micah iii. 6). Now, had all men of this description been collected together, what spirit would have presided over their meeting? Of this we have a notable instance in the council which Ahab convened (1 Kings xxii. 6, 22). Four hundred prophets were present. But because they had met with no other intention than to flatter the impious king, Satan is sent by the Lord to be a lying spirit in all their mouths. The truth is there unanimously condemned. Micaiah is judged a heretic, is smitten, and cast into prison. So was it done to Jeremiah, and so to the other prophets.

7. But there is one memorable example which may suffice for all. In the council which the priests and Pharisees assembled at Jerusalem against Christ (John xi. 47), what is wanting, in so far as external appearance is concerned? Had there been no Church then at Jerusalem, Christ would never have joined in the sacrifices and other ceremonies. A solemn meeting is held; the high priest presides; the whole sacerdotal order take their seats, and yet Christ is condemned, and his doctrine is put to flight. This atrocity proves that the Church was not at all included in that council. But there is no danger that anything of the kind will happen with us. Who has told us so? Too much security in a matter of so great importance lies open to the charge of sluggishness. Nay, when the Spirit, by the mouth of Paul, foretells, in distinct terms, that a defection will take place, a defection which cannot come until pastors first forsake God (2 Thess. ii. 3), why do we spontaneously walk blindfold to our own destruction? Wherefore, we cannot on any account admit that the Church consists in a meeting of pastors, as to whom the Lord has nowhere promised that they would always be good, but has sometimes foretold that they would be wicked. When he warns us of danger, it is to make us use greater caution.

8. What, then, you will say, is there no authority in the definitions of councils? Yes, indeed; for I do not contend that all councils are to be condemned, and all their acts rescinded, or, as it is said, made one complete erasure. But you are bringing them all (it will be said) under subordination, and so leaving every one at liberty to receive or reject the decrees of councils as he pleases. By no means; but whenever the decree of a council is produced, the first thing I would wish to be done is, to examine at what time it was held, on what occasion, with what intention, and who were present at it; next I would bring the subject discussed to the standard of Scripture. And this I would do in such a way that the decision of the council should have its weight, and be regarded in the light of a prior judgment, yet not so as to prevent the application of

the test which I have mentioned. I wish all had observed the method which Augustine prescribes in his Third Book against Maximinus, when he wished to silence the cavils of this heretic against the decrees of councils, "I ought not to oppose the Council of Nice to you, nor ought you to oppose that of Ariminum to me, as prejudging the question. I am not bound by the authority of the latter, nor you by that of the former. Let thing contend with thing, cause with cause, reason with reason, on the authority of Scripture, an authority not peculiar to either, but common to all." In this way, councils would be duly respected, and yet the highest place would be given to Scripture, everything being brought to it as a test. Thus those ancient Councils of Nice, Constantinople, the first of Ephesus, Chalcedon, and the like, which were held for refuting errors, we willingly embrace, and reverence as sacred, in so far as relates to doctrines of faith, for they contain nothing but the pure and genuine interpretation of Scripture, which the holy Fathers with spiritual prudence adopted to crush the enemies of religion who had then arisen. In some later councils, also, we see displayed a true zeal for religion, and moreover unequivocal marks of genius, learning, and prudence. But as matters usually become worse and worse, it is easy to see in more modern councils how much the Church gradually degenerated from the purity of that golden age.. I doubt not, however, that even in those more corrupt ages, councils had their bishops of better character. But it happened with them as the Roman senators of old complained in regard to their decrees. Opinions being numbered, not weighed, the better were obliged to give way to the greater number. They certainly put forth many impious sentiments. There is no need here to collect instances, both because it would be tedious, and because it has been done by others so carefully, as not to leave much to be added.

9. Moreover, why should I review the contests of council with council? Nor is there any ground for whispering to me, that when councils are at variance, one or other of them is not a lawful council. For how shall we ascertain this? Just, if I mistake not, by judging from Scripture that the decrees are not orthodox. For this alone is the sure law of discrimination. It is now about nine hundred years since the Council of Constantinople, convened under the Emperor Leo, determined that the images set up in temples were to be thrown down and broken to pieces. Shortly after, the Council of Nice, which was assembled by Irene, through dislike of the former, decreed that images were to be restored. Which of the two councils shall we acknowledge to be lawful? The latter has usually prevailed, and secured a place for images in churches. But Augustine maintains that this could not be done without the greatest danger of idolatry. Epiphanius, at a later period, speaks much more harshly (Epist. ad Joann. Hierosolym. et Lib. iii. contra Hæres.). For he says, it is an unspeakable abomination to see images in a Christian temple. Could those who speak thus approve of that council if they were alive in

the present day? But if historians speak true, and we believe their acts, not only images themselves, but the worship of them, were there sanctioned. Now it is plain that this decree emanated from Satan: Do they not show, by corrupting and wresting Scripture, that they held it in derision? This I have made sufficiently clear in a former part of the work (see Book I. chap. xi. sec. 14). Be this as it may, we shall never be able to distinguish between contradictory and dissenting councils, which have been many, unless we weigh them all in that balance for men and angels, I mean, the word of God. Thus we embrace the Council of Chalcedon, and repudiate the second of Ephesus, because the latter sanctioned the impiety of Eutyches, and the former condemned it. The judgment of these holy men was founded on the Scriptures, and while we follow it, we desire that the word of God, which illuminated them, may now also illuminate us. Let the Romanists now go and boast after their manner, that the Holy Spirit is fixed and tied to their councils.

10. Even in their ancient and purer councils there is something to be desiderated, either because the otherwise learned and prudent men who attended, being distracted by the business in hand, did not attend to many things beside; or because, occupied with grave and more serious measures, they winked at some of lesser moment; or simply because, as men, they were deceived through ignorance, or were sometimes carried headlong by some feeling in excess. Of this last case (which seems the most difficult of all to avoid) we have a striking example in the Council of Nice, which has been unanimously received, as it deserves, with the utmost veneration. For when the primary article of our faith was there in peril, and Arius, its enemy, was present, ready to engage any one in combat, and it was of the utmost moment that those who had come to attack Arius should be agreed, they nevertheless, feeling secure amid all these dangers, nay, as it were, forgetting their gravity, modesty, and politeness, laying aside the discussion which was before them (as if they had met for the express purpose of gratifying Arius), began to give way to intestine dissensions, and turn the pen, which should have been employed against Arius, against each other. Foul accusations were heard, libels flew up and down, and they never would have ceased from their contention until they had stabbed each other with mutual wounds, had not the Emperor Constantine interfered, and declaring that the investigation of their lives was a matter above his cognisance, repressed their intemperance by flattery rather than censure. In how many respects is it probable that councils, held subsequently to this, have erred? Nor does the fact stand in need of a long demonstration; any one who reads their acts will observe many infirmities, not to use a stronger term.

11. Even Leo, the Roman Pontiff, hesitates not to charge the Council of Chalcedon, which he admits to be orthodox in its doctrines, with ambition and inconsiderate rashness. He denies not that it was lawful, but openly maintains that it might have erred. Some

may think me foolish in labouring to point out errors of this description, since my opponents admit that councils may err in things not necessary to salvation. My labour, however, is not superfluous. For although compelled, they admit this in word, yet by obtruding upon us the determination of all councils, in all matters without distinction, as the oracles of the Holy Spirit, they exact more than they had at the outset assumed. By thus acting what do they maintain but just that councils cannot err, of if they err, it is unlawful for us to perceive the truth, or refuse assent to their errors? At the same time, all I mean to infer from what I have said is, that though councils, otherwise pious and holy, were governed by the Holy Spirit, he yet allowed them to share the lot of humanity, lest we should confide too much in men. This is a much better view than that of Gregory Nanzianzen, who says (Ep. 55), that he never saw any council end well. In asserting that all, without exception, ended ill, he leaves them little authority. There is no necessity for making separate mention of provincial councils, since it is easy to estimate, from the case of general councils, how much authority they ought to have in framing articles of faith, and deciding what kind of doctrine is to be received.

12. But our Romanists, when, in defending their cause, they see all rational grounds slip from beneath them, betake themselves to a last miserable subterfuge. Although they should be dull in intellect and counsel, and most depraved in heart and will, still the word of the Lord remains, which commands us to obey those who have the rule over us (Heb. xiii. 17). Is it indeed so? What if I should deny that those who act thus have the rule over us? They ought not to claim for themselves more than Joshua had, who was both a prophet of the Lord and an excellent pastor. Let us then hear in what terms the Lord introduced him to his office. "This book of the law shall not depart out of thy mouth; but thou shalt meditate therein day and night, that thou mayest observe to do according to all that is written therein: for then shalt thou make thy way prosperous, and thou shalt have good success" (Josh. i. 7, 8). Our spiritual rulers, therefore, will be those who turn not from the law of the Lord to the right hand or the left. But if the doctrine of all pastors is to be received without hesitation, why are we so often and so anxiously admonished by the Lord not to give heed to false prophets? "Thus saith the Lord of Hosts, Hearken not unto the words of the prophets that prophesy unto you; they make you vain: they speak a vision of their own heart, and not out of the mouth of the Lord" (Jer. xxiii. 16). Again, "Beware of false prophets, which come to you in sheep's clothing but inwardly they are ravening wolves" (Matth. vii. 15). In vain also would John exhort us to try the spirits whether they be of God (1 John iv. 1). From this judgment not even angels are exempted (Gal. i. 8); far less Satan with his lies. And what is meant by the expression, "If the blind lead the blind, both shall fall into the ditch"? (Matth. xv. 14.) Does it

not sufficiently declare that there is a great difference among the pastors who are to be heard, that all are not to be heard indiscriminately? Wherefore they have no ground for deterring us by their name, in order to draw us into a participation of their blindness, since we see, on the contrary, that the Lord has used special care to guard us from allowing ourselves to be led away by the errors of others, whatever be the mask under which they may lurk. For if the answer of our Saviour is true, blind guides, whether high priests, prelates, or pontiffs, can do nothing more than hurry us over the same precipice with themselves. Wherefore, let no names of councils, pastors, and bishops (which may be used on false pretences as well as truly), hinder us from giving heed to the evidence both of words and facts, and bringing all spirits to the test of the divine word, that we may prove whether they are of God.

13. Having proved that no power was given to the Church to set up any new doctrine, let us now treat of the power attributed to them in the interpretation of Scripture. We readily admit, that when any doctrine is brought under discussion, there is not a better or surer remedy than for a council of true bishops to meet and discuss the controverted point. There will be much more weight in a decision of this kind, to which the pastors of churches have agreed in common after invoking the Spirit of Christ, than if each, adopting it for himself, should deliver it to his people, or a few individuals should meet in private and decide. Secondly, When bishops have assembled in one place, they deliberate more conveniently in common, fixing both the doctrine and the form of teaching it, lest diversity give offence. Thirdly, Paul prescribes this method of determining doctrine. For when he gives the power of deciding to a single church, he shows what the course of procedure should be in more important cases—namely, that the churches together are to take common cognisance. And the very feeling of piety tells us, that if any one trouble the Church with some novelty in doctrine, and the matter be carried so far that there is danger of a greater dissension, the churches should first meet, examine the question, and at length, after due discussion, decide according to Scripture, which may both put an end to doubt in the people, and stop the mouths of wicked and restless men, so as to prevent the matter from proceeding farther. Thus when Arius arose, the Council of Nice was convened, and by its authority both crushed the wicked attempts of this impious man, and restored peace to the churches which he had vexed, and asserted the eternal divinity of Christ in opposition to his sacrilegious dogma. Thereafter, when Eunomius and Macedonius raised new disturbances, their madness was met with a similar remedy by the Council of Constantinople; the impiety of Nestorius was defeated by the Council of Ephesus. In short, this was from the first the usual method of preserving unity in the Church whenever Satan commenced his machinations. But let us remember, that all ages and places are not favoured with an Athanasius, a Basil, a Cyril, and like vindica-

tors of sound doctrine, whom the Lord then raised up. Nay, let us consider what happened in the second Council of Ephesus when the Eutychian heresy prevailed. Flavianus, of holy memory, with some pious men, was driven into exile, and many similar crimes were committed, because, instead of the Spirit of the Lord, Dioscorus, a factious man, of a very bad disposition, presided. But the Church was not there. I admit it; for I always hold that the truth does not perish in the Church though it be oppressed by one council, but is wondrously preserved by the Lord to rise again, and prove victorious in his own time. I deny, however, that every interpretation of Scripture is true and certain which has received the votes of a council.

14. But the Romanists have another end in view when they say that the power of interpreting Scripture belongs to councils, and that without challenge. For they employ it as a pretext for giving the name of an interpretation of Scripture to everything which is determined in councils. Of purgatory, the intercession of saints, and auricular confession, and the like, not one syllable can be found in Scripture. But as all these have been sanctioned by the authority of the Church, or, to speak more correctly, have been received by opinion and practice, every one of them is to be held as an interpretation of Scripture. And not only so, but whatever a council has determined against Scripture is to have the name of an interpretation. Christ bids all drink of the cup which he holds forth in the Supper. The Council of Constance prohibited the giving of it to the people, and determined that the priest alone should drink. Though this is diametrically opposed to the institution of Christ (Matth. xxvi. 26), they will have it to be regarded as his interpretation. Paul terms the prohibition of marriage a doctrine of devils (1 Tim. iv. 1, 3); and the Spirit elsewhere declares that "marriage is honourable in all" (Heb. xiii. 4). Having afterwards interdicted their priests from marriage, they insist on this as a true and genuine interpretation of Scripture, though nothing can be imagined more alien to it. Should any one venture to open his lips in opposition, he will be judged a heretic, since the determination of the Church is without challenge, and it is unlawful to have any doubt as to the accuracy of her interpretation. Why should I assail such effrontery? to point to it is to condemn it. Their dogma with regard to the power of approving Scripture I intentionally omit. For to subject the oracles of God in this way to the censure of men, and hold that they are sanctioned because they please men, is a blasphemy which deserves not to be mentioned. Besides, I have already touched upon it (Book I. chap. vii. viii. sec. 9). I will ask them one question, however. If the authority of Scripture is founded on the approbation of the Church, will they quote the decree of a council to that effect? I believe they cannot. Why, then, did Arius allow himself to be vanquished at the Council of Nice by passages adduced from the Gospel of John? According to these, he was at liberty to re-

pudiate them, as they had not previously been approved by any general council. They allege an old catalogue, which they call the Canon, and say that it originated in a decision of the Church. But I again ask, In what council was that Canon published? Here they must be dumb. Besides, I wish to know what they believe that Canon to be. For I see that the ancients are little agreed with regard to it. If effect is to be given to what Jerome says (Præf. in Lib. Solom.), the Maccabees, Tobit, Ecclesiasticus, and the like, must take their place in the Apocrypha: but this they will not tolerate on any account.

CHAPTER X.

OF THE POWER OF MAKING LAWS. THE CRUELTY OF THE POPE AND HIS ADHERENTS, IN THIS RESPECT, IN TYRANNICALLY OPPRESSING AND DESTROYING SOULS.

This chapter treats,—I. Of human constitutions in general. Of the distinction between Civil and Ecclesiastical Laws. Of conscience, why and in what sense ministers cannot impose laws on the conscience, sec. 1–8. II. Of traditions or Popish constitutions relating to ceremonies and discipline. The many vices inherent in them, sec. 9–17. Arguments in favour of those traditions refuted, sec. 17-26. III. Of Ecclesiastical constitutions that are good and lawful, sec. 27–32.

Sections.

1. The power of the Church in enacting laws. This made a source of human traditions. Impiety of these traditions.
2. Many of the Papistical traditions not only difficult, but impossible to be observed.
3. That the question may be more conveniently explained, nature of conscience must be defined.
4. Definition of conscience explained. Examples in illustration of the definition.
5. Paul's doctrine of submission to magistrates for conscience sake, gives no countenance to the Popish doctrine of the obligation of traditions.
6. The question stated. A brief mode of deciding it.
7. A perfect rule of life in the Law. God our only Lawgiver.
8. The traditions of the Papacy contradictory to the Word of God.
9. Ceremonial traditions of the Papists. Their impiety. Substituted for the true worship of God.
10. Through these ceremonies the commandment of God made void.
11. Some of these ceremonies useless and childish. Their endless variety. Introduce Judaism.
12. Absurdity of these ceremonies borrowed from Judaism and Paganism.
13. Their intolerable number condemned by Augustine.
14. Injury thus done to the Church. They cannot be excused.
15. Mislead the superstitious. Used as a kind of show and for incantation. Prostituted to gain.
16. All such traditions liable to similar objections.
17. Arguments in favour of traditions answered.
18. Answer continued.
19. Illustration taken from the simple administration of the Lord's Supper, under the Apostles, and the complicated ceremonies of the Papists.
20. Another illustration from the use of Holy Water.
21. An argument in favour of traditions founded on the decision of the Apostles and elders at Jerusalem. This decision explained.
22. Some things in the Papacy may be admitted for a time for the sake of weak brethren.
23. Observance of the Popish traditions inconsistent with Christian liberty, torturing to the conscience, and insulting to God.
24. All human inventions in religion displeasing to God. Reason. Confirmed by an example.
25. An argument founded on the examples of Samuel and Manoah. Answer.
26. Argument that Christ wished such burdens to be borne. Answer.
27. Third part of the chapter, treating of lawful Ecclesiastical arrangements. Their foundation in the general axiom, that all things be done decently and in order. Two extremes to be avoided.

28. All Ecclesiastical arrangements to be thus tested. What Paul means by things done decently and in order.
29. Nothing decent in the Popish ceremonies. Description of true decency. Examples of Christian decency and order.
30. No arrangement decent and orderly, unless founded on the authority of God, and derived from Scripture. Charity the best guide in these matters.
31. Constitutions thus framed not to be neglected or despised.
32. Cautions to be observed in regard to such constitutions.

1. We come now to the second part of power, which, according to them, consists in the enacting of laws, from which source innumerable traditions have arisen, to be as many deadly snares to miserable souls. For they have not been more scrupulous than the Scribes and Pharisees in laying burdens on the shoulders of others, which they would not touch with their finger (Matth xxiii. 4; Luke xi. 16). I have elsewhere shown (Book III. chap. iv. sec. 4–7) how cruel murder they commit by their doctrine of auricular confession. The same violence is not apparent in other laws, but those which seem most tolerable press tyrannically on the conscience. I say nothing as to the mode in which they adulterate the worship of God, and rob God himself, who is the only Lawgiver, of his right. The power we have now to consider is, whether it be lawful for the Church to bind laws upon the conscience? In this discussion, civil order is not touched; but the only point considered is, how God may be duly worshipped according to the rule which he has prescribed, and how our spiritual liberty, with reference to God, may remain unimpaired. In ordinary language, the name of human traditions is given to all decrees concerning the worship of God, which men have issued without the authority of his word. We contend against these, not against the sacred and useful constitutions of the Church, which tend to preserve discipline, or decency, or peace. Our aim is to curb the unlimited and barbarous empire usurped over souls by those who would be thought pastors of the Church, but who are in fact its most cruel murderers. They say that the laws which they enact are spiritual, pertaining to the soul, and they affirm that they are necessary to eternal life. But thus the kingdom of Christ, as I lately observed, is invaded; thus the liberty, which he has given to the consciences of believers, is completely oppressed and overthrown. I say nothing as to the great impiety with which, to sanction the observance of their laws, they declare that from it they seek forgiveness of sins, righteousness and salvation, while they make the whole sum of religion and piety to consist in it. What I contend for is, that necessity ought not to be laid on consciences in matters in which Christ has made them free; and unless freed, cannot, as we have previously shown (Book III. chap. xix.), have peace with God. They must acknowledge Christ their deliverer, as their only king, and be ruled by the only law of liberty—namely, the sacred word of the Gospel—if they would retain the grace which they have once received in Christ: they must be subject to no bondage, be bound by no chains.

2. These Solons, indeed, imagine that their constitutions are laws of liberty, a pleasant yoke, a light burden; but who sees not that this is mere falsehood. They themselves, indeed, feel not the burden of their laws. Having cast off the fear of God, they securely and assiduously disregard their own laws as well as those which are divine. Those, however, who feel any interest in their salvation, are far from thinking themselves free so long as they are entangled in these snares. We see how great caution Paul employed in this matter, not venturing to impose a fetter in any one thing, and with good reason: he certainly foresaw how great a wound would be inflicted on the conscience if these things should be made necessary which the Lord had left free. On the contrary, it is scarcely possible to count the constitutions which these men have most grievously enforced, under the penalty of eternal death, and which they exact with the greatest rigour, as necessary to salvation. And while very many of them are most difficult of observance, the whole taken together are impossible; so great is the mass. How, then, possibly can those, on whom this mountain of difficulty lies, avoid being perplexed with extreme anxiety, and filled with terror? My intention here then is, to impugn constitutions of this description; constitutions enacted for the purpose of binding the conscience inwardly before God, and imposing religious duties, as if they enjoined things necessary to salvation.

3. Many are greatly puzzled with this question, from not distinguishing, with sufficient care, between what is called the external forum and the forum of conscience[1] (Book III. chap. xix. sec 15). Moreover, the difficulty is increased by the terms in which Paul enjoins obedience to magistrates, "not only for wrath, but also for conscience sake" (Rom. xiii. 5); and from which it would follow, that civil laws also bind the conscience. But if this were so, nothing that we have said of spiritual government, in the last chapter, and are to say in this, would stand. To solve this difficulty, we must first understand what is meant by conscience. The definition must be derived from the etymology of the term. As when men, with the mind and intellect, apprehend the knowledge of things, they are thereby said to know, and hence the name of science or knowledge is used; so, when they have, in addition to this, a sense of the divine judgment, as a witness not permitting them to hide their sins, but bringing them as criminals before the tribunal of the judge, that sense is called conscience. For it occupies a kind of middle place between God and man, not suffering man to suppress what he knows in himself, but following him out until it bring him to conviction. This is what Paul means, when he says that conscience bears witness, "our thoughts the meanwhile accusing or else excusing each other" (Rom. ii. 15). Simple knowledge, therefore, might exist in a man, as it were, shut up, and therefore the sense which sists men before the judgment-seat of God has been placed over him as a sentinel, to

1 French, "entre le siege judicial de Dieu, qui est spirituel, et la justice terrestre des hommes;"—between the judgment-seat of God and the terrestrial justice of men.

observe and spy out all his secrets, that nothing may remain buried in darkness. Hence the old proverb, Conscience is a thousand witnesses. For this reason, Peter also uses the "answer of a good conscience towards God" (1 Pet. iii. 21); for tranquillity of mind, when, persuaded of the grace of Christ, we with boldness present ourselves before God. And the author of the Epistle to the Hebrews says, that we have "no more conscience of sins," that we are freed or acquitted, so that sin no longer accuses us (Heb. x. 2).

4. Wherefore, as works have respect to men, so conscience bears reference to God; and hence a good conscience is nothing but inward integrity of heart. In this sense, Paul says, that "the end of the commandment is charity out of a pure heart, and of a good conscience, and of faith unfeigned" (1 Tim. i. 5). He afterwards, in the same chapter, shows how widely it differs from intellect, saying, that "some having put away" a good conscience, "concerning faith have made shipwreck." For by these words he intimates, that it is a living inclination to worship God, a sincere desire to live piously and holily. Sometimes, indeed, it is extended to men also, as when Paul declares, "Herein do I exercise myself, to have always a conscience void of offence toward God, and toward men" (Acts xxiv. 16). But this is said, because the benefits of a good conscience flow forth and reach even to men. Properly speaking, however, it respects God alone, as I have already said. Hence a law may be said to bind the conscience when it simply binds a man without referring to men, or taking them into account. For example, God enjoins us not only to keep our mind chaste and pure from all lust, but prohibits every kind of obscenity in word, and all external lasciviousness. This law my conscience is bound to observe, though there were not another man in the world. Thus he who behaves intemperately not only sins by setting a bad example to his brethren, but stands convicted in his conscience before God. Another rule holds in the case of things which are in themselves indifferent. For we ought to abstain when they give offence, but conscience is free. Thus Paul says of meat consecrated to idols, "If any man say unto you, This is offered in sacrifice unto idols, eat not for his sake that showed it, and for conscience sake;" "conscience, I say, not thine own, but of the other" (1 Cor. x. 28, 29). A believer would sin, if, after being warned, he should still eat such kind of meat. But however necessary abstinence may be in respect of a brother, as prescribed by the Lord, conscience ceases not to retain its liberty. We see how the law, while binding the external work, leaves the conscience free.

5. Let us now return to human laws. If they are imposed for the purpose of forming a religious obligation, as if the observance of them was in itself necessary, we say that the restraint thus laid on the conscience is unlawful. Our consciences have not to do with men but with God only. Hence the common distinction between the

earthly forum and the forum of conscience.[1] When the whole world was enveloped in the thickest darkness of ignorance, it was still held (like a small ray of light which remained unextinguished) that conscience was superior to all human judgments. Although this, which was acknowledged in word, was afterwards violated in fact, yet God was pleased that there should even then exist an attestation to liberty, exempting the conscience from the tyranny of man. But we have not yet explained the difficulty which arises from the words of Paul. For if we must obey princes not only from fear of punishment but for conscience sake, it seems to follow, that the laws of princes have dominion over the conscience. If this is true, the same thing must be affirmed of ecclesiastical laws. I answer, that the first thing to be done here is to distinguish between the genus and the species. For though individual laws do not reach the conscience, yet we are bound by the general command of God, which enjoins us to submit to magistrates. And this is the point on which Paul's discussion turns—viz. that magistrates are to be honoured, because they are ordained of God (Rom. xiii. 1). Meanwhile, he does not at all teach that the laws enacted by them reach to the internal government of the soul, since he everywhere proclaims that the worship of God, and the spiritual rule of living righteously, are superior to all the decrees of men. Another thing also worthy of observation, and depending on what has been already said, is, that human laws, whether enacted by magistrates or by the Church, are necessary to be observed (I speak of such as are just and good), but do not therefore in themselves bind the conscience, because the whole necessity of observing them respects the general end, and consists not in the things commanded. Very different, however, is the case of those which prescribe a new form of worshipping God, and introduce necessity into things that are free.

6. Such, however, are what in the present day are called ecclesiastical constitutions by the Papacy, and are brought forward as part of the true and necessary worship of God. But as they are without number, so they form innumerable fetters to bind and ensnare the soul. Though, in expounding the law, we have adverted to this subject (Book III. chap. iv. 5), yet as this is more properly the place for a full discussion of it, I will now study to give a summary of it as carefully as I can. I shall, however, omit the branch relating to the tyranny with which false bishops arrogate to themselves the right of teaching whatever they please, having already considered it as far as seemed necessary, but shall treat at length of the power which they claim of enacting laws. The pretext, then, on which our

1 French, "Et de fait, tel a eté le sens de cette distinction vulgaire qu'on a tenue par toutes les ecoles; que c'est autre choses des jurisdictions humaines et politiques, que de celles qui touchent à la conscience;"—And in fact, such is the import of the common distinction which has been held by all the schools, that human and civil jurisdictions are quite different from those which touch the conscience.

false bishops burden the conscience with new laws is, that the Lord has constituted them spiritual legislators, and given them the government of the Church. Hence they maintain that everything which they order and prescribe must, of necessity, be observed by the Christian people, that he who violates their commands is guilty of a twofold disobedience, being a rebel both against God and the Church. Assuredly, if they were true bishops, I would give them some authority in this matter, not so much as they demand, but so much as is requisite for duly arranging the polity of the Church; but since they are anything but what they would be thought, they cannot possibly assume anything to themselves, however little, without being in excess. But as this also has been elsewhere shown, let us grant for the present, that whatever power true bishops possess justly belongs to them, still I deny that they have been set over believers as legislators to prescribe a rule of life at their own hands, or bind the people committed to them to their decrees. When I say this, I mean that they are not at all entitled to insist that whatever they devise without authority from the word of God shall be observed by the Church as matter of necessity. Since such power was unknown to the apostles, and was so often denied to the ministers of the Church by our Lord himself, I wonder how any have dared to usurp, and dare in the present day to defend it, without any precedent from the apostles, and against the manifest prohibition of God.

7. Everything relating to a perfect rule of life the Lord has so comprehended in his law, that he has left nothing for men to add to the summary there given. His object in doing this was, first, that since all rectitude of conduct consists in regulating all our actions by his will as a standard, he alone should be regarded as the master and guide of our life; and, secondly, that he might show that there is nothing which he more requires of us than obedience. For this reason James says, "He that speaketh evil of his brother, and judgeth his brother, speaketh evil of the law, and judgeth the law:" "There is one lawgiver, who is able to save and to destroy" (James iv. 11, 12). We hear how God claims it as his own peculiar privilege to rule us by his laws. This had been said before by Isaiah, though somewhat obscurely, "The Lord is our judge, the Lord is our lawgiver, the Lord is our king; he will save us" (Isa. xxxiii. 22). Both passages show that the power of life and death belongs to him who has power over the soul. Nay, James clearly expresses this. This power no man may assume to himself. God, therefore, to whom the power of saving and destroying belongs, must be acknowledged as the only King of souls, or, as the words of Isaiah express it, he is our king and judge, and lawgiver and saviour. So Peter, when he reminds pastors of their duty, exhorts them to feed the flock without lording it over the heritage (1 Pet. v. 2); meaning by heritage the body of believers. If we duly consider that it is unlawful to transfer to man what God declares to belong only to himself,

we shall see that this completely cuts off all the power claimed by those who would take it upon them to order anything in the Church without authority from the word of God.

8. Moreover, since the whole question depends on this, that God being the only lawgiver, it is unlawful for men to assume that honour to themselves, it will be proper to keep in mind the two reasons for which God claims this solely for himself. The one reason is, that his will is to us the perfect rule of all righteousness and holiness, and that thus in the knowledge of it we have a perfect rule of life. The other reason is, that when the right and proper method of worshipping him is in question, he whom we ought to obey, and on whose will we ought to depend, alone has authority over our souls. When these two reasons are attended to, it will be easy to decide what human constitutions are contrary to the word of the Lord. Of this description are all those which are devised as part of the true worship of God, and the observance of which is bound upon the conscience, as of necessary obligation. Let us remember then to weigh all human laws in this balance, if we would have a sure test which will not allow us to go astray. The former reason is urged by Paul in the Epistle to the Colossians against the false apostles who attempted to lay new burdens on the churches. The second reason he more frequently employs in the Epistle to the Galatians in a similar case. In the Epistle to the Colossians, then, he maintains that the doctrine of the true worship of God is not to be sought from men, because the Lord has faithfully and fully taught us in what way he is to be worshipped. To demonstrate this, he says in the first chapter, that in the gospel is contained all wisdom, that the man of God may be made perfect in Christ. In the beginning of the second chapter, he says that all the treasures of wisdom and knowledge are hidden in Christ, and from this he concludes that believers should beware of being led away from the flock of Christ by vain philosophy, according to the constitutions of men (Col. ii. 10). In the end of the chapter, he still more decisively condemns all ἐθελοθρησκείας that is, fictitious modes of worship which men themselves devise or receive from others, and all precepts whatsoever which they presume to deliver at their own hand concerning the worship of God. We hold, therefore, that all constitutions are impious in the observance of which the worship of God is pretended to be placed. The passages in the Galatians in which he insists that fetters are not to be bound on the conscience (which ought to be ruled by God alone), are sufficiently plain, especially chapter v. Let it, therefore, suffice to refer to them.

9. But that the whole matter may be made plainer by examples, it will be proper, before we proceed, to apply the doctrine to our own times. The constitutions which they call ecclesiastical, and by which the Pope, with his adherents, burdens the Church, we hold to be pernicious and impious, while our opponents defend them as sacred and salutary. Now there are two kinds of them, some relating to ceremonies and rites, and others more especially to discipline. Have

we, then, any just cause for impugning both? Assuredly a juster cause than we could wish. First, do not their authors themselves distinctly declare that the very essence of the worship of God (so to speak) is contained in them? For what end do they bring forward their ceremonies but just that God may be worshipped by them? Nor is this done merely by error in the ignorant multitude, but with the approbation of those who hold the place of teachers. I am not now adverting to the gross abominations by which they have plotted the adulteration of all godliness, but they would not deem it to be so atrocious a crime to err in any minute tradition, did they not make the worship of God subordinate to their fictions. Since Paul then declares it to be intolerable that the legitimate worship of God should be subjected to the will of men, wherein do we err when we are unable to tolerate this in the present day? especially when we are enjoined to worship God according to the elements of this world—a thing which Paul declares to be adverse to Christ (Col. ii. 20). On the other hand, the mode in which they lay consciences under the strict necessity of observing whatever they enjoin, is not unknown. When we protest against this, we make common cause with Paul, who will on no account allow the consciences of believers to be brought under human bondage.

10. Moreover, the worst of all is, that when once religion begins to be composed of such vain fictions, the perversion is immediately succeeded by the abominable depravity with which our Lord upbraids the Pharisees of making the commandment of God void through their traditions (Matth. xv. 3). I am unwilling to dispute with our present legislators in my own words;—let them gain the victory if they can clear themselves from this accusation of Christ. But how can they do so, seeing they regard it as immeasurably more wicked to allow the year to pass without auricular confession, than to have spent it in the greatest iniquity: to have infected their tongue with a slight tasting of flesh on Friday, than to have daily polluted the whole body with whoredom: to have put their hand to honest labour on a day consecrated to some one or other of their saintlings, than to have constantly employed all their members in the greatest crimes: for a priest to be united to one in lawful wedlock, than to be engaged in a thousand adulteries: to have failed in performing a votive pilgrimage, than to have broken faith in every promise: not to have expended profusely on the monstrous, superfluous, and useless luxury of churches, than to have denied the poor in their greatest necessities: to have passed an idol without honour, than to have treated the whole human race with contumely: not to have muttered long unmeaning sentences at certain times, than never to have framed one proper prayer? What is meant by making the word of God void by tradition, if this is not done when recommending the ordinances of God only frigidly and perfunctorily, they nevertheless studiously and anxiously urge strict obedience to their own ordinances, as if the whole power of piety was contained in them;—when

vindicating the transgression of the divine Law with trivial satisfactions, they visit the minutest violation of one of their decrees with no lighter punishment than imprisonment, exile, fire, or sword?—When neither severe nor inexorable against the despisers of God, they persecute to extremity, with implacable hatred, those who despise themselves, and so train all those whose simplicity they hold in thraldom, that they would sooner see the whole law of God subverted than one iota of what they call the precepts of the Church infringed. First, there is a grievous delinquency in this, that one contemns, judges, and casts off his neighbour for trivial matters,—matters which, if the judgment of God is to decide, are free. But now, as if this were a small evil, those frivolous elements of this world (as Paul terms them in his Epistle to the Galatians, Gal. iv. 9) are deemed of more value than the heavenly oracles of God. He who is all but acquitted for adultery is judged in meat; and he to whom whoredom is permitted is forbidden to marry. This, forsooth, is all that is gained by that prevaricating obedience, which only turns away from God to the same extent that it inclines to men.

11. There are other two grave vices which we disapprove in these constitutions. First, They prescribe observances which are in a great measure useless, and are sometimes absurd; secondly, by the vast multitude of them, pious consciences are oppressed, and being carried back to a kind of Judaism, so cling to shadows that they cannot come to Christ. My allegation that they are useless and absurd will, I know, scarcely be credited by carnal wisdom, to which they are so pleasing, that the Church seems to be altogether defaced when they are taken away. But this is just what Paul says, that they "have indeed a show of wisdom in will-worship, and humility, and neglecting of the body" (Col. ii. 23); a most salutary admonition, of which we ought never to lose sight. Human traditions, he says, deceive by an appearance of wisdom. Whence this show? Just that being framed by men, the human mind recognises in them that which is its own, and embraces it when recognised more willingly than anything, however good, which is less suitable to its vanity. Secondly, That they seem to be a fit training to humility, while they keep the minds of men grovelling on the ground under their yoke; hence they have another recommendation. Lastly, Because they seem to have a tendency to curb the will of the flesh, and to subdue it by the rigour of abstinence, they seem to be wisely devised. But what does Paul say to all this? Does he pluck off those masks lest the simple should be deluded by a false pretext? Deeming it sufficient for their refutation to say that they were devices of men, he passes all these things without refutation, as things of no value. Nay, because he knew that all fictitious worship is condemned in the Church, and is the more suspected by believers, the more pleasing it is to the human mind—because he knew that this false show of outward humility differs so widely from true humility that it can be easily discerned; —finally, because he knew that this tutelage is valued at no more

than bodily exercise, he wished the very things which commended human traditions to the ignorant to be regarded by believers as the refutation of them.

12. Thus, in the present day, not only the unlearned vulgar, but every one in proportion as he is inflated by worldly wisdom, is wonderfully captivated by the glare of ceremonies, while hypocrites and silly women think that nothing can be imagined better or more beautiful. But those who thoroughly examine them, and weigh them more truly according to the rule of godliness, in regard to the value of all such ceremonies, know, first, that they are trifles of no utility; secondly, that they are impostures which delude the eyes of the spectators with empty show. I am speaking of those ceremonies which the Roman masters will have to be great mysteries, while we know by experience that they are mere mockery. Nor is it strange that their authors have gone the length of deluding themselves and others by mere frivolities, because they have taken their model partly from the dreams of the Gentiles, partly, like apes, have rashly imitated the ancient rites of the Mosaic Law, with which we have nothing more to do than with the sacrifices of animals and other similar things. Assuredly, were there no other proof, no sane man would expect any good from such an ill-assorted farrago. And the case itself plainly demonstrates that very many ceremonies have no other use than to stupify the people rather than teach them. In like manner, to those new canons which pervert discipline rather than preserve it, hypocrites attach much importance; but a closer examination will show that they are nothing but the shadowy and evanescent phantom of discipline.

13. To come to the second fault, who sees not that ceremonies, by being heaped one upon another, have grown to such a multitude, that it is impossible to tolerate them in the Christian Church? Hence it is, that in ceremonies a strange mixture of Judaism is apparent, while other observances prove a deadly snare to pious minds. Augustine complained that in his time, while the precepts of God were neglected, prejudice everywhere prevailed to such an extent, that he who touched the ground barefoot during his octave was censured more severely than he who buried his wits in wine. He complained that the Church, which God in mercy wished to be free, was so oppressed that the condition of the Jews was more tolerable (August. Ep. 119). Had that holy man fallen on our day, in what terms would he have deplored the bondage now existing? For the number is tenfold greater, and each iota is exacted a hundred times more rigidly than then. This is the usual course; when once those perverse legislators have usurped authority, they make no end of their commands and prohibitions until they reach the extreme of harshness. This Paul elegantly intimated by these words,—"If ye be dead with Christ from the rudiments of the world, why, as though living in the world, are ye subject to ordinances? Touch not, taste not, handle not" (Col. ii. 20, 21). For while the word ἅπτεσθαι sig-

nifies both to eat and to touch, it is doubtless taken in the former sense, that there may not be a superfluous repetition. Here, therefore, he most admirably describes the progress of false apostles. The way in which superstition begins is this: they forbid not only to eat, but even to chew gently; after they have obtained this, they forbid even to taste. This also being yielded to them, they deem it unlawful to touch even with the finger.

14. We justly condemn this tyranny in human constitutions, in consequence of which miserable consciences are strangely tormented by innumerable edicts, and the excessive exaction of them. Of the canons relating to discipline, we have spoken elsewhere (*supra*, sec. 12; also chapter xii.). What shall I say of ceremonies, the effect of which has been, that we have almost buried Christ, and returned to Jewish figures? "Our Lord Christ (says Augustine, Ep. 118) bound together the society of his new people by sacraments, very few in number, most excellent in signification, most easy of observance." How widely different this simplicity is from the multitude and variety of rites in which we see the Church entangled in the present day, cannot well be told. I am aware of the artifice by which some acute men excuse this perverseness. They say that there are numbers among us equally rude as any among the Israelitish people, and that for their sakes has been introduced this tutelage, which though the stronger may do without, they, however, ought not to neglect, seeing that it is useful to weak brethren. I answer, that we are not unaware of what is due to the weakness of brethren, but, on the other hand, we object that the method of consulting for the weak is not to bury them under a great mass of ceremonies. It was not without cause that God distinguished between us and his ancient people, by training them like children by means of signs and figures, and training us more simply, without so much external show. Paul's words are, "The heir, as long as he is a child,"—"is under tutors and governors" (Gal. iv. 1, 2). This was the state of the Jews under the law. But we are like adults who, being freed from tutory and curatory, have no need of puerile rudiments. God certainly foresaw what kind of people he was to have in his Church, and in what way they were to be governed. Now, he distinguished between us and the Jews in the way which has been described. Therefore, it is a foolish method of consulting for the ignorant to set up the Judaism which Christ has abrogated. This dissimilitude between the ancient and his new people Christ expressed when he said to the woman of Samaria, "The hour cometh, and now is, when the true worshippers shall worship the Father in spirit and in truth" (John iv. 23). This, no doubt, had always been done; but the new worshippers differ from the old in this, that while under Moses the spiritual worship of God was shadowed, and, as it were, entangled by many ceremonies, these have been abolished, and worship is now more simple. Those, accordingly, who confound this distinction, subvert the order instituted and sanctioned by Christ. Therefore you will ask, Are no ceremonies to

be given to the more ignorant, as a help to their ignorance? I do not say so; for I think that help of this description is very useful to them. All I contend for is the employment of such a measure as may illustrate, not obscure Christ. Hence a few ceremonies have been divinely appointed, and these by no means laborious, in order that they may evince a present Christ. To the Jews a greater number were given, that they might be images of an absent Christ. In saying he was absent, I mean not in power, but in the mode of expression. Therefore, to secure due moderation, it is necessary to retain that fewness in number, facility in observance, and significancy of meaning which consists in clearness. Of what use is it to say that this is not done? The fact is obvious to every eye.

15. I here say nothing of the pernicious opinions with which the minds of men are imbued, as that these are sacrifices by which propitiation is made to God, by which sins are expiated, by which righteousness and salvation are procured. It will be maintained that things good in themselves are not vitiated by errors of this description, since in acts expressly enjoined by God similar errors may be committed. There is nothing, however, more unbecoming than the fact, that works devised by the will of man are held in such estimation as to be thought worthy of eternal life. The works commanded by God receive a reward, because the Lawgiver himself accepts of them as marks of obedience. They do not, therefore, take their value from their own dignity or their own merit, but because God sets this high value on our obedience toward him. I am here speaking of that perfection of works which is commanded by God, but is not performed by men. The works of the law are accepted merely by the free kindness of God, because the obedience is infirm and defective. But as we are not here considering how far works avail without Christ, let us omit that question. I again repeat, as properly belonging to the present subject, that whatever commendation works have, they have it in respect of obedience, which alone God regards, as he testifies by the prophet, "I spake not unto your fathers, nor commanded them in the day that I brought them out of the land of Egypt, concerning burnt-offerings or sacrifices: but this thing commanded I them, saying, Obey my voice" (Jer. vii. 22). Of fictitious works he elsewhere speaks, "Wherefore do you spend your money for that which is not bread"? (Isa. lv. 2; xxix. 13). Again, "In vain do they worship me, teaching for doctrines the commandments of men" (Matth. xv. 9). They cannot, therefore, excuse themselves from the charge of allowing wretched people to seek in these external frivolities a righteousness which they may present to God, and by which they may stand before the celestial tribunal. Besides, it is not a fault deservedly stigmatised, that they exhibit unmeaning ceremonies as a kind of stage-play or magical incantation? For it is certain that all ceremonies are corrupt and noxious which do not direct men to Christ. But the ceremonies in use in the Papacy are separated from doctrine, so that they confine men to signs altogether

devoid of meaning. Lastly (as the belly is an ingenious contriver), it is clear, that many of their ceremonies have been invented by greedy priests as lures for catching money. But whatever be their origin, they are all so prostituted to filthy lucre, that a great part of them must be rescinded if we would prevent a profane and sacrilegious traffic from being carried on in the Church.

16. Although I seem not to be delivering the general doctrine concerning human constitutions, but adapting my discourse wholly to our own age, yet nothing has been said which may not be useful to all ages. For whenever men begin the superstitious practice of worshipping God with their own fictions, all the laws enacted for this purpose forthwith degenerate into those gross abuses. For the curse which God denounces—viz. to strike those who worship him with the doctrines of men with stupor and blindness—is not confined to any one age, but applies to all ages. The uniform result of this blindness is, that there is no kind of absurdity escaped by those who, despising the many admonitions of God, spontaneously entangle themselves in these deadly fetters. But if, without any regard to circumstances, you would simply know the character belonging at all times to those human traditions which ought to be repudiated by the Church, and condemned by all the godly,[1] the definition which we formerly gave is clear and certain—viz. That they include all the laws enacted by men, without authority from the word of God, for the purpose either of prescribing the mode of divine worship, or laying a religious obligation on the conscience, as enjoining things necessary to salvation. If to one or both of these are added the other evils of obscuring the clearness of the Gospel by their multitude, of giving no edification, of being useless and frivolous occupations rather than true exercises of piety, of being set up for sordid ends and filthy lucre, of being difficult of observance, and contaminated by pernicious superstitions, we shall have the means of detecting the quantity of mischief which they occasion.

17. I understand what their answer will be—viz. that these traditions are not from themselves, but from God. For to prevent the Church from erring, it is guided by the Holy Spirit, whose authority resides in them. This being conceded, it at the same time follows, that their traditions are revelations by the Holy Spirit, and cannot be disregarded without impiety and contempt of God. And that they may not seem to have attempted anything without high authority, they will have it to be believed that a great part of their observances is derived from the apostles. For they contend, that in one instance they have a sufficient proof of what the apostles did in other cases. The instance is, when the apostles assembled in council, announced to all the Gentiles as the opinion of the council, that they should "abstain from pollution of idols, and from fornication, and from things strangled, and from blood" (Acts xv. 20, 29). We have

1 Calvin on the Necessity of Reforming the Church.

already explained, how, in order to extol themselves, they falsely assume the name of Church (Chap. viii. sec. 10–13). If, in regard to the present cause, we remove all masks and glosses (a thing, indeed, which ought to be our first care, and also is our highest interest), and consider what kind of Church Christ wishes to have, that we may form and adapt ourselves to it as a standard, it will readily appear that it is not a property of the Church to disregard the limits of the word of God, and wanton and luxuriate in enacting new laws. Does not the law which was once given to the Church endure for ever? "What things soever I command you, observe to do it: thou shalt not add thereto, nor diminish from it" (Deut. xii. 32). And in another place, "Add thou not unto his words, lest he reprove thee, and thou be found a liar" (Prov. xxx. 6). Since they cannot deny that this was said to the Church, what else do they proclaim but their contumacy, when, notwithstanding of such prohibitions, they profess to add to the doctrine of God, and dare to intermingle their own with it? Far be it from us to assent to the falsehood by which they offer such insult to the Church. Let us understand that the name of Church is falsely pretended wherever men contend for that rash human licence which cannot confine itself within the boundaries prescribed by the word of God, but petulantly breaks out, and has recourse to its own inventions. In the above passage there is nothing involved, nothing obscure, nothing ambiguous; the whole Church is forbidden to add to, or take from the word of God, in relation to his worship and salutary precepts. But that was said merely of the Law, which was succeeded by the Prophets and the whole Gospel dispensation! This I admit, but I at the same time add, that these are fulfilments of the Law, rather than additions or diminutions. Now, if the Lord does not permit anything to be added to, or taken from the ministry of Moses, though wrapt up, if I may so speak, in many folds of obscurity, until he furnish a clearer doctrine by his servants the Prophets, and at last by his beloved Son, why should we not suppose that we are much more strictly prohibited from making any addition to the Law, the Prophets, the Psalms, and the Gospel? The Lord cannot forget himself, and it is long since he declared that nothing is so offensive to him as to be worshipped by human inventions. Hence those celebrated declarations of the Prophets, which ought continually to ring in our ears, "I spake not unto your fathers, nor commanded them in the day that I brought them out of the land of Egypt, concerning burnt-offerings or sacrifices; but this thing commanded I them, saying, Obey my voice, and I will be your God, and ye shall be my people: and walk ye in all the ways that I have commanded you" (Jer. vii. 22, 23). "I earnestly protested unto your fathers, in the day that I brought them out of the land of Egypt, even unto this day, rising early and protesting, saying, Obey my voice" (Jer. xi. 7). There are other passages of the same kind, but the most noted of all is, "Hath the Lord as great delight in burnt-offerings and sacrifices, as in obeying the voice of the Lord? Behold, to obey is better than sacrifice, and to hearken than the fat of rams. For rebellion is as the sin of witchcraft, and stubbornness is as iniquity and idolatry" (1 Sam. xv. 22, 23). It is easy, therefore, to prove, that whenever human inventions in this respect are defended by the authority of the Church, they cannot be vindicated from the charge of impiety, and that the name of Church is falsely assumed.

18. For this reason we freely inveigh against that tyranny of human traditions which is haughtily obtruded upon us in the name of the Church. Nor do we hold the Church in derision (as our adversaries, for the purpose of producing obloquy, unjustly accuse us), but we attribute to her the praise of obedience, than which there is none which she acknowledges to be greater. They themselves rather are emphatically injurious to the Church, in representing her as contumacious to her Lord, when they pretend that she goes farther than the word of God allows, to say nothing of their combined impudence and malice, in continually vociferating about the power of the Church, while they meanwhile disguise both the command which the Lord has given her, and the obedience which she owes to the command. But if our wish is as it ought to be, to agree with the Church, it is of more consequence to consider and remember the injunction which the Lord has given both to us and to the Church, to obey him with one consent. For there can be no doubt that we shall best agree with the Church when we show ourselves obedient to the Lord in all things. But to ascribe the origin of the traditions by which the Church has hitherto been oppressed to the apostles is mere imposition, since the whole substance of the doctrine of the apostles is, that conscience must not be burdened with new observances, nor the worship of God contaminated by our inventions. Then, if any credit is to be given to ancient histories and records, what they attribute to the apostles was not only unknown to them, but was never heard by them. Nor let them pretend that most of their decrees, though not delivered in writing, were received by use and practice, being things which they could not understand while Christ was in the world, but which they learned after his ascension, by the revelation of the Holy Spirit. The meaning of that passage has been explained elsewhere (Chap. viii. sec. 14). In regard to the present question, they make themselves truly ridiculous, seeing it is manifest that all those mysteries which so long were undiscovered by the apostles, are partly Jewish or Gentile observances, the former of which had anciently been promulgated among the Jews, and the latter among all the Gentiles, partly absurd gesticulations and empty ceremonies, which stupid priests, who have neither sense nor letters, can duly perform; nay, which children and mountebanks perform so appropriately, that it seems impossible to have fitter priests for such sacrifices. If there were no records, men of sense would judge from the very nature of the case, that such a mass of rites and observances did not rush into the Church all at once, but crept in gradually. For though the venerable bishops, who were nearest in time to the apostles, introduced some things

pertaining to order and discipline, those who came after them, and those after them again, had not enough of consideration, while they had too much curiosity and cupidity, he who came last always vying in foolish emulation with his predecessors, so as not to be surpassed in the invention of novelties. And because there was a danger that these inventions, from which they anticipated praise from posterity, might soon become obsolete, they were much more rigorous in insisting on the observance of them. This false zeal has produced a great part of the rites which these men represent as apostolical. This history attests.

19. And not to become prolix, by giving a catalogue of all, we shall be contented with one example. Under the apostles there was great simplicity in administering the Lord's Supper. Their immediate successors made some additions to the dignity of the ordinance, which are not to be disapproved. Afterwards came foolish imitators, who, by ever and anon patching various fragments together, have left us those sacerdotal vestments which we see in the mass, those altar ornaments, those gesticulations, and whole farrago of useless observances.[1] But they object, that in old time the persuasion was, that those things which were done with the consent of the whole Church proceeded from the apostles. Of this they quote Augustine as a witness. I will give the explanation in the very words of Augustine. "Those things which are observed over the whole world we may understand to have been appointed either by the apostles themselves, or by general councils, whose authority in the Church is most beneficial, as the annual solemn celebration of our Lord's passion, resurrection, and ascension to heaven, and of the descent of the Holy Spirit, and any other occurrence observed by the whole Church wherever it exists" (August. Ep. 118). In giving so few examples, who sees not that he meant to refer the observances then in use to authors deserving of faith and reverence;—observances few and sober, by which it was expedient that the order of the Church should be maintained? How widely does this differ from the view of our Roman masters, who insist that there is no paltry ceremony among them which is not apostolical?

20. Not to be tedious, I will give only one example. Should any one ask them where they get their holy water, they will at once answer, —from the apostles. As if I did not know who the Roman bishop is, to whom history ascribes the invention, and who, if he had admitted the apostles to his council, assuredly never would have adulterated baptism by a foreign and unseasonable symbol; although it does not seem probable to me that the origin of that consecration is

1 French, "Mais depuis sont survenus d'autres singes, qui ont eu une folle affectation de coudre piece sur piece, et ainsi ont composé tant les accoustremens du prestre, que les paremens de l'autel, et le badinage et jeu de farce que nous voyons à present à la Messe, avec tout le reste du borgage."—But other apes have since appeared, who have had a foolish affectation of sewing piece to piece, and thus have formed all the furnishings of the priests, as well as altar ornaments, the trifling and farce play which we now see in the Mass, with all the other garniture.

so ancient as is there recorded. For when Augustine says (Ep. 118) that certain churches in his day rejected the formal imitation of Christ in the washing of feet, lest that rite should seem to pertain to baptism, he intimates that there was then no kind of washing which had any resemblance to baptism. Be this as it may, I will never admit that the apostolic spirit gave rise to that daily sign by which baptism, while brought back to remembrance, is in a manner repeated. I attach no importance to the fact, that Augustine elsewhere ascribes other things to the apostles. For as he has nothing better than conjecture, it is not sufficient for forming a judgment concerning a matter of so much moment. Lastly, though we should grant that the things which he mentions are derived from the apostolic age, there is a great difference between instituting some exercise of piety, which believers may use with a free conscience, or may abstain from if they think the observance not to be useful, and enacting a law which brings the conscience into bondage. Now, indeed, whoever is the author from whom they are derived, since we see the great abuses to which they have led, there is nothing to prevent us from abrogating them without any imputation on him, since he never recommended them in such a way as to lay us under a fixed and immovable obligation to observe them.

21. It gives them no great help, in defending their tyranny, to pretend the example of the apostles. The apostles and elders of the primitive Church, according to them, sanctioned a decree without any authority from Christ, by which they commanded all the Gentiles to abstain from meat offered to idols, from things strangled, and from blood (Acts xv. 20). If this was lawful for them, why should not their successors be allowed to imitate the example as often as occasion requires? Would that they would always imitate them both in this and in other matters! For I am ready to prove, on valid grounds, that here nothing new has been instituted or decreed by the apostles. For when Peter declares in that council, that God is tempted if a yoke is laid on the necks of the disciples, he overthrows his own argument if he afterwards allows a yoke to be imposed on them. But it is imposed if the apostles, on their own authority, prohibit the Gentiles from touching meat offered to idols, things strangled, and blood. The difficulty still remains, that they seem nevertheless to prohibit them. But this will easily be removed by attending more closely to the meaning of their decree. The first thing in order, and the chief thing in importance, is, that the Gentiles were to retain their liberty, which was not to be disturbed, and that they were not to be annoyed with the observances of the Law. As yet, the decree is all in our favour. The reservation which immediately follows is not a new law enacted by the apostles, but a divine and eternal command of God against the violation of charity, which does not detract one iota from that liberty. It only reminds the Gentiles how they are to accommodate themselves to their brother, and to not abuse their liberty for an occasion of offence. Let the second head, therefore, be,

that the Gentiles are to use an innoxious liberty, giving no offence to the brethren. Still, however, they prescribe some certain thing—viz. they show and point out, as was expedient at the time, what those things are by which they may give offence to their brethren, that they may avoid them; but they add no novelty of their own to the eternal law of God, which forbids the offence of brethren.

22. As in the case where faithful pastors, presiding over churches not yet well constituted, should intimate to their flocks not to eat flesh on Friday until the weak among whom they live become strong, or to work on a holiday, or any other similar things, although, when superstition is laid aside, these matters are in themselves indifferent, still, where offence is given to the brethren, they cannot be done without sin; so there are times when believers cannot set this example before weak brethren without most grievously wounding their consciences. Who but a slanderer would say that a new law is enacted by those who, it is evident, only guard against scandals which their Master has distinctly forbidden? But nothing more than this can be said of the apostles, who had no other end in view, in removing grounds of offence, than to enforce the divine Law, which prohibits offence; as if they had said, The Lord hath commanded you not to hurt a weak brother; but meats offered to idols, things strangled, and blood, ye cannot eat, without offending weak brethren; we, therefore, require you, in the word of the Lord, not to eat with offence. And to prove that the apostles had respect to this, the best witness is Paul, who writes as follows, undoubtedly according to the sentiments of the council: "As concerning, therefore, the eating of those things which are offered in sacrifice unto idols, we know that an idol is nothing in the world, and that there is none other God but one."—"Howbeit, there is not in every man that knowledge: for some with conscience of the idol unto this hour eat it as a thing offered unto an idol; and their conscience being weak is defiled."—"But take heed lest by any means this liberty of yours become a stumbling-block to them that are weak" (1 Cor. viii. 4-9). Any one who duly considers these things will not be imposed upon by the gloss which these men employ when, as a cloak to their tyranny, they pretend that the apostles had begun by their decree to infringe the liberty of the Church. But that they may be unable to escape without confessing the accuracy of this explanation, let them tell me by what authority they have dared to abrogate this very decree. It was, it seems, because there was no longer any danger of those offences and dissensions which the apostles wished to obviate, and they knew that the law was to be judged by its end. Seeing, therefore, the law was passed with a view to charity, there is nothing prescribed in it except in so far as required by charity. In confessing that the transgression of this law is nothing but a violation of charity, do they not at the same time acknowledge that it was not some adventitious supplement to the law of God, but a genuine and simple adaptation of it to the times and manners for which it was destined?

23. But though such laws are hundreds of times unjust and injurious to us, still they contend that they are to be heard without exception; for the thing asked of us is not to consent to errors, but only to submit to the strict commands of those set over us,—commands which we are not at liberty to decline (1 Pet. ii. 18). But here also the Lord comes to the succour of his word, and frees us from this bondage by asserting the liberty which he has purchased for us by his sacred blood, and the benefit of which he has more than once attested by his word. For the thing required of us is not (as they maliciously pretend) to endure some grievous oppression in our body, but to be tortured in our consciences, and brought into bondage: in other words, robbed of the benefits of Christ's blood. Let us omit this, however, as if it were irrelevant to the point. Do we think it a small matter that the Lord is deprived of his kingdom which he so strictly claims for himself? Now, he is deprived of it as often as he is worshipped with laws of human invention, since his will is to be sole legislator of his worship. And lest any one should consider this as of small moment, let us hear how the Lord himself estimates it. "Forasmuch as this people draw near me with their mouth, and with their lips do honour me, but have removed their heart far from me, and their fear toward me is taught by the precept of men: therefore, behold, I will proceed to do a marvellous work among the people, even a marvellous work and a wonder; for the wisdom of their wise men shall perish, and the understanding of their prudent men shall be hid" (Isaiah xxix. 13-14). And in another place, "But in vain do they worship me, teaching for doctrines the commandments of men" (Matth. xv. 9). And, indeed, when the children of Israel polluted themselves with manifold idolatries, the cause of the whole evil is ascribed to that impure mixture caused by their disregarding the commandments of God, and framing new modes of worship. Accordingly, sacred history relates that the new inhabitants who had been brought by the king of Assyria from Babylon to inhabit Samaria were torn and destroyed by wild beasts, because they knew not the judgment or statutes of the God of that land (2 Kings xvii. 24-34). Though they had done nothing wrong in ceremonies, still their empty show could not have been approved by God. Meanwhile he ceased not to punish them for the violation of his worship by the introduction of fictions alien from his word. Hence it is afterwards said that, terrified by the punishment, they adopted the rites prescribed in the Law; but as they did not yet worship God purely, it is twice repeated that they feared him and feared not. Hence we infer that part of the reverence due to him consists in worshipping him simply in the way which he commands, without mingling any inventions of our own. And, accordingly, pious princes are repeatedly praised (2 Kings xxii. 1, &c.) for acting according to all his precepts, and not declining either to the right hand or the left. I go further: although there be no open manifestation of impiety in fictitious worship, it is strictly condemned by the Spirit,

inasmuch as it is a departure from the command of God. The altar of Ahaz, a model of which had been brought from Damascus (2 Kings xvi. 10), might have seemed to give additional ornament to the temple, seeing it was his intention there to offer sacrifices to God only, and to do it more splendidly than at the first ancient altar: yet we see how the Spirit detests the audacious attempt, for no other reasons but because human inventions are in the worship of God impure corruptions. And the more clearly the will of God has been manifested to us, the less excusable is our petulance in attempting anything. Accordingly, the guilt of Manasses is aggravated by the circumstance of having erected a new altar at Jerusalem, of which the Lord said, "In Jerusalem will I put my name" (2 Kings xxii. 3, 4), because the authority of God was thereby professedly rejected.

24. Many wonder why God threatens so sternly that he will bring astonishment on the people who worship him with the commandments of men, and declares that it is in vain to worship him with the commandments of men. But if they would consider what it is in the matter of religion, that is, of heavenly wisdom, to depend on God alone, they would, at the same time, see that it is not on slight grounds the Lord abominates perverse service of this description, which is offered him at the caprice of the human will. For although there is some show of humility in the obedience of those who obey such laws in worshipping God, yet they are by no means humble, since they prescribe to him the very laws which they observe. This is the reason why Paul would have us so carefully to beware of being deceived by the traditions of men, and what is called ἐθελοθρησκεία, that is, voluntary worship, worship devised by men without sanction from God. Thus it is, indeed: we must be fools in regard to our own wisdom and all the wisdom of men, in order that we may allow him alone to be wise. This course is by no means observed by those who seek to approve themselves to him by paltry observances of man's devising, and, as it were, against his will obtrude upon him a prevaricating obedience which is yielded to men. This is the course which has been pursued for several ages, and within our own recollection, and is still pursued in the present day in those places in which the power of the creature is more than that of the Creator, where religion (if religion it deserves to be called) is polluted with more numerous, and more absurd superstitions, than ever Paganism was. For what could human sense produce but things carnal and fatuous, and savouring of their authors?

25. When the patrons of superstition cloak them, by pretending that Samuel sacrificed in Ramath, and though he did so contrary to the Law, yet pleased God (1 Sam vii. 17), it is easy to answer, that he did not set up any second altar in opposition to the only true one; but, as the place for the Ark of the Covenant had not been fixed, he sacrificed in the town where he dwelt, as being the most convenient. It certainly never was the intention of the holy prophet to make any innovation in sacred things, in regard to which the Lord had so

strictly forbidden addition or diminution. The case of Manoah I consider to have been extraordinary and special. He, though a private man, offered sacrifice to God, and did it not without approbation, because he did it not from a rash movement of his own mind, but by divine inspiration (Judges xiii. 19). How much God abominates all the devices of men in his worship, we have a striking proof in the case of one not inferior to Manoah—viz. Gideon, whose ephod brought ruin not only on himself and his family, but on the whole people (Judges viii. 27). In short, every adventitious invention, by which men desire to worship God, is nothing else than a pollution of true holiness.

26. Why then, they ask, did Christ say that the intolerable burdens, imposed by Scribes and Pharisees, were to be borne? (Matth. xxiii. 3.) Nay, rather, why did he say in another place that we were to beware of the leaven of the Pharisees? (Matth. xvi. 6,) meaning by leaven, as the Evangelist Matthew explains it, whatever of human doctrine is mingled with the pure word of God. What can be plainer than that we are enjoined to shun and beware of their whole doctrine? From this it is most certain, that in the other passage our Lord never meant that the consciences of his people were to be harassed by the mere traditions of the Pharisees. And the words themselves, unless when wrested, have no such meaning. Our Lord, indeed, beginning to inveigh against the manners of the Pharisees, first instructs his hearers simply, that though they saw nothing to follow in the lives of the Pharisees, they should not, however, cease to do what they verbally taught when they sat in the seat of Moses, that is, to expound the Law. All he meant, therefore, was to guard the common people against being led by the bad example of their teachers to despise doctrine. But as some are not at all moved by reason, and always require authority, I will quote a passage from Augustine, in which the very same thing is expressed. "The Lord's sheepfold has persons set over it, of whom some are faithful, others hirelings. Those who are faithful are true shepherds; learn, however, that hirelings also are necessary. For many in the Church, pursuing temporal advantages, preach Christ, and the voice of Christ is heard by them, and the sheep follow not a hireling, but the shepherd by means of a hireling. Learn that hirelings were pointed out by the Lord himself. The Scribes and Pharisees, says he, sit in Moses' seat; what they tell you, do, but what they do, do ye not. What is this but to say, Hear the voice of the shepherd by means of hirelings? Sitting in the chair, they teach the Law of God, and therefore God teaches by them; but if they choose to teach their own, hear not, do not." Thus far Augustine. (August. in Joann. Tract. 46.)

27. But as very many ignorant persons, on hearing that it is impious to bind the conscience, and vain to worship God with human traditions, apply one blot to all the laws by which the order of the

Church is established, it will be proper to obviate their error. Here, indeed, the danger of mistake is great: for it is not easy to see at first sight how widely the two things differ. But I will, in a few words, make the matter so clear, that no one will be imposed upon by the resemblance. First, then, let us understand that if in every human society some kind of government is necessary to insure the common peace and maintain concord, if in transacting business some form must always be observed, which public decency, and hence humanity itself, require us not to disregard, this ought especially to be observed in churches, which are best sustained by a constitution in all respects well ordered, and without which concord can have no existence. Wherefore, if we would provide for the safety of the Church, we must always carefully attend to Paul's injunction, that all things be done decently and in order (1 Cor. xiv. 40). But seeing there is such diversity in the manners of men, such variety in their minds, such repugnance in their judgments and dispositions, no policy is sufficiently firm unless fortified by certain laws, nor can any rite be observed without a fixed form. So far, therefore, are we from condemning the laws which conduce to this, that we hold that the removal of them would unnerve the Church, deface and dissipate it entirely. For Paul's injunction, that all things be done decently and in order, cannot be observed unless order and decency be secured by the addition of ordinances, as a kind of bonds. In these ordinances, however, we must always attend to the exception, that they must not be thought necessary to salvation, nor lay the conscience under a religious obligation; they must not be compared to the worship of God, nor substituted for piety.

28. We have, therefore, a most excellent and sure mark to distinguish between those impious constitutions (by which, as we have said, true religion is overthrown, and conscience subverted) and the legitimate observances of the Church, if we remember that one of two things, or both together, are always intended—viz. that in the sacred assembly of the faithful, all things may be done decently, and with becoming dignity, and that human society may be maintained in order by certain bonds, as it were, of moderation and humanity. For when a law is understood to have been made for the sake of public decency, there is no room for the superstition into which those fall who measure the worship of God by human inventions. On the the other hand, when a law is known to be intended for common use, that false idea of its obligation and necessity, which gives great alarm to the conscience, when traditions are deemed necessary to salvation, is overthrown; since nothing here is sought but the maintenance of charity by a common office. But it may be proper to explain more clearly what is meant by the decency which Paul commends, and also what is comprehended under order. And the object of decency is, partly that by the use of rites, which produce reverence in sacred matters, we may be excited to piety, and partly that the modesty and gravity which ought to be seen in all honourable actions may here

especially be conspicuous. In order, the first thing is, that those who preside know the law and rule of right government, while those who are governed be accustomed to obedience and right discipline. The second thing is, that by duly arranging the state of the Church, provision be made for peace and tranquillity.

29. We shall not, therefore, give the name of decency to that which only ministers an empty pleasure: such, for example, as is seen in that theatrical display which the Papists exhibit in their public service, where nothing appears but a mask of useless splendour, and luxury without any fruit. But we give the name of decency to that which, suited to the reverence of sacred mysteries, forms a fit exercise for piety, or at least gives an ornament adapted to the action, and is not without fruit, but reminds believers of the great modesty, seriousness, and reverence, with which sacred things ought to be treated. Moreover, ceremonies, in order to be exercises of piety, must lead us directly to Christ. In like manner, we shall not make order consist in that nugatory pomp which gives nothing but evanescent splendour, but in that arrangement which removes all confusion, barbarism, contumacy, all turbulence and dissension. Of the former class we have examples (1 Cor. xi. 5, 21), where Paul says, that profane entertainments must not be intermingled with the sacred Supper of the Lord; that women must not appear in public uncovered. And there are many other things which we have in daily practice, such as praying on our knees, and with our head uncovered, administering the sacraments of the Lord, not sordidly, but with some degree of dignity; employing some degree of solemnity in the burial of our dead, and so forth. In the other class are the hours set apart for public prayer, sermon, and solemn services; during sermon, quiet and silence, fixed places, singing of hymns, days set apart for the celebration of the Lord's Supper, the prohibition of Paul against women teaching in the Church, and such like. To the same list especially may be referred those things which preserve discipline, as catechising, ecclesiastical censures, excommunication, fastings, &c. Thus all ecclesiastical constitutions, which we admit to be sacred and salutary, may be reduced to two heads, the one relating to rites and ceremonies, the other to discipline and peace.

30. But as there is here a danger, on the one hand, lest false bishops should thence derive a pretext for their impious and tyrannical laws, and, on the other, lest some, too apt to take alarm, should, from fear of the above evils, leave no place for laws, however holy, it may here be proper to declare, that I approve of those human constitutions only which are founded on the authority of God, and derived from Scripture, and are therefore altogether divine. Let us take, for example, the bending of the knee which is made in public prayer. It is asked, whether this is a human tradition, which any one is at liberty to repudiate or neglect? I say, that it is human, and that at the same time it is divine. It is of God, inasmuch as it is a part of that decency, the care and observance of which is re-

commended by the apostle; and it is of men, inasmuch as it specially determines what was indicated in general, rather than expounded. From this one example, we may judge what is to be thought of the whole class—viz. that the whole sum of righteousness, and all the parts of divine worship, and everything necessary to salvation, the Lord has faithfully comprehended, and clearly unfolded, in his sacred oracles, so that in them he alone is the only Master to be heard. But as in external discipline and ceremonies, he has not been pleased to prescribe every particular that we ought to observe (he foresaw that this depended on the nature of the times, and that one form would not suit all ages), in them we must have recourse to the general rules which he has given, employing them to test whatever the necessity of the Church may require to be enjoined for order and decency. Lastly, as he has not delivered any express command, because things of this nature are not necessary to salvation, and, for the edification of the Church, should be accommodated to the varying circumstances of each age and nation, it will be proper, as the interest of the Church may require, to change and abrogate the old, as well as to introduce new forms. I confess, indeed, that we are not to innovate rashly or incessantly, or for trivial causes. Charity is the best judge of what tends to hurt or to edify: if we allow her to be guide, all things will be safe.

31. Things which have been appointed according to this rule, it is the duty of the Christian people to observe with a free conscience indeed, and without superstition, but also with a pious and ready inclination to obey. They are not to hold them in contempt, nor pass them by with careless indifference, far less openly to violate them in pride and contumacy. You will ask, What liberty of conscience will there be in such cautious observances? Nay, this liberty will admirably appear when we shall hold that these are not fixed and perpetual obligations to which we are astricted, but external rudiments for human infirmity, which, though we do not all need, we, however, all use, because we are bound to cherish mutual charity towards each other. This we may recognise in the examples given above. What? Is religion placed in a woman's bonnet, so that it is unlawful for her to go out with her head uncovered? Is her silence fixed by a decree which cannot be violated without the greatest wickedness? Is there any mystery in bending the knee, or in burying a dead body, which cannot be omitted without a crime? By no means. For should a woman require to make such haste in assisting a neighbour that she has not time to cover her head, she sins not in running out with her head uncovered. And there are some occasions on which it is not less seasonable for her to speak than on others to be silent. Nothing, moreover, forbids him who, from disease, cannot bend his knees, to pray standing. In fine, it is better to bury a dead man quickly, than from want of grave-clothes, or the absence of those who should attend the funeral, to wait till it rot away unburied. Nevertheless, in those matters the custom and in-

stitutions of the country, in short, humanity and the rules of modesty itself, declare what is to be done or avoided. Here, if any error is committed through imprudence or forgetfulness, no crime is perpetrated; but if this is done from contempt, such contumacy must be disapproved. In like manner, it is of no consequence what the days and hours are, what the nature of the edifices, and what psalms are sung on each day. But it is proper that there should be certain days and stated hours, and a place fit for receiving all, if any regard is had to the preservation of peace. For what a seed-bed of quarrels will confusion in such matters be, if every one is allowed at pleasure to alter what pertains to common order? All will not be satisfied with the same course if matters, placed as it were on debateable ground, are left to the determination of individuals. But if any one here becomes clamorous, and would be wiser than he ought, let him consider how he will approve his moroseness to the Lord. Paul's answer ought to satisfy us, "If any man seem to be contentious, we have no such custom, neither the churches of God."

32. Moreover, we must use the utmost diligence to prevent any error from creeping in which may either taint or sully this pure use. In this we shall succeed, if whatever observances we use are manifestly useful, and very few in number; especially if to this is added the teaching of a faithful pastor, which may prevent access to erroneous opinions. The effect of this procedure is, that in all these matters each retains his freedom, and yet at the same time voluntarily subjects it to a kind of necessity, in so far as the *decency* of which we have spoken or charity demands. Next, that in the observance of these things we may not fall into any superstition, nor rigidly require too much from others, let us not imagine that the worship of God is improved by a multitude of ceremonies: let not church despise church because of a difference in external discipline. Lastly, instead of here laying down any perpetual law for ourselves, let us refer the whole end and use of observances to the edification of the Church, at whose request let us without offence allow not only something to be changed, but even observances which were formerly in use to be inverted. For the present age is a proof that the nature of times allows that certain rites, not otherwise impious or unbecoming, may be abrogated according to circumstances. Such was the ignorance and blindness of former times; with such erroneous ideas and pertinacious zeal did churches formerly cling to ceremonies, that they can scarcely be purified from monstrous superstitions without the removal of many ceremonies which were formerly established, not without cause, and which in themselves are not chargeable with any impiety.

CHAPTER XI.

OF THE JURISDICTION OF THE CHURCH, AND THE ABUSES OF IT, AS EXEMPLIFIED IN THE PAPACY.

This chapter may be conveniently comprehended under two heads,—I. Ecclesiastical jurisdiction, its necessity, origin, description, and essential parts—viz. the sacred ministry of the word, and discipline of excommunication, of which the aim, use, and abuse are explained, sec. 1–8. II. Refutation of the arguments advanced by Papists in defence of the tyranny of Pontiffs, the right of both swords, imperial pomp and dignity, foreign jurisdiction, and immunity from civil jurisdiction, sec. 9–16.

Sections.

1. The power of the Church in regard to jurisdiction. The necessity, origin, and nature of this jurisdiction. The power of the keys to be considered in two points of view. The first view expounded.
2. Second view expounded. How the Church binds and looses in the way of discipline. Abuse of the keys in the Papacy.
3. The discipline of excommunication of perpetual endurance. Distinction between civil and ecclesiastical power.
4. The perpetual endurance of the discipline of excommunication confirmed. Duly ordered under the Emperors and Christian magistrates.
5. The aim and use of ecclesiastical jurisdiction in the primitive Church. Spiritual power was kept entirely distinct from the power of the sword.
6. Spiritual power was not administered by one individual, but by a lawful consistory. Gradual change. First, the clergy alone interfered in the judicial proceedings of the Church. The bishop afterwards appropriated them to himself.
7. The bishops afterwards transferred the rights thus appropriated to their officials, and converted spiritual jurisdiction into a profane tribunal.
8. Recapitulation. The Papal power confuted. Christ wished to debar the ministers of the word from civil rule and worldly power.
9. Objections of the Papists. 1. By this external splendour the glory of Christ is displayed. 2. It does not interfere with the dnties of their calling. Both objections answered.
10. The commencement and gradual progress of the Papistical tyranny. Causes, 1. Curiosity; 2. Ambition; 3. Violence; 4. Hypocrisy; 5. Impiety.
11. Last cause, the mystery of iniquity, and the Satanic fury of Antichrist usurping worldly dominion. The Pope claims both swords.
12. The pretended donation of Constantine. Its futility exposed.
13. When, and by what means, the Roman Pontiffs attained to imperial dignity. Hildebrand its founder.
14. By what acts they seized on Rome and other territories. Disgraceful rapacity.
15. Claim of immunity from civil jurisdiction. Contrast between this pretended immunity and the moderation of the early bishops.
16. What end the early bishops aimed at in steadfastly resisting civil encroachment.

1. It remains to consider the third, and, indeed, when matters are well arranged, the principal part of ecclesiastical power, which, as we have said, consists in jurisdiction. Now, the whole jurisdiction of the Church relates to discipline, of which we are shortly to treat. For as no city or village can exist without a magistrate and government, so the Church of God, as I have already taught, but am again obliged to repeat, needs a kind of spiritual government. This is altogether

distinct from civil government, and is so far from impeding or impairing it, that it rather does much to aid and promote it. Therefore, this power of jurisdiction is, in one word, nothing but the order provided for the preservation of spiritual polity. To this end, there were established in the Church from the first, tribunals which might take cognisance of morals, animadvert on vices, and exercise the office of the keys. This order is mentioned by Paul in the First Epistle to the Corinthians under the name of governments (1 Cor. xii. 28): in like manner, in the Epistle to the Romans, when he says, "He that ruleth with diligence" (Rom. xii. 8). For he is not addressing magistrates, none of whom were then Christians, but those who were joined with pastors in the spiritual government of the Church. In the Epistle to Timothy, also, he mentions two kinds of presbyters, some who labour in the word, and others who do not perform the office of preaching, but rule well (1 Tim. v. 17). By this latter class there is no doubt he means those who were appointed to the inspection of manners, and the whole use of the keys. For the power of which we speak wholly depends on the keys which Christ bestowed on the Church in the eighteenth chapter of Matthew, where he orders, that those who depise private admonition should be sharply rebuked in public, and if they persist in their contumacy, be expelled from the society of believers. Moreover, those admonitions and corrections cannot be made without investigation, and hence the necessity of some judicial procedure and order. Wherefore, if we would not make void the promise of the keys, and abolish altogether excommunication, solemn admonitions, and everything of that description, we must, of necessity, give some jurisdiction to the Church. Let the reader observe that we are not here treating of the general authority of doctrine, as in Matth. xxi. and John xx., but maintaining that the right of the Sanhedrim is transferred to the fold of Christ. Till that time, the power of government had belonged to the Jews. This Christ establishes in his Church, in as far as it was a pure institution, and with a heavy sanction. Thus it behoved to be, since the judgment of a poor and despised Church might otherwise be spurned by rash and haughty men. And lest it occasion any difficulty to the reader, that Christ in the same words makes a considerable difference between the two things, it will here be proper to explain. There are two passages which speak of binding and loosing. The one is Matth. xvi., where Christ, after promising that he will give the keys of the kingdom of heaven to Peter, immediately adds, "Whatsoever thou shalt bind on earth shall be bound in heaven; and whatsoever thou shalt loose on earth shall be loosed in heaven" (Matth. xvi. 19). These words have the very same meaning as those in the Gospel of John, where, being about to send forth the disciples to preach, after breathing on them, he says, "Whose soever sins ye remit, they are remitted unto them; and whose soever sins ye retain, they are retained" (John xx. 23). I will give an interpretation, not subtle, not forced, not wrested, but genuine, natural, and obvious. This command concerning remitting and retaining sins, and that promise made to Peter concerning binding and loosing, ought to be referred to nothing but the ministry of the word. When the Lord committed it to the apostles, he, at the same time, provided them with this power of binding and loosing. For what is the sum of the gospel, but just that all being the slaves of sin and death, are loosed and set free by the redemption which is in Christ Jesus, while those who do not receive and acknowledge Christ as a deliverer and redeemer are condemned and doomed to eternal chains? When the Lord delivered this message to his apostles, to be carried by them into all nations, in order to prove that it was his own message, and proceeded from him, he honoured it with this distinguished testimony, and that as an admirable confirmation both to the apostles themselves, and to all those to whom it was to come. It was of importance that the apostles should have a constant and complete assurance of their preaching, which they were not only to exercise with infinite labour, anxiety, molestation, and peril, but ultimately to seal with their blood. That they might know that it was not vain or void, but full of power and efficacy, it was of importance, I say, that amidst all their anxieties, dangers, and difficulties, they might feel persuaded that they were doing the work of God; that though the whole world withstood and opposed them, they might know that God was for them; that not having Christ the author of their doctrine bodily present on the earth, they might understand that he was in heaven to confirm the truth of the doctrine which he had delivered to them. On the other hand, it was necessary that their hearers should be most certainly assured that the doctrine of the gospel was not the word of the apostles, but of God himself; not a voice rising from the earth, but descending from heaven. For such things as the forgiveness of sins, the promise of eternal life, and message of salvation, cannot be in the power of man. Christ therefore testified, that in the preaching of the gospel the apostles only acted ministerially; that it was he who, by their mouths as organs, spoke and promised all; that, therefore, the forgiveness of sins which they announced was the true promise of God; the condemnation which they pronounced, the certain judgment of God. This attestation was given to all ages, and remains firm, rendering all certain and secure, that the word of the gospel, by whomsoever it may be preached, is the very word of God, promulgated at the supreme tribunal, written in the book of life, ratified firm and fixed in heaven. We now understand that the power of the keys is simply the preaching of the gospel in those places, and in so far as men are concerned, it is not so much power as ministry. Properly speaking, Christ did not give this power to men but to his word, of which he made men the ministers.

2. The other passage, in which binding and loosing are mentioned, is in the eighteenth chapter of Matthew, where Christ says, "If he shall neglect to hear them, tell it unto the Church: but if he neglect to hear the Church, let him be unto thee as an heathen man and

a publican. Verily I say unto you, Whatsoever ye shall bind on earth shall be bound in heaven; and whatsoever ye shall loose on earth shall be loosed in heaven" (Matth. xviii. 17, 18). This passage is not altogether similar to the former, but is to be understood somewhat differently. But in saying that they are different, I do not mean that there is not much affinity between them. First, they are similar in this, that they are both general statements, that there is always the same power of binding and loosing (namely, by the word of God), the same command, the same promise. They differ in this, that the former passage relates specially to the preaching which the ministers of the word perform, the latter relates to the discipline of excommunication which has been committed to the Church. Now, the Church binds him whom she excommunicates, not by plunging him into eternal ruin and despair, but condemning his life and manners, and admonishing him, that, unless he repent, he is condemned. She looses him whom she receives into communion, because she makes him, as it were, a partaker of the unity which she has in Christ Jesus. Let no one, therefore, contumaciously despise the judgment of the Church, or account it a small matter that he is condemned by the suffrages of the faithful. The Lord testifies that such judgment of the faithful is nothing else than the promulgation of his own sentence, and that what they do on earth is ratified in heaven. For they have the word of God by which they condemn the perverse: they have the word by which they take back the penitent into favour. Now, they cannot err nor disagree with the judgment of God, because they judge only according to the law of God, which is not an uncertain or worldly opinion, but the holy will of God, an oracle of heaven. On these two passages, which I think I have briefly, as well as familiarly and truly expounded, these madmen, without any discrimination, as they are borne along by their spirit of giddiness, attempt to found at one time confession, at another excommunication, at another jurisdiction, at another the right of making laws, at another indulgences. The former passage they adduce for the purpose of rearing up the primacy of the Roman See. So well known are the keys to those who have thought proper to fit them with locks and doors, that you would say their whole life had been spent in the mechanic art.

3. Some, in imagining that all these things were temporary, as magistrates were still strangers to our profession of religion, are led astray, by not observing the distinction and dissimilarity between ecclesiastical and civil power. For the Church has not the right of the sword to punish or restrain, has no power to coerce, no prison nor other punishments which the magistrate is wont to inflict. Then the object in view is not to punish the sinner against his will, but to obtain a profession of penitence by voluntary chastisement. The two things, therefore, are widely different, because neither does the Church assume anything to herself which is proper to the magistrate, nor is the magistrate competent to what is done by the Church. This will

be made clearer by an example. Does any one get intoxicated. In a well-ordered city his punishment will be imprisonment. Has he committed whoredom? The punishment will be similar, or rather more severe. Thus satisfaction will be given to the laws, the magistrates, and the external tribunal. But the consequence will be, that the offender will give no signs of repentance, but will rather fret and murmur. Will the Church not here interfere? Such persons cannot be admitted to the Lord's Supper without doing injury to Christ and his sacred institution. Reason demands that he who, by a bad example, gives offence to the Church, shall remove the offence which he has caused by a formal declaration of repentance. The reason adduced by those who take a contrary view is frigid. Christ, they say, gave this office to the Church when there were no magistrates to execute it. But it often happens that the magistrate is negligent, nay, sometimes himself requires to be chastised; as was the case with the Emperor Theodosius. Moreover, the same thing may be said regarding the whole ministry of the word. Now, therefore, according to that view, let pastors cease to censure manifest iniquities, let them cease to chide, accuse, and rebuke. For there are Christian magistrates who ought to correct these things by the laws and the sword. But as the magistrate ought to purge the Church of offences by corporal punishment and coercion, so the minister ought, in his turn, to assist the magistrate in diminishing the number of offenders. Thus they ought to combine their efforts, the one being not an impediment but a help to the other.

4. And, indeed, on attending more closely to the words of Christ, it will readily appear that the state and order of the Church there described is perpetual, not temporary. For it were incongruous that those who refuse to obey our admonitions should be transferred to the magistrate—a course, however, which would be necessary if he were to succeed to the place of the Church. Why should the promise, "Verily I say unto you, What thing soever ye shall bind on earth," be limited to one, or to a few years? Moreover, Christ has here made no new enactment, but followed the custom always observed in the Church of his ancient people, thereby intimating, that the Church cannot dispense with the spiritual jurisdiction which existed from the beginning. This has been confirmed by the consent of all times. For when emperors and magistrates began to assume the Christian name, spiritual jurisdiction was not forthwith abolished, but was only so arranged as not in any respect to impair civil jurisdiction, or be confounded with it. And justly. For the magistrate, if he is pious, will have no wish to exempt himself from the common subjection of the children of God, not the least part of which is to subject himself to the Church, judging according to the word of God; so far is it from being his duty to abolish that judgment. For, as Ambrose says, "What more honourable title can an emperor have than to be called a son of the Church? A good emperor is within the Church, not above the Church" (Ambros. ad Valent. Ep. 32).

Those, therefore, who to adorn the magistrate strip the Church of this power, not only corrupt the sentiment of Christ by a false interpretation, but pass no light condemnation on the many holy bishops who have existed since the days of the apostles, for having on a false pretext usurped the honour and office of the civil magistrate.

5. But, on the other hand, it will be proper to see what was anciently the true use of ecclesiastical discipline, and how great the abuses which crept in, that we may know what of ancient practice is to be abolished, and what restored, if we would, after overthrowing the kingdom of Antichrist, again set up the true kingdom of Christ. First, the object in view is to prevent the occurrence of scandals, and when they arise, to remove them. In the use two things are to be considered: first, that this spiritual power be altogether distinct from the power of the sword; secondly, that it be not administered at the will of one individual, but by a lawful consistory (1 Cor. v. 4). Both were observed in the purer times of the Church. For holy bishops did not exercise their power by fine, imprisonment, or other civil penalties, but as became them, employed the word of God only. For the severest punishment of the Church, and, as it were, her last thunderbolt, is excommunication, which is not used unless in necessity.[1] This, moreover, requires neither violence nor physical force, but is contented with the might of the word of God. In short, the jurisdiction of the ancient Church was nothing else than (if I may so speak) a practical declaration of what Paul teaches concerning the spiritual power of pastors. "The weapons of our warfare are not carnal, but mighty through God to the pulling down of strongholds; casting down imaginations, and every high thing that exalteth itself against the knowledge of God, and bringing into captivity every thought to the obedience of Christ; and having in a readiness to revenge all disobedience" (2 Cor. x. 4–6). As this is done by the preaching of doctrine, so in order that doctrine may not be held in derision, those who profess to be of the household of faith ought to be judged according to the doctrine which is taught. Now this cannot be done without connecting with the office of the ministry a right of summoning those who are to be privately admonished or sharply rebuked, a right, moreover, of keeping back from the communion of the Lord's Supper, those who cannot be admitted without profaning this high ordinance. Hence, when Paul elsewhere asks, "What have I to do to judge them also that are without?" (1. Cor. v. 12), he makes the members of the Church subject to censures for the correction of their vices, and intimates the existence of tribunals from which no believer is exempted.

6. This power, as we have already stated, did not belong to an individual who could exercise it as he pleased, but belonged to the consistory of elders, which was in the Church what a council is in a

1 There is nothing repugnant to this in the statement of Augustine (Ep. 119), that as the teachers of liberal arts and pursuits, so bishops also were often accustomed, in their judicial proceedings, to chastise with the rod.

city. Cyprian, when mentioning those by whom it was exercised in his time, usually associates the whole clergy with the bishop (Cyprian, Lib. iii. Ep. 14, 19). In another place, he shows that though the clergy presided, the people, at the same time, were not excluded from cognisance: for he thus writes:—"From the commencement of my bishopric, I determined to do nothing without the advice of the clergy, nothing without the consent of the people." But the common and usual method of exercising this jurisdiction was by the council of presbyters, of whom, as I have said, there were two classes. Some were for teaching, others were only censors of manners. This institution gradually degenerated from its primitive form, so that, in the time of Ambrose, the clergy alone had cognisance of ecclesiastical causes. Of this he complains in the following terms:—"The ancient synagogue, and afterwards the Church, had elders, without whose advice nothing was done: this has grown obsolete, by whose fault I know not, unless it be by the sloth, or rather the pride, of teachers, who would have it seem that they only are somewhat" (Ambros. in 1 Tim. v.). We see how indignant this holy man was because the better state was in some degree impaired, and yet the order which then existed was at least tolerable. What, then, had he seen those shapeless ruins which exhibit no trace of the ancient edifice? How would he have lamented? First, contrary to what was right and lawful, the bishop appropriated to himself what was given to the whole Church. For this is just as if the consul had expelled the senate, and usurped the whole empire. For as he is superior in rank to the others, so the authority of the consistory is greater than that of one individual. It was, therefore, a gross iniquity, when one man, transferring the common power to himself, paved the way for tyrannical licence, robbed the Church of what was its own, suppressed and discarded the consistory ordained by the Spirit of Christ.

7. But as evil always produces evil, the bishops, disdaining this jurisdiction as a thing unworthy of their care, devolved it on others. Hence the appointment of officials to supply their place. I am not now speaking of the character of this class of persons; all I say is, that they differ in no respect from civil judges. And yet they call it spiritual jurisdiction, though all the litigation relates to worldly affairs. Were there no other evil in this, how can they presume to call a litigious forum a church court? But there are admonitions; there is excommunication. This is the way in which God is mocked. Does some poor man owe a sum of money? He is summoned: if he appears, he is found liable; when found liable, if he pays not, he is admonished. After the second admonition, the next step is excommunication. If he appears not, he is admonished to appear; if he delays, he is admonished, and by-and-by excommunicated. I ask, is there any resemblance whatever between this and the institution of Christ, or ancient custom or ecclesiastical procedure? But there, too, vices are censured. Whoredom, lasciviousness, drunkenness, and similar iniquities, they not only tolerate, but by a kind of tacit ap-

probation encourage and confirm, and that not among the people only, but also among the clergy. Out of many they summon a few, either that they may not seem to wink too strongly, or that they may mulct them in money. I say nothing of the plunder, rapine, peculation, and sacrilege, which are there committed. I say nothing of the kind of persons who are for the most part appointed to the office. It is enough, and more than enough, that when the Romanists boast of their spiritual jurisdiction, we are ready to show that nothing is more contrary to the procedure instituted by Christ, that it has no more resemblance to ancient practice than darkness has to light.

8. Although we have not said all that might here be adduced, and even what has been said is only briefly glanced at, enough, I trust, has been said to leave no man in doubt that the spiritual power on which the Pope plumes himself, with all his adherents, is impious contradiction of the word of God, and unjust tyranny against his people. Under the name of spiritual power, I include both their audacity in framing new doctrines, by which they led the miserable people away from the genuine purity of the word of God, the iniquitous traditions by which they ensnared them, and the pseudo-ecclesiastical jurisdiction which they exercise by suffragans and officials. For if we allow Christ to reign amongst us, the whole of that domination cannot but immediately tumble and fall. The right of the sword which they also claim for themselves, not being exercised against consciences, does not fall to be considered in this place. Here, however, it is worth while to observe, that they are always like themselves, there being nothing which they less resemble than that which they would be thought to be—viz. pastors of the Church. I speak not of the vices of particular men, but of the common wickedness, and, consequently, the pestiferous nature of the whole order, which is thought to be mutilated if not distinguished by wealth and haughty titles. If in this matter we seek the authority of Christ, there can be no doubt that he intended to debar the ministers of his word from civil domination and worldly power when he said, "The princes of the Gentiles exercise dominion over them, and they that are great exercise authority upon them. But it shall not be so among you" (Matth. xx. 25, 26). For he intimates not only that the office of pastor is distinct from the office of prince, but that the things differ so widely that they cannot be united in the same individual. Moses indeed held both (Exod. xviii. 16); but, first, this was the effect of a rare miracle; and, secondly, it was temporary, until matters should be better arranged. For when a certain form is prescribed by the Lord, the civil government is left to Moses, and he is ordered to resign the priesthood to his brother. And justly; for it is more than nature can do, for one man to bear both burdens. This has in all ages been carefully observed in the Church. Never did any bishop, so long as any true appearance of a church remained, think of usurping the right of the sword: so that, in the age of Am-

brose, it was a common proverb, that emperors longed more for the priesthood than priests for imperial power.[1] For the expression which he afterwards adds was fixed in all minds, Palaces belong to the emperor, churches to the priest.

9. But after a method was devised by which bishops might hold the title, honour, and wealth of their office without burden and solicitude, that they might be left altogether idle, the right of the sword was given them, or rather, they themselves usurped it. With what pretext will they defend this effrontery? Was it the part of bishops to entangle themselves with the cognisance of causes, and the administration of states and provinces, and embrace occupations so very alien to them—of bishops, who require so much time and labour in their own office, that though they devote themselves to it diligently and entirely, without distraction from other avocations, they are scarcely sufficient? But such is their perverseness, that they hesitate not to boast that in this way the dignity of Christ's kingdom is duly maintained, and they, at the same time, are not withdrawn from their own vocation. In regard to the former allegation, if it is a comely ornament of the sacred office, that those holding it be so elevated as to become formidable to the greatest monarchs, they have ground to expostulate with Christ, who in this respect has grievously curtailed their honour. For what, according to their view, can be more insulting than these words, "The kings of the Gentiles exercise authority over them"? "But ye shall not be so" (Luke xxii. 25, 26). And yet he imposes no harder law on his servants than he had previously laid on himself. "Who," says he, "made me a judge or divider over you?" (Luke xii. 14.) We see that he unreservedly refuses the office of judging; and this he would not have done if the thing had been in accordance with his office. To the subordination to which the Lord thus reduced himself, will his servants not submit? The other point I wish they would prove by experience as easily as they allege it. But as it seemed to the apostles not good to leave the word of God and serve tables, so these men are thereby forced to admit, though they are unwilling to be taught, that it is not possible for the same person to be a good bishop and a good prince. For if those who, in respect of the largeness of the gifts with which they were endued, were able for much more numerous and weighty cares than any who have come after them, confessed that they could not serve the ministry of the word and of tables, without giving way under the burden, how are these, who are no men at all when compared with the apostles, possibly to surpass them a hundred times in diligence? The very attempt is most impudent and audacious presumption. Still we see the thing done; with what success is plain. The result could not but be that they have deserted their own functions, and removed to another camp.

10. There can be no doubt that this great progress has been made

[1] This is stated by Ambrose, Hom. de Basilic. Tradend. See also August. De Fide et Operibus, cap. 4.

from slender beginnings. They could not reach so far at one step, but at one time by craft and wily art, secretly raised themselves before any one foresaw what was to happen; at another time, when occasion offered, by means of threats and terror, extorted some increase of power from princes; at another time, when they saw princes disposed to give liberally, they abused their foolish and inconsiderate facility. The godly in ancient times, when any dispute arose, in order to escape the necessity of a lawsuit, left the decision to the bishop, because they had no doubt of his integrity. The ancient bishops were often greatly dissatisfied at being entangled in such matters, as Augustine somewhere declares; but lest the parties should rush to some contentious tribunal, unwillingly submitted to the annoyance. These voluntary decisions, which altogether differed from forensic strife, these men have converted into ordinary jurisdiction. As cities and districts, when for some time pressed with various difficulties, betook themselves to the patronage of the bishops, and threw themselves on their protection, these men have, by a strange artifice, out of patrons made themselves masters. That they have seized a good part by the violence of faction cannot be denied. The princes, again, who spontaneously conferred jurisdiction on bishops, were induced to it by various causes. Though their indulgence had some appearance of piety, they did not by this preposterous liberality consult in the best manner for the interests of the Church, whose ancient and true discipline they thus corrupted, nay, to tell the truth, completely abolished. Those bishops who abuse the goodness of princes to their own advantage, gave more than sufficient proof by this one specimen of their conduct, that they were not at all true bishops. Had they had one spark of the apostolic spirit, they would doubtless have answered in the words of Paul, "The weapons of our warfare are not carnal," but spiritual (2 Cor. x. 4). But hurried away by blind cupidity, they lost themselves, and posterity, and the Church.

11. At length the Roman Pontiff, not content with moderate districts, laid hands first on kingdoms, and thereafter on empire. And that he may on some pretext or other retain possession, secured by mere robbery, he boasts at one time that he holds it by divine right, at another, he pretends a donation from Constantine, at another, some different title. First, I answer with Bernard, "Be it that on some ground or other he can claim it, it is not by apostolic right. For Peter could not give what he had not, but what he had he gave to his successors—viz. care of the churches. But when our Lord and Master says that he was not appointed a judge between two, the servant and disciple ought not to think it unbecoming not to be judge of all" (Bernard. de Considerat. Lib. ii.). Bernard is speaking of civil judgments, for he adds, "Your power then is in sins, not in rights of property, since for the former and not the latter you received the keys of the kingdom of heaven. Which of the two seems to you the higher dignity, the forgiving of sins or the dividing of lands? There is no comparison. These low earthly things have for

their judges the kings and princes of the earth. Why do you invade the territories of others?" &c. Again, "You are made superior" (he is addressing Pope Eugenius), "for what? not to domineer, I presume. Let us therefore remember, however highly we think of ourselves, that a ministry is laid upon us, not a dominion given to us. Learn that you have need of a slender rod, not of a sceptre, to do the work of a prophet." Again, "It is plain that the apostles are prohibited to exercise dominion. Go you, therefore, and dare to usurp for yourself, either apostleship with dominion, or dominion with apostleship." Immediately after he says, "The apostolic form is this; dominion is interdicted, ministry is enjoined." Though Bernard speaks thus, and so speaks as to make it manifest to all that he speaks truth, nay, though without a word the thing itself is manifest, the Roman Pontiff was not ashamed at the Council of Arles to decree that the supreme right of both swords belonged to him of divine right.

12. As far as pertains to the donation of Constantine, those who are moderately versant in the history of the time have no need of being told, that the claim is not only fabulous but also absurd. But to say nothing of history, Gregory alone is a fit and most complete witness to this effect. For wherever he speaks of the emperor he calls him His Most Serene Lord, and himself his unworthy servant.[1] Again, in another passage he says, "Let not our Lord in respect of worldly power be too soon offended with priests, but with excellent consideration, on account of him whose servants they are, let him while ruling them also pay them due reverence." We see how in a common subjection he desires to be accounted one of the people. For he there pleads not another's but his own cause. Again, "I trust in Almighty God that he will give long life to pious rulers, and place us under your hand according to his mercy." I have not adduced these things here from any intention thoroughly to discuss the question of Constantine's donation, but only to show my readers by the way, how childishly the Romanists tell lies when they attempt to claim an earthly empire for their Pontiff. The more vile the impudence of Augustine Steuchus, who, in so desperate a cause, presumed to lend his labour and his tongue to the Roman Pontiff. Valla, as was easy for a man of learning and acuteness to do, had completely refuted this fable. And yet, as he was little versant in ecclesiastical affairs, he had not said all that was relevant to the subject. Steuchus breaks in, and scatters his worthless quibbles, trying to bury the clear light. And certainly he pleads the cause of his master not less frigidly than some wit might, under pretence of defending the same view, support that of Valla. But the cause is a worthy one, which the Pope may well hire such patrons to defend; equally worthy are the hired ravers whom the hope of gain may deceive, as was the case with Eugubinus.

13. Should any one ask at what period this fictitious empire began to emerge, five hundred years have not yet elasped since the Roman

1 Gregor. Lib. ii. Ep. 5; Lib. iii. Ep. 20; Lib. ii. Ep. 61; Lib. iv. Ep. 31, 34.

Pontiffs were under subjection to the emperors, and no pontiff was elected without the emperor's authority. An occasion of innovating on this order was given to Gregory VII. by Henry IV., a giddy and rash man, of no prudence, great audacity, and a dissolute life. When he had the whole bishoprics of Germany in his court partly for sale, and partly exposed to plunder, Hildebrand, who had been provoked by him, seized the plausible pretext for asserting his claim. As his cause seemed good and pious, it was viewed with great favour, while Henry, on account of the insolence of his government, was generally hated by the princes. At length Hildebrand, who took the name of Gregory VII., an impure and wicked man, betrayed his sinister intentions. On this he was deserted by many who had joined him in his conspiracy. He gained this much, however, that his successors were not only able to shake off the yoke with impunity, but also to bring the emperors into subjection to them. Moreover, many of the subsequent emperors were liker Henry than Julius Cæsar. These it was not difficult to overcome while they sat at home sluggish and secure, instead of vigorously exerting themselves, as was most necessary, by all legitimate means to repress the cupidity of the pontiffs. We see what colour there is for the grand donation of Constantine, by which the Pope pretends that the western empire was given to him.

14. Meanwhile the pontiff ceased not, either by fraud, or by perfidy, or by arms, to invade the dominions of others. Rome itself, which was then free, they, about a hundred and thirty years ago, reduced under their power. At length they obtained the dominion which they now possess, and to retain or increase which, now for two hundred years (they had begun before they usurped the dominion of the city) they have so troubled the Christian world that they have almost destroyed it. Formerly, when in the time of Gregory, the guardians of ecclesiastical property seized upon lands which they considered to belong to the Church, and, after the manner of the exchequer, affixed their seals in attestation of their claim, Gregory having assembled a council of bishops, and bitterly inveighed against that profane custom, asked whether they would not anathematise the churchman who, of his own accord, attempted to seize some possession by the inscription of a title, and in like manner, the bishop who should order it to be done, or not punish it when done without his order. All pronounced the anathema. If it is a crime deserving of anathema for a churchman to claim a property by the inscription of a title—then, now that for two hundred years, the pontiffs meditate nothing but war and bloodshed, the destruction of armies, the plunder of cities, the destruction or overthrow of nations, and the devastation of kingdoms, only that they may obtain possession of the property of others—what anathemas can sufficiently punish such conduct? Surely it is perfectly obvious that the very last thing they aim at is the glory of Christ. For were they spontaneously to resign every

portion of secular power which they possess, no peril to the glory of God, no peril to sound doctrine, no peril to the safety of the Church ensues; but they are borne blind and headlong by a lust for power, thinking that nothing can be safe unless they rule, as the prophet says, "with force and with cruelty" (Ezek. xxxiv. 4).

15. To jurisdiction is annexed the immunity claimed by the Romish clergy. They deem it unworthy of them to answer before a civil judge in personal causes; and consider both the liberty and dignity of the Church to consist in exemption from ordinary tribunals and laws. But the ancient bishops, who otherwise were most resolute in asserting the rights of the Church, did not think it any injury to themselves and their order to act as subjects. Pious emperors also, as often as there was occasion, summoned clergy to their tribunals, and met with no opposition. For Constantine, in a letter to the Nicomedians, thus speaks:—"Should any of the bishops unadvisedly excite tumult, his audacity shall be restrained by the minister of God, that is, by my executive" (Theodoret. Lib. i. c. 20). Valentinian says, "Good bishops throw no obloquy on the power of the emperor, but sincerely keep the commandments of God, the great King, and obey our laws" (Theodoret. Lib. iv. c. 8). This was unquestionably the view then entertained by all. Ecclesiastical causes, indeed, were brought before the episcopal court; as when a clergyman had offended, but not against the laws, he was only charged by the Canons; and instead of being cited before the civil court, had the bishop for his judge in that particular case. In like manner, when a question of faith was agitated, or one which properly pertained to the Church, cognisance was left to the Church. In this sense the words of Ambrose are to be understood: "Your father, of august memory, not only replied verbally, but enacted by law, that, in a question of faith, the judge should be one who was neither unequal from office, nor incompetent from the nature of his jurisdiction" (Ambros. Ep. 32). Again, "If we attend to the Scriptures, or to ancient examples, who can deny that in a question of faith, a question of faith, I say, bishops are wont to judge Christian emperors, not emperors to judge bishops?" Again, "I would have come before your consistory, O emperor, would either the bishops or the people have allowed me to come: they say that a question of faith should be discussed in the Church before the people." He maintains, indeed, that a spiritual cause, that is, one pertaining to religion, is not to be brought before the civil court, where worldly disputes are agitated. His firmness in this respect is justly praised by all. And yet, though he has a good cause, he goes so far as to say, that if it comes to force and violence, he will yield. "I will not desert the post committed to me, but, if forced, I will not resist: prayers and tears are our weapons" (Ambros. Hom. de Basilic. Traden.). Let us observe the singular moderation of this holy man, his combination of prudence, magnanimity, and boldness. Justina, the mother of the emperor, unable to bring him over to the Arian party, sought to

drive him from the government of the Church. And this would have been the result had he, when summoned, gone to the palace to plead his cause. He maintains, therefore, that the emperor is not fit to decide such a controversy. This both the necessity of the times, and the very nature of the thing, demanded. He thought it were better for him to die than consent to transmit such an example to posterity; and yet if violence is offered, he thinks not of resisting. For he says, it is not the part of a bishop to defend the faith and rights of the Church by arms. But in all other causes he declares himself ready to do whatever the emperor commands. "If he asks tribute, we deny it not: the lands of the Church pay tribute. If he asks lands, he has the power of evicting them; none of us interposes." Gregory speaks in the same manner. "I am not ignorant of the mind of my most serene lord: he is not wont to interfere in sacerdotal causes, lest he may in some degree burden himself with our sins." He does not exclude the emperor generally from judging priests, but says that there are certain causes which he ought to leave to the ecclesiastical tribunal.

16. And hence all that these holy men sought by this exception was, to prevent irreligious princes from impeding the Church in the discharge of her duty, by their tyrannical caprice and violence. They did not disapprove when princes interposed their authority in ecclesiastical affairs, provided this was done to preserve, not to disturb, the order of the Church, to establish, not to destroy discipline. For, seeing the Church has not, and ought not to wish to have, the power of compulsion (I speak of civil coercion), it is the part of pious kings and princes to maintain religion by laws, edicts, and sentences. In this way, when the emperor Maurice had commanded certain bishops to receive their neighbouring colleagues, who had been expelled by the Barbarians, Gregory confirms the order, and exhorts them to obey.[1] He himself, when admonished by the same emperor to return to a good understanding with John, Bishop of Constantinople, endeavours to show that he is not to be blamed; but so far from boasting of immunity from the secular forum, rather promises to comply as far as conscience would permit: he at the same time says, that Maurice had acted as became a religious prince, in giving these commands to priests.

[1] Lib. i. Ep. 43; Lib. iv. Ep. 32, 34; Lib. vii. Ep. 39.

CHAPTER XII.

OF THE DISCIPLINE OF THE CHURCH, AND ITS PRINCIPAL USE IN CENSURES AND EXCOMMUNICATION.

This chapter consists of two parts:—I. The first part of ecclesiastical discipline, which respects the people, and is called common, consists of two parts, the former depending on the power of the keys, which is considered, sec. 1–14; the latter consisting in the appointment of times for fasting and prayer, sec. 14–21. II. The second part of ecclesiastical discipline relating to the clergy, sec. 22–28.

Sections.

1. Of the power of the keys, or the common discipline of the Church. Necessity and very great utility of this discipline.
2. Its various degrees. 1. Private admonition. 2. Rebukes before witnesses. 3. Excommunication.
3. Different degrees of delinquency. Modes of procedure in both kinds of chastisement.
4. Delicts to be distinguished from flagitious wickedness. The last to be more severely punished.
5. Ends of this discipline. 1. That the wicked may not, by being admitted to the Lord's Table, put insult on Christ. 2. That they may not corrupt others. 3. That they themselves may repent.
6. In what way sins public as well as secret are to be corrected. Trivial and grave offences.
7. No person, not even the sovereign, exempted from this discipline. By whom and in what way it ought to be exercised.
8. In what spirit discipline is to be exercised. In what respect some of the ancient Christians exercised it too rigorously. This done more from custom than in accordance with their own sentiments. This shown from Cyprian, Chrysostom, and Augustine.
9. Moderation to be used, not only by the whole Church, but by each individual member.
10. Our Saviour's words concerning binding and loosing wrested if otherwise understood. Difference between anathema and excommunication. Anathema rarely if ever to be used.
11. Excessive rigour to be avoided, as well by private individuals as by pastors.
12. In this respect the Donatists erred most grievously, as do also the Anabaptists in the present day. Portraiture by Augustine.
13. Moderation especially to be used when not a few individuals, but the great body of the people, have gone astray.
14. A second part of common discipline relating to fastings, prayer, and other holy exercises. These used by believers under both dispensations. To what purposes applied. Of Fasting.
15. Three ends of fasting. The first refers more especially to private fasting. Second and third ends.
16. Public fasting and prayer appointed by pastors on any great emergency.
17. Examples of this under the Law.
18. Fasting consists chiefly in three things—viz. time, the quality, and sparing use of food.
19. To prevent superstition, three things to be inculcated. 1. The heart to be rent, not the garments. 2. Fasting not to be regarded as a meritorious work or kind of divine worship. 3. Abstinence must not be immoderately extolled.
20. Owing to an excess of this kind the observance of Lent was established. This superstitious observance refuted by three arguments. It was indeed used by the ancients, but on different grounds.

1. THE discipline of the Church, the consideration of which has been deferred till now, must be briefly explained, that we may be able to pass to other matters. Now discipline depends in a very great measure on the power of the keys and on spiritual jurisdiction. That this may be more easily understood, let us divide the Church into two principal classes—viz. clergy and people. The term clergy I use in the common acceptation for those who perform a public ministry in the Church.[1] We shall speak first of the common discipline to which all ought to be subject, and then proceed to the clergy, who have besides that common discipline one peculiar to themselves. But as some, from hatred of discipline, are averse to the very name, for their sake we observe,—If no society, nay, no house with even a moderate family, can be kept in a right state without discipline, much more necessary is it in the Church, whose state ought to be the best ordered possible. Hence as the saving doctrine of Christ is the life of the Church, so discipline is, as it were, its sinews; for to it it is owing that the members of the body adhere together, each in its own place. Wherefore, all who either wish that discipline were abolished, or who impede the restoration of it, whether they do this of design or through thoughtlessness, certainly aim at the complete devastation of the Church. For what will be the result if every one is allowed to do as he pleases? But this must happen if to the preaching of the gospel are not added private admonition, correction, and similar methods of maintaining doctrine, and not allowing it to become lethargic. Discipline, therefore, is a kind of curb to restrain and tame those who war against the doctrine of Christ, or it is a kind of stimulus by which the indifferent are aroused; sometimes, also, it is a kind of fatherly rod, by which those who have made some more grievous lapse are chastised in mercy with the meekness of the spirit of Christ. Since, then, we already see some beginnings of a fearful devastation in the Church from the total want of care and method in managing the people, necessity itself cries

1 French, "J'use de ce mot de Clercs pource qu'il est commun, combien qu'il soit impropre; par lequel j'entens ceux qui ont office et ministere en l'Eglise."—I use this word Clergy because it is common, though it is improper; by it I mean those who have an office and ministry in the Church.

aloud that there is need of a remedy. Now the only remedy is this which Christ enjoins, and the pious have always had in use.

2. The first foundation of discipline is to provide for private admonition; that is, if any one does not do his duty spontaneously, or behaves insolently, or lives not quite honestly, or commits something worthy of blame, he must allow himself to be admonished; and every one must study to admonish his brother when the case requires. Here especially is there occasion for the vigilance of pastors and presbyters, whose duty is not only to preach to the people, but to exhort and admonish from house to house, whenever their hearers have not profited sufficiently by general teaching; as Paul shows, when he relates that he taught "publicly, and from house to house," and testifies that he is "pure from the blood of all men," because he had not shunned to declare "all the counsel of God" (Acts xx. 20, 26, 27.) Then does doctrine obtain force and authority, not only when the minister publicly expounds to all what they owe to Christ, but has the right and means of exacting this from those whom he may observe to be sluggish or disobedient to his doctrine. Should any one either perversely reject such admonitions, or by persisting in his faults, show that he contemns them, the injunction of Christ is, that after he has been a second time admonished before witnesses, he is to be summoned to the bar of the Church, which is the consistory of elders, and there admonished more sharply, as by public authority, that if he reverence the Church he may submit and obey (Matth. xviii. 15, 17). If even in this way he is not subdued, but persists in his iniquity, he is then, as a despiser of the Church, to be debarred from the society of believers.

3. But as our Saviour is not there speaking of secret faults merely, we must attend to the distinction that some sins are private, others public or openly manifest. Of the former, Christ says to every private individual, "go and tell him his fault between thee and him alone" (Matth. xviii. 15). Of open sins Paul says to Timothy, "Those that sin rebuke before all, that others also may fear" (1 Tim. v. 20). Our Saviour had previously used the words, "If thy brother shall trespass against thee." This clause, unless you would be captious, you cannot understand otherwise than, If this happens *in a manner known to yourself*, others not being privy to it. The injunction which Paul gave to Timothy to rebuke those openly who sin openly, he himself followed with Peter (Gal. ii. 14). For when Peter sinned so as to give public offence, he did not admonish him apart, but brought him forward in face of the Church. The legitimate course, therefore, will be to proceed in correcting secret faults by the steps mentioned by Christ, and in open sins, accompanied with public scandal, to proceed at once to solemn correction by the Church.

4. Another distinction to be attended to is, that some sins are mere delinquencies, others crimes and flagrant iniquities. In correcting the latter, it is necessary to employ not only admonition or

rebuke, but a sharper remedy, as Paul shows when he not only verbally rebukes the incestuous Corinthian, but punishes him with excommunication, as soon as he was informed of his crime (1 Cor. v. 4). Now then we begin better to perceive how the spiritual jurisdiction of the Church, which animadverts on sins according to the word of the Lord, is at once the best help to sound doctrine, the best foundation of order, and the best bond of unity. Therefore, when the Church banishes from its fellowship open adulterers, fornicators, thieves, robbers, the seditious, the perjured, false witnesses, and others of that description; likewise the contumacious, who, when duly admonished for lighter faults, hold God and his tribunal in derision, instead of arrogating to itself anything that is unreasonable, it exercises a jurisdiction which it has received from the Lord. Moreover, lest any one should despise the judgment of the Church, or count it a small matter to be condemned by the suffrages of the faithful, the Lord has declared that it is nothing else than the promulgation of his own sentence, and that that which they do on earth is ratified in heaven. For they act by the word of the Lord in condemning the perverse, and by the word of the Lord in taking the penitent back into favour (John xx. 23). Those, I say, who trust that churches can long stand without this bond of discipline are mistaken, unless, indeed, we can with impunity dispense with a help which the Lord foresaw would be necessary. And, indeed, the greatness of the necessity will be better perceived by its manifold uses.

5. There are three ends to which the Church has respect in thus correcting and excommunicating. The first is, that God may not be insulted by the name of Christians being given to those who lead shameful and flagitious lives, as if his holy Church were a combination of the wicked and abandoned. For seeing that the Church is the body of Christ, she cannot be defiled by such fetid and putrid members, without bringing some disgrace on her Head. Therefore, that there may be nothing in the Church to bring disgrace on his sacred name, those whose turpitude might throw infamy on the name must be expelled from his family. And here, also, regard must be had to the Lord's Supper, which might be profaned by a promiscuous admission.[1] For it is most true, that he who is intrusted with the dispensation of it, if he knowingly and willingly admits any unworthy person whom he ought and is able to repel, is as guilty of sacrilege as if he had cast the Lord's body to dogs. Wherefore, Chrysostom bitterly inveighs against priests, who, from fear of the great, dare not keep any one back. "Blood (says he, Hom. 83, in Matth.) will be required at your hands. If you fear man, he will mock you, but if you fear God, you will be respected also by men. Let us not tremble at fasces, purple, or diadems; our power here is greater. Assuredly I will sooner give up my body to death, and allow my blood to be shed, than be a partaker of that pollution." Therefore, lest this most sacred mystery should be exposed to ignominy, great selection is

1 Vide Cyril in Joann. cap. 50, et Luther, de Commun. Populi, tom. ii.

required in dispensing it, and this cannot be except by the jurisdiction of the Church. A second end of discipline is, that the good may not, as usually happens, be corrupted by constant communication with the wicked. For such is our proneness to go astray, that nothing is easier than to seduce us from the right course by bad example. To this use of discipline the apostle referred when he commanded the Corinthians to discard the incestuous man from their society. " A little leaven leaveneth the whole lump " (1 Cor. v. 6.) And so much danger did he foresee here, that he prohibited them from keeping company with such persons. "If any man that is called a brother be a fornicator, or covetous, or an idolater, or a railer, or a drunkard, or an extortioner; with such an one, no not to eat" (1 Cor. v. 11). A third end of discipline is, that the sinner may be ashamed, and begin to repent of his turpitude. Hence it is for their interest also that their iniquity should be chastised, that whereas they would have become more obstinate by indulgence, they may be aroused by the rod. This the apostle intimates when he thus writes —" If any man obey not our word by this epistle, note that man, and have no company with him, that he may be ashamed" (2 Thess. iii. 14). Again, when he says that he had delivered the Corinthian to Satan, "that the spirit may be saved in the day of the Lord Jesus" (1 Cor. v. 5); that is, as I interpret it, he gave him over to temporal condemnation, that he might be made safe for eternity. And he says that he gave him over to Satan because the devil is without the Church, as Christ is in the Church. Some interpret this of a certain infliction on the flesh, but this interpretation seems to me most improbable. (August. de Verb. Apostol. Serm. 68.)

6. These being the ends proposed, it remains to see in what way the Church is to execute this part of discipline, which consists in jurisdiction. And, first, let us remember the division above laid down, that some sins are public, others private or secret. Public are those which are done not before one or two witnesses, but openly, and to the offence of the whole Church. By secret, I mean not such as are altogether concealed from men, such as those of hypocrites (for these fall not under the judgment of the Church), but those of an intermediate description, which are not without witnesses, and yet are not public. The former class requires not the different steps which Christ enumerates; but whenever anything of the kind occurs, the Church ought to do her duty by summoning the offender, and correcting him according to his fault. In the second class, the matter comes not before the Church, unless there is contumacy, according to the rule of Christ. In taking cognisance of offences, it is necessary to attend to the distinction between delinquencies and flagrant iniquities. In lighter offences there is not so much occasion for severity, but verbal chastisement is sufficient, and that gentle and fatherly, so as not to exasperate or confound the offender, but to bring him back to himself, so that he may rather rejoice than be grieved at the correction. Flagrant iniquities require a sharper

remedy. It is not sufficient verbally to rebuke him who, by some open act of evil example, has grievously offended the Church; but he ought for a time to be denied the communion of the Supper, until he gives proof of repentance. Paul does not merely administer a verbal rebuke to the Corinthian, but discards him from the Church, and reprimands the Corinthians for having borne with him so long (1 Cor. v. 5). This was the method observed by the ancient and purer Church, when legitimate government was in vigour. When any one was guilty of some flagrant iniquity, and thereby caused scandal, he was first ordered to abstain from participation in the sacred Supper, and thereafter to humble himself before God, and testify his penitence before the Church. There were, moreover, solemn rites, which, as indications of repentance, were wont to be prescribed to those who had lapsed. When the penitent had thus made satisfaction to the Church, he was received into favour by the laying on of hands. This admission often receives the name of *peace* from Cyprian, who briefly describes the form.[1] "They act as penitents for a certain time, next they come to confession, and receive the right of communion by the laying on of hands of the bishop and clergy." Although the bishop with the clergy thus superintended the restoration of the penitent, the consent of the people was at the same time required, as he elsewhere explains.

7. So far was any one from being exempted from this discipline, that even princes submitted to it in common with their subjects; and justly, since it is the discipline of Christ, to whom all sceptres and diadems should be subject. Thus Theodosius,[2] when excommunicated by Ambrose, because of the slaughter perpetrated at Thessalonica, laid aside all the royal insignia with which he was surrounded, and publicly in the Church bewailed the sin into which he had been betrayed by the fraud of others, with groans and tears imploring pardon. Great kings should not think it a disgrace to them to prostrate themselves suppliantly before Christ, the King of kings; nor ought they to be displeased at being judged by the Church. For seeing they seldom hear anything in their courts but mere flattery, the more necessary is it that the Lord should correct them by the mouth of his priests. Nay, they ought rather to wish the priests not to spare them, in order that the Lord may spare. I here say nothing as to those by whom the jurisdiction ought to be exercised, because it has been said elsewhere (Chap. xi. sec. 5, 6). I only add, that the legitimate course to be taken in excommunication, as shown by Paul, is not for the elders alone to act apart from others, but with the knowledge and approbation of the Church, so that the body of the people, without regulating the procedure, may, as witnesses and guardians, observe it, and prevent the few from doing anything capriciously. Throughout the whole procedure, in addition to invocation of the name of God, there should be a gravity bespeaking the pre-

1 Cyprian, Lib. i. Ep. 2; Lib. iii. Ep. 14, 26.
2 Ambros. Lib. i. Ep. 3; et Oratio habita in Funere Theodosii.

sence of Christ, and leaving no room to doubt that he is presiding over his own tribunal.

8. It ought not, however, to be omitted, that the Church, in exercising severity, ought to accompany it with the spirit of meekness. For, as Paul enjoins, we must always take care that he on whom discipline is exercised be not "swallowed up with overmuch sorrow" (2 Cor. ii. 7): for in this way, instead of cure there would be destruction. The rule of moderation will be best obtained from the end contemplated. For the object of excommunication being to bring the sinner to repentance and remove bad examples, in order that the name of Christ may not be evil spoken of, nor others tempted to the same evil courses: if we consider this, we shall easily understand how far severity should be carried, and at what point it ought to cease. Therefore, when the sinner gives the Church evidence of his repentance, and by this evidence does what in him lies to obliterate the offence, he ought not on any account to be urged farther. If he is urged, the rigour now exceeds due measure. In this respect it is impossible to excuse the excessive austerity of the ancients, which was altogether at variance with the injunction of our Lord, and strangely perilous. For when they enjoined a formal repentance, and excluded from communion for three, or four, or seven years, or for life, what could the result be, but either great hypocrisy or very great despair? In like manner, when any one who had again lapsed was not admitted to a second repentance, but ejected from the Church, to the end of his life (August. Ep. 54), this was neither useful nor agreeable to reason. Whosoever, therefore, looks at the matter with sound judgment, will here regret a want of prudence. Here, however, I rather disapprove of the public custom, than blame those who complied with it. Some of them certainly disapproved of it, but submitted to what they were unable to correct. Cyprian, indeed, declares that it was not with his own will he was thus rigorous. "Our patience, facility, and humanity (he says, Lib. i. Ep. 3), are ready to all who come. I wish all to be brought back into the Church: I wish all our fellow-soldiers to be contained within the camp of Christ and the mansions of God the Father. I forgive all; I disguise much; from an earnest desire of collecting the brotherhood, I do not minutely scrutinise all the faults which have been committed against God. I myself often err, by forgiving offences more than I ought. Those returning in repentance, and those confessing their sins with simple and humble satisfaction, I embrace with prompt and full delight." Chrysostom, who is somewhat more severe, still speaks thus: "If God is so kind, why should his priest wish to appear austere?" We know, moreover, how indulgently Augustine treated the Donatists; not hesitating to admit any who returned from schism to their bishopric, as soon as they declared their repentance. But, as a contrary method had prevailed, they were compelled to follow it, and give up their own judgment.

9. But as the whole body of the Church are required to act thus

mildly, and not to carry their rigour against those who have lapsed to an extreme, but rather to act charitably towards them, according to the precept of Paul, so every private individual ought proportionately to accommodate himself to this clemency and humanity. Such as have, therefore, been expelled from the Church, it belongs not to us to expunge from the number of the elect, or to despair of, as if they were already lost. We may lawfully judge them aliens from the Church, and so aliens from Christ, but only during the time of their excommunication. If then, also, they give greater evidence of petulance than of humility, still let us commit them to the judgment of the Lord, hoping better of them in future than we see at present, and not ceasing to pray to God for them. And (to sum up in one word) let us not consign to destruction their person, which is in the hand, and subject to the decision, of the Lord alone; but let us merely estimate the character of each man's acts according to the law of the Lord. In following this rule, we abide by the divine judgment rather than give any judgment of our own. Let us not arrogate to ourselves greater liberty in judging, if we would not limit the power of God, and give the law to his mercy. Whenever it seems good to Him, the worst are changed into the best; aliens are ingrafted, and strangers are adopted into the Church. This the Lord does, that he may disappoint the thoughts of men, and confound their rashness; a rashness which, if not curbed, would usurp a power of judging to which it has no title.

10. For when our Saviour promises that what his servants bound on earth should be bound in heaven (Matth. xviii. 18), he confines the power of binding to the censure of the Church, which does not consign those who are excommunicated to perpetual ruin and damnation, but assures them, when they hear their life and manners condemned, that perpetual damnation will follow if they do not repent. Excommunication differs from anathema in this, that the latter completely excluding pardon, dooms and devotes the individual to eternal destruction, whereas the former rather rebukes and animadverts upon his manners; and although it also punishes, it is to bring him to salvation, by forewarning him of his future doom. If it succeeds, reconciliation and restoration to communion are ready to be given. Moreover, anathema is rarely if ever to be used. Hence, though ecclesiastical discipline does not allow us to be on familiar and intimate terms with excommunicated persons, still we ought to strive by all possible means to bring them to a better mind, and recover them to the fellowship and unity of the Church: as the apostle also says, "Yet count him not as an enemy, but admonish him as a brother" (2 Thess. iii. 15). If this humanity be not observed in private as well as public, the danger is, that our discipline shall degenerate into destruction.[1]

[1] French, "Il y a danger, que de discipline nous ne tombions en une maniere de gehene, et que de correcteurs nous ne devenions bourreaux."—There is a danger, lest instead of discipline we fall into a kind of gehenna, and instead of correctors become executioners.

11. Another special requisite to moderation of discipline is, as Augustine discourses against the Donatists, that private individuals must not, when they see vices less carefully corrected by the Council of Elders, immediately separate themselves from the Church; nor must pastors themselves, when unable to reform all things which need correction to the extent which they could wish, cast up their ministry, or by unwonted severity throw the whole Church into confusion. What Augustine says is perfectly true: "Whoever corrects what he can, by rebuking it, or without violating the bond of peace, excludes what he cannot correct, or unjustly condemns while he patiently tolerates what he is unable to exclude without violating the bond of peace, is free and exempted from the curse" (August. contra Parmen. Lib. ii. c. 4). He elsewhere gives the reason. "Every pious reason and mode of ecclesiastical discipline ought always to have regard to the unity of the Spirit in the bond of peace. This the apostle commands us to keep by bearing mutually with each other. If it is not kept, the medicine of discipline begins to be not only superfluous, but even pernicious, and therefore ceases to be medicine" (Ibid. Lib. iii. c. 1). "He who diligently considers these things, neither in the preservation of unity neglects strictness of discipline, nor by intemperate correction bursts the bond of society" (Ibid. cap. 2). He confesses, indeed, that pastors ought not only to exert themselves in removing every defect from the Church, but that every individual ought to his utmost to do so; nor does he disguise the fact, that he who neglects to admonish, accuse, and correct the bad, although he neither favours them, nor sins with them, is guilty before the Lord; and if he conducts himself so that though he can exclude them from partaking of the Supper, he does it not, then the sin is no longer that of other men, but his own. Only he would have that prudence used which our Lord also requires, "lest while ye gather up the tares, ye root up also the wheat with them" (Matth. xiii. 29). Hence he infers from Cyprian, "Let a man then mercifully correct what he can; what he cannot correct, let him bear patiently, and in love bewail and lament."

12. This he says on account of the moroseness of the Donatists, who, when they saw faults in the Church which the bishops indeed rebuked verbally, but did not punish with excommunication (because they did not think that anything would be gained in this way), bitterly inveighed against the bishops as traitors to discipline, and by an impious schism separated themselves from the flock of Christ. Similar, in the present day, is the conduct of the Anabaptists, who, acknowledging no assembly of Christ unless conspicuous in all respects for angelic perfection, under pretence of zeal overthrow everything which tends to edification.[1] "Such (says Augustin. contra Parmen. Lib. iii. c. 4), not from hatred of other men's iniquity, but zeal for their own disputes, ensnaring the weak by the credit of their name, attempt to draw them entirely away, or at least to separate them;

1 See a lengthened refutation in Calv. Instructio adv. Anabap. Art. 2. See also Calv. de Cœna Domini.

swollen with pride, raving with petulance, insidious in calumny, turbulent in sedition. That it may not be seen how void they are of the light of truth, they cover themselves with the shadow of a stern severity: the correction of a brother's fault, which in Scripture is enjoined to be done with moderation, without impairing the sincerity of love or breaking the bond of peace, they pervert to sacrilegious schism and purposes of excision. Thus Satan transforms himself into an angel of light (2 Cor. xi. 14) when, under pretext of a just severity, he persuades to savage cruelty, desiring nothing more than to violate and burst the bond of unity and peace; because, when it is maintained, all his power of mischief is feeble. his wily traps are broken, and his schemes of subversion vanish."

13. One thing Augustine specially commends—viz. that if the contagion of sin has seized the multitude, mercy must accompany living discipline. "For counsels of separation are vain, sacrilegious, and pernicious, because impious and proud, and do more to disturb the weak good than to correct the wicked proud" (August. Ep. 64). This which he enjoins on others he himself faithfully practised. For, writing to Aurelius, Bishop of Carthage, he complains that drunkenness, which is so severely condemned in Scripture, prevails in Africa with impunity, and advises a council of bishops to be called for the purpose of providing a remedy. He immediately adds, "In my opinion, such things are not removed by rough, harsh, and imperious measures, but more by teaching than commanding, more by admonishing than threatening. For thus ought we to act with a multitude of offenders. Severity is to be exercised against the sins of a few" (August. Ep. 64). He does not mean, however, that the bishops were to wink or be silent because they are unable to punish public offences severely, as he himself afterwards explains. But he wishes to temper the mode of correction, so as to give soundness to the body rather than cause destruction. And, accordingly, he thus concludes: "Wherefore, we must on no account neglect the injunction of the apostle, to separate from the wicked, when it can be done without the risk of violating peace, because he did not wish it to be done otherwise (1 Cor. v. 13); we must also endeavour, by bearing with each other, to keep the unity of the Spirit in the bond of peace" (Eph. iv. 2).

14. The remaining part of discipline, which is not, strictly speaking, included in the power of the keys, is when pastors, according to the necessity of the times, exhort the people either to fasting and solemn prayer, or to other exercises of humiliation, repentance, and faith, the time, mode, and form of these not being prescribed by the Word of God, but left to the judgment of the Church. As the observance of this part of discipline is useful, so it was always used in the Church, even from the days of the apostles. Indeed, the apostles themselves were not its first authors, but borrowed the example from the Law and Prophets. For we there see,[1] that as often as any

[1] See a striking instance in Ezra viii. 21, on the appointment of a fast at the river Ahava, on the return of the people from the Babylonish captivity.

weighty matter occurred the people were assembled, and supplication and fasting appointed. In this, therefore, the apostles followed a course which was not new to the people of God, and which they foresaw would be useful. A similar account is to be given of the other exercises by which the people may either be aroused to duty, or kept in duty and obedience. We everywhere meet with examples in Sacred History, and it is unnecessary to collect them. In general, we must hold that whenever any religious controversy arises, which either a council or ecclesiastical tribunal behoves to decide;[1] whenever a minister is to be chosen; whenever, in short, any matter of difficulty and great importance is under consideration: on the other hand, when manifestations of the divine anger appear, as pestilence, war, and famine, the sacred and salutary custom of all ages has been for pastors to exhort the people to public fasting and extraordinary prayer. Should any one refuse to admit the passages which are adduced from the Old Testament, as being less applicable to the Christian Church, it is clear that the apostles also acted thus; although, in regard to prayer, I scarcely think any one will be found to stir the question. Let us, therefore, make some observations on fasting, since very many, not understanding what utility there can be in it, judge it not to be very necessary, while others reject it altogether as superfluous. Where its use is not well known it is easy to fall into superstition.

15. A holy and lawful fast has three ends in view. We use it either to mortify and subdue the flesh, that it may not wanton, or to prepare the better for prayer and holy meditation; or to give evidence of humbling ourselves before God, when we would confess our guilt before him. The first end is not very often regarded in public fasting, because all have not the same bodily constitution, nor the same state of health, and hence it is more applicable to private fasting. The second end is common to both, for this preparation for prayer is requisite for the whole Church, as well as for each individual member. The same thing may be said of the third. For it sometimes happens that God smites a nation with war or pestilence, or some kind of calamity. In this common chastisement it behoves the whole people to plead guilty, and confess their guilt. Should the hand of the Lord strike any one in private, then the same thing is to be done by himself alone, or by his family. The thing, indeed, is properly a feeling of the mind. But when the mind is effected as it ought, it cannot but give vent to itself in external manifestation, especially when it tends to the common edification, that all, by openly confessing their sin, may render praise to the divine justice, and by their example mutually encourage each other.

16. Hence fasting, as it is a sign of humiliation, has a more frequent use in public than among private individuals, although as we

1 French, "Quand il advient quelque different en Chretienté, qui tire grande consequence."—When some difference on a matter of great consequence takes place in Christendom.

have said, it is common to both. In regard, then, to the discipline of which we now treat, whenever supplication is to be made to God on any important occasion, it is befitting to appoint a period for fasting and prayer. Thus when the Christians of Antioch laid hands on Barnabas and Paul, that they might the better recommend their ministry, which was of so great importance, they joined fasting and prayer (Acts xiii. 3). Thus these two apostles afterwards, when they appointed ministers to churches, were wont to use prayer and fasting (Acts xiv. 23). In general, the only object which they had in fasting was to render themselves more alert and disencumbered for prayer. We certainly experience that after a full meal the mind does not so rise toward God as to be borne along by an earnest and fervent longing for prayer, and perseverance in prayer. In this sense is to be understood the saying of Luke concerning Anna, that she "served God with fastings and prayers, night and day" (Luke ii. 37). For he does not place the worship of God in fasting, but intimates that in this way the holy woman trained herself to assiduity in prayer. Such was the fast of Nehemiah, when with more intense zeal he prayed to God for the deliverance of his people (Neh. i. 4). For this reason Paul says, that married believers do well to abstain for a season (1 Cor. vii. 5), that they may have greater freedom for prayer and fasting, when by joining prayer to fasting, by way of help, he reminds us it is of no importance in itself, save in so far as it refers to this end. Again, when in the same place he enjoins spouses to render due benevolence to each other, it is clear that he is not referring to daily prayer, but prayers which require more than ordinary attention.

17. On the other hand, when pestilence begins to stalk abroad, or famine or war, or when any other disaster seems to impend over a province and people (Esther iv. 16), then also it is the duty of pastors to exhort the Church to fasting, that she may suppliantly deprecate the Lord's anger. For when he makes danger appear, he declares that he is prepared and in a manner armed for vengeance. In like manner, therefore, as persons accused were anciently wont, in order to excite the commiseration of the judge, to humble themselves suppliantly with long beard, dishevelled hair, and coarse garments, so when we are charged before the divine tribunal, to deprecate his severity in humble raiment is equally for his glory and the public edification, and useful and salutary to ourselves. And that this was common among the Israelites we may infer from the words of Joel. For when he says, "Blow the trumpet in Zion, sanctify a fast, call a solemn assembly," &c. (Joel ii. 15), he speaks as of things received by common custom. A little before he had said that the people were to be tried for their wickedness, and that the day of judgment was at hand, and he had summoned them as criminals to plead their cause: then he exclaims that they should hasten to sackcloth and ashes, to weeping and fasting; that is, humble themselves before God with external manifestations. The sackcloth and ashes, indeed, were per-

haps more suitable for those times, but the assembly, and weeping and fasting, and the like, undoubtedly belong, in an equal degree, to our age, whenever the condition of our affairs so requires. For seeing it is a holy exercise both for men to humble themselves, and confess their humility, why should we in similar necessity use this less than did those of old? We read not only that the Israelitish Church, formed and constituted by the word of God, fasted in token of sadness, but the Ninevites also, whose only teaching had been the preaching of Jonah.[1] Why, therefore, should not we do the same? But it is an external ceremony, which, like other ceremonies, terminated in Christ. Nay, in the present day it is an admirable help to believers, as it always was, and a useful admonition to arouse them, lest by too great security and sloth they provoke the Lord more and more when they are chastened by his rod. Accordingly, when our Saviour excuses his apostles for not fasting, he does not say that fasting was abrogated, but reserves it for calamitous times, and conjoins it with mourning. "The days will come when the bridegroom shall be taken from them" (Matth. ix. 35; Luke v. 34).

18. But that there may be no error in the name, let us define what fasting is; for we do not understand by it simply a restrained and sparing use of food, but something else. The life of the pious should be tempered with frugality and sobriety, so as to exhibit, as much as may be, a kind of fasting during the whole course of life. But there is another temporary fast, when we retrench somewhat from our accustomed mode of living, either for one day or a certain period, and prescribe to ourselves a stricter and severer restraint in the use of that ordinary food. This consists in three things—viz. the time, the quality of food, and the sparing use of it. By the time I mean, that while fasting we are to perform those actions for the sake of which the fast is instituted. For example, when a man fasts because of solemn prayer, he should engage in it without having taken food. The quality consists in putting all luxury aside, and, being contented with common and meaner food, so as not to excite our palate by dainties. In regard to quantity, we must eat more lightly and sparingly, only for necessity and not for pleasure.

19. But the first thing always to be avoided is, the encroachment of superstition, as formerly happened, to the great injury of the Church. It would have been much better to have had no fasting at all, than have it carefully observed, but at the same time corrupted by false and pernicious opinions, into which the world is ever and anon falling, unless pastors obviate them by the greatest fidelity and prudence. The first thing is constantly to urge the injunction of Joel, "Rend your heart, and not your garments" (Joel ii. 13); that is, to remind the people that fasting in itself is not of great value in the sight of God, unless accompanied with internal affection of the heart, true dissatisfaction with sin and with one's self, true humiliation, and true grief, from the fear of God; nay, that fasting is use-

[1] 1 Sam. vii. 6; xxxi. 13; 2 Kings i. 12; Jonah iii. 5.

ful for no other reason than because it is added to these as an inferior help. There is nothing which God more abominates than when men endeavour to cloak themselves by substituting signs and external appearance for integrity of heart. Accordingly, Isaiah inveighs most bitterly against the hypocrisy of the Jews, in thinking that they had satisfied God when they had merely fasted, whatever might be the impiety and impure thoughts which they cherished in their hearts. "Is it such a fast that I have chosen?" (Isa. lviii. 5.) See also what follows. The fast of hypocrites is, therefore, not only useless and superfluous fatigue, but the greatest abomination. Another evil akin to this, and greatly to be avoided, is, to regard fasting as a meritorious work and species of divine worship. For seeing it is a thing which is in itself indifferent, and has no importance except on account of those ends to which it ought to have respect, it is a most pernicious superstition to confound it with the works enjoined by God, and which are necessary in themselves without reference to anything else. Such was anciently the dream of the Manichees, in refuting whom Augustine clearly shows,[1] that fasting is to be estimated entirely by those ends which I have mentioned, and cannot be approved by God, unless in so far as it refers to them. Another error, not indeed so impious, but perilous, is to exact it with greater strictness and severity as one of the principal duties, and extol it with such extravagant encomiums as to make men imagine that they have done something admirable when they have fasted. In this respect I dare not entirely excuse ancient writers[2] from having sown some seeds of superstition, and given occasion to the tyranny which afterwards arose. We sometimes meet with sound and prudent sentiments on fasting, but we also ever and anon meet with extravagant praises, lauding it as one of the cardinal virtues.

20. Then the superstitious observance of Lent had everywhere prevailed: for both the vulgar imagined that they thereby perform some excellent service to God, and pastors commended it as a holy imitation of Christ; though it is plain that Christ did not fast to set an example to others, but, by thus commencing the preaching of the gospel, meant to prove that his doctrine was not of men, but had come from heaven. And it is strange how men of acute judgment could fall into this gross delusion, which so many clear reasons refute: for Christ did not fast repeatedly (which he must have done had he meant to lay down a law for an anniversary fast), but once only, when preparing for the promulgation of the gospel. Nor does he fast after the manner of men, as he would have done had he meant to invite men to imitation; he rather gives an example, by which he may raise all to admire rather than study to imitate him. In short, the nature of his fast is not different from that which Moses observed

1 August. de Morib. Manich. Lib. ii. c. 13; et cont. Faustum, Lib. xxx.

2 See Chrysostom. Homil. sub. initium Quadragesimæ, where he terms fasting a cure of souls and ablution for sins.

when he received the law at the hand of the Lord (Exod. xxiv. 18; xxxiv. 28). For, seeing that that miracle was performed in Moses to establish the law, it behoved not to be omitted in Christ, lest the gospel should seem inferior to the law. But from that day, it never occurred to any one, under pretence of imitating Moses, to set up a similar form of fast among the Israelites. Nor did any of the holy prophets and fathers follow it, though they had inclination and zeal enough for all pious exercises; for though it is said of Elijah that he passed forty days without meat and drink (1 Kings xix. 8), this was merely in order that the people might recognise that he was raised up to maintain the law, from which almost the whole of Israel had revolted. It was therefore merely false zeal, replete with superstition, which set up a fast under the title and pretext of imitating Christ; although there was then a strange diversity in the mode of the fast, as is related by Cassiodorus in the ninth book of the History of Socrates: "The Romans," says he, "had only three weeks, but their fast was continuous, except on the Lord's day and the Sabbath. The Greeks and Illyrians had, some six, others seven, but the fast was at intervals. Nor did they differ less in the kind of food: some used only bread and water, others added vegetables; others had no objection to fish and fowls; others made no difference in their food." Augustine also makes mention of this difference in his latter epistle to Januarius.

21. Worse times followed. To the absurd zeal of the vulgar were added rudeness and ignorance in the bishops, lust of power, and tyrannical rigour. Impious laws were passed, binding the conscience in deadly chains. The eating of flesh was forbidden, as if a man were contaminated by it. Sacrilegious opinions were added, one after another, until all became an abyss of error. And that no kind of depravity might be omitted, they began, under a most absurd pretence of abstinence, to make a mock of God;[1] for in the most exquisite delicacies they seek the praise of fasting: no dainties now suffice; never was there greater abundance or variety or savouriness of food. In this splendid display they think that they serve God. I do not mention that at no time do those who would be thought the holiest of them wallow more foully. In short, the highest worship of God is to abstain from flesh, and, with this reservation, to indulge in delicacies of every kind. On the other hand, it is the greatest impiety, impiety scarcely to be expiated by death, for any one to taste the smallest portion of bacon or rancid flesh with his bread. Jerome, writing to Nepotian, relates, that even in his day there were some who mocked God with such follies: those who would not even put oil in their food caused the greatest delicacies to be procured from every quarter; nay, that they might do violence to nature, abstained from drinking water, and caused sweet and costly

1 Bernard, in Serm. I. in die Paschæ, censures, among others, princes also, for longing, during the season of Lent, for the approaching festival of our Lord's resurrection, that they might indulge more freely.

potions to be made for them, which they drank, not out of a cup, but a shell. What was then the fault of a few is now common among all the rich: they do not fast for any other purpose than to feast more richly and luxuriously. But I am unwilling to waste many words on a subject as to which there can be no doubt. All I say is, that, as well in fasts as in all other parts of discipline, the Papists are so far from having anything right, anything sincere, anything duly framed and ordered, that they have no occasion to plume themselves as if anything was left them that is worthy of praise.

22. We come now to the second part of discipline, which relates specially to the clergy. It is contained in the canons, which the ancient bishops framed for themselves and their order: for instance, let no clergyman spend his time in hunting, in gaming, or in feasting; let none engage in usury or in trade; let none be present at lascivious dances, and the like. Penalties also were added to give a sanction to the authority of the canons, that none might violate them with impunity. With this view, each bishop was intrusted with the superintendence of his own clergy, that he might govern them according to the canons, and keep them to their duty. For this purpose, certain annual visitations and synods were appointed, that if any one was negligent in his office he might be admonished; if any one sinned, he might be punished according to his fault. The bishops also had their provincial synods once, anciently twice, a-year, by which they were tried, if they had done anything contrary to their duty. For if any bishop had been too harsh or violent with his clergy, there was an appeal to the synod, though only one individual complained. The severest punishment was deposition from office, and exclusion, for a time, from communion. But as this was the uniform arrangement, no synod rose without fixing the time and place of the next meeting. To call a universal council belonged to the emperor alone, as all the ancient summonings testify. As long as this strictness was in force, the clergy demanded no more in word from the people than they performed in act and by example; nay, they were more strict against themselves than the vulgar; and, indeed, it is becoming that the people should be ruled by a kindlier, and, if I may so speak, laxer discipline; that the clergy should be stricter in their censures, and less indulgent to themselves than to others. How this whole procedure became obsolete it is needless to relate, since, in the present day, nothing can be imagined more lawless and dissolute than this order, whose licentiousness is so extreme that the whole world is crying out. I admit that, in order not to seem to have lost all sight of antiquity, they, by certain shadows, deceive the eyes of the simple; but these no more resemble ancient customs than the mimicry of an ape resembles what men do by reason and counsel. There is a memorable passage in Xenophon, in which he mentions, that when the Persians had shamefully degenerated from the customs of their ancestors, and had fallen away from an austere mode of life to luxury and effeminacy, they still, to hide the disgrace,

were sedulously observant of ancient rites (Cyrop. Lib. viii.). For while, in the time of Cyrus, sobriety and temperance so flourished that no Persian required to wipe his nose, and it was even deemed disgraceful to do so, it remained with their posterity, as a point of religion, not to remove the mucus from the nostril, though they were allowed to nourish within, even to putridity, those fetid humours which they had contracted by gluttony. In like manner, according to the ancient custom, it was unlawful to use cups at table; but it was quite tolerable to swallow wine so as to make it necessary to be carried off drunk. It was enjoined to use only one meal a-day: this these good successors did not abrograte, but they continued their surfeit from mid-day to midnight. To finish the day's march, fasting, as the law enjoined it, was the uniform custom; but in order to avoid lassitude, the allowed and usual custom was to limit the march to two hours. As often as the degenerate Papists obtrude their rules that they may show their resemblance to the holy fathers, this example will serve to expose their ridiculous imitation. Indeed, no painter could paint them more to the life.

23. In one thing they are more than rigid and inexorable—in not permitting priests to marry. It is of no consequence to mention with what impunity whoredom prevails among them, and how, trusting to their vile celibacy, they have become callous to all kinds of iniquity. The prohibition, however, clearly shows how pestiferous all traditions are, since this one has not only deprived the Church of fit and honest pastors, but has introduced a fearful sink of iniquity, and plunged many souls into the gulf of despair. Certainly, when marriage was interdicted to priests, it was done with impious tyranny, not only contrary to the word of God, but contrary to all justice. First, men had no title whatever to forbid what God had left free; secondly, it is too clear to make it necessary to give any lengthened proof that God has expressly provided in his Word that this liberty shall not be infringed. I omit Paul's injunction, in numerous passages, that a bishop be the husband of one wife; but what could be stronger than his declaration, that in the latter days there would be impious men "forbidding to marry"? (1 Tim. iv. 3.) Such persons he calls not only impostors, but devils. We have therefore a prophecy, a sacred oracle of the Holy Spirit, intended to warn the Church from the outset against perils, and declaring that the prohibition of marriage is a doctrine of devils. They think that they get finely off when they wrest this passage, and apply it to Montanus, the Tatians, the Encratites, and other ancient heretics. These (they say) alone condemned marriage; we by no means condemn it, but only deny it to the ecclesiastical order, in whom we think it not befitting. As if, even granting that this prophecy was primarily fulfilled in those heretics, it is not applicable also to themselves; or, as if one could listen to the childish quibble that they do not forbid marriage, because they do not forbid it to all. This is just as if a tyrant were to

contend that a law is not unjust because its injustice presses only on a part of the state.

24. They object that there ought to be some distinguishing mark between the clergy and the people; as if the Lord had not provided the ornaments in which priests ought to excel. Thus they charge the apostle with having disturbed the ecclesiastical order, and destroyed its ornament, when, in drawing the picture of a perfect bishop, he presumed to set down marriage among the other endowments which he required of them. I am aware of the mode in which they expound this—viz. that no one was to be appointed a bishop who had a second wife. This interpretation, I admit, is not new; but its unsoundness is plain from the immediate context, which prescribes the kind of wives whom bishops and deacons ought to have. Paul enumerates marriage among the qualities of a bishop; those men declare that, in the ecclesiastical order, marriage is an intolerable vice; and, indeed, not content with this general vituperation, they term it, in their canons, the uncleanness and pollution of the flesh (Siric. ad Episc. Hispaniar.). Let every one consider with himself from what forge these things have come. Christ deigns so to honour marriage as to make it an image of his sacred union with the Church. What greater eulogy could be pronounced on the dignity of marriage? How, then, dare they have the effrontery to give the name of unclean and polluted to that which furnishes a bright representation of the spiritual grace of Christ?

25. Though their prohibition is thus clearly repugnant to the word of God, they, however, find something in the Scriptures to defend it. The Levitical priests, as often as their ministerial course returned, behoved to keep apart from their wives, that they might be pure and immaculate in handling sacred things; and it were therefore very indecorous that our sacred things, which are more noble, and are ministered every day, should be handled by those who are married: as if the evangelical ministry were of the same character as the Levitical priesthood. These, as types, represented Christ, who, as Mediator between God and men, was, by his own spotless purity, to reconcile us to the Father. But as sinners could not in every respect exhibit a type of his holiness, that they might, however, shadow it forth by certain lineaments, they were enjoined to purify themselves beyond the manner of men when they approached the sanctuary, inasmuch as they then properly prefigured Christ appearing in the tabernacle, an image of the heavenly tribunal, as pacificators, to reconcile men to God. As ecclesiastical pastors do not sustain this character in the present day, the comparison is made in vain. Wherefore the apostle declares distinctly, without reservation, "Marriage is honourable in all, and the bed undefiled; but whoremongers and adulterers God will judge" (Heb. xiii. 4). And the apostles showed, by their own example, that marriage is not unbefitting the holiness of any function, however excellent; for Paul de-

clares, that they not only retained their wives, but led them about with them (1 Cor. ix. 5).

26. Then how great the effrontery when, in holding forth this ornament of chastity as a matter of necessity, they throw the greatest obloquy on the primitive Church, which, while it abounded in admirable divine erudition, excelled more in holiness. For if they pay no regard to the apostles (they are sometimes wont strenuously to contemn them), what, I ask, will they make of all the ancient fathers, who, it is certain, not only tolerated marriage in the episcopal order, but also approved it? They, forsooth, encouraged a foul profanation of sacred things when the mysteries of the Lord were thus irregularly performed by them. In the Council of Nice, indeed, there was some question of proclaiming celibacy: as there are never wanting little men of superstitious minds, who are always devising some novelty as a means of gaining admiration for themselves. What was resolved? The opinion of Paphnutius was adopted, who pronounced legitimate conjugal intercourse to be chastity (Hist. Trip. Lib. ii. c. 14). The marriage of priests, therefore, continued sacred, and was neither regarded as a disgrace, nor thought to cast any stain on their ministry.

27. In the times which succeeded, a too superstitious admiration of celibacy prevailed. Hence, ever and anon, unmeasured encomiums were pronounced on virginity, so that it became the vulgar belief that scarcely any virtue was to be compared to it. And although marriage was not condemned as impurity, yet its dignity was lessened, and its sanctity obscured; so that he who did not refrain from it was deemed not to have a mind strong enough to aspire to perfection. Hence those canons which enacted, first, that those who had attained the priesthood should not contract marriage; and, secondly, that none should be admitted to that order but the unmarried, or those who, with the consent of their wives, renounced the marriage-bed. These enactments, as they seemed to procure reverence for the priesthood, were, I admit, received even in ancient times with great applause. But if my opponents plead antiquity, my first answer is, that both under the apostles, and for several ages after, bishops were at liberty to have wives: that the apostles themselves, and other pastors of primitive authority who succeeded them, had no difficulty in using this liberty, and that the example of the primitive Church ought justly to have more weight than allow us to think that what was then received and used with commendation is either illicit or unbecoming. My second answer is, that the age, which, from an immoderate affection for virginity, began to be less favourable to marriage, did not bind a law of celibacy on the priests, as if the thing were necessary in itself, but gave a preference to the unmarried over the married. My last answer is, that they did not exact this so rigidly as to make continence necessary and compulsory on those who were unfit for it. For while the strictest laws were made against

fornication, it was only enacted with regard to those who contracted marriage that they should be superseded in their office.

28. Therefore, as often as the defenders of this new tyranny appeal to antiquity in defence of their celibacy, so often should we call upon them to restore the ancient chastity of their priests, to put away adulterers and whoremongers, not to allow those whom they deny an honourable and chaste use of marriage, to rush with impunity into every kind of lust, to bring back that obsolete discipline by which all licentiousness is restrained, and free the Church from the flagitious turpitude by which it has long been deformed. When they have conceded this, they will next require to be reminded not to represent as necessary that which, being in itself free, depends on the utility of the Church. I do not, however, speak thus as if I thought that on any condition whatever effect should be given to those canons which lay a bond of celibacy on the ecclesiastical order, but that the better-hearted may understand the effrontery of our enemies in employing the name of antiquity to defame the holy marriage of priests. In regard to the Fathers, whose writings are extant, none of them, when they spoke their own mind, with the exception of Jerome, thus malignantly detracted from the honour of marriage. We will be contented with a single passage from Chrysostom, because he being a special admirer of virginity, cannot be thought to be more lavish than others in praise of matrimony. Chrysostom thus speaks: "The first degree of chastity is pure virginity; the second, faithful marriage. Therefore, a chaste love of matrimony is the second species of virginity" (Chrysost. Hom. de Invent. Crucis.).

CHAPTER XIII.

OF VOWS. THE MISERABLE ENTANGLEMENTS CAUSED BY VOWING RASHLY.

This chapter consists of two parts,—I. Of vows in general, sec. 1–8. II. Of monastic vows, and specially of the vow of celibacy, sec. 8–21.

Sections.

1. Some general principles with regard to the nature of vows. Superstitious errors not only of the heathen, but of Christians, in regard to vows.
2. Three points to be considered with regard to vows. First, to whom the vow is made—viz. to God. Nothing to be vowed to him but what he himself requires.
3. Second, Who we are that vow. We must measure our strength, and have regard to our calling. Fearful errors of the Popish clergy by not attending to this. Their vow of celibacy.
4. Third point to be attended to—viz. the intention with which the vow is made. Four ends in vowing. Two of them refer to the past, and two to the future. Examples and use of the former class.
5. End of vows which refer to the future.
6. The doctrine of vows in general. Common vow of Christians in Baptism, &c. This vow sacred and salutary. Particular vows how to be tested.
7. Great prevalence of superstition with regard to vows.
8. Vows of monks. Contrast between ancient and modern monasticism.
9. Portraiture of the ancient monks by Augustine.
10. Degeneracy of modern monks. 1. Inconsiderate rigour. 2. Idleness. 3. False boast of perfection.
11. This idea of monastic perfection refuted.
12. Arguments for monastic perfection. First argument answered.
13. Second argument answered.
14. Absurdity of representing the monastic profession as a second baptism.
15. Corrupt manners of monks.
16. Some defects in ancient monasticism.
17. General refutation of monastic vows.
18. Refutation continued.
19. Refutation continued.
20. Do such vows of celibacy bind the conscience? This question answered.
21. Those who abandon the monastic profession for an honest living, unjustly accused of breaking their faith.

1. It is indeed deplorable that the Church, whose freedom was purchased by the inestimable price of Christ's blood, should have been thus oppressed by a cruel tyranny, and almost buried under a huge mass of traditions; but, at the same time, the private infatuation of each individual shows, that not without just cause has so much power been given from above to Satan and his ministers. It was not enough to neglect the command of Christ, and bear any burdens which false teachers might please to impose, but each individual behoved to have his own peculiar burdens, and thus sink deeper by digging his own cavern. This has been the result when men set about devising vows, by which a stronger and closer obliga-

tion might be added to common ties. Having already shown that the worship of God was vitiated by the audacity of those who, under the name of pastors, domineered in the Church, when they ensnared miserable souls by their iniquitous laws, it will not be out of place here to advert to a kindred evil, to make it appear that the world, in accordance with its depraved disposition, has always thrown every possible obstacle in the way of the helps by which it ought to have been brought to God. Moreover, that the very grievous mischief introduced by such vows may be more apparent, let the reader attend to the principles formerly laid down. First, we showed (Book II. chap. viii. sec. 5) that everything requisite for the ordering of a pious and holy life is comprehended in the law. Secondly, we showed that the Lord, the better to dissuade us from devising new works, included the whole of righteousness in simple obedience to his will. If these positions are true, it is easy to see that all fictitious worship, which we ourselves devise for the purpose of serving God, is not in the least degree acceptable to him, how pleasing soever it may be to us. And, unquestionably, in many passages the Lord not only openly rejects, but grievously abhors such worship. Hence arises a doubt with regard to vows which are made without any express authority from the word of God; in what light are they to be viewed? can they be duly made by Christian men, and to what extent are they binding? What is called a promise among men is a vow when made to God. Now, we promise to men either things which we think will be acceptable to them, or things which we in duty owe them. Much more careful, therefore, ought we to be in vows which are directed to God, with whom we ought to act with the greatest seriousness. Here superstition has in all ages strangely prevailed; men at once, without judgment and without choice, vowing to God whatever came into their minds, or even rose to their lips. Hence the foolish vows, nay, monstrous absurdities, by which the heathen insolently sported with their gods. Would that Christians had not imitated them in this their audacity! Nothing, indeed, could be less becoming; but it is obvious that for some ages nothing has been more usual than this misconduct—the whole body of the people everywhere despising the Law of God,[1] and burning with an insane zeal of vowing according to any dreaming notion which they had formed. I have no wish to exaggerate invidiously, or particularise the many grievous sins which have here been committed; but it seemed right to advert to it in passing, that it may the better appear, that when we treat of vows we are not by any means discussing a superfluous question.

2. If we would avoid error in deciding what vows are legitimate, and what preposterous, three things must be attended to—viz. who

1 See Ps. cxix. 106. "I have sworn, and I will perform it, that I will keep thy righteous judgments." Calvin observes on these words, that the vow and oath to keep the law cannot be charged with rashness, because it trusted to the promises of God concerning the forgiveness of sins, and to the spirit of regeneration.

he is to whom the vow is made; who we are that make it; and, lastly, with what intention we make it. In regard in the first, we should consider that we have to do with God, whom our obedience so delights, that he abominates all will-worship, how specious and splendid soever it be in the eyes of men (Col. ii. 23). If all will-worship, which we devise without authority, is abomination to God, it follows that no worship can be acceptable to him save that which is approved by his word. Therefore, we must not arrogate such licence to ourselves as to presume to vow anything to God without evidence of the estimation in which he holds it. For the doctrine of Paul, that whatsoever is not of faith is sin (Rom. xiv. 23), while it extends to all actions of every kind, certainly applies with peculiar force in the case where the thought is immediately turned towards God. Nay, if in the minutest matters (Paul was then speaking of the distinction of meats) we err or fall, where the sure light of faith shines not before us, how much more modesty ought we to use when we attempt a matter of the greatest weight? For in nothing ought we to be more serious than in the duties of religion. In vows, then, our first precaution must be, never to proceed to make any vow without having previously determined in our conscience to attempt nothing rashly. And we shall be safe from the danger of rashness when we have God going before, and, as it were, dictating from his word what is good, and what is useless.

3. In the second point which we have mentioned as requiring consideration is implied, that we measure our strength, that we attend to our vocation so as not to neglect the blessing of liberty which God has conferred upon us. For he who vows what is not within his means, or is at variance with his calling, is rash, while he who contemns the beneficence of God in making him lord of all things, is ungrateful. When I speak thus, I mean not that anything is so placed in our hand, that, leaning on our own strength, we may promise it to God. For in the Council of Arausica (cap. 11) it was most truly decreed, that nothing is duly vowed to God save what we have received from his hand, since all things which are offered to him are merely his gifts. But seeing that some things are given to us by the goodness of God, and others withheld by his justice, every man should have respect to the measure of grace bestowed on him, as Paul enjoins (Rom. xii. 3; 1 Cor. xii. 11). All then I mean here is, that your vows should be adapted to the measure which God by his gifts prescribes to you, lest by attempting more than he permits, you arrogate too much to yourself, and fall headlong. For example, when the assassins, of whom mention is made in the Acts, vowed "that they would neither eat nor drink till they had killed Paul" (Acts xxiii. 12), though it had not been an impious conspiracy, it would still have been intolerably presumptuous, as subjecting the life and death of a man to their own power. Thus Jephthah suffered for his folly, when with precipitate fervour he made a rash vow (Judges xi. 30). Of this class, the first place of

insane audacity belongs to celibacy. Priests, monks, and nuns, forgetful of their infirmity, are confident of their fitness for celibacy.[1] But by what oracle have they been instructed, that the chastity which they vow to the end of life, they will be able through life to maintain? They hear the voice of God concerning the universal condition of mankind, "It is not good that the man should be alone" (Gen. ii. 18). They understand, and I wish they did not feel that the sin remaining in us is armed with the sharpest stings. How can they presume to shake off the common feelings of their nature for a whole lifetime, seeing the gift of continence is often granted for a certain time as occasion requires? In such perverse conduct they must not expect God to be their helper; let them rather remember the words, "Ye shall not tempt the Lord your God" (Deut. vi. 16). But it is to tempt the Lord to strive against the nature implanted by him, and to spurn his present gifts as if they did not appertain to us. This they not only do, but marriage, which God did not think it unbecoming his majesty to institute, which he pronounced honourable in all, which Christ our Lord sanctified by his presence, and which he deigned to honour with his first miracle, they presume to stigmatise as pollution, so extravagant are the terms in which they eulogise every kind of celibacy; as if in their own life they did not furnish a clear proof that celibacy is one thing and chastity another. This life, however, they most impudently style angelical, thereby offering no slight insult to the angels of God, to whom they compare whoremongers and adulterers, and something much worse and fouler still.[2] And, indeed, there is here very little occasion for argument, since they are abundantly refuted by fact. For we plainly see the fearful punishments with which the Lord avenges this arrogance and contempt of his gifts from overweening confidence. More hidden crimes I spare through shame; what is known of them is too much. Beyond all controversy, we ought not to vow anything which will hinder us in fulfilling our vocation; as if the father of a family were to vow to leave his wife and children, and undertake other burdens; or one who is fit for a public office should, when elected to it, vow to live private. But the meaning of what we have said as to not despising our liberty may occasion some difficulty if not explained. Wherefore, understand it briefly thus: Since God has given us dominion over all things, and so subjected them to us that we may use them for our convenience, we cannot hope that our service will be acceptable to God if we bring ourselves into bondage to external things, which ought to be subservient to us. I say this, because

1 On the vow of celibacy, see Calv. de Fugiend. Micit. sacris, Adv. Theolog. Paris. De Necessit. Reform. Eccl.; Præfat. Antidoti ad Concil. Trident.; Vera Eccles. Reform. Ratio; De Scandalis.

2 Bernard, de Convers. ad Clericos, cap. 29, inveighing against the crimes of the clergy, says, "Would that those who cannot contain would fear to take the vow of celibacy! For it is a weighty saying, that all cannot receive it. Many are either unable to conceal from the multitude, or seek not to do it. They abstain from the remedy of marriage, and thereafter give themselves up to all wickedness.

some aspire to the praise of humility, for entangling themselves in a variety of observances from which God for good reason wished us to be entirely free. Hence, if we would escape this danger, let us always remember that we are by no means to withdraw from the economy which God has appointed in the Christian Church.

4. I come now to my third position—viz. that if you would approve your vow to God, the mind in which you undertake it is of great moment. For seeing that God looks not to the outward appearance but to the heart, the consequence is, that according to the purpose which the mind has in view, the same thing may at one time please and be acceptable to him, and at another be most displeasing. If you vow abstinence from wine, as if there were any holiness in so doing, you are superstitious; but if you have some end in view which is not perverse, no one can disapprove. Now, as far as I can see, there are four ends to which our vows may be properly directed; two of these, for the sake of order, I refer to the past, and two to the future. To the past belong vows by which we either testify our gratitude toward God for favours received, or in order to deprecate his wrath, inflict punishment on ourselves for faults committed. The former, let us if you please call acts of thanksgiving; the latter, acts of repentance. Of the former class, we have an example in the tithes which Jacob vowed (Gen. xxviii. 20), if the Lord would conduct him safely home from exile; and also in the ancient peace-offerings which pious kings and commanders, when about to engage in a just war, vowed that they would give if they were victorious, or, at least, if the Lord would deliver them when pressed by some greater difficulty. Thus are to be understood all the passages in the Psalms which speak of vows (Ps. xxii. 26; lvi. 13; cxvi. 14, 18). Similar vows may also be used by us in the present day, whenever the Lord has rescued us from some disaster or dangerous disease, or other peril. For it is not abhorrent from the office of a pious man thus to consecrate a votive offering to God as a formal symbol of acknowledgment that he may not seem ungrateful for his kindness. The nature of the second class it will be sufficient to illustrate merely by one familiar example. Should any one, from gluttonous indulgence, have fallen into some iniquity, there is nothing to prevent him, with the view of chastising his intemperance, from renouncing all luxuries for a certain time, and in doing so, from employing a vow for the purpose of binding himself more firmly. And yet I do not lay down this as an invariable law to all who have similarly offended; I merely show what may be lawfully done by those who think that such a vow will be useful to them. Thus while I hold it lawful so to vow, I at the same time leave it free.

5. The vows which have reference to the future tend partly, as we have said, to render us more cautious, and partly to act as a kind of stimulus to the discharge of duty. A man sees that he is so prone to a certain vice, that in a thing which is otherwise not bad he cannot restrain himself from forthwith falling into evil: he will

not act absurdly in cutting off the use of that thing for some time by a vow. If, for instance, one should perceive that this or that bodily ornament brings him into peril, and yet allured by cupidity he eagerly longs for it, what can he do better than by throwing a curb upon himself, that is, imposing the necessity of abstinence, free himself from all doubt? In like manner, should one be oblivious or sluggish in the necessary duties of piety, why should he not, by forming a vow, both awaken his memory and shake off his sloth? In both, I confess, there is a kind of tutelage, but inasmuch as they are helps to infirmity, they are used not without advantage by the ignorant and imperfect. Hence we hold that vows which have respect to one of these ends, especially in external things, are lawful, provided they are supported by the approbation of God, are suitable to our calling, and are limited to the measure of grace bestowed upon us.

6. It is not now difficult to infer what view on the whole ought to be taken of vows. There is one vow common to all believers, which taken in baptism we confirm, and as it were sanction, by our Catechism,[1] and partaking of the Lord's Supper. For the sacraments are a kind of mutual contracts by which the Lord conveys his mercy to us, and by it eternal life, while we in our turn promise him obedience. The formula, or at least substance, of the vow is, That renouncing Satan we bind ourselves to the service of God, to obey his holy commands, and no longer follow the depraved desires of our flesh. It cannot be doubted that this vow, which is sanctioned by Scripture, nay, is exacted from all the children of God, is holy and salutary. There is nothing against this in the fact, that no man in this life yields that perfect obedience to the law which God requires of us. This stipulation being included in the covenant of grace, comprehending forgiveness of sins and the spirit of holiness, the promise which we there make is combined both with entreaty for pardon and petition for assistance. It is necessary, in judging of particular vows, to keep the three former rules in remembrance: from them any one will easily estimate the character of each single vow. Do not suppose, however, that I so commend the vows which I maintain to be holy that I would have them made every day. For though I dare not give any precept as to time or number, yet if any one will take my advice, he will not undertake any but what are sober and temporary. If you are ever and anon launching out into numerous vows, the whole solemnity will be lost by the frequency, and you will readily fall into superstition. If you bind yourself by a perpetual vow, you will have great trouble and annoyance in getting free, or, worn out by length of time, you will at length make bold to break it.

7. It is now easy to see under how much superstition the world has laboured in this respect for several ages. One vowed that he would be abstemious, as if abstinence from wine were in itself an acceptable service to God. Another bound himself to fast, another to

1 Latin, "Catechism."—French, "En faisant protestation de notre foy;"—in making profession of our faith.

abstain from flesh on certain days, which he had vainly imagined to be more holy than other days. Things much more boyish were vowed though not by boys. For it was accounted great wisdom to undertake votive pilgrimages to holy places, and sometimes to perform the journey on foot, or with the body half naked, that the greater merit might be acquired by the greater fatigue. These and similar things, for which the world has long bustled with incredible zeal, if tried by the rules which we formerly laid down, will be discovered to be not only empty and nugatory, but full of manifest impiety. Be the judgment of the flesh what it may, there is nothing which God more abhors than fictitious worship. To these are added pernicious and damnable notions, hypocrites, after performing such frivolities, thinking that they have acquired no ordinary righteousness, placing the substance of piety in external observances, and despising all others who appear less careful in regard to them.

8. It is of no use to enumerate all the separate forms. But as monastic vows are held in great veneration, because they seem to be approved by the public judgment of the Church, I will say a few words concerning them. And, first, lest any one defend the monachism of the present day on the ground of the long prescription, it is to be observed, that the ancient mode of living in monasteries was very different. The persons who retired to them were those who wished to train themselves to the greatest austerity and patience. The discipline practised by the monks then resembled that which the Lacedemonians are said to have used under the laws of Lycurgus, and was even much more rigorous. They slept on the ground, their drink was water, their food bread, herbs, and roots, their chief luxuries oil and pulse. From more delicate food and care of the body they abstained. These things might seem hyperbolical were they not vouched by experienced eye witnesses, as Gregory Nazianzen, Basil, and Chrysostom. By such rudimentary training they prepared themselves for greater offices. For of the fact that monastic colleges were then a kind of seminaries of the ecclesiastical order, both those whom we lately named are very competent witnesses (they were all brought up in monasteries, and thence called to the episcopal office), as well as several other great and excellent men of their age. Augustine also shows that in his time the monasteries were wont to furnish the Church with clergy. For he thus addresses the monks of the island of Caprae: "We exhort you, brethren in the Lord, to keep your purpose, and persevere to the end; and if at any time our mother Church requires your labour, you will neither undertake it with eager elation, nor reject it from the blandishment of sloth, but with meek hearts obey God. You will not prefer your own ease to the necessities of the Church. Had no good men been willing to minister to her when in travail, it would have been impossible for you to be born"[1] (August. Ep. 82). He is speak-

1 At the same place, he admirably says, "Dearly beloved, love ease, but with the

ing of the ministry by which believers are spiritually born again. In like manner, he says to Aurelius (Ep. 76), "It is both an occasion of lapse to them, and a most unbecoming injury to the clerical order, if the deserters of monasteries are elected to the clerical warfare, since from those who remain in the monastery our custom is to appoint to the clerical office only the better and more approved. Unless, perhaps, as the vulgar say, A bad chorister is a good symphonist, so, in like manner, it will be jestingly said of us, A bad monk is a good clergyman. There will be too much cause for grief if we stir up monks to such ruinous pride, and deem the clergy deserving of so grave an affront, seeing that sometimes a good monk scarcely makes a good clerk; he may have sufficient continence, but be deficient in necessary learning." From these passages, it appears that pious men were wont to prepare for the government of the Church by monastic discipline, that thus they might be more apt and better trained to undertake the important office: not that all attained to this object, or even aimed at it, since the great majority of monks were illiterate men. Those who were fit were selected.

9. Augustine, in two passages in particular, gives a portraiture of the form of ancient monasticism. The one is in his book, *De Moribus Ecclesiæ Catholicæ* (*On the Manners of the Catholic Church*), where he maintains the holiness of that profession against the calumnies of the Manichees; the other in a treatise, entitled, *De Opere Monachorum* (*On the Work of Monks*), where he inveighs against certain degenerate monks who had begun to corrupt that institution. I will here give a summary of what he there delivers, and, as far as I can, in his own words: "Despising the allurements of this world, and congregated in common for a most chaste and most holy life, they pass their lives together, spending their time in prayer, reading, and discourse, not swollen with pride, not turbulent through petulance, not livid with envy. No one possesses anything of his own: no one is burdensome to any man. They labour with their hands in things by which the body may be fed, and the mind not withdrawn from God. The fruit of their labour they hand over to those whom they call deans. Those deans, disposing of the whole with great care, render an account to one whom they call father. These fathers, who are not only of the purest morals, but most distinguished for divine learning, and noble in all things, without any pride, consult those whom they call their sons, though the former have full authority to command, and the latter a great inclination to obey. At the close of the day they assemble each from his cell, and without having broken their fast, to hear their father, and to the number of three thousand at least (he is speaking of Egypt and the East) they assemble under each father. Then the body is refreshed, so far as suffices for safety and health, every one curbing his concupiscence so as not to be profuse in the scanty and very mean diet which is pro-

view of restraining from all worldly delight, and remember that there is no place where he who dreads our return to God is not able to lay his snares."

vided. Thus they not only abstain from flesh and wine for the purpose of subduing lust, but from those things which provoke the appetite of the stomach and gullet more readily, from seeming to some, as it were, more refined. In this way the desire of exquisite dainties, in which there is no flesh, is wont to be absurdly and shamefully defended. Any surplus, after necessary food (and the surplus is very great from the labour of their hands and the frugality of their meals), is carefully distributed to the needy, the more carefully that it was not procured by those who distribute. For they never act with the view of having abundance for themselves, but always act with the view of allowing no superfluity to remain with them" (August. De Mor. Eccl. Cath. c. 31). Afterwards describing their austerity, of which he had himself seen instances both at Milan and elsewhere, he says, "Meanwhile, no one is urged to austerities which he is unable to bear: no one is obliged to do what he declines, nor condemned by the others, whom he acknowledges himself too weak to imitate. For they remember how greatly charity is commended: they remember that to the pure all things are pure (Tit. i. 15). Wherefore, all their vigilance is employed, not in rejecting kinds of food as polluted, but in subduing concupiscence, and maintaining brotherly love. They remember, 'Meats for the belly, and the belly for meats,' &c. (1 Cor. vi. 13). Many, however strong, abstain because of the weak. In many this is not the cause of action; they take pleasure in sustaining themselves on the meanest and least expensive food. Hence the very persons who in health restrain themselves, decline not in sickness to use what their health requires. Many do not drink wine, and yet do not think themselves polluted by it, for they most humanely cause it to be given to the more sickly, and to those whose health requires it; and some who foolishly refuse, they fraternally admonish, lest by vain superstition they sooner become more weak than more holy. Thus they sedulously practise piety, while they know that bodily exercise is only for a short time. Charity especially is observed: their food is adapted to charity, their speech to charity, their dress to charity, their looks to charity. They go together, and breathe only charity: they deem it as unlawful to offend charity as to offend God; if any one opposes it, he is cast out and shunned; if any one offends it, he is not permitted to remain one day" (August. De Moribus Eccl. Cath. c. 33). Since this holy man appears in these words to have exhibited the monastic life of ancient times as in a picture, I have thought it right to insert them here, though somewhat long, because I perceive that I would be considerably longer if I collected them from different writers, however compendious I might study to be.

10. Here, however, I had no intention to discuss the whole subject. I only wished to show, by the way, what kind of monks the early Church had, and what the monastic profession then was, that from the contrast sound readers might judge how great the effrontery is of those who allege antiquity in support of present monkism. Augus-

tine, while tracing out a holy and legitimate monasticism, would keep away all rigorous exaction of those things which the word of the Lord has left free. But in the present day nothing is more rigorously exacted. For they deem it an inexpiable crime if any one deviates in the least degree from the prescribed form in colour or species of dress, in the kind of food, or in other frivolous and frigid ceremonies. Augustine strenuously contends that it is not lawful for monks to live in idleness on other men's means. (August. De Oper. Monach.) He denies that any such example was to be found in his day in a well-regulated monastery. Our monks place the principal part of their holiness in idleness. For if you take away their idleness, where will that contemplative life by which they glory that they excel all others, and make a near approach to the angels? Augustine, in fine, requires a monasticism which may be nothing else than a training and assistant to the offices of piety which are recommended to all Christians. What? When he makes charity its chief and almost its only rule, do we think he praises that combination by which a few men, bound to each other, are separated from the whole body of the Church? Nay, he wishes them to set an example to others of preserving the unity of the Church. So different is the nature of present monachism in both respects, that it would be difficult to find anything so dissimilar, not to say contrary. For our monks, not satisfied with that piety, on the study of which alone Christ enjoins his followers to be intent, imagine some new kind of piety, by aspiring to which they are more perfect than all other men.

11. If they deny this, I should like to know why they honour their own order only with the title of perfection, and deny it to all other divine callings.[1] I am not unaware of the sophistical solution that their order is not so called because it contains perfection in itself, but because it is the best of all for acquiring perfection. When they would extol themselves to the people; when they would lay a snare for rash and ignorant youth; when they would assert their privileges and exalt their own dignity to the disparagement of others, they boast that they are in a state of perfection. When they are too closely pressed to be able to defend this vain arrogance, they betake themselves to the subterfuge that they have not yet obtained perfection, but that they are in a state in which they aspire to it more than others; meanwhile, the people continue to admire as if the monastic life alone were angelic, perfect, and purified from every vice. Under this pretence they ply a most gainful traffic, while their moderation lies buried in a few volumes.[2] Who sees not that this

1 Laurentius, defending his written assertion, that the monks falsely imagined that by means of their profession they merited more than others, admirably concludes, "There is no safer, no better way than that taught by Christ, and in it no profession is enjoined."

2 French, "Par ce moyen ils attirent farine au moulin et vendent leur sainteté tres cherement; cependant cette glose est cachee et comme ensevelie en peu de livres;"—by this means they bring grist to their mill, and sell their holiness very dear; meanwhile, the gloss is concealed, and is, as it were, buried in a few books.

is intolerable trifling? But let us treat with them as if they ascribed nothing more to their profession than to call it a state for acquiring perfection. Surely by giving it this name, they distinguish it by a special mark from other modes of life. And who will allow such honour to be transferred to an institution of which not one syllable is said in approbation, while all the other callings of God are deemed unworthy of the same, though not only commanded by his sacred lips, but adorned with distinguished titles? And how great the insult offered to God, when some device of man is preferred to all the modes of life which he has ordered, and by his testimony approved?

12. But let them say I calumniated them when I declared that they were not contented with the rule prescribed by God. Still, though I were silent, they more than sufficiently accuse themselves; for they plainly declare that they undertake a greater burden than Christ has imposed on his followers, since they promise that they will keep evangelical counsels regarding the love of enemies, the suppression of vindictive feelings, and abstinence from swearing, counsels to which Christians are not commonly astricted. In this what antiquity can they pretend? None of the ancients ever thought of such a thing: all with one voice proclaim that not one syllable proceeded from Christ which it is not necessary to obey. And the very things which these worthy expounders pretend that Christ only counselled they uniformly declare, without any doubt, that he expressly enjoined. But as we have shown above, that this is a most pestilential error, let it suffice here to have briefly observed that monasticism, as it now exists, founded on an idea which all pious men ought to execrate—namely, the pretence that there is some more perfect rule of life than that common rule which God has delivered to the whole Church. Whatever is built on this foundation cannot but be abominable.

13. But they produce another argument for their perfection, and deem it invincible. Our Lord said to the young man who put a question to him concerning the perfection of righteousness, "If thou wilt be perfect, go and sell that thou hast, and give to the poor" (Matth. xix. 21). Whether they do so, I do not now dispute. Let us grant for the present that they do. They boast, then, that they have become perfect by abandoning their all. If the sum of perfection consists in this, what is the meaning of Paul's doctrine, that though a man should give all his goods to feed the poor, and have not charity, he is nothing? (1 Cor. xiii. 3). What kind of perfection is that which, if charity be wanting, is with the individual himself reduced to nothing? Here they must of necessity answer that it is indeed the highest, but is not the only work of perfection. But here again Paul interposes; and hesitates not to declare that charity, without any renunciation of that sort, is the "bond of perfectness" (Col. iii. 14). If it is certain that there is no disagreement between the scholar and the master, and the latter clearly denies that the perfection of a man consists in renouncing all his goods, and on the other hand asserts that perfection may exist without it, we must see

in what sense we should understand the words of Christ, "If thou wilt be perfect, go and sell that thou hast." Now, there will not be the least obscurity in the meaning if we consider (this ought to be attended to in all our Saviour's discourses) to whom the words are addressed (Luke x. 25). A young man asks by what works he shall enter into eternal life. Christ, as he was asked concerning works, refers him to the law. And justly; for, considered in itself, it is the way of eternal life, and its inefficacy to give eternal life is owing to our depravity. By this answer Christ declared that he did not deliver any other rule of life than that which had formerly been delivered in the law of the Lord. Thus he both bore testimony to the divine law, that it was a doctrine of perfect righteousness, and at the same time met the calumnious charge of seeming, by some new rule of life, to incite the people to revolt from the law. The young man, who was not ill-disposed, but was puffed up with vain confidence, answers that he had observed all the precepts of the law from his youth. It is absolutely certain that he was immeasurably distant from the goal which he boasted of having reached. Had his boast been true, he would have wanted nothing of absolute perfection. For it has been demonstrated above, that the law contains in it a perfect righteousness. This is even obvious from the fact, that the observance of it is called the way to eternal life. To show him how little progress he had made in that righteousness which he too boldly answered that he had fulfilled, it was right to bring before him his besetting sin. Now, while he abounded in riches, he had his heart set upon them. Therefore, because he did not feel this secret wound, it is probed by Christ—"Go," says he, "and sell that thou hast." Had he been as good a keeper of the law as he supposed, he would not have gone away sorrowful on hearing these words. For he who loves God with his whole heart, not only regards everything which wars with his love as dross, but hates it as destruction (Phil. iii. 8). Therefore, when Christ orders a rich miser to leave all that he has, it is the same as if he had ordered the ambitious to renounce all his honours, the voluptuous all his luxuries, the unchaste all the instruments of his lust. Thus consciences, which are not reached by any general admonition, are to be recalled to a particular feeling of their particular sin. In vain, therefore, do they wrest that special case to a general interpretation, as if Christ had decided that the perfection of man consists in the abandonment of his goods, since he intended nothing more by the expression than to bring a youth who was out of measure satisfied with himself to feel his sore, and so understand that he was still at a great distance from that perfect obedience of the law which he falsely ascribed to himself. I admit that this passage was ill understood by some of the Fathers; [1] and hence arose an affectation of voluntary poverty, those only being thought

1 Chrysostom, in his Homily on the words of Paul, "Salute Prisca," &c., says, "All who retire to monasteries separate themselves from the Church, seeing they plainly assert that their monasticism is the form of a second baptism."

blest who abandoned all earthly goods, and in a state of destitution devoted themselves to Christ. But I am confident that, after my exposition, no good and reasonable man will have any dubiety here as to the mind of Christ.

14. Still there was nothing with the Fathers less intended than to establish that kind of perfection which was afterwards fabricated by cowled monks, in order to rear up a speices of double Christianity. For as yet the sacrilegious dogma was not broached which compares the profession of monasticism to baptism, nay, plainly asserts that it is the form of a second baptism. Who can doubt that the Fathers with their whole hearts abhorred such blasphemy? Then what need is there to demonstrate, by words, that the last quality which Augustine mentions as belonging to the ancient monks—viz. that they in all things accommodated themselves to charity—is most alien from this new profession? The thing itself declares that all who retire into monasteries withdraw from the Church. For how? Do they not separate themselves from the legitimate society of the faithful, by acquiring for themselves a special ministry and private administration of the sacraments? What is meant by destroying the communion of the Church if this is not? And to follow out the comparison with which I began, and at once close the point, what resemblance have they in this respect to the ancient monks? These, though they dwelt separately from others, had not a separate Church; they partook of the sacraments with others, they attended public meetings, and were then a part of the people. But what have those men done in erecting a private altar for themselves but broken the bond of unity? For they have excommunicated themselves from the whole body of the Church, and contemned the ordinary ministry by which the Lord has been pleased that peace and charity should be preserved among his followers. Wherefore I hold that as many monasteries as there are in the present day, so many conventicles are there of schismatics, who have disturbed ecclesiastical order, and been cut off from the legitimate society of the faithful. And that there might be no doubt as to their separation, they have given themselves the various names of factions. They have not been ashamed to glory in that which Paul so execrates, that he is unable to express his detestation too strongly. Unless, indeed, we suppose that Christ was not divided by the Corinthians, when one teacher set himself above another (1 Cor. i. 12, 13; iii. 4); and that now no injury is done to Christ when, instead of Christians, we hear some called Benedictines, others Franciscans, others Dominicans, and so called, that while they affect to be distinguished from the common body of Christians, they proudly substitute these names for a religious profession.

15. The differences which I have hitherto pointed out between the ancient monks and those of our age are not in manners, but in profession. Hence let my readers remember that I have spoken of monachism rather than of monks; and marked, not the vices which cleave to a few, but vices which are inseparable from the very mode of life. In regard to

manners, of what use is it to particularise and show how great the difference? This much is certain,[1] that there is no order of men more polluted by all kinds of vicious turpitude; nowhere do faction, hatred, party-spirit, and intrigue, more prevail. In a few monasteries, indeed, they live chastely, if we are to call it chastity, where lust is so far repressed as not to be openly infamous; still you will scarcely find one in ten which is not rather a brothel than a sacred abode of chastity. But how frugally they live? Just like swine wallowing in their sties. But lest they complain that I deal too unmercifully with them, I go no farther; although any one who knows the case will admit, that in the few things which I have said, I have not spoken in the spirit of an accuser. Augustine though he testifies, that the monks excelled so much in chastity, yet complains that there were many vagabonds, who, by wicked arts and impostures, extracted money from the more simple, plying a shameful traffic, by carrying about the relics of martyrs, and vending any dead man's bones for relics, bringing ignominy on their order by many similar iniquities. As he declares that he had seen none better than those who had profited in monasteries; so he laments that he had seen none worse than those who had backslidden in monasteries. What would he say were he, in the present day, to see now almost all monasteries overflowing, and in a manner bursting, with numerous deplorable vices? I say nothing but what is notorious to all; and yet this charge does not apply to all without a single exception; for, as the rule and discipline of holy living was never so well framed in monasteries as that there were not always some drones very unlike the others; so I hold that, in the present day, monks have not so completely degenerated from that holy antiquity as not to have some good men among them; but these few lie scattered up and down among a huge multitude of wicked and dishonest men, and are not only despised, but even petulantly assailed, sometimes even treated cruelly by the others, who, according to the Milesian proverb, think they ought to have no good man among them.

16. By this contrast between ancient and modern monasticism, I trust I have gained my object, which was to show that our cowled monks falsely pretend the example of the primitive Church in defence of their profession; since they differ no less from the monks of that period than apes do from men. Meanwhile I disguise not that even in that ancient form which Augustine commends, there was something which little pleases me. I admit that they were not superstitious in the external exercises of a more rigorous discipline, but I say that they were not without a degree of affectation and false zeal. It was a fine thing to cast away their substance, and free themselves from all worldly cares; but God sets more value on the pious management of a household, when the head of it, discarding all avarice,

[1] See Bernard. ad Guliel. Abbat. "I wonder why there is so much intemperance among monks. O vanity of vanities! but not more vain than insane." See also August. de Opere Monach. in fin

ambition, and other lusts of the flesh, makes it his purpose to serve God in some particular vocation. It is fine to philosophise in seclusion, far away from the intercourse of society; but it ill accords with Christian meekness for any one, as if in hatred of the human race, to fly to the wilderness and to solitude, and at the same time desert the duties which the Lord has especially commanded. Were we to grant that there was nothing worse in that profession, there is certainly no small evil in its having introduced a useless and perilous example into the Church.

17. Now, then, let us see the nature of the vows by which the monks of the present day are initiated into this famous order. First, as their intention is to institute a new and fictitious worship with a view to gain favour with God, I conclude from what has been said above, that everything which they vow is abomination to God. Secondly, I hold that as they frame their own mode of life at pleasure, without any regard to the calling of God, or to his approbation, the attempt is rash and unlawful; because their conscience has no ground on which it can support itself before God; and "whatsoever is not of faith is sin" (Rom. xiv. 23). Moreover, I maintain that in astricting themselves to many perverse and impious modes of worship, such as are exhibited in modern monasticism, they consecrate themselves not to God but to the devil. For why should the prophets have been permitted to say that the Israelites sacrificed their sons to devils and not to God (Deut. xxxii. 17; Ps. cvi. 37), merely because they had corrupted the true worship of God by profane ceremonies; and we not be permitted to say the same thing of monks who, along with the cowl, cover themselves with the net of a thousand impious superstitions? Then what is their species of vows? They offer God a promise of perpetual virginity, as if they had previously made a compact with him to free them from the necessity of marriage. They cannot allege that they make this vow trusting entirely to the grace of God; for, seeing he declares this to be a special gift not given to all (Matth. xix. 11), no man has a right to assume that the gift will be his. Let those who have it use it; and if at any time they feel the infirmity of the flesh, let them have recourse to the aid of him by whose power alone they can resist. If this avails not, let them not despise the remedy which is offered to them. If the faculty of continence is denied, the voice of God distinctly calls upon them to marry. By continence I mean not merely that by which the body is kept pure from fornication, but that by which the mind keeps its chastity untainted. For Paul enjoins caution not only against external lasciviousness, but also burning of mind (1 Cor. vii. 9). It has been the practice (they say) from the remotest period, for those who wished to devote themselves entirely to God, to bind themselves by a vow of continence. I confess that the custom is ancient, but I do not admit that the age when it commenced was so free from every defect that all that was then done is to be regarded as a rule. Moreover, the inexorable rigour of holding that after the vow is conceived there is

no room for repentance, crept in gradually. This is clear from Cyprian. "If virgins have dedicated themselves to Christian faith, let them live modestly and chastely, without pretence. Thus strong and stable, let them wait for the reward of virginity. But if they will not, or cannot persevere, it is better to marry, than by their faults to fall into the fire." In the present day, with what invectives would they not lacerate any one who should seek to temper the vow of continence by such an equitable course? Those, therefore, have wandered far from the ancient custom who not only use no moderation, and grant no pardon when any one proves unequal to the performance of his vow, but shamelessly declare that it is a more heinous sin to cure the intemperance of the flesh by marriage, than to defile body and soul by whoredom.

18. But they still insist and attempt to show that this vow was used in the days of the apostles, because Paul says that widows who marry after having once undertaken a public office, "cast off their first faith" (1 Tim. v. 12). I by no means deny that widows who dedicated themselves and their labours to the Church, at the same time came under an obligation of perpetual celibacy, not because they regarded it in the light of a religious duty, as afterwards began to be the case, but because they could not perform their functions unless they had their time at their own command, and were free from the nuptial tie. But if, after giving their pledge, they began to look to a new marriage, what else was this but to shake off the calling of God? It is not strange, therefore, when Paul says that by such desires they grow wanton against Christ. In further explanation he afterwards adds, that by not performing their promises to the Church, they violate and nullify their first faith given in baptism; one of the things contained in this first faith being, that every one should correspond to his calling. Unless you choose rather to interpret that, having lost their modesty, they afterwards cast off all care of decency, prostituting themselves to all kinds of lasciviousness and pertness, leading licentious and dissolute lives, than which nothing can less become Christian women. I am much pleased with this exposition. Our answer then is, that those widows who were admitted to a public ministry came under an obligation of perpetual celibacy, and hence we easily understand how, when they married, they threw off all modesty, and became more insolent than became Christian women: that in this way they not only sinned by violating the faith given to the Church, but revolted from the common rule of pious women. But, first, I deny that they had any other reason for professing celibacy than just because marriage was altogether inconsistent with the function which they undertook. Hence they bound themselves to celibacy only in so far as the nature of their function required. Secondly, I do not admit that they were bound to celibacy in such a sense that it was not better for them to marry than to suffer by the incitements of the flesh, and fall into uncleanness. Thirdly, I hold that what Paul enjoined was in the common case free from danger,

because he orders the selection to be made from those who, contented with one marriage, had already given proof of continence. Our only reason for disapproving of the vow of celibacy is, because it is improperly regarded as an act of worship, and is rashly undertaken by persons who have not the power of keeping it.

19. But what ground can there be for applying this passage to nuns? For deaconesses were appointed, not to soothe God by chantings or unintelligible murmurs, and spend the rest of their time in idleness; but to perform a public ministry of the Church toward the poor, and to labour with all zeal, assiduity, and diligence, in offices of charity. They did not vow celibacy, that they might thereafter exhibit abstinence from marriage as a kind of worship rendered to God, but only that they might be freer from encumbrance in executing their office. In fine, they did not vow on attaining adolescence, or in the bloom of life, and so afterwards learn, by too late experience, over what a precipice they had plunged themselves, but after they were thought to have surmounted all danger, they took a vow not less safe than holy. But not to press the two former points, I say that it was unlawful to allow women to take a vow of continence before their sixtieth year, since the apostle admits such only, and enjoins the younger to marry and beget children. Therefore, it is impossible, on any ground, to excuse the deduction, first of twelve, then of twenty, and, lastly, of thirty years. Still less possible is it to tolerate the case of miserable girls, who, before they have reached an age at which they can know themselves, or have any experience of their character, are not only induced by fraud, but compelled by force and threats, to entangle themselves in these accursed snares. I will not enter at length into a refutation of the other two vows. This only I say, that besides involving (as matters stand in the present day) not a few superstitions, they seem to be purposely framed in such a manner, as to make those who take them mock God and men. But lest we should seem, with too malignant feeling, to attack every particular point, we will be contented with the general refutation which has been given above.

20. The nature of the vows which are legitimate and acceptable to God, I think I have sufficiently explained. Yet, because some ill-informed and timid consciences, even when a vow displeases, and is condemned, nevertheless hesitate as to the obligation, and are grievously tormented, shuddering at the thought of violating a pledge given to God, and, on the other hand, fearing to sin more by keeping it,—we must here come to their aid, and enable them to escape from this difficulty. And to take away all scruple at once, I say that all vows not legitimate, and not duly conceived, as they are of no account with God, should be regarded by us as null. (See Calv. ad Concil. Trident.) For if, in human contracts, those promises only are binding in which he with whom we contract wishes to have us bound, it is absurd to say that we are bound to perform things which God does not at all require of us, especially since our works can only

be right when they please God, and have the testimony of our consciences that they do please him. For it always remains fixed, that "whatsoever is not of faith is sin" (Rom. xiv. 23). By this Paul means, that any work undertaken in doubt is vicious, because at the root of all good works lies faith, which assures us that they are acceptable to God. Therefore, if Christian men may not attempt anything without this assurance, why, if they have undertaken anything rashly through ignorance, may they not afterwards be freed, and desist from their error? Since vows rashly undertaken are of this description, they not only oblige not, but must necessarily be rescinded. What, then, when they are not only of no estimation in the sight of God, but are even an abomination, as has already been demonstrated? It is needless farther to discuss a point which does not require it. To appease pious consciences, and free them from all doubt, this one argument seems to me sufficient—viz. that all works whatsoever which flow not from a pure fountain, and are not directed to a proper end, are repudiated by God, and so repudiated, that he no less forbids us to continue than to begin them. Hence it follows, that vows dictated by error and superstition are of no weight with God, and ought to be abandoned by us.

21. He who understands this solution is furnished with the means of repelling the calumnies of the wicked against those who withdraw from monasticism to some honest kind of livelihood. They are grievously charged with having perjured themselves, and broken their faith, because they have broken the bond (vulgarly supposed to be indissoluble) by which they had bound themselves to God and the Church. But I say, first, there is no bond when that which man confirms God abrogates; and, secondly, even granting that they were bound when they remained entangled in ignorance and error, now, since they have been enlightened by the knowledge of the truth, I hold that they are, at the same time, free by the grace of Christ. For if such is the efficacy of the cross of Christ, that it frees us from the curse of the divine law by which we were held bound, how much more must it rescue us from extraneous chains, which are nothing but the wily nets of Satan? There can be no doubt, therefore, that all on whom Christ shines with the light of his Gospel, he frees from all the snares in which they had entangled themselves through superstition. At the same time, they have another defence if they were unfit for celibacy. For if an impossible vow is certain destruction to the soul, which God wills to be saved and not destroyed, it follows that it ought by no means to be adhered to. Now, how impossible the vow of continence is to those who have not received it by special gift, we have shown, and experience, even were I silent, declares: while the great obscenity with which almost all monasteries teem is a thing not unknown. If any seem more decent and modest than others, they are not, however, chaste. The sin of unchastity urges, and lurks within. Thus it is that God, by fearful examples, punishes the audacity of men, when, unmindful of their

infirmity, they, against nature, affect that which has been denied to them, and despising the remedies which the Lord has placed in their hands, are confident in their ability to overcome the disease of incontinence by contumacious obstinacy. For what other name can we give it, when a man, admonished of his need of marriage, and of the remedy with which the Lord has thereby furnished, not only despises it, but binds himself by an oath to despise it?

CHAPTER XIV.

OF THE SACRAMENTS.

This chapter consists of two principal parts,—I. Of sacraments in general. The sum of the doctrine stated, sec. 1–6. Two classes of opponents to be guarded against—viz. those who undervalue the power of the sacraments, sec. 7–13; and those who attribute too much to the sacraments, sec. 14–17. II. Of the sacraments in particular, both of the Old and the New Testament. Their scope and meaning. Refutation of those who have either too high or too low ideas of the sacraments.

Sections.

1. Of the sacraments in general. A sacrament defined.
2. Meaning of the word sacrament.
3. Definition explained. Why God seals his promises to us by sacraments.
4. The word which ought to accompany the element, that the sacrament may be complete.
5. Error of those who attempt to separate the word, or promise of God, from the element.
6. Why sacraments are called Signs of the Covenant.
7. They are such signs, though the wicked should receive them, but are signs of grace only to believers.
8. Objections to this view answered.
9. No secret virtue in the sacraments. Their whole efficacy depends on the inward operation of the Spirit.
10. Objections answered. Illustrated by a simile.
11. Of the increase of faith by the preaching of the word.
12. In what way, and how far, the sacraments are confirmations of our faith.
13. Some regard the sacraments as mere signs. This view refuted.
14. Some again attribute too much to the sacraments. Refutation.
15. Refutation confirmed by a passage from Augustine.
16. Previous views more fully explained.
17. The matter of the sacrament always present when the sacrament is duly administered.
18. Extensive meaning of the term sacrament.
19. The ordinary sacraments in the Church. How necessary they are.
20. The sacraments of the Old and of the New Testament. The end of both the same —viz. to lead us to Christ.
21. This apparent in the sacraments of the Old Testament.
22. Apparent also in the sacraments of the New Testament.
23. Impious doctrine of the Schoolmen as to the difference between the Old and the New Testaments.
24. Scholastic objection answered.
25. Another objection answered.
26. Sacraments of the New Testament sometimes excessively extolled by early Theologians. Their meaning explained.

1. Akin to the preaching of the gospel, we have another help to our faith in the sacraments, in regard to which, it greatly concerns us that some sure doctrine should be delivered, informing us both of the end for which they were instituted, and of their present use. First, we must attend to what a sacrament is. It seems to me, then, a simple and appropriate definition to say, that it is an external sign,

by which the Lord seals on our consciences his promises of good-will toward us, in order to sustain the weakness of our faith, and we in our turn testify our piety towards him, both before himself, and before angels as well as men. We may also define more briefly by calling it a testimony of the divine favour toward us, confirmed by an external sign, with a corresponding attestation of our faith towards Him. You may make your choice of these definitions, which in meaning differ not from that of Augustine, which defines a sacrament to be a visible sign of a sacred thing, or a visible form of an invisible grace, but does not contain a better or surer explanation. As its brevity makes it somewhat obscure, and thereby misleads the more illiterate, I wished to remove all doubt, and make the definition fuller by stating it at greater length.

2. The reason why the ancients used the term in this sense is not obscure. The old interpreter, whenever he wished to render the Greek term μυστήριον into Latin, especially when it was used with reference to divine things, used the word *sacramentum*. Thus, in Ephesians, "Having made known unto us the mystery (*sacramentum*) of his will;" and again, "If ye have heard of the dispensation of the grace of God, which is given me to you-wards, how that by revelation he made known unto me the mystery" (*sacramentum*) (Eph. i. 9; iii. 2). In the Colossians, "Even the mystery which hath been hid from ages and from generations, but is now made manifest to his saints, to whom God would make known what is the riches of the glory of this mystery" (*sacramentum*) (Col. i. 26). Also in the First Epistle to Timothy, "Without controversy, great is the mystery (*sacramentum*) of godliness: God was manifest in the flesh" (1 Tim. iii. 16). He was unwilling to use the word *arcanum* (secret), lest the word should seem beneath the magnitude of the thing meant. When the thing, therefore, was sacred and secret, he used the term *sacramentum*. In this sense it frequently occurs in ecclesiastical writers. And it is well known, that what the Latins call *sacramenta*, the Greeks call μυστήρια (mysteries). The sameness of meaning removes all dispute. Hence it is that the term was applied to those signs which gave an august representation of things spiritual and sublime. This is also observed by Augustine, "It were tedious to discourse of the variety of signs; those which relate to divine things are called sacraments" (August. Ep. 5. ad Marcell.).

3. From the definition which we have given, we perceive that there never is a sacrament without an antecedent promise, the sacrament being added as a kind of appendix, with the view of confirming and sealing the promise, and giving a better attestation, or rather, in a manner, confirming it. In this way God provides first for our ignorance and sluggishness, and, secondly, for our infirmity; and yet, properly speaking, it does not so much confirm his word as establish us in the faith of it. For the truth of God is in itself sufficiently stable and certain, and cannot receive a better confirmation from any

other quarter than from itself. But as our faith is slender and weak, so if it be not propped up on every side, and supported by all kinds of means, it is forthwith shaken and tossed to and fro, wavers, and even falls. And here, indeed, our merciful Lord, with boundless condescension, so accommodates himself to our capacity, that seeing how from our animal nature we are always creeping on the ground, and cleaving to the flesh, having no thought of what is spiritual, and not even forming an idea of it, he declines not by means of these earthly elements to lead us to himself, and even in the flesh to exhibit a mirror of spiritual blessings. For, as Chrysostom says (Hom. 60, ad Popul.). "Were we incorporeal, he would give us these things in a naked and incorporeal form. Now because our souls are implanted in bodies, he delivers spiritual things under things visible. Not that the qualities which are set before us in the sacraments are inherent in the nature of the things, but God gives them this signification."

4. This is commonly expressed by saying that a sacrament consists of the word and the external sign. By the word we ought to understand not one which, muttered without meaning and without faith, by its sound merely, as by a magical incantation, has the effect of consecrating the element, but one which, preached, makes us understand what the visible sign means. The thing, therefore, which was frequently done, under the tyranny of the Pope, was not free from great profanation of the mystery, for they deemed it sufficient if the priest muttered the formula of consecration, while the people, without understanding, looked stupidly on. Nay, this was done for the express purpose of preventing any instruction from thereby reaching the people: for all was said in Latin to illiterate hearers. Superstition afterwards was carried to such a height, that the consecration was thought not to be duly performed except in a low grumble, which few could hear. Very different is the doctrine of Augustine concerning the sacramental word. "Let the word be added to the element, and it will become a sacrament. For whence can there be so much virtue in water as to touch the body and cleanse the heart, unless by the agency of the word, and this not because it is said, but because it is believed? For even in the word the transient sound is one thing, the permanent power another. This is the word of faith which we preach says the Apostle (Rom. x. 8). Hence, in the Acts of the Apostles, we have the expression, "Purify their hearts by faith" (Acts xv. 9). And the Apostle Peter says, "The like figure whereunto even baptism doth now save us (not the putting away of the filth of the flesh, but the answer of a good conscience)" (1 Pet. iii. 21). "This is the word of faith which we preach: by which word doubtless baptism also, in order that it may be able to cleanse, is consecrated" (August. Hom. in Joann. 13). You see how he requires preaching to the production of faith. And we need not labour to prove this, since there is not the least room for doubt as to what Christ did, and commanded us to do, as to what the apostles followed, and a purer Church observed. Nay, it is known that, from the very

beginning of the world, whenever God offered any sign to the holy Patriarchs, it was inseparably attached to doctrine, without which our senses would gaze bewildered on an unmeaning object. Therefore, when we hear mention made of the sacramental word, let us understand the promise which, proclaimed aloud by the minister, leads the people by the hand to that to which the sign tends and directs us.

5. Nor are those to be listened to who oppose this view with a more subtle than solid dilemma. They argue thus: We either know that the word of God which precedes the sacrament is the true will of God, or we do not know it. If we know it, we learn nothing new from the sacrament which succeeds. If we do not know it, we cannot learn it from the sacrament, whose whole efficacy depends on the word. Our brief reply is: The seals which are affixed to diplomas, and other public deeds, are nothing considered in themselves, and would be affixed to no purpose if nothing was written on the parchment, and yet this does not prevent them from sealing and confirming when they are appended to writings. It cannot be alleged that this comparison is a recent fiction of our own, since Paul himself used it, terming *circumcision a seal* (Rom. iv. 11), where he expressly maintains that the circumcision of Abraham was not for justification, but was an attestation to the covenant, by the faith of which he had been previously justified. And how, pray, can any one be greatly offended when we teach that the promise is sealed by the sacrament, since it is plain, from the promises themselves, that one promise confirms another? The clearer any evidence is, the fitter is it to support our faith. But sacraments bring with them the clearest promises, and, when compared with the word, have this peculiarity, that they represent promises to the life, as if painted in a picture. Nor ought we to be moved by an objection founded on the distinction between sacraments and the seals of documents—viz. that since both consist of the carnal elements of this world, the former cannot be sufficient or adequate to seal the promises of God, which are spiritual and eternal, though the latter may be employed to seal the edicts of princes concerning fleeting and fading things. But the believer, when the sacraments are presented to his eye, does not stop short at the carnal spectacle, but by the steps of analogy which I have indicated, rises with pious consideration to the sublime mysteries which lie hidden in the sacraments.

6. As the Lord calls his promises covenants (Gen. vi. 18; ix. 9; xvii. 2), and sacraments signs of the covenants, so something similar may be inferred from human covenants. What could the slaughter of a hog effect, unless words were interposed or rather preceded? Swine are often killed without any interior or occult mystery. What could be gained by pledging the right hand, since hands are not unfrequently joined in giving battle? But when words have preceded, then by such symbols of covenant sanction is given to laws, though previously conceived, digested, and enacted by words. Sacra-

ments, therefore, are exercises which confirm our faith in the word of God; and because we are carnal, they are exhibited under carnal objects, that thus they may train us in accommodation to our sluggish capacity, just as nurses lead children by the hand. And hence Augustine calls a sacrament a *visible word* (August. in Joann. Hom. 89), because it represents the promises of God as in a picture, and places them in our view in a graphic bodily form (August. cont. Faust. Lib. xix.). We might refer to other similitudes, by which sacraments are more plainly designated, as when they are called the pillars of our faith. For just as a building stands and leans on its foundation, and yet is rendered more stable when supported by pillars, so faith leans on the word of God as its proper foundation, and yet when sacraments are added leans more firmly, as if resting on pillars. Or we may call them mirrors, in which we may contemplate the riches of the grace which God bestows upon us. For then, as has been said, he manifests himself to us in as far as our dulness can enable us to recognise him, and testifies his love and kindness to us more expressly than by word.

7. It is irrational to contend that sacraments are not manifestations of divine grace toward us, because they are held forth to the ungodly also, who, however, so far from experiencing God to be more propitious to them, only incur greater condemnation. By the same reasoning, the gospel will be no manifestation of the grace of God, because it is spurned by many who hear it; nor will Christ himself be a manifestation of grace, because of the many by whom he was seen and known, very few received him. Something similar may be seen in public enactments. A great part of the body of the people deride and evade the authenticating seal, though they know it was employed by their sovereign to confirm his will; others trample it under foot, as a matter by no means appertaining to them; while others even execrate it: so that, seeing the condition of the two things to be alike, the appropriateness of the comparison which I made above ought to be more readily allowed. It is certain, therefore, that the Lord offers us his mercy, and a pledge of his grace, both in his sacred word and in the sacraments; but it is not apprehended save by those who receive the word and sacraments with firm faith: in like manner as Christ, though offered and held forth for salvation to all, is not, however, acknowledged and received by all. Augustine, when intending to intimate this, said that the efficacy of the word is produced in the sacrament, *not because it is spoken, but because it is believed.* Hence Paul, addressing believers, includes communion with Christ, in the sacraments, as when he says, "As many of you as have been baptized into Christ have put on Christ" (Gal. iii. 27). Again, "For by one Spirit we are all baptized into one body" (1 Cor. xii. 13). But when he speaks of a preposterous use of the sacraments, he attributes nothing more to them than to frigid, empty figures; thereby intimating, that however the ungodly and hypocrites may, by their perverseness, either suppress, or obscure, or impede

the effect of divine grace in the sacraments, that does not prevent them, where and whenever God is so pleased, from giving a true evidence of communion with Christ, or prevent them from exhibiting, and the Spirit of God from performing, the very thing which they promise. We conclude, therefore, that the sacraments are truly termed evidences of divine grace, and, as it were, seals of the good-will which he entertains toward us. They, by sealing it to us, sustain, nourish, confirm, and increase our faith. The objections usually urged against this view are frivolous and weak. They say that our faith, if it is good, cannot be made better; for there is no faith save that which leans unshakingly, firmly, and undividedly, on the mercy of God. It had been better for the objectors to pray, with the apostles, "Lord, increase our faith" (Luke xvii. 5), than confidently to maintain a perfection of faith which none of the sons of men ever attained, none ever shall attain, in this life. Let them explain what kind of faith his was who said, "Lord, I believe; help thou mine unbelief" (Mark ix. 24). That faith, though only commenced, was good, and might, by the removal of the unbelief, be made better. But there is no better argument to refute them than their own consciousness. For if they confess themselves sinners (this, whether they will or not, they cannot deny), then they must of necessity impute this very quality to the imperfection of their faith.

8. But Philip, they say, replied to the eunuch who asked to be baptized, "If thou believest with all thine heart thou mayest" (Acts viii. 37). What room is there for a confirmation of baptism when faith fills the whole heart? I, in my turn, ask them, Do they not feel that a good part of their heart is void of faith—do they not perceive new additions to it every day? There was one who boasted that he grew old while learning. Thrice miserable, then, are we Christians if we grow old without making progress, we whose faith ought to advance through every period of life until it grow up into a perfect man (Eph. iv. 13). In this passage, therefore, to believe *with the whole heart*, is not to believe Christ perfectly, but only to embrace him sincerely with heart and soul; not to be filled with him, but with ardent affection to hunger and thirst, and sigh after him. It is usual in Scripture to say that a thing is done with the whole heart, when it is done sincerely and cordially. Of this description are the following passages:—"With my whole heart have I sought thee" (Ps. cxix. 10); "I will confess unto thee with my whole heart," &c. In like manner, when the fraudulent and deceitful are rebuked, it is said "with flattering lips, and with a double heart, do they speak" (Ps. xii. 2). The objectors next add—"If faith is increased by means of the sacraments, the Holy Spirit is given in vain, seeing it is his office to begin, sustain, and consummate our faith." I admit, indeed, that faith is the proper and entire work of the Holy Spirit, enlightened by whom we recognise God and the treasures of his grace, and without whose illumination our mind is so blind that it can see nothing, so stupid that it has no relish for spiritual things. But

for the one Divine blessing which they proclaim we count three. For, first, the Lord teaches and trains us by his word; next, he confirms us by his sacraments; lastly, he illumines our mind by the light of his Holy Spirit, and opens up an entrance into our hearts for his word and sacraments, which would otherwise only strike our ears, and fall upon our sight, but by no means affect us inwardly.

9. Wherefore, with regard to the increase and confirmation of faith, I would remind the reader (though I think I have already expressed it in unambiguous terms), that in assigning this office to the sacraments, it is not as if I thought that there is a kind of secret efficacy perpetually inherent in them, by which they can of themselves promote or strengthen faith, but because our Lord has instituted them for the express purpose of helping to establish and increase our faith. The sacraments duly perform their office only when accompanied by the Spirit, the internal Master, whose energy alone penetrates the heart, stirs up the affections, and procures access for the sacraments into our souls. If he is wanting, the sacraments can avail us no more than the sun shining on the eyeballs of the blind, or sounds uttered in the ears of the deaf. Wherefore, in distributing between the Spirit and the sacraments, I ascribe the whole energy to him, and leave only a ministry to them; this ministry, without the agency of the Spirit, is empty and frivolous, but when he acts within, and exerts his power, it is replete with energy. It is now clear in what way, according to this view, a pious mind is confirmed in faith by means of the sacraments—viz. in the same way in which the light of the sun is seen by the eye, and the sound of the voice heard by the ear; the former of which would not be at all affected by the light unless it had a pupil on which the light might fall; nor the latter reached by any sound, however loud, were it not naturally adapted for hearing. But if it is true, as has been explained, that in the eye it is the power of vision which enables it to see the light, and in the ear the power of hearing which enables it to perceive the voice, and that in our hearts it is the work of the Holy Spirit to commence, maintain, cherish, and establish faith, then it follows, both that the sacraments do not avail one iota without the energy of the Holy Spirit; and that yet in hearts previously taught by that preceptor, there is nothing to prevent the sacraments from strengthening and increasing faith. There is only this difference, that the faculty of seeing and hearing is naturally implanted in the eye and ear; whereas, Christ acts in our minds above the measure of nature by special grace.

10. In this way, also, we dispose of certain objections by which some anxious minds are annoyed. If we ascribe either an increase or confirmation of faith to creatures, injustice is done to the Spirit of God, who alone ought to be regarded as its author. But we do not rob him of the merit of confirming and increasing faith; nay, rather, we maintain that that which confirms and increases faith, is nothing else than the preparing of our minds by his internal illumination to re-

ceive that confirmation which is set forth by the sacraments. But if the subject is still obscure, it will be made plain by the following similitude: Were you to begin to persuade a person by word to do something, you would think of all the arguments by which he may be brought over to your view, and in a manner compelled to serve your purpose. But nothing is gained if the individual himself possess not a clear and acute judgment, by which he may be able to weigh the value of your arguments; if, moreover, he is not of a docile disposition, and ready to listen to doctrine; if, in fine, he has no such idea of your faith and prudence as in a manner to prejudice him in your favour, and secure his assent. For there are many obstinate spirits who are not to be bent by any arguments; and where faith is suspected, or authority contemned, little progress is made even with the docile. On the other hand, when opposite feelings exist, the result will be, that the person whose interests you are consulting will acquiesce in the very counsels which he would otherwise have derided. The same work is performed in us by the Spirit. That the word may not fall upon our ear, or the sacraments be presented to our eye in vain, he shows that it is God who there speaks to us, softens our obdurate hearts, and frames them to the obedience which is due to his word; in short, transmits those external words and sacraments from the ear to the soul. Both word and sacraments, therefore, confirm our faith, bringing under view the kind intentions of our heavenly Father, in the knowledge of which the whole assurance of our faith depends, and by which its strength is increased; and the Spirit also confirms our faith when, by engraving that assurance on our minds, he renders it effectual. Meanwhile, it is easy for the Father of lights, in like manner as he illumines the bodily eye by the rays of the sun, to illumine our minds by the sacraments, as by a kind of intermediate brightness.

11. This property our Lord showed to belong to the external word, when, in the parable, he compared it to seed (Matth. xiii. 4; Luke viii. 15). For as the seed, when it falls on a deserted and neglected part of the field, can do nothing but die, but when thrown into ground properly laboured and cultivated, will yield a hundred-fold; so the word of God, when addressed to any stubborn spirit, will remain without fruit, as if thrown upon the barren waste, but when it meets with a soul which the hand of the heavenly Spirit has subdued, will be most fruitful. But if the case of the seed and of the word is the same, and from the seed corn can grow and increase, and attain to maturity, why may not faith also take its beginning, increase, and completion from the word? Both things are admirably explained by Paul in different passages. For when he would remind the Corinthians how God had given effect to his labours, he boasts that he possessed the ministry of the Spirit (1 Cor. ii. 4); just as if his preaching were inseparably connected with the power of the Holy Spirit, in inwardly enlightening the mind, and stimulating it. But in another passage, when he would remind them what the power of the word is

in itself, when preached by man, he compares ministers to husbandmen, who, after they have expended labour and industry in cultivating the ground, have nothing more that they can do. For what would ploughing, and sowing, and watering avail, unless that which was sown should, by the kindness of Heaven, vegetate? Wherefore he concludes, that he that planteth, and he that watereth is nothing, but that the whole is to be ascribed to God, who alone gives the increase. The apostles, therefore, exert the power of the Spirit in their preaching, inasmuch as God uses them as instruments which he has ordained for the unfolding of his spiritual grace. Still, however, we must not lose sight of the distinction, but remember what man is able of himself to do, and what is peculiar to God.

12. The sacraments are confirmations of our faith in such a sense, that the Lord, sometimes, when he sees meet to withdraw our assurance of the things which he had promised in the sacraments, takes away the sacraments themselves. When he deprives Adam of the gift of immortality, and expels him from the garden, "lest he put forth his hand and take also of the tree of life, and live for ever" (Gen. iii. 22). What is this we hear? Could that fruit have restored Adam to the immortality from which he had already fallen? By no means. It is just as if he had said, Lest he indulge in vain confidence, if allowed to retain the symbol of my promise, let that be withdrawn which might give him some hope of immortality. On this ground, when the apostle urges the Ephesians to remember, that they "were without Christ, being aliens from the commonwealth of Israel, and strangers from the covenants of promise, having no hope, and without God in the world" (Eph. ii. 12), he says that they were not partakers of circumcision. He thus intimates metonymically, that all were excluded from the promise who had not received the badge of the promise. To the other objection—viz. that when so much power is attributed to creatures, the glory of God is bestowed upon them, and thereby impaired—it is obvious to reply, that we attribute no power to the creatures. All we say is, that God uses the means and instruments which he sees to be expedient, in order that all things may be subservient to his glory, he being the Lord and disposer of all. Therefore, as by bread and other aliment he feeds our bodies, as by the sun he illumines, and by fire gives warmth to the world, and yet bread, sun, and fire are nothing, save inasmuch as they are instruments under which he dispenses his blessings to us; so in like manner he spiritually nourishes our faith by means of the sacraments, whose only office is to make his promises visible to our eye, or rather, to be pledges of his promises. And as it is our duty in regard to the other creatures which the divine liberality and kindness has destined for our use, and by whose instrumentality he bestows the gifts of his goodness upon us, to put no confidence in them, nor to admire and extol them as the causes of our mercies; so neither ought our confidence to be fixed on the sacraments, nor ought the glory of God to be transferred to them, but passing beyond them all, our faith and

confession should rise to Him who is the Author of the sacraments and of all things.

13. There is nothing in the argument which some found on the very term *sacrament.* This term, they say, while it has many significations in approved authors, has only one which is applicable to signs—namely, when it is used for the formal oath which the soldier gives to his commander on entering the service. For as by that military oath recruits bind themselves to be faithful to their commander, and make a profession of military service; so by our signs we acknowledge Chirst to be our commander, and declare that we serve under his standard. They add similitudes, in order to make the matter more clear. As the toga distinguished the Romans from the Greeks, who wore the pallium; and as the different orders of Romans were distinguished from each other by their peculiar insignia; *e. g.*, the senatorial from the equestrian by purple, and crescent shoes, and the equestrian from the plebeian by a ring, so we wear our symbols to distinguish us from the profane. But it is sufficiently clear from what has been said above, that the ancients, in giving the name of sacraments to signs, had not at all attended to the use of the term by Latin writers, but had, for the sake of convenience, given it this new signification, as a means of simply expressing sacred signs. But were we to argue more subtilely, we might say that they seem to have given the term this signification in a manner analogous to that in which they employ the term faith in the sense in which it is now used. For while faith is truth in performing promises, they have used it for the certainty or firm persuasion which is had of the truth. In this way, while a sacrament is the act of the soldier when he vows obedience to his commander, they made it the act by which the commander admits soldiers to the ranks. For in the sacraments the Lord promises that he will be our God, and we that we will be his people. But we omit such subtleties, since I think I have shown by arguments abundantly plain, that all which ancient writers intended was to intimate, that sacraments are the signs of sacred and spiritual things. The similitudes which are drawn from external objects (chap. xv. sec. 1), we indeed admit; but we approve not, that that which is a secondary thing in sacraments is by them made the first, and indeed the only thing. The first thing is, that they may contribute to our faith in God; the secondary, that they may attest our confession before men. These similitudes are applicable to the secondary reason. Let it therefore remain a fixed point, that mysteries would be frigid (as has been seen) were they not helps to our faith, and adjuncts annexed to doctrine for the same end and purpose.

14. On the other hand, it is to be observed, that as these objectors impair the force, and altogether overthrow the use of the sacraments, so there are others who ascribe to the sacraments a kind of secret virtue, which is nowhere said to have been implanted in them by God. By this error the more simple and unwary are perilously deceived,

while they are taught to seek the gifts of God where they cannot possibly be found, and are insensibly withdrawn from God, so as to embrace instead of his truth mere vanity. For the schools of the Sophists have taught with general consent that the sacraments of the new law, in other words, those now in use in the Christian Church, justify, and confer grace, provided only that we do not interpose the obstacle of mortal sin. It is impossible to describe how fatal and pestilential this sentiment is, and the more so, that for many ages it has, to the great loss of the Church, prevailed over a considerable part of the world. It is plainly of the devil: for, first, in promising a righteousness without faith, it drives souls headlong on destruction; secondly, in deriving a cause of righteousness from the sacraments, it entangles miserable minds, already of their own accord too much inclined to the earth, in a superstitious idea, which makes them acquiesce in the spectacle of a corporeal object rather than in God himself. I wish we had not such experience of both evils as to make it altogether unnecessary to give a lengthened proof of them. For what is a sacrament received without faith, but most certain destruction to the Church? For, seeing that nothing is to be expected beyond the promise, and the promise no less denounces wrath to the unbeliever than offers grace to the believer, it is an error to suppose that anything more is conferred by the sacraments than is offered by the word of God, and obtained by true faith. From this another thing follows—viz. that assurance of salvation does not depend on participation in the sacraments, as if justification consisted in it. This, which is treasured up in Christ alone, we know to be communicated, not less by the preaching of the Gospel than by the seal of the sacrament, and may be completely enjoyed without this seal. So true is it, as Augustine declares, that there may be invisible sanctification without a visible sign, and, on the other hand, a visible sign without true sanctification (August. de Quæst. Vet. Test. Lib. iii.). For, as he elsewhere says, "Men put on Christ, sometimes to the extent of partaking in the sacrament, and sometimes to the extent of holiness of life" (August. de Bapt. Cont. Donat. cap. xxiv.). The former may be common to the good and the bad, the latter is peculiar to the good.

15. Hence the distinction, if properly understood, repeatedly made by Augustine between the *sacrament* and the *matter of the sacrament*. For he does not mean merely that the figure and truth are therein contained, but that they do not so cohere as not to be separable, and that in this connection it is always necessary to distinguish the thing from the sign, so as not to transfer to the one what belongs to the other. Augustine speaks of the separation when he says that in the elect alone the sacraments accomplish what they represent (Augustin. de Bapt. Parvul.). Again, when speaking of the Jews, he says, "Though the sacraments were common to all, the grace was not common: yet grace is the virtue of the sacraments. Thus, too, the laver of regeneration is now common to all, but the grace by which

the members of Christ are regenerated with their head is not common to all" (August. in Ps. 78). Again, in another place, speaking of the Lord's Supper, he says, "We also this day receive visible food; but the sacrament is one thing, the virtue of the sacrament another. Why is it that many partake of the altar and die, and die by partaking? For even the cup of the Lord was poison to Judas, not because he received what was evil, but being wicked he wickedly received what was good" (August. in Joann. Hom. 26). A little after, he says, "The sacrament of this thing, that is, of the unity of the body and blood of Christ, is in some places prepared every day, in others at certain intervals at the Lord's table, which is partaken by some unto life, by others unto destruction. But the thing itself, of which there is a sacrament, is life to all, and destruction to none who partake of it." Some time before he had said, "He who may have eaten shall not die, but he must be one who attains to the virtue of the sacrament, not to the visible sacrament; who eats inwardly, not outwardly; who eats with the heart, and not with the teeth." Here you are uniformly told that a sacrament is so separated from the reality by the unworthiness of the partaker, that nothing remains but an empty and useless figure. Now, in order that you may have not a sign devoid of truth, but the thing with the sign, the Word which is included in it must be apprehended by faith. Thus, in so far as by means of the sacraments you will profit in the communion of Christ, will you derive advantage from them.

16. If this is obscure from brevity, I will explain it more at length. I say that Christ is the matter, or, if you rather choose it, the substance of all the sacraments, since in him they have their whole solidity, and out of him promise nothing. Hence the less toleration is due to the error of Peter Lombard, who distinctly makes them causes of the righteousness and salvation of which they are parts (Sent. Lib. iv. Dist. 1). Bidding adieu to all other causes of righteousness which the wit of man devises, our duty is to hold by this only. In so far, therefore, as we are assisted by their instrumentality in cherishing, confirming, and increasing the true knowledge of Christ, so as both to possess him more fully, and enjoy him in all his richness, so far are they effectual in regard to us. This is the case when that which is there offered is received by us in true faith. Therefore, you will ask, Do the wicked, by their ingratitude, make the ordinance of God fruitless and void? I answer, that what I have said is not to be understood as if the power and truth of the sacrament depended on the condition or pleasure of him who receives it. That which God instituted continues firm, and retains its nature, however men may vary; but since it is one thing to offer, and another to receive, there is nothing to prevent a symbol, consecrated by the word of the Lord, from being truly what it is said to be, and preserving its power, though it may at the same time confer no benefit on the wicked and ungodly. This question is well solved by Augustine in a few words: "If you receive carnally, it ceases not to

be spiritual, but it is not spiritual to you" (August. Hom. in Joann. 26). But as Augustine shows in the above passages that a sacrament is a thing of no value if separated from its truth; so also, when the two are conjoined, he reminds us that it is necessary to distinguish, in order that we may not cleave too much to the external sign. "As it is servile weakness to follow the latter, and take the signs for the thing signified, so to interpret the signs as of no use is an extravagant error" (August. de Doct. Christ. Lib. iii. c. 9). He mentions two faults which are here to be avoided; the one when we receive the signs as if they had been given in vain, and by malignantly destroying or impairing their secret meanings, prevent them from yielding any fruit—the other, when by not raising our minds beyond the visible sign, we attribute to it blessings which are conferred upon us by Christ alone, and that by means of the Holy Spirit, who makes us to be partakers of Christ, external signs assisting if they invite us to Christ; whereas, when wrested to any other purpose, their whole utility is overthrown.

17. Wherefore, let it be a fixed point, that the office of the sacraments differs not from the word of God; and this is to hold forth and offer Christ to us, and, in him, the treasures of heavenly grace. They confer nothing, and avail nothing, if not received in faith, just as wine and oil, or any other liquor, however large the quantity which you pour out, will run away and perish unless there be an open vessel to receive it. When the vessel is not open, though it may be sprinkled all over, it will nevertheless remain entirely empty. We must be aware of being led into a kindred error by the terms, somewhat too extravagant, which ancient Christian writers have employed in extolling the dignity of the sacraments. We must not suppose that there is some latent virtue inherent in the sacraments by which they, in themselves, confer the gifts of the Holy Spirit upon us, in the same way in which wine is drunk out of a cup, since the only office divinely assigned them is to attest and ratify the benevolence of the Lord towards us; and they avail no farther than accompanied by the Holy Spirit to open our minds and hearts, and make us capable of receiving this testimony, in which various distinguished graces are clearly manifested. For the sacraments, as we lately observed (chap. xiii. sec. 6; and xiv. sec. 6, 7), are to us what messengers of good news are to men, or earnests in ratifying pactions. They do not of themselves bestow any grace, but they announce and manifest it, and, like earnests and badges, give a ratification of the gifts which the divine liberality has bestowed upon us. The Holy Spirit, whom the sacraments do not bring promiscuously to all, but whom the Lord specially confers on his people, brings the gifts of God along with him, makes way for the sacraments, and causes them to bear fruit. But though we deny not that God, by the immediate agency of his Spirit, countenances his own ordinance, preventing the administration of the sacraments which he has instituted from being fruitless and vain, still we maintain that the internal grace of the Spirit, as

it is distinct from the external ministration, ought to be viewed and considered separately. God, therefore, truly performs whatever he promises and figures by signs; nor are the signs without effect, for they prove that he is their true and faithful author. The only question here is, whether the Lord works by proper and intrinsic virtue (as it is called), or resigns his office to external symbols? We maintain, that whatever organs he employs detract nothing from his primary operation. In this doctrine of the sacraments, their dignity is highly extolled, their use plainly shown, their utility sufficiently proclaimed, and moderation in all things duly maintained; so that nothing is attributed to them which ought not to be attributed, and nothing denied them which they ought to possess. Meanwhile, we get rid of that fiction by which the cause of justification and the power of the Holy Spirit are included in elements as vessels and vehicles, and the special power which was overlooked is distinctly explained. Here, also, we ought to observe, that what the minister figures and attests by outward action, God performs inwardly, lest that which God claims for himself alone should be ascribed to mortal man. This Augustine is careful to observe: "How does both God and Moses sanctify? Not Moses for God, but Moses by visible sacraments through his ministry, God by invisible grace through the Holy Spirit. Herein is the whole fruit of visible sacraments; for what do these visible sacraments avail without that sanctification of invisible grace?"

18. The term sacrament, in the view we have hitherto taken of it, includes, generally, all the signs which God ever commanded men to use, that he might make them sure and confident of the truth of his promises. These he was pleased sometimes to place in natural objects—sometimes to exhibit in miracles. Of the former class we have an example, in his giving the tree of life to Adam and Eve, as an earnest of immortality, that they might feel confident of the promise as often as they ate of the fruit. Another example was, when he gave the bow in the cloud to Noah and his posterity, as a memorial that he would not again destroy the earth by a flood. These were to Adam and Noah as sacraments: not that the tree could give Adam and Eve the immortality which it could not give to itself; or the bow (which is only a reflection of the solar rays on the opposite clouds) could have the effect of confining the waters; but they had a mark engraven on them by the word of God, to be proofs and seals of his covenant. The tree was previously a tree, and the bow a bow; but when they were inscribed with the word of God, a new form was given to them: they began to be what they previously were not. Lest any one suppose that these things were said in vain, the bow is even in the present day a witness to us of the covenant which God made with Noah (Calv. in Gen. ix. 6). As often as we look upon it, we read this promise from God, that the earth will never be destroyed by a flood. Wherefore, if any philosophaster, to deride the simplicity of our faith, shall contend that the variety of

colours arises naturally from the rays reflected by the opposite cloud, let us admit the fact; but, at the same time, deride his stupidity in not recognising God as the Lord and governor of nature, who, at his pleasure, makes all the elements subservient to his glory. If he had impressed memorials of this description on the sun, the stars, the earth, and stones, they would all have been to us as sacraments. For why is the shapeless and the coined silver not of the same value, seeing they are the same metal? Just because the former has nothing but its own nature, whereas the latter, impressed with the public stamp, becomes money, and receives a new value. And shall the Lord not be able to stamp his creatures with his word, that things which were formerly bare elements may become sacraments? Examples of the second class were given when he showed light to Abraham in the smoking furnace (Gen. xv. 17), when he covered the fleece with dew while the ground was dry; and, on the other hand, when the dew covered the ground while the fleece was untouched, to assure Gideon of victory (Judges vi. 37); also, when he made the shadow go back ten degrees on the dial, to assure Hezekiah of his recovery (2 Kings xx. 9; Isa. xxxviii. 7). These things, which were done to assist and establish their faith, were also sacraments.

19. But my present purpose is to discourse especially of those sacraments which the Lord has been pleased to institute as ordinary sacraments in his Church, to bring up his worshippers and servants in one faith, and the confession of one faith. For, to use the words of Augustine, "In no name of religion, true or false, can men be assembled, unless united by some common use of visible signs or sacraments" (August. cont. Faustum, Lib. ix. c. 11). Our most merciful Father, foreseeing this necessity, from the very first appointed certain exercises of piety to his servants; these, Satan, by afterwards transferring to impious and superstitious worship, in many ways corrupted and depraved. Hence those initiations of the Gentiles into their mysteries, and other degenerate rites. Yet, although they were full of error and superstition, they were, at the same time, an indication that men could not be without such external signs of religion. But, as they were neither founded on the word of God, nor bore reference to that truth which ought to be held forth by all signs, they are unworthy of being named when mention is made of the sacred symbols which were instituted by God, and have not been perverted from their end—viz. to be helps to true piety. And they consist not of simple signs, like the rainbow and the tree of life, but of ceremonies, or (if you prefer it) the signs here employed are ceremonies. But since, as has been said above, they are testimonies of grace and salvation from the Lord, so, in regard to us, they are marks of profession by which we openly swear by the name of God, binding ourselves to be faithful to him. Hence Chrysostom somewhere shrewdly gives them the name of pactions, by which God enters into covenant with us, and we become bound to holiness and purity of life, because a mutual stipulation is here interposed be-

tween God and us. For as God there promises to cover and efface any guilt and penalty which we may have incurred by transgression, and reconciles us to himself in his only begotten Son, so we, in our turn, oblige ourselves by this profession to the study of piety and righteousness. And hence it may be justly said, that such sacraments are ceremonies, by which God is pleased to train his people, first, to excite, cherish, and strengthen faith within; and, secondly, to testify our religion to men.

20. Now these have been diffierent at diffierent times, according to the dispensation which the Lord has seen meet to employ in manifesting himself to men. Circumcision was enjoined on Abraham and his posterity, and to it were afterwards added purifications and sacrifices, and other rites of the Mosaic Law. These were the sacraments of the Jews even until the advent of Christ. After these were abrogated, the two sacraments of Baptism and the Lord's Supper, which the Christian Church now employs, were instituted. I speak of those which were instituted for the use of the whole Church. For the laying on of hands, by which the ministers of the Church are initiated into their office, though I have no objection to its being called a sacrament, I do not number among ordinary sacraments. The place to be assigned to the other commonly reputed sacraments we shall see by-and-by. Still the ancient sacraments had the same end in view as our own—viz. to direct and almost lead us by the hand to Christ, or rather, were like images to represent him and hold him forth to our knowledge. But as we have already shown that sacraments are a kind of seals of the promises of God, so let us hold it as a most certain truth, that no divine promise has ever been offered to man except in Christ, and that hence when they remind us of any divine promise, they must of necessity exhibit Christ. Hence that heavenly pattern of the tabernacle and legal worship which was shown to Moses in the mount. There is only this difference, that while the former shadowed forth a promised Christ while he was still expected, the latter bear testimony to him as already come and manifested.

21. When these things are explained singly and separately, they will be much clearer. Circumcision was a sign by which the Jews were reminded that whatever comes of the seed of man—in other words, the whole nature of man—is corrupt, and requires to be cut off; moreover, it was a proof and memorial to confirm them in the promise made to Abraham, of a seed in whom all the nations of the earth should be blessed, and from whom they themselves were to look for a blessing. That saving seed, as we are taught by Paul (Gal. v. 16), was Christ, in whom alone they trusted to recover what they had lost in Adam. Wherefore circumcision was to them what Paul says it was to Abraham—viz. a sign of the righteousness of faith (Rom. iv. 11):—viz. a seal by which they were more certainly assured that their faith in waiting for the Lord would be accepted by God for righteousness. But we shall have a better opportunity elsewhere (chap. xvi. sec. 3, 4) of following out the comparison between circum-

cision and baptism.[1] Their washings and purifications placed under their eye the uncleanness, defilement, and pollution with which they were naturally contaminated, and promised another laver in which all their impurities might be wiped and washed away. This laver was Christ, washed by whose blood we bring his purity into the sight of God, that he may cover all our defilements. The sacrifices convicted them of their unrighteousness, and at the same time taught that there was a necessity for paying some satisfaction to the justice of God; and that, therefore, there must be some high priest, some mediator between God and man, to satisfy God by the shedding of blood, and the immolation of a victim which might suffice for the remission of sins. The high priest was Christ: he shed his own blood, he was himself the victim: for in obedience to the Father, he offered himself to death, and by this obedience abolished the disobedience by which man had provoked the indignation of God (Phil. ii. 8; Rom. v. 19).

22. In regard to our sacraments, they present Christ the more clearly to us, the more familiarly he has been manifested to man, ever since he was exhibited by the Father, truly as he had been promised. For Baptism testifies that we are washed and purified; the Supper of the Eucharist that we are redeemed. Ablution is figured by water, satisfaction by blood. Both are found in Christ, who, as John says, "came by water and blood;" that is, to purify and redeem. Of this the Spirit of God also is a witness. Nay, there are three witnesses in one, water, Spirit, and blood. In the water and blood we have an evidence of purification and redemption, but the Spirit is the primary witness who gives us a full assurance of this testimony. This sublime mystery was illustriously displayed on the cross of Christ, when water and blood flowed from his sacred side (John xix. 34); which, for this reason, Augustine justly termed the fountain of our sacraments (August. Hom. in Joann. 26). Of these we shall shortly treat at greater length. There is no doubt that, if you compare time with time, the grace of the Spirit is now more abundantly displayed. For this forms part of the glory of the kingdom of Christ, as we gather from several passages, and especially from the seventh chapter of John. In this sense are we to understand the words of Paul, that the law was "a shadow of good things to come, but the body is of Christ" (Col. ii. 17). His purpose is not to declare the inefficacy of those manifestations of grace in which God was pleased to prove his truth to the patriarchs, just as he proves it to us in the present day in Baptism and the Lord's Supper, but to contrast the two, and show the great value of what is given to us, that no one may think it strange that by the advent of Christ the ceremonies of the law have been abolished.

23. The Scholastic dogma (to glance at it in passing), by which the difference between the sacraments of the old and the new dispensa-

[1] Heb. ix. 1-14; 1 John i. 7; Rev. i. 5; Heb. iv. 14; v, 5; ix. 11.

tion is made so great, that the former did nothing but shadow forth the grace of God, while the latter actually confer that it, must be altogether exploded. Since the apostle speaks in no higher terms of the one than of the other, when he says that the fathers ate of the same spiritual food, and explains that that food was Christ (1 Cor. x. 3), who will presume to regard as an empty sign that which gave a manifestation to the Jews of true communion with Christ? And the state of the case which the apostle is there treating militates strongly for our view. For to guard against confiding in a frigid knowledge of Christ, an empty title of Christianity and external observances, and thereby daring to contemn the judgment of God, he exhibits signal examples of divine severity in the Jews, to make us aware that if we indulge in the same vices, the same punishments which they suffered are impending over us. Now, to make the comparison appropriate, it was necessary to show that there is no inequality between us and them in those blessings in which he forbade us to glory. Therefore, he first makes them equal to us in the sacraments, and leaves us not one iota of privilege which could give us hopes of impunity. Nor can we justly attribute more to our baptism than he elsewhere attributes to circumcision, when he terms it a seal of the righteousness of faith (Rom. iv. 11). Whatever, therefore, is now exhibited to us in the sacraments, the Jews formerly received in theirs—viz. Christ, with his spiritual riches. The same efficacy which ours possess they experienced in theirs—viz. that they were seals of the divine favour toward them in regard to the hope of eternal salvation. Had the objectors been sound expounders of the Epistle to the Hebrews, they would not have been so deluded, but reading therein that sins were not expiated by legal ceremonies, nay, that the ancient shadows were of no importance to justification, they overlooked the contrast which is there drawn, and fastening on the single point, that the law in itself was of no avail to the worshipper, thought that they were mere figures, devoid of truth. The purpose of the apostle is to show that there is nothing in the ceremonial law until we arrive at Christ, on whom alone the whole efficacy depends.

24. But they will found on what Paul says of the circumcision of the letter,[1] and object that it is in no esteem with God; that it confers nothing, is empty; that passages such as these seem to set it far beneath our baptism. But by no means. For the very same thing might justly be said of baptism. Indeed, it is said; first by Paul himself, when he shows that God regards not the external ablution by which we are initiated into religion, unless the mind is purified inwardly, and maintains its purity to the end; and, secondly, by Peter, when he declares that the reality of baptism consists not in external ablution, but in the testimony of a good conscience. But it seems that in another passage he speaks with the greatest contempt of circumcision made with hands, when he contrasts it with the cir-

1 Rom. ii. 25–29; 1 Cor. vii. 19; Gal. vi. 15; 1 Cor. x. 5; 1 Pet. iii. 21; Col. ii. 11.

cumcision made by Christ. I answer, that not even in that passage is there anything derogatory to its dignity. Paul is there disputing against those who insisted upon it as necessary, after it had been abrogated. He therefore admonishes believers to lay aside ancient shadows, and cleave to truth. These teachers, he says, insist that your bodies shall be circumcised. But you have been spiritually circumcised both in soul and body. You have, therefore, a manifestation of the reality, and this is far better than the shadow. Still any one might have answered, that the figure was not to be despised because they had the reality, since among the fathers also was exemplified that putting off of the old man of which he was speaking, and yet to them external circumcision was not superfluous. This objection he anticipates, when he immediately adds, that the Colossians were buried together with Christ by baptism, thereby intimating that baptism is now to Christians what circumcision was to those of ancient times; and that the latter, therefore, could not be imposed on Christians without injury to the former.

25. But there is more difficulty in explaining the passage which follows, and which I lately quoted[1]—viz. that all the Jewish ceremonies were shadows of things to come, but the body is of Christ (Col. ii. 17). The most difficult point of all, however, is that which is discussed in several chapters of the Epistle to the Hebrews—namely, that the blood of beasts did not reach to the conscience; that the law was a shadow of good things to come, but not the very image of the things (Heb. x. 1); that worshippers under the Mosaic ceremonies obtained no degree of perfection, and so forth. I repeat what I have already hinted, that Paul does not represent the ceremonies as shadowy because they had nothing solid in them, but because their completion was in a manner suspended until the manifestation of Christ. Again, I hold that the words are to be understood not of their efficiency, but rather of the mode of significancy. For until Christ was manifested in the flesh, all signs shadowed him as absent, however he might inwardly exert the presence of his power, and consequently of his person on believers. But the most important observation is, that in all these passages Paul does not speak simply but by way of reply. He was contending with false apostles, who maintained that piety consisted in mere ceremonies, without any respect to Christ; for their refutation it was sufficient merely to consider what effect ceremonies have in themselves. This, too, was the scope of the author of the Epistle to the Hebrews. Let us remember, therefore, that he is here treating of ceremonies not taken in their true and native signification, but when wrested to a false and vicious interpretation, not of the legitimate use, but of the superstitious abuse of them. What wonder, then, if ceremonies, when separated from Christ, are devoid of all virtue? All signs become null when the thing signified is taken away. Thus Christ, when addressing those who thought that manna

[1] French, "Mais on fera encore un autre argument."—But there is still another argument which they will employ.

was nothing more than food for the body, accommodates his language to their gross opinion, and says, that he furnished a better food, one which fed souls for immortality. But if you require a clearer solution, the substance comes to this: First, the whole apparatus of ceremonies under the Mosaic law, unless directed to Christ, is evanescent and null. Secondly, these ceremonies had such respect to Christ, that they had their fulfilment only when Christ was manifested in the flesh. Lastly, at his advent they behoved to disappear, just as the shadow vanishes in the clear light of the sun. But I now touch more briefly on the point, because I defer the future consideration of it till I come to the place where I intend to compare baptism with circumcision.

26. Those wretched sophists are perhaps deceived by the extravagant eulogiums on our signs which occur in ancient writers: for instance, the following passage of Augustine: "The sacraments of the old law only promised a Saviour, whereas ours give salvation" (August. Proem. in Ps. 73). Not perceiving that these and similar figures of speech are hyperbolical, they too have promulgated their hyperbolical dogmas, but in a sense altogether alien from that of ancient writers. For Augustine means nothing more than in another place where he says, "The sacraments of the Mosaic law foretold Christ, ours announce him" (Quæst. sup. Numer. c. 33). And again, "Those were promises of things to be fulfilled, these indications of the fulfilment" (Contra Faustum, Lib. xix. c. 14); as if he had said, Those figured him when he was still expected, ours, now that he has arrived, exhibit him as present. Moreover, with regard to the mode of signifying, he says, as he also elsewhere indicates, "The Law and the Prophets had sacraments foretelling a thing future, the sacraments of our time attest that what they foretold as to come has come" (Cont. Liter. Petil. Lib. ii. c. 37). His sentiments concerning the reality and efficacy, he explains in several passages, as when he says, "The sacraments of the Jews were different in the signs, alike in the things signified; different in the visible appearance, alike in spiritual power" (Hom. in Joann. 26). Again, "In different signs there was the same faith: it was thus in different signs as in different words, because the words change the sound according to times, and yet words are nothing else than signs. The fathers drank of the same spiritual drink, but not of the same corporeal drink. See then, how, while faith remains, signs vary. There the rock was Christ; to us that is Christ which is placed on the altar. They as a great sacrament drank of the water flowing from the rock: believers know what we drink. If you look at the visible appearance there was a difference; if at the intelligible signification, they drank of the same spiritual drink." Again, "In this mystery their food and drink are the same as ours; the same in meaning, not in form, for the same Christ was figured to them in the rock; to us he has been manifested in the flesh" (in Ps. 77). Though we grant that in this respect also there is some difference. Both testify that

the paternal kindness of God, and the graces of the Spirit, are offered us in Christ, but ours more clearly and splendidly. In both there is an exhibition of Christ, but in ours it is more full and complete, in accordance with that distinction between the Old and New Testaments of which we have discoursed above. And this is the meaning of Augustine (whom we quote more frequently, as being the best and most faithful witness of all antiquity), where he says that after Christ was revealed, sacraments were instituted, fewer in number, but of more august significancy and more excellent power (De Doct. Christ. Lib. iii. ; et Ep. ad Janur.). It is here proper to remind the reader, that all the trifling talk of the sophists concerning the *opus operatum*,[1] is not only false, but repugnant to the very nature of sacraments, which God appointed in order that believers, who are void and in want of all good, might bring nothing of their own, but simply beg. Hence it follows, that in receiving them they do nothing which deserves praise, and that in this action (which in respect of them is merely passive [2]) no work can be ascribed to them.

1 The French adds, "Qu'ils appellent en leur gergon."—So called in their jargon.

2 The French adds, "J'appel le acte passif, pourceque Dieu fait le tout, et seulement nous recevons."—I call the act passive, because God does the whole, and we only receive.

CHAPTER XV.

OF BAPTISM.

There are two parts of this chapter,—I. Dissertation on the two ends of Baptism, sec, 1–13. II. The second part may be reduced to four heads. Of the use of Baptism, sec. 14, 15. Of the worthiness or unworthiness of the minister, sec. 16–18. Of the corruptions by which this sacrament was polluted, sec. 19. To whom reference is had in the dispensation, sec. 20–22.

Sections.

1. Baptism defined. Its primary object. This consists of three things. 1. To attest the forgiveness of sins.
2. Passages of Scripture proving the forgiveness of sins.
3. Forgiveness not only of past but also of future sins. This no encouragement to license in sin.
4. Refutation of those who share forgiveness between Baptism and Repentance.
5. Second thing in Baptism—viz. to teach that we are ingrafted into Christ for mortification and newness of life.
6. Third thing in Baptism—viz. to teach us that we are united to Christ so as to be partakers of all his blessings. Second and third things conspicuous in the baptism both of John and the apostles.
7. Identity of the baptism of John and the apostles.
8. An objection to this refuted.
9. The benefits of baptism typified to the Israelites by the passage of the Red Sea and the pillar of cloud.
10. Objection of those who imagine that there is some kind of perfect renovation after baptism. Original depravity remains after baptism. Its existence in infants. The elect after baptism are righteous in this life only by imputation.
11. Original corruption trying to the pious during the whole course of their lives. They do not, on this account, seek a licence for sin. They rather walk more cautiously and safely in the ways of the Lord.
12. The trouble occasioned by corruption, shown by the example and testimony of the Apostle Paul.
13. Another end of baptism is to serve as our confession to men.
14. Second part of the chapter. Of baptism as a confirmation of our faith.
15. This illustrated by the examples of Cornelius and Paul. Of the use of baptism as a confession of faith.
16. Baptism not affected by the worthiness or unworthiness of the minister. Hence no necessity to rebaptise those who were baptised under the Papacy.
17. Nothing in the argument that those so baptised remained some years blind and unbelieving. The promise of God remains firm. God, in inviting the Jews to repentance, does not enjoin them to be again circumcised.
18. No ground to allege that Paul rebaptised certain of John's disciples. The baptism of John. What it is to be baptised in the name of Christ.
19. The corruptions introduced into baptism. The form of pure Christian baptism. Immersion or sprinkling should be left free.
20. To whom the dispensation of baptism belongs. Not to private individuals or women, but to the ministers of the Church. Origin of the baptism of private individuals and women. An argument in favour of it refuted.
21. Exploded also by Tertullian and Epiphanius.
22. Objection founded on the case of Zipporah. Answer. Children dying before baptism not excluded from heaven, provided the want of it was not caused by negligence or contempt.

1. Baptism is the initiatory sign by which we are admitted to the fellowship of the Church, that being ingrafted into Christ we may be accounted children of God. Moreover, the end for which God has given it (this I have shown to be common to all mysteries) is, first, that it may be conducive to our faith in him; and, secondly, that it may serve the purpose of a confession among men. The nature of both institutions we shall explain in order. Baptism contributes to our faith three things, which require to be treated separately. The first object, therefore, for which it is appointed by the Lord, is to be a sign and evidence of our purification, or (better to explain my meaning) it is a kind of sealed instrument by which he assures us that all our sins are so deleted, covered, and effaced, that they will never come into his sight, never be mentioned, never imputed. For it is his will that all who have believed, be baptised for the remission of sins. Hence those who have thought that baptism is nothing else than the badge and mark by which we profess our religion before men, in the same way as soldiers attest their profession by bearing the insignia of their commander, having not attended to what was the principal thing in baptism; and this is, that we are to receive it in connection with the promise, "He that believeth and is baptised shall be saved" (Mark xvi. 16).

2. In this sense is to be understood the statement of Paul, that "Christ loved the Church, and gave himself for it, that he might sanctify and cleanse it with the washing of water by the word" (Eph. v. 25, 26); and again, "not by works of righteousness which we have done, but according to his mercy he saved us, by the washing of regeneration and renewing of the Holy Ghost" (Titus iii. v.). Peter also says that "baptism also doth now save us" (1 Peter iii. 21). For he did not mean to intimate that our ablution and salvation are perfected by water, or that water possesses in itself the virtue of purifying, regenerating, and renewing; nor does he mean that it is the cause of salvation, but only that the knowledge and certainty of such gifts are perceived in this sacrament. This the words themselves evidently show. For Paul connects together the word of life and baptism of water, as if he had said, by the gospel the message of our ablution and sanctification is announced; by baptism this message is sealed. And Peter immediately subjoins, that that baptism is "not the putting away of the filth of the flesh, but the answer of a good conscience toward God, which is of faith." Nay, the only purification which baptism promises is by means of the sprinkling of the blood of Christ, who is figured by water from the resemblance to cleansing and washing. Who, then, can say that we are cleansed by that water which certainly attests that the blood of Christ is our true and only laver? So that we cannot have a better argument to refute the hallucination of those who ascribe the whole to the virtue of water than we derive from the very meaning of baptism, which leads us away as well from the visible element which is

presented to our eye, as from all other means, that it may fix our minds on Christ alone.

3. Nor is it to be supposed that baptism is bestowed only with reference to the past, so that, in regard to new lapses into which we fall after baptism, we must seek new remedies of expiation in other so-called sacraments, just as if the power of baptism had become obsolete. To this error, in ancient times, it was owing that some refused to be initiated by baptism until their life was in extreme danger, and they were drawing their last breath, that they might thus obtain pardon for all the past. Against this preposterous precaution ancient bishops frequently inveigh in their writings. We ought to consider that at whatever time we are baptised, we are washed and purified once for the whole of life. Wherefore, as often as we fall, we must recall the remembrance of our baptism, and thus fortify our minds, so as to feel certain and secure of the remission of sins. For though, when once administered, it seems to have passed, it is not abolished by subsequent sins. For the purity of Christ was therein offered to us, always is in force, and is not destroyed by any stain: it wipes and washes away all our defilements. Nor must we hence assume a licence of sinning for the future (there is certainly nothing in it to countenance such audacity), but this doctrine is intended only for those who, when they have sinned, groan under their sins burdened and oppressed, that they may have wherewith to support and console themselves, and not rush headlong into despair. Thus Paul says that Christ was made a propitiation for us for the remission of sins that are past (Rom. iii. 25). By this he denies not that constant and perpetual forgiveness of sins is thereby obtained even till death: he only intimates that it is designed by the Father for those poor sinners who, wounded by remorse of conscience, sigh for the physician. To these the mercy of God is offered. Those who, from hopes of impunity, seek a licence for sin, only provoke the wrath and justice of God.

4. I know it is a common belief that forgiveness, which at our first regeneration we receive by baptism alone, is after baptism procured by means of penitence and the keys (see chap. xix. sec. 17). But those who entertain this fiction err from not considering that the power of the keys, of which they speak, so depends on baptism, that it ought not on any account to be separated from it. The sinner receives forgiveness by the ministry of the Church; in other words, not without the preaching of the gospel. And of what nature is this preaching? That we are washed from our sins by the blood of Christ. And what is the sign and evidence of that washing if it be not baptism? We see, then, that that forgiveness has reference to baptism. This error had its origin in the fictitious sacrament of penance, on which I have already touched. What remains will be said at the proper place. There is no wonder if men who, from the grossness of their minds, are excessively attached to external things, have nere also betrayed the defect,—if not contented with the pure

institution of God, they have introduced new helps devised by themselves, as if baptism were not itself a sacrament of penance. But if repentance is recommended during the whole of life, the power of baptism ought to have the same extent. Wherefore, there can be no doubt that all the godly may, during the whole course of their lives, whenever they are vexed by a consciousness of their sins, recall the remembrance of their baptism, that they may thereby assure themselves of that sole and perpetual ablution which we have in the blood of Christ.

5. Another benefit of baptism is, that it shows us our mortification in Christ and new life in him. "Know ye not," says the apostle, "that as many of us as were baptised into Jesus Christ, were baptised into his death? Therefore we are buried with him by baptism into death," that we "should walk in newness of life" (Rom. vi. 3, 4). By these words, he not only exhorts us to imitation of Christ, as if he had said, that we are admonished by baptism, in like manner as Christ died, to die to our lusts, and as he rose, to rise to righteousness; but he traces the matter much higher, that Christ by baptism has made us partakers of his death, ingrafting us into it. And as the twig derives substance and nourishment from the root to which it is attached, so those who receive baptism with true faith truly feel the efficacy of Christ's death in the mortification of their flesh, and the efficacy of his resurrection in the quickening of the Spirit. On this he founds his exhortation, that if we are Christians we should be dead unto sin, and alive unto righteousness. He elsewhere uses the same argument—viz. that we are circumcised, and put off the old man, after we are buried in Christ by baptism (Col. ii. 12). And in this sense, in the passage which we formerly quoted, he calls it "the washing of regeneration, and renewing of the Holy Ghost" (Tit. iii. 5). We are promised, first, the free pardon of sins and imputation of righteousness; and, secondly, the grace of the Holy Spirit, to form us again to newness of life.

6. The last advantage which our faith receives from baptism is its assuring us not only that we are ingrafted into the death and life of Christ, but so united to Christ himself as to be partakers of all his blessings. For he consecrated and sanctified baptism in his own body, that he might have it in common with us as the firmest bond of union and fellowship which he deigned to form with us; and hence Paul proves us to be the sons of God, from the fact that we put on Christ in baptism (Gal. iii. 27). Thus we see the fulfilment of our baptism in Christ, whom for this reason we call the proper object of baptism. Hence it is not strange that the apostles are said to have baptised in the name of Christ, though they were enjoined to baptise in the name of the Father and Spirit also (Acts viii. 16; xix. 5; Matth. xxviii. 19). For all the divine gifts held forth in baptism are found in Christ alone. And yet he who baptises into Christ cannot but at the same time invoke the name of the Father and the Spirit. For we are cleansed by his blood, just because our

gracious Father, of his incomparable mercy, willing to receive us into favour, appointed him Mediator to effect our reconciliation with himself. Regeneration we obtain from his death and resurrection only, when sanctified by his Spirit we are imbued with a new and spiritual nature. Wherefore we obtain, and in a manner distinctly perceive, in the Father the cause, in the Son the matter, and in the Spirit the effect of our purification and regeneration. Thus first John baptised, and thus afterwards the apostles by the baptism of repentance for the remission of sins, understanding by the term *repentance*, regeneration, and by the *remission* of sins, ablution.

7. This makes it perfectly certain that the ministry of John was the very same as that which was afterwards delegated to the apostles. For the different hands by which baptism is administered do not make it a different baptism, but sameness of doctrine proves it to be the same. John and the apostles agreed in one doctrine. Both baptised unto repentance, both for remission of sins, both in the name of Christ, from whom repentance and remission of sins proceed. John pointed to him as the Lamb of God who taketh away the sins of the world (John i. 29), thus describing him as the victim accepted of the Father, the propitiation of righteousness, and the author of salvation. What could the apostles add to this confession? Wherefore, let no one be perplexed because ancient writers labour to distinguish the one from the other. Their views ought not to be in such esteem with us as to shake the certainty of Scripture. For who would listen to Chrysostom denying that remission of sins was included in the baptism of John (Hom. in Matth. i. 14), rather than to Luke asserting, on the contrary, that John preached "the baptism of repentance for the remission of sins"? (Luke iii. 3). Nor can we admit Augustine's subtlety, that by the baptism of John sins were forgiven in hope, but by the baptism of Christ are forgiven in reality. For seeing the Evangelist clearly declares that John in his baptism promised the remission of sins, why detract from this eulogium when no necessity compels it? Should any one ask what difference the word of God makes, he will find it to be nothing more than that John baptised in the name of him who was to come, the apostles in the name of him who was already manifested (Luke iii. 16; Acts xix. 4).

8. This fact, that the gifts of the Spirit were more liberally poured out after the resurrection of Christ, does not go to establish a diversity of baptisms. For baptism, administered by the apostles while he was still on the earth, was called his baptism, and yet the Spirit was not poured out in larger abundance on it than on the baptism of John. Nay, not even after the ascension did the Samaritans receive the Spirit above the ordinary measure of former believers, till Peter and John were sent to lay hands on them (Acts viii. 14–17). I imagine that the thing which imposed on ancient writers, and made them say that the one baptism was only a preparative to the other, was, because they read that those who had received the baptism of

John were again baptised by Paul (Acts xix. 3–5; Matth. iii. 11). How greatly they are mistaken in this will be most clearly explained in its own place. Why, then, did John say that he baptised with water, but there was one coming who would baptise with the Holy Ghost and with fire? This may be explained in a few words. He did not mean to distinguish the one baptism from the other, but he contrasted his own person with the person of Christ, saying, that while he was a minister of water, Christ was the giver of the Holy Spirit, and would declare this virtue by a visible miracle on the day on which he would send the Holy Spirit on the apostles, under the form of tongues of fire. What greater boast could the apostles make, and what greater those who baptise in the present day? For they are only ministers of the external sign, whereas Christ is the Author of internal grace, as those same ancient writers uniformly teach, and, in particular, Augustine, who, in his refutation of the Donatists, founds chiefly on this axiom, Whoever it is that baptises, Christ alone presides.

9. The things which we have said, both of mortification and ablution, were adumbrated among the people of Israel, who, for that reason, are described by the apostle as having been baptised in the cloud and in the sea (1 Cor. x. 2). Mortification was figured when the Lord, vindicating them from the hand of Pharaoh and from cruel bondage, paved a way for them through the Red Sea, and drowned Pharaoh himself and their Egyptian foes, who were pressing close behind, and threatening them with destruction. For in this way also he promises us in baptism, and shows by a given sign that we are led by his might, and delivered from the captivity of Egypt, that is, from the bondage of sin, that our Pharaoh is drowned; in other words, the devil, although he ceases not to try and harass us. But as that Egyptian was not plunged into the depth of the sea, but cast out upon the shore, still alarmed the Israelites by the terror of his look, though he could not hurt them, so our enemy still threatens, shows his arms and is felt, but cannot conquer. The cloud was a symbol of purification (Num. ix. 18). For as the Lord then covered them by an opposite cloud, and kept them cool, that they might not faint or pine away under the burning rays of the sun; so in baptism we perceive that we are covered and protected by the blood of Christ, lest the wrath of God, which is truly an intolerable flame, should lie upon us. Although the mystery was then obscure, and known to few, yet as there is no other method of obtaining salvation than in those two graces, God was pleased that the ancient fathers, whom he had adopted as heirs, should be furnished with both badges.

10. It is now clear how false the doctrine is which some long ago taught, and others still persist in, that by baptism we are exempted and set free from original sin, and from the corruption which was propagated by Adam to all his posterity, and that we are restored to the same righteousness and purity of nature which Adam would have had if he had maintained the integrity in which he was created. This

class of teachers never understand what is meant by original sin, original righteousness, or the grace of baptism. Now, it has been previously shown (Book II. chap. i. sec. 8), that original sin is the depravity and corruption of our nature, which first makes us liable to the wrath of God, and then produces in us works which Scripture terms *the works of the flesh* (Gal. v. 19). The two things, therefore, must be distinctly observed—viz. that we are vitiated and perverted in all parts of our nature, and then, on account of this corruption, are justly held to be condemned and convicted before God, to whom nothing is acceptable but purity, innocence, and righteousness. And hence, even infants bring their condemnation with them from their mother's womb ; for although they have not yet brought forth the fruits of their unrighteousness, they have its seed included in them. Nay, their whole nature is, as it were, a seed of sin, and, therefore, cannot but be odious and abominable to God. Believers become assured by baptism, that this condemnation is entirely withdrawn from them, since (as has been said) the Lord by this sign promises that a full and entire remission has been made, both of the guilt which was imputed to us, and the penalty incurred by the guilt. They also apprehend righteousness, but such righteousness as the people of God can obtain in this life—viz. by imputation only, God, in his mercy, regarding them as righteous and innocent.

11. Another point is, that this corruption never ceases in us, but constantly produces new fruits—viz. those works of the flesh which we previously described, just as a burning furnace perpetually sends forth flame and sparks, or a fountain is ever pouring out water. For concupiscence never wholly dies or is extinguished in men, until, freed by death from the body of death, they have altogether laid aside their own nature (Book III. chap. iii. sec. 10-13). Baptism, indeed, tells us that our Pharaoh is drowned and sin mortified ; not so, however, as no longer to exist, or give no trouble, but only so as not to have dominion. For as long as we live shut up in this prison of the body, the remains of sin dwell in us, but if we faithfully hold the promise which God has given us in baptism, they will neither rule nor reign. But let no man deceive himself, let no man look complacently on his disease, when he hears that sin always dwells in us. When we say so, it is not in order that those who are otherwise too prone to sin may sleep securely in their sins, but only that those who are tried and stung by the flesh may not faint and despond. Let them rather reflect that they are still on the way, and think that they have made great progress when they feel that their concupiscence is somewhat diminished from day to day, until they shall have reached the point at which they aim—viz. the final death of the flesh ; a death which shall be completed at the termination of this mortal life. Meanwhile, let them cease not to contend strenuously, and animate themselves to further progress, and press on to complete victory. Their efforts should be stimulated by the consideration, that after a lengthened struggle much still remains to be done. We ought to

hold that we are baptised for the mortification of our flesh, which is begun in baptism, is prosecuted every day, and will be finished when we depart from this life to go to the Lord.

12. Here we say nothing more than the apostle Paul expounds most clearly in the sixth and seventh chapters of the Epistle to the Romans. He had discoursed of free justification, but as some wicked men thence inferred that they were to live as they listed, because their acceptance with God was not procured by the merit of works, he adds, that all who are clothed with the righteousness of Christ are at the same time regenerated by the Spirit, and that we have an earnest of this regeneration in baptism. Hence he exhorts believers not to allow sin to reign in their members. And because he knew that there is always some infirmity in believers, lest they should be cast down on this account, he adds, for their consolation, that they are not under the law. Again, as there may seem a danger that Christians might grow presumptuous because they were not under the yoke of the law, he shows what the nature of the abrogation is, and at the same time what the use of the law is. This question he had already postponed a second time. The substance is, that we are freed from the rigour of the law in order that we may adhere to Christ, and that the office of the law is to convince us of our depravity, and make us confess our impotence and wretchedness. Moreover, as this malignity of nature is not so easily apparent in a profane man who, without fear of God, indulges his passions, he gives an example in the regenerate man, in other words, in himself. He therefore says that he had a constant struggle with the remains of his flesh, and was kept in miserable bondage, so as to be unable to devote himself entirely to the obedience of the divine law. Hence he is forced to groan and exclaim, "O wretched man that I am! who shall deliver me from the body of this death?" (Rom. vii. 24). But if the children of God are kept captive in prison as long as they live, they must necessarily feel very anxious at the thought of their danger, unless their fears are allayed. For this single purpose, then, he subjoins the consolation, that there is "now no condemnation to them which are in Christ Jesus" (Rom. viii. 1). Hence he teaches that those whom the Lord has once admitted into favour, and ingrafted into communion with Christ, and received into the fellowship of the Church by baptism, are freed from guilt and condemnation while they persevere in the faith of Christ, though they may be beset by sin and thus bear sin about with them. If this is the simple and genuine interpretation of Paul's meaning, we cannot think that there is anything strange in the doctrine which he here delivers.[1]

1 French, "Nous suivons donc de mot à mot la doctrine de Sainct Paul, en ce que nous disons que le peché est remis au Baptesme, quant à la coulpe, mais qu'il demeure toujours quant à la matière, en tous Chretiens jusques à la mort."—We therefore follow the doctrine of St Paul, word for word, when we say that in Baptism, sin is forgiven as to the guilt, but that it always remains as to the matter in all Christians until death.

13. Baptism serves as our confession before men, inasmuch as it is a mark by which we openly declare that we wish to be ranked among the people of God, by which we testify that we concur with all Christians in the worship of one God, and in one religion; by which, in short, we publicly assert our faith, so that not only do our hearts breathe, but our tongues also, and all the members of our body, in every way they can, proclaim the praise of God. In this way, as is meet, everything we have is made subservient to the glory of God, which ought everywhere to be displayed, and others are stimulated by our example to the same course. To this Paul referred when he asked the Corinthians whether or not they had been baptised in the name of Christ (1 Cor. i. 13); intimating, that by the very circumstance of having been baptised in his name, they had devoted themselves to him, had sworn and bound themselves in allegiance to him before men, so that they could no longer confess any other than Christ alone, unless they would abjure the confession which they had made in baptism.

14. Now that the end to which the Lord had regard in the institution of baptism has been explained, it is easy to judge in what way we ought to use and receive it. For inasmuch as it is appointed to elevate, nourish, and confirm our faith, we are to receive it as from the hand of its author, being firmly persuaded that it is himself who speaks to us by means of the sign; that it is himself who washes and purifies us, and effaces the remembrance of our faults; that it is himself who makes us the partakers of his death, destroys the kingdom of Satan, subdues the power of concupiscence, nay, makes us one with himself, that being clothed with him we may be accounted the children of God. These things, I say, we ought to feel as truly and certainly in our mind as we see our body washed, immersed, and surrounded with water. For this analogy or similitude furnishes the surest rule in the sacraments—viz. that in corporeal things we are to see spiritual, just as if they were actually exhibited to our eye, since the Lord has been pleased to represent them by such figures; not that such graces are included and bound in the sacrament, so as to be conferred by its efficacy, but only that by this badge the Lord declares to us that he is pleased to bestow all these things upon us. Nor does he merely feed our eyes with bare show; he leads us to the actual object, and effectually performs what he figures.

15. We have a proof of this in Cornelius the centurion, who, after he had been previously endued with the graces of the Holy Spirit, was baptised for the remission of sins, not seeking a fuller forgiveness from baptism, but a surer exercise of faith; nay, an argument for assurance from a pledge. It will, perhaps, be objected, Why did Ananias say to Paul that he washed away his sins by baptism (Acts xxii. 16), if sins are not washed away by the power of baptism? I answer, we are said to receive, procure, and obtain, whatever according to the perception of our faith is exhibited to us by the Lord, whether he then attests it for the first time, or gives additional con-

firmation to what he had previously attested. All then that Ananias meant to say was, Be baptised, Paul, that you may be assured that your sins are forgiven you. In baptism, the Lord promises forgiveness of sins: receive it, and be secure. I have no intention, however, to detract from the power of baptism. I would only add to the sign the substance and reality, inasmuch as God works by external means. But from this sacrament, as from all others, we gain nothing, unless in so far as we receive in faith. If faith is wanting, it will be an evidence of our ingratitude, by which we are proved guilty before God, for not believing the promise there given. In so far as it is a sign of our confession, we ought thereby to testify that we confide in the mercy of God, and are pure, through the forgiveness of sins which Christ Jesus has procured for us; that we have entered into the Church of God, that with one consent of faith and love we may live in concord with all believers. This last was Paul's meaning, when he said that "by one Spirit are we all baptised into one body" (1 Cor. xii. 13).

16. Moreover, if we have rightly determined that a sacrament is not to be estimated by the hand of him by whom it is administered, but is to be received as from the hand of God himself, from whom it undoubtedly proceeded, we may hence infer that its dignity neither gains nor loses by the administrator. And, just as among men, when a letter has been sent, if the hand and seal is recognised, it is not of the least consequence who or what the messenger was; so it ought to be sufficient for us to recognise the hand and seal of our Lord in his sacraments, let the administrator be who he may. This confutes the error of the Donatists, who measured the efficacy and worth of the sacrament by the dignity of the minister. Such in the present day are our Catabaptists, who deny that we are duly baptised, because we were baptised in the Papacy by wicked men and idolaters; hence they furiously insist on anabaptism. Against these absurdities we shall be sufficiently fortified if we reflect that by baptism we were initiated not into the name of any man, but into the name of the Father, and the Son, and the Holy Spirit; and, therefore, that baptism is not of man, but of God, by whomsoever it may have been administered. Be it that those who baptised us were most ignorant of God and all piety, or were despisers, still they did not baptise us into a fellowship with their ignorance or sacrilege, but into the faith of Jesus Christ, because the name which they invoked was not their own but God's, nor did they baptise into any other name. But if baptism was of God, it certainly included in it the promise of forgiveness of sin, mortification of the flesh, quickening of the Spirit, and communion with Christ. Thus it did not harm the Jews that they were circumcised by impure and apostate priests. It did not nullify the symbol so as to make it necessary to repeat it. It was enough to return to its genuine origin. The objection that baptism ought to be celebrated in the assembly of the godly, does not prove that it loses its whole efficacy because it is partly defective. When we show what

ought to be done to keep baptism pure and free from every taint, we do not abolish the institution of God though idolaters may corrupt it. Circumcision was anciently vitiated by many superstitions, and yet ceased not to be regarded as a symbol of grace; nor did Josiah and Hezekiah, when they assembled out of all Israel those who had revolted from God, call them to be circumcised anew.

17. Then, again, when they ask us what faith for several years followed our baptism, that they may thereby prove that our baptism was in vain, since it is not sanctified unless the word of the promise is received with faith, our answer is, that being blind and unbelieving, we for a long time did not hold the promise which was given us in baptism, but that still the promise, as it was of God, always remained fixed, and firm, and true. Although all men should be false and perfidious, yet God ceases not to be true (Rom. iii. 3, 4); though all were lost, Christ remains safe. We acknowledge, therefore, that at that time baptism profited us nothing, since in us the offered promise, without which baptism is nothing, lay neglected. Now, when by the grace of God we begin to repent, we accuse our blindness and hardness of heart in having been so long ungrateful for his great goodness. But we do not believe that the promise itself has vanished, we rather reflect thus: God in baptism promises the remission of sins, and will undoubtedly perform what he has promised to all believers. That promise was offered to us in baptism, let us therefore embrace it in faith. In regard to us, indeed, it was long buried on account of unbelief; now, therefore, let us with faith receive it. Wherefore, when the Lord invites the Jewish people to repentance, he gives no injunction concerning another circumcision, though (as we have said) they were circumcised by a wicked and sacrilegious hand, and had long lived in the same impiety. All he urges is conversion of heart. For how much soever the covenant might have been violated by them, the symbol of the covenant always remained, according to the appointment of the Lord, firm and inviolable. Solely, therefore, on the condition of repentance, were they restored to the covenant which God had once made with them in circumcision, though this which they had received at the hand of a covenant-breaking priest, they had themselves as much as in them lay polluted and extinguished.

18. But they seem to think the weapon which they brandish irresistible, when they allege that Paul rebaptised those who had been baptised with the baptism of John (Acts xix. 3, 5). For if, by our confession, the baptism of John was the same as ours, then, in like manner as those who had been improperly trained, when they learned the true faith, were rebaptised into it, ought that baptism which was without true doctrine to be accounted as nothing, and hence we ought to be baptised anew into the true religion with which we are now, for the first time, imbued? It seems to some that it was a foolish imitator of John, who, by a former baptism, had initiated them into vain superstition. This, it is thought, may be conjectured

from the fact, that they acknowledge their entire ignorance of the Holy Spirit, an ignorance in which John never would have left his disciples. But it is not probable that the Jews, even though they had not been baptised at all, would have been destitute of all knowledge of the Spirit, who is celebrated in so many passages of Scripture. Their answer, therefore, that they knew not whether there was a Spirit, must be understood as if they had said, that they had not yet heard whether or not the gifts of the Spirit, as to which Paul questioned them, were given to the disciples of Christ. I grant that John's was a true baptism, and one and the same with the baptism of Christ. But I deny that they were rebaptised (see Calv. Instruct. adv. Anabapt.). What then is meant by the words, "They were baptised in the name of the Lord Jesus"? Some interpret that they were only instructed in sound doctrine by Paul; but I would rather interpret more simply, that the baptism of the Holy Spirit, in other words, the visible gifts of the Holy Spirit, were given by the laying on of hands. These are sometimes designated under the name of baptism. Thus, on the day of Pentecost, the apostles are said to have remembered the words of the Lord concerning the baptism of the Spirit and of fire. And Peter relates that the same words occurred to him when he saw these gifts poured out on Cornelius and his family and kindred. There is nothing repugnant to this interpretation in its being afterwards added, "When Paul had laid his hands upon them, the Holy Ghost came on them" (Acts xix. 6). For Luke does not narrate two different things, but follows the form of narrative common to the Hebrews, who first give the substance, and then explain more fully. This any one may perceive from the mere context. For he says, "When they heard this they were baptised in the name of the Lord Jesus. And when Paul laid his hands upon them, the Holy Ghost came on them." In this last sentence is described what the nature of the baptism was. But if ignorance vitiates a former, and requires to be corrected by a second baptism, the apostles should first of all have been rebaptised, since for more than three full years after their baptism they had scarcely received any slender portion of purer doctrine. Then so numerous being the acts of ignorance which by the mercy of God are daily corrected in us, what rivers would suffice for so many repeated baptisms?

19. The force, dignity, utility, and end of the sacrament must now, if I mistake not, be sufficiently clear. In regard to the external symbol, I wish the genuine institution of Christ had been maintained as fit to repress the audacity of men. As if to be baptised with water, according to the precept of Christ, had been a contemptible thing, a benedicion, or rather incantation, was devised to pollute the true consecration of water. There was afterwards added the taper and chrism, while exorcism[1] was thought to open the door for baptism. Though I am not unaware how ancient the origin of this

[1] Latin, "Exsufflatio."—French, "Le souffle pour conjurer le diable."

adventitious farrago is, still it is lawful for me and all the godly to reject whatever men have presumed to add to the institution of Christ. When Satan saw that by the foolish credulity of the world his impostures were received almost without objection at the commencement of the gospel, he proceeded to grosser mockery: hence spittle and other follies, to the open disgrace of baptism, were introduced with unbridled licence.[1] From our experience of them, let us learn that there is nothing holier, or better, or safer, than to be contented with the authority of Christ alone. How much better, therefore, is it to lay aside all theatrical pomp, which dazzles the eyes of the simple, and dulls their minds, and when any one is to be baptised to bring him forward and present him to God, the whole Church looking on as witnesses, and praying over him; to recite the Confession of Faith, in which the catechumen has been instructed, explain the promises which are given in baptism, then baptise in the name of the Father, and the Son, and the Holy Spirit, and conclude with prayer and thanksgiving. In this way, nothing which is appropriate would be omitted, and the one ceremony, which proceeded from its divine Author, would shine forth most brightly, not being buried or polluted by extraneous observances. Whether the person baptised is to be wholly immersed, and that whether once or thrice, or whether he is only to be sprinkled with water, is not of the least consequence: churches should be at liberty to adopt either, according to the diversity of climates, although it is evident that the term *baptise* means to immerse, and that this was the form used by the primitive Church.[2]

20. It is here also pertinent to observe, that it is improper for private individuals to take upon themselves the administration of baptism; for it, as well as the dispensation of the Supper, is part of the ministerial office. For Christ did not give command to any men or women whatever to baptise, but to those whom he had appointed apostles. And when, in the administration of the Supper, he ordered his disciples to do what they had seen him do (he having done the part of a legitimate dispenser), he doubtless meant that in this they should imitate his example. The practice which has been in use for many ages, and even almost from the very commencement of the Church, for laics to baptise, in danger of death, when a minister

1 Vid. Calv. in Epist. de Fugiendis illicitis sacris. Item, Vera Ecclesia Reformandæ Ratio. See also infra, chap. xvii. sec. 43. As to the form of baptism, see Cyprian, Lib. iv. Ep. 7.

2 French, "Au reste, c'est une chose de nulle importance, si on baptise en plongeant du tout dans l'eau celui qui est baptisé, ou en repandant seulement de l'eau sur lui: mais selon la diversité des regions cela doit demeura en la liberté des Eglises. Car le signe est representé en l'un et en l'autre. Combien que le mot mesme de Baptiser signifie du tout plonger et qu'il soit certain que la coustume d'ainsi totalement plonger, ait eté anciennement observée en l'Eglise."—Moreover, it is a matter of no importance whether we baptise by entirely immersing the person baptised in the water, or only by sprinkling water upon him, but, according to the diversity of countries, this should remain free to the churches. For the sign is represented in either. Although the mere term Baptise means to immerse entirely, and it is certain that the custom of thus entirely immersing was anciently observed in the Church.

could not be present in time, cannot, it appears to me, be defended on sufficient grounds. Even the early Christians who observed or tolerated this practice were not clear whether it were rightly done. This doubt is expressed by Augustine when he says, "Although a laic have given baptism when compelled by necessity, I know not whether any one can piously say that it ought to be repeated. For if it is done without any necessity compelling it, it is usurpation of another's office; but if necessity urges, it is either no fault, or a venial one" (August. Cont. Epist. Parmen. Lib. ii. c. 13). With regard to women, it was decreed, without exception, in the Council of Carthage (cap. 100), that they were not to presume to baptise at all. But there is a danger that he who is sick may be deprived of the gift of regeneration if he decease without baptism! By no means. Our children, before they are born, God declares that he adopts for his own when he promises that he will be a God to us, and to our seed after us. In this promise their salvation is included. None will dare to offer such an insult to God as to deny that he is able to give effect to his promise. How much evil has been caused by the dogma, ill expounded, that baptism is necessary to salvation, few perceive, and therefore think caution the less necessary. For when the opinion prevails that all are lost who happen not to be dipped in water, our condition becomes worse than that of God's ancient people, as if his grace were more restrained than under the Law. In that case, Christ will be thought to have come not to fufil, but to abolish the promises, since the promise, which was then effectual in itself to confer salvation before the eighth day, would not now be effectual without the help of a sign.

21. What the custom was before Augustine's day is gathered, first, from Tertullian, who says, that a woman is not permitted to speak in the Church, nor yet to teach, or baptise, or offer. that she may not claim to herself any office of the man, not to say of the priest (Tertull. Cont. Hæres. Lib. i.). Of the same thing we have a sufficient witness in Epiphanius, when he upbraids Marcian with giving permission to women to baptise. I am not unaware of the answer given by those who take an opposite view—viz. that common use is very different from an extraordinary remedy used under the pressure of extreme necessity—but since he declares it mockery to allow women to baptise, and makes no exception, it is sufficiently plain that the corruption is condemned as inexcusable on any pretext. In his Third Book, also, when he says that it was not even permitted to the holy mother of Christ, he makes no reservation.

22. The example of Zipporah (Exod. iv. 25) is irrelevantly quoted. Because the angel of God was appeased after she took a stone and circumcised her son, it is erroneously inferred that her act was approved by God. Were it so, we must say that God was pleased with a worship which Gentiles brought from Assyria, and set up in Samaria.[1] But other valid reasons prove, that what a foolish woman

1 French, "Car par une mesme raison il faudroit dire, le service meslé que dres-

did is ignorantly drawn into a precedent. Were I to say that there was something special in the case, making it unfit for a precedent—and especially as we nowhere read that the command to circumcise was specially given to priests, the cases of baptism and circumcision are different—I should give a sufficient refutation. For the words of Christ are plain: "Go ye, therefore, and teach all nations, baptising them" (Matth. xxviii. 19). Since he appointed the same persons to be preachers of the Gospel, and dispensers of baptism—and in the Church, "no man taketh this honour unto himself," as the apostle declares (Heb. v. 4), "but he that is called of God, as was Aaron"—any one who baptises without a lawful call usurps another's office. Paul declares, that whatever we attempt with a dubious conscience, even in the minutest matters, as in meat and drink, is sin (Rom. xiv. 23). Therefore, in baptism by women, the sin is the greater, when it is plain that the rule delivered by Christ is violated, seeing we know it to be unlawful to put asunder what God has joined. But all this I pass; only I would have my readers to observe, that the last thing intended by Zipporah was to perform a service to God. Seeing her son in danger, she frets and murmurs, and, not without indignation, throws down the foreskin on the ground; thus upbraiding her husband, and taking offence at God. In short, it is plain that her whole procedure is dictated by passion: she complains both against her husband and against God, because she is forced to spill the blood of her son. We may add, that however well she might have conducted herself in all other respects, yet her presumption is inexcusable in this, in circumcising her son while her husband is present, and that husband not a mere private individual, but Moses, the chief prophet of God, than whom no greater ever arose in Israel. This was no more allowable in her, than it would be for women in the present day under the eye of a bishop. But this controversy will at once be disposed of when we maintain, that children who happen to depart this life before an opportunity of immersing them in water, are not excluded from the kingdom of heaven. Now, it has been seen, that unless we admit this position, great injury is done to the covenant of God, as if in itself it were weak, whereas its effect depends not either on baptism, or on any accessaries. The sacrament is afterwards added as a kind of seal, not to give efficacy to the promise, as if in itself invalid, but merely to confirm it to us. Hence it follows, that the children of believers are not baptised, in order that though formerly aliens from the Church, they may then, for the first time, become children of God, but rather are received into the Church by a formal sign, because, in virtue of the promise, they previously belonged to the body of Christ. Hence if, in omitting the sign, their is neither sloth, nor

serent en Samarie ceux qui etoient la envoyés d'Orient, eut eté agreable a Dieu, veu que depuis ils ne furent plus molestes des betes sauvages."—For the same reason it would be necessary to say, that the mongrel worship set up in Samaria by those who came from the East was agreeable to God, seeing that thereafter they were not molested by wild beasts.

contempt, nor negligence, we are safe from all danger. By far the better course, therefore, is to pay such respect to the ordinance of God as not to seek the sacraments in any other quarter than where the Lord has deposited them. When we cannot receive them from the Church, the grace of God is not so inseparably annexed to them that we cannot obtain it by faith, according to his word.

CHAPTER XVI.

PÆDOBAPTISM. ITS ACCORDANCE WITH THE INSTITUTION OF CHRIST, AND THE NATURE OF THE SIGN.

Divisions of this chapter,—I. Confirmation of the orthodox doctrine of Pædobaptism, sec. 1–9. II. Refutation of the arguments which the Anabaptists urge against Pædobaptism, sec. 10–30. III. Special objections of Servetus refuted, sec. 31, 32.

Sections.

1. Pædobaptism. The consideration of the question necessary and useful. Pædobaptism of divine origin.
2. This demonstrated from a consideration of the promises. These explain the nature and validity of Pædobaptism.
3. Promises annexed to the symbol of water cannot be better seen than in the institution of circumcision.
4. The promise and thing figured in circumcision and baptism one and the same. The only difference in the external ceremony.
5. Hence the baptism of the children of Christian parents as competent as the circumcision of Jewish children. An objection founded on a stated day for circumcision refuted.
6. An argument for Pædobaptism founded on the covenant which God made with Abraham. An objection disposed of. The grace of God not diminished by the advent of Christ.
7. Argument founded on Christ's invitation to children. Objection answered.
8. Objection, that no infants were baptised by the apostles. Answer. Objection, that pædobaptism is a novelty. Answer.
9. Twofold use and benefit of pædobaptism. In respect, 1. Of parents. 2. Of children baptised.
10. Second part of the chapter, stating the arguments of Anabaptists. Alleged dissimilitude between baptism and circumcision. First answer.
11. Second answer. The covenant in baptism and circumcision not different.
12. Third answer.
13. Infants, both Jewish and Christian, comprehended in the covenant.
14. Objection considered.
15. The Jews being comprehended in the covenant, no substantial difference between baptism and circumcision.
16. Another argument of the Anabaptists considered.
17. Argument that children are not fit to understand baptism, and therefore should not be baptised.
18. Answer continued.
19. Answer continued.
20. Answer continued.
21. Answer continued.
22. Argument, that baptism being appointed for the remission of sins, infants, not having sinned, ought not to be baptised. Answer.
23. Argument against pædobaptism, founded on the practice of the apostles. Answer.
24. Answer continued.
25. Argument founded on a saying of our Lord to Nicodemus. Answer.
26. Error of those who adjudge all who die unbaptised to eternal destruction.
27. Argument against pædobaptism, founded on the precept and example of our Saviour, in requiring instruction to precede baptism. Answer.
28. Answer continued.
29. Answer continued.

1. But since, in this age, certain frenzied spirits have raised, and even now continue to raise, great disturbance in the Church on account of pædobaptism, I cannot avoid here, by way of appendix, adding something to restrain their fury. Should any one think me more prolix than the subject is worth, let him reflect that, in a matter of the greatest moment, so much is due to the peace and purity of the Church, that we should not fastidiously object to whatever may be conducive to both. I may add, that I will study so to arrange this discussion, that it will tend, in no small degree, still farther to illustrate the subject of baptism.[1] The argument by which pædobaptism is assailed is, no doubt, specious—viz. that it is not founded on the institution of God, but was introduced merely by human presumption and depraved curiosity, and afterwards, by a foolish facility, rashly received in practice; whereas a sacrament has not a thread to hang upon, if it rest not on the sure foundation of the word of God. But what if, when the matter is properly attended to, it should be found that a calumny is falsely and unjustly brought against the holy ordinance of the Lord? First, then, let us inquire into its origin. Should it appear to have been devised merely by human rashness, let us abandon it, and regulate the true observance of baptism entirely by the will of the Lord; but should it be proved to be by no means destitute of his sure authority, let us beware of discarding the sacred institutions of God, and thereby insulting their Author.

2. In the first place, then, it is a well-known doctrine, and one as to which all the pious are agreed,—that the right consideration of signs does not lie merely in the outward ceremonies, but depends chiefly on the promise and the spiritual mysteries, to typify which the ceremonies themselves are appointed. He, therefore, who would thoroughly understand the effect of baptism—its object and true character—must not stop short at the element and corporeal object.

1 The French from the beginning of the chapter is as follows :—"Or d'autant que nous voyons l'observation que nous tenons de baptiser les petits enfans etre impugnée et debatue par aucuns esprits malins, comme si elle n'avoit point eté instituée de Dieu mais inventée nouvellement des hommes, ou pour le moins quelques années apres le tems des Apostres; j'estime qu'il viendra bien à propos, de confermer en cest endroit les consciences imbecilles, et refuter les objections mensonges qui pourroient faire teis seducteurs, pour renverser le verité de Dieu aux cœur des simples, qui ne seraient pas exercités pour repondre a leur cauteles et cavillations."—Now, inasmuch as we see that the practice which we have of baptising little children is impugned and assailed by some malignant spirits, as if it had not been appointed by God, but newly invented by men, or at least some years after the days of the Apostles, I think it will be very seasonable to confirm weak consciences in this matter, and refute the lying objections which such seducers might make, in order to overthrow the truth of God in the hearts of the simple, who might not be skilled in answering their cavils and objections.

but look forward to the divine promises which are therein offered to us, and rise to the internal secrets which are therein represented. He who understands these has reached the solid truth, and, so to speak, the whole substance of baptism, and will thence perceive the nature and use of outward sprinkling. On the other hand, he who passes them by in contempt, and keeps his thoughts entirely fixed on the visible ceremony, will neither understand the force, nor the proper nature of baptism, nor comprehend what is meant, or what end is gained by the use of water. This is confirmed by passages of Scripture too numerous and too clear to make it necessary here to discuss them more at length. It remains, therefore, to inquire into the nature and efficacy of baptism, as evinced by the promises therein given. Scripture shows, *first*, that it points to that cleansing from sin which we obtain by the blood of Christ; and, *secondly*, to the mortification of the flesh, which consists in participation in his death, by which believers are regenerated to newness of life, and thereby to the fellowship of Christ. To these general heads may be referred all that the Scriptures teach concerning baptism, with this addition, that it is also a symbol to testify our religion to men.

3. Now, since prior to the institution of baptism, the people of God had circumcision in its stead, let us see how far these two signs differ, and how far they resemble each other. In this way it will appear what analogy there is between them. When the Lord enjoins Abraham to observe circumcision (Gen. xvii. 10), he premises that he would be a God unto him and to his seed, adding, that in himself was a perfect sufficiency of all things, and that Abraham might reckon on his hand as a fountain of every blessing. These words include the promise of eternal life, as our Saviour interprets when he employs it to prove the immortality and resurrection of believers: "God," says he, "is not the God of the dead, but of the living" (Matth. xxii. 32). Hence, too, Paul, when showing to the Ephesians how great the destruction was from which the Lord had delivered them, seeing that they had not been admitted to the covenant of circumcision, infers that at that time they were aliens from the covenant of promise, without God, and without hope (Eph. ii. 12), all these being comprehended in the covenant. Now, the first access to God, the first entrance to immortal life, is the remission of sins. Hence it follows, that this corresponds to the promise of our cleansing in baptism. The Lord afterwards covenants with Abraham, that he is to walk before him in sincerity and innocence of heart: this applies to mortification or regeneration. And lest any should doubt whether circumcision were the sign of mortification, Moses explains more clearly elsewhere when he exhorts the people of Israel to circumcise the foreskin of their heart, because the Lord had chosen them for his own people, out of all the nations of the earth. As the Lord, in choosing the posterity of Abraham for his people, commands them to be circumcised, so Moses declares that they are to be circumcised in heart, thus explaining what is typified by that carnal

circumcision. Then, lest any one should attempt this in his own strength, he shows that it is the work of divine grace. All this is so often inculcated by the prophets, that there is no occasion here to collect the passages which everywhere occur. We have, therefore, a spiritual promise given to the fathers in circumcision, similar to that which is given to us in baptism, since it figured to them both the forgiveness of sins and the mortification of the flesh. Besides, as we have shown that Christ, in whom both of these reside, is the foundation of baptism, so must he also be the foundation of circumcision. For he is promised to Abraham, and in him all nations are blessed. To seal this grace, the sign of circumcision is added.

4. There is now no difficulty in seeing wherein the two signs agree, and wherein they differ. The promise, in which we have shown that the power of the signs consists, is one in both—viz. the promise of the paternal favour of God, of forgiveness of sins, and eternal life. And the thing figured is one and the same—viz. regeneration. The foundation on which the completion of these things depends is one in both. Wherefore, there is no difference in the internal meaning, from which the whole power and peculiar nature of the sacrament is to be estimated. The only difference which remains is in the external ceremony, which is the least part of it, the chief part consisting in the promise and the thing signified. Hence we may conclude, that everything applicable to circumcision applies also to baptism, excepting always the difference in the visible ceremony. To this analogy and comparison we are led by that rule of the apostle, in which he enjoins us to bring every interpretation of Scripture to the analogy of faith (Rom. xii. 3, 6). And certainly in this matter the truth may almost be felt. For just as circumcision, which was a kind of badge to the Jews, assuring them that they were adopted as the people and family of God, was their first entrance into the Church, while they, in their turn, professed their allegiance to God, so now we are initiated by baptism, so as to be enrolled among his people, and at the same time swear unto his name. Hence it is incontrovertible, that baptism has been substituted for circumcision, and performs the same office.

5. Now, if we are to investigate whether or not baptism is justly given to infants, will we not say that the man trifles, or rather is delirious, who would stop short at the element of water, and the external observance, and not allow his mind to rise to the spiritual mystery? If reason is listened to, it will undoubtedly appear that baptism is properly administered to infants as a thing due to them. The Lord did not anciently bestow circumcision upon them without making them partakers of all the things signified by circumcision. He would have deluded his pepole with mere imposture, had he quieted them with fallacious symbols: the very idea is shocking. He distinctly declares, that the circumcision of the infant will be instead of a seal of the promise of the covenant. But if the covenant remains firm and fixed, it is no less applicable to the children of Christians

in the present day, than to the children of the Jews under the Old Testament. Now, if they are partakers of the thing signified, how can they be denied the sign? If they obtain the reality, how can they be refused the figure? The external sign is so united in the sacrament with the word, that it cannot be separated from it: but if they can be separated, to which of the two shall we attach the greater value? Surely, when we see that the sign is subservient to the word, we shall say that it is subordinate, and assign it the inferior place. Since, then, the word of baptism is destined for infants, why should we deny them the sign, which is an appendage of the word? This one reason, could no other be furnished, would be amply sufficient to refute all gainsayers. The objection, that there was a fixed day for circumcision, is a mere quibble. We admit that we are not now, like the Jews, tied down to certain days; but when the Lord declares, that though he prescribes no day, yet he is pleased that infants shall be formally admitted to his covenant, what more do we ask?

6. Scripture gives us a still clearer knowledge of the truth. For it is most evident that the covenant, which the Lord once made with Abraham, is not less applicable to Christians now than it was anciently to the Jewish people, and therefore that word has no less reference to Christians than to Jews. Unless, indeed, we imagine that Christ, by his advent, diminished, or curtailed the grace of the Father—an idea not free from execrable blasphemy. Wherefore, both the children of the Jews, because, when made heirs of that covenant, they were separated from the heathen, were called a holy seed, and for the same reason the children of Christians, or those who have only one believing parent, are called holy, and, by the testimony of the apostle, differ from the impure seed of idolaters. Then, since the Lord, immediately after the covenant was made with Abraham, ordered it to be sealed in infants by an outward sacrament, how can it be said that Christains are not to attest it in the present day, and seal it in their children? Let it not be objected, that the only symbol by which the Lord ordered his covenant to be confirmed was that of circumcision, which was long ago abrogated. It is easy to answer, that, in accordance with the form of the old dispensation, he appointed circumcision to confirm his covenant, but that it being abrogated, the same reason for confirmation still continues, a reason which we have in common with the Jews. Hence it is always necessary carefully to consider what is common to both, and wherein they differed from us. The covenant is common, and the reason for confirming it is common. The mode of confirming it is so far different, that they had circumcision, instead of which we now have baptism. Otherwise, if the testimony by which the Jews were assured of the salvation of their seed is taken from us, the consequence will be, that, by the advent of Christ, the grace of God. which was formerly given to the Jews, is more obscure and less perfectly attested to us. If this cannot be said without extreme insult to Christ, by whom the infinite goodness of the Father has

been more brightly and benignly than ever shed upon the earth, and declared to men, it must be confessed that it cannot be more confined, and less clearly manifested, than under the obscure shadows of the law.

7. Hence our Lord Jesus Christ, to give an example from which the world might learn that he had come to enlarge rather than to limit the grace of the Father, kindly takes the little children in his arms, and rebukes his disciples for attempting to prevent them from coming (Matth. xix. 13), because they were keeping those to whom the kingdom of heaven belonged away from him, through whom alone there is access to heaven. But it will be asked, What resemblance is there between baptism and our Saviour embracing little children? He is not said to have baptised, but to have received, embraced, and blessed them; and, therefore, if we would imitate his example, we must give infants the benefit of our prayers, not baptise them. But let us attend to the act of our Saviour a little more carefully than these men do. For we must not lightly overlook the fact, that our Saviour, in ordering little children to be brought to him, adds the reason, "of such is the kingdom of heaven." And he afterwards testifies his good-will by act, when he embraces them, and with prayer and benediction commends them to his Father. If it is right that children should be brought to Christ, why should they not be admitted to baptism, the symbol of our communion and fellowship with Christ? If the kingdom of heaven is theirs, why should they be denied the sign by which access, as it were, is opened to the Church, that being admitted into it they may be enrolled among the heirs of the heavenly kingdom? How unjust were we to drive away those whom Christ invites to himself, to spoil those whom he adorns with his gifts, to exclude those whom he spontaneously admits. But if we insist on discussing the difference between our Saviour's act and baptism, in how much higher esteem shall we hold baptism (by which we testify that infants are included in the divine covenant), than the taking up, embracing, laying hands on children, and praying over them, acts by which Christ, when present, declares both that they are his, and are sanctified by him. By the other cavils by which the objectors endeavour to evade this passage, they only betray their ignorance: they quibble that, because our Saviour says, "Suffer little children to come," they must have been several years old, and fit to come. But they are called by the Evangelists βρέφη καὶ παιδία, terms which denote infants still at their mothers' breasts. The term "come" is used simply for "approach." See the quibbles to which men are obliged to have recourse when they have hardened themselves against the truth! There is nothing more solid in their allegation, that the kingdom of heaven is not assigned to children, but to those like children, since the expression is, "of such," not "of themselves." If this is admitted, what will be the reason which our Saviour employs to show that they are not strangers to him from nonage? When he orders that little children shall be allowed to

come to him, nothing is plainer than that mere infancy is meant. Lest this should seem absurd, he adds, "Of such is the kingdom of heaven." But if infants must necessarily be comprehended, the expression, "of such," clearly shows that infants themselves, and those like them, are intended.

8. Every one must now see that pædobaptism, which receives such strong support from Scripture, is by no means of human invention. Nor is there anything plausible in the objection, that we nowhere read of even one infant having been baptised by the hands of the apostles. For although this is not expressly narrated by the Evangelists, yet as they are not expressly excluded when mention is made of any baptised family (Acts xvi. 15, 32), what man of sense will argue from this that they were not baptised? If such kinds of argument were good, it would be necessary, in like manner, to interdict women from the Lord's Supper, since we do not read that they were ever admitted to it in the days of the apostles. But here we are contented with the rule of faith. For when we reflect on the nature of the ordinance of the Lord's Supper, we easily judge who the persons are to whom the use of it is to be communicated. The same we observe in the case of baptism. For, attending to the end for which it was instituted, we clearly perceive that it is not less applicable to children than to those of more advanced years, and that, therefore, they cannot be deprived of it without manifest fraud to the will of its divine Author. The assertion which they disseminate among the common people, that a long series of years elapsed after the resurrection of Christ, during which pædobaptism was unknown, is a shameful falsehood, since there is no writer, however ancient, who does not trace its origin to the days of the apostles.

9. It remains briefly to indicate what benefit redounds from the observance, both to believers who bring their children to the church to be baptised, and to the infants themselves, to whom the sacred water is applied, that no one may despise the ordinance as useless or superfluous: though any one who would think of ridiculing baptism under this pretence, would also ridicule the divine ordinance of circumcision: for what can they adduce to impugn the one, that may not be retorted against the other? Thus the Lord punishes the arrogance of those who forthwith condemn whatever their carnal sense cannot comprehend. But God furnishes us with other weapons to repress their stupidity. His holy institution, from which we feel that our faith derives admirable consolation, deserves not to be called superfluous. For the divine symbol communicated to the child, as with the impress of a seal, confirms the promise given to the godly parent, and declares that the Lord will be a God not to him only, but to his seed; not merely visiting him with his grace and goodness, but his posterity also to the thousandth generation. When the infinite goodness of God is thus displayed, it, in the first place, furnishes most ample materials for proclaiming his glory, and fills pious

breasts with no ordinary joy, urging them more strongly to love their affectionate Parent, when they see that, on their account, he extends his care to their posterity. I am not moved by the objection, that the promise ought to be sufficient to confirm the salvation of our children. It has seemed otherwise to God, who, seeing our weakness, has herein been pleased to condescend to it. Let those, then, who embrace the promise of mercy to their children, consider it as their duty to offer them to the Church, to be sealed with the symbol of mercy, and animate themselves to surer confidence, on seeing with the bodily eye the covenant of the Lord engraven on the bodies of their children. On the other hand, children derive some benefit from their baptism, when, being ingrafted into the body of the Church, they are made an object of greater interest to the other members. Then when they have grown up, they are thereby strongly urged to an earnest desire of serving God, who has received them as sons by the formal symbol of adoption, before, from nonage, they were able to recognise him as their Father. In fine, we ought to stand greatly in awe of the denunciation, that God will take vengeance on every one who despises to impress the symbol of the covenant on his child (Gen. xvii. 15), such contempt being a rejection, and, as it were, abjuration of the offered grace.

10. Let us now discuss the arguments by which some furious madmen cease not to assail this holy ordinance of God. And, first, feeling themselves pressed beyond measure by the resemblance between baptism and circumcision, they contend that there is a wide difference between the two signs, that the one has nothing in common with the other. They maintain that the things meant are different, that the covenant is altogether different, and that the persons included under the name of children are different. When they first proceed to the proof, they pretend that circumcision was a figure of mortification, not of baptism. This we willingly concede to them, for it admirably supports our view, in support of which the only proof we use is, that baptism and circumcision are signs of mortification. Hence we conclude that the one was substituted for the other, baptism representing to us the very thing which circumcision signified to the Jews. In asserting a difference of covenant, with what barbarian audacity do they corrupt and destroy Scripture? and that not in one passage only, but so as not to leave any passage safe and entire. The Jews they depict as so carnal as to resemble brutes more than men, representing the covenant which was made with them as reaching no farther than a temporary life, and the promises which were given to them as dwindling down into present and corporeal blessings. If this dogma is received, what remains but that the Jewish nation was overloaded for a time with divine kindness (just as swine are gorged in their sty), that they might at last perish eternally? Whenever we quote circumcision and the promises annexed to it, they answer, that circumcision was a literal sign, and that its promises were carnal.

11. Certainly, if circumcision was a literal sign, the same view must be taken of baptism, since, in the second chapter to the Colossians, the apostle makes the one to be not a whit more spiritual than the other. For he says that in Christ we "are circumcised with the circumcision made without hands, in putting off the body of the sins of the flesh, by the circumcision of Christ." In explanation of his sentiment he immediately adds, that we are "buried with him in baptism." What do these words mean, but just that the truth and completion of baptism is the truth and completion of circumcision, since they represent one thing? For his object is to show that baptism is the same thing to Christians that circumcision formerly was to the Jews. Now, since we have already clearly shown that the promises of both signs, and the mysteries which are represented by them, agree, we shall not dwell on the point longer at present. I would only remind believers to reflect, without anything being said by me, whether that is to be regarded as an earthly and literal sign, which has nothing heavenly or spiritual under it. But lest they should blind the simple with their smoke, we shall, in passing, dispose of one objection by which they cloak this most impudent falsehood. It is absolutely certain that the original promises comprehending the covenant which God made with the Israelites under the old dispensation were spiritual, and had reference to eternal life, and were, of course, in like manner spiritually received by the fathers, that they might thence entertain a sure hope of immortality, and aspire to it with their whole soul. Meanwhile, we are far from denying that he testified his kindness to them by carnal and earthly blessings; though we hold that by these the hope of spiritual promises was confirmed. In this manner, when he promised eternal blessedness to his servant Abraham, he, in order to place a manifest indication of favour before his eye, added the promise of possession of the land of Canaan. In the same way we should understand all the terrestrial promises which were given to the Jewish nation, the spiritual promise, as the head to which the others bore reference, always holding the first place. Having handled this subject fully when treating of the difference between the old and the new dispensations, I now only glance at it.

12. Under the appellation of *children* the difference they observe is this, that the children of Abraham, under the old dispensation, were those who derived their origin from his seed, but that the appellation is now given to those who imitate his faith, and therefore that carnal infancy, which was ingrafted into the fellowship of the covenant by circumcision, typified the spiritual children of the new covenant, who are regenerated by the word of God to immortal life. In these words we indeed discover a small spark of truth, but these giddy spirits err grievously in this, that laying hold of whatever comes first to their hand, when they ought to proceed farther, and compare many things together, they obstinately fasten upon one single word. Hence it cannot but happen that they are every now

and then deluded, because they do not exert themselves to obtain a full knowledge of any subject. We certainly admit that the carnal seed of Abrahan for a time held the place of the spiritual seed, which is ingrafted into him by faith (Gal. iv. 28; Rom. iv. 12). For we are called his sons, though we have no natural relationship with him. But if they mean, as they not obscurely show, that the spiritual promise was never made to the carnal seed of Abraham, they are greatly mistaken. We must, therefore, take a better aim, one to which we are directed by the infallible guidance of Scripture. The Lord therefore promises to Abraham that he shall have a seed in whom all the nations of the earth will be blessed, and at the same time assures him that he will be a God both to him and his seed. All who in faith receive Christ as the author of the blessing are the heirs of this promise, and accordingly are called the children of Abraham.

13. Although, after the resurrection of Christ, the boundaries of the kingdom began to be extended far and wide into all nations indiscriminately, so that, according to the declaration of Christ, believers were collected from all quarters to sit down with Abraham, Isaac, and Jacob, in the kingdom of heaven (Matth. viii. 11), still, for many ages before, the Jews had enjoyed this great mercy. And as he had selected them (while passing by all other nations) to be for a time the depositaries of his favour, he designated them as his peculiar purchased people (Exod. xix. 5). In attestation of this kindness, he appointed circumcision, by which symbol the Jews were taught that God watched over their safety, and they were thereby raised to the hope of eternal life. For what can ever be wanting to him whom God has once taken under his protection? Wherefore the apostle, to prove that the Gentiles, as well as the Jews, were the children of Abraham, speaks in this way: "Faith was reckoned to Abraham for righteousness. How was it then reckoned? when he was in circumcision, or in uncircumcision? Not in circumcision, but in uncircumcision. And he received the sign of circumcision, a seal of the righteousness of the faith which he had yet being uncircumcised; that he might be the father of all them that believe, though they be not circumcised: that righteousness might be imputed to them also: and the father of circumcision to them who are not of the circumcision only, but who also walk in the steps of that faith of our father Abraham, which he had yet being uncircumcised" (Rom. iv. 9-12). Do we not see that both are made equal in dignity? For, to the time appointed by the divine decree, he was the father of circumcision. But when, as the apostle elsewhere writes (Eph. ii. 14), the wall of partition which separated the Gentiles from the Jews was broken down, to them, also, access was given to the kingdom of God, and he became their father, and that without the sign of circumcision, its place being supplied by baptism. In saying expressly that Abraham was not the father of those who were of the circumcision only, his object was to repress the superciliousness of some who, laying aside all regard to godliness, plumed themselves

on mere ceremonies. In like manner, we may, in the present day, refute the vanity of those who, in baptism, seek nothing but water.

14. But in opposition to this is produced a passage from the Epistle to the Romans, in which the apostle says, that those who are of the flesh are not the children of Abraham, but that those only who are the children of promise are considered as the seed (Rom. ix. 7). For he seems to insinuate, that carnal relationship to Abraham, which we think of some consequence, is nothing. But we must attend carefully to the subject which the apostle is there treating. His object being to show to the Jews that the goodness of God was not restricted to the seed of Abraham, nay, that of itself it contributes nothing, produces, in proof of the fact, the cases of Ishmael and Esau. These being rejected, just as if they had been strangers, although, according to the flesh, they were the genuine offspring of Abraham, the blessing resides in Isaac and Jacob. This proves what he afterwards affirms—viz. that salvation depends on the mercy which God bestows on whomsoever he pleases, but that the Jews have no ground to glory or plume themselves on the name of the covenant, unless they keep the law of the covenant, that is, obey the word. On the other hand, after casting down their vain confidence in their origin, because he was aware that the covenant which had been made with the posterity of Abraham could not properly prove fruitless, he declares, that due honour should still be paid to carnal relationship to Abraham, in consequence of which, the Jews were the primary and native heirs of the gospel, unless in so far as they were, for their ingratitude, rejected as unworthy, and yet rejected so as not to leave their nation utterly destitute of the heavenly blessing. For this reason, though they were contumacious breakers of the covenant, he styles them holy (such respect does he pay to the holy generation which God had honoured with his sacred covenant), while we, in comparison of them, are termed posthumous, or abortive children of Abraham, and that not by nature, but by adoption, just as if a twig were broken from its own tree, and ingrafted on another stock. Therefore, that they might not be defrauded of their privilege, it was necessary that the gospel should first be preached to them. For they are, as it were, the first-born in the family of God. The honour due, on this account, must therefore be paid them, until they have rejected the offer, and, by their ingratitude, caused it to be transferred to the Gentiles. Nor, however great the contumacy with which they persist in warring against the gospel, are we therefore to despise them. We must consider, that in respect of the promise, the blessing of God still resides among them; and, as the apostle testifies, will never entirely depart from them, seeing that "the gifts and calling of God are without repentance" (Rom. xi. 29).

15. Such is the value of the promise given to the posterity of Abraham,—such the balance in which it is to be weighed. Hence, though we have no doubt that in distinguishing the children of God from bastards and foreigners, that the election of God reigns freely,

we, at the same time, perceive that he was pleased specially to embrace the seed of Abraham with his mercy, and, for the better attestation of it, to seal it by circumcision. The case of the Christian Church is entirely of the same description; for as Paul there declares that the Jews are sanctified by their parents, so he elsewhere says that the children of Christians derive sanctification from their parents. Hence it is inferred, that those who are chargeable with impurity are justly separated from others. Now, who can have any doubt as to the falsehood of their subsequent averment—viz. that the infants who were formerly circumcised only typified the spiritual infancy which is produced by the regeneration of the word of God? When the apostle says, that "Jesus Christ was a minister of the circumcision for the truth of God, to confirm the promises made unto the fathers" (Rom. xv. 8), he does not philosophise subtilely, as if he had said, Since the covenant made with Abraham has respect unto his seed, Christ, in order to perform and discharge the promise made by the Father, came for the salvation of the Jewish nation. Do you see how he considers that, after the resurrection of Christ, the promise is to be fulfilled to the seed of Abraham, not allegorically, but literally, as the words express? To the same effect is the declaration of Peter to the Jews: "The promise is unto you and to your children" (Acts ii. 39); and in the next chapter, he calls them *the children of the covenant*, that is, heirs. Not widely different from this is the other passage of the apostle, above quoted, in which he regards and describes circumcision performed on infants as an attestation to the communion which they have with Christ. And, indeed, if we listen to the absurdities of those men, what will become of the promise by which the Lord, in the second commandment of his law, engages to be gracious to the seed of his servants for a thousand generations? Shall we here have recourse to allegory? This were the merest quibble. Shall we say that it has been abrogated? In this way, we should do away with the law which Christ came not to destroy, but to fulfil, inasmuch as it turns to our everlasting good. Therefore, let it be without controversy, that God is so good and liberal to his people, that he is pleased, as a mark of his favour, to extend their privileges to the children born to them.

16. The distinctions which these men attempt to draw between baptism and circumcision are not only ridiculous, and void of all semblance of reason, but at variance with each other. For, when they affirm that baptism refers to the first day of spiritual contest, and circumcison to the eighth day, mortification being already accomplished, they immediately forget the distinction, and change their song, representing circumcision as typifying the mortification of the flesh, and baptism as a burial, which is given to none but those who are already dead. What are these giddy contradictions but frenzied dreams? According to the former view, baptism ought to precede circumcision; according to the latter, it should come after it. It is not the first time we have seen the minds of men wander

to and fro when they substitute their dreams for the infallible word of God. We hold, therefore, that their former distinction is a mere imagination. Were we disposed to make an allegory of the eighth day, theirs would not be the proper mode of it. It were much better with the early Christians to refer the number eight to the resurrection, which took place on the eighth day, and on which we know that newness of life depends, or to the whole course of the present life, during which, mortification ought to be in progress, only terminating when life itself terminates; although it would seem that God intended to provide for the tenderness of infancy by deferring circumcision to the eighth day, as the wound would have been more dangerous if inflicted immediately after birth. How much more rational is the declaration of Scripture, that we, when already dead, are buried by baptism (Rom. vi. 4); since it distinctly states, that we are buried into death that we may thoroughly die, and thenceforth aim at that mortification? Equally ingenious is their cavil, that women should not be baptised if baptism is to be made conformable to circumcision. For if it is most certain that the sanctification of the seed of Israel was attested by the sign of circumcision, it cannot be doubted that it was appointed alike for the sanctification of males and females. But though the right could only be performed on males, yet the females were, through them, partners and associates in circumcision. Wherefore, disregarding all such quibbling distinctions, let us fix on the very complete resemblance between baptism and circumcision, as seen in the internal office, the promise, the use, and the effect.

17. They seem to think they produce their strongest reason for denying baptism to children, when they allege, that they are as yet unfit, from nonage, to understand the mystery which is there sealed—viz. spiritual regeneration, which is not applicable to earliest infancy. Hence they infer, that children are only to be regarded as sons of Adam until they have attained an age fit for the reception of the second birth. But all this is directly opposed to the truth of God. For if they are to be accounted sons of Adam, they are left in death, since, in Adam, we can do nothing but die. On the contrary, Christ bids them be brought to him. Why so? Because he is life. Therefore, that he may quicken them, he makes them partners with himself; whereas these men would drive them away from Christ, and adjudge them to death. For if they pretend that infants do not perish when they are accounted the sons of Adam, the error is more than sufficiently confuted by the testimony of Scripture (1 Cor. xv. 22). For seeing it declares that in Adam all die, it follows, that no hope of life remains unless in Christ. Therefore, that we may become heirs of life, we must communicate with him. Again, seeing it is elsewhere written that we are all by nature the children of wrath (Eph. ii. 3), and conceived in sin (Ps. li. 5), of which condemnation is the inseparable attendant, we must part with our own nature before we have any access to the kingdom of God. And what can be clearer than the expression, "Flesh and blood cannot inherit the kingdom of God"? (1 Cor. xv. 50.) Therefore, let

everything that is our own be abolished (this cannot be without regeneration), and then we shall perceive this possession of the kingdom. In fine, if Christ speaks truly when he declares that he is life, we must necessarily be ingrafted into him by whom we are delivered from the bondage of death. But how, they ask, are infants regenerated, when not possessing a knowledge of either good or evil? We answer, that the work of God, though beyond the reach of our capacity, is not therefore null. Moreover, infants who are to be saved (and that some are saved at this age is certain) must, without question, be previously regenerated by the Lord. For if they bring innate corruption with them from their mother's womb, they must be purified before they can be admitted into the kingdom of God, into which shall not enter anything that defileth (Rev. xxi. 27). If they are born sinners, as David and Paul affirm, they must either remain unaccepted and hated by God, or be justified. And why do we ask more, when the Judge himself publicly declares, that "except a man be born again, he cannot see the kingdom of God"? (John iii. 3.) But to silence this class of objectors, God gave, in the case of John the Baptist, whom he sanctified from his mother's womb (Luke i. 15), a proof of what he might do in others. They gain nothing by the quibble to which they here resort—viz. that this was only once done, and therefore it does not forthwith follow that the Lord always acts thus with infants. That is not the mode in which we reason. Our only object is to show, that they unjustly and malignantly confine the power of God within limits, within which it cannot be confined. As little weight is due to another subterfuge. They allege that, by the usual phraseology of Scripture, "from the womb," has the same meaning as "from childhood." But it is easy to see that the angel had a different meaning when he announced to Zacharias that the child not yet born would be filled with the Holy Spirit. Instead of attempting to give a law to God, let us hold that he sanctifies whom he pleases, in the way in which he sanctified John, seeing that his power is not impaired.

18. And, indeed, Christ was sanctified from earliest infancy, that he might sanctify his elect in himself at any age, without distinction. For as he, in order to wipe away the guilt of disobedience which had been committed in our flesh, assumed that very flesh, that in it he might, on our account, and in our stead, perform a perfect obedience, so he was conceived by the Holy Spirit, that, completely pervaded with his holiness in the flesh which he had assumed, he might transfuse it into us. If in Christ we have a perfect pattern of all the graces which God bestows on all his children, in this instance we have a proof that the age of infancy is not incapable of receiving sanctification. This, at least, we set down as incontrovertible, that none of the elect is called away from the present life without being previously sanctified and regenerated by the Spirit of God. As to their objection that, in Scripture, the Spirit acknowledges no sanctification save that from incorruptible seed, that is, the word of God, they erron-

eously interpret Peter's words, in which he comprehends only believers who had been taught by the preaching of the gospel (1 Pet. i. 23). We confess, indeed, that the word of the Lord is the only seed of spiritual regeneration ; but we deny the inference that, therefore, the power of God cannot regenerate infants. This is as possible and easy for him, as it is wondrous and incomprehensible to us. It were dangerous to deny that the Lord is able to furnish them with the knowledge of himself in any way he pleases.

19. But *faith*, they say, *cometh by hearing*, the use of which infants have not yet obtained, nor can they be fit to know God, being, as Moses declares, without the knowledge of good and evil (Deut. i. 39). But they observe not that where the apostle makes hearing the beginning of faith, he is only describing the usual economy and dispensation which the Lord is wont to employ in calling his people, and not laying down an invariable rule, for which no other method can be substituted. Many he certainly has called and endued with the true knowledge of himself, by internal means, by the illumination of the Spirit, without the intervention of preaching. But since they deem it very absurd to attribute any knowledge of God to infants, whom Moses makes void of the knowledge of good and evil, let them tell me where the danger lies if they are said now to receive some part of that grace, of which they are to have the full measure shortly after. For if fulness of life consists in the perfect knowledge of God, since some of those whom death hurries away in the first moments of infancy pass into life eternal, they are certainly admitted to behold the immediate presence of God. Those, therefore, whom the Lord is to illumine with the full brightness of his light, why may he not, if he so pleases, irradiate at present with some small beam, especially if he does not remove their ignorance, before he delivers them from the prison of the flesh ? I would not rashly affirm that they are endued with the same faith which we experience in ourselves, or have any knowledge at all resembling faith (this I would rather leave undecided) ; but I would somewhat curb the stolid arrogance of those men who, as with inflated cheeks, affirm or deny whatever suits them.

20. In order to gain a stronger footing here, they add, that baptism is a sacrament of penitence and faith, and as neither of these is applicable to tender infancy, we must beware of rendering its meaning empty and vain, by admitting infants to the communion of baptism. But these darts are directed more against God then against us ; since the fact that circumcision was a sign of repentance is completely established by many passages of Scripture (Jer. iv. 4). Thus Paul terms it a seal of the righteousness of faith (Rom. iv. 11). Let God, then, be demanded why he ordered circumcision to be performed on the bodies of infants ? For baptism and circumcision being here in the same case, they cannot give anything to the latter without conceding it to the former. If they recur to their usual evasion, that, by the age of infancy, spiritual infants were then figured, we have already

closed this means of escape against them. We say, then, that since God imparted circumcision, the sign of repentance and faith, to infants, it should not seem absurd that they are now made partakers of baptism, unless men choose to clamour against an institution of God. But as in all his acts, so here also, enough of wisdom and righteousness shines forth to repress the slanders of the ungodly. For although infants, at the moment when they were circumcised, did not comprehend what the sign meant, still they were truly circumcised for the mortification of their corrupt and polluted nature—a mortification at which they afterwards aspired when adults. In fine, the objection is easily disposed of by the fact, that children are baptised for future repentance and faith. Though these are not yet formed in them, yet the seed of both lies hid in them by the secret operation of the Spirit. This answer at once overthrows all the objections which are twisted against us out of the meaning of baptism; for instance, the title by which Paul distinguishes it when he terms it the "washing of regeneration and renewing" (Tit. iii. 5). Hence they argue, that it is not to be given to any but to those who are capable of such feelings. But we, on the other hand, may object, that neither ought circumcision, which is designated regeneration, to be conferred on any but the regenerate. In this way, we shall condemn a divine institution. Thus, as we have already hinted, all the arguments which tend to shake circumcision are of no force in assailing baptism. Nor can they escape by saying, that everything which rests on the authority of God is absolutely fixed, though there should be no reason for it, but that this reverence is not due to pædobaptism, nor other similar things which are not recommended to us by the express word of God. They always remain caught in this dilemma. The command of God to circumcise infants was either legitimate and exempt from cavil, or deserved reprehension. If there was nothing incompetent or absurd in it, no absurdity can be shown in the observance of pædobaptism.

21. The charge of absurdity with which they attempt to stigmatise it, we thus dispose of. If those on whom the Lord has bestowed his election, after receiving the sign of regeneration, depart this life before they become adults, he, by the incomprehensible energy of his Spirit, renews them in the way which he alone sees to be expedient. Should they reach an age when they can be instructed in the meaning of baptism, they will thereby be animated to greater zeal for renovation, the badge of which they will learn that they received in earliest infancy, in order that they might aspire to it during their whole lives. To the same effect are the two passages in which Paul teaches, that we are buried with Christ by baptism (Rom. vi. 4; Col. ii. 12). For by this he means not that he who is to be initiated by baptism must have previously been buried with Christ; he simply declares the doctrine which is taught by baptism, and that to those already baptised: so that the most senseless cannot maintain from this passage that it ought to precede baptism. In this way, Moses

and the prophets reminded the people of the thing meant by circumcision, which however infants received. To the same effect, Paul says to the Galatians, "As many of you as have been baptised into Christ have put on Christ" (Gal. iii. 27). Why so? That they might thereafter live to Christ, to whom previously they had not lived. And though, in adults, the receiving of the sign ought to follow the understanding of its meaning, yet, as will shortly be explained, a different rule must be followed with children. No other conclusion can be drawn from a passage in Peter, on which they strongly found. He says, that baptism is "not the putting away of the filth of the flesh, but the answer of a good conscience toward God by the resurrection of Jesus Christ" (1 Pet. iii. 21). From this they contend that nothing is left for pædobaptism, which becomes mere empty smoke, as being altogether at variance with the meaning of baptism. But the delusion which misleads them is, that they would always have the thing to precede the sign in the order of time. For the truth of circumcision consisted in the same answer of a good conscience; but if the truth must necessarily have preceded, infants would never have been circumcised by the command of God. But he himself, showing that the answer of a good conscience forms the truth of circumcision, and, at the same time, commanding infants to be circumcised, plainly intimates that, in their case, circumcision had reference to the future. Wherefore, nothing more of present effect is to be required in pædobaptism, than to confirm and sanction the covenant which the Lord has made with them. The other part of the meaning of the sacrament will follow at the time which God himself has provided.

22. Every one must, I think, clearly perceive, that all arguments of this stamp are mere perversions of Scripture. The other remaining arguments akin to these we shall cursorily examine. They object, that baptism is given for the remission of sins. When this is conceded, it strongly supports our view; for, seeing we are born sinners, we stand in need of forgiveness and pardon from the very womb. Moreover, since God does not preclude this age from the hope of mercy, but rather gives assurance of it, why should we deprive it of the sign, which is much inferior to the reality? The arrow, therefore, which they aim at us, we throw back upon themselves. Infants receive forgiveness of sins; therefore, they are not to be deprived of the sign. They adduce the passage from the Ephesians, that Christ gave himself for the Church, "that he might sanctify and cleanse it with the washing of water by the word" (Eph. v. 26). Nothing could be quoted more appropriate than this to overthrow their error: it furnishes us with an easy proof. If, by baptism, Christ intends to attest the ablution by which he cleanses his Church, it would seem not equitable to deny this attestation to infants, who are justly deemed part of the Church, seeing they are called heirs of the heavenly kingdom. For Paul comprehends the whole Church when he says that it was cleansed by the washing of water. In like

manner, from his expression in another place, that by baptism we are ingrafted into the body of Christ (1 Cor. xii. 13), we infer, that infants, whom he enumerates among his members, are to be baptised, in order that they may not be dissevered from his body. See the violent onset which they make with all their engines on the bulwarks of our faith.

23. They now come down to the custom and practice of the apostolic age, alleging that there is no instance of any one having been admitted to baptism without a previous profession of faith and repentance. For when Peter is asked by his hearers, who were pricked in their heart, "What shall we do?" his advise is, "Repent and be baptised, every one of you, in the name of Jesus Christ, for the remission of sins" (Acts ii. 37, 38). In like manner, when Philip was asked by the eunuch to baptise him, he answered, "If thou believest with all thine heart, thou mayest." Hence they think they can make out that baptism cannot be lawfully given to any one without previous faith and repentance. If we yield to this argument, the former passage, in which there is no mention of faith, will prove that repentance alone is sufficient, and the latter, which makes no requirement of repentance, that there is need only of faith. They will object, I presume, that the one passage helps the other, and that both, therefore, are to be connected. I, in my turn, maintain that these two must be compared with other passages which contribute somewhat to the solution of this difficulty. There are many passages of Scripture whose meaning depends on their peculiar position. Of this we have an example in the present instance. Those to whom these things are said by Peter and Philip are of an age fit to aim at repentance, and receive faith. We strenuously insist that such men are not to be baptised unless their conversion and faith are discerned, at least in as far as human judgment can ascertain it. But it is perfectly clear that infants must be placed in a different class. For when any one formerly joined the religious communion of Israel, he behoved to be taught the covenant, and instructed in the law of the Lord, before he received circumcision, because he was of a different nation; in other words, an alien from the people of Israel, with whom the covenant, which circumcision sanctioned, had been made.

24. Thus the Lord, when he chose Abraham for himself, did not commence with circumcision, in the meanwhile concealing what he meant by that sign, but first announced that he intended to make a covenant with him, and, after his faith in the promise, made him partaker of the sacrament. Why does the sacrament come after faith in Abraham, and precede all intelligence in his son Isaac? It is right that he who, in adult age, is admitted to the fellowship of a covenant by one from whom he had hitherto been alienated, should previously learn its conditions; but it is not so with the infant born to him. He, according to the terms of the promise, is included in the promise by hereditary right from his mother's womb. Or, to

state the matter more briefly and more clearly, If the children of believers, without the help of understanding, are partakers of the covenant, there is no reason why they should be denied the sign, because they are unable to swear to its stipulations. This undoubtedly is the reason why the Lord sometimes declares that the children born to the Israelites are begotten and born to him (Ezek. xvi. 20; xxiii. 37). For he undoubtedly gives the place of sons to the children of those to whose seed he has promised that he will be a Father. But the child descended from unbelieving parents is deemed an alien to the covenant until he is united to God by faith. Hence, it is not strange that the sign is withheld when the thing signified would be vain and fallacious. In that view, Paul says that the Gentiles, so long as they were plunged in idolatry, were strangers to the covenant (Eph. ii. 11). The whole matter may, if I mistake not, be thus briefly and clearly expounded: Those who, in adult age, embrace the faith of Christ, having hitherto been aliens from the covenant, are not to receive the sign of baptism without previous faith and repentance. These alone can give them access to the fellowship of the covenant, whereas children, deriving their origin from Christians, as they are immediately on their birth received by God as heirs of the covenant, are also to be admitted to baptism. To this we must refer the narrative of the Evangelist, that those who were baptised by John confessed their sins (Matth. iii. 6). This example, we hold, ought to be observed in the present day. Were a Turk to offer himself for baptism, we would not at once perform the rite without receiving a confession which was satisfactory to the Church.

25. Another passage which they adduce is from the third chapter of John, where our Saviour's words seem to them to imply that a present regeneration is required in baptism, "Except a man be born of water, and of the Spirit, he cannot enter into the kingdom of God" (John iii. 5). See, they say, how baptism is termed regeneration by the lips of our Lord himself, and on what pretext, therefore, with what consistency is baptism given to those who, it is perfectly obvious, are not at all capable of regeneration? First, they are in error in imagining that there is any mention of baptism in this passage, merely because the word water is used. Nicodemus, after our Saviour had explained to him the corruption of nature, and the necessity of being born again, kept dreaming of a corporeal birth, and hence our Saviour intimates the mode in which God regenerates us—viz. by water and the Spirit; in other words, by the Spirit, who, in irrigating and cleansing the souls of believers, operates in the manner of water. By "water and the Spirit," therefore, I simply understand the Spirit, which is water. Nor is the expression new. It perfectly accords with that which is used in the third chapter of Matthew, "He that cometh after me is mightier than I;" "he shall baptise you with the Holy Ghost, and with fire" (Matth. iii. 11). Therefore, as to baptise with the Holy Spirit, and with fire, is to

confer the Holy Spirit, who, in regeneration, has the office and nature of fire, so to be born again of water, and of the Spirit, is nothing else than to receive that power of the Spirit, which has the same effect on the soul that water has on the body. I know that a different interpretation is given, but I have no doubt that this is the genuine meaning, because our Saviour's only purpose was to teach, that all who aspire to the kingdom of heaven must lay aside their own disposition. And yet were we disposed to imitate these men in their mode of cavilling, we might easily, after conceding what they wish, reply to them, that baptism is prior to faith and repentance, since, in this passage, our Saviour mentions it before the Spirit. This certainly must be understood of spiritual gifts, and if they follow baptism, I have gained all I contend for. But, cavilling aside, the simple interpretation to be adopted is that which I have given—viz. that no man, until renewed by living water, that is, by the Spirit, can enter the kingdom of God.

26. This, moreover, plainly explodes the fiction of those who consign all the unbaptised to eternal death.[1] Let us suppose, then, that, as they insist, baptism is administered to adults only. What will they make of a youth who, after being embued duly and properly with the rudiments of piety, while waiting for the day of baptism, is unexpectedly carried off by sudden death? The promise of our Lord is clear, " He that heareth my word, and believeth on him that sent me, hath everlasting life, and shall not come into condemnation, but is passed from death unto life" (John v. 24). We nowhere read of his having condemned him who was not yet baptised. I would not be understood as insinuating that baptism may be contemned with impunity. So far from excusing this contempt, I hold that it violates the covenant of the Lord. The passage only serves to show, that we must not deem baptism so necessary as to suppose that every one who has lost the opportunity of obtaining it has forthwith perished. By assenting to their fiction, we should condemn all, without exception, whom any accident may have prevented from procuring baptism, how much soever they may have been endued with the faith by which Christ himself is possessed. Moreover, baptism being, as they hold, necessary to salvation, they, in denying it to infants, consign them all to eternal death. Let them now consider what kind of agreement they have with the words of Christ, who says, that " of such is the kingdom of heaven" (Matth. xix. 14). And though we were to concede everything to them, in regard to the meaning of this passage, they will extract nothing from it, until they have previously overthrown the doctrine which we have already established concerning the regeneration of infants.

27. But they boast of having their strongest bulwark in the very

[1] See Calv. Cont. Articulos Theologorum Paris. Art 4. Item, Ad. Concil. Trident. Item, Vera Eccles. Reformand. Ratio, et in Append. Nævus in August. Lib. i. ad Bonifac. et Epist. 28. Ambros. de Vocat. Gentium, Lib. ii. cap. 8, de Abraham. Lib. ii. cap. 11.

institution of baptism, which they find in the last chapter of Matthew, where Christ, sending his disciples into all the world, commands them to teach and then baptise. Then, in the last chapter of Mark, it is added, "He that believeth, and is baptised, shall be saved" (Mark xvi. 16). What more (say they) do we ask, since the words of Christ distinctly declare, that teaching must precede baptism, and assign to baptism the place next to faith? Of this arrangement our Lord himself gave an example, in choosing not to be baptised till his thirtieth year. In how many ways do they here entangle themselves, and betray their ignorance! They err more than childishly in this, that they derive the first institution of baptism from this passage, whereas Christ had, from the commencement of his ministry, ordered it to be administered by the apostles. There is no ground, therefore, for contending that the law and rule of baptism is to be sought from these two passages, as containing the first institution. But to indulge them in their error, how nerveless is this mode of arguing? Were I disposed to evasion, I have not only a place of escape, but a wide field to expatiate in. For when they cling so desperately to the order of the words, insisting that because it is said, "Go, preach and baptise," and again, "Whosoever believes and is baptised," they must preach before baptising, and believe before being baptised, why may not we in our turn object, that they must baptise before teaching the observance of those things which Christ commanded, because it is said, "Baptise, teaching whatsoever I have commanded you"? The same thing we observed in the other passage in which Christ speaks of the regeneration of water and of the Spirit. For if we interpret as they insist, then baptism must take precedence of spiritual regeneration, because it is first mentioned. Christ teaches that we are to be born again, not of the Spirit and of water, but of water and of the Spirit.

28. This unassailable argument, in which they confide so much, seems already to be considerably shaken; but as we have sufficient protection in the simplicity of truth, I am unwilling to evade the point by paltry subtleties. Let them, therefore, have a solid answer. The command here given by Christ relates principally to the preaching of the gospel: to it baptism is added as a kind of appendage. Then he merely speaks of baptism in so far as the dispensation of it is subordinate to the function of teaching. For Christ sends his disciples to publish the gospel to all nations of the world, that by the doctrine of salvation they may gather men, who were previously lost, into his kingdom. But who or what are those men? It is certain that mention is made only of those who are fit to receive his doctrine. He subjoins, that such, after being taught, were to be baptised, adding the promise, Whosoever believeth and is baptised, shall be saved. Is there one syllable about infants in the whole discourse? What, then, is the form of argument with which they assail us? Those who are of adult age are to be instructed and brought to the faith before being baptised, and therefore it is unlawful to make

baptism common to infants. They cannot, at the very utmost, prove any other thing out of this passage, than that the gospel must be preached to those who are capable of hearing it before they are baptised; for of such only the passage speaks. From this let them, if they can, throw an obstacle in the way of baptising infants.

29. But I will make their fallacies palpable even to the blind, by a very plain similitude. Should any one insist that infants are to be deprived of food, on the pretence that the apostle permits none to eat but those who labour (2 Thess. iii. 10), would he not deserve to be scouted by all? Why so? Because that which was said of a certain class of men, and a certain age, he wrests and applies to all indifferently. The dexterity of these men in the present instance is not greater. That which every one sees to be intended for adult age merely, they apply to infants, subjecting them to a rule which was laid down only for those of riper years. With regard to the example of our Saviour, it gives no countenance to their case. He was not baptised before his thirtieth year. This is indeed true, but the reason is obvious; because he then determined to lay the solid foundation of baptism by his preaching, or rather to confirm the foundation which John had previously laid. Therefore, when he was pleased with his doctrine to institute baptism, that he might give the greater authority to his institution, he sanctified it in his own person, and that at the most befitting time, namely, the commencement of his ministry. In fine, they can prove nothing more than that baptism received its origin and commencement with the preaching of the gospel. But if they are pleased to fix upon the thirtieth year, why do they not observe it, but admit any one to baptism according to the view which they may have formed of his proficiency? Nay, even Servetus, one of their masters, although he pertinaciously insisted on this period, had begun to act the prophet in his twenty-first year; as if any man could be tolerated in arrogating to himself the office of a teacher in the Church before he was a member of the Church.

30. At length they object, that there is not greater reason for admitting infants to baptism than to the Lord's Supper, to which, however, they are never admitted: as if Scripture did not in every way draw a wide distinction between them. In the early Church, indeed, the Lord's Supper was frequently given to infants, as appears from Cyprian and Augustine (August. ad Bonif. Lib. i.); but the practice justly became obsolete. For if we attend to the peculiar nature of baptism, it is a kind of entrance, and as it were initiation into the Church, by which we are ranked among the people of God, a sign of our spiritual regeneration, by which we are again born to be children of God; whereas, on the contrary, the Supper is intended for those of riper years, who, having passed the tender period of infancy, are fit to bear solid food. This distinction is very clearly pointed out in Scripture. For there, as far as regards baptism, the Lord makes no selection of age, whereas he does not admit all to

partake of the Supper, but confines it to those who are fit to discern the body and blood of the Lord, to examine their own conscience, to show forth the Lord's death, and understand its power. Can we wish anything clearer than what the apostle says, when he thus exhorts, "Let a man examine himself, and so let him eat of that bread, and drink of that cup"? (1 Cor. xi. 28.) Examination, therefore, must precede, and this it were vain to expect from infants. Again, "He that eateth and drinketh unworthily, eateth and drinketh damnation to himself, not discerning the Lord's body." If they cannot partake worthily without being able duly to discern the sanctity of the Lord's body, why should we stretch out poison to our young children instead of vivifying food? Then what is our Lord's injunction? "Do this in remembrance of me." And what the inference which the apostle draws from this? "As often as ye eat this bread, and drink this cup, ye do show the Lord's death till he come." How, pray, can we require infants to commemorate any event of which they have no understanding; how require them "to show forth the Lord's death," of the nature and benefit of which they have no idea? Nothing of the kind is prescribed by baptism. Wherefore, there is the greatest difference between the two signs. This also we observe in similar signs under the old dispensation. Circumcision, which, as is well known, corresponds to our baptism, was intended for infants, but the passover, for which the Supper is substituted, did not admit all kinds of guests promiscuously, but was duly eaten only by those who were of an age sufficient to ask the meaning of it (Exod. xii. 26). Had these men the least particle of soundness in their brain, would they be thus blind as to a matter so very clear and obvious?

31. Though I am unwilling to annoy the reader with the series of conceits which Servetus, not the least among the Anabaptists, nay, the great honour of this crew, when girding himself for battle, deemed, when he adduced them, to be specious arguments, it will be worth while briefly to dispose of them.[1] He pretends that as the symbols of Christ are perfect, they require persons who are perfect, or at least capable of perfection. But the answer is plain. The perfection of baptism, which extends even to death, is improperly restricted to one moment of time; moreover, perfection, in which baptism invites us to make continual progress during life, is foolishly exacted by him all at once. He objects, that the symbols of Christ were appointed for remembrance, that every one may remember that he was buried together with Christ. I answer, that what he coined out of his own brain does not need refutation, nay, that which he transfers to baptism properly belongs to the Supper, as appears from Paul's words, "Let a man examine

[1] French, "Combien qu'il me fasche d'amasser tant de reveries frivoles que pourront ennuyer les lecteurs, toutesfois pource que Servet, se meslant aussi de mesdire du baptesme des petis enfans, a cuide amener de fort belles raisons, il sera raison de les rabattre brievement."—Although I am sorry to amass so many frivolous reveries which may annoy the reader, yet as Servetus, taking it upon him to calumniate baptism also, has seemed to adduce very fine arguments, it will be right briefly to dispose of them.

himself," words similar to which are nowhere used with reference to baptism. Whence we infer, that those who from nonage are incapable of examination are duly baptised. His third point is, That all who believe not in the Son remain in death, the wrath of God abideth on them (John iii. 36); and, therefore, infants who are unable to believe lie under condemnation. I answer, that Christ does not there speak of the general guilt in which all the posterity of Adam are involved, but only threatens the despisers of the gospel, who proudly and contumaciously spurn the grace which is offered to them. But this has nothing to do with infants. At the same time, I meet him with the opposite argument. Every one whom Christ blesses is exempted from the curse of Adam, and the wrath of God. Therefore, seeing it is certain that infants are blessed by him, it follows that they are freed from death. He nexts falsely quotes a passage which is nowhere found, Whosoever is born of the Spirit, hears the voice of the Spirit. Though we should grant that such a passage occurs in Scripture, all he can extract from it is, that believers, according as the Spirit works in them, are framed to obedience. But that which is said of a certain number, it is illogical to apply to all alike. His fourth objection is, As that which precedes is animal (1 Cor. xv. 46), we must wait the full time for baptism, which is spiritual. But while I admit that all the posterity of Adam, born of the flesh, bear their condemnation with them from the womb, I hold that this is no obstacle to the immediate application of the divine remedy. Servetus cannot show that by divine appointment, several years must elapse before the new spiritual life begins. Paul's testimony is, that though lost by nature, the children of believers are holy by supernatural grace. He afterwards brings forward the allegory that David, when going up into mount Zion, took with him neither the blind nor the lame, but vigorous soldiers (2 Sam. v. 8). But what if I meet this with the parable in which God invites to the heavenly feast the lame and the blind? In what way will Servetus disentangle this knot? I ask, moreover, whether the lame and the maimed had not previously served with David? But it is superfluous to dwell longer on this argument, which, as the reader will learn from the sacred history, is founded on mere misquotation. He adds another allegory—viz. that the apostles were fishers of men, not of children. I ask, then, What does our Saviour mean when he says that in the net are caught all kinds of fishes? (Matth. iv. 19; xiii. 47.) But as I have no pleasure in sporting with allegory, I answer, that when the office of teaching was committed to the apostles, they were not prohibited from baptising infants. Moreover, I should like to know why, when the Evangelist uses the term ἀνθρώπους (which comprehends the whole human race without exception), he denies that infants are included. His seventh argument is, Since spiritual things accord with spiritual (1 Cor ii. 13), infants, not being spiritual, are unfit for baptism. It is plain how perversely he wrests this passage of Paul. It relates to doctrine. The Corinthians, pluming themselves excessively on a vain acuteness, Paul rebukes their folly, because they still require to be imbued with the first rudiments of heavenly doctrine. Who can infer from this that baptism is to be denied to infants, whom, when begotten of the flesh, the Lord consecrates to himself by gratuitous adoption? His objection, that if they are new men, they must be fed with spiritual food, is easily obviated. By baptism they are admitted into the fold of Christ, and the symbol of adoption is sufficient for them, until they grow up and become fit to bear solid food. We must, therefore, wait for the time of examination, which God distinctly demands in the sacred Supper. His next objection is, that Christ invites all his people to the sacred Supper. But as it is plain that he admits those only who are prepared to celebrate the commemoration of his death, it follows that infants, whom he honoured with his embrace, remain in a distinct and peculiar position until they grow up, and yet are not aliens. When he objects, that it is strange why the infant does not partake of the Supper, I answer, that souls are fed by other food than the external eating of the Supper, and that accordingly Christ is the food of infants, though they partake not of the symbol. The case is different with baptism, by which the door of the Church is thrown open to them. He again objects, that a good householder distributes meat to his household in due season (Matth. xxiv. 45). This I willingly admit; but how will he define the time of baptism, so as to prove that it is not seasonably given to infants? He, moreover, adduces Christ's command to the apostles to make haste, because the fields are already white to the harvest (John iv. 35). Our Saviour only means that the apostles, seeing the present fruit of their labour, should bestir themselves with more alacrity to teach. Who will infer from this, that harvest only is the fit time for baptism? His eleventh argument is, That in the primitive Church, Christians and disciples were the same; but we have already seen that he argues unskilfully from the part to the whole. The name of disciples is given to men of full age, who had already been taught, and had assumed the name of Christ, just as the Jews behoved to be disciples under the law of Moses. Still none could rightly infer from this that infants, whom the Lord declared to be of his household, were strangers. Moreover, he alleges that all Christians are brethren, and that infants cannot belong to this class, so long as we exclude them from the Supper. But I return to my position, first, that none are heirs of the kingdom of heaven but those who are the members of Christ; and, secondly, that the embracing of Christ was the true badge of adoption, in which infants are joined in common with adults, and that temporary abstinence from the Supper does not prevent them from belonging to the body of the Church. The thief on the cross, when converted, became the brother of believers, though he never partook of the Lord's Supper. Servetus afterwards adds, that no man becomes our brother unless by the Spirit of adoption, who is only conferred by the hearing of faith. I answer, that he always falls back into the same paralogism, because he preposterously applies to infants what is said only of adults.

Paul there teaches that the ordinary way in which God calls his elect, and brings them to the faith, is by raising up faithful teachers, and thus stretching out his hand to them by their ministry and labours. Who will presume from this to give the law to God, and say that he may not ingraft infants into Christ by some other secret method? He objects, that Cornelius was baptised after receiving the Holy Spirit; but how absurdly he would convert a single example into a general rule, is apparent from the case of the Eunuch and the Samaritans, in regard to whom the Lord observed a different order, baptism preceding the gifts of the Holy Spirit. The fifteenth argument is more than absurd. He says that we become gods by regeneration, but that they are gods to whom the word of God is sent (John x. 35; 2 Pet. i. 4), a thing not possible to infant children. The attributing of deity to believers is one of his ravings, which this is not the proper place to discuss; but it betrays the utmost effrontery to wrest the passage in the psalm (Ps. lxxxii. 6) to a meaning so alien to it. Christ says, that kings and magistrates are called gods by the prophet, because they perform an office divinely appointed them. This dexterous interpreter transfers what is addressed by special command to certain individuals to the doctrine of the Gospel, so as to exterminate infants from the Church. Again, he objects, that infants cannot be regarded as new men, because they are not begotten by the word. But what I have said again and again I now repeat, that, for regenerating us, doctrine is an incorruptible seed, if indeed we are fit to perceive it; but when, from nonage, we are incapable of being taught, God takes his own methods of regenerating. He afterwards returns to his allegories, and says, that under the law, the sheep and the goat were not offered in sacrifice the moment they were dropt (Exod. xii. 5). Were I disposed to deal in figures, I might obviously reply, first, that all the first-born, on opening the matrix, were sacred to the Lord (Exod. xiii. 12); and, secondly, that a lamb of a year old was to be sacrificed: whence it follows, that it was not necessary to wait for mature age, the young and tender offspring having been selected by God for sacrifice. He contends, moreover, that none could come to Christ but those who were previously prepared by John; as if John's ministry had not been temporary. But, to omit this, assuredly there was no such preparation in the children whom Christ took up in his arms and blessed. Wherefore, let us have done with his false principle. He at length calls in the assistance of Trismegistus and the Sybils, to prove that sacred ablutions are fit only for adults. See how honourably he thinks of Christian baptism, when he tests it by the profane rites of the Gentiles, and will not have it administered except in the way pleasing to Trismegistus. We defer more to the authority of God, who has seen it meet to consecrate infants to himself, and initiate them by a sacred symbol, the significancy of which they are unable from nonage to understand. We do not think it lawful to borrow from the expiations of the Gentiles, in order to change, in our baptism, that eternal and inviolable law which God enacted in circumcision. His last argument is, If infants, without understanding, may be baptised, baptism may be mimicked and jestingly administered by boys in sport. Here let him plead the matter with God, by whose command circumcision was common to infants before they received understanding. Was it, then, a fit matter for ridicule or boyish sport, to overthrow the sacred institution of God? But no wonder that these reprobate spirits, as if they were under the influence of frenzy, introduce the grossest absurdities in defence of their errors, because God, by this spirit of giddiness, justly avenges their pride and obstinacy. I trust I have made it apparent how feebly Servetus has supported his friends the Anabaptists.

32. No sound man, I presume, can now doubt how rashly the Church is disturbed by those who excite quarrels and disturbances because of pædobaptism. For it is of importance to observe what Satan means by all this craft—viz. to rob us of the singular blessing of confidence and spiritual joy, which is hence to be derived, and in so far to detract from the glory of the divine goodness. For how sweet is it to pious minds to be assured not only by word, but even by ocular demonstration, that they are so much in favour with their heavenly Father, that he interests himself in their prosperity! Here we may see how he acts towards us as a most provident parent, not ceasing to care for us even after our death, but consulting and providing for our children. Ought not our whole heart to be stirred up within us, as David's was (Ps. xlviii. 11), to bless his name for such a manifestation of goodness? Doubtless the design of Satan in assaulting pædobaptism with all his forces is to keep out of view, and gradually efface, that attestation of divine grace which the promise itself presents to our eyes. In this way, not only would men be impiously ungrateful for the mercy of God, but be less careful in training their children to piety. For it is no slight stimulus to us to bring them up in the fear of God, and the observance of his law, when we reflect, that from their birth they have been considered and acknowledged by him as his children. Wherefore, if we would not maliciously obscure the kindness of God, let us present to him our infants, to whom he has assigned a place among his friends and family, that is, the members of the Church.

CHAPTER XVII.

OF THE LORD'S SUPPER, AND THE BENEFITS CONFERRED BY IT.

This chapter is divided into two principal heads.—I. The first part shows what it is that God exhibits in the Holy Supper, sec. 1–4; and then in what way and how far it becomes ours, sec. 5–11. II. The second part is chiefly occupied with a refutation of the errors which superstition has introduced in regard to the Lord's Supper. And, first, Transubstantiation is refuted, sec. 12–15. Next, Consubstantiation and Ubiquity, sec. 16–19. Thirdly, It is shown that the institution itself is opposed to those hyperbolical doctors, sec. 20–25. Fourth, The orthodox view is confirmed by other arguments derived from Scripture, sec. 26-27. Fifth, The authority of the Fathers is shown to support the same view. Sixth, The presence for which opponents contend is overthrown, and another presence established, sec. 29–32. Seventh, What the nature of our communion ought to be, sec. 33, 34. Eighth, The adoration introduced by opponents refuted. For what end the Lord's Supper was instituted, sec. 35–39. Lastly, The examination of communicants is considered, sec. 40–42. Of the external rites to be observed. Of frequent communion in both kinds. Objections refuted, sec. 43–50.

Sections.

1. Why the Holy Supper was instituted by Christ. The knowledge of the sacrament, how necessary. The signs used. Why there are no others appointed.
2. The manifold uses and advantages of this sacrament to the pious.
3. The Lord's Supper exhibits the great blessings of redemption, and even Christ himself. This even evident from the words of the institution. The thing specially to be considered in them. Congruity of the signs and the things signified.
4. The chief parts of this sacrament.
5. How Christ, the Bread of Life, is to be received by us. Two faults to be avoided. The receiving of it must bear reference both to faith and the effect of faith. What meant by eating Christ. In what sense Christ the bread of life.
6. This mode of eating confirmed by the authority of Augustine and Chrysostom.
7. It is not sufficient, while omitting all mention of flesh and blood, to recognise this communion merely as spiritual. It is impossible fully to comprehend it in the present life.
8. In explanation of it, it may be observed,—I. There is no life at all save in Christ. II. Christ has life in a twofold sense; first, in himself, as he is God; and, secondly, by transfusing it into the flesh which he assumed, that he might thereby communicate life to us.
9. This confirmed from Cyril, and by a familiar example. How the flesh of Christ gives life, and what the nature of our communion with Christ.
10. No distance of place can impede it. In the Supper it is not presented as an empty symbol, but, as the apostle testifies, we receive the reality. Objection, that the expression is figurative. Answer. A sure rule with regard to the sacraments.
11. Conclusion of the first part of the chapter. The sacrament of the Supper consists of two parts—viz. corporeal signs, and spiritual truth. These comprehend the meaning, matter, and effect. Christ truly exhibited to us by symbols.
12. Second part of the chapter, reduced to nine heads. The transubstantiation of the Papists considered and refuted. Its origin and absurdity. Why it should be exploded..
13. Transubstantiation as feigned by the Schoolmen. Refutation. The many superstitions introduced by their error.

14. The fiction of transubstantiation why invented contrary to Scripture, and the consent of antiquity. The term of transubstantiation never used in the early Church. Objection. Answer.
15. The error of transubstantiation favoured by the consecration, which was a kind of magical incantation. The bread is not a sacrament to itself, but to those who receive it. The changing of the rod of Moses into a serpent gives no countenance to Popish transubstantiation. No resemblance between it and the words of institution in the Supper. Objection. Answer.
16. Refutation of consubstantiation; whence the idea of ubiquity.
17. This ubiquity confounds the natures of Christ. Subtleties answered.
18. Absurdities connected with consubstantiation. Candid exposition of the orthodox view.
19. The nature of the true presence of Christ in the Supper The true and substantial communion of the body and blood of the Lord. This orthodox view assailed by turbulent spirits.
20. This view vindicated from their calumnies. The words of the institution explained in opposition to the glosses of transubstantiators and consubstantiators. Their subterfuges and absurd blasphemies.
21. Why the name of the thing signified is given to the sacramental symbols. This illustrated by passages of Scripture; also by a passage of Augustine.
22. Refutation of an objection founded on the words, *This is.* Objection answered.
23. Other objections answered.
24. Other objections answered. No question here as to the omnipotence of God.
25. Other objections answered.
26. The orthodox view further confirmed. I. By a consideration of the reality of Christ's body. II. From our Saviour's declaration that he would always be in the world. This confirmed by the exposition of Augustine.
27. Refutation of the sophisms of the Ubiquitists. The evasion of visible and invisible presence refuted.
28. The authority of Fathers not in favour of these errors as to Christ's presence. Augustine opposed to them.
29. Refutation of the invisible presence maintained by opponents. Refutation from Tertullian, from a saying of Christ after his resurrection, from the definition of a true body, and from different passages of Scripture.
30. Ubiquity refuted by various arguments.
31. The imaginary presence of Transubstantiators, Consubstantiators, and Ubiquitists, contrasted with the orthodox doctrine.
32. The nature of our Saviour's true presence explained. The mode of it incomprehensible.
33. Our communion in the blood and flesh of Christ. Spiritual not oral, and yet real. Erroneous view of the Schoolmen.
34. This view not favoured by Augustine. How the wicked eat the body of Christ. Cyril's sentiments as to the eating of the body of Christ.
35. Absurdity of the adoration of sacramental symbols.
36. This adoration condemned. I. By Christ himself. II. By the Council of Nice. III. By ancient custom. IV. By Scripture. This adoration is mere idolatry.
37, This adoration inconsistent with the nature and institution of the sacrament. Ends for which the sacrament was instituted.
38. Ends for which the sacrament was instituted.
39. True nature of the sacrament, contrasted with the Popish observance of it.
40. Nature of an unworthy approach to the Lord's table. The great danger of it. The proper remedy in serious self-examination.
41. The spurious examination introduced by the Papists. Refutation.
42. The nature of Christian examination.
43. External rites in the administration of the Supper. Many of them indifferent.
44. Duty of frequent communion. This proved by the practice of the Church in its purer state, and by the canons of the early bishops.
45. Frequent communion in the time of Augustine. The neglect of it censured by Chrysostom.
46. The Popish injunction to communicate once a-year an execrable invention.
47. Communion in one kind proved to be an invention of Satan.
48. Subterfuges of the Papists refuted.
49. The practice of the early Church further considered.
50. Conclusion.

1. AFTER God has once received us into his family, it is not that he may regard us in the light of servants, but of sons, performing the part of a kind and anxious parent, and providing for our maintenance during the whole course of our lives. And, not contented with this, he has been pleased by a pledge to assure us of his continued liberality. To this end, he has given another sacrament to his Church by the hand of his only-begotten Son—viz. a spiritual feast, at which Christ testifies that he himself is living bread (John vi. 51), on which our souls feed, for a true and blessed immortality. Now, as the knowledge of this great mystery is most necessary, and, in proportion to its importance, demands an accurate exposition, and Satan, in order to deprive the Church of this inestimable treasure, long ago introduced, first, mists, and then darkness, to obscure its light, and stirred up strife and contention to alienate the minds of the simple from a relish for this sacred food, and in our age, also, has tried the same artifice, I will proceed, after giving a simple summary adapted to the capacity of the ignorant, to explain those difficulties by which Satan has tried to ensnare the world. First, then, the signs are bread and wine, which represent the invisible food which we receive from the body and blood of Christ. For as God, regenerating us in baptism, ingrafts us into the fellowship of his Church, and makes us his by adoption, so we have said that he performs the office of a provident parent, in continually supplying the food by which he may sustain and preserve us in the life to which he has begotten us by his word. Moreover, Christ is the only food of our soul, and, therefore, our heavenly Father invites us to him, that, refreshed by communion with him, we may ever and anon gather new vigour until we reach the heavenly immortality. But as this mystery of the secret union of Christ with believers is incomprehensible by nature, he exhibts its figure and image in visible signs adapted to our capacity, nay, by giving, as it were, earnests and badges, he makes it as certain to us as if it were seen by the eye; the familiarity of the similitude giving it access to minds however dull, and showing that souls are fed by Christ just as the corporeal life is sustained by bread and wine. We now, therefore, understand the end which this mystical benediction has in view—viz. to assure us that the body of Christ was once sacrificed for us, so that we may now eat it, and, eating, feel within ourselves the efficacy of that one sacrifice,—that his blood was once shed for us so as to be our perpetual drink. This is the force of the promise which is added, "Take, eat; this is my body, which is broken for you" (Matth. xxvi. 26, &c.). The body which was once offered for our salvation we are enjoined to take and eat, that, while we see ourselves made partakers of it, we may safely conclude that the virtue of that death will be efficacious in us. Hence he terms the cup the covenant in his blood. For the covenant which he once sanctioned by his blood he in a manner renews, or rather continues, in so far as

regards the confirmation of our faith, as often as he stretches forth his sacred blood as drink to us.

2. Pious souls can derive great confidence and delight from this sacrament, as being a testimony that they form one body with Christ, so that everything which is his they may call their own. Hence it follows, that we can confidently assure ourselves, that eternal life, of which he himself is the heir, is ours, and that the kingdom of heaven, into which he has entered, can no more be taken from us than from him; on the other hand, that we cannot be condemned for our sins, from the guilt of which he absolves us, seeing he has been pleased that these should be imputed to himself as if they were his own. This is the wondrous exchange made by his boundless goodness. Having become with us the Son of Man, he has made us with himself sons of God. By his own descent to the earth he has prepared our ascent to heaven. Having received our mortality, he has bestowed on us his immortality. Having undertaken our weakness, he has made us strong in his strength. Having submitted to our poverty, he has transferred to us his riches. Having taken upon himself the burden of unrighteousness with which we were oppressed, he has clothed us with his righteousness.

3. To all these things we have a complete attestation in this sacrament, enabling us certainly to conclude that they are as truly exhibited to us as if Christ were placed in bodily presence before our view, or handled by our hands. For these are words which can never lie nor deceive—Take, eat, drink. This is my body, which is broken for you: this is my blood, which is shed for the remission of sins. In bidding us take, he intimates that it is ours: in bidding us eat, he intimates that it becomes one substance with us: in affirming of his body that it was broken, and of his blood that it was shed for us, he shows that both were not so much his own as ours, because he took and laid down both, not for his own advantage, but for our salvation. And we ought carefully to observe, that the chief, and almost the whole energy of the sacrament, consists in these words, It is broken for you: it is shed for you. It would not be of much importance to us that the body and blood of the Lord are now distributed, had they not once been set forth for our redemption and salvation. Wherefore they are represented under bread and wine, that we may learn that they are not only ours, but intended to nourish our spiritual life; that is, as we formerly observed, by the corporeal things which are produced in the sacrament, we are by a kind of analogy conducted to spiritual things. Thus when bread is given as a symbol of the body of Christ, we must immediately think of this similitude. As bread nourishes, sustains, and protects our bodily life, so the body of Christ is the only food to invigorate and keep alive the soul. When we behold wine set forth as a symbol of blood, we must think that such use as wine serves to the body, the same is spiritually bestowed by the blood of Christ; and the use is to foster, refresh, strengthen, and exhilarate. For if we duly consider

what profit we have gained by the breaking of his sacred body, and the shedding of his blood, we shall clearly perceive that these properties of bread and wine, agreeably to this analogy, most appropriately represent it when they are communicated to us.

4. Therefore, it is not the principal part of a sacrament simply to hold forth the body of Christ to us without any higher consideration, but rather to seal and confirm that promise by which he testifies that his flesh is meat indeed, and his blood drink indeed, nourishing us unto life eternal, and by which he affirms that he is the bread of life, of which, whosoever shall eat, shall live for ever—I say, to seal and confirm that promise, and in order to do so, it sends us to the cross of Christ, where that promise was performed and fulfilled in all its parts. For we do not eat Christ duly and savingly unless as crucified, while with lively apprehension we perceive the efficacy of his death. When he called himself the bread of life, he did not take that appellation from the sacrament, as some perversely interpret; but such as he was given to us by the Father, such he exhibited himself when becoming partaker of our human mortality, he made us partakers of his divine immortality; when offering himself in sacrifice, he took our curse upon himself, that he might cover us with his blessing, when by his death he devoured and swallowed up death, when in his resurrection he raised our corruptible flesh, which he had put on, to glory and incorruption.

5. It only remains that the whole become ours by application. This is done by means of the gospel, and more clearly by the sacred Supper, where Christ offers himself to us with all his blessings, and we receive him in faith. The sacrament, therefore, does not make Christ become for the first time the bread of life; but, while it calls to remembrance that Christ was made the bread of life that we may constantly eat him, it gives us a taste and relish for that bread, and makes us feel its efficacy. For it assures us, first, that whatever Christ did or suffered was done to give us life; and, secondly, that this quickening is eternal; by it we are ceaselessly nourished, sustained, and preserved in life. For as Christ would not have not been the bread of life to us if he had not been born, if he had not died and risen again; so he could not now be the bread of life, were not the efficacy and fruit of his nativity, death, and resurrection, eternal. All this Christ has elegantly expressed in these words, "The bread that I will give is my flesh, which I will give for the life of the world" (John vi. 51); doubtless intimating, that his body will be as bread in regard to the spiritual life of the soul, because it was to be delivered to death for our salvation, and that he extends it to us for food when he makes us partakers of it by faith. Wherefore he once gave himself that he might become bread, when he gave himself to be crucified for the redemption of the world; and he gives himself daily, when in the word of the gospel he offers himself to be partaken by us, inasmuch as he was crucified, when he seals that offer by the sacred mystery of the Supper, and when he accomplishes inwardly

what he externally designates. Moreover, two faults are here to be avoided. We must neither, by setting too little value on the signs, dissever them from their meanings to which they are in some degree annexed, nor by immoderately extolling them, seem somewhat to obscure the mysteries themselves. That Christ is the bread of life by which believers are nourished unto eternal life, no man is so utterly devoid of religion as not to acknowledge. But all are not agreed as to the mode of partaking of him. For there are some who define the eating of the flesh of Christ, and the drinking of his blood, to be, in one word, nothing more than believing in Christ himself. But Christ seems to me to have intended to teach something more express and more sublime in that noble discourse, in which he recommends the eating of his flesh—viz. that we are quickened by the true partaking of him, which he designated by the terms eating and drinking, lest any one should suppose that the life which we obtain from him is obtained by simple knowledge. For as it is not the sight but the eating of bread that gives nourishment to the body, so the soul must partake of Christ truly and thoroughly, that by his energy it may grow up into spiritual life. Meanwhile, we admit that this is nothing else than the eating of faith, and that no other eating can be imagined. But there is this difference between their mode of speaking and mine. According to them, to eat is merely to believe; while I maintain that the flesh of Christ is eaten by believing, because it is made ours by faith, and that that eating is the effect and fruit of faith; or, if you will have it more clearly, according to them, eating is faith, whereas it rather seems to me to be a consequence of faith. The difference is little in words, but not little in reality. For, although the apostle teaches that Christ dwells in our hearts by faith (Eph. iii. 17), no one will interpret that dwelling to be faith. All see that it explains the admirable effect of faith, because to it it is owing that believers have Christ dwelling in them. In this way, the Lord was pleased, by calling himself the bread of life, not only to teach that our salvation is treasured up in the faith of his death and resurrection, but also, by virtue of true communication with him, his life passes into us and becomes ours, just as bread when taken for food gives vigour to the body.

6. When Augustine, whom they claim as their patron, wrote, that we eat by believing, all he meant was to indicate that that eating is of faith, and not of the mouth. This I deny not; but I at the same time add, that by faith we embrace Christ, not as appearing at a distance, but as uniting himself to us, he being our head, and we his members. I do not absolutely disapprove of that mode of speaking; I only deny that it is a full interpretation, if they mean to define what it is to eat the flesh of Christ. I see that Augustine repeatedly used this form of expression, as when he said (De Doct. Christ. Lib. iii.), "Unless ye eat the flesh of the Son of Man" is a figurative expression enjoining us to have communion with our Lord's passion, and sweetly and usefully to treasure in our memory

that his flesh was crucified and wounded for us. Also when he says, "These three thousand men who were converted at the preaching of Peter (Acts ii. 41), by believing, drank the blood which they had cruelly shed."[1] But in very many other passages he admirably commends faith for this, that by means of it our souls are not less refreshed by the communion of the blood of Christ, than our bodies with the bread which they eat. The very same thing is said by Chrysostom, "Christ makes us his body, not by faith only, but in reality." He does not mean that we obtain this blessing from any other quarter than from faith: he only intends to prevent any one from thinking of mere imagination when he hears the name of faith. I say nothing of those who hold that the Supper is merely a mark of external profession, because I think I sufficiently refuted their error when I treated of the sacraments in general (Chap. xiv. sec. 13). Only let my readers observe, that when the cup is called the covenant in blood (Luke xxii. 20), the promise which tends to confirm faith is expressed. Hence it follows, that unless we have respect to God, and embrace what he offers, we do not make a right use of the sacred Supper.

7. I am not satisfied with the view of those who, while acknowledging that we have some kind of communion with Christ, only make us partakers of the Spirit, omitting all mention of flesh and blood. As if it were said to no purpose at all, that his flesh is meat indeed, and his blood is drink indeed; that we have no life unless we eat that flesh and drink that blood; and so forth. Therefore, if it is evident that full communion with Christ goes beyond their description, which is too confined, I will attempt briefly to show how far it extends, before proceeding to speak of the contrary vice of excess. For I shall have a longer discussion with these hyperbolical doctors, who, according to their gross ideas, fabricate an absurd mode of eating and drinking, and transfigure Christ, after divesting him of his flesh, into a phantom: if, indeed, it be lawful to put this great mystery into words, a mystery which I feel, and therefore freely confess that I am unable to comprehend with my mind, so far am I from wishing any one to measure its sublimity by my feeble capacity. Nay, I rather exhort my readers not to confine their apprehension within those too narrow limits, but to attempt to rise much higher than I can guide them. For whenever this subject is considered, after I have done my utmost, I feel that I have spoken far beneath its dignity. And though the mind is more powerful in thought than the tongue in expression, it too is overcome and overwhelmed by the magnitude of the subject. All then that remains is to break forth in admiration of the mystery, which it is plain that the mind is inadequate to comprehend, or the tongue to express. I will, however, give a summary of my view as I best can,

[1] See August. Hom. in Joann. 31 et 40, &c.; Chrysost. Hom. ad Popul. Antioch., 60, 61; et Hom. in Marc. 89.

not doubting its truth, and therefore trusting that it will not be disapproved by pious breasts.

8. First of all, we are taught by the Scriptures that Christ was from the beginning the living Word of the Father, the fountain and origin of life, from which all things should always receive life. Hence John at one time calls him the Word of life, and at another says, that in him was life; intimating, that he, even then pervading all creatures, instilled into them the power of breathing and living. He afterwards adds, that the life was at length manifested, when the Son of God, assuming our nature, exhibited himself in bodily form to be seen and handled. For although he previously diffused his virtue into the creatures, yet as man, because alienated from God by sin, had lost the communication of life, and saw death on every side impending over him, he behoved, in order to regain the hope of immortality, to be restored to the communion of that Word. How little confidence can it give you, to know that the Word of God, from which you are at the greatest distance, contains within himself the fulness of life, whereas in yourself, in whatever direction you turn, you see nothing but death? But ever since that fountain of life began to dwell in our nature, he no longer lies hid at a distance from us, but exhibits himself openly for our participation. Nay, the very flesh in which he resides he makes vivifying to us, that by partaking of it we may feed for immortality. "I," says he, "am that bread of life;" "I am the living bread which came down from heaven;" "And the bread that I will give is my flesh, which I will give for the life of the world" (John vi. 48, 51). By these words he declares, not only that he is life, inasmuch as he is the eternal Word of God who came down to us from heaven, but, by coming down, gave vigour to the flesh which he assumed, that a communication of life to us might thence emanate. Hence, too, he adds, that his flesh is meat indeed, and that his blood is drink indeed: by this food believers are reared to eternal life. The pious, therefore, have admirable comfort in this, that they now find life in their own flesh. For they not only reach it by easy access, but have it spontaneously set forth before them. Let them only throw open the door of their hearts that they may take it into their embrace, and they will obtain it.

9. The flesh of Christ, however, has not such power in itself as to make us live, seeing that by its own first condition it was subject to mortality, and even now, when endued with immortality, lives not by itself. Still it is properly said to be life-giving, as it is pervaded with the fulness of life for the purpose of transmitting it to us. In this sense I understand our Saviour's words as Cyril interprets them, "As the Father hath life in himself, so hath he given to the Son to have life in himself" (John v. 26). For there properly he is speaking not of the properties which he possessed with the Father from the beginning, but of those with which he was invested in the flesh in which he appeared. Accordingly, he shows that in his humanity also

fulness of life resides, so that every one who communicates in his flesh and blood, at the same time enjoys the participation of life. The nature of this may be explained by a familiar example. As water is at one time drunk out of the fountain, at another drawn, at another led away by conduits to irrigate the fields, and yet does not flow forth of itself for all these uses, but is taken from its source, which, with perennial flow, ever and anon sends forth a new and sufficient supply; so the flesh of Christ is like a rich and inexhaustible fountain, which transfuses into us the life flowing forth from the Godhead into itself. Now, who sees not that the communion of the flesh and blood of Christ is necessary to all who aspire to the heavenly life? Hence those passages of the apostle: The Church is the "body" of Christ; his "fulness." He is "the head," "from whence the whole body fitly joined together, and compacted by that which every joint supplieth," "maketh increase of the body" (Eph. i. 23; iv. 15, 16). Our bodies are the "members of Christ" (1 Cor. vi. 15). We perceive that all these things cannot possibly take place unless he adheres to us wholly in body and spirit. But the very close connection which unites us to his flesh, he illustrated with still more splendid epithets, when he said that we "are members of his body, of his flesh, and of his bones" (Eph. v. 30). At length, to testify that the matter is too high for utterance, he concludes with exclaiming, "This is a great mystery" (Eph. v. 32). It were, therefore, extreme infatuation not to acknowledge the communion of believers with the body and blood of the Lord, a communion which the apostle declares to be so great, that he chooses rather to marvel at it than to explain it.

10. The sum is, that the flesh and blood of Christ feed our souls just as bread and wine maintain and suport our corporeal life. For there would be no aptitude in the sign, did not our souls find their nourishment in Christ. This could not be, did not Christ truly form one with us, and refresh us by the eating of his flesh, and the drinking of his blood. But though it seems an incredible thing that the flesh of Christ, while at such a distance from us in respect of place, should be food to us, let us remember how far the secret virtue of the Holy Spirit surpasses all our conceptions, and how foolish it is to wish to measure its immensity by our feeble capacity. Therefore, what our mind does not comprehend let faith conceive—viz. that the Spirit truly unites things separated by space. That sacred communion of flesh and blood by which Christ transfuses his life into us, just as if it penetrated our bones and marrow, he testifies and seals in the Supper, and that not by presenting a vain or empty sign, but by there exerting an efficacy of the Spirit by which he fulfils what he promises. And truly the thing there signified he exhibits and offers to all who sit down at that spiritual feast, although it is beneficially received by believers only who receive this great benefit with true faith and heartfelt gratitude. For this reason the apostle said, "The cup of blessing which we bless, is it not the communion of the blood of Christ? The bread which we break, is it not the communion of

the body of Christ"? (1 Cor. x. 16.) There is no ground to object that the expression is figurative, and gives the sign the name of the thing signified. I admit, indeed, that the breaking of bread is a symbol, not the reality. But this being admitted, we duly infer from the exhibition of the symbol that the thing itself is exhibited. For unless we would charge God with deceit, we will never presume to say that he holds forth an empty symbol. Therefore, if by the breaking of bread the Lord truly represents the partaking of his body, there ought to be no doubt whatever that he truly exhibits and performs it. The rule which the pious ought always to observe is, whenever they see the symbols instituted by the Lord, to think and feel surely persuaded that the truth of the thing signified is also present. For why does the Lord put the symbol of his body into your hands, but just to assure you that you truly partake of him? If this is true let us feel as much assured that the visible sign is given us in seal of an invisible gift as that his body itself is given to us.

11. I hold then (as has always been received in the Church, and is still taught by those who feel aright), that the sacred mystery of the Supper consists of two things—the corporeal signs, which, presented to the eye, represent invisible things in a manner adapted to our weak capacity, and the spiritual truth, which is at once figured and exhibited by the signs. When attempting familiarly to explain its nature, I am accustomed to set down three things—the thing meant, the matter which depends on it, and the virtue or efficacy consequent upon both. The thing meant consists in the promises which are in a manner included in the sign. By the matter, or substance, I mean Christ, with his death and resurrection. By the effect, I understand redemption, justification, sanctification, eternal life, and all other benefits which Christ bestows upon us. Moreover, though all these things have respect to faith, I leave no room for the cavil, that when I say Christ is conceived by faith, I mean that he is only conceived by the intellect and imagination. He is offered by the promises, not that we may stop short at the sight or mere knowledge of him, but that we may enjoy true communion with him. And, indeed, I see not how any one can expect to have redemption and righteousness in the cross of Christ, and life in his death, without trusting first of all to true communion with Christ himself. Those blessings could not reach us, did not Christ previously make himself ours. I say then, that in the mystery of the Supper, by the symbols of bread and wine, Christ, his body and his blood, are truly exhibited to us, that in them he fulfilled all obedience, in order to procure righteousness for us—first that we might become one body with him; and, secondly, that being made partakers of his substance, we might feel the result of this fact in the participation of all his blessings.

12. I now come to the hyperbolical mixtures which superstition has introduced. Here Satan has employed all his wiles, withdrawing the minds of men from heaven, and imbuing them with the perverse error that Christ is annexed to the element of bread. And, first, we are not to

dream of such a presence of Christ in the sacrament as the artificers of the Romish court have imagined, as if the body of Christ, locally present, were to be taken into the hand, and chewed by the teeth, and swallowed by the throat. This was the form of Palinode, which Pope Nicholas dictated to Berengarius, in token of his repentance, a form expressed in terms so monstrous, that the author of the Gloss exclaims, that there is danger, if the reader is not particularly cautious, that he will be led by it into a worse heresy than was that of Berengarius (Distinct. ii. c. Ego Berengarius). Peter Lombard, though he labours much to excuse the absurdity, rathers inclines to a different opinion. As we cannot at all doubt that it is bounded according to the invariable rule in the human body, and is contained in heaven, where it was once received, and will remain till it return to judgment, so we deem it altogether unlawful to bring it back under these corruptible elements, or to imagine it everywhere present. And, indeed, there is no need of this, in order to our partaking of it, since the Lord by his Spirit bestows upon us the blessing of being one with him in soul, body, and spirit. The bond of that connection, therefore, is the Spirit of Christ, who unites us to him, and is a kind of channel by which everything that Christ has and is, is derived to us. For if we see that the sun, in sending forth its rays upon the earth, to generate, cherish, and invigorate its offspring, in a manner transfuses its substance into it, why should the radiance of the Spirit be less in conveying to us the communion of his flesh and blood? Wherefore the Scripture, when it speaks of our participation with Christ, refers its whole efficacy to the Spirit. Instead of many, one passage will suffice. Paul, in the Epistle to the Romans (Rom. viii. 9–11), shows that the only way in which Christ dwells in us is by his Spirit. By this, however, he does not take away that communion of flesh and blood of which we now speak, but shows that it is owing to the Spirit alone that we possess Christ wholly, and have him abiding in us.

13. The Schoolmen, horrified at this barbarous impiety, speak more modestly, though they do nothing more than amuse themselves with more subtle delusions. They admit that Christ is not contained in the sacrament circumscriptively, or in a bodily manner, but they afterwards devise a method which they themselves do not understand, and cannot explain to others. It, however, comes to this, that Christ may be sought in what they call the species of bread. What? When they say that the substance of bread is converted into Christ, do they not attach him to the white colour, which is all they leave of it? But they say, that though contained in the sacrament, he still remains in heaven, and has no other presence there than that of abode. But, whatever be the terms in which they attempt to make a gloss, the sum of all is, that that which was formerly bread, by consecration becomes Christ: so that Christ thereafter lies hid under the colour of bread. This they are not ashamed distinctly to express. For Lombard's words are, "The body of Christ, which is visible in itself, lurks and lies covered after the

act of consecration under the species of bread" (Lombard. Sent. Lib. iv. Dist. 12). Thus the figure of the bread is nothing but a mask which conceals the view of the flesh from our eye. But there is no need of many conjectures to detect the snare which they intended to lay by these words, since the thing itself speaks clearly. It is easy to see how great is the superstition under which not only the vulgar but the leaders also, have laboured for many ages, and still labour, in Popish Churches. Little solicitous as to true faith (by which alone we attain to the fellowship of Christ, and become one with him), provided they have his carnal presence, which they have fabricated without authority from the word, they think he is sufficiently present. Hence we see, that all which they have gained by their ingenious subtlety is to make bread to be regarded as God.

14. Hence proceeded that fictitious transubstantiation for which they fight more fiercely in the present day than for all the other articles of their faith. For the first architects of local presence could not explain, how the body of Christ could be mixed with the substance of bread, without forthwith meeting with many absurdities. Hence it was necessary to have recourse to the fiction, that there is a conversion of the bread into body, not that properly instead of bread it becomes body, but that Christ, in order to conceal himself under the figure, reduces the substance to nothing. It is strange that they have fallen into such a degree of ignorance, nay, of stupor, as to produce this monstrous fiction not only against Scripture, but also against the consent of the ancient Church. I admit, indeed, that some of the ancients occasionally used the term *conversion*, not that they meant to do away with the substance in the external signs, but to teach that the bread devoted to the sacrament was widely different from ordinary bread, and was now something else. All clearly and uniformly teach that the sacred Supper consists of two parts, an earthly and a heavenly. The earthly they without dispute interpret to be bread and wine. Certainly, whatever they may pretend, it is plain that antiquity, which they often dare to oppose to the clear word of God, gives no countenance to that dogma. It is not so long since it was devised; indeed, it was unknown not only to the better ages, in which a purer doctrine still flourished, but after that purity was considerably impaired. There is no early Christian writer who does not admit in distinct terms that the sacred symbols of the Supper are bread and wine, although, as has been said, they sometimes distinguish them by various epithets, in order to recommend the dignity of the mystery. For when they say that a secret conversion takes place at consecration, so that it is now something else than bread and wine, their meaning, as I already observed, is, not that these are annihilated, but that they are to be considered in a different light from common food, which is only intended to feed the body, whereas in the former the spiritual food and drink of the mind are exhibited. This we deny not. But, say our opponents, if there is conversion, one thing must become another. If

they mean that something becomes different from what it was before, I assent. If they will wrest it in support of their fiction, let them tell me of what kind of change they are sensible in baptism. For here, also, the Fathers make out a wonderful conversion, when they say that out of the corruptible element is made the spiritual laver of the soul, and yet no one denies that it still remains water. But say they, there is no such expression in Baptism as that in the Supper, *This is my body;* as if we were treating of these words, which have a meaning sufficiently clear, and not rather of that term *conversion*, which ought not to mean more in the Supper than in Baptism. Have done, then, with those quibbles upon words, which betray nothing but their silliness. The meaning would have no congruity, unless the truth which is there figured had a living image in the external sign. Christ wished to testify by an external symbol that his flesh was food. If he exhibited merely an empty show of bread, and not true bread, where is the analogy or similitude to conduct us from the visible thing to the invisible? For, in order to make all things consistent, the meaning cannot extend to more than this, that we are fed by the species of Christ's flesh; just as, in the case of baptism, if the figure of water deceived the eye, it would not be to us a sure pledge of our ablution; nay, the fallacious spectacle would rather throw us into doubt. The nature of the sacrament is therefore overthrown, if in the mode of signifying the earthly sign corresponds not to the heavenly reality; and, accordingly, the truth of the mystery is lost if true bread does not represent the true body of Christ. I again repeat, since the Supper is nothing but a conspicuous attestation to the promise which is contained in the sixth chapter of John—viz. that Christ is the bread of life, who came down from heaven, that visible bread must intervene, in order that that spiritual bread may be figured, unless we would destroy all the benefits with which God here favours us for the purpose of sustaining our infirmity. Then on what ground could Paul infer that we are all one bread, and one body in partaking together of that one bread, if only the semblance of bread, and not the natural reality, remained?

15. They could not have been so shamefully deluded by the impostures of Satan had they not been fascinated by the erroneous idea, that the body of Christ included under the bread is transmitted by the bodily mouth into the belly. The cause of this brutish imagination was, that consecration had the same effect with them as magical incantation. They overlooked the principle, that bread is a sacrament to none but those to whom the word is addressed, just as the water of baptism is not changed in itself, but begins to be to us what it formerly was not, as soon as the promise is annexed. This will better appear from the example of a similar sacrament. The water gushing from the rock in the desert was to the Israelites a badge and sign of the same thing that is figured to us in the Supper by wine. For Paul declares that they drank the same spiritual drink (1 Cor. x. 4.) But the water was common to the herds and

flocks of the people. Hence it is easy to infer, that in the earthly elements, when employed for a spiritual use, no other conversion takes place than in respect of men, inasmuch as they are to them seals of promises. Moreover, since it is the purpose of God, as I have repeatedly inculcated, to raise us up to himself by fit vehicles, those who indeed call us to Christ, but to Christ lurking invisibly under bread, impiously, by their perverseness, defeat this object. For it is impossible for the mind of man to disentangle itself from the immensity of space, and ascend to Christ even above the heavens. What nature denied them, they attempted to gain by a noxious remedy. Remaining on the earth, they felt no need of a celestial proximity to Christ. Such was the necessity which impelled them to transfigure the body of Christ. In the age of Bernard, though a harsher mode of speech had prevailed, transubstantiation was not yet recognised. And in all previous ages, the similitude in the mouths of all was, that a spiritual reality was conjoined with bread and wine in this sacrament. As to the terms, they think they answer acutely, though they adduce nothing relevant to the case in hand. The rod of Moses (they say), when turned into a serpent, though it acquires the name of a serpent, still retains its former name, and is called a rod; and thus, according to them, it is equally probable that though the bread passes into a new substance, it is still called by catachresis, and not inaptly, what it still appears to the eye to be. But what resemblance, real or apparent, do they find between an illustrious miracle and their fictitious illusion, of which no eye on the earth is witness? The magi by their impostures had persuaded the Egyptians, that they had a divine power above the ordinary course of nature to change created beings. Moses comes forth, and after exposing their fallacies, shows that the invincible power of God is on his side, since his rod swallows up all the other rods. But as that conversion was visible to the eye, we have already observed, that it has no reference to the case in hand. Shortly after the rod visibly resumed its form. It may be added, that we know not whether this was an extemporary conversion of substance.[1] For we must attend to the illusion to the rods of the magicians, which the prophet did not choose to term serpents, lest he might seem to insinuate a conversion which had no existence, because those impostors had done nothing more than blind the eyes of the spectators. But what resemblance is there between that expression and the following? "The bread which we break;"—"As often as ye eat this bread;"—"They communicated in the breaking of bread;" and so forth. It is certain that the eye only was deceived by the incantation of the magicians. The matter is more doubtful with regard to Moses, by whose hand it was not more difficult for God to make a serpent out of a rod, and again to make a rod out of a serpent, than to clothe angels with corporeal

1 Compare together Ambrose on those who are initiated in the sacraments (cap. 9), and Augustine, De Trinitate, Lib. iii. cap. 10, and it will be seen that both are opposed to transubstantiation.

bodies, and a little after unclothe them. If the case of the sacrament were at all akin to this, there might be some colour for their explanation. Let it, therefore, remain fixed that there is no true and fit promise in the Supper, that the flesh of Christ is truly meat, unless there is a correspondence in the true substance of the external symbol. But as one error gives rise to another, a passage in Jeremiah has been so absurdly wrested, to prove transubstantiation, that it is painful to refer to it. The prophet complains that wood was placed in his bread, intimating that by the cruelty of his enemies his bread was infected with bitterness, as David by a similar figure complains, "They gave me also gall for my meat: and in my thirst they gave me vinegar to drink" (Psalm lxix. 21). These men would allegorise the expression to mean, that the body of Christ was nailed to the wood of the cross. But some of the Fathers thought so! As if we ought not rather to pardon their ignorance and bury the disgrace, than to add impudence, and bring them into hostile conflict with the genuine meaning of the prophet.

16. Some, who see that the analogy between the sign and the thing signified cannot be destroyed without destroying the truth of the sacrament, admit that the bread of the Supper is truly the substance of an earthly and corruptible element, and cannot suffer any change in itself, but must have the body of Christ included under it. If they would explain this to mean, that when the bread is held forth in the sacrament, an exhibition of the body is annexed, because the truth is inseparable from its sign, I would not greatly object. But because fixing the body itself in the bread, they attach to it an ubiquity contrary to its nature, and by adding *under* the bread, will have it that it lies hid under it, I must employ a short time in exposing their craft, and dragging them forth from their concealments. Here, however, it is not my intention professedly to discuss the whole case; I mean only to lay the foundations of a discussion which will afterwards follow in its own place. They insist, then, that the body of Christ is invisible and immense, so that it may be hid under bread, because they think that there is no other way by which they can communicate with him than by his descending into the bread, though they do not comprehend the mode of descent by which he raises us up to himself. They employ all the colours they possibly can, but after they have said all, it is sufficiently apparent that they insist on the local presence of Christ. How so? Because they cannot conceive any other participation of flesh and blood than that which consists either in local conjunction and contact, or in some gross method of enclosing.

17. Some, in order obstinately to maintain the error which they have once rashly adopted, hesitate not to assert that the dimensions of Christ's flesh are not more circumscribed than those of heaven and earth. His birth as an infant, his growth, his extension on the cross, his confinement in the sepulchre, were effected, they say, by a kind of dispensation, that he might perform the offices of being

born, of dying, and of other human acts: his being seen with his wonted bodily appearance after the resurrection, his ascension into heaven, his appearance, after his ascension, to Stephen and Paul, were the effect of the same dispensation, that it might be made apparent to the eye of man that he was constituted King in heaven. What is this but to call forth Marcion from his grave? For there cannot be a doubt that the body of Christ, if so constituted, was a phantasm, or was phantastical. Some employ a rather more subtle evasion, That the body which is given in the sacrament is glorious and immortal, and that, therefore, there is no absurdity in its being contained under the sacrament in various places, or in no place, and in no form. But, I ask, what did Christ give to his disciples the day before he suffered? Do not the words say that he gave the mortal body, which was to be delivered shortly after? But, say they, he had previously manifested his glory to the three disciples on the mount (Matth. xvii. 2). This is true; but his purpose was to give them for the time a taste of immortality. Still they cannot find there a twofold body, but only the one which he had assumed, arrayed in new glory. When he distributed his body in the first Supper, the hour was at hand in which he was "stricken, smitten of God, and afflicted" (Isa. liii. 4). So far was he from intending at that time to exhibit the glory of his resurrection. And here what a door is opened to Marcion, if the body of Christ was seen humble and mortal in one place, glorious and immortal in another! And yet, if their opinion is well-founded, the same thing happens every day, because they are forced to admit that the body of Christ, which is in itself visible, lurks invisibly under the symbol of bread. And yet those who send forth such monstrous dogmas, so far from being ashamed at the disgrace, assail us with virulent invectives for not subscribing to them.

18. But assuming that the body and blood of Christ are attached to the bread and wine, then the one must necessarily be dissevered from the other. For as the bread is given separately from the cup, so the body, united to the bread, must be separated from the blood, included in the cup. For since they affirm that the body is in the bread, and the blood is in the cup, while the bread and wine are, in regard to space, at some distance from each other, they cannot, by any quibble, evade the conclusion that the body must be separated from the blood. Their usual pretence—viz. that the blood is in the body, and the body again in the blood, by what they call concomitance, is more than frivolous, since the symbols in which they are included are thus distinguished. But if we are carried to heaven with our eyes and minds, that we may there behold Christ in the glory of his kingdom, as the symbols invite us to him in his integrity, so, under the symbol of bread, we must feed on his body, and, under the symbol of wine, drink separately of his blood, and thereby have the full enjoyment of him. For though he withdrew his flesh from us, and with his body ascended to heaven, he, however, sits at the right hand of the

Father; that is, he reigns in power and majesty, and the glory of the Father. This kingdom is not limited by any intervals of space, nor circumscribed by any dimensions. Christ can exert his energy wherever he pleases, in earth and heaven, can manifest his presence by the exercise of his power, can always be present with his people, breathing into them his own life, can live in them, sustain, confirm, and invigorate them, and preserve them safe, just as if he were with them in the body; in fine, can feed them with his own body, communion with which he transfuses into them. After this manner, the body and blood of Christ are exhibited to us in the sacrament.

19. The presence of Christ in the Supper we must hold to be such as neither affixes him to the element of bread, nor encloses him in bread, nor circumscribes him in any way (this would obviously detract from his celestial glory); and it must, moreover, be such as neither divests him of his just dimensions, nor dissevers him by differences of place, nor assigns to him a body of boundless dimensions, diffused through heaven and earth. All these things are clearly repugnant to his true human nature. Let us never allow ourselves to lose sight of the two restrictions. First, Let there be nothing derogatory to the heavenly glory of Christ. This happens whenever he is brought under the corruptible elements of this world, or is affixed to any earthly creatures. Secondly, Let no property be assigned to his body inconsistent with his human nature. This is done when it is either said to be infinite, or made to occupy a variety of places at the same time. But when these absurdities are discarded, I willingly admit anything which helps to express the true and substantial communication of the body and blood of the Lord, as exhibited to believers under the sacred symbols of the Supper, understanding that they are received not by the imagination or intellect merely, but are enjoyed in reality as the food of eternal life. For the odium with which this view is regarded by the world, and the unjust prejudice incurred by its defence, there is no cause, unless it be in the fearful fascinations of Satan. What we teach on the subject is in perfect accordance with Scripture, contains nothing absurd, obscure, or ambiguous, is not unfavourable to true piety and solid edification; in short, has nothing in it to offend, save that, for some ages, while the ignorance and barbarism of sophists reigned in the Church, the clear light and open truth were unbecomingly suppressed. And yet as Satan, by means of turbulent spirits, is still, in the present day, exerting himself to the utmost to bring dishonour on this doctrine by all kinds of calumny and reproach, it is right to assert and defend it with the greatest care.

20. Before we proceed farther, we must consider the ordinance itself, as instituted by Christ, because the most plausible objection of our opponents is, that we abandon his words. To free ourselves from the obloquy with which they thus load us, the fittest course will be to begin with an interpretation of the words. Three Evangelists and Paul relate that our Saviour took bread, and after giving

thanks, brake it, and gave it to his disciples, saying, Take, eat: this is my body which is given or broken for you. Of the cup, Matthew and Mark say, "This is my blood of the new testament, which is shed for many for the remission of sins" (Matth. xxvi. 26; Mark xiv. 22). Luke and Paul say, "This cup is the new testament in my blood" (Luke xxii. 20; 1 Cor. xi. 25). The advocates of transubstantiation insist, that by the pronoun, *this*, is denoted the appearance of bread, because the whole complexion of our Saviour's address is an act of consecration, and there is no substance which can be demonstrated. But if they adhere so religiously to the words, inasmuch as that which our Saviour gave to his disciples he declared to be his body, there is nothing more alien from the strict meaning of the words than the fiction, that what was bread is now body. What Christ takes into his hands, and gives to the apostles, he declares to be his body; but he had taken bread, and, therefore, who sees not that what is given is still bread? Hence, nothing can be more absurd than to transfer what is affirmed of bread to the species of bread. Others, in interpreting the particle *is*, as equivalent to being transubstantiated, have recourse to a gloss which is forced and violently wrested. They have no ground, therefore, for pretending that they are moved by a reverence for the words. The use of the term *is*, for being converted into something else, is unknown to every tongue and nation. With regard to those who leave the bread in the Supper, and affirm that it is the body of Christ, there is great diversity among them. Those who speak more modestly, though they insist upon the letter, This is my body, afterwards abandon this strictness, and observe that it is equivalent to saying that the body of Christ is with the bread, in the bread, and under the bread. To the reality which they affirm, we have already adverted, and will by-and-by, at greater length. I am not only considering the words by which they say they are prevented from admitting that the bread is called body, because it is a sign of the body. But if they shun everything like metaphor, why do they leap from the simple demonstration of Christ to modes of expression which are widely different? For there is a great difference between saying that the bread is the body, and that the body is with the bread. But seeing it impossible to maintain the simple proposition that the bread is the body, they endeavoured to evade the difficulty by concealing themselves under those forms of expression. Others, who are bolder, hesitate not to assert that, strictly speaking, the bread is body, and in this way prove that they are truly of the letter. If it is objected that the bread, therefore, is Christ, and, being Christ, is God,—they will deny it, because the words of Christ do not expressly say so. But they gain nothing by their denial, since all agree that the whole Christ is offered to us in the Supper. It is intolerable blasphemy to affirm, without figure, of a fading and corruptible element, that it is Christ. I now ask them, if they hold the two propositions to be identical, Christ is the Son of God, and Bread is the body of

Christ? If they concede that they are different (and this, whether they will or not, they will be forced to do), let them tell wherein is the difference. All which they can adduce is, I presume, that the bread is called body in a sacramental manner. Hence it follows, that the words of Christ are not subject to the common rule, and ought not to be tested grammatically. I ask all these rigid and obstinate exactors of the letter, whether, when Luke and Paul call the cup *the testament in blood*, they do not express the same thing as in the previous clause, when they call bread the body? There certainly was the same solemnity in the one part of the mystery as in the other, and, as brevity is obscure, the longer sentence better elucidates the meaning. As often, therefore, as they contend, from the one expression, that the bread is body, I will adduce an apt interpretation from the longer expression, That it is a testament in the body. What? Can we seek for surer or more faithful expounders than Luke and Paul? I have no intention, however, to detract, in any respect, from the communication of the body of Christ, which I have acknowledged. I only meant to expose the foolish perverseness with which they carry on a war of words. The bread I understand, on the authority of Luke and Paul, to be the body of Christ, because it is a covenant in the body. If they impugn this, their quarrel is not with me, but with the Spirit of God. However often they may repeat, that reverence for the words of Christ will not allow them to give a figurative interpretation to what is spoken plainly, the pretext cannot justify them in thus rejecting all the contrary arguments which we adduce. Meanwhile, as I have already observed, it is proper to attend to the force of what is meant by a testament in the body and blood of Christ. The covenant, ratified by the sacrifice of death, would not avail us without the addition of that secret communication, by which we are made one with Christ.

21. It remains, therefore, to hold, that on account of the affinity which the things signified have with their signs, the name of the thing itself is given to the sign figuratively, indeed, but very appropriately. I say nothing of allegories and parables, lest it should be alleged that I am seeking subterfuges, and slipping out of the present question. I say that the expression which is uniformly used in Scripture, when the sacred mysteries are treated of, is metonymical. For you cannot otherwise understand the expressions, that circumcision is a "covenant"—that the lamb is the Lord's "passover"—that the sacrifices of the law are expiations—that the rock from which the water flowed in the desert was Christ,—unless you interpret them metonymically."[1] Nor is the name merely transferred from the superior to the inferior, but, on the contrary, the name of the visible sign is given to the thing signified, as when God is said to have appeared to Moses in the bush; the ark of the covenant is called God, and the face of God, and the dove is called the Holy Spirit.[2]

[1] Gen. xvii. 10; Exod. xii. 11; xvii. 6; 1 Cor. x. 4.
[2] Exod. iii. 2; Psalm lxxxiv. 8; xlii. 3; Matth. iii. 16.

For although the sign differs essentially from the thing signified, the latter being spiritual and heavenly, the former corporeal and visible,—yet, as it not only figures the thing which it is employed to represent as a naked and empty badge, but also truly exhibits it, why should not its name be justly applied to the thing? But if symbols humanly devised, which are rather the images of absent than the marks of present things, and of which they are very often most fallacious types, are sometimes honoured with their names,—with much greater reason do the institutions of God borrow the names of things, of which they always bear a sure, and by no means fallacious signification, and have the reality annexed to them. So great, then, is the similarity, and so close the connection between the two, that it is easy to pass from the one to the other. Let our opponents, therefore, cease to indulge their mirth in calling us Tropists, when we explain the sacramental mode of expression according to the common use of Scripture. For, while the sacraments agree in many things, there is also, in this metonymy, a certain community in all respects between them. As, therefore, the apostle says that the rock from which spiritual water flowed forth to the Israelites was Christ (1 Cor. x. 4), and was thus a visible symbol under which, that spiritual drink was truly perceived, though not by the eye, so the body of Christ is now called bread, inasmuch as it is a symbol under which our Lord offers us the true eating of his body. Lest any one should despise this as a novel invention, the view which Augustine took and expressed was the same: "Had not the sacraments a certain resemblance to the things of which they are sacraments, they would not be sacraments at all. And from this resemblance, they generally have the names of the things themselves. This, as the sacrament of the body of Christ, is, after a certain manner, the body of Christ, and the sacrament of Christ is the blood of Christ; so the sacrament of faith is faith" (August. Ep. 23, ad Bonifac.). He has many similar passages, which it would be superfluous to collect, as that one may suffice. I need only remind my readers, that the same doctrine is taught by that holy man in his Epistle to Evodius. Where Augustine teaches that nothing is more common than metonymy in mysteries, it is a frivolous quibble to object that there is no mention of the Supper. Were this objection sustained, it would follow, that we are not entitled to argue from the genus to the species; *e. g.*, Every animal is endued with motion; and, therefore, the horse and the ox are endued with motion.[1] Indeed, longer discussion is rendered unnecessary by the words of the Saint himself, where he says, that when Christ gave the symbol of his body, he did not hesitate to call it his body (August. Cont. Adimantum, cap. 12). He elsewhere says, "Wonderful was the patience of Christ in admitting Judas to the

1 French, "Certes si on ne veut abolir toute raison, on ne peut dire que ce qui est commun à tous sacremens n'appartienne aussi à la Cene."—Certainly if we would not abolish reason altogether, we cannot say that that which is common to all the sacraments belongs not also to the Supper.

feast, in which he committed and delivered to the disciples the symbol of his body and blood" (August. in. Ps. iii).

22. Should any morose person, shutting his eyes to everything else, insist upon the expression, *This is*, as distinguishing this mystery from all others, the answer is easy. They say that the substantive verb is so emphatic, as to leave no room for interpretation. Though I should admit this, I answer, that the substantive verb occurs in the words of Paul (1 Cor. x. 16), where he calls the bread the *communion* of the body of Christ. But communion is something different from the body itself. Nay, when the sacraments are treated of, the same word occurs: "My covenant shall be in your flesh for an everlasting covenant" (Gen. xvii. 13). "This is the ordinance of the passover" (Exod. xii. 43). To say no more, when Paul declares that the rock was Christ (1 Cor. x. 4), why should the substantive verb, in that passage, be deemed less emphatic than in the discourse of Christ? When John says, "The Holy Ghost was not yet given, because that Jesus was not yet glorified" (John vii. 39), I should like to know what is the force of the substantive verb? If the rule of our opponents is rigidly observed, the eternal essence of the Spirit will be destroyed, as if he had only begun to be after the ascension of Christ. Let them tell me, in fine, what is meant by the declaration of Paul, that baptism is "the washing of regeneration, and renewing of the Holy Ghost" (Tit. iii. 5); though it is certain that to many it was of no use. But they cannot be more effectually refuted than by the expression of Paul, that the Church is Christ. For, after introducing the similitude of the human body, he adds, "So also is Christ" (1 Cor. xii. 12), when he means not the only-begotten Son of God in himself, but in his members. I think I have now gained this much, that all men of sense and integrity will be disgusted with the calumnies of our enemies, when they give out that we discredit the words of Christ; though we embrace them not less obediently than they do, and ponder them with greater reverence. Nay, their supine security proves that they do not greatly care what Christ meant, provided it furnishes them with a shield to defend their obstinacy, while our careful investigation should be an evidence of the authority which we yield to Christ. They invidiously pretend that human reason will not allow us to believe what Christ uttered with his sacred mouth; but how naughtily they endeavour to fix this odium upon us, I have already, in a great measure, shown, and will still show more clearly. Nothing, therefore, prevents us from believing Christ speaking, and from acquiescing in everything to which he intimates his assent. The only question here is, whether it be unlawful to inquire into the genuine meaning?

23. Those worthy masters, to show that they are of the letter, forbid us to deviate, in the least, from the letter. On the contrary, when Scripture calls God a man of war, as I see that the expression would be too harsh if not interpreted, I have no doubt that the similitude is taken from man. And, indeed, the only pretext which enabled

the Anthropomorphites to annoy the orthodox Fathers was by fastening on the expressions, "The eyes of God see;" "It ascended to his ears;" "His hand is stretched out;" "The earth is his footstool;" and exclaimed, that God was deprived of the body which Scripture assigns to him. Were this rule admitted, complete barbarism would bury the whole light of faith. What monstrous absurdities shall fanatical men not be able to extract, if they are allowed to urge every knotty point in support of their dogmas? Their objection, that it is not probable that when Christ was providing special comfort for the apostles in adversity, he spoke enigmatically or obscurely, —supports our view. For, had it not occurred to the apostles that the bread was called the body figuratively, as being a symbol of the body, the extraordinary nature of the thing would doubtless have filled them with perplexity. For, at this very period, John relates, that the slightest difficulties perplexed them (John xiv. 5, 8; xvi. 17). They debate, among themselves, how Christ is to go to the Father, and not understanding that the things which were said referred to the heavenly Father, raise a question as to how he is to go out of the world until they shall see him? How, then, could they have been so ready to believe what is repugnant to all reason—viz. that Christ was seated at table under their eye, and yet was contained invisible under the bread? As they attest their consent by eating this bread without hesitation, it is plain that they understood the words of Christ in the same sense as we do, considering what ought not to seem unusual when mysteries are spoken of, that the name of the thing signified was transferred to the sign. There was therefore to the disciples, as there is to us, clear and sure consolation, not involved in any enigma; and the only reason why certain persons reject our interpretation is, because they are blinded by a delusion of the devil to introduce the darkness of enigma, instead of the obvious interpretation of an appropriate figure. Besides, if we insist strictly on the words, our Saviour will be made to affirm erroneously something of the bread different from the cup. He calls the bread body, and the wine blood. There must either be a confusion in terms, or there must be a division separating the body from the blood. Nay, "This is my body," may be as truly affirmed of the cup as of the bread; and it may in turn be affirmed that the bread is the blood.[1] If they answer, that we must look to the end or use for which symbols were instituted, I admit it: but still they will not disencumber themselves of the absurdity which their error drags along with it—viz. that the bread is blood, and the wine is body. Then I know not what they mean when they concede that bread and body are different things, and yet maintain that the one is predicated of the other, properly and without figure, as if one were to say that a garment is different from a man, and yet is properly called a man. Still, as if the victory depended on obstinacy and invective, they say that Christ

[1] The French adds, "Je di si Jesus Christ est enclos sous chacun des deux signes." —I mean, if Jesus Christ is included under each of the two signs.

is charged with falsehood, when it is attempted to interpret his words. It will now be easy for the reader to understand the injustice which is done to us by those carpers at syllables, when they possess the simple with the idea that we bring discredit on the words of Christ; words which, as we have shown, are madly perverted and confounded by them, but are faithfully and accurately expounded by us.

24. This infamous falsehood cannot be completely wiped away without disposing of another charge. They give out that we are so wedded to human reason, that we attribute nothing more to the power of God than the order of nature admits, and common sense dictates.[1] From these wicked calumnies, I appeal to the doctrine which I have delivered,—a doctrine which makes it sufficiently clear that I by no means measure this mystery by the capacity of human reason, or subject it to the laws of nature. I ask, whether it is from physics we have learned that Christ feeds our souls from heaven with his flesh, just as our bodies are nourished by bread and wine? How has flesh this virtue of giving life to our souls? All will say, that it is not done naturally. Not more agreeable is it to human reason to hold that the flesh of Christ penetrates to us, so as to be our food. In short, every one who may have tasted our doctrine, will be carried away with admiration of the secret power of God. But these worthy zealots fabricate for themselves a miracle, and think that without it God himself and his power vanish away. I would again admonish the reader carefully to consider the nature of our doctrine, whether it depends on common apprehension, or whether, after having surmounted the world on the wings of faith, it rises to heaven. We say that Christ descends to us, as well by the external symbol as by his Spirit, that he may truly quicken our souls by the substance of his flesh and blood. He who feels not that in these few words are many miracles, is more than stupid; since nothing is more contrary to nature than to derive the spiritual and heavenly life of the soul from flesh, which received its origin from the earth, and was subjected to death, nothing more incredible than that things separated by the whole space between heaven and earth should, notwithstanding of the long distance, not only be connected, but united, so that souls receive aliment from the flesh of Christ. Let preposterous men, then, cease to assail us with the vile calumny, that we malignantly restrict the boundless power of God. They either foolishly err, or wickedly lie. The question here is not, What could God do? but, What has he been pleased to do? We affirm that he has done what pleased him, and it pleased him that Christ should be in all respects like his brethren, "yet without sin" (Heb. iv. 15). What is our flesh? Is it not that which consists of certain dimensions? is confined within a certain place? is touched and seen? And why,

1 The French adds, "En lisant nos ecrits, on verra incontinent combien ces calomnies sont vilaines et puantes."—In reading our writings, it will at once be seen how vile and foul these calumnies are.

say they, may not God make the same flesh occupy several different places, so as not to be confined to any particular place, and so as to have neither measure nor species? Fool! why do you require the power of God to make a thing to be at the same time flesh and not flesh? It is just as if you were to insist on his making light to be at the same time light and darkness. He wills light to be light, darkness to be darkness, flesh to be flesh. True, when he so chooses, he will convert darkness into light, and light into darkness: but when you insist that there shall be no difference between light and darkness, what do you but pervert the order of the divine wisdom? Flesh must therefore be flesh, and spirit spirit; each under the law and condition on which God has created them. Now, the condition of flesh is, that it should have one certain place, its own dimensions, its own form. On that condition, Christ assumed the flesh, to which, as Augustine declares (Ep. ad Dardan.), he gave incorruption and glory, but without destroying its nature and reality.

25. They object that they have the word by which the will of God has been openly manifested; that is if we permit them to banish from the Church the gift of interpretation, which should throw light upon the word. I admit that they have the word, but just as the Anthropomorphites of old had it, when they made God corporeal; just as Marcion and the Manichees had it when they made the body of Christ celestial or phantastical. They quoted the passages, "The first man is of the earth, earthy; the second man is the Lord from heaven" (1 Cor. xv. 47): Christ "made himself of no reputation, and took upon him the form of a servant, and was made in the likeness of men" (Phil. ii. 7). But these vain boasters think that there is no power of God unless they fabricate a monster in their own brains, by which the whole order of nature is subverted. This rather is to circumscribe the power of God, to attempt to try, by our fictions, what he can do. From this word, they have assumed that the body of Christ is visible in heaven, and yet lurks invisible on the earth under innumerable bits of bread. They will say that this is rendered necessary, in order that the body of Christ may be given in the Supper. In other words, because they have been pleased to extract a carnal eating from the words of Christ, carried away by their own prejudice, they have found it necessary to coin this subtlety, which is wholly repugnant to Scripture. That we detract, in any respect, from the power of God, is so far from being true, that our doctrine is the loudest in extolling it. But as they continue to charge us with robbing God of his honour, in rejecting what, according to common apprehension, it is difficult to believe, though it had been promised by the mouth of Christ; I answer, as I lately did, that in the mysteries of faith we do not consult common apprehension, but, with the placid docility and spirit of meekness which James recommends (James i. 21), receive the doctrine which has come from heaven. Wherein they perniciously err, I am confident that we follow a proper moderation. On hearing the words of Christ, this

is my body, they imagine a miracle most remote from his intention; and when, from this fiction, the grossest absurdities arise, having already, by their precipitate haste, entangled themselves with snares, they plunge themselves into the abyss of the divine omnipotence, that, in this way, they may extinguish the light of truth.[1] Hence the supercilious moroseness. We have no wish to know how Christ is hid under the bread: we are satisfied with his own words, "This is my body." We again study, with no less obedience than care, to obtain a sound understanding of this passage, as of the whole of Scripture. We do not, with preposterous fervour, rashly, and without choice, lay hold on whatever first presents itself to our minds; but, after careful meditation, embrace the meaning which the Spirit of God suggests. Trusting to him, we look down, as from a height, on whatever opposition may be offered by earthly wisdom. Nay, we hold our minds captive, not allowing one word of murmur, and humble them, that they may not presume to gainsay. In this way, we have arrived at that exposition of the words of Christ, which all who are moderately versant in Scripture know to be perpetually used with regard to the sacraments. Still, in a matter of difficulty, we deem it not unlawful to inquire, after the example of the blessed Virgin, "How shall this be?" (Luke i. 34).

26. But as nothing will be more effectual to confirm the faith of the pious than to show them that the doctrine which we have laid down is taken from the pure word of God, and rests on its authority, I will make this plain with as much brevity as I can. The body with which Christ rose is declared, not by Aristotle, but by the Holy Spirit, to be finite, and to be contained in heaven until the last day. I am not unaware how confidently our opponents evade the passages which are quoted to this effect. Whenever Christ says that he will leave the world and go away (John xiv. 2, 28), they reply, that that departure was nothing more than a change of mortal state. Were this so, Christ would not substitute the Holy Spirit, to supply, as they express it, the defect of his absence, since he does not succeed in place of him, nor, on the other hand, does Christ himself descend from the heavenly glory to assume the condition of a mortal life. Certainly the advent of the Spirit and the ascension of Christ are set against each other, and hence it necessarily follows that Christ dwells with us according to the flesh, in the same way as that in which he sends his Spirit. Moreover, he distinctly says that he would not always be in the world with his disciples (Matth. xxvi. 11). This saying, also, they think they admirably dispose of, as if it were a denial by Christ that he would always be poor and mean, or liable to the necessities of a fading life. But this is plainly repugnant to the context, since reference is made not to poverty and want, or the wretched condition of an earthly life, but to worship and honour.

1 Thus Augustine, speaking of certain persons, says: "It is strange, when they are confined in their straits, over what precipices they plunge themselves, fearing the nets of truth" (Aug. Ep. 105).

The disciples were displeased with the anointing by Mary, because they thought it a superfluous and useless expenditure, akin to luxury, and would therefore have preferred that the price which they thought wasted should have been expended on the poor. Christ answers, that he will not be always with them to receive such honour. No different exposition is given by Augustine, whose words are by no means ambiguous. When Christ says, "Me ye have not always," he spoke of his bodily presence. In regard to his majesty, in regard to his providence, in regard to his ineffable and invisible grace, is fulfilled what he said: "Lo, I am with you alway, even unto the end of the world" (Matth. xxviii. 20); but in regard to the flesh which the Word assumed—in regard to that which was born of the Virgin—in regard to that which was apprehended by the Jews, nailed to the tree, suspended on the cross, wrapt in linen clothes, laid in the tomb, and manifested in the resurrection,—"Me ye have not always." Why? Since he conversed with his disciples in bodily presence for forty days, and, going out with them, ascended, while they saw but followed not. He is not here, for he sits there, at the right hand of the Father. And yet he is here: for the presence of his majesty is not withdrawn. Otherwise, as regards the presence of his majesty, we have Christ always; while, in regard to his bodily presence, it was rightly said, "Me ye have not always." In respect of bodily presence, the Church had him for a few days: now she holds him by faith, but sees him not with the eye (August. Tract. in Joann. 50). Here (that I may briefly note this) he makes him present with us in three ways—in majesty, providence, and ineffable grace; under which I comprehend that wondrous communion of his body and blood, provided we understand that it is effected by the power of the Holy Spirit, and not by that fictitious enclosing of his body under the element, since our Lord declared that he had flesh and bones which could be handled and seen. *Going away*, and *ascending*, intimate, not that he had the appearance of one going away and ascending, but that he truly did what the words express. Some one will ask, Are we then to assign a certain region of heaven to Christ? I answer with Augustine, that this is a curious and superfluous question, provided we believe that he is in heaven.

27. What? Does not the very name of ascension, so often repeated, intimate removal from one place to another? This they deny, because by height, according to them, the majesty of empire only is denoted. But what was the very mode of ascending? Was he not carried up while the disciples looked on? Do not the Evangelists clearly relate that he was carried into heaven? These acute Sophists reply, that a cloud intervened, and took him out of their sight, to teach the disciples that he would not afterwards be visible in the world. As if he ought not rather to have vanished in a moment, to make them believe in his invisible presence, or the cloud to have gathered around him before he moved a step. When he is carried aloft into the air, and the interposing cloud shows that he is no more

to be sought on earth, we safely infer that his dwelling now is in the heavens, as Paul also asserts, bidding us look for him from thence (Phil. iii. 20). For this reason, the angels remind the disciples that it is vain to keep gazing up into heaven, because Jesus, who was taken up, would come in like manner as they had seen him ascend. Here the adversaries of sound doctrine escape, as they think, by the ingenious quibble, that he will come in visible form, though he never departed from the earth, but remained invisible among his people. As if the angels had insinuated a two-fold presence, and not simply made the disciples eye-witnesses of the ascent, that no doubt might remain. It was just as if they had said, By ascending to heaven, while you looked on, he has asserted his heavenly power: it remains for you to wait patiently until he again arrive to judge the world. He has not entered into heaven to occupy it alone, but to gather you and all the pious along with him.

28. Since the advocates of this spurious dogma are not ashamed to honour it with the suffrages of the ancients, and especially of Augustine, how perverse they are in the attempt I will briefly explain. Pious and learned men have collected the passages, and therefore I am unwilling to plead a concluded cause: any one who wishes may consult their writings. I will not even collect from Augustine what might be pertinent to the matter,[1] but will be contented to show briefly, that without all controversy he is wholly ours. The pretence of our opponents, when they would wrest him from us, that throughout his works the flesh and blood of Christ are said to be dispensed in the Supper—namely, the victim once offered on the cross, is frivolous, seeing he, at the same time, calls it either the eucharist or sacrament of the body. But it is unnecessary to go far to find the sense in which he uses the terms *flesh* and *blood*, since he himself explains, saying (Ep. 23, ad Bonif.) that the sacraments receive names from their similarity to the things which they designate; and that, therefore, the sacrament of the body is after a certain manner the body. With this agrees another well-know passage, "The Lord hesitated not to say, This is my body, when he gave the sign" (Cont. Adimant. Manich. cap. 12). They again object that Augustine says distinctly that the body of Christ falls upon the earth, and enters the mouth. But this is in the same sense in which he affirms that it is consumed, for he conjoins both at the same time. There is nothing regugnant to this in his saying that the bread is consumed after the mystery is performed: for he had said a little before, "As these things are known to men, when they are done by men they may receive honour as being religious, but not as being wonderful" (De Trinit. Lib. iii. c. 10). His meaning is not different in the passage which our opponents too rashly appropriate to themselves—viz. that

[1] That the dogma of those who place the body of Christ in the bread is not aided by passages from Augustine, or the authority of Scripture, is proved here and sec. 29–31. There is no ambiguity in what he says, De Civit. Dei, 16, cap. 27. In Psal. 26 et 46. In Joann. Tract. 13, 102, 106, 107, &c.

Christ in a manner carried himself in his own hands, when he held out the mystical bread to his disciples. For by interposing the expression, *in a manner*, he declares that he was not really or truly included under the bread. Nor is it strange, since he elsewhere plainly contends, that bodies could not be without particular localities, and being nowhere, would have no existence. It is a paltry cavil that he is not there treating of the Supper, in which God exerts a special power. The question had been raised as to the flesh of Christ, and the holy man professedly replying, says, "Christ gave immortality to his flesh, but did not destroy its nature. In regard to this form, we are not to suppose that it is everywhere diffused: for we must beware not to rear up the divinity of the man, so as to take away the reality of the body. It does not follow that that which is in God is everywhere as God" (Ep. ad Dardan.). He immediately subjoins the reason, "One person is God and man, and both one Christ, everywhere, inasmuch as he is God, and in heaven, inasmuch as he is man." How careless would it have been not to except the mystery of the Supper, a matter so grave and serious, if it was in any respect adverse to the doctrine which he was handling? And yet, if any one will attentively read what follows shortly after, he will find that under that general doctrine the Supper also is comprehended, that Christ, the only-begotten Son of God, and also Son of man, is everywhere wholly present as God, in the temple of God, that is, in the Church, as an inhabiting God, and in some place in heaven, because of the dimensions of his real body. We see how, in order to unite Christ with the Church, he does not bring his body out of heaven. This he certainly would have done had the body of Christ not been truly our food, unless when included under the bread. Elsewhere, explaining how believers now possess Christ, he says, "You have him by the sign of the cross, by the sacrament of baptism, by the meat and drink of the altar" (Tract. in Joann. 50). How rightly he enumerates a superstitious rite, among the symbols of Christ's presence, I dispute not; but in comparing the presence of the flesh to the sign of the cross, he sufficiently shows that he has no idea of a twofold body of Christ, one lurking concealed under the bread, and another sitting visible in heaven. If there is any need of explanation, it is immediately added, "In respect of the presence of his majesty, we have Christ always: in respect of the presence of his flesh, it is rightly said, 'Me ye have not always.'" They object that he also adds, "In respect of ineffable and invisible grace is fulfilled what was said by him, 'I am with you always, even to the end of the world.'" But this is nothing in their favour. For it is at length restricted to his majesty, which is always opposed to body, while the flesh is expressly distinguished from grace and virtue. The same antithesis elsewhere occurs, when he says that "Christ left the disciples in bodily presence, that he might be with them in spiritual presence." Here it is clear that the essence of the flesh is distinguished from the virtue of the Spirit, which conjoins us with Christ, when, in respect of space, we are at a great distance from him. He repeatedly uses the same mode of expression, as when he says, "He is to come to the quick and the dead in bodily presence, according to the rule of faith and sound doctrine: for in spiritual presence he was to come to them, and to be with the whole Church in the world until its consummation. Therefore, this discourse is directed to believers, whom he had begun already to save by corporeal presence, and whom he was to leave in coporeal absence, that by spiritual presence he might preserve them with the Father." By corporeal to understand visible is mere trifling, since he both opposes his body to his divine power, and by adding, that he might "preserve them with the Father," clearly expresses that he sends his grace to us from heaven by means of the Spirit.

29. Since they put so much confidence in his hiding-place of invisible presence, let us see how well they conceal themselves in it. First, they cannot produce a syllable from Scripture to prove that Christ is invisible; but they take for granted what no sound man will admit, that the body of Christ cannot be given in the Supper, unless covered with the mask of bread. This is the very point in dispute; so far is it from occupying the place of the first principle. And while they thus prate, they are forced to give Christ a twofold body, because, according to them, it is visible in itself in heaven, but in the Supper is invisible, by a special mode of dispensation. The beautiful consistency of this may easily be judged, both from other passages of Scripture, and from the testimony of Peter. Peter says that the heavens must receive, or contain Christ, till he come again (Acts iii. 21). These men teach that he is in every place, but without form. They say that it is unfair to subject a glorious body to the ordinary laws of nature. But this answer draws along with it the delirious dream of Servetus, which all pious minds justly abhor, that his body was absorbed by his divinity. I do not say that this is their opinion; but if it is considered one of the properties of a glorified body to fill all things in an invisible manner, it is plain that the corporeal substance is abolished, and no distinction is left between his Godhead and his human nature. Again, if the body of Christ is so multiform and diversified, that it appears in one place, and in another is invisible, where is there anything of the nature of body with its proper dimensions, and where is its unity? Far more correct is Tertullian, who contends that the body of Christ was natural and real, because its figure is set before us in the mystery of the Supper, as a pledge and assurance of spiritual life (Tertull. Cont. Marc. Lib. iv.).[1] And certainly Christ said of his glorified body, "Handle me, and see; for a spirit hath not flesh and bones, as ye see me have" (Luke xxiv. 39). Here, by the lips of Christ himself, the reality of his flesh is proved, by its admitting of being seen and handled. Take these away, and it will cease to be flesh. They always betake themselves to their lurking-place of dispensation, which they have fabri-

1 The French adds, "Car la figure seroit fausse, si ce qu'elle represente n'estoit vray." —For the figure would be false, if the thing which it represents were not real.

cated. But it is our duty so to embrace what Christ absolutely declares, as to give it an unreserved assent. He proves that he is not a phantom, because he is visible in his flesh. Take away what he claims as proper to the nature of his body, and must not a new definition of body be devised? Then, however they may turn themselves about, they will not find any place for their fictitious dispensation in that passage, in which Paul says, that "our conversation is in heaven; from whence we look for the Saviour, the Lord Jesus Christ: who shall change our vile body, that it may be fashioned like unto his glorious body" (Phil. iii. 20, 21). We are not to hope for conformity to Christ in these qualities which they ascribe to him as a body, without bounds, and invisible. They will not find any one so stupid as to be persuaded of this great absurdity. Let them not, therefore, set it down as one of the properties of Christ's glorious body, that it is, at the same time, in many places, and in no place. In short, let them either openly deny the resurrection of his flesh, or admit that Christ, when invested with celestial glory, did not lay aside his flesh, but is to make us, in our flesh, his associates, and partakers of the same glory, since we are to have a common resurrection with him. For what does Scripture throughout deliver more clearly than that, as Christ assumed our flesh when he was born of the Virgin, and suffered in our true flesh when he made satisfaction for us, so on rising again he resumed the same true flesh, and carried it with him to heaven? The hope of our resurrection, and ascension to heaven, is, that Christ rose again and ascended, and, as Tertullian says (De Resurrect. Carnis), "Carried an earnest of our resurrection along with him into heaven." Morever, how weak and fragile would this hope be, had not this very flesh of ours in Christ been truly raised up, and entered into the kingdom of heaven. But the essential properties of a body are to be confined by space, to have dimension and form. Have done, then, with that foolish fiction, which affixes the minds of men, as well as Christ, to bread. For to what end this occult presence under the bread, save that those who wish to have Christ conjoined with them may stop short at the symbol? But our Lord himself wished us to withdraw not only our eyes, but all our senses, from the earth, forbidding the woman to touch him until he had ascended to the Father (John xx. 17). When he sees Mary, with pious reverential zeal, hastening to kiss his feet, there could be no reason for his disapproving and forbidding her to touch him before he had ascended to heaven, unless he wished to be sought nowhere else. The objection, that he afterwards appeared to Stephen, is easily answered. It was not necessary for our Saviour to change his place, as he could give the eyes of his servant a power of vision which could penetrate to heaven. The same account is to be given of the case of Paul. The objection, that Christ came forth from the closed sepulchre, and came in to his disciples while the doors were shut (Matth. xxviii. 6; John xx. 19), gives no better support to their error. For as the water, just as if it had been a solid pavement, furnished a path to our Saviour when he walked on it (Matth. xiv.), so it is not strange that the hard stone yielded to his step; although it is more probable that the stone was removed at his command, and forthwith, after giving him a passage, returned to its place. To enter while the doors were shut, was not so much to penetrate through solid matter, as to make a passage for himself by divine power, and stand in the midst of his disciples in a most miraculous manner. They gain nothing by quoting the passage from Luke, in which it is said, that Christ suddenly vanished from the eyes of the disciples, with whom he had journed to Emmaus (Luke xxiv. 31). In withdrawing from their sight, he did not become invisible: he only disappeared. Thus Luke declares that, on the journeying with them, he did not assume a new form, but that "their eyes were holden." But these men not only transform Christ that he may live on the earth, but pretend that there is another elsewhere of a different description. In short, by thus trifling, they, not in direct terms indeed, but by a circumlocution, make a spirit of the flesh of Christ; and, not contented with this, give him properties altogether opposite. Hence it necessarily follows that he must be twofold.

30. Granting what they absurdly talk of the invisible presence, it will still be necessary to prove the immensity, without which it is vain to attempt to include Christ under the bread. Unless the body of Christ can be everywhere without any boundaries of space, it is impossible to believe that he is hid in the Supper under the bread. Hence, they have been under the necessity of introducing the monstrous dogma of ubiquity. But it has been demonstrated by strong and clear passages of Scripture, first, that it is bounded by the dimensions of the human body; and, secondly, that its ascension into heaven made it plain that it is not in all places, but on passing to a new one, leaves the one formerly occupied. The promise to which they appeal, "I am with you always, even to the end of the world," is not to be applied to the body. First, then, a perpetual connection with Christ could not exist, unless he dwells in us corporeally, independently of the use of the Supper; and, therefore, they have no good ground for disputing so bitterly concerning the words of Christ, in order to include him under the bread in the Supper.[1] Secondly, the context proves that Christ is not speaking at all of his flesh, but promising the disciples his invincible aid to guard and sustain them against all the assaults of Satan and the world. For, in appointing them to a difficult office, he confirms them by the assurance of his presence, that they might neither hesitate to undertake it, nor be timorous in the discharge of it; as if he had said, that his invincible protection would not fail them. Unless we would throw everything into confusion, must it not be necessary to distinguish the mode of presence? And, indeed, some, to their great disgrace, choose rather to betray their ignorance than give up one iota of their error. I

1 The French adds, "veu qu'ils confessent que nous l'avons aussi bien sans la Cene;"—seeing they acknowledge that we have him as well without the Supper.

speak not of Papists, whose doctrine is more tolerable, or at least more modest; but some are so hurried away by contention as to say, that on account of the union of natures in Christ, wherever his divinity is, there his flesh, which cannot be separated from it, is also; as if that union formed a kind of medium of the two natures, making him to be neither God nor man. So held Eutyches, and after him Servetus. But it is clearly gathered from Scripture that the one person of Christ is composed of two natures, but so that each has its peculiar properties unimpaired. That Eutyches was justly condemned, they will not have the hardihood to deny. It is strange that they attend not to the cause of condemnation—viz. that destroying the distinction between the natures, and insisting only on the unity of person, he converted God into man and man into God.[1] What madness, then, is it to confound heaven with earth, sooner than not withdraw the body of Christ from its heavenly sanctuary? In regard to the passages which they adduce, "No man has ascended up to heaven, but he that came down from heaven, even the Son of man which is in heaven" (John iii. 13); "The only-begotten Son, who is in the bosom of the Father, he hath declared him" (John i. 18), they betray the same stupidity, scouting the communion of properties (*idiomatum*, κοινωνιαν), which not without reason was formerly invented by holy Fathers. Certainly when Paul says of the princes of this world that they "crucified the Lord of glory" (1 Cor. ii. 8), he means not that he suffered anything in his divinity, but that Christ, who was rejected and despised, and suffered in the flesh, was likewise God and the Lord of glory. In this way, both the Son of man was in heaven because he was also Christ; and he who, according to the flesh, dwelt as the Son of man on earth, was also God in heaven. For this reason, he is said to have descended from heaven in respect of his divinity, not that his divinity quitted heaven to conceal itself in the prison of the body, but because, although he filled all things, it yet resided in the humanity of Christ coporeally, that is, naturally, and in an ineffable manner. There is a trite distinction in the schools which I hesitate not to quote. Although the whole Christ is everywhere, yet everything which is in him is not eveywhere. I wish the Schoolmen had duly weighed the force of this sentence, as it would have obviated their absurd fiction of the corporeal presence of Christ. Therefore, while our whole Mediator is everywhere, he is always present with his people, and in the Supper exhibits his presence in a special manner; yet so, that while he is wholly present, not everything which is in him is present, because, as has been said, in his flesh he will remain in heaven till he come to judgment.

31. They are greatly mistaken in imagining that there is no presence of the flesh of Christ in the Supper, unless it be placed in the bread. They thus leave nothing for the secret operation of the Spirit, which

[1] French, "Il faisoit Jesus Christ homme en tant qu'il est Dieu, et Dieu en tant qu'il est homme."—He made Jesus Christ man, in so far as he is God, and God in so far as he is man.

unites Christ himself to us. Christ does not seem to them to be present unless he descends to us, as if we did not equally gain his presence when he raises us to himself. The only question, therefore, is as to the mode, they placing Christ in the bread, while we deem it unlawful to draw him down from heaven. Which of the two is more correct, let the reader judge. Only have done with the calumny that Christ is withdrawn from his Supper if he lurk not under the covering of bread. For seeing this mystery is heavenly, there is no necessity to bring Christ on the earth that he may be connected with us.

32. Now, should any one ask me as to the mode, I will not be ashamed to confess that it is too high a mystery either for my mind to comprehend or my words to express; and to speak more plainly, I rather feel than understand it. The truth of God, therefore, in which I can safely rest, I here embrace without controversy. He declares that his flesh is the meat, his blood the drink, of my soul; I give my soul to him to be fed with such food. In his sacred Supper he bids me take, eat, and drink his body and blood under the symbols of bread and wine. I have no doubt that he will truly give and I receive. Only, I reject the absurdities which appear to be unworthy of the heavenly majesty of Christ, and are inconsistent with the reality of his human nature. Since they must also be repugnant to the word of God, which teaches both that Christ was received into the glory of the heavenly kingdom, so as to be exalted above all the circumstances of the world (Luke xxiv. 26), and no less carefully ascribes to him the properties belonging to a true human nature. This ought not to seem incredible or contradictory to reason (Iren. Lib. iv. cap. 34); because, as the whole kingdom of Christ is spiritual, so whatever he does in his Church is not to be tested by the wisdom of this world; or, to use the words of Augustine, "this mystery is performed by man like the others, but in a divine manner, and on earth, but in a heavenly manner." Such, I say, is the corporeal presence which the nature of the sacrament requires, and which we say is here displayed in such power and efficacy, that it not only gives our minds undoubted assurance of eternal life, but also secures the immortality of our flesh, since it is now quickened by his immortal flesh, and in a manner shines in his immortality. Those who are carried beyond this with their hyperboles, do nothing more by their extravagancies than obscure the plain and simple truth. If any one is not yet satisfied, I would have him here to consider with himself that we are speaking of the sacrament, every part of which ought to have reference to faith. Now by participation of the body, as we have explained, we nourish faith not less richly and abundantly than do those who drag Christ himself from heaven. Still I am free to confess that that mixture or transfusion of the flesh of Christ with our soul, which they teach, I repudiate, because it is enough for us, that Christ, out of the substance of his flesh, breathes life into our souls, nay, diffuses his own life into us, though

the real flesh of Christ does not enter us.[1] I may add, that there can be no doubt that the analogy of faith by which Paul enjoins us to test every interpretation of Scripture, is clearly with us in this matter. Let those who oppose a truth so clear, consider to what standard of faith they conform themselves: "Ever spirit that confesseth not that Jesus Christ is come in the flesh is not of God" (1 John iv. 23; 2 John ver. 7). These men, though they disguise the fact, or perceive it not, rob him of his flesh.

33. The same view must be taken of communion, which, according to them, has no existence unless they swallow the flesh of Christ under the bread. But no slight insult is offered to the Spirit if we refuse to believe that it is by his incomprehensible agency that we communicate in the body and blood of Christ. Nay, if the nature of the mystery, as delivered to us, and known to the ancient Church for four hundred years, had been considered as it deserves, there was more than enough to satisfy us; the door would have been shut against many disgraceful errors. These have kindled up fearful dissensions, by which the Church, both anciently and in our own times, has been miserably vexed; curious men insisting on an extravagant mode of presence to which Scripture gives no countenance. And for a matter thus foolishly and rashly devised they keep up a turmoil, as if the including of Christ under the bread were, so to speak, the beginning and end of piety. It was of primary importance to know how the body of Christ once delivered to us becomes ours, and how we become partakers of his shed blood, because this is to possess the whole of Christ crucified, so as to enjoy all his blessings. But overlooking these points, in which there was so much importance, nay, neglecting and almost suppressing them, they occupy themselves only with this one perplexing question, How is the body of Christ hidden under the bread, or under the appearance of bread? They falsely pretend that all which we teach concerning spiritual eating is opposed to true and what they call real eating, since we have respect only to the mode of eating. This, according to them, is carnal, since they include Christ under the bread, but according to us is spiritual, inasmuch as the sacred agency of the Spirit is the bond of our union with Christ. Not better founded is the other objection, that we attend only to the fruit or effect which believers receive from eating the flesh of Christ. We formerly said, that Christ himself is the matter of the Supper, and that the effect follows from this, that by the sacrifice of his death our sins are expiated, by his blood we are washed, and by his resurrection we are raised to the hope of life in heaven. But a foolish imagination, of which Lombard was the author, perverts their minds, while they think that the sacrament is the eating of the flesh of Christ. His words are, "The sacrament and not the thing are the forms of bread and wine; the sacrament and the thing are the flesh and blood of Christ; the thing and not the sacrament is his mystical flesh" (Lombard,

1 See Bernard in Cant. Serm. 74, 75; et Trad. de Gratia et Liber. Arbit.

Lib. iv. Dist. 8). Again a little after, "The thing signified and contained is the proper flesh of Christ; the thing signified and not contained is his mystical body." To his distinction between the flesh of Christ and the power of nourishing which it possesses, I assent; but his maintaining it to be a sacrament, and a sacrament contained under the bread, is an error not to be tolerated. Hence has arisen that false interpretation of sacramental eating, because it was imagined that even the wicked and profane, however much alienated from Christ, eat his body. But the very flesh of Christ in the mystery of the Supper is no less a spiritual matter than eternal salvation. Whence we infer, that all who are devoid of the Spirit of Christ can no more eat the flesh of Christ than drink wine that has no savour. Certainly Christ is shamefully lacerated, when his body, as lifeless and without any vigour, is prostituted to unbelievers. This is clearly repugnant to his words, "He that eateth my flesh, and drinketh my blood, dwelleth in me, and I in him" (John vi. 56). They object that he is not there speaking of sacramental eating; this I admit, provided they will not ever and anon stumble on this stone, that his flesh itself is eaten without any benefit. I should like to know how they confine it after they have eaten. Here, in my opinion, they will find no outlet. But they object, that the ingratitude of man cannot in any respect detract from, or interfere with, faith in the promises of God. I admit and hold that the power of the sacrament remains entire, however the wicked may labour with all their might to annihilate it. Still, it is one thing to be offered, another to be received. Christ gives this spiritual food and holds forth this spiritual drink to all. Some eat eagerly, others superciliously reject it. Will their rejection cause the meat and drink to lose their nature? They will say that this similitude supports their opinion—viz. that the flesh of Christ, though it be without taste, is still flesh. But I deny that it can be eaten without the taste of faith, or (if it is more agreeable to speak with Augustine), I deny that men carry away more from the sacrament than they collect in the vessel of faith. Thus nothing is detracted from the sacrament, nay, its reality and efficacy remain unimpaired, although the wicked, after externally partaking of it, go away empty. If, again, they object, that it derogates from the expression, "This is my body," if the wicked receive corruptible bread and nothing besides, it is easy to answer, that God wills not that his truth should be recognised in the mere reception, but in the constancy of his goodness, while he is prepared to perform, nay, liberally offers to the unworthy what they reject. The integrity of the sacrament, an integrity which the whole world cannot violate, lies here, that the flesh and blood of Christ are not less truly given to the unworthy than to the elect believers of God; and yet it is true, that just as the rain falling on the hard rock runs away because it cannot penetrate, so the wicked by their hardness repel the grace of God, and prevent it from reaching them. We may add, that it is no more possible to receive Christ without faith, than it is for seed to germinate in the fire. They ask how Christ can have come for the condemnation of some, unless they unworthily receive him; but this is absurd, since we nowhere read that they bring death upon themselves by receiving Christ unworthily, but by rejecting him. They are not aided by the parable in which Christ says, that the seed which fell among thorns sprung up, but was afterwards choked (Matth. xiii. 7), because he is there speaking of the effect of a temporary faith, a faith which those who place Judas in this respect on a footing with Peter, do not think necessary to the eating of the flesh and the drinking of the blood of Christ. Nay, their error is refuted by the same parable, when Christ says that some seed fell upon the wayside, and some on stony ground, and yet neither took root. Hence it follows that the hardness of believers is an obstacle which prevents Christ from reaching them. All who would have our salvation to be promoted by this sacrament, will find nothing more appropriate than to conduct believers to the fountain, that they may draw life from the Son of God. The dignity is amply enough commended when we hold, that it is a help by which we may be ingrafted into the body of Christ, or, already ingrafted, may be more and more united to him, until the union is completed in heaven. They object, that Paul could not have made them guilty of the body and blood of the Lord if they had not partaken of them (1 Cor. xi. 27); I answer, that they were not condemned for having eaten, but only for having profaned the ordinance by trampling under foot the pledge, which they ought to have reverently received, the pledge of sacred union with God.

34. Moreover, as among ancient writers, Augustine especially maintained [1] this head of doctrine, that the grace figured by the sacraments is not impaired or made void by the infidelity or malice of men, it will be useful to prove clearly from his words, how ignorantly and erroneously those who cast forth the body of Christ to be eaten by dogs, wrest them to their present purpose. Sacramental eating, according to them, is that by which the wicked receive the body and blood of Christ without the agency of the Spirit, or any gracious effect. Augustine, on the contrary, prudently pondering the expression, "Whoso eateth my flesh, and drinketh my blood, hath eternal life" (John vi. 54), says: "That is the virtue of the sacrament, and not merely the visible sacrament: the sacrament of him who eats inwardly, not of him who eats outwardly, or merely with the teeth" (Hom. in Joann. 26). Hence he at length concludes, that the sacrament of this thing, that is, of the unity of the body and blood of Christ in the Lord's Supper, is set before some for life, before others for destruction: while the matter itself, of which it is the sacrament, is to all for life, to none for destruction, whoever may have been the partaker. Lest any one should here cavil that by *thing* is not meant body, but the grace of the Spirit, which may be separated from it, he dissipates these mists by the antithetical epithets, Visible and Invisible. For the body of Christ cannot be

1 See August. Cont. Liter. Petiliani, Lib. ii. c. 47, et Tract. in Joann.

included under the former. Hence it follows, that unbelievers communicate only in the visible symbol; and the better to remove all doubt, after saying that this bread requires an appetite in the inner man, he adds (Hom. in Joann. 59), "Moses, and Aaron, and Phinehas, and many others who ate manna, pleased God. Why? Because the visible food they understood spiritually, hungered for spiritually, tasted spiritually, and feasted on spiritually. We, too, in the present day, have received visible food: but the sacrament is one thing, the virtue of the sacrament is another." A little after, he says: "And hence, he who remains not in Christ, and in whom Christ remains not, without doubt neither spiritually eats his flesh, nor drinks his blood, though with his teeth he may carnally and visibly press the symbol of his body and blood." Again, we are told that the visible sign is opposed to spiritual eating. This refutes the error that the invisible body of Christ is sacramentally eaten in reality, although not spiritually. We are told, also, that nothing is given to the impure and profane beyond the visible taking of the sign. Hence his celebrated saying, that the other disciples ate *bread which was the Lord*, whereas Judas ate *the bread of the Lord* (Hom. in Joann. 62). By this, he clearly excludes unbelievers from participation in his body and blood. He has no other meaning when he says, "Why do you wonder that the bread of Christ was given to Judas, though he consigned him to the devil, when you see, on the contrary, that a messenger of the devil was given to Paul to perfect him in Christ?" (August. de Bapt. Cont. Donat. Lib. v.). He indeed says elsewhere, that the bread of the Supper was the body of Christ to those to whom Paul said, "He that eateth and drinketh unworthily, eateth and drinketh damnation to himself; and that it does not follow that they received nothing because they received unworthily." But in what sense he says this, he explains more fully in another passage (De Civit. Dei, Lib. xxi. c. 25). For undertaking professedly to explain how the wicked and profane, who, with the mouth, profess the faith of Christ, but in act deny him, eat the body of Christ; and, indeed, refuting the opinion of some who thought that they ate not only sacramentally, but really, he says: "Neither can they be said to eat the body of Christ, because they are not to be accounted among the members of Christ. For, not to mention other reasons, they cannot be at the same time the members of Christ and the members of a harlot. In fine, when Christ himself says, 'He that eateth my flesh, and drinketh my blood, dwelleth in me, and I in him' (John vi. 56), he shows what it is to eat the body of Christ, not sacramentally, but in reality. It is to abide in Christ, that Christ may abide in him. For it is just as if he had said, Let not him who abides not in me, and in whom I abide not, say or think that he eats my body or drinks my blood." Let the reader attend to the antithesis between eating sacramentally and eating really, and there will be no doubt. The same thing he confirms not less clearly in these words: "Prepare not the jaws, but the heart; for which alone the Supper is appointed. We believe in Christ when we receive him in faith: in receiving, we know what we think: we receive a small portion, but our heart is filled: it is not therefore that which is seen, but that which is believed, that feeds (August. Cont. Faust. Lib. xiii. c. 16). Here, also, he restricts what the wicked take to be the visible sign, and shows that the only way of receiving Christ is by faith. So, also, in another passage, declaring distinctly that the good and the bad communicate by signs, he excludes the latter from the true eating of the flesh of Christ. For had they received the reality, he would not have been altogether silent as to a matter which was pertinent to the case. In another passage, speaking of eating, and the fruit of it, he thus concludes: "Then will the body and blood of Christ be life to each, if that which is visibly taken in the sacrament is in reality spiritually eaten, spiritually drunk" (De Verb. Apost. Serm. ii.) Let those, therefore, who make unbelievers partakers of the flesh and blood of Christ, if they would agree with Augustine, set before us the visible body of Christ, since, according to him, the whole truth is spiritual. And certainly his words imply that sacramental eating, when unbelief excludes the entrance of the reality, is only equivalent to visible or external eating. But if the body of Christ may be truly and yet not spiritually eaten, what could he mean when he elsewhere says: "Ye are not to eat this body which you see, nor to drink the blood which will be shed by those who are to crucify me? I have committed a certain sacrament to you: it is the spiritual meaning which will give you life" (August. in Ps. xcviii.). He certainly meant not to deny that the body offered in the Supper is the same as that which Christ offered in sacrifice; but he adverted to the mode of eating—viz. that the body, though received into the celestial glory, breathes life into us by the secret energy of the Spirit. I admit, indeed, that he often uses the expression, "that the body of Christ is eaten by unbelievers;" but he explains himself by adding, "in the sacrament." And he elsewhere speaks of a spiritual eating, in which our teeth do not chew grace (Hom. in Joann. 27). And, lest my opponents should say that I am trying to overwhelm them with the mass of my quotations, I would ask how they get over this one sentence: "In the elect alone, the sacraments effect what they figure." Certainly they will not venture to deny, that by the bread in the Supper, the body of Christ is figured. Hence it follows, that the reprobate are not allowed to partake of it. That Cyril did not think differently is clear from these words: "As one in pouring melted wax on melted wax mixes the whole together, so it is necessary, when one receives the body and blood of the Lord, to be conjoined with him, that Christ may be found in him, and he in Christ." From these words, I think it plain that there is no true and real eating by those who only eat the body of Christ sacramentally, seeing the body cannot be separated from its virtue, and that the promises of God do not fail, though, while he ceases not to rain from heaven, rocks and stones are not penetrated by the moisture.

35. This consideration will easily dissuade us from that carnal adoration which some men have, with perverse temerity, introduced into the sacrament, reasoning thus with themselves: If it is body, then it is also soul and divinity which go along with the body, and cannot be separated from it; and, therefore, Christ must there be adored. First, if we deny their pretended concomitance, what will they do? For, as they chiefly insist on the absurdity of separating the body of Christ from his soul and divinity, what sane and sober man can persuade himself that the body of Christ is Christ? They think that they completely establish this by their syllogisms. But since Christ speaks separately of his body and blood, without describing the mode of his presence, how can they in a doubtful matter arrive at the certainty which they wish? What then? Should their consciences be at any time exercised with some more grievous apprehension, will they forthwith set them free, and dissolve the apprehensions by their syllogisms? In other words, when they see that no certainty is to be obtained from the word of God, in which alone our minds can rest, and without which they go astray the very first moment when they begin to reason, when they see themselves opposed by the doctrine and practice of the apostles, and that they are supported by no authority but their own, how will they feel? To such feelings other sharp stings will be added. What? Was it a matter of little moment to worship God under this form without any express injunction? In a matter relating to the true worship of God, were we thus lightly to act without one word of Scripture? Had all their thoughts been kept in due subjection to the word of God, they certainly would have listened to what he himself has said, "Take, eat, and drink," and obeyed the command by which he enjoins us to receive the sacrament, not worship it. Those who receive, without adoration, as commanded by God, are secure that they deviate not from the command. In commencing any work, nothing is better than this security. They have the example of the apostles, of whom we read not that they prostrated themselves and worshipped, but that they sat down, took and ate. They have the practice of the apostolic Church, where, as Luke relates, believers communicated not in adoration, but in the breaking of bread (Acts ii. 42). They have the doctrine of the apostles as taught to the Corinthian Church by Paul, who declares that what he delivered he had received of the Lord (1 Cor. xi. 23).

36. The object of these remarks is to lead pious readers to reflect how dangerous it is in matters of such difficulty to wander from the simple word of God to the dreams of our own brain. What has been said above should free us from all scruple in this matter. That the pious soul may duly apprehend Christ in the sacrament, it must rise to heaven. But if the office of the sacrament is to aid the infirmity of the human mind, assisting it in rising upwards, so as to perceive the height of spiritual mysteries, those who stop short at the

external sign stray from the right path of seeking Christ. What then? Can we deny that the worship is superstitious when men prostrate themselves before bread that they may therein worship Christ? The Council of Nice undoubtedly intended to meet this evil when it forbade us to give humble heed to the visible signs. And for no other reason was it formerly the custom, previous to consecration, to call aloud upon the people to raise their hearts, *sursum corda.* Scripture itself, also, besides carefully narrating the ascension of Christ, by which he withdrew his bodily presence from our eye and company, that it might make us abandon all carnal thoughts of him, whenever it makes mention of him, enjoins us to raise our minds upwards and seek him in heaven, seated at the right hand of the Father (Col. iii. 2). According to this rule, we should rather have adored him spiritually in the heavenly glory, than devised that perilous species of adoration replete with gross and carnal ideas of God. Those, therefore, who devised the adoration of the sacrament, not only dreamed it of themselves, without any authority from Scripture, where no mention of it can be shown (it would not have been omitted, had it been agreeable to God); but, disregarding Scripture, forsook the living God, and fabricated a god for themselves, after the lust of their own hearts. For what is idolatry if it is not to worship the gifts instead of the giver? Here the sin is twofold. The honour robbed from God is transferred to the creature, and God, moreover, is dishonoured by the pollution and profanation of his own goodness, while his holy sacrament is converted into an execrable idol. Let us, on the contrary, that we may not fall into the same pit, wholly confine our eyes, ears, hearts, minds, and tongues, to the sacred doctrine of God. For this is the school of the Holy Spirit, that best of masters, in which such progress is made, that while nothing is to be acquired anywhere else, we must willingly be ignorant of whatever is not there taught.

37. Then, as superstition, when once it has passed the proper bounds, has no end to its errors, men went much farther; for they devised rites altogether alien from the institution of the Supper, and to such a degree that they paid divine honours to the sign. They say that their veneration is paid to Christ. First, if this were done in the Supper, I would say that that adoration only is legitimate which stops not at the sign, but rises to Christ sitting in heaven. Now, under what pretext do they say that they honour Christ in that bread, when they have no promise of this nature? They consecrate the host, as they call it, and carry it about in solemn show, and formally exhibit it to be admired, reverenced, and invoked. I ask by what virtue they think it duly consecrated? They will quote the words, "This is my body." I, on the contrary, will object, that it was at the same time said, "Take, eat." Nor will I count the other passage as nothing; for I hold that since the promise is annexed to the command, the former is so included under the latter, that it cannot possibly be separated from it. This will be made clearer by

an example. God gave a command when he said, "Call upon me," and added a promise, "I will deliver thee" (Psal. l. 15). Should any one invoke Peter or Paul, and found on this promise, will not all exclaim that he does it in error? And what else, pray, do those do who, disregarding the command to eat, fasten on the mutilated promise, "This is my body," that they may pervert it to rites alien from the institution of Christ? Let us remember, therefore, that this promise has been given to those who observe the command connected with it, and that those who transfer the sacrament to another end, have no countenance from the word of God. We formerly showed how the mystery of the sacred Supper contributes to our faith in God. But since the Lord not only reminds us of this great gift of his goodness, as we formerly explained, but passes it, as it were, from hand to hand, and urges us to recognise it, he, at the same time, admonishes us not to be ungrateful for the kindness thus bestowed, but rather to proclaim it with such praise as is meet, and celebrate it with thanksgiving. Accordingly, when he delivered the institution of the sacrament to the apostles, he taught them to do it in remembrance of him, which Paul interprets, "to show forth his death" (1 Cor. xi. 26). And this is, that all should publicly and with one mouth confess that all our confidence of life and salvation is placed in our Lord's death, that we ourselves may glorify him by our confession, and by our example excite others also to give him glory. Here, again, we see what the aim of the sacrament is—namely, to keep us in remembrance of Christ's death. When we are ordered to show forth the Lord's death till he come again, all that is meant is, that we should, with confession of the mouth, proclaim what our faith has recognised in the sacrament—viz. that the death of Christ is our life. This is the second use of the sacrament, and relates to outward confession.

38. Thirdly, The Lord intended it to be a kind of exhortation, than which no other could urge or animate us more strongly, both to purity and holiness of life, and also to charity, peace, and concord. For the Lord there communicates his body so that he may become altogether one with us, and we with him. Moreover, since he has only one body of which he makes us all to be partakers, we must necessarily, by this participation, all become one body. This unity is represented by the bread which is exhibited in the sacrament. As it is composed of many grains, so mingled together, that one cannot be distinguished from another; so ought our minds to be so cordially united, as not to allow of any dissension or division. This I prefer giving in the words of Paul: "The cup of blessing which we bless, is it not the communion of the blood of Christ? The bread which we break, is it not the communion of the body of Christ? For we being many, are one bread and one body, for we are all partakers of that one bread" (1 Cor. x. 15, 16). We shall have profited admirably in the sacrament, if the thought shall have been impressed and engraven on our minds, that none of our brethren is hurt, despised,

rejected, injured, or in any way offended, without our, at the same time, hurting, despising, and injuring Christ; that we cannot have dissension with our brethren, without at the same time dissenting from Christ; that we cannot love Christ without loving our brethren; that the same care we take of our own body we ought to take of that of our brethren, who are members of our body; that as no part of our body suffers pain without extending to the other parts, so every evil which our brother suffers ought to excite our compassion. Wherefore Augustine not inappropriately often terms this sacrament *the bond of charity.* What stronger stimulus could be employed to excite mutual charity, than when Christ, presenting himself to us, not only invites us by his example to give and devote ourselves mutually to each other, but inasmuch as he makes himself common to all, also makes us all to be one in him.

39. This most admirably confirms what I elsewhere said—viz. that there cannot be a right administration of the Supper without the word. Any utility which we derive from the Supper requires the word. Whether we are to be confirmed in faith, or exercised in confession, or aroused to duty, there is need of preaching. Nothing, therefore, can be more preposterous than to convert the Supper into a dumb action. This is done under the tyranny of the Pope, the whole effect of consecration being made to depend on the intention of the priest, as if it in no way concerned the people, to whom especially the mystery ought to have been explained. This error has originated from not observing that those promises by which consecration is effected are intended, not for the elements themselves, but for those who receive them. Christ does not address the bread and tell it to become his body, but bids his disciples eat, and promises them the communion of his body and blood. And, according to the arrangement which Paul makes, the promises are to be offered to believers along with the bread and the cup. Thus, indeed, it is. We are not to imagine some magical incantation, and think it sufficient to mutter the words, as if they were heard by the elements; but we are to regard those words as a living sermon, which is to edify the hearers, penetrate their minds, being impressed and seated in their hearts, and exert its efficacy in the fulfilment of that which it promises. For these reasons, it is clear that the setting apart of the sacrament, as some insist, that an extraordinary distribution of it may be made to the sick, is useless. They will either receive it without hearing the words of the institution read, or the minister will conjoin the true explanation of the mystery with the sign. In the silent dispensation, there is abuse and defect. If the promises are narrated, and the mystery is expounded, that those who are to receive may receive with advantage, it cannot be doubted that this is the true consecration. What then becomes of that other consecration, the effect of which reaches even to the sick? But those who do so have the example of the early Church. I confess it; but in so important

a matter, where error is so dangerous, nothing is safer than to follow the truth.

40. Moreover, as we see that this sacred bread of the Lord's Supper is spiritual food, is sweet and savoury, not less than salutary, to the pious worshippers of God, on tasting which they feel that Christ is their life, are disposed to give thanks, and exhorted to mutual love; so, on the other hand, it is converted into the most noxious poison to all whom it does not nourish and confirm in the faith, nor urge to thanksgiving and charity. For, just as corporeal food, when received into a stomach subject to morbid humours, becomes itself vitiated and corrupted, and rather hurts than nourishes, so this spiritual food also, if given to a soul polluted with malice and wickedness, plunges it into greater ruin, not indeed by any defect in the food, but because to the "defiled and unbelieving is nothing pure" (Titus i. 15), however much it may be sanctified by the blessing of the Lord. For, as Paul says, "Whosoever shall eat this bread, and drink this cup of the Lord, unworthily, shall be guilty of the body and blood of the Lord;" "eateth and drinketh damnation to himself, not discerning the Lord's body" (1 Cor. xi. 27, 29). For men of this description, who without any spark of faith, without any zeal for charity, rush forward like swine to seize the Lord's Supper, do not at all discern the Lord's body. For, inasmuch as they do not believe that body to be their life, they put every possible affront upon it, stripping it of all its dignity, and profane and contaminate it by so receiving; inasmuch as while alienated and estranged from their brethren, they dare to mingle the sacred symbol of Christ's body with their dissensions. No thanks to them if the body of Christ is not rent and torn to pieces. Wherefore they are justly held guilty of the body and blood of the Lord, which, with sacrilegious impiety, they so vilely pollute. By this unworthy eating, they bring judgment on themselves. For while they have no faith in Christ, yet, by receiving the sacrament, they profess to place their salvation only in him, and abjure all other confidence. Wherefore they themselves are their own accusers; they bear witness against themselves; they seal their own condemnation. Next being divided and separated by hatred and ill-will from their brethren, that is, from the members of Christ, they have no part in Christ, and yet they declare that the only safety is to communicate with Christ, and be united to him. For this reason Paul commands a man to examine himself before he eats of that bread, and drinks of that cup (1 Cor. xi. 28). By this, as I understand, he means that each individual should descend into himself, and consider, first, whether, with inward confidence of heart, he leans on the salvation obtained by Christ, and with confession of the mouth, acknowledges it; and, secondly, whether with zeal for purity and holiness he aspires to imitate Christ; whether, after his example, he is prepared to give himself to his brethren, and to hold himself in common with those with whom he has Christ in common; whether, as he himself is

regarded by Christ, he in his turn regards all his brethren as members of his body, or, like his members, desires to cherish, defend, and assist them, not that the duties of faith and charity can now be perfected in us, but because it behoves us to contend and seek, with all our heart, daily to increase our faith.

41. In seeking to prepare for eating worthily, men have often dreadfully harassed and tortured miserable consciences, and yet have in no degree attained the end. They have said that those *eat worthily* who are in a state of grace. *Being in a state of grace*, they have interpreted to be pure and free from all sin. By this definition, all the men that ever have been, and are upon the earth, were debarred from the use of this sacrament. For if we are to seek our worthiness from ourselves, it is all over with us; only despair and fatal ruin await us. Though we struggle to the utmost, we will not only make no progress, but then be most unworthy after we have laboured most to make ourselves worthy. To cure this ulcer, they have devised a mode of procuring worthiness—viz. after having, as far as we can, made an examination, and taken an account of all our actions, to expiate our unworthiness by contrition, confession, and satisfaction. Of the nature of this expiation we have spoken at the proper place (Book III. chap. iv. sec. 2, 17, 27). As far as regards our present object, I say that such things give poor and evanescent comfort to alarmed and downcast consciences, struck with terror at their sins. For if the Lord, by his prohibition, admits none to partake of his Supper but the righteous and innocent, every man would require to be cautious before feeling secure of that righteousness of his own which he is told that God requires. But how are we to be assured that those who have done what in them lay have discharged their duty to God? Even were we assured of this, who would venture to assure himself that he had done what in him lay? Thus there being no certain security for our worthiness, access to the Supper would always be excluded by the fearful interdict, "He that eateth and drinketh unworthily, eateth and drinketh damnation to himself."

42. It is now easy to judge what is the nature, and who is the author, of that doctrine which prevails in the Papacy, and which, by its inhuman austerity, deprives and robs wretched sinners, oppressed with sorrow and trembling, of the consolation of this sacrament, a sacrament in which all that is delightful in the gospel was set before them. Certainly the devil could have no shorter method of destroying men than by thus infatuating them, and so excluding them from the taste and savour of this food with which their most merciful Father in heaven had been pleased to feed them. Therefore, lest we should rush over such a precipice, let us remember that this sacred feast is medicine to the sick, comfort to the sinner, and bounty to the poor; while to the healthy, the righteous, and the rich, if any such could be found, it would be of no value. For while Christ is therein given us for food, we perceive that without him we fail, pine,

and waste away, just as hunger destroys the vigour of the body. Next, as he is given for life, we perceive that without him we are certainly dead. Wherefore, the best and only worthiness which we can bring to God, is to offer him our own vileness, and, if I may so speak, unworthiness, that his mercy may make us worthy; to despond in ourselves, that we may be consoled in him; to humble ourselves, that we may be elevated by him; to accuse ourselves, that we may be justified by him; to aspire, moreover, to the unity which he recommends in the Supper; and, as he makes us all one in himself, to desire to have all one soul, one heart, one tongue. If we ponder and meditate on these things, we may be shaken, but will never be overwhelmed by such considerations as these, how shall we, who are devoid of all good, polluted by the defilements of sin, and half dead, worthily eat the body of the Lord? We shall rather consider that we, who are poor, are coming to a benevolent giver, sick to a physician, sinful to the author of righteousness, in fine, dead to him who gives life; that worthiness which is commanded by God, consists especially in faith, which places all things in Christ, nothing in ourselves, and in charity, charity which, though imperfect, it may be sufficient to offer to God, that he may increase it, since it cannot be fully rendered. Some, concurring with us in holding that worthiness consists in faith and charity, have widely erred in regard to the measure of worthiness, demanding a perfection of faith to which nothing can be added, and a charity equivalent to that which Christ manifested towards us. And in this way, just as the other class, they debar all men from access to this sacred feast. For, were their view well founded, every one who receives must receive unworthily, since all, without exception, are guilty, and chargeable with imperfection. And certainly it were too stupid, not to say idiotical, to require to the receiving of the sacrament a perfection which would render the sacrament vain and superfluous, because it was not instituted for the perfect, but for the infirm and weak, to stir up, excite, stimulate, exercise the feeling of faith and charity, and at the same time correct the deficiency of both.

43. In regard to the external form of the ordinance, whether or not believers are to take into their hands and divide among themselves, or each is to eat what is given to him: whether they are to return the cup to the deacon or hand it to their neighbour; whether the bread is to be leavened or unleavened, and the wine to be red or white, is of no consequence. These things are indifferent, and left free to the Church, though it is certain that it was the custom of the ancient Church for all to receive into their hand. And Christ said, "Take this, and divide it among yourselves" (Luke xxii. 17). History relates that leavened and ordinary bread was used before the time of Alexander the Bishop of Rome, who was the first that was delighted with unleavened bread: for what reason I see not, unless it was to draw the wondering eyes of the populace by the novelty of the spectacle, more than to train them in sound religion.

I appeal to all who have the least zeal for piety, whether they do not evidently perceive both how much more brightly the glory of God is here displayed, and how much more abundant spiritual consolation is felt by believers than in these rigid and histrionic follies, which have no other use than to impose on the gazing populace. They call it restraining the people by religion, when, stupid and infatuated, they are drawn hither and thither by superstition. Should any one choose to defend such inventions by antiquity, I am not unaware how ancient is the use of chrism and exorcism in baptism, and how, not long after the age of the apostles, the Supper was tainted with adulteration; such, indeed, is the forwardness of human confidence, which cannot restrain itself, but is always sporting and wantoning in the mysteries of God. But let us remember that God sets so much value on obedience to his word, that, by it, he would have us to judge his angels and the whole world. All this mass of ceremonies being abandoned, the sacrament might be celebrated in the most becoming manner, if it were dispensed to the Church very frequently, at least once a-week. The commencement should be with public prayer; next, a sermon should be delivered: then the minister, having placed bread and wine on the table, should read the institution of the Supper. He should next explain the promises which are therein given; and, at the same time, keep back from communion all those who are debarred by the prohibition of the Lord. He should afterwards pray that the Lord, with the kindness with which he has bestowed this sacred food upon us, would also form and instruct us to receive it with faith and gratitude; and, as we are of ourselves unworthy, would make us worthy of the feast by his mercy. Here, either a psalm should be sung, or something read, while the faithful, in order, communicate at the sacred feast, the minister breaking the bread, and giving it to the people. The Supper being ended, an exhortation should be given to sincere faith, and confession of faith, to charity, and lives becoming Christians. Lastly, thanks should be offered, and the praises of God should be sung. This being done, the Church should be dismissed in peace.

44. What we have hitherto said of the sacrament, abundantly shows that it was not instituted to be received once a-year and that perfunctorily (as is now commonly the custom); but that all Christians might have it in frequent use, and frequently call to mind the sufferings of Christ, thereby sustaining and confirming their faith: stirring themselves up to sing the praises of God, and proclaim his goodness; cherishing and testifying towards each other that mutual charity, the bond of which they see in the unity of the body of Christ. As often as we communicate in the symbol of our Saviour's body, as if a pledge were given and received, we mutually bind ourselves to all the offices of love, that none of us may do anything to offend his brother, or omit anything by which he can assist him when necessity demands, and opportunity occurs. That such was the practice of the Apostolic Church, we are informed by Luke in the Acts, when he says, that

"they continued stedfastly in the apostles' doctrine and fellowship, and in breaking of bread, and in prayers" (Acts ii. 42). Thus we ought always to provide that no meeting of the Church is held without the word, prayer, the dispensation of the Supper, and alms. We may gather from Paul that this was the order observed by the Corinthians, and it is certain that this was the practice many ages after. Hence, by the ancient canons, which are attributed to Anacletus and Calixtus, after the consecration was made, all were to communicate who did not wish to be without the pale of the Church. And in those ancient canons, which bear the name of Apostolical, it is said that those who continue not to the end, and partake not of the sacred communion, are to be corrected, as causing disquiet to the Church. In the Council of Antioch it was decreed, that those who enter the Church, hear the Scriptures, and abstain from communion, are to be removed from the Church until they amend their fault. And although, in the first Council of Tholouse, this was mitigated, or at least stated in milder terms, yet there also it was decreed, that those who, after hearing the sermon, never communicated, were to be admonished, and if they still abstained after admonition, were to be excluded.

45. By these enactments, holy men wished to retain and ensure the use of frequent communion, as handed down by the apostles themselves; and which, while it was most salutary to believers, they saw gradually falling into desuetude by the negligence of the people. Of his own age, Augustine testifies: "The sacrament of the unity of our Lord's body is, in some places, provided daily, and in others at certain intervals, at the Lord's table; and at that table some partake to life, and others to destruction" (August. Tract. 26, in Joann. 6). And in the first Epistle to Januarius he says: "Some communicate daily in the body and blood of the Lord; others receive it on certain days: in some places, not a day intervenes on which it is not offered: in others, it is offered only on the Sabbath and the Lord's day: in others, on the Lord's day only." But since, as we have said, the people were sometimes remiss, holy men urged them with severe rebukes, that they might not seem to connive at their sluggishness. Of this we have an example in Chrysostom, on the Epistle to the Ephesians (Hom. 26). "It was not said to him who dishonoured the feast, Why have you not taken your seat? 'But how camest thou in?' (Matth. xxii. 12). Whoever partakes not of the sacred rites is wicked and impudent in being present: should any one who was invited to a feast come in, wash his hands, take his seat, and seem to prepare to eat, and thereafter taste nothing, would he not, I ask, insult both the feast and the entertainer? So you, standing among those who prepare themselves by prayer to take the sacred food, profess to be one of the number by the mere fact of your not going away, and yet you do not partake,—would it not have been better not to have made your appearance? I am unworthy, you say. Then neither were you worthy of the communion of prayer, which is the preparation for taking the sacred mystery."

46. Most assuredly, the custom which prescribes communion once a-year is an invention of the devil, by what instrumentality soever it may have been introduced. They say that Zephyrinus was the author of the decree, though it is not possible to believe that it was the same as we now have it. It may be, that as times then were, he did not, by his ordinance, consult ill for the Church. For there cannot be a doubt that at that time the sacred Supper was dispensed to the faithful at every meeting; nor can it be doubted that a great part of them communicated. But as it scarcely ever happened that all could communicate at the same time, and it was necessary that those who were mingled with the profane and idolaters, should testify their faith by some external symbol, this holy man, with a view to order and government, had appointed that day, that on it the whole of Christendom might give a confession of their faith by partaking of the Lord's Supper. The ordinance of Zephyrinus, which was otherwise good, posterity perverted, when they made a fixed law of one communion in the year. The consequence is, that almost all, when they have once communicated, as if they were discharged as to all the rest of the year, sleep on secure. It ought to have been far otherwise. Each week, at least, the table of the Lord ought to have been spread for the company of Christians, and the promises declared on which we might then spiritually feed. No one, indeed, ought to be forced, but all ought to be exhorted and stimulated; the torpor of the sluggish, also, ought to be rebuked, that all, like persons famishing, should come to the feast. It was not without cause, therefore, I complained, at the outset, that this practice had been introduced by the wile of the devil; a practice which, in prescribing one day in the year, makes the whole year one of sloth. We see, indeed, that this perverse abuse had already crept in in the time of Chrysostom; but we, also, at the same time, see how much it displeased him. For he complains in bitter terms, in the passage which I lately quoted, that there is so great an inequality in this matter, that they did not approach often, at other times of the year, even when prepared, but only at Easter, though unprepared. Then he exclaims: "O custom! O presumption! In vain, then, is the daily oblation made: in vain do we stand at the altar. There is none who partakes along with us." So far is he from having approved the practice by interposing his authority to it.

47. From the same forge proceeded another constitution, which snatched or robbed a half of the Supper from the greater part of the people of God—namely, the symbol of blood, which, interdicted to laics and profane (such are the titles which they give to God's heritage), became the peculiar possession of a few shaven and anointed individuals. The edict of the eternal God is, that all are to drink. This an upstart dares to antiquate and abrogate by a new and contrary law, proclaiming that all are not to drink. And that such legislators may not seem to fight against their God without any ground, they make a pretext of the dangers which might happen if

the sacred cup were given indiscriminately to all: as if these had not been observed and provided for by the eternal wisdom of God. Then they reason acutely, forsooth, that the one is sufficient for the two. For if the body is, as they say, the whole Christ, who cannot be separated from his body, then the blood includes the body by concomitance. Here we see how far our sense accords with God, when to any extent whatever it begins to rage and wanton with loosened reins. The Lord, pointing to the bread, says, "This is my body." Then pointing to the cup, he calls it his blood. The audacity of human reason objects and says, The bread is the blood, the wine is the body, as if the Lord had without reason distinguished his body from his blood, both by words and signs; and it had ever been heard that the body of Christ or the blood is called God and man. Certainly, if he had meant to designate himself wholly, he might have said, It is I, according to the Scriptural mode of expression, and not, "This is my body," "This is my blood." But wishing to succour the weakness of our faith, he placed the cup apart from the bread, to show that he suffices not less for drink than for food. Now, if one part be taken away, we can only find the half of the elements in what remains. Therefore, though it were true, as they pretend, that the blood is in the bread, and, on the other hand, the body in the cup, by concomitance, yet they deprive the pious of that confirmation of faith which Christ delivered as necessary. Bidding adieu, therefore, to their subtleties, let us retain the advantage which, by the ordinance of Christ, is obtained by a double pledge.

48. I am aware, indeed, how the ministers of Satan, whose usual practice is to hold the Scriptures in derision, here cavil.[1] First, they allege that from a simple fact we are not to draw a rule which is to be perpetually obligatory on the Church. But they state an untruth when they call it a simple fact. For Christ not only gave the cup, but appointed that the apostles should do so in future. For his words contain the command, "Drink ye all of it." And Paul relates, that it was so done, and recommends it as a fixed institution. Another subterfuge is, that the apostles alone were admitted by Christ to partake of this sacred Supper, because he had already selected and chosen them to the priesthood. I wish they would answer the five following questions, which they cannot evade, and which easily refute them and their lies. First, By what oracle was this solution so much at variance with the word of God revealed to them? Scripture mentions twelve who sat down with Jesus, but it does not so derogate from the dignity of Christ as to call them priests. Of this appellation we shall afterwards speak in its own place. Although he then gave to twelve, he commanded them to "do this;" in other words, to distribute thus among themselves. Secondly, Why during that purer age, from the days of the apostles downward for a thousand years, did all, without exception, partake of both symbols?

1 See Calvin de Cœna Domini. Item, Adv. Theol. Paris. Item, Vera Eccles. Reform. Ratio.

Did the primitive Church not know who the guests were whom Christ would have admitted to his Supper? It were the most shameless impudence to carp and quibble here. We have extant ecclesiastical histories, we have the writings of the Fathers, which furnish clear proofs of this fact. "The flesh," says Tertullian, "feeds on the body and blood of Christ, that the soul may be satiated by God" (Tertull. de Resurr. Carnis.). "How," says Ambrose to Theodosius, "will you receive the sacred body of the Lord with such hands? how will you have the boldness to put the cup of precious blood to your lips?" Jerome speaks of "the priests who perform the Eucharist and distribute the Lord's blood to the people" (Hieron. in Malach. cap. 2). Chrysostom says, "Not as under the ancient law the priest ate a part and the people a part, but one body and one cup is set before all. All the things which belong to the Eucharist are common to the priest and the people" (Chrysost. in Cor. cap. 8, Hom. 18). The same thing is attested by Augustine in numerous passages.

49. But why dispute about a fact which is perfectly notorious? Look at all Greek and Latin writers. Passages of the same kind everywhere occur. Nor did this practice fall into desuetude so long as there was one particle of integrity in the Church. Gregory, whom you may with justice call the last Bishop of Rome, says that it was observed in his age. "What the blood of the Lamb is you have learned, not by hearing, but by drinking it. His blood is poured into the mouths of the faithful." Nay, four hundred years after his death, when all things had degenerated, the practice still remained. Nor was it regarded as the custom merely, but as an inviolable law. Reverence for the divine institution was then maintained, and they had no doubt of its being sacrilege to separate what the Lord had joined. For Gelasius thus speaks: "We find that some taking only a portion of the sacred body, abstain from the cup. Undoubtedly let those persons, as they seem entangled by some strange superstition, either receive the whole sacrament, or be debarred from the whole. For the division of this mystery is not made without great sacrilege" (De Consec. Dist. 2). Reasons were given by Cyprian, which surely ought to weigh with Christian minds. "How," says he, "do we teach or incite them to shed their blood in confessing Christ, if we deny his blood to those who are to serve; or how do we make them fit for the cup of martyrdom, if we do not previously admit them by right of communion in the Church, to drink the cup of the Lord?" (Cyprian, Serm. 5, de Lapsis). The attempt of the Canonists to restrict the decree of Gelasius to priests is a cavil too puerile to deserve refutation.

50. Thirdly, Why did our Saviour say of the bread simply, "Take, eat," and of the cup, "drink ye all of it;" as if he had purposely intended to provide against the wile of Satan? Fourthly, If, as they will have it, the Lord honoured priests only with his Supper, what man would ever have dared to call strangers, whom the Lord had ex-

cluded, to partake of it, and to partake of a gift which he had not in his power, without any command from him who alone could give it? Nay, what presumption do they show in the present day in distributing the symbol of Christ's body to the common people, if they have no command or example from the Lord? Fifthly, Did Paul lie when he said to the Corinthians, "I have received of the Lord that which also I delivered unto you?" (1 Cor. xi. 23). The thing delivered, he afterwards declares to be, that all should communicate promiscuously in both symbols. But if Paul received of the Lord that all were to be admitted without distinction, let those who drive away almost the whole people of God see from whom they have received, since they cannot now pretend to have their authority from God, with whom there is not "yea and nay" (2 Cor. i. 19, 20). And yet these abominations they dare to cloak with the name of the Church, and defend under this pretence, as if those Antichrists were the Church who so licentiously trample under foot, waste, and abrogate the doctrine and institutions of Christ, or as if the Apostolic Church, in which religion flourished in full vigour, were not the Church.

CHAPTER XVIII.[1]

OF THE POPISH MASS. HOW IT NOT ONLY PROFANES, BUT ANNIHILATES THE LORD'S SUPPER.

The principal heads of this chapter are,—I. The abomination of the Mass, sec. 1. Its manifold impiety included under five heads, sec. 2–7. Its origin described, sec. 8, 9. II. Of the name of sacrifice which the ancients gave to the holy Supper, sec. 10-12. An apposite discussion on sacrifice, refuting the arguments of the Papists for the sacrifice of the Mass, sec. 13–18. III. A summary of the doctrine of the Christian Church respecting sacraments, paving the way for the subsequent discussion of the five sacraments, falsely so called, sec. 19, 20.

Sections.

1. The chief of all the abominations set up in opposition to the Lord's Supper is the Papal Mass. A description of it.
2. Its impiety is five-fold. 1. Its intolerable blasphemy in substituting priests to him the only Priest. Objections of the Papists answered.
3. Impiety of the Mass continued. 2. It overthrows the cross of Christ by setting up an altar. Objections answered.
4. Other objections answered.
5. Impiety of the Mass continued. 3. It banishes the remembrance of Christ's death. It crucifies Christ afresh. Objections answered.
6. Impiety of the Mass continued. 4. It robs us of the benefit of Christ's death.
7. Impiety of the Mass continued. 5. It abolishes the Lord's Supper. In the Supper the Father offers Christ to us; in the Mass, priestlings offer Christ to the Father. The Supper is a sacrament common to all Christians; the Mass confined to one priest.
8. The origin of the Mass. Private masses an impious profanation of the Supper.
9. This abomination unknown to the purer Church. It has no foundation in the word of God.
10. Second part of the chapter. Some of the ancients call the Supper a sacrifice, but not propitiatory, as the Papists do the Mass. This proved by passages from Augustine.
11. Some of the ancients seem to have declined too much to the shadows of the law.
12. Great distinction to be made between the Mosaic sacrifices and the Lord's Supper, which is called a eucharistic sacrifice. Same rule in this discussion.
13. The terms *sacrifice* and *priest*. Different kinds of sacrifices. 1. Propitiatory. 2. Eucharistic. None propitiatory but the death of Christ.
14. The Lord's Supper not properly called a propitiatory sacrifice, still less can the Popish Mass be so called. Those who mutter over the mass cannot be called priests.
15. Their vanity proved even by Plato.
16. To the eucharistic class of sacrifice belong all offices of piety and charity. This species of sacrifice has no connection with the appeasing of God.
17. Prayer, thanksgiving, and other exercises of piety, called sacrifices. In this sense the Lord's Supper called the eucharist. In the same sense all believers are priests.
18. Conclusion. Names given to the Mass.
19. Last part of the chapter, recapitulating the views which ought to be held concerning baptism and the Lord's Supper. Why the Lord's Supper is, and Baptism is not, repeated.
20. Christians should be contented with these two sacraments. They are abolished by the sacraments decreed by men.

1 Vid. Calv. Ep. de Fugiend. Illic. Sacris. Item, De Sacerdotiis Eccles. Papal. Item, De Necessitate Reform. Eccles. Item, Epist. ad Sadoletum.

1. By these and similar inventions, Satan has attempted to adulterate and envelop the sacred Supper of Christ as with thick darkness, that its purity might not be preserved in the Church. But the head of this horrid abomination was, when he raised a sign by which it was not only obscured and perverted, but altogether obliterated and abolished, vanished away and disappeared from the memory of man—namely, when, with most pestilential error, he blinded almost the whole world into the belief that the Mass was a sacrifice and oblation for obtaining the remission of sins. I say nothing as to the way in which the sounder Schoolmen at first received this dogma.[1] I leave them with their puzzling subtleties, which, however they may be defended by cavilling, are to be repudiated by all good men, because, all they do is to envelop the brightness of the Supper in great darkness. Bidding adieu to them, therefore, let my readers understand that I am here combating that opinion with which the Roman Antichrist and his prophets have imbued the whole world—viz. that the mass is a work by which the priest who offers Christ, and the others who in the oblation receive him, gain merit with God, or that it is an expiatory victim by which they regain the favour of God. And this is not merely the common opinion of the vulgar, but the very act has been so arranged as to be a kind of propitiation, by which satisfaction is made to God for the living and the dead. This is also expressed by the words employed, and the same thing may be inferred from daily practice. I am aware how deeply this plague has struck its roots; under what a semblance of good it conceals its true character, bearing the name of Christ before it, and making many believe that under the single name of Mass is comprehended the whole sum of faith. But when it shall have been most clearly proved by the word of God, that this mass, however glossed and splendid, offers the greatest insult to Christ, suppresses and buries his cross, consigns his death to oblivion, takes away the benefit which it was designed to convey, enervates and dissipates the sacrament, by which the remembrance of his death was retained, will its roots be so deep that this most powerful axe, the word of God, will not cut it down and destroy it? Will any semblance be so specious that this light will not expose the lurking evil?

2. Let us show, therefore, as was proposed in the first place, that in the mass intolerable blasphemy and insult are offered to Christ. For he was not appointed Priest and Pontiff by the Father[2] for a time merely, as priests were appointed under the Old Testament. Since their life was mortal, their priesthood could not be immortal, and hence there was need of successors, who might ever and anon be substituted in the room of the dead. But Christ being immortal, had not the least occasion to have a vicar substituted for him.

[1] The French adds, "qui ont parlé un petit plus passablement que leur successeurs qui sont venus depuis;"—who have spoken somewhat more tolerably than their successors who have come since.

[2] Heb. v. 5–10; vii. 17, 21; ix. 11; x. 21; Ps. cx, 4; Gen. xiv. 18.

Wherefore he was appointed by his Father a priest for ever, after the order of Melchizedek, that he might eternally exercise a permanent priesthood. This mystery had been typified long before in Melchizedek, whom Scripture, after once introducing as the priest of the living God, never afterwards mentions, as if he had had no end of life. In this way Christ is said to be a priest after his order. But those who sacrifice daily must necessarily give the charge of their oblations to priests, whom they surrogate as the vicars and successors of Christ. By this surrogation they not only rob Christ of his honour, and take from him the prerogative of an eternal priesthood, but attempt to remove him from the right hand of his Father, where he cannot sit immortal without being an eternal priest. Nor let them allege that their priestlings are not substituted for Christ, as if he were dead, but are only substitutes in that eternal priesthood, which therefore ceases not to exist. The words of the apostle are too stringent to leave them any means of evasion—viz. "They truly were many priests, because they were not suffered to continue by reason of death: but this man, because he continueth ever, hath an unchangeable priesthood" (Heb. vii. 23, 24). Yet such is their dishonesty, that to defend their impiety they arm themselves with the example of Melchizedek. As he is said to have "brought forth (*obtulisse*) bread and wine" (Gen. xiv. 18), they infer that it was a prelude to their mass, as if there was any resemblance between him and Christ in the offering of bread and wine. This is too silly and frivolous to need refutation. Melchizedek gave bread and wine to Abraham and his companions, that he might refresh them when worn out with the march and the battle. What has this to do with sacrifice? The humanity of the holy king is praised by Moses: these men absurdly coin a mystery of which there is no mention. They, however, put another gloss upon their error, because it is immediately added, he was "priest of the most high God." I answer, that they erroneously wrest to bread and wine what the apostle refers to blessing. "This Melchizedek, king of Salem, priest of the most high God, who met Abraham," "and blessed him." Hence the same apostle (and a better interpreter cannot be desired) infers his excellence. "Without all contradiction, the less is blessed of the better." But if the oblation of Melchizedek was a figure of the sacrifice of the mass, I ask, would the apostle, who goes into the minutest details, have forgotten a matter so grave and serious? Now, however they quibble, it is in vain for them to attempt to destroy the argument which is adduced by the apostle himself—viz. that the right and honour of the priesthood has ceased among mortal men, because Christ, who is immortal, is the one perpetual priest.

3. Another iniquity chargeable on the mass is, that it sinks and buries the cross and passion of Christ. This much, indeed, is most certain,—the cross of Christ is overthrown the moment an altar is erected. For if, on the cross, he offered himself in sacrifice that he

might sanctify us for ever, and purchase eternal redemption for us,[1] undoubtedly the power and efficacy of his sacrifice continues without end. Otherwise, we should not think more honourably of Christ than of the oxen and calves which were sacrificed under the law, the offering of which is proved to have been weak and inefficacious because often repeated. Wherefore, it must be admitted, either that the sacrifice which Christ offered on the cross wanted the power of eternal cleansing, or that he performed this once for ever by his one sacrifice. Accordingly, the apostle says, "Now once in the end of the world hath he appeared to put away sin by the sacrifice of himself." Again: "By the which act we are sanctified through the offering of the body of Jesus Christ once for all." Again: "For by one offering he hath perfected for ever them that are sanctified." To this he subjoins the celebrated passage: "Now, where remission of these is, there is no more offering for sin." The same thing Christ intimated by his latest voice, when, on giving up the ghost, he exclaimed, "It is finished." We are accustomed to observe the last words of the dying as oracular. Christ, when dying, declares, that by his one sacrifice is perfected and fulfilled whatever was necessary to our salvation. To such a sacrifice, whose perfection he so clearly declared, shall we, as if it were imperfect, presume daily to append innumerable sacrifices? Since the sacred word of God not only affirms, but proclaims and protests, that this sacrifice was once accomplished, and remains eternally in force, do not those who demand another, charge it with imperfection and weakness? But to what tends the mass which has been established, that a hundred thousand sacrifices may be performed every day, but just to bury and suppress the passion of our Lord, in which he offered himself to his Father as the only victim? Who but a blind man does not see that it was Satanic audacity to oppose a truth so clear and transparent? I am not unaware of the impostures by which the father of lies is wont to cloak his fraud—viz. that the sacrifices are not different or various, but that the one sacrifice is repeated. Such smoke is easily dispersed. The apostle, during his whole discourse, contends not only that there are no other sacrifices, but that that one was once offered, and is no more to be repeated. The more subtle try to make their escape by a still narrower loophole—viz. that it is not repetition, but application. But there is no more difficulty in confuting this sophism also. For Christ did not offer himself once, in the view that his sacrifice should be daily ratified by new oblations, but that by the preaching of the gospel and the dispensation of the sacred Supper, the benefit of it should be communicated to us. Thus Paul says, that "Christ, our passover, is sacrificed for us," and bids us "keep the feast" (1 Cor. v. 7, 8). The method, I say, in which the cross of Christ is duly applied to us is when the enjoyment is communicated to us, and we receive it with true faith.

[1] Heb. ix. 11, 12, 26; x. 10. 14, 16.

4. But it is worth while to hear on what other foundation besides they rear up their sacrifice of the mass. To this end they drag in the prophecy of Malachi, in which the Lord promises that "in every place incense shall be offered unto my name, and a pure offering" (Mal. i. 11). As if it were new or unusual for the prophets, when they speak of the calling of the Gentiles, to designate the spiritual worship of God to which they call them, by the external rites of the law, more familiarly to intimate to the men of their age that they were to be called into the true fellowship of religion, just as in general they are wont to describe the truth which has been exhibited by the gospel by the types of their own age. Thus they use going up to Jerusalem for conversion to the Lord, the bringing of all kinds of gifts for the adoration of God—dreams and visions for the more ample knowledge with which believers were to be endued in the kingdom of Christ. The passage they quote from Malachi resembles one in Isaiah, in which the prophet speaks of three altars to be erected in Assyria, Egypt, and Judea. First, I ask, whether or not they grant that this prophecy is fulfilled in the kingdom of Christ? Secondly, Where are those altars, or when were they ever erected? Thirdly, Do they suppose that a single temple is destined for a single kingdom, as was that of Jerusalem? If they ponder these things, they will confess, I think, that the prophet, under types adapted to his age, prophesied concerning the propagation of the spiritual worship of God over the whole world. This is the answer which we give them; but, as obvious examples everywhere occur in the Scripture, I am not anxious to give a longer enumeration; although they are miserably deluded in this also, that they acknowledge no sacrifice but that of the mass, whereas in truth believers now sacrifice to God and offer him a pure offering, of which we shall speak by-and-by.

5. I now come to the third part of the mass, in regard to which, we are to explain how it obliterates the true and only death of Christ, and drives it from the memory of men. For as among men, the confirmation of a testament depends upon the death of the testator, so also the testament by which he has bequeathed to us remission of sins and eternal righteousness, our Lord has confirmed by his death. Those who dare to make any change or innovation on this testament deny his death, and hold it as of no moment. Now, what is the mass but a new and altogether different testament? What? Does not each mass promise a new forgiveness of sins, a new purchase of righteousness, so that now there are as many testaments as there are masses? Therefore, let Christ come again, and, by another death, make this new testament; or rather, by innumerable deaths, ratify the innumerable testaments of the mass. Said I not true, then, at the outset, that the only true death of Christ is obliterated by the mass? For what is the direct aim of the mass but just to put Christ again to death, if that were possible? For, as the apostle says, "Where a testament is, there must also of necessity be the death of the testator" (Heb. ix. 16). The novelty of the mass bears,

on the face of it, to be a testament of Christ, and therefore demands his death. Besides, it is necessary that the victim which is offered be slain and immolated. If Christ is sacrificed at each mass, he must be cruelly slain every moment in a thousand places. This is not my argument, but the apostle's: "Nor yet that he should offer himself often;" "for then must he often have suffered since the foundation of the world" (Heb. ix. 25, 26). I admit that they are ready with an answer, by which they even charge us with calumny; for they say that we object to them what they never thought, and could not even think. We know that the life and death of Christ are not at all in their hand. Whether they mean to slay him, we regard not: our intention is only to show the absurdity consequent on their impious and accursed dogma. This I demonstrate from the mouth of the apostle. Though they insist a hundred times that this sacrifice is bloodless (ἀναίμακτον), I will reply, that it depends not on the will of man to change the nature of sacrifice, for in this way the sacred and inviolable institution of God would fall. Hence it follows, that the principle of the apostle stands firm, "without shedding of blood is no remission" (Heb. ix. 22).

6. The fourth property of the mass which we are to consider is, that it robs us of the benefit which redounded to us from the death of Christ, while it prevents us from recognising it and thinking of it. For who can think that he has been redeemed by the death of Christ when he sees a new redemption in the mass? Who can feel confident that his sins have been remitted when he sees a new remission? It will not do to say that the only ground on which we obtain forgiveness of sins in the mass is, because it has been already purchased by the death of Christ. For this is just equivalent to saying that we are redeemed by Christ on the condition that we redeem ourselves. For the doctrine which is disseminated by the ministers of Satan, and which, in the present day, they defend by clamour, fire, and sword, is, that when we offer Christ to the Father in the mass, we, by this work of oblation, obtain remission of sins, and become partakers of the sufferings of Christ. What is now left for the sufferings of Christ, but to be an example of redemption, that we may thereby learn to be our own redeemers? Christ himself, when he seals our assurance of pardon in the Supper, does not bid his disciples stop short at that act, but sends them to the sacrifice of his death; intimating, that the Supper is the memento, or, as it is commonly expressed, the memorial from which they may learn that the expiatory victim by which God was to be appeased was to be offered only once. For it is not sufficient to hold that Christ is the only victim, without adding that his is the only immolation, in order that our faith may be fixed to his cross.

7. I come now to the crowning point—viz. that the sacred Supper, on which the Lord left the memorial of his passion formed and engraved, was taken away, hidden, and destroyed, when the mass was erected. While the supper itself is a gift of God, which was to be

received with thanksgiving, the sacrifice of the mass pretends to give a price to God to be received as satisfaction. As widely as giving differs from receiving, does sacrifice differ from the sacrament of the Supper. But herein does the wretched ingratitude of man appear,—that when the liberality of the divine goodness ought to have been recognised, and thanks returned, he makes God to be his debtor. The sacrament promised, that by the death of Christ we were not only restored to life once, but constantly quickened, because all the parts of our salvation were then completed. The sacrifice of the mass uses a very different language—viz. that Christ must be sacrificed daily, in order that he may lend something to us. The Supper was to be dispensed at the public meeting of the Church, to remind us of the communion by which we are all united in Christ Jesus. This communion the sacrifice of the mass dissolves, and tears asunder. For after the heresy prevailed, that there behoved to be priests to sacrifice for the people, as if the Supper had been handed over to them, it ceased to be communicated to the assembly of the faithful according to the command of the Lord. Entrance has been given to private masses, which more resemble a kind of excommunication than that communion ordained by the Lord, when the priestling, about to devour his victim apart, separates himself from the whole body of the faithful. That there may be no mistake, I call it a private mass whenever there is no partaking of the Lord's Supper among believers, though, at the same time, a great multitude of persons may be present.

8. The origin of the name of Mass I have never been able certainly to ascertain. It seems probable that it was derived from the offerings which were collected. Hence the ancients usually speak of it in the plural number. But without raising any controversy as to the name, I hold that private masses are diametrically opposed to the institution of Christ, and are, therefore, an impious profanation of the sacred Supper. For what did the Lord enjoin? Was it not to take and divide amongst ourselves? What does Paul teach as to the observance of this command? Is it not that the breaking of bread is the communion of body and blood? (1 Cor. x. 16). Therefore, when one person takes without distributing, where is the resemblance? But that one acts in the name of the whole Church. By what command? Is it not openly to mock God when one privately seizes for himself what ought to have been distributed among a number? But as the words, both of our Saviour and of Paul, are sufficiently clear, we must briefly conclude, that wherever there is no breaking of bread for the communion of the faithful, there is no Supper of the Lord, but a false and preposterous imitation of the Supper. But false imitation is adulteration. Moreover, the adulteration of this high ordinance is not without impiety. In private masses, therefore, there is an impious abuse: and as in religion, one fault ever and anon begets another, after that custom of offering without communion once crept in, they began gradually to make innumerable masses

in all the separate corners of the churches, and to draw the people hither and thither, when they ought to have formed one meeting, and thus recognised the mystery of their unity. Let them now go and deny their idolatry when they exhibit the bread in their masses, that it may be adored for Christ. In vain do they talk of those promises of the presence of Christ, which, however they may be understood, were certainly not given that impure and profane men might form the body of Christ as often as they please, and for whatever abuse they please; but that believers, while, with religious observance, they follow the command of Christ in celebrating the Supper, might enjoy the true participation of it.

9. We may add, that this perverse course was unknown to the purer Church. For however the more impudent among our opponents may attempt to gloss the matter, it is absolutely certain that all antiquity is opposed to them, as has been above demonstrated in other instances, and may be more surely known by the diligent reading of the Fathers.[1] But before I conclude, I ask our missal doctors, seeing they know that obedience is better than sacrifice, and God commands us to listen to his voice rather than to offer sacrifice (1 Sam. xv. 22),—how they can believe this method of sacrificing to be pleasing to God, since it is certain that he does not command it, and they cannot support it by one syllable of Scripture? Besides, when they hear the apostle declaring that "no man taketh this honour to himself, but he that is called of God, as was Aaron," so also Christ glorified not himself to be made an high priest, but he that said unto him, "Thou art my Son: this day have I begotten thee" (Heb. v. 4, 5). They must either prove God to be the author and founder of their priesthood, or confess that there is no honour from God in an office, into which, without being called, they have rushed with wicked temerity. They cannot produce one iota of Scripture in support of their priesthood. And must not the sacrifices be vain, since they cannot be offered without a priest?

10. Should any one here obtrude concise sentences of the ancients, and contend, or their authority, that the sacrifice which is performed in the Supper is to be understood differently from what we have explained it, let this be our brief reply,—that if the question relates to the approval of the fiction of sacrifice, as imagined by Papists in the mass, there is nothing in the Fathers to countenance the sacrilege. They indeed use the term sacrifice, but they, at the same time, explain that they mean nothing more than the commemoration of that one true sacrifice which Christ, our only sacrifice (as they themselves

[1] The French of this sentence is, "Car combien que ceux qui sont les plus effrontés entre les Papistes fassent un bouclier des anciens docteurs, abusant faussement de leurs tesmoignages, toutesfois c'est une chose claire comme le soleil en plein midi, que ce qu'ils font est tout contraire a l'usage ancien: et que c'est un abus qui est venu en avant du temps que tout etoit depravé et corrompu en l'Eglise."—For although those who have the most effrontery among the Papists make a shield of the ancient doctors, falsely abusing their testimony, it is clear as the sun at noon-day, that what they do is quite contrary to ancient practice, and that is an abuse which immediately preceded the time when everything was depraved and corrupted in the Church.

everywhere proclaim), performed on the cross. "The Hebrews," says Augustine (Cont. Faust. Lib. xx. c. 18), "in the victims of beasts which they offered to God, celebrated the prediction of the future victim which Christ offered: Christians now celebrate the commemoration of a finished sacrifice by the sacred oblation and participation of the body of Christ." Here he certainly teaches the same doctrine which is delivered at greater length in the Treatise on Faith, addressed to Peter the deacon, whoever may have been the author. The words are, "Hold most firmly, and have no doubt at all, that the Only-Begotten became incarnate for us, that he offered himself for us, an offering and sacrifice to God for a sweet-smelling savour; to whom, with the Father and the Holy Spirit, in the time of the Old Testament, animals were sacrificed, and to whom now, with the Father and the Holy Spirit (with whom there is one God-head), the holy Church, throughout the whole world, ceases not to offer the sacrifice of bread and wine. For, in those carnal victims, there was a typifying of the flesh of Christ, which he himself was to offer for our sins, and of the blood which he was to shed for the forgiveness of sins. But in that sacrifice there is thanksgiving and commemoration of the flesh of Christ which he offered for us, and of the blood which he shed for us." Hence Augustine himself, in several passages (Ep. 120, ad Honorat. Cont. Advers. Legis.), explains, that it is nothing else than a sacrifice of praise. In short, you will find in his writings, *passim*, that the only reason for which the Lord's Supper is called a sacrifice is, because it is a commemoration, an image, a testimonial of that singular, true, and only sacrifice by which Christ expiated our guilt. For there is a memorable passage (De Trinitate, Lib. iv. c. 24), where, after discoursing of the only sacrifice, he thus concludes: "Since, in a sacrifice, four things are considered—viz. to whom it is offered, by whom, what and for whom, the same one true Mediator, reconciling us to God by the sacrifice of peace, remains one with him to whom he offered, made himself one with those for whom he offered, is himself the one who offered, and the one thing which he offered." Chrysostom speaks to the same effect. They so strongly claim the honour of the priesthood for Christ alone, that Augustine declares it would be equivalent to Antichrist for any one to make a bishop to be an intercessor between God and man (August. Cont. Parmen. Lib. ii c. 8).[1]

11. And yet we deny not that in the Supper the sacrifice of Christ is so vividly exhibited as almost to set the spectacle of the cross before our eyes, just as the apostle says to the Galatians, that Jesus Christ had been evidently set forth before their eyes, when the preaching of the cross was delivered to them (Gal. iii. 1). But because I see that those ancient writers have wrested this commemoration to a different purpose than was accordant to the divine institution (the Supper somehow seemed to them to present the appearance of a re-

1 This last sentence forms, in the French, the first of sec. 11.

peated, or at least renewed, immolation), nothing can be safer for the pious than to rest satisfied with the pure and simple ordinance of God, whose Supper it is said to be, just because his authority alone ought to appear in it. Seeing that they retained a pious and orthodox view of the whole ordinance—and I cannot discover that they wished to derogate in the least from the one sacrifice of the Lord—I cannot charge them with any impiety, and yet I think they cannot be excused from having erred somewhat in the mode of action. They imitated the Jewish mode of sacrificing more closely than either Christ had ordained, or the nature of the gospel allowed. The only thing, therefore, for which they may be justly censured is, that preposterous analogy, that not contented with the simple and genuine institution of Christ, they declined too much to the shadows of the law.

12. Any who will diligently consider, will perceive that the word of the Lord makes this distinction between the Mosaic sacrifices and our eucharist—that while the former represented to the Jewish people the same efficacy of the death of Christ which is now exhibited to us in the Supper, yet the form of representation was different. There the Levitical priests were ordered to typify the sacrifice which Christ was to accomplish; a victim was placed to act as a substitute for Christ himself; an altar was erected on which it was to be sacrificed; the whole, in short, was so conducted as to bring under the eye an image of the sacrifice which was to be offered to God in expiation. But now that the sacrifice has been performed, the Lord has prescribed a different method to us—viz. to transmit the benefit of the sacrifice offered to him by his Son to his believing people. The Lord, therefore, has given us a table at which we may feast, not an altar on which a victim may be offered; he has not consecrated priests to sacrifice, but ministers to distribute a sacred feast. The more sublime and holy this mystery is, the more religiously and reverently ought it to be treated. Nothing, therefore, is safer than to banish all the boldness of human sense, and adhere solely to what Scripture delivers. And certainly, if we reflect that it is the Supper of the Lord and not of men, why do we allow ourselves to be turned aside one nail's-breadth from Scripture, by any authority of man or length of prescription?[1] Accordingly, the apostle, in desiring completely to remove the vices which had crept into the Church of Corinth, as the most expeditious method, recalls them to the institution itself, showing that thence a perpetual rule ought to be derived.

13. Lest any quarrelsome person should raise a dispute with us as to the terms *sacrifice* and *priest*, I will briefly explain what in the whole of this discussion we mean by sacrifice, and what by priest. Some, on what rational ground I see not, extend the term *sacrifice* to all sacred ceremonies and religious acts. We know that by the uniform

1 French, " n'aucun authorite humaine, ne longeur de temps, ne toutes autres apparences;"—no human authority, no length of time, nor any other appearnces.

use of Scripture, the name of sacrifice is given to what the Greeks call at one time θυσια, at another προσφορὰ, at another τελετὴ. This, in its general acceptation, includes everything whatever that is offered to God. Wherefore, we ought to distinguish, but so that the distinction may derive its analogy from the sacrifices of the Mosaic Law, under whose shadows the Lord was pleased to represent to his people the whole reality of sacrifices. Though these were various in form, they may all be referred to two classes. For either an oblation for sin was made by a certain species of satisfaction, by which the penalty was redeemed before God, or it was a symbol and attestation of religion and divine worship, at one time in the way of supplication to demand the favour of God; at another, by way of thanksgiving, to testify gratitude to God for benefits received; at another, as a simple exercise of piety, to renew the sanction of the covenant, to which latter branch, burnt-offerings, and libations, oblations, first-fruits, and peace offerings, referred. Hence let us also distribute them into two classes. The other class, with the view of explaining, let us call λατρευτικὸν, and σεβαστικὸν, as consisting of the veneration and worship which believers both owe and render to God; or, if you prefer it, let us call it ευχαριστικὸν, since it is exhibited to God by none but those who, enriched with his boundless benefits, offer themselves and all their actions to him in return. The other class let us call *propitiatory* or *expiatory*. A sacrifice of expiation is one whose object is to appease the wrath of God, to satisfy his justice, and thereby wipe and wash away the sins, by which the sinner being cleansed and restored to purity, may return to favour with God. Hence the name which was given in the Law to the victims which were offered in expiation of sin (Exod. xxix. 36); not that they were adequate to regain the favour of God, and wipe away guilt, but because they typified the true sacrifice of this nature, which was at length performed in reality by Christ alone; by him alone, because no other cculd, and once, because the efficacy and power of the one sacrifice performed by Christ is eternal, as he declared by his voice, when he said, "It is finished;" that is, that everything necessary to regain the favour of the Father, to procure forgiveness of sins, righteousness, and salvation, that all this was performed and consummated by his one oblation, and that hence nothing was wanting. No place was left for another sacrifice.

14. Wherefore, I conclude, that it is an abominable insult and intolerable blasphemy, as well against Christ as the sacrifice, which, by his death, he performed for us on the cross, for any one to think of repeating the oblation, of purchasing the forgiveness of sins, of propitiating God, and obtaining justification. But what else is done in the mass than to make us partakers of the sufferings of Christ by means of a new oblation? And that there might be no limit to their extravagance, they have deemed it little to say, that it properly becomes a common sacrifice for the whole Church, without adding, that it is at their pleasure to apply it specially to this one or

that, as they choose; or rather, to any one who is willing to purchase their merchandise from them for a price paid. Moreover, as they could not come up to the estimate of Judas, still, that they might in some way refer to their author, they make the resemblance to consist in the number. He sold for thirty pieces of silver: they, according to the French method of computation, sell for thirty pieces of brass. He did it once: they as often as a purchaser is met with. We deny that they are priests in this sense—namely, that by such oblations they intercede with God for the people, that by propitiating God they make expiation for sins. Christ is the only Pontiff and Priest of the New Testament: to him all priestly offices were transferred, and in him they closed and terminated. Even had Scripture made no mention of the eternal priesthood of Christ, yet, as God, after abolishing those ancient sacrifices, appointed no new priest, the argument of the apostle remains invincible, "No man taketh this honour unto himself, but he that is called of God, as was Aaron" (Heb. v. 4). How, then, can those sacrilegious men, who by their own account are murderers of Christ, dare to call themselves the priests of the living God?

15. There is a most elegant passage in the second book of Plato's Republic. Speaking of ancient expiations, and deriding the foolish confidence of wicked and iniquitous men, who thought that by them, as a kind of veils, they concealed their crimes from the gods; and, as if they had made a paction with the gods, indulged themselves more securely, he seems accurately to describe the use of the expiation of the mass, as it exists in the world in the present day. All know that it is unlawful to defraud and circumvent another. To do injustice to widows, to pillage pupils, to molest the poor, to seize the goods of others by wicked arts, to get possession of any man's succession by fraud and perjury, to oppress by violence and tyrannical terror, all admit to be impious. How then do so many, as if assured of impunity, dare to do all those things? Undoubtedly, if we duly consider, we will find that the only thing which gives them so much courage is, that by the sacrifice of the mass as a price paid, they trust that they will satisfy God, or at least will easily find a means of transacting with him. Plato next proceeds to deride the gross stupidity of those who think by such expiations to redeem the punishments which they must otherwise suffer after death. And what is meant by anniversaries and the greater part of masses in the present day, but just that those who through life have been the most cruel tyrants, or most rapacious plunderers, or adepts in all kinds of wickedness, may, as if redeemed at this price, escape the fire of purgatory?

16. Under the other kind of sacrifice, which we have called eucharistic, are included all the offices of charity, by which, while we embrace our brethren, we honour the Lord himself in his members; in fine, all our prayers, praises, thanksgivings, and every act of worship which we perform to God. All these depend on the greater

sacrifice with which we dedicate ourselves, soul and body, to be a holy temple to the Lord. For it is not enough that our external acts be framed to obedience, but we must dedicate and consecrate first ourselves, and, secondly, all that we have, so that all which is in us may be subservient to his glory, and be stirred up to magnify it. This kind of sacrifice has nothing to do with appeasing God, with obtaining remission of sins, with procuring justification, but is wholly employed in magnifying and extolling God, since it cannot be grateful and acceptable to God unless at the hand of those who, having received forgiveness of sins, have already been reconciled and freed from guilt. This is so necessary to the Church, that it cannot be dispensed with. Therefore, it will endure for ever, so long as the people of God shall endure, as we have already seen above from the prophet. For in this sense we may understand the prophecy, "From the rising of the sun, even unto the going down of the same, my name shall be great among the Gentiles; and in every place incense shall be offered unto my name, and a pure offering: for my name shall be great among the heathen, said the Lord of hosts" (Malachi i. 11); so far are we from doing away with this sacrifice. Thus Paul beseeches us by the mercies of God, to present our bodies "a living sacrifice, holy, acceptable unto God," our "reasonable service" (Rom. xii. 1). Here he speaks very significantly when he adds, that this service is reasonable, for he refers to the spiritual mode of worshipping God, and tacitly opposes it to the carnal sacrifices of the Mosaic Law. Thus to do good and communicate are called sacrifices with which God is well pleased (Heb. xiii. 16). Thus the kindness of the Philippians in relieving Paul's want is called "an odour of a sweet smell, a sacrifice acceptable, well pleasing to God" (Phil. iv. 18); and thus all the good works of believers are called spiritual sacrifices.

17. And why do I enumerate? This form of expression is constantly occurring in Scripture. Nay, even while the people of God were kept under the external tutelage of the law, the prophets clearly expressed that under these carnal sacrifices there was a reality which is common both to the Jewish people and the Christian Church. For this reason David prayed, "Let my prayer ascend forth before thee as incense" (Ps. cxli. 2). And Hosea gives the name of "calves of the lips" (Hos. xiv. 3) to thanksgivings, which David elsewhere calls "sacrifices of praise;" the apostle, imitating him, speaks of offering "the sacrifice of praise," which he explains to mean, "the fruit of our lips, giving thanks to his name" (Heb. xiii. 15). This kind of sacrifice is indispensable in the Lord's Supper, in which, while we show forth his death, and give him thanks, we offer nothing but the sacrifice of praise. From this office of sacrificing, all Christians are called "a royal priesthood," because by Christ we offer that sacrifice of praise of which the apostle speaks, the fruit of our lips, giving thanks to his name (1 Pet. ii. 9; Heb. xiii. 15). We do not appear with our gifts in the presence of God without an intercessor.

Christ is our Mediator, by whose intervention we offer ourselves and our all to the Father; he is our High Priest, who, having entered into the upper sanctuary, opens up an access for us; he is the altar on which we lay our gifts, that whatever we do attempt, we may attempt in him; he it is, I say, who "hath made us kings and priests unto God and his Father" (Rev. i. 6).

18. What remains but for the blind to see, the deaf to hear, children even to perceive this abomination of the mass, which, held forth in a golden cup,[1] has so intoxicated all the kings and nations of the earth, from the highest to the lowest; so struck them with stupor and giddiness, that, duller than the lower animals, they have placed the vessel of their salvation in this fatal vortex. Certainly Satan never employed a more powerful engine to assail and storm the kingdom of Christ. This is the Helen for whom the enemies of the truth in the present day fight with so much rage, fury, and atrocity; and truly the Helen with whom they commit spiritual whoredom, the most execrable of all. I am not here laying my little finger on those gross abuses by which they might pretend that the purity of their sacred mass is profaned; on the base traffic which they ply; the sordid gain which they make; the rapacity with which they satiate their avarice. I only indicate, and that in few and simple terms, how very sacred the sanctity of the mass is, how well it has for several ages deserved to be admired and held in veneration! It were a greater work to illustrate these great mysteries as they deserve, and I am unwilling to meddle with their obscene impurities, which are daily before the eyes and faces of all, that it may be understood that the mass, taken in the most choice form in which it can be exhibited, without any appendages, teems from head to foot with all kinds of impiety, blasphemy, idolatry, and sacrilege.

19. My readers have here a compendious view of all that I have thought it of importance to know concerning these two sacraments, which have been delivered to the Christian Church, to be used from the beginning of the new dispensation to the end of the world, Baptism being a kind of entrance into the Church, an initiation into the faith, and the Lord's Supper the constant aliment by which Christ spiritually feeds his family of believers. Wherefore, as there is but one God, one faith, one Christ, one Church, which is his body, so Baptism is one, and is not repeated. But the Supper is ever and anon dispensed, to intimate, that those who are once allured into the Church are constantly fed by Christ. Besides these two, no other has been instituted by God, and no other ought to be recognised by the assembly of the faithful. That sacraments are not to be instituted and set up by the will of men, is easily understood by him who remembers what has been above with sufficient plainness expounded—viz. that the sacraments have been appointed by God to instruct

1 The French explains, "c'est à dire, sous le nom de la parole de Dieu;"—that is to say, under the name of the word of God.

us in his promise, and testify his goodwill towards us; and who, moreover, considers, that the Lord has no counsellor (Isa. xl. 13; Rom. xi. 34); who can give us any certainty as to his will, or assure us how he is disposed towards us, what he is disposed to give, and what to deny? From this it follows, that no one can set forth a sign which is to be a testimonial of his will, and of some promise. He alone can give the sign, and bear witness to himself. I will express it more briefly, perhaps in homelier, but also in clearer terms,—There never can be a sacrament without a promise of salvation. All men collected into one cannot, of themselves, give us any promise of salvation, and, therefore, they cannot, of themselves, give out and set up a sacrament.

20. With these two, therefore, let the Christian Church be contented, and not only not admit or acknowledge any third at present, but not even desire or expect it even until the end of the world. For though to the Jews were given, besides his ordinary sacraments, others differing somewhat according to the nature of the times (as the manna, the water gushing from the rock, the brazen serpent, and the like),[1] by this variety they were reminded not to stop short at such figures, the state of which could not be durable, but to expect from God something better, to endure without decay and without end. Our case is very different. To us Christ has been revealed. In him are hidden all the treasures of wisdom and knowledge (Col. ii. 3), in such richness and abundance, that to ask or hope for any new addition to these treasures is truly to offend God and provoke him against us. It behoves us to hunger after Christ only, to seek him, look to him, learn of him, and learn again, until the arrival of the great day on which the Lord will fully manifest the glory of his kingdom, and exhibit himself as he is to our admiring eye (1 John iii. 2). And, for this reason, this age of ours is designated in Scripture[2] by the last hour, the last days, the last times, that no one may deceive himself with the vain expectation of some new doctrine or revelation. Our heavenly Father, who "at sundry times, and in divers manners, spake in time past unto the fathers by the prophets, hath in these last days spoken unto us" by his beloved Son, who alone can manifest, and, in fact, has fully manifested, the Father, in so far as is of importance to us, while we now see him through a mirror. Now, since men have been denied the power of making new sacraments in the Church of God, it were to be wished, that in those which are of God, there should be the least possible admixture of human invention. For just as when water is infused, the wine is diluted, and when leaven is put in, the whole mass is leavened, so the purity of the ordinances of God is impaired, whenever man makes any addition of his own. And yet we see how far the sacraments as at present used have degenerated from their genuine purity. There is everywhere more than enough of pomp,

[1] Exod. xvi. 13–15; xvii. 6; Num. xx. 8; xxi. 9; 1 Cor. x. 4; John iii. 14.
[2] 1 John ii. 18; 1 Pet. i. 20; Luke x. 22; Heb. i. 1; 1 Cor. xiii. 12.

ceremony, and gesticulation, while no account is taken, or mention made, of the word of God, without which, even the sacraments themselves are not sacraments. Nay, in such a crowd, the very ceremonies ordained by God cannot raise their head, but lie as it were oppressed. In Baptism, as we have elsewhere justly complained, how little is seen of that which alone ought to shine and be conspicuous there, I mean Baptism itself? The Supper was altogether buried when it was turned into the Mass. The utmost is, that it is seen once a year, but in a garbled, mutilated, and lacerated form.[1]

1 French, "deschiree, decouppee, departie, brisee, divisee, et toute difformee.

CHAPTER XIX.

OF THE FIVE SACRAMENTS, FALSELY SO CALLED. THEIR SPURIOUSNESS PROVED, AND THEIR TRUE CHARACTER EXPLAINED.

There are two divisions of this chapter,—I. A general discussion of these five sacraments, sec. 1–3. II. A special consideration of each. 1. Of Confirmation, sec. 4–13. 2. Of Penance, sec. 14–17. 3. Of Extreme Unction, sec. 18–21. 4 Of Order, in which the seven so-called sacraments have originated, sec. 22–23. 5. Of Marriage, sec. 34–37.

Sections.

1. Connection of the present discussion with that concerning Baptism and the Lord's Supper. Impiety of the popish teachers in attributing more to human rites than to the ordinances of God.
2. Men cannot institute sacraments. Necessary to keep up a distinction between sacraments and other ceremonies.
3. Seven sacraments not to be found in ecclesiastical writers. Augustine, who may represent all the others, acknowledged two sacraments only.
4. Nature of confirmation in ancient times. The laying on of hands.
5. This kind of confirmation afterwards introduced. It is falsely called a sacrament.
6. Popish argument for confirmation answered.
7. Argument confirmed by the example of Christ. Absurdity and impiety of Papists in calling their oil the oil of salvation.
8. Papistical argument, that Baptism cannot be complete without Confirmation. Answered.
9. Argument, that without confirmation we cannot be fully Christians. Answer.
10. Argument, that the Unction in confirmation is more excellent than Baptism. Answer.
11. Answer continued. Argument, that confirmation has greater virtue.
12. Argument from the practice of antiquity. Augustine's view of confirmation.
13. The ancient confirmation very praiseworthy. Should be restored in churches in the present day.
14. Of Penitence. Confused and absurd language of the Popish doctors. Imposition of hands in ancient times. This made by the Papists a kind of foundation of the sacrament of Penance.
15. Disagreement among Papists themselves, as to the grounds on which penance is regarded as a sacrament.
16. More plausibility in calling the absolution of the priest, than in calling penance a sacrament.
17. Penance not truly a sacrament. Baptism the sacrament of penitence.
18. Extreme Unction described. No foundation for it in the words of James.
19. No better ground for making this unction a sacrament, than any of the other symbols mentioned in Scripture.
20. Insult offered by this unction to the Holy Spirit. It cannot be a sacrament, as it was not instituted by Christ, and has no promise annexed to it.
21. No correspondence between the unction enjoined by James and the anointing of the Papists.
22. Of ecclesiastical orders. Two points for discussion. Absurdities here introduced. Whether ecclesiastical order is a sacrament. Papists not agreed as to holy orders.
23. Insult to Christ in attempting to make him their colleague.
24. The greater part of these orders empty names implying no certain office. Popish exorcists.
25. Absurdity of the tonsure.

26. The Judaizing nature of the tonsure. Why Paul shaved his head in consequence of a vow.
27. Origin of this clerical tonsure as given by Augustine. Absurd ceremonies in consecrating Doorkeepers, Readers, Exorcists, and Acolytes.
28. Of the higher class of orders called Holy Orders. Insult offered to Christ when ministers are regarded as priests. Holy orders have nothing of the nature of a sacrament.
29. Absurd imitation of our Saviour in breathing on his apostles.
30. Absurdity of the anointing employed.
31. Imposition of hands. Absurdity of, in Papistical ordination.
32. Ordination of deacons. Absurd forms of Papists.
33. Of sub-deacons.
34. Marriage not a sacrament.
35. Nothing in Scripture to countenance the idea that marriage is a sacrament.
36. Origin of the notion that marriage is a sacrament.
37. Practical abuses from this erroneous idea of marriage. Conclusion.

1. THE above discourse concerning the sacraments might have the effect, among the docile and sober-minded, of preventing them from indulging their curiosity, or from embracing, without authority from the word, any other sacraments than those two, which they know to have been instituted by the Lord. But since the idea of seven sacraments, almost common in the mouths of all, and circulated in all schools and sermons, by mere antiquity, has struck its roots, and is even now seated in the minds of men, I thought it might be worth while to give a separate and closer consideration of the other five, which are vulgarly classed with the true and genuine sacraments of the Lord, and, after wiping away every gloss, to hold them up to the view of the simple, that they may see what their true nature is, and how falsely they have hitherto been regarded as sacraments. Here, at the outset, I would declare to all the pious, that I engage not in this dispute about a word for love of wrangling, but am induced, by weighty causes, to impugn the abuse of it. I am not unaware that Christians are the masters of words, as they are of all things, and that, therefore, they may at pleasure adapt words to things, provided a pious meaning is retained, though there should be some impropriety in the mode of expression. All this I concede, though it were better to make words subordinate to things than things to words. But in the name of sacrament, the case is different. For those who set down seven sacraments, at the same time give this definition to all—viz. that they are visible forms of invisible grace; and at the same time, make them all vehicles of the Holy Spirit, instruments for conferring righteousness, causes of procuring grace. Accordingly, the Master of Sentences himself denies that the sacraments of the Mosaic Law are properly called by this name, because they exhibited not what they figured. Is it tolerable, I ask, that the symbols which the Lord has consecrated with his own lips, which he has distinguished by excellent promises, should be regarded as no sacraments, and that, meanwhile, this honour should be transferred to those rites which men have either devised of themselves, or at least observe without any express command from God? Therefore, let them either change the definition, or refrain from this use of the word, which may after-

wards give rise to false and absurd opinions. Extreme unction, they say, is a figure and cause of invisible grace, because it is a sacrament. If we cannot possibly admit the inference, we must certainly meet them on the subject of the name, that we may not receive it on terms which may furnish occasion for such an error. On the other hand, when they prove it to be a sacrament, they add the reason, because it consists of the external sign and the word. If we find neither command nor promise, what else can we do than protest against it?

2. It now appears that we are not quarrelling about a word, but raising a not unnecessary discussion as to the reality. Accordingly, we most strenuously maintain what we formerly confirmed by invincible argument, that the power of instituting a sacrament belongs to God alone, since a sacrament ought, by the sure promise of God, to raise up and comfort the consciences of believers, which could never receive this assurance from men. A sacrament ought to be a testimony of the good-will of God toward us. Of this no man or angel can be witness, since God has no counsellor (Isa. xl. 13; Rom. xi. 34). He himself alone, with legitimate authority, testifies of himself to us by his word. A sacrament is a seal of attestation or promise of God. Now, it could not be sealed by corporeal things, or the elements of this world, unless they were confirmed and set apart for this purpose by the will of God. Man, therefore, cannot institute a sacrament, because it is not in the power of man to make such divine mysteries lurk under things so abject. The word of God must precede to make a sacrament to be a sacrament, as Augustine most admirably shows (Hom. in Joann. 80). Moreover, it is useful to keep up some distinction between sacraments and other ceremonies, if we would not fall into many absurdities. The apostles prayed on their bended knees; therefore our knees may not be bent without a sacrament (Acts ix. 20; xx. 36). The disciples are said to have prayed toward the east; thus looking at the east is a sacrament. Paul would have men in every place to lift up pure hands (1 Tim. ii. 8); and it is repeatedly stated that the saints prayed with uplifted hands, let the outstretching, therefore, of hands also become a sacrament; in short, let all the gestures of saints pass into sacraments, though I should not greatly object to this, provided it was not connected with those greater inconveniences.

3. If they would press us with the authority of the ancient Church, I say that they are using a gloss. This number seven is nowhere found in the ecclesiastical writers, nor is it well ascertained at what time it crept in. I confess, indeed, that they sometimes use freedom with the term *sacrament*, but what do they mean by it? all ceremonies, external writs, and exercises of piety. But when they speak of those signs which ought to be testimonies of the divine favour toward us, they are contented with those two, Baptism and the Eucharist. Lest any one suppose that this is falsely alleged by me, I will here give a few passages from Augustine. "First, I wish you to hold that the principle point in this discussion is, that our Lord Jesus

Christ (as he himself says in the gospel) has placed us under a yoke which is easy, and a burden which is light. Hence he has knit together the society of his new people by sacraments, very few in number, most easy of observance, and most excellent in meaning; such is baptism consecrated by the name of the Trinity: such is the communion of the body and blood of the Lord, and any other, if recommended in the canonical Scriptures" (August. ad. Januar. Ep. 118). Again, "After the resurrection of our Lord, our Lord himself, and apostolic discipline, appointed, instead of many, a few signs, and these most easy of performance, most august in meaning, most chaste in practice; such is baptism and the celebration of the body and blood of the Lord" (August. De. Doct. Christ. Lib. iii. cap. 9). Why does he here make no mention of the sacred number, I mean seven? Is it probable that he would have omitted it if it had then been established in the Church, especially seeing he is otherwise more curious in observing numbers than might be necessary? Nay, when he makes mention of Baptism and the Supper, and is silent as to others,[1] does he not sufficiently intimate that these two ordinances excel in special dignity, and that other ceremonies sink down to an inferior place? Wherefore, I say, that those sacramentary doctors are not only unsupported by the word of God, but also by the consent of the early Church, however much they may plume themselves on the pretence that they have this consent. But let us now come to particulars.

OF CONFIRMATION.[2]

4. It was anciently customary for the children of Christians, after they had grown up, to appear before the bishop to fulfil that duty which was required of such adults as presented themselves for baptism. These sat among the catechumens until they were duly instructed in the mysteries of the faith, and could make a confession of it before bishop and people. The infants, therefore, who had been initiated by baptism, not having then given a confession of faith to the Church, were again, toward the end of their boyhood, or on adolescence, brought forward by their parents, and were examined by the bishop in terms of the Catechism which was then in common use. In order that this act, which otherwise justly required to be grave and holy, might have more reverence and dignity, the ceremony of laying on of hands was also used. Thus the boy, on his faith being approved, was dismissed with a solemn blessing. Ancient writers often make mention of this custom. Pope Leo says (Ep. 39), "If any one returns from heretics, let him not be baptised

1 Ambros. de iis qui init. Mysteriis et de Sacrament.

2 Calv. adv. Concil. Trident. Præfat. in Catechis. Latinum. Viret. de Adulter. Sacrament. cap. 2–5.

again, but let that which was there wanting to him—viz. the virtue of the Spirit, be conferred by the laying on of the hands of the bishop." Our opponents will here exclaim, that the name of sacrament is justly given to that by which the Holy Spirit is conferred. But Leo elsewhere explains what he means by these words (Ep. 77); "Let not him who was baptised by heretics be rebaptised, but be confirmed by the laying on of hands with the invocation of the Holy Spirit, because he received only the form of baptism without sanctification." Jerome also mentions it (Contra Luciferian). Now though I deny not that Jerome is somewhat under delusion when he says that the observance is apostolical, he is, however, very far from the follies of these men. And he softens the expression when he adds, that this benediction is given to bishops only, more in honour of the priesthood than from any necessity of law. This laying on of hands, which is done simply by way of benediction, I commend, and would like to see restored to its pure use in the present day.

5. A later age having almost obliterated the reality, introduced a kind of fictitious confirmation as a divine sacrament. They feigned that the virtue of confirmation consisted in conferring the Holy Spirit, for increase of grace, on him who had been prepared in baptism for righteousness, and in confirming for contest those who in baptism were regenerated to life. This confirmation is performed by unction, and the following form of words: "I sign thee with the sign of the holy cross, and confirm thee with the chrism of salvation, in the name of the Father, and of the Son, and of the Holy Spirit." All fair and venerable. But where is the word of God which promises the presence of the Holy Spirit here? Not one iota can they allege. How will they assure us that their chrism is a vehicle of the Holy Spirit? We see oil, that is, a thick and greasy liquid, but nothing more. "Let the word be added to the element," says Augustine, "and it will become a sacrament." Let them, I say, produce this word if they would have us to see anything more in the oil than oil. But if they would show themselves to be ministers of the sacraments as they ought, there would be no room for further dispute. The first duty of a minister is not to do anything without a command. Come, then, and let them produce some command for this ministry, and I will not add a word. If they have no command, they cannot excuse their sacrilegious audacity. For this reason our Saviour interogated the Pharisees as to the baptism of John, "Was it from heaven, or of men?" (Matth. xxi. 25). If they had answered, Of men, he held them confessed that it was frivolous and vain; if Of heaven, they were forced to acknowledge the doctrine of John. Accordingly, not to be too contumelious to John, they did not venture to say that it was of men. Therefore, if confirmation is of men, it is proved to be frivolous and vain; if they would persuade us that it is of heaven, let them prove it.

6. They indeed defend themselves by the example of the apostles,

who, they presume, did nothing rashly. In this they are right, nor would they be blamed by us if they showed tnemselves to be imitators of the apostles. But what did the apostles do? Luke narrates (Acts viii. 15, 17), that the apostles who were at Jerusalem, when they heard that Samaria had received the word of God, sent thither Peter and John, that Peter and John prayed for the Samaritans, that they might receive the Holy Spirit, who had not yet come upon any of them, they having only been baptised in the name of Jesus; that after prayer they laid their hands upon them, and that by this laying on of hands the Samaritans received the Holy Spirit. Luke repeatedly mentions this laying on of hands. I hear what the apostles did, that is, they faithfully executed their ministry. It pleased the Lord that those visible and admirable gifts of the Holy Spirit, which he then poured out upon his people, should be administered and distributed by his apostles by the laying on of hands. I think that there was no deeper mystery under this laying on of hands, but I interpret that this kind of ceremony was used by them to intimate, by the outward act, that they commended to God, and, as it were, offered him on whom they laid hands. Did this ministry, which the apostles then performed, still remain in the Church, it would also behove us to observe the laying on of hands; but since that gift has ceased to be conferred, to what end is the laying on of hands? Assuredly the Holy Spirit is still present with the people of God; without his guidance and direction the Church of God cannot subsist. For we have a promise of perpetual duration, by which Christ invites the thirsty to come to him, that they may drink living water (John vii. 37). But those miraculous powers and manifest operations, which were distributed by the laying on of hands, have ceased. They were only for a time. For it was right that the new preaching of the gospel, the new kingdom of Christ, should be signalised and magnified by unwonted and unheard-of miracles. When the Lord ceased from these, he did not forthwith abandon his Church, but intimated that the magnificence of his kingdom, and the dignity of his word, had been sufficiently manifested. In what respect then can these stage-players say that they imitate the apostles? The object of the laying on of hands was, that the evident power of the Holy Spirit might be immediately exerted. This they effect not. Why then do they claim to themselves the laying on of hands, which is indeed said to have been used by the apostles, but altogether to a different end?

7. The same account is to be given were any one to insist that the breathing of our Lord upon his disciples (John xx. 22) is a sacrament by which the Holy Spirit is conferred. But the Lord did this once for all, and did not also wish us to do it. In the same way, also, the apostles laid their hands, agreeably to that time at which it pleased the Lord that the visible gifts of the Spirit should be dispensed in answer to their prayers; not that posterity might, as those apes do, mimic the empty and useless sign without the reality. But

if they prove that they imitate the apostles in the laying on of hands (though in this they have no resemblance to the apostles, except it be in manifesting some absurd false zeal),[1] where did they get their oil which they call the oil of salvation? Who taught them to seek salvation in oil? Who taught them to attribute to it the power of strengthening? Was it Paul, who draws us far away from the elements of this world, and condemns nothing more than clinging to such observances? This I boldly declare, not of myself, but from the Lord: Those who call oil the oil of salvation abjure the salvation which is in Christ, deny Christ, and have no part in the kingdom of God. Oil for the belly, and the belly for oil, but the Lord will destroy both. For all these weak elements, which perish even in the using, have nothing to do with the kingdom of God, which is spiritual, and will never perish. What, then, some one will say, do you apply the same rule to the water by which we are baptised, and the bread and wine under which the Lord's Supper is exhibited? I answer, that in the sacraments of divine appointment, two things are to be considered: the substance of the corporeal thing which is set before us, and the form which has been impressed upon it by the word of God, and in which its whole force lies. In as far, then, as the bread, wine, and water, which are presented to our view in the sacraments, retain their substance, Paul's declaration applies, "meats for the belly, and the belly for meats: but God shall destroy both it and them" (1 Cor. vi. 13). For they pass and vanish away with the fashion of this world. But in as far as they are sanctified by the word of God to be sacraments, they do not confine us to the flesh, but teach truly and spiritually.

8. But let us make a still closer inspection, and see how many monsters this greasy oil fosters and nourishes. Those anointers say that the Holy Spirit is given in baptism for righteousness, and in confirmation, for increase of grace, that in baptism we are regenerated for life, and in confirmation, equipped for contest. And, accordingly, they are not ashamed to deny that baptism can be duly completed without confirmation. How nefarious! Are we not, then, buried with Christ by baptism, and made partakers of his death, that we may also be partners of his resurrection? This fellowship with the life and death of Christ, Paul interprets to mean the mortification of our flesh, and the quickening of the Spirit, our old man being crucified in order that we may walk in newness of life (Rom vi. 6). What is it to be equipped for contest, if this is not? But if they deemed it as nothing to trample on the word of God, why did they not at least reverence the Church, to which they would be thought to be in everything so obedient? What heavier charge can be brought against their doctrine than the decree of the Council of

[1] French, "en laquelle toutesfois ils n'ont rien semblable a eux, sinon une folle et perverse singerie;—in which, however, they have nothing like them but a foolish and perverse aping.

Melita?[1] "Let him who says that baptism is given for the remission of sins only, and not in aid of future grace, be anathema." When Luke, in the passage which we have quoted, says, that the Samaritans were only "baptised in the name of the Lord Jesus" (Acts viii. 16), but had not received the Holy Spirit, he does not say absolutely that those who believed in Christ with the heart, and confessed him with the mouth, were not endued with any gift of the Spirit. He means that receiving of the Spirit by which miraculous power and visible graces were received. Thus the apostles are said to have received the Spirit on the day of Pentecost (Acts ii. 4), whereas Christ had long before said to them, "It is not ye that speak, but the Spirit of your Father which speaketh in you" (Matth. x. 20). Ye who are of God see the malignant and pestiferous wile of Satan. What was truly given in baptism, is falsely said to be given in the confirmation of it, that he may stealthily lead away the unwary from baptism. Who can now doubt that this doctrine, which dissevers the proper promises of baptism from baptism, and transfers them elsewhere, is a doctrine of Satan? We have discovered on what foundation this famous unction rests. The word of God says, that as many as have been baptised into Christ, have put on Christ with his gifts (Gal. iii. 27). The word of the anointers says that they received no promise in baptism to equip them for contest (De Consecr. Dist. 5, cap. Spir. Sanct). The former is the word of truth, the latter must be the word of falsehood. I can define this baptism more truly than they themselves have hitherto defined it—viz. that it is a noted insult to baptism, the use of which it obscures—nay, abolishes: that it is a false suggestion of the devil, which draws us away from the truth of God; or, if you prefer it, that it is oil polluted with a lie of the devil, deceiving the minds of the simple by shrouding them, as it were, in darkness.

9. They add, moreover, that all believers ought, after baptism, to receive the Holy Spirit by the laying on of hands, that they may become complete Christians, inasmuch as there never can be a Christian who has not been *chrismed* by episcopal confirmation. These are their exact words.[2] I thought that everything pertaining to Christianity was prescribed and contained in Scripture. Now I see that the true form of religion must be sought and learned elsewhere than in Scripture. Divine wisdom, heavenly truth, the whole doctrine of Christ, only begins the Christian; it is the oil that perfects him. By this sentence are condemned all the apostles and the many martyrs who, it is absolutely certain, were never chrismed, the oil not yet being made, besmeared with which, they might fufil all the parts of Christianity, or rather become Christians, which, as yet, they were not. Though I were silent, they abundantly refute themselves. How small the proportion of the people whom they anoint after baptism! Why, then, do they allow among their flock so many

[1] The French adds, "du temps de Sainct Augustin;"—of the time of St Augustine.
[2] De Consecr. Dist. 5, Concil. Aurel. cap. Ut Jejuni de Consecr. Dist. 5.

half Christians, whose imperfection they might easily remedy? Why, with such supine negligence, do they allow them to omit what cannot be omitted without grave offence? Why do they not more rigidly insist on a matter so necessary, that, without it, salvation cannot be obtained unless, perhaps, when the act has been anticipated by sudden death? When they allow it to be thus licentiously despised, they tacitly confess that it is not of the importance which they pretend.

10. Lastly, they conclude that this sacred unction is to be held in greater veneration than baptism, because the former is specially administered by the higher order of priests, whereas the latter is dispensed in common by all priests whatever (Distinct. 5, De his vero). What can you here say, but that they are plainly mad in thus pluming themselves on their own inventions, while, in comparison with these, they carelessly contemn the sacred ordinances of God? Sacrilegious mouth! dare you oppose oil merely polluted with your lewd breath, and charmed by your muttered words, to the sacrament of Christ, and compare it with water sanctified by the word of God? But even this was not enough for your improbity: you must also prefer it. Such are the responses of the holy see, such the oracles of the apostolic tripod. But some of them have begun to moderate this madness, which, even in their own opinion, was carried too far (Lombard. Sent. Lib. iv. Dist. 7, c. 2). It is to be held in greater veneration, they say, not perhaps because of the greater virtue and utility which it confers, but because it is given by more dignified persons, and in a more dignified part of the body, the forehead; or because it gives a greater increase of virtue, though baptism is more effectual for forgiveness. But do they not, by their first reason, prove themselves to be Donatists, who estimate the value of the sacrament by the dignity of the minister? Grant, however, that confirmation may be called more dignified from the dignity of the bishop's hand, still should any one ask how this great perrogative was conferred on the bishops, what reason can they give but their own caprice? The right was used only by the apostles, who alone dispensed the Holy Spirit. Are bishops alone apostles? Are they apostles at all? However, let us grant this also; why do they not, on the same grounds, maintain that the sacrament of blood in the Lord's Supper is to be touched only by bishops? Their reason for refusing it to laics is, that it was given by our Lord to the apostles only. If to the apostles only, why not infer then to bishops only? But in that place, they make the apostles simple Presbyters, whereas here another vertigo seizes them, and they suddenly elect them bishops. Lastly, Ananias was not an apostle, and yet Paul was sent to him to receive his sight, to be baptised and filled with the Holy Spirit (Acts ix. 17). I will add, though cumulatively, if, by divine right, this office was peculiar to bishops, why have they dared to transfer it to plebeian Presbyters, as we read in one of the Epistles of Gregory? (Dist. 95, cap. Pervenis).

11. How frivolous, inept, and stolid the other reason, that their confirmation is worthier than the baptism of God, because in confirmation it is the forehead that is besmeared with oil, and in baptism the cranium. As if baptism were performed with oil, and not with water! I take all the pious to witness, whether it be not the one aim of these miscreants to adulterate the purity of the sacraments by their leaven. I have said elsewhere, that what is of God in the sacraments, can scarcely be got a glimpse of among the crowd of human inventions. If any did not then give me credit for the fact, let them now give it to their own teachers. Here, passing over water, and making it of no estimation, they set a great value on oil alone in baptism. We maintain, against them, that in baptism also the forehead is sprinkled with water, in comparison with which, we do not value your oil one straw, whether in baptism or in confirmation. But if any one alleges that oil is sold for more, I answer, that by this accession of value any good which might otherwise be in it is vitiated, so far is it from being lawful fraudulently to vend this most vile imposture. They betray their impiety by the third reason, when they pretend that a greater increase of virtue is conferred in confirmation than in baptism. By the laying on of hands the apostles dispensed the visible gifts of the Spirit. In what respect does the oil of these men prove its fecundity? But have done with these guides, who cover one sacrilege with many acts of sacrilege. It is a Gordian knot, which it is better to cut than to lose so much labour in untying.

12. When they see that the word of God, and everything like plausible argument, fail them, they pretend, as usual, that the observance is of the highest antiquity, and is confirmed by the consent of many ages. Even were this true, they gain nothing by it. A sacrament is not of earth, but of heaven; not of men, but of God only. They must prove God to be the author of their confirmation, if they would have it to be regarded as a sacrament. But why obtrude antiquity, seeing that ancient writers, whenever they would speak precisely, nowhere mention more than two sacraments? Were the bulwark of our faith to be sought from men, we have an impregnable citadel in this, that the fictitious sacraments of these men were never recognised as sacraments by ancient writers. They speak of the laying on of hands, but do they call it a sacrament? Augustine distinctly affirms that it is nothing but prayer (De Bapt. cont. Donat. Lib. iii. cap. 16). Let them not here yelp out one of their vile distinctions, that the laying on of hands to which Augustine referred was not the confirmatory, but the curative or reconciliatory. His book is extant and in men's hands; if I wrest it to any meaning different from that which Augustine himself wrote it, they are welcome not only to load me with reproaches after their wonted manner, but to spit upon me. He is speaking of those who returned from schism to the unity of the Church. He says that they have no need of a repetition of baptism, for the laying on of hands is sufficient, that the Lord may bestow the Holy Spirit upon them by the bond of

peace. But as it might seem absurd to repeat laying on of hands more than baptism, he shows the difference: "What," he asks, "is the laying on of hands but prayer over the man?" That this is his meaning is apparent from another passage, where he says, "Because of the bond of charity, which is the greatest gift of the Holy Spirit, without which all the other holy qualities which a man may possess are ineffectual for salvation, the hand is laid on reformed heretics" (Lib. v. cap. 23).

13. I wish we could retain the custom, which, as I have observed, existed in the early Church, before this abortive mask of a sacrament appeared. It would not be such a confirmation as they pretend, one which cannot even be named without injury to baptism, but catechising by which those in boyhood, or immediately beyond it, would give an account of their faith in the face of the Church. And the best method of catechising would be, if a form were drawn up for this purpose, containing, and briefly explaining, the substance of almost all the heads of our religion, in which the whole body of the faithful ought to concur without controversy. A boy of ten years of age would present himself to the Church, to make a profession of faith, would be questioned on each head, and give answers to each. If he was ignorant of any point, or did not well understand it, he would be taught. Thus, while the whole Church looked on and witnessed, he would profess the one true sincere faith with which the body of the faithful, with one accord, worship one God. Were this discipline in force in the present day, it would undoubtedly whet the sluggishness of certain parents, who carelessly neglect the instruction of their children, as if it did not at all belong to them, but who could not then omit it without public disgrace; there would be greater agreement in faith among the Christian people, and not so much ignorance and rudeness; some persons would not be so readily carried away by new and strange dogmas; in fine, it would furnish all with a methodical arrangement of Christian doctrine.

OF PENITENCE.

14. The next place they give to Penitence, of which they discourse so confusedly and unmethodically, that consciences cannot derive anything certain or solid from their doctrine. In another place (Book III. chap. iii. and iv.), we have explained at length, first, what the Scriptures teach concerning repentance, and, secondly, what these men teach concerning it. All we have now to advert to is the grounds of that opinion of it as a sacrament which has long prevailed in schools and churches. First, however, I will speak briefly of the rite of the early Church, which those men have used as a pretext for establishing their fiction. By the order observed in public repentance, those who had performed the satisfactions imposed upon them were reconciled by the formal laying on of hands. This was

the symbol of absolution by which the sinner himself regained his confidence of pardon before God, and the Church was admonished to lay aside the remembrance of the offence, and kindly receive him into favour. This Cyprian often terms *to give peace.* In order that the act might have more weight and estimation with the people, it was appointed that the authority of the bishop should always be interposed. Hence the decree of the second Council of Carthage, "No presbyter may publicly at mass reconcile a penitent;" and another, of the Council of Arausica, "Let those who are departing this life, at the time of penitence, be admitted to communion without the reconciliatory laying on of hands; if they recover from the disease, let them stand in the order of penitents, and after they have fulfilled their time, receive the reconciliatory laying on of hands from the bishop." Again, in the third Council of Carthage, "A presbyter may not reconcile a penitent without the authority of the bishop." The object of all these enactments was to prevent the strictness, which they wished to be observed in that matter, from being lost by excessive laxity. Accordingly, they wished cognisance to be taken by the bishop, who, it was probable, would be more circumspect in examining. Although Cyprian somewhere says that not the bishop only laid hands, but also the whole clergy. For he thus speaks, "They do penitence for a proper time; next they come to communion, and receive the right of communion by the laying on of the hands of the bishop and clergy" (Lib. iii. Ep 14). Afterwards, in process of time, the matter came to this, that they used the ceremony in private absolutions also without public penitence. Hence the distinction in Gratian (Decret. 26, Quæst. 6) between public and private reconciliation. I consider that ancient observance of which Cyprian speaks to have been holy and salutary to the Church, and I could wish it restored in the present day. The more modern form, though I dare not disapprove, or at least strongly condemn, I deem to be less necessary. Be this as it may, we see that the laying on of hands in penitence was a ceremony ordained by men, not by God, and is to be ranked among indifferent things, and external exercises, which indeed are not to be despised, but occupy an inferior place to those which have been recommended to us by the word of the Lord.

15. The Romanists and Schoolmen, whose wont it is to corrupt all things by erroneous interpretation, anxiously labour to find a sacrament here, and it cannot seem wonderful, for they seek a thing where it is not. At best, they leave the matter involved, undecided, uncertain, confused, and confounded by the variety of opinions. Accordingly, they say (Sent. Lib. iv. Dist. 22, cap. 3), either that external penitence is a sacrament, and, if so, ought to be regarded as a sign of internal penitence; *i. e.*, contrition of heart, which will be the matter of the sacrament, or that both together make a sacrament, not two, but one complete; but that the external is the sacrament merely, the internal, the matter, and the sacrament, whereas the

forgiveness of sins is the matter only, and not the sacrament. Let those who remember the definition of a sacrament, which we have given above, test by it that which they say is a sacrament, and it will be found that it is not an external ceremony appointed by God for the confirmation of our faith. But if they allege that my definition is not a law which they are necessarily bound to obey, let them hear Augustine, whom they pretend to regard as a saint.[1] "Visible sacraments were instituted for the sake of carnal men, that by the ladder of sacraments they may be conveyed from those things which are seen by the eye, to those which are perceived by the understanding" (August. Quæst. Vet. Test. Lib. iii). Do they themselves see, or can they show to others, anything like this in that which they call the sacrament of penance? In another passage, he says, "It is called a sacrament, because in it one thing is seen, another thing is understood. What is seen has bodily appearance, what is understood has spiritual fruit" (Serm. de Bapt. Infant). These things in no way apply to the sacrament of penance, as they feign it; there, there is no bodily form to represent spiritual fruit.

16. And (to despatch these beasts in their own arena) if any sacrament is sought here, would it not have been much more plausible to maintain that the absolution of the priest is a sacrament, than penitence either external or internal? For it might obviously have been said that it is a ceremony to confirm our faith in the forgiveness of sins, and that it has the promise of the keys, as they describe them: "Whatsoever ye shall bind or loose on earth, shall be bound or loosed in heaven." But some one will object that to most of those who are absolved by priests nothing of the kind is given by the absolution, whereas, according to their dogma, the sacraments of the new dispensation ought to effect what they figure. This is ridiculous. As in the eucharist, they make out a twofold eating—a sacramental, which is common to the good and bad alike, and a spiritual, which is proper only to the good; why should they not also pretend that absolution is given in two ways? And yet I have never been able to understand what they meant by their dogma. How much it is at variance with the truth of God, we showed when we formally discussed that subject. Here I only wish to show that no scruple should prevent them from giving the name of a sacrament to the absolution of the priest. For they might have answered by the mouth of Augustine,[2] that there is a sanctification without a visible sacrament, and a visible sacrament without internal sanctification. Again, that in the elect alone sacraments effect what they figure. Again, that some put on Christ so far as the receiving of the sacrament, and others so far as sanctification; that the former is done equally by the good and the bad, the latter by the good only. Surely they were more deluded than children, and blind in the full light of the sun when

1 French, "Auquel ils font semblant de porter une reverence inviolable;"—for whom they pretend to have an inviolable respect.

2 August. Quæst. Vet. Test. Lib. iii. De Bapt. Parvul. De Bapt. Cont. Donat. Lib. v

they toiled with so much difficulty, and perceived not a matter so plain and obvious to every man.

17. Lest they become elated, however, whatever be the part in which they place the sacrament, I deny that it can justly be regarded as a sacrament; first, because there exists not to this effect any special promise of God, which is the only ground of a sacrament;[1] and, secondly, because whatever ceremony is here used is a mere invention of man; whereas, as has already been shown, the ceremonies of sacraments can only be appointed by God. Their fiction of the sacrament of penance, therefore, was falsehood and imposture. This fictitious sacrament they adorned with the befitting eulogium, that it was the second plank in the case of shipwreck, because if any one had, by sin, injured the garment of innocence received in baptism, he might repair it by penitence.[2] This was a saying of Jerome. Let it be whose it may, as it is plainly impious, it cannot be excused if understood in this sense; as if baptism were effaced by sin, and were not rather to be recalled to the mind of the sinner whenever he thinks of the forgiveness of sins, that he may thereby recollect himself, regain courage, and be confirmed in the belief that he shall obtain the forgiveness of sins which was promised him in baptism. What Jerome said harshly and improperly—viz. that baptism, which is fallen from by those who deserve to be excommunicated from the Church, is repaired by penitence, these worthy expositors wrest to their own impiety. You will speak most correctly, therefore, if you call baptism the sacrament of penitence, seeing it is given to those who aim at repentance to confirm their faith and seal their confidence. But lest you should think this our invention, it appears, that besides being conformable to the words of Scripture, it was generally regarded in the early Church as an indubitable axiom. For in the short Treatise on Faith addressed to Peter, and bearing the name of Augustine, it is called, *The sacrament of faith and repentance.* But why have recourse to doubtful writings, as if anything can be required more distinct than the statement of the Evangelist, that John preached "the baptism of repentance for the remission of sins"? (Mark i. 4; Luke iii. 3).

1 The French adds, "Car, comme nous avons assez declairé ci dessus, la promesse des clefs n'appartient nullement a faire quelque estat particulier d'absolution, mais seulement à la predication de l'Evangile soit qu'elle soit faite ou a plusieurs, ou a un seul, sans y mettre difference; c'est a dire, que par icelle promesse notre Seigneur ne fonde point une absolution speciale qui soit faite distinctement à un chacun mais celle qui se fait indifferement a tous pecheurs, sans addresse particuliere."—For, as we have sufficiently shown above, the promise of the keys pertains not to the making of any particular state of absolution, but only to the preaching of the Gospel, whether it is made to several or to one only, without making any difference; that is to say, that by this promise our Lord does not found a special absolution which is given separately to each, but one which is given indifferently to all sinners, without particular application.

2 Sent. Lib. iv. Dist. 14, cap. 1. De Pœnit. Dist. 1, cap. 2. August. Dictum in Decret. 15. Quæst. 1, Cap. Fermissime.

OF EXTREME UNCTION, SO CALLED.

18. The third fictitious sacrament is Extreme Unction, which is performed only by a priest, and, as they express it, *in extremis*, with oil consecrated by the bishop, and with this form of words, "By this holy unction, and his most tender mercy, may God forgive you whatever sin you have committed, by the eye, the ear, the smell, the touch, the taste" (see Calv. Epist. de Fugiend. Illicit. Sac.). They pretend that there are two virtues in it—the forgiveness of sins, and relief of bodily disease, if so expedient; if not expedient, the salvation of the soul. For they say, that the institution was set down by James, whose words are, "Is any sick among you? let him send for the elders of the Church; and let them pray over him, anointing him with oil in the name of the Lord; and the prayer of faith shall save the sick, and the Lord shall raise him up: and if he have committed sins, they shall be forgiven him" (James v. 14). The same account is here to be given of this unction as we lately gave of the laying on of hands; in other words, it is mere hypocritical stage-play, by which, without reason or result, they would resemble the apostles. Mark relates that the apostles, on their first mission, agreeably to the command which they had received of the Lord, raised the dead, cast out devils, cleansed lepers, healed the sick, and, in healing, used oil. He says, they "anointed with oil many that were sick, and healed them" (Mark vi. 13). To this James referred when he ordered the presbyters of the Church to be called to anoint the sick. That no deeper mystery lay under this ceremony will easily be perceived by those who consider how great liberty both our Lord and his apostles used in those external things.[1] Our Lord, when about to give sight to the blind man, spat on the ground, and made clay of the spittle; some he cured by a touch, others by a word. In like manner the apostles cured some diseases by word only, others by touch, others by anointing. But it is probable that neither this anointing nor any of the other things were used at random. I admit this; not, however, that they were instruments of the cure, but only symbols to remind the ignorant whence this great virtue proceeded, and prevent them from ascribing the praise to the apostles. To designate the Holy Spirit and his gifts by oil is trite and common (Ps. xlv. 8). But the gift of hearing disappeared with the other miraculous powers which the Lord was pleased to give for a time, that it might render the new preaching of the gospel for ever wonderful. Therefore, even were we to grant that anointing was a sacrament of those powers which were then administered by the hands of the apostles, it pertains not to us, to whom no such powers have been committed.

19. And what better reason have they for making a sacrament of

[1] John ix. 6; Matth. ix. 29; Luke xviii. 42: Acts iii. 6; v. 16; xix. 12.

this unction, than of any of the other symbols which are mentioned in Scripture? Why do they not dedicate some pool of Siloam, into which, at certain seasons the sick may plunge themselves? That, they say, were done in vain. Certainly not more in vain than unction. Why do they not lay themselves on the dead, seeing that Paul, in raising up the dead youth, lay upon him? Why is not clay made of dust and spittle a sacrament? The other cases were special, but this is commanded by James. In other words, James spake agreeably to the time when the Church still enjoyed this blessing from God. They affirm, indeed, that there is still the same virtue in their unction, but we experience differently. Let no man now wonder that they have with so much confidence deluded souls, which they knew to be stupid and blind, because deprived of the word of God, that is, of his light and life, seeing they blush not to attempt to deceive the bodily perceptions of those who are alive, and have all their senses about them. They make themselves ridiculous, therefore, by pretending that they are endued with the gift of healing. The Lord, doubtless, is present with his people in all ages, and cures their sicknesses as often as there is need, not less than formerly; and yet he does not exert those manifest powers, nor dispense miracles by the hands of apostles, because that gift was temporary, and owing, in some measure, to the ingratitude of men, immediately ceased.

20. Wherefore, as the apostles, not without cause, openly declared, by the symbol of oil, that the gift of healing committed to them was not their own, but the power of the Holy Spirit; so, on the other hand, these men insult the Holy Spirit by making his power consist in a filthy oil of no efficacy. It is just as if one were to say that all oil is the power of the Holy Spirit, because it is called by that name in Scripture, and that every dove is the Holy Spirit, because he appeared in that form. Let them see to this: it is sufficient for us that we perceive, with absolute certainty, that their unction is no sacrament, as it is neither a ceremony appointed by God, nor has any promise. For when we require, in a sacrament, these two things, that it be a ceremony appointed by God, and have a promise from God, we at the same time demand that that ceremony be delivered to us, and that that promise have reference to us. No man contends that circumcision is now a sacrament of the Christian Church, although it was both an ordinance of God, and had his promise annexed to it, because it was neither commanded to us, nor was the promise annexed to it given us on the same condition. The promise of which they vaunt so much in unction, as we have clearly demonstrated, and they themselves show by experience, has not been given to us. The ceremony behoved to be used only by those who had been endued with the gift of healing, not by those murderers, who do more by slaying and butchering than by curing.

21. Even were it granted that this precept of unction, which has nothing to do with the present age, were perfectly adapted to it, they

will not even thus have advanced much in support of their unction, with which they have hitherto besmeared us. James would have all the sick to be anointed: these men besmear, with their oil, not the sick, but half-dead carcasses, when life is quivering on the lips, or, as they say, *in extremis.* If they have a present cure in their sacrament, with which they can either alleviate the bitterness of disease, or at least give some solace to the soul, they are cruel in never curing in time. James would have the sick man to be anointed by the elders of the Church. They admit no anointer but a priestling. When they interpret the elders of James to be priests, and allege that the plural number is used for honour, the thing is absurd; as if the Church had at that time abounded with swarms of priests, so that they could set out in long procession, bearing a dish of sacred oil. James, in ordering simply that the sick be anointed, seems to me to mean no other anointing than that of common oil, nor is any other mentioned in the narrative of Mark. These men deign not to use any oil but that which has been consecrated by a bishop, that is warmed with much breath, charmed by much muttering, and saluted nine times on bended knee, Thrice Hail, holy oil! thrice Hail, holy chrism! thrice Hail, holy balsam! From whom did they derive these exorcisms? James says, that when the sick man shall have been anointed with oil, and prayer shall have been made over him, if he have committed sins, they shall be forgiven him—viz. that his guilt being forgiven, he shall obtain a mitigation of the punishment, not meaning that sins are effaced by oil, but that the prayers by which believers commended their afflicted brother to God would not be in vain. These men are impiously false in saying that sins are forgiven by their sacred, that is, abominable unction. See how little they gain, even when they are allowed to abuse the passage of James as they list. And to save us the trouble of a laborious proof, their own annals relieve us from all difficulty; for they relate that Pope Innocent, who presided over the church of Rome in the age of Augustine, ordained, that not elders only, but all Christians, should use oil in anointing, in their own necessity, or in that of their friends.[1] Our authority for this is Sigebert, in his Chronicles.

OF ECCLESIASTICAL ORDERS.

22. The fourth place in their catalogue is held by the sacrament of Orders, one so prolific, as to beget of itself seven lesser sacraments. It is very ridiculous that, after affirming that there are seven sacraments, when they begin to count, they make out thirteen. It cannot be alleged that they are one sacrament, because they all tend to one priesthood, and are a kind of steps to the same thing. For while it is certain that the ceremonies in each are different, and they them-

1 The French adds, "Comment accorderont ils cela avec ce qu'ils veulent faire accroire"?—How will they reconcile this with what they wish to be believed?

selves say that the graces are different, no man can doubt that if their dogmas are admitted, they ought to be called seven sacraments. And why debate it as a doubtful matter, when they themselves plainly and distinctly declare that they are seven? First, then, we shall glance at them in passing, and show to how many absurdities they introduce us when they would recommend their orders to us as sacraments; and, secondly, we shall see whether the ceremony which churches use in ordaining ministers ought at all to be called a sacrament. They make seven ecclesiastical orders, or degrees, which they distinguish by the title of a sacrament. These are Doorkeepers, Readers, Exorcists, Acolytes, Subdeacons, Deacons, and Priests. And they say that they are seven, because of the seven kinds of graces of the Holy Spirit with which those who are promoted to them ought to be endued. This grace is increased and more liberally accumulated on promotion. The mere number has been consecrated by a perversion of Scripture, because they think they read in Isaiah that there are seven gifts of the Holy Spirit, whereas truly not more than six are mentioned by Isaiah, who, however, meant not to include all in that passage. For, in other passages are mentioned the spirit of life, of sanctification, of the adoption of sons, as well as there, the spirit of wisdom and understanding, the spirit of counsel and might, the spirit of knowledge, and of the fear of the Lord.[1] Although others who are more acute make not seven orders, but nine, in imitation, as they say, of the Church triumphant. But among these, also, there is a contest; because some insist that the clerical tonsure is the first order of all, and the episcopate the last; while others, excluding the tonsure, class the office of archbishop among the orders. Isiodorus distinguishes differently, for he makes Psalmists and Readers different.[2] To the former, he gives the charge of chanting; to the latter, that of reading the Scriptures for the instruction of the common people. And this distinction is observed by the canons. In this great variety, what would they have us to follow or to avoid? Shall we say that there are seven orders? So the master of the school teaches, but the most illuminated doctors determine otherwise. On the other hand, they are at variance among themselves. Besides, the most sacred canons call us in a different direction. Such, indeed, is the concord of men when they discuss divine things apart from the word of God.

23. But the crowning folly of all is, that in each of these they make Christ their colleague. First, they say[3] he performed the office of Doorkeeper when, with a whip of small cords, he drove the buyers and sellers from the temple. He intimates that he is a Doorkeeper when he says, "I am the door." He assumed the office of Reader,

1 Isa. xi. 2; Ezek. i. 20; Rom. i. 4; viii. 15.

2 Isidor. Lib. vii., Etymolog. allegatim, cap. Cleros. Dist. 21, 33, cap. Lector, et cap. Ostier.

3 John ii. 15; x. 7; Luke iv. 17; Matth. vii. 33; John viii. 12; xiii. 5; Matth. xxvi. 26; xxvii. 50.

when he read Isaiah in the synagogue. He performed the office of Exorcist when, touching the tongue and ears of the deaf and dumb man with spittle, he restored his hearing. He declared that he was an Acolyte by the words, "He that followeth me shall not walk in darkness." He performed the office of Subdeacon, when, girding himself with a towel, he washed the feet of his disciples. He acted the part of a Deacon, when he distributed his body and blood in the Supper. He performed the part of a Priest, when, on the cross, he offered himself in sacrifice to the Father. As these things cannot be heard without laughter, I wonder how they could have been written without laughter, if, indeed, they were men who wrote them. But their most noteable subtlety is that in which they speculate on the name of Acolyte, calling him Ceroferarius—a magical term, I presume, one certainly unknown to all nations and tongues; ἀκόλουθος, in Greek, meaning simply *attendant*. Were I to stop and seriously refute these things, I might myself justly be laughed at, so frivolous are they and ludicrous.

24. Still, lest they should be able to impose on silly women, their vanity must be exposed in passing. With great pomp and solemnity they elect their readers, psalmists, doorkeepers, acolytes, to perform those services which they give in charge, either to boys, or at least to those whom they call laics. Who, for the most part, lights the tapers, who pours wine and water from the pitcher, but a boy or some mean person among laics, who gains his bread by so doing? Do not the same persons chant? Do they not open and shut the doors of Churches? Who ever saw, in their churches, either an acolyte or doorkeeper performing his office? Nay, when he who as a boy performed the office of acolyte, is admitted to the order of acolyte, he ceases to be the very thing he begins to be called, so that they seem professedly to wish to cast away the office when they assume the title. See why they hold it necessary to be consecrated by sacraments, and to receive the Holy Spirit! It is just to do nothing. If they pretend that this is the defect of the times, because they neglect and abandon their offices, let them, at the same time, confess that there is not in the Church, in the present day, any use or benefit of these sacred orders which they wondrously extol, and that their whole Church is full of anathema, since the tapers and flagons, which none are worthy to touch but those who have been consecrated acolytes, she allows to be handled by boys and profane persons; since her chants, which ought to be heard only from consecrated lips, she delegates to children. And to what end, pray, do they consecrate exorcists? I hear that the Jews had their exorcists, but I see they were so called from the exorcisms which they practised (Acts xix. 13). Who ever heard of those fictitious exorcists having given one specimen of their profession? It is pretended that power has been given them to lay their hands on energumens, catechumens, and demoniacs, but they cannot persuade demons that they are endued with such power, not only because demons do not

submit to their orders, but even command themselves. Scarcely will you find one in ten who is not possessed by a wicked spirit. All, then, which they babble about their paltry orders is a compound of ignorant and stupid falsehoods. Of the ancient acolytes, door-keepers, and readers, we have spoken when explaining the government of the Church. All that we here proposed was to combat that novel invention of a sevenfold sacrament in ecclesiastical orders of which we nowhere read except among silly raving Sorbonnists and Canonists.

25. Let us now attend to the ceremonies which they employ. And first, all whom they enrol among their militia they initiate into the clerical status by a common symbol. They shave them on the top of the head, that the crown may denote regal honour, because clergy ought to be kings in governing themselves and others. Peter thus speaks of them: "Ye are a chosen generation, a royal priesthood, a holy nation, a peculiar people" (1 Pet. ii. 9). But it was sacrilege in them to arrogate to themselves alone what is given to the whole Church, and proudly to glory in a title of which they had robbed the faithful. Peter addresses the whole Church: these men wrest it to a few shaven crowns, as if it had been said to them alone, Be ye holy: as if they alone had been purchased by the blood of Christ: as if they alone had been made by Christ kings and priests unto God. Then they assign other reasons (Sent. Lib. iv. Dist. 24). The top of the head is bared, that their mind may be shown to be free, with unveiled face, to behold the glory of God; or that they may be taught to cut off the vices of the eye and the lip. Or the shaving of the head is the laying aside of temporal things, while the circumference of the crown is the remnants of good which are retained for support. Everything is in figure, because forsooth, the veil of the temple is not yet rent. Accordingly, persuaded that they have excellently performed their part because they have figured such things by their crown, they perform none of them in reality. How long will they delude us with such masks and impostures? The clergy, by shaving off some hair, intimate (Sent. loco cit.) that they have cast away abundance of temporal good—that they contemplate the glory of God—that they have mortified concupiscence of the ear and the eye: but no class of men is more rapacious, more stupid, more libidinous. Why do they not rather exhibit true sanctity, than give a hypocritical semblance of it in false and lying signs?

26. Moreover, when they say that the clerical crown has its origin and nature from the Nazarenes, what else do they say than that their mysteries are derived from Jewish ceremonies, or rather are mere Judaism? When they add that Priscilla, Aquila, and Paul himself, after they had taken a vow, shaved their head that they might be purified, they betray their gross ignorance. For we nowhere read this of Priscilla, while, with regard to Aquila, it is uncertain, since that tonsure may refer equally well to Paul as to Aquila (Acts xviii.

18). But not to leave them in possession of what they ask—viz. that they have an example in Paul, it is to be observed, to the more simple, that Paul never shaved his head for any sanctification, but only in subservience to the weakness of brethren. Vows of this kind I am accustomed to call vows of charity, not of piety; in other words, vows not undertaken for divine worship, but only in deference to the infirmity of the weak, as he himself says, that to the Jews he became a Jew (1 Cor. ix. 20). This, therefore, he did, and that once and for a short time, that he might accommodate himself for a little to the Jews. When these men would, for no end, imitate the purifications of the Nazarenes (Num. vi. 18), what else do they than set up a new, while they improperly affect to rival the ancient Judaism? In the same spirit the Decretal Epistle was composed, which enjoins the clergy, after the apostle, not to nourish their hair, but to shave it all round (Cap. Prohibitur, Dist. 24); as if the apostle, in showing what is comely for all men, had been solicitous for the spherical tonsure of the clergy. Hence, let my readers consider what kind of force or dignity there can be in the subsequent mysteries, to which this is the introduction.

27. Whence the clerical tonsure had its origin, is abundantly clear from Augustine alone (De Opera. Monach. et Retract). While in that age none wore long hair but the effeminate, and those who affected an unmanly beauty and elegance, it was thought to be of bad example to allow the clergy to do so. They were therefore enjoined either to cut or shave their hair, that they might not have the appearance of effeminate indulgence. And so common was the practice, that some monks, to appear more sanctimonious than others by a notable difference in dress, let their locks hang loose.[1] But when hair returned to use, and some nations, which had always worn long hair, as France, Germany, and England, embraced Christianity, it is probable that the clergy everywhere shaved the head, that they might not seem to affect ornament. At length, in a more corrupt age, when all ancient customs were either changed, or had degenerated into superstition, seeing no reason for the clerical tonsure (they had retained nothing but a foolish imitation), they betook themselves to mystery, and now superstitiously obtrude it upon us in support of their sacrament. The Doorkeepers, on consecration, receive the keys of the Church, by which it is understood that the custody of it is committed to them; the Readers receive the Holy Bible; the Exorcists, forms of exorcism which they use over the possessed and catechumens; the Acolytes, tapers and the flagon. Such are the ceremonies which, it would seem, possess so much secret virtue, that they cannot only be signs and badges, but even causes of invisible grace. For this, according to their definition, they demand, when they would have them to be classed among sacraments. But to despatch the

1 The French adds, "Voila comment la tonsure n'estoit point une chose speciale aux clercs, mais estoit en usance quasi à tous."—See how the tonsure was not a thing peculiar to the clergy, but was used, as it were, by all.

matter in a few words, I say that it is absurd for schools and canons to make sacraments of those minor orders, since, even by the confession of those who do so, they were unknown to the primitive Church, and were devised many ages after. But sacraments as containing a divine promise ought not to be appointed, either by angels or men, but by God only, to whom alone it belongs to give the promise.

28. There remain the three orders which they call major. Of these, what they call the subdeaconate was transferred to this class, after the crowd of minor began to be prolific. But as they think they have authority for these from the word of God, they honour them specially with the name of Holy Orders. Let us see how they wrest the ordinances of God to their own ends. We begin with the order of presbyter or priest. To these two names they give one meaning, understanding by them, those to whom, as they say, it pertains to offer the sacrifice of Christ's body and blood on the altar, to frame prayers, and bless the gifts of God. Hence, at ordination, they receive the patena with the host, as symbols of the power conferred upon them of offering sacrifices to appease God, and their hands are anointed, this symbol being intended to teach that they have received the power of consecrating. But of the ceremonies afterwards. Of the thing itself, I say that it is so far from having, as they pretend, one particle of support from the word of God, that they could not more wickedly corrupt the order which he has appointed. And first, it ought to be held as confessed (this we maintained when treating of the Papal Mass), that all are injurious to Christ who call themselves priests in the sense of offering expiatory victims. He was constituted and consecrated Priest by the Father, with an oath, after the order of Melchisedek, without end and without successor (Psalm cx. 4; Heb. v. 6; vii. 3). He once offered a victim of eternal expiation and reconciliation, and now also having entered the sanctuary of heaven, he intercedes for us. In him we all are priests, but to offer praise and thanksgiving, in fine, ourselves, and all that is ours, to God. It was peculiar to him alone to appease God and expiate sins by his oblation. When these men usurp it to themselves, what follows, but that they have an impious and sacrilegious priesthood? It is certainly wicked over much to dare to distinguish it with the title of sacrament. In regard to the true office of presbyter, which was recommended to us by the lips of Christ, I willingly give it that place. For in it there is a ceremony which, first, is taken from the Scriptures; and, secondly, is declared by Paul to be not empty or superfluous, but to be a faithful symbol of spiritual grace (1 Tim. iv. 14). My reason for not giving a place to the third is, because it is not ordinary or common to all believers, but is a special rite for a certain function. But while this honour is attributed to the Christian ministry, Popish priests may not plume themselves upon it. Christ ordered dispensers of his gospel and his sacred mysteries to be ordained, not sacrificers to be inaugurated, and his command was to preach the gospel and feed the flock, not to immolate victims. He

promised the gift of the Holy Spirit, not to make expiation for sins, but duly to undertake and maintain the government of the Church (Matt. xxviii. 19; Mark xvi. 15; John xxi. 15).

29. With the reality the ceremonies perfectly agree. When our Lord commissioned the apostles to preach the gospel, he breathed upon them (John xx. 22). By this symbol he represented the gift of the Holy Spirit which he bestowed upon them. This breathing these worthy men have retained; and, as they were bringing the Holy Spirit from their throat, mutter over their priestlings, "Receive the Holy Spirit." Accordingly, they omit nothing which they do not preposterously mimic. I say not in the manner of players (who have art and meaning in their gestures), but like apes who imitate at random without selection. We observe, say they, the example of the Lord. But the Lord did many things which he did not intend to be examples to us. Our Lord said to his disciples, "Receive the Holy Spirit" (John xx. 22). He said also to Lazarus, "Lazarus, come forth" (John xi. 43). He said to the paralytic, "Rise, take up thy bed, and walk" (John v. 8). Why do they not say the same to all the dead and paralytic? He gave a specimen of his divine power when, in breathing on the apostles, he filled them with the gift of the Holy Spirit. If they attempt to do the same, they rival God, and do all but challenge him to the contest. But they are very far from producing the effect, and only mock Christ by that absurd gesture. Such, indeed, is the effrontery of some, that they dare to assert that the Holy Spirit is conferred by them; but what truth there is in this, we learn from experience, which cries aloud that all who are consecrated priests, of horses become asses, and of fools, madmen. And yet it is not here that I am contending against them; I am only condemning the ceremony itself, which ought not to be drawn into a precedent, since it was used as the special symbol of a miracle, so far is it from furnishing them with an example for imitation.

30. But from whom, pray, did they receive their unction? They answer, that they received it from the sons of Aaron, from whom also their order derived its origin (Sent. Lib. iv. Dist. 14, cap. 8, et in Canon. Dist. 21, cap. 1). Thus they constantly choose to defend themselves by perverse examples, rather than confess that any of their rash practices is of their own devising. Meanwhile, they observe not that in professing to be the successors of the sons of Aaron, they are injurious to the priesthood of Christ, which alone was adumbrated and typified by all ancient priesthoods. In him, therefore, they were all concluded and completed, in him they ceased, as we have repeatedly said, and as the Epistle to the Hebrews, unaided by any gloss, declares. But if they are so much delighted with Mosaic ceremonies, why do they not hurry oxen, calves, and lambs, to their sacrifices? They have, indeed, a great part of the ancient tabernacle, and of the whole Jewish worship. The only thing wanted to their religion is, that they do not sacrifice oxen and calves. Who sees not that this

practice of unction is much more pernicious than circumcision, especially when to it is added superstition and a Pharisaical opinion of the merit of the work? The Jews placed their confidence of justification in circumcision, these men look for spiritual gifts in unction. Therefore, in desiring to be rivals of the Levites, they become apostates from Christ, and discard themselves from the pastoral office.

31. It is, if you please, the sacred oil which impresses an indelible character. As if oil could not be washed away by sand and salt, or if it sticks the closer, with soap. But that character is spiritual. What has oil to do with the soul? Have they forgotten what they quote from Augustine, that if the word be withdrawn from the water, there will be nothing but water, but that it is owing to the word that it is a sacrament? What word can they show in their oil? Is it because Moses was commanded to anoint the sons of Aaron? (Exod. xxx. 30). But he there receives command concerning the tunic, the ephod, the breastplate, the mitre, the crown of holiness with which Aaron was to be adorned; and concerning the tunics, belts, and mitres which his sons were to wear. He receives command about sacrificing the calf, burning its fat, about cutting and burning rams, about sanctifying ear-rings and vestments with the blood of one of the rams, and innumerable other observances. Having passed over all these, I wonder why the unction of oil alone pleases them. If they delight in being sprinkled, why are they sprinkled with oil rather than with blood? They are attempting, forsooth, an ingenious device; they are trying, by a kind of patchwork, to make one religion out of Christianity, Judaism, and Paganism. Their unction, therefore, is without savour; it wants salt, that is, the word of God. There remains the laying on of hands, which, though I admit it to be a sacrament in true and legitimate ordination, I do deny to have any such place in this fable, where they neither obey the command of Christ, nor look to the end to which the promise ought to lead us. If they would not have the sign denied them, they must adapt it to the reality to which it is dedicated.

32. As to the order of the diaconate, I would raise no dispute, if the office which existed under the apostles, and a purer Church, were restored to its integrity. But what resemblance to it do we see in their fictitious deacons? I speak not of the men, lest they should complain that I am unjustly judging their doctrine by the vices of those who profess it; but I contend that those whom their doctrine declares to us, derive no countenance from those deacons whom the apostolic Church appointed. They say that it belongs to their deacons to assist the priests, and minister at all the things which are done in the sacraments, as in baptism, in chrism, the patena, and chalice, to bring the offerings and lay them on the altar, to prepare and dress the table of the Lord, to carry the cross, announce and read out the gospel and epistle to the people (Sent. Lib. iv. Dist. 24, cap. 8; Item, Cap. Perlectis, Dist. 25). Is there here one word about

the true office of deacon? Let us now attend to the appointment. The bishop alone lays hands on the deacon who is ordained; he places the prayer-book and stole upon his left shoulder, that he may understand that he has received the easy yoke of the Lord, in order that he may subject to the fear of the Lord every thing pertaining to the left side: he gives him a text of the gospel, to remind him that he is its herald. What have these things to do with deacons? But they act just as if one were to say he was ordaining apostles, when he was only appointing persons to kindle the incense, clean the images, sweep the churches, set traps for mice, and put out dogs. Who can allow this class of men to be called apostles, and to be compared with the very apostles of Christ? After this, let them not pretend that those whom they appoint to mere stage-play are deacons. Nay, they even declare, by the very name, what the nature of the office is. For they call them Levites, and wish to trace their nature and origin to the sons of Levi. As far as I am concerned, they are welcome, provided they do not afterwards deck themselves in borrowed feathers.

33. What use is there in speaking of subdeacons? For, whereas in fact they anciently had the charge of the poor, they attribute to them some kind of nugatory function, as carrying the chalice and patena, the pitcher with water, and the napkin to the altar, pouring out water for the hands, &c. Then, by the offerings which they are said to receive and bring in, they mean those which they swallow up, as if they had been destined to anathema. There is an admirable correspondence between the office and the mode of inducting to it—viz. receiving from the bishop the patena and chalice, and from the archdeacon the pitcher with water, the manual and trumpery of this kind. They call upon us to admit that the Holy Spirit is included in these frivolities. What pious man can be induced to grant this? But to have done at once, we may conclude the same of this as of the others, and there is no need to repeat at length what has been explained above. To the modest and docile (it is such I have undertaken to instruct), it will be enough that there is no sacrament of God, unless where a ceremony is shown annexed to a promise, or rather where a promise is seen in a ceremony. Here there is not one syllable of a certain promise, and it is vain, therefore, to seek for a ceremony to confirm the promise. On the other hand, we read of no ceremony appointed by God in regard to those usages which they employ, and, therefore, there can be no sacrament.

OF MARRIAGE.

The last of all is marriage, which, while all admit it to be an institution of God, no man ever saw to be a sacrament, until the time of Gregory. And would it ever have occurred to the mind of any sober man? It is a good and holy ordinance of God. And agriculture, architecture, shoemaking, and shaving, are lawful ordinances of God; but they are not sacraments. For in a sacrament, the thing required is not only that it be a work of God, but that it be an external ceremony appointed by God to confirm a promise. That there is nothing of the kind in marriage, even children can judge. But it is a sign, they say, of a sacred thing, that is, of the spiritual union of Christ with the Church. If by the term sign they understand a symbol set before us by God to assure us of our faith, they wander widely from the mark. If they mean merely a sign because it has been employed as a similitude, I will show how acutely they reason. Paul says, "One star differeth from another star in glory. So also is the resurrection of the dead" (1 Cor. xv. 41, 42). Here is one sacrament. Christ says, "The kingdom of heaven is like to a grain of mustard-seed" (Matth. xiii. 31). Here is another sacrament. Again, "The kingdom of heaven is like unto leaven" (Matth. xiii. 33). Here is a third sacrament. Isaiah says, "He shall feed his flock like a shepherd" (Isaiah xl. 11). Here is a fourth sacrament. In another passage he says, "The Lord shall go forth as a mighty man" (Isaiah xlii. 13). Here is a fifth sacrament. And where will be the end or limit? Everything in this way will be a sacrament. All the parables and similitudes in Scripture will be so many sacraments. Nay, even theft will be a sacrament, seeing it is written, "The day of the Lord so cometh as a thief in the night" (1 Thess. v. 2). Who can tolerate the ignorant garrulity of these sophists? I admit, indeed, that whenever we see a vine, the best thing is to call to mind what our Saviour says, "I am the true vine, and my father is the husbandman." "I am the vine, ye are the branches" (John xv. 1, 5). And whenever we meet a shepherd with his flock, it is good also to remember, "I am the good shepherd, and know my sheep, and am known of mine" (John x. 14). But any man who would class such similitudes with sacraments should be sent to bedlam.

35. They adduce the words of Paul, by which they say that the name of a sacrament is given to marriage, "He that loveth his wife loveth himself. For no man ever yet hated his own flesh; but nourisheth and cherisheth it, even as the Lord the Church: for we are members of his body, of his flesh, and of his bones. For this cause shall a man leave his father and mother, and shall be joined unto his wife, and they two shall be one flesh. This is a great mystery: but I speak concerning Christ and the Church" (Eph. v. 28, 32). To treat Scripture thus is to confound heaven and earth. Paul, in order to show husbands how they ought to love their wives, sets Christ before them as an example. As he shed his bowels of affection for the Church, which he has espoused to himself, so he would have every one to feel affected toward his wife. Then he adds, "He that loveth his wife loveth himself," "even as the Lord the Church." Moreover, to show how Christ loved the Church as himself, nay, how he made himself one with his spouse the Church, he

applies to her what Moses relates that Adam said of himself. For after Eve was brought into his presence, knowing that she had been formed out of his side, he exclaimed, "This is now bone of my bones, and flesh of my flesh" (Gen. ii. 23). That all this was spiritually fulfilled in Christ, and in us, Paul declares, when he says, that we are members of his body, of his flesh, and of his bones, and so one flesh with him. At length he breaks out into the exclamation, "This is a great mystery;" and lest any one should be misled by the ambiguity, he says, that he is not speaking of the connection between husband and wife, but of the spiritual marriage of Christ and the Church. And truly it is a great mystery that Christ allowed a rib to be taken from himself, of which we might be formed; that is, that when he was strong, he was pleased to become weak, that we might be strengthened by his strength, and should no longer live ourselves, but he live in us (Gal. ii. 20).

36. The thing which misled them was the term *sacrament*.[1] But, was it right that the whole Church should be punished for the ignorance of these men? Paul called it a mystery. When the Latin interpreter might have abandoned this mode of expression as uncommon to Latin ears, or converted it into "secret," he preferred calling it *sacramentum*, but in no other sense than the Greek term μυστηριον was used by Paul. Let them go now and clamour against skill in languages, their ignorance of which leads them most shamefully astray in a matter easy and obvious to every one. But why do they so strongly urge the term sacrament in this one passage, and in others pass it by with neglect? For both in the First Epistle to Timothy (1 Tim. iii. 9, 16), and also in the Epistle to the Ephesians, it is used by the Vulgate interpreter, and in every instance, for mystery. Let us, however, pardon them this lapsus, though liars ought to have good memories. Marriage being thus recommended by the title of a sacrament,[2] can it be anything but vertiginous levity afterwards to call it uncleanness, and pollution, and carnal defilement? How absurd is it to debar priests from a sacrament! If they say that they debar not from a sacrament but from carnal connection, they will not thus escape me. They say that this connection is part of the sacrament, and thereby figures the union which we have with Christ in conformity of nature, inasmuch as it is by this connection that husband and wife become one flesh; although some have here found two sacraments, the one of God and the soul, in bridegroom and bride, another of Christ and the Church, in husband and wife. Be this as it may, this connection is a sacrament from which no Christian can lawfully be debarred, unless, indeed, the sacraments of Christians accord so ill that they cannot stand together. There is

1 French, "Ils ont eto trompé du mot de Sacrement qui est en la translation commune."—They have been misled by the word Sacrament, which is in the common translation.

2 Lat. Lib. iv. Dist. 26, cap. 6, et in Decret 27, Quæst. 2, cap. Quæ Societas, etc. Gloss. eod. c. Lex Divina. Ibid. Lib. iv. Dist. 33, cap. 2. et in Decret. 32, Quæst. 2, cap. Quicquid, &c.

also another absurdity in these dogmas. They affirm that in a sacrament the gift of the Holy Spirit is conferred; this connection they hold to be a sacrament, and yet they deny that in it the Holy Spirit is ever present.

37. And, that they might not delude the Church in this matter merely, what a long series of errors, lies, frauds, and iniquities have they appended to one error? So that you may say they sought nothing but a hiding-place for abominations when they converted marriage into a sacrament. When once they obtained this, they appropriated to themselves the cognisance of conjugal causes: as the thing was spiritual, it was not to be intermeddled with by profane judges. Then they enacted laws by which they confirmed their tyranny,—laws partly impious toward God, partly fraught with injustice toward men; such as, that marriages contracted between minors, without the consent of their parents, should be valid; that no lawful marriages can be contracted between relations within the seventh degree, and that such marriages, if contracted, should be dissolved. Moreover, they frame degrees of kindred contrary to the laws of all nations, and even the polity of Moses, and enact that a husband who has repudiated an adulteress may not marry again—that spiritual kindred cannot be joined in marriage—that marriage cannot be celebrated from Septuagesimo to the Octaves of Easter, three weeks before the nativity of John, nor from Advent to Epiphany, and innumerable others, which it were too tedious to mention. We must now get out of their mire, in which our discourse has stuck longer than our inclination. Methinks, however, that much has been gained if I have, in some measure, deprived these asses of their lion's skin.

CHAPTER XX.

OF CIVIL GOVERNMENT.

This chapter consists of two principal heads,—I. General discourse on the necessity, dignity, and use of Civil Government, in opposition to the frantic proceedings of the Anabaptists, sec. 1–3. II. A special exposition of the three leading parts of which Civil Government consists, sec. 4–32.

The first part treats of the function of Magistrates, whose authority and calling is proved, sec. 4–7. Next, the three forms of civil government are added, sec. 8. Thirdly, Consideration of the office of the civil magistrate in respect of piety and righteousness. Here, of rewards and punishments—viz. punishing the guilty, protecting the innocent, repressing the seditious, managing the affairs of peace and war, sec. 9–13. The second part treats of Laws, their utility, necessity, form, authority, constitution, and scope; sec. 14–16. The last part relates to the People, and explains the use of laws, courts, and magistrates, to the common society of Christians, sec. 17–21. Deference which private individuals owe to magistrates, and how far obedience ought to be carried, sec. 22–32.

Sections.

1. Last part of the whole work, relating to the institution of Civil Government. The consideration of it necessary, 1. To refute the Anabaptists. 2. To refute the flatterers of princes. 3. To excite our gratitude to God. Civil government not opposed to Christian liberty. Civil government to be distinguished from the spiritual kingdom of Christ.
2. Objections of the Anabaptists, 1. That civil government is unworthy of a Christian man. 2. That it is diametrically repugnant to the Christian profession. Answer.
3. The answer confirmed. Discourse reduced to three heads, 1. Of Laws. 2. Of Magistrates. 3. Of the People.
4. The office of Magistrates approved by God. 1. They are called Gods. 2. They are ordained by the wisdom of God. Examples of pious Magistrates.
5. Civil government appointed by God for Jews, not Christians. This objection answered.
6. Divine appointment of Magistrates. Effect which this ought to have on Magistrates themselves.
7. This consideration should repress the fury of the Anabaptists.
8. Three forms of civil government, Monarchy, Aristocracy, Democracy. Impossible absolutely to say which is best.
9. Of the duty of Magistrates. Their first care the preservation of the Christian religion and true piety. This proved.
10. Objections of Anabaptists to this view. These answered.
11. Lawfulness of War.
12. Objection, that the lawfulness of war is not taught in Scripture. Answer.
13. Right of exacting tribute and raising revenues.
14. Of Laws, their necessity and utility. Distinction between the Moral, Ceremonial, and Judicial Law of Moses.
15. Sum and scope of the Moral Law. Of the Ceremonial and Judicial Law. Conclusion.
16. All Laws should be just. Civil Law of Moses; how far in force, and how far abrogated.
17. Of the People, and of the use of laws as respects individuals.
18. How far litigation lawful.
19. Refutation of the Anabaptists, who condemn all judicial proceedings.
20. Objection, that Christ forbids us to resist evil. Answer.
21. Objection, that Paul condemns law-suits absolutely. Answer.

22. Of the respect and obedience due to Magistrates.
23. Same subject continued.
24. How far submission due to tyrants.
25. Same continued.
26. Proof from Scripture.
27. Proof continued.
28. Objections answered.
29. Considerations to curb impatience under tyranny.
30. Considerations considered.
31. General submission due by private individuals.
32. Obedience due only in so far as compatible with the word of God.

1. HAVING shown above that there is a twofold government in man, and having fully considered the one which, placed in the soul or inward man, relates to eternal life, we are here called to say something of the other, which pertains only to civil institutions and the external regulation of manners. For although this subject seems from its nature to be unconnected with the spiritual doctrine of faith, which I have undertaken to treat, it will appear as we proceed, that I have properly connected them, nay, that I am under the necessity of doing so, especially while, on the one hand, frantic and barbarous men are furiously endeavouring to overturn the order established by God, and, on the other, the flatterers of princes, extolling their power without measure, hesitate not to oppose it to the government of God. Unless we meet both extremes, the purity of the faith will perish. We may add, that it in no small degree concerns us to know how kindly God has here consulted for the human race, that pious zeal may the more strongly urge us to testify our gratitude. And first, before entering on the subject itself, it is necessary to attend to the distinction which we formerly laid down (Book III. Chap. xix. sec. 16, et supra, Chap. x.), lest, as often happens to many, we imprudently confound these two things, the nature of which is altogether different. For some, on hearing that liberty is promised in the gospel, a liberty which acknowledges no king and no magistrate among men, but looks to Christ alone, think that they can receive no benefit from their liberty so long as they see any power placed over them. Accordingly, they think that nothing will be safe until the whole world is changed into a new form, when there will be neither courts, nor laws, nor magistrates, nor anything of the kind to interfere, as they suppose, with their liberty. But he who knows to distinguish between the body and the soul, between the present fleeting life and that which is future and eternal, will have no difficulty in understanding that the spiritual kingdom of Christ and civil government are things very widely separated. Seeing, therefore, it is a Jewish vanity to seek and include the kingdom of Christ under the elements of this world, let us, considering, as Scripture clearly teaches, that the blessings which we derive from Christ are spiritual, remember to confine the liberty which is promised and offered to us in him within its proper limits. For why is it that the very same apostle who bids us "stand fast in the liberty wherewith Christ hath made us free, and be not again entangled with the yoke of bondage" (Gal. v. 1), in another

passage forbids slaves to be solicitous about their state (1 Cor. vii, 21), unless it be that spiritual liberty is perfectly compatible with civil servitude? In this sense the following passages are to be understood: "There is neither Jew nor Greek, there is neither bond nor free, there is neither male nor female" (Gal. iii. 28). Again, "There is neither Greek nor Jew, circumcision nor uncircumcision, barbarian, Scythian, bond nor free: but Christ is all and in all" (Col. iii. 11). It is thus intimated, that it matters not what your condition is among men, nor under what laws you live, since in them the kingdom of Christ does not at all consist.

2. Still the distinction does not go so far as to justify us in supposing that the whole scheme of civil government is matter of pollution, with which Christian men have nothing to do. Fanatics, indeed, delighting in unbridled license, insist and vociferate that, after we are dead by Christ to the elements of this world, and being translated into the kingdom of God sit among the celestials, it is unworthy of us, and far beneath our dignity, to be occupied with those profane and impure cares which relate to matters alien from a Christian man. To what end, they say, are laws without courts and tribunals? But what has a Christian man to do with courts? Nay, if it is unlawful to kill, what have we to do with laws and courts? But as we lately taught that that kind of government is distinct from the spiritual and internal kingdom of Christ, so we ought to know that they are not adverse to each other. The former, in some measure, begins the heavenly kingdom in us, even now upon earth, and in this mortal and evanescent life commences immortal and incorruptible blessedness, while to the latter it is assigned, so long as we live among men, to foster and maintain the external worship of God, to defend sound doctrine and the condition of the Church, to adapt our conduct to human society, to form our manners to civil justice, to conciliate us to each other, to cherish common peace and tranquillity. All these I confess to be superfluous, if the kingdom of God, as it now exists within us, extinguishes the present life. But if it is the will of God that while we aspire to true piety we are pilgrims upon the earth, and if such pilgrimage stands in need of such aids, those who take them away from man rob him of his humanity. As to their allegation that there ought to be such perfection in the Church of God that her guidance should suffice for law, they stupidly imagine her to be such as she never can be found in the community of men. For while the insolence of the wicked is so great, and their iniquity so stubborn, that it can scarcely be curbed by any severity of laws, what do we expect would be done by those whom force can scarcely repress from doing ill, were they to see perfect impunity for their wickedness?

3. But we shall have a fitter opportunity of speaking of the use of civil government. All we wish to be understood at present is, that it is perfect barbarism to think of exterminating it, its use among men being not less than that of bread and water, light and air, while its dignity is much more excellent. Its object is not merely, like

those things, to enable men to breathe, eat, drink, and be warmed (though it certainly includes all these, while it enables them to live together); this, I say, is not its only object, but it is, that no idolatry, no blasphemy against the name of God, no calumnies against his truth, nor other offences to religion, break out and be disseminated among the people; that the public quiet be not disturbed, that every man's property be kept secure, that men may carry on innocent commerce with each other, that honesty and modesty be cultivated; in short, that a public form of religion may exist among Christians, and humanity among men. Let no one be surprised that I now attribute the task of constituting religion aright to human polity, though I seem above to have placed it beyond the will of man, since I no more than formerly allow men at pleasure to enact laws concerning religion and the worship of God, when I approve of civil order which is directed to this end—viz. to prevent the true religion, which is contained in the law of God, from being with impunity openly violated and polluted by public blasphemy. But the reader, by the help of a perspicuous arrangement, will better understand what view is to be taken of the whole order of civil government, if we treat of each of its parts separately. Now these are three: The Magistrate, who is president and guardian of the laws; the Laws, according to which he governs; and the People, who are governed by the laws, and obey the magistrate. Let us consider, then, first, What is the function of the magistrate? Is it a lawful calling approved by God? What is the nature of his duty? What the extent of his power? Secondly, What are the laws by which Christian polity is to be regulated? And, lastly, What is the use of laws as regards the people? And, What obedience is due to the magistrate?

4. With regard to the function of magistrates, the Lord has not only declared that he approves and is pleased with it, but, moreover, has strongly recommended it to us by the very honourable titles which he has conferred upon it. To mention a few.[1] When those who bear the office of magistrate are called gods, let no one suppose that there is little weight in that appellation. It is thereby intimated that they have a commission from God, that they are invested with divine authority, and, in fact, represent the person of God, as whose substitutes they in a manner act. This is not a quibble of mine, but is the interpretation of Christ. "If Scripture," says he, "called them Gods, to whom the word of God came." What is this but that the business was committed to them by God, to serve him in their office, and (as Moses and Jehoshaphat said to the judges whom they were appointing over each of the cities of Judah) to exercise judgment, not for man, but for God? To the same effect Wisdom affirms, by the mouth of Solomon, "By me kings reign, and princes decree justice. By me princes rule, and nobles, even all the judges of the earth" (Prov. viii. 15, 16). For it is just as if it had

[1] Exod. xxii. 8, 9; Ps. lxxxii. 1, 6; John x. 34, 35; Deut. i. 16, 17; 2 Chron. xix. 6, 7; Prov. viii. 15.

been said, that it is not owing to human perverseness that supreme power on earth is lodged in kings and other governors, but by Divine Providence, and the holy decree of Him to whom it has seemed good so to govern the affairs of men, since he is present, and also presides in enacting laws and exercising judicial equity. This Paul also plainly teaches when he enumerates offices of rule among the gifts of God, which, distributed variously, according to the measure of grace, ought to be employed by the servants of Christ for the edification of the Church (Rom. xii. 8). In that place, however, he is properly speaking of the senate of grave men who were appointed in the primitive Church to take charge of public discipline. This office, in the Epistle to the Corinthians, he calls κυβερνήσεις, *governments* (1 Cor. xii. 28). Still, as we see that civil power has the same end in view, there can be no doubt that he is recommending every kind of just government. He speaks much more clearly when he comes to a proper discussion of the subject. For he says that "there is no power but of God: the powers that be are ordained of God;" that rulers are the ministers of God, "not a terror to good works, but to the evil" (Rom. xiii. 1, 3). To this we may add the examples of saints, some of whom held the offices of kings, as David, Josiah, and Hezekiah; others of governors, as Joseph and Daniel; others of civil magistrates among a free people, as Moses, Joshua, and the Judges. Their functions were expressly approved by the Lord. Wherefore no man can doubt that civil authority is, in the sight of God, not only sacred and lawful, but the most sacred, and by far the most honourable, of all stations in mortal life.

5. Those who are desirous to introduce anarchy[1] object that, though anciently kings and judges presided over a rude people, yet that, in the present day, that servile mode of governing does not at all accord with the perfection which Christ brought with his gospel. Herein they betray not only their ignorance, but their devilish pride, arrogating to themselves a perfection of which not even a hundredth part is seen in them. But be they what they may, the refutation is easy. For when David says, "Be wise now therefore, O ye kings: be instructed, ye judges of the earth;" "Kiss the Son, lest he be angry" (Psalm ii. 10, 12), he does not order them to lay aside their authority and return to private life, but to make the power with which they are invested subject to Christ, that he may rule over all. In like manner, when Isaiah predicts of the Church, "Kings shall be thy nursing-fathers, and their queens thy nursing-mothers" (Isaiah xlix. 23), he does not bid them abdicate their authority; he rather gives them the honourable appellation of patrons of the pious worshippers of God; for the prophecy refers to the advent of Christ. I intentionally omit very many passages which occur throughout Scripture, and especially in the Psalms, in which the due authority of all rulers is asserted. The most celebrated passage of all is that in which Paul,

1 French, "Ceux qui voudroyent que les hommes vesquissent pesle mesle comme rats en paille;"—Those who would have men to live pell-mell like rats among straw.

admonishing Timothy, that prayers are to be offered up in the public assembly for kings, subjoins the reason, "that we may lead a quiet and peaceable life in all godliness and honesty" (1 Tim. ii. 2). In these words, he recommends the condition of the Church to their protection and guardianship.

6. This consideration ought to be constantly present to the minds of magistrates, since it is fitted to furnish a strong stimulus to the discharge of duty, and also afford singular consolation, smoothing the difficulties of their office, which are certainly numerous and weighty. What zeal for integrity, prudence, meekness, continence, and innocence, ought to sway those who know that they have been appointed ministers of the divine justice! How will they dare to admit iniquity to their tribunal, when they are told that it is the throne of the living God? How will they venture to pronounce an unjust sentence with that mouth which they understand to be an ordained organ of divine truth? With what conscience will they subscribe impious decrees with that hand which they know has been appointed to write the acts of God? In a word, if they remember that they are the vicegerents of God, it behoves them to watch with all care, diligence, and industry, that they may in themselves exhibit a kind of image of the Divine Providence, guardianship, goodness, benevolence, and justice. And let them constantly keep the additional thought in view, that if a curse is pronounced on him that "doeth the work of the Lord deceitfully," a much heavier curse must lie on him who deals deceitfully in a righteous calling. Therefore, when Moses and Jehoshaphat would urge their judges to the discharge of duty, they had nothing by which they could more powerfully stimulate their minds than the consideration to which we have already referred,—"Take heed what ye do: for ye judge not for man, but for the Lord, who is with you in the judgment. Wherefore now let the fear of the Lord be upon you; take heed and do it: for there is no iniquity with the Lord our God, nor respect of persons, nor taking of gifts" (2 Chron. xix. 6, 7, compared with Deut. i. 16, &c.). And in another passage it is said, "God standeth in the congregation of the mighty; he judgeth among the gods" (Psalm lxxxii. 1; Isaiah iii. 14), that they may be animated to duty when they hear that they are the ambassadors of God, to whom they must one day render an account of the province committed to them. This admonition ought justly to have the greatest effect upon them; for if they sin in any respect, not only is injury done to the men whom they wickedly torment, but they also insult God himself, whose sacred tribunals they pollute. On the other hand, they have an admirable source of comfort when they reflect that they are not engaged in profane occupations, unbefitting a servant of God, but in a most sacred office, inasmuch as they are the ambassadors of God.

7. In regard to those who are not debarred by all these passages of Scripture from presuming to inveigh against this sacred ministry, as if it were a thing abhorrent from religion and Christian piety, what

else do they than assail God himself, who cannot but be insulted when his servants are disgraced? These men not only speak evil of dignities, but would not even have God to reign over them (1 Sam. vii. 7). For if this was truly said of the people of Israel, when they declined the authority of Samuel, how can it be less truly said in the present day of those who allow themselves to break loose against all the authority established by God? But it seems that when our Lord said to his disciples, "The kings of the gentiles exercise lordship over them; and they that exercise authority upon them are called benefactors. But ye shall not be so: but he that is greatest among you, let him be as the younger; and he that is chief, as he that doth serve" (Luke xxii. 25, 26); he by these words prohibited all Christians from becoming kings or governors. Dexterous expounders! A dispute had arisen among the disciples as to which of them should be greatest. To suppress this vain ambition, our Lord taught them that their ministry was not like the power of earthly sovereigns, among whom one greatly surpasses another. What, I ask, is there in this comparison disparaging to royal dignity? nay, what does it prove at all unless that the royal office is not the apostolic ministry? Besides, though among magisterial offices themselves there are different forms, there is no difference in this respect, that they are all to be received by us as ordinances of God. For Paul includes all together when he says that "there is no power but of God," and that which was by no means the most pleasing of all, was honoured with the highest testimonial—I mean the power of one. This, as carrying with it the public servitude of all (except the one to whose despotic will all is subject), was anciently disrelished by heroic and more excellent natures. But Scripture, to obviate these unjust judgments, affirms expressly that it is by divine wisdom that "kings reign," and gives special command "to honour the king" (1 Peter ii. 17).

8. And certainly it were a very idle occupation for private men to discuss what would be the best form of polity in the place where they live, seeing these deliberations cannot have any influence in determining any public matter. Then the thing itself could not be defined absolutely without rashness, since the nature of the discussion depends on circumstances. And if you compare the different states with each other, without regard to circumstances, it is not easy to determine which of these has the advantage in point of utility, so equal are the terms on which they meet. Monarchy is prone to tyranny. In an aristocracy, again, the tendency is not less to the faction of a few, while in popular ascendancy there is the strongest tendency to sedition.[1] When these three forms of government, of

[1] French, "On conte trois especes de regime civil: c'est assavoir Monarchie, qui est la domination d'un seul, soit qu'on le nomme Roy ou Duc, ou autrement: Aristocratie, qui est une domination gouvernee par les principaux et gens d'apparence: et Democratie, qui est une domination populaire, en laquelle chacun du peuple a puissance."—There are three kinds of civil government; namely, Monarchy, which is the domination

which philosophers treat, are considered in themselves, I, for my part, am far from denying that the form which greatly surpasses the others is aristocracy, either pure or modified by popular government, not indeed in itself, but because it very rarely happens that kings so rule themselves as never to dissent from what is just and right, or are possessed of so much acuteness and prudence as always to see correctly. Owing, therefore, to the vices or defects of men, it is safer and more tolerable when several bear rule, that they may thus mutually assist, instruct, and admonish each other, and should any one be disposed to go too far, the others are censors and masters to curb his excess. This has already been proved by experience, and confirmed also by the authority of the Lord himself, when he established an aristocracy bordering on popular government among the Israelites, keeping them under that as the best form, until he exhibited an image of the Messiah in David. And as I willingly admit that there is no kind of government happier than where liberty is framed with becoming moderation, and duly constituted so as to be durable, so I deem those very happy who are permitted to enjoy that form, and I admit that they do nothing at variance with their duty when they strenuously and constantly labour to preserve and maintain it. Nay, even magistrates ought to do their utmost to prevent the liberty, of which they have been appointed guardians, from being impaired, far less violated. If in this they are sluggish or little careful, they are perfidious traitors to their office and their country. But should those to whom the Lord has assigned one form of government, take it upon them anxiously to long for a change, the wish would not only be foolish and superfluous, but very pernicious. If you fix your eyes not on one state merely, but look around the world, or at least direct your view to regions widely separated from each other, you will perceive that Divine Providence has not, without good cause, arranged that different countries should be governed by different forms of polity. For as only elements of unequal temperature adhere together, so in different regions a similar inequality in the form of government is best. All this, however, is said unnecessarily to those to whom the will of God is a sufficient reason. For if it has pleased him to appoint kings over kingdoms, and senates or burgomasters over free states, whatever be the form which he has appointed in the places in which we live, our duty is to obey and submit.

9. The duty of magistrates, its nature, as described by the word of God, and the things in which it consists, I will here indicate in passing. That it extends to both tables of the law, did Scripture not teach, we might learn from profane writers; for no man has discoursed of the duty of magistrates, the enacting of laws, and the common weal, without beginning with religion and divine worship.

of one only, whether he be called King or Duke, or otherwise; Aristocracy, which is a government composed of the chiefs and people of note; and Democracy, which is a popular government, in which each of the people has power.

Thus all have confessed that no polity can be successfully established unless piety be its first care, and that those laws are absurd which disregard the rights of God, and consult only for men. Seeing then that among philosophers religion holds the first place, and that the same thing has always been observed with the universal consent of nations, Christian princes and magistrates may be ashamed of their heartlessness if they make it not their care. We have already shown that this office is specially assigned them by God, and indeed it is right that they exert themselves in asserting and defending the honour of him whose vicegerents they are, and by whose favour they rule. Hence in Scripture holy kings are especially praised for restoring the worship of God when corrupted or overthrown, or for taking care that religion flourished under them in purity and safety. On the other hand, the sacred history sets down anarchy among the vices, when it states that there was no king in Israel, and, therefore, every one did as he pleased (Judges xxi. 25). This rebukes the folly of those who would neglect the care of divine things, and devote themselves merely to the administration of justice among men; as if God had appointed rulers in his own name to decide earthly controversies, and omitted what was of far greater moment, his own pure worship as prescribed by his law. Such views are adopted by turbulent men, who, in their eagerness to make all kinds of innovations with impunity, would fain get rid of all the vindicators of violated piety. In regard to the second table of the law, Jeremiah addresses rulers, "Thus saith the Lord, Execute ye judgment and righteousness, and deliver the spoiled out of the hand of the oppressor: and do no wrong, do no violence to the stranger, the fatherless, nor the widow, neither shed innocent blood" (Jer. xxii. 3). To the same effect is the exhortation in the Psalm, "Defend the poor and fatherless; do justice to the afflicted and needy. Deliver the poor and needy; rid them out of the hand of the wicked" (Psalm lxxxii. 3, 4). Moses also declared to the princes whom he had substituted for himself, "Hear the causes between your brethren, and judge righteously between every man and his brother, and the stranger that is with him. Ye shall not respect persons in judgment; but ye shall hear the small as well as the great: ye shall not be afraid of the face of man, for the judgment is God's" (Deut. i. 16). I say nothing as to such passages as these, "He shall not multiply horses to himself, nor cause the people to return to Egypt;" "neither shall he multiply wives to himself; neither shall he greatly multiply to himself silver and gold;" "he shall write him a copy of this law in a book;" "and it shall be with him, and he shall read therein all the days of his life, that he may learn to fear the Lord his God;" "that his heart be not lifted up above his brethren" (Deut. xvii. 16–20). In here explaining the duties of magistrates, my exposition is intended not so much for the instruction of magistrates themselves, as to teach others why there are magistrates, and to what end they have been appointed by God. We say, therefore, that they are the ordained guardians and vindicators of public innocence, modesty, honour, and tranquillity, so that it should be their only study to provide for the common peace and safety. Of these things David declares that he will set an example when he shall have ascended the throne. " A froward heart shall depart from me: I will not know a wicked person. Whoso privily slandereth his neighbour, him will I cut off: him that hath an high look and a proud heart will not I suffer. Mine eyes shall be upon the faithful of the land, that they may dwell with me: he that walketh in a perfect way, he shall serve me" (Psalm ci. 4–6). But as rulers cannot do this unless they protect the good against the injuries of the bad, and give aid and protection to the oppressed, they are armed with power to curb manifest evil-doers and criminals, by whose misconduct the public tranquillity is disturbed or harassed. For we have full experience of the truth of Solon's saying, that all public matters depend on reward and punishment; that where these are wanting, the whole discipline of states totters and falls to pieces. For in the minds of many the love of equity and justice grows cold, if due honour be not paid to virtue, and the licentiousness of the wicked cannot be restrained, without strict discipline and the infliction of punishment. The two things are comprehended by the prophet when he enjoins kings and other rulers to execute "judgment and righteousness" (Jer. xxi. 12; xxii. 3). It is righteousness (justice) to take charge of the innocent, to defend and avenge them, and set them free: it is judgment to withstand the audacity of the wicked, to repress their violence, and punish their faults.

10. But here a difficult, and, as it seems, a perplexing question arises. If all Christians are forbidden to kill, and the prophet predicts concerning the holy mountain of the Lord, that is, the Church,[1] "They shall not hurt or destroy," how can magistrates be at once pious and yet shedders of blood? But if we understand that the magistrate, in inflicting punishment, acts not of himself, but executes the very judgments of God, we shall be disencumbered of every doubt. The law of the Lord forbids to kill; but, that murder may not go unpunished, the Lawgiver himself puts the sword into the hands of his ministers, that they may employ it against all murderers. It belongs not to the pious to afflict and hurt; but to avenge the afflictions of the pious, at the command of God, is neither to afflict nor hurt.[2] I wish it could always be present to our mind, that nothing is done here by the rashness of man, but all in obedience to the authority of

1 Exod. xx. 13; Deut. v. 17; Matth. v. 21; Isa. xi. 9; lxv. 25.

2 The French adds, "Pourtant il est facile de conclure, qu'en cette partie il ne sont sujets a la loy commune; par laquelle combien que le Seigneur lie les mains de tous les hommes, toutes fois il ne lie pas sa justice laquelle il exerce par les mains des magistrats. Tout ainsi que quand un prince defend à tou sses sujets de porter baston, ou blesser aucun, il n'empeche pas neantmoins ses officiers d'executer la justice, laquelle il leur a specialement commise."—Therefore, it is easy to conclude, that in this respect they are not subject to the common law, by which, although the Lord ties the hands of all men, still he ties not his justice which he exercises by the hands of magistrates. Just as when a prince forbids all his subjects to beator hnrt any oue, he nevertheless prohibits not his officers from executing the justice which he has specially committed to them.

God. When it is the guide, we never stray from the right path, unless, indeed, divine justice is to be placed under restraint, and not allowed to take punishment on crimes. But if we dare not give the law to it, why should we bring a charge against its ministers? "He beareth not the sword in vain," says Paul, "for he is the minister of God, a revenger to execute wrath on him that doeth evil" (Rom. xiii. 4). Wherefore, if princes and other rulers know that nothing will be more acceptable to God than their obedience, let them give themselves to this service if they are desirous to improve their piety, justice, and integrity to God. This was the feeling of Moses[1] when, recognising himself as destined to deliver his people by the power of the Lord, he laid violent hands on the Egyptian, and afterwards took vengeance on the people for sacrilege, by slaying three thousand of them in one day. This was the feeling of David also, when, towards the end of his life, he ordered his son Solomon to put Joab and Shimei to death. Hence, also, in an enumeration of the virtues of a king, one is to cut off the wicked from the earth, and banish all workers of iniquity from the city of God. To the same effect is the praise which is bestowed on Solomon, "Thou lovest righteousness, and hatest wickedness." How is it that the meek and gentle temper of Moses becomes so exasperated, that, besmeared and reeking with the blood of his brethren, he runs through the camp making new slaughter? How is it that David, who, during his whole life, showed so much mildness, almost at his last breath, leaves with his son the bloody testament, not to allow the grey hairs of Joab and Shimei to go to the grave in peace? Both, by their sternness, sanctified the hands which they would have polluted by showing mercy, inasmuch as they executed the vengeance committed to them by God. Solomon says,[2] "It is an abomination to kings to commit wickedness; for the throne is established by righteousness." Again, "A king that sitteth in the throne of judgment, scattereth away all evil with his eyes." Again, "A wise king scattereth the wicked, and bringeth the wheel over them." Again, "Take away the dross from the silver, and there shall come forth a vessel for the finer. Take away the wicked men from before the king, and his throne shall be established in righteousness." Again, "He that justifieth the wicked, and he that condemneth the just, even they both are an abomination to the Lord." Again, "An evil man seeketh only rebellion, therefore an evil messenger shall be sent against him." Again, "He that saith unto the wicked, Thou art righteous; him shall the people curse, nations shall abhor him." Now, if it is true justice in them to pursue the guilty and impious with drawn sword, to sheath the sword, and keep their hands pure from blood, while nefarious men wade through murder and slaughter, so far from redounding to the praise of their goodness and justice, would be to incur the guilt of the greatest impiety; provided always they eschew reckless and cruel

1 Exod. ii. 12; Acts vii. 21; Exod. xxxii. 26; 1 Kings ii. 5; Ps. ci. 8; xlv. 8.
2 Prov. xvi. 12; xx. 26; xxv. 4, 5; xvii. 15; xvii. 14; xxiv. 24.

ssperity, and that tribunal which may be justly termed a rock on which the accused must founder. For I am not one of those who would either favour an unseasonable severity, or think that any tribunal could be accounted just that is not presided over by mercy, that best and surest counsellor of kings, and, as Solomon declares, "upholder of the throne" (Prov. xx. 28). This, as was truly said by one of old, should be the primary endowment of princes. The magistrate must guard against both extremes; he must neither, by excessive severity, rather wound than cure, nor by a superstitious affectation of clemency, fall into the most cruel inhumanity, by giving way to soft and dissolute indulgence to the destruction of many. It was well said by one under the empire of Nerva, It is indeed a bad thing to live under a prince with whom nothing is lawful, but a much worse to live under one with whom all things are lawful.

11. As it is sometimes necessary for kings and states to take up arms in order to execute public vengeance, the reason assigned furnishes us with the means of estimating how far the wars which are thus undertaken are lawful. For if power has been given them to maintain the tranquillity of their subjects, repress the seditious movements of the turbulent, assist those who are violently oppressed, and animadvert on crimes, can they use it more opportunely than in repressing the fury of him who disturbs both the ease of individuals and the common tranquillity of all; who excites seditious tumult, and perpetrates acts of violent oppression and gross wrongs? If it becomes them to be the guardians and maintainers of the laws, they must repress the attempts of all alike by whose criminal conduct the discipline of the laws is impaired. Nay, if they justly punish those robbers whose injuries have been afflicted only on a few, will they allow the whole country to be robbed and devastated with impunity? Since it makes no difference whether it is by a king or by the lowest of the people that a hostile and devastating inroad is made into a district over which they have no authority, all alike are to be regarded and punished as robbers. Natural equity and duty, therefore, demand that princes be armed not only to repress private crimes by judicial inflictions, but to defend the subjects committed to their guardianship whenever they are hostilely assailed. Such even the Holy Spirit, in many passages of Scripture, declares to be lawful.

12. But if it is objected, that in the New Testament there is no passage or example teaching that war is lawful for Christians, I answer, first, that the reason for carrying on war, which anciently existed, still exists in the present day, and that, on the other hand, there is no ground for debarring magistrates from the defence of those under them; and, secondly, that in the Apostolical writings we are not to look for a distinct exposition of those matters, their object being not to form a civil polity, but to establish the spiritual kingdom of Christ; lastly, that there also it is indicated, in passing, that our Saviour, by his advent, made no change in this respect. For (to use the words of Augustine) "if Christian discipline con-

demned all wars, when the soldiers ask counsel as to the way of salvation, they would have been told to cast away their arms, and withdraw altogether from military service. Whereas it was said (Luke iii. 14), Concuss no one, do injury to no one, be contented with your pay. Those whom he orders to be contented with their pay he certainly does not forbid to serve" (August. Ep. v. ad Marcell.) But all magistrates must here be particularly cautious not to give way, in the slightest degree, to their passions. Or rather, whether punishments are to be inflicted, they must not be borne headlong by anger, nor hurried away by hatred, nor burn with implacable severity; they must, as Augustine says (De Civit. Dei. Lib. v. cap. 24), "even pity a common nature in him in whom they punish an individual fault;" or whether they have to take up arms against an enemy, that is, an armed robber, they must not readily catch at the opportunity, nay, they must not take it when offered, unless compelled by the strongest necessity. For if we are to do far more than that heathen demanded, who wished war to appear as desired peace, assuredly all other means must be tried before having recourse to arms. In fine, in both cases, they must not allow themselves to be carried away by any private feeling, but be guided solely by regard for the public. Acting otherwise, they wickedly abuse their power which was given them, not for their own advantage, but for the good and service of others. On this right of war depends the right of garrisons, leagues, and other civil munitions. By garrisons, I mean those which are stationed in states for defence of the frontiers; by leagues, the alliances which are made by neighbouring princes, on the ground that if any disturbance arise within their territories, they will mutually assist each other, and combine their forces to repel the common enemies of the human race; under civil munitions, I include everything pertaining to the military art.

13. Lastly, we think it proper to add, that taxes and imposts are the legitimate revenues of princes, which they are chiefly to employ in sustaining the public burdens of their office. These, however, they may use for the maintenance of their domestic state, which is in a manner combined with the dignity of the authority which they exercise. Thus we see that David, Hezekiah, Josiah, Jehoshaphat, and other holy kings, Joseph also, and Daniel, in proportion to the office which they sustained, without offending piety, expended liberally of the public funds; and we read in Ezekiel, that a very large extent of territory was assigned to kings (Ezek. xlviii. 21). In that passage, indeed, he is depicting the spiritual kingdom of Christ, but still he borrows his representation from lawful dominion among men. Princes, however, must remember, in their turn, that their revenues are not so much private chests as treasuries of the whole people (this Paul testifies, Rom. xiii. 6), which they cannot, without manifest injustice, squander or dilapidate; or rather, that they are almost the blood of the people, which it were the harshest inhumanity not to spare. They should also consider that their levies and contributions,

and other kinds of taxes, are merely subsidies of the public necessity, and that it is tyrannical rapacity to harass the poor people with them without cause. These things do not stimulate princes to profusion and luxurious expenditure (there is certainly no need to inflame the passions, when they are already, of their own accord, inflamed more than enough), but seeing it is of the greatest consequence that, whatever they venture to do, they should do with a pure conscience, it is necessary to teach them how far they can lawfully go, lest, by impious confidence, they incur the divine displeasure. Nor is this doctrine superfluous to private individuals, that they may not rashly and petulantly stigmatise the expenditure of princes, though it should exceed the ordinary limits.

14. In states, the thing next in importance to the magistrates is laws, the strongest sinews of government, or, as Cicero calls them after Plato, the soul, without which, the office of the magistrate cannot exist; just as, on the other hand, laws have no vigour without the magistrate. Hence nothing could be said more truly than that the law is a dumb magistrate, the magistrate a living law. As I have undertaken to describe the laws by which Christian polity is to be governed, there is no reason to expect from me a long discussion on the best kind of laws. The subject is of vast extent, and belongs not to this place. I will only briefly observe, in passing, what the laws are which may be piously used with reference to God, and duly administered among men. This I would rather have passed in silence, were I not aware that many dangerous errors are here committed. For there are some who deny that any commonwealth is rightly framed which neglects the law of Moses, and is ruled by the common law of nations. How perilous and seditious these views are, let others see: for me it is enough to demonstrate that they are stupid and false. We must attend to the well known division which distributes the whole law of God, as promulgated by Moses, into the moral, the ceremonial, and the judicial law, and we must attend to each of these parts, in order to understand how far they do, or do not, pertain to us. Meanwhile, let no one be moved by the thought that the judicial and ceremonial laws relate to morals. For the ancients who adopted this division, though they were not unaware that the two latter classes had to do with morals, did not give them the name of moral, because they might be changed and abrogated without affecting morals. They give this name specially to the first class, without which, true holiness of life and an immutable rule of conduct cannot exist.

15. The moral law, then (to begin with it), being contained under two heads, the one of which simply enjoins us to worship God with pure faith and piety, the other to embrace men with sincere affection, is the true and eternal rule of righteousness prescribed to the men of all nations and of all times, who would frame their life agreeably to the will of God. For his eternal and immutable will is, that we are all to worship him and mutually love one another. The ceremonial

law of the Jews was a tutelage by which the Lord was pleased to exercise, as it were, the childhood of that people, until the fulness of the time should come when he was fully to manifest his wisdom to the world, and exhibit the reality of those things which were then adumbrated by figures (Gal. iii. 24; iv. 4). The judicial law, given them as a kind of polity, delivered certain forms of equity and justice, by which they might live together innocently and quietly. And as that exercise in ceremonies properly pertained to the doctrine of piety, inasmuch as it kept the Jewish Church in the worship and religion of God, yet was still distinguishable from piety itself, so the judicial form, though it looked only to the best method of preserving that charity which is enjoined by the eternal law of God, was still something distinct from the precept of love itself. Therefore, as ceremonies might be abrogated without at all interfering with piety, so, also, when these judicial arrangements are removed, the duties and precepts of charity can still remain perpetual. But if it is true that each nation has been left at liberty to enact the laws which it judges to be beneficial, still these are always to be tested by the rule of charity, so that while they vary in form, they must proceed on the same principle. Those barbarous and savage laws, for instance, which conferred honour on thieves, allowed the promiscuous intercourse of the sexes, and other things even fouler and more absurd, I do not think entitled to be considered as laws, since they are not only altogether abhorrent to justice, but to humanity and civilised life.

16. What I have said will become plain if we attend, as we ought, to two things connected with all laws—viz. the enactment of the law, and the equity on which the enactment is founded and rests. Equity, as it is natural, cannot be the same in all, and therefore ought to be proposed by all laws, according to the nature of the thing enacted. As constitutions have some circumstances on which they partly depend, there is nothing to prevent their diversity, provided they all alike aim at equity as their end. Now, as it is evident that the law of God which we call moral, is nothing else than the testimony of natural law, and of that conscience which God has engraven on the minds of men, the whole of this equity of which we now speak is prescribed in it. Hence it alone ought to be the aim, the rule, and the end of all laws. Wherever laws are formed after this rule, directed to this aim, and restricted to this end, there is no reason why they should be disapproved by us, however much they may differ from the Jewish law, or from each other (August. de Civit. Dei, Lib. xix. c. 17). The law of God forbids to steal. The punishment appointed for theft in the civil polity of the Jews may be seen in Exodus xxii. Very ancient laws of other nations punished theft by exacting the double of what was stolen, while subsequent laws made a distinction between theft manifest and not manifest. Other laws went the length of punishing with exile, or with branding, while others made the punishment capital. Among the Jews, the punishment of the false witness was to " do unto him as he had thought to have done

with his brother" (Deut. xix. 19). In some countries, the punishment is infamy, in others hanging, in others crucifixion. All laws alike avenge murder with blood, but the kinds of death are different. In some countries, adultery was punished more severely, in others more leniently. Yet we see that amidst this diversity they all tend to the same end. For they all with one mouth declare against those crimes which are condemned by the eternal law of God—viz. murder, theft, adultery, and false witness; though they agree not as to the mode of punishment. This is not necessary, nor even expedient. There may be a country which, if murder were not visited with fearful punishments, would instantly become a prey to robbery and slaughter. There may be an age requiring that the severity of punishments should be increased. If the state is in troubled condition, those things from which disturbances usually arise must be corrected by new edicts. In time of war, civilisation would disappear amid the noise of arms, were not men overawed by an unwonted severity of punishment. In sterility, inpestilence, were not stricter discipline employed, all things would grow worse. One nation might be more prone to a particular vice, were it not most severely repressed. How malignant were it, and invidious of the public good, to be offended at this diversity, which is admirably adapted to retain the observance of the divine law. The allegation, that insult is offered to the law of God enacted by Moses, where it is abrogated, and other new laws are preferred to it, is most absurd. Others are not preferred when they are more approved, not absolutely, but from regard to time and place, and the condition of the people, or when those things are abrogated which were never enacted for us. The Lord did not deliver it by the hand of Moses to be promulgated in all countries, and to be everywhere enforced; but having taken the Jewish nation under his special care, patronage, and guardianship, he was pleased to be specially its legislator, and as became a wise legislator, he had special regard to it in enacting laws.

17. It now remains to see, as was proposed in the last place, what use the common society of Christians derive from laws, judicial proceedings, and magistrates. With this is connected another question—viz. What difference ought private individuals to pay to magistrates, and how far ought obedience to proceed? To very many it seems that among Christians the office of magistrate is superfluous, because they cannot piously implore his aid, inasmuch as they are forbidden to take revenge, cite before a judge, or go to law. But when Paul, on the contrary, clearly declares that he is the minister of God to us for good (Rom. xiii. 4), we thereby understand that he was so ordained of God, that, being defended by his hand and aid against the dishonesty and injustice of wicked men, we may live quiet and secure. But if he would have been appointed over us in vain, unless we were to use his aid, it is plain that it cannot be wrong to appeal to it and implore it. Here, indeed, I have to do with two classes of men. For there are very many who boil with

such a rage for litigation, that they never can be quiet with themselves unless they are fighting with others. Law-suits they prosecute with the bitterness of deadly hatred, and with an insane eagerness to hurt and revenge, and they persist in them with implacable obstinacy, even to the ruin of their adversary. Meanwhile, that they may be thought to do nothing but what is legal, they use this pretext of judicial proceedings as a defence of their perverse conduct. But if it is lawful for brother to litigate with brother, it does not follow that it is lawful to hate him, and obstinately pursue him with a furious desire to do him harm.

18. Let such persons then understand that judicial proceedings are lawful to him who makes a right use of them; and the right use, both for the pursuer and for the defender, is for the latter to sist himself on the day appointed, and, without bitterness, urge what he can in his defence, but only with the desire of justly maintaining his right; and for the pursuer, when undeservedly attacked in his life or fortunes, to throw himself upon the protection of the magistrate, state his complaint, and demand what is just and good; while, far from any wish to hurt or take vengeance—far from bitterness or hatred—far from the ardour of strife, he is rather disposed to yield and suffer somewhat than to cherish hostile feelings towards his opponent. On the contrary, when minds are filled with malevolence, corrupted by envy, burning with anger, breathing revenge, or, in fine, so inflamed by the heat of the contest, that they, in some measure, lay aside charity, the whole pleading, even of the justest cause, cannot but be impious. For it ought to be an axiom among all Christians, that no plea, however equitable, can be rightly conducted by any one who does not feel as kindly towards his opponent as if the matter in dispute were amicably transacted and arranged. Some one, perhaps, may here break in and say, that such moderation in judicial proceedings is so far from being seen, that an instance of it would be a kind of prodigy. I confess that in these times it is rare to meet with an example of an honest litigant; but the thing itself, untainted by the accession of evil, ceases not to be good and pure. When we hear that the assistance of the magistrate is a sacred gift from God, we ought the more carefully to beware of polluting it by our fault.

19. Let those who distinctly condemn all judicial distinction know, that they repudiate the holy ordinance of God, and one of those gifts which to the pure are pure, unless, indeed, they would charge Paul with a crime,[1] because he repelled the calumnies of his accusers, exposing their craft and wickedness, and, at the tribunal, claimed for himself the privilege of a Roman citizen, appealing, when necessary, from the governor to Cæsar's judgment-seat. There is nothing contrary to this in the prohibition, which binds all Christians to refrain from revenge, a feeling which we drive far away from all Christian tribunals. For whether the action be of a civil nature, he only takes

1 Acts xxii. xxiv. 12; xvi. 37; xxii. 25; xxv. 10; Lev. xix. 18; Matth. v. 39; Deut. xxxii. 35; Rom. xii. 19.

the right course who, with innocuous simplicity, commits his cause to the judge as the public protector, without any thought of returning evil for evil (which is the feeling of revenge); or whether the action is of a graver nature, directed against a capital offence, the accuser required is not one who comes into court, carried away by some feeling of revenge or resentment from some private injury, but one whose only object is to prevent the attempts of some bad men to injure the commonweal. But if you take away the vindictive mind, you offend in no respect against that command which forbids Christians to indulge revenge. But they are not only forbidden to thirst for revenge, they are also enjoined to wait for the hand of the Lord, who promises that he will be the avenger of the oppressed and afflicted. But those who call upon the magistrate to give assistance to themselves or others, anticipate the vengeance of the heavenly Judge. By no means, for we are to consider that the vengeance of the magistrate is the vengeance not of man, but of God, which, as Paul says, he exercises by the ministry of man for our good (Rom. xiii. 8).

20. No more are we at variance with the words of Christ, who forbids us to resist evil, and adds, "Whosoever shall smite thee on thy right cheek, turn to him the other also. And if any man will sue thee at the law, and take away thy coat, let him have thy cloak also" (Matth. v. 39, 40). He would have the minds of his followers to be so abhorrent to everything like retaliation, that they would sooner allow the injury to be doubled than desire to repay it. From this patience we do not dissuade them. For verily Christians were to be a class of men born to endure affronts and injuries, and be exposed to the iniquity, imposture, and derision of abandoned men, and not only so, but were to be tolerant of all these evils; that is, so composed in the whole frame of their minds, that, on receiving one offence, they were to prepare themselves for another, promising themselves nothing during the whole of life but the endurance of a perpetual cross. Meanwhile, they must do good to those who injure them, and pray for those who curse them, and (this is their only victory) strive to overcome evil with good (Rom. xii. 20, 21). Thus affected, they will not seek eye for eye, and tooth for tooth (as the Pharisees taught their disciples to long for vengeance), but (as we are instructed by Christ), they will allow their body to be mutilated, and their goods to be maliciously taken from them, prepared to remit and spontaneously pardon those injuries the moment they have been inflicted. This equity and moderation, however, will not prevent them, with entire friendship for their enemies, from using the aid of the magistrate for the preservation of their goods, or, from zeal for the public interest, to call for the punishment of the wicked and pestilential man, whom they know nothing will reform but death. All these precepts are truly expounded by Augustine, as tending to prepare the just and pious man patiently to sustain the malice of those whom he desires to become good, that he may thus increase the number of the good, not add himself to the number of the bad

by imitating their wickedness. Moreover, it pertains more to the preparation of the heart which is within, than to the work which is done openly, that patience and good-will may be retained within the secret of the heart, and that may be done openly which we see may do good to those to whom we ought to wish well (August. Ep. v. ad. Marcell.).

21. The usual objection, that law-suits are universally condemned by Paul (1 Cor. vi. 6), is false. It may easily be understood from his words, that a rage for litigation prevailed in the Church of Corinth to such a degree, that they exposed the gospel of Christ, and the whole religion which they professed, to the calumnies and cavils of the ungodly. Paul rebukes them, first for traducing the gospel to unbelievers by the intemperance of their dissensions; and, secondly, for so striving with each other while they were brethren. For so far were they from bearing injury from another, that they greedily coveted each other's effects, and voluntarily provoked and injured them. He inveighs, therefore, against that madness for litigation, and not absolutely against all kinds of disputes. He declares it to be altogether a vice or infirmity, that they do not submit to the loss of their effects, rather than strive, even to contention, in preserving them; in other words, seeing they were so easily moved by every kind of loss, and on every occasion, however slight, ran off to the forum and to law-suits, he says, that in this way they showed that they were of too irritable a temper, and not prepared for patience. Christians should always feel disposed rather to give up part of their right than to go into court, out of which they can scarcely come without a troubled mind, a mind inflamed with hatred of their brother. But when one sees that his property, the want of which he would grievously feel, he is able, without any loss of charity, to defend, if he should do so, he offends in no respect against that passage of Paul. In short, as we said at first, every man's best adviser is charity. Everything in which we engage without charity, and all the disputes which carry us beyond it, are unquestionably unjust and impious.

22. The first duty of subjects towards their rulers, is to entertain the most honourable views of their office, recognising it as a delegated jurisdiction from God, and on that account receiving and reverencing them as the ministers and ambassadors of God. For you will find some who show themselves very obedient to magistrates, and would be unwilling that there should be no magistrates to obey, because they know this is expedient for the public good, and yet the opinion which those persons have of magistrates is, that they are a kind of necessary evils. But Peter requires something more of us when he says, "Honour the king" (1 Pet. ii. 17); and Solomon, when he says, "My son, fear thou the Lord and the king" (Prov. xxiv. 21). For, under the term honour, the former includes a sincere and candid esteem, and the latter, by joining the king with God, shows that he is invested with a kind of sacred veneration and dignity. We have

also the remarkable injunction of Paul, "Be subject not only for wrath, but also for conscience sake" (Rom. xiii. 5). By this he means, that subjects, in submitting to princes and governors, are not to be influenced merely by fear (just as those submit to an armed enemy who see vengeance ready to be executed if they resist), but because the obedience which they yield is rendered to God himself, inasmuch as their power is from God. I speak not of the men as if the mask of dignity could cloak folly, or cowardice, or cruelty, or wicked or flagitious manners, and thus acquire for vice the praise of virtue; but I say that the station itself is deserving of honour and reverence, and that those who rule should, in respect of their office, be held by us in esteem and veneration.

23. From this, a second consequence is, that we must with ready minds prove our obedience to them, whether in complying with edicts, or in paying tribute, or in undertaking public offices and burdens, which relate to the common defence, or in executing any other orders. "Let every soul," says Paul, "be subject unto the higher powers." "Whosoever, therefore, resisteth the power, resisteth the ordinance of God" (Rom. xiii. 1, 2). Writing to Titus, he says, "Put them in mind to be subject to principalities and powers, to obey magistrates, to be ready to every good work" (Tit. iii. 1). Peter also says, "Submit yourselves to every human creature" (or rather, as I understand it, "ordinance of man"), "for the Lord's sake: whether it be to the king, as supreme; or unto governors, as unto them that are sent by him for the punishment of evil-doers, and for the praise of them that do well" (1 Pet. ii. 13). Moreover, to testify that they do not feign subjection, but are sincerely and cordially subject, Paul adds, that they are to commend the safety and prosperity of those under whom they live to God. "I exhort, therefore," says he, "that, first of all, supplications, prayers, intercessions, and giving of thanks, be made for all men; for kings, and for all that are in authority: that we may lead a quiet and peaceable life in all godliness and honesty" (1 Tim. ii. 1, 2). Let no man here deceive himself, since we cannot resist the magistrate without resisting God. For, although an unarmed magistrate may seem to be despised with impunity, yet God is armed, and will signally avenge this contempt. Under this obedience, I comprehend the restraint which private men ought to impose on themselves in public, not interfering with public business, or rashly encroaching on the province of the magistrate, or attempting anything at all of a public nature. If it is proper that anything in a public ordinance should be corrected, let them not act tumultuously, or put their hands to a work where they ought to feel that their hands are tied, but let them leave it to the cognisance of the magistrate, whose hand alone here is free. My meaning is, let them not dare to do it without being ordered. For when the command of the magistrate is given, they too are invested with public authority. For as, according to the common saying, the eyes and ears of the prince are his counsellors,

so one may not improperly say that those who, by his command, have the charge of managing affairs, are his hands.

24. But as we have hitherto described the magistrate who truly is what he is called—viz. the father of his country, and (as the Poet speaks) the pastor of the people, the guardian of peace, the president of justice, the vindicator of innocence, he is justly to be deemed a madman who disapproves of such authority. And since in almost all ages we see that some princes, careless about all their duties on which they ought to have been intent, live, without solicitude, in luxurious sloth; others, bent on their own interest, venally prostitute all rights, privileges, judgments, and enactments; others pillage poor people of their money, and afterwards squander it in insane largesses; others act as mere robbers, pillaging houses, violating matrons, and slaying the innocent; many cannot be persuaded to recognise such persons for princes, whose command, as far as lawful, they are bound to obey. For while in this unworthy conduct, and among atrocities so alien, not only from the duty of the magistrate, but also of the man, they behold no appearance of the image of God, which ought to be conspicuous in the magistrate, while they see not a vestige of that minister of God, who was appointed to be a praise to the good and a terror to the bad, they cannot recognise the ruler whose dignity and authority Scripture recommends to us. And, undoubtedly, the natural feeling of the human mind has always been not less to assail tyrants with hatred and execration, than to look up to just kings with love and veneration.

25. But if we have respect to the word of God, it will lead us farther, and make us subject not only to the authority of those princes who honestly and faithfully perform their duty toward us, but all princes, by whatever means they have so become, although there is nothing they less perform than the duty of princes. For though the Lord declares that a ruler to maintain our safety is the highest gift of his beneficence, and prescribes to rulers themselves their proper sphere, he at the same time declares, that of whatever description they may be, they derive their power from none but him. Those, indeed, who rule for the public good, are true examples and specimens of his beneficence, while those who domineer unjustly and tyrannically are raised up by him to punish the people for their iniquity. Still all alike possess that sacred majesty with which he has invested lawful power. I will not proceed further without subjoining some distinct passages to this effect.[1] We need not labour to prove that an impious king is a mark of the Lord's anger, since I presume no one will deny it, and that this is not less true of a king than of a robber who plunders your goods, an adulterer who defiles your bed, and an assassin who aims at your life, since all such calamities are classed by Scripture among the curses of God. But let us insist at greater length in proving what does not so easily fall in with

[1] Job xxxiv. 30; Hos. xiii. 11; Isa. iii 4; x. 5; Deut. xxviii. 29.

the views of men, that even an individual of the worst character, one most unworthy of all honour, if invested with public authority, receives that illustrious divine power which the Lord has by his word devolved on the ministers of his justice and judgment, and that, accordingly, in so far as public obedience is concerned, he is to be held in the same honour and reverence as the best of kings.

26. And, first, I would have the reader carefully to attend to that Divine Providence which, not without cause, is so often set before us in Scripture, and that special act of distributing kingdoms, and setting up as kings whomsoever he pleases. In Daniel it is said, "He changeth the times and the seasons: he removeth kings, and setteth up kings" (Dan. ii. 21, 37). Again, "That the living may know that the Most High ruleth in the kingdom of men, and giveth it to whomsoever he will" (Dan. iv. 17, 25). Similar sentiments occur throughout Scripture, but they abound particularly in the prophetical books. What kind of king Nebuchadnezzar, he who stormed Jerusalem, was, is well known. He was an active invader and devastator of other countries. Yet the Lord declares in Ezekiel that he had given him the land of Egypt as his hire for the devastation which he had committed. Daniel also said to him, "Thou, O king, art a king of kings: for the God of heaven hath given thee a kingdom, power, and strength, and glory. And wheresoever the children of men dwell, the beasts of the field and the fowls of the heaven hath he given into thine hand, and hath made thee ruler over them all" (Dan. ii. 37, 38). Again, he says to his son Belshazzar, "The most high God gave Nebuchadnezzar thy father a kingdom, and majesty, and glory, and honour: and for the majesty that he gave him, all people, nations, and languages, trembled and feared before him" (Dan. v. 18, 19). When we hear that the king was appointed by God, let us, at the same time, call to mind those heavenly edicts as to honouring and fearing the king, and we shall have no doubt that we are to view the most iniquitous tyrant as occupying the place with which the Lord has honoured him. When Samuel declared to the people of Israel what they would suffer from their kings, he said, "This will be the manner of the king that shall reign over you: He will take your sons, and appoint them for himself, for his chariots, and to be his horsemen; and some shall run before his chariots. And he will appoint him captains over thousands, and captains over fifties; and will set them to ear his ground, and to reap his harvest, and to make his instruments of war, and instruments of his chariots. And he will take your daughters to be confectionaries, and to be cooks, and to be bakers. And he will take your fields, and your vineyards, and your oliveyards, even the best of them, and give them to his servants. And he will take the tenth of your seed, and of your vineyards, and give to his officers, and to his servants. And he will take your men-servants, and your maid-servants, and your goodliest young men, and your asses, and put them to his work. He will take the tenth of your sheep: and ye shall be his servants" (1

Sam. viii. 11–17). Certainly these things could not be done legally by kings, whom the law trained most admirably to all kinds of restraint ; but it was called justice in regard to the people, because they were bound to obey, and could not lawfully resist: as if Samuel had said, To such a degree will kings indulge in tyranny, which it will not be for you to restrain. The only thing remaining for you will be to receive their commands, and be obedient to their words.

27. But the most remarkable and memorable passage is in Jeremiah. Though it is rather long, I am not indisposed to quote it, because it most clearly settles this whole question. "I have made the earth, the man and the beast that are upon the ground, by my great power, and by my outstretched arm, and have given it unto whom it seemed meet unto me. And now have I given all these lands into the hand of Nebuchadnezzar the king of Babylon, my servant: and the beasts of the field have I given him also to serve him. And all nations shall serve him, and his son, and his son's son, until the very time of his land come: and then many nations and great kings shall serve themselves of him. And it shall come to pass, that the nation and kingdom which will not serve the same Nebuchadnezzer the king of Babylon, and that will not put their neck under the yoke of the king of Babylon, that nation will I punish, saith the Lord, with the sword, and with famine, and with pestilence, until I have consumed them by his hand" (Jer. xxvii. 5–8). Therefore "bring your necks under the yoke of the king of Babylon, and serve him and his people, and live" (v. 12). We see how great obedience the Lord was pleased to demand for this dire and ferocious tyrant, for no other reason than just that he held the kingdom. In other words, the divine decree had placed him on the throne of the kingdom, and admitted him to regal majesty, which could not be lawfully violated. If we constantly keep before our eyes and minds the fact, that even the most iniquitous kings are appointed by the same decree which establishes all regal authority, we will never entertain the seditious thought, that a king is to be treated according to his deserts, and that we are not bound to act the part of good subjects to him who does not in his turn act the part of a king to us.

28. It is vain to object, that that command was specially given to the Israelites. For we must attend to the ground on which the Lord places it—"I have given the kingdom to Nebuchadnezzar; therefore serve him and live." Let us doubt not that on whomsoever the kingdom has been conferred, him we are bound to serve. Whenever God raises any one to royal honour, he declares it to be his pleasure that he should reign. To this effect we have general declarations in Scripture. Solomon says—"For the transgression of a land, many are the princes thereof" (Prov. xxviii. 2). Job says—"He looseth the bond of kings, amd girdeth their loins with a girdle" (Job. xii. 18). This being confessed, nothing remains for us but to serve and live. There is in Jeremiah another command in which the Lord thus orders his people—"Seek the peace of the city whither I

have caused you to be carried away captives, and pray unto the Lord for it: for in the peace thereof shall ye have peace" (Jer. xxix. 7). Here the Israelites, plundered of all their property, torn from their homes, driven into exile, thrown into miserable bondage, are ordered to pray for the prosperity of the victor, not as we are elsewhere ordered to pray for our persecutors, but that his kingdom may be preserved in safety and tranquillity, that they too may live prosperously under him. Thus David, when already king elect by the ordination of God, and anointed with his holy oil, though causelessly and unjustly assailed by Saul, holds the life of one who was seeking his life to be sacred, because the Lord had invested him with royal honour. "The Lord forbid that I should do this thing unto my master, the Lord's anointed, to stretch forth mine hand against him, seeing he is the anointed of the Lord." "Mine eyes spare thee; and I said, I will not put forth mine hand against my lord; for he is the Lord's anointed" (1 Sam. xxiv. 6, 11). Again,—"Who can stretch forth his hand against the Lord's anointed, and be guiltless"? "As the Lord liveth the Lord shall smite him, or his day shall come to die, or he shall descend into battle, and perish. The Lord forbid that I should stretch forth mine hand against the Lord's anointed" (1 Sam. xxiv. 9–11).

29. This feeling of reverence, and even of piety, we owe to the utmost to all our rulers, be their characters what they may. This I repeat the oftener, that we may learn not to consider the individuals themselves, but hold it to be enough that by the will of the Lord they sustain a character on which he has impressed and engraven inviolable majesty. But rulers, you will say, owe mutual duties to those under them. This I have already confessed. But if from this you conclude that obedience is to be returned to none but just governors, you reason absurdly. Husbands are bound by mutual duties to their wives, and parents to their children. Should husbands and parents neglect their duty; should the latter be harsh and severe to the children whom they are enjoined not to provoke to anger, and by their severity harass them beyond measure; should the former treat with the greatest contumely the wives whom they are enjoined to love and to spare as the weaker vessels; would children be less bound in duty to their parents, and wives to their husbands? They are made subject to the froward and undutiful. Nay, since the duty of all is not to look behind them, that is, not to inquire into the duties of one another, but to submit each to his own duty, this ought especially to be exemplified in the case of those who are placed under the power of others. Wherefore, if we are cruelly tormented by a savage, if we are rapaciously pillaged by an avaricious or luxurious, if we are neglected by a sluggish, if, in short, we are persecuted for righteousness' sake by an impious and sacrilegious prince, let us first call up the remembrance of our faults, which doubtless the Lord is chastising by such scourges. In this way humility will

curb our impatience. And let us reflect that it belongs not to us to cure these evils, that all that remains for us is to implore the help of the Lord, in whose hands are the hearts of kings, and inclinations of kingdoms.[1] "God standeth in the congregation of the mighty; he judgeth among the gods." Before his face shall fall and be crushed all kings and judges of the earth, who have not kissed his anointed, who have enacted unjust laws to oppress the poor in judgment, and do violence to the cause of the humble, to make widows a prey, and plunder the fatherless.

30. Herein is the goodness, power, and providence of God wondrously displayed. At one time he raises up manifest avengers from among his own servants, and gives them his command to punish accursed tyranny, and deliver his people from calamity when they are unjustly oppressed; at another time he employs, for this purpose, the fury of men who have other thoughts and other aims. Thus he rescued his people Israel from the tyranny of Pharaoh by Moses; from the violence of Chusa, king of Syria, by Othniel; and from other bondage by other kings or judges. Thus he tamed the pride of Tyre by the Egyptians; the insolence of the Egyptians by the Assyrians; the ferocity of the Assyrians by the Chaldeans; the confidence of Babylon by the Medes and Persians,—Cyrus having previously subdued the Medes, while the ingratitude of the kings of Judah and Israel, and their impious contumacy after all his kindness, he subdued and punished,—at one time by the Assyrians, at another by the Babylonians. All these things, however, were not done in the same way. The former class of deliverers being brought forward by the lawful call of God to perform such deeds, when they took up arms against kings, did not at all violate that majesty with which kings are invested by divine appointment, but armed from heaven, they, by a greater power, curbed a less, just as kings may lawfully punish their own satraps. The latter class, though they were directed by the hand of God, as seemed to him good, and did his work without knowing it, had nought but evil in their thoughts.

31. But whatever may be thought of the acts of the men themselves,[2] the Lord by their means equally executed his own work, when he broke the bloody sceptres of insolent kings, and overthrew their intolerable dominations. Let princes hear and be afraid; but let us at the same time guard most carefully against spurning or violating the venerable and majestic authority of rulers, an authority which God has sanctioned by the surest edicts, although those invested with it should be most unworthy of it, and, as far as in them lies, pollute it by their iniquity. Although the Lord takes vengeance on unbridled domination, let us not therefore suppose that that vengeance is committed to us, to whom no command has been given but

1 Dan. ix. 7; Prov. xxi. 1; Psalm lxxxii. 1; ii. 10; Isaiah x. 1.

2 The French adds, "Car les uns les faisoyent estans asseurez qu'ils faisoyent bien, et les autres par autre zele (comme nous avons dit)."—For the former acted under the full conviction, that they were doing right, and the latter, from a different feeling, as we have said.

to obey and suffer. I speak only of private men. For when popular magistrates have been appointed to curb the tyranny of kings (as the Ephori, who were opposed to kings among the Spartans, or Tribunes of the people to consuls among the Romans, or Demarchs to the senate among the Athenians; and perhaps there is something similar to this in the power exercised in each kingdom by the three orders, when they hold their primary diets). So far am I from forbidding these officially to check the undue license of kings, that if they connive at kings when they tyrannise and insult over the humbler of the people, I affirm that their dissimulation is not free from nefarious perfidy, because they fradulently betray the liberty of the people, while knowing that, by the ordinance of God, they are its appointed guardains.

32. But in that obedience which we hold to be due to the commands of rulers, we must always make the exception, nay, must be particularly careful that it is not incompatible with obedience to Him to whose will the wishes of all kings should be subject, to whose decrees their commands must yield, to whose majesty their sceptres must bow. And, indeed, how preposterous were it, in pleasing men, to incur the offence of Him for whose sake you obey men! The Lord, therefore, is King of kings. When he opens his sacred mouth, he alone is to be heard, instead of all and above all. We are subject to the men who rule over us, but subject only in the Lord. If they command anything against Him let us not pay the least regard to it, nor be moved by all the dignity which they possess as magistrates—a dignity to which no injury is done when it is subordinated to the special and truly supreme power of God. On this ground Daniel denies that he had sinned in any respect against the king when he refused to obey his impious decree (Dan. vi. 22), because the king had exceeded his limits, and not only been injurious to men, but, by raising his horn against God, had virtually abrogated his own power. On the other hand, the Israelites are condemned for having too readily obeyed the impious edict of the king. For, when Jeroboam made the golden calf, they forsook the temple of God, and, in submissiveness to him, revolted to new superstitions (1 Kings xii. 28). With the same facility posterity had bowed before the decrees of their kings. For this they are severely upbraided by the Prophet (Hosea. v. 11). So far is the praise of modesty from being due to that pretence by which flattering courtiers cloak themselves, and deceive the simple, when they deny the lawfulness of declining anything imposed by their kings, as if the Lord had resigned his own rights to mortals by appointing them to rule over their fellows, or as if earthly power were diminished when it is subjected to its author, before whom even the principalities of heaven tremble as suppliants. I know the imminent peril to which subjects expose themselves by this firmness, kings being most indignant when they are contemned. As Solomon says, "The wrath of a king is as messengers of death" (Prov. xvi. 14). But since Peter, one of heaven's heralds, has pub-

lished the edict, "We ought to obey God rather than men" (Acts v. 29), let us console ourselves with the thought, that we are rendering the obedience which the Lord requires, when we endure anything rather than turn aside from piety. And that our courage may not fail, Paul stimulates us by the additional consideration (1 Cor. vii. 23), that we were redeemed by Christ at the great price which our redemption cost him, in order that we might not yield a slavish obedience to the depraved wishes of men, far less do homage to their impiety.

END OF THE INSTITUTES.

ONE HUNDRED APHORISMS,*

CONTAINING,

WITHIN A NARROW COMPASS, THE SUBSTANCE AND ORDER OF

THE FOUR BOOKS OF THE

INSTITUTES OF THE CHRISTIAN RELIGION.

BOOK I.

1. THE true wisdom of man consists in the knowledge of God the Creator and Redeemer.

2. This knowledge is naturally implanted in us, and the end of it ought to be the worship of God rightly performed, or reverence for the Deity accompanied by fear and love.

3. But this seed is corrupted by ignorance, whence arises superstitious worship; and by wickedness, whence arise slavish dread and hatred of the Deity.

4. It is also from another source that it is derived—namely, from the structure of the whole world, and from the Holy Scriptures.

5. This structure teaches us what is the goodness, power, justice, and wisdom of God in creating all things in heaven and earth, and in preserving them by ordinary and extraordinary government, by which his Providence is more clearly made known. It teaches also what are our wants, that we may learn to place our confidence in the goodness, power, and wisdom of God,—to obey his commandments, —to flee to him in adversity,—and to offer thanksgiving to him for the gifts which we enjoy.

6. By the Holy Scriptures, also, God the Creator is known. We ought to consider what these Scriptures are; that they are true, and have proceeded from the Spirit of God; which is proved by the testimony of the Holy Spirit, by the efficacy and antiquity of the Scriptures, by the certainty of the Prophecies, by the miraculous preservation of the Law, by the calling and writings of the Apostles, by the consent of the Church, and by the steadfastness of the martyrs,

* THE ONE HUNDRED APHORISMS, with the various TABLES and INDICES, which must greatly facilitate reference, and enhance the utility and value of the present translation of THE INSTITUTES OF THE CHRISTIAN RELIGION, have been kindly furnished by the Rev. WILLIAM PRINGLE of Auchterarder.

whence it is evident that all the principles of piety are overthrown by those fanatics who, laying aside the Scripture, fly to revelations.

7. Next, what they teach; or, what is the nature of God in himself, and in the creation and government of all things.

8. The nature of God in himself is infinite, invisible, eternal, almighty; whence it follows that they are mistaken who ascribe to God a visible form. In his one essence there are three persons, the Father, the Son, and the Holy Spirit.

9. In the creation of all things there are chiefly considered, 1. Heavenly and spiritual substances, that is, angels, of which some are good and the protectors of the godly, while others are bad, not by creation, but by corruption; 2. Earthly substances, and particularly man, whose perfection is displayed in soul and in body.

10. In the government of all things the nature of God is manifested. Now his government is, in one respect, universal, by which he directs all the creatures according to the properties which he bestowed on each when he created them.

11. In another respect, it is special; which appears in regard to contingent events, so that if any person is visited either by adversity or by any prosperous result, he ought to ascribe it wholly to God; and with respect to those things which act according to a fixed law of nature, though their peculiar properties were naturally bestowed on them, still they exert their power only so far as they are directed by the immediate hand of God.

12. It is viewed also with respect to time past and future. *Past*, that we may learn that all things happen by the appointment of God, who acts either by means, or without means, or contrary to means; so that everything which happens yields good to the godly and evil to the wicked. *Future*, to which belong human deliberations, and which shows that we ought to employ lawful means; since that Providence on which we rely furnishes its own means.

13. Lastly, by attending to the advantage which the godly derive from it. For we know certainly, 1. That God takes care of the whole human race, but especially of his Church. 2. That God governs all things by his will, and regulates them by his wisdom. 3. That he has most abundant power of doing good; for in his hand are heaven and earth, all creatures are subject to his sway, the godly rest on his protection, and the power of hell is restrained by his authority. That nothing happens by chance, though the causes may be concealed, but by the will of God; by his secret will which we are unable to explore, but adore with reverence, and by his will which is conveyed to us in the Law and in the Gospel.

BOOK II.

14. The knowledge of God the Redeemer is obtained from the fall of man, and from the material cause of redemption.

15. In the fall of man, we must consider what he ought to be, and what he may be.

16. For he was created after the image of God; that is, he was made a partaker of the divine Wisdom, Righteousness, and Holiness, and, being thus perfect in soul and in body, was bound to render to God a perfect obedience to his commandments.

17. The immediate causes of the fall were—Satan, the Serpent, Eve, the forbidden fruit; the remote causes were—unbelief, ambition, ingratitude, obstinacy. Hence followed the obliteration of the image of God in man, who became unbelieving, unrighteous, liable to death.

18. We must now see what he may be, in respect both of soul and of body. The understanding of the soul in divine things, that is, in the knowledge and true worship of God, is blinder than a mole; good works it can neither contrive nor perform. In human affairs, as in the liberal and mechanical arts, it is exceedingly blind and variable. Now the will, so far as regards divine things, chooses only what is evil. So far as regards lower and human affairs, it is uncertain, wandering, and not wholly at its own disposal.

19. The body follows the depraved appetites of the soul, is liable to many infirmities, and at length to death.

20. Hence it follows that redemption for ruined man must be sought through Christ the Mediator; because the first adoption of a chosen people, the preservation of the Church, her deliverance from dangers, her recovery after dispersions, and the hope of the godly, always depended on the grace of the Mediator. Accordingly, the law was given, that it might keep their minds in suspense till the coming of Christ; which is evident from the history of a gracious covenant frequently repeated, from ceremonies, sacrifices, and washings, from the end of adoption, and from the law of the priesthood.

21. The material cause of redemption is Christ, in whom we must consider three things; 1. How he is exhibited to men; 2. How he is received; 3. How men are retained in his fellowship.

22. Christ is exhibited to men by the Law and by the Gospel.

23. The Law is threefold: Ceremonial, Judicial, Moral. The use of the Ceremonial Law is repealed, its effect is perpetual. The Judicial or Political Law was peculiar to the Jews, and has been set aside, while that universal justice which is described in the Moral Law remains. The latter, or Moral Law, the object of which is to cherish and maintain godliness and righteousness, is perpetual, and is incumbent on all.

24. The use of the Moral Law is threefold. The first use shows our weakness, unrighteousness, and condemnation; not that we may despair, but that we may flee to Christ. The second is, that those who are not moved by promises, may be urged by the terror of threatenings. The third is, that we may know what is the will of God; that we may consider it in order to obedience; that our minds

may be strengthened for that purpose; and that we may be kept from falling.

25. The sum of the Law is contained in the Preface, and in the two Tables. In the Preface we observe, 1. The power of God, to constrain the people by the necessity of obedience; 2. A promise of grace, by which he declares himself to be the God of the Church; 3. A kind act, on the ground of which he charges the Jews with ingratitude, if they do not requite his goodness.

26. The first Table, which relates to the worship of God, consists of four commandments.

27. The design of the First Commandment is, that God alone may be exalted in his people. To God alone, therefore, we owe adoration, trust, invocation, thanksgiving.

28. The design of the Second Commandment is, that God will not have his worship profaned by superstitious rites. It consists of two parts. The former restrains our licentious daring, that we may not subject God to our senses, or represent him under any visible shape. The latter forbids us to worship any images on religious grounds, and, therefore, proclaims his power, which he cannot suffer to be despised,—his jealousy, for he cannot bear a partner,—his vengeance on children's children,—his mercy to those who adore his majesty.

29. The Third Commandment enjoins three things: 1. That whatever our mind conceives, or our tongue utters, may have a regard to the majesty of God; 2. That we may not rashly abuse his holy word and adorable mysteries for the purposes of ambition or avarice; 3. That we may not throw obloquy on his works, but may speak of them with commendatians of his Wisdom, Long-suffering, Power, Goodness, Justice. With these is contrasted a threefold profanation of the name of God, by perjury, unnecessary oaths, and idolatrous rites; that is, when we substitute in the place of God saints, or creatures animate or inanimate.

30. The design of the Fourth Commandment is, that, being dead to our own affections and works, we may meditate on the kingdom of God. Now there are three things here to be considered: 1. A spiritual rest, when believers abstain from their own works, that God may work in them; 2. That there may be a stated day for calling on the name of God, for hearing his word, and for performing religious rites; 3. That servants may have some remission from labour.

31. The Second Table, which relates to the duties of charity towards our neighbour, contains the last Six Commandments. The design of the Fifth Commandment is, that, since God takes pleasure in the observance of his own ordinance, the degrees of dignity appointed by him must be held inviolable. We are therefore forbidden to take anything from the dignity of those who are above us, by contempt, obstinacy, or ingratitude; and we are commanded to pay them reverence, obedience, and gratitude.

32. The design of the Sixth Commandment is, that, since God has bound mankind by a kind of unity, the safety of all ought to be

considered by each person; whence it follows that we are forbidden to do violence to private individuals, and are commanded to exercise benevolence.

33. The design of the Seventh Commandment is, that, because God loves purity, we ought to put away from us all uncleanness. He therefore forbids adultery in mind, word, and deed.

34. The design of the Eighth Commandment is, that, since injustice is an abomination to God, he requires us to render to every man what is his own. Now men steal, either by violence, or by malicious imposture, or by craft, or by sycophancy, &c.

35. The design of the Ninth Commandment is, that, since God, who is truth, abhors falsehood, he forbids calumnies and false accusations, by which the name of our neighbour is injured,—and lies, by which any one suffers loss in his fortunes. On the other hand, he requires every one of us to defend the name and property of our neighbour by asserting the truth.

36. The design of the Tenth Commandment is, that, since God would have the whole soul pervaded by love, every desire averse to charity must be banished from our minds; and therefore every feeling which tends to the injury of another is forbidden.

37. We have said that Christ is revealed to us by the Gospel. And, first, the agreement between the Gospel, or the New Testament, and the Old Testament is demonstrated: 1. Because the godly, under both dispensations, have had the same hope of immortality; 2. They have had the same covenant, founded not on the works of men, but on the mercy of God; 3. They have had the same Mediator between God and men—Christ.

38. Next, five points of difference between the two dispensations are pointed out. 1. Under the Law the heavenly inheritance was held out to them under earthly blessings; but under the Gospel our minds are led directly to meditate upon it. 2. The Old Testament, by means of figures, presented the image only, while the reality was absent; but the New Testament exhibits the present truth. 3. The former, in respect of the Law, was the ministry of condemnation and death; the latter, of righteousness and life. 4. The former is connected with bondage, which begets fear in the mind; the latter is connected with freedom, which produces confidence. 5. The word had been confined to the single nation of the Jews; but now it is preached to all nations.

39. The sum of evangelical doctrine is, to teach, 1. What Christ is; 2. Why he was sent; 3. In what manner he accomplished the work of redemption.

40. Christ is God and man: *God*, that he may bestow on his people righteousness, sanctification, and redemption; *Man*, because he had to pay the debt of man.

41. He was sent to perform the office, 1. Of a Prophet, by preaching the truth, by fulfilling the prophecies, by teaching and doing the will of his Father; 2. Of a King, by governing the whole Church

and every member of it, and by defending his people from every kind of adversaries; 3. Of a Priest, by offering his body as a sacrifice for sins, by reconciling God to us though his obedience, and by perpetual intercession for his people to the Father.

42. He performed the office of a Redeemer by dying for our sins, by rising again for our justification, by opening heaven to us through his ascension, by sitting at the right hand of the Father whence he will come to judge the quick and the dead; and, therefore, he procured for us the grace of God and salvation.

BOOK III.

43. We receive Christ the Redeemer by the power of the Holy Spirit, who unites us to Christ; and, therefore, he is called the Spirit of sanctification and adoption, the earnest and seal of our salvation, water, oil, a fountain, fire, the hand of God.

44. Faith is the hand of the soul, which receives, through the same efficacy of the Holy Spirit, Christ offered to us in the Gospel.

45. The general office of faith is, to assent to the truth of God, whenever, whatever, and in what manner soever he speaks; but its peculiar office is, to behold the will of God in Christ, his mercy, the promises of grace, for the full conviction of which the Holy Spirit enlightens our minds and strengthens our hearts.

46. Faith, therefore, is a steady and certain knowledge of the divine kindness towards us, which is founded on a gracious promise through Christ, and is revealed to our minds and sealed on our hearts by the Holy Spirit.

47. The effects of faith are four: 1. Repentance; 2. A Christian life; 3. Justification; 4. Prayer.

48. True repentance consists of two parts: 1. Mortification, which proceeds from the acknowledgment of sin, and a real perception of the divine displeasure; 2. Quickening, the fruits of which are—piety towards God, charity towards our neighbour, the hope of eternal life, holiness of life. With this true repentance is contrasted false repentance, the parts of which are, Contrition, Confession, and Satisfaction. The two former may be referred to true repentance, provided that there be contrition of heart on account of the acknowledgment of sin, and that it be not separated from the hope of forgiveness through Christ; and provided that the confession be either *private* to God alone, or made to the pastors of the Church willingly and for the purpose of consolation, not for the enumeration of offences, and for introducing a torture of the conscience; or *public*, which is made to the whole Courch, or to one or many persons in presence of the whole Church. What was formerly called Ecclesiastical Satisfaction, that is, what was made for the edification of the Church on account of repentance and public confession of sins, was introduced as due to God by the Sophists; whence sprung the supplements of

Indulgences in this world, and the fire of Purgatory after death. But that Contrition of the Sophists, and auricular Confession (as they call it), and the Satisfaction of actual performance, are opposed to the free forgiveness of sins.

49. The two parts of a Christian life are laid down: 1. The love of righteousness; that we may be holy, because God is holy, and because we are united to him, and are reckoned among his people; 2. That a rule may be prescribed to us, which does not permit us to wander in the course of righteousness, and that we may be conformed to Christ. A model of this is laid down to us, which we ought to copy in our whole life. Next are mentioned the blessings of God, which it will argue extreme ingratitude if we do not requite.

50. The sum of the Christian life is denial of ourselves.

51. The ends of this self-denial are four. 1. That we may devote ourselves to God as a living sacrifice. 2. That we may not seek our own things, but those which belong to God and to our neighbour. 3. That we may patiently bear the cross, the fruits of which are—acknowledgment of our weakness, the trial of our patience, correction of faults, more earnest prayer, more cheerful meditation on eternal life. 4. That we may know in what manner we ought to use the present life and its aids, for necessity and delight. Necessity demands that we possess all things as though we possessed them not; that we bear poverty with mildness, and abundance with moderation; that we know how to endure patiently fulness, and hunger, and want; that we pay regard to our neighbour, because we must give account of our stewardship; and that all things correspond to our calling. The delight of praising the kindness of God ought to be with us a stronger argument.

52. In considering Justification, which is the third effect of faith, the first thing that occurs is an explanation of the word. He is said to be justified who, in the judgment of God, is deemed righteous. He is justified by works, whose life is pure and blameless before God; and no such person ever existed except Christ. They are justified by faith who, shut out from the righteousness of works, receive the righteousness of Christ. Such are the elect of God.

53. Hence follows the strongest consolation; for instead of a severe Judge, we have a most merciful Father. Justified in Christ, and having peace, trusting to his power, we aim at holiness.

54. Next follows Christian liberty, consisting of three parts. 1. That the consciences of believers may rise above the Law, and may forget the whole righteousness of the Law. 2. That the conscience, free from the yoke of the Law, may cheerfully obey the will of God. 3. That they may not be bound by any religious scruples before God about things indifferent. But here we must avoid two precipices. 1. That we do not abuse the gifts of God. 2. That we avoid giving and taking offence.

55. The fourth effect of faith is Prayer; in which are considered its fruits, laws, faults, and petitions.

56. The fruit of prayer is fivefold. 1. When we are accustomed to flee to God, our heart is inflamed with a stronger desire to seek, love, and adore him. 2. Our heart is not a prey to any wicked desire, of which we would be ashamed to make God our witness. 3. We receive his benefits with thanksgiving. 4. Having obtained a gift, we more earnestly meditate on the goodness of God. 5. Experience confirms to us the Goodness, Providence, and Truth of God.

57. The laws are Four. 1. That we should have our heart framed as becomes those who enter into converse with God; and therefore the lifting up of the hands, the raising of the heart, and perseverance, are recommended. 2. That we should feel our wants. 3. That we should divest ourselves of every thought of our own glory, giving the whole glory to God. 4. That while we are prostrated amidst overwhelming evils, we should be animated by the sure hope of succeeding, since we rely on the command and promise of God.

58. They err who call on the Saints that are placed beyond this life. 1. Because Scripture teaches that prayer ought to be offered to God alone, who alone knows what is necessary for us. He chooses to be present, because he has promised. He can do so, for he is Almighty. 2. Because he requires that he be addressed in faith, which rests on his word and promise. 3. Because faith is corrupted as soon as it departs from this rule. But in calling on the saints there is no word, no promise; and therefore there is no faith; nor can the saints themselves either hear or assist.

59. The summary of prayer, which has been delivered to us by Christ the Lord, is contained in a Preface and two Tables.

60. In the Preface, the Goodness of God is conspicuous, for he is called *our Father*. It follows that we are his children, and that to seek supplies from any other quarter would be to charge God either with poverty or with cruelty; that sins ought not to hinder us from humbly imploring mercy; and that a feeling of brotherly love ought to exist amongst us. The power of God is likewise conspicuous in this Preface, for he is *in Heaven*. Hence we infer that God is present everywhere, and that when we seek him, we ought to rise above perceptions of the body and the soul; that he is far beyond all risk of change or corruption; that he holds the whole universe in his grasp, and governs it by his power.

61. The First Table is entirely devoted to the glory of God, and contains Three petitions. 1. That the *name* of God, that is, his power, goodness, wisdom, justice, and truth, *may be hallowed;* that is, that men may neither speak nor think of God but with the deepest veneration. 2. That God may correct, by the agency of his Spirit, all the depraved lusts of the flesh; may bring all our thoughts into obedience to his authority; may protect his children; and may defeat the attempts of the wicked. The use of this petition is threefold. (1). It withdraws us from the corruptions of the world. (2). It inflames us with the desire of mortifying the flesh. (3). It ani-

mates us to endure the cross. 3. The Third petition relates not to the secret will of God, but to that which is made known by the Scriptures, and to which voluntary obedience is the counterpart.

62. The Second Table contains the Three remaining petitions, which relate to ourselves and our neighbours. 1. It asks everything which the body needs in this sublunary state; for we commit ourselves to the care and providence of God, that he may feed, foster, and preserve us. 2. We ask those things which contribute to the spiritual life, namely, *the forgiveness of sins*, which implies satisfaction, and to which is added a condition, that when we have been offended by deed or by word, we nevertheless forgive them their offences against us. 3. We ask *deliverance from temptations*, or, that we may be furnished with armour and defended by the Divine protection, that we may be able to obtain the victory. *Temptations* differ in their *cause*, for God, Satan, the world, and the flesh *tempt;* in their *matter*, for we are tempted, on the right hand, in respect of riches, honours, beauty, &c., and on the left hand, in respect of poverty, contempt, and afflictions: and in their *end*, for God tempts the godly for good, but Satan, the flesh, and the world, tempt them for evil.

63. Those Four effects of faith bring us to the certainty of election, and of the final resurrection.

64. The causes of election are these. The *efficient* cause is—the free mercy of God, which we ought to acknowledge with humility and thanksgiving. The *material* cause is—Christ, the well-beloved Son. The *final* cause is—that, being assured of our salvation, because we are God's people, we may glorify him both in this life and in the life which is to come, to all eternity. The effects are, in respect either of many persons, or of a single individual; and that by electing some, and justly reprobating others. The elect are called by the preaching of the word and the illumination of the Holy Spirit, are justified, and sanctified, that they may at length be glorified.

65. The final resurrection will take place. 1. Because on any other supposition we cannot be perfectly glorified. 2. Because Christ rose in our flesh. 3. Because God is Almighty.

BOOK IV.

66. God keeps us united in the fellowship of Christ by means of Ecclesiastical and Civil government.

57. In Ecclesiastical government Three things are considered. 1. What is the Church? 2. How is it governed? 3. What is its power?

68. The Church is regarded in two points of view; as Invisible and Universal, which is the communion of saints; and as Visible and Particular. The Church is discerned by the pure preaching of the word, and by the lawful administration of the sacraments.

69. As to the government of the Church, there are Five points of inquiry. 1. Who rule? 2. What are they? 3. What is their calling? 4. What is their office? 5. What was the condition of the ancient Church?

70. They that rule are not Angels, but Men. In this respect, God declares his condescension towards us: we have a most excellent training to humility and obedience, and it is singularly fitted to bind us to mutual charity.

71. These are Prophets, Apostles, Evangelists, whose office was temporary; Pastors and Teachers, whose office is of perpetual duration.

72. Their calling is twofold; *internal* and *external*. The *internal* is from the Spirit of God. In the *external* there are Four things to be considered. 1. What sort of persons ought to be chosen? Men of sound doctrine and holy lives. 2. In what manner? With fasting and prayer. 3. By whom? Immediately, by God, as Prophets and Apostles. Mediately, with the direction of the word, by Bishops, by Elders, and by the people. 4. With what rite of ordination? By the laying on of hands, the use of which is threefold. 1. That the dignity of the ministry may be commended. 2. That he who is called may know that he is devoted to God. 3. That he may believe that the Holy Spirit will not desert this holy ministry.

73. The duty of Pastors in the Church is, to preach the Word, to administer the Sacraments, to exercise Discipline.

74. The condition of the ancient Church was distributed into Presbyters, Elders, Deacons, who dispensed the funds of the Church to the Bishops, the Clergy, the poor, and for repairing churches.

75. The power of the Church is viewed in relation to Doctrine, Legislation, and Jurisdiction.

76. Doctrine respects the articles of faith, none of which must be laid down without the authority of the word of God, but all must be directed to the glory of God and the edification of the Church. It respects also the application of the articles, which must agree with the analogy of faith.

77. Ecclesiastical laws, in precepts necessary to be observed, must be in accordance with the written word of God. In things indifferent, regard must be had to places, persons, times, with a due attention to order and decorum. Those constitutions ought to be avoided which have been laid down by pretended pastors instead of the pure worship of God, which bind the consciences by rigid necessity, which make void a commandment of God, which are useless and trifling, which oppress the consciences by their number, which lead to theatrical display, which are considered to be propitiatory sacrifices, and which are turned to the purposes of gain.

78. Jurisdiction is twofold. 1. That which belongs to the Clergy, which was treated of under the head of Provincial and General Synods. 2. That which is common to the Clergy and the people, the design of which is twofold, that scandals may be prevented, and

that scandal which has arisen may be removed. The exercise of it consists in private and public admonitions, and likewise in excommunication, the object of which is threefold. 1. That the Church may not be blamed; 2. That the good may not be corrupted by intercourse with the bad; 3. That they who are excommunicated may be ashamed, and may begin to repent.

79. With regard to Times, Fasts are appointed, and Vows are made. The design of Fasts is, that the flesh may be mortified, that we may be better prepared for prayer, and that they may be evidences of humility and obedience. They consist of Three things, the time, the quality, and the quantity of food. But here we must beware lest we rend our garments only, and not our hearts, as hypocrites do, lest those actions be regarded as a meritorious performance, and lest they be too rigorously demanded as necessary to salvation.

80. In Vows we must consider; 1. To whom the vow is made—namely, to God. Hence it follows that nothing must be attempted but what is approved by his word, which teaches us what is pleasing and what is displeasing to God. 2. Who it is that vows—namely, a man. We must, therefore, beware lest we disregard our liberty, or promise what is beyond our strength or inconsistent with our calling. 3. What is vowed. Here regard must be had to time; to the *past*, such as a vow of thanksgiving and repentance; to the *future*, that we may afterwards be more cautious, and may be stimulated by them to the performance of duty. Hence it is evident what opinion we ought to form respecting Popish vows.

81. In explaining the Sacraments, there are Three things to be considered. 1. What a sacrament is;—namely, an external sign, by which God seals on our consciences the promises of his good-will towards us, in order to sustain the weakness of our faith. We in our turn testify our piety towards him. 2. What things are necessary;—namely, the Sign, the Thing signified, the Promise, and the general Participation. 3. What is the number of them;—namely, Baptism and the Lord's Supper.

82. The Sign in Baptism is water; the Thing Signified is the blood of Christ; the Promise is eternal life; the Communicants or Partakers are, adults, after making a confession of their faith, and likewise infants; for Baptism came in the place of Circumcision, and in both the mystery, promise, use, and efficacy, are the same. Forgiveness of sins also belongs to infants, and therefore it is likewise a sign of this forgiveness.

83. The end of Baptism is twofold. 1. To promote our faith towards God. For it is a sign of our washing by the blood of Christ, and of the mortification of our flesh, and the renewal of our souls in Christ. Besides, being united to Christ, we believe that we shall be partakers of all his blessings, and that we shall never fall under condemnation. 2. To serve as our confession before our neighbour; for it is a mark that we choose to be regarded as the people of God,

and we testify that we profess the Christian religion, and that our desire is, that all the members of our body may proclaim the praise of God.

84. The Lord's Supper is a spiritual feast, by which we are preserved in that life into which God hath begotten us by his word.

85. The design of the Lord's Supper is threefold. 1. To aid in confirming our faith towards God. 2. To serve as a confession before men. 3. To be an exhortation to charity.

86. We must beware lest, by undervaluing the signs, we separate them too much from their mysteries, with which they are in some measure connected; and lest, on the other hand, by immoderately extolling them, we appear to obscure the mysteries themselves.

87. The parts are two. 1. The *spiritual truth* in which the meaning is beheld, consists in the promises; the *matter*, or substance, is Christ dead and risen; and the *effect* is our redemption and justification. 2. The visible signs are, bread and wine.

88. With the Lord's Supper is contrasted the Popish Mass. 1. It offers insult and blasphemy to Christ. 2. It buries the cross of Christ. 3. It obliterates his death. 4. It robs us of the benefits which we obtain in Christ. 5. It destroys the Sacraments in which the memorial of his death was left.

89. The Sacraments, falsely so called, are enumerated, which are, Confirmation, Penitence, Extreme Unction, Orders [which gave rise to the (seven) less and the (three) greater], and Marriage.

90. Next comes Civil government, which belongs to the external regulation of manners.

91. Under this head are considered Magistrates, Laws, and the People.

92. The Magistrate is God's vicegerent, the father of his country, the guardian of the laws, the administrator of justice, the defender of the Church.

93. By these names he is excited to the performance of duty. 1. That he may walk in holiness before God, and before men may maintain uprightness, prudence, temperance, harmlessness, and righteousness. 2. That by wonderful consolation it may smooth the difficulties of his office.

94. The kinds of Magistracy or Civil Government are, Monarchy, Aristocracy, Democracy.

95. As to Laws, we must see what is their constitution in regard to God and to men: and what is their equity in regard to times, places, and nations.

96. The People owe to the Magistrate, 1. Reverence heartily rendered to him as God's ambassador. 2. Obedience, or compliance with edicts, or paying taxes, or undertaking public offices and burdens. 3. That love which will lead us to pray to God for his prosperity.

97. We are enjoined to obey not only good magistrates, but all who possess authority, though they may exercise tyranny; for it

was not without the authority of God that they were appointed to be princes.

98. When tyrants reign, let us first remember our faults, which are chastised by such scourges; and, therefore, humility will restrain our impatience. Besides, it is not in our power to remedy these evils, and all that remains for us is to implore the assistance of the Lord, in whose hand are the hearts of men and the revolutions of kingdoms.

99. In Two ways God restrains the fury of tyrants; either by raising up from among their own subjects open avengers, who rid the people of their tyranny, or by employing for that purpose the rage of men whose thoughts and contrivances are totally different, thus overturning one tyranny by means of another.

100. The obedience enjoined on subjects does not prevent the interference of any popular Magistrates whose office it is to restrain tyrants and to protect the liberty of the people. Our obedience to Magistrates ought to be such, that the obedience which we owe to the King of kings shall remain entire and unimpaired.

GENERAL INDEX.

THE REFERENCES ARE TO THE VOLUMES AND PAGES.